Gödel:
N. J. O.
3/8/72

a phrase and sentence dictionary of spoken

SPANISH

Spanish-English
English-Spanish

Dover Publications, Inc.
New York

Published in Canada by General Publishing Company, Ltd., 30 Lesmill Road, Don Mills, Toronto, Ontario.

Published in the United Kingdom by Constable and Company, Ltd., 10 Orange Street, London W. C. 2.

This new Dover edition first published in 1958 is an unabridged republication of the War Department Technical Manual TM 30-900, *Dictionary of Spoken Spanish*.

Standard Book Number: 486-20495-2
Library of Congress Catalog Card Number: 58-14487

Manufactured in the United States of America

Dover Publications, Inc.
180 Varick Street
New York 14, N. Y.

CONTENTS

ABBREVIATIONS AND SYMBOLS USED IN THIS DICTIONARY

Abbreviations

abbr	abbreviated		*n*	noun
adj	adjective		*neu*	neuter
adv	adverb			
Am	America			
Ant	Antilles		*obj*	object, objective
Arg	Argentina			
art	article			
			part.	participle
C.A.	Central America		*pl*	plural
Col	Colombia		*prep*	preposition
Com	commerce, commercial		*pret.*	preterite
condit.	conditional		*pres.*	present
conj	conjunction		*pron*	pronoun
f	feminine			
Fam	familiar			
fut.	future		*rad-ch*	radical-changing
imperf.	imperfect			
interj	interjection		*S.A.*	South America
irr	irregular		*sg*	singular
			Sp	Spain
lit.	literally		*subj.*	subjunctive
m	masculine			
Math	mathematics, mathematical			
Mex	Mexico		*v*	verb
Mil	military		*Ven*	Venezuela

Symbols

In the vocabularies the symbol ▲ denotes an additional translation of the preceding boldface term. The symbol ° denotes idiomatic phrases and reflexive forms. The symbol ‖ introduces idiomatic sentences in which the boldface term is not translatable alone.

PART I

Spanish-English

GRAMMATICAL INTRODUCTION

I. Sounds and Spelling

Both the sounds and the spelling of Spanish are simple, and will be described together, with the Spanish letters as a starting point.

0.1 Vowels are five in number:

SPELLING	DESCRIPTION	EXAMPLES
i	like English *i* in *machine* or *ee* in *beet*	*fino* "fine"; *mí* "me"
u	like English *oo* in *boot*	*puro* "pure"; *tú* "you"

These two vowels may occur unstressed before or after a stressed vowel, in which case they are pronounced like English *y* and *w* respectively: *bien* "well"; *bueno* "good"; *automóvil* "automobile".

e	like the *e* of English *they*, if no consonant follows in the same syllable; like *e* in *bed*, if a consonant follows in the same syllable	*pero* "but"; *puesto* "put"
o	like the *o* of English *know*, if no consonant follows in the same syllable; like *au* in *taut*, if a consonant follows in the same syllable	*todo* "all"; *corte* "court"
a	like the *a* of English *father*	*mano* "hand" *parte* "part"

0.2 Consonants are:

p	like English *p*	*Pepe* "Joe"
t	like English *t*, but with tongue against upper teeth instead of gum ridge	*tanto* "so much"
qu (before *e, i*), *c* (elsewhere)	like English *k* or "hard *c*"	*que* "that"; *carro* "cart"

1

These three sounds are never pronounced with the puff of breath after them, as the corresponding English sounds often are.

SPELLING	DESCRIPTION	EXAMPLES
b, v	like English *b*	*bebe* "he drinks"
d	like English *d*	*dedo* "finger"
gu (before *e, i*), *g* (elsewhere)	like English "hard *g*"	*pague Usted* "(you) pay"; *pagar* "pay"

The above three sounds, when they come between two vowels, are not pronounced with a full closure of lips or tongue (as are English *b, d, g*) but with the breath forcing its way out between the lips, or between the tongue and teeth, or between the tongue and top of the mouth.

m	like English *m*	*mano* "hand"
n	like English *n*, but with the tip of the tongue against the front teeth	*nada* "nothing"
ñ	like *ni* in English *onion*, but a single sound (beginning like *n* and ending like *y*)	*año* "year"
f	like English *f*	*fuerte* "strong"
c (before *e, i*), *z* (elsewhere)	like *th* in English *thick*	*cierto* "certain"; *zorra* "fox"; *conozco* "I know"

The above sound is not used by speakers of American Spanish, who replace it by "s".

s	like English *s*	*seso* "brain"
l	like English *l*, but with the tip of the tongue against the front teeth	*lado* "side"
ll	like *lli* in English *million*, but a single sound beginning like *l* and ending like *y;* in Latin America, generally like English *y*	*llano* "plain"; *milla* "mile"
r	single flap of the tongue against the front teeth, somewhat like our American English *d*	*caro* "dear"
rr	several repeated flaps of the tongue against the front teeth, like the telephone operator's "th-r-r-ee"	*carro* "cart"
y	like English *y*	*reyes* "kings"
g (before *e, i*), *j* (elsewhere)	like English *h*	*gente* "people"; *junto* "together"

2

Spelling	Description	Examples
h	stands for no sound at all, but is written in a number of words	*haba* "bean"; *hierba* "grass"

0.3 Syllables. A single consonant sound (and, in writing, two letters representing a single sound), or a consonant followed by *l* or *r*, belongs to the same syllable as the vowel following it: *ca-ro, ca-rro, mi-lla*. Other groups of two consonants are broken up, the first consonant belonging with the preceding vowel and the second with the following vowel: *juz-gar* "to judge"; *rec-tor* "rector".

0.4 Stress. Words ending in a vowel or in *-n* or *-s* are normally stressed on the next to the last syllable; words ending in any other consonant are stressed on the last syllable. Words having this type of stress bear no written accent mark: *cosa* "thing"; *cantan* "they sing"; *cantas* "you sing" (Fam); *cantar* "to sing". If a word does not conform to this pattern, an accent mark is written over the vowel letter of the syllable which is stressed: *vámonos* "let's go"; *jardín* "garden". In a few cases, a written accent serves only to mark the difference between one word and another written like it but having a different meaning: *¿cuándo?* "when?" (interrogative), but *cuando* "when" (relative).

II. Forms

1.1 Nouns and adjectives are inflected alike, and will be discussed together. A noun is an inflected form that may follow *el/la* and precede a verb; an adjective is a form that may follow *el/la* and precede a noun. (For the definite article, cf §1.22.)

1.11 The **plural** of nouns and adjectives is formed in one of three ways:

1. By leaving the singular unchanged (words ending in *-s*, family names, and a few others): *jueves* "Thursday, Thursdays"; *López* "López, Lópezes"; *déficit* "deficit, deficits".

2. By adding *-s* to nouns ending in an unstressed vowel or stressed *-é*: *libro* "book", *libros* "books"; *cara* "face", *caras* "faces"; *café* "coffee", *cafés* "coffees".

3. By adding *-es* to most other nouns: *rubí* "ruby", pl *rubíes; buey* "ox", pl *bueyes; papel* "paper", pl *papeles*. The letter *c* is replaced by *qu*, and *z* by *c*, before *-es: frac* "frock coat", pl *fraques; lápiz* "pencil", pl *lápices*.

1.12 Gender. Nouns belong either to the masculine or the feminine gender; adjectives to both. The feminine of an adjective is formed on the masculine in one of the following three ways:

1. By substituting *-a* for *-o* of the masculine: *bueno* m, *buena* f "good".

2. By adding *-a* to the masculine: *inglés* m, *inglesa* f "English".

3. By leaving the masculine unchanged: *interesante* m, f "interesting"; *fácil* m, f "easy".

1.13 Reduced forms of adjectives. Certain adjectives are used in shortened or **reduced** forms when they stand before a noun they modify, e.g. *un buen libro* "a good book". The following adjectives have reduced forms in the masculine singular only: *buen(o)* "good"; *mal(o)* "bad"; *primer(o)* "first"; *tercer(o)* "third";

3

un(o) "one" and its compounds. *Santo* "Saint" has the form *San* before a masculine name in the singular: *San Francisco* "St. Francis". *Gran* takes the place of *grande* "great" (but *un gran hombre* is "an important man" while *un hombre grande* is "a large man"), and *cien* takes the place of *ciento* "100", before either masculine or feminine.

1.2 Pronouns are of five classes: personal, demonstrative, interrogative, relative, and indefinite.

1.21 Personal pronouns are of two main types: those which can be used apart from verbs, called **disjunctive** pronouns, and those which can be used only with verbs, called **conjunctive** pronouns.

1. Disjunctive pronouns are:

SINGULAR	PLURAL
NOMINATIVE	
1. *yo* "I"	1. *nosotros* (m), *nosotras* (f) "we"
2. *tú* "you" (Fam)	2. *vosotros* (m), *vosotras* (f) "you" (Fam)
3. *usted* "you"	3. *ustedes* "you"
él "he", *ella* "she"	*ellos* (m), *ellas* (f) "they"

PREPOSITIONAL	
1. *mí* "me"	1. *nosotros* (m), *nosotras* (f) "us"
2. *ti* "you" (Fam)	2. *vosotros* (m), *vosotras* (f) "you" (Fam)
3. *usted* "you"	3. *ustedes* "you"
él "him", *ella* "her"	*ellos* (m), *ellas* (f) "they"

REFLEXIVE PREPOSITIONAL	
sí "himself, herself, itself"	*sí* "themselves"

When the pronouns *mí*, *ti*, and *sí* (sg) are used as objects of the preposition *con* "with", the following forms result: *conmigo*, *contigo*, and *consigo*.

The word *usted* (abbreviated *Ud.* or *Vd.*) is used when speaking to persons with whom one is not well acquainted, and takes a verb in the third person singular; the plural *ustedes* (abbreviated *Uds.* or *Vds.*) is used in the same way. In Spanish America, *ustedes* is often used instead of *vosotros*, as the plural corresponding to *tú*. *Tú* is used only between relatives, young people, intimate friends, and in addressing children, servants, and pets. In South America, especially Argentina, *vos* is generally used for *tú*.

2. Conjunctive pronouns are:

SINGULAR	PLURAL
DIRECT OBJECT	
1. *me* "me"	1. *nos* "us"
2. *te* "you" (Fam)	2. *os* "you" (Fam)
3. *le* "you" (m), "him"	3. *los* "you, them" (m)
la "you" (f), "her", "it" (f)	*las* "you, them" (f)
lo "it"	

4

REFLEXIVE

se "yourself, himself, herself, itself"   *se* "yourselves, themselves"

INDIRECT OBJECT

1. *me* "to me"
2. *te* "to you" (Fam)
3. *le* "to you, to him, to her, to it"

1. *nos* "to us"
2. *os* "to you" (Fam)
3. *les* "to you, to them"

These conjunctive pronouns may occur either singly or in groups of two. The occurrence of groups of two conjunctive pronouns is determined by the following rules:

a¹) If the pronoun *se* is present in the group, it always comes before the other conjunctive pronoun. When *se* is used in this way, it may have the meaning of:

aa) An unspecified actor: *se dice* "it is said"; *se la trató bien* "she was treated well".

bb) A third person object, either reflexive or not: *se lo dice* "he says it to him (her)", or "he (she) says it to himself (herself)".

b¹) If the pronoun *se* is not present, the first pronoun of the group has the meaning of an indirect object, and the second that of a direct object: *me lo da* "he gives it to me". *Le, les* may not occur as the first member of a group of conjunctive pronouns, their place being taken by *se* (see a¹. bb, above).

The conjunctive pronouns are placed after the verb they modify, and written together with it, in the following circumstances:

a²) After an infinitive or gerund: *dárselo* "to give it to him"; *diciéndolo* "saying it".

b²) After other verb forms, only in literary style or (to save money) in telegrams: *fuíme* "I went away".

With other verb forms than the infinitive and gerund, the conjunctive pronouns are usually placed before the verb and written as separate words: *se lo da* "he gives it to him"; *me fuí* "I went away".

1.22 Demonstrative pronouns have three genders: masculine, feminine, and neuter. The neuter occurs only in the singular and is used only to refer to something abstract or already spoken of. The demonstrative pronouns are *éste* "this", *ése* "that" (near you), *aquél* "that" (over there), and the definite article (*el, la, los, las, lo*) with *de* and *que*, meaning respectively "that (those) of", "the one (ones) with (in, on)", "that (those) which", and "the one (ones) which".

The forms of these pronouns are:

sg	m	*éste*	*ése*	*aquél*	*el de, el que*
	f	*ésta*	*ésa*	*aquélla*	*la de, la que*
	neu	*esto*	*eso*	*aquello*	*lo de, lo que*
pl	m	*éstos*	*ésos*	*aquéllos*	*los de, los que*
	f	*éstas*	*ésas*	*aquéllas*	*las de, las que*

The demonstrative adjectives are the same as the demonstrative pronouns but do not bear a written accent and they usually precede the noun.

Yo escribo con esta pluma.	"I'm writing with this pen."
Esta pluma y ésa.	"This pen and that one."

There is no neuter adjective in Spanish and the neuter demonstrative pronouns *esto, eso, aquello,* and *lo* bear no written accent. They are used to refer to a general idea or object without a determined gender.

Eso es verdad.	"That (what has been said) is true."
Esto me alarma.	"This (situation, outlook) alarms me."

When used before a noun or noun phrase (cf §2.14.1), *el, la,* etc, have about the meaning of English "the", and in this use are termed the **definite article.** The form *el* is used before a masculine singular noun or noun phrase: *el hombre* "the man", *el gran diccionario* "the great dictionary"; and also directly before a feminine noun beginning with the stressed sound *a: el alma* "the soul", *el hambre* "the hunger". Before other feminines, *la* is used: *la persona* "the person", *la otra persona* "the other person". In the plural, *los* is used before masculine and *las* before feminine nouns or noun phrases: *los hombres* "the men", *los grandes diccionarios* "the great dictionaries", *las almas* "the souls", *las otras personas* "the other persons".

1.23 **Interrogative pronouns** are: *¿qué?* "what?", *¿quién?* "who?", *¿quiénes?* (pl), *¿de quién?* "whose?", *¿de quiénes?* (pl), *¿cuál?* "which one?", *¿cuáles?* "which ones?", *¿cuánto?* "how much?", *¿cuántos?* "how many?"

All interrogative adjectives and pronouns bear a written accent mark to distinguish them from the corresponding relative.

qué is not inflected. *¿de quién?* is always followed immediately by *ser: ¿De quién es este libro?* "Whose book is this?"

When translating from English into Spanish, the interrogative *¿de quién?* should not be confused with the possessive relative *cuyo* "whose, of which"· "This book, whose influence has been so beneficial." *Ese libro, cuya influencia ha sido tan beneficiosa.* But "Whose book is this?" *¿De quién es este libro?*

1.24 **Relative pronouns** are: *que* "that, which, who", *quien, quienes* "who, whom", *el que* "he who, the one who, the one which, that which", *la que* "she who, the one who, the one which, that which", *lo que* "that which, what", *los que* "those who, those which", *las que* "those who, those which", *el cual, la cual* "he who (she who), the one who, that which", *los cuales, las cuales* "they who, the ones who, those which", *lo cual* "that, which, what", *cuanto* "all that, as much as", *cuantos* "all that, as many as".

A simple relative (1, below) has an antecedent in the main clause and the compound relative (2, below) contains its own antecedent. This distinction concerns the use and not the form.

(1) *El libro que está sobre la mesa es suyo.*	"The book which is on the table is yours."
(2) *Quien trabaja mejor es María.*	"The one who works best is Mary."

lo que is used when reference is made to a phrase, a sentence, or to a specific thing without a specific gender: *Lo que Ud. pide es imposible.* "What (That which) you ask is impossible."

lo cual is used in supplementary clauses when the antecedent is a clause, a phrase, or an idea: *Se negó a recibirme, lo cual lamento mucho.* "He refused to receive me, which I regret very much."

1.25 Indefinite pronouns are: *alguien* "someone", *alguno, -a, -os, -as* "somebody, some", *algo* "something", *nadie* "no one", *ninguno, -a, -os, -as* "nobody, none", *nada* "nothing", *cualquiera* "whichever", and *quienquiera* "whoever"··

1.26 Possessive adjectives are·

SINGULAR	PLURAL
1. *mi, mis* "my"	1 *nuestro, -a(s)* "our"
2. *tu, tus* "your" (Fam)	2. *vuestro, -a(s)* "your" (Fam)
3. *su, sus* "his, her, its, your"	3. *su, sus* "their"
1. *mío, -ía, -íos, -ías* "mine"	1. *nuestro, -a, -os, -as* "ours"
2. *tuyo, -a, -os, -as* "yours" (Fam)	2. *vuestro, -a, -os, -as* "yours" (Fam)
3. *suyo, -a, -os, -as* "yours, his, hers, its"	3. *suyo, -a, -os, -as* "theirs"

Possessives agree in gender and number with the thing possessed. Possessive pronouns are formed by adding *el* to *mío, tuyo, suyo, nuestro,* and *vuestro. El suyo* is usually replaced (to avoid ambiguity) by *el de él, el de ella, el de ustedes, el de ellos: Mi libro, el suyo y el de él.* "My book, yours, and his." *El* is omitted after the verb *ser: El libro es mío.* "The book's mine."

The English possessive case ("-'s") is rendered by *de* and possessor noun or pronoun: *Ese es el libro de mi amigo.* "This is my friend's book."

1.3 Prepositions and conjunctions: *a, de, en, por,* and *para* are the most frequently used prepositions in Spanish.

1. *a* "to" implies motion, in contrast with *en,* which corresponds to English "in" or "at" (place where or state). Bear this distinction in mind in translating English "at".

Voy a Valencia.	"I'm going to Valencia."
Estoy en casa.	"I'm at home."

a) *a* is used as a sign of personal object, and as such is not translated into English:

Yo amo a María.	"I love Mary."
María enseña a su hija.	"Mary teaches her daughter."

It is also used with the infinitive after verbs of motion (see §2.44.3)

b) *al* (*a*+*el*) followed by the infinitive corresponds to English "on" and "when": *al partir* "on leaving"

2. *de* "of, from" is replaced by *que* "that" and *estar* "be" when the position of a noun is purely accidental and not permanent or customary: *la casa de enfrente* "the house across the street", *el hombre que está delante de la casa* "the man who is in front of the house".

7

3. *por* points to the cause, motive, or reason for an action and corresponds to the English "through" (along, around), "by" (expressing agency, means, manner, unit of measure) and "for" (meaning "on account of", "because of", "in exchange for", "during", "as").

4. *para* points to the end or objective of an action and corresponds to the English "for" denoting purpose or destination.

5. *por* and *para* are frequently misused by foreign students of Spanish. English "for" is translated in each case into Spanish according to its specific meaning:

"This present's for you."	*Este regalo es PARA Ud.*
"Do it for me."	*Hágalo POR mi.*

1.31 Coordinate conjunctions are: *y* "and", *o* "or", *ni* "nor", *pero* "but" (nevertheless), and *sino* "but" (on the contrary).

1. *y* "and" is replaced by *e* when the word immediately following begins with *i* or *hi: franceses e italianos* "Frenchmen and Italians"; *padre e hijo* "father and son".

2. *o* "or" is replaced by *u* before *o* or *ho: siete u ocho* "seven or eight"; *mujer u hombre* "woman or man".

1.32 Subordinate conjunctions are: *que* "that", *como* "as, since" (causal), *cuando* "when", *mientras* "while", *pues(que)* "for, since", *porque* "because", and *si* "if, whether".

1. *que*, the most widely used subordinate conjunction, introduces noun clauses. In addition to its conjunctive uses, *que* is also a relative pronoun (§1.24) or a comparative adverb ("than"). Unlike Spanish, "that" is very often omitted in English:

Quiero que venga.	"I want him to come."
Creo que se ha ido	"I think he's gone."
Me parece que sí.	"I think so."

2. *si* "if, whether" is used to introduce adverb clauses of condition.

3. *sí* "yes" bears a written accent to differentiate it from the conjunction *si*, and is an adverb of affirmation: *Le pregunté si iba y me dijo que sí.* "I asked him if he was going and he said yes."

1.4 Adverbs of manner may be formed by adding *-mente* (which is the equivalent of English "-ly") to the feminine singular of the adjective: *lento, -a* "slow"; *lentamente* "slow, slowly".

Prepositional phrases are preferable in Spanish to the adverbs ending in *-mente: con lentitud* or *de una manera lenta* instead of *lentamente*.

1.41 Adverbs are placed as near as possible to the verb they modify: *Habla bien el español.* "He speaks Spanish well."

1.42 *aquí* "here", *ahí, allí* "there", *allá* "over there" correspond respectively to the demonstratives *este, ese*, and *aquel*.

1.43 *no* "not" corresponds to English "do not", "is not", etc, and the adjective "no".

1. *no* is placed before the verb: *No oigo.* "I don't hear."

8

2. If another negative is used after the verb, *no* must always precede: *No oigo nada.* "I hear nothing."

3. When another negative word precedes the verb, *no* is omitted: *Nada oigo.* "I hear nothing."

1.44 When no verb is present, *no* usually follows pronouns and adverbs: *todos no* "not all of them"; *todavía no* "not yet". *sí* is similarly used.

1.45 In a negative sentence all forms are negative (§1.43).

1.5 **Diminutives and augmentatives:** The suffixes *-ito, -illo, -cito, -cillo* added to nouns, adjectives, or adverbs imply small size or affectionate interest: *Pedrito* "little Peter", *chiquillo* "kid", *mujercita* "little woman, dear little wife", *pequeñito* "very small, tiny", *piececito* "tiny little foot".

The more frequent augmentative suffixes are *-ón, -ote, -azo, -acho*, give the idea of large size or comic effect: *mujerona* "large woman, ward woman", *grandote* "very large", *manaza* "huge hand", *ricacho* "rich ...n".

1.6 The **absolute superlative** ending is regularly *-ísimo*, corresponding to English "most, very, highly, exceedingly": *Es un hombre rarísimo.* "He's a most peculiar man." *Una mujer simpatiquísima.* "A most charming woman."

1.61 There are a number of other ways of expressing a high degree of quality in Spanish (see §§2.21, 2.5). The same idea expressed by the suffix *-ísimo* may be conveyed by *muy* "very" or *sumamente* "exceedingly, a most", with the exception of *muchísimo* (never *muy mucho*), regular form for "very much."

1.62 When *-ísimo* is added, adjectives and adverbs ending in *-co* or *-ca, -z, -go*, and *-able* change their ending to *-qui, -c, -gui*, and *-bil* respectively: *cerca, cerquísimo; feroz, ferocísimo; largo, larguísimo; amable, amabilísimo.*

1.7 **Verbs** have ten tenses, or sets of **finite forms** which show the person and number of the actor; and three **non-finite forms,** or forms which do not show person and number. The non-finite forms are: infinitive, gerund, and past participle. The ten tenses are formed on three stems, the "present" stem, the "future" stem, and the "preterite" stem, as follows:

PRESENT STEM	FUTURE STEM	PRETERITE STEM
Present Indicative	Future	Preterite
Imperfect	Conditional	Past Subjunctive, *-se* form
Present Subjunctive		Past Subjunctive, *-ra* form
Imperative		

1.71. There are four classes of verbs, according to the ending of the infinitive:

I. *-ar: cantar* "sing"   III. *-ir: vivir* "live"

II. *-er: aprender* "learn"   IV. *-r: ver* "see"*

In the following paragraphs, we shall give examples of the normal forms of these four conjugations, as shown in the four model verbs listed above.

1. **Present tense.** The present tense is generally used to refer to the present but it is often used as a graphic substitute for other tenses, as: a) em-

---

* This manual lists as "Class IV verbs" certain verbs usually designated elsewhere as simply "irregular verbs." For irregular verbs of all classes see page 12.

phatic future: *Mañana le escribo.* "I'll write him tomorrow." b) when immediate future time is involved: *¿Vamos ahora?* "Shall we go now?" c) for the perfect conditional in contrary-to-fact conditions: *Si dice algo en aquel momento, le pego.* "I'd have hit him if he'd said something at that moment." d) for the simple past in historical narrative: *Por poco le cojo.* "I almost caught him." The forms of the present are:

1. sg	"I"	*canto*	*aprendo*	*vivo*	*veo*
2. sg	"you" (Fam)	*cantas*	*aprendes*	*vives*	*ves*
3. sg	"you, he, she, it"	*canta*	*aprende*	*vive*	*ve*
1. pl	"we"	*cantamos*	*aprendemos*	*vivimos*	*vemos*
2. pl	"you" (Fam)	*cantáis*	*aprendéis*	*vivís*	*veis*
3. pl	"you, they"	*cantan*	*aprenden*	*viven*	*ven*

2. Imperfect tense. This tense refers to past action that was going on at the same time as some other action ("I was singing") or that was habitual ("I used to sing").

1. sg	*cantaba*	*aprendía*	*vivía*	*veía*
2. sg	*cantabas*	*aprendías*	*vivías*	*veías*
3. sg	*cantaba*	*aprendía*	*vivía*	*veía*
1. pl	*cantábamos*	*aprendíamos*	*vivíamos*	*veíamos*
2. pl	*cantábais*	*aprendíais*	*vivíais*	*veíais*
3. pl	*cantaban*	*aprendían*	*vivían*	*veían*

3. Present subjunctive. This tense is used either to express a command (in the first person plural, or third person singular or plural) or in certain types of dependent clauses (see §§3.5–3.52).

1. sg	*cante*	*aprenda*	*viva*	*vea*
2. sg	*cantes*	*aprendas*	*vivas*	*veas*
3. sg	*cante*	*aprenda*	*viva*	*vea*
1. pl	*cantemos*	*aprendamos*	*vivamos*	*veamos*
2. pl	*cantéis*	*aprendáis*	*viváis*	*veáis*
3. pl	*canten*	*aprendan*	*vivan*	*vean*

4. Imperative. This tense is used to give commands; it has only the second person singular and plural forms.

2. sg	*canta*	*aprende*	*vive*	*ve*
2. pl	*cantad*	*aprended*	*vivid*	*ved*

5. Future. This tense refers to action in future time ("I'll sing") or probability.

1 sg	*cantaré*	*aprenderé*	*viviré*	*veré*
2. sg	*cantarás*	*aprenderás*	*vivirás*	*verás*
3. sg	*cantará*	*aprenderá*	*vivirá*	*verá*
1. pl	*cantaremos*	*aprenderemos*	*viviremos*	*veremos*
2. pl	*cantaréis*	*aprenderéis*	*viviréis*	*veréis*
3. pl	*cantarán*	*aprenderán*	*vivirán*	*verán*

6. Conditional. This tense refers to hypothetical action or to future action viewed from past time ("I'd sing").

1. sg	cantaría	aprendería	viviría	vería
2. sg	cantarías	aprenderías	vivirías	verías
3. sg	cantaría	aprendería	viviría	vería
1. pl	cantaríamos	aprenderíamos	viviríamos	veríamos
2. pl	cantaríais	aprenderíais	viviríais	veríais
3. pl	cantarían	aprenderían	vivirían	verían

7. Past absolute. This tense refers to action at a specific point in past time ("I sang"). The past absolute of most verbs is as follows:

1. sg	canté	apprendí	viví	vi
2. sg	cantaste	aprendiste	viviste	viste
3. sg	cantó	apprendió	vivió	vió
1. pl	cantamos	aprendimos	vivimos	vimos
2. pl	cantasteis	aprendisteis	vivisteis	visteis
3. pl	cantaron	aprendieron	vivieron	vieron

Certain irregular verbs, called "strong" verbs, have special changes in the stem for the past absolute and the two past subjunctive tenses, e.g.: *venir* "to come"; *vine* "I came"; and *viniera, viniese* "(that) I might come". The past absolute of these strong verbs is inflected as follows:

	SINGULAR	PLURAL
1.	vine	vinimos
2.	viniste	vinisteis
3.	vino	vinieron

8. Past subjunctive. Each Spanish verb has two forms of the past subjunctive, one ending in the singular in *-se* and the other in *-ra*. The forms of these tenses are always built on the same stem as the past absolute or preterite tense:

a) Past subjunctive in *-se:*

1. sg	cantase	aprendiese	viviese	viese
2. sg	cantases	aprendieses	vivieses	vieses
3. sg	cantase	aprendiese	viviese	viese
1. pl	cantásemos	aprendiésemos	viviésemos	viésemos
2. pl	cantaseis	aprendiéseis	vivieseis	vieseis
3. pl	cantasen	aprendiesen	viviesen	viesen

b) Past subjunctive in *-ra:*

1. sg	cantara	aprendiera	viviera	viera
2. sg	cantaras	aprendieras	vivieras	vieras
3. sg	cantara	aprendiera	viviera	viera
1. pl	cantáramos	aprendiéramos	viviéramos	viéramos
2. pl	cantarais	aprendierais	vivierais	vierais
3. pl	cantaran	aprendieran	vivieran	vieran

1.72 Non-finite forms are such as are based on verbs, but do not show distinction of person and number and belong to other than verbal word classes. Verbs normally have:

1. Gerund—an adverb formed by adding *-ando* to the root of I-conjugation verbs; *-endo* to roots ending in *-y, -ll, -ñ;* and *-iendo* to others: *cantando, aprendiendo, viviendo, viendo; oyendo* "hearing" (*oír* "hear"), *bullendo* "boiling" (*bullir* "boil"), *riñendo* "wrangling" (*reñir* "wrangle").

2. Past participle—an adjective formed by adding *-ado* to the root of I-conjugation verbs, *-ido* to the root of II- and III-conjugation verbs, and *-do* to the root of IV-conjugation verbs. Irregular past participles are all those that have other endings than these, as: *abierto* "opened", *cubierto* "covered", *dicho* "said", *escrito* "written", *hecho* "done", *impreso* "printed", *muerto* "dead", *provisto* "provided", *resuelto* "resolved", *roto* "broken", *visto* "seen", *vuelto* "returned".

3. Infinitive—a masculine singular noun ending in *-r*. Occasionally an infinitive is used in the plural, which then ends in *-es*.

1.73 Irregular verbs. A number of verbs vary in one way or another from the patterns set forth above. Some of them fall into regular patterns of irregularities:

1. **Radical-changing verbs** are such as have the regular endings of the conjugation to which they belong, but have certain changes in the vowel of the last syllable of the root, depending on the form involved. There are three main types of radical-changing verbs:

a) Type I, in which a diphthong is substituted for a vowel (*ie* for *e* or *i; ue* for *o* or *u*) when it is stressed. (At the beginning of a verb, the sounds *ie* are spelled *ye*, and the sounds *ue* are spelled *hue*.) These forms are (with *contar* "count" and *pensar* "think" as examples):

PRESENT	1. sg	cuento	pienso
	2. sg	cuentas	piensas
	3. sg	cuenta	piensa
	3. pl	cuentan	piensan
PRESENT SUBJUNCTIVE	1. sg	cuente	piense
	2. sg	cuentes	pienses
	3. sg	cuente	piense
	3. pl	cuenten	piensen
IMPERATIVE	2. sg	cuenta	piensa

b) Type II, in which *ie* is substituted for *e*, and *ue* for *o*, in all forms where stress falls on this vowel, and *i* is substituted for *e*, and *u* for *o*, wherever the root is unstressed but followed by *a, ie,* or *ió*.

c) Type III, in which *i* is substituted for *e* both in forms where the last syllable of the root is stressed and where the root is unstressed but followed by *a, ie,* or *ió*.

12

Examples of types II and III are *sentir* "feel", *dormir* "sleep", *pedir* "ask":

PRESENT					
	1. sg	*siento*	*duermo*	*pido*
	2. sg	*sientes*	*duermes*	*pides*
	3. sg	*siente*	*duerme*	*pide*
	3. pl	*sienten*	*duermen*	*piden*

PRESENT SUBJUNCTIVE					
	1. sg	*sienta*	*duerma*	*pida*
	2. sg	*sientas*	*duermas*	*pidas*
	3. sg	*sienta*	*duerma*	*pida*
	1. pl	*sintamos*	*durmamos*	*pidamos*
	2. pl	*sintáis*	*durmáis*	*pidáis*
	3. pl	*sientan*	*duerman*	*pidan*

IMPERATIVE					
	2. sg	*siente*	*duerme*	*pide*

PRETERITE					
	3. sg	*sintió*	*durmió*	*pidió*
	3. pl	*sintieron*	*durmieron*	*pidieron*

PAST SUBJUNCTIVE					
	1, 3. sg	*sintiese*	*durmiese*	*pidiese*
	1, 3. sg	*sintiera*	*durmiera*	*pidiera*

PRESENT PARTICIPLE					
		sintiendo	*durmiendo*	*pidiendo*

2. Roots ending in *-y* lose this *y* wherever it would come before stressed *i*, and unstressed *i* of an ending is lost after this *y*. Thus, from the root *distribuy-* (III) "distribute" we have: infinitive *distribuir;* present 1. pl *distribuimos*, 2. pl *distribuís;* imperfect *distribuía*, etc; imperative 2. pl *distribuíd;* future *distribuiré*, etc; conditional *distribuiría*, etc; preterite 1. sg *distribuí*, 2. sg *distribuiste*, 3. sg *distribuyó*, 1. pl *distribuimos*, 2. pl *distribuisteis*, 3. pl *distribuyeron;* past participle *distribuido;* present participle *distribuyendo*. All verbs with infinitive in *-uir* are of this type.

3. Certain verbs, which we shall term the *-zc-* verbs, substitute *-zc-* for *-c-* wherever *-o* or *-a* follows. Thus *conocer* (II) "know" has:

PRESENT INDICATIVE	1. sg	*conozco*		
PRESENT SUBJUNCTIVE	1. sg	*conozca*	1. pl	*conozcamos*
	2. sg	*conozcas*	2. pl	*conozcáis*
	3. sg	*conozca*	3. pl	*conozcan*

4. Other irregular verbs, which do not fall into regular sub-patterns, are the following, here listed with indication of the class of verb to which they belong and with the individual forms which are irregular:

abrir III "open": past part. *abierto.*
andar I "walk": preterite *anduve* etc; past subj. *anduviese, anduviera.*
atenerse II "depend": like *tener.*
atraer II "attract": like *traer.*
avenirse III "agree": like *venir.*
bendecir III "bless": like *decir*, but past part. *bendito.*

13

caber II "be contained, fit": pres. 1. sg *quepo;* pres. subj. *quepa* etc; fut. *cabré;* condit. *cabría;* pret. *cupe* etc; past subj. *cupiese, cupiera.*

caer II "fall": pres. 1.sg *caigo;* pres. subj. *caiga* etc; pret. 3. sg *cayó,* 3. pl *cayeron;* past subj. *cayese, cayera;* pres. part. *cayendo.*

componer II "compose": like *poner.*

contener II "contain": like *tener.*

contradecir III "contradict": like *decir.*

contraer II "contract": like *traer.*

convenir III "agree": like *venir.*

cubrir III "cover": past part. *cubierto.*

dar IV "give": pres. 1.sg *doy;* imperf. *daba* etc; pres. subj. 1.sg *dé,* 3.sg *dé;* pret. *di, diste, dió, dimos, disteis, dieron;* past subj. *diese, diera.*

decaer II "decay": like *caer.*

decir III "say": radical-changing type III and: pres. 1.sg *digo;* pres. subj. *diga* etc; imperative 2.sg *di;* fut. 1.sg *diré* etc; condit. *diría* etc; pret. *dije* etc; past subj. *dijese, dijera;* past part. *dicho.*

descubrir III "discover": like *cubrir.*

desenvolver II "unroll, unwrap": like *volver.*

detener II "hold back, detain": like *tener.*

disolver II "dissolve": rad-ch I and past part. *disuelto.*

disponer II "dispose": like *poner.*

distraer II "distract": like *traer.*

entretener II "entertain": like *tener.*

escribir III "write": past part. *escrito.*

estar IV "be": pres. 1.sg *estoy,* 2.sg *estás,* 3.sg *está,* 3.pl *están;* imperf. *estaba* etc; pres. subj. *esté, estés, esté, estemos, estéis, estén;* pret. *estuve* etc; past subj. *estuviese, estuviera.*

exponer II "expose": like *poner.*

haber II "have, for there to be" (normally used in verbal phrases to form perfect tenses or in 3.sg meaning "there is, there was" etc): pres. *he, has, ha, hemos, habéis, han;* pres. subj. *haya* etc; fut. *habré;* condit. *habría;* pret. *hube* etc; past subj. *hubiese, hubiera.* The special form *hay* is used in pres. 3.sg in the meaning "there is, there are".

hacer II "do, make": pres. 1.sg *hago;* pres. subj. *haga* etc; fut. *haré;* condit. *haría;* pret. *hice* etc; past subj. *hiciese, hiciera;* past part. *hecho.*

imponer II "impose": like *poner.*

indisponer II "indispose": like *poner.*

interponer II "interpose": like *poner.*

intervenir III "intervene": like *venir.*

ir IV "go": pres. *voy, vas, va, vamos, váis, van;* imperf. *iba* etc; pres. subj. *vaya* etc; fut. *iré;* condit. *iría;* pret. and past subj. same as those of *ser.*

maldecir III "curse": like *decir,* but past part. *maldito.*

mantener II "maintain": like *tener.*

morir III "die": rad-ch I and past part. *muerto.*

obtener II "obtain": like *tener.*

oponer II "oppose": like *poner.*

poder II "be able": rad-ch I and: fut. *podré;* condit. *podría;* pret. *pude* etc; past subj. *pudiese, pudiera.*

poner II "place": pres. 1.sg *pongo;* pres. subj. *ponga* etc; fut. *pondré;* condit. *pondría;* pret. *puse* etc; past subj. *pusiese, pusiera;* past part. *puesto.*

prevenir III "prepare, warn": like *venir.*

proponer II "propose": like *poner.*

retener II "retain": like *tener.*

saber II "know": pres. 1.sg *sé;* pres. subj. *sepa* etc; fut. *sabré;* condit. *sabría;* pret. *supe* etc; past subj. *supiese, supiera.*

salir III "go out": pres. 1.sg *salgo;* pres. subj. *salga* etc; fut. *saldré;* condit. *saldría.*

satisfacer II "satisfy": like *hacer.*

ser IV "be": pres. *soy, eres, es, somos, sóis, son;* imperf. *era* etc; pres. subj. *sea* etc; pret. *fuí, fuiste, fué, fuimos, fuisteis, fueron;* past subj. *fuese, fuera;* pres. part. *siendo;* past part. *sido.*

sostener II "uphold, sustain": like *tener.*

suponer II "suppose": like *poner.*

tener II "have, hold": rad-ch I and: pres. 1.sg *tengo;* pres. subj. *tenga* etc; fut. *tendré;* condit. *tendría;* pret. *tuve* etc; past subj. *tuviese, tuviera.*

traer II "bring": pres. 1.sg *traigo;* pres. subj. *traiga* etc; pret. *traje* etc; past subj. *trajese, trajera.*

valer II "be worth": pres. 1.sg *valgo;* pres. subj. *valga* etc; fut. *valdré;* condit. *valdría.*

venir III "come": rad-ch I and: pres. 1.sg *vengo;* pres. subj. *venga* etc; fut. *vendré;* condit. *vendría;* pret. *vine* etc; past subj. *viniese, viniera.*

ver IV "see": pret. *ví, viste, vió, vimos, visteis, vieron;* past subj. *viese, viera;* past part. *visto.*

volver II "turn": rad-ch I and past part. *vuelto.*

1.8 Special uses of some important verbs:

1. *ser* "be" is used with a noun or adjective denoting permanent condition, inherent characteristic or quality, origin, material, or ownership, and also in impersonal expressions and expressions of time:

¿Quién es?	"Who is it?"
Soy yo.	"It's me."
¿De dónde es?	"Where's he from?"
Es de Cuba.	"He's from Cuba."
Yo soy español.	"I'm a Spaniard."
Ella es pintora.	"She's a painter."
Esa mesa es de madera.	"That table's made of wood."
¿De quién es?	"Whose is it?"
Es de ella.	"It's hers."

Es para ti.	"It's for you."
¿Qué hora es?	"What time is it?"
Son las cinco.	"It's five o'clock."
Es tarde.	"It's late."
Pero es necesario ir.	"But it's necessary to **go**."
Es evidente.	"It's evident."

2. *estar* "be" is used to express a temporary condition, location, and also as the auxiliary of the progressive tense:

¿Cómo está Ud.?	"How are you?"
¿Dónde está el libro?	"Where's the book?"
Está sobre la mesa.	"It's on the table."
Ellos están en Chile.	"They're in Chile."
¿Quién está hablando?	"Who's speaking?"
El niño está jugando.	"The child's playing."
Ella está enferma.	"She's sick."

a) In order to determine whether to use *ser* or *estar* when the predicate is an adjective, the following rule should be kept in mind: *ser* is used when the predicate adjective indicates the nature of an object or an inherent characteristic (1, below); *estar* is used when the predicate adjective indicates a temporary condition (2, below):

(1) *La lechuga es verde.*	"Lettuce is green." (by nature)
(2) *La fruta está verde.*	"The fruit's green." (a state of the fruit)
(1) *María es pálida.*	"Mary's pale." (by nature)
(2) *María está pálida.*	"Mary looks pale."
(1) *Es un hombre raro.*	"He's a queer man."
(2) *Está muy raro hoy.*	"He acts very queer today."

b) *estar* should never be used with a predicate noun.

c) *ser* should never be used with the past participle except to form an unequivocal passive voice:

La ventana está abierta.	"The window's open."
La ventana fué abierta por María.	"The window was opened by Mary."
La casa está bien construida.	"The house is well built."
La casa fué construida en 1945.	"The house was built in 1945."

3. *haber* never means "have" in the sense of "possess". This meaning is rendered by *tener: el tiene el libro* "he has the book".

a) When *haber* is not used as an auxiliary verb to form the compound tenses, it is an impersonal verb corresponding to English "there is, there are, there was, there were", etc., and as such has the form *hay* in the present tense:

Hay tres libros sobre la mesa.	"There are three books on the table."
Hay un hombre en la habitación.	"There's a man in the room."

16

b) In all other tenses the impersonal form is identical with the **third** person singular of the auxiliary:

había	"there was, there were"
hubo	"there was, there were"
habrá	"there'll be"
habría	"there'd be"

4. *tener*, which means "have" in the sense of "possess", used with *que* + infinitive expresses a strong obligation equivalent to English "have to, must":

Tenemos que hacerlo hoy. "We must do it today."

a) *hay que* is substituted for *tener que* in impersonal constructions **and** is translated into English as "must, it's necessary":

Hay que decir la verdad. "It's necessary to (One must) tell the truth."

b) *tener* as used in many idioms is translated "be" in English. In **such** cases the Spanish adjective *mucho* is rendered in English by the adverb **"very"**:

Tengo hambre.	"I'm hungry."
Tengo mucha hambre.	"I'm very hungry."
Tengo sed.	"I'm thirsty."
Tengo frío.	"I'm cold."
Tengo miedo.	"I'm afraid."
Tengo prisa.	"I'm in a hurry."

5. The pronoun "it", which is used in the impersonal construction **in** English, is never required in Spanish:

Llueve.	"It's raining."	*Escampa.*	"It's clearing off."
Truena.	"It's thundering."	*Hace fresco.*	"It's cool."

6. *hacer* is used impersonally in expressions of weather:

Hace calor.	"It's warm."	*Hace frío.*	"It's cold."

a) *hace . . . que, hacía . . . que*, and *hace (hacía)* preceded by *desde* **may** be used to indicate time elapsed:

Hace dos días que llegó.	"It's two days since he arrived."
Está aquí desde hace dos días.	"He's been here two days."
No la había visto desde hacía dos años.	"I hadn't seen her for two years."

III. Phrase Structure

Two or more words may be combined into groups of words, or **phrases,** which are used in sentences to take the place of, and fulfill the functions of, the various parts of speech. In this section we shall list the main types of phrases which occur in Spanish, according to the parts of speech whose place they take. We shall use the term **head** to refer to the central word of the phrase, and **modifier** to refer to a word modifying the head: thus, in English "good boy", the noun "boy" is the head of the phrase and "good" is a modifier.

2.0 **Universal phrase types** are such as occur with all parts of speech. In them two or more heads, usually belonging to the same part of speech, are

17

placed next to each other, either not connected at all or connected by conjunctions.

1. No conjunction is present in some phrases which serve to enumerate things, actions, etc:

Se lo dije una, dos, tres veces. "I told him once, twice, three times."

Museos, escuelos, templos, todo "Museums, schools, and churches— *lo saquearon.* they pillaged everything."

2. A conjunction is used in other phrases:

a) Before the last head: *el hambre, el frío, la fatiga, y demás dolores* "hunger, cold, fatigue, and other sorrows".

b) Before each head: *ni esto ni aquello* "neither this nor that".

2.1 Noun phrases normally contain a noun as their head, and an adjective or other element as modifier. This modifier may occur either before or after the head of the phrase, giving two main types of noun phrases:

2.11 Modifier+head. This order occurs primarily when the modifier is:

1. One of the adjectives mentioned in §1.13: *buen(o)* "good", *gran(de)* "great", *cien(to)* "100", *mal(o)* "bad", *postrer(o)* "last", *primer(o)* "first", *San(to)* "Saint", *tercer(o)* "third", and *un(o)** "one"; or one of certain others: *pequeño* "little", *viejo* "old", *bonito* "pretty".

2. A numeral: *diez hombres* "ten men".

3. An interrogative or indefinite adjective: *¿cuáles libros?* "which books?"; *otras personas* "other persons"; *los demás libros* "the other books".

2.12 Head+modifier. This order is the normal one when the modifier is:

1. An adjective other than the types mentioned in §2.11: *un hombre fuerte* "a strong man"; *una puerta abierta* "an open door".

2. An adjective phrase (adverb+adjective), or a phrase consisting of preposition+noun, pronoun, or verb: *un hombre muy fuerte* "a very strong man"; *un vaso de agua* "a glass of water"; *su libro de él* "his book"; *la casualidad de haberse encontrado con ella* "the chance of having met her".

3. A clause, normally introduced by a relative pronoun or adjective: *un caballero que desea hablarle* "a gentleman who wants to talk to you".

2.13 Reversal of normal order of adjective and head in a noun phrase (placing the adjective before the noun when it would normally follow, or vice versa) gives to the adjective an added meaning of emphasis, rhetorical ornament, or figurative speech: *la blanca nieve* "the white, white snow"; *cierta ciudad* "a certain city"; *un hombre malo* "a very bad man".

2.14 Phrase markers are certain types of words which may precede any noun or noun phrase and mark it as such. They are:

1. The definite article (§1.22): *la infeliz madre* "the unhappy mother"; *los libros escritos en español* "the books written in Spanish".

2. The indefinite article *un, una*, which in the singular has the meaning "a, an" and in the plural "some": *un libro interesante* "an interesting book"; *unos libros interesantes* "some interesting books".

---

* *Uno* used as a pronoun does not drop the *o*.

3. A possessive adjective: *mi viejo amigo* "my old friend".

4. A demonstrative adjective: *estos cinco libros* "these five books".

2.2 Adjective phrases are of the following types:

2.21 Modifier+head. The modifier in this type of phrase is normally an adverb· *muy bonito* "very pretty". A special formation of this type is the comparative and superlative of adjectives: *más* "more" or *menos* "less" placed before an adjective makes a phrase with comparative meaning: *más interesante* "more interesting"; *menos útil* "less useful". The definite article placed before a phrase containing a comparative adjective gives it the meaning of a superlative: *el más interesante* "the most interesting"; *el menos útil* "the least useful".

2.22 Head+modifier. The modifier may be one of the following:

1. A phrase introduced by a preposition: *esta agua es buena para beber* "this water's good to drink".

2. A clause introduced by *que* or *de* "than" or *como* "as" (often elliptical) after a comparative phrase (§2.21): *más habladora que su madre* "more talkative than her mother"; *tiene tantas tarjetas como ella* "he has as many cards as she".

2.3 Pronoun phrases have the structure head+modifier. The modifier may be:

1. An adjective: *yo solo* "I alone".

2. A phrase introduced by a preposition: *el de mi padre* "the one of my ather, my father's".

3. A clause: *lo que me gusta* "that which pleases me, what I like".

2.4 Verb phrases are of the following types:

2.41 Verb+verb. These may be classified according to the form of the second verb in the phrase:

1. Past participle. The first verb may be:

a) *haber* "have", which forms perfect tenses with the past participle of other verbs. In such phrases, the past participle is always in the masculine singular: *ha enviado los libros* "he's sent the books"; *los libros que ha enviado* "the books he's sent"; *los ha enviado* "he's sent them".

b) *ser* "be", which forms passive tenses with the past participle of other verbs. This type of phrase is chiefly literary in use; the past participle agrees in gender and number with the subject: *este libro fué escrito por Pérez Galdós* "this book was written by Pérez Galdós".

c) *estar* "be", *tener* "have", *quedarse* "remain", and similar verbs. The past participle agrees in gender and number with the noun to which it refers: *la puerta está abierta* "the door's open"; *los niños estaban sentados en el suelo* "the children were sitting on the floor"; *tengo escrita la carta* "I have the letter written".

2. Gerund, with *estar* "be", *seguir* "keep on", etc, as the first verb. This construction is equivalent to the English present progressive, which consists of a form of "be"+a verb form in "-ing": *está hablando* "he's talking".

3. Infinitive. The first verb is one which indicates desire, ability, obligation, cause, intention, or emotion: *debo irme* "I have to go away"; *creía haberlo* *visto* "he thought he'd seen it". Among the many verbs which occur in this construction are·

acostumbrar "be accustomed to"	*mandar* "order to, command to"
bastar "be enough to"	*necesitar* "need to"
conseguir "succeed in"	*parecer* "seem to, appear to"
creer "believe, think"	*pensar* "intend to"
deber "ought, should"	*poder* "be able to"
decidir "decide to"	*procurar* "try to"
dejar "let, allow to"	*querer* "wish to"
desear "wish to, desire to"	*resolver* "decide to"
gustar "like, be pleasing to"	*saber* "know how to"
hacer "cause to, have done"	*servirse* "be so kind as to"
intentar "attempt to, try to"	*temer* "fear, be afraid"
lograr "succeed in"	*ver* "see"

2.42 Verb+direct object, which is normally a noun, pronoun, or clause: *no tenemos libros* "we haven't any books"; *no me tratan bien* "they don't treat me well"; *quiero que estén contentos* "I want them to be happy". But this construction is normally replaced by that of verb+indirect object (cf §2.44.3) with proper nouns or nouns referring to specific persons (or personified objects or animals), and with disjunctive personal pronouns, relative, demonstrative, and indefinite pronouns referring to persons (except *que*).

2.43 Verb+predicate complement, which is normally a noun or pronoun used after *ser* or *estar* "be" and certain other verbs indicating identity or development, and agreeing with the subject in gender and number: *mi amigo es abogado* "my friend's a lawyer"; *estamos cansados* "we're tired".

2.44 Verb+adverbial complement. This latter may be:

1. An adverb: *habla muy bien* "he speaks very well".

2. An adjective or noun used as an adverb: *el enemigo atacó duro* "the enemy attacked hard".

3. A phrase introduced by a preposition: *sigue viviendo a la antigua* "he continues to live in the old way"; *nos entendimos por fin* "we understood each other at last". This type of adverbial complement, with the preposition *a*, is normal instead of a direct object, in referring to a person (cf 2.42, above). Furthermore, the preposition *a* is normally used to introduce an infinitive after most verbs indicating motion, beginning, teaching, and learning, among others the following:

acostumbrarse "become accustomed"	*empezar* "begin"
acudir "come up, run"	*enseñar* "teach"
aprender "learn"	*invitar* "invite"
atreverse "dare"	*ir* "go"
ayudar "help"	*llegar* "come, succeed"
comenzar "begin"	*negarse* "refuse"
correr "run"	*obligar* "oblige"
decidirse "decide"	*ponerse* "start, begin"
disponerse "get ready"	*probar* "try"

resistirse "resist"
subir "go up, come up"
tornar "return, do again"

venir "come"
volver "return, come back"

The preposition *de* is normally used to introduce an infinitive after the following verbs:

> *acabar* "finish, have just . . ."
> *acordarse* "remember (to)"
> *cansarse* "get tired (of)"
> *cesar* "stop"
> *dejar* "stop, fail (to)"
> *guardarse* "take care not (to)"
> *haber* "have (to), be going (to)"
> *olvidarse* "forget (to)"
> *quejarse* "complain (of)"
> *tratar* "try (to)"; (reflexive) "be a question (of)"

The preposition *en* is used after the following (and other) verbs:

complacerse "take pleasure (in)"
consentir "consent (to)"
consistir "consist (of)"
convenir "agree (to)'
empeñarse "insist (on)"

insistir "insist (on)"
pensar "think (of, about)"
persistir "persist (in)"
tardar "delay (in)"

4. A clause: *Antes venía porque me obligaban.* "I used to come because they forced me to."

2.5 Adverb phrases are normally of the structure modifier+head, with the modifier another adverb: *muy bien* "very well". An adverb phrase with *más* "more" or *menos* "less" as modifier has the meaning of the English comparative or superlative of an adverb: *más tarde* "later"; *menos bien* "less well".

Phrases consisting of preposition+noun, pronoun, or verb may also be used adverbially: *en el zaguán saludó a la portera* "he greeted the janitress in the main entrance".

2.6 Preposition phrases normally consist of an adverb (or equivalent phrase) followed by a preposition: *junto a* "together with"; *a pesar de* "in spite of".

2.61 Prepositional phrases are used in Spanish where in English two or more nouns can be combined to form compound nouns*: *máquina de coser* "sewing machine"; *ropa para caballeros* "men's wear"; *neumático de repuesto* "spare tire".

2.7 Conjunction phrases usually consist of an adverb or preposition or equivalent phrase followed by a subordinate conjunction (normally *que* "that"): *para que* "in order that"; *sin que* "without".

IV. Clause Structure

3.0 The **clause** is the basic unit of the sentence in Spanish as in English. Clauses are either **major** or **minor**; major clauses are the customary normal

---

* In Spanish there are only a few genuine compounds of the type of *ferrocarril* "railroad", *radiodifusión* "broadcasting", which generally have an initial member ending in -*o*.

type, and minor clauses are all others. The structure of major clauses and their combinations will be discussed in §§3.1–3.53; of minor clauses, in §§3.6–3.62. A major clause always contains a predicate and may or may not contain a subject as well.

3.1 The **predicate** always has as its main element a verb or verb phrase: *nos inclinamos para ver mejor* "we bent over to see better"; *estoy cansado* "I'm tired"; *han matado a la señora* "they've killed the lady". Since the verb indicates by its endings the person and number of the agent, a predicate often occurs alone (as in the above examples), where English would have a pronoun subject.

3.2 The **subject** may be one of the following:

1. A noun or noun phrase: *Inglaterra es grande y bella* "England is great and beautiful"; *las antiguas explotaciones petrolíferas han sido abandonadas* "the old oil drillings have been abandoned".

2. An adjective or other part of speech serving as noun: *todo le ayudaba* "everything helped him"; *lo mejor y más granado* "the finest and most select type".

3. A pronoun: *él iba delante* "he went first"; *me gusta éste* "I like this one".

3.21 **Agreement in number.** The subject normally agrees in number with the verb of the predicate: *lo hago yo* "I'll do it"; *lo hacemos nosotros* "we'll do it".

3.22 **Agreement in person.** The verb of the predicate is normally in the grammatical person of the lowest-numbered person represented in the subject. (*usted, ustedes* "you" naturally count as third person in this respect.) If the subject contains heads belonging to two different grammatical persons, the verb is in the first person if the first person element is present, otherwise in the second: *nos casaremos, tú y yo* "we'll get married, you and I".

3.23 **Agreement in gender.** A predicate complement (§2.43) agrees in number and gender with the subject: *él estaba cansado* "he was tired"; *las señoritas estaban cansadas* "the young ladies were tired".

3.3 **Order of subject and predicate** is much freer in Spanish than in English. In general, the normal order is subject+predicate; inversion of this order implies emphasis or rhetorical force, but is very frequent: *eso lo hago yo* "I'll do that"; *así continuaba el joven* "the young man continued thus". Inverted order is normal in a clause containing a subjunctive used as an imperative: *quítese usted el sombrero* "take off your hat".

Likewise the direct object, predicate complement, or adverbial complement is often placed before the verb and subject, giving a meaning of greater emphasis than does the normal order: *eso es* "that's it" (literally, "it is that"); *el que no se entera de nada soy yo* "I'm the one who doesn't understand"; *mejor será avisar a la policía* "it'll be better to notify the police"; *mucho lo siento* "I'm very sorry". In a sentence containing a specifically interrogative word, the phrase containing this word comes first: *¿qué quiere usted?* "what do you want?"; *¿desde cuándo le conoces?* "since when have you known him?"

3.4 **Coordination** is the relation to each other of two or more clauses of equal rank in a sentence. Of two coordinate clauses, the second is usually joined to the first by a coordinating conjunction, such as *pero* "but", *y* "and".

The conjunction *que* may introduce an independent or coordinate clause when followed by a verb in the subjunctive indicating a command: *que lo haga él* "let him do it".

3.5 Subordination. If a clause has, in another clause, the function of one of the parts of speech, and modifies some element of that clause, it is said to be **subordinate** to or **dependent** on the element it modifies. Subordinate clauses are normally introduced by a subordinating conjunction, often one formed with *que* "that". The use of a clause in a subordinate position often requires the use of a subjunctive form in the main verb of the subordinate clause. The use of the subjunctive may be automatic, i.e. obligatory in certain constructions. In others, the use of the subjunctive is not obligatory, and its use is significant, i.e. it gives the clause a different meaning than the use of the indicative would.

3.51 Automatic use of the subjunctive is found in the following types of subordinate clauses:

1. Those containing certain verbs:

a) Verbs whose general meaning is that of desire, command, judgment or opinion, emotion, or doubt. The chief of these verbs are:

agradecer "be grateful"	*mandar* "command"
alegrarse "be glad"	*pedir* "ask"
dejar "let, allow"	*perdonar* "forgive"
deplorar "regret"	*permitir* "permit, allow"
desear "desire"	*preferir* "prefer"
estar "be" + certain adjectives (e.g.	*prohibir* "forbid"
contento (de) "glad", *enojado*	*querer* "want, wish"
"annoyed")	*sentir* "be sorry"
gustar "like"	*sorprenderse* "be surprised"
impedir "hinder"	*sugerir* "suggest"
insistir (en) "insist (on)"	*tener miedo (de)* "be afraid"

b) Impersonal expressions (used only in the third person singular) in which *ser* "be" is followed by any of a number of adjectives, among them:

bueno "good"	*malo* "bad"
difícil "difficult"	*mejor* "better"
extraño "strange"	*necesario* "necessary"
fácil "easy"	*peor* "worse"
importante "important"	*posible* "possible"
justo "right"	*probable* "probable"

c) Verbs, usually when they are in the negative or interrogative, whose general meaning is that of perceiving, thinking, knowing, declaring; the meaning given by use of the subjunctive is that of uncertainty or doubt. The most important of the determining verbs are:

concebir "conceive, imagine"	*juzgar* "judge"
creer "believe"	*pensar* "think"
decir "say"	*saber* "know"
estimar "consider"	*suponer* "suppose"

But after such verbs as *dudar* "doubt" and *negar* "deny", with essentially negative meaning, the subjunctive is used when the main verb is in the positive, and the indicative when it is in the negative: *dudo que sea posible* "I doubt that it's possible".

2. Clauses serving as adverbs: after a number of conjunctions, such as:

a condición que "on condition that"	*aun cuando* "even if"
a fin (de) que "in order that"	*para que* "so that"
a menos que "unless"	*supuesto que* "supposing that"

3.52 Significant use of the subjunctive is found in the following types of clauses:

1. Clauses used as adjectives, giving the clauses the meaning of:

a) A desired characteristic or purpose: *busco un libro que sea interesante* "I'm looking for a book that'll be interesting".

b) Uncertainty or doubt: *las expresiones que Uds. hayan olvidado* "the expressions you may have forgotten". This type of clause is especially frequent after indefinite and concessive expressions: *cualquier libro que escriba* "whatever book he may write"; *por rico que sea* "no matter how rich he may be". It is also found after superlatives or equivalent expressions: *el libro más interesante que haya* "the most interesting book there is".

2. Clauses used as adverbs, giving the meaning of:

a) Intent, purpose, or anticipation: *hable Ud. de manera que todos le oigan* "talk in such a way that all can hear you"; *aunque venga, no nos lo enseñará* "even though he may come, he won't show it to us".

b) Futurity: *cuando venga, dígaselo* "when he comes, tell it to him".

3.53 Conditional sentences. If a sentence contains a clause beginning with *si* "if", the tense of the verb in this clause is determined by the tense of the verb in the main clause, normally as follows:

IF THE MAIN CLAUSE HAS A VERB IN THE:	THE "IF"-CLAUSE HAS A VERB IN THE:
Present ⎫	
Imperative ⎬	Present
Future ⎭	
Imperfect	Imperfect
Preterite	Preterite
Conditional	Past Subjunctive (*-ra* or *-se*)

Thus: *si está aquí, trabaja* "if he's here, he's working"; *si estaba aquí, trabajaba* "if he was here, he was working"; *si está aquí mañana, trabajará* "if he's here tomorrow, he'll be working"; *si estuviera aquí, trabajaría* "if he were here, he'd be working". A main verb indicating a condition contrary to fact may also be in the *-ra* form of the subjunctive: *si estuviera aquí, trabajara* "if he were here, he'd be working".

3.6 Minor clauses, which do not conform to the customary structure of clauses, are chiefly of the following two types:

24

3.61 Fragmentary or elliptical clauses: a phrase or single word, such as could enter into the structure of a full clause if the rest of a full clause were uttered. Under this type come most cases of incomplete sentences in normal conversation, answers to questions, etc: *¿Qué le dijo?—Nada.* "What did he say to him?—Nothing."; *Buenos días. ¿Cómo está Ud.?—Muy bien, gracias. ¿Y Ud.?* "Hello. How are you?—Very well, thanks. And you?"

3.62 Interjectional clauses, consisting of words which do not have the inflection or function of any of the parts of speech, and may be used as separate utterances or joined with other clauses: *¡Ah!* "Ah!"; *¡Ay!* "Ouch!"; *¡Hola!* "Hello!"; *¡Oh!* "Oh!"; etc.

A

a to *Voy a Barcelona.* I'm going to Barcelona.—*Vamos a casa.* Let's go home. —*Se lo dimos al hombre.* We gave it to the man. ▲at *Vengan Uds. a las dos.* Come at two o'clock. ▲on, upon *Al salir de la casa, la vimos.* We saw her on leaving the house. ▲later *Nos marchamos a los cuatro días.* We left four days later. ▲by *La carta estaba escrita a mano.* The letter was written by hand. ▲on *Fuimos a pie.* We went on foot. ▲from *Se lo compré a Juan.* I bought it from John.
○**a no ser que** if . . . not *Le veré, a no ser que venga demasiado tarde.* I'll see him if he doesn't come too late. ‖ *Quiero ver a Nueva York* [*Am*]. I want to see New York. ‖ *¡A que no sabes donde estuve anoche!* I bet you can't guess where I was last night!

abajo below, down, downstairs *Estoy aquí abajo.* I'm down here.
○**boca abajo** face down. ○**cuesta abajo** downhill *No vaya Ud. tan de prisa en la cuesta abajo.* Don't drive so fast downhill. ○**de abajo** lower *Los pisos de abajo son muy oscuros.* The lower floors are very dark. ○**de arriba abajo** from top to bottom, from head to foot *Lo examinó de arriba abajo.* He examined it from top to bottom. ○**desde abajo** from below *Desde abajo la casa parecía muy alta.* From below, the house seemed very tall. ○**hacia abajo** downward, down *Cuando pase el puente no mire hacia abajo.* When you cross the bridge, don't look down. ○**por abajo** at *or* around the bottom, down there *El pantalón estaba gastado por abajo.* The trousers were worn at the bottom.

abandonado (see **abandonar**) [*adj*] negligent, sloppy *Es muy abandonado en su manera de vestir.* He's very sloppy in his dress.

abandonar to abandon, leave *Abandonó a su mujer.* He left his wife. ▲to neglect *Abandona su trabajo a menudo.* He frequently neglects his work.

abanicar(se) to fan (oneself) *Como hacía calor, se abanicaba.* As it was warm, she was fanning herself.

abanico fan *Compró un abanico chino.* She bought a Chinese fan.

abarrotes [*m pl*] ○**tienda de abarrotes** grocery store [*Mex*].

abatir to depress *Las noticias le han abatido mucho.* The news depressed him very much.

abeja bee.

abertura opening (of material) *La abertura de este jersey es pequeña y no me cabe la cabeza.* The opening in this sweater's small and my head won't go through.

abierto (see **abrir**) open *Las ventanas están abiertas.* The windows are open.

ablandar to soften *El asfalto se ablandó con el calor.* The asphalt was softened by the heat.

abogado lawyer.

abolir to abolish.

abollar to dent, batter *El guardabarros quedó todo abollado.* The fender was badly dented.

abonar to pay *Abonaremos la diferencia.* We'll pay the difference. ▲to fertilize *Esta es la mejor época de abonar los campos.* This is the best time to fertilize the fields.
○**abonarse** to subscribe *Me voy a abonar a estos conciertos de música de cámara.* I'm going to subscribe to these chamber-music concerts.

abono commutation ticket; subscription; fertilizer.

abrasar to burn *La casa se abrasó.* The house burned to the ground.

abrazar to embrace, hug.

abrazo embrace, hug.

abrelatas [*m sg*] can opener.

abreviar to shorten; to abbreviate.

abreviatura abbreviation.

abrigar to warm *Estas mantas abrigan mucho.* These blankets are very warm. ▲ to shelter, protect *La pared me abrigaba de la lluvia.* The wall protected me from the rain.

○ **abrigarse** to wrap oneself, dress warmly *Abríguese bien antes de salir.* Wrap up well before you go out.

abrigo overcoat.

abril [m] April.

abrir [irr] to open *Haga el favor de abrir la puerta.* Please open the door.— *¿Cuándo han abierto el cajón?* When was the box opened? ▲ to unlock *Con esta llave abra Ud. el armario.* Unlock the cabinet with this key.

○ **abrirse** to withdraw, back out [Am] *Si se abren Uds. no se hará el negocio.* If you back out the deal won't go through. ○ **abrirse paso, abrirse camino** to make one's way *Se abría paso entre la multitud.* He was making his way through the crowd.

abrochar to buckle, button *Abróchale el cinturón al niño.* Buckle the child's belt.—*Tengo que abrocharme la chaqueta.* I have to button my jacket.

absoluto ○ **en absoluto** (not) at all *"¿Le molesta a Ud.?" "No, en absoluto."* "Do you mind?" "Not at all."—*"¿Rehusó Ud. hacerlo?" "¡En absoluto!"* "Did you refuse to do it?" "Not at all!"

absorber to absorb.

absurdo absurd; absurdity.

abuela grandmother.

abuelo grandfather.

abundancia abundance.

abundante abundant.

aburrir to bore *Aburre a todo el mundo.* He bores everybody.

abusar de to abuse *El gobernador abusó de su autoridad.* The governor abused his authority. ▲ to betray *Abusó de mi confianza.* He betrayed my confidence.

abuso abuse (of power); betrayal (of confidence).

acá here, this way *Venga Ud. acá.* Come here.

○ **por acá** around here *Espero que le veamos por acá pronto.* I hope we'll be seeing you around here soon.

acabado (see **acabar**) [adj] *Este mueble está muy bien acabado.* This piece of furniture has a fine finish. ▲ exhausted, worn out [Am] *Estoy acabado.* I'm worn out. ▲ [m] finish *El acabado de la mesa era perfecto.* The finish of the table was perfect.

acabar to finish, end, terminate *Acabe Ud. su trabajo pronto.* Finish your work quickly. ▲ to put an end to *Acabemos esta discusión.* Let's put an end to this discussion.

○ **acabar con** to exhaust, use up *Han acabado con todos los recursos del país.* They exhausted all the resources of the country. ▲ to wipe out *Acabaron con el enemigo.* They wiped out the enemy. ○ **acabar de** to have just *Acabo de llegar.* I've just arrived. ○ **acabar por** to end by *Acabaré por volverme loco.* I'll end up by going crazy. ○ **acabarse** to run out of *Se me acabó el dinero.* I ran out of money.

academia academy.

acalenturado feverish [Am] *El enfermo está acalenturado esta tarde.* The patient's feverish this afternoon.

acalorarse to become heated *or* excited *La discusión se acaloró.* The argument became heated. ▲ to get overheated *Me acaloré jugando al beisbol.* I got overheated playing baseball.

acariciar to caress, pet *Acariciaba al perro.* He was petting the dog.

acarrear to carry (a load).

acaso perhaps, maybe *Acaso venga mañana.* Maybe he'll come tomorrow. ▲ by chance *¿Acaso lo tiene Ud.?* Do you have it by any chance?

○ **por si acaso** just in case *Por si acaso lo necesita, lleve Ud. dinero.* Take some money just in case you need it.

accidental accidental.

accidente [m] accident, mishap, chance.

acción [f] action *Esas tropas van a entrar en acción.* Those troops are going into action. ▲ plot (of a drama) *La acción se desarrolla rápidamente.* The plot develops rapidly.

aceite [m] oil.

aceituna olive.

acento stress, accent *Esta palabra tiene el acento en la última sílaba.* This word's stressed on the last syllable. ▲ accent, pronunciation *Tiene buen acento.* He has a good accent.

acentuar to accent.

aceptar to accept.

acera sidewalk.

acerca de about, concerning *No sé nada acerca de eso.* I don't know anything about that.

acercar to bring near *Acérqueme una silla, por favor.* Bring up a chair for me, please.

○ **acercarse a** to approach *Se acercó a la puerta.* He approached the door.

acero steel.

acertar [*rad-ch I*] to guess right *Gana el que acierte el número.* Whoever guesses the number wins.

○ **acertar con** to locate, find *No acertó con la casa.* He couldn't find the house.

○ **acertar en** to hit (a mark) *Acertó en el centro del blanco.* He hit the bull's-eye.

ácido sour *Estas naranjas son muy ácidas.* These oranges are very sour. ▲ [*m*] acid.

acierto good judgment, good choice *Es un acierto este traje que se ha comprado Ud.* That suit you bought's a good choice.

aclamación [*f*] acclamation *Fué elegido por aclamación.* He was elected by acclamation.

aclamar to acclaim, applaud.

aclaración [*f*] explanation.

aclarar to make clear, clarify *Hay que aclarar este asunto.* This matter must be clarified. ▲ to brighten, clear up *Parece que el día aclara.* It seems to be clearing up.

acogida reception *Tuvieron una calurosa acogida.* They got a warm reception.

acometer to attack.

acomodado (see **acomodar**) well-to-do *Es una familia acomodada.* It's a well-to-do family.

acomodador [*m*] usher.

acomodar to put, place *Acomode bien las maletas en la red.* Put the suitcases carefully on the rack.

○ **acomodarse** to adapt oneself *Se acomoda a las circunstancias.* She adapts herself to circumstances. ▲ to make oneself comfortable *Acomódense, que tenemos tiempo de sobra.* Make yourselves comfortable, for we have plenty of time.

acomodo job, position *Está buscando acomodo.* He's looking for a job.

acompañar to accompany.

aconsejar to advise.

acontecimiento event.

acorazado battleship.

acordar [*rad-ch I*] to agree to, on, *or* upon *Lo acordaron por unanimidad.* They agreed to it unanimously.

○ **acordarse de** to remember, recollect *¿Se acuerda Ud. de esto?* Do you remember this?

acortar to shorten *Haga el favor de acortar la chaqueta.* Would you please shorten the jacket.

○ **acortar la marcha** to slow down.

acostar [*rad-ch I*] to put to bed *Ya es hora de acostar a los niños.* It's time

to put the children to bed. ▲ to lay *Se puso enfermo y lo acostaron en un banco.* He became sick and they laid him on a bench.

○ **acostarse** to go to bed *Se acuesta temprano pero tarda en dormirse.* He goes to bed early but it takes him a long time to get to sleep. ○ **estar acostado** to be lying down *Estaba acostado en el diván.* He was lying on the couch.

acostumbrarse a to get accustomed to.

acrecentar [*rad-ch I*] to increase.

acreditado accredited *Es un representante acreditado del gobierno francés.* He's an accredited representative of the French government. ▲ of good reputation *Es un médico acreditado.* He's a doctor of good reputation. ▲ solvent *Es una firma acreditada.* It's a solvent firm.

acreedor [*m*] creditor *Le persiguen los acreedores.* His creditors are after him.

actitud [*f*] attitude.

actividad [*f*] activity *En la oficina ha habido mucha actividad esta mañana.* There's been a lot of activity around the office this morning.

○ **actividades** activities *Además de su empleo tiene otras muchas actividades.* In addition to his regular job, he has a lot of other activities.

activo active.

acto act *Fué un acto de valor.* It was an act of courage. ▲ ceremony *El acto tuvo lugar por la tarde.* The ceremony took place in the afternoon. ▲ act (of a play) *Ahora va a empezar el tercer acto.* The third act is about to begin.

○ **en el acto** right away *Lo hizo en el acto.* He did it right away.

actor [*m*] actor.

actriz [*f*] actress.

actual present, current *Las circunstancias actuales son desfavorables.* Present circumstances are unfavorable.

actualidad [*f*] present time *En la actualidad escasea el café.* Nowadays coffee is scarce.

actualmente at present, at the present time *Actualmente está en Chicago.* At the present time he's in Chicago.

actuar to act.

acudir to rush *Acudieron en su ayuda.* They rushed to his aid. ▲ to keep (an appointment) *No acudió a la cita.* He didn't keep his appointment.

acuerdo agreement *Llegaron a un acuerdo.* They came to an agreement.

○ **de acuerdo** of the same opinion *Estamos de acuerdo.* We're of the same opinion. ○ **de acuerdo con** in accordance with *Lo hice de acuerdo con sus instrucciones.* I did it according to your instructions.

acumular to accumulate.

acusación [*f*] accusation.

acusado (see **acusar**) [*adj*] accused. ▲ [*n*] defendant.

acusar to accuse *Le acusaron de homicidio.* They accused him of manslaughter. ▲ to acknowledge (in business correspondence) *Acusamos recibo de su carta.* We acknowledge receipt of your letter.

adaptar to adapt.

adecuado adequate, suitable.

adelantado (see **adelantar**) ○ **por adelantado** in advance *En ese hotel hay que pagar por adelantado.* You have to pay in advance in that hotel.

adelantar to surpass, take the lead *Este muchacho adelanta al resto de la clase.* This boy surpasses the rest of the class. —*Adelantaron a todos los demás.* They went ahead of all the others. ▲ to pass *Iban a ochenta kilómetros y nos adelantaron.* They were doing eighty kilometers and they passed us. ▲ to gain time *Su reloj adelanta.* Your watch gains time. ▲ to put ahead *Adelante Ud. su reloj porque está atrasado.* Put your watch ahead; it's slow. ▲ to be fast *Mi reloj está adelantado cinco minutos.* My watch is five minutes fast. ▲ to improve, advance *Su español adelanta poco a poco.* His Spanish is improving little by little.

○ **adelantarse** to beat (someone) to, steal a march on *Yo quería invitarle, pero su amigo se me adelantó.* I wanted to invite you, but your friend beat me to it.

adelante *Siga Ud. adelante.* Go ahead. ○ **en adelante** from now on *De ahora en adelante lo haremos así.* From now on we'll do it this way. ○ **más adelante** later on *Más adelante lo comprenderás.* You'll understand it later on. ▲ farther on *Más adelante encontramos una casa.* Farther on we came upon a house.

‖ *¡Adelante!* Come in! or Forward!

adelanto improvement *Esta casa tiene todos los adelantos.* This house has all the latest improvements.

adelgazar to make thin; to lose weight.

además moreover, furthermore *No tengo ganas de ir y además ya es muy tarde.*

I don't want to go, and besides it's too late.

○ **además de** in addition to, besides *Además de fruta vamos a tomar helado.* Besides fruit we're going to have ice cream.

adentro within, inside *Voy a ir adentro.* I'm going inside.

‖ *¡Adentro!* Come in!

adiós good-by, so long.

adivinar to guess *¿A qué no adivina Ud. lo que me ha ocurrido hoy?* I'll bet you can't guess what happened to me today.

adjunto enclosed. (Used in correspondence.)

administración [*f*] administration, management.

administrador [*m*] manager; superintendent (of a building).

administrar to manage, administer.

admirable admirable, excellent, wonderful.

admiración [*f*] admiration, wonder.

admirar to amaze *Me admira su descaro.* I'm amazed at his nerve. ▲ to admire *Admiraba el trabajo de su amigo.* He admired his friend's work.

○ **admirarse de** to be surprised or amazed at *Se admiraron de su resistencia.* They were amazed at his courage.

admitir to admit *Le han admitido en la escuela de ingenieros.* He was admitted to the engineering school. ▲ to accept *No se admiten propinas.* Tips not accepted. ▲ to let, allow *No admite interrupciones.* He doesn't allow interruptions.

adolescencia adolescence, youth.

adolescente [*adj; n*] adolescent.

adonde where, to what place *Adonde voy tú no puedes ir.* You can't go where I'm going.

○ **¿adónde?** where? where to? *¿Adónde va Ud.?* Where are you going?

adoptar to adopt *Adoptaron una niña.* They adopted a little girl.—*Han adoptado un nuevo plan.* They've adopted a new plan. ▲ to assume *Adoptó un aire de gran importancia.* He assumed an air of great importance.

adorar to worship, adore.

adornar to decorate, fix up *El salón está muy bien adornado para la fiesta.* The room's nicely fixed up for the party. ▲ to trim *El traje estaba adornado con* *encajes.* The dress was trimmed with lace.

adorno ornament, trimming.

adquirir to acquire.

adquisición [*f*] acquisition.

aduana customhouse. ▲ customs *Pagaron derechos de aduana(s).* They paid customs duties.

adulación [*f*] flattery.

adular to flatter.

adulto [*n; adj*] adult.

adversario opponent.

adversidad [*f*] adversity, misfortune.

advertencia warning.

advertir [*rad-ch II*] to notice, observe *Advertí algunos errores en su informe.* I noticed some mistakes in his report. ▲ to advise, warn *Te advierto que no lo hagas otra vez.* I'm warning you not to do it again.—*Ya se lo advertí a Ud.* I told you so.

aéreo aerial, (of the) air *Envíelo por correo aéreo.* Send it airmail.

aeródromo airport.

aeroplano airplane.

afable affable, pleasant.

afán [*m*] anxiety, eagerness.

afanarse to be eager *Muchachos, no se afanen tanto.* Don't be so eager, boys.

afectado (see afectar) affected, unnatural.

afectar to move *La noticia le afectó mucho.* The news moved him deeply.

afecto affection, regard *Les tiene afecto a todos sus compañeros de oficina.* He has regard for all his office companions.

afeitar to shave.
    ○ **afeitarse** to shave (oneself).

afición [*f*] fondness; inclination.

aficionado, aficionada fan *Soy un gran aficionado al beisbol.* I'm a great baseball fan. ▲ amateur *Esta es una compañía de aficionados.* This is an amateur company.
    ○ **aficionado a** fond of *Es muy aficionado a la lectura.* He's very fond of reading.

aficionarse a to become fond of *Se ha aficionado a los deportes.* He's become fond of sports.

afilar to sharpen.

afinidad [*f*] relationship by marriage *Es pariente mío por afinidad.* He's one of my in-laws.

afirmar to affirm, assert, maintain.

afirmativo [*adj*] affirmative.

aflicción [*f*] affliction, sorrow, grief.

afligir to grieve (someone) *Les afligió mucho la pérdida de su madre.* The loss of their mother grieved them very much.
    ○ **afligirse** to grieve *Se afligieron por la desgracia de su amigo.* They grieved over their friend's misfortune.

aflojar to loosen, relax *Afloje Ud. un poco la venda.* Loosen the bandage a little. ▲ to slacken *No aflojen el trabajo en tiempo de guerra.* Don't slacken in your work in war time. ▲ to decrease, let up, subside *La tormenta aflojó.* The storm let up.

afortunadamente fortunately.

afortunado fortunate, lucky.

afuera out, outside *Vamos afuera.* Let's go out.
    ○ **afueras** [*f pl*] suburbs, outskirts *Viven en las afueras de la ciudad.* They live in the suburbs.
    ‖ *¡Afuera!* Get out!

agachar to lower, bend down *Agachen la cabeza que el techo es muy bajo.* Bend down; the ceiling's very low.

agarradero handle.

agarrar to hold, grasp *Agarre Ud. bien la cuerda.* Hold the rope tight. ▲ to catch or contract (illness) *He agarrado un catarro atroz.* I caught an awful cold. ▲ to take [*Arg*].
    ○ **agarrarse** to hold on, catch hold *Se agarró de mi brazo para no caerse.* She caught hold of my arm so she wouldn't fall.

agencia agency (except governmental).

agente [*m*] agent *Es agente de una gran compañía de seguros.* He's agent for a big insurance company. ▲ representative *La compañía ha enviado varios agentes para tratar el asunto.* The company's sent several representatives to discuss the matter.
    ○ **agente (de policia)** policeman [*Am*] *Pregunte al agente dónde está la plaza de Santiago.* Ask the policeman where St. James Square is.

ágil quick, agile *Es ágil de movimientos.* He's quick in his movements.—*Tiene una inteligencia muy ágil.* She has a very quick mind.

agitación [*f*] excitement, agitation.

agitar to shake *Agítese bien antes de usarlo.* Shake well before using. ▲ to stir up, excite *El político agitó a los trabajadores.* The politician stirred up the workers.
    ○ **agitarse** to become excited *Cuando lo oyó se agitó mucho.* When she heard it she got very excited.

agosto August.

agotar to run through, use up, exhaust *Agotaron rápidamente la herencia.* They ran through the inheritance.

O agotarse to wear oneself out *Con tanto trabajo se está agotando.* He's wearing himself out working so much. ▲ to go out of print *La edición se agotó rápidamente.* The edition went out of print quickly. ▲ to give out *Se agotaron las provisiones en poco tiempo.* The provisions gave out in a short time.

agradable agreeable, pleasant.

agradar to be pleasing to *Es un tipo que no me agrada.* I don't like his type.

agradecer [-zc-] to appreciate *Le agradezco mucho su amabilidad.* I appreciate your kindness. ▲ to thank for *Le agradecí mucho su ayuda.* I thanked him very much for his help.

agradecimiento gratitude.

agrado liking *Esto no es de su agrado.* This is not to his liking.

agrandar to enlarge *Van a agrandar su tienda.* They're going to enlarge their store. ▲ to let out (a garment).

agravar to aggravate, make worse *Esto agrava la situación.* This makes the situation worse.

O agravarse to get worse *El enfermo se agravó.* The patient got worse.

agregado See agregar. ▲ [m] attaché *Vimos al agregado militar de la Embajada Americana.* We saw the military attaché of the American Embassy.

agregar to add *Hace falta agregar más detalles al informe.* You have to add more details to the report.

agresión [f] aggression.

agresivo aggressive.

agresor [m] aggressor.

agricultor [m] farmer.

agricultura agriculture.

agrio sour *La toronja está muy agria.* The grapefruit tastes very sour.

agrupar to group.

agua water *Quiere un vaso de agua fresca.* He wants a glass of cold water. ▲ rain *Ahora hace un tiempo de agua.* We're having a rainy spell.

O agua de coco coconut milk. O aguas termales hot springs. O más claro que el agua clear as crystal *Tiene Ud. razón, eso está más claro que el agua.* You're right, that's as clear as crystal.

‖ *¡Hombre al agua!* Man overboard!

aguacate [m] avocado, alligator pear.

aguacero [m] rainstorm *El aguacero de anoche ha cortado el camino.* Last night's storm washed out the road.

aguado O manos aguadas butterfingers [Am] *¡Tienes las manos aguadas!* You have butterfingers.

aguafiestas [m, f; sg] wet blanket, killjoy *No seas aguafiestas.* Don't be a wet blanket.

aguantar to bear, endure, stand *Es asombroso como puede aguantar tanto.* It's amazing how much he can stand.— *Esto no se puede aguantar.* This is unbearable. ▲ to hang on, not give up *¡Aguante duro!* Hang on tight!

O aguantarse to be patient, take it *Hay que aguantarse.* You have to take it.

aguardar to expect *Le aguardamos mañana a las diez.* We expect him tomorrow at ten o'clock. ▲ to wait for *Te estoy aguardando hace horas.* I've been waiting for you for hours.

aguardiente [m] brandy, whiskey.

agudo sharp, keen *El cuchillo tenía la punta muy aguda.* The knife had a very sharp point. ▲ clever *Es un muchacho muy agudo.* He's a very clever boy. ▲ high-pitched *Tiene una voz muy aguda.* She has a very high-pitched voice. ▲ witty *¡Siempre tiene dichos tan agudos!* He's always making such witty remarks! ▲ acute (of an angle) *Las calles forman un ángulo agudo.* The two streets form an acute angle.

águila [f] eagle.

agüita agüita (water flavored with aromatic leaves) [Am] *¿Qué quiere Ud. después de la comida, café, té o agüita de menta?* What would you like after dinner—coffee, tea, or mint water?

aguja needle *¿Tiene Ud. una aguja para coser estos botones?* Do you have a needle to sew on these buttons? ▲ hand (of watch, compass) *A mi reloj se le ha caído una aguja.* One of the hands has fallen off my watch.

O agujas [pl] switch *El tren ha entrado en agujas.* The train's passed the switch.

agujero hole.

aguzar to sharpen to a point *Aguce un poco la estaca.* Sharpen the end of the stick a little.

‖ *Aguzó el oído.* He pricked up his ears.

¡ah! oh!

ahí there *Ahí está su amigo.* There's your friend.—*Qué tiene Ud. ahí en el bolsillo?* What have you got there in your pocket?

O por ahí that way *Por ahí, haga el*

favor. That way, please. ▲ around here *Por ahí anda su sombrero.* Your hat's somewhere around here.
‖ *¿Y de ahí, qué hubo?* Hello there, what's new? [*C.A.*]

ahijada goddaughter.

ahijado godson.

ahogar to choke *Trató de ahogarle.* He tried to choke him.

○ **ahogarse** to drown, to be drowned *Muchos animales se ahogaron en la inundación.* Many animals were drowned in the flood. ▲ to be suffocated *Me ahogo en esta habitación tan pequeña y tan caliente.* This room's so small and hot that I'm suffocating.

ahora now, right now *Ahora voy a casa.* I'm going home now. ▲ now *¿Ahora, qué piensa Ud.?* Now, what do you think?

○ **ahora bien** now, now then *Ahora bien, hay que aclarar este problema.* Now then, let's get this problem cleared up. ○ **ahora mismo** at once, right away *Hágalo ahora mismo.* Do it right away. ▲ just, just now *Salió ahora mismo.* He just left. ○ **de ahora en adelante** from now on *Lo haremos así de ahora en adelante.* We'll do it this way from now on. ○ **hasta ahora** up to now, so far *Hasta ahora nunca hemos tenido este problema.* Up to now we've never had this problem. ○ **por ahora** for the present *Por ahora tenemos bastante comida.* We have enough food for the present.

ahorcar to hang (execute) *Lo ahorcaron el mismo día.* They hanged him the same day.

ahorita right now [*Am*] *Ahorita vamos a verle.* We're going to see him right now.

ahorrar to save *¿Cuánto dinero hemos ahorrado este mes?* How much have we saved this month?

aire [*m*] air *El aire de esta habitación está muy cargado.* The air in this room's very stuffy. ▲ wind *Sopla un aire muy fuerte.* There's a very strong wind blowing. ▲ look, a p p e a r a n c e *Tiene aire de millonario.* He looks like a millionaire.—*Tenía un aire muy cansado.* He looked very tired.

○ **al aire libre** in the open air *Pasamos tres horas al aire libre.* We spent three hours in the open air. ○ **tomar el aire** to get some fresh air.

‖ *Se da aires de persona importante.* He puts on airs.

aislamiento isolation.

aislar to isolate, cut off.

¡ajá! ‖ *¡Ajá! ¿Conque esas tenemos?* So that's what's going on!

ajedrez [*m*] chess.

ajeno another's, someone else's *No se meta en vidas ajenas.* Don't meddle in other people's affairs.

ajo garlic.

○ **echar ajos** to swear *Empezó a echar ajos.* He started swearing. ○ **estar en el ajo** to be in the know.

ajustar to tighten *Tiene Ud. que ajustar esos tornillos.* You have to tighten those screws. ▲ to fit *Esta tapadera no ajusta.* This cover doesn't fit. ▲ to agree about, decide (on) *Se reunieron para ajustar las condiciones de la paz.* They met to decide peace terms. ▲ to settle *Vamos a ajustar las cuentas.* Let's settle accounts.

al (a + el) See **a.**

ala wing; brim (of a hat).

alabanza praise.

alabar to praise.

alacrán [*m*] scorpion.

alambrada wire fence.

alambre [*m*] wire.

alameda mall, public walk (lined with poplars).

álamo poplar.

alarde [*m*] boast.

○ **hacer alarde de** to show off *Levantó el baúl para hacer alarde de fuerza.* He lifted the trunk to show off his strength.

alardear to boast.

alargar to lengthen, extend *Hay que alargar las mangas de este abrigo.* The sleeves of this coat have to be lengthened. ▲ to hand *Haga el favor de alargarme la maleta.* Would you hand me the suitcase, please?

alarma alarm.

alba dawn.

albañil [*m*] mason, bricklayer.

albaricoque [*m*] apricot [*Sp*].

alborotar to disturb, make noise *Los niños están alborotando mucho.* The children are making a lot of noise.

alboroto disturbance, excitement; [*C.A.*] popcorn.

alcachofa artichoke.

alcalde [*m*] mayor.

alcance [*m*] reach *Estaba fuera de su alcance.* It was out of his reach.

alcancía toy bank; collection box.

alcanzado short (of money) *Siempre anda alcanzado de dinero.* He's always short of money.

alcanzar to catch up with, overtake *Nos alcanzaron muy pronto.* They caught up with us quickly. ▲to reach *No puedo alcanzar esa lata de tomate.* I can't reach that can of tomatoes. ▲to attain, reach *Alcanzó el grado de general.* He reached the rank of general.
○ **alcanzar a** to succeed in, can *Desde aquí no alcanzo a verlo.* From here I can't see it.

alcoba bedroom.

alcohol [*m*] alcohol.

alcohólico [*adj; n*] alcoholic.

aldea village.

alegar to allege, state, assert.

alegrar to brighten (up) *Las flores alegrarán la mesa.* The flowers will brighten up the table. ▲to cheer up.
○ **alegrarse** to rejoice, be glad *Me alegro mucho de verla.* I'm very glad to see you.

alegre glad, happy *¿Por qué está Ud. tan alegre hoy?* Why are you so happy today? ▲cheerful *Son gente muy alegre.* They're very cheerful people. ▲brilliant, bright *¡Qué traje tan alegre!* What a bright-colored suit that is! ▲drunk, tipsy *Está un poco alegre.* He's a little tipsy.

alegría delight, joy, pleasure *Mostró gran alegría cuando le vió.* He showed great joy when he saw him.

alejarse to go away *No se aleje demasiado.* Don't go too far away.

alentado well, all right [*Am*] *Estaba enfermo, pero hoy ya está alentado.* He was ill, but today he's all right.

alentar [*rad-ch I*] to comfort, cheer up *Hay que alentarla un poco.* She needs a little cheering up. ▲to encourage *Aliéntele Ud. a que lo haga ahora.* Encourage him to do it.

alfabeto alphabet.

alfiler [*m*] pin.

alfombra carpet, rug.

algo something *¿Tiene Ud. algo que decirme?* Have you something to tell me? ▲rather, somewhat *Me parece algo caro.* It seems rather expensive to me.
○ **algo de** some *¿Tiene Ud. algo de dinero?* Have you got some money?
○ **por algo** for some reason *Por algo me dice Ud. eso.* You must have a reason for telling me. ○ **servir para algo** to be useful, be good for something *No sé si esto le servirá para algo.* I don't know whether this'll be of any use to you.

algodón [*m*] cotton.

alguien somebody, someone *Alguien llama a la puerta.* Somebody's knocking at the door. ▲anybody, anyone *¿Ha venido alguien?* Has anybody come?

algún (see **alguno**) some *Espero que Ud. vuelva algún día.* I hope you'll come again some day.

alguno some, any *Quiero hacerle algunas preguntas.* I want to ask you some questions.—*¿Quiere Ud. hacerme alguna pregunta?* Do you want to ask me any questions?
○ **alguna cosa más** anything else *¿Necesita Ud. alguna cosa más?* Do you need anything else? ○ **alguna vez** now and then, sometimes *Nos visita algunas veces.* He visits us now and then. ○ **algunos** some people *Algunos no tienen paciencia.* Some people have no patience.

alhaja jewel.

aliado allied. ▲ [*n*] ally.

alianza union, alliance.

aliarse to form an alliance, ally oneself.

aliento breath *Llegó sin aliento.* He was out of breath when he got here.
‖ *Es una persona de muchos alientos.* He's a very energetic person.

aligerar to lighten *Tenemos que aligerar la carga.* We have to lighten the load. ▲to hasten, hurry *Aligera porque es tarde.* Hurry up, it's late.

alimentar to feed, nourish *Esta comida no alimenta bastante.* This food's not nourishing enough.

alimento food, nourishment.

alistarse to enlist *Se alistó en la Legión Extranjera.* He enlisted in the Foreign Legion.

alistarse to get ready [*Am*] *Hay que alistarse temprano porque el tren no espera.* We'd better get ready early because the train won't wait.

aliviar to relieve, alleviate.

allá there *¡Allá está!* There it is!
○ **allá arriba** up there, way up *Está allá arriba esperándole.* He's up there waiting for you. ○ **allá dentro** in there, inside *Allá dentro están sus amigos.* Your friends are in there.
○ **hacia allá, para allá** that way *Vamos hacia allá.* Let's go that way. ○ **más allá** farther on, beyond *El pueblo está más allá de aquellos árboles.* The village is beyond those trees. ○ **por allá** over there *Les ví por allá hace un rato.* I saw 'em over there a while ago.

allí there *Póngalo allí.* Put it over there. —*Su casa está allí a la derecha.* His house is there on the right.

○ **de allí** from there *Vive lejos de allí.* She lives far from there. ○ **desde allí** from there *Desde allí se veía perfectamente.* From there one could see perfectly. ○ **por allí** that way *Dice que vayamos por allí.* He says we should go that way.

alma soul.

○ **almas** people *Es un pueblo de tres mil almas.* It's a town of 3000 people. ○ **de mi alma** (term of affectionate address used in Spanish-speaking countries) *¡Hijo de mi alma!* My dear child! ‖ *Lo siento en el alma.* I'm terribly sorry.

almacén [*m*] warehouse, stockroom; store, shop; department store; [*Arg*] grocery store.

almendra almond.

almidón [*m*] starch.

almidonar to starch.

almirante [*m*] admiral.

almohada pillow.

‖ *Lo voy a consultar con la almohada.* I'm going to sleep on it (*i.e.,* think it over).

almohadón [*m*] cushion.

almorzar [*rad-ch I*] to lunch, breakfast.

almuerzo lunch, noon meal; breakfast.

alocado reckless *Es un muchacho muy alocado.* He's a reckless young fellow.

alojamiento lodging.

alojar to put up, lodge, quarter.

alpargata espadrille (sandal with fiber sole and canvas upper).

alquilar to rent, hire *Alquilaron una casa.* They rented a house. ▲ to let *Se alquilan habitaciones.* Rooms for rent.

alquiler [*m*] rent, price of rent.

alrededor ○ **alrededor de** around *Estaban sentados alrededor de la mesa.* They were sitting around the table. ▲ about *Costó alrededor de treinta pesos.* It cost about thirty pesos. ○ **alrededores** [*m pl*] outskirts, surroundings.

altar [*m*] altar.

altavoz [*m*] loudspeaker.

alteración [*f*] alteration, change *Tenemos que hacer algunas alteraciones en nuestros planes.* We have to make some changes in our plans. ▲ strong emotion *Daba muestras de gran alteración.* He showed signs of great emotion.

○ **alteración del orden** tumult, public disorder *Hubo alteraciones del orden en todo el país.* There were disorders all over the country.

alterar to change, transform *Su venida alteró completamente nuestra vida.* His coming changed our lives completely.

○ **alterarse** to get excited *No se altere Ud. que no es nada.* Don't get excited; it's nothing.

alternar to alternate, take turns.

alternativa [*f*] alternative.

alto high, tall *¿Qué es aquel edificio tan alto?* What's that very tall building? ▲ high (in rank) *Habló con un alto empleado del Ministerio de Hacienda.* He talked to a high official of the Treasury Department. ▲ high *Los precios son muy altos en esta tienda.* Prices are very high in this store. ▲ loud *No hables tan alto.* Don't talk so loud.

○ **a altas horas de la noche** very late at night *Volvió a altas horas de la noche.* He returned very late at night. ○ **altos** upper story *Viven en los altos de aquella casa.* They live in the upper story of that house. ○ **lo alto** top *La casa está en lo alto de la colina.* The house is on top of the hill. ○ **pasar por alto** to overlook, forget *Hemos pasado por alto muchos puntos importantes.* We've overlooked many important facts.

alto ○ **hacer alto** to stop, halt *Hicimos alto en el camino para almorzar.* We stopped along the way to have lunch.— *Los soldados hicieron alto a la entrada del pueblo.* The soldiers halted at the entrance to the town.

‖ *¡Alto!* Halt! *or* Stop!

altura height, altitude, elevation *No me encuentro bien a tanta altura.* I don't feel well at such a high altitude.

aludir a to allude to, refer to.

alumbrado See **alumbrar.** ▲ lighting, lighting system *Hay muy poco alumbrado en esta parte de la ciudad.* The lighting's poor in this part of the city.

alumbrar to give light *Los faroles de la calle no alumbran bastante.* The street lamps don't give enough light. ▲ to light, illuminate *¿Puede alumbrar el camino?* Can you light the way?

alumno pupil, student.

alusión [*f*] allusion, reference; hint.

alzar to lift, raise *No alzó los ojos del libro.* He didn't raise his eyes from the book.

○ **alzarse** to rise, revolt *Se alzaron contra el gobierno.* They revolted against the government. ▲ to get up. ○ **alzarse con** to lift, steal, swipe *Se alzó con el dinero.* He stole the money.

amabilidad [*f*] kindness.

amable kind, amiable.

amanecer to dawn *En verano amanece más temprano que en invierno.* In the summer it dawns earlier than in winter.

amanecer [*m*] daybreak, dawn.

amanecida ○ **a la amanecida** at daybreak, at dawn.

amante [*adj*] loving. ▲ [*n*] lover; mistress.

amapola poppy.

amar to love.

amargado (see **amargar**) embittered *Ese tipo está amargado.* That guy's very embittered.

amargar to make bitter, make miserable *Amarga la vida de todos los que le rodean.* He makes life miserable for everyone around him.

amargo bitter.

amargor [*m*] bitterness *No podía soportar el amargor del café.* He couldn't stand the bitterness of the coffee.

amargura bitterness *Sus desgracias le causaron una gran amargura.* His misfortunes caused him great bitterness.

amarillo yellow.

amarrar to tie, fasten.

ambición [*f*] (excessive) ambition.

ambicioso overambitious.

ambiente [*m*] atmosphere, environment.

ambulancia ambulance.

amén amen.

‖ *Dice a todo amén.* He's a yes-man.

amenaza threat, menace.

amenazar to threaten, menace.

americana coat (of a man's suit) [*Sp*].

amigo, amiga friend *Es una amiga mía.* She's a friend of mine.

amistad [*f*] friendship.

○ **hacer amistad** to become friends, make friends (with) *Pronto hicieron amistad.* They soon became friends.— *Hizo amistad con Juan.* He made friends with John. ○ **hacer amistades** to get acquainted *En poco tiempo hizo amistades allí.* He got acquainted there in a short time.

amistoso friendly.

amo, ama owner, proprietor *Hablamos con el amo de la casa.* We talked with the owner of the house. ▲ boss *No se lo digas al amo.* Don't tell the boss.

amontonar to heap, pile up.

amor [*m*] love *Le gusta hablar de amor.* He likes to talk of love. ▲ love, heartthrob *Ha encontrado un nuevo amor.*

He's found a new love. ▲ love, darling *Sí, mi amor.* Yes, darling.

○ **amor propio** self-esteem, pride *Tiene un amor propio excesivo.* He has too much pride.

amoscarse to become peeved *or* irked *Se ha amoscado con tus palabras.* He was peeved by what you said.

amotinarse to mutiny.

amparo aid; protection.

ampliación [*f*] enlargement *Quiero una ampliación de esta fotografía.* I want an enlargement of this photograph.

ampliar to enlarge, amplify, extend.

amplio ample, roomy, large.

amueblar to furnish, supply with furniture *Amueblaron la casa con todo lujo.* They furnished the house very luxuriously.

analfabeto [*adj, n*] illiterate.

análisis [*m or f*] analysis.

analizar to analyze.

anarquía anarchy.

ancho wide, broad *¿Cree Ud. que el camino es bastante ancho para automóviles?* Do you think the road's wide enough for cars? ▲ too big, too wide *Este traje me está ancho.* This suit's too big for me. ▲ width, breadth *¿Qué ancho tiene la tela?* What's the width of the material?

○ **a sus anchas** at ease, comfortable.

anciano aged, very old (of people).

ancla anchor.

andada hike [*Am*] *Dimos la gran andada para llegar a la cumbre.* We took a long hike up to the summit.

andalón [*m*] wanderer, gadabout [*Am*] *Eres muy andalón, muchacho.* You're a great gadabout, my boy.

andar [*irr*] to walk, go on foot *Es demasiado lejos para ir andando.* It's too far to walk. ▲ to go, move *El tren echó a andar.* The train began to move. ▲ to run, go, work *¿Anda ese reloj?* Is that clock going?

○ **andar andando** to roam around [*Mex, Col*] *He andado andando todo el día.* I've been chasing around all day. ○ **andar cerca** to come close to *No se sacó el premio, pero le anduvo cerca.* He didn't win the prize, but he came close to it. ○ **andar en** to be going on [*Am*] *El niño anda en siete años.* The child's going on seven. ○ **andarse por las ramas** to beat around the bush.

‖ *¡Anda!* Move on! *or* Get up! *or* Go ahead! ‖ *¡Ándale!* Go on! *or* Go to it! [*Am*]

andarivel [*m*] cable ferry, aerial cable car [*Am*]. ▲ rail, fence [*Arg*] *El jinete cayó cerca del andarivel.* The jockey fell right by the rail.

andén [*m*] (railroad) platform.

angosto narrow.

ángulo angle.

anillo ring *Le regaló un anillo de brillantes.* He gave her a diamond ring.

animación [*f*] animation, liveliness *La animación de la reunión me sorprendió.* The liveliness of the gathering surprised me.

animado (see **animar**) lively, animated.

animal [*m*] animal. ▲ jackass, stupid person *¡No seas animal!* Don't be a jackass!

animar to cheer, encourage *Vamos a animar a los jugadores.* Let's encourage the players. ▲ to pep up *Su llegada animó la fiesta.* His arrival pepped up the party.

○ **animar a** to encourage to, urge to *Le estoy animando a que venga con nosotros.* I'm urging him to come with us.

ánimo (state of) mind, spirits *Estaba de buen ánimo.* He was in good spirits. ▲ courage.

○ **dar ánimos** to encourage, cheer up *Le dió ánimos porque estaba decaído.* She cheered him up because he was depressed.

aniversario [*m*] anniversary.

anoche last night.

anochecer [-*zc*-] to grow dark, get dark *Ahora anochece a las cinco.* It gets dark at five now.

anochecer [*m*] dusk, nightfall.

ansiedad [*f*] anxiety.

ansioso anxious, eager, impatient *Estoy ansioso de conocerla.* I'm anxious to meet her.

anteanoche night before last.

anteayer day before yesterday.

anteojos [*m pl*] eyeglasses, spectacles.

antepasado [*adj*] before last *El año antepasado fuimos a Europa.* The year before last we went to Europe. ▲ [*n*] ancestor, ancestress.

anterior previous, last.

antes before *Ya se lo dije a Ud. antes.* I told you that before. ▲ formerly *Esta calle tenía otro nombre antes.* This street used to have another name.

○ **antes de** before *Comamos antes de ir.* Let's eat before we go. ○ **antes que** before *Salieron antes que nosotros llegásemos.* They left before we arrived.

ante todo above all, first of all *Ante todo no olvide escribirme.* Above all, don't forget to write me.

anticipar to advance, lend *Me anticipó treinta pesos.* He lent me 30 pesos. ▲ to advance *Anticiparon la fecha de la fiesta.* They advanced the date of the party.

○ **anticiparse** to arrive ahead of time *Se anticiparon media hora.* They arrived half an hour early. ▲ to get ahead of *Se me anticipó.* He got ahead of me.

antiguo former; old, ancient.

○ **a la antigua** in an old-fashioned way *Le gusta vestir a la antigua.* She likes to dress in an old-fashioned way.

antipatía dislike *Me tiene antipatía.* He dislikes me.

antipático disagreeable *Es un hombre muy antipático.* He's a very disagreeable man.

antojarse ‖ *Hace todo lo que se le antoja.* She does whatever comes into her mind. ‖ *Lo hago porque se me antoja.* I do it because I take a notion to.

anunciar to announce; to advertise.

anuncio advertisement; announcement; notice.

añadir to add (to).

año year.

○ **año bisiesto** leap year. ○ **año nuevo** new year *Feliz año nuevo.* Happy New Year. ○ **tener . . . años** to be . . . years old *Tengo veinte años.* I'm twenty years old.

apagar to put out, extinguish *Apague Ud. la luz.* Put out the light.

○ **apagarse** to go out *Se apagaron las luces.* The lights went out.

apagón [*m*] blackout.

aparato apparatus, set *Vende aparatos de radio.* He sells radio sets.

aparecer [-*zc*-] to show up, turn up *No apareció.* He didn't show up.

aparición [*f*] appearance (presence) *Le sorprendió la aparición repentina de su amigo.* He was surprised by the sudden appearance of his friend. ▲ apparition.

apariencia appearance, looks *No me gusta su apariencia.* I don't like his looks.

apartado (see **apartar**) distant, far away.

○ **apartado (de correos)** post office box.

apartamiento apartment [*Am*].

apartar to separate, divide.

aparte separate *Eso es cuestión aparte.* That's a separate question. ▲ aside.

separately *Ponga este paquete aparte.*
Put this package aside.

apearse to get off *Se prohibe apearse en
marcha.* Don't get off while the vehicle's in motion.

apellido (family) name.

apenado sorry, grieved *Estaban apenados
por la enfermedad de su tía.* They
were grieved by the illness of their
aunt. ▲ worried [*Am*] *Estábamos apenados porque no recibíamos noticias.*
We were worried because we weren't
getting any news.

apenas scarcely, hardly *Apenas puede
andar.* He can hardly walk. ▲ as soon
as *Apenas llegue, avíseme.* Let me
know as soon as he comes.

apertura opening (of exhibition, public
event).

apetito appetite.

apiñado gathered in a crowd *La gente
está apiñada para ver el desfile.* A
crowd of people gathered to see the
parade.

apio celery.

aplanar to smooth, flatten.
　○ **aplanarse** to be in low spirits, get
depressed *Se aplanó después del fracaso.* He got very depressed after his
failure.

aplastar to crush *Aplastaron toda resistencia.* They crushed all resistance.
▲ to flatten *Le aplastaron las narices.*
They flattened his nose.
　○ **aplastarse** to flatten oneself *Se
aplastaron contra la pared.* They flattened themselves against the wall.

aplaudir to applaud.

aplauso applause.

aplicado (see aplicar) studious, industrious *Es un estudiante muy aplicado.*
He's very studious.

aplicar to apply, put on *Le aplicaron a
la silla una capa de pintura.* They
put a coat of paint on the chair.
　○ **aplicarse** to apply oneself.

aplomo self-possession, poise *Tiene mucho aplomo.* He has a lot of poise.

apoderarse de to take possession of, seize.

apodo nickname.

aporrear to beat up, club.

apostar to bet *¿Cuánto apuesta Ud.?*
How much do you bet?
　○ **apostar a que** to bet that *Apuesto
a que llego yo antes de Ud.* I bet I
get there before you.

apoyar to rest, prop *Apoye el pie en ese
escalón.* Rest your foot on that step.
▲ to back, support, second *Nadie apoyó
su proposición.* No one supported his

motion.—*Apoyo la proposición.* I
second the motion.
　○ **apoyarse** to support oneself, lean
Se apoya en un bastón. He's leaning
on a cane.

apoyo prop, support.

aprecio esteem, respect, liking *Le tengo
mucho aprecio.* I have great respect
for him.

aprender to learn.

apresurar to hasten, hurry *No apresure
el paso; llegaremos a la hora.* Don't
walk so fast; we'll get there on time.
　○ **apresurarse** to hurry up *Haga el
favor de apresurarse; ya llegamos
tarde.* Please hurry; we're late already.

apretar [*rad-ch I*] to tighten *Apriete
este tornillo.* Tighten this screw. ▲ to
be too tight on *Me aprieta mucho este
cuello.* This collar's too tight. ▲ to
press down on, put pressure on, compress *Apretó para cerrar la maleta.*
He pressed down on the suitcase to
close it. ▲ to grip *Me apretó la mano.*
He gripped my hand. ▲ to clench
(fist or teeth). ▲ to go faster, sprint
El corredor apretó en la última vuelta.
The runner sprinted on the last lap.

apretazón [*f*] crowd [*Am*] *Era tanta la
apretazón que nadie vió nada.* There
was such a crowd that nobody saw
anything.

aprieto jam, tight spot *Se vió en un
aprieto.* He found himself in a tight
spot.

aprisa swiftly, fast, quickly *Hace todo
muy aprisa.* He does everything very
quickly.

aprobación [*f*] approval.

aprobar to approve of *No apruebo su
conducta.* I don't approve of his conduct. ▲ to pass (an examination)
*¿Aprobó Ud. en el examen de matemá-
ticas?* Did you pass your math exam?

aprontar to advance [*Am*] *El patrón
tuvo que aprontarle algún dinero.* The
boss had to advance him some money.

aprovechar to profit by, make use of
Aprovechaba todos los restos. She
made use of all the left-overs.
　○ **aprovecharse de** to take advantage
of *No dejes que se aproveche de tí.*
Don't let him take advantage of you.

aprovisionar to supply, provision.

aproximarse to approach, move near *No
se aproxime Ud. demasiado al fuego.*
Don't go too near the fire.

apuesta bet, wager.

apunarse to become ill from altitude [*Am*].

apuntar to aim *Apunta demasiado bajo para dar en el blanco.* You're aiming too low to hit the target. ▲ to jot down, make a note of *Apúntelo en su cuaderno de notas.* Jot it down in your notebook.

apurar to drain, drink up, consume *Apuraron las copas.* They drained their glasses. ▲ to smoke to the end.

O **apurar(se)** to worry *La situación me apura mucho.* The situation worries me very much.—*No se apure Ud.* Don't worry. ▲ to hurry *¡Apúrate niña!* Hurry up, child!—*¡Apúrale!* Hurry up! [*Am*].

apuro jam, tight spot, fix *Estoy en gran apuro.* I'm in a jam.

aquel, aquella, aquellos, aquellas [*adj*] that, these *Compré aquella bufanda que vimos ayer.* I bought that scarf we looked at yesterday.

aquél, aquélla, aquéllos, aquéllas [*pron*] that (one), these *Prefiero este libro a aquél.* I like this book better than that one.

aquello [*neu pron*] that (thing) *¿Qué es aquello?* What's that?

aquí here *No está aquí.* He isn't here. O **aquí dentro** in here *Les espero aquí dentro.* I'll wait for you in here. O **de aquí en adelante** from now on *De aquí en adelante tendremos que gastar menos.* From now on we'll have to spend less money. O **por aquí** here, this way *Venga Ud. por aquí.* Come this way.

arado plow.

araña spider.

arañar to scratch.

arañazo scratch.

arar to plow.

araucano [*adj, n*] Araucanian.

árbitro arbitrator, umpire, referee.

árbol tree.

arbusto bush, shrub.

archivar to file, put in a file.

arco arch; bow (for arrows). O **arco iris** rainbow.

arder to burn (be in flames) *La leña mojada no arde bien.* Wet firewood doesn't burn well. ▲ to burn (with fever).

ardido burned up, sore [*Am*] *Me tiene ardido con lo que me dijo.* I was burned up by what he said.

ardiente [*adj*] burning.

ardilla squirrel.

arena sand.

arenoso sandy.

arenque [*m*] herring.

arepa arepa (corn griddle cake) [*Am*].

argumento argument, logic, premises *No me convencen sus argumentos.* His arguments don't convince me. ▲ plot, story *No me gustó el argumento de la película.* I didn't like the plot of the movie.

árido arid, dry, barren.

aristocracia aristocracy.

arma weapon *Se prohíbe llevar armas.* It's forbidden to carry arms.

armadura armor; framework.

armar to arm *Armaron al pueblo.* They armed the people. ▲ to assemble, put together *Hay que armar esta máquina.* The machine has to be assembled.

O **armar jaleo** to make a racket *Anoche armaron mucho jaleo.* They made a big racket last night. O **armarse** to balk [*Am*] *Las mulas se armaron a medio camino.* The mules balked halfway there. O **armarse de** to arm *or* provide oneself with *Se armó de una pistola.* He armed himself with a pistol. ▲ to build up [*Am*] *Se armó de un buen negocio en poco tiempo.* He built up a good business in a short time.

‖ *Siempre arma líos.* He's always making a mess of things.

armario closet, wardrobe.

armonía harmony.

arqueo balance (in accounting).

arquitecto architect.

arquitectura architecture.

arrabal [*m*] suburb, outskirts.

arrancado broke [*Am*] *Siempre está arrancado a fin de mes.* He's always broke at the end of the month.

arrancar to root out, pull out, tear out *Han arrancado tres páginas.* Three pages have been torn out. ▲ to start *Vimos arrancar el automóvil.* We saw the car start.

arranque [*m*] sudden impulse *En un arranque me volví a mi pueblo.* On a sudden impulse I returned to my home town. ▲ starter *Este automóvil tiene arranque automático.* This car has a self-starter.

arrastrado (see **arrastrar**) low, contemptible *¡Qué tipo tan arrastrado!* What a heel! ▲ bootlicker, yes-man [*Am*] *Consigue todo porque es muy arrastrado.* He gets everything because he's a bootlicker.

arrastrar to drag, drag along *Le arrastró la corriente.* He was dragged along by the current. ▲ to touch the floor *or* ground, drag *Cuidado, le arrastra el abrigo.* Be careful, your coat's dragging.

O **arrastrarse** to crawl, creep, drag oneself *Salieron de la cueva arrastrándose.* They crawled out of the cave.

arreglar to arrange, adjust, settle *¿Está todo arreglado para el viaje?* Is everything arranged for the trip? ▲ to fix *Creo que arreglarán el radio esta tarde.* I think they'll fix the radio this afternoon.

O **arreglarse** to tidy up, dress, put make-up on *Arréglate un poco y vámonos al cine.* Tidy up a bit and we'll go to the movies. O **arreglárselas para** to manage to *¿Cómo me las arreglaré para terminar a tiempo?* How can I manage to finish on time?

arreglo arrangement, settlement, agreement; alteration.

O **con arreglo a** according to, in accordance with *Lo hicimos con arreglo a sus instrucciones.* We did it according to your instructions.

arrendar [*rad-ch I*] to rent, let *¿Quiere Ud. arrendar su casa?* Do you want to rent your house? ▲ to rent, hire *Necesito arrendar una habitación.* I want to rent a room.

arrepentirse [*rad-ch II*] to be sorry for, regret *Se arrepentirá Ud. de esto.* You'll be sorry for this.

arrestar to arrest, imprison.

arriba up, above *Viven dos pisos más arriba.* They live two flights up. ▲ upstairs *Los dormitorios están arriba.* The bedrooms are upstairs.

O **arriba de** beyond, past (on higher level) *Es más arriba de la plaza.* It's past the square. O **boca arriba, panza arriba, patas arriba** face up, on one's *or* its back. O **cuesta arriba** uphill. O **de arriba abajo** from top to bottom, from head to foot *Le miró de arriba abajo.* He looked him up and down. O **desde arriba** from above *Desde arriba se veía el río.* From above one could see the river. ▲ **hacia arriba** up, upwards *El coche iba hacia arriba.* The car was going up. O **para arriba** up, upward *Vamos para arriba.* Let's go up. O **por arriba** at *or* around the top, up there *El sombrero estaba sucio por arriba.* The hat was dirty around the top.

arriesgar to risk, hazard *No le importa arriesgar la vida.* He doesn't mind risking his life.

O **arriesgarse** to take risks *Si no nos arriesgamos no haremos nada.* If we don't take risks we'll never get anything done.

arrimar to place *or* put near *or* close *No arrimes tanto la mesa a la pared.* Don't put the table so close to the wall.

‖ *¡Arrima el hombro!* Give me a hand!

arrinconar to neglect; to pigeonhole; to corner.

arrodillarse to kneel.

arrogante arrogant, haughty, proud.

arrojar to throw, hurl, cast *Se prohibe arrojar objetos por la ventanilla.* Don't throw things out the window.

arrollar to coil *Hay que arrollar esa cuerda.* That rope has to be coiled. ▲ to trample, run over *Fueron arrollados por la multitud.* They were trampled by the crowd.

arroyo brook.

arroz [*m*] rice.

arrugar to wrinkle, crumple.

arruinar to ruin (financially) *Ese hombre los ha arruinado completamente.* That man ruined them completely.

O **arruinarse** to be ruined (financially) *Con esos negocios se ha arruinado.* He was ruined by that business.

arte [*m or f*] art *¿Le interesa el arte?* Are you interested in art?—*Las bellas artes.* Fine arts. ▲ skill *Presenta sus argumentos con mucho arte.* He presents his arguments with great skill. ▲ craft, cunning.

arteria artery.

articulación [*f*] joint.

artículo article, news article *Lea el artículo de la página dos.* Read the article on page two.

O **artículos** things, goods *Venden artículos de deportes.* They sell sporting goods.

artificial artificial.

artista [*m, f*] artist.

artístico artistic.

arveja green pea [*Am*].

as [*m*] ace, star; ace (cards).

asado See **asar**. ▲ [*m*] roast.

asaltar to assault, attack, hold up.

asamblea assembly, convention.

asar to roast *Vamos a asar las castañas.* Let's roast the chestnuts.

○ **asarse** to be roasting, be uncomfortably warm *Se asa uno en este cuarto.* It's roasting in this room.

ascender [*rad-ch I*] to ascend, go up *El globo ascendió lentamente.* The balloon went up slowly. ▲ to be promoted *Ascendió tres veces en un año.* He was promoted three times in one year.

○ **ascender a** to amount to *La cuenta ascendía a cuatrocientos pesos.* The bill amounted to 400 pesos.

ascensor [*m*] (passenger) elevator.

ascensorista [*m, f*] elevator operator.

asco nausea, disgust *Rechazó la comida con asco.* He refused the food with disgust.

○ **dar asco** to disgust *Esas cosas me dan asco.* Those things disgust me. ○ **estar hecho un asco** to be very dirty, be filthy *No te acerques, estás hecho un asco.* Don't come near me; you're filthy. ○ **hacer ascos** to turn up one's nose *Le hace ascos a todo.* He turns up his nose at everything.

asegurar to secure, fasten (with rope or strap) *Aseguró con una cuerda la carga del caballo.* He fastened the horse's pack with a rope. ▲ to assure *Le aseguro que todo estará preparado a tiempo.* I assure you everything will be ready on time. ▲ to affirm, maintain *Asegura que es cierto.* He maintains it's true. ▲ to insure *El equipaje está asegurado.* The baggage is insured.

○ **asegurarse** to make sure *Asegúrense primero de que la información es cierta.* First make sure the information's correct. ▲ to get insured *Se aseguró contra accidentes.* He took out accident insurance.

asesinar to murder.

asesinato murder.

asesino assassin, murderer.

así so, that way *Así es.* That's the way it is. ▲ in this manner, this way *Lo debe Ud. hacer así.* You must do it this way. ▲ therefore, and so *Así, decidieron actuar inmediatamente.* And so they decided to act immediately.

○ **así, así** so so *"¿Cómo está Ud.?" "Así, así." "How are you?" "So so."* ○ **así como así** without reason *No lo digo así como así.* I don't say it without reason. ○ **así que** as soon as, after *Así que llegue le avisaré.* I'll let you know as soon as I get there.

asiento seat, chair *Tome Ud. asiento.* Take a seat.

asilo orphanage; home (for aged).

asimismo likewise, too, in the same way *Asimismo lo creo yo.* I think so too.

asistencia attendance, presence *Su asistencia no es necesaria.* Your attendance isn't necessary. ▲ assistance, help.

asistir to assist, help, take care of *Le asistí en su enfermedad.* I took care of him during his illness.

○ **asistir a** to attend, be present at *¿Asistió Ud. a la reunión?* Were you present at the meeting?

asno ass, donkey.

asociación [*f*] association, club.

asociado See **asociar**. ▲ [*n*] associate, partner.

asociar to associate.

asolear to dry in the sun *Hay que asolear la ropa.* The wash'll have to be put in the sun to dry.

○ **asolearse** to take a sun bath [*Am*] *Estuvieron asoleándose en la playa.* They were taking a sun bath on the beach.

asomar to put out (one's head, hand, etc) *Asomó la cabeza por la ventana.* He put his head out of the window.

○ **asomarse a** to lean out of *Se prohíbe asomarse al exterior.* It's forbidden to lean out of windows.

asombrar to astonish, amaze *Asombra a todo el mundo por su ingenio.* He amazes everybody by his cleverness.

○ **asombrarse de** to wonder at, be astonished by, be amazed at *Me asombra que diga Ud. eso.* I'm amazed that you say that.

asombroso wonderful, astonishing.

áspero rough, harsh *Esa tela es muy áspera.* That cloth's very rough.

aspiración [*f*] ambition.

aspirar to aspire.

asqueroso filthy, nasty, mean, low.

astilla chip; splinter.

○ **astillas** [*pl*] kindling.

astucia [*f*] cunning.

astuto astute, crafty.

asumir to assume, take on *Asumió todas las responsabilidades.* He assumed full responsibility.

asunto subject *¿Cuál es el asunto de esa comedia?* What's the subject of that play? ▲ affair, business *No se meta Ud. en mis asuntos.* Don't meddle in my affairs. *or* Mind your own business.

asustar to frighten *Me asustaron sus gritos.* Your screams frightened me.

○ **asustarse** to be frightened *Se asusta de los ruidos fuertes.* She's frightened by loud noises.

atacar to attack.

atado See **atar.** ▲ [*m*] bundle, parcel [*Am*].
atajar to overtake, catch up with *Por este camino les atajaremos.* If we go this way we'll catch up with 'em. ▲ to interrupt, cut short *Le atajó diciéndole que no.* He cut him short by saying no.
atajo short cut, shorter road.
ataque [*m*] attack, assault; attack, fit.
atar to tie, lace, bind *Átate bien los zapatos.* Lace your shoes up tight.
　○ **atar cabos** to put two and two together *Aoírlo, até cabos.* When I heard that I put two and two together.
atarantado dizzy *He bailado tanto que estoy atarantada.* I've danced so much that I'm dizzy.
atareado busy.
ataúd [*m*] coffin, casket.
atención [*f*] attention *El anunciador pidió atención.* The announcer called for attention.
　○ **atenciones** [*pl*] kindness *Nunca olvidaré sus atenciones.* I'll never forget your kindness. ○ **llamar la atención** to attract attention *Le gusta llamar la atención.* She likes to attract attention. ▲ to reprimand *Le llamé la atención por su falta de respeto.* I reprimanded him for his insolence.
atender [*rad-ch I*] to attend, wait on *El dependiente los atendió en seguida.* The clerk waited on them immediately. ▲ to pay attention *Haz el favor de atender a lo que te digo.* Please pay attention to what I'm saying. ▲ to look after, take care of *Atiende muy bien a sus invitados.* He takes very good care of his guests.
atenerse a [*irr*] to depend on, rely on (accept as valid) *No sé a que atenerme.* I don't know what to depend on.
atentado assassination (attempted or successful); attempt (to overthrow by violence) *Se cometió un atentado contra la vida del presidente.* There was an attempt on the life of the president.
atento polite, courteous; attentive.
　‖ *Su atento seguro servidor.* Very truly yours.
aterrar to terrify.
atinar to hit the mark. ▲ to guess (right) *Atinó el dinero que yo tenía en el bolsillo.* He guessed the amount of money I had in my pocket.
　○ **atinar a** to succeed in *No atinó a explicar lo que quería.* He didn't succeed in explaining what he wanted. ○ **atinar con** to find (hit upon) *No atino con el ojo de la cerradura.* I can't find the keyhole.

atleta [*m, f*] athlete.
atlético athletic.
atmósfera atmosphere.
atol, atole [*m*] atol, atole (a hot nonalcoholic drink widely used in Mexico and Central America).
atolondrado scatter-brained *No he visto una persona más atolondrada.* I've never seen such a scatterbrain.
atontado foolish, stupid *No seas atontado.* Don't be so foolish.
atormentar to torment, torture.
atornillar to screw, turn a screw.
atracción [*f*] attraction.
atractivo attractive, charming *¡Que mujer tan atractiva!* What an attractive woman! ▲ [*m*] charm, appeal *Es muy bonita pero no tiene atractivo.* She's very pretty but she has no appeal.
atraer [*irr*] to attract, charm.
atrás back *Está allí atrás con unos amigos.* She's back there with some friends.
　○ **dar marcha atrás** to go into reverse, back up *No dé marcha atrás que hay un árbol.* Don't back up; there's a tree behind you. ○ **hacia atrás** back, backward *Miró hacia atrás.* He looked back. ○ **quedarse atrás** to stay behind, fall behind *Se ha quedado atrás con unos amigos.* She stayed behind with some friends.
atrasado (see **atrasar**) backward, behind (in work, studies, etc).
atrasar to delay, detain *Esto atrasa mucho mi viaje.* This'll delay my trip a long time. ▲ to put back (watch or clock) *Tengo que atrasar mi reloj, está muy adelantado.* I have to set my watch back; it's very fast. ▲ to go *or* be slow, lose time *Mi reloj atrasa diez minutos al día.* My watch loses ten minutes a day.
　○ **atrasarse** to remain *or* get behind, lose time *Creo que nos atrasamos en este trabajo.* I think we're getting behind in this work.
atraso backwardness *El atraso de ese país es bien conocido.* The backwardness of that country's well known. ▲ delay.
atravesar [*rad-ch I*] to pierce *La bala le atravesó el brazo.* The bullet pierced his arm. ▲ to cross *He atravesado el Atlántico varias veces.* I've crossed the Atlantic several times.
　○ **atravesarse** to stop crosswise *Se atravesó un camión en la carretera.* A truck stopped crosswise in the middle of the road.

atreverse to dare, venture *No se atreve a decírmelo.* He doesn't dare to tell me.

atribuir to attribute.

atrocidad [*f*] atrocity; horrible *or* terrible thing *¡Qué atrocidad!* What a horrible thing!

atropellar to run over, knock down *Le atropelló un auto.* An automobile ran over him.

○ **atropellarse** to rush through *Si quiere Ud. hacer el trabajo bien, no se atropelle.* If you want to do a good job, don't rush through it.

atropello abuse, outrage *No podemos tolerar tal atropello.* We can't tolerate such an outrage. ▲ accident (in which a pedestrian is injured) *Tres peatones fueron víctimas de un atropello.* Three pedestrians were victims of an accident.

atroz terrible, atrocious *¡Fué una cosa atroz!* It was a terrible thing!

aturdir to rattle *Me aturde tanto ruido.* So much noise rattles me.

○ **aturdirse** to be stunned *Se aturdió y no supo que contestar.* He was stunned and didn't know what to answer.

audacia audacity, boldness.

audaz bold, daring.

auditorio audience, listeners.

aumentar to increase *Han aumentado los sueldos.* They've increased the salaries.

aumento increase.

aun, aún still *Aun podemos llegar a tiempo.* We can still get there on time. ▲ even *Ni aun ahora sería posible.* Even now it wouldn't be possible. ▲ yet *No ha venido aún.* He hasn't come yet.

○ **aun cuando** even though, even if *Aun cuando no venga tendremos que empezar.* Even if he doesn't come we'll have to begin.

aunque though, even if *Aunque no he nacido en el país, lo conozco muy bien.* Though I wasn't born in the country, I know it very well.

ausencia absence.

ausentarse to leave, absent oneself *Se ausentó de la clase porque se sentía enfermo.* He left the class because he was feeling sick.

ausente absent. ▲ [*n*] one who is absent.

auténtico authentic.

auto auto, car *¿Hay bastante sitio en el auto para todos?* Is there enough room in the car for everybody?

autobús [*m*] bus *¿Qué es más barato, el autobús o el tranvía?* Which is cheaper, the bus or the street car?

automático automatic. ▲ [*m*] snap (for clothing).

automóvil [*m*] automobile.

autor [*m*] author.

autora authoress.

autoridad [*f*] authority, power *No supo mantener su autoridad.* He couldn't maintain his authority.

○ **autoridades** authorities, government *Han dado parte a las autoridades.* They reported it to the authorities.

autorizar to authorize.

auxiliar to aid, help, assist.

avanzar to move forward *El coche avanzaba muy despacio.* The car moved very slowly. ▲ to advance, make progress, get ahead *No avanzamos nada en nuestro trabajo.* We're not making any progress in our work.

avaro stingy, miserly. ▲ [*n*] miser.

ave [*m*] bird, fowl.

avena oats.

avenida avenue. ▲ flood *Las avenidas han estropeado la cosecha.* The floods ruined the crops.

avenirse [*irr*] to agree *Se avino a lo que le dijeron.* He agreed to what they said.

aventajado promising *Es un muchacho muy aventajado.* He's a very promising young man.

aventajar to get ahead, to surpass *Aventaja a todos en el trabajo.* He gets ahead of everybody in his work.

aventura adventure; risk, chance.

aventurar to risk, hazard *¡No se aventure!* Don't risk it!

aventurero adventurous; adventurer.

avergonzar [*rad-ch I*] to shame, to make (someone) ashamed *Avergonzó a toda su familia con su conducta.* He shamed his whole family by his conduct.

○ **avergonzarse** to be ashamed *Después de decirlo se avergonzó.* After he said it, he was ashamed.

avería damage *El mecánico arregló la avería sin demora.* The mechanic repaired the damage without delay.

averiarse to be damaged, be spoiled *Con la lluvia se averió el cargamento.* The shipment was damaged by the rain.

averiguar to find out.

aviación [*f*] aviation.

aviador [*m*] aviator.

ávido eager, anxious *Estaba ávido de noticias.* He was eager for news.

avión [*m*] airplane, plane.

avisar to notify, inform *Hay que avisar
a la policía* We have to notify the
police. ▲to warn, advise, counsel *Es
la última vez que te aviso* I'm warning you for the last time.

aviso announcement, notice, warning
Aviso al público. Notice to the public.

avispa wasp.

avivar to revive (make bright) *Avivaron
el fuego echando más leña.* They re-
vived the fire by putting on more wood.
○ avivar el ojo to keep one's eyes
open, look sharp *¿Por qué no avivas
el ojo?* Why don't you keep your eyes
open? ○ avivar el paso to step lively
Avive el paso; es muy tarde. Step
lively; it's very late. ○ avivarse to
wake up, to cheer up *Avívate; estás
como dormido.* Wake up; you're half
asleep.

¡ay! oh! ouch!

ayer yesterday.

ayuda help, aid, assistance *Necesito
ayuda en esto.* I need help with this.

ayudar to aid, help, assist *Quiero ayudarle a llevar los paquetes.* I want to
help him carry the packages.

ayunar to fast.

ayunas ○ en ayunas hungry, fasting, on
an empty stomach *No fume en ayunas.*
Don't smoke on an empty stomach.

azada hoe.

azafate [m] tray [Am].

azafrán [m] saffron.

azahar [m] orange blossom.

azar [m] chance, risk *Corramos ese azar.*
Let's take that chance. ▲chance *Le
gustan los juegos de azar.* He likes
games of chance.
○ al azar at random *Los escogió al
azar.* He chose them at random.

azarar to embarrass, confuse *Esto azara
a cualquiera.* This would embarrass
anyone.
○ azararse to be embarrassed *Cuando
se lo dije se azaró mucho.* When I told
him that he was very much embarrassed.

azote [m] whipping; spank; lash.

azteca [adj; n] Aztec.

azúcar [m or f] sugar.

azucarera sugar bowl. ▲[adj] pertaining to sugar *La industria azucarera.*
The sugar industry.

azucena white lily.

azufre [m] sulfur.

azul [adj; n] blue

B

babucha slipper.

bacalao codfish.

bachiller [m] graduate, holder of a bachelor's degree (person possessing a Spanish degree equivalent in the U.S. to a
high-school diploma plus two years of
college).

bagazo pulp [Am].

bahía bay (arm of sea).

bailar to dance.

bailarín [m] dancer.

bailarina [f] dancer.

baile [m] dance, ball.

baja (military) casualty *El enemigo sufrió muchas bajas.* The enemy suffered many casualties. ▲fall (in price)
Hubo una baja en todos los precios.
There was a general fall in prices.
○ dar de baja to drop out (from a
list of members or subscribers) *Se dió
de baja del club.* He dropped out of
the club.—*Por falta de pago, lo dieron
de baja de la lista de subscriptores.*
For lack of payment they dropped him
from the subscription list.

bajada descent, slope.

bajamar [f] low tide.

bajar to go down, descend *Bajemos la
escalera despacio.* Let's go down the
stairs slowly. ▲to fall, drop *La temperatura bajó.* The temperature fell.
▲to lower; to bring down *Baje Ud. la
maleta de mi cuarto.* Bring the suitcase down from my room. ▲to take
down *¿Quiere ayudarme a bajar las
maletas de la red?* Will you help me
take the suitcases down from the
rack?
○ bajarse to get down, get off *Nos
vieron al bajarse del tren.* They saw
us as they were getting off the train.
▲to bend over *Se bajó para atarse un
zapato.* He bent over to tie his shoe.

bajo low *Quiero una mesa baja.* I want
a low table. ▲short *Es más bajo que
su hermano.* He's shorter than his
brother. ▲low, soft *Hablaban en voz
baja.* They were speaking in a low
voice. ▲bass (voice, instrument) *Vamos a colocar los bajos a la izquierda.*
Let's put the basses on the left. ▲be-
low *La temperatura ha llegado a bajo*

cero. The temperature's fallen below
zero. ▲ street floor, ground floor *El
portero vive en el bajo* The superintendent lives on the ground floor.
bala bullet, ball.
balance [*m*] balance; balance sheet *¿Cuál
es mi balance de este mes en el banco?*
What's my bank balance this month?
balancearse to sway, rock, swing *No se
balancee en la silla; se va a romper.*
Don't rock in the chair; it's going to
break.
balanceo [*m*] rocking, wobbling.
balanza scales, balance.
balazo shot *Se oyeron tres balazos.* Three
shots were heard. ▲ bullet wound
Tenía tres balazos en el pecho. He
had three bullet wounds in his chest.
balcón [*m*] balcony.
balde [*m*] bucket, pail *Este balde se sale.*
This bucket leaks.
  O **de balde** gratis, free *Dan boletos
de balde.* They're giving tickets free.
  O **en balde** in vain, without success
*Trató en balde de hablar con ella por
teléfono.* He tried to get her on the
phone without success.
balear to wound by gunshot [*Am*] *Lo
balearon ayer.* They shot him yesterday.
balneario bathing resort.
balón [*m*] football.
banana banana.
banco bank *¿Puedo cobrar mi cheque en
este banco?* Can I cash my check in
this bank? ▲ bench *Todos los bancos
están ocupados.* All the benches are
taken.
banda sash, band (wide strip of material)
La falda tenía tres bandas rojas. The
skirt had three red bands.—*Llevaba
una banda roja cruzada al pecho.* He
wore a red sash across his chest.
▲ band (music) *Esa banda (de música)
me da dolor de cabeza.* That band
gives me a headache. ▲ gang *Una
banda de ladrones actúa por esta región.* A gang of thieves works these
parts.
bandeja tray.
bandera flag.
bandido bandit.
banquero banker.
banqueta sidewalk [*Mex*]; stool.
bañar to bathe *Haga el favor de bañar a
los niños.* Please bathe the children.
  O **bañarse** to take a bath *Voy a
bañarme.* I'm going to take a bath.
bañera bathtub.
bañero lifeguard.

baño bath; bathroom; bathtub.
baraja deck of cards.
barajar to shuffle (cards).
baranda banister.
barata cockroach [*Ch, Peru*].
barato cheap, inexpensive *Es muy bonito
y además barato.* It's very pretty and
besides it's cheap. ▲ cheaply, cheap
En este almacén venden muy barato.
They sell things very cheap in this
store. ▲ [*m*] sale *Hoy hay un barato
en ese almacén.* There's a sale today
in that department store.
barba beard; chin.
barbaridad [*f*] any excess in speech *or*
action *Come una barbaridad.* He eats
too much.—*No diga Ud. barbaridades.*
Don't talk nonsense.—*Lo que hizo fué
una barbaridad.* What he did was an
outrage.—*Me gusta una barbaridad.* I
like her an awful lot.
bárbaro crude *Es un hombre bárbaro.*
He's a crude man.
barbería barbershop.
barbero barber.
barca (small) boat.
barco boat, ship *¿Cuántas veces ha hecho
Ud. el viaje por barco?* How many
times have you made the trip by boat?
barniz [*m*] varnish.
barnizar to varnish.
barquinazo tumble, fall [*Am*].
barra bar, rod *Necesitamos una barra de
hierro.* We need an iron bar. ▲ public,
spectators [*Am*] *La barra animaba a
los jugadores.* The spectators cheered
the players on.
barranco gorge, ravine.
barrer to sweep.
barril [*m*] barrel, cask.
barrio quarter, section, district.
barro mud; pimple.
base [*f*] basis; base.
¡basta! (See **bastar**) enough! stop!
¡Basta ya! He dicho que te calles.
That's enough! I told you to shut up!
bastante enough, sufficient *¿Tiene Ud.
bastante dinero?* Do you have enough
money? ▲ enough, rather *Es una
mujer bastante bonita.* She's a rather
pretty woman.
bastar to be enough *No bastó la comida
para todos.* There wasn't enough food
for all.
bastidores [*m pl*] O **entre bastidores**
behind the scenes, backstage.
basto coarse, rough *El traje está hecho
de material muy basto.* The suit's made
of very rough material.
bastón [*m*] cane, walking stick.

basura garbage, refuse.
bata robe, bathrobe; house coat.
batalla battle.
batata sweet potato.
bate [*m*] baseball bat [*Am*].
batería battery.
batir to beat *Haga el favor de batir los huevos.* Please beat the eggs. ▲ to defeat *Batió a su enemigo.* He defeated his enemy.
batirse to fight; to fight a duel.
baúl [*m*] trunk *No han deschecho todavía los baúles.* They haven't unpacked their trunks yet.
bautismo baptism.
bautizar to baptize.
bebé [*m*] baby.
beber to drink *¿Qué van a beber Uds.?* What are you going to drink?
bebida drink, beverage.
becerro calf; calfskin.
beisbol [*m*] baseball (game) [*Am*].
beisbolista [*m*] baseball player [*Am*].
belleza beauty.
bello beautiful.
bendecir [*irr*] to bless *¡Qué Dios le bendiga!* God bless you!
bendición [*f*] blessing.
bendito (see **bendecir**) blessed, holy.
beneficencia public charity; department of welfare.
beneficio favor *No agradece los beneficios.* He doesn't appreciate favors. ▲ profit *Los beneficios fueron muy altos.* The profits were very high.
benevolencia kindness, good will.
berenjena eggplant.
besar to kiss.
beso kiss.
bestia beast.
betabel [*f*] beet [*Mex*].
Biblia Bible.
biblioteca library.
bicarbonato bicarbonate of soda.
bicha snake.
bicicleta bicycle, bike.
bien [*m*] good *No distingue el bien del mal.* He doesn't know the difference between good and evil. ▲ [*adv*] well *Habló muy bien.* He spoke very well. ▲ very *La cerveza está bien fría.* The beer's very cold.
　○ **ahora bien** now then. ○ **bienes** [*m pl*] property, estate *Tiene muchos bienes.* He has a great deal of property. ○ **más bien que** rather *Es más bien rico que pobre.* He's rich rather than poor.
　¶ *Está bien.* All right *or* Correct.

¶ *Fíjese bien en lo que le digo.* **Pay** close attention to what I tell you.
bienestar [*m*] well-being, comfort.
bienvenido [*adj*] welcome *¡Bienvenido a mi casa!* Welcome to my house!
biftec [*m*] see **bistec**.
bigote [*m*] mustache.
billar [*m*] billiards, pool.
billete [*m*] ticket *¿Ha comprado Ud. los billetes?* Have you bought the tickets?
　○ **billete (de banco)** bill *Déme el dinero en billetes de a cinco y de a diez.* Give me the money in fives and tens. ○ **billete de ida y vuelta** round-trip ticket.
biombo screen *Hay que poner un biombo delante de la puerta.* You have to put a screen in front of the door.
bisabuela great-grandmother.
bisabuelo great-grandfather.
bistec, biftec [*m*] beefsteak.
bizco cross-eyed.
bizcocho sponge cake.
blanco white *¡Ojalá hubiera comprado un traje blanco!* I wish I'd bought a white dress! ▲ [*n*] white (person) *En esta ciudad hay blancos, indios y negros.* There are white people, Indians, and Negroes in this city. ▲ [*m*] target *Dieron en el blanco.* They hit the target.
　○ **en blanco** blank *Deje Ud. esta hoja en blanco.* Leave this sheet blank. ○ **hacer blanco** to hit the mark *Hicieron blanco tres veces.* They hit the mark three times. ○ **tirar al blanco** to shoot at the target, have target practice *Los soldados tiraron al blanco por la mañana.* The soldiers had target practice in the morning.
blando soft; tender.
blanquillo egg [*Mex*].
bloque [*m*] block, piece.
blusa blouse.
bobo fool; foolish *¡Hijo, no seas bobo!* Son, don't be foolish!
boca mouth *No abrió la boca en toda a tarde.* He didn't open his mouth all afternoon. ▲ entrance (of subway, cave, etc) *En la esquina está la boca del metro.* The subway entrance is on the corner.
　○ **boca abajo** on one's stomach, face down *El niño duerme boca abajo.* The child's sleeping on his stomach. ○ **boca arriba** on one's back, upside down *Estaba echado en la playa boca arriba.* He was lying on his back on the beach.
bocacalle [*f*] street intersection.
bocado mouthful; bit.

bochorno embarrassment *¡Qué bochorno pasamos!* What an embarrassing situation that was! ▲ sultry weather *¡Qué bochorno hace!* What sultry weather we're having!

bochornoso embarrassing; shameful *¡Qué acción bochornosa!* What a shameful action! ▲ sultry.

bocina horn *Toque la bocina para que ese auto nos deje pasar.* Blow the horn so that car'll let us pass.

boda wedding.

bodega (wine) cellar, winery; storehouse; [*Am*] grocery store.

bofe lung.
   ○ **echar los bofes** to pant, be out of breath *Estoy echando los bofes.* I'm out of breath.

bofetada slap.

bohemio [*adj; n*] Bohemian.

boina beret.

bola ball, round body *or* mass *Deme Ud. esa bola de hierro.* Give me that iron ball. ▲ ball (to play with) [*Am*] *Compramos unas bolas de tenis.* We bought some tennis balls. ▲ crowd [*Mex*] *Había una bola de gente a la entrada del teatro.* There was a crowd of people at the entrance of the theater.

boleador [*m*] bootblack [*Mex*].

boletería box office [*Am*].

boleto ticket [*Am*].

bolo drunkard [*Am*].
   ○ **jugar a los bolos** to bowl.

bolsa purse *Llevaba una bolsa de seda.* She carried a silk purse. ▲ bag *Necesito una bolsa de papel para guardarlo.* I need a paper bag to put it in. ▲ stock exchange *No sé como están hoy las cotizaciones en la bolsa.* I don't know what the quotations are on the exchange today.

bolsillo pocket; [*Sp*] (woman's) handbag, purse.

bomba pump *Usaron una bomba para sacar el agua.* They used a pump to take out the water. ▲ bomb *La bomba destruyó tres casas.* The bomb destroyed three houses.—*¡Cayó como una bomba!* It struck like a bombshell!
   ○ **bomba de gasolina** gasoline pump; filling station *¿Dónde hay una bomba de gasolina?* Where is there a filling station? ○ **bomba de incendios** fire engine.
   ‖ *Se puso una bomba.* He got drunk [*Am*].

bombero fireman (fire department).

bombilla (electric) bulb *Se han fundido tres bombillas.* Three bulbs have burned out.

bonaerense [*adj; n*] (native) of Buenos Aires.

bondad [*f*] kindness, goodness *Le agradezco su bondad.* Thank you for your kindness.
   ○ **tener la bondad (de)** please *Tenga la bondad de esperar un momento.* Please wait a moment.

bondadoso [*adj*] kind.

boniato sweet potato [*Sp, Cuba*].

bonito pretty.

bono government bond.

boquilla cigarette holder.

bordar to embroider.

borde [*m*] edge, border.

bordo ○ **a bordo** aboard (ship).

borrachera drunkenness.
   ○ **coger una borrachera** to get drunk.

borracho [*n, adj*] drunkard; drunk.

borrar to rub out, erase.

bosque [*m*] forest, woods.

bostezar to yawn.

bostezo yawn.

bota boot; wine bag.

botado (See **botar**) cheap, inexpensive [*Am*] *Está botado.* It's dirt-cheap. ▲ lying (down) [*Am*] *Estaba botado en la cama.* He was lying on the bed.

botar to throw away [*Am*] *Tenga cuidado, no bote esos papeles.* Be careful, don't throw away those papers. ▲ to throw out, fire *Le han botado de su empleo.* They've fired him. ▲ to bounce [*Sp*] *Mire cuanto bota esa pelota.* Look how that ball bounces.

bote [*m*] boat. ▲ can, box *Quiero un bote de tomates.* I want a can of tomatoes.
   ○ **dar un bote** to jump *Cuando lo oyó dió un bote.* When he heard it he jumped. ○ **de bote en bote** crowded, jammed *El teatro estaba de bote en bote.* The theater was jammed.

botella bottle.

botica pharmacy.

botón [*m*] button.

botones [*m sg*] bellboy.

boxeador [*m*] boxer, prize fighter.

bozal [*m*] muzzle (for animals).

bravo fierce, wild *Cuidado, es un toro bravo.* Be careful, it's a fierce bull. ▲ angry, mad [*Am*] *Se puso muy bravo.* He got very mad.
   ‖ *¡Bravo!* Bravo!

brazo arm (of body).
   ○ **ir del brazo** to go arm in arm.

brea pitch, tar.

breve brief, short.
   O **en breve** in a little while, shortly.
brillante shiny *No me gusta este papel; es muy brillante.* I don't like this paper; it's too shiny. ▲ [*m*] diamond *Le regaló una pulsera de brillantes.* He gave her a diamond bracelet.
brillantina brilliantine.
brillar to shine.
brillo gloss, shine.
brincar to leap, jump.
brindar to drink to a person's health, toast *¡Brindemos a su salud!* Let's drink to your health!
brindis [*m sg*] toast (ceremony).
brisa breeze.
brocha paint brush; shaving brush.
broma joke, jest *Siempre está diciendo bromas.* He's always joking.
   O **en broma** as a joke *Lo dije en broma.* I said it as a joke. O **tomar a broma** to take lightly, take as a joke *Todo lo toma a broma.* He takes everything lightly.
bromear to joke *Está siempre bromeando.* He's always joking.
bronca fight, quarrel.
   O **armar una bronca** to pick a quarrel, start a fight.
bronce [*m*] bronze.
brotar to bud, sprout.
brújula (mariner's) compass.
brusco abrupt, rough *Es brusco en su manera de hablar.* He's abrupt in his way of speaking.
brutal brutal.
bruto beast, brute *No seas bruto.* Don't be a brute.
budín [*m*] pudding.
buen good, kind *Es un buen hombre.* He's a good man.
bueno good *Ese automóvil es muy bueno.* That's a very good car. ▲ appropriate, good *Era una buena ocasión.* It was a good opportunity. ▲ well, all right

No estoy muy bueno. I'm not feeling very well. ▲ well, all right, O.K. *Bueno, nos veremos a las cinco.* All right, we'll meet at five.
   O **por las buenas** willingly *Me lo dió por las buenas.* He gave it to me willingly.
   ‖ *¡Está bueno!* That's enough! [*Am*]
   ‖ *Buenos días.* Good morning.
buey [*m*] ox.
bufanda muffler, scarf.
buho owl.
bujía candle; spark plug; watt.
bulla noise, racket.
   O **armar bulla** to make a racket *Armaron una bulla terrible.* They made a terrible racket.
bulto bundle *Salió con un bulto de ropa en la mano.* He went out with a bundle of clothes in his hand. ▲ swelling, lump *Tiene un bulto en la cabeza.* He has a swelling on his head.
   O **escurrir, huir,** *or* **sacar el bulto** to duck out *En cuanto vió lo que había que hacer escurrió el bulto.* As soon as he saw what he had to do, he ducked out.
buque [*m*] ship, steamer.
burla mockery, jest.
   O **hacer burla** to make fun of, make a fool of *Le estaban haciendo burla.* They were making fun of him.
burlarse de to make fun of *Se burla de todo el mundo.* He makes fun of everybody.
burro donkey, ass. ▲ jackass, dope *¡Qué burro eres!* What a dope!
busca O **en busca de** in search of.
buscar to look for, seek.
busto bust.
butaca arm chair; orchestra seat.
buzón [*m*] mail box *Eche Ud. estas cartas en el buzón.* Put these letters in the mail box.

C

¡ca! oh no! no sir!
cabal complete *El juego de té no está cabal.* The tea set isn't complete.
caballería cavalry; saddle horse.
caballero gentleman *Es todo un caballero.* He's a perfect gentleman. ▲ sir *Caballero, aquí está la cuenta.* Here's your bill, sir.

caballete [*m*] sawhorse; easel.
caballo horse.
   O **a caballo** on horseback.
cabaña cabin, hut.
cabaret [*m*] cabaret, night club.
cabecera head (of a bed, table); seat of honor.
cabecilla ringleader.

cabello hair (of the head) *Lleva el cabello suelto.* She wears her hair loose.

caber [*irr*] to fit, be contained in *No caben más cosas en el baúl.* Nothing else will fit in the trunk. ▲to go through *El piano no cabe por esa puerta.* The piano won't go through that door.

○ **no cabe duda (de que)** there's no doubt (that) *No cabe duda de que es inglés.* There's no doubt that he's English.

cabeza head *Ese chico tiene la cabeza muy grande.* That child has a very large head. ▲chief, leader, head *Fué la cabeza del movimiento.* He was the leader of the movement. ▲mind, brains *Este trabajo hay que hacerlo con cabeza.* You have to use your brains in this work.

○ **de cabeza** headlong, head first *Se tiró de cabeza al agua.* He plunged into the water head first. ▲topsy-turvy, in a mess *Los negocios andan de cabeza.* Business is in a mess. ○ **dolor de cabeza** headache. ○ **perder la cabeza** to lose one's head *Nunca pierde la cabeza.* He never loses his head.

‖ *Ese proyecto no tiene pies ni cabeza.* There's no rhyme or reason to that plan.

cabildo city hall.

cable [*m*] cable; cablegram.

cablegrama [*m*] cablegram.

cabo end *De cabo a cabo.* From end to end.—*No podemos dejar cabos sueltos.* We can't leave any loose ends. ▲cape *Pasaron el cabo de Buena Esperanza.* They passed the Cape of Good Hope. ▲corporal *Tiene galones de cabo.* He has corporal's stripes.

○ **dar cabo a** to end, put an end to, finish *Dieron cabo a la conversación.* They put an end to the conversation. ○ **de cabo a rabo** from beginning to end *Conozco la historia de cabo a rabo.* I know the story from beginning to end. ○ **llevar a cabo** to carry out *En seguida llevaron a cabo el proyecto.* They carried out the plan right away.

cabra goat.

cacahuate [*m*] peanut [*Am*].

cacahuete [*m*] peanut [*Sp*].

cacao cacao tree; cocoa bean.

cacerola casserole.

cachivache(s) [*m*] junk, trash *Quite de aquí estos cachivaches.* Take this junk out of here.

cacho piece, hunk *Deme Ud. un cacho de pan.* Give me a piece of bread.

cactus [*m*] cactus.

cada every, each *Cada día dice una cosa distinta.* Every day he says something different.

○ **cada cual, cada uno** every one *Cada cual pagó su comida.* Every one paid for his own meal. ○ **cada vez que** every time, whenever *Me lo pide cada vez que me ve.* He asks me for it every time he sees me.

cadáver [*m*] corpse.

cadena chain; range (of mountains).

cadera hip.

cadete [*m*] cadet.

caer [*irr*] to fall *Cayó una lluvia torrencial.* A heavy rain fell. ▲to drop *Cayó de rodillas.* He dropped to his knees. ▲to be becoming to *El traje le cae bien.* The suit's becoming to him. ▲to fall, come *Su cumpleaños cae en domingo.* His birthday falls on Sunday.

○ **caer enfermo (en cama)** to be taken sick, fall sick *Cayó enfermo hace unos días.* He was taken sick a few days ago. ○ **caer en la cuenta** to realize, notice, think of *No caí en la cuenta hasta mucho después.* I didn't realize it until much later. ○ **caerse** to fall *Se cayó por la escalera.* She fell down the stairs. ○ **dejar caer** to drop *Tenga cuidado, no deje caer la bandeja.* Be careful, don't drop the tray.

café [*m*] coffee; café.

cafetera coffee pot.

caída fall, drop *Se quedó cojo después de la caída.* He was lame after the fall. ▲fall, collapse *La oposición de la Cámara causó la caída del gobierno.* The opposition of the House caused the fall of the government.

caja box, case *Le regaló una caja.* He gave her a box.

○ **caja de ahorros** savings bank *Ha ingresado mucho dinero en la caja de ahorros.* He put a lot of money in the savings bank. ○ **caja de caudales, caja de hierro** safe *Tienen sus alhajas en la caja de caudales.* They keep their jewelry in the safe. ○ **caja (registradora)** cash register *Mire lo que marca la caja.* Look and see how much the cash register rings up. ○ **en caja** on hand (of cash) *Hay que ver lo que tenemos en caja.* We have to see how much cash we have on hand.

cajero cashier.

cajetilla pack of cigarettes *Voy a comprar una cajetilla.* I'm going to buy a pack of cigarettes.

cajón [*m*] drawer *Han perdido la llave del cajón.* They've lost the key to the drawer. ▲ box *Recibieron un cajón de libros.* They received a box of books.

cal [*f*] lime.

calabaza pumpkin, squash.

○ **dar calabazas** to refuse, turn down, reject (a declaration of love) *Le dió calabazas.* She turned him down. ▲ to flunk *Le dieron calabazas en geometría.* They flunked him in geometry.

calabozo prison, cell.

calamar [*m*] squid.

calambre [*m*] cramp *Le dió un calambre mientras nadaba.* He got a cramp while he was swimming.

calamidad [*f*] disaster, calamity, misfortune.

calar to penetrate *El puñal le caló hasta el corazón.* The dagger penetrated to his heart. ▲ to soak through, drench *Llegué a casa calado.* I got home drenched.

○ **calarse** to put on *or* pull down (a hat) *Se caló el sombrero hasta las cejas.* He pulled his hat down to his eyes.

calavera skull; madcap, rake.

calcetín [*m*] sock.

calcular to calculate, figure out *Vamos a calcular los gastos del viaje.* Let's figure out the cost of the trip.

cálculo calculation.

caldera boiler, large kettle.

caldo broth, bouillon.

calefacción [*f*] heating (system).

calendario calendar.

calentar to heat, warm *Caliente el agua, por favor.* Please heat the water.

○ **calentarse** to get warm *Se calentaron al sol.* They warmed themselves in the sun.

calentura fever *Está con calentura desde hace días.* He's had a fever for the past few days.

calidad [*f*] quality *¿Es de buena calidad esta tela?* Is this good material?

○ **en calidad de** in one's capacity of, as.

caliente hot, warm *Cuidado, la sopa está muy caliente.* Be careful, the soup's very hot.

callado (See **callar**) silent, quiet *¿Por qué está Ud. tan callado?* Why are you so quiet?

callar to keep quiet *Calló mientras nosotros hablábamos.* He kept quiet while

we were talking. ▲ to conceal, keep from someone *Había callado la verdad.* He kept the truth from us.

○ **callarse** to shut up *Cállate, ya has hablado bastante.* Shut up! You're talking too much. ▲ to stop talking, playing, singing, etc *Se callaron de repente.* All of a sudden they stopped talking.

calle [*f*] street *¿En qué calle vive Ud.?* What street do you live on?

○ **echar a la calle** to throw out, to fire *No tuve más remedio que echarle a la calle.* I had no choice but to throw him out. ○ **quedar(se) en la calle** to be left penniless *Al fracasar el negocio se quedó en la calle.* When his business failed he was left penniless.

callejón [*m*], **calleja** alley, lane *Estamos en un callejón sin salida.* We're in a blind alley.

calma calm, quiet *Después de la tempestad vino la calma.* There was a calm after the storm.

○ **con calma** slowly, taking one's time *Trabaja con mucha calma.* He takes his time when he works.

calmar to calm, soothe, ease *Estas píldoras le calmarán el dolor.* These pills will ease the pain.

○ **calmarse** to calm down *No se calmó hasta mucho después.* He didn't calm down until much later.

calor [*m*] heat *No me gusta el calor.* I don't like the heat.

○ **hacer calor** to be warm (of weather) *Hoy hace mucho calor.* It's very warm today. ○ **tener calor** to feel warm *Tengo calor.* I'm warm.

calumnia slander, false charge *Todo lo que dice son calumnias.* Everything he's saying is slander.

calumniar to slander.

caluroso warm, hot *¡Qué días más caluroso!* What a hot day!

calva bald head; baldness.

calvicie [*f*] baldness (loss of hair).

calvo bald *Estoy quedándome calvo.* I'm getting bald.

calzada paved highway; [*Am*] sidewalk.

calzado shoes, footwear.

calzador [*m*] shoe-horn.

calzar to put on *or* wear (shoes) *¿Qué número calza Ud.?* What size shoe do you wear? ▲ to block, chock *Voy a calzar las ruedas para que no se mueva el coche.* I'm going to chock the wheels so the car won't move.

calzoncillos [*m pl*] shorts (underwear).

cama bed *Hágame la cama por favor.* Please make my bed.

○ **guardar cama, estar en cama** to be confined to bed *Está enfermo en cama desde hace tres meses.* He's been confined to bed for the past three months.

cámara camera *¿Qué clase de cámara tiene Ud.?* What kind of a camera do you have?

○ **cámara de comercio** chamber of commerce. ○ **cámara de diputados** chamber of deputies, house of representatives.

camarada [*m, f*] comrade, pal *Charlaban como viejos camaradas.* They were talking together like old pals.

camarera maid, chambermaid *La camarera todavía no ha arreglado el cuarto.* The maid hasn't made up the room yet. ▲ waitress *Pídale el menú a la camarera.* Ask the waitress for the menu.

camarero waiter; valet.

camarote [*m*] cabin, stateroom *Quiero reservar un camarote de primera clase.* I want to reserve a first-class stateroom.

cambiar to change *No ha cambiado nada desde que le ví.* He hasn't changed a bit since I saw him. ▲ to change (money) *¿Puede cambiarme un billete de diez pesos?* Can you change a ten-peso bill for me?

cambio change *¿Ha habido algún cambio de política?* Has there been any change in policy? ▲ small change, coins *¿Tiene Ud. cambio?* Do you have any change? ▲ rate of exchange *¿Cuál es el cambio del dólar hoy?* What's the rate of exchange on the dollar today?

○ **a cambio de** in exchange for *Le daré este libro a cambio de ese otro.* I'll give you this book in exchange for the other one. ○ **en cambio** on the other hand.

camilla stretcher, litter.

caminar to walk *Es muy aficionado a caminar.* He's very fond of walking.

○ **caminar con pies de plomo** to move cautiously *En este asunto hay que caminar con pies de plomo.* You have to move cautiously in this matter.

caminata long walk, hike.

camino road, way, highway *¿Está bien el camino para ir en auto?* Is the road all right to drive on? ▲ method, way *No sé qué camino seguir para conseguirlo.* I don't know how to go about getting it.

○ **ponerse en camino** to start out,

set out *Se pusieron en camino al día siguiente.* They started out the following day.

camión [*m*] truck; [*Mex*] bus.

camisa shirt.

○ **en mangas de camisa** in one's shirt sleeves *Estaba en mangas de camisa.* He was in his shirt sleeves.

camisería haberdashery, store for men's wear.

camiseta undershirt.

camisón [*m*] nightgown.

camote [*m*] sweet potato [*Mex, C.A.*].

campamento camp *Los soldados volverán pronto al campamento.* The soldiers will soon return to camp.

campana bell *Oímos las campanas de la iglesia.* We heard the church bells.

campanada stroke of a bell *or* clock *No he oído cuántas campanadas eran.* I didn't hear how many times the clock struck.

campanilla small bell, hand bell.

campaña campaign.

campeón [*m*] champion.

campeonato championship.

campesino, campesina peasant.

campo country, field *Vivimos durante muchos años en el campo.* We lived in the country for many years.

○ **campo de batalla** battlefield.

cana gray hair *Se encontró la primera cana.* She found her first gray hair.— *Tiene muchas canas.* She has a lot of gray hair.

canal [*m*] canal *Pasamos por el canal de Panamá.* We passed through the Panama Canal. ▲ strait, channel *El barco se acercaba al canal de la Mancha.* The boat was approaching the English Channel.

canario canary.

canasta wide basket *Nos trajeron una canasta de fruta.* They brought us a basket of fruit.

cancha court *En este parque hay canchas de tenis.* There are tennis courts in this park. ▲ popcorn [*Am*].

canción [*f*] song *¿Cuál es la canción que está más de moda?* What's the latest song hit?

candado padlock.

candela candle *Encienda la candela.* Light the candle. ▲ light *Déme candela para encender el cigarrillo.* Give me a light for my cigarette.

candidato candidate, applicant.

cándido simple-minded, innocent, gullible.

canela cinnamon.

cangrejo crab (shellfish).

canje [*m*] exchange (publications, prisoners).

canjear to exchange *Decidieron canjear los prisioneros.* They decided to exchange prisoners.

canoa canoe.

cansado (see **cansar**) tired *Estoy cansada.* I'm tired. ▲tiresome, boring *Ese hombre es muy cansado.* This man's very tiresome.

cansancio tiredness, fatigue *Está muerto de cansancio.* He's dead-tired.

cansar to tire *Es un trabajo que cansa mucho.* It's a very tiring job.
○ **cansarse** to get tired *Se cansa en seguida.* She gets tired quickly.

cantaleta ‖ *Siempre está con la misma cantaleta.* He's always harping on the same string.

cantante [*m, f*] singer.

cantar [*m*] song *Quiero aprender ese cantar.* I want to learn that song. ▲[*v*] to sing *El tenor ha cantado muy bien esta noche.* The tenor sang very well tonight.
○ **cantar claro** *Tendré que cantárselo claro.* I'll have to tell it to him straight from the shoulder.

cantidad [*f*] amount, quantity *¿Qué cantidad le debo?* How much do I owe you?

cantimplora canteen, water bottle.

cantina tavern, saloon [*Am*]; railroad restaurant [*Sp*].

canto singing *Es profesor de canto.* He's a singing teacher. ▲song *Me gustan los cantos populares.* I like folk songs.

canto edge.
○ **de canto** on edge, on its side *Ponga el libro de canto.* Stand the book on edge.

caña reed, cane *En Cuba se cultiva mucha caña de azúcar.* A lot of sugar cane is grown in Cuba. ▲walking stick, cane (of bamboo) *Llevaba una caña.* He carried a cane.
○ **caña de pescar** fishing rod.

cañada ravine.

cañería water pipe, pipe line *Tienen que arreglar la cañería; está atrancada.* They have to fix the water pipe; it's clogged.

cañón [*m*] barrel (of a gun) *Compró una escopeta de dos cañones.* He bought a double-barreled shotgun. ▲cannon, gun. ▲canyon, gorge *¿Conoce Ud. el cañón del Colorado?* Have you seen the Grand Canyon?

caoba mahogany.

capa cape (clothing) *Usa capa española.* He wears a Spanish cape. ▲coat *La puerta necesita otra capa de pintura.* The door needs another coat of paint.
○ **andar** (*or* **ir**) **de capa caída** to be on the downgrade *¡Pobrecillos, andan de capa caída!* Poor people, they're on the downgrade!

capacidad [*f*] capacity *Este tanque tiene una capacidad de treinta litros.* This tank has a capacity of thirty liters. ▲capability *Es un hombre de gran capacidad para los negocios.* He's a very capable business man.

capataz [*m*] foreman *Querría hablar con el capataz.* I'd like to talk to the foreman.

capaz large *Es una habitación bastante capaz para biblioteca.* It's a room large enough for a library. ▲capable *No es capaz de una acción tan baja.* He's not capable of such a low trick. ▲able, competent *Me han dicho que es una persona muy capaz.* I've been told that he's a very competent person.

capellán [*m*] chaplain.

capilla chapel.

capital [*m*] capital *La compañía tiene un capital de un millón de dólares.* The company has a capital of a million dollars. ▲[*f*] capital (city) *Hicieron un viaje a la capital.* They took a trip to the capital.
○ **pena capital** capital punishment.

capitán [*m*] captain.

capítulo chapter *He leído sólo los tres primeros capítulos.* I've read only the first three chapters.

capotera hat *or* clothes rack [*Am*].

capricho whim, fancy *No haga Ud. caso de sus caprichos.* Don't pay any attention to her whims.

caprichoso fickle, capricious.

cápsula capsule; shell (for short firearms).

capturar to capture.

capullo bud; cocoon.

cara face *Tiene una cara muy bonita.* She has a very pretty face. ▲face, front *No entiendo las palabras que hay en la cara de la moneda.* I don't understand the words on the face of the coin.
○ **cara a cara** right to a person's face *Se lo dijo cara a cara.* He told

him right to his face. ○ **cara o cruz** heads or tails. ○ **dar la cara** to face the music *Tuvo que dar la cara.* He had to face the music.

caracol [m] snail.

○ **escalera de caracol** winding staircase.

carácter [m] character *Es un hombre de muy buen carácter.* He's a man of very good character. ▲ firmness, character *En todo muestra que tiene carácter.* Everything she does shows she has character.

característica [f] characteristic.

¡caramba! gosh darn! heavens! *¡Caramba que frío hace!* Heavens, how cold it is!

caramelo candy *¿Tiene caramelos de menta?* Do you have any peppermint candy?

carbón [m] coal *Hay que poner más carbón en la estufa.* You have to put more coal in the stove.

carbonera coal bin *La carbonera está llena.* The coal bin's full.

carbonero coal dealer.

carburador [m] carburetor.

carcajada burst of laughter, loud laughter *Se estaban riendo a carcajadas.* They were splitting their sides.

cárcel [f] jail, prison *Le metieron en la cárcel.* They put him in jail.

carecer [-zc-] to lack, not to have *Carece del dinero necesario para viajar.* He doesn't have enough money to travel.

carey [m] tortoise shell.

carga load *Este mulo no puede llevar más carga.* This mule can't carry a heavier load. ▲ cargo *Es un barco de carga.* It's a cargo ship. ▲ freight *Están sacando la carga del vagón.* They're taking the freight out of the car.

cargamento load; shipment.

cargar to load *Cargaron el camión.* They loaded the truck. ▲ to charge *Hay que cargar la batería.* The battery has to be charged.—*La caballería cargó sobre el enemigo.* The cavalry charged the enemy. ▲ to charge (to one's account) *Cargo esta cantidad en su cuenta.* I'm charging this amount to your bill.

caricatura caricature, cartoon.

caridad [f] charity.

cariño affection, love *Le tienen mucho cariño.* They're very fond of him.

cariñoso affectionate *Era muy cariñoso con sus padres.* He was very affectionate with his parents.

‖ *Recuerdos cariñosos a su familia.* My best regards to your family.

carne [f] meat *Generalmente como carne una vez al día.* I usually eat meat once a day.

○ **carne de gallina** goose flesh *Con este frío se me pone la carne de gallina.* This cold weather gives me goose flesh. ○ **carne de res** beef [Am]. ○ **carne de vaca** beef *¿Quieren Uds. carne de vaca o de cerdo?* Do you want beef or pork?

carnero sheep; mutton, lamb.

carnicería meat market, butcher shop.

carnicero butcher.

caro dear, expensive *Estas corbatas son muy caras.* These ties are very expensive.

carpeta briefcase [Am] *Necesito una carpeta de cuero.* I need a leather briefcase. ▲ letter file, folder *La correspondencia está guardada en varias carpetas.* The correspondence is kept in several files.

carpintero carpenter.

carrera race *Me gustan las carreras de caballos.* I like horse races. ▲ avenue, broad street [Col] *Viven en la Carrera Tercera.* They live on Third Avenue. ▲ career *Está preparándose para la carrera diplomática.* He's preparing for a diplomatic career.

○ **a la carrera** hastily, hurriedly *Lo escribió a la carrera.* He wrote it hurriedly. ○ **dar una carrera** to sprint *Dió una carrera para alcanzarlos.* He sprinted to catch up to them.

carreta wagon.

carretera highway, road *En este país las carreteras son magníficas.* The highways in this country are excellent.

carro cart *Por la carretera iba un carro de mulas.* There was a mule cart on the road. ▲ car, automobile [Am] *Vamos a ir en carro a la casa.* We're going home by car.

carruaje [m] carriage (vehicle).

carta letter *Voy a echar esta carta al correo.* I'm going to mail this letter.

○ **a carta cabal** thoroughly, in every respect *Es honrado a carta cabal.* He's thoroughly honest. ○ **a la carta** á la carte. ○ **carta certificada** registered letter *Recibió una carta certificada.* He received a registered letter. ○ **carta de crédito** letter of credit. ○ **carta de presentación** letter of introduction. ○ **carta de recomendación** letter of recommendation. ○ **jugar a las cartas** [Sp], **jugar cartas** [Am] to play cards

Vamos a jugar un rato a las cartas.
Let's play cards a while.

cartel [*m*] placard, bill, poster.

cartera bag *Llevaba bajo el brazo una gran cartera de cuero.* She was carrying a large leather bag under her arm. ▲ wallet *Sacó la cartera del bolsillo.* He took his wallet out of his pocket. ▲ briefcase *¿Caben muchos libros en esa cartera?* Will that briefcase hold many books?

cartero mailman, postman *¿A qué hora viene el cartero?* What time does the mailman come?

cartón [*m*] cardboard.

casa house. ▲ home *¿Estará Ud. en casa esta tarde?* Will you be at home this afternoon?
○ **casa de comercio** commercial house, firm. ○ **casa de empeño(s)** pawnshop. ○ **casa de huéspedes** boarding house. ○ **casa de maternidad** maternity hospital (charitable institution). ○ **casa de socorro** emergency hospital.

casado (see **casar**) married *¿Es Ud. casado o soltero?* Are you married or single?

casamiento wedding, marriage.

casar to marry *Este es el cura que los casó.* This is the priest who married them. ▲ to match *Estos colores no casan bien.* These colors don't match well.
○ **casarse** to marry, get married *Se casará el domingo próximo.* He'll be married next Sunday. ○ **casarse con** to marry *Se casó con una muchacha muy joven.* He married a very young girl.

cascar to crack *¿Tiene Ud. algo con que cascar estas nueces?* Have you got something to crack these nuts?

cáscara rind, peel *Esta naranja tiene una cáscara muy gruesa.* This orange has a thick rind. ▲ shell (of nuts, eggs, etc) *¿Dónde tiro estas cáscaras de huevos?* Where do I throw these eggshells?

cascarrabias [*adj; m & f sg*] irritable (person), crab(by) *Te estás volviendo muy cascarrabias.* You're getting to be an old crab.

casco helmet *Los soldados llevaban casco de acero.* The soldiers were wearing steel helmets. ▲ hull (of a ship) *El casco del buque está averiado.* The ship's hull is damaged.
○ **calentarse los cascos** to rack one's brains *Aunque se caliente Ud. los cascos no lo resolverá.* Though you rack

your brains over it, you won't solve it. ○ **casco de caballo** horse's hoof.

caserío small village, settlement.

casero, casera landlord, landlady; building superintendent. ▲ [*adj*] homemade *Son dulces caseros.* They're homemade candies.

caseta de baños locker, bath house.

casi almost, nearly.
○ **casi, casi** very nearly *Casi, casi lo ha acertado.* You very nearly guessed it.

caso case *Ha habido varios casos de parálisis infantil.* There have been several cases of infantile paralysis. ▲ occurrence, event *Les voy a contar un caso curioso.* I'm going to tell you about a strange incident.
○ **en tal caso** in such a case *En tal caso avise a su familia.* In such a case, notify his family. ○ **en todo caso** at all events, anyway *En todo caso nos vemos mañana.* Anyway, we'll see each other tomorrow. ○ **hacer caso a** to pay attention to, heed, obey (a person) *No hace caso a sus padres.* He doesn't obey his parents. ○ **hacer caso de** to mind, heed, pay attention to *No hagas caso de lo que te cuente.* Don't pay any attention to what he tells you.

castaña chestnut.

castaño chestnut tree. ▲ [*adj*] brown *Tiene el pelo castaño.* He has brown hair.

castañuela castanet.

castigar to punish *No castigue a los niños.* Don't punish the children.

castigo punishment.

castillo castle.

castizo correct, pure *Habla un español castizo.* He speaks a pure Spanish. ▲ genuine, real *Es un español castizo.* He's a real Spaniard.

casual accidental, chance *Fué un encuentro casual.* It was a chance meeting.

casualidad [*f*] coincidence *¡Qué casualidad encontrarle aquí!* What a coincidence meeting you here!
○ **por casualidad** by chance, by any chance *¿Por casualidad le conoce Ud.?* Do you know him, by any chance?

catalogar to catalog, list.

catálogo catalog, list.

catarata cataract, waterfall; cataract (of eye).

catarro cold *He cogido un catarro horrible.* I've caught a terrible cold.

catástrofe [*f*] catastrophe.

catedral [*f*] cathedral.

catedrático professor *Es catedrático en la Universidad Nacional.* He's a professor at the National University.

categoría class, category *Los dos no son de la misma categoría.* The two are not in the same category. ▲ rank *No tiene categoría para ese puesto.* His rank isn't high enough for that position.
○ **de categoría** of importance *Es un hombre de categoría.* He's a man of importance.

catolicismo Catholicism.

católico [*adj, n*] Catholic.

catorce fourteen.

catre [*m*] cot.

caucho rubber (material).

caudal [*m*] fortune, wealth, means *Ha aumentado mucho el caudal de esa familia.* The family fortune has increased a great deal. ▲ volume (of water) *El río lleva un gran caudal.* The river carries a huge volume of water.

caudillo leader, chief *Fué uno de los caudillos de la revolución.* He was one of the leaders of the revolution.

causa cause *¿Cuál fué la causa de su retraso?* What was the cause of his delay? ▲ case, trial, lawsuit *Fué una de las causas célebres de su época.* It was one of the famous cases of his time.

causar to cause, occasion *Me ha causado muchos disgustos.* She's caused me a lot of trouble.

cauto cautious, careful *Uno tiene que ser cauto en los negocios.* You have to be careful in business.

cavar to dig.

caverna cavern, cave.

cayuco dugout canoe [*Am*].

caza hunt, hunting *Ahora está prohibida la caza.* Hunting's forbidden now. ▲ game *En esa selva hay mucha caza mayor.* There's a lot of big game in that forest.
○ **andar a caza de** to go hunting for, go in search of *Los periodistas andaban a caza de noticias.* The reporters were hunting for news.

cazador [*m*] hunter.

cazar to hunt.

cazuela earthen cooking pot.

cebada barley.

cebo bait.

cebolla onion; bulb.

cecear to lisp.

cedazo sifter (utensil).

ceder to transfer, turn over, cede *Cedió todos sus bienes a su hijo.* He transferred his whole estate to his son. ▲ to yield, give in *No cedió en su empeño.* He wouldn't give in.

cedro cedar.

cédula personal identification card.

cegar [*rad-ch I*] to blind *Me ciega esa luz tan fuerte.* That strong light blinds me.

ceja eyebrow.
○ **tener entre ceja y ceja** to dislike, have a grudge against *Mi jefe me tiene entre ceja y ceja.* My boss has a grudge against me.

celebrar to celebrate, commemorate *Celebraron su cumpleaños en una gran fiesta.* They celebrated his birthday with a big party. ▲ to praise, applaud, approve *Todos celebran sus éxitos.* They all applauded his success. ▲ to be glad, rejoice *Celebro mucho verle a Ud.* I'm certainly glad to see you.

célebre famous *Fué el escritor más célebre de su tiempo.* He was the most famous writer of his day.

celebridad [*f*] celebrity.

celo zeal, enthusiasm *Trabaja con mucho celo.* He's a very zealous worker.
○ **estar en celo** to be in heat (of animals). ○ **tener celos** to be jealous *Tiene muchos celos de su mujer.* He's very jealous of his wife.

celoso jealous.

cementerio cemetery, graveyard.

cemento cement, concrete.

cena supper *¿Qué vamos a tomar de cena?* What are we having for supper?

cenar to dine, eat *¿Dónde cenaron Uds. anoche?* Where did you eat last night? ▲ to have for supper *Cenamos pescado anoche.* We had fish for supper last night.

cenicero ash tray.

ceniza ashes, cinders.

censura censorship *La correspondencia tiene que pasar por la censura.* Mail has to go through censorship. ▲ office of censor *Hay que enviar este artículo a la censura.* This article has to go through the censor's office. ▲ reproach, criticism *Es una censura injusta la que Ud. me hace.* Your criticism's unfair.

censurar to blame, criticize *No se la puede censurar por lo que ha hecho.* You can't blame her for what she did.

centavo cent [*Am*].

centenar [*m*] a hundred *Había un cen-*

tenar de personas en el local. There were a hundred people in the hall.

○ **a centenares** by hundreds *Murieron las gentes a centenares.* People died by the hundreds.

centenario centenary.

centeno rye.

centímetro centimeter.

céntimo cent [*Sp*].

centinela [*m*] sentry, guard.

○ **de centinela** on sentry duty *Está de centinela.* He's on sentry duty.

central [*adj; f*] central.

○ **central eléctrica** electric power plant, power house.

centro center *Vivimos en el centro (de la ciudad).* We live in the center of the city. ▲ business district, downtown *Vamos al centro.* Let's go downtown. ▲ club *Hubo un baile en nuestro centro.* There was a dance at our club.

ceñir [*rad-ch III*] to fit tightly *Esta cinturón me ciñe demasiado.* This belt fits me too tightly.

○ **ceñirse** to confine *or* limit oneself *Cíñase Ud. al asunto.* Confine yourself to the facts.

‖ *No se ciña tanto en la curva.* Don't hug the inside of the curve.

ceño ○ **mirar con ceño** to frown.

ceñudo [*adj*] scowling, frowning *Siempre está ceñudo.* He's always scowling.

cepillar to brush *Tengo que cepillar el sombrero.* I have to brush my hat. ▲ to plane, make smooth *Estas tablas no están bien cepilladas.* These boards haven't been planed right.

cepillo brush (flat, with bristles on one side) *¿Dónde puedo comprar un cepillo?* Where can I buy a brush?

○ **cepillo de cabeza** hairbrush. ○ **cepillo de carpintero** carpenter's plane. ○ **cepillo de dientes** toothbrush. ○ **cepillo de ropa** clothes brush.

cera wax.

cerca fence *La huerta tiene una cerca de madera.* The garden has a wooden fence.

cerca de near (in place) *La estación está cerca del hotel.* The station's near the hotel. ▲ nearly, about, almost *Son cerca de las once.* It's about eleven o'clock.

○ **por aquí cerca** near here, somewhere near here *¿Hay un buen restaurante por aquí cerca?* Is there a good restaurant somewhere near here?

cercado fenced in, enclosed.

cercano near, close *Viven en una casa*

cercana a la nuestra. They live in a house close to ours.

cercar to surround, fence in *Cercaron la finca con alambrado.* They fenced in the property with wire.

cerdo pig, hog; pork.

○ **chuletas de cerdo** pork chops.

cereal [*adj; m*] cereal.

ceremonia ceremony *La ceremonia fué muy solemne.* The ceremony was very impressive.

cereza cherry.

cerilla match *Voy a comprar una caja de cerillas.* I'm going to buy a box of matches.

cerillo match [*Mex*].

cero zero *La temperatura está a cuarenta grados bajo cero.* The temperature's forty below.

cerradura lock.

cerrar to close, shut *Cierre Ud. la puerta, por favor.* Please close the door. ▲ to seal *Añade unas palabras antes de que yo cierre la carta.* Add a few words before I seal the letter.

cerro hill *Desde ese cerro hay muy buena vista.* There's a very good view from that hill.

cerrojo bolt, latch.

certero well-aimed *Fué un disparo certero.* It was a well-aimed shot.

certeza assurance, certainty *Tengo la certeza de que vendrá.* I'm certain he's coming.

certificado (see **certificar**) certificate *¿Necesita Ud. un certificado médico?* Do you need a doctor's certificate? ▲ piece of registered mail.

certificar to register (a letter) *Voy a certificar estas cartas.* I'm going to register these letters.

cervecería bar, saloon.

cerveza beer, ale *Vamos a tomar unos vasos de cerveza.* Let's drink a few glasses of beer.

cesar to stop, cease *El ruido no ha cesado en todo el día.* The noise hasn't stopped all day. ▲ to dismiss, fire *Ayer cesaron a siete empleados.* Yesterday they fired seven employees.

césped [*m*] lawn, grass.

cesta basket *Compraron una cesta de fruta.* They bought a basket of fruit.

cesto large basket.

chabacano vulgar, in bad taste *Siempre hace chistes chabacanos.* He always tells vulgar jokes. ▲ [*m*] apricot [*Mex*].

chacra small farm [*S.A.*].

chal [*m*] shawl.

chaleco vest.

chalet [*m*] chalet.

chamaco youngster [*Mex*].

chambergo soft hat.

champú [*m*] shampoo.

chancearse to jest, joke, fool *Se chancea de todo el mundo.* He makes fun of everybody.

chancho pig, hog [*Am*].

chanchullo something u n d e r h a n d e d, racket *Siempre anda metido en chanchullos.* He's always in something underhanded.

chanclos [*m pl*] rubbers.

chanza joke *Déjate de chanzas porque la cosa es muy seria.* Stop joking; it's a serious matter.

chapa plate, sheet (of metal) *El tejado está cubierto de chapas metálicas.* The roof's covered with sheet metal. ▲ lock [*Am*] *Hay que cambiar la chapa de la puerta.* You have to change the lock on the door.

○ **chapas** rosy cheeks [*Am*] *Tiene unas lindas chapas.* She has beautiful rosy cheeks.

chaparro short person [*Mex*].

chaparrón [*m*] heavy shower, downpour.

chapetón [*m*] Spaniard (fresh from Spain) [*S. A.*].

chapetonada illness caused by change of climate [*S. A.*].

chapucería botched job, hurried job *Hágalo Ud. con cuidado, no me gustan les chapucerías.* Do it carefully. I don't like botched jobs.

chapurrear to speak (a language) brokenly *Chapurrea el español.* He speaks broken Spanish.

chaqueta jacket, coat.

charco puddle.

charlar to talk, chatter.

charol [*m*] patent leather.

charro cowboy [*Mex*].

chasco ○ **darle a uno un chasco** to fool, play a joke on *Le dimos un chasco dejándole la cuenta.* We played a joke on him by leaving him the bill. ○ **llevarse un chasco** to be disappointed *or* disconcerted *Con esa muchacha nos llevamos un chasco terrible.* We were very disappointed in that girl.

chato flat-nosed, pug-nosed.

cheque [*m*] check (money).

chequear to check, put a check next to [*Am*].

chica girl.

chicha chicha (alcoholic drink made from corn) [*Am*].

chícharo green pea [*Mex*].

chicharrón [*m*] thick crisp bacon.

chichón [*m*] bump, lump (on the head).

chicle [*m*] chewing gum.

chico little, small *El cuarto en que vive es muy chico.* He lives in a very small room. ▲ boy, kid *Tiene tres chicos.* She has three kids.

chifladura eccentricity.

chiflón [*m*] draft [*Am*] *Por esa ventana entra un chiflón muy fuerte.* A strong draft's blowing in at that window.

chile [*f*] chili, red pepper.

chillar to screech, scream.

chillido screech, scream.

chimenea smokestack *Desde la ventana se ven las chimeneas de la fábrica.* From the window you can see the smokestacks of the factory. ▲ chimney *Se subieron al tejado para limpier la chimenea.* They climbed up on the roof to clean the chimney. ▲ fireplace *Se sentaron junto a la chimenea.* They sat by the fireplace.

china pebble, small stone *Se me ha metido una china en el zapato.* I have a pebble in my shoe. ▲ peasant girl, maid, servant [*Am*] *La china lo llevará a su casa.* The maid'll take it to your house. ▲ china, porcelain *¿Son de china estas tazas?* Are these cups porcelain? ▲ orange [*Antilles*] *Deme una docena de chinas.* Give me a dozen oranges.

chinche [*f*] bedbug; thumbtack.

chiquilín [*m*] small child.

chiquillo, chiquilla small child.

chiripa chance *or* unexpected event [*Fam*] *Me ha salido bien por chiripa.* I got it right by accident.

¡chis! sh!

chisme gossip, malicious remark *Siempre anda metiendo chismes.* He's always gossiping.

chispa spark *¡Cuidado con las chispas que saltan de la chimenea!* Watch out for the sparks that are flying out of the fireplace. ▲ little bit, small amount *No tiene chispa de tonto.* He's not at all stupid.

○ **echar chispas** [*Fam*] to rage, be furious *Cuando se lo dije echó chispas.* When I told him that, he got furious.

chistar to keep quiet.

○ **no,** *or* **ni, chistar** not to say a word *Cuando vió a su padre ni chistó.* When he saw his father, he didn't even say a word.

chiste [*m*] joke *Contó un chiste muy gracioso.* He told a very funny joke.

chistoso funny, witty.

chocante surprising, witty [*Sp*]; annoying, unpleasant [*Mex*].

chocar to collide, crash *Chocaron los dos autos.* The two cars crashed. ▲ to clash *Han chocado varias veces por sus opiniones políticas.* They often clashed over their political beliefs. ▲ to surprise unpleasantly, to vex *Me choca que diga Ud. eso.* I'm surprised to hear you say that.

choclo green ear of corn [*S.A.*].

chocolate [*m*] chocolate.

chofer, chófer [*m*] chauffeur.

cholo, chola half-breed [*S.A.*].

choque [*m*] collision, crash.

chorizo Spanish sausage.

chorrear to gush, drip.

chorro jet, spurt *Abrió el grifo y salió un chorro de agua.* He turned on the faucet and a jet of water came out. ○ **a chorros** abundantly [*Fam*]. ○ **llover a chorros** to pour (rain).

choza hut, cabin.

chuchería trinket; tidbit; trifle.

chueco crooked, bent [*Am*] *Este zapato está chueco.* This shoe is crooked.

chuleta chop.

chupar to suck.

churro a kind of cruller.

chusco funny, amusing.

cicatriz [*f*] scar.

ciclón [*m*] cyclone.

ciego blind *Se está quedando ciego.* He's going blind. ▲ [*n*] blind person *Han construído un asilo para ciegos.* They built an asylum for the blind. ○ **a ciegas** in the dark, blindly *Se metió en ese negocio a ciegas.* He went into that business blindly.

cielo sky *El cielo estaba lleno de aviones.* The sky was filled with airplanes. ▲ paradise, heaven. ▲ dear, darling. *Ven aquí, mi cielo.* Come here, darling. ○ **llovido del cielo** out of the clear sky *Apareció como llovido del cielo.* He appeared out of a clear sky.

cien (see **ciento**) one hundred.

ciencia science.

científico scientist; scientific.

ciento one hundred. ○ **por ciento** per cent *Gana el cinco por ciento sobre lo que vende.* He makes five per cent on what he sells.

cierto sure, certain, true *¿Es cierto que vendrá mañana?* Is it true he's coming tomorrow? ▲ certain, some *A cierta gente le gusta.* Some people like it. ▲ [*adv*] certainly *Cierto, tiene Ud. razón.* Certainly, you're right. ○ **no por cierto** certainly not *No por cierto, no estoy de acuerdo con Ud.* Certainly not, I don't agree with you.

ciervo deer.

cifra figure, digit (number) *¿Cuántas cifras tiene ese número?* How many digits does that number have? ▲ code *La carta estaba escrita en cifra.* The letter was written in code.

cigarrera cigarette case [*Am*]; woman cigar maker.

cigarrería place where cigars and cigarettes are made or sold [*Am*].

cigarrillo cigarette.

cigarro (see **puro**) cigar *Le regaló una caja de cigarros habanos.* She presented him with a box of Havana cigars. ▲ cigarette *Voy a comprar un paquete de cigarros.* I'm going to buy a pack of cigarettes.

cilindro cylinder.

cima summit, peak.

cimiento foundation *Han comenzado los cimientos de la casa.* They laid the foundation of the house.

cinc [*m*] zinc.

cinco five.

cincuenta fifty.

cine [*m*] moving pictures, movies *Me gusta mucho el cine americano.* I like American movies very much. ▲ movie theater *Es un nuevo cine.* It's a new movie theater.

cinematógrafo movie house.

cínico cynic; cynical.

cinta ribbon *Llevaba una cinta atada a la cabeza.* She wore a ribbon tied around her hair. ▲ film (moving picture) *Es la mejor cinta del año.* It's the best film of the year.

cintura waist *Tiene una cintura muy pequeña.* She has a small waist. ○ **meter en cintura** to discipline, restrain *Hay que meter en cintura ese chico.* That child has to be restrained.

cinturón [*m*] belt *Voy a comprar un cinturón de cuero.* I'm going to buy a leather belt.

circo circus *Este año el circo tiene diez elefantes.* This year the circus has ten elephants.

circulación [*f*] circulation *Este periódico tiene mucha circulación.* This paper has a large circulation. ▲ traffic *No conozco el reglamento de la circulación aquí.* I don't know the traffic regulations here.

circular [*f*] circular, letter *He recibido una circular del banco.* I've received a circular from the bank.

circular to move about, get around *Era casi imposible circular por esa calle.* It was almost impossible to get around

on that street. ▲ to circulate, get
around *Ha circulado esa noticia.* That
news got around.

círculo circle *Estábamos sentados en círculo.* We were seated in a circle.
▲ club, social circle *Comimos juntos en el círculo.* We ate together at the club.

circunstancia circumstance.

circunstante [*m*] bystander.

ciruela plum.
   ○ **ciruela pasa** prune.

ciruelo plum tree.

cita engagement, appointment, date *¿Acudió Ud. a la cita?* Did you keep your appointment? ▲ quotation *Es una cita del Quijote.* It's a quotation from Don Quixote.

citar to call, summon *Todavía no nos han citado para la reunión.* We haven't been called to the meeting yet. ▲ to make (*or* give) an appointment *El dentista me citó para las siete.* The dentist gave me an appointment for seven o'clock. ▲ to quote, refer to *En mi artículo cité muchas veces su libro.* In my article, I referred to your book a great deal.

ciudad [*f*] city.

ciudadano, ciudadana citizen *¿De qué país es Ud. ciudadano?* What country are you a citizen of?

civil civil.
   ○ **derechos civiles** civil rights.

civilización [*f*] civilization, culture.

civilizar to civilize *Los misioneros civilizaron a los indígenas.* The missionaries civilized the natives.

claramente clearly, openly, frankly *Dígamelo claramente.* Tell me frankly.

claridad [*f*] clearness, distinctness *La claridad de la explicación lo convenció.* The clearness of the explanation satisfied him.

clarín [*m*] trumpet.

claro clear, transparent *Es tan claro como el agua.* It's as clear as crystal. ▲ thin *En las sienes tiene el pelo muy claro.* His hair's thin at the temples. ▲ cloudless, fair *Es un día muy claro.* It's a very clear day. ▲ light *Lleva un traje azul claro.* She's wearing a light blue suit. ▲ plain, clear *La explicación es clara.* The explanation is clear.

clase [*f*] class, kind, sort. ▲ class *Era uno de los dirigentes de la clase trabajadora.* He was a leader of the working class.—*Sólo asisto a dos clases este curso.* I have only two classes this

year. ▲ classroom *Esa clase es demasiado pequeña.* That classroom's too small.
   ○ **dar clase** to give a class, hold class *Tengo que dar una clase mañana a las ocho.* I have to give a class tomorrow at eight.

clásico classical *Anoche asistimos a un concierto de música clásica.* Last night we attended a concert of classical music. ▲ [*m*] classic *¿Ha leído los clásicos latinos?* Have you read the Latin classics?

clasificar to sort out, classify *Todavía no han clasificado la correspondencia.* They haven't sorted the mail yet.

claustro cloister *En esa iglesia hay un claustro muy bonito.* There's a very beautiful cloister in that church.

clavar to nail *Necesito un martillo para clavar las tablas.* I need a hammer to nail the boards. ▲ to stick, pin *Tenga cuidado donde clava el alfiler.* Be careful where you stick the pin.
   ○ **clavarse** to stick, prick *Me clavé una espina en el dedo.* I got a thorn in my finger.

clave [*f*] key (of a code) *Necesito la clave para descifrar esta comunicación.* I need the key to decode this message. ▲ key *Esta canción está en clave de sol.* This song's in the key of G.

clavel [*m*] carnation.

clavo nail *Necesito una caja de clavos.* I need a box of nails.
   ○ **dar en el clavo** to hit the nail on the head.

clemencia mercy.

clerical clerical (church).

clero clergy.

cliente [*m, f*] client, customer.

clientela clientele.

clima [*m*] climate.

clínica clinic.

cobarde [*m, f*] coward *¡Anímese Ud.! ¡No sea cobarde!* Come on, don't be a coward! ▲ [*adj*] cowardly *Lo que hizo fué muy cobarde.* It was a cowardly thing he did.

cobardía cowardice.

cobija cover, blanket [*Am*] *¿Cuántas cobijas tiene la cama?* How many blankets are there on the bed?

cobrador [*m*] collector (bills, taxes) *Les visitó el cobrador de contribuciones.* The tax collector called on them. ▲ conductor (of bus or trolley) *Se lo preguntaremos al cobrador (del tranvía).* We'll ask the conductor (of the trolley).

cobranza collection *La cobranza de impuestos está bien organizada.* The collection of taxes is well organized.

cobrar to collect, receive *¿Cobró Ud. el dinero que le debían?* Did you collect the money they owed you? ▲ to cash *En esta ventanilla puede cobrar su cheque.* You can cash your check at this window. ▲ to charge *Cobran muy caro en esa tienda.* They charge high prices at that store.

cobre [*m*] copper.

cobro collection (of money due) *Presentó la factura al cobro.* He presented the bill for collection.

coca coca (plant from which cocaine is obtained) [*Am*].

cocal [*m*] coconut plantation [*Am*].

cocer [*rad-ch I*] to boil *Cueza Ud. esas papas.* Boil those potatoes. ▲ to bake *El pan se está cociendo en el horno.* The bread's baking in the oven.

coche [*m*] carriage, coach *Tienen un coche de dos caballos.* They have a two-horse carriage. ▲ car *Acaban de comprar un coche nuevo.* They've just bought a new car.

○ **coche-cama** sleeping car, Pullman *¿Lleva coche-cama este tren?* Does this train have a sleeping car? ○ **coche-comedor** dining car *El coche-comedor va a la cabeza del tren.* The dining car's at the forward end of the train.

cochero coachman *Déle la dirección al cochero.* Give the address to the coachman.

cochino hog, pig. ▲ swine (insult). ▲ dirty, filthy, vile *¡Qué cochinos están estos niños!* How filthy these children are!

cocina kitchen *La cocina de esa casa es muy bonita.* The kitchen in that house is very nice. ▲ cuisine, cooking *Me gusta la cocina francesa.* I like French cooking.

cocinar to cook *Su mujer cocina muy bien.* His wife cooks very well.

cocinero, cocinera cook.

coco coconut; coconut tree.

cocotero coconut tree.

coctelera cocktail shaker.

codicioso greedy *Es un hombre codicioso.* He's a greedy man.

código code (of laws).

○ **código civil** civil law. ○ **código militar** military law.

codo elbow *Se está rompiendo la chaqueta por los codos.* The jacket's wearing through at the elbows.—*Se sale el agua por el codo de la cañería.* The water's leaking from the elbow of the pipe.

cofre [*m*] (see also **baúl**) trunk [*Am*]; chest [*Sp*] *Cerró el cofre con llave.* He locked the trunk with a key.

coger [*should not be used in Arg*] to catch *Cogieron al ladrón.* They caught the thief. ▲ to pick, gather *Van a empezar a coger las naranjas.* They're going to start picking oranges.

coincidencia coincidence.

coincidir to coincide, agree *Los dos relatos no coinciden.* The two statements don't agree.

cojear (*not used in Arg; see* **renguear**) to limp, hobble *Cojea un poco del pie derecho.* He limps slightly on his right foot.

cojín [*m*] pad, cushion *Ponga esos cojines en el diván.* Put those cushions on the couch.

col [*f*] cabbage.

cola tail *El perro movía la cola.* The dog was wagging his tail. ▲ train (of dress) *Llevaba un vestido de cola.* She wore a dress with a train. ▲ line of people *Esta es la cola para sacar los billetes.* This is the ticket line.

○ **hacer cola** to stand in line *He estado haciendo cola más de dos horas.* I was standing in line for more than two hours.

colaboración [*f*] collaboration, working together *Escribe en colaboración con su hermano.* He writes in collaboration with his brother.

colaborador [*m*] collaborator, co-worker. ▲ contributor (to a periodical, etc) *Es uno de los mejores colaboradores de este periódico.* He's one of the best contributors to this newspaper.

colaborar to collaborate, cooperate; to contribute.

colador [*m*] colander, strainer *Ponga las verduras en el colador.* Put the vegetables in the strainer.

colar to strain *El jugo de naranja no está bien colado.* The orange juice isn't well strained.

colcha bedspread *Tienen una colcha azul sobre la cama.* They have a blue bedspread on the bed.

colchón [*m*] mattress.

colección [*f*] collection (of things) *Tiene una buena colección de cuadros modernos.* He has a good collection of modern paintings.

coleccionar to collect (stamps, coins, etc).

colecta collection (charity).

colectivo collective *Los intereses colectivos deben protegerse.* Collective interests must be protected. ▲ organized.
colega [*m*] fellow worker, colleague.
colegio school (private) *Acaba de entrar en el colegio.* He's just entered school. ▲ association, college *Es miembro del colegio de médicos.* He's a member of the medical association.
cólera [*f*] anger, rage, fury *Eso le dió mucha cólera.* That made him very angry.
cólera [*m*] cholera.
colgado (See **colgar**) hanging *El sombrero está colgado en la percha.* The hat's hanging on the rack.
colgando (See **colgar**) dangling *Llevaba el reloj colgando del bolsillo.* His watch was dangling from his pocket.
colgar [*rad-ch I*] to hang *Cuelgue Ud. aquí sus ropas.* Hang your clothes here. ▲ to hang (by the neck) *Merecía que lo colgaran.* He deserved to be hanged.
colina hill.
collar [*m*] necklace; collar.
colmena beehive.
colocación [*f*] job, position *¿Le gusta su nueva colocación?* Do you like your new job? ▲ arrangement *¿Le agrada la colocación de los muebles?* Do you like the arrangement of the furniture?
colocar to put, arrange *Voy a colocar estas flores.* I'm going to arrange these flowers. ▲ to take on *Colocaron muchos empleados nuevos.* They took on many new employees.
○ **colocar dinero** to invest (money) *Voy a colocar dinero en este negocio.* I'm going to invest (money) in this business. ○ **colocarse** to take a job *Me he colocado en un banco.* I've taken a job in a bank.
colonia colony *Jamaica es una colonia inglesa.* Jamaica's an English colony. ▲ suburb, (real estate) development *Hay lindas colonias en los alrededores de la capital.* There are beautiful developments on the outskirts of the capital.
○ **(agua de) Colonia** toilet water.
colonial [*adj*] colonial.
colonizador [*m*] colonizer.
colono tenant farmer *Tiene muchos colonos en la hacienda.* He has many tenants on his land. ▲ colonist *Los primeros colonos americanos llegaron en el siglo diecisiete.* The first American colonists arrived in the 17th century.

color [*m*] color *Todo lo ve color de rosa.* He sees the world through rose-colored glasses. ▲ blush, flush *Le hizo salir los colores (a la cara).* He made her blush. ▲ slant *Este periódico no tiene color político.* This newspaper has no political slant.
colorado [*adj*] red.
○ **ponerse colorado** to blush.
colorear to color (a map, etc).
colorido colors, coloring *El colorido de este cuadro es muy brillante.* The colors of this painting are very bright.
colosal huge, gigantic, colossal; "terrific."
columna column.
coma comma.
comadre [*f*] (term of address between mother and godmother of a child); gossip; old woman (among country people).
comandante [*m*] commander; major.
combate [*m*] combat, battle, fight.
combatir to combat, fight, oppose, attack.
combinación [*f*] combination; (woman's) slip.
combinar to combine, join, unite.
combustible [*m*] fuel *¿Con qué clase de combustible funciona esta máquina?* What kind of fuel do you use in this machine?
comedia comedy; play.
comedor [*m*] dining room.
comentar to comment on *Comentaban su nuevo libro.* They were commenting on his new book.
comentario remark, comment, commentary *No hay que hacer comentarios.* One should not make comments.
comenzar [*rad-ch I*] to begin, commence *¿Cuándo comienza la función?* When does the performance begin?
comer to eat. ▲ to dine *¿A qué hora comen Uds.?* What time do you have dinner? ▲ to fade *El sol come los colores.* The sun fades colors.
○ **comerse** to eat up *Se han comido todo el pastel.* They ate up all the cake. ▲ to omit, skip *Se ha comido un renglón.* He skipped a line. ▲ to run through, squander *Se comieron rápidamente el dinero.* They squandered their money.
comercial commercial.
comercio commerce, trade, business *Ha hecho mucho dinero en el comercio de frutas.* He's made a lot of money in the fruit business. ▲ store, shop *Tienen un comercio de trajes.* They own a dress shop.

○ **cámara de comercio** chamber of commerce. ○ **comercio exterior** foreign trade. ○ **comercio interior** domestic trade.

comestible edible, good to eat.
○ **comestibles** [*m pl*] provisions, groceries *En esta calle hay una tienda de comestibles.* There's a grocery store on this street.

cometa [*m*] comet; [*f*] kite.

cómico comic, funny, amusing *¡Qué situación más cómica!* What an amusing situation! ▲ [*n*] actor, actress *Son unos cómicos malísimos.* They're very bad actors.

comida food *La comida es muy buena en este hotel.* The food in this hotel's very good. ▲ dinner *¿A qué hora es la comida?* When's dinner served?

comienzo beginning, start.

comilón [*m*] glutton.

comisaría police station.

comisario de policía chief of police.

comisión [*f*] assignment *Le han dado una comisión difícil.* They gave him a difficult assignment. ▲ committee, delegation *Ha llegado una comisión de diputados.* A committee of congressmen has arrived.

comisionado agent.

comisionar to commission *Han sido comisionados por el Gobierno.* They've been commissioned by the Government.

como how *Voy a decirle como lo tiene que hacer.* I'll tell you how to do it. ▲ as *Como Ud. quiera.* As you like. ▲ as, since *Como no me lo dijo, no fui.* Since he didn't tell me, I didn't go. ▲ like *Nada como un pez.* He swims like a fish. ▲ if *Como Ud. no se lo diga, él no lo hará.* If you don't tell him, he won't do it.
○ **¿cómo?** why? how come? *¿Cómo no me lo dijo?* Why didn't you tell me?
○ **tan ... como** as ... as *¿Es Ud. tan alto como yo?* Are you as tall as I?
○ **tanto como** as much as *No creo que Ud. trabaje tanto como él.* I don't believe you do as much work as he does.

cómoda chest of drawers.

comodidad [*f*] convenience *La casa tiene todas las comodidades.* The house has all the conveniences. ▲ ease, comfort *Viven con mucha comodidad.* They live very comfortably.

cómodo convenient, suitable, handy *Una maleta de este tamaño es muy cómoda.* A valise of this size is very handy. ▲ comfortable *¿Está Ud. cómodo?* Are you comfortable?

compadecer [-*zc*-] to pity, sympathize with *Le compadezco a Ud.* I sympathize with you.

compadre [*m*] (term of address between father and godfather of a child); pal (among country people).

compañero, compañera companion, pal, schoolmate *Fueron compañeros de estudios.* They were schoolmates.

compañía company *Trabaja en una compañía de seguros.* He works for an insurance company. ▲ company of actors, stock company *¿Le gusta la compañía que hay en ese teatro?* Do you like the company at that theater?
○ **hacer compañía (a)** to keep company (with) *Está sola; hágale compañía.* She's lonely; keep her company.

comparable comparable.

comparación [*f*] comparison.

comparar to compare *Compare Ud. esta copia con el original.* Compare this copy with the original.

comparecer [-*zc*-] to appear (in answer to summons) *Los testigos comparecieron ante el juez.* The witnesses appeared before the judge.

compartir to share *Compartieron lo que tenían.* They shared what they had. —*No comparto su opinión.* I don't share his opinion.

compás [*m sg*] compass *Es difícil dibujar un círculo sin un compás.* It's hard to draw a circle without a compass. ▲ beat, rhythm, time *No sabe llevar el compás.* He can't keep time.

compasión [*f*] compassion, pity, sympathy *No tiene compasión de nadie.* He has no pity for anybody.

compatriota [*m, f*] (fellow) countryman, fellow citizen.

compensar to balance, compensate *Las ganancias compensan los gastos.* The income balances the expenses.

competencia competition, rivalry *Hay mucha competencia en el comercio.* There's a lot of competition in business.

competir [*rad-ch III*] to compete *No va a competir en el campeonato.* He's not going to compete for the championship.

complacer [-*zc*-] to please, accommodate *¿En qué puedo complacerla?* How can I help you?

complaciente pleasing, accommodating, kind *Es una persona complaciente.* She's a very accommodating person.

completar to complete, finish *No han completado el informe.* They haven't completed the report.

completo complete *¿Está completo este juego de té?* Is this tea set complete? ▲ full *El tranvía va completo.* The trolley's full.

complicación [*f*] complication.

complicar to complicate *No complique Ud. la cuestión.* Don't complicate the matter.

cómplice [*m, f*] accomplice.

componer [*irr*] to repair, fix *¿Compusieron el reloj?* Did they repair the watch? ▲ to compose *Ha compuesto una sonata.* He's composed a sonata.

○ **componerse** to fix bneself, to doll up *Se compuso mucho para ir al baile.* She dolled up a lot to go to the dance.

composición [*f*] composition.

compositor [*m*] composer *¿Quién es el compositor de esta sinfonía?* Who's the composer of this symphony?

compostura mending, repair(s), repairing *Hacemos toda clase de compostura.* We make all kinds of repairs.

compota stewed fruit.

compra purchase, buy *Hicimos una buena compra.* We made a good buy.

○ **hacer la compra** to do the day's marketing *La criada salió a hacer la compra.* The maid went out to do the day's marketing. ○ **ir de compras** to go shopping.

comprador, compradora buyer, purchaser *Tiene varios compradores para la finca.* He has several buyers for the property.

comprar to buy, purchase.

comprender to understand, comprehend *¿Comprende Ud. español?* Do you understand Spanish? ▲ to include, comprise, cover *Esta historia comprende también la época contemporánea.* This history also includes the contemporary period.

comprensión [*f*] comprehension, understanding.

comprimir to compress.

comprobar [*rad-ch I*] to verify, confirm, check *Comprobaron las cuentas.* They checked the accounts.—*Compruebe Ud. esta traducción con el original.* Check this translation with the original. ▲ to substantiate, verify *No se pudo comprobar la inocencia del acusado.* The defendant's innocence could not be verified.

comprometer to risk *No comprometan Uds. su fortuna en eso.* Don't risk your fortune on that. ▲ to expose, jeopardize, endanger *Está comprometi-*

endo su carrera política. He's jeopardizing his political career.

○ **comprometerse** to get involved *No se comprometa Ud. en eso.* Don't get yourself involved in that. ▲ to become engaged *Se comprometieron ayer.* They became engaged yesterday.

compromiso obligation, engagement *No puedo ir con Ud., tengo un compromiso.* I can't go with you, I have an engagement. ▲ predicament, plight, fix *Se encontró en un compromiso terrible.* He found himself in a terrible fix.

○ **compromiso matrimonial** engagement *Rompió su compromiso matrimonial.* She broke her engagement.

compuesto See **componer.**

común common, usual, general *Fué la opinión común.* It was the general opinion.

comunicación [*f*] communication.

comunicar to communicate, transmit, send, issue *Comunique Ud. esta orden a sus empleados.* Issue this order to your employees.

○ **comunicarse** to connect *Las dos habitaciones se comunican.* The two rooms are connected. ▲ to communicate, tell one another *Se comunican todo lo que ocurre.* They tell each other about everything that happens.

comunicativo communicative *Es un persona muy comunicativa.* He's very communicative.

con with *Salió con su hermano.* She left with her brother.

○ **con tal que** provided that.

concebir [*rad-ch III*] to imagine *No concibo que motivo puede tener para hacer eso.* I can't imagine what reason he has for doing that.

conceder to give, grant *Le han concedido una pensión.* They've granted him a pension.

concejal [*m*] councilman.

concejo board of aldermen.

concentrar to concentrate.

concepto judgment, opinion, thought *Tengo buen concepto de él.* I have a good opinion of him.

concesión [*f*] concession, grant.

conciencia conscience *Me remuerde la conciencia.* My conscience bothers me. ▲ scruples *Es un hombre sin conciencia.* He's a man without scruples. ▲ religion *En este país no hay libertad de conciencia.* There's no freedom of religion in this country. ▲ consciousness *Con el golpe perdió la conciencia.*

He lost consciousness as a result of the blow.

○ **a conciencia** conscientiously *Lo hizo a conciencia.* He did it conscientiously. ▲ painstakingly *Hizo su trabajo a conciencia.* He did his work painstakingly.

concierto concert *¿Va Ud. al concierto esta noche?* Are you going to the concert tonight?

conciliar to conciliate, reconcile *Es difícil conciliar todas las opiniones.* It's difficult to reconcile all the opinions.

concisión [f] conciseness *La concisión es una virtud.* Conciseness is a virtue.

concluir to conclude, end, finish, close *¿A qué hora concluyó la sesión?* What time did the meeting end?

conclusión [f] conclusion *¿Se ha llegado a alguna conclusión?* Has any conclusion been reached?

concretar to express concretely *Concrete Ud. su idea.* Express your idea concretely.

○ **concretarse** to limit *or* confine oneself *Concrétese al tema.* Confine yourself to the subject.

concreto definite, concrete *¿Le ha dicho a Ud. algo concreto?* Has he told you anything definite?

○ **en concreto** concretely, in so many words *Dígame en concreto lo que necesita.* Tell me in so many words what you need.

concurrir to attend *Mucha gente concurrió a la sesión.* Many people attended the meeting.

concurso competition, contest *¿Quiénes se presentaron al concurso?* Who took part in the contest?

condado county.

conde [m] count (title).

condena sentence, term of imprisonment, penalty *Cumplió su condena en el penal de Alcatraz.* He served his sentence at Alcatraz.

condenar to prove, find, *or* declare guilty *¿Ud. cree que lo condenarán?* Do you think they'll find him guilty? ▲ to sentence *Le condenaron a treinta años de cárcel.* They sentenced him to thirty years in prison. ▲ to condemn, blame *Condenaron su conducta.* They condemned his behavior.

condensar to condense *Tienen un nuevo procedimiento para condensar la leche.* They have a new process for condensing milk.

condición [f] condition, character *Es un*

hombre de mala condición. He's a man of bad character.

○ **a condición de que, con la condición de que** on the understanding that, on condition that, provided (that) *Iré a condición de que Ud. vaya conmigo.* I'll go provided you go with me. ○ **condiciones** qualities *Tiene buenas condiciones, pero está mal educada.* She has good qualities, but she's badly brought up. ▲ terms *¿Cuáles son las condiciones del contrato?* What are the terms of the contract? ▲ condition, quality, state *¿En qué condiciones está el edificio?* What condition is the building in?

condiscípulo, condiscípula schoolfellow, schoolmate, fellow student.

cóndor [m] condor.

conducir [-zc-] to lead *¿A dónde conduce este camino?* Where does this road lead? ▲ to take, accompany *Conduzca a este señor a mi oficina.* Take this gentleman to my office. ▲ to drive *Ud. conduce a demasiada velocidad.* You drive too fast.

○ **conducirse** to act, behave *Se conduce como una persona educada.* She acts like a well-bred person.

conducta conduct, behavior.

conductor [m] driver, motorman *Se prohíbe hablar al conductor.* Don't talk to the driver. ▲ conductor of train [*Mex*].

conectar to connect *¿Han conectado la antena del radio?* Have they connected the radio antenna?

conejo rabbit.

conexión [f] connection *No tiene conexión una cosa con la otra.* There's no connection between the two things.

confección [f] workmanship, finish *La confección del traje es muy mala.* The workmanship on the dress is very bad.

confederación [f] confederacy, federation.

conferencia conference, meeting *Hubo muchas conferencias entre los ministros y senadores.* The Ministers and the Senators held many conferences. ▲ public lecture *Está dando unas conferencias sobre literatura.* He's giving some lectures on literature.

conferenciar to confer, consult together, hold an interview *Después de conferenciar varias horas hicieron públicos los acuerdos.* After conferring for several hours, they made the agreements public.

confesar [rad-ch I] to admit, confess *Confesó su delito.* He confessed his crime.

confesión [f] confession, acknowledgment.

confiado (See **confiar**) trusting, unsuspecting *Son unas personas muy confiadas.* They're very trusting people.

confianza confidence, faith *Han perdido la confianza en él.* They've lost confidence in him.

○ **de confianza** informal, intimate *Fué una reunión de confianza.* It was an informal meeting. ○ **en confianza** confidentially, in confidence *Le digo esto en confianza.* I'm telling you this confidentially. ○ **hombre de confianza** right-hand man *Es su hombre de confianza.* He's his right-hand man. ○ **tener confianza con** to be on intimate terms with *No tengo suficiente confianza con él para eso.* I'm not sufficiently intimate with him for that. ○ **tener confianza en** to trust *¿Por qué no tiene Ud. confianza en mí?* Why don't you trust me?

confiar to entrust to, put in charge of *Le confiaron la administración de sus negocios.* They put him in charge of their business.

○ **confiar en** to rely on, trust in, count on *Ud. puede confiar en él.* You can rely on him.

confidencia ○ **hacer confidencias** to confide *Me ha estado haciendo confidencias.* He's been confiding in me.

confidencial confidential.

confirmación [f] confirmation.

confirmar to confirm, corroborate *La prensa confirmó los rumores.* The press confirmed the rumors.

confitería candy store, confectionery; candy.

conflicto conflict, struggle.

conforme as *Todo queda conforme estaba.* Everything remains as it was.—*Conforme leía, más me interesaba.* As I was reading, I became more interested.

○ **conforme a** in accordance with, in line with *Conforme a su petición. . . .* In accordance with your request. . . . ○ **estar conforme con** to be resigned to *Está conforme con su suerte.* He's resigned to his fate. ▲ to be in agreement with *Estoy conforme con lo que Ud. dice.* I agree with you.

confundido confused, mistaken.

○ **estar confundido** to be mistaken, confused. ○ **quedar confundido** to be extremely embarrassed *Al ver lo que había hecho, quedó confundido.* On seeing what he had done, he was extremely embarrassed.

confundir to confound, jumble, mix up *Han confundido todas las tarjetas.* They've mixed up all the cards. ▲ to mistake *Ud. me confunde con mi hermano.* You're mistaking me for my brother.

○ **confundirse** to make a mistake *Me he confundido muchas veces al copiar esta carta.* I made many mistakes in copying this letter.

confusión [f] confusion, disorder *Hubo unos momentos de confusión.* There were a few moments of confusion. ▲ embarrassment, confusion.

confuso confusing, not clear *Los informes eran confusos.* The reports were confusing. ▲ hard to read *or* understand *Su letra es confusa.* His handwriting's hard to read. ▲ hazy, vague *Tengo un recuerdo confuso.* I have a vague recollection. ▲ confused, mixed up, embarrassed *Se quedaron muy confusos.* They were completely confused.

congestión [f] stroke (sun, etc) *Le dió una congestión.* He had a stroke.

congestionado congested *El tráfico está congestionado.* The traffic's congested.

congraciarse to get into one's good graces *Quería congraciarse con la madre de su novia.* He wanted to get into the good graces of his sweetheart's mother.

congregación [f] congregation.

congregar to congregate, assemble *El cura congregó a los fieles en la iglesia.* The priest assembled the parishioners in the church.

○ **congregarse** to gather, assemble *Los manifestantes se congregaron en la plaza.* The demonstrators gathered in the square.

congreso congress, convention.

○ **Congreso de los Diputados** House of Representatives.

conjetura conjecture, guess *Se hacían muchas conjeturas sobre lo que iba a ocurrir.* There was a great deal of conjecture as to what would happen.

conjunto joint, unified *Acción conjunta.* Joint action. ▲ [m] whole, entirety *Vale más el conjunto que las partes.* The whole is worth more than the parts.

○ **en conjunto** as a whole *En conjunto el plan me parece bien.* As a whole, the plan seems good to me.

conmemorativo commemorative.

conmigo with me *Fueron conmigo de paseo.* They went for a walk with me.

conocer [-*zc*-] to know, understand *Conoce muy bien el problema.* He knows the problem very well. ▲ to know, be acquainted with *¿Conoce Ud. al Sr. López?* Do you know Mr. López?

○ **conocerse** to meet, become acquainted *Nos conocimos la semana pasada.* We met last week. ▲ to know each other *Se conocen muy bien.* They know each other very well.

conocido (see **conocer**) prominent, well known *Era muy conocido en su país.* He was well known in his country. ▲ [*n*] acquaintance *Es un conocido nuestro.* He's an acquaintance of ours.

conocimiento knowledge, understanding *Tiene muy pocos conocimientos de geografía.* He has very little knowledge of geography. ▲ consciousness *Todavía no ha recobrado el conocimiento.* He still hasn't regained consciousness.

conquista conquest.

conquistador [*m*] conqueror *Alejandro fué un gran conquistador.* Alexander was a great conqueror. ▲ Don Juan, lady-killer *Tenga Ud. cuidado con él; es un conquistador.* Be careful with him; he's a Don Juan.

conquistar to conquer, overcome, subdue *Conquistaron la ciudad.* They conquered the city. ▲ to win *No pude conquistar su amistad.* I wasn't able to win his friendship.

consagrar to devote, dedicate; to consecrate *Consagró toda su vida a la ciencia.* He devoted his whole life to science.

○ **consagrarse** to devote oneself *Se consagra a su trabajo.* He devotes himself to his work.

consciente conscious.

consecuencia consequence *La disputa tuvo malas consecuencias.* The quarrel had unfortunate consequences.

conseguir [*rad-ch III*] to attain, get, obtain *Conseguí lo que quería.* I got what I wanted. ▲ to succeed in *Consiguió salir de la casa.* He succeeded in getting out of the house.

consejero adviser, counselor.

consejo advice, counsel *No necesito sus consejos.* I don't need your advice. ▲ council *Lo acordó el consejo.* The council agreed on it.

○ **consejo de ministros** cabinet (of a government).

consentimiento consent *No ha dado su*

consentimiento. He hasn't given his consent.

consentir [*rad-ch II*] to allow, permit, tolerate *¿Cómo lo consiente Ud.?* Why do you permit it? ▲ to coddle, spoil *Consentían demasiado a sus nietos.* They spoiled their grandchildren.

conserva ○ **conservas** preserves; canned food. ○ **en conserva** canned *Me gustan las frutas en conserva.* I like canned fruits.

conservación [*f*] conservation, maintenance.

conservador [*adj; m*] conservative.

○ **el partido conservador** the conservative party.

conservar to conserve, preserve, keep *Ponga Ud. esta fruta en la nevera para que se conserve bien.* Put this fruit in the ice box so it will keep. ▲ to keep *Conservó el retrato durante muchos años.* He kept the picture for many years.

○ **conservarse** to keep (oneself) young, be well preserved *Se conserva muy joven.* He keeps himself very young.

considerable considerable, great, large *Es una cantidad considerable.* It's a large amount.

consideración [*f*] consideration, account *Lo tomaré en consideración.* I'll take it into consideration. ▲ respect *No tuvo ninguna consideración con ella.* He showed her no respect.

considerado thoughtful, tactful.

considerar to consider, think over *Considere de nuevo el problema.* Consider the problem again. ▲ to show consideration *Lo consideran mucho.* They show him every consideration.

consigo with him(self), with her(self), with it(self), etc *Lleve Ud. el dinero consigo.* Take the money with you.

○ **consigo mismo** to oneself *Hablaba consigo misma.* She was talking to herself.

consiguiente ○ **por consiguiente** consequently, therefore.

consistir en to be a question *or* matter of *La felicidad consiste en la moderación.* Happiness is a question of moderation.

consolar [*rad-ch I*] to console, comfort.

consolidar to strengthen, consolidate *Hay que consolidar la República.* It's necessary to strengthen the Republic.

conspiración [*f*] conspiracy, plot.

conspirador, conspiradora conspirator.

conspirar to conspire, plot.

constancia perseverance *Todo lo consigue por su constancia.* He gets everything through perseverance. ▲ record, statement *No hay constancia de lo que ha dicho.* There's no record of what he said.

constante firm, faithful, constant.

constar to be evident, be clear, be certain *Consta que es así.* It's clear that it's so. ▲ to be recorded *or* registered *Eso consta en las actas.* That is recorded in the minutes.

○ **constar de** to be composed of, consist of *La obra consta de treinta capítulos.* The book consists of thirty chapters. ○ **constarle a uno** to be evident to one, be positive *Me consta que no salió ayer.* I'm positive he didn't go out yesterday. ○ **conste que** let it be understood that *Conste que yo no lo he hecho.* Let it be clearly understood that I didn't do it.

constitución [*f*] constitution *La constitución del país es muy democrática.* The constitution of the country is very democratic.—*Es un hombre de una constitución muy fuerte.* He has a strong constitution.

constitucional constitutional.

constituir to constitute, be *Esto constituye la parte esencial de la obra.* This is the essential part of the work. ▲ to establish, organize, constitute *Constituyeron una nueva firma comercial.* They established a new firm.

construcción [*f*] construction *Han empezado la construcción del nuevo ferrocarril.* They've begun the construction of the new railroad. ▲ structure, building *Es la mayor construcción de la ciudad.* It's the biggest building in the city.

constructor [*m*] builder.

construir to build, construct.

consuelo consolation, comfort.

cónsul [*m*] consul.

consulado consulate.

consulta consultation, conference *Se reunieron en consulta.* They met in conference. ▲ office hours *¿A qué hora tiene el doctor la consulta?* What are the doctor's office hours?

consultar to consult (about) *Tengo que consultarle una cosa.* I want to consult you about something.

○ **consultar con la almohada** to sleep on, think over *Antes de decidirlo consúltelo con la almohada.* Sleep on it before deciding.

consumado complete, perfect, accomplished *Es un nadador consumado.* He's an accomplished swimmer.

consumar to carry out, commit (an evil action) *Consumaron el crimen.* They committed the crime.

consumidor, consumidora consumer.

consumirse to be used up, run out *Se consumieron todas las provisiones.* All the supplies ran out.

○ **consumirse de** to be consumed with *Se consume de curiosidad.* He's consumed with curiosity.

consumo consumption *No es grande el consumo diario.* Daily consumption isn't large.

contabilidad [*f*] bookkeeping, accounting.

contable [*m, f*] bookkeeper, accountant.

contacto contact, touch. ▲ ignition (of motors) *Encienda el contacto.* Turn on the ignition.

contado (see **contar**) few *Son contadas las personas que lo saben.* Very few people know it.

○ **al contado** (for) cash *¿Va Ud. a pagar al contado?* Will you pay cash?

contador [*m*] accountant, bookkeeper. ▲ meter (for gas, water, electricity, or taxi).

contagiar to infect.

contagio contagion.

contagioso contagious *El tifus es una enfermedad contagiosa.* Typhus is a contagious disease.

contaminar to contaminate, pollute.

contar [*rad-ch I*] to count *Cuente Ud. el cambio.* Count your change. ▲ to relate, tell *Contaron muy bien la historia.* They told the story very well.

○ **contar con** to depend upon, count on *Cuento con su ayuda.* I'm counting on your help.

contemplación [*f*] contemplation (in visual sense).

contemporáneo [*adj, n*] contemporary.

contener [*irr*] to check, curb, control *No podía contener el caballo.* He couldn't control the horse. ▲ to contain *La botella contenía vino.* The bottle contained wine.

○ **contenerse** to control oneself *Se contiene admirablemente.* He controls himself admirably.

contenido See **contener**. [*m*] contents *¿Puedo ver el contenido del paquete?* May I see the contents of the package?

contentar to satisfy, please *Es muy difícil de contentar.* He's very hard to please.

○ **contentarse** to be satisfied *No se contenta con nada.* He isn't satisfied with anything. ▲ to become reconciled, make up *Se han contentado ya.* They've already made up.

contento happy, glad *Estaba muy contento.* He was very happy.

contestación [*f*] reply, answer *No he recibido contestación a mi carta.* I haven't received a reply to my letter.

contestar to answer, reply *No ha contestado a mi carta.* He hasn't answered my letter yet.

contigo with you *No sabía que tu madre vivía contigo.* I didn't know that your mother lived with you.

contiguo adjacent, next *Se oían voces en el cuarto contiguo.* They heard voices in the next room.

continente [*m*] continent.

continuación [*f*] continuation; sequence.
○ **a continuación** immediately, right away *Entró a continuación se sentó.* He came in and immediately sat down.
‖ *Continuación de la primera página.* Continued from page one.

continuar to continue, pursue, carry on *Continúa sus estudios.* He's pursuing his studies. ▲ to remain *Su estado continúa lo mismo.* His condition remains the same. ▲ to be still (in same place or condition) *Juan continúa enfermo y en el mismo hospital.* John is still sick and in the same hospital. ▲ to go on, keep on *Continuó hablando dos horas.* He kept on talking for two hours.

continuo continuous, uninterrupted.

contorno neighborhood *Es conocido en todo el contorno.* He's known in the whole neighborhood. ▲ contour, outline *El contorno de la figura no es claro.* The outline of the figure isn't clear.

contra against *¡Apoye Ud. la escalera contra la pared!* Put the ladder against the wall! ▲ against, in opposition to *Los Diputados votaron contra la proposición.* The Representatives voted against the proposition.
○ **contra viento y marea** against all odds *Contra viento y marea consiguió lo que quería.* He got what he wanted against all odds. ○ **en pro y en contra** for and against. ○ **llevar la contra** to oppose, object, raise objections *Le gusta llevar la contra.* He likes to raise objections.

contrabando contraband, smuggling.

contradecir [*irr*] to contradict *Se enfada si le contradicen.* He gets angry if he's contradicted.
○ **contradecirse** to contradict oneself *Se contradijo varias veces en su decla-* *ración.* He contradicted himself several times in his testimony.

contradicción [*f*] contradiction.

contraer [*irr*] to contract *Contrajo esa enfermedad hace muchos años.* He contracted that illness many years ago. ▲ to incur, run into *Contrajeron deudas.* They ran into debt.
○ **contraer matrimonio** to marry, get married *Contraerán matrimonio el próximo sábado.* They'll get married next Saturday. ○ **contraerse** to contract, diminish *Se contrae con el frío.* It contracts with the cold.

contrahecho deformed, crippled (from birth).

contraorden [*m*] countermand.

contrariar to thwart, change, spoil (a plan) *Esto contraría todos mis planes.* This spoils all my plans. ▲ to annoy *Esto me contraría mucho.* This annoys me very much.

contrariedad [*f*] disappointment *Fué una contrariedad no verle.* It was a disappointment not to see him.

contrario contrary *Esto es contrario a la ley.* This is against the law. ▲ adverse, unfavorable *El fallo fué contrario.* The verdict was unfavorable. ▲ [*n*] opponent *Ganaron el pleito sus contrarios.* His opponents won the lawsuit.
○ **al contrario** on the contrary *"¿Ha dicho eso?" "Al contrario, no la ha dicho."* "Did he say that?" "On the contrary, he didn't say that." ○ **de lo contrario** otherwise, if not *Saldré a las seis; de lo contrario llegaré tarde.* I'll leave at six; otherwise, I'll be late. ○ **todo la contrario** just the opposite, the other way around *No es lo que Ud. dice, sino todo lo contrario.* It isn't what you say, but just the opposite.

contraseña countersign; pass, check (for hat, baggage, or for readmittance).

contrastar to contrast, be opposed *Sus ideas contrastaban con la mías.* His ideas were opposed to mine.
○ **contrastar bien** to harmonize, go well together *Esos colores contrastan muy bien.* Those colors go well together. ○ **contrastar mal** to clash *Esos colores contrastan mal.* Those colors clash.

contraste [*m*] contrast.

contratar to engage, hire *Le han contratado por un año.* They hired him for one year.

contratista [*m*] contractor.

contrato contract.

contribución [f] contribution. ▲tax *Han aumentado mucho las contribuciones.* They've raised the taxes considerably.
contribuir to contribute.
control [m] control.
controlar to control.
convalecencia convalescence.
convencer to convince.
　O convencerse to become (or be) convinced *No se convence fácilmente.* He's not easily convinced.
convencido (see convencer) convinced.
conveniencia self-interest, good, advantage *No mira más que su propia conveniencia.* He only looks out for his own good.
　O ser de la mayor conveniencia to be highly desirable *Seriá de la mayor conveniencia que viniese Ud.* It would be highly desirable for you to come.
conveniente suitable *Este clima es muy conveniente para él.* This climate's very suitable for him. ▲convenient *¿Será esta hora conveniente para Ud.?* Will this time be convenient for you? ▲desirable, advisable *Es conveniente para su salud.* It's advisable for his health.
convenir [irr] to agree *Convengo con Ud. en ese punto.* I agree with you on that point.
　O convenirle a uno to be to one's advantage, be advisable, suit *No le conviene aceptar ese empleo.* It isn't advisable for him to take that position.
convento convent; [Arg] tenement house.
conversación [f] conversation, talk.
conversar to talk, converse *Le gusta conversar.* He likes to talk.
convertir [rad-ch I] to convert, turn *Han convertido la casa en un museo.* They've converted their house into a museum.
　O convertirse to be converted *Se convirtió al catolicismo.* He became a Catholic.
convicción [f] conviction, belief.
convidado (see convidar) invited. ▲[n] guest *¿Había muchos convidados en la cena?* Were there many guests at the dinner?
convidar to invite *Me convidaron a pasar unos días en su casa.* They invited me to spend a few days at their house.
　O convidarse to invite oneself, come uninvited *Se convida siempre a comer.* He always invites himself for dinner.
convite [m] treat; invitation *¿Esto es un convite o tenemos que pagar?* Is this a treat or do we have to pay?
convocar to convoke, call *¿Han convocado*

ya la reunión? Have they called the meeting yet?
coñac [m] cognac, brandy.
cooperativa [f] cooperative (enterprise).
cooperativo [adj] cooperative.
copa glass, stem glass, goblet *Llenó las copas de vino.* He filled the glasses with wine. ▲drink *Se fueron a tomar unas copas.* They went out to get a few drinks. ▲tree-top *Las copas de los árboles estaban llenas de pájaros.* The trees were full of birds. ▲crown (of a hat) *La copa de este sombrero es demasiado alta.* The crown of this hat's too high. ▲heart (of playing cards) *Tengo el as de copas.* I have the ace of hearts.
　O sombrero de copa top hat.
copia copy *Necesito tres copias de esta carta.* I need three copies of this letter.—*Este cuadro es una buena copia del original.* This painting's a good copy of the original.
copiar to copy, make a copy of; to imitate.
copla popular song.
copo flake (of snow, soap, etc).
coqueta coquette, flirt *Es la mujer más coqueta que he conocido.* She's the biggest flirt I've ever known.
coquetear to flirt *Coquetea con todo el mundo.* She flirts with everybody.
coraje [m] anger; courage, bravery.
　O darle a uno coraje to make one angry or mad *Lo que le dijeron le dió mucho coraje.* What they told him made him very mad.
coral [m] coral.
corazón [m] heart. ▲core (of fruits).
　O dar el corazón, decir el corazón to have a premonition or hunch *Me da el corazón que no vendrá.* I've a hunch he isn't coming. O de buen corazón kind-hearted *Es un hombre de buen corazón.* He's a kind-hearted man. O de (todo) corazón heartily, sincerely *Lo dijo de (todo) corazón.* He said it very sincerely.
corazonada presentiment, hunch.
corbata necktie, tie *¿Qué tipo de corbata quiere Ud., de lazo o de nudo?* What kind of tie do you want, a bow tie or a four-in-hand?
corcho cork.
cordel [m] thin rope, cord.
cordero lamb.
cordial cordial, hearty.
cordillera mountain range.
cordón [m] cord, twine, lace *Quiero comprar unos cordónes de zapatos.* I want

to buy some shoe laces. ▲ cordon (of police or soldiers).

corneta [*f*] bugle; cornet.

corneta [*m*] bugler.

coro chorus, choir.

corona crown; wreath.

coronar to crown *Aquel rey fué coronado a los quince años.* That king was crowned when he was fifteen years old. —*Sus esfuerzos fueron coronados por el éxito.* Their efforts were crowned with success.

coronel [*m*] colonel.

coronilla top of the head, crown. ○ **estar hasta la coronilla de** to be fed up with *¡Estoy hasta la coronilla de sus bromas!* I'm fed up with his jokes!

corporación [*f*] (non-profit) corporation.

corral [*m*] animal enclosure, corral. ○ **aves de corral** domestic fowls.

correa strap, belt.

corrección [*f*] correction *He tardado mucho en la corrección de estas páginas.* The correction of these pages has taken me a long time.—*La carta tiene muchas correcciones.* The letter has many corrections. ▲ good manners *Es un hombre malo pero de gran corrección.* He's a bad man, but with very good manners.

correcto correct, right *El libro estaba escrito en correcto español.* The book was written in correct Spanish. ▲ irreproachable *Su conducta es muy correcta.* His conduct is irreproachable.

corredor [*m*] runner, racer; corridor.

corregir [*rad-ch III*] to correct *Corrija Ud. los errores.* Correct the errors. ▲ to discipline, correct *No le han corregido cuando era malo.* They didn't discipline him when he was bad.

correo mail *¿Ha venido el correo?* Has the mail come? ▲ post office *¿Está cerca de aquí el correo* (or *la oficina de correos*)*?* Is the post office near here? ○ **administrador de correos** postmaster. ○ **correo aéreo** air mail *Envíe Ud. sus cartas por correo aéreo.* Send your letters by air mail. ○ **correo certificado** registered mail. ○ **echar al correo** to mail *¿Echó Ud. las cartas al correo?* Did you mail the letters? ○ **lista de correos** general delivery.

correr to run *Tenemos que correr para llegar a tiempo.* We'll have to run to get there on time. ▲ to race *Su caballo correrá mañana.* His horse is racing tomorrow. ▲ to flow *El río corre hacia el sur.* The river flows towards the south. ▲ to blow *Corre un viento muy fresco.* A very cool wind's blowing. ▲ to move, push *Corre esa silla para aquí.* Push that chair over here. ▲ to slide, draw *Corre la cortina.* Draw the curtain. ▲ to go over, travel over *Han corrido medio mundo.* They've traveled over half the world. ○ **correr el rumor** to be rumored *Corre el rumor de que se va a casar.* It's rumored that he's going to get married. ○ **correr por cuenta de uno** to be one's affair, to be up to one *Eso corre por mi cuenta.* I'll take care of that. *or* That's up to me.

correspondencia correspondence *Hemos mantenido correspondencia desde hace años.* We've kept up a correspondence for years. ▲ mail *Voy a abrir la correspondencia.* I'm going to open the mail. ○ **en justa correspondencia** in reciprocation, to get even *Lo hice en justa correspondencia.* I did it to get even.

corresponder to correspond, match *Estos botones no corresponden.* These buttons don't match. ▲ to concern, be up to *Eso le corresponde a Ud.* That's up to you. ▲ to return, reciprocate, respond to *Correspondió a sus atenciones.* She responded to his attentions.

corresponsal [*m*] correspondent.

corrida ○ **corrida de toros** bullfight.

corrido corrido (typical Latin American song and dance).

corriente current, common *No es de uso corriente.* It's not current usage. ▲ ordinary *Está hecho con tela corriente.* It's made of ordinary cloth. ▲ running, flowing *¿Hay agua corriente en este cuarto?* Does this room have running water? ▲ instant, present (month or year) *Contesté a su carte el veinte del corriente* (*mes*). I answered your letter on the twentieth instant (*or* on the twentieth of the present month). ▲ [*f*] current (of electricity, air, river) *Cuidado, la corriente es muy fuerte.* Be careful, the current's very strong. ○ **al corriente** informed, posted *Le tendré al corriente de lo que pase.* I'll keep you informed of what happens. ○ **contra corriente** upstream, against the tide. ○ **corriente y moliente** commonplace *Es una expresión corriente y moliente.* It's a commonplace expression. ○ **dejarse llevar de la corriente** to follow the current, follow the crowd *En todo se deja llevar de la corriente.* He always follows the crowd.

corromper to corrupt.

corrupción [*f*] corruption.

cortada cut, wound [*Mex*] *Tengo una cortada en la mano.* I have a cut on my hand.

cortado [*adj*] cut *El traje estaba muy bien cortado.* The suit was well cut. ▲ chapped *Tengo las manos cortadas por el frío.* My hands are chapped from the cold. ▲ confused, abashed *Se quedó cortado y no pudo seguir hablando.* He became confused and couldn't continue talking.

cortador [*m*] cutter (tailoring).

cortadura cut (wound) *Tiene una cortadura muy profunda en el pie.* He has a very deep cut on his foot.

cortapapeles [*m sg*] paper knife.

cortaplumas [*m sg*] penknife, pocket-knife.

cortar to cut *¿Tiene Ud. algo con que cortar esta cuerda?* Have you anything to cut this string? ▲ to interrupt, stop, cut short *Su entrada cortó la conversación.* His entrance interrupted the conversation.—*Por favor, no me cortes el relato.* Please don't interrupt my story. ▲ to cut off *Tiene Ud. que cortar los tallos de esas flores.* You'll have to cut off the stems of these flowers. ▲ to cut out *El sastre todavía no ha cortado el traje.* The tailor still hasn't cut out the suit. ▲ to shut off, cut off (steam, water, electricity) *Han cortado la electricidad.* They shut off the electricity. ▲ to cut out, abridge *Han cortado algunas escenas importantes de la película.* They cut out several important scenes in the picture.

○ **cortar al prójimo** to criticize [*Am*] *Le gusta mucho cortar el prójima.* He likes to criticize others. ○ **cortar el hilo** to interrupt, break the thread (of a story) *Por favor, no me cortes el hilo.* Please don't interrupt my story. ○ **cortársele a uno** to get chapped *Se me ha cortado la cara con el viento.* My face has got chapped in the cold wind.

corte [*m*] cut *Tenía un pequeño corte en la mano.* He had a small cut on his hand. ▲ cut (style) *Este traje tiene buen corte.* This suit's well cut. ▲ length (of material) *Le regaló un corte de vestido.* He presented her with a dress length.

corte [*f*] court [*Am*] *El pleito será juzgado en la Corte Suprema.* The case will be tried in the Supreme Court.

○ **hacer la corte** to court, woo *Le está haciendo la corte desde hace tiempo.* He's been courting her for some time. ○ **las cortes** [*pl*] the Spanish parliament.

cortedad [*f*] bashfulness, shyness, timidity.

cortés polite, courteous *No es una respuesta muy cortés.* It's not a very courteous answer.

cortesía courtesy.

corteza bark (of tree); crust (of bread).

cortijo ranch [*Andalusia*].

cortina curtain.

corto short *La chaqueta me está demasiado corta.* The jacket's too short for me. ▲ bashful, shy.

○ **a la corta o a la larga** sooner or later *Les veremos a la corta o a la larga.* We'll see 'em sooner or later. ○ **corto de vista** near-sighted *Tiene que usar gafas porque es muy corto de vista.* He has to wear glasses because he's very nearsighted.

cosa thing *Eso ya es otra cosa.* That's quite another thing.

○ **como si tal cosa** as if nothing had happened. ○ **cosa de** about, more or less *Serían cosa de veinte personas.* There must have been about twenty people. ○ **cosa de ver** thing worth seeing. ○ **cosa nunca vista** something unheard of. ○ **cosas** ideas, notions *¡Qué cosas tiene Ud.!* What ideas you have! ○ **cosas de** of the nature of, pertaining to. ○ **cosas de niños** childish things (doings or sayings). ○ **no . . . gran cosa** not . . . much *No vale gran cosa.* It isn't worth much.—*No dijo gran cosa.* He didn't say much. ○ **no hay tal cosa** no such thing.

coscorrón [*m*] blow on the head.

cosecha crop, harvest.

cosechar to reap, harvest.

coser to sew.

cosmopolita [*adj*] cosmopolitan.

cosquilla tickle.

○ **buscarle a uno las cosquillas** to pick on one. ○ **hacer cosquillas** to tickle. ○ **tener cosquillas** to be ticklish.

cosquilloso ticklish.

costa coast *Viven en un pueblecito de la costa.* They live in a little village on the coast.

○ **a costa de** by dint of, at the expense of *Lo hizo a costa de su salud.* He did it at the expense of his health. —*A costa de mucho trabajo consiguió lo que quería.* By dint of hard work he got what he wanted. ○ **a poca costa** with little effort *Lo consiguió a poca costa.* He got it with little effort.

○ **a toda costa** at all hazards, at any cost *Lo hará a toda costa.* He'll do it at any cost.

costado side, flank.

costar [*rad-ch I*] to cost *Eso cuesta demasiado.* That costs too much.

coste [*m*] cost, price.

costilla rib *Se rompió una costilla montando en bicicleta.* He broke a rib riding his bike. ▲ better half, wife *Tengo que ver a mi costilla.* I must see my better half.

costo cost, price.

costoso costly, expensive.

costumbre [*f*] custom; habit.

costura sewing; seam.

cotidiano [*adj*] daily.

cotorra parrot.

coyuntura joint (of body) *Le duelen las coyunturas.* His joints hurt. ▲ opportunity, chance *Es una buena coyuntura para hacer dinero.* It's a good chance to make money.

coz [*f*] kick (of animals).

cráneo skull (of living person or animal).

cráter [*m*] crater.

creación [*f*] creation.

creador [*m*] creator.

crear to create *¿Quien creó el mundo?* Who created the world? ▲ to create, design *Están creando nuevos modelos de aeroplanos.* They're designing new airplane models. ▲ to create, cause *Creó muchos disgustos su actuación.* His actions caused a lot of trouble.

crecer [*-zc-*] to increase *Su capital ha crecido en los últimos años.* His capital's increased in the last few years. ▲ to grow *¡Cómo crece ese niño!* How that child's growing!

crecimiento growth.

crédito credit *Puedo comprar a crédito en esta tienda.* I can buy on credit at this store.

   ○ **dar crédito a** to believe *No dí ningún crédito al relato.* I didn't believe the story at all.

creencia belief.

creer to believe *Creyó lo que Ud. le dijo.* He believed what you told him. ▲ to think, believe *No lo creo.* I don't think so.

   ¶ *¡Ya lo creo!* Of course!

crema cream (of milk); cream (cosmetic).

crespo curly.

cretona cretonne.

cría breeding, stock breeding *Se dedicó a la cría de caballos.* He devoted himself to horse breeding. ▲ the young (of animals) *La gata tuvo una cría.*

The cat had a litter.—*Esa cerdo tiene buena cría.* That sow has a fine litter.

   ○ **ama de cría** wet nurse.

criada maid, servant.

criado servant.

criar to raise, bring up.

criatura baby, infant *¡Cómo llora esta criatura!* How this baby cries!—*¡No seas criatura!* Don't be a baby!

crimen [*m*] crime (spilling of blood).

criminal [*adj, n*] criminal.

crío baby (fretful).

criollo [*adj, n*] Creole.

crisis [*f*] crisis.

cristal [*m*] crystal, glass *¿Cuánto vale este juego de cristal?* How much is this set of crystal worth? ▲ window pane *El cristal de esta ventana está roto.* The pane of this window's broken. ▲ crystal, lens *Se me han roto los cristales de las gafas y el del reloj.* I've broken my lenses and my watch crystal.

cristianismo Christianity.

cristiano [*adj, n*] Christian.

Cristo Christ.

criterio criterion *No tenemos los dos el mismo criterio.* The two of us don't have the same criterion. ▲ judgment *Es un hombre de buen criterio.* He's a man of good judgment.

crítica criticism.

criticar to criticize.

crítico critical ▲ [*n*] critic.

cruda hangover [*Mex*].

crudo raw, not cooked enough *Estas patatas están muy crudas.* These potatoes weren't cooked long enough. ▲ crude *Habla de una manera muy cruda.* He speaks very crudely.

cruel cruel.

crueldad [*f*] cruelty.

cruz [*f*] cross.

cruzar to cross, go across *Cuidado al cruzar la calle.* Be careful when you cross the street.

   ○ **cruzarse con** to pass (a person) *Me crucé con él en la calle.* I passed him in the street. ○ **cruzarse de brazos** to fold one's arms; to be idle.

cuaderno notebook.

cuadra stable; [*Am*] block of houses.

cuadrado [*adj; n m*] square (shape).

cuadro painting *Es un cuadro de Velázquez.* It's a painting by Velázquez. ▲ scene *La obra está dividida en tres actos y ocho cuadros.* The play's divided into three acts and eight scenes.

   ○ **a cuadros** plaid, checked *Llevaba un traje a cuadros.* She was wearing a checked dress.

cuajado de filled with *La calle estaba cuajada de gente.* The street was filled with people.

cuajar to materialize *No cuajó su plan.* His plan didn't materialize.

○ **cuajarse** to coagulate *La sangre se cuajó en el suelo.* The blood coagulated on the ground. ○ **leche cuajada** junket.

¿cuál? which? which one? what? *¿Cuál de los dos lo hizo?* Which one of the two did it?—*¿Cual es el número de su casa?* What's the number of your house?

○ **por lo cual** for that reason, that's why *Me dijo que estabas enfermo, por lo cual te he llamado.* He told me you were ill and that's why I'm calling.

‖ *Cual el padre, tal el hijo.* Like father, like son.

cualidad [*f*] quality, trait.

cualquier(a) any, whatever, whatsoever *Llegarán cualquier día.* They'll come any day now.—*Deme un libro cualquiera.* Give me any book whatsoever. ▲ any, any one *Deme Ud. cualquiera de esos libros.* Give me any (one) of those books. ▲ anyone (at all) *Cualquiera puede hacer eso.* Anyone can do that.

○ **un cualquiera** a nobody, low-down fellow *Es un cualquiera.* He's a low-down fellow.

cuando when *Cuando Ud. venga se lo diré.* When you come I'll tell you. ▲ if *Cuando Ud. lo dice será verdad.* If you say so, it must be true.

○ **¿cuándo?** when? *¿Cuándo vendrá Ud.?* When will you come? ○ **cuando más** at most *Cuando más, costará treinta pesos.* It'll cost, at the most, thirty pesos. ○ **cuando quiera** when you please, when you're ready *Cuando Ud. quiera, empezamos.* When you're ready, we'll begin. ○ **de cuando en cuando** from time to time *Vendré a verle de cuando en cuando.* I'll come to see you from time to time.

cuanto all that, as much as *Le daré a Ud. cuanto necesite.* I'll give you all that you need.

○ **cuánto** how much? *¿Cuánto cuesta?* How much does it cost? ▲ how *¡Cuánto me alegro de verle!* How glad I am to see you! ○ **cuanto antes** as soon as possible *Venga cuanto antes.* Come as soon as possible. ○ **cuanto más . . . menos** the more . . . the less *Cuanto más me lo digas menos te creeré.* The more you tell me, the less I'll believe you. ○ **¿cuántos?** how

many? *¿Cuántos vendrán?* How many will come? ○ **en cuanto** as soon as *En cuanto llegue avíseme.* Let me know as soon as he arrives.

cuarenta forty.

cuaresma Lent.

cuarta span (of the hand).

cuartel [*m*] barracks.

cuarto room *Está en su cuarto.* He's in his room. ▲ quarter, one fourth *Le he esperado más de un cuarto de hora.* I waited for him for more than a quarter of an hour. ▲ fourth *Carlos IV* (cuarto). Charles the Fourth. ▲ **cuarto** (old Spanish coin) *No tengo un cuarto.* I don't have any money.

○ **cuarto de baño** bathroom.

‖ *Son las tres y cuarto.* It's a quarter past three.

cuatro four.

cuatrocientos four hundred.

cuba barrel, cask.

cubeta pail, bucket [*Am*].

cubierta wrapping *El paquete tenía una cubierta de papel grueso.* The package was wrapped in thick paper. ▲ cover (of book, magazine). ▲ deck (of ship) *Estuvimos paseando sobre cubierta.* We were walking on the deck.

cubierto (see **cubrir**) covered. ▲ [*m*] place at table.

○ **cubiertos** set of silver; cover.

cubrir [*irr*] to cover *Cúbralo con un plato.* Cover it with a plate. ▲ to cover, balance *Sus ingresos cubrían sus gastos.* His earnings covered his expenses.

○ **cubrirse** to put on one's hat *Cúbrase Ud.* Put on your hat.

cucaracha cockroach.

cuchara soup spoon, tablespoon.

cucharada tablespoonful.

cucharadita teaspoonful.

cucharilla teaspoon.

cucharón [*m*] ladle.

cuchichear to whisper.

cuchicheo whisper, whispering.

cuchilla wide blade; razor blade.

cuchillo knife.

cuelgo See **colgar**.

cuello neck *Tiene un cuello muy largo.* He has a long neck. ▲ neck (of a bottle) *Se le ha roto en cuello a la botella.* The neck of the bottle was broken. ▲ collar *Necesito una camisa de cuello duro.* I need a shirt with a stiff collar.

cuenta account *Póngalo en la cuenta.* Put it on my account. ▲ bill *¿Le ha pedido la cuenta al camarero?* Did you ask the waiter for the bill?

○ **a cuenta y riesgo** at one's own risk *Lo hizo a su cuenta y riesgo.* He did it at his own risk. ○ **caer en la cuenta** to figure out, catch on *No caigo en la cuenta de lo que quiere Ud. decirme.* I can't figure out what you're trying to tell me. ○ **dar cuenta de** to account for, report *Hay que dar cuenta de este dinero.* You must account for this money. ▲ to exhaust, finish up *Dió cuenta de todo el tabaco.* He finished up all the tobacco. ○ **darse cuenta de** to realize *Se dió cuenta de su error.* He realized his mistake. ○ **en resumidas cuentas** in short, in a word *En resumidas cuentas, no quiso venir.* In short, he wouldn't come. ○ **hacer cuentas de** to compute, calculate, figure out *Estaba haciendo las cuentas de la casa.* She was figuring out her household expenses. ○ **tener en cuenta** to keep in mind *Tenga en cuenta lo que le digo.* Keep in mind what I tell you. ○ **tomar por su cuenta** to take upon oneself *Ese asunto lo tomo yo por mi cuenta.* I'll take that matter upon myself.
‖ *Eso no me tiene cuenta.* That isn't convenient for me.

cuento story, tale *Compró un libro de cuentos.* He bought a book of stories. ○ **dejarse de cuentos** to stop beating around the bush, come to the point. ○ **no venir a cuento** not to have bearing on the question *Lo que dice Ud. ahora no viene a cuento.* What you're saying now has nothing to do with the question.

cuerda cord *¿Tiene Ud. una cuerda para atar este paquete?* Do you have a cord to tie this package with? ▲ string *Tengo que cambiar una cuerda a la guitarra.* I have to change a string on the guitar. ▲ spring, mainspring *Se le rompió la cuerda al reloj.* The watch spring broke.
○ **dar cuerda a** to wind (a watch *or* clock) *No le dí cuerda al reloj anoche.* I didn't wind the clock last night.

cuerno horn (of an animal).

cuero tanned skin, leather *La maleta es de cuero.* It's a leather valise. ▲ skin *El elefante tiene el cuero muy duro.* The elephant's skin is very tough.
○ **cuero cabelludo** scalp *Es una enfermedad del cuero cabelludo.* It's a scalp disease. ○ **en cueros** stark-naked.

cuerpo body. ▲ corps *Pertenece al cuerpo diplomático.* He belongs to the diplomatic corps. ▲ corpse, body *Encontra-*

ron el cuerpo en el río. They found the body in the river.
○ **tomar cuerpo** to take shape *El proyecto va tomando cuerpo.* The project's taking shape.

cuervo crow.

cuesta slope, hill *Al otro lado de la cuesta está el río.* The river's on the other side of the hill.
○ **a cuestas** on one's back *Llevaba la carga a cuestas.* He was carrying the load on his back. ○ **cuesta abajo** downhill. ○ **cuesta arriba** uphill.

cuestión [f] question (problem) *Esta es la cuestión que tenemos que resolver.* That's the question we have to solve. ▲ argument *Tuve una cuestión con él.* I had an argument with him.

cueva cave; cellar.

cuidado care *El cuidado de la piel es importante.* Care of the skin is important. ▲ keeping, care *Considera muy importante el cuidado de su casa.* She considers the care of her home very important.
○ **estar con cuidado** to be anxious *or* worried *Tardan tanto que estoy con cuidado.* They're so late that I'm worried. ○ **tener cuidado** to be careful *Tenga cuidado al bajar.* Be careful going down.
‖ *¡Cuidado!* Look out!

cuidadoso careful, painstaking.

cuidar to take care of, mind *Cuida muy bien de los niños.* She takes very good care of the children.

culebra snake.

culpa fault, blame *Eso no ha ocurrido por mi culpa.* It isn't my fault that it happened. ▲ sin *Confesó todas sus culpas.* He confessed all his sins.
○ **echar la culpa a** to blame *No me eches la culpa a mí.* Don't blame me. ○ **tener la culpa** to be to blame *Ella tiene la culpa de todo.* She's to blame for everything.

culpable guilty.

culpar to blame, accuse.

cultivado (see **cultivar**) cultured, cultivated *Es un hombre muy cultivado.* He's a very cultured man.

cultivar to cultivate.

cultivo cultivation, growing *Se dedican al cultivo del algodón.* They devote themselves to the growing of cotton. ▲ cultivated fields, crops *La inundación arruinó los cultivos.* The flood ruined the crops.

culto cultured, educated *Es un hombre muy culto.* He's a very cultured man. ▲ [m] worship *Acaban de abrir al culto* *esta iglesia.* They've just opened this church for worship.

cultura culture (of the mind).

cumbre [*f*] top, summit.

cumpleaños [*m sg*] birthday *¡Feliz cumpleaños!* Happy birthday!

cumplido polite *Es un hombre muy cumplido.* He's a very polite man.

cumplidor reliable *Es muy cumplidor en su trabajo.* He's very reliable in his work.

cumplidos formalities *¡Basta de cumplidos!* Enough of formalities!

cumplimiento performance, fulfillment *Murió en el cumplimiento de su deber.* He died in the performance of his duty. ▲ compliment *Me llenó de cumplimientos.* He paid me many compliments.

cumplir to carry out, execute *¡Cumpla Ud. mis órdenes!* Carry out my orders! ▲ to keep (a promise) *Cumplirá lo que nos ha prometido.* He'll keep his promise to us. ○ **cumplir** ... (años) to reach one's ... birthday *Mañana cumpliré veinte y cinco.* I'll be twenty-five tomorrow. ○ **cumplirse** to mature, fall due *Hoy se cumple el plazo.* The installment falls due today.

cuna cradle.

cuneta gutter (along highway).

cuña wedge.

cuñada sister-in-law.

cuñado brother-in-law.

cuota share, quota; dues.

cúpula dome.

cura [*m*] priest, minister *Es el cura de esta parroquia.* He's the priest of this parish. ▲ [*f*] cure, treatment *El médico venía a hacerle la(s) cura(s).* The doctor came to dress his wound. ○ **cura de urgencia** first aid.

curación [*f*] healing, recovery.

curar to treat, dress the wounds of *Los médicos estuvieron curando a los heridos.* The doctors were treating the wounded. ▲ to salt, cure, preserve *No han curado bien estos jamones.* They haven't cured these hams well. ○ **curarse** to recover *Se ha curado muy bien de la pulmonía.* He's completely recovered from pneumonia.

curiosidad [*f*] curiosity; curio.

curioso curious, inquisitive. ▲ odd, strange, quaint, rare *Es un tipo curioso.* He's very odd.

cursi unsuccessfully pretentious.

curso course (direction) *Seguimos el curso del río.* We followed the course of the river. ▲ course (of studies) *Estudia un curso de historia.* He's taking a history course. ▲ course (development) *La enfermedad sigue su curso.* The ailment's taking its course.

curtido (see **curtir**) experienced, hardened (by life) *Es un hombre curtido por la vida.* He's a man hardened by life.

curtir to tan (hides). ○ **curtirse** to become tanned *or* weatherbeaten.

curva curve.

cutis [*m*] complexion.

cuyo whose *Este es el hombre cuya hija conociste ayer.* This is the man whose daughter you met yesterday.

D

dados dice. ○ **jugar a los dados** to shoot dice.

dama lady. *Primero las damas.* Ladies first.

danza dance (spectacle) *Ha escrito un libro sobre la historia de la danza.* He's written a book on the history of the dance.

danzar to dance (as a performance).

dañar to damage. ○ **dañarse** to damage *Al aterrizar se le dañó un ala al avión.* The plane damaged a wing in landing.

daño damage *El temporal causó gran daño.* The storm caused a lot of damage. ○ **daños** damages *Tuvo que pagar los daños.* He had to pay the damages. ○ **hacerle daño a uno** to be harmful to one, not to agree with one *Me hace daño la comida picante.* Highly spiced food doesn't agree with me. ○ **hacerse daño** to get hurt, hurt oneself *Me hice daño en el pie.* I hurt my foot.

dar [*irr*] to give. ▲ to bear *Este árbol da muy buena fruta.* This tree bears good fruit. ▲ to show *No da señales de vida.* He doesn't show any sign of life. ▲ to show (movies or plays) *¿Dónde dan esa película?* Where's that movie showing? ○ **dar a** to face, overlook *Las ventanas dan a la calle.* The windows face the street. ○ **dar a conocer** to make known *Dió a conocer su opinión.* He made his opinion known. ○ **dar a**

entender to pretend *El da a entender que no le interesa.* He pretends that it doesn't interest him. ▲ to insinuate, drive at *¿Qué quiere dar a entender?* What are you driving at? ○ **dar (al) fiado** to sell *or* give on credit *Se lo podemos dar fiado.* We can let you have it on credit. ○ **dar calabazas** See **calabaza.** ○ **dar con** to find, locate *No puedo dar con él.* I can't locate him. ○ **dar de baja** to dismiss *Le han dado de baja del equipo.* They've dropped him from the team. ○ **dar de sí** to stretch, give *Estos calcetines no dan de sí cuando se lavan.* These socks don't stretch when you wash 'em. ○ **dar el golpe** to create a sensation, make a hit *Darás el golpe con ese vestido.* You'll make a hit with that dress. ○ **dar en** to hit *¡Al fin ha dado Ud. en el clavo!* At last you've hit the nail on the head! ▲ to take to *Dió en coleccionar sellos.* He took to stamp collecting. ○ **dar fin** a to complete, finish *Dimos fin a la obra.* We finished the work. ○ **dar guerra** to make trouble *or* a rumpus *Dile a los chicos que no den guerra.* Tell the boys not to make a rumpus. ○ **dar la hora** to strike *El reloj de la catedral acaba de dar las tres.* The cathedral's clock just struck three. ○ **dar la razón** to agree, be of the same opinion *Le doy la razón.* I agree with you. ○ **dar las gracias** to thank *No le dieron las gracias.* They didn't thank him. ○ **darle a uno** to be stricken with, come down with (illness) *Me dió el sarampión.* I came down with measles. ○ **darle a uno gana(s)** to want, desire *Me dan ganas de comprar un automóvil.* I want to buy an automobile. ○ **dar . . . manos de** to put on . . . coats (as of paint) *Dió dos manos de pintura a la pared.* He put two coats of paint on the wall. ○ **dar parte** to report *¿Dieron ya parte a la policía?* Have they reported it to the police yet? ○ **dar por cierto** *or* **seguro** to feel sure *Doy por seguro que vendrá.* I feel sure he'll come. ○ **dar por hecho** to assume, take for granted *Lo dimos por hecho.* We took it for granted. ○ **dar que decir** *or* **hablar** to cause criticism *Eso dará mucho que decir.* That'll cause a lot of criticism. ○ **dar que hacer** to give *or* cause trouble *or* work *¡Estos niños me dan tanto qué hacer!* These children give me so much trouble! ○ **dar que pensar** to make suspicious *Su conducta extraña me dió*

que pensar. His queer behavior made me suspicious. ○ **dar recuerdos** to give regards *Déle recuerdos de mi parte.* Give him my regards. ○ **dar saltos** to jump *Al ver a su padre los niños dieron saltos de alegría.* When they saw their father, the children jumped for joy. ○ **darse la mano** to shake hands *¡Ea, dénse la mano, muchachos!* Come on, shake hands, boys! ○ **darse prisa** to hurry *¡Dése prisa que perdemos el tren!* Hurry up or we'll miss the train! ○ **(no) darle a uno la gana** (not) to feel like *No me da la gana (de) hacerlo.* I don't feel like doing it. *or* I refuse to do it.

datos data.

de of, -'s *Viven en casa de mi madre.* They live in my mother's house. ▲ of *Haga el favor de darme un vaso de agua.* Please give me a glass of water. ▲ from *Soy de Madrid.* I'm from Madrid. ▲ about *¿Habla Ud. de mi amiga?* Are you talking about my friend? ▲ in *Se lo bebió de un trago.* He drank it in one gulp. ▲ with *¿Quién es esa señora del sombrero rojo?* Who's the woman with the red hat? ▲ to *Es la hora de salir.* It's time to leave.

debajo de beneath, under *Encontrará Ud. la carta debajo de estos papeles.* You'll find the letter under these papers.

debate [*m*] debate.

deber to owe *Nos debe mucho dinero.* He owes us a lot of money. ▲ to have to, must *Debemos irnos.* We have to go. ○ **deber de** must be (probability) *Debe de hacer frío.* It must be pretty cold.

deber [*m*] duty, obligation *Cumple con su deber.* He does his duty.

débil weak *Después de su enfermedad se ha quedado muy débil.* Since his illness he's been very weak.

debilidad [*f*] weakness.

debilitar to weaken.

debut [*m*] debut.

decadencia decline.

decaer [*irr*] to fail *Su salud decae.* His health's failing. ▲ to lessen, fall off *Ha decaído mucho el interés del público.* Public interest has fallen off a lot.

decano dean.

decente nice, decent *A ese lugar no va gente decente.* No decent people go to that place. ▲ honest *Creo que son personas decentes.* I think they're honest people.

decepción [*f*] disappointment.

decepcionar to disappoint.
decidido (see **decidir**) determined *Es una persona muy decidida.* He's a very determined person.
decidir to decide *Decidieron hacer el viaje en seguida.* They decided to make the trip right away.
○ **decidirse a** to make up one's mind to *Se decidió a casarse con ella.* He made up his mind to marry her.
décimo tenth. ▲ [*m*] one-tenth of a lottery ticket.
decir [*irr*] to tell *No dijo la verdad.* He didn't tell the truth. ▲ to say *¿Qué dice hoy el periódico?* What does the paper say today?
○ **como quien no dice nada** as if it were of no importance *Habló de ganar miles de dólares como quien no dice nada.* He spoke of earning thousands of dollars as if it were nothing. ○ **decir bien** to be right *Dice Ud. bien.* That's right. ○ **decir para sí** to say to oneself. ○ **decir por decir** to talk for the sake of talking, talk to make conversation *No hace más que decir por decir.* He just talks for the sake of talking. ○ **el qué dirán** gossip, what people will say *No hay que preocuparse del qué dirán.* One shouldn't worry about what people are going to say. ○ **es decir** that is to say, that is. ○ **querer decir** to mean *¿Qué quiere decir eso?* What does that mean? ○ **ser un decir** to be a manner of speaking *Todo esto es un decir.* All this is a manner of speaking.
‖ *¡Diga!* Hello! (telephone) [*Sp, Cuba*].
decisión [*f*] determination *Muestra siempre mucha decisión en todo lo que emprende.* He always shows great determination in everything he undertakes. ▲ decision *¿Han hecho ya pública la decisión del tribunal?* Have they announced the decision of the court yet?
decisivo decisive, final.
declaración [*f*] declaration *¿Fué después de la declaración de guerra?* Was it after the declaration of war? ▲ statement *Lea Ud. su declaración antes de firmarla.* Read your statement before you sign it.
declarar to testify *Después declararon los testigos.* Afterwards the witnesses testified.
○ **declararse** to declare one's love *No se me ha declarado todavía.* He hasn't told me he loves me yet. ○ **declararse en huelga** to declare a strike.

decoración [*f*] decoration. ▲ (stage) setting, props *Las decoraciones de la obra eran muy acertadas.* The settings of the play were very appropriate.
decorar to decorate.
decoro dignity, decorum.
decretar to decree.
decreto decree.
dedal [*m*] thimble.
dedicar to devote *Dedica todo su tiempo al trabajo.* He devotes all his time to his work. ▲ to inscribe, autograph *El autor me ha dedicado su libro.* The author has autographed his book for me. ▲ to dedicate *El libro está dedicado al Presidente.* The book's dedicated to the President.
dedillo ○ **saber al dedillo** to know perfectly.
dedo finger; toe.
○ **dedo anular** ring finger. ○ **dedo gordo** thumb; big toe. ○ **dedo índice** index finger. ○ **dedo medio** middle finger. ○ **dedo meñique** little finger, pinky. ○ **dedo pulgar** thumb.
deducir [-*zc*-] to deduce, imagine *Se pueden deducir las consecuencias.* You can imagine the consequences. ▲ subtract, deduct *Deduzca Ud. esa cantidad del total.* Subtract this amount from the total.
defecto defect, imperfection, shortcoming *No tiene defectos físicos.* He has no physical defects.
defectuoso defective, faulty.
defender [*rad-ch I*] to defend *Defendió su opinión con energía.* He defended his opinion with vigor. ▲ to protect *La pared nos defendía del viento.* The wall protected us from the wind.
defensa defense, protection.
defensor [*m*] defender *Era uno de los defensores de Bataan.* He was one of the defenders of Bataan. ▲ champion *Siempre ha sido uno de mis defensores.* He's always been one of my champions. ▲ [*adj*] for the defense *Después habló el abogado defensor.* Then the attorney for the defense spoke.
deficiencia deficiency.
definir to define.
definitivo final, definite.
deformar to deform.
degenerar to degenerate.
dejado (see **dejar**) sloppy *¡Anda siempre tan dejado!* He's always so sloppy!
dejar to leave *Dejó el libro sobre la mesa.* He left the book on the table. ▲ to let, leave *Déjale tranquilo.* Let him alone.
▲ to leave, abandon *Dejó a su mujer*

y a sus hijos. He left his wife and children. ▲ to intrust, leave, turn over *Dejó sus negocios a su hijo por un año.* He turned the business over to his son for a year. ▲ to yield, produce, pay (income, dividends, profit) *Es un negocio que deja muchas ganancias.* It's a business that pays big dividends. ▲ to give up, leave *Ha dejado ese empleo.* He's left that job. ▲ to permit, allow, let *Déjeme Ud. que se lo explique.* Let me explain it to you. ○ dejar caer to drop *Cuidado, no dejes caer la botella.* Be careful, don't drop the bottle. ○ dejar de to stop *Dejó de comer.* He stopped eating. ○ dejar dicho to leave word *Dejó dicho que vendría a las cuatro.* He left word that he'd come at four. ○ dejar en paz to leave alone *Déjeme en paz porque estoy trabajando.* Leave me alone; I'm working. ○ dejar sin efecto to cancel. ○ no dejar de not to fail to *No dejes de venir a verme.* Don't fail to come and see me.

del (de + el; see de) *Es el padre del abogado.* He's the lawyer's father. —*Acaba de llegar del extranjero.* He's just arrived from abroad.

delantal [m] apron.

delante de before, in front of *Mi casa está delante de la catedral.* My house is in front of the cathedral. ▲ before, in front of, in the presence of *No digas esas cosas delante de una señora.* Don't say such things in front of a lady.

delantera start, lead *El caballo blanco ha tomado la delantera.* The white horse has taken the lead. ▲ front row (of seats). ▲ front, façade (of building).

delantero front *Hay que arreglar el delantero de la chaqueta.* You have to fix the front of the jacket. ▲ forward (basketball, soccer).

delegación [f] delegation *Es un miembro de la delegación española.* He's a member of the Spanish delegation. ○ delegación de policía police station *Lo llevaron a la delegación de policía.* They took him to the police station.

delegado delegated. ▲ [n] delegate.

deletrear to spell (out) *¿Quiere Ud. hacer el favor de deletrear su apellido?* Would you spell your name, please?

delgado thin, slim *Se ha quedado muy delgado.* He's become very thin. ▲ thin, light *Ese abrigo es muy delgado.* That coat's too thin.

deliberar to deliberate *El jurado está todavía deliberando.* The jury's still deliberating.

delicadeza delicacy.

delicado delicate.

delicia delight.

delicioso delightful *Hemos pasado un rato delicioso.* We had a delightful time. ▲ delicious *El postre está delicioso.* The dessert's delicious.

delincuente [adj; n] delinquent.

delirio delirium *El delirio le duró toda la noche.* The delirium lasted all night. ○ con delirio madly *La quiere con delirio.* He's madly in love with her. ○ delirio de grandeza delusions of grandeur.

delito misdemeanor, crime.

demanda claim, demand, request *Han aceptado nuestra demanda.* They've accepted our demand. ▲ demand, call (Com) *Ahora hay mucha demanda de este artículo.* There's a great demand for this article now. ○ demanda (judicial) legal proceeding, court action *Entablaré demanda contra ellos.* I'll take court action against them. ○ oferta y demanda supply and demand.

demás ○ lo demás the rest *Luego contaré la demás.* I'll tell you the rest later. ○ los demás, las demás others, the others, the rest *Esperemos a los demás.* Let's wait for the others. ○ por demás too, too much *Eso es por demás.* That's too much. ○ por lo demás aside from this, as to the rest *Por lo demás me parece bien.* Aside from this, it seems all right to me. ○ todo lo demás everything else.

demasiado [adj] too much, too many *Había demasiada gente.* There were too many people there. ▲ [adv] too much *Cuesta demasiado.* It costs too much.

demente mad, insane. ▲ [n] insane person.

democracia democracy.

demócrata [m, f] democrat.

democrático democratic.

demoler [rad-ch I] to demolish.

demonio devil *¿Para qué demonios lo quiere?* What the devil does he want it for? ○ ¡demonio! damn (it)! *¡Demonio, qué frío hace!* Damn it, it's cold!

demora delay.

demorar to delay *Se demoraron en el camino.* They were delayed on the way.

demostración [f] proof *Eso no necesita demostración.* That doesn't need any proof. ▲ demonstration *Se le recibió con grandes demostraciones de alegría.* He was received with great demonstrations of joy.

demostrar [rad-ch I] to prove *Demostró que tenía razón.* He proved he was right. ▲ to show *Demostró mucho talento.* He showed great talent.

densidad [f] density.

dentadura set of teeth.

dentífrico toothpaste, toothpowder.

dentista [m, f] dentist.

dentro inside, into, within *Le espero dentro.* I'll wait for you inside.

○ **a dentro** See adentro. ○ **dentro de** inside (of) *Está dentro del cajón.* It's inside the drawer. ▲ in, within *Vendrá dentro de dos meses.* He'll be here in two months. ○ **dentro de poco** soon, in a little while *Nos veremos dentro de poco.* I'll see you again soon. ○ **por dentro** inside, on the inside *La caja está pintada por dentro.* The box is painted on the inside.

denunciar to denounce.

departamento section, department. ▲ apartment [Am] *Viven en una casa de departamentos.* They live in an apartment house.

depender to depend, be dependent *No le gusta depender de nadie.* He doesn't like to be dependent on anyone.

○ **depende** it depends *Depende de lo que quiera Ud. hacer.* It depends on what you want to do.

dependiente [m, f] clerk, salesman.

deplorar to deplore, regret, lament.

deponer [irr] to depose.

deportar to deport, exile.

deporte [m] sport *¿Le gustan a Ud. los deportes?* Do you like sports?

deportista [m, f] sportsman, sportswoman. ▲ [adj] fond of sports.

deportivo [adj] sport, athletic.

depositar to deposit *Depositaron su dinero en el banco.* They deposited their money in the bank. ▲ to put, have *Deposité en él toda mi confianza.* I put all my trust in him.

depósito deposit, bond *Para entrar en el país hay que dejar un depósito.* You must leave a deposit in order to enter the country. ▲ warehouse *Estos edificios son los depósitos de la fábrica.* These buildings are the warehouses of the factory.

○ **depósito de agua** water tank; reservoir. ○ **en depósito** on deposit.

depravado depraved, lewd.

depreciado depreciated *Esa mercadería está depreciada.* That merchandise has depreciated.

depresión [f] depression.

deprimir to depress.

derecha right (hand), right (side) *Tomamos el camino de la derecha.* We took the road to the right.—*Conserve* (or *lleve*) *la derecha.* Keep to the right.

○ **a derechas** right, well *No hace nada a derechas.* He doesn't do anything right. ○ **a la derecha** to the right. ○ **de derecha** conservative *Pertenece a un partido de derecha.* He belongs to a conservative party.

derecho [adj] right (opposed to left) *Llevaba un anillo en la mano derecha.* He wore a ring on his right hand. ▲ straight *Póngase Ud. la corbata derecha.* Straighten your tie. ▲ [m] right *Ud. no tiene derecho a decirme eso.* You have no right to say that to me. ▲ law *Es estudiante de derecho.* He's a law student.

○ **del derecho** right side out *Fíjese que esté del derecho.* Make sure it's right side out. ○ **derechos de aduana** customs duties *No tiene Ud. que pagar derechos de aduana.* You don't have to pay duty. ○ **derechos de autor** copyright; royalties. ○ **hecho y derecho** grown-up, full-fledged *Es un hombre hecho y derecho.* He's a real man now. ○ **ponerse derecho** to stand up straight.

derecho [adv] straight, right *Siga Ud. todo derecho hasta la plaza.* Go straight ahead to the square.

derramar to spill *Derramó el agua en el mantel.* He spilled water on the tablecloth.

derretir [rad-ch III] to melt *El sol está derritiendo la nieve.* The sun's melting the snow.

○ **derretirse** to melt *La mantequilla se está derritiendo.* The butter's melting.

derribar to demolish, tear down *Han derribado muchas casas viejas.* Many old houses have been torn down. ▲ to throw down, knock down *De un golpe lo derribó al suelo.* He knocked him down with one blow. ▲ to overthrow *Derribaron al gobierno.* They overthrew the government.

derrochar to waste, squander.

derrota defeat, rout.

derrotar to defeat, rout.

derrumbarse to collapse, tumble down *El*

puente se derrumbó. The bridge collapsed.

derrumbe [*m*] landslide *Hay un derrumbe en el camino.* There's a landslide on the road.

desabrigarse to take off outer clothing, to expose oneself (to cold).

desabrochar to unclasp, unbutton, unfasten.

desacierto error, mistake, blunder.

desacreditar to discredit.

desacuerdo disagreement.

desafiar to challenge *Le desafío a una partida de ajedrez.* I challenge you to a game of chess. ▲ to defy *Desafiaba el peligro.* He defied the danger.

desafinar to be out of tune.

desafío duel; challenge; match (sports).

desagradable disagreeable, unpleasant.

desagradar to displease *Me desagrada mucho lo que Ud. ha hecho.* I'm very much displeased with what you did.

desagrado displeasure.

desaguar to drain, draw liquid off.

desagüe [*m*] drain (plumbing).

desahogado comfortable *Viven de una manera muy desahogada.* They live very comfortably. ▲ cheeky, nervy *¡Qué tío más desahogado!* What a nervy guy.

desahogo relief, breathing spell, rest *No he tenido un momento de desahogo desde que empecé este trabajo.* I haven't had a moment's rest since I began this work. ▲ cheek, nerve *Tiene un desahogo terrible.* He has an awful nerve.

desairar to scorn, disregard, slight *No quiero desairarle.* I don't mean to slight him.

desalentar [*rad-ch I*] to discourage *No le desaliente en su trabajo.* Don't discourage him about his work.

desaliento discouragement.

desalmado inhuman, merciless.

desalquilado unrented, vacant *¿Tienen algún apartamento desalquilado?* Do you have a vacant apartment?

desalquilarse to become vacant *Me han dicho que este piso se desalquilará el mes próximo.* I've been told this apartment will be vacant next month.

desamparar to abandon, desert.

desamueblado unfurnished.

desandar to retrace (one's steps).

desangrarse to bleed, lose blood.

desanimación [*f*] lack of enthusiasm *Hubo gran desanimación en el público.* There was a great lack of enthusiasm on the part of the public.

desanimado poorly attended *La fiesta es-*

tuvo muy desanimada. The fiesta was very poorly attended.

desanimar to dishearten, discourage *¿Por qué me desanima Ud. a hacer el viaje?* Why are you discouraging me from taking the trip?

○ **desanimarse** to become discouraged *Se desanima con la menor dificultad.* He gets discouraged at the least difficulty.

desaparecer [*-zc-*] to disappear.

desaparición [*f*] disappearance.

desaprobar to disapprove of *Desapruebo su actitud.* I disapprove of his attitude.

desarmar to disarm *Desarmaron a los soldados.* They disarmed the soldiers. ▲ to take apart *Desarmé la máquina de escribir para limpiarla.* I took the typewriter apart to clean it.

desarreglar to disarrange.

desarrollar to develop *Están desarrollando una nueva industria.* They're developing a new industry.

○ **desarrollarse** to develop *El niño se ha desarrollado muy de prisa.* The child's developed very quickly.

desarrollo development.

desaseado slovenly, not clean.

desastrado untidy, slovenly.

desastre [*m*] disaster, catastrophe.

desastroso unfortunate, disastrous.

desatar to untie.

desatento discourteous.

desatinado foolish *Me dió un consejo desatinado.* He gave me foolish advice. ▲ [*n*] idiot, fool.

desatino nonsense.

desavenencia discord, disagreement.

desayunarse to breakfast *¿Se ha desayunado Ud. ya?* Have you had your breakfast yet?

desayuno breakfast.

desbaratar to destroy, ruin *Estos niños desbaratan todo lo que cogen.* These children destroy everything they get hold of.

○ **desbaratarse** to fall to pieces *Se han desbaratado todos nuestros planes.* All our plans went to pieces.

desbordarse to overflow.

descabellado preposterous, absurd *¡Qué ideas tan descabelladas tiene Ud.!* What absurd ideas you have!

descalabro setback, misfortune.

descalificar to disqualify.

descalzarse to take off one's shoes.

descalzo [*adj*] barefoot.

descamisado ragamuffin [*Am*].

descansar to rest *Cuando termine este*

trabajo, descanse Ud. un rato. When you finish this work, rest for a while.

descanso rest, let-up *Trabaja sin descanso.* He works without let-up. ▲ relief *¡Qué descanso me da haber terminado eso!* What a relief to be finished with that! ▲ intermission *Iremos a su palco en el descanso.* We'll come to your box during the intermission. ▲ landing (of staircase).

descarado impudent, saucy, fresh.

descargar to unload *Varios hombres descargaban el camión.* Several men were unloading the truck. ▲ to free (from an obligation or debt) *Le han descargado de esas obligaciones.* They've freed him from those obligations. ▲ to burst, strike (as a storm) *La tormenta va a descargar de un momento a otro.* The storm's going to strike any minute.

descargo unloading, unburdening.

descartar to discard, eliminate *Hay que descartar esa posibilidad.* You have to eliminate that possibility.

○ **descartarse (de)** to discard (at cards) *Me he descartado de un rey.* I discarded a king.

descendencia descendants *Su descendencia llegó a ser ilustre.* His descendants came to be well known.

descender [*rad-ch I*] to go down, descend *Esa carretera desciende hasta el mar.* That road goes down to the sea. ▲ to be descended *Creo que descienden de una familia francesa.* I think they're descended from a French family. ▲ to descend, come down *El avión descendió rápidemente.* The airplane came down rapidly. ▲ to drop, decrease *La temperatura está descendiendo.* The temperature's dropping.

descendiente [*m, f*] descendant.

descenso descent, going down *El descenso era muy peligroso.* The descent was very dangerous. ▲ fall, decrease *Durante varios años hubo un descenso en la natalidad.* There was a fall in the birth rate for several years.

descifrar to decipher, make out.

descolgar to take down *Ayúdeme a descolgar este cuadro.* Help me take down this picture.

descolorido faded *La tela está muy descolorida.* The cloth's very faded. ▲ pale *Después de la enfermedad se quedó muy descolorido.* He was very pale after his illness.

descomedido impolite, rude *Es un muchacho muy descomedido.* He's very impolite.

descomponer [*irr*] to upset *Eso descom-* *puso todos nuestros planes.* That upset all our plans. ▲ to put out of order *Los niños descompusieron el radio.* The children put the radio out of order.

○ **descomponerse** to dislocate *Se ha descompuesto un brazo.* He's dislocated his arm. ▲ to get out of order *El teléfono se descompuso.* The telephone got out of order. ▲ to spoil, rot *Por el calor se ha descompuesto la comida.* The food's spoiled because of the heat. ▲ to get very angry, lose one's temper *Al oír aquello, se descompuso.* When he heard that he got very angry. ▲ to lose one's looks [*Mex*] *Con la enfermedad se ha descompuesto mucho.* On account of her illness she's lost a lot of her good looks.

descompuesto (see **descomponer**) out of order; spoiled.

desconcertar [*rad-ch I*] to disturb, confuse *La pregunta le desconcertó mucho.* The question confused him.

desconfianza distrust.

desconfiar de to distrust, suspect *No tiene Ud. razón para desconfiar de él.* You have no reason to distrust him. ▲ to have little hope of *El médico desconfiaba de poder salvarlo.* The doctor had little hope of saving him.

desconocer [*-zc-*] to disregard, ignore *Desconoce las reglas de la etiqueta.* He ignores the rules of etiquette.

desconocido (see **desconocer**) unknown, strange *Es difícil orientarse en una ciudad desconocida.* It's difficult to find one's way around in a strange city. ▲ [*n*] stranger *Se le acercó un desconocido.* A stranger approached him.

desconsideración [*f*] inconsiderateness *¡Eso es mucha desconsideración!* That's very inconsiderate.

desconsolado disconsolate.

descontado See **descontar**. ○ **dar por descontado** to take for granted.

descontar [*rad-ch I*] to deduct *Descuente Ud. de esa cantidad los gastos de viaje.* Deduct the traveling expenses from that amount.

descontento dissatisfied, displeased *Estaban muy descontentos de su trabajo.* They were dissatisfied with his work. ▲ [*m*] dissatisfaction.

descortés discourteous, rude.

describir to describe.

descripción [*f*] description.

descrito See **describir**.

descubierto See **descubrir**.

descubrimiento discovery.

descubrir [*irr*] to discover *Descubrimos que todo era mentira.* We discovered that it was all a lie. ▲ to disclose, show, make clear *Descubrió sus intenciones.* He disclosed his intentions. ○ **descubrirse** to take off one's hat.

descuento discount; deduction.

descuidado (see **descuidar**) sloppy, slovenly, unclean. ▲ unaware, off guard. ▲ careless, negligent *No seas tan descuidado en tu trabajo.* Don't be careless in your work.

descuidar to neglect *Descuidó mucho su trabajo.* He neglected his work. ‖ *Descuida, yo me encargo de eso.* Don't worry, I'll take care of that.

descuido carelessness, negligence. ○ **al descuido** carelessly *Hace todo al descuido.* He does everything carelessly. ○ **en un descuido** when least expected [*Mex*] *En un descuido llega.* He turns up when least expected.

desde from *Le ví desde lejos.* I saw him from a distance. ▲ since *Vivo en esta casa desde el mes pasado.* I've been living in this house since last month. ○ **desde ahora** from now on. ○ **desde entonces** since then *Desde entonces he cambiado mucho.* I've changed a lot since then. ○ **desde hace** for *Le conozco desde hace muchos años.* I've known him for many years. ○ **desde luego** of course *¡Desde luego Uds. vendrán con nosotros!* Of course you're coming with us! ○ **desde que** (ever) since *Desde que la conocí la quiero.* I've loved her ever since I met her. ○ **desde un principio** from the beginning *Desde un principio me pareció que estaba equivocado.* It seemed to me from the beginning that he was mistaken.

desdén [*m*] scorn.

desdicha misfortune.

desdichado unhappy, unfortunate *Fué un accidente desdichado.* It was an unfortunate accident.

desdoblar to unfold.

desear to desire, want, like *Deseo verle cuanto antes.* I want to see you as soon as possible.

desechar to reject *Desecharon su propuesta.* They rejected his proposal. ▲ to put aside *Deseche Ud. esos temores.* Put aside those fears.

desembarcar to unload, put ashore *Estaban desembarcando las mercancías.* They were unloading the goods. ▲ to land, disembark *Cuando desembarcamos vimos a nuestro amigo en el muelle.* When we landed we saw our friend on the pier.

desembarco landing, disembarkation.

desembocar to flow, *or* empty, into *Ese río desemboca en el Pacífico.* That river flows into the Pacific. ▲ to end, lead *No sé donde desemboca esa calle.* I don't know where that street leads.

desembolsar to pay out.

desempacar to unpack [*Am*] *Tengo que desempacar el equipaje.* I have to unpack my luggage.

desempeñar to carry out *Desempeñó muy bien su misión.* He carried out his mission very well.

desenfrenado wild *Lleva una vida desenfrenada.* He leads a wild life.

desengañar to set right, undeceive. ○ **desengañarse** to be disillusioned, not to fool oneself *Desengáñate, no te quiere.* Don't fool yourself, he doesn't love you. ○ **estar desengañado** to be disappointed *or* disillusioned *Están muy desengañados después de lo ocurrido.* They were disillusioned after what happened.

desengaño disappointment, disillusion.

desentendido ○ **hacerse el desentendido** to pretend not to know.

desenterrar [*rad-ch I*] to dig up.

desenvolver [*rad-ch I*] to unwrap *Voy a desenvolver el paquete.* I'm going to unwrap the package.

desenvuelto (see **desenvolver**) forward; free and easy.

deseo desire, wish *No puede refrenar sus deseos.* He can't control his desires. ○ **tener deseo de** to be eager to *Tengo muchos deseos de verle.* I'm very eager to see him.

deseoso desirous, eager.

desertor [*m*] deserter.

desesperación [*f*] desperation.

desesperanza despair.

desesperar to despair, lose hope *El médico desespera de salvarle.* The doctor's losing hope of saving him. ▲ to drive crazy *Me desesperó con su insistencia.* He drove me crazy with his insistence.

desespero despair.

desfallecer [*-zc-*] to be on the verge of collapse, grow weak, break down.

desfavorable unfavorable.

desfigurar to disfigure, deform.

desfilar to parade.

desfile [*m*] parade.

desganado having no appetite.

desgarrar to tear, rip.

desgracia misfortune *Tuvo la desgracia de perder todo su dinero.* He had the misfortune to lose all his money. ▲ sorrow, grief *Trataban de consolarla en* *su desgracia.* They tried to console her in her grief.

○ **por desgracia** unfortunately *Por desgracia no lo supimos a tiempo.* Unfortunately we didn't find it out in time.

desgraciadamente unfortunately.

desgraciado [*should not be used in Ecuador*] unfortunate *Han sido muy desgraciados durante los últimos años.* They've been very unfortunate during the past few years. ▲ [*n*] wretch *No es más que un desgraciado.* He's nothing but a miserable wretch.

deshacer [*irr*] to undo *Tenemos que deshacer lo hecho.* We have to undo what was done. ▲ to untie, unwrap *No puedo deshacer este nudo.* I can't untie this knot. ▲ to dissolve *Deshaga la pastilla en un vaso de agua.* Dissolve the tablet in a glass of water. ▲ to spoil, upset *Su llegada deshizo nuestros planes.* His arrival spoiled our plans.

○ **deshacerse** to wear oneself out *Se deshace con tanto trabajo.* He's wearing himself out with so much work. ○ **deshacerse de** to dispose of, get rid of *Me deshice de mis alhajas.* I got rid of my jewels. ○ **deshacerse en** to outdo oneself in *Se deshizo en amabilidades con las señoras.* He outdid himself in courteous attentions to the ladies. ○ **deshacerse en lágrimas** to burst into tears.

deshecho (see **deshacer**) undone, not made. ▲ worn out, exhausted *Estoy deshecho.* I'm exhausted.

deshonesto dishonest, dishonorable; lewd.

deshonra dishonor, disgrace.

deshonrar to disgrace.

desierto deserted; uninhabited *La estación estaba desierta.* The station was deserted. ▲ [*m*] desert *La última parte del viaje fué a través del desierto.* The last part of the trip was across the desert.

designar to name, appoint (a person).

desigual unequal *La lucha era muy desigual.* It was an unequal struggle. ▲ uneven *El terreno era muy desigual.* The ground was very uneven.

desigualdad [*f*] difference, inequality.

desilusión [*f*] disillusionment.

desinfectante [*adj; m*] disinfectant.

desinfectar to disinfect.

desinteresado impartial; disinterested.

desistir de to give up, call off *Desistió de hacer el viaje.* He called off the trip.

desleal disloyal.

deslizarse to slip, slide, glide *Los patinadores se deslizaban rápidamente por la pista.* The skaters glided rapidly around the rink.

deslucido worn, faded *Este traje está muy deslucido.* This dress is too worn. ▲ unsuccessful *La fiesta fué muy deslucida.* The party was a failure.

deslumbrar to dazzle.

desmayar to be dismayed *or* depressed *or* discouraged *No desmayó en su intento.* He wasn't discouraged in his plan.

○ **desmayarse** to faint *Al saber la noticia se desmayó.* When she learned the news she fainted.

desmejorado ○ **estar desmejorado** to look sickly.

desmentir [*rad-ch II*] to disprove *Pude desmentirle en todo lo que decía.* I was able to disprove every statement he made.

○ **desmentirse** to take back, retract *Después de haberlo dicho trató de desmentirse.* After he had said it, he tried to take it back.

desnudar to undress *Está desnudando a los niños.* She's undressing the children.

○ **desnudarse** to take off one's clothes, get undressed *Se desnudó y se tiró al agua.* He took off his clothes and dove into the water.

desnudo naked, nude, bare.

desobedecer [-*zc*-] to disobey *No desobedezca Ud. mis órdenes.* Don't disobey my orders.

desocupado unoccupied, vacant *¿Hay algún piso desocupado?* Do you have an apartment vacant? ▲ not busy, not occupied *Hablaré con Ud. cuando esté desocupado.* I'll talk with you when you're not busy. ▲ [*n*] idler *Toda su vida no ha sido más que un desocupado.* He's been an idler all his life.

desocupar to vacate *Tenemos que desocupar la casa antes del mes próximo.* We must vacate the house before next month. ▲ to empty *Voy a desocupar este armario para que Ud. lo use.* I'm going to empty this cabinet so that you can use it.

desolación [*f*] desolation.

desolado desolate, disconsolate; disappointed.

desollar to skin *Después de matar el carnero tendrá Ud. que desollarlo.* After you kill the sheep you'll have to skin it. ‖ *Queda el rabo por desollar.* The most difficult part's still to be done.

desorden [*m*] disorder, confusion, mess *El cuarto estaba en el más completo desorden.* The room was a complete mess.

○ **desórdenes** riots, disturbance *En los últimos desórdenes hubo varios heridos.* There were several people hurt in the recent riots.

desordenado disorderly.

desordenar to upset.

desorganizar to disorganize.

desorientar to confuse *Me desorienta su manera de presentar el asunto.* His way of presenting the matter confuses me.

○ **desorientarse** to lose one's bearings, get lost *Me desorienté al salir del metro.* I lost my bearings when I came out of the subway.

despachar to ship, send out *Despacharon un vagón de géneros.* They shipped a carload of goods. ▲ to attend to, take care of *No he despachado todavía la correspondencia de hoy.* I haven't taken care of today's mail yet. ▲ to wait on, take care of *Señorita, ¿quiere Ud. despacharme, por favor?* Will you please wait on me, miss? ▲ to fire, dismiss *Le despacharon por inútil.* They fired him because he was useless.

despacho dispatch. ▲ office *¿Quiere Ud. pasar a su despacho?* Will you go into his office?

○ **despacho de billetes** ticket office, ticket window *Tuvo que hacer cola en el despacho de billetes.* He had to stand in line at the ticket office. ○ **despacho de mercancía** shipment of goods *Se ha retrasado mucho el despacho de esa mercancía.* That shipment's been very much delayed.

despacio slowly *¿Quiere Ud. hablar más despacio?* Would you speak more slowly?

despedazar to tear up, mangle.

despedida farewell, send-off *Les dieron una comida de despedida.* They gave them a farewell dinner.

despedir [*rad-ch III*] to dismiss, discharge *Tuvieron que despedir a la mitad del personal.* They had to dismiss half their personnel. ▲ to see (someone) off *Iremos a despedirle a la estación.* We'll go to the station to see him off.

○ **despedirse a la francesa** to take French leave, sneak away. ○ **despedirse (de)** to take leave (of), say goodby (to) *Tengo que despedirme de unos amigos.* I have to say good-by to some friends. ○ **ser despedido, salir despedido** to be thrown out *A consecuencia del choque uno de los pasajeros salió despedido.* As a result of the collision one of the passengers was thrown out.

despegar to unglue, take off *Voy a despegar este sello con agua caliente.* I'm going to take off this stamp with hot water. ▲ to rise, take off *El avión todavía no ha despegado.* The plane still hasn't taken off.

○ **despegarse** to come off *El sello se despegó.* The stamp came off. ○ **no despegar los labios** to keep silent, keep one's mouth shut.

despejado (see **despejar**) smart, bright *¡Qué muchacho tan despejado!* What a bright boy!

despejar to clear *La policía ha despejado la plaza.* The police have cleared the square.

○ **despejarse** to clear up (of the weather or sky) *Me parece que el tiempo se está despejando.* I think it's clearing up.

despensa pantry.

desperdiciar to waste *No se debe desperdiciar la comida.* Food shouldn't be wasted.

desperdicio [*m*] waste *Esta carne no tiene desperdicio.* This meat has no waste.

○ **desperdicios** refuse, garbage.

desperezarse to stretch (oneself).

despertador [*m*] alarm clock *Ponga el despertador a las siete.* Set the alarm clock for seven o'clock.

despertar [*rad-ch I*] to wake up *Despiérteme a las ocho.* Wake me up at eight o'clock. ▲ to arouse, sharpen, excite *Todo lo que ve despierta su curiosidad.* Everything he sees arouses his curiosity.

○ **despertarse** to wake up *Me desperté al amanecer.* I woke up at sunrise.

despierto (see **despertar**) awake. ▲ smart, wide-awake *Es un chico muy despierto.* He's a very wide-awake boy.

despintar to remove paint; to remove make-up.

desplegar [*rad-ch I*] to unfold *Estaban desplegando el mapa sobre la mesa.* They were unfolding the map on the table. ▲ to deploy (*Mil*).

○ **desplegar los labios** to open one's mouth *Estuvo allí sin desplegar los labios.* He sat there without opening his mouth.

desplomarse to fall, collapse.

despoblado uninhabited place, wilderness.

despojar to strip (of property), despoil *Le han despojado hasta del último centavo.* They stripped him of his last penny.

○ **despojarse de** to take off (clothing)

Al entrar se despojó del abrigo. On entering he took off his coat.
despojo spoils.
  ○ **despojos** remains.
déspota [*m*] tyrant, despot.
despotismo tyranny, despotism.
despreciable despicable, low-down.
despreciar to look down on, despise *No tiene Ud. ninguna razón para despreciarle.* You have no reason to look down on him. ▲ to scorn, reject *Despreció todos mis consejos.* He scorned all my advice.
desprecio contempt.
desprender to unfasten *Desprenda Ud. el broche.* Unfasten the pin.
  ○ **desprenderse** to loosen, fall off *Se ha desprendido un botón del saco.* A button's fallen off the jacket. ○ **desprenderse de** to give away *Se ha desprendido de toda su fortuna.* He gave away his whole fortune.
desprendido (see **desprender**) generous *Siempre ha sido muy desprendido.* He's always been very generous.
desprestigiado having lost one's prestige *or* reputation *Es un hombre completamente desprestigiado.* He's a man who's completely lost his reputation.
desprestigiar to slander.
despropósito nonsense.
después later *Tendremos una reunión y después podemos dar un paseo.* We'll have a meeting and later we can take a walk. ▲ then *Después fuimos al teatro.* Then we went to the theater. ▲ afterwards *Se lo contaré después.* I'll tell you afterwards.
  ○ **después de** after *Iremos después de comer.* We'll go after we eat. ○ **después de todo** after all *Después de todo es lo razonable.* After all, it's reasonable.
despuntar to be outstanding *Ese alumno despunta mucho.* That student's very outstanding.
desquitarse to get even *Vamos a jugar otra partida, a ver si me desquito.* Let's play another game to see if I can get even.
desquite [*m*] revenge, getting even *Entonces se le presentó la ocasión de su desquite.* Then he had a chance for revenge.
destacar to stand out *Destacaban por su estatura.* They stood out because of their height.
  ○ **destacarse** to be noted, be famous, distinguish oneself *Se destacaron por su valor.* They distinguished themselves by their courage.

destapar to take the lid *or* cover off *¿Puede Ud. destapar esta caja?* Can you take the lid off this box? ▲ to open *Destape Ud. otra botella de Coca-Cola.* Open another bottle of Coca-Cola.
desternillarse to split (one's sides with laughter).
desterrar [*rad-ch I*] to banish, exile *Lo van a desterrar.* They're going to exile him.
destilar to distill.
destinado (see **destinar**) addressed *La carta venía destinada a mí.* The letter was addressed to me.
  ○ **estar destinado a** to be bound to, be destined to *Ese proyecto está destinado a fracasar.* That plan's bound to fail.
destinar to appoint, assign *Le destinaron a otra sucursal del banco.* They appointed him to another branch of the bank.
destinatario, destinataria addressee.
destino job *Tiene un destino en el ministerio de Hacienda.* He has a job in the Treasury Department. ▲ destiny, fate *Su destino fué trágico.* He had a tragic fate. ▲ destination *Esta carta no llegará a su destino.* This letter won't reach its destination.
  ○ **con destino a** bound for, going to *Salió con destino a Buenos Aires.* He was bound for Buenos Aires.
destituir to dismiss (from office).
destornillador [*m*] screw driver.
destornillar to unscrew.
destreza skill.
destrozar to destroy, tear down.
destrucción [*f*] destruction.
destruir to destroy.
desunir to separate, take apart *Tendremos que desunir los alambres.* We'll have to separate the wires. ▲ to estrange *La política desunió a las dos familias.* Politics estranged the two families.
desvalido destitute.
desván [*m*] attic.
desvanecerse to vanish, disappear *Con el viento, el humo se desvaneció.* The smoke vanished with the wind. ▲ to faint *Al oír la mala noticia se desvaneció.* When she heard the bad news she fainted.
desvelar to keep awake *El café me desvela mucho.* Coffee keeps me awake.
  ○ **desvelarse** to outdo oneself *Se desvelaban por sernos agradables.* They outdid themselves in being kind to us.
desventaja disadvantage; handicap.
desventura misfortune, mishap.

desvergüenza impudence; shamelessness.
desviación [f] detour *Había una desviación en el camino.* There was a detour on the road.
desviar to change the course of *Desviaron la carretera para hacerla más corta.* They changed the course of the road to make it shorter.
○ **desviar la mirada** to avoid someone's eyes, look away. ○ **desviarse** to deviate, get away (from) *No se desvíe Ud. del tema.* Don't get away from the subject. ▲ to drift *El avión se ha desviado de su ruta.* The plane drifted from its course.
desvío indifference *Su desvío me molesta.* Her indifference annoys me.
detallar to tell in detail, to detail.
detalle [m] detail *Cuénteme Ud. todos los detalles.* Tell me all the details.
○ **con detalle** in detail *Explíquenme Uds. con detalle como ha ocurrido eso.* Explain to me in detail how it happened.
detener [irr] to stop, detain *Por favor, deténgale un momento.* Please detain him for a minute. ▲ to arrest *La policía detenuvo a los cómplices del asesino.* The police have arrested the accomplices of the murderer.
○ **detenerse** to stop, halt *El automóvil se detuvo.* The automobile stopped. ▲ to stop, restrain oneself *Detente un momento a pensarlo.* Stop and think it over for a minute.
detenido (see **detener**) [adj; n] (person) under arrest *Los detenidos esperaban a que se les interrogara.* Those under arrest were waiting to be questioned.
determinación [f] determination; decision *Tenemos que tomar una determinación.* We have to make a decision.
determinado determined [Am] *Triunfó porque era muy determinado.* He succeeded because he was very determined.
determinar to fix, determine *Determinaron las condiciones del negocio.* They fixed the terms of the deal. ▲ to decide *¿Determinó Ud. lo que quiere hacer?* Did you decide what you want to do?
○ **determinarse** to make up one's mind *¿Se determinó a hacer el viaje?* Did he make up his mind to make the trip?
detestable hateful, detestable, awful.
detrás behind *Vienen detrás.* They're coming along behind.
○ **detrás de** behind, in back of *Detrás de los árboles hay una casa.* There's a house behind the trees. ○ **por**

detrás from behind *El enemigo atacó por detrás.* The enemy attacked from behind. ▲ behind one's back *Por detrás hablaba mal de él.* He talked about him behind his back.
deuda debt *Pagó todas sus deudas.* He paid all his debts.
○ **estar en deuda** to be indebted *Estoy en deuda con Ud.* I'm indebted to you.
deudo, deuda relative, kin.
deudor, deudora debtor.
devanar to wind *Estaba devanando un ovillo de lana.* She was winding up a spool of wool.
○ **devanarse** to double up (with pain) [Am]. ○ **devanarse los sesos** to rack one's brains *Me estoy devanando los sesos para encontrar una solución.* I'm racking my brains to find a solution.
devastar to lay waste.
devoción [f] piety, devoutness; devotion.
devolver [rad-ch I] to return, give back *¿No ha devuelto Ud. todavía esos libros?* Haven't you returned those books yet? ▲ to pay back *¿Te ha devuelto el dinero que le prestaste?* Has he paid back the money you lent him? ▲ to restore *Aquella noticia le devolvió la tranquilidad.* That news restored her peace of mind.
devorar to devour.
devoto devout, pious.
devuelto See **devolver**.
día [m] *¿A qué día estamos hoy?* What day's today?
○ **al día** a day, per day *Producen cien automóviles al día.* They produce a hundred automobiles a day. ▲ up to date *Ponga Ud. Esa correspondencia al día.* Bring that correspondence up to date. ○ **al día siguiente** the following day. ▲ **buenos días** good morning *Buenos días. ¿Cómo está Ud.?* Good morning. How are you? ○ **darle a uno los días** to congratulate one on his saint's day *or* birthday *Fuí a dar los días a mi hermano.* I went to congratulate my brother on his birthday.
○ **de día** before dark *¿Cree Ud. que volveremos de día?* Do you think we'll return before dark? ▲ by day, when it's light *Llegó a casa cuando ya era de día.* It was daylight when he got home. ○ **de día en día** from day to day, as time goes by *De día en día la situación va empeorando.* The situation's getting worse from day to day.
○ **de hoy en ... días** ... days from today

Iremos de hoy en ocho días. We'll go a week from today. ○ **de un día para otro** from day to day *Está dejando esa visita de un día para otro.* He keeps putting off that visit from day to day. ○ **día de Año Nuevo** New Year's Day. ○ **día de fiesta** holiday *¿Es mañana un día de fiesta?* Is tomorrow a holiday? ○ **día del santo** saint's day. ○ **el día menos pensado** when one least expects. ○ **el mejor día** some fine day *El mejor día se presenta aquí.* Some fine day he'll show up here. ○ **hoy (en) día** today, these days *Hoy día es muy difícil encontrar eso.* It's very hard to find that today. ○ **ocho días** a week *Voy al cine cada ocho días.* I go to the movies every week. ○ **quince días** two weeks *Estaré en el campo quince días.* I'll be in the country two weeks. ○ **todos los días** daily, every day *Le veo todos los días.* I see him every day. ○ **un día sí y otro no, día de por medio** every other day *Tengo clase un día sí y otro no.* I have a class every other day.

diablo devil *¡Qué diablo estás haciendo!* What the devil are you doing? ○ **irse al diablo** to go to the devil.

diáfano transparent.

dialecto dialect.

diálogo dialogue.

diamante [m] diamond.

¡diantre! the deuce! the devil!

diario [adj] daily *Salió a dar su paseo diario.* He went out for his daily walk. ▲ [m] journal, diary *Escribía por las noches su diario.* He used to write his diary in the evening. ▲ paper, journal *¿Qué trae el diario?* What's new in the paper today? ○ **a diario** daily, every day *Nos vemos a diario.* We see each other every day.

dibujar to draw, sketch.

dibujo drawing.

diccionario dictionary.

dicha happiness.

dicho See **decir.** ▲ [m] saying, saw *Ese es un dicho muy antiguo.* That's a very old saying. ▲ witty remark *Tiene unos dichos muy graciosos.* He makes some very witty remarks. ‖ *Dicho y hecho.* No sooner said than done.

dichoso happy, fortunate, lucky.

diciembre [m] December.

dictador [m] dictator.

dictadura dictatorship.

dictar to dictate *Le voy a dictar unas cartas.* I'm going to dictate some let-

ters to him.—*Hizo lo que le dictó su conciencia.* He did what his conscience dictated. ▲ to give, issue (by decree) *Acerca de esto no se han dictado órdenes.* They haven't given any orders about this.

diente [m] tooth *Tengo un diente picado.* I have a cavity in my tooth. ▲ tine *El tenedor tiene torcidos los dientes.* The tines of the fork are bent. ▲ cog *Se cogió el brazo entre los dientes de la rueda.* His arm was caught between the cogs of the wheel. ○ **decir** (*or* hablar) **entre dientes** to mumble, mutter. ○ **tener buen diente** to be a hearty eater *Este chico tiene muy buen diente.* This boy's a hearty eater.

diestro able, skillful. ▲ [m] bull fighter.

dieta diet.

diez ten.

diferencia difference.

diferenciar to distinguish between.

diferente different.

diferido (see **diferir**) deferred *Pusieron un cable diferido.* They sent a deferred cablegram.

diferir [rad-ch II] to postpone, put off *No difiera Ud. esos asuntos.* Don't put off those matters. ▲ to differ *Difiero de Ud. en ese punto.* I differ with you on that point.

difícil difficult, hard.

dificultad [f] difficulty.

dificultar to make difficult.

difundir to spread, tell *¿Quién habrá difundido esa noticia?* Who could have spread that news? ▲ to broadcast *Esa emisión será difundida a toda América.* That program'll be broadcast throughout America.

difunto [adj] dead, deceased ▲ [n] deceased person, corpse.

difusora (radio) broadcasting station.

digerir [rad-ch II] to digest *Es una comida que se digiere muy mal.* That food's hard to digest.

digestión [f] digestion.

dignidad [f] dignity; high rank (office).

digno dignified *¡Que hombre tan digno!* What a dignified man! ▲ worthy *No es digno del puesto que tiene.* He's not worthy of his position. ▲ worthwhile. ○ **digno de confianza** reliable *Es una persona digna de confianza.* He's a reliable person.

dije [m] trinket, charm, pendant.

dilatación [f] expansion, enlargement.

dilatar to expand, dilate *Tiene las pupilas dilatadas.* The pupils of his eyes are dilated. ▲ to delay [Am] *No dila-*

ten Uds. más la resolución del negocio.
Don't delay finishing the business.
diligencia diligence *Trabaja con mucha diligencia.* He works diligently. ▲ speed *Hay que resolverlo con toda la diligencia posible.* You must solve it with all possible speed.
○ **hacer una diligencia** to attend to some business, do an errand.
diligente industrious.
diluvio flood, deluge.
dimensión [*f*] dimension.
diminuto diminutive, tiny.
dineral [*m*] large sum of money.
dinero money *En ese cajón he dejado el dinero.* I've left the money in that drawer.—*No venturen Uds. su dinero en eso.* Don't risk your money in that.
○ **dinero suelto** small change. ○ **persona** (*or* **gente**) **de dinero** wealthy person (*or* people).
Dios, dios [*m sg*] God, god.
○ **a Dios gracias, gracias a Dios** thank God *A Dios gracias, tenemos lo que necesitamos.* Thank God, we have what we need. ○ **¡Dios mío!** My God! Goodness! ○ **¡por Dios!** for goodness' sake *¡Por Dios! No diga Ud. eso.* For goodness' sake, don't say that!
‖ *Que Dios se lo pague.* May God reward you.
diplomacia diplomacy.
diplomático diplomatic *Su respuesta no fué diplomática.* His answer wasn't diplomatic. ▲ [*m*] diplomat *Era un buen diplomático.* He was a good diplomat.
diputado a cortes congressman.
dirección [*f*] direction *¿En qué dirección va Ud.?* Which way are you going? ▲ address (mail, etc) *Escriba Ud. la dirección con claridad.* Write the address clearly. ▲ board of directors. ▲ management.
○ **de dirección única** one-way *Esta calle es de dirección única.* This is a one-way street.
directo [*adj*] direct.
director [*m*] director, manager *Hable Ud. con el director de la empresa.* Speak to the manager of the firm.
○ **director de escena** stage manager. ○ **director (de escuela)** principal (of a school). ○ **director de orquesta** orchestra conductor. ○ **director (de un periódico)** editor (of a newspaper).
dirigible [*m*] dirigible.
dirigir to direct. ▲ to address *¿A quién tengo que dirigir la carta?* Who should I address the letter to? ▲ to manage

Dirigió la campaña política. He managed the political campaign. ▲ to lead *Diríjanos Ud. que sabe el camino.* Lead us, since you know the road. ▲ to steer *Dirigieron el barco hacia el muelle.* They steered the boat toward the wharf.
○ **dirigir la palabra** to speak, address *No me dirigió la palabra en varios días.* He didn't speak to me for several days.
○ **dirigirse (a, hacia)** to go, make one's way (to *or* toward) *Se dirigieron hacia la puerta.* They went toward the door.
disciplina discipline.
discípulo, discípula student, pupil.
disco disk. ▲ phonograph record *Ponga Ud. un disco de música de baile.* Put on a dance record.
discordia discord.
discreción [*f*] discretion.
discrepar to differ, disagree *Discrepo de su opinión.* I differ from your opinion.
discreto fair (fairly good) *Es un actor discreto.* He's a fair actor. ▲ discreet *Lo que dijo no era discreto.* What he said wasn't discreet.
disculpa apology *Sus disculpas no me interesan.* I'm not interested in his apologies. ▲ excuse *Lo que ha hecho no tiene disculpa.* There's no excuse for what he did.
disculpar to pardon, excuse *Tenemos que disculpar sus faltas.* We must excuse his mistakes.
○ **disculparse** to apologize *Tengo que disculparme por lo tarde que he venido.* I must apologize for coming late.
discurrir to think *Es un hombre que discurre muy bien en una emergencia.* He's a man who thinks well in an emergency.
discurso speech.
discusión [*f*] discussion.
discutir to discuss (involving difference of opinion between two or more persons) *Estuvieron varias horas discutiendo el asunto.* They discussed the matter for several hours. ▲ to argue *Discute todo lo que se le manda.* He argues about everything he's told to do.
disfraz [*m*] disguise.
disfrazar(se) to disguise (oneself).
disfrutar ○ **disfrutar de** to enjoy (good health) *Disfruta de muy buena salud.* He enjoys good health. ○ **disfrutar en** *or* **de** to enjoy *Disfrutamos mucho en la excursión.* We enjoyed the excursion very much.
disgustar to displease, grieve *Aquello*

disgustó a todos. That displeased everyone.

○ **disgustarse** to be displeased *or* hurt *Se disgustó por lo que le dije.* She was hurt by what I said to her.

disgusto quarrel *He tenido un disgusto con unos amigos.* I had a quarrel with some friends. ▲ grief, sorrow *Cuando se enteró de la muerte de su amigo se llevó un disgusto terrible.* When he found out about the death of his friend, he was very much grieved.

○ **dar disgustos** to distress, grieve *Ese muchacho le dio muchos disgustos a sus padres.* That boy distressed his parents very much. ○ **estar a disgusto** to be uncomfortable, be ill at ease *Estaba muy a disgusto con aquella gente.* I was very ill at ease with those people.

disimular to conceal, dissimulate *Siempre disimula sus intenciones.* He always conceals his intentions. ▲ to tolerate, overlook *Como la quiere tanto disimula todas sus faltas.* Since he likes her so much, he overlooks her faults.

disimulo dissimulation.

disipar to squander *Disiparon su fortuna en un par de años.* They squandered their fortune in a couple of years. ▲ to dispel, drive away *Quiero disipar sus dudas.* I want to dispel his doubts.

disminución [*f*] decrease, diminution.

disminuir to decline, lessen *En unas horas disminuirá el dolor.* The pain'll be lessened in a few hours. ▲ to decrease *En estos días han disminuido las ventas.* Sales have decreased these days. ▲ to die down, diminish *Si disminuye el viento, iremos.* If the wind dies down, we'll go.

disolución [*f*] dissolution.

disolver [*irr*] to dissolve *Disuelva Ud. la pastilla en un vaso de agua.* Dissolve the tablet in a glass of water. ▲ to break up *La policía disolvió la reunión.* The police broke up the meeting.

disparado (see **disparar**) ○ **a la disparada** [*Am*] at full speed. ○ **salir disparado** to beat it *Al llegar la policía salieron disparados.* When the police arrived they beat it.

disparar to shoot, fire *Dispararon al aire.* They fired into the air.

○ **dispararse** to go off *Se disparó la escopeta.* The shotgun went off.

disparate [*m*] nonsense; mistake.

disparo discharge, shooting (of weapon).

dispensar to excuse *Le han dispensado de hacer ese trabajo.* They've excused him from doing that work. ▲ to excuse,

pardon *Dispense Ud. que le interrumpa.* Pardon me for interrupting you. —*Dispénseme.* Excuse me. *or* Beg pardon. ▲ to distribute, dispense.

dispersar to scatter, disperse *Los guardias dispersaron a la multitud.* The police dispersed the crowd.

disponer [*irr*] to place, arrange *Han dispuesto mal los muebles.* They arranged the furniture badly. ▲ to arrange *Disponga Ud. lo que quiera.* Make any arrangements you like. ▲ to order, decree *El gobierno ha dispuesto la movilización general.* The government's ordered total mobilization.

○ **disponer de** to spend [*Am*] *Dispuso de todo el dinero que le dí.* He spent all the money I gave him. ▲ to have at one's disposal *Dispongo de muy poco tiempo.* I have very little time at my disposal. ○ **disponerse a** to get ready to *Me dispongo a salir mañana.* I'm getting ready to leave tomorrow.

disponible available.

disposición [*f*] disposal, service *Estoy a su disposición.* I'm at your service. ▲ provision, order *Han cambiado las disposiciones.* They changed the orders. ▲ arrangement *La disposición de los cuadros.* The arrangement of the pictures.

○ **estar en buena disposición** to be in a good frame of mind. ○ **tener disposición** to have aptitude *or* talent *Tiene mucha disposición para el dibujo.* She has a great talent for drawing.

dispuesto (see **disponer**) disposed, ready; zealous.

○ **bien dispuesto** favorably disposed. ○ **mal dispuesto** ill-disposed.

disputa dispute.

○ **sin disputa** undoubtedly, doubtless.

disputar to dispute, argue *Disputaban por cualquier cosa.* They argued over anything at all.

○ **disputarse** to fight for *or* over *Los dos se disputaron el premio.* The two of them fought for the prize.

distancia distance *¿Qué distancia hay de su casa al pueblo?* How far is it from your house to town?

○ **a distancia** at a distance. ○ **a larga distancia** long-distance [*Am*] *¿Cuánto tiempo hay que esperar para una llamada a larga distancia?* How long must one wait for a long-distance call?

distante far, distant.

distar to be distant *¿Dista mucho de aquí?* Is it far from here? ▲ to be far *Distaba mucho de ser cierto.* It was far from certain.

distinción [*f*] distinction *Era una mujer de mucha distinción.* She was a woman of great distinction. ▲ difference, distinction *Hay que hacer una distinción entre los dos sonidos.* It's necessary to make a distinction between the two sounds. ▲ distinction, honor *Aquella distinción era merecida.* That distinction was well-deserved.

distinguir to distinguish, tell apart *Era muy difícil distinguir a los gemelos.* It was very difficult to tell the twins apart. ▲ to make out *¿Distingue Ud. a lo lejos una luz?* Can you make out a light in the distance? ▲ to esteem, show regard for *La distingue de un modo especial.* He has a special regard for her.

○ **distinguirse** to distinguish oneself.

distinto different.

distracción [*f*] absent-mindedness *Lo hizo por distracción.* He did it absent-mindedly. ▲ diversion, pastime, amusement *El cine es una gran distracción.* Movies are a great diversion.

distraer [*irr*] to distract *Ese ruido me distrae.* That noise distracts me. ▲ to entertain, divert *Me ha distraído mucho esta novela.* I've enjoyed this novel very much.

○ **distraerse** to be distracted, not to be able to concentrate *Ese chico se distrae fácilmente.* That child's easily distracted.

distribución [*f*] distribution.

distribuir to distribute *Distribuyeron víveres.* They distributed food. ▲ to sort *¿Han distribuido el correo?* Has the mail been sorted?

distrito district.

divagar to digress.

diván [*m*] couch.

diversidad [*f*] diversity.

diversión [*f*] pastime, diversion.

diverso different *Tenían opiniones diversas.* They had different opinions.

○ **diversos** various, several *Le he visto en diversas ocasiones.* I've seen him on several occasions.

divertir [*rad-ch II*] to amuse, entertain, divert *Esa película le divertirá mucho.* That picture will amuse you.

○ **divertirse** to be entertained, have a good time. *¿Se divirtieron Uds. anoche?* Did you have a good time last night?

dividendo dividend.

dividir to divide.

divinidad [*f*] divinity.

divino divine. ▲ very beautiful *Era una mujer divina.* She was a very beautiful woman.

○ **culto divino** public worship in churches.

divisar to make out, perceive indistinctly.

división [*f*] division. ▲ compartment *El cajón de la cómoda tiene varias divisiones.* The bureau drawer has several compartments. ▲ disunity, discord *Hay una gran división en el partido.* There's a serious split ▪in the party. ▲ division [*Mil*] *Se han rendido dos divisiones.* Two divisions have surrendered.

divorciarse to get a divorce.

divorcio divorce.

divulgación [*f*] diffusion, spread.

divulgar to reveal, let out *No sé quien divulgó la noticia.* I don't know who let out the news. ▲ to popularize, make popular *Ese libro ha contribuido mucho a divulgar la química.* That book's done a lot to popularize chemistry.

○ **divulgarse** to become widespread *Se ha divulgado mucho el uso de ese tipo de radio.* The use of this type of radio has become widespread.

doblar to fold *Está doblando el mantel.* She's folding the tablecloth. ▲ to double *Doblaron las apuestas.* They doubled their bets.

○ **doblar la cabeza** to give in, yield.

○ **doblar la esquina** to turn the corner.

○ **doblarse** to bend, sag *Con tanto peso se doblará la barra.* The rod'll bend under so much weight.

doble double *Tendrá Ud. que pagar el doble.* You'll have to pay double. ▲ thick, heavy *Quiero una tela doble.* I want some heavy cloth. ▲ deceitful, two-faced *No se fíe Ud. de él, es muy doble.* Don't trust him, he's very two-faced.

‖ *Ponga la manta doble.* Double the blanket.

doblez [*m*] fold, crease *Tiene que hacer el doblez bien derecho.* You have to make the crease very straight.

doce twelve.

docena dozen.

dócil docile, obedient.

doctor [*m*] doctor (academic title) *Acaba de obtener el grado de doctor en Filosofía.* He's just received his Ph.D. ▲ doctor (of medicine) *El doctor dijo que será necesario operar.* The doctor said it'll be necessary to operate.

doctrina doctrine; Sunday school.

documento document, paper.

dólar [*m*] dollar.

dolencia pain; disease.

doler [*rad-ch I*] to hurt, pain *Esta inyección no duele nada.* This injection doesn't hurt a bit. ▲ to hurt, grieve *Les dolió mucho lo que dijo.* What he said hurt their feelings.

dolor [*m*] pain, ache *Tomó un calmante para el dolor de muelas.* He took a sedative for his toothache. ▲ sorrow, grief, affliction *Trataba de consolarla en su dolor.* He tried to console her in her sorrow.

dolorido sore, painful.

domar to tame; to subdue, overcome.

doméstico [*adj*] domestic. ▲ [*n*] domestic, servant.

domicilio residence *Avise Ud. si cambia de domicilio.* Let us know if you change your residence.

dominar to have a command *or* mastery of *Domina el español.* He has an excellent command of Spanish. ▲ to dominate *No deje que ese hombre le domine.* Don't let that man dominate you. ▲ to overlook, command a view of *Esta colina domina la ciudad.* This hill overlooks the city. ▲ to predominate *Entre los productos de esta región domina el algodón.* Among the products of this region, cotton predominates.
  ○ **dominarse** to control oneself *Dominese, no se ponga Ud. así.* Control yourself; don't get excited.

domingo Sunday.

dominico Dominican friar.

dominio power, rule, control *Tiene un gran dominio sobre sí mismo.* He's very self-controlled. ▲ domination, authority *Estos territorios estuvieron bajo el dominio extranjero.* These lands were under foreign domination. ▲ dominion *El rey salió a visitar sus dominios.* The king went to visit his dominions.

dominó [*m*] game of dominoes.

Don [*m*] Mr. (used before a man's first name or full name).

don [*m*] gift *Tiene un don natural para hablar.* He has a natural gift for speaking.
  ○ **don de gentes** winning manners.

donación [*f*] donation, gift, grant.

donativo donation, gift.

doncella maid, servant [*Sp*] *La doncella sirvió el té.* The maid served the tea. ▲ girl *¡Qué doncella tan linda!* What a pretty girl!

donde where *Aquí es donde murió.* This is where he died.
  ○ **¿a dónde?** where? *¿A dónde va*

Ud.? Where are you going? ○ **¿de dónde?** how? *¿De dónde va a saberlo si nadie se lo ha dicho?* How's he going to know if no one's told him? ○ **¿dónde?** where? *¿Dónde estuvo Ud. ayer?* Where were you yesterday? ○ **¿por dónde?** which way? where? *¿Por dónde está la salida?* Where's the exit?
  ‖ **¡De dónde!** Nonsense! ‖ *Fuí donde mi hermano.* I went to my brother's.

dondequiera wherever; anywhere.

Doña Mrs. (used before a woman's first name or full name) *¿Conoce Ud. a Doña María López?* Do you know Mrs. María López? ▲ Miss [*Col*] *¿Ha llegado Doña Juanita?* Has Miss Janet arrived?

dorado gold, gilded.

dormilón, dormilona sleepyhead.

dormir [*rad-ch II*] to sleep. ▲ **to rest**, be inactive *Deje que duerma el asunto hasta que yo vuelva.* Let the matter rest until I get back. ▲ to put to sleep *Duerme al niño.* Put the child to sleep.
  ○ **dormirse** to fall asleep *Se durmió en la conferencia.* He fell asleep at the lecture. ▲ to go to bed, retire *Nunca se duerme antes de las doce.* He never goes to bed before midnight.

dormitorio bedroom; dormitory.

dos two. ▲ second *Saldré el dos o el tres del mes próximo.* I'll leave the second or third of next month. ▲ [*m*] deuce *Echó el dos del triunfo.* He played the deuce of trumps.
  ○ **de dos en dos** in pairs, by twos, two abreast *Las niñas iban de dos en dos por el paseo.* The girls went down the walk in pairs. ○ **de dos en fondo** two abreast *Los soldados marchaban de dos en fondo.* The soldiers were marching two abreast. ○ **entre los dos** between you and me *Esto queda entre los dos.* This is just between you and me. ○ **en un dos por tres** in a jiffy *En un dos por tres lo arregló todo.* He fixed it all up in a jiffy.

doscientos two hundred.

dosis [*f*] dose (of medicine).

dotación [*f*] allotment *La dotación no es suficiente.* The allotment's inadequate. ▲ endowment, foundation; donation. ▲ crew *Ya está completa la dotación del buque.* The ship's crew is now complete.

dotado (see **dotar**) gifted *Es un muchacho muy bien dotado.* He's a very gifted boy.

dotar to give a dowry to *Su padre la dotó muy bien.* Her father gave her a good dowry.

dote [*f*] dowry *Se gastó la dote de su mujer.* He spent his wife's dowry. ▲ talent *Con tan buenas dotes tenía que triunfar.* With such talents he was bound to succeed.

draga dredge.

drama [*m*] play, drama.

dramático dramatic.

droga drug.

droguería drug store.

ducha shower, shower bath.

duda doubt.

　O **sin duda** certainly, without doubt *"¿Vendrá Ud. mañana?" "Sin duda."* "Will you come tomorrow?" "Certainly."

dudar to doubt *Dudo que venga.* I doubt that he'll come. ▲ to hesitate *Dudó al darme la respuesta.* He hesitated before he answered me.

　O **dudar de** to doubt, distrust, question *No dudamos de lo que Ud. dice.* We don't question what you say.

dudoso doubtful. ▲ dubious, suspicious *Ese es un tipo dudoso.* He's a suspicious character.

duelo mourning *Se cerraron las tiendas en señal de duelo.* The stores were closed as a sign of mourning. ▲ sorrow *La muerte del presidente causó gran duelo.* The president's death caused great sorrow. ▲ duel *Su abuelo murió en un duelo.* His grandfather was killed in a duel.

duende [*m*] hobgoblin.

dueño, dueña owner, landlord, landlady *Es el dueño de la propiedad.* He's the owner of the property. ▲ master, mistress *El perro miraba a su dueño.* The dog looked at his master.

　O **dueño de sí mismo** self-controlled *Siempre es dueño de sí mismo.* He's always self-controlled.

dulce [*adj*] sweet. ▲ [*m*] a piece of candy; *pl* candy *Compró una caja de dulces.* He bought a box of candy.

　O **agua dulce** fresh water.

dulzura sweetness; mildness *El clima es de una gran dulzura.* The climate's very mild.

duodécimo twelfth.

duplicado (see duplicar) [*adj; m*] duplicate *Este ejemplar está duplicado.* This is a duplicate copy.

　O **por duplicado** in duplicate *Envíelo por duplicado.* Send it in duplicate.

duplicar to double; to duplicate; to repeat.

duque [*m*] duke.

duquesa duchess.

duración [*f*] duration, term, length *La duración de la guerra perjudica al comercio.* The length of the war's harmful to trade.

　O **ser de duración** to wear well, last *Este género es de mucha duración.* This material will wear very well.

duradero lasting, durable.

durante during.

durar to last *¿Cuanto dura la película?* How long does the picture last? ▲ to wear, last *El abrigo me ha durado tres años.* This overcoat's lasted me three years.

dureza hardness, solidity *La dureza del ébano es bien conocida.* The hardness of ebony is well known. ▲ hardness, harshness *¡Qué dureza de corazón!* How hard-hearted!—*Debe evitarse la dureza en esos casos.* Harshness should be avoided in those cases. ▲ callus *Me ha salido una dureza en la planta del pie.* I have a callus on the sole of my foot.

durmiente [*m*] (railroad) tie [*Am*].

duro hard *Este colchón es muy duro.* This is a very hard mattress. ▲ hard, rough *¡Llevan una vida tan dura!* They lead such a hard life. ▲ hard, stubborn *¿Por qué tienes la cabeza tan dura?* Why are you so hard-headed? ▲ [*adv*] hard *Trabajó muy duro para conseguirlo.* He worked very hard to accomplish it. ▲ [*m*] duro (Spanish coin equal to five pesetas).

　O **a duras penas** with difficulty, hardly *A duras penas se hacía entender.* He could hardly make himself understood.

E

e and (before **i** or **hi**) *María e Inés irán conmigo.* Mary and Inez will go with me.

¡ea pues! come on! *¡Ea pues! Sigamos adelante.* Come on, let's get going.

echar to throw *Echaremos esto en el cajón.* We'll throw this into the drawer. ▲ to discharge, dismiss, fire *Echaron a muchos empleados.* They fired many employees. ▲ to pour *Puede echar el vino en el vaso.* You can pour the wine into the glass.

○ **echar a** (followed by verb of motion) to begin to, start to *Echaron a correr al ver al policía.* They began to run when they saw the police. ○ **echar a perder** to spoil, ruin *Ha echado a perder el trabajo.* He's spoiled the work. ○ **echar a pique** to sink *Los submarinos echaron a pique muchos barcos.* The submarines sank a lot of ships. ○ **echar de menos** to miss (notice the lack of) *Echa de menos a sus amigos.* He misses his friends. ○ **echar de ver** to notice, observe *No echó de ver el cambio.* He didn't notice the change. ○ **echar en cara** to throw in one's teeth, throw up to one *Siempre me echaba en cara sus favores.* He was always throwing his favors up to me. ○ **echar la llave** to lock the door *Eche Ud. la llave al salir.* Lock the door when you go out. ○ **echar por tierra** to overthrow, spoil *Le echaron por tierra sus proyectos.* They overthrew his plans. ○ **echarse** to lie down *Se echó en la arena.* He lay down in the sand. ○ **echarse a perder** to spoil *La carne se echó a perder.* The meat spoiled. ○ **echarse a (reír, llorar)** to begin *or* start to (laugh, cry). ○ **echarse atrás** to back out, withdraw *Cuento con Ud., no se vaya a echar atrás.* I'm counting on you not to back out.

eclipsar to eclipse.

eco echo.

economía economy.
     ○ **economía política** economics. ○ **economías** savings *Perdió todas sus economías.* He lost all his savings.

económico economical.

economizar to save *Economizaba la mitad de lo que ganaba.* He saved half of what he earned.—*Por aquel camino economizaba tiempo.* He saved time by taking that road.

ecuador [m] equator.

edad [f] age.

edificar to build *Edificarán una ciudad moderna.* They'll build a modern city.

edificio building.

editor [m] publisher *Los editores de ese periódico son muy liberales.* The publishers of that newspaper are very liberal.

edredón [m] comforter (cover); feather-bed.

educación [f] breeding, upbringing *Es un hombre sin educación.* He's ill-bred. ▲ education (intellectual, physical, and moral training).

educar to educate *Hay que educar al* *pueblo.* The people must be educated. ▲ to train *Han educado muy bien a su perro.* They've trained their dog very well.

efectivo effective.
     ○ **en efectivo** in cash *Quiero que me paguen en efectivo.* I want to be paid in cash.

efecto effect. ▲ impression *Su actuación causó mal efecto.* His behavior made a bad impression.
     ○ **en efecto** in fact *¡En efecto, no sabe nada!* In fact, he doesn't know anything.

efectuar to carry out, put into effect.

eficaz efficient, effective *Tomaron una medida muy eficaz.* They took a very effective measure.

efusión [f] effusion, warmth *La efusión de su acogida le emocionó.* The warmth of his reception moved him.

egoísta selfish *Es un hombre muy egoísta; no piensa en los demás.* He's a very selfish man; he never thinks of others.

¡eh! hey! *¡Eh! Aquí estoy.* Hey, here I am!

eje [m] axle *El eje está roto.* The axle's broken. ▲ main point *Este es el eje de la cuestión.* That's the crux of the matter.

ejecución [f] execution *Se hará cargo de la ejecución del proyecto.* He'll be in charge of carrying out the plan. ▲ performance *La ejecución del programa musical fué excelente.* The performance of the musical program was excellent.

ejecutar to execute, carry out *Se están ejecutando cambios en el Gabinete.* They're making changes in the Cabinet.

ejecutivo [adj] executive; efficient.

ejemplar exemplary *Es de una conducta ejemplar.* His conduct is exemplary. ▲ [m] copy *No pude conseguir otro ejemplar del libro.* I couldn't get another copy of the book.

ejemplo example *Sirve de ejemplo a los demás.* He sets an example for the others.—*Déme Ud. un ejemplo porque no etiendo.* Give me an example; I don't understand.

ejercer to handle, hold, practice *Ha ejercido ese cargo por mucho tiempo.* He's handled that job for a long time.

ejercicio exercise, drill.

ejercitar to exercise, drill *Está ejercitando su caballo.* He's exercising his horse.

ejército army.

ejote [m] string bean [Am].
el the.
él he El llegó tarde. He arrived late.
elástico [adj; m] elastic.
elección [f] election; choice.
electo See elegir.
electricidad [f] electricity.
electricista [m, f] electrician.
eléctrico electric.
elefante [m] elephant.
elegancia elegance Estaba vestida con elegancia. She was elegantly dressed.
elegante stylish, smart.
elegir [rad-ch III] to choose, select Sabe elegir sus amigos. He knows how to choose his friends. ▲ to elect ¿A quién han elegido presidente del club? Who did they elect president of the club?
elemental elementary.
elemento element, factor Es un elemento perturbador. He's a disturbing element. ▲ element Cuando baila está en su elemento. He's in his element when he's dancing.
elevación [f] elevation, height, altitude.
elevar to erect Van a elevar un monumento a los héroes. They're going to erect a monument to the heroes.
○ **elevarse** to climb, ascend Los aviones se elevaron a gran altura. The airplanes climbed very high.
eliminar to eliminate.
ella she.
ello it, that Hablemos de ello. Let's talk about that.
ellos [m] they.
elocuencia eloquence.
elocuente eloquent.
elogiar to praise Nunca elogia a nadie. He never praises anyone.
elogio praise.
elote [m] ear of green corn (for roasting) [Am].
emanación [f] fumes.
embajada embassy; delegation.
embajador [m] ambassador.
embanderar to decorate with banners La calle está embanderada. The street's decorated with banners.
embarcar to ship, send by boat Embarcaré mi equipaje primero. I'll ship my baggage first.
○ **embarcar(se)** to embark Se embarcó para Buenos Aires. He embarked for Buenos Aires.
embargar to seize, attach Les embargarán todas sus propiedades. They'll seize all their property.
embargo ○ **sin embargo** however, nevertheless Aunque es el estado más pequeño, es, sin embargo, el más poblado.

Though it's the smallest estate, nevertheless it's the most densely populated.
embarque [m] shipment; boarding (a ship).
embestir [rad-ch III] to attack, charge (head first) El enemigo embistió con furia. The enemy attacked furiously.
emblema [m] emblem, insignia.
embriagar to make drunk, intoxicate Este vino embriaga muy fácilmente. This wine's very intoxicating. ▲ to overcome Estaba embriagado por la emoción. He was overcome with emotion.
○ **embriagarse** to get drunk Se embriagaron en la fiesta. They got drunk at the party.
embrollar to muddle, mess up No embrolle Ud. las cosas. Don't mess things up.
embrollo muddle, mess ¡Esto es un embrollo! This is a mess.
embromar to play jokes on Se pasa el tiempo embromando a todo el mundo. He spends his time playing jokes on everybody.
embuste [m] lie Todos creyeron su embuste. Everyone believed his lie.
embustero, embustera liar.
emergencia emergency.
emigración [f] emigration.
emigrante [m, f; adj] emigrant.
emigrar to emigrate.
eminencia summit, top; hill Desde una eminencia se divisaba el valle. From a hill one could see the valley. ▲ outstanding person (in science, letters, arts).
eminente famous, eminent Es un escritor eminente. He's a famous writer.
emoción [f] emotion Me quedé mudo de la emoción. I was speechless with emotion. ▲ feeling El actor hizo su papel con emoción. The actor played the part with feeling.
emocionarse to be moved Se emociona fácilmente. He's easily moved.
empacar to pack.
empalizada (wooden) fence.
empalizar to fence Empalizaron el jardín. They fenced the garden.
empalme [m] junction.
empañar to blur, dim La humedad empaña los vidrios. Moisture blurs the glass.
empapar to soak Empape esta esponja en agua. Soak this sponge in water.
○ **empaparse** to be soaked, be drenched Llueve tanto que me he empapado al cruzar la calle. It's raining so hard I got soaked crossing the street.

emparejar to make level, make even [*Am*]; to match [*Sp*].

empatar to equal. ▲to tie *Los dos equipos empataron en el primer partido.* The two teams tied in the first game.

empate [*m*] tie, draw.

empedrado cobblestone pavement.

empedrar to pave with cobblestones.

empellón [*m*] push, shove *Me dió un empellón y pasó delante de mí.* He gave me a push and got ahead of me.
    ○ **entrar a empellones** to push one's way in *La gente entraba a empellones.* The people pushed their way in.

empeñar to pledge, give *Empeñé mi palabra.* I gave my word. ▲to pawn *Tuvo que empeñar su reloj.* He had to pawn his watch.
    ○ **empeñarse en** to be bent on *Se empeña en hacerlo a pesar de los obstáculos.* He's bent on doing it in spite of all obstacles.

empeño determination, firmness *Trabajó con tanto empeño que se hizo rico.* He worked with such determination that he became rich. ▲pawn; pawning.
    ○ **casa de empeños** pawnshop.

empeorarse to grow worse.

empezar [*rad-ch I*] to begin *¿A qué hora empieza la función?* When does the performance begin?

empinado steep.

empinar ○ **empinar el codo** to drink *Le gusta empinar el codo.* He likes to drink. ○ **empinarse** to stand on one's toes *Tendrá que empinarse para poder ver.* You'll have to stand on your toes to see.

empleado See **emplear.** ▲[*n*] employee.

emplear to use, employ *Emplearemos otro material.* We'll use other material. ▲to employ, hire *¿Van a emplear más gente?* Are they going to employ more people? ▲to invest *Empleó su dinero en negocios.* He invested his money in business.

empleo employment; job *Tengo un buen empleo.* I have a good job. ▲use *El empleo de esa palabra no es común.* That word isn't in common use.

empobrecerse [-*zc*-] to become poor.

empolvarse to powder oneself *Se empolva demasiado.* She uses too much powder. ▲to get dusty *En este tiempo se empolva mucho la carretera.* The road gets very dusty in this weather.

emprender to undertake.

empresa undertaking, project, enterprise *Es muy difícil realizar esa empresa.* It's very difficult to carry out that project. ▲company *Ha quebrado la empresa.* The company's failed.

empresario manager (theatrical), promoter.

empujar to push *Haga el favor de empujar la mesa hacia aquí.* Please push the table over this way.

empujón [*m*] push *Le dieron un empujón.* They gave him a push.
    ○ **a empujones** by pushing.

en in. ▲at *La vi en la estación.* I saw her at the station. ▲on *¿En cuál tren vino Ud.?* What train did you come on?
    ○ **en vano** in vain *Esperé en vano toda la tarde.* I waited all afternoon in vain.

enamorado in love. ▲[*n*] one in love, lover, sweetheart.

enamorar to flirt with, make love to *Enamora a todas las chicas.* He makes love to all the girls.
    ○ **enamorarse de** to fall in love with.

encadenar to chain.

encajar to fit *La tapa no encaja bien.* The cover doesn't fit well. ▲to fit in *Ella no encaja bien aquí.* She doesn't fit in here.

encaminar to direct *Los encaminamos a la estación.* We directed them to the station.
    ○ **encaminarse** to make one's way, go *Se encaminó hacia su casa.* He went toward his house.

encantador [*adj*] charming. ▲[*n*] charmer.

encantar to charm, delight *Esta escena me encanta.* This scene delights me.

encanto charm.

encarado ○ **mal encarado** tough-looking *Es un tío muy mal encarado.* He's a very tough-looking guy.

encaramarse to climb *Se encaramó al árbol.* He climbed the tree.

encarcelar to imprison.

encarecer [-*zc*-] to raise, make expensive *Han encarecido el precio de la carne.* They've raised the price of meat. ▲to beg *Le encarezco que lo haga con cuidado.* I beg you to do it carefully.
    ○ **encarecerse** to become more expensive, go up *Los víveres se han encarecido.* The price of food's gone up.

encargado (see **encargar**) in charge *Está encargado de la organización de la fiesta.* He's in charge of preparations for the party. ▲[*n*] manager, person in charge *Hable Ud. con el encargado.* Speak to the manager.

encargar to entrust *Le encargaron una misión muy delicada.* They entrusted him with a very delicate mission. ▲ to ask, urge *Me encargó que no lo dijese.* He urged me not to say it.

○ **encargarse** to take charge *Me encargaré del trabajo.* I'll take charge of the work.

encargo job, assignment *Me ha dado un encargo que no me gusta.* He's given me an assignment that I don't like. ▲ errand *Salió a hacer unos encargos.* He went out on some errands.

encarnado [*adj*] red.

encarnizado cruel, pitiless.

encendedor [*m*] cigarette lighter.

encender [*rad-ch I*] to light, put on *Haga el favor de encender la luz.* Please put on the light.

○ **encenderse** to light up, go on *Se encendieron los faroles.* The street lights went on.

encendido (see **encender**) bright-colored.

○ **ponerse encendido** to blush.

encerrar [*rad-ch I*] to lock up *Los encerraron en un calabozo.* They locked them up in a cell. ▲ to include, contain *Ese libro encierra ideas útiles.* That book contains useful ideas.

○ **encerrarse** to shut oneself (up), lock oneself (up) *Se ha encerrado en su cuarto.* He locked himself in his room.

encía gum (of the mouth).

encima on *¿Quiere Ud. que ponga esto encima de la mesa?* Do you want me to put this on the table?

○ **por encima** superficially, sketchily *He leído el diario por encima.* I skimmed through the paper. ○ **por encima de** above *El avión volaba por encima de las nubes.* The airplane was flying above the clouds.

encina evergreen oak (tree).

encinta pregnant.

encoger to shrink *Esa tela va a encoger si se lava.* That material's going to shrink if it's washed.

○ **encogerse de hombros** to shrug one's shoulders *Se encogió de hombros por toda contestación.* His only answer was to shrug his shoulders.

encogido (see **encoger**) bashful *Era un chico muy encogido.* He was a very bashful boy.

encolerizar to anger.

○ **encolerizarse** to become angry.

encomendar to charge with, entrust to *Le encomendarán la ejecución del proyecto.* They'll entrust the completion of the project to him.

encomienda ○ **encomienda postal** parcel, package, parcel post [*Am*].

enconado (see **enconarse**) rankling *Se tenían un odio enconado.* They had a rankling hatred for each other.

enconarse to become infected *Se le ha enconado la herida.* His wound has become infected.

encontrar [*rad-ch I*] to find *Encontré este reloj en la estación.* I found this watch at the station.—*¿Cómo encuentra Ud. el trabajo?* How do you find the work? ▲ to meet *Anoche encontré a mi amigo en la biblioteca.* I met my friend in the library last night.

○ **encontrarse** to meet *Nos encontraremos en el teatro.* We'll meet in the theater. ▲ to collide *Los dos camiones se encontraron con gran estrépito.* The two trucks collided with a great crash. ▲ to be *Mi mujer se encontraba allí.* My wife was there. ▲ to come upon *Al doblar la esquina nos encontramos con el desfile.* We came upon the parade when we turned the corner. ▲ to feel *¿Cómo se encuentra el enfermo esta mañana?* How's the patient feeling this morning?

encontronazo bump, collision.

encorvar to bend, curve.

○ **encorvarse** to bend, stoop.

encrucijada street *or* road intersection.

encuentro meeting *Fué un encuentro muy afortunado.* It was a very fortunate meeting. ▲ match *Después de vencer en todos los encuentros, obtuvo el título de campeón.* After winning all the matches, he got the title of champion.

○ **salir al encuentro de** to go to meet *Salió al encuentro de los invitados.* He went to meet the guests.

encurtido pickle [*Am*].

enderezar to straighten.

○ **enderezarse** to straighten up, sit up.

endiablado devilish, mischievous.

endoso indorsement.

endulzar to sweeten.

endurecer(se) [*-zc-*] to harden.

enemigo [*n; adj*] enemy.

enemistad [*f*] enmity.

energía energy.

○ **energía eléctrica** electric power.

enérgico energetic.

enero January.

enfadar to anger, annoy.

○ **enfadarse** to get angry *No hay motivo para enfadarse.* There's no reason to get angry.

enfado anger, annoyance.

énfasis [*m*] emphasis.

enfermar(se) to fall ill, to get sick.

enfermedad [*f*] illness, sickness, disease.
enfermera nurse.
enfermo [*adj*] sick *Ayer operaron al niño enfermo.* They operated on the sick child yesterday. ▲ [*n*] patient *El enfermo está en el hospital.* The patient's in the hospital.
enflaquecer(se) [*-zc-*] to become thin.
enfrente opposite, across *Enfrente hay una casa blanca.* Across (the street) there's a white house. ○ **de enfrente** across the street *Viven en la casa de enfrente.* They live in the house across the street. ○ **enfrente de** opposite *El auto está parado enfrente de aquel edificio.* The car's parked opposite that building.
enfriamiento [*m*] cold (illness).
enfriar to cool *Debemos enfriar el agua en la nevera.* We must cool the water in the ice box. ○ **enfriarse** to cool off, become cold *Deje el café ahí para que se enfríe.* Leave your coffee there so it can cool off. ▲ to get chilled *Abríguese bien, no se vaya a enfriar.* Dress warmly so you won't get chilled.
engañar to deceive *Engañó a su amigo.* He deceived his friend. ○ **engañarse** to make a mistake, be wrong *Se engañaron a causa de la niebla.* They made a mistake because of the fog.
engaño deceit.
engordar to fatten; to get fat.
enhorabuena congratulations.
enjuagar to rinse.
enlace [*m*] marriage *Han anunciado su próximo enlace.* They've announced their coming marriage. ○ connection(s) *El enlace de trenes es excelente en esta estación.* The train connections at this station are excellent.
enlazar to connect *Esos dos trenes enlazan en la próxima estación.* Those two trains connect at the next station.
enlodarse to get muddy *Las ruedas se enlodaron completamente.* The wheels got all muddy.
enloquecer [*-zc-*] to become insane *A consecuencia del golpe enloqueció.* As a result of the blow he became insane. ▲ to drive crazy *Este trabajo me está enloqueciendo.* This work's driving me crazy. ○ **enloquecerse** to get furious *or* mad *Con la discusión se enloqueció.* He got furious as a result of the argument.
enmendar [*rad-ch I*] to amend, correct *Hágame el favor de enmendar esta copia.* Please correct this copy for me. ○ **enmendarse** to mend one's ways, reform *Si no no se enmienda, no podrá triunfar nunca.* If he doesn't mend his ways, he'll never succeed.
enmohecido rusty.
enojar to anger *La suspensión del espectáculo enojó al público.* The public was angered by the suspension of the show. ○ **enojarse** to get angry *Enojándose no arreglará nada.* Nothing will be gained by getting angry.
enojo anger.
enorme enormous.
enormidad [*f*] outrage *Lo que ha hecho ese hombre es una enormidad.* What that man's done is an outrage. ▲ great number, great quantity *En la fiesta hubo una enormidad de gente.* There was a great crowd at the party.
enredadera climbing vine.
enredar to snarl, tangle up *El gato enredó todos los hilos.* The cat tangled up all the threads. ▲ to snarl, mess up *El gerente enredó todos los negocios de la compañía.* The manager messed up all the company's business. ○ **enredarse** to get snarled *Se enredó la cuerda.* The string got snarled. ○ **enredarse con** to get involved with *Se enredó con una mala mujer.* He got involved with a bad woman. ○ **enredarse en** to get involved in *Se enredó en negocios sucios.* He got involved in shady business affairs.
enredo tangle, intrigue.
enriquecer [*-zc-*] to enrich. ▲ to enhance *Ese adorno enriquece mucho el traje.* That trimming enhances the dress. ○ **enriquecerse** to get rich *Se enriqueció de repente.* He got rich quickly.
enrollar to roll up *Enrolle Ud. esas revistas.* Roll up those magazines.
enronquecer(se) [*-zc-*] to get hoarse *Se enronqueció de tanto gritar.* He got hoarse from so much shouting.
ensalada salad.
ensanchar to widen *Estaban ensanchando el camino cuando pasamos.* They were widening the road when we passed. ▲ to let out, enlarge *Tiene Ud. que ensancharme la chaqueta.* You'll have to let out my jacket.
ensayar to try, test *Vamos a ensayar el nuevo material.* We're going to test the new material. ▲ to rehearse *No han tenido tiempo de ensayar la comedia.* They haven't had time to rehearse the play.
ensayo test, trial; rehearsal.
ensenada cove.

enseñanza instruction, teaching.
enseñar to teach *Un mejicano le enseñó español.* A Mexican taught him Spanish. ▲ to show *Me enseñó el retrato de su novia.* He showed me a picture of his sweetheart. ▲ to show, point out *Enseñe Ud. el camino al señor.* Show this gentleman the way.
ensillar to saddle.
ensordecer [-zc-] to deafen.
ensuciar to soil, to dirty.
ensueño pipe dream, day dream.
entablar to board up *Entablaron las ventanas.* They boarded up the windows. ▲ to begin, start *Han entablado negociaciones.* They've started negotiations.
entablillar to put splints on *Se rompió un brazo y tuvieron que entablillárselo.* He broke his arm and they had to put splints on it.
entender [*rad-ch I*] to understand *Ya entiendo lo que Ud. quiere decir.* Now I understand what you mean.
○ **a** (*or* **según**) **mi entender** in my opinion *A mi entender es mejor cambiar de procedimiento.* In my opinion it's better to change the policy. ○ **entender de** to be familiar with, be good at *¿Entiende Ud. de mecánica?* Are you good at mechanics? ○ **entenderse con** to deal with *Tendrán que entenderse con el jefe.* They'll have to deal with the boss. ○ **entender(se) en** to be in charge of *¿Quién se entiende en este asunto?* Who's in charge of this matter?
entendido (see **entender**) ○ **estar** (*or* **quedar**) **entendido** to be understood *Está entendido que empezaremos mañana.* It's understood that we'll start tomorrow. ○ **no darse por entendido** to pretend not to understand *No me dí por entendido.* I pretended I'm sorry I understand. ○ **ser (muy) entendido en** to be skilled *or* informed in *Es un obrero muy entendido en su oficio.* He's very skilled in his trade.
entendimiento understanding; mind.
enterar to inform, report *Debemos enterar a la dirección de lo que pasa.* We must inform the management of what's going on.
○ **enterarse** to pay attention *No te enteras de lo que te estoy diciendo.* You aren't listening to what I'm saying. ○ **enterarse (de)** to learn *Acabo de enterarme de la noticia.* I've just learned the news. ▲ to find out, inquire *Entérese del hotel en que viven.* Find out what hotel they're living at.

entereza fortitude; presence of mind.
entero entire, whole.
enterrar [*rad-ch I*] to bury.
entierro burial.
entonación [*f*] intonation.
entonar to sing in tune; to begin to sing. ▲ to harmonize, blend (of colors) *Estos colores entonan muy bien.* These colors harmonize very well.
entonces at the time, then *Entonces vivía con sus padres.* He was living with his parents at the time. ▲ then *¿Entonces ya no me necesita Ud.?* Then you don't need me now, do you?—*¿Y entonces que pasó?* And then what happened?
‖ *¿Entonces?* Then what? *or* And then? [*Am*].
entrada entrance *Adornaron la entrada con banderas.* They decorated the entrance with flags. ▲ admission *La entrada será gratis.* Admission will be free. ▲ attendance *La función tuvo una buena entrada.* The show was well attended. ▲ ticket, seat *Debemos comprar las entradas ahora mismo.* We have to buy the tickets right now. ▲ admittance *Se prohibe la entrada.* No admittance. ▲ beginning *A la entrada del invierno saldré de viaje.* I'm leaving on a trip at the beginning of winter. ▲ entrée *¿Qué desea Ud. como entrada?* What do you want for an entrée?
○ **entradas** receding hair at temples *A pesar de su juventud ya tiene entradas.* In spite of his youth his hair's already receding at the temples. ▲ income *Las entradas superan a las salidas.* The income exceeds the outgo.
‖ *Entrada pública.* Admission free.
entrar to enter, come in, go in *¿Se puede entrar?* May I come in? ▲ to fit *El zapato no me entra, es muy chico.* The shoe doesn't fit me; it's too small. ▲ to join *Quiero entrar en un club deportivo.* I want to join an athletic club.
○ **entrar a trabajar** to go to work, be employed *Entraron a trabajar en una fábrica.* They went to work in a factory. ○ **entrar en** (*or* **a**) to enter *Entrará en la Universidad el año próximo.* He'll enter the University next year.
‖ *A este chico no le entra la aritmética.* This child can't get arithmetic through his head.
entre between *La mujer estaba sentada entre dos hombres.* The woman was sitting between two men. ▲ among

Repartiremos las ganancias entre todos. We'll divide the profits among all of us.—*Es muy alegre la vida entre estudiantes.* Life among students is very gay.—*Entre los cuatro levantaron la carga.* Among the four of them, they picked up the load.

entreabierto (see **entreabrir**) ajar, half-open.

entreabrir to open halfway, open part way.

entreacto intermission.

entrega delivery *Ud. tendrá que pagar a la entrega del paquete.* You'll have to pay for the package on delivery.

entregar to deliver, hand over *No han entregado la mercadería todavía.* They haven't delivered the goods yet. ▲to hand *Entrégueme la carta.* Hand me the letter. ▲to give up, surrender, turn over *Lo entregaron a la policía.* They turned him over to the police.

○ **entregarse** to give in, yield *Se entregó a la bebida.* He gave in to drink. ▲to surrender *El batallón se entregó al enemigo.* The battalion surrendered to the enemy.

entrenador [m] trainer, coach.

entrenamiento training, coaching.

entrenar to train.

entrepaño shelf.

entretanto meanwhile.

entretener [irr] to entertain, amuse *Hay que entretener al niño con algo.* You have to amuse the child with something. ▲to delay, tie up *Mis asuntos me entretuvieron hasta muy tarde.* My affairs tied me up until very late.

○ **entretenerse** to amuse oneself *Nos entretuvimos jugando a las cartas.* We amused ourselves playing cards. ▲to be tied up, be delayed *Me entretuve hasta muy tarde arreglando unas cosas.* I was tied up until very late getting some things in order.

entretenido (see **entretener**) entertaining, amusing.

entretenimiento pastime.

entrevista interview.

entrevistar to interview.

entristecer [-zc-] to sadden, be depressing *Lo negro entristece.* Black is depressing.

○ **entristecerse** to become sad *Se entristeció mucho al saberlo.* He became sad when he found out.

entumecer to numb *El frío entumece los miembros.* Cold numbs the limbs.

○ **entumecerse** [-zc-] to become numb.

enturbiar to roil, make muddy *El temporal enturbió las aguas.* The storm

roiled the water. ▲to dim (vision) *La fiebre le enturbió la vista.* The fever dimmed his vision.

○ **enturbiarse** to become muddy *El agua se enturbió con la lluvia.* The water became muddy because of the rain.

entusiasmar to make enthusiastic *Las noticias entusiasmaron al público.* The news made the public enthusiastic.

○ **entusiasmarse** to be enthusiastic *Los muchachos se entusiasmaron con la música.* The boys were enthusiastic about the music.

entusiasmo enthusiasm.

entusiasta [m, f] enthusiast.

envejecer [-zc-] to age, become old.

envenenamiento poisoning.

envenenar to poison.

enviado envoy.

enviar to send *Envíe Ud. la carta por correo aéreo.* Send the letter airmail.

○ **enviarle a uno a paseo** to send one about his business, tell someone to go chase himself.

envidia envy.

envidiable enviable.

envidiar to envy *Envidia a todos sus amigos.* He envies all his friends.

envidioso envious.

envío shipment.

envolver [rad-ch I] to wrap *No envolvieron bien la caja.* They didn't wrap the box well.

envuelto (see **envolver**) involved *Siempre está envuelto en líos.* He's always involved in some sort of a mess.

epidemia epidemic.

episodio episode.

época epoch, time, times, period.

equilibrio balance.

equipaje [m] baggage, luggage *Si va Ud. en avión no podrá llevar mucho equipaje.* If you go by plane you won't be able to take much luggage.—*En la frontera van a registrar el equipaje.* They're going to examine the baggage at the border.

equipo team; equipment.

equivalencia equivalent *Déme Ud. la equivalencia en dólares.* Give me the equivalent in dollars.

equivocación [f] mistake *Se llevó mi abrigo por equivocación.* He took my coat by mistake.

equivocar to mistake, confuse *Equivocó los paquetes.* He mixed up the packages.

○ **equivocarse** to make a mistake, be wrong *Se equivoca Ud.* You're wrong.
○ **equivocarse de** to . . . the wrong . . .

Me equivoqué de autobús. I took the wrong bus.—*Me equivoqué de puerta.* I went to the wrong door.

error [m] mistake *Esta copia está llena de errores.* This copy's full of mistakes.
○ **error de imprenta** typographical error (in printed matter). ○ **error de máquina** typographical error (in typewriting). ○ **estar en un error** to be mistaken *Dispénseme, pero está Ud. en un error.* Excuse me, but you're mistaken.

esa (see **ese**) that.

escabroso rough, uneven *Bajamos por un camino muy escabroso.* We went down a very rough road. ▲ off-color, risqué *Nos contó un chiste escabroso.* He told us an off-color story.

escala (rope) ladder *Cayó al romperse la escala.* He fell when the ladder broke. ▲ scale *¿A qué escala está este mapa?* What's the scale of this map?—*Estaba haciendo escalas en el piano.* He was playing scales on the piano.
○ **hacer escala** to make a stop *El barco hará escala en Cádiz.* The ship'll make a stop at Cadiz.

escalera stair, stairway *Subió las escaleras corriendo.* He ran up the stairs. ▲ ladder *Apoye la escalera contra la pared.* Put the ladder against the wall.

escalón [m] step *¿Cuántos escalones tiene esta escalera?* How many steps has this staircase?

escampar to clear up, stop raining *Al escampar podremos seguir.* We'll be able to go on when it clears up.

escandalizar to shock, scandalize *La noticia escandalizó al público.* The news shocked the public.

escándalo scandal.

escapada escapade.
○ **en una escapada** in a jiffy *Aun no lo he hecho pero lo haré en una escapada.* I haven't done it yet, but I'll do it in a jiffy.

escapar to escape *Escapamos de un gran peligro.* We escaped from a great danger.
○ **escaparse** to escape, run away *Se nos escapó el perro.* The dog ran away from us.—*Se han escapado unos presos de la cárcel.* Some prisoners have escaped from the jail. ▲ to slip out *Siento haberlo dicho, se me escapó.* I'm sorry I said it; it slipped out.

escapatoria escapade, prank *Las escapatorias de ese niño preocupan a sus padres.* That child's pranks worry his parents.

escape [m] escape.
○ **a escape** hastily, in a hurry.

escarbar to scratch, dig, pick.

escasear to be scarce *La gasolina escasea por aquí.* Gasoline is scarce around here.

escasez [f] shortage, scarcity.

escaso scarce, short *La carne está escasa.* Meat's scarce.

escena scene *No me hagas escenas.* Don't make scenes. ▲ stage *Al levantarse el telón, la escena estaba oscura.* When the curtain went up, the stage was dark.

escenario stage (of a theater).

esclavo, esclava slave.

escoba broom.

escoger to choose, take, select *Escogimos el camino más corto.* We took the shortest road.

escolar scholastic. ▲ [n] student.

esconder to hide *No sé en dónde escondieron la llave.* I don't know where they hid the key.

escopeta shotgun.

escribiente [m, f] clerk.

escribir [irr] to write.
○ **escribir a máquina** to type, typewrite.

escrito (see **escribir**) written.

escritor, escritora writer, author.

escritorio desk.

escuadra fleet (naval); carpenter's square.

escuchar to listen *Escuche Ud. un momento.* Listen a minute.

escuela school.

escultura sculpture.

escupir to spit *Se prohibe escupir.* Spitting prohibited.

escurrir to wring *Escurra bien esa ropa antes de tenderla.* Wring those clothes well before you hang them up. ▲ to drain *Escurre las espinacas.* Drain the spinach.
○ **escurrir el bulto** to sneak away, to make a get-away *Escurrió el bulto cuando menos lo pensábamos.* He sneaked away when we least expected it. ○ **escurrirse** to slip *Se escurrió en una monda de plátano.* He slipped on a banana peel.—*El plato se me escurrió de las manos.* The plate slipped out of my hands. ▲ to slip away *Se escurrió de la reunión sin que lo viesen.* He slipped away from the meeting without anyone seeing him.

ese, esa; *pl* **esos, esas** [adj] that, those *¿Quién es ese chico?* Who's that boy?

ése, ésa; *pl* **ésos, ésas** [pron] that, that one, those *Esos no son los míos.* Those aren't mine.

esencia essence.

esfera sphere.

esfuerzo effort *Haré un esfuerzo para terminar el trabajo hoy.* I'll make an effort to complete the work today.

eso [*neu pron*] that *Eso es.* That's right. ○ **eso mismo** the same *Eso mismo creía yo.* That's exactly what I used to think.

espacio space *El avión se perdio en el espacio.* The plane disappeared in the sky. ▲ space, line *Escriba Ud. el informe a un espacio.* Single-space the report. ▲ blank, space *Deje Ud. un espacio.* Leave a blank.

espada sword; spade (cards).

espalda back (of the body) *Le duele la espalda.* His back hurts. ○ **a espaldas** behind one's back *Lo hicieron a espaldas de sus padres.* They did it behind their parents' back.

espantapájaros [*m sg*] scarecrow.

espantar to scare, frighten *Se espanta por muy poca cosa.* She gets scared over nothing at all.

espanto fear, fright.

espantoso terrible, frightful.

espárrago asparagus.

especial [*adj*] special.

espectáculo spectacle, show *La corrida de toros es un espectáculo muy interesante.* Bull fighting's a very interesting spectacle. ▲ spectacle, scene *No des un espectáculo llorando en la calle.* Don't make a spectacle of yourself crying in the street.

espectador, espectadora spectator. ○ **espectadores** [*m pl*] audience.

espejo mirror.

espera wait *Después de una espera larga pudimos entrar.* We got in after a long wait. ○ **estar en** (*or* **estar a la**) **espera de** to be waiting for *Estuvimos en espera del barco muchas horas.* We were waiting for the boat for many hours. ○ **sala de espera** waiting room.

esperanza hope. ○ **tener (la) esperanza (de)** to hope *Tengo esperanza de que venga.* I hope he'll come.

esperar to expect *Espero una llamada telefónica esta mañana.* I expect a phone call this morning. ▲ to hope *Esperaban que no muriese.* They hoped he wouldn't die. ▲ to wait *Espero a mi amiga.* I'm waiting for my friend.

espeso thick *No me gusta la sopa espesa.* I don't like thick soup. ▲ heavy *Aceite espeso.* Heavy oil.

espesor [*m*] thickness.

espesura thickness, density; thicket.

espía [*m, f*] spy.

espiar to spy (on).

espina thorn *Tengo una espina en el dedo.* I have a thorn in my finger. ▲ bone *Este pescado tiene muchas espinas.* This fish has a lot of bones.

espinacas [*f pl*] spinach.

espinazo spine.

espíritu [*m*] spirit, soul.

espléndido splendid, wonderful, swell *Después del baile sirvieron una cena espléndida.* They served a wonderful dinner after the dance. ▲ generous *Son espléndidos con sus amigos.* They're generous with their friends.

esponja sponge.

esposa wife. ○ **esposas** [*f pl*] handcuffs.

esposo husband.

espuela spur.

espuma foam; lather.

esqueleto skeleton. ▲ blank (to be filled out) [*Am*].

esquina corner (outward angle) *Viven en la casa de la esquina.* They live in the house on the corner.

esquinazo ○ **dar esquinazo** to evade, avoid *Le ví venir pero le dí esquinazo.* I saw him coming but I avoided him.

establecer [-*zc*-] to establish *Establecieron un nuevo régimen.* They established a new regime. ○ **establecerse** to settle *Se establecerán en Méjico.* They'll settle in Mexico. ▲ to set up a business *Se establecieron en la Quinta Avenida.* They set up a business on Fifth Avenue.

establecimiento establishment.

estaca stake (post).

estacada ○ **dejarle a uno en la estacada** to leave one holding the bag.

estación [*f*] station *Fueron a recibirnos a la estación.* They went to the station to meet us. ▲ season *En los trópicos hay sólo dos estaciones.* There are only two seasons in the tropics. ▲ stop [*Am*] *Este tren es directo, no hará muchas estaciones.* This is a through train; it won't make many stops.

estacionar to park (car, etc). ○ **estacionarse** to park *¿Dónde podemos estacionarnos?* Where can we park? ▲ to station oneself.

estadio stadium.

estado condition *El camino está en mal estado.* The road's in bad condition. ▲ status *"¿Estado?" "Soltero." "Mar-*

ital status?" "Single." ▲ state *Hizo un viaje por todos los estados del país.* He took a trip through all the states in the country. ▲ state, government *Está al servicio del estado.* He works for the government.

estallar to break out, start *Temen que estalle una insurrección.* They're afraid a revolt'll break out. ▲ to explode *Al estallar la bomba causó muchos daños.* The bomb caused a lot of damage when it exploded.

estampilla postage stamp [*Am*].

estanco cigar store.

estanque [*m*] pond.

estanquillo cigar store [*Mex*].

estante [*m*] shelf.

estar [*irr*] to be (in a place) *La casa está en la colina.* The house is on the hill. ▲ to be (in a condition at a given moment) *La sopa está muy caliente.* The soup's very hot. ▲ to look, seem *Está Ud. muy linda hoy.* You look very pretty today. ○ **estamos a** it's (a date or day of the week) "*¿A cuántos estamos?*" "*Estamos a 5 de junio.*" "What's the date?" "It's the fifth of June." ○ **estar con** to have (an illness) *Estoy con dolor de cabeza.* I have a headache. ○ **estar con prisa** to be in a hurry *No puedo esperar porque estoy con prisa.* I can't wait because I'm in a hurry. ○ **estar de** to act as, act in the capacity of *¿Quién está de telefonista hoy?* Who's at the switchboard today? ○ **estar de acuerdo** to agree *Estuvieron de acuerdo en todo.* They agreed on everything. ○ **estar de viaje** to be traveling *Estuvimos de viaje durante el verano.* We were traveling during the summer. ○ **estar para** to be about to *Cuando llegamos estaban para salir.* When we arrived they were about to leave. ○ **estar por** to be in favor of *Yo estaba por ir y ellos por quedarse.* I was in favor of going and they were in favor of staying.

‖ *¡Está bien!* or *Está bueno.* All right.

estatua statue.

estatura stature, height.

este [*m*] east.

este, esta; estos, estas [*adj*] this, these *Este chico nos da mucha guerra.* This boy gives us a lot of trouble.

éste, ésta; éstos, éstas [*pron*] this one, those *Este fué el que llegó primero.* He was the first to arrive.

estilo style *¿Qué estilo de muebles le gus-*

taría? What style of furniture would you like?

estimar to value, respect, hold dear *Estima mucho a sus amigos.* He values his friends highly.

estirar to stretch, pull *Al estirar la tela se rompió.* The material tore when it was stretched. ○ **estirarse** to stretch (oneself). ▲ to stretch *Esta tela se estira mucho al lavarla.* This cloth stretches a great deal when it's washed.

esto [*neu pron*] this *Esto no lo entiendo.* I don't understand this. ○ **en esto** at this point *En esto llegó él.* At this point he arrived.

estofado stew.

estómago stomach.

estorbar to block, obstruct *Este mueble estorba el paso.* This furniture's in the way. ▲ to bother, be in one's way *No se vaya Ud., no nos estorba.* Don't go away, you're not bothering us. ▲ to impede, hinder *Las huelgas estorban la producción de guerra.* Strikes hinder war production.

estornudar to sneeze.

estrechar to take in, make narrower *Me tiene Ud. que estrechar la chaqueta.* You have to take in my jacket. ○ **estrechar la mano (a)** to shake hands (with).

estrecho narrow *Pasamos por un camino estrecho.* We went along a narrow road. ▲ tight *El traje le está muy estrecho.* The dress is very tight on her. ▲ close *Su amistad es muy estrecha.* Their friendship's very close. ○ [*m*] strait(s) *¿Ha pasado Ud. por el estrecho de Magallanes?* Have you ever gone through the Straits of Magellan?

estrella star; leading actor *or* actress.

estrellado (see estrellar) ○ **cielo estrellado** starry sky. ○ **huevos estrellados** eggs sunny side up.

estrellar to smash (up) *Cualquier día va a estrellar el automóvil.* He's going to smash up his car any day. ○ **estrellarse** to crash *El avión se estrelló contra la casa.* The plane crashed against the house.

estremecer [*-zc-*] to shake *La detonación estremeció el suelo.* The explosion shook the ground. ○ **estremecerse** to start, shudder, tremble *Se estremeció al oír el ruido.* He started when he heard the noise.

estremecimiento shudder, shuddering.

estrenar to open (a play) *Mañana estrenarán una nueva obra en el Teatro Na-*

cional. Tomorrow they'll open a new play at the National Theater. ▲ to wear for the first time *¿Está Ud. estrenando ese traje?* Are you wearing that dress for the first time?

○ **estrenarse** to open (of a play) *Esa obra se estrenó en Broadway la semana pasada.* That play opened on Broadway last week.

estropear to ruin, damage *Los niños han estropeado el radio.* The boys have ruined the radio. ▲ to spoil *Su dimisión estropeó nuestros planes.* His resignation spoiled our plans.

○ **estropearse** to be out of order *La plancha eléctrica se ha estropeado.* The electric iron's out of order.

estruendo deafening noise.

estudiante [*m, f*] student.

estudiar to study.

estufa stove, heater.

estupendo wonderful *Anoche ví una película estupenda.* I saw a wonderful movie last night.

estupidez [*f*] stupidity.

estúpido stupid. ▲ [*n*] stupid person.

etcétera, etc. and so forth, etc.

éter [*m*] ether.

eterno eternal, endless.

etiqueta label *Lea Ud. lo que dice la etiqueta.* Read what's on the label.

○ **de etiqueta** formal *Habrá un baile de etiqueta en el Casino.* There'll be a formal dance at the Casino.

evangelio gospel.

evitar to avoid *Evitaba encontrarse con él.* He avoided meeting him. ▲ to prevent *Lograron evitar la explosión.* They succeeded in preventing the explosion.

exactitud [*f*] accuracy *Este trabajo está hecho con mucha exactitud.* This work's very accurately done. ▲ punctuality *La exactitud es su cualidad característica.* Punctuality is his distinguishing characteristic.

exacto exact, correct *La cuenta está exacta, gracias.* The bill's correct, thank you. ▲ accurate *Hizo un relato exacto.* He gave an accurate report.

exagerar to exaggerate *No le puedo creer porque siempre exagera.* I can't believe him because he always exaggerates.

examen [*m*] examination, test.

examinar to inspect *No han examinado todavía el equipaje.* They haven't inspected the baggage yet. ▲ to examine *El médico examinó al enfermo.* The doctor examined the patient. ▲ to observe *Examinaba con mucha atención*

todos sus movimientos. He observed all his movements closely.

○ **examinarse** to be examined, take (an) examination(s) *Tendrán que examinarse de español e inglés.* They'll have to take examinations in Spanish and English.

excelente excellent. ▲ fine *¡Excelente! Iremos juntos.* Fine! We'll go together.

excepción [*f*] exception.

excursión [*f*] excursion, picnic.

excusa excuse.

excusado washroom, toilet.

excusar to excuse, pardon *Debe Ud. excusar sus faltas.* You should excuse his faults. ▲ to decline *Excusó la invitación porque no le gustaba la gente.* He declined the invitation because he didn't like the people.

○ **excusarse** to apologize *Si no va tendrá Ud. que excusarse.* If you don't go you'll have to apologize.

exhibición [*f*] exhibition, showing [*Am*].

exhibir to exhibit, show.

exigir to require *Exigen que se pague por adelantado.* Payment is required in advance. ▲ to demand *Le exigieron que declarase.* They demanded that he testify.

existencia existence, life *Me amarga la existencia.* He makes my life miserable. ▲ stock *Tenían grandes existencias de mercadería.* They had a large stock of merchandise.

éxito success *El éxito de la empresa sorprendió a todos.* The success of the enterprise astonished everybody.

exótico foreign, exotic.

experiencia experience *No tengo experiencia en este trabajo.* I haven't any experience in this work.

experto expert, skilled.

expirar to expire *El plazo del contrato expira hoy.* The contract expires today.

explicar to explain *¡Déjeme Ud. que se lo explique!* Let me explain it to you!

○ **explicarse** to understand *No puedo explicarme lo ocurrido.* I can't understand what happened.

explorador [*m*] explorer; Boy Scout.

explosión [*f*] explosion, blast.

explotar to work, exploit *Están explotando una mina de plata.* They're working a silver mine. ▲ to exploit, use *Explotaba siempre a sus amigos.* He was always using his friends.

exponer [*irr*] to expose *No hay que exponer esto al sol.* This mustn't be exposed to the sun. ▲ to explain *Exponga Ud. su idea con más claridad.*

Explain your idea more clearly.

○ **exponerse** to expose oneself *Se expone Ud. a que le critiquen mucho.* You're exposing yourself to a lot of criticism.

exportación [*f*] export *Trabaja en una oficina de exportación.* He works in an export house.

exportar to export.

exposición [*f*] exhibition; risk.

expresar to express.

○ **expresarse** to express oneself, speak *Se expresa con mucha corrección.* He expresses himself very correctly.

expresión [*f*] expression.

expresivo affectionate *Escribió una carta muy expresiva.* He wrote a very affectionate letter. ▲ expressive *Tiene facciones muy expresivas.* She has very expressive features.

expreso ○ **tren expreso** express train.

expuesto (see **exponer**) exhibited, on display *Esos libros estaban expuestos en el escaparate.* Those books were on display in the window. ▲ dangerous *En aquel tiempo era muy expuesto viajar.* Traveling was very dangerous at that time.

expulsar to expel.

exquisito delicious *El pastel está exquisito.* The pie's delicious. ▲ exquisite *Tiene un gusto exquisito para vestir.* She has exquisite taste in clothes.

extender [*rad-ch I*] to spread out, extend *Extendieron el mapa sobre la mesa.* They spread the map out on the table. ▲ to issue *La biblioteca le extenderá una tarjeta de lector.* The library will issue you a reader's card. ▲ to enlarge *Extenderán el campo de aterrizaje.* They'll enlarge the landing field. ▲ to expand *Han extendido sus negocios por*

todo el país. They've expanded their business throughout the country.

○ **extenderse** to spread, become common *or* widespread *Se ha extendido mucho esa costumbre.* That custom's become very widespread.

exterior [*adj; m*] outside *El exterior de la casa estaba muy deteriorado.* The outside of the house was very run down.

externo external *Para uso externo solamente.* For external use only.

extra [*adv*] extra *El desayuno se paga extra.* Extra charge for breakfast. ▲ [*f*] extra [*Am*] *¿Leyó Ud. la extra de esta mañana?* Did you read this morning's extra?

extranjero foreign *Hablaban una lengua extranjera.* They spoke a foreign language. ▲ [*n*] foreigner *El hotel está lleno de extranjeros.* The hotel's full of foreigners.

○ **en el extranjero** abroad *Ha vivido mucho tiempo en el extranjero.* He's lived abroad for a long time.

extrañar to miss *Extraño mucho a mi madre.* I miss my mother very much.

○ **extrañarle a uno** to seem strange (to) *Me extraña que no haya llegado aún.* It seems strange to me that he hasn't arrived yet.

extraño strange *Tiene un nombre extraño.* He has a strange name. ▲ [*n*] stranger *No lo conozco, es un extraño.* I don't know him; he's a stranger.

extraordinario extraordinary.

extravagante queer, unusual.

extraviarse to be off course, get lost *or* misplaced *Los aviadores se extraviaron.* The aviators were off their course.

extremo end *Siéntese Ud. al extremo de la mesa.* Sit at the end of the table.

F

fábrica factory.

fabricación [*f*] manufacture.

fabricante [*m*] manufacturer.

fabricar to manufacture.

fábula fable. ▲ fabrication, lies *Todo lo que nos contó es una fábula.* Everything he told us was pure fabrication.

fabuloso fabulous.

facción [*f*] faction.

○ **facciones** features (of the face) *Tiene las facciones muy correctas.* He has very regular features.

facha appearance, looks *No me gustaba*

la facha que tenía aquel hombre. I didn't like that man's looks. ▲ sight, mess *Vestido de aquella manera, era una facha.* He was a sight, dressed that way.

fachada front (of a building).

fácil easy. ▲ loose *Aquella mujer era muy fácil.* She was a loose woman. ▲ probable, likely *Es muy fácil que vaya el domingo.* It's very likely he'll go Sunday.

○ **fácil de** easy to *Eso es muy fácil de hacer.* That's very easy to do.

facilidad [f] facility, ease. ▲ aptitude *Mostró gran facilidad para aprender música.* He showed great aptitude for music.

○ **con facilidad** with ease, fluently *Hablaba inglés con mucha facilidad.* He speaks English very fluently. ○ **dar facilidades** to facilitate; to offer assistance *El gobierno nos dió toda clase de facilidades para la investigación.* The government offered us every assistance in the investigation.

facilitar to supply *Facilitó los fondos necesarios para aquel negocio.* He supplied the necessary funds for that deal. ▲ to facilitate, make easier *Estos libros facilitarán su trabajo.* These books will make your work easier.

factor [m] factor, element; baggageman.

factoría trading post; [Mex] factory.

factura bill, invoice *Mándeme la factura a casa.* Send the bill to my house.

facturar to check (baggage).

facultad [f] faculty *No tenía completas sus facultades.* He didn't have all his faculties. ▲ authority *Se le dió facultad para resolver la cuestión.* He was given authority to settle the dispute. ▲ branch of a university, school *Se licenció en la Facultad de Derecho.* He graduated from Law School.

faena work, task *Se dedicaban a las faenas del campo.* They were engaged in farm work. ▲ trick *Me hizo una mala faena.* He played a dirty trick on me.

faja sash (worn around waist); girdle (underwear).

falda skirt *Lleva la falda muy corta.* She's wearing a very short skirt. ▲ slope, side *El pueblo está en la falda de la colina.* The village is on the side of the hill. ▲ lap *Tenía el niño en la falda.* She had the child on her lap.

fallar to pass sentence *El juez está dispuesto a fallar.* The judge is ready to pass sentence. ▲ to fail *Me ha fallado uno de mis mejores amigos.* One of my best friends has failed me. ▲ to miss, fail *El motor falla siempre al subir las cuestas.* The motor always misses going uphill.

fallecer [-zc-] to die, pass away.

fallo verdict, decision.

falsear to falsify *Ha falseado los hechos.* He's falsified the facts. ▲ to open with a skeleton key *or* pass key [Am] *Los ladrones falsearon la puerta.* The thieves opened the door with a pass key.

falsedad [f] falsehood, lie *Estoy seguro*

de que ha dicho una falsedad. I'm sure he's told a lie.

falsificar to forge, counterfeit.

falso false, untrue. ▲ forged *La firma era falsa.* The signature was forged. ▲ counterfeit *Me dieron un peso falso.* They gave me a counterfeit peso. ▲ imitation *Usaba joyas falsas.* She was wearing imitation jewelry. ▲ dishonest *Fué muy falso conmigo.* He was dishonest with me.

○ **dar un paso en falso** to make a misstep. ○ **en falso** falsely *Juró en falso.* He swore falsely.

falta error, mistake *Hay muchas faltas en esta traducción.* There are a lot of mistakes in this translation. ▲ fault *Todos tenemos nuestras faltas.* We all have our faults. ▲ misdemeanor, petty crime.

○ **a falta de** for lack of *Tomaremos esto a falta de cosa mejor.* We'll take this for lack of something better. ○ **hacer falta** to be necessary, be needed *Hace falta dinero.* Money is needed. ○ **hacerle falta a uno** to need *Me hace falta un lápiz.* I need a pencil. ▲ to miss *Ud. me hace mucha falta.* I miss you very much. ○ **sin falta** without fail *Venga Ud. sin falta a las once.* Come at eleven without fail.

faltar to lack *Le faltan condiciones para tener éxito en el teatro.* He lacks the qualifications for success in the theater. ▲ to be missing *¿Le falta a Ud. algo en su cartera?* Is anything missing from your pocketbook? ▲ to be needed *Faltan cuatro para completar los cincuenta.* Four more are needed to make fifty. ▲ to be lacking *Faltan diez minutos para las dos.* It's ten minutes to two. ▲ to offend *No le he querido faltar.* I didn't want to offend him.

○ **faltar a** to be absent from *Faltó a la clase el lunes.* He was absent from class Monday. ▲ to break, ignore *No puede Ud. faltar a la cita.* You can't break the appointment. ○ **¡No faltaba más!** Of course; by all means *"¿Va Ud. a quedarse?" "¡No faltaba más!"* "Are you going to stay?" "Of course!"

fama fame. ▲ reputation *Ese hombre tiene mala fama.* That man has a bad reputation.

○ **tener fama de** to have the reputation of *Tiene fama de sabio.* He has the reputation of being very wise.

familia family.

familiar familiar *Su apellido me es familiar.* His name's familiar to me. ▲ [*m*] relative *Invitaron solamente a los familiares.* They invited only their relatives.

famoso famous.

fanático [*adj*] fanatic, fanatical. ▲ [*n*] fanatic.

fango mud.

fantasía imagination *Toda esa historia es un producto de su fantasía.* That whole story's a product of his imagination. ▲ whim *No debe Ud. consentirle todas sus fantasías.* You shouldn't give in to all her whims. ▲ fantasy, fairy tale *No le crea, todo eso es una fantasía.* Don't believe that; it's all a fairy tale.

fantasma [*m*] ghost.

fantástico fantastic, unbelievable *Explicó de una manera fantástica su retraso.* He told a fantastic story to explain his delay. ▲ extravagant *Daba unas propinas fantásticas.* He gave extravagant tips.

fardo big bundle, bale.

farmacéutico pharmacist.

farmacia pharmacy.

faro beacon, lighthouse; headlight.

farol [*m*] lantern *Encienda Ud. el farol para que veamos.* Light the lantern so we can see. ▲ street lamp *A la luz del farol de la calle leyó la carta.* He read the letter by the light of the street lamp. ▲ bluff *Se echó un farol diciendo que le conocía.* He was bluffing when he said he knew him.

farola street lamp.

farra ○ ir de farra to paint the town red, to go on a spree.

fascinar to fascinate.

fastidiar to annoy, bother *¡Hombre, no fastidies con esas bromas!* Don't annoy me with those jokes.

fastidioso annoying, tiresome.

fatal fatal.

fatalidad [*f*] fate.

fatiga fatigue, tiredness *El trabajo produce fatiga.* Work produces fatigue. ▲ hardship *No hay vida sin fatigas.* There's no life without hardships.

○ **pasar fatigas** to have a hard time *Pasaba fatigas para ganarse la vida.* He had a hard time making a living.

fatigar to tire *Fatigó al caballo de tanto galopar.* He tired the horse with so much galloping.

○ **fatigarse** to get tired *¡Se fatiga Ud. demasiado con este trabajo!* You're getting too tired doing this work.

fatuo pompous, vain.

favor [*m*] favor *Le hicieron muchos favores.* They did him many favors.

○ **a favor de** with, aided by *Remaba a favor de la corriente.* He rowed with the current. ▲ on behalf of, for, in favor of *Hizo testamento a favor de sus hijos.* He made his will in favor of his children. ○ **en favor** in behalf (of someone) *Fué el único que habló en su favor.* He was the only one who spoke in his behalf. ○ **favor de** please [*Am*] *Favor de pasarme el azúcar.* Please pass me the sugar. ○ **hacer el favor de** please *¿Quiere Ud. hacer el favor de pasarme su plato?* Will you please pass me your plate? ○ **por favor** please *Por favor, ¿Quiere decirme qué hora es?* Would you tell me the time, please?

favorable favorable.

favorecer [-*zc*-] to grant favors to, help *Ese hombre ha favorecido mucha a mi familia.* That man's helped my family a lot. ▲ to flatter *Ud. me favorece.* You flatter me. ▲ to become *No creo que ese color le favorezca a Ud.* I don't think that color becomes you.

favorito [*adj; n*] favorite.

fe [*f*] faith.

○ **de buena fe, de mala fe** in good faith, in bad faith *Lo hizo de buena fe.* He did it in good faith. ○ **tener fe en** to believe in, have faith in *Tengo mucha fe en él.* I have great faith in him.

fealdad [*f*] ugliness.

febrero February.

febril feverish.

fecha date *¿Qué fecha tiene la carta?* What's the date on the letter?

fechar to date (a letter, etc).

fecundo prolific, fruitful.

federación [*f*] federation.

federal federal.

felicidad [*f*] happiness *Es difícil conseguir la felicidad.* It's hard to achieve happiness. ▲ safety *Salió de aquella prueba con toda felicidad.* He came through that experience safely.

felicitación [*f*] congratulations *Cuando le escriba envíele mi felicitación por su éxito.* When you write to him, send my congratulations on his success.

felicitar to congratulate.

feliz happy *No creo que será muy feliz viviendo con su suegra.* I don't think she'll be happy living with her mother-in-law.—*Deseamos a Ud. Feliz Año*

Nuevo. We wish you a Happy New Year.

femenino feminine.

fenómeno phenomenon; freak. ▲ prodigy *Era un fenómeno en las matemáticas.* He was a prodigy in mathematics.

feo homely, ugly *Era un hombre muy feo.* He was a very homely man. ▲ serious *El asunto tomó un cariz muy feo.* The matter took a serious turn. ○ **hacer un feo** to be impolite to, to slight *Vaya Ud. a visitarlo, no le haga Ud. un feo.* Go and visit him; don't slight him.

feria country market, fair *Compró dos caballos en la feria.* He bought two horses at the fair. ▲ small change [*Mex*] *¿Tiene Ud. feria?* Do you have any small change?

feriado ○**día feriado** holiday [*Am*].

fermentar to ferment, sour.

feroz ferocious.

ferretería hardware store.

ferrocarril [*m*] railroad, railway.

fértil fertile.

festivo humorous. ○ **día festivo** holiday.

fiado (see **fiar**) ○ **al fiado** on credit.

fiambre cold, served cold (of food). ○ **fiambres** [*m pl*] cold meat, cold cuts.

fiambrera lunch pail.

fianza bail, bond. ○ **bajo fianza** on bail *Le han puesto en libertad bajo fianza.* They've freed him on bail.

fiar to give credit *El Banco le fió hasta cien mil pesetas.* The bank gave him a hundred thousand pesetas' credit. ▲ to sell on trust, sell on credit *Hoy no se fía mañana sí.* Cash today, credit tomorrow. ○ **fiarse de** to trust, rely on *No me fío de lo que dice.* I don't trust what he says. ○ **ser de fiar** to be trustworthy *Ese hombre no es de fiar.* That man's not to be trusted.

fibra fiber. ▲ stamina, energy *Es un hombre de mucha fibra.* He's a man of great energy.

ficha chip (card games); domino; filing card.

fidelidad [*f*] loyalty, faithfulness *La fidelidad es una virtud.* Faithfulness is a virtue. ▲ exactness *El documento se copió con toda fidelidad.* The document was copied exactly.

fiebre [*f*] fever.

fiel faithful *Le era fiel como un perro.* He was as faithful to him as a dog. ▲ correct, accurate *El relato que hizo*

era fiel. The account he gave was correct. ○ **estar en el fiel** to balance, be balanced *La balanza estaba en el fiel.* The scales were balanced.

fieltro felt (material).

fiera wild animal *En el circo tienen una magnífica colección de fieras.* The circus has a wonderful collection of wild animals. ○ **como una fiera** furious, like a wild beast *Se puso como una fiera.* He became furious. ○ **trabajar como una fiera** to work like a horse.

fiesta holiday *El lunes es día de fiesta.* Monday's a holiday. ▲ party *Hubo una gran fiesta en su casa.* There was a big party at his house. ○ **hacerle fiestas a uno** to play with (an infant) *Le hizo fiestas al niño.* He played with the child.

figura figure, build *Ese hombre tiene muy buena figura.* That man has a very good build.

figurar to figure, be *Entre los concurrentes figuraba el Duque de X.* The Duke of X was among those present. ▲ to be in the limelight, be conspicuous *Le gustaba mucho figurar.* He liked to be in the limelight. ○ **figurarse** to imagine, think *Se figura que puede hacer todo lo que quiere.* She imagines she can get away with anything.

fijar to drive in *Fijaron estacas para asegurar la tienda.* They drove in stakes to hold the tent down. ▲ to post *Se prohibe fijar carteles.* Post no bills. ▲ to establish *Han fijado su residencia en Paris.* They've established their residence in Paris. ▲ to fix, set *Fijaron la fecha de la boda.* They set the date for the wedding. ○ **fijar los ojos en** to stare at. ○ **fijarse** to imagine *¡Fíjate (en) lo que me pasó!* Imagine what happened to me! ○ **fijarse en** to pay attention to *Fíjese Ud. en lo que le digo.* Pay close attention to what I'm telling you.

fijo permanent *Su puesto no es fijo.* His job isn't permanent. ▲ fixed, set *No hacemos rebajas, nuestros precios son fijos.* We don't make reductions; our prices are fixed. ▲ fast *No se puede quitar. Está fijo.* It can't be removed. It's fast. ○ **a punto fijo** exactly *No lo sé a punto fijo.* I don't know exactly. ○ **de fijo** surely *De fijo llueve hoy.* It'll surely rain today. ○ **hora fija** exact time, time agreed upon.

fila row *Deme una butaca de primera fila.* Give me a seat in the first row, orchestra. ▲ line, rank *Había dos filas de soldados.* There were two lines of soldiers.

   ○ **en fila** in (a) line *Los niños estaban en fila.* The children were standing in line.

filete [*m*] steak *Comió un filete con papas fritas.* He had steak and fried potatoes.

filial filial.

filo (cutting) edge.

filosofía philosophy.

filtrar to filter.

fin [*m*] end *¿Llegaremos antes del fin de la película?* Will we get there before the end of the movie? ▲ purpose *No sé con qué fin lo dice.* I don't know what his purpose is in saying it.

   ○ **a fin de que** so (that) *A fin de que pudiera volver le mandé dinero.* I sent him money so he'd be able to come back. ○ **a fines de** toward the end of, late in (the week, etc) *A fines de mes volveré a mi casa.* I'll be back home toward the end of the month. ○ **al fin** at last, finally *Al fin se quedaron solos.* They were alone at last. ○ **al fin y al cabo** after all *Al fin y al cabo no era tan mala la comedia.* After all the play wasn't so bad. ○ **en fin** in short *En fin, ella no le quería.* In short, she didn't love him. ▲ well *En fin, ya veremos.* Well, we'll see. ○ **por fin** at last *Por fin pude encontrarle.* At last I managed to find him. ○ **sin fin (de)** endless, no end (of), numberless *Tenía un sin fin de cosas que hacer.* He had no end of things to do.

final [*adj*] final. ▲ [*m*] end, conclusion.

   ○ **punto final** period (punctuation).

financiar to finance [*Am*].

finca country estate, property, farm.

fineza courtesy, politeness, kindness *Me hizo muchas finezas.* He extended many courtesies to me.

fingir to pretend *¡No finja Ud. lo que no siente!* Don't pretend what you don't feel.

   ○ **fingirse** to feign, pretend *Se fingió enfermo para no trabajar.* He feigned illness to get out of working.

fino thin, fine, sharp *Me gusta una pluma fina.* I like a pen with a fine point. ▲ fine, delicate (of features, etc) *Esa muchacha tiene las facciones muy finas.* That girl has very delicate features. ▲ refined, fine *La pulsera es de oro fino.* The bracelet's of fine gold.

▲ courteous *Era un hombre muy fino.* He was a very courteous man. ▲ sheer, thin *Llevaba unas medias muy finas.* She wore very sheer hose.

finura courtesy.

firma signature *Escriba Ud. la firma al pie.* Sign it at the bottom.

   ○ **buena firma** reliable firm *or* house *Trabajaba para una buena firma.* He worked for a reliable firm.

firmar to sign.

firme firm, steady, sturdy *Tome esta silla que es muy firme.* Take this chair; it's sturdy.

   ○ **en firme** definite, firm *Hicieron una oferta en firme.* They made a definite offer. ○ **estar en lo firme** to be in the right *Creo que estoy en lo firme.* I believe I'm in the right. ○ **firmes** [*mpl*] roadbed *La carretera se hizo con firmes especiales.* The road was built with a special roadbed.

firmeza firmness.

fiscal fiscal. ▲ [*m*] attorney-general; district attorney.

física physics.

físico physical. ▲ [*n*] physicist.

fisonomía physiognomy, countenance, looks.

flaco thin, lean *Cada día se le veía más flaco.* He appeared thinner every day. ▲ weak *Encontré su punto flaco.* I discovered his weak spot.

   ○ **hacerle a uno un flaco servicio** to play a dirty trick on one *Le hizo un flaco servicio.* He played a dirty trick on him.

flamenco flamingo; flamenco (type of Spanish songs and dances).

flan [*m*] custard.

flaqueza failing, weakness.

flauta flute.

flecha arrow.

flete [*m*] freight; freight rate.

flexibilidad [*f*] flexibility.

flexible flexible. ▲ [*m*] electric cord [*Sp*]; soft hat.

flirtear to flirt.

flojo lazy, slack *Es muy flojo para el trabajo.* He's very slack about his work. ▲ loose *Ese nudo está flojo.* That knot's loose.

flor [*f*] flower. ▲ compliment *Al verla pasar le echó una flor.* When he saw her pass, he paid her a compliment.

florecer [-*zc*-] to bloom *No creo que florezcan tan pronto los rosales.* I don't think the roses will bloom so soon.

florero flower vase.

florido florid, flowery. ▲ in bloom *Los*

almendros están floridos. The almond trees are in bloom.

flota fleet (of ships).

flotación [*f*] buoyancy.

○ **línea de flotación** waterline.

flotar to float.

foco focus; headlight.

fogón [*m*] fire box (of locomotive, etc); stove, cooking range.

fogonero stoker, fireman.

folleto pamphlet.

fomentar to foment, promote *El gobierno debe fomentar las artes.* The government ought to promote the arts. ▲ to foment, instigate *Los agitadores fomentaban la rebelión.* The agitators instigated the rebellion.

fomento encouragement, promotion *El fomento de las artes.* Promotion of the arts.

fonda inn.

fondo bottom *Lo guardaba en el fondo del cajón.* He kept it in the bottom of the drawer. ▲ background *El retrato tenía un fondo oscuro.* The portrait had a dark background. ▲ back *El fondo de la casa.* The back of the house.

○ **a fondo** thoroughly *Era necesario estudiar el asunto a fondo.* It was necessary to study the matter thoroughly. ○ **andar mal de fondos** to be short of money. ○ **artículo de fondo** editorial *Escribió un buen artículo de fondo.* He wrote a good editorial. ○ **en el fondo** at bottom, at heart *En el fondo era una excelente persona.* He was an excellent person at heart. ○ **fondos** funds *No tengo fondos en el banco.* I have no funds in the bank.

fonógrafo phonograph.

forastero, forastera stranger (from another city or town).

forjado (see **forjar**) ○ **hierro forjado** wrought iron.

forjar to forge, hammer.

○ **forjarse ilusiones** to delude oneself, build castles in the air.

forma shape, form *No me gusta la forma de este sombrero.* I don't like the shape of this hat. ▲ way, manner *No había forma de entenderlo.* There was no way of understanding it.

○ **con buenas** (*or* **malas**) **formas** politely (*or* impolitely) *Lo dijo con muy buenas formas.* He said it very politely. ○ **dar forma a** to put in final form *or* shape *Había que dar forma al artículo.* The article had to be put in final form. ○ **en forma** in order *El*

pasaporte estaba en forma. The passport was in order.

formación [*f*] formation.

○ **en formación** in formation.

formal reliable *Es un hombre muy formal.* He's a very reliable man. ▲ serious, sedate, settled *Desde que se casó se ha vuelto muy formal.* He's become very settled since his marriage.

formalidad [*f*] earnestness, seriousness *Hablemos con formalidad.* Let's talk seriously.

○ **formalidades** red tape *Perdieron mucho tiempo en todas las formalidades.* They lost a lot of time, with all the red tape.

formalizar to arrange, legalize *Formalizaron el contrato.* They legalized the contract.

formar to form, make, be *Formaban un grupo muy alegre.* They made a very merry group.

○ **formar parte de** to be a member *or* part of *Formó parte de esa organización.* He was a member of that organization.

formidable formidable *Se enfrentaban con una competición formidable.* They were up against some very formidable competition.

fórmula formula. ▲ solution *Había que encontrar una fórmula.* A solution had to be found.

○ **por fórmula** as a matter of form *Le saludó por fórmula.* He greeted him as a matter of form.

formular to draw up, formulate *Formuló sus ideas en una memoria.* He formulated his ideas in a report.

forro lining (in clothing).

fortaleza fortitude, strength *Su fortaleza era notable.* His fortitude was remarkable. ▲ fortress.

fortuna fortune *Hizo una fortuna especulando en la bolsa.* He made a fortune playing the stock market. ▲ luck *Tuve la fortuna de encontrarle.* I had the luck to find him.

○ **por fortuna** fortunately *Por fortuna pudieron escapar.* Fortunately, they were able to escape.

forzado See **forzar**. ▲ [*m*] convict.

○ **trabajo forzado** forced labor.

forzar [*rad-ch I*] to force, compel; to rape. ▲ to break down *Forzaron la puerta.* They broke down the door.

forzoso compulsory, unavoidable *La decisión era forzosa.* The decision was unavoidable.

○ **paro forzoso** unemployment.

fosa grave *Lo llevaron a la fosa.* They took him to the grave.

fósforo match *¿Tiene Ud. fósforos?* Have you any matches?

fotografía photography; photograph.

fracasar to fail *La comedia fracasó.* The play failed.

fracaso failure, flop *El negocio fué un fracaso.* The business was a failure.

fracción [*f*] fraction; fragment.

fragancia fragrance.

frágil fragile.

fragmento fragment.

fraile [*m*] monk, friar.

franco free, exempt *Se estableció un puerto franco.* A free port was established. ▲ frank *¡Sea Ud. franco conmigo!* Be frank with me! ○ **franco de porte** prepaid *Envió la mercancía franco de porte.* He sent the merchandise prepaid.

franqueo postage, amount of postage *¿Cuánto es el franqueo de esta carta?* What's the postage on this letter?

franqueza frankness *Me gusta la franqueza de Ud.* I like your frankness. ○ **con franqueza** frankly *¿Habla Ud. con franqueza?* Are you speaking frankly?

frasco bottle, flask.

frase [*f*] phrase.

fraternal brotherly, fraternal.

frazada blanket *Ponga Ud. dos frazadas en la cama.* Put two blankets on the bed.

frecuencia frequency.

frecuente frequent.

fregadero *or* **fregadera** kitchen sink.

fregar [*rad-ch I*] to scour, scrub *Hace falta que frieguen este piso.* The floor has to be scrubbed. ▲ to wash (dishes) *No me gusta fregar los platos.* I don't like to wash dishes. ▲ to annoy [*Am*] *¡Hombre no friegues más!* Stop annoying me!

freír [*rad-ch III*] to fry *Fríe el pescado con aceite.* He's frying the fish in oil.

frenar to (put on the) brake; to restrain.

frenesí [*m*] madness; frenzy.

frenético very angry; frenzied.

freno bit (for horses); brake.

frente [*f*] forehead. ▲ [*m*] front, battlefield *Los soldados marcharon al frente.* The soldiers left for the front. ○ **al frente de** in charge of *No sé quien está al frente del negocio.* I don't know who's in charge of the business. ○ **en frente de** opposite *Vive en la casa que está en frente de la nuestra.* He lives in the house opposite ours.

○ **frente a** in front of *El coche paró frente a la puerta.* The coach stopped in front of the door. ○ **frente a frente** face to face *Los dos enemigos estaban frente a frente.* The two enemies were face to face. ○ **hacer frente** to face *Había que hacer frente a aquel conflicto.* The problem had to be faced.

fresa strawberry.

fresco cool (of weather, wind, etc) *La noche estaba fresca.* The night was cool. ▲ fresh (of food) *El pescado estaba muy fresco.* The fish was very fresh. ▲ fresh, cheeky, nervy *Ese tipo es muy fresco.* That guy has a lot of nerve. ▲ [*m*] cooling drink [*Am*] *¿Le gusta el fresco de piña?* Do you like pineapple drinks? ▲ fresco *Los frescos de la catedral son muy interesantes.* The frescoes of the cathedral are very interesting. ○ **quedarse tan fresco** to show no concern, to remain unmoved *¡Y se quedó tan fresco!* He was completely unconcerned! ○ **tomar el fresco** to get some fresh air *Estaban en el jardín tomando el fresco.* They were in the garden getting some fresh air.

frescura coolness *Notamos frescura al llegar al río.* We felt the coolness when we arrived at the river. ▲ nerve, cheek *La frescura de aquel hombre indignaba.* The nerve of that man was irritating.

frialdad [*f*] coldness (of weather); coolness, unconcern.

frijol [*m*] bean.

frío [*adj*] cold *La sopa está fría.* The soup's cold. ▲ cold, unemotional *Era de temperamento muy frío.* He was a very cold person. ○ **hacer frío** to be cold (of weather) *Aquel invierno hizo mucho frío.* It was very cold that winter. ○ **no darle a uno frío ni calor** to leave one indifferent *No me daba frío ni calor.* It left me indifferent. ○ **tener frío** to feel (or be) cold *Tengo mucho frío.* I'm very cold.

friolento sensitive to cold.

friolera trifle, something unimportant *Eso es una friolera.* That's a trifle.

friolero chilly, sensitive to cold *Es muy friolero.* He's very sensitive to cold. ▲ (ironically) extremely important.

frito (see **freír**) fried. ○ **estar frito** to be annoyed *Estaba frito con esas preguntas.* He was annoyed by those questions. ○ **traerle a**

uno frito to pester *or* annoy *Aquel hombre me traía frito.* That man was pestering me.

fritura fritter.

frívolo frivolous.

frontera frontier, boundary.

frotación [*f*] rub, rubbing.

frotar to rub *Le frotó la espalda con alcohol.* She rubbed his back with alcohol.

fruncir to shir, gather (material).
○ fruncir el ceño *or* entrecejo to frown.

frustrar to thwart, frustrate.

fruta (edible) fruit *De postre siempre tomaba fruta.* He always ate fruit for dessert.

frutal [*m*], árbol frutal fruit tree.

frutero greengrocer; fruit bowl.

fruto fruit (edible or inedible) *El fruto de ese arbusto es venenoso.* The fruit of that shrub's poisonous. ▲ fruit, reward *Aquel esfuerzo no dió fruto.* That effort bore no fruit. ▲ profit *El negocio no dió fruto.* The business didn't produce a profit.
○ frutos produce *Inglaterra importa frutos españoles.* England imports Spanish produce.

fuego fire *Atice Ud. el fuego que se apaga.* Poke the fire; it's going out.
○ hacer fuego to fire (a weapon) *Los soldados hicieron fuego.* The soldiers fired.

fuente [*f*] fountain *El agua de esta fuente está muy fría.* The water of this fountain's very cold. ▲ source *Su información es de buena fuente.* His information comes from a reliable source. ▲ dish, platter *Sirva Ud. el pescado en esa fuente.* Serve the fish on that platter.

fuera out, outside *Los enviaron fuera.* They sent them out. ▲ out *¡Fuera de aquí!* Get out!
○ desde fuera from the outside *Desde fuera no se ve el jardín.* The garden can't be seen from the outside.
○ fuera de out of *Estará tres días fuera de la ciudad.* He'll be out of the city for three days. ○ fuera de sí beside oneself *Estaba fuera de sí de cólera.* He was beside himself with anger. ○ por fuera on the outside *Por fuera la casa es muy bonita.* On the outside the house is very pretty.

fuerte strong *Era un hombre muy fuerte.* He was a very strong man. ▲ bad, severe *Ha cogido un catarro muy fuerte.* He's caught a very bad cold.

▲ severe, intense *Hace un frío muy fuerte.* The cold's intense. ▲ heavy, warm, thick *Lleve calzado fuerte para la excursión.* Wear heavy shoes for the outing. ▲ heavy *La lluvia era muy fuerte.* The rainfall was very heavy. ▲ harsh, unbearable *Lo que le dijo fué demasiado fuerte.* What she told him was too harsh. ▲ [*adv*] loud *Habla demasiado fuerte.* He speaks too loud. ▲ [*m*] fort.

fuerza power *Ese motor no tiene fuerza suficiente.* That motor doesn't have enough power.
○ a fuerza de by dint of *Lo consiguió a fuerza de trabajo.* He got it by dint of hard work. ○ a la fuerza forcibly *Habrá que hacerlo a la fuerza.* It'll have to be done forcibly. ○ fuerza(s) strength. ○ fuerzas forces *Nuestras fuerzas ocuparon la ciudad.* Our forces occupied the city. ○ por (la) fuerza by force, forcibly *Lo metieron al automóvil por la fuerza.* They put him into the car forcibly.

fuete [*m*] quirt, riding whip [*Am*].

fuga flight, escape.

fugarse to run away, flee, escape.

fullero shady, not on the level *Su juego es un poco fullero.* He plays a shady game. ▲ stuck-up, conceited, pompous [*Am*] *Es un tipo muy fullero.* He's a pompous ass.

fumar to smoke *Se prohibe fumar.* No smoking.

función [*f*] function, duty, position *¿Cuáles son sus funciones?* What are your duties? ▲ show, performance *¿A qué hora empieza la función?* What time does the show start?

funcionamiento [*m*] working, functioning.

funcionar to work, function, run (of machines) *El ascensor no funciona.* The elevator isn't running.

funcionario public official, public servant.

funda case, pillowcase; slipcover; sheath.

fundación [*f*] foundation, founding *Hoy se celebra la fundación de la ciudad.* Today they're celebrating the founding of the city.

fundamental [*adj*] fundamental.

fundamento basis *Sus ideas no tienen fundamento.* His ideas have no basis.

fundar to found, establish.
○ fundarse to base oneself *En eso me fundo para decirlo.* That's my basis for saying so.

fundición [*f*] melting; foundry. ▲ casting *La fundición de la estatua se re-*

trasó. The casting of the statue was delayed.

fundir to smelt *Fundieron todo el hierro.* They smelted all the iron.

○ **fundirse** to combine, merge *Se fundieron los dos negocios en uno.* They merged the two businesses into one. ▲ to be ruined [*Am*].

funeral(es) [*m*] funeral service *Los funerales se celebrarán en la catedral.* Funeral services will take place in the cathedral.

furia fury.

furioso furious.

furor [*m*] fury, anger; rage, fashion.

fusil [*m*] army rifle.

fusilar to shoot (execute by shooting).

fuste [*m*] substance, importance *Una dama de alto fuste.* A lady of great importance.

fútbol [*m*] soccer, football (game).

futuro [*adj; m*] future.

○ **en lo futuro** in (the) future, hereafter *Procure Ud. en lo futuro venir puntualmente a la oficina.* In the future, try to get to the office on time.

G

gabán [*m*] coat, overcoat.

gabinete [*m*] cabinet *Se han encargado de formar gabinete.* They've undertaken to form a cabinet. ▲ study, small living room *La casa tiene comedor, alcoba y gabinete.* The house has a dining room, a bedroom, and a study.

gaceta gazette, newspaper; record.

gacho slouched, turned down, stooped *Lleva el sombrero gacho.* He wears his hat turned down.

gachupín, gachupina Spaniard who settles in Mexico.

gafas [*f pl*] eye-glasses, spectacles.

gajo small bunch [*Am*] *Quiero un gajo de uvas.* I want a small bunch of grapes. ▲ section, piece *Pele la naranja y deme un gajo.* Peel the orange and give me a piece.

gala ○ **función de gala** gala performance. ○ **tener a gala** to be proud *Tenía a gala ser inglés.* He was proud to be an Englishman. ○ **traje de gala** dress suit (uniform).

galán juvenile lead (in a movie or theatrical performance) *El galán de esa compañía es muy malo.* The juvenile lead of that company is very bad.

○ **galán, galán** easily, without effort [*Mex*] *Galán, galán subió las escaleras.* He climbed the stairs easily.

galante attentive *Sea Ud. galante con ella.* Be attentive to her.

galantear to court, make love to.

galantería compliment *Me dijo una galantería.* He paid me a compliment. ▲ courtesy.

galápago fresh-water tortoise. ▲ side saddle [*Am*].

galera shed [*Am*] *El carro estaba debajo de la galera.* The cart was under the shed. ▲ wagon; van.

galería gallery (art) *La galería de pintura estaba muy concurrida.* The art gallery was very crowded. ▲ gallery (theater) *Los espectadores de la galería hacían mucho ruido.* The spectators in the gallery were making a lot of noise. ▲ glass-covered sun porch *Vamos a tomar el sol en la galería.* Let's sun ourselves on the sun porch. ▲ underground passageway, gallery *Abrieron otra galería en la mina.* They opened another passageway in the mine.

galgo greyhound.

gallardía fine bearing *Los soldados mostraban gran gallardía.* The soldiers had a very fine bearing.

gallego, gallega Spaniard [*Am*].

galleta cookie *¿Quiere Ud. galletas con el té?* Would you like cookies with your tea? ▲ slap *Le dió una galleta.* She gave him a slap.

gallina [*f*] hen. ▲ [*m*] coward *¡Es Ud. un gallina!* You're a coward!

gallinero hen coop; top gallery.

gallo cock, rooster. ▲ bully [*Sp*]. ▲ match, equal [*Am*] *Ese no es gallo para él.* That fellow's no match for him.

○ **llevar un gallo** to serenade [*Mex*].

galón [*m*] gallon.

galope [*m*] gallop, canter.

galpón [*m*] toolshed [*Arg*].

gana ○ **dar ganas** to feel like *No me dan ganas de trabajar.* I don't feel like working. ○ **darle a uno la gana** [*Fam*] to feel like, want to *Me da la gana de ir.* I'm going because I want to. ○ **de buena gana** willingly *Lo hizo de buena gana.* He did it willingly. ○ **de mala gana** unwillingly. ○ **no darle a uno la gana** to refuse to, not to feel like *No me da la gana de hacerlo.* I refuse to do it. ○ **tener ganas de** to feel like *Tengo ganas de pasear.* I feel like taking a walk.

ganado cattle, livestock *Tenía doscientas cabezas de ganado.* He had two hundred head of cattle.

ganador, ganadora winner.

ganancia profit, gain.

ganar to win *¿No ganó Ud. la apuesta?* Didn't you win the bet? ▲ to gain *No ganó nada con decirme eso.* He gained nothing by telling me that. ▲ to earn *¿Cuánto gana Ud. a la semana?* How much do you earn per week?

○ **ganar de mano** to beat (someone) to it [*Arg*] *Los dos queríamos comprar el caballo pero él me ganó de mano.* We both wanted to buy the horse but he beat me to it. ○ **ganarse la vida** to earn a living *Me gano la vida como puedo.* I earn my living as best I can. ○ **ganar tiempo** to save time.

ganchada ○ **hacer una ganchada** to do a favor [*Arg*].

gancho hook *Colgó la chaqueta en un gancho.* He hung his jacket on a hook. ○ **gancho de cabeza** hairpin [*Am*]. ○ **tener gancho** to be attractive, charming *Esa muchacha tiene mucho gancho.* That girl is very attractive.

ganga bargain *Estos calcetines son una ganga.* These socks are a bargain.

ganso goose, gander.

garaje [*m*] garage.

garantía security *Antes de prestarle el dinero pidió garantía.* Before lending him the money he asked for security.

garantizar to guarantee *El reloj estaba garantizado.* The watch was guaranteed. ▲ to vouch for *Quiero que Ud. le garantice.* I want you to vouch for him.

garbanzo chickpea.

garbo grace *Baila con garbo.* He dances gracefully.

garfio hook, gaff.

garganta throat.

gárgaras [*f pl*] gargle (act of gargling). ○ **hacer gárgaras** to gargle.

garra claw. ○ **caer en las garras de** to fall into the clutches of.

garrafa decanter; straw-covered bottle.

garrote [*m*] club (weapon); gallows.

garúa drizzle [*Arg*].

gas [*m*] gas (vapor) *Encienda Ud. el gas.* Turn on the gas. ○ **llevar gas** to go at high speed, go fast *Llevaba mucho gas aquel automó-*

vil. That automobile was going very fast.

gasa gauze.

gasolina gasoline.

gastar to spend *Gastó casi todo su sueldo.* He spent almost all his salary. ▲ to waste *Me está Ud. haciendo gastar el tiempo.* You're making me waste time. ▲ to wear, use *Nunca gasta sombrero.* He never wears a hat.

○ **gastar bromas pesadas** to play practical jokes *Siempre está gastando bromas pesadas.* He is always playing practical jokes. ○ **gastarse** to wear out *Se ha gastado muy pronto esa tela.* That cloth has worn out very rapidly.

gasto expense *Cuando pagó los gastos quedó limpio.* When he paid the expenses, he had nothing left. ○ **hacer el gasto** to be the life of the party *Fué él quien hizo el gasto de la fiesta.* He was the life of the party. ○ **pagar los gastos** to pay the expenses, foot the bill.

gata cat, she-cat. ○ **andar a gatas** to walk on all fours, creep.

gatillo trigger.

gato cat, tom-cat. ▲ jack *Nos hace falta el gato para cambiar la rueda.* We need a jack to change the wheel.

○ **dar gato por liebre** to cheat, to deceive.

‖ *Aquí hay gato encerrado.* There is more here than meets the eye.

gaucho gaucho, man of the pampas, cowboy [*Am*].

gaveta drawer [*Am*] *Los pañuelos están en la gaveta.* The handkerchiefs are in the drawer.

gemelo twin *Parecían gemelos.* They looked like twins. ▲ cuff link. ○ **gemelos** binoculars, opera glasses *Préstame los gemelos para verlo mejor.* Lend me the binoculars so I can see it better.

gemido moan, whine.

general [*adj*] general *Tomaron billetes de entrada general.* They bought general admission tickets. ▲ [*m*] general [*Mil*].

○ **en general** usually, generally *En general se va a casa a las cinco.* He generally goes home at five o'clock. ○ **por lo general** usually *¿Que bebe Ud. por lo general, vino o cerveza?* What do you usually drink, wine or beer? ○ **por regla general** as a general rule.

generalidad [*f*] greatest part, majority

*La generalidad de los niños son jugue-
tones.* Most children are playful.
generalizar to generalize *Generaliza al
hablar de los norteamericanos.* He
generalizes when he speaks of Americans.

○ **generalizarse** to become general *El
uso del chicle se ha generalizado.* The
use of chewing gum has become general.

género cloth *Ese sastre usa siempre muy
buenos géneros.* That tailor always
uses very good material. ▲ kind *¿Qué
género de trabajo le gusta?* What kind
of work do you like?

○ **género humano** mankind. ○ **género
masculino, género femenino** masculine
gender, feminine gender.

‖ *Sin ningún género de duda.* Without any doubt. *or* Beyond a shadow of
a doubt.

generosidad [*f*] generosity.
genial brilliant *Es un músico genial.* He
is a brilliant musician.
genio genius *Es un hombre de genio.*
He's a genius.

○ **buen genio** good nature *Tiene buen
genio.* He's good-natured. ○ **mal
genio** bad temper.

gente [*f*] people *¿Cuánta gente hay en
esta oficina?* How many people are
there in this office? ▲ folks *¿Cómo está
su gente?* How are your folks?

○ **gente bien** upper class. ○ **gente
de bien** honest people. ○ **gente menuda** children, small fry.

gentil gracious, kind.
gentileza graciousness, kindness.
geografía geography.
geográfico geographical.
gerencia management *Mudaron la gerencia de la fábrica.* They changed the
management of the factory.
gerente [*m*] manager.
germen [*m*] germ.
gesto gesture; expression of the face
Tenía mal gesto. He had an unpleasant
expression on his face. ▲ gesture *Su
dimisión fué un gesto muy noble.* His
resignation was a very noble gesture.

○ **hacer gestos** to make gestures, to
signal, make (a) sign(s) *Hizo gestos
de aprobación.* He made signs of approval.

giganta giantess.
gigante huge, gigantic. ▲ [*m*] giant.
gimnasia physical exercise, calisthenics.
gimnasio gymnasium.
gimotear to whine.
girar to revolve, turn *La rueda no gira.*
The wheel doesn't turn. ▲ to turn

*Llegando a la esquina el coche giró a
la derecha.* The car turned right when
it reached the corner. ▲ to draw *Puede
Ud. girar contra mí cuenta.* You can
draw against my account.

giro turn *El asunto ha tomado un nuevo
giro.* The matter has taken a new
turn. ▲ draft *Ayer le mandamos un
giro de veinte dólares.* We sent him a
draft yesterday for fifty dollars.

○ **giro (postal)** money order *Mándeme la cantidad por giro (postal).*
Send me the amount by money order.

gitano, gitana gypsy.
glacial icy *El frío es glacial en este país.*
It's freezing cold in this country.
globo globe, sphere, balloon.
gloria glory *En la batalla el general se
cubrió de gloria.* In the battle the
general covered himself with glory.
▲ heaven.

○ **saber a gloria** to be delicious *Comimos un pastel que sabía a gloria.* We
ate a very delicious pie.

glotón [*adj; n*] gluttonous; glutton.
gobernador [*m*] governor (political).
gobernar to govern *Es un pueblo difícil
de gobernar.* It is a difficult country
to govern.

○ **gobernarse** to manage *Se gobierna
muy bien.* He manages his affairs
very well.

gobierno cabinet *El primer ministro está
formando un nuevo gobierno.* The pre-
mier is forming a new cabinet. ▲ government *Es un gobierno democrático.*
It's a democratic government. ▲ control *Perdió el gobierno del volante.* He
lost control of the steering wheel.

golfo gulf.
golondrina swallow (bird).
golpe [*m*] blow *El golpe no le hizo daño.*
The blow didn't harm him.

○ **al primer golpe de vista** at first
sight *Al primer golpe de vista me
pareció más grande.* At first sight it
seemed larger to me. ○ **dar golpes** to
knock, pound *Dió varios golpes en la
puerta.* He knocked on the door several times. ○ **de golpe** suddenly, all of
a sudden *Me lo dijo de golpe.* He told
me all of a sudden. ○ **golpe de estado**
coup d'état.

golpear to pound *Estaba golpeando con
el martillo.* He was pounding with the
hammer.

goma glue; rubber, eraser. ▲ hang-over
[*Am*] *¡Qué goma tengo!* What a hangover I have!

gordo fat *Era demasiado gordo.* He was
too fat.

○ **agua gorda** hard water [*Sp*].
○ **hacer la vista gorda** to pretend not to see, wink at *Los niños robaban la fruta pero el guarda hacía la vista gorda.* The children were stealing the fruit but the keeper pretended not to see. ○ **llevarse un susto gordo** to get a bad scare.

gordura stoutness, fatness.

gorro cap (for head).

○ **ir de gorra** to sponge *Le gustaba ir de gorra.* He liked to sponge on people.

gorrión [*m*] sparrow.

gorro cap (for head).

gota drop *No dejó gota en el vaso.* He didn't leave a drop in the glass. ▲ gout.
○ **gota a gota** drop by drop. ○ **sudar la gota gorda** to sweat blood.

gotear to rain, to drizzle. ▲ to leak *Esa cañería gotea.* That water pipe leaks.

gotera leak (in roof, wall) *¡Tape Ud. esa gotera!* Plug up that leak!

gótico Gothic.

gozar to enjoy oneself, have a good time [*Am*] *Gozamos mucho en la fiesta.* We had a very good time at the party.
○ **gozar de** to enjoy *¿Goza Ud. de buena salud?* Are you enjoying good health?

gozo joy.

grabado (see **grabar**) engraved *Sus iniciales están grabados en la pulsera.* Her initials are engraved on the bracelet. ▲ fixed *La idea quedó grabado en su imaginación.* The idea became fixed in his mind. ▲ [*m*] engraving, etching *Era un experto en el grabado en cobre.* He was an expert in copper engraving. ▲ picture (illustration) *El periódico tenía muy buenos grabados.* The newspaper had very good pictures.

grabar to engrave; to cut (a record).

gracejada crude joke.

gracia wit, charm, grace. ▲ mercy *El abogado defensor pidió gracia para el condenado.* The defense attorney asked mercy for the condemned man. ▲ joke *Se reía de todas sus gracias.* He laughed at all her jokes. ▲ name *¿Cual es su gracia de Ud.?* What is your name?
○ **gracias** thanks *Estoy bien, muchas gracias.* I am well, thank you. ○ **gracias a** thanks to *Gracias a Ud. llegué a tiempo.* Thanks to you I arrived on time. ○ **hacer gracia** to strike one (as) funny *Me hace gracia lo que dice.* What he says strikes me (as) funny.
○ **tener gracia** to be funny, be witty.

‖ *¡Qué gracia!* How swell! *or* How funny! (*Ironical*)

gradas wide steps leading to the entrance of a building; bleachers.

grado degree *Obtuvo el grado de doctor en filosofía.* He got his doctor's degree. —*La temperatura bajó tres grados.* The temperature went down three degrees.
○ **de mal grado** unwillingly, reluctantly *Aceptó de mal grado.* He accepted reluctantly.

graduar to set *Había que graduar la espoleta.* It was necessary to set the fuse.
○ **graduarse** to graduate, be graduated *Se graduó en la Universidad de Harvard.* He was graduated from Harvard University.

gráfico [*adj*] graphic *Habla de una manera gráfica.* He speaks very graphically. ▲ pictorial, picture *¿Hay aquí revistas gráficas?* Are there any picture magazines here? ▲ [*m*] time table *Ese gráfico marca las horas de entrada y salida.* That time table gives the hours of arrival and departure.

grama lawn (grass) [*Am*].

gramática grammar.

gramo gram (weight).

gran (see **grande**) great *Ha tenido Ud. una gran idea.* You've had a great idea. ▲ fine, good, grand *Es una gran persona.* He is a fine person.

granada grenade; pomegranate.

granado ripe, mature *Es un hombre granado.* He's a mature man. ▲ [*m*] pomegranate tree.

grande large *Un cigarro grande.* A large cigar. ▲ tall *Es un hombre grande.* He's a big man. ▲ old [*Am*] *Es el más grande de los tres.* He is the oldest of the three.
○ **a lo grande** in (great) style *Le gustaba vivir a lo grande.* He liked to live in style. ○ **en grande** on a large scale *Las fábricas están produciendo en grande.* The factories are producing on a large scale.

grandeza greatness.

grandioso grandiose, magnificent.

granero granary.

granito granite; pimple.

granizo hail.

granja farm.

grano grain *El grano maduró bien aquel año.* The grain ripened well that year. ▲ pimple *Tiene la cara llena de granos.* His face is covered with pimples.
○ **ir al grano** to get to the point

¡*Vamos al grano!* Let's get to the point!

grasa grease *Una mancha de grasa.* A grease spot. ▲fat *La carne de cerdo tiene mucha grasa.* Pork has a lot of fat.

grasiento greasy, oily *Tiene el pelo muy grasiento.* Her hair is very oily.

gratificar to reward *Lo gratificaron esplendidamente.* They rewarded him generously.

gratis gratis, free *La entrada es gratis.* Admission free.

gratitud [*f*] gratitude.

gratuito free *La entrada es gratuita.* Admission free.

grave grave, serious *El estado de mi amigo es muy grave.* My friend's condition is very grave. ▲deep *Tiene la voz grave.* He has a deep voice.

gravedad [*f*] seriousness, gravity.

grieta crack *La pared tenía una grieta.* The wall had a crack in it.
   ○ **grietas en las manos** chapped hands *Tengo grietas en las manos.* My hands are chapped.

grifo having hair *or* fur bristling *or* standing on end *El gato está grifo.* The cat's fur is bristling. ▲[*m*] faucet *El grifo del baño está estropeado.* The faucet in the bathroom's out of order.

grillo cricket (insect).
   ○ **grillos** fetters (for prisoners) *Le pusieron grillos en los pies.* They put fetters on his feet.

grima ○ **darle grima a uno** to set one's teeth on edge, get on one's nerves *El chirrido de la puerta me da grima.* The squeaking of the door gets on my nerves.

gringo gringo, American [*Am*]; foreigner [*Am*].

gripa grippe, influenza [*Mex*].

gripe [*f*] grippe, influenza.

gris gray.

gritar to shout, scream.

grito scream, shout.
   ○ **a grito pelado** at the top of one's lungs *Nos llamó a grito pelado.* He called us at the top of his lungs. ○ **alzar el grito** to raise the voice, shout. ○ **poner el grito en el cielo** to hit the ceiling, make a great fuss.

grosero rude, coarse *Era un hombre grosero.* He was a coarse man.

grotesco grotesque.

gruesa gross (twelve dozen).

grueso [*adj*] stout, heavy set *Era demasiado grueso.* He was too stout. ▲thick *Esta tela es muy gruesa.* This cloth

is very thick. ▲[*m*] main body (of troops) *El grueso del ejército atravesó el río.* The main body of the army crossed the river.

gruñido growl; grunt.

gruñir to growl *El perro gruñó cuando nos acercamos.* The dog growled when we approached. ▲to grunt. ▲to grumble *Gruñía porque no le pagaban bastante.* He grumbled because they didn't pay him enough.

gruñón cranky, irritable.

grupo group *¿En qué grupo está su amigo?* Which group is your friend in? ▲clump *En lo alto había un grupo de árboles.* At the top there was a clump of trees.

guacho odd (only one of a pair) [*Chile*] *Tengo un guante guacho.* I have an odd glove.

guagua bus [*Ant*] *¿Para dónde va esa guagua?* Where does that bus go to? ▲baby [*Am*] *La guagua lloró toda la noche.* The baby cried all night.

guajolote [*m*] turkey [*Mex*].

guante [*m*] glove.

guapo handsome *Era un hombre guapo.* He was a handsome man. ▲brave *Se las da de guapo.* He acts like a tough guy.

guarango rough, vulgar [*Arg*].

guarda [*m*] guard; [*Arg*] conductor.

guardar to keep *Guarde Ud. copia de ese documento.* Keep a copy of that document. ▲to guard *Guardaba la entrada.* He was guarding the entrance.
   ○ **guardarse de** to avoid *Guardese de las malas compañías.* Avoid bad company. ○ **guardar silencio** to keep quiet.

guardarropa [*m*] wardrobe, clothes closet, checkroom.

guardia [*m*] policeman *Llame Ud. a un guardia.* Call a policeman. ▲[*f*] guard, guard duty *Le tocó hacer la guardia.* It was his turn for guard duty.
   ○ **en guardia** on guard *Ante el peligro me pongo en guardia.* I put myself on guard against the danger. ○ **estar de guardia** to be on guard duty. ○ **guardia-civil** [*f*] civil guard (body of rural police). ▲[*m*] member of civil guard [*Sp*].

guardián [*m*] watchman.

guarida den.

guarnición [*f*] garrison; trimming, edging.

guasa kidding, joking *A los andaluces les gusta la guasa.* Andalusians are fond of kidding.
   ○ **de guasa** jokingly.

guasón [*m*] wag, joker.

guerra war.

○ dar guerra to cause trouble *Ese niño da mucha guerra.* That child caused a lot of trouble. ○ **Departamento de** (*or* **Ministerio de la**) **Guerra** War Department.

guía [*m, f*] guide *Hubo que buscar un guía para el viaje.* It was necessary to find a guide for the trip. ▲ [*f*] guide (book), directory. ○ **guía de ferrocarriles** railroad guide. ○ **guía de turismo** tourists' guide book. ○ **guía telefónica** telephone directory.

guiar to guide *Iba delante para guiar a los soldados.* He went ahead to guide the soldiers. ▲ to drive *Aprendió a guiar un automóvil.* Hè learned to drive a car.

○ **guiarse por** to follow *Quiso guiarse por los consejos de su amigo.* He wanted to follow his friend's advice.

guillotina guillotine.

guisante [*m*] pea [*Sp*].

guisar to cook.

gustar to like, be fond of *Le gustaba mucho viajar.* He was very fond of traveling.—*Como Ud. guste.* As you like.

gusto taste *Esto tiene buen gusto.* This tastes good.—*Viste con muy buen gusto.* She dresses in very good taste. ▲ liking *Eso ne es de mi gusto.* That isn't to my liking.

○ **a gusto** comfortable *¿Esta Ud. a gusto?* Are you comfortable? ○ **con mucho gusto** gladly, willingly, with much pleasure *Lo haré con mucho gusto.* I shall do it gladly. ○ **dar gusto a** to please *Mi deseo es darles gusto a Uds.* My wish is to please you. ‖ *Tengo mucho gusto en conocerle.* I'm very glad to meet you.

H

haba Lima bean.

haber to have (auxiliary). ▲ [*m*] credit *Asiente Ud. esa cantidad en el haber.* Enter that amount on the credit side.

○ **haber de** to be to *He de salir mañana.* I'm to leave tomorrow. ○ **hay** there is, there are. *Hay uno.* There's one.—*Ayer hubo un accidente en la Quinta Avenida.* There was an accident on Fifth Avenue yesterday.—*Habrá tres.* There'll be three. ○ **hay que** it's necessary *Hay que hacerlo.* It has to be done.—*Habrá que hacerlo mañana.* It'll have to be done tomorrow. ○ **no hay de qué** you're welcome, don't mention it *"¡Muchas gracias!" "No hay de qué."* "Thank you!" "You're welcome."

‖ *¿Qué hubo?* How goes it? [*Mex*]

habichuela kidney bean.

○ **habichuela verde** (green) string bean.

hábil skillful *Era muy hábil como mecánico.* He was a very skillful mechanic.

○ **día hábil** work day *¿Cuántos días hábiles hay este mes?* How many work days are there this month?

habilidad [*f*] ability.

habilitado paymaster.

habitación [*f*] room *Mi habitación es el número catorce del tercer piso.* My room is number fourteen on the third floor.

habitante [*m, f*] inhabitant *Es un pueblecito de doscientos habitantes.* It is a village of two hundred inhabitants.

habitar to inhabit.

hábito habit (of a religious). ▲ habit, custom *Tenía por hábito levantarse temprano.* It was his custom to get up early.

○ **tomar el hábito** to become a monk or nun.

habitual habitual.

habituarse to become accustomed *Se habituó a trabajar en la oficina.* He became accustomed to working in the office.

habla speech *Su habla es clara y precisa.* His speech is clear and precise.—*Ese hombre no es de habla española.* That man's not of Spanish speech.—*El mundo de habla española.* The Spanish-speaking world.

○ **perder el habla** to be speechless *Con la emoción perdió el habla.* He was speechless with emotion.

hablador [*adj*] talkative *Es muy hablador.* He's very talkative.

hablar to speak *¿Habla Ud. inglés?* Do you speak English? ▲ to talk *Habla, pero no sabe lo que dice.* He talks, but he doesn't know what he's saying.

○ **hablar (hasta) por los codos** to chatter *Ese muchacho habla por los codos.* That boy is a chatterbox. ○ **hablar por hablar** to be just talking *Ne le* *creas, habla por hablar.* Don't believe him, he's just talking (to hear himself talk). ○ **hablarse** to speak to each other, be on speaking terms *Hace dos días que no se hablan.* They haven't been speaking to each other for two days.—*Aunque eran hermanos no se hablaban.* Although they were brothers they were not on speaking terms.

hacendado rancher; landowner [*Am*] *Su padre es un rico hacendado.* His father's a wealthy rancher.

hacendoso industrious.

hacer [*irr*] to make *Le han hecho un traje nuevo.* They have made him a new suit. ▲ to have *Hágales entrar ahora mismo.* Have them come in right now. ▲ to do *¿Qué hace Ud. para ganar tanto dinero?* What do you do to make so much money? ▲ to be *Hace un buen día.* It is a beautiful day.

○ **hacer alarde** to boast, brag *Hizo alarde de valor.* He boasted of his courage. ○ **hacer caso** a to pay attention to *No le haga caso.* Don't pay any attention to him. ○ **hacer de cuenta** to pretend, act [*Am*] *Haga de cuenta que nada ha ocurrido.* Just act as if nothing has happened. *or* Think nothing of it. ○ **hacer de las suyas** to be up to one's old tricks *Otra vez está haciendo de las suyas.* He's up to his old tricks again. ○ **hacer el amor** to pay court to, make love to *Le estuvo haciendo el amor durante la fiesta.* He was making love to her during the party. ○ **hacer el favor** please *¿Quiere hacer el favor de acompañarme?* Will you please come with me? ○ **hacer el honor de** to do the honor of *¿Me hará Ud. el honor de comer conmigo?* Will you do me the honor of dining with me? ○ **hacer frío** *or* **calor** to be cold *or* hot (of weather) *Hoy hace mucho calor.* It's very hot today. ○ **hacer furor** to make a hit *Está haciendo furor esta nueva canción.* This new song is making a big hit. ○ **hacer gimnasia** to do exercises (calisthenics) *Hago gimnasia por la mañana.* I do exercises in the morning. ○ **hacer los honores** to play *or* act as host(ess) *Nos hizo honores de la casa.* She played hostess to us. ○ **hacerse** to become *Se ha hecho muy famoso.* He's become very famous. ○ **hacerse el sueco** to pretend not to understand. ○ **hacerse el tonto** to play dumb *No te hagas el tonto, que te conozco.* Don't play dumb; I know you. ○ **hacerse ilusiones** to fool oneself *No nos hagamos ilusiones con ese proyecto.*

Let's not fool ourselves about that project. ○ **hacerse rogar** to be coaxed *Le gusta hacerse rogar.* He likes to be coaxed. ○ **hacer un barro** to make a break, to put one's foot in it [*Arg*]. ○ **hacer un paréntesis** to digress *Después de hacer un paréntesis, volvió al tema.* After digressing, he returned to the subject. ○ **tener (algo) que hacer** to have (something) to do *¿Tiene Ud. algo que hacer hoy?* Have you anything to do today?

‖ *No le hace.* Never mind. *or* Skip it.

hacha ax.

hacia toward *Iba hacia su casa.* He was going toward his house.

○ **hacia acá** this way *¡Mire Ud. hacia acá!* Look this way! ○ **hacia adelante** forward *El coche iba hacia adelante.* The car was going forward. ○ **hacia allá** that way *¡Mire hacia allá, a la derecha!* Look that way, to the right! ○ **hacia atrás** backward(s) *Remaban hacia atrás.* They rowed backwards.

hacienda fortune *Perdió toda su hacienda.* He lost his whole fortune. ▲ ranch, large estate [*Am*]. ▲ Treasury (government) *Ministro (or Secretario) de Hacienda.* Secretary of the Treasury.

halagar to flatter.

halagüeño promising, bright *Las perspectivas no son halagüeñas.* The prospects aren't very bright.

halar [*today usually written* **jalar**] to pull [*Am*] *Halaban la cuerda con fuerza.* They pulled hard on the rope.

hallar to find *Se registró los bolsillos y halló un peso.* He searched his pockets and found one peso.

○ **hallarse** to be *No ha podido venir porque se halla enfermo.* He hasn't been able to come because he is sick.

hallazgo thing found *Entre los hallazgos hubo paraguas, zapatos y pañuelos.* Among the things found were umbrellas, shoes, and handkerchiefs.

hamaca hammock [*Am*].

hambre [*f*] hunger *Tenía mucha hambre.* He was very hungry.

hambriento hungry, starved.

harapo rag *Iba vestido de harapos.* He went around dressed in rags.

harina flour, meal.

hartarse to gorge, stuff oneself *Tomó helado hasta hartarse.* He gorged himself on ice cream.

harto full, stuffed; fed up *¡Estoy harto de sus cuentos!* I'm fed up with your stories!

hasta until *No regresarán hasta después*

de las seis. They won't return until after six.—*Hasta mañana.* Until tomorrow. *or* See you tomorrow. ▲ as far as *Fueron hasta la última calle del pueblo.* They went as far as the last street in town.

O **hasta aquí** so far *Hasta aquí todo está bien.* So far everything is all right. ‖ *Hasta la vista.* So long. ‖ *Hasta luego.* So long.

hay See **haber.**

haya beech tree.

hazaña feat, exploit, deed *El soldado fué condecorado por sus hazañas.* The soldier was decorated for his deeds.

hebilla buckle (fastener).

hebra thread.

hechicero bewitching *Tiene una cara hechicera.* She has a bewitching face.

hechizo domestic, made in (a given country) [*Am*].

hecho (see **hacer**) done. ▲ ready-made *Prefiero un traje hecho.* I prefer a ready-made suit. ▲ [*m*] deed *Fué recordado por sus nobles hechos.* He was remembered for his noble deeds. ▲ fact *El periódico publica los hechos más importantes.* The newspaper publishes the most important facts.

O **de hecho** in fact, as a matter of fact *De hecho quedó convencido.* As a matter of fact he was convinced.

hechura workmanship, making *No me gusta la hechura de ese traje.* I don't like the workmanship of that suit. ▲ style.

hectárea hectare (10,000 sq. meters).

hediondo foul, stinking.

hedor [*m*] stench, stink.

helado (see **helar**) frozen *El estanque amaneció completamente helado.* The pond was completely frozen in the morning. ▲ shocked *La noticia me dejó helado.* The news shocked me. ▲ [*m*] ice cream *Me gusta el helado de chocolate.* I like chocolate ice cream.

helar [*rad-ch I*] to freeze.

helecho fern.

hélice [*f*] (screw) propeller (of ship).

hembra female *No es macho, es hembra.* It's not a male, it's a female.

hemisferio hemisphere.

heredad [*f*] (inherited) country estate *or* farm *Mi padre me dejó una heredad.* My father left me some property.

heredar to inherit *A la muerte de sus padres heredó una gran fortuna.* He inherited a large fortune when his parents died.

heredero, heredera heir.

hereditario hereditary.

hereje [*m, f*] heretic.

herejía heresy.

herencia inheritance.

herida wound *La herida se curó.* The wound healed.

herido wounded man *El herido se curó en tres días.* The wounded man recovered in three days.

herir [*rad-ch II*] to wound, hurt *Fué herido en la guerra.* He was wounded in the war.

hermana sister. ▲ nun, sister *Una hermana de la caridad le cuidaba.* A Sister of Charity took care of him.

hermano brother.

hermoso beautiful, handsome *Es una mujer muy hermosa.* She's a very beautiful woman.

hermosura beauty, handsomeness.

héroe [*m*] hero.

heroico heroic.

heroína heroine.

heroísmo heroism.

herrador [*m*] horseshoer.

herradura horseshoe *Le pusieron la herradura al caballo.* They shod the horse.

herramienta tool; set of tools.

herrar [*rad-ch I*] to shoe (horses); to brand (cattle).

herrería iron works, blacksmith's shop.

herrero blacksmith.

herrumbre [*f*] rust.

hervir [*rad-ch III*] to boil *El agua empezó a hervir.* The water began to boil.

híbrido [*adj; n*] hybrid.

hidalga noble(woman); lady.

hidalgo noble(man); gentleman.

hidrógeno hydrogen.

hiel [*f*] gall; bitterness, malice.

hielo ice *Haga el favor de darme hielo para el agua.* Please give me some ice for the water.

hiena hyena.

hierba grass.

O **mala hierba** weed *La dehesa está llena de mala hierba.* The pasture is full of weeds. ▲ bad influence *Ese niño es mala hierba.* That boy is a bad influence.

hierro iron *Toda el armazón era de hierro.* The whole framework was made of iron.

O **machacar en hierro frío** to work in vain, be useless *Tratar de corregir a ese niño es machacar en hierro frío.* Trying to correct that boy is useless.

hígado liver.

higiene [*f*] hygiene.

higo fig.

hija daughter.

hijo son.

hila row, line.

hilar to spin (wool, silk, etc).

hilera row, line.
hilo thread *Cuidado no se rompa el hilo.* Be careful that the thread doesn't break.—*Me hace falta hilo para coser este botón.* I need thread to sew on this button. ▲ linen *Me regaló media docena de pañuelos de hilo.* He gave me a half dozen linen handkerchiefs.
hilvanar to baste (in sewing).
himno hymn.
hincar to drive *Hincaron en el suelo estacas para asegurar la tienda.* They drove stakes into the ground to make the tent secure. ▲ to sink *El perro me hincó los dientes en el brazo.* The dog sank his teeth into my arm.
○ **hincarse de rodillas** to kneel down *Lo primero que hizo fué hincarse de rodillas.* The first thing he did was to kneel down.
hincha [f] fan *Es una hincha del equipo argentino.* He's a fan of the Argentine team. (When referring to a sport as a whole, the word used in *aficionado*).
hinchar to swell *Se le hinchó la pierna.* His leg swelled up.
hinchazón [m] swelling (lump).
hipocresía hypocrisy.
hipócrita hypocritical. ▲ [n] hypocrite.
hipoteca mortgage.
hipótesis [f] hypothesis.
hispanoamericano [adj; n] Spanish-American.
histérico hysterical.
historia history, story *Conocía a fonda la historia de América.* He knew the history of America thoroughly. ▲ tale *No me vengas con historias.* Don't come to me with tales.
historiador [m] historian.
histórico historic(al) *Visitamos los lugares históricos del país.* We visited the historic sites of the country.
historieta short story; the comics [Sp].
hocico muzzle, snout, nose *El gato metió el hocico en el puchero.* The cat put its nose in the pot.
○ **estar de hocicos con** to be on the outs with *Estaba de hocicos con su novia.* He was on the outs with his sweetheart.
hogar [m] fireplace *¿Tiene Ud. un hogar en su casa?* Do you have a fireplace in your home? ▲ home *Abandonó el hogar cuando era muy joven.* He left home when he was very young.
hogaza (large) loaf of bread.
hoguera bonfire *Encendieron una hoguera.* They lit a bonfire.
hoja leaf *El suelo estaba cubierto de hojas.* The ground was covered with leaves. ▲ blade *La hoja estaba muy afilada.* The blade was very sharp. ▲ page *¿En qué hoja está Ud.?* What page are you on? ▲ record *¿Presentó Ud. su hoja de servicios?* Did you show your record of service?
○ **hoja de lata** tin plate. ○ **poner le a uno como hoja de perejil** to give one a tongue lashing *Le puso como hoja de perejil.* He gave him a tongue lashing. ○ **tener hoja** to be counterfeit (have more than legal proportion of tin) *Esta plata tiene hoja.* That coin is counterfeit.
‖ *Doblemos la hoja.* Let's change the subject.
hojear to thumb through, glance (*or* skim) through (a book, etc).
¡hola! Hello! (informal) *¡Hola! ¿Cómo estás?* Hello, how are you?
holgazán lazy.
hombre [m] man *Vino a buscarle un hombre.* A man came to see him.
○ **¡hombre!** man! man alive! *¡Hombre, no digas eso!* Man, don't say that! ○ **hombre de Estado** statesman.
hombría manliness, courage *En la lucha demostró su hombría.* He showed his courage in the fight.
○ **hombría (de bien)** honesty *Todos lo estimaban por su hombría.* They all esteemed him for his honesty.
hombro shoulder *Cargó el equipaje al hombro.* He loaded the baggage on his shoulder.
○ **encogerse de hombros** to shrug the shoulders *Por toda contestación se encogió de hombros.* The only answer he gave was a shrug of his shoulders.
homenaje [m] homage *Han venido a rendirle homenaje al autor.* They have come to pay homage to the author.
homicida [m, f] killer, slayer *El homicida se refugió en la montaña.* The slayer hid in the mountains. ▲ [adj] homicidal *El arma homicida no fué hallada.* The homicidal weapon wasn't found.
homogéneo homogeneous.
honda sling (for hurling stones).
hondo deep *Este pozo es muy hondo.* This well is very deep.
honestidad [f] modesty, decorum *Se enamoró de ella por su honestidad.* He fell in love with her for her modesty.
honesto decent, honest *El cajero era un hombre muy honesto.* The cashier was a very honest man.
honor [m] honor *Era un hombre de honor.* He was a man of honor.
○ **honores** honors *Al morir le hicieron honores militares.* When he died he was given military honors.
honradez [f] honesty, integrity.

honrado (see **honrar**) honest *Es un hombre honrado.* He's an honest man.

honrar to honor *Nos honra mucho su presencia.* We're very much honored by your presence.

hora hour *Empezó la fiesta a la hora en punto.* The party began exactly on the hour. ▲ time *¿Qué hora es?* What time is it?

○ **a primeras horas de la mañana** in the early morning. ○ **a última hora** at the last moment *A última hora todo se solucionó.* Everything was solved at the last moment. ○ **a últimas horas de la tarde** in the late afternoon.

horca gallows.

horizontal horizontal.

horizonte [*m*] horizon.

hormiga ant.

horno oven.

horrible horrid, horrible *Hizo una escena horrible.* She made a horrible scene.

horror [*m*] horror *Tiene horror a la guerra.* He has a horror of war.

horroroso horrible, frightful *Fué una escena horrorosa.* It was a horrible scene.

hortalizas [*f pl*] vegetables.

hospital [*m*] hospital.

hospitalidad [*f*] hospitality.

hostilidad [*f*] hostility.

hotel [*m*] hotel.

hoy today *Hoy empezamos a trabajar.* We're starting to work today.

○ **hoy por hoy** for the time being, under present circumstances *Hoy por hoy no pienso regresar a mi país.* Under present circumstances I don't intend to return to my country. ○ **por hoy** for the present *Por hoy lo dejaremos pasar.* We'll let it go for the present.

hoyo hole, depression; ditch.

hoyuelo dimple.

hoz [*f*] sickle.

hueco [*adj*] hollow, empty *El tronco del árbol estaba hueco.* The tree trunk was hollow. ▲ [*m*] hole *Cuidado, hay un hueco en el piso.* Be careful, there's a hole in the floor.

huelga strike (of workers).

huella track *Siguieron las huellas del otro automóvil.* They followed the tracks of the other car. ▲ trace, sign *En la América del Sur hay muchas huellas de la cultura india.* In South America there are many traces of Indian culture. ▲ footprint, fingerprint *Aquí están sus huellas.* Here are his footprints.

○ **huella dactilar** fingerprint *Se detuvo el asesino por sus huellas dacti-*

lares. The assassin was arrested through his fingerprints.

huérfano, huérfana orphan.

huerta large vegetable garden.

huerto orchard.

hueso bone.

○ **estar en los huesos** to be nothing but skin and bones.

‖ *¡A otro perro con ese hueso!* Tell it to the Marines!

huésped [*m*] guest.

huevo egg *¿Cómo quiere Ud. los huevos, fritos o revueltos?* How do you like your eggs, fried or scrambled?

huída flight, escape.

huir to flee *Los prisioneros huyeron del campo de concentración.* The prisoners fled from the concentration camp.

humanidad [*f*] humanity. ▲ humaneness *La humanidad de sus sentimientos era bien conocida.* The humaneness of his sentiments was well known.

humano [*adj*] human. ▲ humane *Era una persona muy humana.* He was a very humane person.

humear to smoke, give off smoke *Las cenizas todavía humeaban.* The cinders were still smoking.

humedad [*f*] dampness, humidity, moisture *La humedad del tiempo me hace daño a la salud.* The dampness of the weather is bad for my health.

humedecer [-*zc*-] to moisten.

húmedo damp, humid.

humilde poor; humble, unaffected.

humillar to humiliate.

humo smoke *Por la ventana se veía salir el humo.* Smoke could be seen pouring out of the window.

○ **darse humos de grandeza** to put on airs of grandeur. ○ **humos** airs, affected manner *Lo dijo con muchos humos.* He said it in an affected manner.

humor [*m*] humor, mood *Está siempre de buen humor.* He's always in good humor. ▲ humor, wit.

hundirse to sink *Se hundió en el barro hasta las rodillas.* He sank in mud up to his knees. ▲ to cave in *La casa se hundió.* The house caved in. ▲ to fall off, diminish *Empezó a hundirse su negocio por no atenderlo.* His business began to fall off because he didn't take care of it.

huracán [*m*] hurricane.

hurtar to steal, pilfer.

○ **hurtar el cuerpo** to shy away, dodge *Hurtó el cuerpo al toro.* He dodged the bull.

huye See **huir**.

I

iberoamericano [*adj; n*] Latin American.
ida leaving, going, trip out *A la ida, el viaje fué mas agradable que a la vuelta.* The trip out was more pleasant than the return.
   ○ **billete de ida y vuelta** round-trip ticket.
idea idea.
ideal [*adj*] ideal, perfect. ▲ [*m*] ideal, principle.
idear to plan, invent *Ideó un mecanismo para pelar fruta.* He invented an instrument for peeling fruit.
idéntico identical.
identidad [*f*] identity. ▲ identification *¿Tiene Ud. documentos de identidad?* Have you any identification?
identificar to identify.
   ○ **identificarse con** to identify oneself with.
idioma [*m*] language, tongue *El Consul habla muchos idiomas.* The Consul speaks many languages.
idolatrar to worship, idolize, adore *Te idolatro.* I adore you.
ídolo idol.
iglesia church; clergy.
ignorancia ignorance.
ignorante ignorant.
ignorar not to know, lack knowledge *Ignora las cosas más elementales.* He doesn't know the most elementary things.
igual same, similar *La madre y la hija tienen los ojos iguales.* Mother and daughter have the same eyes. ▲ even *Tiene un carácter muy igual.* He has a very even disposition. ▲ [*m*] equal, peer *Era un hombre sin igual.* He was a man without (an) equal.—*Solo se trata con sus iguales.* He only deals with his equals.
   ○ **de igual a igual** as one equal to another, man to man *Le habló de igual a igual.* He spoke to him man to man.
   ○ **igual a** equal to, the same as *Esta mesa es igual a aquélla.* This table's the same as that one. ○ **igual que** *Pienso igual que Ud.* I think the same as you. ○ **por igual** evenly *Extienda Ud. la arena por igual.* Spread the sand evenly. ○ **serle a uno igual** to be all the same to one *Que venga o no venga me es igual.* Whether he comes or not it's all the same to me.
igualar to equal *No iguala a su hermano.* He doesn't equal his brother. ▲ to level *No han igualado la carretera.*

The road hasn't been leveled.
   ○ **igualar con** *or* **a** to put oneself on the same plane as, compare oneself with *No te iguales a tu hermano porque vale más que tú.* Don't compare yourself with your brother because he's a better man than you. ○ **igualarse** to be equal, to be tied (score) *Los dos equipos se igualaron al final.* The two teams were tied at the finish.
igualdad [*f*] equality *Libertad, igualdad y fraternidad.* Liberty, equality, and fraternity. ▲ evenness, smoothness.
ilegal illegal, unlawful.
ilícito illicit, immoral.
ilimitado boundless, unlimited *Su audacia es ilimitada.* His audacity is boundless.
iluminar to light, illumine *Iluminaron el salón con todas las luces.* They turned on all the lights in the salon.—*Han iluminado muy bien el estadio.* They've lighted the stadium very well.
ilusión [*f*] illusion, delusion.
   ○ **hacerse ilusiones** to kid oneself. ▲ to bank on *No se haga Ud. ilusiones sobre ese negocio.* Don't bank too much on that business. ○ **tener ilusiones (de)** to have hopes *or* illusions *Tiene ilusiones de casarse algún día.* She has hopes of getting married some day.
ilusionar to thrill *La idea de ver a mi madre me ilusiona mucho.* The idea of seeing my mother thrills me very much.
   ○ **ilusionarse (con)** to get excited, thrilled *Se ilusiona con cualquier cosa.* She gets excited over anything.
ilustración [*f*] learning *Es un hombre de mucha ilustración.* He's a very learned man. ▲ illustration, picture *Las ilustraciones del libro son muy buenas.* The illustrations of the book are very good.
ilustrado learned *Era un hombre muy ilustrado.* He was a very learned man. ▲ illustrated, with pictures *Pidió una revista ilustrada para distraerse.* He asked for a picture magazine to amuse himself.
ilustrar to illustrate *Es un buen artista el que ha ilustrado este libro.* The artist who illustrated this book is very good.
   ○ **ilustrarse** to educate oneself *Le gustaba ilustrarse viajando.* He liked to educate himself by traveling.
ilustre illustrious, distinguished.
imagen [*f*] image, representation; image, reflection.
imaginar to think of, figure out *Imagine*

Ud. algo para resolver nuestro proble-
ma. Figure out something to solve our
problem.

○ **imaginarse** to imagine, suspect *No*
puedo imaginarme lo que pretende. I
can't imagine what he's driving at.—
¡Imagíne(se) Ud. que sorpresa tuvi-
mos! Just imagine what a surprise we
had!

imán [*m*] magnet.

imbécil [*n*] imbecile, fool. ▲ [*adj*] stupid.

imborrable indelible, unforgettable *Es*
una impresión imborrable. It's an unforgettable impression.

imitar to imitate, impersonate *Imita muy*
bien a esa actriz. She imitates that
actress very well.

impaciencia impatience.

impaciente impatient; anxious, eager.

imparcial impartial.

impasible impassive, unmoved, indifferent
Tiene una cara impasible. He has an
impassive face.

impedimento hindrance, impediment.

impedir [*rad-ch III*] to prevent *¿Quién*
lo puede impedir? Who can prevent
it?

○ **impedir el paso** to block the way
Retírese de ahí, está Ud. impidiendo
el paso. Step aside; you're blocking
the way.

imperar to prevail, reign *En la calle im-*
pera el desorden. Disorder prevails in
the street.

imperativo imperative *Es imperativo*
salir. It's imperative to go out. ▲ bossy
Es un hombre muy imperativo. He's a
very bossy man.

imperdible [*m*] safety pin [*Sp*].

imperio empire; command. ▲ spell *Ese*
hombre está bajo el imperio de ese
mujer. That man is under that
woman's influence.

imperioso imperative; arrogant, haughty.

impermeable [*adj*] waterproof. ▲ [*m*]
raincoat.

impertenencia impertinence *Su imperti-*
nencia me molesta. His impertinence
annoys me.

impertinente impertinent.

○ **impertinentes** [*m pl*] lorgnettes.

ímpetu [*m*] impetus, impulse.

impío impious, irreligious.

implacable implacable, relentless.

implicar to involve, implicate *No me im-*
plique Ud. en ese asunto. Don't involve me in that matter.

implorar to beg, implore.

imponente imposing *La ceremonia fué*
imponente. The ceremony was imposing.

imponer [*irr*] to impose, levy *Le impusie-*
ron una multa. They imposed a fine on
him.

○ **imponerse** to assert oneself, command respect *Supo imponerse por su*
talento. He was able to command respect because of his ability. ▲ to dominate, get one's way *Es un hombre que*
siempre se impone a todo el mundo.
He's a man who always gets his way.

importación [*f*] import(s), importation.

importante important.

importar to import *Importó cien mil tone-*
ladas de trigo. He imported one hundred thousand tons of wheat.

○ **importarle a uno** to matter (to),
concern *Eso no me importa.* That
doesn't matter to me.

‖ *importa no.* No matter. *or* Never
mind.

importe [*m*] cost.

importuno annoying (of a person) *Me*
molesta la gente importuna. Annoying
people irritate me.

imposible impossible.

imposición [*f*] deposit (of money in a
bank); imposition (of will on another); tax.

impotencia impotence, weakness.

imprenta printing shop; press; print.

○ **error de imprenta** printer's error.

○ **libertad de imprenta** freedom of the
press.

imprescindible essential, indispensable,
imperative.

impresión [*f*] impression *Me causó muy*
buena impresión lo que me dijo. What
he said made a good impression on
me. ▲ imprint. ▲ printing *La impre-*
sión del libro era perfecta. The printing of the book was perfect.

impresionar to impress *Le impresionó*
mucho esa novela. She was very much
impressed by the novel. ▲ to make *or*
cut (a record) *Fué contratado para*
impresionar discos. He was under
contract to make records.

○ **impresionarse** to be moved *Se im-*
presionaron cuando le vieron. They
were moved when they saw him.—*Se*
impresionaron con la noticia. They
were moved by the news.

impreso (see **imprimir**) printed matter,
pamphlet; blank (paper to be filled).

imprevisión [*f*] lack of foresight,
thoughtlessness *Dejar a los niños solos*
fué una gran imprevisión. Leaving the
children alone was sheer thoughtlessness.

imprevisto unforeseen, unexpected.

imprimir to print.

improbable improbable.

impropio inappropriate, unfitting.

improvisado makeshift *Un pupitre improvisado.* A makeshift desk.

improvisar to improvise.

imprudente imprudent, unwise.

impuesto (see **imponer**) [*m*] tax.

impulsar to urge; to encourage; to push.

inaccesible inaccessible.

inactivo inactive.

inadvertencia oversight *No lo incluyeron en la lista por inadvertencia.* He was left off the list through an oversight.

inagotable inexhaustible.

inaguantable unbearable *El dolor era inaguantable.* The pain was unbearable.

inaudito unheard of, strange, unexpected *Obró de una manera inaudita.* He behaved in a strange manner.

inauguración [*f*] unveiling, dedication, (ceremony of) opening (a building) *Ayer fué la inauguración de la estatua del fundador y del edificio de la escuela.* Yesterday the unveiling of the founder's statue and the opening of the school building took place.

inaugurar to unveil, dedicate, open (exhibition, courses, etc).

incansable untiring.

incapacidad [*f*] incapacity; incompetence.

incapaz incompetent; incapable.

incauto [*adj*] unwary, gullible. ▲ [*n*] easy mark *Por ser incauto le robaron el dinero.* Since he was an easy mark they stole his money.

incendiar to set on fire.

incendio fire (conflagration) *El incendio destruyó tres casas.* The fire destroyed three houses.

incertidumbre [*f*] uncertainty.

incesante continual, ceaseless *El ruido era incesante.* The noise was ceaseless.

incidente [*m*] incident, disturbance.

incierto uncertain, doubtful *El resultado del partido es incierto.* The result of the game is doubtful.

inclemencia severity, inclemency.

inclinación [*f*] slant, slope *La inclinación del terreno hacia difícil la construcción de la carretera.* The slope of the ground made it difficult to construct the road. ▲ bent, inclination *Desde niño tuvo inclinación por el arte.* He had a bent for art from childhood.

inclinar to bend, bow *Inclinó la cabeza.* He bowed his head.

○ **inclinarse** to bow. ▲ to yield, give in *Hubo que inclinarse ante aquella verdad.* He had to yield in the face

of that truth. ○ **inclinarse a** to be inclined to *Me parece que se inclina a hacerlo.* I think he's inclined to do it.

incluir to include *Incluya Ud. su nombre en la lista.* Include his name in the list. ▲ to enclose *Incluí el recibo en la carta.* I enclosed the receipt in the letter.

incomodar to disturb, inconvenience, bother *¿Le incomoda a Ud. esta maleta?* Does this suitcase bother you?

○ **incomodarse** to become angry, to be upset *Se incomoda por cualquier cosa.* He gets angry at the slightest thing.

incomodidad [*f*] inconvenience.

incómodo uncomfortable (of position) *Esta silla es incómoda.* This chair is uncomfortable.—*En esta postura estoy incómodo.* In this position I'm uncomfortable.

incomparable incomparable.

incompatible incompatible.

incomprensible incomprehensible.

inconsciente unconscious *El golpe lo dejó inconsciente.* The blow left him unconscious. ▲ irresponsible *Es un hombre muy inconsciente.* He's a very irresponsible person.

inconveniente [*m*] disadvantage *Ese plan tiene algunos inconvenientes.* That plan has certain disadvantages. ▲ objection *No tiene inconveniente en que salgamos.* He has no objection to our leaving.

incorporar to incorporate, unite. ▲ to add *Incorporó su dinero al fondo común.* He added his money to the common fund.

○ **incorporarse** to sit up (in bed). ▲ to join (a military unit) *Recibió orden de incorporarse en su batallón.* He got orders to join his battalion.

incorrecto incorrect; ill-mannered.

increíble incredible, unbelievable.

inculto uncultivated.

incumplido unfulfilled *Sus promesas quedaron incumplidas.* His promises were unfulfilled.

incurable incurable.

indagar to investigate.

indecente indecent, obscene.

indeciso vacillating, hesitant *Es un hombre muy indeciso.* He's a very hesitant man. ▲ indefinite, not clear *Su oferta es indecisa.* His offer is indefinite.

indefinido indefinite.

indemnización [*f*] indemnity, compensation.

indescriptible indescribable.

indiano, indiana Spaniard who returns to

birthplace after long residence on the American continent.

indicación [*f*] suggestion *Siguió las indicaciones del médico.* He followed the doctor's suggestions. ▲ hint *Una indicación de Ud. es bastante.* A hint from you is enough.

○ **indicaciones** directions *Para usarlo siga Ud. las indicaciones siguientes.* To use this, follow these instructions.

indicado (see **indicar**) indicated. ▲ logical, appropriate *Su madre es la persona más indicada para decírselo.* Her mother is the most logical person to tell it to her.

○ **lo indicado** that which is stated, directed, *or* requested *Haga Ud. lo indicado en el prospecto.* Do what's directed in the prospectus.

indicar to indicate, to hint, to show.

índice [*m*] index; forefinger, index finger.

indicio indication, evidence, clue *No se encontraron indicios del asesino.* They found no clues of the murderer.

indiferente indifferent *Se mostró indiferente a cualquier sugerencia.* He was indifferent to any suggestion.

○ **serle a uno indiferente** to make no difference to one *Eso me es indiferente.* That makes no difference to me.

indigena [*adj*] native, aboriginal ▲ [*n*] native, aborigine.

indigestión [*f*] indigestion.

indignación [*f*] indignation.

indignar to make indignant *Sus palabras la indignaron.* His words made her indignant.

○ **indignarse** to become indignant *Ante aquella injusticia se indignó.* He became indignant in the face of that injustice.

indigno despicable, unworthy.

indio [*adj*; *n*] Indian; Hindu.

indirecta insinuation, hint.

○ **echar indirectas** to make insinuations.

‖ *Suprima Ud. esas indirectas.* Stop insinuating.

indirecto indirect.

indiscreto indiscreet.

indiscutible unquestionable, indisputable.

indispensable essential, indispensable.

indisponer [*irr*] to set against (of persons), prejudice *Su mala lengua nos indispuso.* Her sharp tongue set us against each other.

○ **indisponerse** to fall out (with a person) *Se indispuso con sus compañeros.* He had a falling out with his friends. ▲ to become ill, sick *A*

consecuencia del viaje se indispuso. As a result of the trip she became sick.

indispuesto (see **indisponer**) set against; indisposed, ill.

individual [*adj*] individual, separate.

individuo individual, person, guy *¿Quién es ese individuo?* Who is that guy?

índole [*f*] (inner) nature *Es un hombre de mala índole.* He's an evil man. ▲ class, kind.

indolencia indolence.

inducir [-*zc*-] to induce.

indudable indubitable, certain, evident.

indulgente indulgent, lenient.

indulgencia leniency *La indulgencia de ese profesor es conocida.* The leniency of that teacher is known.

indulto pardon (legal).

industria industry (manufacturing).

industrial [*adj*] industrial. ▲ [*m*] manufacturer.

ineficaz inefficient.

inesperado unexpected.

inestimable invaluable.

inevitable unavoidable, inevitable.

inexplicable inexplicable.

infalible infallible.

infame infamous. ▲ [*m*] scoundrel.

infancia infancy, childhood.

infantería infantry.

infantil infantile, childlike.

infatigable untiring.

infección [*f*] infection.

infeliz unhappy *Su vida fué muy infeliz.* His life was very unhappy. ▲ [*n*] poor devil *Ese es un infeliz.* He's a poor devil.

inferior lower, inferior *En la parte inferior iba el depósito de gasolina.* The gasoline tank was underneath. ▲ [*n*] inferior *Trata a sus inferiores con brutalidad.* He treats his inferiors brutally.

inferioridad [*f*] inferiority.

infernal infernal, terrible.

infidelidad [*f*] infidelity, unfaithfulness.

infiel unfaithful *Fué infiel a sus deberes.* He didn't fulfill his obligations.

infierno hell.

infinidad [*f*] endless number, a lot *Había una infinidad de personas en el parque.* There were a lot of people in the park.

infinito infinite. ▲ [*m*] infinity.

inflamar to set on fire *Una chispa del cigarro inflamó el depósito.* A cigarette spark set the warehouse on fire.

○ **inflamarse** to catch fire *Tenga Ud. cuidado porque se inflama muy fácilmente.* Be careful, it's very inflammable. ▲ to swell *Los bordes de la* *herida se inflamaron.* The edges of the wound swelled.

influir (en) to influence, to have influence (on) *Influye en los que le rodean.* He influences everyone around him.

influyente influential, having pull.

información [*f*] information *Necesito más información sobre este asunto.* I need more information on this matter.

○ **fuente de información** source of information, contact *Este periódico tiene muy buenas fuentes de información.* This newspaper has very good sources of information.

informar to tell, to inform *Necesitaba informar a sus lectores de lo sucedido.* He had to tell his readers what happened.

○ **informarse** to get information, to inform oneself *Pudo informarse leyendo la carta.* He could get the information by reading the letter. ○ **informarse de** to find out, get information on *¿Se ha informado Ud. de lo que necesita para entrar en el país?* Did you find out what you need to enter the country?—*Infórmese Ud. de que clase de persona es.* Find out what kind of a person he is.—*Por el periódico puede Ud. informarse de la marcha de la guerra.* Through the newspaper you can get information on the progress of the war.

informe [*m*] report *Presentó un informe a sus superiores.* He presented a report to his superiors.

○ **informes** data, information.

infortunio great misfortune *La muerte de su padre fué un infortunio para él.* The death of his father was a great misfortune.

ingeniero engineer (holder of a degree in engineering).

ingenio talent *Fué un escritor de mucho ingenio.* He was a writer of great talent. ▲ wit *Esa frase tiene mucho ingenio.* That's a very witty phrase. ▲ wits, ingenuity *Vivía de su ingenio.* He lived by his wits.

○ **ingenio de azúcar** sugar plantation; sugar mill.

ingenuo ingenuous, candid, innocent.

ingrato ungrateful, thankless *Es un trabajo muy ingrato.* It's a thankless job. ▲ [*n*] ingrate.

ingresar (en) to enter, to join *Cuando ingresó en el Ejército tenía viente años.* He was twenty when he joined the Army. ▲ to deposit *Ingresaba cada mes su dinero en la Caja de Ahorros.*

He put his money in a savings bank every month.

ingreso entrance (joining) *Su ingreso en el partido fué muy comentado.* His joining the party caused a lot of comment.

○ **ingresos** earnings, income *Sus ingresos eran escasos.* His earnings were small.

íngrimo alone [*Am*] *Se quedó íngrimo.* He was left all alone.

inicial [*adj; f*] initial *¿Cuáles son sus iniciales?* What are your initials?

iniciar to initiate, begin; to initiate (in societies or religious orders).

iniciativa initiative.

inhábil incompetent, unskillful, clumsy.

injuria insult.

injusticia injustice.

inmediato adjoining, next.

inmenso immense.

inmigrante [*m, f*] immigrant.

inmoral immoral.

inmortal [*adj*] immortal.

inmóvil motionless *El miedo lo dejó inmóvil.* He was motionless with fright.

inmundo filthy, unclean.

innoble ignoble.

inocente innocent; not guilty; guilible, unsophisticated.

inofensivo inoffensive, harmless.

inolvidable unforgettable.

inoportuno inopportune, inconvenient *Era un momento muy inoportuno para tratar el asunto.* That was a very inconvenient time to bring up the subject.

inquietar to worry, to trouble *La falta de noticias le inquietaba.* The lack of news worried him.

○ **inquietarse** to become restless, to become worried *Empezó a inquietarse con aquel ruido.* He began to get restless because of that noise.

inquilino, inquilina tenant.

inquieto restless *Es un niño muy inquieto.* He's a very restless child. ▲ worried *Estoy inquieto por su ausencia.* I'm worried over his absence.

insaciable greedy, insatiable.

insano unhealthy, unsanitary; insane *Un clima insano.* An unhealthy climate.

inscribir to register, enroll *Se inscribieron en la lista de votantes.* They registered for voting.

inscripción [*f*] inscription *La medalla tenía una inscripción.* The medal had an inscription. ▲ registration *El plazo de inscripción acaba a las cuatro.* Registration is over at four o'clock.

insecto insect.

inseguro insecure, unsafe, unsteady.

insensato senseless, stupid, foolish.
insensible heartless, insensitive. ▲ numb *Tenía los dedos insensibles.* His fingers were numb.
inseparable inseparable.
insigne famous, noted, outstanding (of persons).
insignificancia insignificance; trifle *Se preocupa por cualquier insignificancia.* He worries over every trifle.
insignificante insignificant.
insinuación [f] insinuation.
insinuar to insinuate, hint.
insistir to insist *Insistió pero no consiguió nada.* He insisted but he didn't get anything.
○ **insistir en** to insist on *Insistió en salir a la calle.* He insisted on going out into the street.
insolente insolent.
insoportable unbearable.
inspección [f] inspection, examination *Hicieron una inspección en la oficina.* They made an inspection in the office. ▲ inspector's office *Fuí a la Inspección por los documentos.* I went to the inspector's office for the documents.
inspeccionar to inspect, to examine.
inspector, inspectora inspector.
instalar to install, set up *¿Quién le ha instalado la radio?* Who installed your radio?
○ **instalarse** to establish oneself, to take quarters *Apenas llegó a la capital se instaló en un hotel.* As soon as he arrived in the capital he got settled at a hotel.
instancia petition, application (written).
○ **a instancia de** at the request of.
instante [m] instant, moment.
instintivo instinctive.
instinto instinct *Su instinto le decía que iba a ocurrir algo.* His instinct told him that something was going to happen.
institución [f] institution.
instituto institute; school (equivalent to high school plus two years of college).
instrucción [f] education *Creo que tiene poca instrucción.* I don't think he has much education.
○ **instrucciones** instructions, directions *Todavía no ha recibido instrucciones.* He hasn't yet received instructions.
instruir to teach, instruct.
instrumento instrument.
insuficiente insufficient.
insufrible unbearable, intolerable.
insultar to insult.
insurrección [f] insurrection, rebellion.

insurrecto [adj; n] insurgent.
intacto intact, untouched.
integridad [f] integrity; entirety.
íntegro complete, whole *Estaba íntegro el dinero, nadie lo tocó.* The money was all there; nobody touched it. ▲ upright *Es un hombre serio y muy íntegro.* He's a serious and upright man.
intelectual [adj; n] intellectual.
inteligencia intelligence.
inteligente intelligent.
intención [f] intention, purpose *No sé con que intención me lo dijo.* I don't know what his purpose was in telling me that.
○ **tener buenas intenciones** to be well meaning. ○ **tener la intención de** to intend to, mean to *Tenía la intención de decírselo pero se me olvidó.* I meant to tell him that, but I forgot. ○ **tener malas intenciones** to be malicious.
intensidad [f] intensity.
intenso intense.
intentar to attempt, try.
interés [m] interest *Pone mucho interés en todo lo que hace.* He takes a lot of interest in everything he does. ▲ rate of interest *Tenía que pagar mucho interés.* I had to pay a high interest.
○ **intereses** affairs *Administraba los intereses de su amigo.* He administered his friend's affairs. ○ **por (el) interés** for money *Se casó por (el) interés.* He married for money.
interesado (see **interesar**) interested; mercenary.
interesar to interest *Su conversación me interesaba.* His conversation interested me.
○ **interesarse** to be interested *Llegó a interesarse en las matemáticas.* He became interested in mathematics.
interior [adj] interior, inside *Esas habitaciones son interiores.* Those are inside rooms. ▲ domestic *El correo interior se distribuía cuatro veces por día.* Domestic mail was delivered four times a day. ▲ [m] inside *El interior de la casa es muy fresco.* The inside of the house's very cool.
○ **para el interior de uno** to oneself *Lo dijo para su interior.* He said it to himself.
interjección [f] interjection.
intermedio intermediate, medium *Quisier una talla intermedia.* I'd like an intermediate size. ▲ [m] intermission *Le veré en el intermedio.* I'll see him during the intermission.
○ **por intermedio de** through (the intervention of) *Lo consiguió por inter-*

medio de su tío. He got it through his uncle.

interminable endless.

internacional [*adj*] international.

interno internal *Esto es para uso interno.* This is for internal use. ▲ boarding *Es un alumno interno.* He's a boarding pupil.

interponer [*irr*] to interpose, place (between) *Interpusieron un tabique entre las dos partes de la habitación.* They placed a partition between the two parts of the room.
  ○ **interponerse** to block *Esa mujer se interpuso en mi camino.* That woman blocked my way.

interpretar to interpret *Procure Ud. interpretar bien mis palabras.* Try to interpret my words properly.

intérprete [*m, f*] interpreter.

interrogación [*f*] interrogation; question mark.

interrogar to question, interrogate.

interrogatorio interrogation, questioning.

interrumpir to interrupt *Por favor, no me interrumpa.* Please don't interrupt me.
  ○ **interrumpirse** to be interrupted, to be blocked *El tráfico se interrumpió por la aglomeración de automóviles.* The traffic was blocked by the jam of automobiles.

intervalo interval.

intervención [*f*] intervention *Su intervención fué muy oportuna.* He intervened at a very opportune moment. ▲ mediation *El sindicato ha pedido la intervención del Estado en la cuestión.* The union has asked for the mediation of the government in the dispute. ▲ (surgical) operation *Después de la caída hubo que hacerle una rápida intervención.* He had to undergo an operation immediately after his fall.

intervenir [*irr*] to intervene *Para evitar el conflicto tuvo que intervenir.* He had to intervene to prevent the conflict. ▲ to audit, check *Se le intervino la cuenta en el Banco.* His bank account was audited.

intestino [*adj; m*] intestine.

intimar to become an intimate friend.

intimidar to frighten, intimidate.

íntimo [*adj*] intimate. ▲ [*n*] intimate (friend).

intolerable intolerable.

intoxicar to poison; to drug.

intranquilo restless, worried.

intratable unsociable.

intrépido brave, fearless.

intrigar to scheme *¿Cuándo terminará Ud. de intrigar?* When will you stop

scheming? ▲ to intrigue, interest *Aquello intrigó a todos.* That intrigued everybody.
  ○ **intrigarse** to be intrigued *Me intriga lo que Ud. dice.* I'm intrigued by what you say.

introducir [-*zc*-] to put (in), insert *Introdujo la llave en la cerradura.* He put the key in the keyhole. ▲ to present (a person) *Era el encargado de introducir los embajadores ante el rey.* He was the one in charge of presenting the ambassadors to the king.

intuición [*f*] intuition.

inundación [*f*] flood.

inundar to flood *El agua inundó la calles.* The water flooded the streets.
  ○ **inundarse** to be flooded *Se inundó el piso bajo.* The ground floor was flooded.

inútil useless. ▲ [*n*] useless person.

invadir to invade.

invariable constant, unchanging.

invasión [*f*] invasion.

invencible invincible, unconquerable.

inventar to invent; to lie, fib.

inventario inventory.

invento invention; lie.

invernal wintry.

inverosímil unlikely, improbable.

invertido See **invertir**. ▲ [*adj; n*] homosexual.

invertir [*rad-ch II*] to invest *Invirtió su dinero en una casa.* He invested his money in a house. ▲ to reverse, turn upside down *No invierta Ud. el orden de esas cantidades.* Don't reverse the order of those amounts. ▲ to spend (time) *Invirtió dos horas en recorrer veinte millas.* He spent two hours traveling twenty miles.

investigación [*f*] investigation, inquiry; research.

investigar to investigate *Investigue Ud. cuál es la causa.* Investigate the cause of it. ▲ to do research work *Investigaba en un laboratorio.* He was doing research work in a laboratory.

invierno winter.

invisible invisible.

invitación [*f*] invitation.

invitado See **invitar**. ▲ [*n*] guest *Estaban recibiendo a los invitados.* They were receiving their guests.

invitar to invite.

involuntario involuntary.

inyección [*f*] injection, shot.

inyectado bloodshot *Tenía los ojos inyectados.* His eyes were bloodshot.

inyectar to inject, give an injection *Le*

inyectó una dosis de morfina. He gave him an injection of morphine.

ir [*irr*] to go. ▲ to lead *¿A dónde va ese camino?* Where does that road lead?

○ **ir a caballo** to ride on horseback *Fuimos a caballo a la hacienda.* We rode to the ranch on horseback. ○ **ir a pie** to walk, go on foot *Si vamos a pie tardaremos mucho.* If we walk we'll be very late. ○ **ir del brazo** to walk arm in arm *Iban del brazo.* They were walking arm in arm. ○ **ir de paseo** to go for a walk *¿Va Ud. de paseo?* Are you going for a walk? ○ **ir en auto** to drive *Yendo en auto llegaremos en tres horas.* We'll arrive in three hours if we drive. ○ **irle a uno (bien)** to be becoming *Ese color le va muy bien.* That color is very becoming to you. ○ **ir para** (*or* **con**) to be meant for (of remarks) *Lo que he dicho no va con Ud.* What I've said isn't meant for you. ○ **irse** to leave, to go away *Ya se fueron.* They've already left.

‖ *Ahora va de veras.* Now it's the real thing. ‖ *¿Cómo le va?* How are you?

ira anger.

ironía irony, sarcasm.

irónico ironical, sarcastic.

irregular irregular, improper *Su conducta es bastante irregular.* His conduct is quite irregular. ▲ irregular, uneven *Tiene unas facciones muy irregulares.* He has very irregular features.

irremediable irreparable, hopeless.

irresoluto irresolute, wavering, hesitant.

irritable irritable.

irritación [*f*] irritation *Tiene irritación en la garganta.* He has an irritation in his throat. ▲ irritation, peevishness *Su irritación molestó a todos.* His peevishness annoyed everyone.

irritar to irritate; to peeve.

isla island, isle.

isleño, isleña islander.

itinerario itinerary.

izquierda left hand *Escribía con la izquierda.* He wrote with his left hand. ▲ left *En política, militaba en la izquierda.* In politics, he belonged to the left.

○ **a la izquierda** on the left, to the left *Estaba sentado a mi izquierda.* He was sitting on my left.

izquierdo [*adj*] left *Recibió un balazo en el pie izquierdo.* He got a bullet wound in his left foot.

J

jaba crate [*Am*].

jabón [*m*] soap *¿Puede darme un jabón y una toalla?* Can you give me a piece of soap and a towel?

jalar (see **halar**) to pull, haul [*Am*].

jalea jelly *Deseo café, tostadas y jalea.* I want coffee, toast, and jelly.

jamás never, not ever.

jamón [*m*] ham (cured pork).

jamona buxom woman (middle-aged) [*Sp*]; old maid [*Antilles*].

jaqueca headache, megrim *Estoy con jaqueca desde ayer.* I've had a headache since yesterday.

jarabe [*m*] syrup; jarabe (a Mexican dance).

jardín [*m*] garden (of flowers).

jaripeo bronco-busting, rodeo [*Mex*].

jarra pitcher *Hágame el favor de poner una jarra con agua en mi cuarto.* Please put a pitcher of water in my room.

jaula cage.

jefatura headquarters, chief's office *Los* *llevaron a la jefatura de Policía.* They took them to Police Headquarters.

jefe [*m*] chief, leader, head *Lograron capturar al jefe.* They managed to capture the leader. ▲ boss *Tendré que avisar a mi jefe que no vendré mañana.* I'll have to tell my boss that I won't be in tomorrow.

jerga slang.

jícara small cup.

jinete [*m*] horseman.

jitomate [*m*] tomato [*Mex*].

jornada journey; day's work; day's walk.

jornalero day laborer, casual worker.

jota letter "j"; Aragonese folk dance.

joven [*adj*] young. ▲ [*n*] young person.

joya gem; piece of jewelry.

judía bean [*Sp*].

○ **judías verdes** string beans.

judío Jewish. ▲ [*n*] Jew.

judía bean [*Sp*]. ○ **judías verdes** string

juego game *El ajedrez es un juego muy difícil.* Chess is a very difficult game. ▲ set *Compré un juego de manteles.* I bought a set of table linen. ▲ play, playing *La hora de juego en isa escuela es de la una a las dos.* The hour for play in that school is from one to two. ▲ gambling *Es un hombre aficionado al juego.* He's a man fond of gambling. ○ **hacer juego** to match *Ese sombrero hace juego con el traje.* That hat matches the suit. ○ **juego de palabras** pun, play on words. ○ **no ser cosa de juego** not to be a laughing matter.

jueves [m] Thursday.

juez [m] judge.

jugador [m] gambler; player, contestant.

jugar [rad-ch I] to play *¿Sabe Ud. jugar tenis?* Do you play tennis? ▲ to play, gamble *Jugó y perdió.* He played and lost.

jugo juice. ○ **sacar jugo de** to get a lot out of *Saca jugo de todo lo que hace.* He gets a lot out of everything he does.

juguete [m] toy.

juicio judgment *Esta chica tiene muy buen juicio.* This girl has very good judgment. ▲ trial (law).

julepe [m] card game; [Am] dread, fear. ○ **tener julepe** to be scared stiff [Am].

julio July.

juma drinking spree.

junio June.

junta meeting; board *La Junta de Reclutamiento.* Draft Board. ▲ joint, joining (carpentry).

juntar to join, connect *Juntaron los dos cordones eléctricos.* They connected the two electric wires. ▲ to pool *Junta-* mos todo el dinero.* Let's pool all our money. ○ **juntarse** to meet, gather *Nos juntamos a la puerta de casa.* We met at the door of my house. ○ **juntarse con** to associate with.

junto together *¿Quiere Ud. que vayamos juntos al teatro?* Let's go to the theater together. ○ **junto a** next to, beside *Se sentó junto a ella.* He sat down next to her. ○ **junto con** with *Llegó junto conmigo.* He arrived with me.

jurado jury.

juramento oath (law); oath, swearing.

jurar to swear (oath); to swear, curse.

justicia justice (fairness); administration of justice; the law.

justo [adj] right, just *Creo que la decisión es justa.* I believe that the decision is just. ▲ exact, on the dot *La corrida empezó a la hora justa.* The bullfight began on the dot. ▲ [n] good person *Siempre pagan justos por pecadores.* The good always pay for the wicked. ○ **estar justo** to fit tightly *Este anillo me está muy justo.* This ring is too tight for me. ▲ to be correct *Esta cuenta está justa.* This account is correct.

juvenil juvenile.

juventud [f] youth, youthfulness.

juzgar to judge *No me gusta juzgar los actos ajenos.* I don't like to judge the acts of others. ▲ to try *Juzgarán a los reos inmediatamente.* They'll try the criminals immediately.

K

kilo kilogram.

kilogramo kilogram.

kilométrico mileage ticket, book (railroad mileage purchased in quantity at cut rate) [Sp].

kilómetro kilometer.

kiosco pavilion; newsstand; bandstand.

L

la; pl **las** the. ▲ her, it; [pl] them *¿Dónde la encontró Ud.?* Where did you meet her?

labio lip.

labor [f] work, task.

labrador [m] farmer.

labrar to plow, farm.

lado side *Se sentó a mi lado.* He sat by my side. ▲ edge, margin *Escribió una nota en el lado de la página.* He made a note in the margin. ○ **al lado (de)** near(by), next door to *El restaurante está al lado del teatro.* The restaurant is next door to the theater. ○ **al lado derecho, al lado izquierdo** on (or to) the right side, on (or to) the left side *La casa estaba al lado derecho del camino.* The house was on the right side of the road. ○ a un **lado** aside *¿Quiere hacerse a un lado?* Would you step aside? ○ **de lado** sideways, on its side *Hay que poner el piano de lado para que entre.* We have to put the piano on its side in order to get it in. ○ **lado a lado** side by side *Trabajaron lado a lado.* They worked side by side. ○ **lado flaco** weak side, weak spot *Conozco muy bien su lado flaco.* I know his weakness very well. ○ **mirar de lado** to look out of the corner of the eye, look askance *Aquella mujer me miró de lado.* That woman looked askance at me. ○ **por el lado** around, in the general direction of *Estan por el lado del río.* They're around the river. ○ **por todos lados** on all sides *El edificio tiene salidas por todos lados.* The building has exits on all sides. ○ **por un lado ... por otro** on the one side *or* hand ... on the other; in a way ... in a way *Por un lado me gusta, pero por otro no.* In a way I like it, in a way I don't.

ladrar to bark.

ladrillo brick.

ladrón, ladrone thief, robber.

lagarto lizard [*Sp*]; alligator [*Am*].

lago lake.

lágrima tear *Nɔ derramó ni una lágrima.* He didn'ᵗ shed a tear.

lamentable lamentable, pitiful, sorry *Estaba en un estado lamentable.* She was in a pitiful state.

lamentar to be sorry *Lamento que Ud. no pueda acompañarnos.* I'm sorry you can't join us.

○ **lamentarse** to lament, wail, moan *Se lamentaba por la muerte de su perro.* She moaned over the death of her dog.

lamento moan.

lamer to lick, lap.

lámina sheet, plate *Hoy hay muchos objetos hechos con lámina de metal.* Today there are many things made of sheet metal. ▲ plate (illustration) *¿Tiene láminas de colores ese libro?* Does that book have colored plates?

lámpara lamp, bulb; radio tube.

lana wool.

lancha (small) boat *Alquilemos una lancha de remos.* Let's hire a row boat.

lanchón [*m*] barge.

langosta lobster; locust (insect).

lanzar to throw, hurl, fling *Lanzó la pelota.* He threw the ball.

○ **lanzarse (a)** to throw oneself, rush to *Se lanzó al agua.* He threw himself into the water.

lápida memorial tablet, plaque; headstone.

lápiz [*m*] pencil.

larga ○ **a la larga** in the long run, eventually *A la larga se convencerá Ud.* Eventually you'll be convinced. ○ **dar largas** to put off. ▲ to give one the run-around *Siempre me está dando largas.* He's always giving me the run-around.

largar to let loose, loosen [*Am*] *Ya van a largar los caballos.* They're going to let the horses loose now.

○ **largarse** to scram, beat it *¡Lárguese de aquí!* Scram!

largo long *Recibí una larga carta de mis padres.* I got a long letter from my folks. ▲ [*m*] length *¿Cuál es el largo de ese trozo de tela?* What is the length of this piece of cloth?

○ **a lo largo** at full length *Se tumbó a lo largo sobre el sofá.* He stretched out full length on the couch. ○ **a lo largo de** along *Hay un bosque a lo largo del río.* There's a forest along the river. ○ **de largo** long *Este terreno tiene doscientos metros de largo.* This piece of ground is two hundred meters long. ○ **largos años** many years *Vivió en Nueva York largos años.* He lived in New York (for) many years. ▲ long life *Vivió largos años.* He lived to a ripe old age. ○ **pasar de largo** to pass right by *Pasó de largo sin mirarme.* He passed right by without looking at me. ○ **traje largo** evening dress *Las damas estaban de traje largo.* The ladies were in evening dress.

‖ *¡Largo de aquí!* Get out of here!

las See **la.**

lástima pity *¡Es látima que Ud. no haya venido anoche!* It's a pity you didn't come last night.—*¡Qué lástima!* What a pity!

○ **dar lástima** to inspire pity, be pitiful *Su estado daba lástima.* His condition was pitiful.

lastimadura sore, superficial wound.

lastimar to hurt *Estos zapatos me lastiman.* These shoes hurt me.—*Me dijo una cosa que me lastimó.* He told me something that hurt me. ▲ to injure, hurt *El golpe no le lastimó.* The blow didn't hurt him.

○ **lastimarse** to hurt oneself *Se lastimó al caer.* He hurt himself when he fell.

lata tin (plate) *Esta caja está hecha de lata.* This box is made of tin. ▲ can *Quisier dos latas de tomate.* I'd like two cans of tomatoes. ▲ annoyance, nuisance *El ruido era una lata.* The noise was a nuisance.

○ **dar la lata** to annoy, bother, pester *Nos daba la lata con sus quejas.* He annoyed us with his complaints.

latido beat, beating, throb.

látigo whip, lash.

latín [*m*] Latin (language).

latino [*adj; n*] Latin.

latir to beat, throb *El corazón le latía rápidamente.* His heart was beating rapidly.

latón [*m*] brass.

laucha mouse [*Am*].

laurel [*m*] laurel.

lavabo washstand; washroom.

lavadero washtub.

lavamanos [*m sg*] washbowl, lavatory [*Am*].

lavandera laundress.

lavandería laundry [*Am*].

lavar to wash *Tenemos que lavar la ropa.* We have to wash the clothes.

lavatorio lavatory, wash basin [*Am*].

laxante [*adj; m*] laxative.

lazareto hospital for contagious diseases; quarantine (of ports of entry).

lazo bow, loop *¿Puede Ud. hacer un lazo?* Can you tie a bow? ▲ lasso, lariat.

○ **echar el lazo** to lasso.

le [*obj pron*] him, to him, to her, to you, to it; [*pl*] them, to them, to you.

leal loyal.

lección [*f*] lesson.

leche [*f*] milk.

lechería dairy store (place where only milk is sold).

lecho bed, couch.

lechuga lettuce.

lector [*m*] reader, one who reads.

lectura reading *¿Qué clase de lectura le gusta a Ud.?* What kind of reading do you like?

leer to read *¿Ha leído Ud. el diario de esta mañana?* Have you read this morning's paper?

legación [*f*] legation.

legal legal, lawful.

legible legible, readable.

legítimo lawful, legitimate.

legua league (measure of length).

legumbre [*f*] vegetable.

lejano distant, far.

lejos far *¿Es muy lejos de aquí?* Is it very far from here? ▲ far away *Están muy lejos.* They are very far away.

○ **a lo lejos** in the distance *A lo lejos vimos unas casas.* We saw some houses in the distance. ○ **desde lejos** from a distance *Desde lejos le reconocimos.* We recognized him from a distance. ○ **lejos de** far from *Vive demasiado lejos de la ciudad.* He lives too far from the city.—*Lejos de enmendarse está cada día peor.* Far from getting better he gets worse every day.

lengua tongue *Me mordí la lengua.* I bit my tongue. ▲ language, tongue *En Centro y Sur América se habla la la lengua castellana.* Spanish is spoken in Central and South America.

○ **írsele a uno la lengua** to let something out (by talking); to give oneself away *Se le va la lengua muy fácilmente.* He gives himself away very easily. ○ **morderse la lengua** to hold *or* control one's tongue. ○ **no morderse la lengua** not to mince words, speak straight from the shoulder.

lenguado sole, flounder.

lenguaje [*m*] language, speech.

lente [*m or f*] lens (optical).

○ **lente (de aumento)** magnifying glass *Estas letras tan pequeñas se pueden leer solamente con una lente.* These small letters can only be read with a magnifying glass. ○ **lentes** [*m pl*] eyeglasses *Deseo comprar unos lentes oscuros.* I want to buy some dark glasses.

lentitud [*f*] slowness.

lento slow.

leña firewood.

león [*m*] lion.

les See **le.**

letra letter (of alphabet). ▲ handwriting *Mi hermana tiene muy buena letra.* My sister has a very good handwriting. ▲ words (of a song) *¿Sabe Ud. la letra de esa canción?* Do you know the words of that song?

○ **cuatro letras** a few lines *Le he escrito cuatro letras.* I wrote him a few lines. ○ **letra (de cambio)** draft *¿Dónde puedo cobrar esta letra (de cambio)?* Where can I cash this draft? ○ **letra (de imprenta)** type *¿Qué estilo de letra (de imprenta) es esa?* What style of type is that?

letrero sign *¿Quí dice este letrero?* What does this sign say?

levantar to raise *Si Ud. quiere hablar levante la mano.* If you want to speak, raise your hand.—*Empezó a levantar la voz.* He began to raise his voice. ▲ to lift *No puedo levantar esto, pesa* *demasiado.* I can't lift this, it's too heavy. ▲ to pick up *Levanta ese papel del suelo.* Pick up that paper there on the floor. ▲ to rise up *El pueblo se levantó contra los invasores.* The people rose up against the invaders. ▲ to build *Están levantando muchas casas nuevas en esa calle.* They are building many new houses on that street.

O **levantar cabeza** to get on one's feet *Después de la bancarrota no pudo levantar cabeza.* After his bankruptcy, he wasn't able to get back on his feet. O **levantar planos** to draw up plans *Los ingenieros levantaron un plano para un nuevo muelle.* The engineers drew up plans for a new dock. O **levantarse** to get up *Yo me levanto temprano.* I get up early.

ley [*f*] law.

leyenda legend.

libelo libel.

liberación [*f*] liberation.

liberal [*adj; m*] liberal.

liberar to free, liberate.

libertad [*f*] liberty, freedom *Los pueblos luchan por su libertad.* Nations are fighting for freedom.

O **dejar en libertad** to free *Dejaron en libertad a los presos.* They freed the prisoners.

libertador [*m*] liberator.

libertar to free.

libra pound (weight).

O **libra (esterlina)** pound (sterling).

libranza O **libranza postal** money order [*Am*].

librar to free, deliver *Los actos del gobernador libraron al pueblo de la miseria.* The acts of the governor delivered the people from their misery.

O **librar (una letra) contra** to draw (a draft) on. O **librarse de** to get rid of *Al fin nos libramos de él.* At last we got rid of him. ▲ to avoid, get out of *Quiso librarse de pagar los impuestos.* He wanted to get out of paying his taxes.

libre free *Abrió la jaula para dejar libre al pájaro.* He opened the cage to set the bird free.—*Esta mercadería está libre de impuestos.* This merchandise is tax free.—*Es muy libre para hablar.* He's very free-spoken.—*La entrada es libre.* Admission (is) free. ▲ free, unencumbered, disengaged, off *¿Tiene Ud. libre el sábado?* Do you have Saturday off? ▲ dissolute, loose *Es una mujer (de vida) libre.* She's a loose woman.

librería bookshop.

libreta O **libreta de banco** bankbook, pass book. O **libreta de direcciones** address book *Ya he apuntado su dirección en mi libreta.* I have already put your address in my book.

libro book.

O **libro de apuntes** notebook. O **libro de caja** cashbook. O **libro de cuentas** account book.

licencia license, permit *¿Tiene Ud. licencia para vender licor?* Do you have a license to sell liquor? ▲ furlough *El cabo está con licencia.* The corporal is on furlough.

O **licencia absoluta** discharge *Le dieron licencia absoluta del ejército.* He got his discharge from the army.

licenciado See **licenciar.** O **licenciado del ejército** veteran. O **licenciado de presidio** discharged convict. O **licenciado en filosofía** Master of Arts.

licenciar to discharge (from army or prison).

O **licenciarse** to get a master's degree.

licor [*m*] liqueur, cordial.

liga garter *Estas ligas son de buen elástico.* These garters are made of good elastic.

ligar to tie, bind *Le ligaron las manos a la espalda.* They tied his hands behind his back. ▲ to join, to connect *Ligaron los dos alambres.* They connected the two wires.

O **ligarse** to join, band together *Se ligaron contra el peligro común.* They joined together against the common danger.

ligero light, thin *Quiero un abrigo ligero de primavera.* I want a light spring coat. ▲ fast *¡No vaya tan ligero!* Don't go so fast! ▲ light *Comeré algo ligero.* I'll eat something light.—*La comedia que vimos era muy ligera.* We saw a very light comedy. ▲ unimportant, trifling *Su contribución era muy ligera.* His contribution was unimportant.

O **a la ligera** quickly, superficially *Lo hice a la ligera.* I did it quickly. O **una mujer ligera de cascos** featherbrained woman.

lima lime (fruit); file (tool).

limitar to restrict, to limit *Quieren limitar el número de boletos.* They want to limit the number of tickets.

O **limitar con** to be bounded by *México limita al norte con los Estados*

Unidos. Mexico is bounded on the north by the United States.

límite [*m*] limit, boundary.

limón [*m*] lemon.

limonada lemonade.

limonar [*m*] lemon grove.

limonero lemon tree.

limosna alms.

limpiabotas [*m sg*] bootblack.

limpiar to clean *¿Cuánto cuesta limpiar un traje de lana?* How much do you charge for cleaning a woolen dress? ▲ to clean out (of money) *Lo limpiaron (de dinero).* They cleaned him out.

○ **limpiarse** to clean, wash (one's face, hands, etc); to brush (one's teeth) *Tengo que limpiarme las manos y los dientes.* I have to wash my hands and brush my teeth.

limpieza cleanliness.

limpio clean *Estos cristales no están limpios.* These windows aren't clean. ▲ clear *El cielo está limpio hoy.* The sky's clear today. ▲ free *Está limpio de culpa.* He's free from guilt.

○ **poner en limpio** to make a final copy *Ponga Ud. la carta en limpio.* Make a final copy of the letter. ○ **sacar en limpio** to make head or tail of, to understand *No he podido sacar nada en limpio de ese discurso.* I couldn't make head or tail of that speech.

lindo lovely *Viven en una linda casa.* They live in a lovely house.—*¡Qué lindo!* How lovely! ▲ pretty *¡Qué linda mujer!* What a pretty woman! ▲ fine *Ha hecho un lindo trabajo.* He's done a fine job.

○ **de lo lindo** very much *Gozamos de lo lindo en la fiesta.* We enjoyed the party very much.

línea line *Trace Ud. una línea aquí.* Draw a line here. ▲ lines, figure *La muchacha no quiere perder la línea.* The girl doesn't want to lose her figure.

○ **descendiente en línea directa** (*or* **recta**) direct descendant, lineal descendant. ○ **en línea** in a row *Los árboles estaban en línea.* The trees were in a row. ○ **entre líneas** between the lines *Sabe leer entre líneas.* He knows how to read between the lines. ○ **línea férrea** railway line.

lino linen (material).

linterna lantern; [*Sp*] flashlight.

lío bundle *Llevaba un lío de ropa.* He carried a bundle of clothes. ▲ jam, trouble *No quiero meterme en un lío.* I don't want to get into a jam. ▲ mess *¡Qué lío!* What a mess!

liquidación [*f*] bargain sale, selling out

En aquel comercio hay una liquidación. There is a bargain sale at that store.

liquidar to pay, pay up *Liquida sus cuentas todos los meses.* He pays his bills every month. ▲ to squander *Liquidó la fortuna de su padre.* He squandered his father's fortune. ▲ to sell out *Este almacén está liquidando.* This store is selling out.

líquido [*adj*] exactly, just *Me quedan tres pesos líquidos.* I have just three dollars left. ▲ [*m*] liquid *Sólo toma líquidos.* He can only take liquids. ▲ net (balance) *Hecho el inventario, quedó un líquido de trescientos pesos.* After inventory, there was a net balance of three hundred pesos.

lirio lily.

liso smooth *Quiero un papel liso.* I want a smooth piece of paper. ▲ straight *Tiene el pelo liso.* She has straight hair. ▲ plain *Prefiero las telas lisas.* I prefer plain materials. ▲ slippery *El suelo está muy liso.* The floor is very slippery.

lista [*f*] list *¿Esta su nombre en la lista?* Is your name on the list? ▲ stripe *Lleva un traje a listas.* She is wearing a striped dress.

○ **lista (de teléfonos)** (telephone) directory.

listo ready *Todo estaba listo para el viaje.* Everything was ready for the trip. ▲ clever *Es muy lista.* She's very clever.

literal literal.

literatura literature.

litro liter.

liviano light (not heavy) [*Am*]; free and easy (of women) [*Sp*].

lívido livid.

llaga open sore.

llama flame; llama.

llamada call *¿Ha habido algunas llamadas pari mí?* Have there been any calls for me?

llamar to call *Haga Ud. el favor de llamar un taxi.* Please call a taxi. ▲ to knock *Llame Ud. antes de entrar.* Knock before entering. ▲ to ring (a bell) *Abra Ud. la puerta están llamando (el timbre).* Open the door, they are ringing (the bell).

○ **llamar a** call upon, summon *El gobierno le llama a defender la patria.* The government calls upon him to defend his country. ○ **llamar la atención** to warn, scold *Los niños pisaron el césped y el guarda les llamó la atención.* The children trampled on the grass and the guard scolded them. ▲ to call *or* attract attention *Quiso llamar la atención sobre sí mismo todo el tiempo.* He always wanted to call attention to himself. ○ **llamar por teléfono** to phone, to telephone *La han llamado a Ud. por teléfono varias veces.* They've phoned you several times. ○ **llamarse** to be called *or* named *"¿Cómo se llama su amigo?" "Se llama Jorge."* "What's your friend's name?" "His name's George."—*¿Cómo se llama esto?* What's the name of this?

llanero cowboy, plainsman [*Ven, Col*].

llano level, even *La casa está en la parte más llana del terreno.* The house is on the most level part of the ground. ▲ simple, plain *Dígalo en lenguaje llano.* Say it in plain terms. ▲ frank, unaffected *Es un tipo llano y sincero.* He is a frank and sincere fellow.

llanta tire *Llevamos dos llantas de repuesta.* We are taking two spare tires.

llanura plain *La ciudad está en una llanura.* The city is on a plain.

llave key *Olvidé la llave de mi cuarto.* I forgot the key to my room. ▲ jet (gas stove) *Dejaron abierta la llave del gas.* They left the gas jet on. ▲ switch *¿Dónde está la llave de la luz?* Where's the light switch? ▲ faucet, tap *Cierre Ud. la llave del baño.* Turn off the faucet in the bath tub.

○ **echar (la) llave** to lock the door *Debemos echar llave al salir.* We should lock the door when we leave. ○ **llave inglesa** monkey wrench.

llavero key ring.

llegada arrival.

llegar to arrive *Cuándo llegaremos a la Habana?* When will we arrive in Havana? ▲ to come *Lo haré cuando llegue mi turno.* I'll do it when my turn comes. ▲ to reach *El traje le llegaba hasta los pies.* The dress reached to her feet. ▲ to extend, go as far as *Este camino llega hasta Bogotá.* This road goes as far as Bogotá. ▲ to amount *El gasto llegó a doce pesos.* The cost amounted to twelve pesos.

○ **llegar a** to succeed in *No llegó a oír lo que decíamos.* He didn't succeed in hearing what we were saying. ○ **llegar a ser** to get to be *Era muy joven cuando llegó a ser coronel.* He was very young when he became a colonel. ○ **llegar a suceder** to come to pass, happen *Si eso llega a suceder me alegraré mucho.* If that happens I'll be very glad.

llenar to fill (up) *Llenó la copa de vino.* He filled the glass with wine. ▲ to cover

Se llenaron las manos de pintura. They covered their hands with paint. ▲ to satisfy, please fully *No me llena ese espectáculo.* That show doesn't please me fully. ▲ to fill out *Llene Ud. el pliego de solicitud.* Fill out the application.

lleno full *La piscina está llena de agua limpia.* The pool is full of clean water. —*Esta noche habrá luna llena.* There will be a full moon tonight. ▲ [*m*] full house *En el teatro hubo un lleno.* The theater had a full house.

○ **de lleno** fully *Su libro trataba el asunto de lleno.* His book treated the subject fully. ▲ squarely *El golpe le dió de lleno en la cara.* The blow hit him squarely in the face. ○ **lleno de** covered with *¡Todo está lleno de polvo!* Everything is covered with dust. ○ **lleno de bote en bote** full, full to the brim *La sala estaba llena de bote en bote.* The room was full of people.

llevar to take, carry *Llevaron al enfermo al hospital.* They took the patient to the hospital. ▲ to have (with or on one), carry *¿Lleva Ud. los boletos?* Have you the tickets? ▲ to wear *Llevaré un traje blanco.* I'll wear a white dress. ▲ to be (for a certain time) *Llevo mucho tiempo esperando.* I have been waiting for a long time. —*¿Cuánto tiempo lleva Ud. en los Estados Unidos?* How long have you been in the United States? ▲ to take, guide, lead *Nos llevaron por un lugar peligroso.* They took us through a dangerous place. ▲ to charge *¿Cuánto me llevará Ud. por el traje?* How much will you charge me for the suit? ▲ to lead *¿A dónde lleva este camino?* Where does this road lead? ▲ to conduct *Lleva muy bien sus negocios.* He conducts his business very well.

○ **llevar a cabo** to carry through, accomplish *Llevó a cabo su misión diplomática con éxito.* He carried through his diplomatic mission with success. ○ **llevar la contra** to oppose, contradict *Le gusta llevar la contra.* He likes to contradict. ▲ to antagonize. ○ **llevar la delantera** to be ahead *Nos llevan la delantera.* They're ahead of us. ○ **llevar (mala) vida** to lead a (bad) life *Lleva una vida desordenada.* He leads a disorderly life. ○ **llevarse** to carry off *or* away, take, steal *Los ladrones se llevaron las joyas.* The thieves carried off the jewels. ○ **llevarse bien** to get along well *Se lleva muy bien con sus amigos.* He gets

along very well with his friends.
○ **llevarse (el premio)** to win, carry off (the prize) *Se llevó el premio grande.* He won the first prize.
○ **llevarse un chasco** to be disappointed, get it in the neck *¡Qué chasco me he llevado!* I certainly got it in the neck!
llorar to˙ weep, cry.
llover [*rad-ch I*] to rain *Está lloviendo mucho.* It's raining very hard.
○ **como llovido del cielo** like manna from heaven *Llegó el dinero como llovido del cielo.* The money came like manna from heaven. ○ **llover a cántaros** to pour (rain) *Espere un momento, llueve a cántaros.* Wait a while, it's pouring.
lloviznar to drizzle.
lluvia rain.
lluvioso rainy.
lo [*neut art*] the *Es lo mejor que tenemos.* It's the best we have.▲ [*obj pron; pl* **los**] him, it; *pl* them *Mándemelo.* Send him to me.—*Mándemelos.* Send them to me.
loba female wolf.
lobo wolf.
local [*adj*] local *Este es uno de los mejores periódicos locales.* This is one of the best local newspapers. ▲ [*m*] place (indoors) *No me gusta este local.* I don't like this place.
localidad [*f*] locality, place *¿Qué localidad es esta?* What place is this? ▲ seat (in a theater) *¿Quédan buenas localidades para esta noche?* Are there any good seats left for tonight?
localizar to locate. ▲ to find out *Primero, tenemos que localizer donde viven.* First we have to find out where they live. ▲ to localize *Los bomberos localizaron el fuego.* The firemen localized the fire.
loco insane, crazy *¡No seas loco!* Don't be crazy! ▲ [*n*] madman, lunatic *Es un loco.* He's a lunatic.
locomotora locomotive.
locura insanity, madness *Su locura era hereditaria.* His insanity was hereditary. ▲ folly *Esas son locuras de la juventud.* Those are the follies of youth.
lodo mud.
lógica logic.
lógico logical, reasonable.
lograr to get, obtain *Lograba todo lo que quería.* He got all he wanted. ▲ to succeed in *No logramos convencerle.* We didn't succeed in convincing him.
lomo loin *¿Le gusta el lomo de cerdo?* Do you like loin of pork?

lona canvas.
longitud [*f*] length; longitude.
loquero attendant in an insane asylum.
loro parrot.
los See **le, el, lo.**
lotería lottery.
loza crockery.
lucero any bright star.
lucha struggle, fight *La lucha por la existencia.* The struggle for existence.
luchador [*m*] fighter; wrestler.
luchar to fight, struggle *Los dos hombres lucharon largo rato.* The two men fought for a long time. ▲ to wrestle.
lucir [*-zc-*] to shine, glitter, sparkle *Las joyas lucían en sus dedos.* The jewels glittered on her fingers. ▲ to wear, show off *Se empeñó en lucir su traje nuevo.* She insisted on wearing her new dress. ▲ to look, appear *Luce Ud. muy bien hoy.* You look very well today.
○ **lucirse** to do splendidly *Se lució en el examen.* He did splendidly in the examination. ▲ to show off *Le gusta mucho lucirse.* He likes to show off.
luego immediately, right away *Vengo luego.* I'm coming right away. ▲ afterwards *¿Qué haremos luego?* What shall we do afterwards? ▲ next *¿Qué pasó luego?* What happened next? ▲ then *Cenaremos juntos y luego iremos al teatro.* We'll dine together and then go to the theater. ▲ later *Luego lo haré.* I'll do it later.
○ **desde luego** naturally, of course *¡Desde luego lo haré!* Of course I'll do it! ○ **luego, luego** right away [*Mex*]. ○ **tan luego** as soon as [*Am*] *Tan luego como llegue se lo diré.* As soon as he arrives I'll tell him.
‖ *¡Hasta luego!* So long!
lugar [*m*] place *Nos encontraremos en el lugar acostumbrado.* We'll meet at the usual place. ▲ place, city, town *¿De qué lugar es Ud.?* Where are you from? ▲ room, space *No hay lugar donde sentarnos.* There's no room for us to sit down. ▲ position, office *Tiene un buen lugar en el banco.* He has a good position in the bank.
○ **dar lugar a** to cause, give rise to *Lo que dijo dió lugar a muchas controversias.* What he said gave rise to much controversy. ○ **en lugar de** instead of *En lugar de comer aquí vamos a casa.* Instead of eating here, let's go home. ○ **en primer lugar** in the first place *En primer lugar tengo que*

hacer, además hace calor. In the first place I'm busy, and besides it's too hot. ○ **tener lugar** to take place *La ceremonia tuvo lugar en el cementerio.* The services took place at the cemetery.

lujo luxury.
　　○ **de lujo** de luxe, luxurious.

lujoso luxurious, showy.

lumbre [*f*] fire (in stove, fireplace) *Se sentaron cerca de la lumbre.* They sat near the fire. ▲ light *Se me apagó el cigarro. ¿Quiere Ud. darme lumbre?* My cigar went out. Will you give me a light?

luminoso bright, luminous *Una idea luminosa.* A bright idea.

luna moon *Estaban paseando a la luz de la luna.* They were walking in the moonlight.
　　○ **estar en la luna** to be distracted. ○ **luna de miel** honeymoon. ○ **luna llena** full moon.

lunar [*m*] mole, beauty mark *Tenía un lunar en el cuello.* She had a mole on her neck. ▲ polka dot *Llevaba un traje de lunares.* She was wearing a polka dot dress.

lunes [*m*] Monday.

lunfardo Argentine slang.

lustrar to polish, shine *Tengo que lustrarme los zapatos.* I have to shine my shoes.

lustre [*m*] luster, shine, polish; splendor.
　　○ **dar lustre** to shine, polish.

luto mourning; grief; mourning garments.
　　○ **estar de luto** to be in mourning.

luz [*f*] light *No puedo ver con esta luz.* I can't see in this light.—*Hizo luz en el asunto.* He shed some light on the matter.
　　○ **a todas luces** any way you look at it *A todas luces es cierto.* It's true any way you look at it. ○ **dar a la luz** to publish. ○ **dar a luz** to give birth (to a child). ○ **entre dos luces** in the twilight *Llegaron entre dos luces.* They arrived at twilight. ○ **luces** intelligence *Es un hombre de muchas luces.* He's a man of great intelligence.

M

macana fib, tall tale, exaggeration [*Arg*]. ‖ *¡Qué macana!* How annoying! [*Arg*]

macanudo excellent, wonderful, super [*Am*].

maceta flowerpot; potted plant.

machacar to crush *Machacó la piedra completamente.* He crushed the stone completely. ▲ to harp (on a subject) *Es inútil, no machaque Ud. más.* It's useless, don't harp on it any longer.

macho [*adj; m*] male (animals).

macizo [*adj*] solid *Era una barra de oro macizo.* It was a solid gold bar. ▲ [*m*] flower bed *En medio del jardín había un macizo (de flores).* There was a flower bed in the middle of the garden.

madera wood *La caja estaba hecha de madera de sándalo.* The box was made of sandalwood. ▲ lumber, timber *La madera no está todavía seca.* The lumber is still green. ▲ qualities, talent *Tiene madera de actor.* He has a talent for acting.

madero beam; timber.

madrastra stepmother.

madre [*f*] mother. ▲ origin, source, cradle *Grecia fué la madre de la civilización occidental.* Greece was the cradle of western civilization.
　　○ **madre política** mother-in-law *Le voy a presentar a mi madre política.* I'm going to introduce you to my mother-in-law. ○ **salirse de madre** to overflow *El río se salió de madre.* The river overflowed. ▲ to lose control of oneself.

madrina godmother.

madrugada dawn.
　　○ **de madrugada** at daybreak, at dawn.

madrugar to rise early.

madurar to ripen *La uva maduró bien aquel verano.* The grapes ripened well that summer. ▲ to think out, develop (an idea) *Maduró la idea antes de realizarla.* He thought out the idea thoroughly before putting it into practice. ▲ to mature *Maduró con los años.* He became more mature with the passing of the years.

madurez [*f*] maturity, ripeness.

maduro ripe; mature (of persons).

maestro teacher *Los chicos escuchaban al maestro.* The children were listening to the teacher. ▲ master, craftsman *Era maestro en su oficio.* He was master of his trade.

magistrado magistrate; judge (higher courts).

magnífico magnificent, excellent, grand.
mago wizard.
maguey [*m*] maguey (plant).
maíz [*m*] corn, maize.
majadero silly, foolish. ▲ [*n*] blockhead.
majestad [*f*] majesty.
majestuoso [*adj*] grand, majestic.
mal (see **malo**) bad *Hemos pasado un mal rato.* We have had a bad time. ▲ [*m*] illness *Su mal era incurable.* His illness was incurable. ▲ harm *Gozaba haciendo el mal.* He enjoyed doing harm. ▲ [*adv*] badly *Todo va muy mal.* Everything is going very badly.
    ○ **de mal en peor** from bad to worse *Vamos de mal en peor.* We are going from bad to worse. ○ **estar mal de** to be badly off (*or* in a bad way) as regards *Estoy mal de dinero.* I'm badly in need of money. ○ **mal hecho** poorly done *Ese trabajo está mal hecho.* That work is poorly done. ▲ wrong.
    ‖ *No hay mal que por bien no venga.* It's an ill wind that blows nobody good. ‖ *Quien canta su mal espanta.* He who sings drives away his grief.
malcriado ill-bred, spoiled.
maldad [*f*] wickedness, evil deed; harm.
maldecir [*irr*] to damn, to curse.
maldición [*f*] curse.
maldito [*adj*] cursed, damned.
malestar [*m*] indisposition; discontent, dissatisfaction.
maleta suitcase. ▲ bundle [*Am*] *Haga una maleta con esta ropa.* Make a bundle of these clothes.
    ○ **hacer la maleta** to pack the suitcase; to get ready to leave.
maletero porter (carrier).
maletín [*m*] overnight bag, small case.
maleza weeds.
malicia malice *Lo hizo sin malicia.* He did it without malice.
    ○ **tener malicia** to be malicious *Aquellas palabras parecían tener malicia.* Those seemed to be malicious words.
malicioso malicious; risqué.
maligno malignant.
malo bad, unpleasant *El tiempo está muy malo.* The weather is very bad. ▲ difficult, hard, bad *¡Qué rato tan malo hemos pasado!* What a bad time we've had! ▲ naughty *Este niño es demasiado malo.* This child's very naughty. ▲ ill *Tan malo se puso que murió a las dos horas.* He became so ill that he died two hours later.
    ○ **por las malas o por las buenas** whether you like it or not *Lo harás*

por las malas o por las buenas. You will do it whether you like it or not. ‖ *Ese es un tipo muy malo.* He's a bad egg.
malograr to waste, to miss, fail to take advantage of (as time, opportunity, etc) *Malograron la ocasión.* They failed to take advantage of the opportunity.
    ○ **malograrse** to fail *La empresa se malogró.* The business failed.
malsano unhealthy, unhealthful, unsanitary, unwholesome.
maltratar to mistreat, to abuse.
malvado wicked. ▲ [*n*] wicked person, villain.
mamá [*f*] mamma, mom.
mameluco overalls [*Am*].
manantial [*m*] spring, source of stream.
manar to flow out, spring *De la roca manaba una fuente.* A spring flowed out of the rock.
mancha spot, stain *Le cayó una mancha en el traje.* She got a spot on her dress. ▲ patch (of ground or vegetation) *Sólo había algunas manchas de vegetación cerca del río.* There were only a few patches of vegetation near the river.
manchado (see **manchar**) spotted, mottled *Un perro manchado.* A spotted dog.
manchar to stain, soil.
manco one-armed.
mandadero messenger; errand boy.
mandado See **mandar.** ▲ [*m*] errand; message.
mandamiento order, command; commandment.
mandar to order, direct *Mandó salir a la criada.* He ordered the maid to leave. ▲ to send *Al llegar mandaron el equipaje al hotel.* When they arrived they sent their luggage to the hotel. ▲ to send, transmit *Mande Ud. recuerdos a nuestro amigo.* Send my regards to our friend.
    ○ **mandar a paseo** to tell someone to go fly a kite.
mandato order, mandate, command.
mando order *El general dió el mando de retirarse.* The general gave the order to retreat. ▲ leadership, sternness *Era hombre de mucho mando.* He was a man of great leadership. ▲ control *Los mandos del avión no funcionaban.* The controls of the plane were out of order.
    ○ **(alto) mando** high command *El mando decidió atacar de madrugado.* The high command decided to attack at dawn. ○ **estar al mando** to be in com-

mand *Está al mando del sector.* He's in command of the sector. ○ **tomar el mando** to take command *Un comandante tuvo que tomar el mando de la división.* A major had to take command of the division.

manecilla hand (of a watch, clock, or gage).

manejar to manage, handle *Manejó bien el dinero y aumentó los ingresos.* He handled the money well and increased the income from it. ▲ to drive [*Am*] *¿Ha aprendido Ud. a manejar el coche?* Have you learned to drive the car?

○ **manejarse** to move about *Se manejaba ya sin las muletas.* He was already moving about without crutches. ▲ to get along *Se maneja bien.* He gets along all right. ▲ to manage, succeed in *¿Cómo se maneja Ud. para hacer esto?* How do you manage to do this?

manejo handling *El manejo de esto ofrece peligro.* This is a dangerous thing to handle.—*El manejo de la dinamita es peligroso.* The handling of dynamite is dangerous. ▲ driving (a car) [*Am*]. ▲ management, control *Lleva todo el manejo de la tienda.* He is in complete charge of the shop. ▲ intrigue *Con sus manejos consiguió lo que quería.* He got what he wanted by intrigue.

manera way, manner *¿Qué manera es esa de contestar?* Is that the way to answer?

○ **de (esta) manera** this way, in this manner *Hágalo Ud. de esta manera.* Do it this way. ○ **de mala manera** rudely *Lo dijo de mala manera.* He said it in a rude way. ○ **de manera que** so, as a result *Ayer no fuí, de manera que tengo que ir hoy.* I didn't go yesterday, so I have to go today. ○ **de ninguna manera** by no means *De ninguna manera lo aceptaré.* By no means will I accept it. ○ **de otra manera** in another way *No se lo puedo decir de otra manera.* I can't tell him any other way. ▲ otherwise *Estaba allí de otra manera no le hubiera hablado.* He was there, otherwise I wouldn't have spoken to him. ○ **de todas maneras** at any rate *De todas maneras iremos.* In any case we'll go. ○ **en cierta manera** in a way *En cierta manera, tiene Ud. razón.* In a way you are right. ○ **maneras** manners *No tiene buenas maneras.* He hasn't got good manners. ○ **no hay manera de** there's no way to *No hay manera de traducirlo.* There's no way to translate it.

manga sleeve *Las mangas le estaban cortas.* His sleeves were short for him. ○ **andar manga por hombro** to be in a mess *En aquella casa todo andaba manga por hombro.* Everything was in a mess in that house. ○ **de manga ancha** indulgent *Es hombre de manga ancha con sus hijos.* He's very indulgent with his children. ▲ not too scrupulous. ○ **en mangas de camisa** in shirt sleeves *Por el calor estaban en mangas de camisa.* They were in their shirt sleeves because of the heat. ○ **manga (de riego)** hose *La manga (de riego) no funcionaba.* The hose didn't work.

mango handle; mango (fruit).

manguito muff.

maní [*m*] peanut [*Am*].

manía madness; mania; hobby. ○ **tomar manía (a)** to dislike, have a grudge (against).

manifestación [*f*] demonstration (parade).

manifestar [*rad-ch I*] to express, show *En la carta manifestaba estar conforme.* In the letter he expressed his agreement.

○ **manifestarse** to make a demonstration *Los obreros quisieron manifestarse, pero no pudieron.* The workers wanted to make a demonstration, but couldn't.

manifiesto manifest, plain, obvious. ▲ [*m*] manifesto.

manilla hand (of watch, clock, gage).

mano [*f*] hand. ▲ coat (of paint, varnish, etc) *Hay que una mano de barniz.* We must give it a coat of varnish. ▲ first player (next to dealer) *La mano echó un triunfo.* The first player led a trump. ▲ mishap, misfortune [*Am*] *Nos pasó una mano.* We had a slight accident.

○ **a mano** by hand *La carta estaba escrita a mano.* The letter was written by hand. ▲ near by, within reach *Póngalo Ud. a mano.* Put it within reach. ○ **a mano derecha** *or* **izquierda** on the right *or* left *Su habitación está a mano derecha.* His room is on the right. ○ **de la mano** by the hand *Llevaba el niño de la mano.* She was leading the child by the hand. ○ **de segunda mano** second-hand. ○ **echar una mano** to lend a hand. ○ **hecho a mano** handmade. ○ **mano a mano** tête à tête *Se pusieron a hablar mano a mano.* They had a tête à tête.

manojo bunch (of flowers or vegetables).

mansedumbre [*f*] meekness, humility, tameness.

manso tame; calm; meek.

manta blanket.

manteca lard, fat.

mantel [*m*] table-cloth.

mantener [*irr*] to support, provide for, make a living for *Mantenía a su madre y tres hermanos.* He supported his mother and three brothers. ▲to hold *Mantenga firme la cuerda.* Hold the rope tight. ▲to maintain, defend (an opinion) *Mantendrá su opinión contra todos.* He will defend his opinion against anyone. ▲to keep up *Costaba trabajo mantener la conversación.* It was difficult to keep up the conversation. ○**mantenerse** to support oneself *Para mantenerse durante aquel mes no tenía dinero.* During that month he had no money on which to live. ○**mantenerse (en)** to hold (to) *No creo que se mantenga en su decisión.* I don't think he will hold to his decision.

mantenimiento maintenance, support; upkeep.

mantequilla butter.

mantilla mantilla; baby clothes. ○**estar en mantillas** to be innocent as a child, not to know anything about *En cuanto a la política, está todavía en mantillas.* As far as politics is concerned, he's still as innocent as a child.

manual [*adj*] manual, physical. ▲[*m*] manual, handbook.

manufactura manufacture.

manufacturar to manufacture.

manuscrito handwritten. ▲[*m*] manuscript.

manzana apple. ▲block *¿En qué manzana está su casa?* What block is your house in?

manzano apple tree.

maña skill; craftiness. ○**darse maña** to contrive, manage *Se da maña para conseguir lo que quiere.* He manages to get what he wants.

mañana [*f*] morning *La mañana estaba clara.* The morning was clear. ▲[*m*] future *Trabaja con ilusión para el mañana.* He works hopefully for the future. ▲[*adv*] tomorrow *Le espero a Ud. mañana en el hotel.* I'll wait for you in the hotel tomorrow. ○**a la mañana siguiente** on the morning after *Le vi a la mañana siguiente.* I saw him the morning after. ○**de la mañana** A.M. *Vendrá a las seis de la mañana.* He's coming at 6 A.M. ○**de**

mañana early in the morning *Salió muy de mañana.* He went out very early in the morning. ○**por (or en) la mañana** in the morning *Nos veremos el jueves por la mañana.* We'll meet on Thursday morning. ○**de mañanita** very early in the morning. ‖ *¡Hasta mañana!* See you tomorrow!

mapa [*m*] map.

máquina machine *La máquina se puso en movimiento.* The machine began to run. ▲car (automobile) [*Arg*]. ○**a toda máquina** at full speed *Llevaba el trabajo a toda máquina.* He worked at full speed. ○**máquina (de escribir)** typewriter *Escribe muy bien a máquina.* She types very well.

mar [*m or f*] sea. ○**alta mar** high sea, open sea. ○**hablar de la mar** to talk idly *Eso es hablar de la mar.* That's idle talk. ○**la mar** a lot, lots *En su casa había la mar de gente.* There were a lot of people at his house. ○**meterse mar adentro** to go beyond one's depth (in swimming).

maravilla wonder, marvel.

maravillar to amaze *La fiesta maravillaba por su riqueza.* The lavishness of the party amazed everybody. ○**maravillarse** to be astonished *Me maravillo de que llegue a tiempo.* I'm astonished that he's on time.

maravilloso wonderful.

marca mark, characteristic *¿Hay alguna marca que lo distinga?* Has it any distinguishing mark? ▲mark *Ponga Ud. una marca en está página.* Put a mark on this page. ○**marca (de fábrica)** trademark, brand *La marca de fábrica es muy conocida.* The trademark is very well-known.—*¿Qué marca de cigarrillos fuma Ud.?* What brand of cigarettes do you smoke?

marcar to mark *Marcaba con un lápiz los nombres de los que asistían.* With a pencil he marked off the names of those who attended. ○**marcar el compás** to keep time *Aprenda Ud. a marcar el compás.* Learn to keep time.

marcha speed *El barco llevaba muy buena marcha.* The ship traveled at a good speed. ▲march *Tocaban una marcha militar.* They played a military march. ○**apresurar la marcha** to hurry, speed up *Hay que apresurar la marcha.* We must hurry. ○**poner en marcha**

to start, put in motion *No podía poner en marcha el motor.* He couldn't start the motor. O **sobre la marcha** at once *El trabajo hay que terminarlo sobre la marcha.* The work must be completed at once.

‖ *¡En marcha!* Let's go! or Forward, march!

marchar to run *El tren marchaba a toda velocidad.* The train was running at full speed. ▲ to progress, go along *¡Esto marcha muy bien!* This is coming along fine! ▲ to go, run, work *¿Marcha el reloj de Ud.?* Is your watch running?

O **marcharse** to leave, go away *¿A qué hora se marcha Ud.?* When are you leaving?

marchitar to wither *El calor marchitó la flores.* The heat withered the flowers.

O **marchitarse** to fade, wither *Su belleza empezó a marchitarse.* Her beauty began to fade.

marchito faded, withered.

marco frame (of door, window, picture); mark (German monetary unit).

marea tide.

marear to bother *¡No me maree Ud. más!* Don't bother me any more!

O **marearse** to get seasick, get carsick, get dizzy *Al empezar a andar el barco, se mareó.* As soon as the ship began to move, he got seasick.

mareo seasickness, carsickness, dizziness.

marfil [*m*] ivory.

margen [*m or f*] margin *Deje Ud. margen en el papel cuando escriba.* Leave a margin on the paper when you write. ▲ edge, border, bank *Llegó hasta la margen del río.* He reached the edge of the river.

O **dar margen** to give an opportunity *Le dió margen para ganar dinero.* He gave him an opportunity to earn money.

mariachi [*m*] Mexican street singer.

marido husband.

marihuana marihuana.

marimba marimba [*Am*].

marina seascape, marine painting.

O **marina (de guerra)** navy *Era un oficial de la marina de guerra.* He was a naval officer. O **marina mercante** merchant marine.

marinero sailor, seaman.

marino marine, of the sea, maritime. ▲ [*m*] seaman *Ese almirante era un buen marino.* That admiral was a good seaman.

mariposa butterfly.

marítimo maritime.

marmita large cooking pot.

mármol [*m*] marble (stone).

marrano hog. ▲ [*adj*] piggish.

marrón [*adj*] brown.

martes [*m*] Tuesday.

martillar, martillear to hammer.

martillo hammer.

martirio torture, martyrdom.

marzo March.

más more. ▲ plus *Cuatro más tres son siete.* Four plus three is seven. ▲ longer *No puedo esperarle más.* I can't wait any longer for him.

O **a lo más** at most *A lo más, costará diez pesos.* At most it'll cost ten pesos. O **a más tardar** at the latest *A más tardar llegará esta noche.* He'll arrive tonight at the latest. O **de más** too much, too many *Le dieron seis libras de más.* They gave him six pounds too much. O **el** (*or* **la, los, las**) **más** the more, the most *Esta muchacha es la más inteligente.* This girl is the most intelligent. O **en más de** for more than *Lo ha vendido en más de lo que lo compró.* He's sold it for more than he paid for it. O **estar de más** to be in excess, be unnecessary *Estoy de más.* I'm unnecessary here. O **lo más . . . que** as . . . as *Llegó lo más pronto que pudo.* He arrived as soon as he could. O **los** (*or* **las**) **más** the majority *Los más de aquellos hombres trabajaban en la mina.* The majority of those men worked in the mine. O **más adelante** later on, farther (*or* further) on *Más adelante se lo explicaré.* Later on I'll explain it to you. O **más allá** farther on *La casa está más allá.* The house is farther on. O **más bien** rather *Llegó más bien tarde.* He arrived rather late. O **más de** (before numerals) more than *El pueblo tenía más de mil habitantes.* The village had more than a thousand inhabitants. O **más que** more than *Me importa más que a Ud.* It's more important to me than to you. O **más tarde o más temprano** sooner or later *Se sabrá más tarde o más temprano.* It'll be known sooner or later. O **no más que** only *No tiene más que cuatro pesos.* He has only four pesos. O **por más que** however much, no matter how much *Por más que diga Ud. no logrará convencerle.* No matter how much you say you won't succeed in convincing him.

masa dough *Se hizo la masa para el pan.*

The dough was made for the bread. ▲ mass (of people) *Su discurso iba dirigido a las masas.* His speech was directed to the masses.
  O **con las manos en la masa** in the act, red-handed *Le cogieron con las manos en la masa.* They caught him in the act. O **masa de la sangre** inner nature, blood *Eso lo tiene en la masa de la sangre.* It's in his blood.

masacre [*m*] massacre.

mascar to chew *Tráguelo, no lo masque.* Swallow it, don't chew it.

máscara [*f*] mask. ▲ [*m, f*] masquerader.
  O **baile de máscaras** masquerade ball.
  O **máscara contra gases** gas mask.
  O **vestido de máscara** in costume.

mascota mascot, good-luck charm.

masculino masculine.

mástil [*m*] mast, pole, post.

mata plant, bush, shrub.

matanza slaughter.

matar to kill. ▲ to trump *Me mató el rey.* He trumped my king.
  O **estar a matar con** to have a feud with, be on bad terms with *No me hables de Pérez, estoy a matar con él.* Don't speak to me about Pérez; we're on bad terms. O **matar de aburrimiento** to bore to death *Ese trabajo me mata de aburrimiento.* That job bores me to death. O **matar de hambre** to starve *En aquel hotel nos mataban de hambre.* They starved us at that hotel. O **matar dos pájaros en un tiro** to kill two birds with one stone. O **matar el tiempo** to kill time *Mató el tiempo leyendo el periódico.* He killed time reading the paper. O **matarse** to kill oneself *Intentó matarse con una pistola.* He tried to kill himself with a pistol. ▲ to get killed *Se mató en un accidente de automóvil.* He got killed in an automobile accident.

mate [*m*] maté (South American tea).

matemáticas [*f pl*] mathematics.

materia material, substance *¿De qué materia está hecho esto?* What material's this made of? ▲ matter, topic *La materia que discutimos es interesante.* The matter we're discussing is interesting. ▲ subject *Enseñaba varias materias.* He taught several subjects.
  O **entrar en materia** to come to the point, get down to business. O **materia prima** raw material.

material [*m*] material *¿Con qué material se hace esto?* What material's used to make this? ▲ equipment *Tiene una fábrica de material eléctrico.* He has an electrical equipment factory.

maternal maternal, motherly.

materno maternal, on the mother's side.

matiz [*m*] shade, tint.

matón [*m*] bully, overbearing person.

matorral [*m*] thicket, brush.

matrimonio marriage *Contrajo matrimonio hace tres días.* He got married three days ago. ▲ married couple *Era un matrimonio bien avenido.* They were a harmonious couple.

maullar to meow.

máxima maxim, proverb.

máximo [*adj; m*] maximum.

mayo May.

mayor larger, largest; bigger, biggest *Juan es mayor que su hermano.* John's bigger than his brother. ▲ older, oldest *¿Cómo se llama su hermana mayor?* What's your older (*or* oldest) sister's name? ▲ main (of streets) *Viven en la calle mayor.* They live on the main street. ▲ [*m*] major *Fué mayor en el Ejército.* He was a major in the Army.
  O **al por mayor** wholesale *Sólo vendemos al por mayor.* We sell wholesale only. O **la mayor parte (de)** the majority (of), the greater part (of). O **ser mayor de edad** to be of age.

mayoría majority, greater part.
  O **mayoría de edad** majority (of age). O **llegar a la mayoría de edad** to come of age.

mayorista [*m*] wholesale merchant [*Am*].

me [*obj pron*] me, to me; myself, to (*or* for) myself *Cuando me vieron anoche me estaba afeitando.* When they saw me last night I was shaving.

mecánica mechanics.

mecánico mechanical *Este juguete es mecánico.* This is a mechanical toy. ▲ [*m*] mechanic *Trabajó de mecánico en una fábrica.* He worked as a mechanic in a factory.

mecanismo mechanism, works (of machines).

mecanógrafo, mecanógrafa typist.

mecedora rocking chair.

mecer to rock *Mecía al niño en la cuna.* He rocked the child in the cradle.
  O **mecerse** to rock (oneself), swing, sway *Las flores se mecían en el viento.* The flowers were swaying in the wind.

medalla medal.

media stocking *Llevaba medias negras.* She wore black stockings. ▲ sock [*Am*] *Entró a comprarse unas medias.* He went in to buy some socks.

mediación [*f*] mediation.

mediado (see **mediar**) half-filled, half-full *La jarra estaba mediada.* The pitcher was half-filled. ▲ half-gone, half-over.

○ **a mediados de** in (*or* about) the middle of (a period of time) *Estamos a mediados de mes.* We're in the middle of the month.

medianería partition (wall).

mediano [*adj*] medium *Es de estatura mediana.* He's of medium height. ▲ mediocre *Su trabajo era muy mediano.* His work was very mediocre.

mediante through, by means of *Mediante influencia pudo embarcar.* He was able to book passage because he had pull.

○ **Dios mediante** God willing.

mediar to mediate *Quiso mediar en la discusión.* He wanted to mediate in the argument.

medicina medicine *¿Qué año de medicina cursa Ud.?* What year of medical school are you in?—*El doctor le recetó una medicina.* The doctor prescribed a medicine for him.

médico [*adj*] medical. ▲ [*n*] physician.

medida measure, measurements *Voy a tomarle la medida.* I'm going to take your measurements. ▲ rule, measure *Aquella medida afectaba a todo el mundo.* That rule applied to everybody. ▲ number, size *¿Cuál es su medida de calzado?* What's your shoe size?

○ **a la medida** to order, to measure, custom-made *El traje está hecho a la medida.* The suit's custom-made. ○ **a medida que** as *A medida que lleguen, dígales Ud. que pasen.* As they arrive, tell them to come in. ○ **llenar** (*or* **colmar**) **la medida** to be the last straw *Eso colma la medida.* That's the last straw. ○ **sin medida** without moderation *Bebe sin medida.* He drinks to excess. ○ **tener medida** to have a sense of proportion *or* moderation *No tiene medida en lo que hace.* He has no sense of proportion in what he does. ○ **tomar medidas** to take measurements *Me tomaron medidas para el traje.* They took my measurements for the suit. ▲ to take measures *or* steps *Tomaron medidas para evitar la rebelión.* They took steps to prevent the revolt.

medio [*adj*] half, half a *¿Quiere Ud. medio pollo?* Would you like half a chicken? ▲ mid, middle of *Podemos vernos a media tarde.* We can meet in the middle of the afternoon. ▲ [*m*] middle *El auto se paró en medio de la carretera.* The car stopped in the

middle of the road. ▲ means *No veo medio de solucionar esto.* I see no means of solving this.

○ **a medias** fifty-fifty, halves *Iremos a medias en el negocio.* We'll go fifty-fifty in the business. ○ **a medio camino** halfway to a place *Ya estamos a medio camino.* We're halfway there. ○ **a medio hacer** half-done *Este trabajo está a medio hacer.* This work's half-done. ○ **hacer algo a medias** to do something poorly, do a half-baked job *No haga Ud. las cosas a medias.* Don't do a half-baked job. ○ **ir a medias** to go fifty-fifty, to go halves.

mediocre mediocre.

mediodía [*m*] noon, midday.

medir [*rad-ch III*] to measure *Midió el ancho y el largo de la habitación.* He measured the length and width of the room. ▲ to measure, weigh *No mide lo que dice.* He doesn't weigh his words.

meditación [*f*] meditation, thought.

meditar to meditate, think.

mejilla cheek.

mejor [*adj*] better *Esta casa es mejor que la otra.* This is a better house than the other one. ▲ best *Es la mejor casa del pueblo.* It's the best house in town.

○ **a lo mejor** perhaps, maybe *A lo mejor mañana no llueve.* Maybe it won't rain tomorrow. ○ **mejor dicho** or rather, or better *Iré a las tres, mejor dicho a las tres y cuarto.* I'll go at three, or rather at a quarter past three. ○ **mejor que** rather than, instead of *Mejor que escribir, ponga Ud. un telegrama.* Instead of writing, send a telegram. ○ **mejor que mejor** all the better, so much the better *Si viene, mejor que mejor.* If he comes, so much the better.

mejora improvement, getting better; renovation, alteration.

mejorar to improve, recover *Se le veía mejorar rápidamente.* He was obviously improving fast. ▲ to improve, get better *Han mejorado los negocios.* Business has improved. ▲ to improve, make better *Con las obras mejoraron la casa.* With the alterations, the house was improved.

melancolía gloom, blues.

melancólico melancholy, sad.

melena long hair.

melocotón [*m*] peach.

melodía melody.

melón [*m*] melon, cantaloupe.

meloso honeylike, sweet.

memorable memorable.
memoria memory (not used for things remembered) *Su memoria era magnífica.* He had a wonderful memory. ▲ memorandum, report *Escribió una memoria con los gastos hechos.* He made a memorandum of the expenses. ○ **de memoria** by heart *Me lo aprendí de memoria.* I learned it by heart. ○ **hacer memoria** to recall, remember *Haga Ud. memoria y recuerde lo que pasó.* Try to recall what happened. ○ **memorias** regards *Muchas memorias a su familia.* My regards to your family. ▲ memoirs.
mencionar to mention.
mendigo, mendiga beggar.
menear to stir *Hay que menearlo mientras cuece.* It has to be stirred while it's cooking. ▲ to shake *No menee Ud. la mesa.* Don't shake the table. ▲ to wag *El perro meneaba la cola.* The dog was wagging his tail.
menester [*m*] occupation, duty *Los menesteres de la casa.* Household duties.
○ **ser menester** to be necessary *No es menester que venga a verme.* You don't have to come to see me.
menesteroso needy, poor. ▲ [*n*] beggar.
menguar to diminish, decrease.
menor smaller, smallest *María es la menor de las tres.* Mary's the smallest of the three. ▲ younger, youngest *Es de la misma edad que mi hermano menor.* She's the same age as my younger brother. ▲ less, least, slightest *No tengo la menor idea.* I haven't the least idea. ▲ [*n*] minor *No es apto para menores.* It isn't suitable for minors. ○ **al por menor** at retail *Vendía sólo al por menor.* He sold only at retail. ▲ minutely, in great detail *Refirió al por menor todo lo sucedido.* He reported in great detail everything that happened. ○ **menor de edad** under age, minor.
menoría ○ **menoría de edad** minority (of age).
menorista [*m*] retail merchant [*Am*].
menos less, least *Mi hermano tiene seis años menos que yo.* My brother's six years younger than I am.—*Es el menos caro de todos.* It's the least expensive of all. ▲ [*prep*] except, but *Puede Ud. usar todos los libros, menos éste.* You may use all the books but this one.
○ **al menos** at least *Procure Ud. al menos llegar a la hora.* At least try to come on time. ○ **a menos que** unless *Le espero mañana a menos que Ud.*

me avise. I'll expect you tomorrow unless you let me know otherwise.
○ **echar de menos** to miss *Echaba mucho de menos a sus amigos.* He missed his friends very much. ○ **lo de menos** the least of it *Eso es lo de menos.* That's the least of it. ○ **lo menos** at least *En el combate perecieron le menos seiscientos hombres.* At least six hundred men died in the action. ○ **menos de** (before a numeral) less than *Tengo menos de quince.* I have less than fifteen. ○ **por lo menos** at least *Por lo menos costará cien pesos.* It'll cost at least a hundred pesos. ○ **venir a menos** to lose social position *Esa familia ha venido mucho a menos.* That family's lost its social position.
mensaje [*m*] message [*Am*]; dispatch [*Sp*].
mensajero, mensajera messenger [*Am*]; courier [*Sp*].
○ **paloma mensajera** carrier pigeon.
mensual [*adj*] monthly.
menta mint, peppermint.
mental mental.
mente [*f*] mind (mental faculties).
mentir [*rad-ch II*] to lie, tell lies.
mentira lie.
○ **parece mentira** it seems impossible *Parece mentira que tenga tanta edad.* It seems impossible that you're that old.
‖ ¡*Mentira!* That's a lie!
menudeo ○ **al menudeo** at retail.
menudo tiny, very small *Era una mujer muy menuda.* She was a very small woman. ▲ [*m*] coins, change [*Am*] *Deme cambio en billetes y menudo.* Give me change in bills and coins.
○ **a menudo** often *Iba a verle a menudo.* He used to go to see him often.
menudillo giblets.
mercado market *En este mercado hay fruta y hay carne.* There's fruit and meat in this market.
○ **mercado de valores** stock market. ○ **tener mercado con** to trade with *Tenemos mercado con toda América.* We trade with all America.
mercancía merchandise, goods.
mercantil commercial, mercantile.
merced [*f*] favor *Tenga Ud. la merced de . . . .* Please . . . .
○ **estar a merced de** to be at the mercy of. ○ **su merced** you (courteous and familiar) [*Col*] *Si su merced quiere, iremos.* If you want to, we'll go.
merecer [*-zc-*] to deserve *La cuestión*

merecía estudio. The question deserved study.

○ **merecer la pena** to be worthwhile.
merecimiento value, merit.
merendar [*rad-ch I*] to have a snack *or* refreshments in the afternoon.
meridional southern.
merienda afternoon snack.

○ **merienda en el campo** picnic.
mérito merit, worth.

○ **hacer méritos** to build up good will, make oneself deserving.
mero pure, simple; mere.
mes [*m*] month.
mesa table.

○ **poner la mesa** to set the table.
meseta plateau.
mesón [*m*] country inn (for lower classes).
mestizo [*adj; n*] half-breed, (one) of mixed blood (white and Indian).
meta aim, goal; finish line.
metal [*m*] metal; brass.

○ **metal de voz** tone, timbre (of voice).
metálico metallic. ▲ [*m*] coin(s) *¿Quiere Ud. su dinero en metálico?* Do you want your money in coins?
meter to put *Meta Ud. el dinero dentro del bolsillo.* Put the money in your pocket. ▲ to take in *Haga el favor de meter un poco las costuras de la chaqueta.* Please take in the seams of the jacket a little.

○ **meter embustes** to tell fibs. ○ **meter miedo** to frighten *Ud. trata de meternos miedo.* You're trying to frighten us. ○ **meter ruido** to make noise *No meta Ud. tanto ruido.* Don't make so much noise. ○ **meterse a** to become (without previous thought or training) *Decidió meterse a literato.* He decided to become an author. ○ **meterse con** to pick a fight with *¿Por qué se mete Ud. conmigo?* Why are you picking a fight with me? ○ **meterse en** to get into *Se metió en la cama.* He got into bed. ○ **meterse fraile** *or* **monja** to become a monk *or* nun. ○ **meterse uno en lo que no le importa** to be nosy *No se meta Ud. en lo que no le importa.* Don't be (so) nosy.
metódico systematic, methodical.
método method.
metro meter *Compre Ud. seis metros de esa tela.* Buy six meters of that cloth. ▲ subway [*Sp*] *Tome Ud. el metro aquí mismo.* Take the subway right here.
mezclar to mix *¿Quiere Ud. wiskey puro o lo mezclo con agua?* Do you want

your whiskey straight or shall I mix it with water? ▲ to blend *Aquí mezclan el café del Brasil con el de Colombia.* They blend Brazilian and Colombian coffee here.

○ **mezclarse** to get mixed up *No se mezcle Ud. en eso.* Don't get mixed up in that.
mezquino mean, petty; stingy, skimpy.
mi; *pl* **mis** [*adj*] my *¿Dónde están mi sombrero y mis guantes?* Where are my hat and my gloves? ▲ [*obj pron*] me *Esta carta es para mí.* This letter's for me.
‖ *¡A mí qué!* I don't care!
miedo fear.

○ **tener miedo** to be afraid *Tenía mucho miedo a estar enfermo.* He was very much afraid of being ill.
miedoso fearful, afraid.
miel [*f*] honey.
miembro limb *Se le paralizaron los miembros.* His limbs got paralyzed. ▲ member *Es miembro de varias sociedades.* He's a member of several societies.
mientras while *Lea Ud. el periódico mientras yo recibo la visita.* Read the paper while I receive the visitor.

○ **mientras más** (*or* **menos**) . . . **más** (*or* **menos**) the more (*or* less) . . . the more (*or* less) *Mientras más duermo, menos ganas tengo de trabajar.* The more I sleep, the less I feel like working. ○ **mientras no** unless *Mientras no estudie Ud. no aprenderá esto.* Unless you study you won't learn this. ○ **mientras tanto** meanwhile *Volverán pronto, mientras tanto juguemos una partida.* They'll be back soon; meanwhile let's play a game.
miércoles [*m*] Wednesday.
miga crumb *Quitaba las migas de pan del mantel.* She brushed the bread crumbs from the tablecloth.

○ **hacer buenas migas** to get on well together *Los dos amigos hacían buenas migas.* The two friends got on well together. ○ **hacerse migas** to be smashed to bits *El jarrón al caerse al suelo se hizo migas.* The jar was smashed to bits when it hit the floor. ○ **tener miga** to have a point, be pithy *Todo lo que dijo tenía miga.* Everything he said was pithy.
mil (one) thousand.
milico soldier, "G.I." [*Am*].
militar [*adj*] military *Fué llamado al servicio militar.* He was called up for military service. ▲ [*m*] military man

Es un club de militares. It's a military club.

milonga party and dance, "shindig", kind of dance music [*Arg*].

milla mile.

millar [*m*] one thousand.

millón [*m*] million.

millonario,. millonaria millionaire.

mimar to pamper, spoil (a child).

mina mine (excavation) *Los obreros no bajaron a la mina aquella noche.* The workmen didn't go down into the mine that night.—*Aquel negocio era una mina (de oro).* That business was a gold mine. ▲ mine (explosive) *La navegación era difícil porque había minas.* Navigation was difficult because there were mines.

minero miner.

mínimo [*adj; m*] minimum.

ministerio department (government) *¿Es este el Ministerio de Trabajo?* Is this the Department of Labor? ▲ cabinet *Dimitió el ministerio.* The cabinet resigned.

ministro minister (member of a cabinet).

minoría minority *Habló en nombre de la minoría.* He spoke on behalf of the minority.

minorista [*m*] retail merchant [*Am*].

minucioso minute, precise, thorough.

minuta memorandum; minutes (of a meeting).

○ **a la minuta** short-order [*Arg*].

minuto [*adj*] minute. ▲ [*m*] minute.

○ **al minuto** right away.

mío, mía; *pl* **míos, mías** [*adj*] mine, of mine *Estas corbatas no son mías.* These ties aren't mine.—*Fué un gran amigo mío.* He was a great friend of mine.

○ **el mío, la mía; los míos, las mías** [*pron*] mine *Este lápiz es de Ud.; el mío está en la mesa.* This pencil's yours; mine's on the desk.

mira intention, aim, goal *¿Cuáles son sus miras?* What are your intentions? ▲ sight (of gun).

○ **estar a la mira** to be on the lookout *Procura estar a la mira por si vienen.* Try to be on the lookout in case they come. ○ **tener la mira puesta en** to aim at *Tiene la mira puesta en esa colocación.* He's aiming for that job.

mirada look, expression *Su mirada es inteligente.* He has an intelligent expression. ▲ glance, look *Su mirada de mostraba odio.* His look showed hatred.

○ **echar una mirada** to glance, cast a glance *Echó una mirada al libro.* He glanced at the book.

mirar to look at *¿Qué mira Ud.?* What are you looking at? ▲ to glance *Miraba a uno y a otro procurando una respuesta.* He glanced from one to the other, hoping for an answer. ▲ to regard, look at *Debemos mirar este asunto con más calma.* We must look at this matter more calmly. ▲ to consider, think *Mire Ud. bien lo que hace.* Consider well what you're doing. ▲ to watch, be careful *Mire Ud. donde pisa.* Watch your step. ▲ to watch *Miraba lo que estábamos haciendo.* He watched what we were doing.

○ **mirar a** to face *Tres de las habitaciones miran a la calle.* Three of the rooms face the street. ▲ to look towards (in the direction of) *Estaba mirando al mar.* He was looking towards the sea. ○ **mirar alrededor** to look around *Miró alrededor para ver si estaban allí.* He looked around to see if they were there. ○ **mirar de hito en hito** to stare at *Se quedó mirándole de hito en hito.* He kept staring at him. ○ **mirar de reojo** to look out of the corner of one's eye *Le miraba de reojo mientras hablaba.* He was looking at him out of the corner of his eye while he was speaking. ○ **mirar por** to look after *¿No tienen a nadie que mire por ellos?* Don't they have anyone to look after them? ○ **mirarse** to look at each other *Se miraron y se echaron a reír.* They looked at each other and burst out laughing. ▲ to look at oneself *Le gustaba mirarse en el espejo.* He liked to look at himself in the mirror.

‖ *¡Mire!* Look here! *or* Listen!

misa Mass.

miserable miserable, unhappy, wretched *Llevaba una vida miserable.* He lead a miserable life. ▲ contemptible, rotten *Fué una acción miserable.* It was a contemptible thing to do. ▲ [*n*] cur, cad *Aquel hombre era un miserable.* That man was a cad.

miseria poverty *La familia estaba en la miseria.* The family lived in poverty. ▲ trifle, pittance *Lo que le pagan es una miseria.* They pay him a pittance.

misericordia mercy, compassion.

misia, misiá title of respect used with first name of old ladies [*Col, Arg, Ven*].

misión [*f*] mission *Le envió el gobierno en misión a Rusia.* The government sent him on a mission to Russia.—*Esas iglesias las construyeron las misiones* *franciscanas.* The Franciscan missions built those churches.

mismo same, identical *Es el mismo sombrero.* It's the same hat.

○ **aquí mismo** right here *Nos encontraremos aquí mismo.* We'll meet right here. ○ **darle a uno lo mismo** to be all the same to one *Todo le da lo mismo.* It's all the same to him. ○ **eso mismo** that very thing *Eso mismo le dije yo.* That's just what I told him. ○ **mismo(s)** -self, -selves *Yo mismo puedo hacer esto.* I can do this myself.—*Que lo hagan ellos mismos.* Let 'em do it themselves.

misterio mystery.

mitad [*f*] half *¿Quiere Ud. la mitad de este pastel?* Do you want half of this cake? ▲ better half, wife *Allí estaba el señor Gómez con su cara mitad.* Mr. Gómez was there with his better half.

○ **en la mitad** in the middle *El auto estaba en la mitad del camino.* The auto was in the middle of the road. ○ **por la mitad** in half *Parta Ud. esto por la mitad.* Divide this in half. ‖ *Estamos a mitad de camino.* We're half-way there. ‖ *Estamos a (la) mitad del trabajo.* We're half-way through.

mitin [*m*] political meeting, rally.

mixto mixed.

○ **parejas mixtas** mixed doubles (games). ○ **tren mixto** mixed train (freight and passenger train).

mobiliario furniture.

mochila knapsack.

moda fashion, style *Viste a la última moda.* She dresses in the latest fashion.

○ **a la moda** fashionable *Siempre lleva trajes a la moda.* She always wears fashionable dresses. ○ **estar de moda** to be popular, be in fashion *Ese artista está muy de moda.* That artist's very popular. ○ **pasado de moda** out of style *Se ha pasado de moda.* It's gone out of style.

modales [*m pl*] manners.

modelo [*adj*] model, perfect *Era una esposa modelo.* She was a model wife. ▲ [*n*] model, one who poses *Es un buen modelo para una escultura.* He's a good model for sculpture. ▲ (clothes) model *Es una de la modelas de la tienda.* She's one of the models in the store. ▲ [*m*] thing to be copied, model *Tenga Ud. esto como modelo.* Use this as a model. ▲ model, style, pattern *Me gusta este modelo.* I like this model.

‖ *No tiene modelo.* She has no equal.

moderación [*f*] moderation.

moderado (see **moderar**) [*adj*] conservative *El partido moderado.* The conservative party.

moderar to restrain *Modere Ud. sus ímpetus.* Restrain your impulses.

○ **moderarse** to become moderate, moderate, control oneself *Se moderó en la bebida.* He cut down on drinking. —*¡Modérese Ud.!* Control yourself!

moderno modern.

modestia modesty, humbleness *La modestia era su mejor cualidad.* Modesty was his greatest attribute. ▲ modesty, lack of display *Vestía con mucha modestia.* He dressed very modestly.

modesto simple.

modificación [*f*] modification.

modificar to modify.

modista dressmaker.

modo method, way *Ese es el mejor modo de arreglarlo.* That's the best way of settling it.

○ **a mi** (*or* **su**) **modo** in my (*or* his) own way *Yo hago las cosas a mi modo.* I do things in my own way. ○ **con buenos modos** politely. ○ **con malos modos** rudely *Contestó con muy malos modos.* He replied very rudely. ○ **de este modo** (in) this way *Creo que es mejor hacerlo de este modo.* I think it's better to do it this way. ○ **de modo que** so *¿De modo que es Ud. americano?* So you're an American? ▲ so, therefore *Tenemos mucha prisa, de modo que vamos a tomar un taxi.* We're in a hurry, so let's take a taxi. ○ **de ningún modo** by no (*or* any) means, under no (*or* any) circumstances *No iré de ningún modo.* I won't go under any circumstances. ○ **de todos modos** anyhow.

moho mold, mildew.

mojar to wet, moisten; to drench.

molde [*m*] mold, form.

○ **de molde** fitting, to the purpose, to the point *Viene de molde.* It's to the point.

moldura molding.

moler [*rad-ch I*] to grind, mill.

molestar to disturb *¡No me moleste!* Don't disturb me! ▲ to annoy *Molestaba a sus amigos con sus palabras.* His words annoyed his friends. ▲ to bother, inconvenience *¿Le molesta a Ud. que fume?* Will it bother you if I smoke? ▲ to hurt *Me molestan un poco estos zapatos.* These shoes hurt me a little.

○ **molestarse** to be annoyed *Ten cui-*

dado con lo que dices porque se molesta muy fácilmente. Be careful of what you say, for he's easily annoyed. ○ **molestarse (en)** to bother (to), take the trouble (to) *No se moleste en hacer tantos viajes.* Don't bother making so many trips.

molestia trouble *Perdone Ud. tantas molestias.* I'm sorry to trouble you so much. ▲ discomfort *No se encontraba muy bien, tenía algunas molestias.* She wasn't very well; she suffered some discomfort.

molesto uncomfortable *¿Está Ud. molesto?* Are you uncomfortable? ▲ annoyed *Se sentía molesto y dejó de hablarle.* He was annoyed and stopped speaking to her.

molete [m] disorder, mix-up, confusion [Am].

molino mill.

momento moment. ○ **al momento** right away, immediately. ○ **por momentos** any moment, soon.

mona female monkey. ▲ hangover *Tiene una mona horrible.* He has a terrible hangover. ○ **como la mona** terrible, lousy [Arg] *Me siento como la mona.* I feel terrible.

mondar to peel.

mondas [f pl] peelings.

moneda coin *Dejó algunas monedas sobre la mesa.* He left some coins on the table. ▲ currency *¿Dónde podré cambiar moneda extranjera?* Where can I exchange foreign currency? ○ **pagar en la misma moneda** to pay back in one's own coin, give tit for tat.

monja nun.

monje [m] monk.

mono [adj] cute *¡Qué mona es esta muchacha!* What a cute girl! ▲ [m] monkey *El mono está metido dentro de la jaula.* The monkey's in the cage. ○ **mono (de mecánico)** overalls [Sp] *Llevaba puesto un mono de mecánico.* He was wearing overalls.

monótono monotonous.

monstruo monster.

monstruoso monstrous.

montado (see **montar**) astride.

montador [m] assembler (of machinery).

montaña mountain.

montañoso mountainous.

montar to ride (horseback) *No monte Ud. ese caballo porque le tirará a Ud.* Don't ride that horse; he'll throw you. ▲ to set up, assemble, install *Hubo que montar una máquina en la fábrica.* A machine had to be installed in the factory. ▲ to set (a precious stone) *Montaron en el anillo cinco diamantes.* They set five diamonds in the ring. ○ **montar a** to amount to (in money) *¿A cuánto monta mi deuda?* How much does my debt amount to? ○ **montar a caballo** to ride horseback *Montaba a caballo todas las mañanas.* He went horseback riding every morning. ○ **montar en** to get on or in, board (a vehicle) *Al montar en el automóvil me hice daño en un pie.* I hurt my foot getting in the automobile. ○ **montar en cólera** to get furious *Al oír aquello, montó en cólera.* When he heard that he got furious. ○ **montarse** to get up onto, mount *Se montaron a caballo y se fueron.* They mounted their horses and left.

monte [m] mountain *Subió hasta lo más alto del monte.* He climbed to the very top of the mountain. ▲ woods, forest *El monte era tan espeso que casi no se podía andar por él.* The forest was so thick that one could hardly walk through it.

montón [m] heap, pile *Tengo un montón de cosas que hacer.* I have a lot of things to do.

monumental monumental, tremendous.

monumento monument.

moño knot, bun (of hair).

mora blackberry; Moorish woman.

moral [adj] moral *No es un libro muy moral.* It's not a very moral book. ▲ [f] morale *La moral de aquellos hombres era magnífica.* The morale of those men was excellent. ▲ [m] black mulberry tree.

moralidad [f] morals, morality.

morder [rad-ch I] to bite.

moreno dark-skinned, brunet(te). ▲ [n] colored person [Antilles].

morir [irr] to die *Cuando murió lo rodeaba toda su familia.* All his family was around him when he died. ○ **estarse muriendo por** to be dying to, be very anxious to *Me estoy muriendo por verla.* I'm dying to see her. ○ **morirse** to die *Se murió el año pasado.* He died last year.—*Se moría de miedo.* He was scared to death. ○ **morirse de hambre** to starve to death *Por no morirse de hambre aceptó aquel trabajo.* He took the job to keep from starving to death. ○ **morirse por** to like very much, be crazy about *Se muere por la cerveza.* He's crazy about beer. ○ **¡Muera...!** Down with...! *¡Muera el rey!* Down with the king!

moro [adj] Moorish. ▲ [n] Moor.

morocho dark-skinned [Am].

mortal [adj] fatal La herida que recibió era mortal. The wound he received was fatal. ▲ deadly, terrible Un enemigo mortal. A deadly enemy. ▲ [n] mortal being Eso les ocurre a todos los mortales. That happens to all mortals.

mortificar to mortify, humiliate Lo que dije me mortifica. What I said mortifies me. ▲ to hurt, bother Estos zapatos me mortifican. These shoes hurt.
   ○ **mortificarse** to torment oneself.

mosca fly.

mosquito mosquito.

mostaza mustard.

mostrador [m] counter (in a shop).

mostrar [rad-ch I] to show Le mostró la herida al médico. He showed the doctor his wound. ▲ to show, display Mostraba una gran tristeza. He showed great sadness.
   ○ **mostrarse** to appear, show oneself Quiso mostrarse indulgente en ese momento. He wanted to appear lenient at that moment.

mote [m] nickname; alias.

motín [m] uprising, revolt, riot.

motivar to cause.

motivo motive, reason.
   ○ **por ningún motivo** under no circumstances.

motor [m] motor.

mover [rad-ch I] to move Mueva Ud. esta mesa hacia el rincón. Move this table toward the corner. ▲ to make use of Movió sus influencias para conseguir un puesto. He made use of his connections to get a job. ▲ to motivate No le movía al interés de la ganancia. He wasn't motivated by gain. ▲ to stir Mueva Ud. la sopa hasta que hierva. Stir the soup until it boils.
   ○ **mover la cola** to wag the tail.
   ○ **moverse** to move Procure no moverse tanto. Try not to move so much.

movible [adj] movable.

móvil mobile Pertenece a una brigada móvil. He belongs to a mobile brigade. [m] motive ¿Qué móvil tuvo Ud. para venir aquí? What made you come here?

movilización [f] mobilization.

movilizar to mobilize.

movimiento movement, move A la hora en punto el tren se puso en movimiento. The train pulled out exactly on time. ▲ movement Pertenecía a un movimiento progresista. He belonged to a progressive movement. ▲ traffic

Hay mucho movimiento en esa calle. There's a lot of traffic in that street. ▲ animation, action La primera escena tiene mucho movimiento. The first scene has a lot of action.

mozo lad, young man (of peasant class). ▲ waiter ¡Mozo, tráigame la lista del almuerzo! Waiter, bring me the luncheon menu! ▲ porter, red-cap.
   ○ **buen mozo** good-looking [Am]; well-built [Sp].

mucamo, mucama servant [Am].

muchacha girl Me parece una excelente muchacha. She seems like a fine girl. ▲ young girl (in her teens) Sus hijas son ya unas muchachas. Her daughters are already in their teens. ▲ maid Dígale a la muchacha que haga las camas. Tell the maid to make the beds.

muchachada boyish action, prank; [Arg] gang of boys.

muchacho boy Estaba jugando con otros muchachos. He was playing with other boys.

mucho [adj] much No tiene mucha fuerza. He hasn't much strength. ▲ long, extended Hace mucho tiempo que le estoy esperando. I've been waiting a long time for you. ▲ [adv] much, a lot Bebía mucho. He used to drink a lot. ▲ often Esas cosas ocurren mucho. Those things happen often. ▲ long No me haga Ud. aguardar mucho. Don't make me wait long.
   ○ **muchos** many Había muchos niños en la plaza. There were many children in the square. ○ **ni mucho menos** nor anything like it, far from it No es tonto, ni mucho menos. He's not stupid; far from it. ○ **sentir mucho** to be very sorry Siento mucho lo que le sucede. I'm very sorry about what happened to him.

mudanza moving, changing residence; change, evolution.

muda change of underwear.

mudar (de) to change Mudaba de opinión cada día. He changed his mind daily. —Hubo que mudar toda la instalación eléctrica. All the electric installations had to be changed.
   ○ **mudarse (de)** to change (clothes) ¿Se mudó Ud. de traje? Did you change your clothes? ○ **mudarse (de casa, piso,** or **habitación)** to move, change residence Decidió mudarse (de casa) aquel mismo día. He decided to move that very day.

mudo dumb, mute; speechless. ▲ [n] mute (person unable to talk).
   ○ **cine mudo** silent films.

mueble [*adj*] movable. ▲ [*m*] piece of furniture *Me gusta mucho ese mueble.* I like that piece of furniture very much.
○ **muebles** furniture *Los muebles del salón eran de estilo moderno.* The living-room furniture was modern in style. ○ **propiedad mueble** movable property, personal property.
muela molar, molar tooth; millstone.
○ **dolor de muelas** toothache.
muelle soft *Una vida muelle.* A soft life. ▲ [*m*] spring (wire); pier.
muerte [*f*] death.
○ **de mala muerte** worthless, crumby.
○ **guerra a muerte** fight to the death.
muerto (see **morir**) dead.
muestra sample *Mande Ud. muestras de tela.* Send samples of cloth. ▲ (shop) sign *¿Leyó Ud. bien la muestra?* Did you read the sign correctly?
○ **dar muestras de** to show signs of *Daba muestras de no entender nada.* She showed no signs of understanding.
mugre [*f*] grime, dirt, filth.
mujer [*f*] woman; wife.
mula female mule.
mulato [*adj; n*] mulatto.
muleta crutch.
multa fine (punishment).
multiplicar to multiply.
multitud [*f*] crowd *Abrió el balcón para ver la multitud.* He opened the balcony window to see the crowd. ▲ masses *En su discurso se dirigía a la multitud.* His speech was addressed to the masses.
○ **multitud de** a great many, a great deal of *Se me ocurren una multitud de ideas.* I've a great many ideas.
mundano worldly.
mundial global, universal, world *La guerra mundial.* The World War.
mundo world *Ha viajado por todo el mundo.* He's traveled all over the world. ▲ world, environment, circle(s) *Frecuentaba el mundo de las letras.* He moved in literary circles.
○ **gran mundo** high society. ○ **tener**

(**mucho**) **mundo** to be sophisticated *or* experienced. ○ **todo el mundo** everybody *Todo el mundo estaba reunido en el salón.* Everybody was gathered in the living room. ○ **vida del mundo** world, worldly life *Abandonó la vida del mundo y entró en el convento.* She gave up the world and entered the convent.
munición, municiones [*f*] ammunition.
municipal municipal.
muñeca wrist; doll.
muralla wall (of a city).
murmullo murmur, whisper.
murmuración [*f*] gossip, slander.
murmurar to mutter *Murmuró unas palabras ininteligibles.* He muttered some unintelligible words. ▲ to murmur, whisper *Le murmuró al oído unas palabras.* She murmured some words in his ear. ▲ to gossip *Se pasaron la tarde murmurando de todo el mundo.* They spent the afternoon gossiping about everybody.
muro outside wall (of a house or garden).
músculo muscle.
museo museum.
música music *Estuvimos oyendo música clásica.* We were listening to classical music. ▲ band (of musicians) *La música venía a la cabeza del desfile.* The band came at the head of the parade. ▲ sheet music *No puedo tocar de memoria, haga el favor de darme la música.* I can't play from memory, please give me the music.
musical [*adj*] musical.
músico musical. ▲ [*n*] musician.
muslo thigh.
mustio withered; depressed.
mutuo mutual, reciprocal.
muy very *Estoy muy mal de salud.* My health's very bad.—*Lo he escrito muy de prisa.* I've written it very quickly.
○ **es muy de lamentar** it's to be deeply regretted *Es muy de lamentar que ocurra esto.* It's to be deeply regretted that this should happen.

N

nabo turnip.
nacer [-*zc*-] to be born *El nació en España.* He was born in Spain. ▲ to start, originate *La idea nació durante la fiesta.* The idea started at the party. ▲ to sprout *Ya nacieron las cebollas.* The onions have already

sprouted. ▲ to rise, appear *El sol nace más temprano en el verano.* The sun rises earlier in the summer. ▲ to rise, spring, have its source *El río hace en las montañas rococas.* The river has its source in the Rocky Mountains.
○ **nacer de pie** to be born lucky *Ese*

hombre nació de pie. That man was born lucky.

nacimiento birth. ▲ beginning, source *¿Dónde está el nacimiento de este río?* Where's the source of this river?

nación [*f*] nation.

nacional national.

nacionalidad [*f*] nationality.

nada nothing, not anything *No hay nada en esta caja.* There's nothing in this box.—*No me ha dado nada.* He hasn't given me anything. ▲ [*adv*] not at all *No es nada fácil.* It's not at all easy. ○ **De nada** You're welcome *"Muchas gracias." "De nada."* "Thank you very much." "You're welcome."

nadador, nadadora swimmer.

nadar to swim *¿Sabe Ud. nadar?* Can you swim? ○ **nadar en la abundancia** to live in luxury *Desde joven nadó en la abundancia.* From youth he lived in luxury.

nadie nobody, no one, not anybody, not anyone *No vino nadie.* Nobody came. —*No he visto a nadie.* I haven't seen anybody.—*Nadie lo conoce.* No one knows him.

naipe [*m*] (playing) card.

nalga buttock(s).

nana grandmother; nurse; lullaby; [*Am*] mamma.

naranja orange. ○ **media naranja** better half *Es ella su media naranja.* She's his better half.

naranjada orangeade.

naranjal [*m*] orange grove.

naranjero, naranjera orange seller; orange grower.

naranjo orange tree.

narcótico [*adj*] narcotic. ▲ [*m*] narcotic, dope.

nariz [*f*] nose.

nativo [*adj*] native.

natural [*adj*] natural. ▲ [*n*] native *Es un natural del Uruguay.* He's a native of Uruguay. ▲ [*m*] disposition, nature *Tiene un natural triste.* He has a sad disposition.

naturaleza nature *La naturaleza es variada en los países tropicales.* Nature is varied in tropical countries. ▲ constitution *El enfermo no tenía muy buena naturaleza.* The patient didn't have a very good constitution. ▲ temperament, disposition *Era muy nervioso por naturaleza.* He had a nervous temperament.

naturalidad [*f*] naturalness *Se conduce con mucha naturalidad.* He behaves very naturally.

naturalización [*f*] naturalization.

naufragar to be (ship)wrecked *Aquel barco naufragó en las costas de Chile.* That boat was wrecked on the coast of Chile. ▲ to fail, fall through *Las negociaciones naufragaron.* The negotiations fell through.

naufragio shipwreck.

náufrago, náufraga shipwrecked person, castaway.

náusea nausea.

navaja pen knife, clasp knife. ○ **navaja de afeitar** razor.

naval naval.

nave [*f*] ship *A pesar del huracán la nave llegó al puerto.* In spite of the hurricane the ship reached port.

navegación [*f*] navigation. ▲ voyage *Tuvimos una navegación difícil.* We had a rough voyage.

navegante [*m*] navigator.

navegar to navigate, sail.

navidad [*f*] Christmas.

neblina mist, fog.

necesario [*adj*] necessary.

necesidad [*f*] need, necessity *Sintió la necesidad de un cambio de clima.* He felt the need of a change of climate.

necesitar to need *Necesitamos más obreros.* We need more workers.

negar [*rad-ch I*] to deny *Negó que conociera a aquel hombre.* He denied that he knew that man. ▲ to refuse *Le negaron el aumento de sueldo.* They refused him a raise in salary. ▲ to disclaim *Negó toda responsabilidad en el accidente.* He disclaimed all responsibility for the accident. ○ **negarse a** to refuse to *Se negó a ayudarme.* He refused to help me.

negativo [*adj*] negative, in the negative *Su respuesta fué negativa.* His reply was in the negative. ▲ [*m*] negative *¿Quiere Ud. prestarme los negativos de esas fotografías?* Will you lend me the negatives of those photographs?

negligente negligent.

negociación [*f*] negotiation.

negociante [*m*] business man.

negociar to negotiate *Se reunieron para negociar las condiciones de paz.* They met to negotiate peace terms. ▲ to do business *Mi amigo quiere negociar con casas sudamericanas.* My friend wants to do business with South American firms.

negocio business, interest *Tienen negocios de petróleo.* They have oil interests. ○ **negocio redondo** good bargain *Esa* *compra fué un negocio redondo.* That purchase was a good bargain.

negro [*adj*] black. ▲ gloomy, dark *El porvenir parecía muy negro.* The future looked very gloomy. ▲ [*n*] Negro, Negress *Oímos algunos cantos religiosos de los negros.* We heard some Negro spirituals. ▲ [*m*] black (color).

○ **suerte negra** very bad luck *Tiene una suerte negra.* He has very bad luck.

nene, nena baby.

neoyorquino, neoyorquina New Yorker.

nervio nerve.

nervioso nervous.

neto [*adj*] net.

○ **peso neto** net weight.

neumático (pneumatic) tire.

neumonía pneumonia.

neutral [*adj*] neutral.

nevada snowfall.

nevar [*rad-ch I*] to snow *En este país no nieva nunca.* It never snows in this country.

nevera icebox, refrigerator.

ni neither, nor. ▲ not even *No dijo ni adiós.* He didn't even say good-by.

○ **ni . . . ni** neither . . . nor *No sabe ni inglés ni español.* He knows neither English nor Spanish. ○ **ni siquiera** not even, not a single *No dijo ni siquiera una palabra.* He didn't say a single word.

nicotina nicotine.

nido nest.

niebla fog, mist, haze.

nieta granddaughter.

nieto grandson.

nieve [*f*] snow.

ningún no, not a, not one *Ningún hombre entre ellos pudo levantar el peso.* Not a man among them could lift the weight. ▲ no, none *¿No hay ningún cuarto libre?* Are there no vacant rooms?

ninguno none *Ninguna de mis amigas lo sabe.* None of my friends know. ▲ not any *¿No le agrada ninguno de estos?* Don't you like any of these? ▲ no *or* none (whatever *or* at all) *No tiene criado ninguno.* He has no servants at all.

○ **de ninguna manera** under no circumstances, by no means *De ninguna manera iría.* I wouldn't go under any circumstances. ○ **de ningún modo** under no circumstances, by no means *De ningún modo debe Ud. irse hoy.* Under no circumstances should you go away today. ○ **por ningún lado** nowhere *No lo encontré por ningún lado.* I couldn't find it anywhere.

niña girl *Con ese traje parece una niña.* You look like a little girl in that dress. ▲ baby *No seas niña.* Don't be a baby. ▲ young lady, girl [*Am*]. ▲ Miss (used by servants) [*Am*] *Pregúntele Ud. a la niña María.* Ask Miss Mary.

○ **niña bien** glamour girl. ○ **niña del ojo** pupil (of the eye). ▲ apple of the eye *La quiere como a la niña de sus ojos.* She's the apple of his eye.

niñada childishness. ▲ childish action *Eso es una niñada.* That's childish.

niñez [*f*] childhood.

niño [*adj*] young *Yo era muy niño cuando sucedió eso.* I was very young when that happened. ▲ childish *Es muy niño todavía.* He's still very childish. ▲ [*m*] boy *Tiene dos niños y una niña.* He has two boys and a girl.

○ **niños** children *Había un grupo de niños jugando en el parque.* There was a group of children playing in the park.

nivel [*m*] level.

nivelar to level *Nivelaron el terreno en muy poco tiempo.* They leveled the ground in a very short time. ▲ to balance *Tenemos que nivelar nuestro presupuesto.* We must balance our budget.

no no, not "*¿Hará Ud. eso?*" "*No, no lo haré.*" "Will you do that?" "No, I won't."

○ **así no más** [*Am*] just like this *Hágalo así no más.* Do it just like this. ○ **no más** only, no more *Esto y no más.* This and no more. ○ **no sea que** or else *Tenemos que darnos prisa no sea que cierren la tienda.* We must hurry or else the shop'll be closed.

noble [*adj*] noble.

nobleza nobility, nobleness.

noche [*f*] night. ▲ evening (after sunset), night *¡Buenas noches!* Good evening! *or* Good night!

○ **ayer noche** last night *Ayer noche hizo mucho frío.* It was very cold last night. ○ **de la noche a la mañana** overnight *Se hizo rico de la noche a la mañana.* He became rich overnight. ○ **esta noche** tonight *Esta noche vamos al cine.* We're going to the movies tonight. ○ **hacerse de noche** to get dark *Tengo que irme proque se hace de noche.* I must go; it's getting dark. ○ **muy de noche** late at night *Era muy de noche cuando regresamos.* It was late at night when we got back.

Nochebuena Christmas Eve *Pasaré la*

Nochebuena con mi familia. I'm spending Christmas Eve with my family.

noción [*f*] notion, idea.

nombramiento nomination; appointment.

nombrar to name, mention *En la conversación nombramos a ese señor.* We mentioned that gentleman in the conversation. ▲ to appoint *Le nombraron presidente de la comisión.* They appointed him chairman of the committee.

nombre [*m*] name *¿Cuál es su nombre?* What's your name? ▲ fame, renown *Su libro le dió mucho nombre.* His book brought him great fame. ▲ reputation *Esa empresa tiene muy buen nombre.* That firm has a good reputation. ▲ noun *En este caso el adjetivo va antes del nombre.* In this case the adjective goes before the noun.
○ **nombre de familia** family name, surname. ○ **nombre y apellido** full name *Escriba Ud. su nombre y apellido.* Write your full name. ○ **no tener nombre** to be unspeakable *Lo que ha hecho no tiene nombre.* What he did is unspeakable. ○ **poner nombre (a)** to name, call *¿Qué nombre le van a poner?* What are they going to name him?

nordeste [*m*] northeast.

normal [*adj*] normal; standard.

norte [*m*] north. ▲ north wind *Sopla un norte muy fuerte.* A very strong north wind's blowing.

norteamericano [*adj; n*] North American (specifically, in all Spanish-speaking countries, used to designate persons or things of or from the United States).

nos us *No nos invitaron a la fiesta.* They didn't invite us to the party. —*Vinieron a buscarnos.* They came to look for us. ▲ one another, each other *Nos vimos en la calle.* We saw each other on the street.

nosotros we *Nosotros estamos listos.* We're ready.
○ **nosotros mismos** we (...) ourselves *Lo hicimos nosotros mismos.* We did it ourselves.

nota note *¿Tiene Ud. muchas notas en su cuaderno?* Do you have many notes in your notebook?—*Desafina en las notas altas.* She goes flat on the high notes.—*Hemos recibido una nota del Consulado Español.* We've received a note from the Spanish Consulate. ▲ mark, grade *Sacó muy buena nota en el examen de castellano.* He got a

very good mark on the Spanish exam. ▲ note, renown *Es un escritor de nota.* He's a writer of note. ▲ footnote, marginal note.
○ **dar la nota discordante** to be the disturbing element *Dó la nota discordante.* She was out of place. *or* She spoke out of turn. ○ **tomar nota de** to take note of, jot down *Tomé nota de todo lo que había ocurrido en el viaje.* I took note of everything that happened on the trip.

notable remarkable, notable; distinguished.

notar to notice, note, see *No notamos el cambio de altura.* We didn't notice the change in altitude.

notario notary public.

noticia news; news item *¿Cómo supo Ud. la noticia?* How did you find out the news? ▲ notice *Ponga Ud. una noticia en el periódico.* Put a notice in the paper.
○ **atrasado de noticias** behind the times *Me parece que está Ud. atrasado de noticias.* I think you're behind the times.

notificar to notify, inform.

novedad [*f*] novelty, latest fashion *Esta tienda ofrece las últimas novedades en artículos para caballero.* This shop has the latest things in men's wear. ▲ news *¡Eso es una novedad para mí!* That's news to me! ▲ surprise *¡Eso es una novedad!* That's a surprise!
○ **sin novedad** as usual; nothing new, no news "*¿Hay noticias?*" "*Sin novedad.*" "Any news?" "Nothing new."

novela novel.

novelista [*m, f*] novelist.

novena novena (nine days' devotion).

noveno [*adj*] ninth.

noventa ninety.

novia sweetheart, fiancée; bride.

noviembre [*m*] November.

novio sweetheart, fiancé; bridegroom.

nube [*f*] cloud. ▲ crowd *Le rodeaba una nube de gente.* A crowd of people surrounded him.
○ **esta en las nubes** to daydream *Siempre está en las nubes.* He's always daydreaming. ○ **por las nubes** sky-high *¡Los precios están por las nubes!* Prices are sky-high.

nublado cloudy, overcast.

nudo knot.

nuera daughter-in-law.

nuestro our *Nuestro maestro de español es madrileño.* Our Spanish teacher's from Madrid. ▲ of ours *Un amigo nuestro nos lo regaló.* A friend of ours (or One of our friends) gave it to us. ▲ours *Esta no es la nuestra, es la de Ud.* This isn't ours, it's yours.

nueve nine *Ahora son las nueve.* It's now nine o'clock.

nuevo new *La mesa era nueva.* The table was new.—*¿Qué hay de nuevo por aquí?* What's new around here? ▲new, different *Ya ha llegado el nuevo director.* The new director's already arrived.

○ **de nuevo** again *Tendrá que hacerlo de nuevo.* He'll have to do it again. ‖ *Eso es nuevo para mí.* That's news to me.

nuez [f] walnut.

nulo void, null.

numerar to number, put numbers on *Numeraron los asientos.* They numbered the seats.

número number *¿Cuál es el número de su teléfono?* What's your phone number? ▲size (of wearing apparel) *¿Cuál es el número de camisa que usa Ud.?* What size shirt do you wear? ▲number, edition *¿Tiene Ud. el último número de esta revista?* Do you have the latest number of this magazine?

nunca never, not ever *Nunca me habló.* He never spoke to me.—*No la he visto nunca.* I've never seen her.

Ñ

ñame [m] yam [Antilles].

ñapa See yapa.

ñato pug-nosed [Am].

ñeque [m] ‖ *Es hombre de ñeque.* He's a real he-man [Am].

ñoño silly.

ñudo ○ **al ñudo** in vain [Arg].

O

o or *Vienen tres o cuatro amigos.* Three or four friends are coming.

○ **o...o** either...or *O lo hace Ud. o lo mato.* Either you do it or I'll kill you. ○ **o sea** that is *La fiesta será el lunes próximo, o sea el 25 de agosto.* The party will be next Monday, that is, August 25th.

oasis [m] oasis.

obedecer [-zc-] to obey *Tendrán Uds. que obedecer mis órdenes.* You'll have to obey my orders. ▲to be the reason for, to arise from *¿A qué obedece todo eso?* What's the reason for all that?

obediencia obedience.

obediente obedient.

obispo bishop.

objeción [f] objection.

objeto object *Había varios objetos sobre la mesa.* There were several objects on the table. ▲purpose *El objeto de su visita era estrictamente comercial.* The purpose of his call was strictly business.

oblicuo [adj] oblique.

obligación [f] duty *Tiene Ud. la obligación de contestar.* It's your duty to reply. ▲obligation, responsibility *Con una familia tan numerosa tiene muchas obligaciones.* With such a large family he has a great many responsibilities.

obligar to oblige, force, compel *Le obligaron a firmarlo.* He was forced to sign it.

○ **obligarse** to obligate oneself, bind oneself *Se obligó a pagarlo.* He bound himself to pay it.

obligatorio obligatory, binding, compulsory.

obra work *Pongámonos a la obra.* Let's get to work. ▲book(s), work(s) *La obra de Cervantes es universalmente admirada.* The works of Cervantes are universally admired. ▲show, performance *¿Qué tal era la obra que vieron Uds. anoche?* How was the show last night?

○ **en obras** under construction, undergoing repairs *Esa casa está en obras.* That house is undergoing repairs. ○ **obra maestra** masterpiece. ‖ *¡Manos a la obra!* Let's get to work!

obrar to do, act *Obre Ud. como quiera.* Do as you please. ▲to act, behave *Obró Ud. ligeramente.* You acted without thinking.

○ **obrar en poder de** to be in the

possession of, be in one's hands *La carta obra en mi poder.* The letter's in my possession.

obrero, obrera worker, laborer.

o(b)scurecer [-*zc*-] to get dark *En el invierno o(b)scurece pronto.* It gets dark early in winter.

  ○ **o(b)scurecerse** to get dark *El cielo se o(b)scureció.* The sky got dark.

o(b)scuridad [*f*] obscurity, darkness.

o(b)scuro [*adj*] dark *A las cinco ya está o(b)scuro.* It's already dark at five o'clock.—*Quiero un traje azul o(b)scuro.* I want a dark-blue suit. ▲ obscure, not clear *El significado de esta frase es más bien o(b)scuro.* The meaning of this sentence is rather obscure.

  ○ **a o(b)scuras** in the dark, in darkness *La habitación estaba a o(b)scuras.* The room was in darkness.

obsequiar to lavish attentions on, entertain lavishly *Todo el tiempo que estuvo en casa de sus amigos le obsequiaron mucho.* During the whole time he was in his friends' home, they entertained him lavishly. ▲ to present with *La obsequiaron (con) un ramo de flores.* They presented her with a bouquet of flowers.

obsequio gift, present.

observación [*f*] observation, suggestion *¿Le puedo hacer a Ud. una observación?* May I make a suggestion?

  ○ **en observación** under observation *Estaba en observación en un sanatorio.* He was under observation in a sanatorium.

observador [*adj*] observing *Es un muchacho muy observador.* He's a very observing fellow. ▲ [*m*] observer *El gobierno francés envió un observador.* The French government sent an observer.

observar to notice *¿Observa Ud. algún cambio en el enfermo?* Do you notice any change in the patient? ▲ to watch *Observe Ud. lo que hacen.* Watch what they're doing.

  ○ **observar buena conducta** to behave well.

obstáculo obstacle, hindrance.

obstinación [*f*] obstinacy, stubbornness.

obstinado stubborn.

obstinarse en to insist on *Se obstina en quedarse en casa.* He insists on staying home.

obstruir to obstruct, block *Aquel automóvil estaba obstruyendo el tráfico.* That car was blocking traffic.

  ○ **obstruirse** to be blocked up *or* clogged up *La cañería se obstruía con frecuencia.* The pipe was often clogged.

obtener [*irr*] to get, obtain *¿Dónde obtuvo Ud. esos informes?* Where did you get that information?

obtuso obtuse.

ocasión [*f*] chance, opportunity *Aquí puede tener ocasión de encontrar trabajo.* You may have a chance of finding work here. ▲ time, occasion *No es esta la mejor ocasión para preguntárselo.* This isn't the best time to ask him about it.

  ○ **aprovechar la ocasión** to take advantage of a situation. ○ **de ocasión** second-hand *Compró un automóvil de ocasión.* He bought a second-hand car.

ocasionar to cause *Aquel descuido pudo ocasionar un incendio.* That carelessness could have caused a fire.

occidental [*adj*] western; Occidental. ▲ [*n*] Occidental.

occidente [*m*] west; Occident.

océano ocean.

ocio idleness, leisure.

  ○ **ratos de ocio** spare time *Lo haré en mis ratos de ocio.* I'll do it in my spare time.

ocioso lazy, idle *Era un hombre ocioso.* He was a lazy fellow.

octavo [*adj*] eighth.

octubre [*m*] October.

ocultar to hide.

oculto concealed, hidden.

ocupación [*f*] business *Si no tiene ocupación mañana, venga por aquí.* If you have nothing to do tomorrow, come on over. ▲ occupation *La ocupación se hizo con orden.* The occupation was carried out in an orderly way.

ocupado (see **ocupar**) busy *Hoy estaré ocupado todo el día.* I'll be busy all day today. ▲ occupied, taken *¿Está ocupado ese piso?* Is that apartment occupied?

ocupar to occupy, take possession of *Han ocupado una nueva ciudad.* They've occupied a new city. ▲ to take *Puede Ud. ocupar esa silla.* You may take that chair. ▲ to live in *Ocupó una habitación en el piso tercero.* He lived in a room on the third floor.

  ○ **ocuparse de** to take care of, pay attention to *Se ocupa muy poco de su familia.* He pays very little attention to his family.

ocurrencia witticism, wisecrack *Las ocurrencias de aquel hombre hacían reír a todos.* That fellow's wisecracks made everyone laugh.

ocurrir to occur, happen *Salga Ud. a ver qué ocurre.* Go out and see what's happening.

○ **ocurrírsele a uno** to occur to one *Se me ocurrió una buena idea.* A good idea occurred to me.

ochavo penny.

○ **no tener ni un ochavo** to be penniless.

ochenta eighty.

ocho eight; eighth (day of the month).

odiar to hate.

odio hatred.

odioso mean, nasty *¡Qué odioso!* How nasty!

oeste [*m*] west.

ofenderse to take offense *Se lo dije y no se ofendió.* I told him and he didn't take offense.

ofensa insult, offense (personal).

ofensivo [*adj*] offensive.

oferta offer.

oficial [*adj*] official *Fué en misión oficial.* He went on an official mission. ▲ [*m*] officer *Fué oficial del Ejército.* He was an army officer.

○ **oficial mayor** chief clerk (government or civil service).

oficina office (room).

oficinista [*m, f*] office worker, white-collar worker; clerk.

oficio manual work, occupation, trade *¿Qué oficio tiene Ud.?* What's your occupation?—*Es carpintero de oficio.* He's a carpenter by trade.

○ **oficio(s) divino(s)** church service(s).

ofrecer [*-zc-*] to offer *Me ofrecen un nuevo empleo.* They're offering me a new job.

○ **ofrecerse** to offer oneself, be at the service of *Me ofrezco a Ud. para todo.* I'm completely at your service.

ofrecimiento offer, offering.

ofrenda offering (religious).

¡oh! O! oh!

oída hearing.

○ **de** (*or* **por**) **oídas** by hearsay.

oído (inner) ear *Le duelen los oídos.* He has an earache. ▲ hearing *Era muy duro de oído.* He was very hard of hearing.

○ **al oído** in the ear, whispering *Le murmuró algo al oído.* She whispered something in his ear. ○ **dar oídos** to listen, lend an ear *No quiso dar oídos a aquello.* He didn't want to listen

to that. ○ **de oído** by ear *Tocaba el piano de oído.* He played the piano by ear. ○ **tener buen oído** to have a good ear (for music); to have good hearing.

oír [*irr*] to hear *No oigo bien; hable más alto.* I don't hear well; speak louder. ▲ to listen *Oígame, por favor, tengo que hacerle una pregunta.* Listen, please, I have to ask you a question.

‖ *¡Oiga!* Hello! (telephone) [*Sp*].

ojal [*m*] buttonhole.

¡ojalá! ‖ *¡Ojalá (que) venga!* I wish he'd come!

ojeada glance.

○ **echar una ojeada** to cast a glance.

ojear to glance through *Ojeó rápidamente el periódico.* He quickly glanced through the paper.

ojo eye *El médico le examinó los ojos.* The doctor examined his eyes.

○ **costar un ojo de la cara** to cost plenty *Nos costó un ojo de la cara.* It's cost us plenty. ○ **en un abrir y cerrar de ojos** in the twinkling of an eye. ○ **¡ojo!** look out! *¡Ojo! Que se va a caer.* Look out! It's going to fall. ○ **ojo de agua** spring of water. ○ **ojo de la llave** keyhole. ○ **ojo morado, ojo negro** black eye *Le pusieron un ojo negro.* They gave him a black eye. ○ **poner ojo** to pay (close) attention *¡Ponga Ud. ojo en esto!* Pay attention to this! ○ **tener buen ojo** to have a good eye *or* good foresight *Ha tenido Ud. buen ojo.* You've shown good foresight.

ola wave (of water).

oleaje [*m*] ground swell, motion of waves.

oler [*rad-ch I*] to smell *Esto huele muy bien.* This smells very good.—*Olió el peligro y decidió no salir.* He smelled danger and decided not to go out.

olfato sense of smell.

olivar [*m*] olive grove.

oliva olive.

olivo olive tree.

olla pot.

olor [*m*] smell, odor.

oloroso fragrant.

olvidar to forget *¿Ha olvidado Ud. algo?* Have you forgotten something?

○ **olvidarse (de)** to forget *Olvídese de lo ocurrido.* Forget what's happened.

olvido forgetfulness.

omisión [*f*] omission.

omitir to omit.

ómnibus [m] bus.
once eleven; eleventh (day of month).
onda wave (of hair); ripple (of water).
○ onda corta, onda larga short wave, long wave (radio).
ondulación [f] wave, waiving.
○ ondulación permanente permanent wave.
ondulado (see ondular) wavy. ▲ [m] wave, waving.
ondular to ripple. wave.
onza ounce.
opaco opaque.
ópera opera.
operación [f] operation Los médicos decidieron hacer la operación. The doctors agreed to perform the operation. ▲ operation (Math), calculation ¿Quiere Ud. comprobar las operaciones? Do you want to check the calculations? ▲ operation (Mil) El general dirigía las operaciones. The general directed the operations.
operar to operate on Le han operado de apendicitis. They operated on him for appendicitis.
operario, operaria operator, skilled worker.
opinar to judge, hold (or be of) the opinion.
opinión [f] opinion ¿Qué opinión tiene Ud. de esto? What's your opinion about this?
oponer [irr] to set up Opusieron toda clese de obstáculos. They set up all kinds of obstacles.
○ oponerse (a) to oppose Nadie se opuso a aquel proyecto. No one opposed that project.
oportunidad [f] opportunity.
oportuno opportune, fitting, appropriate Su intervención fué oportuna. His intervention was opportune.
oposición [f] opposition.
oprimir to oppress Oprimía a los débiles. He oppressed the weak. ▲ to be tight El cinturón le oprimía demasiado. The belt was too tight on him.
óptico optometrist Voy al óptico para comprar unos lentes. I'm going to the optometrist to get glasses.
optimismo optimism.
optimista optimistic. ▲ [n] optimist.
opuesto (see oponer) [adj] opposed. ▲ opposite Estaba situado en el lado opuesto. It was situated on the opposite side.
opulento rich, opulent.
oración [f] sentence Escribe oraciones muy cortas. He writes very short sentences. ▲ prayer Rezó sus oraciones. He said his prayers.
orador [m] orator.
órbita [f] orbit.
orden [f] order(s), command, instruction No he recibido ninguna(s) orden(es) de mis superiores. I haven't received any order(s) from my superiors. ▲ order (commercial) Despacharemos su orden vía Nueva Orleans. We'll ship your order via New Orleans. ▲ order (religious) La orden franciscana. The Franciscan order. ▲ [m] order Trabajaba sin ningún orden. He had no order in his work.
○ a sus órdenes at your service.
○ en orden in order Todo estaba en orden. Everything was in order.
○ orden del día agenda, order of the day.
ordenar to put in order Tenemos que ordenar estos papeles. We must put these papers in order. ▲ to order Ordenó que le sirvieran la comida. He ordered them to serve his dinner.
○ ordenarse to be ordained.
ordinario usual ¿Cuál es el precio ordinario de esto? What's the usual price of this? ▲ ordinary Era un hombre ordinario. He was an ordinary man. ▲ vulgar Es un tipo muy ordinario. He's a very vulgar fellow.
○ correo ordinario regular mail.
○ de ordinario usually De ordinario viene por la mañana. He usually comes in the morning.
oreja ear Tiene las orejas grandes. He has big ears. ▲ handle [Am] Se le rompió la oreja a la taza. The handle of the cup broke.
○ descubrir la oreja to give oneself away.
orgánico organic.
organismo organism.
organización [f] organization.
organizador [adj] organizing. ▲ [m] organizer.
○ comité organizador, comisión organizadora committee on arrangements.
organizar to organize Van a organizar el club la semana que viene. They're going to organize the club next week. ▲ to arrange, organize Organizó una fiesta. She arranged a party.
órgano organ La cantante fué acompañada por un órgano. The singer was accompanied by an organ.—No tiene órgano sano. He hasn't a healthy organ in his body.—Ese periódico es el

órgano de un partido político. That paper's the organ of a political party.
orgía drunken revel, orgy.
orgullo pride.
orgulloso proud, haughty.
oriental [adj] eastern; Oriental. ▲ [n] Oriental.
orientarse to find one's bearings, to orient oneself.
oriente [m] east; Orient.
origen [m] origin Sé el origen de toda la historia. I know the origin of the whole story. ▲ descent, extraction Es de origen francés. He's of French descent.
original original; eccentric, odd Es un tipo muy original. He's a very eccentric person. ▲ [m] original Haga Ud. el original y tres copias. Make an original and three copies.
originalidad [f] originality; oddity, eccentricity.
originar to start Aquella frase originó una discusión. That sentence started a discussion.
orilla bank Las orillas del río estaban cubiertas de árboles. The banks of the river were heavily wooded. ▲ edge, rim La orilla de la taza está rota. The rim of the cup's chipped. ○ orilla del mar seashore.
oro gold.
orquesta orchestra (musicians).
ortografía spelling (in writing).

os you, to you [Fam pl, Sp; see vosotros] Os he dicho que no lo hagáis más. I told you not to do it again.
osadía audacity, daring, boldness.
oso, osa bear.
ostentación [f] ostentation.
ostentar to boast, show off.
ostión [m] oyster [Mex].
ostra oyster.
otoño autumn, fall.
otro another, other Este otro me gusta más. I like this other one better. ▲ another ¿Quiere Ud. otro? Would you like another? ○ alguna otra cosa something (or anything) else ¿Quiere Ud. alguna otra cosa? Do you want anything else? ○ (el) uno a(l) otro each other Se miraron (el) uno a(l) otro con sorpresa. They looked at each other in surprise. ○ otra cosa something else, something different Eso es otra cosa. That's something else. ○ otra vez again ¿Volverá Ud. otra vez por aquí? Will you come here again? ○ por otra parte on the other hand. ○ unos a otros one another Se miraron unos a otros. They looked at each other.
ovación [f] ovation, cheering.
oveja sheep.
oxígeno oxygen.
oyente [m, f] hearer, listener.

P

paciencia patience, forbearance.
paciente [adj] patient ¡Qué niño más paciente! What a patient child! ▲ [n] patient No se puede visitar a los pacientes después de las seis. Patients may not be visited after six o'clock.
pacto agreement, pact.
padecer [-zc-] to suffer Padezco de jaquecas. I suffer from headaches.
padre [m] father. ▲ priest Llamaron a un padre. They called a priest. ○ padres [m] parents Sus padres son franceses. His parents are French.
padrino godfather Fué a ver a su padrino. He went to see his godfather. ▲ patron, sponsor Tiene muy buenos padrinos. He has very good sponsors.
paella dish of rice with meat or chicken.
paga wages, pay.
pagador [m] paying teller, paymaster.
pagar to pay Hay que pagar por antici-

pado. You have to pay in advance. ▲ to pay for Pagaron el traje a plazos. They paid for the suit in installments. ○ pagar contra recepción C.O.D. ○ pagar el pato to be the scapegoat, take the rap Siempre me toca pagar el pato. I'm always the one who takes the rap. ○ pagarlas to pay for (atone for) ¡Tarde o temprano me las pagarás! Sooner or later you'll pay for it. or I'll get even with you! ○ pagarse de uno mismo to be conceited Se paga mucho de si mismo. He's very conceited.
página page (of a book).
pago payment.
país [m] country Esa parte del país está llena de bosques. That part of the country's heavily wooded. ○ del país domestic ¿Le gusta Ud. el vino del país? Do you like the domestic wine?
paisaje [m] landscape, scenery.

paisano, paisana person from same province *or* city *Este señor es gallego; es paisano mío.* This gentleman's a Galician; he's from my province. ▲civilian *En la plaza había algunos militares y muchos paisanos.* In the square there were some army men and many civilians.
○ **de paisano** in civilian clothes, in mufti *Iba vestido de paisano.* He was wearing civilian clothes.

paja straw.
○ **echarlo a pajas** to draw straws *Vamos a echarlo a pajas para ver quien paga.* Let's draw straws to see who pays.

pájaro, pájara bird *Más vale pájaro en mano que ciento volando.* A bird in the hand's worth two in the bush.

pala spade, shovel; dust pan.

palabra word *¿Cómo se escribe esa palabra?* How do you spell that word?
○ **decir de palabra** to tell in person, to tell by word of mouth *Es mejor que se lo diga de palabra que no por escrito.* It's better to tell him in person than in writing. ○ **¡palabra!** honestly! no fooling! no kidding! *Lo que le dijo es cierto ¡palabra!* No kidding! What he told him's true.
○ **palabra de honor** word of honor *Dió su palabra de honor.* He gave his word of honor. ○ **palabras mayores** no joking matter, insulting *Esas son palabras mayores.* That's no joking matter. *or* It's insulting. ○ **pedir** (*or* **tener**) **la palabra** *"¡Pido la palabra!" "Un momento, por favor. Ahora la tiene el presidente." "May I have the floor?" "One moment, please. The president has the floor now."*

palacio palace.

palco box (theater).

pálido pale.

paliza beating, spanking.

palma palm (leaf, tree) *La avenida estaba bordeada de palmas.* The avenue was lined with palms. ▲palm (hand) *Conozco este lugar como la palma de la mano.* I know this place like the palm of my hand.
○ **llevar la palma** to win the prize, carry the day *Me parece que te has llevado la palma.* I think you've won the prize.

palmada clapping; pat (on the back).
○ **dar palmadas** to clap, applaud.

palmo span (measure of length: 8 inches).

palo stick *Tenía un palo en la mano.* He had a stick in his hand. ▲pole *El palo del telégrafo cayó en tierra.* The telegraph pole fell on the ground. ▲wood *La cuchara y el tenedor eran de palo.* The spoon and fork were made of wood. ▲tree [*Am*] *Los palos están en flor.* The trees are in bloom. ▲suit (in cards) *¿Qué palo es el triunfo?* What's trumps?
○ **dar de palos** to club, beat *Le dieron de palos.* They gave him a beating.

paloma pigeon, dove.

palpitante [*adj*] throbbing, beating.

palpitar to beat, throb, quiver.

pampa pampa, plain [*Arg*].
○ **estar a la pampa** to be outdoors, camp [*Am*].

pan [*m*] bread.
○ **pan integral** whole-wheat bread.
○ **pan seco, pan duro** stale bread.
○ **pan tierno** fresh bread.

panadería bakery.

panadero, panadera baker.

panamericano Pan-American.

pandereta tambourine.

pandillero gangster [*Am*].

panecillo roll (bread) *Los panecillos están muy tiernos.* The rolls are very soft.

pánico panic, fright.

panorama [*m*] panorama.

pantalla lamp shade *Cambie la pantalla de esta lámpara.* Change the shade on this lamp. ▲film, screen, movie *Conocía a muchas estrellas de la pantalla.* He knew many movie stars.

pantalones [*m pl*] trousers, pants.

pantano swamp, marsh, bog.

pantomima pantomime.

pantorrilla calf (of the leg).

panza belly, paunch.

pañal [*m*] diaper.

pañito small cloth.

paño cloth, woolen goods.

pañuelo handkerchief, kerchief; shawl.

Papa [*m*] Pope *El Papa reside en el Vaticano.* The Pope lives in the Vatican.

papa [*f*] potato [*Am*] *Nos dieron puré de papas.* They gave us mashed potatoes.

papá [*m*] papa, pop, dad.

papaya papaya (fruit).

papel [*m*] paper *¿Está hecho de papel o de tela?* Is it made of paper or cloth? ▲paper, document *Guarda esos papeles, son importantes.* Keep those papers; they're important. ▲role, part *Tendrá a su cargo el pa-*

pel principal. He'll have the leading role.

○ **papel de cartas** stationery *He comprado una caja de papel de cartas.* I bought a box of stationery. ○ **papel de seda** tissue paper *Envuélvalo primero en papel de seda.* Wrap it first in tissue paper. ○ **papel moneda** paper money, bills *Démelo en papel moneda.* Give it to me in bills.

papelería stationery store.

papeleta slip of paper.

○ **papeleta electoral** ballot.

papera mumps.

par [*adj*] even (of numbers) *Las casas con números pares están al norte.* The houses with even numbers are on the north side. ▲ [*m*] equal *Es una mujer sin par.* She has no equal. ▲ pair *Un par de zapatos.* A pair of shoes. ▲ couple *Llegará dentro de un par de días.* He'll arrive in a couple of days.

○ **abierto de par en par** wide open *La puerta estaba abierta de par en par.* The door was wide open. ○ **a la par** at par *La peseta estaba a la par.* The peseta was at par. ▲ in a tie, in a dead heat *Los caballos llegaban a la par.* The horses finished in a dead heat. ○ **pares y** (*or* o) **nones** odds and (*or* or) evens *¿Toma Ud. pares o nones?* Do you take odds or evens?

para to, in order to *Debemos salir ya para llegar a tiempo.* We must leave now to get there on time.

○ **estar para** (followed by infinitive) to be about to *Estoy para salir.* I'm about to leave. ○ **¿para dónde?** where (to)? *¿Para dónde va este tren?* Where does this train go? ○ **para que** so (that) *Abra la ventana para que no entre el aire fresco.* Open the window so we can get some fresh air. ○ **¿para qué?** what for? what good? what use? *¿Para qué sirve esta máquina?* What's this machine for? ▲ why? *¿Para qué lo despertó?* Why did you wake him?

parachoques [*m sg*] bumper (of car).

parada stop *¿Cuántas paradas hace este tren?* How many stops does this train make? ▲ parade (military) *Vió Ud. la parada esta mañana?* Did you see the parade this morning?

paradero whereabouts *¿Sabe Ud. el paradero de Juan?* Do you know John's whereabouts?

parado (see **parar**) shy, timid *El chico es parado.* The boy's shy. ▲ sus-

pended, shut down *Está parada la fábrica.* The factory's shut down. ▲ unemployed *¿Hay muchos obreros parados estos días?* Are there many unemployed workers at present? ▲ standing [*Am*] *He estado parado mucho rato.* I've been standing quite a while.

paraguas [*m sg*] umbrella.

paraíso paradise, heaven; upper gallery (in a theater).

paralelo parallel, corresponding.

paralizar to paralyze.

parar to stop *Tuvieron que parar a medio camino.* They had to stop halfway there. ▲ to stake, bet [*Am*] *Con estas cartas yo voy a parar cincuenta pesos.* With these cards I'm going to bet fifty pesos. ▲ to stop (over), stay *¿En qué hotel pararán sus amigos?* What hotel will your friends stay at? ▲ to end up, turn out *No paró bien aquel negocio.* That business didn't turn out very well.

○ **ir** (*or* **venir**) **a parar** to land finally, end up *¿Cómo ha venido a parar esto aquí?* How in the world did this get here? ○ **parar de** to stop *No para de llover desde ayer.* It hasn't stopped raining since yesterday. ○ **parar la oreja** to prick up one's ears *Paró la oreja para oír lo que decíamos.* He pricked up his ears to hear what we were saying. ○ **pararse** to stop, halt *Al llegar a la puerta se paró.* When he got to the door he stopped. ▲ to stand up, get up [*Am*] *Se pararon al verla llegar.* They got up when they saw her coming.

parcial partial.

pardo dark-gray; brown *Tiene ojos pardos.* He has brown eyes. ▲ [*n*] mulatto [*Am*].

parecer [-*zc*-] to look, appear *Parece que va a llover hoy.* It looks as though it'd rain today. ▲ to seem *Me parece muy bien.* It seems all right to me. ▲ [*m*] opinion *Me gustaría saber cuál es su parecer en este asunto.* I'd like to know what your opinion is in this matter.

○ **al parecer** apparently *Al parecer vendrá la semana próxima.* Apparently he's coming next week. ○ **parecerse** to be alike *Los dos se parecen mucho.* The two of them are very much alike. ○ **según parece** as it seems, apparently *Según parece lloverá toda la tarde.* Apparently it'll rain all afternoon.

parecido like, similar *Los dos trabajos son muy parecidos.* The two jobs are very similar. ▲ [m] resemblance *El parecido entre padre e hijo es muy claro.* The resemblance between father and son is very clear.
○ **bien parecido** good-looking *Su hijo es muy bien parecido.* Your son's very good-looking. ○ **parecido a** like, similar to *Yo tengo un traje muy parecido al suyo.* I have a suit very much like yours.

pared [f] wall.

pareja pair *¡Gano, tengo dos parejas!* I win; I have two pairs. ▲ team *Esos dos tenistas hacen muy buena pareja.* Those two tennis players make a very good team. ▲ couple *Ví una pareja de soldados en el parque.* I saw a couple of soldiers in the park. —*Hacen muy buena pareja.* They make a good couple. ▲ dancing partner *Su pareja baila muy bien.* Your partner dances very well.

parejo [adj] neck and neck *Los dos caballos iban parejos en la carrera.* The two horses were running neck and neck. ▲ equal, the same *Sus carácteres son parejos.* Their characters are the same.

pariente [m, f] relative.

parlamento parliament; parley.

paro stoppage; unemployment; strike.

parpadear to blink, wink.

párpado eyelid.

parque [m] park *Paseamos por el parque.* We strolled through the park. ▲ ammunition [Am] *Se les acabó el parque.* They ran out of ammunition.

párrafo paragraph.

parranda binge *Se pasaron toda la noche de parranda.* We were on a binge all night.

parte [f] part *¿En qué parte de la ciudad vive Ud.?* What part of the city do you live in?—*¿Qué parte del pollo le gusta más?* What part of the chicken do you like best? ▲ share *Cada uno pagó su parte.* Each paid his share. ▲ party (legal) *Hicieron comparecer a ambas partes ante el juez.* They summoned both parties before the judge. ▲ [m] report *Envíeme el parte mañana.* Send me the report tomorrow.
○ **dar parte** to inform, notify *Dieron parte del robo a la policía.* They notified the police of the robbery. ○ **de mi parte** on my behalf *Déle recuerdos de mi parte.* Remember me

to him. ○ **de parte de** in the name of, on behalf of *Telefoneo de parte del Sr. Gómez.* I'm calling on behalf of Mr. Gómez. ○ **en alguna otra parte** somewhere else *He debido dejar mi billete en alguna otra parte.* I must have left my ticket somewhere else. ○ **en parte** partly, in part *Tiene Ud. razón sólo en parte.* You're only partly right. ○ **en todas partes** everywhere *Se le ve siempre en todas partes.* He's seen everywhere. ○ **parte de guerra** (war) communiqué *¿Ha leído Ud. el parte de guerra?* Have you read the communiqué? ○ **por mi parte** as for me, as far as I'm concerned *Por mi parte no hay inconveniente.* It's all right as far as I'm concerned. ○ **por** (or **a**) **partes** in parts *Hagamos el trabajo por partes iguales.* Let's do the work in equal parts. ○ **tomar parte** to take part *¿Tomará parte Ud. en el próximo campeonato de golf?* Are you taking part in the next golf tournament?

participante participating. ▲ [n] participant.

participar to announce *Participaron a las amistades su próximo matrimonio.* They announced to their friends their coming marriage.
○ **participar de** to share, share in *Participaremos de las ganancias.* We'll share the profits.—*Los hijos participaron de la fortuna de su padre.* The children shared in their father's fortune. ○ **participar en** to take part in *Participó en las olimpiadas de 1936.* He took part in the 1936 Olympic games.

particular special, particular *Es un caso muy particular.* It's a very special case. ▲ private *Esta es una casa particular.* This is a private house. ▲ odd, peculiar *Es una persona muy particular.* He's a very peculiar person.
○ **en particular** particularly, especially *Me gustan todos los deportes, pero el tenis en particular.* I like all sports, but particularly tennis. ○ **nada de particular** nothing special, nothing unusual *Esa casa no tiene nada de particular.* There's nothing unusual about that house.

partida departure *La hora de la partida de los trenes está indicada en el horario.* Train departures are listed in the timetable. ▲ item (in an account) *Asiente Ud. Esta partida en* *el libro correspondiente.* Enter this item in the right book. ▲ game *¿Echamos una partida de cartas?* Shall we play a game of cards? ▲ certificate (of birth, marriage, death) *Partida de nacimiento.* Birth certificate.—*Partida de casamiento* or *boda.* Marriage license.—*Partida de defunción.* Death certificate. ▲ band, gang *Fueron atacados por una partida de ladrones.* They were attacked by a band of thieves.

○ **jugarle una mala partida** to play a dirty trick on, double-cross *Le jugó una mala partida.* She played a dirty trick on him.

partidario follower *Este señor es uno de sus partidarios más antiguos.* This gentleman's one of his oldest followers.

partido broken, divided *La cuerda está partida en dos.* The string's broken in two. ▲ [m] party, faction *Pertenecen al mismo partido.* They belong to the same party. ▲ match, game *¿Quiere Ud. ver el partido de fútbol?* Would you like to see the football game?

○ **sacar partido de** to profit by *Ese hombre saca partido de todo.* That man profits by everything.

partir to split *Partió la manzana en dos.* He split the apple in two. ▲ to divide *Partieron el terreno en varios lotes.* They divided the land into several lots. ▲ to cut *Partamos un poco de leña para el fuego.* Let's cut some wood for the fire. ▲ to break, crush *Esta máquina sirve para partir las piedras.* This machine's for crushing stones. ▲ to divide (mathematics) *Parta Ud. 250 entre 3.* Divide 250 by 3. ▲ to leave *Si partimos por la noche llegaremos durante el día.* If we leave at night, we'll arrive during the day. ▲ to start, reckon *Ud. parte de un supuesto equivocado.* You're starting with a false assumption.

○ **partirse** to break *Al partirse el hielo, cayeron al agua.* When the ice broke they fell into the water.

pasa (see **paso**) raisin.

pasado last *Estas cartas llegaron la semana pasada.* These letters came last week. ▲ spoiled *La fruta está pasado.* The fruit's spoiled. ▲ [m] past *Esa mujer tiene un pasado muy romántico.* That woman has a very romantic past.

○ **pasado de moda** out of date, out of style *Está pasado de moda.* It's

out of date. ○ **pasado mañana** day after tomorrow *Me dijeron que vendrían pasado mañana.* They told me they'd come day after tomorrow.

pasaje [m] crossing, journey, voyage *Hicimos el pasaje a Europa en siete días.* We made the crossing to Europe in seven days. ▲ fare *¿Cuánto cuesta un pasaje en primera a La Habana?* How much is the fare to Havana, first-class? ▲ passage *Citó un pasaje del Quijote.* He quoted a passage from Don Quixote. ▲ arcade *Dentro de este edificio hay un pasaje.* There's an arcade in this building. ▲ number of passengers on a ship, plane, etc *El pasaje del avión estaba completo.* All seats on the plane were taken.

pasajero passing, transitory *Es solamente una lluvia pasajera.* It's only a passing shower. ▲ [n] passenger *Los pasajeros tienen que enseñar sus billetes a la entrada.* Passengers must show their tickets at the gate.

pasamanos [m sg] rail, banister.

pasaporte [m] passport.

pasar to pass, overtake *Pasemos ese carro, nos retrasa mucho.* Let's pass that car, he's holding us up. ▲ to pass, hand *Haga el favor de pasarme el azúcar.* Please pass me the sugar. ▲ to pass, go through *Tuvimos que pasar muchos túneles.* We had to go through a number of tunnels. ▲ to cross *Debemos pasar el puente durante la noche.* We must cross the bridge at night. ▲ to move, transfer *Tienen que pasar al enfermo a otro cuarto.* They have to move the patient to another room. ▲ to happen *¿Qué pasó anoche?* What happened last night? ▲ to spend *Pasa los domingos en la playa.* He spends his Sundays at the beach. ▲ to come (*or* go) in *Pase Ud. y siéntese.* Come in and sit down. ▲ to tolerate, overlook *Ella le pasa todas sus faltas.* She overlooks all his faults. ▲ to get along, make out *Pasa muy bien con lo que gana.* He gets along very well on what he earns. ▲ to pass (at cards) *Paso.* I pass. ▲ to pass, stop (of rain, snow, etc) *La lluvia pasará pronto.* The rain'll stop soon.

○ **pasar de largo** to go (*or* pass) right by, pass by without stopping *No se demore, pase Ud. de largo.* Don't delay. Pass by without stopping. ○ **pasar de moda** to go out of style. ○ **pasar el rato** to kill time, pass the time away *¿Cómo pasaremos el rato?* How shall we kill time? ○ **pasar (la) lista** to call the roll *Dentro de un momento pasarán (la) lista.* In a moment they'll call the roll. ○ **pasarlo bien** to have a good time *La otra noche lo pasamos muy bien.* We had a very good time the other night. ○ **pasar por alto** to skip, overlook *Pasé por alto esa página.* I skipped that page. ○ **pasarse** to go over *Se pasó al partido contrario.* He went over to the other party. ▲ to slip one's mind *¡Se me pasó completamente!* It completely slipped my mind. ○ **pasarse de ...** to be too ... *Se pasa de listo.* He thinks he's smart. ○ **pasársele a uno** to get over (a state of mind), pass from *Se enfadó, pero se le pasó pronto.* He got angry but he soon got over it. ○ **pasarse sin** to do (or get along) without *Podemos pasar muy bién sin automóvil.* We can get along very well without a car.

pasatiempo pastime, amusement.

Pascua ○ **Pascua florida, Pascua de resurrección** Easter *Celebran mucho la Pascua de resurrección.* They have a big Easter celebration. ○ **pascuas** Christmas *¡Felices Pascuas!* Merry Christmas!
○ **estar como unas pascuas** to be beaming all over.

pase [m] pass, permit.

pasear to stroll, take a walk *Ibamos paseando por el parque cuando la vimos.* We were taking a walk through the park when we saw her. ▲ to go for a ride (car, horse, bicycle) *Le gustaba pasear a caballo.* She liked to go horseback riding.
○ **pasearse** to pace the floor *Estuvo paseandose toda la noche.* He paced the floor all night.

paseo walk *En este lugar hay lindos paseos.* There are beautiful walks here.
○ **dar un paseo** to stroll, take a walk *¿Le gustaría dar un paseo por el parque?* Would you like to take a walk in the park?

pasillo passage, corridor.

pasión [f] emotion, passion.

paso dried (of fruits).
○ **ciruela pasa** prune.

paso step *Dió unos cuantos pasos y se paró.* He took a few steps and stopped. ▲ gait *Este caballo tiene un paso excelente.* This horse has a fine gait. ▲ progress *Ha dado un gran*

paso en sus estudios. He's made great progress in his studies. ▲ pass (mountain) *El paso es peligroso por la noche.* The pass is dangerous at night.
○ **abrir paso** to open a passage, make way *Los policías abrieron paso para el coche del Presidente.* The policemen opened a passage for the President's car. ○ **abrirse paso** to get through *Hay tanta gente que es muy difícil abrirse paso.* There's such a crowd that it's very hard to get through. ○ **apretar el paso** to hurry, hasten *Apretemos el paso para llegar a tiempo.* Let's hurry and get there on time. ○ **de paso** in passing *Aludió a la situación política solamente de paso.* He referred to the political situation only in passing. ○ **paso a paso** step by step, little by little *Paso a paso se hizo una posición.* Little by little he made a place for himself. ○ **salir del paso** to get by *Estudia sólo lo suficiente para salir del paso.* He only studies enough to get by. ○ **salir de un paso** to get out of a tough spot *Será difícil que Ud. salga de ese paso.* It'll be hard for you to get out of that tough spot.
‖ *Prohibido el paso.* No trespassing. or Keep out.

pasta paste, batter *Hicieron una pasta de harina de maíz.* They made a paste of corn meal. ▲ pie crust *La pasta es muy buena.* The pie crust's very good. ▲ plastic *El cenicero era de pasta.* The ashtray was made of plastic. ▲ "dough" (money) *Ese muchacho tiene mucha pasta.* That fellow has a lot of dough. ▲ tea cake *Tomaron té con pastas.* They had tea and cakes. ▲ binding, cover (of a book) *Leía un libro de pasta roja.* He was reading a book with a red cover.
○ **de buena pasta** good-natured *Ese hombre es de muy buena pasta.* He's a very good-natured man. ○ **pasta de dientes** toothpaste *¿Venden Uds. pasta de dientes?* Do you sell toothpaste? ○ **sopa de pasta** noodle soup.

pastel [m] pie *Nos sirvieron pastel de cerezas.* They served us cherry pie.

pastelería pastry shop; pastry.

pasteurizado pasteurized.

pastilla tablet, drop *¿Tiene Ud. algunas pastillas contra la tos?* Do you have any cough drops?

pasto pasture; grass.
○ **a (todo) pasto** aplenty, galore

Teníamos comida a todo pasto. We had food galore.

pastor [m] shepherd.

pata foot, leg (of an animal) *Cogieron al perro de una pata.* They caught the dog by the leg. ▲ leg (furniture) *La pata de la mesa está quebrada.* The table leg's broken.

○ **a cuatro patas** on all fours, creeping. ○ **meter la pata** to pull a boner, to put one's foot in it *Ten cuidado no metas la pata.* Be careful not to put your foot in it.

patada kick.

patata potato [Sp].

patente evident *Era patente que quería pedirle a Ud. dinero.* It was evident that he wanted to borrow some money from you. ▲ [f] patent *Deberá sacar una patente de su invento.* You should take out a patent on your invention.

patinador, patinadora skater.

patinar to skate; to skid, slip.

patio patio, courtyard *El patio es característico en las casas españolas.* The patio's characteristic of Spanish houses.

○ **patio de butacas** orchestra (theater).

patizambo bow-legged.

pato, pata duck.

patojo lame, crippled [Am] *Quedó patojo después de la caída.* His fall left him lame. ▲ [n] kid, urchin [Am] *Un patojo me enseñó el camino.* A kid showed me the way.

patria fatherland, native land.

patriota [m, f] patriot.

patriótico patriotic.

patriotismo patriotism.

patrón [m] boss *Lo ha ordenado el patrón.* The boss has ordered it. ▲ employer. ▲ patron saint *Santiago, patrón de España.* Saint James, patron saint of Spain. ▲ pattern *Estos patrones para hacer vestidos son muy prácticos.* These dress patterns are very practical.

○ **patrón de barca** skipper (of small boat).

patronal [adj] of the employers *Las representaciones patronales y obreras han llegado a un acuerdo.* The representatives of the employers and workers have reached an agreement.

patrono employer; patron saint.

pausa rest; break.

○ **hacer una pausa** to take a break, to pause *Vamos a hacer una pausa de cinco minutos.* Let's take a five-minute break.

pausar to pause, hesitate.

pava pot, kettle [Arg]; turkey hen.

pavada nonsense, foolishness [Arg].

pavimentar to pave.

pavimento pavement.

pavo turkey cock.

○ **pavo real** peacock.

payar to sing to the accompaniment of a guitar [Arg].

payaso clown.

paz [f] peace *Que en paz descanse.* May he rest in peace.

○ **estar** (or **quedar**) **en paz** to be even, be quits *Cuando le dé tres dólares estaremos en paz.* When I give you three dollars, we'll be square. ○ **hacer las paces** to make up, patch up (differences), become reconciled *Me alegra que hayan hecho las paces.* I'm glad they've made up.

pecado sin.

pecar to sin.

pecho chest, bosom.

pedazo piece, bit *Le dió un pedazo de pan.* She gave him a piece of bread.

○ **hacerse pedazos** to break into pieces, shatter *El florero se hizo pedazos al caer al suelo.* The vase broke into pieces when it fell on the floor.

pedido order, shipment.

pedir [rad-ch III] to ask for *Tengo que pedirle permiso.* I have to ask him for permission. ▲ to ask, request *¿Por qué no pide que le sirvan más temprano?* Why don't you ask them to serve you earlier? ▲ to order *He pedido mil copias.* I've ordered a thousand copies.

○ **pedir de boca** according to desire *Todo salió a pedir de boca.* Everything worked out according to our desires. ○ **pedir limosna** to beg for alms.

pegadizo catchy *Es una música muy pegadiza.* It's a very catchy tune.

pegajoso sticky.

pegar to stick, glue, cement *¿Con qué pegaron esto?* What did they glue this with? ▲ to post *Pegaron un cartel en la pared.* They posted a sign on the wall. ▲ to sew (on) *Tiene Ud. que pegarle botones a esta camisa.* You have to sew buttons on this shirt. ▲ to infect with, communicate *Me pegó el catarro.* He infected me with his cold. or I caught his cold. ▲ to hit, beat, strike *Le pegó con un bastón.* He beat him with a cane.

○ **pegar** (le) **fuego** a to set fire to *Le pegaron fuego a la casa.* They set fire to the house. ○ **pegarse** to be catching *Todo se pega menos la* *belleza.* Everything's catching except beauty. ▲to adhere, stick *Este papel se ha pegado a la mesa.* This paper's stuck to the table.

peinado (see **peinar**) combed. ▲[*m*] hair-do.

peinador [*m*] hairdresser; hairdressing cape.

peinar to comb, do the hair of *Peinó a la niña con trenzas.* She did the child's hair in braids.

○ **peinarse** to comb one's hair, fix one's hair *Está peinándose.* She's fixing her hair.

peine [*m*] comb (for hair).

peineta comb (for hair).

pelado (see **pelar**) picked, plucked; "skinned." ▲[*n*] peasant [*Mex*].

pelar to peel *Esta fruta no se puede comer sin pelar.* You can't eat this fruit without peeling it. ▲to pick, pluck (fowl) *La cocinera peló los pollos.* The cook picked the chickens. ▲to fleece, skin *En ese negocio me pelaron.* They skinned me in that deal.

○ **pelarse** to peel off *Esta pintura se está pelando.* This paint's peeling off. ▲to get one's hair cut *Hoy tengo que ir a pelarme.* I have to get my hair cut today.

pelea fight, brawl, quarrel; bout.

pelear to fight *Pelearon durante muchas horas.* They fought for hours. ▲to quarrel *Son amigos, pero pelean mucho.* They're friends, but they often quarrel.

película film *Necesito un rollo de película.* I need a roll of film. ▲picture, movie *Hoy dan una película muy buena.* There's a very good picture today.

peligro danger *Hubo peligro de que se incendiara la casa.* There was danger of the house catching fire.

○ **correr peligro** to run a risk *Corrió peligro de perder todo su dinero.* He ran the risk of losing all his money.

peligroso dangerous, risky.

pellejo skin, hide (of animals); wine skin.

○ **estar en el pellejo de otro** to be in another's shoes *No querría yo estar en su pellejo.* I wouldn't like to be in his shoes. ○ **jugarse el pellejo** to risk one's life. ○ **quitarle a uno el pellejo** to gossip about, flay *Le quitan el pellejo a todo el mundo.* They gossip about everybody.

pellizcar to pinch.

pelo hair *Tiene el pelo negro y los ojos castaños.* He has black hair and brown eyes.

○ **en pelo** bareback *Sabía montar en pelo.* He could ride bareback. ○ **ne tener pelos en la lengua** to be outspoken *Esa muchacha no tiene pelos en la lengua.* That girl's very outspoken. ○ **pelos y señales** minute details *Lo contó con pelos y señales.* He told it in minute detail. ○ **tomar el pelo** to pull one's leg *Creo que me estás tomando el pelo.* I think you're pulling my leg. ○ **venir a pelo** to be to the point *Lo que dijo no venía muy a pelo.* What he said wasn't to the point.

pelota ball (for games).

peluca wig, toupee.

peluquería barber shop; beauty parlor.

peluquero barber, hairdresser.

pena penalty *Sufrieron una severa pena por lo que hicieron.* They paid a severe penalty for what they did. ▲pain, sorrow *Le dió mucha pena la muerte de su primo.* His cousin's death caused him great sorrow. ▲trouble *Han pasado muchas penas.* They've suffered a great deal of trouble. ▲embarrassment, chagrin [*Am*] *Me da mucha pena.* It's very embarrassing.

○ **a duras penas** with great difficulty *Llegaron a duras penas.* They had a hard time getting here. ○ **pena capital, pena de muerte** death, capital punishment *Lo condenaron a la pena capital.* They condemned him to death. ○ **tener la pena de** to have the misfortune to *Tuvo la pena de perder a su padre.* He had the misfortune to lose his father. ○ **valer la pena** to be worth(while) *No vale la pena hacerlo.* It's not worth doing.

pendiente pending *Tenemos un asunto pendiente con ellos.* We have some unfinished business with them. ▲[*f*] drop, slope *La pendiente era muy pronunciada.* The slope was very steep.

○ **pendientes** [*m pl*] earrings *Le regaló unos pendientes de brillantes.* He gave her diamond earrings.

penetrante penetrating, piercing.

penetrar to penetrate, go in *La bala penetró hasta el hueso.* The bullet penetrated to the bone. ▲to determine, make out *Es difícil penetrar sus pensamientos.* It's hard to make out what he thinks.

península peninsula.

penoso arduous, hard *Aquel trabajo era muy penoso.* That was very hard work. ▲embarrassing, unpleasant *Sería penoso decírselo.* It'd be embarrassing to tell him.

pensamiento thought, idea *Sus pensamientos son muy elevados.* His thoughts are very lofty. ▲pansy (flower).

pensar [*rad-ch I*] to think *¡Yo pensaba que Ud. estaba en Chile!* I thought you were in Chile! ▲to intend, plan *¿Adónde piensa Ud. ir mañana?* Where do you intend to go tomorrow? ○**pensar de** to think of, have an opinion of *¿Qué piensa Ud. de Juan?* What do you think of John? ○**pensar en** to think of, about, *or* over *¿En qué piensas?* What are you thinking about?

pensativo pensive, thoughtful.

pensión [*f*] pension; boarding house.

peña rock, boulder. ▲group of friends *La peña se reunía en el Café Universal.* The group of friends used to meet in Café Universal.

peón [*m*] workman, day laborer [*Am*]. ▲pawn (chess). ▲top (plaything). ○**jugar al peón** to spin the top.

peonza top (plaything). ○**bailar como una peonza** to dance well, be light on one's feet.

peor worse *Hoy me encuentro peor.* I'm worse today. ▲worst *Es el peor de todos.* He's the worst of all. ○**de mal en peor** from bad to worse. ○**tanto peor** so much the worse *Tanto peor para él.* So much the worse for him.

pepa seed, stone, pit [*Am*].

pepino cucumber.

pequeño small, little *Vive en un cuarto muy pequeño.* He lives in a very small room. ▲ [*n*] child *Los pequeños están en la escuela.* The children are in school.

pera pear.

percha rack (for hat or clothes); hanger, coat hanger.

perder [*rad-ch I*] to lose *Tenga mucho cuidado no pierda esos papeles.* Be careful you don't lose those papers. —*Jugó y perdió.* He gambled and lost. ▲to miss *Perdimos el tren.* We missed the train. ▲to ruin, disgrace (morally, socially) *A esa muchacha la perdió su amor al lujo.* Love of luxury ruined that girl. ○**echar a perder** to ruin, spoil *Me ha echado Ud. a perder el traje.* You've ruined my suit. ○**echarse a**

perder to spoil *La carne se echó a perder con el calor.* The meat spoiled because of the heat. ▲to become spoiled *El niño se echó a perder con las malas compañías.* The boy was spoiled by the bad company he kept. ○**perder de vista** to lose sight of *Al volver la esquina le perdimos de vista.* When we turned the corner we lost sight of him. ○**perder la vista** to go blind. ○**perderse** to go to the dogs *Se perdió con la bebida.* He went to the dogs because he liked to drink. ▲to get sour, turn, become spoiled *La fruta se va a perder porque está demasiado madura.* The fruit's going to spoil because it's overripe. ▲to get lost *Se perdió porque no conocía bien la ciudad.* He got lost because he didn't know the city very well. ○**perderse de vista** to drop out of sight.

pérdida loss *El enemigo sufrió muchas pérdidas.* The enemy suffered great losses.

perdido (see **perder**) lost. ▲ [*m*] black sheep (person). ▲**perdida** [*f*] loose woman.

perdón [*m*] forgiveness *Me pidió perdón por no haber contestado a mi carta.* He asked my forgiveness for not having answered my letter. ▲pardon, reprieve *El perdón del gobernador le salvó la vida.* The governor's pardon saved his life.

‖ *¡Perdón!* Pardon me! *or* Excuse me!

perdonar to pardon *Han perdonado a los criminales.* They've pardoned the criminals. ▲to forgive *¡Dios me perdone!* God forgive me! ▲to excuse, pardon *¡Perdone Ud.!* Excuse me!

perecer [*-zc-*] to perish *En la mina perecieron cincuenta hombres.* Fifty men perished in the mine.

peregrino exotic, strange *Tiene ideas muy peregrinas.* He has very strange ideas.

perejil [*m*] parsley.

pereza laziness.

perezoso lazy.

perfección [*f*] perfection.

perfecto perfect.

perfil [*m*] profile; outline.

perfumar to perfume.

perfume [*m*] perfume.

pericia skill, expertness.

periódico [*adj*] periodic(al). ▲ [*m*] newspaper *Lo he leído en el periódico de esta mañana.* I read it in this morning's paper.

periodista [*m, f*] journalist, newspaperman, newspaperwoman.

período period, term.

perito [*adj; n*] expert.

perjudicar to damage, hurt, injure.

perjudicial harmful, injurious.

perjuicio prejudice; damage, injury, harm; financial loss.

perla pearl.

  ○ **ser una perla** to be a jewel *Esa criada es una perla.* That maid's a jewel.

permanecer [-*zc*-] to stay, remain.

permanente [*adj*] permanent. ▲ [*f*] permanent (wave).

permiso permission, license, permit.

  ‖ *Con permiso* (lit., with your permission) If you don't mind. *or* Excuse me, please.

permitir to permit, allow.

pero [*conj*] but *La ciudad es grande, pero no es muy hermosa.* The city's large but it's not very attractive. ▲ [*m*] shortcoming, defect.

  ○ **no tener pero(s)** to be faultless *or* flawless *Ese trabajo no tiene peros.* That work's flawless. ○ **poner pero(s)** to find fault, object *A este trabajo no se le puede poner ningún pero.* You can't find fault with this job.

  ‖ *¡No hay pero que valga!* No buts about it!

perra female dog, bitch, slut.

perro dog.

persecución [*f*] persecution; pursuit.

perseguir [*rad-ch III*] to pursue *Persiguieron a los fugitivos.* They pursued the fugitives. ▲ to aim at *¿Qué fin persigue Ud.?* What are you aiming at?

perseverancia perseverance.

persona person.

personaje [*m*] personage, big shot *Debe ser un personaje.* He must be an important person. ▲ character (in a play) *El personaje principal es un viejo.* The main character's an old man.

personal [*adj*] personal *Esos son asuntos personales.* Those are personal matters. ▲ [*m*] personnel *Vaya Ud. a la oficina de personal.* Go to the personnel office.

  ○ **cuestión personal** personal quarrel *Tuve una cuestión personal con él.* I had a personal quarrel with him.

personalidad [*f*] personality, prominent person *A la fiesta concurrieron muchas personalidades.* Many prominent people attended the party.

persuadir to persuade, convince *Le persuadió a que se quedasen.* He persuaded them to stay.

pertenecer [-*zc*-] to pertain to, concern. ▲ to belong to *Este dinero no nos pertenece.* This money doesn't belong to us.

perturbar to perturb, disturb.

perverso perverse, wicked.

pesa weight (object).

pesadez [*f*] boringness, dullness. ▲ persistence *La pesadez de ese hombre me molesta.* The persistence of that man annoys me.

pesadilla nightmare.

pesado (see **pesar**) heavy *Esta maleta es muy pesada.* This suitcase is very heavy. ▲ boring, dull, tiresome; persistent *Es uno de esos tipos pesados.* He's one of those boring people. ▲ sultry (of weather) *¡Qué tiempo tan pesado!* What sultry weather! ▲ sound (of sleep) *Tenía un sueño muy pesado.* She slept soundly. ▲ stuffy *En esta habitación hay una atmósfera muy pesada.* The air in this room's very stuffy.

pesar to weigh *Esta carta pesa demasiado.* This letter weighs too much. ▲ to be weighty, important, count *Su opinión pesa mucho.* Your opinion counts a lot.

  ○ **pesarle a uno** to regret, be sorry for *No me pesa haberlo dicho.* I don't regret having said it. ○ **pesarse** to weigh oneself, get weighed *Es aconsejable pesarse a menudo.* It's advisable to get weighed frequently.

pesar [*m*] sorrow, remorse *Su muerte causó gran pesar.* His death caused great sorrow.

  ○ **a pesar de** in spite of *A pesar de todo, lo haremos.* In spite of everything, we'll do it. ○ **tener pesar** to be sorry *Tengo gran pesar por lo que hice.* I'm very sorry for what I did.

pesca fishing *La pesca es un deporte agradable.* Fishing's a pleasant sport. ▲ catch (of fish) *Fué una gran pesca.* It was a big catch.

  ○ **ir de pesca** to go fishing.

pescado fish (caught).

pescador [*m*] fisherman.

pescar to fish *¿Le gusta a Ud. pescar?* Do you like fishing? ▲ to catch, get, "hook" *Ha pescado un buen marido.* She hooked a good husband.

peseta peseta (monetary unit of Spain).

pesimista [*adj*] pessimistic. ▲ [*n*] pessimist.

pésimo [*adj*] the very worst.

peso weight *¿Puede Ud. darme el peso en libras?* Can you give me the weight in pounds? ▲load *Es demasiado peso para tí.* That's too big a load for you. ▲weight, burden, load *Se me ha quitado un gran peso de encima.* That's a big load off my mind. ▲peso (monetary unit).

○ **caerse de su peso** to be self-evident, go without saying *Eso se cae de su peso.* That goes without saying. ○ **de peso** weighty, important *La razón es de peso.* The reason's important. ○ **exceso de peso** excess weight.

pestaña eyelash.

pestañear to wink, blink.

peste [*f*] plague.

pestillo door latch, bolt *Corre el pestillo.* Bolt the door.

petaca cigarette case; [*Am*] suitcase.

petate [*m*] straw mat [*Mex*].

petición [*f*] petition; request.

petróleo petroleum.

pez [*m*] fish (in the water). ▲[*f*] tar.

pianista [*m, f*] pianist.

piano piano.

pibe [*m*] kid, child [*Arg*].

picante spiced *La comida mexicana es muy picante.* Mexican food's highly spiced. ▲ risqué, off-color *Las historias que él cuenta son siempre un poco picantes.* His stories are always a little off-color.

picar to sting, bite, eat (of insects) *Lo picaron bien las avispas.* The wasps stung him good and proper.—*Esta tela está picada.* This material's moth-eaten. ▲to chop, grind up *Hay que picar muy bien la carne.* The meat has to be well ground up. ▲to nibble *El pez picó el cebo.* The fish nibbled at the bait. ▲to itch *Me pica todo el cuerpo.* I'm itching all over. ▲to crush (stone). ▲to burn *Pica mucho el sol hoy.* The sun burns today.

○ **picarse** to be hurt, be offended *Se picó por lo que le dijo él.* She was hurt by what he said. ▲to begin to spoil *Está picándose la fruta.* The fruit's beginning to spoil. ▲to get rough *El mar empieza a picarse.* The sea's beginning to get rough.

pícaro mischievous. ▲[*n*] rascal, rogue.

picazón [*m*] itching, itch *Tengo un picazón en la espalda.* I have an itch on my back.

pichel [*m*] pitcher [*Am*].

pícher [*m*] baseball pitcher [*Am*].

pichón [*m*] young pigeon, squab.

pico beak, bill *¡Qué pico más tremendo el de ese pájaro!* What a huge bill that bird has! ▲sharp point, corner *Me dí un golpe con el pico de la mesa.* I bumped against the corner of the table. ▲pick, pickax *Llevaba al hombro un pico y una pala.* He was carrying a pick and shovel on his shoulder. ▲spout *Está roto el pico del jarro.* The spout of the pitcher's broken. ▲summit, peak *Subimos hasta el pico más alto.* We climbed up to the highest point. ▲small amount over *Me costó diez pesos y pico.* It cost a little over ten pesos.

pie [*m*] foot *Se lastimó un pie durante el juego.* He hurt his foot during the game.—*Un metro tiene un poco más de tres pies.* A meter's a little over three feet.—*Estaba sentado al pie de la cama.* He was sitting at the foot of the bed. ▲base *El pie de esa lámpara está roto.* The base of that lamp's broken.

○ **al pie de la letra** thoroughly *Sabe el asunto al pie de la letra.* He knows the subject thoroughly. ○ **a pie** on foot *Iremos a pie.* We'll go on foot. ○ **de pie** standing *Tuvieron que ir de pie en el tren.* They had to stand in the train. ○ **en pie** pending, undecided *Aun están en pie nuestros proyectos.* Our plans are still up in the air.

‖ *A los pies de Ud., señora.* At your service, madam.

piedad [*f*] piety; pity.

piedra stone.

piel [*f*] skin *Tiene la piel muy delicada.* He has a very delicate skin. ▲leather *Este calzado está hecho con una piel muy fina.* These shoes are made of very fine leather. ▲fur *La piel de zorro es muy cara.* Fox fur's very expensive. ▲skin, peel *A esta fruta es muy difícil quitarle la piel.* This fruit's hard to peel.

○ **abrigo de pieles** fur coat *Me gustaría tener un abrigo de pieles.* I'd like to have a fur coat.

pierna leg *Perdió una pierna en la guerra.* He lost a leg in the war.

pieza part (of a machine) *Se ha perdido una pieza de la máquina.* A part of the machine's been lost. ▲bolt (of cloth) *Necesitamos una pieza de esa tela para las cortinas.* We need a bolt of that material for the curtains. ▲room *La casa tiene varias piezas grandes.* The house has several large rooms. ▲play *Vimos una pieza muy* *graciosa anoche.* We saw a very amusing play last night. ▲piece (of music) *Toque Ud. una pieza en el piano.* Play a piece on the piano. ▲man (piece in games) *Falta una pieza en este juego.* One of the men's missing in this game.

○**buena pieza** fine guy (ironical) *¡Ud. es una buena pieza!* You're a fine guy!

pijama [*m in Sp, f in Am*] pajamas.

pila stone trough, basin. ▲sink *Vacíe Ud. la pila.* Empty the sink. ▲battery (electrical) *Hay que cambiar las pilas a esta linterna.* The batteries in this flashlight have to be changed. ▲pile *Había una pila de cosas en el cuarto.* There was a pile of things in the room.

○**pila de bautismo** baptismal font. ○**nombre de pila** Christian name, given name.

pilar [*m*] pillar, column, post.

píldora pill, pellet.

pillo petty thief; rascal.

piloto pilot.

pimentón [*m*] red pepper; paprika.

pimienta pepper (spice).

pimiento pepper (vegetable).

pino pine, pine tree.

pintado (see pintar) ○**como el más pintado** as (or with) the best of them *Puede hacerlo como el más pintado.* He can hold his own with the best of them.

pintar to paint *Van a pintar esta habitación.* They're going to paint this room.

○**pintarse** to make up *Esa muchacha se pinta demasiado.* That girl uses too much make-up. ○**pintarse solo para** to have great talent for *Se pinta solo para ganar dinero.* He has great talent for making money.

pintor [*m*], **pintora** painter.

pintoresco picturesque.

pintura painting, picture *Las pinturas que se exhiben aquí son muy valiosas.* The paintings exhibited here are very valuable. ▲paint *Dé Ud. dos manos de pintura.* Put on two coats of paint.

piña pineapple.

piojo louse.

pipa pipe (smoking); cask, hogshead.

pique [*m*] resentment.

○**echar a pique** to sink *Echaron a pique muchas naves de guerra.* Many warships were sunk. ○**tener un pique con** to have a grudge against.

piquete [*m*] bite, small wound.

piropo compliment, flattery.

pisar to step on, tread on.

piscina pool, swimming pool.

piso floor, flooring *Los pisos de esta casa son de madera.* This house has wood floors. ▲floor, story *Vive en el tercer piso.* He lives on the third floor.

○**piso bajo** ground floor *El piso bajo está desalquilado.* The ground floor's vacant.

pistola pistol.

pita string, cord [*Am*].

pitar to whistle *La locomotora pitó al entrar en la estación.* The engine whistled as it entered the station.

pito whistle.

○**tocar un pito** to blow a whistle. ‖ *No me importa un pito.* I don't give a hoot.

pizarra slate; blackboard.

placa plaque.

placer [*v*] to please, be pleasing to *Puede Ud. hacer lo que le plazca.* You can do what you please. ▲[*m*] pleasure *He tenido un gran placer en conocerle a Ud.* It's been a great pleasure to meet you.

plaga plague, epidemic.

plan [*m*] plan *¿Cuáles son sus planes?* What are your plans?

○**estar en plan de** to be out for, be in the mood for *Están en plan de divertirse.* They're out for a good time. ○**plan de estudios** curriculum *Han cambiado el plan de estudios en la Universidad.* They've changed the curriculum at the University.

plancha plate *Las planchas estaban soldadas.* The plates were welded together. ▲iron, flatiron *El último modelo de planchas eléctricas está ya a la venta.* The latest model electric irons are now on sale.

○**hacer planchas** to put one's foot in it *Siempre está haciendo planchas.* He's always putting his foot in it. ○**tirarse una plancha** to pull a boner.

planilla payroll [*Am*] *La planilla de esa compañía es muy elevada.* That company has a very large payroll. ▲bus (or streetcar) ticket. ▲list of candidates, ticket [*Am*] *Votaremos por esta planilla.* We'll vote this ticket.

plano flat *El terreno aquí es muy plano* The ground here's very flat. ▲[*m*] plan, drawing *El arquitecto trazó un plano muy bonito.* The architect drew a very fine plan.

planta sole *Me duele la planta del pie.* The sole of my foot hurts. ▲ plant *Esta planta es del Brasil.* This plant comes from Brazil.

○ **buena planta** fine physique, good build *Tiene muy buena planta.* He has a very good build.

plantado ○ **dejarle a uno plantado** to leave one in the lurch, leave one high and dry; to stand someone up.

plantear to pose, present, *or* state (a problem) *Eso plantea una dificultad.* That presents a difficulty.

plástico [*adj*] plastic, pliable.

plata silver *En México y Perú hay muchas minas de plata.* There are many silver mines in Mexico and Peru.

○ **quedarse sin plata** to be broke *Me he quedado sin plata.* I'm broke.

plataforma platform.

platal [*m*] great quantity of money [*Am*] *Le ha costado un platal.* It cost him a fortune.

plátano banana.

platea orchestra (theater section).

plateado silver-plated, silvered.

plática talk, conversation.

platillo dish (of food) [*Mex*].

plato plate, dish *La criada rompió tres platos.* The maid broke three plates. ▲ dish (of food) *Hubo unos platos deliciosos en la cena.* There were several delicious dishes for supper. ▲ course *¿Qué desea como plato fuerte?* What would you like for the main course?

○ **ser plato de segunda mesa** to play second fiddle.

playa beach, shore.

plaza plaza, square *En el centro de la plaza hay un gran monumento.* There's a big monument in the center of the square. ▲ market *En la plaza encontrará Ud. todo lo que desea.* You'll find everything you need in the market. ▲ job, position *Hay una plaza vacante en la oficina.* There's a job open in the office.

○ **plaza de toros** bull ring. ○ **sacar plaza** to get a position *Sacó plaza en una compañía de seguros.* He got a position with an insurance company.

plazo time limit *Si Ud. desea, podemos fijar un nuevo plazo.* If you wish, we can set a new time limit. ▲ installment *El primer plazo es de cien pesos.* The first installment is one hundred pesos.

○ **a plazos** in installments.

plebiscito plebiscite.

plegar [*rad-ch I*] to fold; to plait.

pleito lawsuit *Siguen un pleito sobre su herencia.* They're having a lawsuit over their inheritance. ▲ dispute *Hubo un pleito entre los estudiantes.* There was a dispute among the students.

○ **poner pleito** to sue, bring suit against.

plenitud [*f*] plenty, abundance.

pleno full, complete.

○ **en pleno invierno** *or* **verano** *or* **día** in the middle of winter *or* summer *or* the day.

pliego sheet (of paper, usually folded)

pliegue [*m*] fold, crease.

plomero plumber.

plomo lead (metal). ▲ fuse *Se ha fundido un plomo.* A fuse was blown out.

pluma feather. ▲ pen *Vive de su pluma.* He lives by his pen.

○ **pluma-fuente** fountain pen *¿Podría arreglarme esta pluma-fuente?* Could you fix this fountain pen for me?

plural [*adj; m*] plural.

población [*f*] population *¿Qué población tiene este país?* What's the population of this country? ▲ town, village *Pasamos por muchas poblaciones pintorescas durante el viaje.* We went through many picturesque towns on the trip.

pobre [*adj*] poor *En este distrito vive gente muy pobre.* Very poor people live in this section. ▲ poor, humble *La casa de su madre es muy pobre.* Her mother's house is very humble. ▲ poor, pitiful *¡Pobre muchacho!* Poor fellow! ▲ [*n*] poor person *Ayudan a los pobres.* They help the poor. ▲ beggar *Déle algo a ese pobre.* Give something to that beggar.

‖ *¡Pobre de mí!* Poor me!

pobreza poverty.

poco little *Queda muy poca gasolina en el tanque.* There's very little gasoline left in the tank. ▲ small *Tienen muy poca existencia de vinos.* They have a very small stock of wines.

○ **a poco (de)** shortly after *A poco de llegar nosotros a la estación, llegó el tren.* The train arrived shortly after we reached the station. ○ **dentro de poco** soon, in a short time *Llegará dentro de poco.* He'll be here soon. ○ **poco a poco** little by little, gradually *Poco a poco aprenderá Ud. a hablar español.* Little by little

you'll learn to speak Spanish. ○ **poco
después de** soon after *Poco después de
la terminación de la guerra, me casé.*
Soon after the end of the war, I got
married. ○ **poco más o menos** more
or less, about *Saldremos poco más o
menos a las ocho de la mañana.*
We'll leave about eight in the morning. ○ **pocos** a few *Saldré dentro de
pocos días.* I'll leave in a few days.
○ **por poco** almost, nearly *No miré por
donde iba y por poco me perdí.* I
didn't look where I was going and
nearly got lost. ○ **un poco de** a little, small amount of *¿Le pongo un
poco de vino?* May I give you a little wine?
∥ *¡Eh, poco a poco!* Hey, not so
fast! *or* Take it easy! *or* Easy
there!

pocho, pocha Mexican born in the U. S.
[*Mex*].

poder [*irr*] to be able, can *¿No puede
Ud. correr más?* Can't you run any
faster? ▲ to be possible, may *Puede
que vaya a Europa el próximo año.*
I may go to Europe next year. ▲ [*m*]
power, influence *Tenía un poder muy
grande entre los obreros.* He had
great influence among the workers.
○ **a más no poder** to the utmost
Estudia a más no poder. He studies
as hard as he possibly can. ○ **no
poder con** not to be able to stand, endure, carry, control, manage *No puedo
con él.* I can't stand him. ○ **no poder
más** to be exhausted, be all in *¡No
puedo más!* I'm all in! ○ **no poder
menos de** not to be able to help *No
puedo menos de ir.* I can't help going. ○ **no poder ver** not to be able to
stand *No puedo verle.* I can't stand
him. ○ **poder general** power of attorney *Ha dado poder general a su padre.* He's given his father power of
attorney.

poderío power, might.

poderoso powerful, mighty.

podrido rotten, spoiled.

poema [*m*] poem.

poesía poetry.

poeta [*m*] poet.

polar polar.

policía [*f*] police *Dieron parte a la
policía inmediatamente.* They informed the police immediately. ▲ [*m*]
policeman *Se lo preguntaré al policía
de la esquina.* I'll ask the policeman
on the corner.

polilla moth.

política policy *Ese país ha cambiado su
política exterior.* That country's
changed its foreign policy. ▲ politics
*Ha dejado todo para dedicarse a la
política.* He's given up everything to
devote himself to politics.

político political *Este periódico no representa a ningún partido político.*
This newspaper doesn't represent any
political party. ▲ [*n*] politician *Fué
uno de los políticos más distinguidos
de su época.* He was one of the most
distinguished politicians of his time.

póliza de seguro insurance policy.

pollo chicken *Los pollos están muy caros
en este tiempo.* Chickens are very
high right now.

polo pole *Hicieron una expedición al
polo norte.* They made an expedition
to the North Pole. ▲ pole (electrical).
▲ polo *¿Le interesaría ver un partido
de polo?* Would you like to see a
polo match?

polvareda cloud of dust; dust storm.

polvera powder box.

polvo dust *Cerraremos la ventana para
que no entre polvo.* We'll close the
window to keep the dust out.
○ **en polvo** powdered *¿Quiere Ud.
azúcar en polvo o en terrón?* Do you
want powdered or lump sugar?
○ **polvos** powder *Uso polvos de talco
después de afeitarme.* I use talcum
powder after I shave. ○ **polvos para
dientes** tooth powder.

pólvora powder, gunpowder.

pompa pomp, show, display.
○ **pompas de jabón** soap bubbles *El
niño hace pompas de jabón.* The
child's blowing soap bubbles.

ponche [*m*] punch (liquor).

poncho poncho (South American blanket
with slit in middle for the head).

poner [*irr*] to put, place, lay *Ponga sus
cosas aquí.* Put your things here.
▲ to suppose, assume *Pongamos que
eso sea cierto.* Let's suppose that's
true. ▲ to impose, keep *Aquí se necesita alguien que ponga orden.* We
need someone to keep order around
here. ▲ to put down, write down
Ponga Ud. lo que yo le voy a dictar.
Put down what I'm going to dictate
to you.
○ **poner al corriente** to inform, tell,
bring one up to date *Le puse al corriente de lo que había sucedido.* I
informed him of what had happened.
○ **poner de mi** (*or* tu, su *etc*) **parte**
to do all one can *Ponga Ud. de su
parte todo lo que pueda.* Do all you
can. ○ **poner en claro** to clear up,

make clear *Tenemos que poner en claro este lío.* We've got to clear up this mess. ○ **poner en duda** to question, doubt *Pone en duda todo lo que le dicen.* He questions everything they tell him. ○ **poner la mesa** to set the table *Ya dije que pusieran la mesa para cenar.* I've already told them to set the table for supper. ○ **ponerle a uno** to cause one to become, make *Este calor me pone mala.* This heat makes me ill. ○ **ponerse** to put on, wear *Hoy me pondré el vestido azul.* I'll put on my blue dress today. ▲ to get, become (with adjective denoting physical condition or state of mind) *Se pondrán muy disgustados si lo saben.* They'll get very angry if they find out. ▲ to place oneself *Póngase Ud. en esa ventana.* Place yourself at that window. ▲ to set (of the sun) *El sol se pone más temprano en invierno.* The sun sets earlier in winter. ○ **ponerse a** to begin to, start to *De repente se puso a correr.* Suddenly he began to run. ○ **ponerse (a) mal con** to get in bad with *Se pone (a) mal con todos.* He gets in bad with everybody. ○ **ponerse colorado** to blush *Al oírlo se puso colorada.* She blushed when she heard it. ○ **ponerse de acuerdo** to come to an agreement *Después de discutir mucho se pusieron de acuerdo.* After much discussion they came to an agreement. ○ **ponerse en** to reach *Se puso en la frontera en unas cuantas horas.* He reached the border in a few hours. ○ **ponerse en camino** to set out *Nos pusimos en camino muy temprano.* We set out very early. ○ **ponerse en contra de** to be against, oppose *La mayoría de los diputados se pusieron en contra del proyecto.* The majority of deputies were against the measure. ○ **ponerse en marcha** to start, start out, pull out *El tren se puso en marcha lentamente.* The train started out slowly. ○ **ponerse en (or de) pie** to get up, rise *Cuando entró el presidente se pusieron todos en pie.* When the president entered they all stood up.

poniente [*m*] west.
popote [*m*] straw (for drinking) [*Mex*].
popular popular; folkloric.
popularidad [*f*] popularity.
poquito [*adj*] little. ▲ [*m*] little bit.
por by *América fué descubierta por Colón.* America was discovered by Columbus.—*Hice el viaje por avión.* I made the trip by plane. ▲ for (in behalf of) *Nunca olvidaré lo que Ud. hizo por mí.* I'll never forget what you did for me. ▲ around, about *Regresará por la Navidad.* He'll come back around Christmas. ▲ through *Pasaron por el túnel.* They went through the tunnel. ▲ for, (in order) to get *Vaya Ud. por una botella de leche.* Go get a bottle of milk. ▲ to, in order to *Lo hicimos por ayudarle.* We did it to help him. ▲ still (or yet) to (be)... *¿Tiene trabajo por hacer?* Do you still have work to do? —*Quedan tres cartas por escribir.* There are three letters still to be written. ▲ by way of, via *Este autobús va por la calle central.* This bus goes by way of Center Street. ▲ across, over *Se pasó la mano por los ojos.* He passed his hand across his eyes. ▲ in, during *Estudio por la mañana.* I study in the morning. ▲ per, a(n) *¿Cuánto paga Ud. por hora?* How much do you pay an hour?

○ **al por mayor** wholesale. ○ **al por menor** retail. ○ **por ahí** around there, near there *Viven por ahí cerca.* They live near there. ○ **por aquí** around here *Venga Ud. por aquí mañana temprano.* Come around early tomorrow morning. ○ **por ciento** per cent. ○ **por docena** by the dozen. ○ **por donde** wherever *Por donde voy lo encuentro.* Wherever I go I meet him. ○ **por encima** superficially, hastily *Leí el documento por encima.* I glanced over the document. ○ **por entre** through, among, between *La vi por entre los árboles.* I saw her through the trees. ○ **por escrito** in writing. ○ **por eso** for that reason, therefore *Por eso quiero salir temprano.* For that reason I want to leave early. ○ **por más que** however much, no matter how much *Por más que llame Ud. nadie contestará.* No matter how much you knock, no one'll answer. ○ **por qué** why *No sé por qué me gusta tanto.* I don't know why I like him so much.—*¿Por qué me lo preguntas?* Why do you ask me? ○ **por si acaso** in case *Llevemos paraguas por si acaso llueve.* Let's take umbrellas in case it rains. ○ **por supuesto** of course.

‖ *¡Por Dios!* Goodness! *or* For heaven's sake!
porcelana chinaware; enamelware.
porción [*f*] portion, part.

porfiar to persist, insist *No profíe tanto.* Don't insist so much. ▲ to argue, contend *No porfíen más sobre eso.* Don't argue any more over that.

pormenor [m] detail, particular.

poroto bean [*Arg*].

porque because, for, as.

porqué [m] reason *No ha explicado el porqué de su ausencia.* He hasn't explained the reason for his absence.

porqué [*adv*] why.

porquería dirty trick, filthy action *or* saying.

porra club, bludgeon.

‖ *¡Váyase a la porra!* Go to the devil!

porrazo blow, knock; fall.

portada entrance, lintel (of door in front part of house) *La portada está pintada de rojo.* The entrance is painted red. ▲ front, façade *La portada del edificio es muy hermosa.* The building has a beautiful façade. ▲ cover (of book, magazine, etc) *Dibujaba portadas para revistas.* He drew covers for magazines.

portal [m] entry, vestibule, hallway.

portamonedas [m sg] purse, pocketbook.

portarse to behave, conduct oneself *Se portó muy mal.* He behaved very badly.

porte [m] postage *¿Cuánto será el porte de esta carta?* How much is the postage on this letter? ▲ bearing (of a person).

portería superintendent's *or* janitor's room.

portero doorman, janitor.

portezuela door (of a vehicle).

porvenir [m] future.

posada lodging house; inn (low-class).

posar to pose *¿Quién posa para ese cuadro?* Who's posing for that painting?
○ **posarse** to light *Los pájaros se posaron en las líneas del teléfono.* The birds lighted on the telephone wires.

posdata postscript.

poseedor, poseedora owner, possessor.

poseer to hold, possess, own.

posesión [f] possession; property.

posibilidad [f] possibility.

posible possible *No me fué posible venir más temprano.* It wasn't possible for me to come earlier.
○ **en lo posible** as far as possible.
○ **lo más ... posible** as ... as possible *Lo más pronto posible.* As soon as possible.—*Lo más tarde posible.* As late as possible. ○ **todo lo posible** everything possible *Hace todo lo posible por terminar el trabajo.* He's doing everything possible to finish the work.

posición [f] position *Cambiaré de posición para estar más cómodo.* I'm going to change to a more comfortable position. ▲ position, place *Me gustaría cambiar la posición de la cama.* I'd like to change the position of the bed. ▲ position, status *Es una persona de alta posición.* He's a man of high position. ▲ position (military).

positivo positive, certain *Eso es un hecho positivo.* That's positive. ▲ practical *Es un hombre muy positivo.* He's a very practical man. ▲ real *No hace un trabajo positivo.* He doesn't do a real job.

poso sediment, dregs.

postal [*adj*] postal, mail *¿Tienen Uds. servicio postal aquí?* Do you have mail service out here? ▲ [f] postcard, postal card *Me escribió una postal.* He wrote me a postcard.
○ **giro postal** money order *Deseo enviar un giro postal.* I want to send a money order.

poste [m] post, pillar; pole.

posterior [*adj*] rear. ▲ later *Eso ocurrió en una época posterior.* That happened in a later period. ▲ back *Salga Ud. por la puerta posterior.* Leave by the back door.

postizo artificial, false *Tiene los dientes postizos.* He has false teeth.

postre [m] dessert *Aquí sirven muy buenos postres.* They serve very good desserts here.

postre ○ **a la postre** at last.

postura position, posture *Estaba incómodo en aquella postura.* I was uncomfortable in that position. ▲ position *¿Cuál es su postura política?* What's your political position? ▲ stake, bet *Mi postura es de diez pesos.* My bet's ten pesos.

potable [*adj*] drinkable, potable.

pote [m] pot, jar.

potencia power, capacity, potency *El motor tiene gran potencia.* It's a high-powered motor. ▲ power, large nation *No sabemos qué decidirán las potencias extranjeras.* We don't know what the foreign powers will decide.

potente powerful, strong, potent.

pozo well (for water).

práctica practice; exercise.

practicar to practice, go in for *¿Practica Ud. algún deporte?* Do you go in for any sport? ▲ to carry out, perform, make *Practicaron una inspección general.* They made a general inspection.

práctico practical; experienced, skillful. ○ **práctico de puerto** harbor pilot.

prado lawn; field; meadow.

precaución [*f*] precaution.

preceder to precede.

preciar to value, prize *Precia mucho este recuerdo.* She prizes this souvenir very highly. ○ **preciarse de** to take pride in, boast of *Se precia de su habilidad.* He takes pride in his ability.

precio price *Los precios han bajado en los últimos días.* Prices have gone down in the last few days. ○ **no tener precio** to be priceless. ○ **precios fijos** fixed prices.

precioso beautiful *Llevaba un traje precioso.* She wore a beautiful dress. ▲ precious *Me gustan las piedras preciosas.* I like precious stones.

precipicio cliff, precipice.

precipitación [*f*] rash haste; precipitation.

precipitarse to rush, hurry, hurl oneself.

precisar to fix, set *Hay que precisar la fecha de salida.* We must fix the date of departure. ▲ to be necessary, must *Precisa hacer eso pronto.* That must be done soon. ▲ to be urgent [*Am*] *Me precisa hablar con Ud.* I must speak with you. ▲ to make clear *Precise Ud. lo que quiere decir.* Make clear what you mean.

precisión [*f*] necessity *Hay precisión de terminar la carretera pronto.* The highway must be completed soon. ▲ precision *Es admirable la precisión de la máquina.* The precision of that machine's wonderful. ○ **tener precisión** to need, have *Tengo precisión de salir.* I have to go out.

preciso accurate *El reloj es muy preciso.* The watch is very accurate. ▲ exact *Dígame la hora precisa.* Tell me the exact time. ○ **ser preciso** to be necessary *Es preciso llegar temprano.* It's necessary to get there early. ○ **tiempo preciso** just time enough *Tenemos el tiempo preciso para llegar a la estación.* We've just enough time to get to the station.

precoz precocious.

predecesor [*m*] predecessor.

predispuesto predisposed.

predominar to predominate, prevail.

preferencia preference *Debemos dar preferencia al estudio del español y del inglés.* We ought to give preference to the study of Spanish and English.

preferible preferable.

preferir [*rad-ch II*] to prefer.

pregunta question *Me hizo muchas preguntas.* He asked me a lot of questions. ○ **estar a la cuarta pregunta** to be broke *Siempre está a la cuarta pregunta.* He's always broke. ○ **hacer una pregunta** to ask a question *¿Puedo hacerle una pregunta?* May I ask you a question?

preguntar to ask *Pregúntele Ud. dónde vive.* Ask him where he lives. ○ **preguntar por** to inquire or ask about or for (a person) *Preguntaron por Ud. esta mañana.* They inquired for you this morning. ○ **preguntarse** to wonder *Me pregunto cuando volverá.* I wonder when he'll be back.

premiar to reward, give a prize to.

premio prize, reward.

prenda security *Lo dejaron en prenda.* They left it as security. ▲ personal quality *Una muchacha de muchas prendas.* A girl of many fine qualities. ○ **juego de prendas** game of forfeits *¿Conoce Ud. algún juego de prendas?* Do you know any game of forfeits? ○ **prenda de vestir** garment *He comprado algunas prendas de vestir.* I've bought some clothes.

prendedor [*m*] pin, brooch; [*Sp*] clothes pin.

prender to fix, catch, pin *Prenda esto con un alfiler.* Fix this with a pin. ▲ to arrest *Lo prendió la policía.* The police arrested him. ○ **prender fuego a** to set on fire *Prendieron fuego a los bosques.* They set the woods on fire.

prensa press *Las prensas funcionan muy bien.* The presses are working very well. ▲ press, newspapers *Libertad de prensa.* Freedom of the press.

prensar to press, compress *Prensaron las uvas en la bodega.* They pressed the grapes in the winery.

preocupación [*f*] preoccupation. ▲ cares, worries *Tiene mucha preocupación.* He has many cares.

preocupar to preoccupy. ▲ to worry *Aquello le preocupó mucho.* That worried him a lot. ○ **preocuparse** to worry *No se pre-*

ocupe Ud. por eso. Don't worry about that. O **preocuparse de** to care for, take care (of) *Preocúpese Ud. de que los niños beban la leche.* Take care that the children drink their milk.

preparación [*f*] preparation.

preparado (see **preparar**) preparation.

preparar to prepare *Le prepararé el desayuno.* I'll get your breakfast. ▲to arrange, prepare *Vamos a preparar una fiesta de despedida.* Let's arrange a farewell party.
O **prepararse** to get ready *Está preparándose para hacer un viaje.* He's getting ready for a trip.

preparativos [*m pl*] preparations.

presa prey *El león devoraba su presa.* The lion devoured his prey. ▲dam (for water) *Tomamos una fotografía de la presa.* We took a photograph of the dam.

prescribir to prescribe.

prescrito (see **prescribir**) prescribed.

presencia presence *Será muy de agradecer su presencia en ese acto.* Your presence at that function will be greatly appreciated. ▲appearance *Tiene muy buena presencia.* He has a very good appearance.
O **en presencia de** in front of, in the presence of *Lo dijo en presencia de todos.* He said it in front of everybody. O **presencia de ánimo** presence of mind *Su presencia de ánimo nos evitó el peligro.* His presence of mind saved us from danger.

presenciar to see, witness.

presentación [*f*] exhibition, display *Ese escaparate tiene presentación muy bonita.* That window has a very pretty display. ▲introduction *La presentación del orador fué hecha por el presidente.* The speaker was introduced by the president.
O **a la presentación** on presentation *Lo pagaré a la presentación de la cuenta.* I'll pay it on presentation of the bill.

presentar to present, introduce, submit *El comité presentará mañana un nuevo plan.* The committee will present a new plan tomorrow. ▲to present, put on *Presentarán un nuevo programa la semana próxima.* They'll put on a new program next week.
O **presentarse** to present oneself, report *Preséntese Ud. a la oficina de inmigración.* Report to the Immigration Department. ▲to appear, turn up *Se presentó inesperadamente.* He turned up unexpectedly. O **presentar**

una queja to complain *Presentaron una queja a la directiva.* They complained to the management.

presente present, current *Hay cinco fiestas en el presente mes.* There are five holidays in the current month. ▲present *Todos los niños presentes se levantaron.* All the children present got up.
O **al presente** at present *Al presente no tenemos ninguna noticia.* At present we have no news. O **la presente** this, the present writing *La presente es para saudarle y decirle....* This is to greet you and say.... O **tener presente** to bear in mind *Tengo presente lo que me dijo.* I'm bearing in mind what he told me.
‖ *¡Presente!* Present! (roll call).

presentimiento feeling, premonition.

presentir [*rad-ch II*] to have a feeling *or* premonition.

preservar to preserve, guard, keep.

presidencia presidency; chairmanship.

presidente [*m*] president *El presidente de la compañía es un hombre muy joven.* The president of the company's a very young man. ▲chairman *Cada año nuestra comisión elige un nuevo presidente.* Every year our committee elects a new chairman.

presidio penitentiary.

presión [*f*] pressure.

preso fastened; arrested. ▲[*n*] convict, jailbird.

préstamo loan.

prestado (see **prestar**) lent; borrowed.
O **pedir prestado** to borrow *¿Puedo pedirle prestado su coche el proximo domingo?* May I borrow your car next Sunday?

prestar to lend, loan *Me prestó un libro muy interesante.* He lent me a very interesting book.
O **prestar atención** to pay attention *Se ruega prestar atención.* Please pay attention. O **prestar ayuda** to help *¿Quiere Ud. prestarnos ayuda?* Will you help us? O **prestarse** to lend itself *Lo que dijo se prestaba a malas interpretaciones.* What he said lent itself to misinterpretation. ▲to offer *Se prestó a ayudarnos.* He offered to help us.

prestigio prestige.

presumir to presume *Presumo que es así.* I presume it's so. ▲to be conceited, show off *Presume mucho.* She shows off too much.
O **presumir de** to think of oneself

as *Presume de elegante.* He thinks he's pretty stylish.

presunción [*f*] conceit, presumption, vanity.

presupuesto budget.

pretender to intend, try *Esa persona pretende aprovecharse de Ud.* That person intends to take advantage of you. ▲ to court *Pretendía a una chica rica.* He was courting a rich girl. ▲ to pretend *Pretendió no haberme visto.* He pretended not to have seen me. ▲ to aim for, aspire to *Varias personas pretendían el puesto.* Several people aspired to the job. ○ **pretender decir** to mean, drive at *¿Qué pretende Ud. decir?* What are you driving at? ○ **pretender demasiado (de)** to make unreasonable demands (on), ask too much (of) *Esa señora pretende demasiado de su cocinera.* That lady demands too much of her cook.

pretendiente [*m*] suitor; pretender (to throne).

pretensión [*f*] (unreasonable) claim *No había justificación alguna en su pretensión.* There was no justification at all for his claim. ▲ pretension *Tiene muchas pretensiones descabelladas.* He has many foolish pretensions.

pretexto pretext, excuse.

prevención [*f*] prevention; police precinct.

prevenido (see **prevenir**) forewarned. ○ **estar prevenido** to be ready, be prepared, be forewarned *Como estaba prevenido, no lo sorprendieron.* As he was prepared, they didn't catch him unawares.

prevenir to prepare, arrange *Será necesario prevenir algo para la fiesta.* It'll be necessary to prepare something for the party. ▲ to prevent, avoid *Tendremos que tomar medidas para prevenir la propagación de la enfermedad.* We'll have to take measures to prevent the spread of the disease. ▲ to forewarn *Le previnieron del peligro.* They forewarned him of the danger. ○ **prevenirse (contra)** to take precautions (against) *Hay que prevenirse contra las enfermedades.* One must take precautions against diseases.

previo previous. ○ **examen previo** preliminary *or* entrance examination.

previsión [*f*] foresight. ○ **previsión social** social security.

prieto dark, brunet(te) [*Am*].

prever to foresee, anticipate *Previeron la desgracia.* They foresaw the mishap.

previsto (see **prever**) foreseen.

prima female cousin.

primavera spring (season).

primer See **primero**. ○ **en primer lugar** in the first place. ○ **Primer Ministro** Prime Minister. ○ **primer plano** foreground.

primero [*adj*] first *Es el primero de la fila.* He's the first in line. ▲ [*adv*] first, in the first place *Primero es un tonto; segundo no me gusta.* In the first place, he's a fool; in the second place, I don't like him. ▲ first *Haga esto primero.* Do this first. ○ **de buenas a primeras** suddenly, unexpectedly *De buenas a primeras, empezó a llorar.* Suddenly she began to cry. ○ **por primera vez** for the first time.

primitivo [*adj*] primitive.

primo male cousin.

primor [*m*] something lovely *Ese abrigo es un primor.* That coat's lovely. ▲ neatness *Ese trabajo está hecho con primor.* That job's very beautifully done.

primoroso exquisite; neat; dexterous.

princesa princess.

principal [*adj*] main, principal *Es la persona principal en la oficina.* He's the main person in the office. ▲ [*m*] principal *Hable Ud. con el principal.* Speak to the principal. ○ **el piso principal** the second floor.

príncipe [*m*] prince.

principiar to begin, start *Hay que principiar el trabajo inmediatamente.* The work must be started immediately.

principio principle *¿En qué principio basa Ud. su teoría?* On what principle do you base your theory? ▲ principle, standard *Eso no está de acuerdo con sus principios.* That doesn't agree with your principles. ▲ beginning *El principio del libro era muy interesante.* The beginning of the book was very interesting. ▲ entrée, main dish. ○ **al principio** at first *Al principio me parecía fácil el trabajo.* The work seemed easy to me at first. ○ **a principios de** at the beginning of *Reunámonos a principios de la semana entrante.* Let's get together the beginning of next week. ○ **en principio** in principle *En principio no me* *parece mal la idea.* That idea doesn't seem bad to me in principle.

prisa hurry. ▲urgency *Hay prisa de terminar este trabajo hoy.* It's urgent that this work be finished today. ○**andar de prisa** to be in a hurry *Siempre anda de prisa.* He's always in a hurry. ○**a toda prisa** at full speed *Iban a toda prisa.* They were going at full speed. ○**darse prisa** to hurry *¡Démonos prisa, que es tarde!* Let's hurry, it's late! ○**de prisa** quickly. ○**tener prisa** to be in a hurry *Tenía tanta prisa que se olvidó el sombrero.* He was in such a hurry that he forgot his hat.

prisión [*f*] prison.

prisionero prisoner (military).

privado [*adj*] private *Todos los cuartos tienen baño privado.* All rooms have a private bath. ○**en privado** privately, in private *Lo resolvieron en privado.* They settled it privately.

privado (see **privar**) deprived. ▲unconscious *De la impresión, quedó privada.* She became unconscious from the shock.

privar to deprive *Lo privaron de sus derechos.* They deprived him of his rights. ○**privarse** to deprive oneself *Se priva Ud. de demasiadas cosas.* You deprive yourself of too many things.

privilegio privilege.

proa bow, prow; nose (of an airplane).

probabilidad [*f*] probability.

probable probable.

probar to try, test *Probaremos el avión esta tarde.* We'll test the airplane this afternoon. ▲to taste *Pruebe Ud. este dulce.* Taste this candy. ▲to prove *Probó su inocencia.* He proved his innocence. ▲to agree with, suit *Este clima me prueba muy bien.* This climate agrees with me. ○**probarse** to try on *¿Puedo probarme el vestido?* May I try on the dress?

problema [*m*] problem.

proceder to proceed, begin *Después de examinar a los muchachos procedieron a calificarlos.* After testing the children they proceeded to classify them. ▲to come, be the result *Esto procede de su ignorancia.* This is the result of his ignorance. ▲to come *¿De dónde proceden sus padres?* Where do your parents come from? ▲to act *Procedió sin reflexionar.* He acted without thinking. ▲to behave. ▲[*m*] con-

duct, behavior *No me gusta su proceder.* I don't like your behavior. ○**proceder contra** to take action against.

procedimiento method, procedure *Su procedimiento de enseñanza es muy bueno.* Your method of teaching's very good.

procesión [*f*] procession.

proceso process; trial (court).

proclamar to proclaim.

procurar to try *Procuraré llegar al teatro a tiempo.* I'll try to get to the theater on time. ▲to see *Procure Ud. que no falte nada.* See that nothing is lacking. ○**procurarse** to get, obtain *Procúrese Ud. un buen asiento.* Get a good seat.

pródigo prodigal, extravagant.

producción [*f*] production.

producir [*irr*] to produce *Ese país produce mucho café.* That country produces a lot of coffee. ▲to produce, cause *Un descuido de alguien produjo el incendio.* The fire was caused by somebody's carelessness. ▲to produce, yield, give *No creo que el alquiler de la casa le produzca a Ud. mucho.* I don't think the rent from the house will yield you much. ○**producirse** to arise, break out *Se produjo una huelga.* A strike broke out.

productivo productive.

producto product. ○**productos agrícolas** (farm) produce.

profecía prophecy, forecast.

profesión [*f*] profession.

profesional [*adj*] professional.

profesar to profess; to join (a religious order).

profesor [*m*] professor.

profeta [*m*] prophet.

profundidad [*f*] depth.

profundo deep *¿Es muy profunda esta parte del lago?* Is this part of the lake very deep? ▲profound *Eso es un pensamiento muy profundo.* That's a very profound thought.

programa [*m*] program *¿Tiene Ud. el programa del concierto?* Do you have the program of the concert? ▲plans *¿Cuál es su programa para el domingo?* What are your plans for Sunday?

progresar to progress, make progress, advance *Ese país ha progresado mucho en los ultimos años.* That country's made great progress in the last

few years. ▲to progress, improve *Su
español progresa mucho.* His Spanish is improving a great deal.
progreso progress.
prohibición [*f*] prohibition.
prohibir to forbid *Te prohibo comer entre horas.* I forbid you to eat between meals.
‖ *Se prohibe fumar.* No smoking.
‖ *Se prohibe fijar carteles.* Post no
bills.
prólogo prologue; preface.
prolongar to prolong.
promedio [*m*] average.
promesa promise.
prometer to promise *Le he prometido ir
a visitarla.* I've promised to visit
her.—*La fiesta promete estar muy
alegre.* It promises to be a very gay
party. ▲to be promising *Este niño
promete mucho.* He's a very promising child.
prometido (see **prometer**) engaged.
pronto [*adj*] ready *Estoy pronto para
empezar.* I'm ready to begin. ▲[*adv*]
quickly *Hizo muy pronto el trabajo.*
He did the work very quickly. ▲soon
*Llegó más pronto de lo que yo espe-
raba.* He came sooner than I expected. ▲[*m*] sudden impulse *Todavía siente aquel pronto que tuvo.* He
still regrets that sudden impulse.
○ **al pronto** at first *Al pronto no lo
reconocí.* At first I didn't recognize
him. ○ **de pronto** suddenly *De pronto
apareció.* Suddenly he appeared.
○ **por de pronto** in the meantime, for
the time being *Por de pronto trabaje
Ud. en esto.* For the time being,
work on this. ○ **tan pronto como** as
soon as *Tan pronto como lo haga,
avíseme.* Let me know as soon as
you do it.
pronunciación [*f*] pronunciation.
pronunciamiento pronouncement; insurrection (in army).
pronunciar to pronounce.
propaganda advertising; propaganda.
propiedad [*f*] property.
propietario, propietaria owner, proprietor, proprietress.
propina tip, gratuity.
propio own *Lo ví con mis propios ojos.*
I saw it with my own eyes. ▲typical
Eso es muy propio de él. That's typical of him. ▲proper, right *Era el
hombre propio para aquel trabajo.*
He was the right man for that job.
▲oneself *Ella propia lo hizo.* She did
it herself.

proponer [*irr*] to propose (suggest)
Propondremos un cambio. We'll propose a change.
○ **proponerle algo a alquien** to make
a proposition *Le propuso un negocio
a mi padre.* He made a business
proposition to my father. ○ **proponerse** to plan, intend *Se propuso estudiar mucho.* He planned to study
a lot.
proporción [*f*] proportion.
proporcionar to provide with, supply
with *Le voy a proporcionar a Ud.
todo lo que necesita.* I'm going to
provide you with everything you need.
proposición [*f*] proposition.
propósito purpose *¿Cuál es su propósito?*
What's your purpose? ▲intention *El
infierno está empedrado de buenos
propósitos.* The road to hell is paved
with good intentions.
○ **a propósito** on purpose *Lo hice a
propósito.* I did it on purpose. ○ **a
propósito de** in connection with *A
propósito de lo que dicen les contaré
esto....* In connection with what
you're saying, I'll tell you this....
‖ *¡A propósito!* By the way!
propuesta proposal, proposition, motion.
prorrogar to extend (expiration date).
prosa prose.
prosperar to prosper.
prosperidad [*f*] prosperity.
protección [*f*] protection.
protector [*m*] protector.
proteger to protect *La madre protege a
sus hijos.* The mother protects her
children.
○ **protegerse** to protect oneself *Para
protegernos de la lluvia entramos en
una tienda.* We went into a store
to get out of the rain.
protesta protest *El juez no dió importancia a la protesta del público.* The
judge ignored the public protest.
protestar to protest.
○ **protestar de** to protest against
Protestaron de la injusticia. They
protested against the injustice.
provecho profit *No sacó ningún provecho de aquel negocio.* He didn't
make any profit on that deal.
○ **de provecho** useful *Es hombre de
provecho.* He's a useful man. ○ **ser
de provecho** to be good (for) *Esta
comida no es de provecho para Ud.*
This food isn't good for you.
‖ *Buen provecho.* Enjoy your meal.
or I hope you've enjoyed your meal.
(customary greeting before or after
a meal)

provechoso profitable.
providencia providence.
provincia province.
provinciano [*adj; n*] provincial.
provisión [*f*] provision.
provisional provisional.
provocación [*f*] provocation.
provocar to provoke *¡No me provoque Ud.¡* Don't provoke me!
proximidad [*f*] vicinity *Naufragaron en la proximidad de aquella costa.* They were shipwrecked in the vicinity of that coast.
próximo [*adj*] next *Empezaré el año próximo.* I'll begin next year. ▲close *Son parientes muy próximos.* They're very close relatives.
○ **estar próximo a** to almost.... *Estuvo próximo a caer al río.* He almost fell in the river.
proyectar to plan *Proyectan hacer más carreteras.* They plan to build more highways. ▲to project, show *Proyectaron una película científica.* They showed a scientific movie.
proyecto plan *El proyecto del nuevo edificio está listo.* The plan of the new building's ready. ▲project, plan *Mis hijos tienen muchos proyectos para el futuro.* My sons have many plans for the future.
prudencia prudence.
prudente prudent, wise.
prueba proof *¿Qué prueba tiene Ud.?* What proof do you have? ▲evidence *No hay prueba(s) para condenarlo.* There's no evidence to condemn him. ▲test *El aparato se rompió en la prueba.* The apparatus broke down during the test. ▲proof (printing, photography) *Me han enviado las pruebas de la imprenta.* They've sent me the printers' proofs. ▲trick [*Am*] *Hizo una prueba can las barajas.* He did a card trick.
○ **a prueba de** proof against, -proof *Este refugio está a prueba de bombas.* This shelter's bomb-proof.
‖ *Haga Ud. la prueba.* Try it.
psicología psychology.
publicación [*f*] publication.
publicar to publish.
publicidad [*f*] publicity.
público [*adj*] public *¿Hay aquí un teléfono público?* Is there a public telephone here? ▲[*m*] public; audience *El público estaba impaciente.* The audience was impatient.
puchero cooking pot.
pudín [*m*] pudding.
pueblo town, village *Este es un pueblo muy pintoresco.* This is a very picturesque village. ▲people *Es un hombre del pueblo.* He's a man of the people.
puente [*m*] bridge.
puerco pig, hog; pork.
puerta door; gate.
○ **dar con la puerta en las narices** to slam the door in one's face *Me dió con la puerta en las narices.* He slammed the door in my face.
puerto port.
pues because, as, since *Vaya, pues lo han llamado.* Go, since they've called you. ▲anyhow *Pues yo me voy.* I'm going anyhow. ▲well *Pues, si no quieres no vayas.* Well, if you don't want to, don't go. ▲certainly [*Am*] *Sí, pues.* Yes, certainly.
○ **pues bien** all right then *¡Pues bien, iré!* All right then, I'll go!
○ **pues no** not at all, not so.
‖ *¿Pues qué?* So what? ‖ *¿Y pues?* So? *or* Is that so? *or* And so?
puesto (see **poner**) set *La mesa está puesta.* The table's set. ▲[*m*] place *Tengo el tercer puesto en la cola.* I have the third place in the line. ▲stall, stand, booth *Lo compré en un puesto del mercado.* I bought it at a stand in the market. ▲position, job *Tiene un buen puesto.* He has a good job.
○ **bien puesto** well dressed *Iba muy bien puesto.* He was very well dressed. ○ **mal puesto** out of place.
○ **puesto que** since, as long as *Puesto que temes aburrirte, no vayas.* Since you're afraid you'll be bored, don't go.
pulga flea.
pulgada inch.
pulgar [*m*] thumb.
pulmón [*m*] lung.
pulmonía pneumonia.
pulpería grocery store, general store [*Am*].
pulque [*m*] pulque (fermented juice of the maguey plant; a Mexican drink).
pulsera bracelet.
○ **reloj de pulsera** wrist watch.
pulso pulse.
○ **tomarle a uno el pulso** to take one's pulse *El médico le tomó el pulso.* The doctor took his pulse.
punta point *Este lápiz no tiene punta.* This pencil has no point. ▲end, tip *Caminamos hasta la punta del muelle.* We walked to the end of the pier ▲top *En la punta del volcán se veía humo.* Smoke could be seen at the top

of the volcano.

○ **de punta en blanco** all dressed up *Iban de punta en blanco.* They were all dressed up.

puntada stitch.

○ **echar puntadas** to stitch.

puntal [*m*] snack [*Am*].

puntiagudo sharp-pointed.

puntilla ○ **de puntillas** on tiptoe.

punto point, dot *El avión se veía como un punto en el cielo.* The airplane looked like a dot in the sky. ▲ period (in writing) *¿Dónde está el punto en esta máquina de escribir?* Where's the period on this typewriter? ▲ place, spot *Nos veremos en el mismo punto.* We'll meet at the same place. ▲ point (in sports) *Ganó por pocos puntos.* He won by a few points.

○ **al punto** instantly *Se presentó al punto.* He appeared instantly. ○ **a punto fijo** exactly *No lo sé a punto fijo.* I don't know exactly. ○ **a tal punto** that far *A tal punto no quiero llegar.* I don't want to go that far. ○ **coche de punto** taxi, car for hire [*Sp*]. ○ **dar en el punto** to hit the nail on the head *Ha dado Ud. en el punto.* You've hit the nail on the head. ○ **de punto** by the minute *Su cólera subía de punto.* He became angrier by the minute. ▲ knitted *Compraré un chaleco de punto.* I'll buy a knitted vest. ○ **desde cierto punto de vista** from a certain standpoint *Desde cierto punto de vista Ud. tiene razón.* You're right from a certain standpoint. ○ **en punto** on the dot, sharp *Debemos llegar a las seis en punto.* We must arrive at six on the dot. ○ **en punto a** in regard to *En punto a los precios que Ud. indica, estamos completamente de acuerdo.* In regard to the prices you mention, we're in complete agreement. ○ **estar a punto de** to be about to *Estábamos a punto de salir cuando llegaron.* We were about to leave when they arrived. ○ **hasta cierto punto** to a certain extent *Hasta cierto punto es cierto.* To a certain extent it's true. ○ **punto de gracia** funny side *Tiene su punto de gracia.* It has its funny side. ○ **punto final** stop *Hay que poner punto final a esto.* We must put a stop to this. ○ **punto por punto** step by step, in detail *Lo contó todo punto por punto.* He told everything step by step.

‖ *¿Hasta qué punto del programa han estudiado?* How far did they get in their studies?

puntual prompt, punctual.

puñado handful.

puñalada stab, knife wound.

puño fist *Cerró los puños.* He clenched his fists. ▲ handle *El puño del paraguas está roto.* The umbrella handle's broken. ▲ cuff *Están mal planchados los puños de la camisa.* The shirt cuffs are poorly ironed.

pupila pupil (of eye).

pupitre [*m*] (school) desk.

pureza purity.

purgante [*m*] purgative, physic.

puro pure *Esta leche es pura.* This milk's pure. ▲ clear *Tiene una voz muy pura.* She has a very clear voice. ▲ [*m*] cigar *Le gusta fumar puros.* He likes to smoke cigars. ○ **de pura casualidad** purely by chance *Me encontré con él de pura casualidad.* I met him purely by chance. ○ **de pura sangre** thoroughbred *Ese caballo es de pura sangre.* That horse is a thoroughbred. ○ **la pura verdad** absolute *or* unvarnished truth *Lo que le dijo es la pura verdad.* What he told her's the unvarnished truth.

‖ *Apenas podía andar de puro fatigado.* He was so exhausted he could hardly walk.

Q

que that, which *Tomaré el tren que llegue primero.* I'll take the first train that arrives. ▲ that, on which, when *El día que vino era miércoles.* The day he came was Wednesday. ▲ who *Ud., que es una experta, debe seguramente saberlo.* You're an expert; you should certainly know. ▲ whom *Ese es el muchacho de que le hablé.* That's the boy I spoke to you about. ▲ what *No sé qué haré mañana.* I don't know what I'll do tomorrow.—*¿Qué ha sido de su hermano?* What's become of your brother? ▲ that *Estaba tan cambiado que no le conocí.* He looked so changed that I didn't recognize him. ▲ that *Dudo que venga.* I doubt that he'll come. ▲ than *La otra es mejor que ésta.* The other's better than this.

○ **el** (*or* **la, los, las**) **que** he (*or* she, they) who, the one(s) who, anyone who *El que quiera beber que venga conmigo.* Anyone who wants a drink, come with me. ○ **¿qué? which?** *¿Qué libro le gusta a Ud. más?* Which book do you like better? ▲ **what kind of?** *¿Dime qué gente es esa?* Tell me, what kind of people are they? ○ **¡qué! how!** *¡Qué bonito es ese cuadro!* How pretty that picture is! ▲ **what! what a!** *¡Qué tontería!* What nonsense!—*¡Qué niño!* What a child! ○ **¡qué de! how many!** *¡Qué de cosas me contó!* How many things he told me! ○ **¡qué va!** go on! come on! how come? (expressing disbelief) *¡Qué va! Eso no es cierto.* Go on! That's not true. ○ **sin qué ni para qué** without cause or motive. ○ **un no sé qué** a certain something *Tiene un no sé qué que atrae.* She has a certain something that's attractive. ‖ *¿Qué más da?* What's the difference? ‖ *¿Pues qué?* So what?

quebrado rough, rugged *Estos últimos días hemos viajado por terrenos muy quebrados.* We've been through some very rough country in the last few days. ▲ **broken** *Trace una línea quebrada.* Draw a broken line. ○ **estar quebrado** to be ruptured. ○ **número quebrado** fraction (mathematics).

quebrar to break *Quebró un vaso.* He broke a glass. ▲ **to fail** *El banco quebró cuando nadie lo esperaba.* The bank failed when no one expected it. ○ **quebrarse** to break *El plato se quebró.* The plate broke. ▲ **to break** (a bone) *Al caer se quebró un brazo.* He broke his arm when he fell.

quedar to be left *El bolso quedó sobre la mesa.* The purse was left on the table.—*Sólo me quedan unos centavos.* I have only a few cents left. ▲ **to remain** *La carta quedó sin contestar.* The letter remained unanswered. ▲ **to be** *Queda lejos de aquí.* It's far from here. ○ **quedar (bien)** to come out (well) *Quedó muy bien el trabajo.* The work came out very well. ○ **quedar bien con** to make a hit with, get along well with *Está quedando bien con ella.* He's making a hit with her. ○ **quedar de** to promise to [*Am*] *Quedamos de llegar el domingo.* We promised to come Sunday. ○ **quedar en** to agree, have an understanding *Quedamos en que vendría a las ocho.* We agreed

that he'd come at eight. ○ **quedarse** to remain, stay *Nuestro amigo se quedó en Europa.* Our friend stayed in Europe. ○ **quedarse atrás** to stay behind. ○ **quedarse con** to take *Me quedo con el azul.* I'll take the blue one. ○ **quedarse limpio** to get cleaned out *Jugó a las cartas y se quedó limpio.* He played cards and was cleaned out.
‖ *¿Se puede saber en qué quedamos?* Can we find out where we stand?

quehaceres *(m pl]* **de casa** household chores.

queja complaint.

quejarse to complain *No tiene Ud. de qué quejarse.* You have nothing to complain about.

quema burning *La quema de las hojas.* The burning of the leaves.
○ **huir de la quema** to get away from trouble, beat it *Al ver lo que iba a ocurrir, huyó de la quema.* When he saw what was going to happen, he beat it.

quemado (see **quemar**) burnt *Huele a quemado.* It smells burnt.
○ **quemado por el sol** sunburned.

quemadura burn, scald.

quemar to burn *¿Quién quemó esta cortina?* Who burned this curtain?
○ **quemarse** to burn oneself *Cuidado, puede Ud. quemarse.* Be careful, you'll burn yourself.

querer [*irr*] to want, wish *¿Qué quiere Ud. comer?* What do you want to eat? ▲ **to love** *La quiere mucho.* He loves her very much.
○ **como quiera que sea** in any case *Como quiera que sea, iremos.* In any case, we'll go. ○ **donde quiera** anywhere, wherever. ○ **querer decir** to mean *¿Qué quiere decir esta palabra?* What does this word mean? ○ **sin querer** unwillingly; unintentionally *Lo hizo sin querer.* He did it unwillingly.

querido [*adj*] dear, beloved *Querido hijo:*... Dear son:...

queso cheese.

quiebra bankruptcy, failure.

quien who, whom *¿Quién llamó?* Who called?—*Son los muchachos de quienes le hablé.* They're the boys I spoke to you about.—*Es la muchacha a quien más quiero.* She's the girl I like best of all. ▲ **whoever, anyone who** *Quien así piense se equivoca.* Whoever thinks so is wrong.
○ **¿quién sabe?** who knows? "*¿Crees*

que va a llover?" "¿Quién sabe?" "Do you think it'll rain?" "Who knows?"

quienquiera whoever *Deja pasar a quienquiera que venga.* Whoever comes, let him in.

quieto [*adj*] still *Estése quieto un momento.* Stand (*or* Sit) still a moment. ▲calm *El lago ha estado quieto todo el día.* The lake's been calm all day. ▲quiet *Es una chica muy quieta.* She's a very quiet girl.

quietud [*f*] quiet, repose.

quijada jaw.

química chemistry.

químico chemical. ▲ [*n*] chemist.

quince fifteen.

quincena ○por quincena(s) every two weeks, semi-monthly.

quinientos five hundred.

quinina quinine.

quinta country house.

quintal [*m*] a hundred pounds.

quinto [*adj*] fifth. ▲ [*m*] nickel (coin) [*Mex*].

quitar to take away *Quitaremos esta mesa de aquí.* We'll take this table away from here. ▲to subtract *Hay que quitar esta cantidad del total.* You have to subtract this amount from the total.

○**quitarse** to take off (clothing) *No se quite el abrigo.* Don't take off your overcoat. ▲to come out *Estas manchas no se quitan.* These stains won't come out. ▲to give up *Se ha quitado el vicio de la bebida.* He's given up drinking. ○**quitarse de en medio** to get out of the way. ○**quitarse el agua** to stop raining [*Am*] *Cuando se quite el agua saldremos.* When it stops raining we'll go out. ○**quitarse un peso de encima** to take a load off one's mind. ○**quitar tiempo** to take (too much) time *Este trabajo le quita mucho tiempo.* This work's taking too much of his time.

quizá, quizás perhaps, maybe.

R

rábano radish.

○**tomar el rábano por las hojas** to misinterpret.

rabia rabies *El perro tiene rabia.* The dog has rabies. ▲rage, fury.

○**dar rabia** to make furious, to anger *Me da rabia no haber ido.* It makes me furious that I didn't go. ○**tener rabia** to have a grudge against *Le tengo una rabia tremenda.* I've a terrible grudge against him. ○**tomar rabia** to develop a grudge against *Le tomó rabia sin tener porqué.* He developed a grudge against him for no reason at all.

rabiar to be mad, be furious, to rage.

rabioso furious, enraged; rabid.

rabo tail (without hair or feathers) *El ratón se cogió el rabo en la ratonera.* The mouse's tail got caught in the trap.

○**(con el) rabo entre (las) piernas** crestfallen *Volvió con el rabo entre las piernas.* He came back crestfallen.

rabona ○**hacer rabona** to cut *or* skip (class, etc); to play hookey.

racha streak, string, series *Ha habido una racha de crímenes.* There's been a series of crimes.

○**buena racha** streak of good luck.

racimo cluster, bunch.

radiador [*m*] radiator.

radio [*f in Sp & Arg, m in rest of Am*] radio *El radio dió la noticia.* The news came over the radio. ▲ [*m*] radium.

○**radio de acción** range *El radio de acción de aquella emisora era muy extenso.* That transmitter had a very long range.

radiograma [*m*] radiogram.

raído frayed, threadbare.

raíz [*f*] root *Este árbol tiene las raíces muy hondas.* This tree has very deep roots.

○**arrancar de raíz** to uproot.

raja split, crack; slice (of food).

rajar to split, rend. ▲to slice *Hay que rajar el melón.* The melon has to be sliced. ▲to chatter, gossip [*Slang*].

○**rajarse** to crack *El cristal del reloj se rajó.* My watch crystal cracked. ▲to hold back *Siempre se raja a última hora.* He always holds back at the last moment.

ralo thin, sparse; [*Antilles*] weak (of infusions).

rama branch, twig, bough *¡No te cuelgues de esa rama!* Don't hang from that branch! ▲branch *Aquel apellido era de otra rama de la familia.* That name came from another branch of the family.

○ **andarse por las ramas** to beat about the bush.

ramo bough (cut off tree). ▲ bouquet, bunch *Le ofreció un ramo de flores.* He gave her a bouquet of flowers. ▲ branch *La química es un ramo de la ciencia.* Chemistry's a branch of science. ▲ (line of) business *El ramo de ferretería.* The hardware business.

rancho mess (of food), chow ¿*A qué hora dan el rancho?* What time's chow? ▲ hut [*Am*] *Viven en ranchos de paja.* They live in thatched huts. ▲ ranch [*Am*] *Tiene un rancho muy grande.* He has a very big ranch. ▲ man's flat straw hat [*Am*].

rancio rancid; old (of wine, nobility). ▲ old-fashioned, antiquated *Es un hombre muy rancio.* He's a very old-fashioned man.

rapidez [*f*] rapidity, swiftness.

rápido [*adj*] rapid, quick *Era muy rápido en sus decisiones.* He was very quick in his decisions. ▲ [*m*] express (train) *A las nueve pasó el rápido.* The express went by at nine.

raqueta racket (tennis).

raro rare, unusual *Era raro que recibiera carta.* It was unusual for him to get a letter.—*Los muebles coloniales son muy raros hoy día.* Colonial furniture's rare nowadays. ▲ odd, strange ¡*Qué cosa más rara!* What a strange thing!

rascacielos [*m sg*] skyscraper.

rascar to scratch.

rasgar to tear *Se rasgó los pantalones.* He tore his pants.

rasgo stroke *Los rasgos de ese dibujo son muy acentuados.* The strokes in that drawing are very heavy. ▲ impulse *Tuvo un rasgo muy digno de alabanza.* He had a very worthy impulse.

○ **a grandes rasgos** briefly, in outline, in a few words *Se lo contaré a grandes rasgos.* I'll tell it to you in a few words. ○ **rasgos** features *Sus rasgos me eran familiares.* His features were familiar to me. ○ **rasgos (de carácter)** characteristics *Tiene rasgos (de carácter) muy desagradables.* He has very unpleasant characteristics.

rasgón [*m*] tear *Llevaba un rasgón en el traje.* He had a tear in his clothes.

rasguño scratch *Se hizo un rasguño en la cara.* He got a scratch on his face.

raspadura bruise *Tengo una raspadura en el brazo.* I have a bruise on my arm.

raspar to scrape, scratch out.

raspón [*m*] bruise.

rastreador [*m*] scout.

rastrear to scout, track down.

rastro track, trail *Los perros perdieron el rastro al llegar al río.* When they reached the river, the dogs lost the track. ▲ trace *Después del huracán no quedó ni rastro de la casa.* After the hurricane not a trace of the house was left.

○ **seguir el rastro** to track down, follow the scent.

rata rat.

ratero pickpocket.

rato (short) while *Espere Ud. un rato.* Wait a while.

○ **al poco rato** very soon, after a little while *Nuestros amigos llegarán al poco rato.* Our friends will come after a little while. ○ **a ratos perdidos** in one's spare time *Leía a ratos perdidos.* He read in his spare time. ○ **pasar el rato** to while away the time, pass the time away. ○ **pasar un buen rato** to have a good time.

ratón [*m*] mouse.

raya dash, line; crease (in trousers); part (in hair); ray fish. ▲ line (sports) *La pelota cayó fuera la raya.* The ball fell outside of the line.

○ **tener a raya** to keep within bounds, control, restrain.

rayar to draw lines on, rule. ▲ to scratch (make scratches on) *Está Ud. rayando la mesa.* You're scratching the table.

rayo flash (*or* bolt) of lightning *Cayó un rayo e incendió la casa.* A bolt of lightning struck the house and set it on fire. ▲ ray *Los rayos del sol queman en verano.* The rays of the sun burn in summer.—*Todavía quedaba un rayo de esperanza.* There was still a ray of hope left.

raza race (anthropological).

razón [*f*] reason (reasoning power). ▲ reason, sanity *Ha perdido la razón.* He's lost his reason. ▲ reason, explanation *Dé Ud. algunas razones si quiere convencerme.* Give me some reasons if you want to convince me. ▲ reason, cause *Lo hizo sin razón.* He did it without reason. ▲ message [*Am*] *Le daré la razón a la señora.* I'll give her the message.

○ **a razón de** at the rate of *Pagará a razón de un seis por ciento al año.* He'll pay at the rate of six per cent a year. ○ **atender a razones** to listen to reason. ○ **dar razón** to give information *Se alquila. Darán razón en la portería.* For rent. See the janitor for information. ○ **tener razón** to be right. ○ **no tener razón** to be wrong. ○ **tomar razón de** to make a record of.

razonable reasonable.

razonar to reason.

reacción [*f*] reaction; political conservatism; reactionary force.

○ **entrar en reacción** to warm oneself, warm up *Encendió la estufa para entrar en reacción.* He lit the stove to warm himself.

real real, actual *La situación real no ha cambiado.* The actual situation hasn't changed. ▲ royal *Pertenecía a la familia real.* He belonged to the royal family. ▲ [*m*] real (Sp coin worth about 25 cents) *Esta revista cuesta un real.* This magazine costs one real.

realidad [*f*] reality, fact.

realización [*f*] realization, execution *La realización de los planes durará por lo menos un año.* The execution of the plans will take at least a year. ▲ sale *El lunes pasado hubo una realización de todas las mercancías.* There was a sale of all the merchandise last Monday.

realizar to accomplish *Esto no es difícil de realizar.* This isn't hard to accomplish. ▲ to carry out *Realizaron el plan con todos sus detalles.* They carried out the plan in every detail. ▲ to sell out *Realizaron todas las existencias.* They sold out all the goods in stock.

reanimar to cheer up, encourage; to revive.

rebaja reduction.

rebajar to reduce, lower *Han rebajado un poco los precios.* They've reduced the prices a little. ▲ to reduce (in weight) *He rebajado diez libras.* I've reduced ten pounds.

○ **rebajarse** to lower oneself *No me rebajaré a hacer tal cosa.* I won't lower myself to do such a thing.

rebelde rebellious. ▲ [*n*] rebel.

recadero, recadera messenger.

recado message; errand.

recaída relapse.

recámara bedroom [*Mex*].

recambio ○ **pieza de recambio** spare part.

receloso distrustful, suspicious.

recepción [*f*] reception, formal gathering *La recepción fué muy lucida.* It was a very brilliant reception. ▲ reception *Les hicieron una recepción muy calurosa.* They were given a very warm reception.

receta prescription (medicine). ○ **receta de cocina** recipe (cooking).

rechazar to discard, reject, turn down *Rechazó la idea de ir al campo.* He turned down the idea of going to the country. ▲ to drive back *El enemigo fué rechazado a sus posiciones.* The enemy was driven back to his positions.

recibir to receive *Recibió Ud. ayer alguna visita?* Did you receive any visitors yesterday?

○ **recibirse** to graduate [*Am*] *Se recibió de doctor.* He graduated as a doctor. ○ **ser bien** (*or* **mal**) **recibido** to be (*or* not to be) well-taken *Fué mal recibida su opinión.* His opinion wasn't well-taken.

recibo receipt.

recién recently, newly *Ese café está recién hecho.* That coffee hasn't been made very long. ▲ just, recently [*Am*] *Recién me entero.* I just found out. ○ **recién casados** newlyweds. ○ **recién llegado** newcomer.

reciente new, fresh *La pintura estaba reciente.* The paint was fresh. ▲ recent *¿Son estas noticias recientes?* Is this news recent?

reclamación [*f*] reclamation; complaint; claim.

reclamar to claim *Ud. ya no puede reclamar ese dinero.* You can no longer claim that money. ○ **reclamar en juicio** to sue.

reclamo advertising; claim [*Am*]; decoy.

recluta [*m*] recruit, rookie.

recobrar to recover, regain.

recoger to get *Voy a recoger los papeles que dejé en mi despacho.* I'm going to get the papers I left in my office. ▲ to collect *Han recogido mucho dinero para la Cruz Roja.* They've collected a lot of money for the Red Cross. ▲ to collect, gather up *Recoja Ud. todas esas cosas y póngalas en orden.* Gather up all those things and put them in order. ▲ to pick up *Recoja Ud. eso que se le ha caído.* Pick up what you dropped. ▲ to take in, shelter *Han recogido varios huérfanos.* They've taken in several orphans.

○ **recogerse** to go home, retire *Se recoge muy tarde.* He keeps late hours.

recomendación [*f*] recommendation.

recomendar to recommend *¿Me puede Ud. recomendar un buen restaurant?* Can you recommend a good restaurant to me? ▲ to recommend, advise *Le recomiendo a Ud. que lo haga de prisa.* I advise you to do it quickly.

reconocer to inspect, examine *El paciente fué reconocido cuidadosamente.* The patient was carefully examined. ▲ to recognize *Cuando le ví de nuevo, no le reconocí.* When I saw him again, I didn't recognize him. ▲ to acknowledge, admit *¿Reconoce Ud. su falta?* Do you acknowledge your mistake? ▲ to acknowledge, be grateful for *Estoy reconocido a sus atenciones.* I'm grateful for your kindness.

reconstruir to rebuild, reconstruct.

recordar [*rad-ch I*] to remember *¿Recuerda Ud. lo que le dije?* Do you remember what I told you? ▲ to remind *Me recuerda mucho a su padre.* He reminds me very much of his father.

recorrer to cover, travel *Ayer recorrimos diez millas.* Yesterday we covered ten miles.

recorrido route, course, run *Ese cartero tiene un recorrido muy largo.* That postman has a very long route.

recorte [*m*] scrap, cutting; clipping (newspaper).

recreo recreation.

recto [*adj*] straight *Todo el camino era recto.* The road was straight all the way. ▲ just, fair *Era un hombre recto.* He was a just man.

○ **ángulo recto** right angle.

recuerdo remembrance, memory *Guardo muy buenos recuerdos de mi amistad con él.* I have very happy memories of my friendship with him. ▲ souvenir, memento *Estos son recuerdos de nuestro viaje por Italia.* These are souvenirs of our trip through Italy.

○ **recuerdos** regards *Dé Ud. recuerdos a su familia de mi parte.* Give my regards to your family.

recurso means, argument *Empleó todos los recursos para convencerle.* He used every argument to convince him.

○ **recursos** resources, means *Estaba materialmente sin recursos.* He was practically without means.

red [*f*] net *Los pescadores tendieron la red.* The fishermen spread out the net. ▲ snare, trap *Cayó en la(s) red(es) que le tendieron.* He fell into the snare they set for him.

redacción [*f*] editorial staff *Entró en la redacción de una revista.* He joined

the editorial staff of a magazine. ▲ composition *La redacción de esta carta es mala.* This letter's badly written.

redactar to compose, frame in writing *Esta carta está muy bien redactada.* This letter's very well put.

redondo [*adj*] round.

○ **en números redondos** in round numbers.

reducción [*f*] reduction, decrease.

reducir [*-zc-*] to reduce *Redujo el presupuesto en su departamento.* He reduced the budget in his department.

○ **quedar reducido a** to be reduced to, be brought to a condition of *El edificio quedó reducido a escombros.* The building was reduced to rubble. ○ **reducir a la obediencia** to compel to obey.

reemplazar to replace.

reexpedir to forward (mail).

referencia reference *¿Cuáles son sus referencias?* What are your references?

○ **dar referencias** to inform. ○ **hacer referencia a** to refer to, mention *Hizo referencia a un autor muy famoso.* He referred to a very famous author.

referir [*rad-ch II*] to relate *Refirió el caso con muchos detalles.* He related the matter in great detail.

○ **referirse a** to refer to *¿A qué se refiere Ud. cuando dice eso?* What are you referring to when you say that?

reforma alteration.

○ **cerrado por reformas** closed for alterations.

refrán [*m*] proverb, saying.

refrescar to cool *Hay que refrescar el agua.* The water must be cooled. ▲ to get cool *or* cooler *Esta refrescando la tarde.* The afternoon's getting cooler.

○ **refrescar la memoria** to refresh one's memory. ○ **refrescarse** to cool off *Vamos a refrescarnos a la sombra de los árboles.* Let's cool off in the shade of the trees.

refresco refreshment, cold drink *Tomó un refresco para aplacar la sed.* He took a cold drink to quench his thirst.

refrigerador [*m*] refrigerator.

refugiarse to take shelter.

regalar to present, give (gift) *¿Qué me vas a regalas por mi cumpleaños?* What are you going to give me for my birthday?

regalo present, gift *Recibió un buen regalo.* He received a nice gift.

○ **con regalo** in luxury *Vivía con regalo.* He lived in luxury.

regañar to scold *Siempre me esta regañando.* He's always scolding me.

regaño scolding, reprimand.

regar [*rad-ch I*] to water, irrigate.

regateo bargaining, haggling.

régimen [*m*] regime, political system *El régimen de aquel país era muy democrático.* The political system of that country was very democratic. ▲ diet *El médico lo puso a régimen.* The doctor put him on a diet.

región [*f*] region.

regir [*rad-ch III*] to rule, govern *¿Quién rige esos territorios?* Who rules those territories? ▲ to be in effect *Aun rige ese decreto.* That decree's still in effect.

registrar to search *La policía registró su casa.* The police searched his house. ▲ to examine (baggage). ▲ to record, keep a record of *Registraba en aquel libro las compras y ventas.* He kept a record of purchases and sales in that book.

○ **registrarse** to register (oneself) *Es preciso registrarse en el Consulado.* You have to register at the Consulate.

regla rule, regulation *Tiene Ud. que obedecer las reglas.* You have to obey the rules. ▲ ruler (for drawing lines) *¿Puede dejarme la regla?* Can you leave me the ruler?

○ **en regla** in order *¿Todo está en regla?* Is everything in order? ○ **por regla general** as a general rule.

regocijo joy, gladness.

regreso return, coming *or* going back.

regular regular, orderly, regulated *Llevaba una vida muy regular.* He led a very regular life. ▲ moderate, so-so *Esta mañana me siento regular nada más.* This morning I only feel so-so.

○ **por lo regular** as a rule, ordinarily *Por lo regular le veía todos los días.* Ordinarily I saw him every day.

regularidad [*f*] regularity.

reina queen.

reinar to reign *Luis diez y seis reinó en Francia en el siglo dieciocho.* Louis the Sixteenth reigned in France in the eighteenth century. ▲ to prevail, reign *Durante la guerra reinó el terror.* Terror reigned during the war.

reino kingdom.

reír(se) [*rad-ch III*] to laugh *No se ría Ud.* Don't laugh.

○ **reírse a carcajadas** to laugh heart-ily, guffaw. ○ **reírse de** to laugh at *¿De qué se ríe Ud.?* What are you laughing at? ▲ to make fun of, ridicule *Estaban riéndose de él.* They were making fun of him.

reja bars, iron window grating.

relación [*f*] story, account *Toda aquella relación era interesante.* The whole story was interesting.

○ **con relación a** about, with regard to *No sé nada con relación a ese asunto.* I don't know anything about that matter. ○ **entrar en** (*or* **establecer**) **relaciones con** to establish (business) relations with. ○ **relaciones** relations, dealings *No existían entre ellos ningunas relaciones.* They had no dealings with each other. ○ **tener relación con** to have connection with, have relation to *Eso no tiene ninguna relación con el asunto que estamos tratando.* That has no relation to the subject we're discussing. ○ **tener relaciones** to have connections *Tiene muy buenas relaciones.* He has very good connections.

relacionar to relate, connect, establish a relation between *En su conferencia relacionó los dos hechos históricos.* In his lecture he established a relation between the two historical facts. ▲ to introduce (make acquainted) *Mi prima nos relacionó.* My cousin introduced us.

○ **relacionarse con** to have dealings with *No se relacione con tales gentes.* Don't have any dealings with such people.

relajamiento laxness, laxity, looseness.

relajo disorder, confusion, mix-up [*Am*].

relámpago lightning.

relatar to relate, tell.

religión [*f*] religion.

religioso religious. ▲ [*n*] member of a religious order.

reloj [*m*] clock, watch.

○ **andar** (*or* **marchar**) **como un reloj** to be in perfect trim. ○ **reloj de pulsera** wrist watch.

relucir [*-zc-*] to shine, glisten, glitter.

rellenar to refill; to fill up; to stuff.

relleno stuffed, filled. ▲ [*m*] stuffing.

○ **pimientos rellenos** stuffed peppers.

remar to row (a boat).

remate [*m*] auction.

○ **de remate** completely *Estaba loco de remate.* He was completely crazy.

remediar to remedy, repair *Tenemos que remediar el daño.* We'll have to repair the damage.

○ **no poder remediar** not to be able to help *No pudo remediar lo que pasó.* He couldn't help what happened.

remedio remedy, medicine *Se le dieron al enfermo varios remedios caseros.* Various home remedies were given to the patient.

○ **ni para un remedio** for love or money *No pude encontrar un taxi ni para un remedio.* I couldn't get a taxi for love or money. ○ **no hay más remedio que** there's nothing to do but *No hay más remedio que dejarle marchar.* There's nothing to do but let him go. ○ **no tener más remedio que** to have no recourse but *No tuve más remedio que ir.* I had no recourse but to go. ○ **no tener remedio** to be beyond repair *Lo que has hecho no tiene remedio.* What you've done's beyond repair. ○ **sin remedio** hopeless, beyond hope *Es un caso sin remedio.* He's a hopeless case.

remendar [*rad-ch I*] to mend, patch, repair.

remiendo patch.

remitir to remit, send.

remo oar; [*Slang*] leg.

remolacha beet.

remolcar to tow.

remontar to go up *Remontaron el curso del río.* They went up the river.

○ **remontarse** to get excited, be excited *Procure Ud. no remontarse tanto.* Try not to be so excited. ○ **remontarse a** to go back to *En su conferencia el profesor se remontó a fechas muy lejanas.* The professor went back to very early times in his lecture. ▲ to date from, date back to *Ese hecho se remonta al siglo dieciseis.* That event dates back to the sixteenth century.

remordimiento remorse.

remover [*rad-ch I*] to dig up, loosen (soil) *Removió la tierra para sembrar la semilla.* He dug up the ground to plant the seeds. ▲ to stir *Remueva Ud. la sopa.* Stir the soup. ▲ to shake *La explosión removió la casa.* The explosion shook the house.

○ **remover (de un cargo** *or* **puesto)** to dismiss (from a post *or* office) *Removieron a todos los empleados.* All the employees were dismissed.

rendir [*rad-ch III*] to yield, produce *Esta hacienda rinde muy poco.* This farm produces very little. ▲ to conquer, win (over) *Con sus amabilidades la rindió.* With his attentions, he conquered her. ▲ to surrender *El general rindió la plaza al enemigo.* The general surrendered the city to the enemy.

○ **estar rendido** to be all in. ○ **rendir cuentas** to give (*or* render) an account *Tuvo que rendir cuentas.* He had to render an account. ○ **rendirse** to become exhausted, be worn out *Se rindió de tanto correr.* He became exhausted from running so hard. ▲ to surrender, give up *Después de seis días se rindió la plaza.* After six days the garrison surrendered. ▲ to yield, give in *No quería rendirse a la evidencia.* He didn't want to yield to the evidence.

rengo lame [*Arg*].

renguear to limp, hobble [*Arg*].

renquear to limp, hobble.

renta rent *No hemos pagado la renta de la casa este mes.* We haven't paid this month's rent on the house. ▲ income; interest (from a bank account) *¿Qué renta anual le produce su capital?* What's the annual income on your capital?

rentar to rent for *¿Cuánto renta ese cuarto?* How much does that room rent for? ▲ to produce, yield *Estos valores rentarán mucho en el futuro.* These stocks will yield a great deal in the future.

renuncia resignation; renunciation.

renunciar to resign *Tuvo que renunciar a su puesto.* He had to resign from his position. ▲ to refuse, reject *Renunció a aquel honor.* He refused that honor. ▲ to give up, renounce *Hay que renunciar a esos planes.* Those plans have to be given up.

reñido (see **reñir**) on bad terms *Estamos reñidos.* We're on bad terms.

reñir [*rad-ch III*] to wrangle, quarrel, argue *Le gustaba reñir por cualquier cosa.* He'd quarrel about anything. ▲ to scold *No le riña Ud. más.* Don't scold him any more.

reorganizar to reorganize.

reparar to repair *Había que reparar el edificio.* The building had to be repaired.

○ **reparar en** to consider *No reparó en las consecuencias.* He didn't consider the consequences. ▲ to notice *No reparó en el saludo que le hice.* He didn't notice my greeting.

reparo objection *Los reparos de Ud. no son razonables.* Your objections aren't reasonable.

○ **poner reparo(s)** to make objection(s) *¿Puso algún reparo a aquella*

carta? Did he make any objections to that letter?
‖ *Es un hombre de muchos reparos.* He's a very discreet man.

repartir to distribute.
  ○ **repartirse** to share, divide *Nos repartimos el pastel.* We divided the cake among ourselves.

reparto sharing, distribution; delivery (of goods, mail).

repasar to check *Repase Ud. esa cuenta detenidamente.* Check that account carefully. ▲ to review *Repase Ud. las lecciones.* Review your lessons. ▲ to mend *Había que repasar aquella ropa.* Those clothes had to be mended.

repaso review (of a lesson); mending.

repente [*m*] sudden impulse *Tuvo un repente y se declaró.* He had a sudden impulse and proposed to her.
  ○ **de repente** suddenly, unexpectedly *Llegó de repente.* He arrived unexpectedly.

repentino sudden.

repetición [*f*] repetition *El informe estaba lleno de repeticiones.* The report was full of repetitions. ▲ encore *El público entusiasmado pidió la repetición.* The enthusiastic audience asked for an encore.

repetir [*rad-ch III*] to repeat *Haga el favor de repetir esa palabra.* Please repeat that word.

replicar to reply, answer back; to argue.

replicón insolent (of children or servants).

reponer [*irr*] to replace *Repuso de fondos su cuenta corriente.* He replaced the funds in his current account. ▲ to repair *Hay que reponer este ventilador.* This electric fan has to be repaired.
  ○ **reponerse** to recover (health) *Se marchó al campo para reponerse.* He went to the country to recover his health.

reposar to rest.

reposo rest.
  ○ **sin reposo** ceaselessly, endlessly *Habla sin reposo.* He talks endlessly.

representación [*f*] performance (usually of a play) *¿A qué hora empieza la representación?* What time does the play begin?
  ○ **en representación de** representing, as a representative of *Fué a México en representación de su país.* He went to Mexico as his country's representative.

representante [*adj*] representative. ▲ [*m*] traveling salesman, agent.

representar to represent; to perform.

represión [*f*] repression, suppression *Medidas de represión.* Repressive measures.

reprimir to suppress, repress *Reprimieron la sublevación.* They suppressed the revolt.
  ○ **reprimirse** to repress oneself, control oneself *No pudo reprimirse por más tiempo.* He could control himself no longer.

reprochar to reproach.

reproducción [*f*] reproduction (biology). ▲ reproduction *Aquel instrumento servía para la reproducción del sonido.* That instrument was used to reproduce the sound. ▲ reproduction, copy *Hizo una buena reproducción de un cuadro de Velázquez.* He made a good copy of a Velázquez painting.

reproducir [*-zc-*] to reproduce.

república republic.

republicano [*adj; n*] republican.

repuesto See **reponer**.
  ○ **de repuesto** extra, spare (of a part).

repugnante repugnant; repulsive.

repugnar to cause disgust (*or* loathing) in *Me repugna esa sopa.* I loathe that soup.—*Me repugna hacerlo.* I hate to do it.

requerir [*rad-ch II*] to summon *Lo requirieron para declarar.* They summoned him to testify. ▲ to require *Este trabajo requiere cuidado.* This work requires care.

requisito requisite, requirement.

res [*f*] head of cattle.

resaltar to stand out (by contrast).

resbaladizo slippery.

resbalar(se) to slip *Tenga cuidado no vaya a resbalarse.* Be careful you don't slip.

resbaloso slippery [*Am*] *El camino era muy resbaloso.* The road was very slippery.

rescate [*m*] ransom; exchange (of prisoners).

reserva secrecy, discretion *Se aconseja reserva en este asunto.* Discretion's advisable in this matter. ▲ reserve *Estaba en la reserva militar.* He was in the military reserve.
  ○ **guardar reserva** to use discretion, be discreet *Por favor, guarde Ud. reserva en esto.* Please be discreet about this.

reservado (See **reservar**) reserved *Era muy reservado.* He was very reserved.

reservar to reserve *Le reservó la habi-*

tación hasta su regreso. She reserved the room for him until his return. ▲ to keep in reserve *Reserve Ud. ese dinero, puede hacerle falta.* Keep that money in reserve; you may need it.
○ reservarse to keep for oneself *Se reservó el mejor asiento.* He kept the best seat for himself.
‖ *Reservado el derecho de admisión.* Catering to a restricted clientele.

resfriado cold (sickness).

resfriarse to catch cold.

residencia residence, house; student's boarding house.

residente [*adj*] resident.

residir to reside, live.

resignarse to be resigned.

resistencia resistance; strength, stamina.

resistente strong; resistant.

resistir to resist, put up resistance *Resistieron en la ciudad durante un mes.* They resisted in the city for a month.
○ resistirse a to refuse to *Se resistió a comer.* He refused to eat.

resolución [*f*] decision, resolution; courage, resoluteness.

resolver [*rad-ch I*] to decide *Era necesario resolver con toda urgencia.* A decision had to be made immediately. ▲ to solve *Resolvió el problema.* He solved the problem.
○ resolverse to bring oneself to the point (of) *No se resuelve a tomar una decisión.* He can't bring himself to the point of making a decision.

respaldar to indorse *Respalde Ud. este documento.* Indorse this document. ▲ to back, support *El jefe respaldaba sus actos.* The chief supported his actions.

respaldo back (of a seat).

respecto ○ (con) respecto a with respect to, with regard to.

respetable respectable *Era un hombre respetable.* He was a respectable man. ▲ considerable *Le debía una cantidad respetable.* I owed him a considerable sum.

respeto respect.

respiración [*f*] respiration *Le faltó la respiración.* He got short of breath.

respirar to breathe *Respire Ud. fuerte.* Breathe deeply.

responder to answer, respond *No respondió nada.* He didn't answer anything. ▲ to respond, react *Ha respondido muy bien al tratamiento.* He responded very well to the treatment. ▲ to be the result, be due *Esa ley responde a una necesidad pública.* That law's the result of a public need. ▲ to repay, requite.
○ responder de to answer for *¿Quién responde de los daños?* Who answers for the damages? ▲ to back (up) *¿Quién responde de él?* Who backs him up?

responsable responsible, reliable *Es un hombre muy responsable.* He's a very responsible man.
○ ser responsable to be in charge *¿Quién es la persona responsable aquí?* Who's in charge here? ○ ser responsable de to be responsible for, be to blame for *Ese hombre es responsable del incendio.* That man's responsible for the fire.

responsabilidad [*f*] responsibility.

respuesta answer, reply.

resquebrajado cracked.

resta subtraction.

restar to subtract. ▲ to be left, remain *No resta nada que hacer.* Nothing remains to be done.

restaurante [*m*] restaurant.

resto remainder, balance, rest *Es el resto del dinero.* It's the rest of the money. ▲ pile, stack (of chips in playing cards) *Le juego mi resto.* I bet my pile.
○ echar el resto to do one's best *Echó el resto por conseguir trabajo.* He did his best to get a job. ○ restos leftovers *Esa cocinera sabe aprovechar los restos.* That cook knows how to use leftovers. ○ restos (mortales) (mortal) remains *Trasladaron los restos al cementerio.* They took the remains to the cemetery.

restorán [*m*] restaurant.

resuelto (see **resolver**) determined, resolute *Es un hombre muy resuelto.* He's a very determined man.

resultado result.

resultar to result, turn out *La fiesta resultó muy bien.* The party turned out very well. ▲ to wear, last *¿Qué traje le ha resultado mejor?* Which suit wore better?

resumen [*m*] summary, abstract, résumé.
○ en resumen in brief, in short.

retener [*irr*] to withhold *Le retuvieron el sueldo aquel mes.* They withheld his salary that month. ▲ to keep, remember, retain (in one's mind) *No podía retener las fechas en la cabeza.* He couldn't remember dates. ▲ to hold, keep *Retuvieron aquella colina* *dos días más.* They held that hill two more days.

retirada retreat, retirement, withdrawal.

retirar to withdraw *Puede Ud. retirar esa cantidad del Banco.* You may withdraw that amount from the bank. ▲ to pull back, put aside *Retire un poco la silla para que se pueda pasar.* Pull the chair aside a little so there'll be room to pass. ▲ to retire *Lo retiraron a los setenta años.* They retired him at seventy.

○ **retirarse** to withdraw, retreat *Las fuerzas se retiraron.* The forces withdrew. ▲ to retire *Se ha retirado de los negocios.* He's retired from business.

retiro retirement (from social life, business, or profession).

retrasar to postpone *Retrasaron la fecha de la reunión.* They postponed the date of the meeting. ▲ to delay *Ciertos asuntos me retrasaron.* Some business delayed me. ▲ to set back *Retrasó el reloj.* He set back his watch.

○ **retrasarse** to run slow *El reloj se retrasa.* That clock runs slow. ▲ to be late *Siento haberme retrasado tanto.* I'm sorry to be so late.

retratar to portray; to take a picture of.

retrato portrait, painting, photograph.

retrete [m] toilet (room) [Sp].

retroceder to go back, come back *Retrocedió unos pasos para reunirse con nosotros.* He came back a few steps to join us. ▲ to back up *El auto retrocedió hasta quedar enfrente de la puerta.* The car backed up until it was in front of the door. ▲ to draw back, go back (on) *No podía retroceder de su decisión.* He couldn't go back on his decision.

reunión [f] meeting, gathering, assembly, party.

reunir to unite, gather, bring together *Reunió todos sus amigos en una fiesta.* He brought all his friends together at a party. ▲ to collect *Reunieron mucho dinero en la función benéfica.* They collected a lot of money at the benefit.

○ **reunirse** to meet *Se reunen en su casa todos los miércoles.* They meet at his home every Wednesday. ▲ to unite, gang up *Se han reunido todos contra mí.* They've all ganged up on me.

revelación [f] revelation.

revelar to reveal, show *Revela gran talento.* He shows great talent. ▲ to

develop *¿Reveló Ud. ya las fotografías?* Have you developed the pictures yet?

reventar [rad-ch I] to burst, bust *La cañería reventó.* The water main busted. ▲ to annoy (to death), irritate *Ese tipo me revienta.* That fellow annoys me to death. ▲ to burst, be full *Reventaba de salud.* He was bursting with health. ▲ to exhaust, knock out *La caminata me reventó.* The long walk exhausted me.

○ **estar reventado** to be exhausted, be knocked out *Después de esa caminata estoy reventado.* After that long walk I'm knocked out. ○ **reventarse** to blow out, explode *Se reventó un neumático.* A tire blew out.

revés [m] wrong side, reverse side *Ese es el revés de la tela.* This is the wrong side of the material. ▲ slap (with back of hand). ▲ backhand shot *Fué un buen revés.* It was a good backhand shot.

○ **al revés** the contrary, the opposite *No es así, precisamente es al revés.* It's not like this; it's just the opposite. ▲ the wrong way, wrong *Todo le salía al revés.* Everything he did went wrong. ○ **del revés** inside out, wrong side out *La chaqueta está del revés.* The jacket's wrong side out.

revisar to revise; to review, examine.

revisor [m] conductor (on train) [Sp].

revista review *Se pasó revista a los soldados.* The soldiers were reviewed. ▲ magazine *Es una revista muy cara.* It's a very expensive magazine.

revolución [f] revolution, revolt; revolution, turn.

revolucionario [adj; n] revolutionary.

revólver [m] revolver, pistol.

revolver [rad-ch I] to revolve. ▲ to stir *Revuélvalo Ud. con una cuchara.* Stir it with a spoon. ▲ to turn upside down *El niño lo revolvía todo en la casa.* The child was turning the house upside down.

revuelta revolt *Lo revuelta empezó en un cuartel.* The revolt started in one of the barracks. ▲ turn *Al llegar a la revuelta del camino, paró.* He stopped when he reached the turn in the road.

revuelto (see **revolver**) [adj] topsy-turvy.

rey [m] king.

rezar to pray, say (prayers) *Rezaba todos los días sus oraciones.* He said his prayers every day.

○ **rezar con** to concern *or* affect *La*

orden no reza conmigo. The order doesn't concern me.

rezo [*m*] praying.

rico rich, wealthy *Era el más rico del pueblo.* He was the richest man in the town. ▲ rich (in) *Hay vegetales muy ricos en vitaminas.* Some vegetables are very rich in vitamins. ▲ delicious *¡Qué más rico el sabor de esta carne!* What a delicious flavor this meat has! ▲ cute *¡Qué niño más rico!* What a cute child!

ridículo ridiculous *Su aspecto era ridículo.* His appearance was ridiculous.

○ **poner en ridículo** to put in a ridiculous position *La conducta de su mujer lo puso en ridículo.* The conduct of his wife put him in a ridiculous position.

ridiculizar to ridicule.

rienda rein *Sujete Ud. bien las riendas.* Hold on to the reins.

○ **a rienda suelta** without restraint *Se rió a rienda suelta.* He laughed without restraint. ○ **dar rienda suelta a** to give free rein to *Dió rienda al llanto.* She gave free rein to her tears.

riesgo danger, risk *Corrió mucho riesgo.* He ran a big risk.

rifar to raffle.

rígido stiff, rigid; severe, stern.

rigor [*m*] rigor, severity.

○ **en rigor** in fact. ○ **ser de rigor** to be indispensable.

riguroso rigorous, strict, severe.

rincón [*m*] (inside) corner *Ponga Ud. la silla en el rincón.* Put the chair in the corner. ▲ remote spot *Buscó un rincón donde vivir tranquilo.* He looked for a remote spot where he could live quietly.

riñón [*m*] kidney.

río river.

riqueza wealth; abundance.

risa laugh, laughter *La risa es contagiosa.* Laughter's contagious.

○ **cosa de risa** a laughing matter *No es cosa de risa.* It's not a laughing matter.

risueño smiling, cheerful.

rizador [*m*] curler, curling iron.

rizo curl.

robar to rob, plunder *Ese hombre roba a todo el mundo.* That man robs everybody. ▲ to steal *Robó el dinero.* He stole the money. ▲ to draw (in cards) *Ahora le toca a Ud. robar.* Now it's your turn to draw.

roble [*m*] oak.

robo robbery, theft.

robusto robust, vigorous, hale.

roca rock; cliff.

rodar [*rad-ch I*] to roll *La piedra rodaba cuesta abajo.* The stone was rolling downhill. ▲ to wander about, roam *Empezó a rodar por el mundo.* He began to roam around the world. ▲ to roll in *Ahora rueda el dinero más que nunca.* Now the money rolls in more than ever.

○ **rodar una película** to shoot a movie *Se empezó a rodar la película.* They started shooting the picture.

rodear to surround, encircle *El río rodeaba la ciudad.* The river surrounded the city.—*La casa está rodeada de árboles.* The house is surrounded with trees. ▲ to take the long way around.

○ **rodearse** to surround oneself *Procuró rodearse de buenos amigos.* He tried to surround himself with good friends.

rodeo turn, winding *Ese camino da un rodeo muy grande.* The road makes a wide turn. ▲ roundup *Hubo rodeo la semana pasada.* There was a roundup last week.

○ **dejarse de rodeos** to stop beating around the bush *Déjese de rodeos y conteste claramente.* Stop beating around the bush and give me a straight answer.

rodilla knee *Póngase Ud. de rodillas.* Get down on your knees. ▲ dusting cloth, rag *Limpie Ud. con esa rodilla.* Clean it with that rag.

rogar [*rad-ch I*] to request, beg *Me rogó que le esperara.* He begged me to wait for him. ▲ to plead *Le rogó y le rogó pero no consiguió convencerle.* He pleaded and pleaded but couldn't convince him.

rojo red.

○ **al rojo** red-hot, to red heat.

rollo roll, anything rolled up.

romance [*m*] ballad, poem.

romántico romantic.

romper [*irr*] to break *Rompió el vaso.* He broke the glass. ▲ to break, break off relations *Han roto con esa familia.* They've broken with that family.

○ **al romper el día, al romper el alba** at dawn, at daybreak. ○ **romper a** to start to *Rompió a hablar cuando nadie lo esperaba.* He started to talk when nobody expected it. ○ **romper la marcha** to lead the march *Rompía la marcha un escuadrón de caballería.*

A squadron of cavalry led the march. ○ **romperse** to break *¡Cuidado que puede romperse!* Be careful, it may break! ▲ to fracture, break (bone) *Se rompió una pierna.* He broke his leg. ▲ to be torn *Se le ha roto el traje.* Your dress is torn.

roncar to snore.

ronco hoarse.

ropa clothes *Voy a planchar la ropa.* I'm going to iron the clothes. ○ **a quema ropa** point-blank *Le disparó a quema ropa.* He fired at him point-blank. ○ **ropa blanca** linen. ○ **ropa hecha** ready-made clothes. ○ **ropa limpia** clean laundry. ○ **ropa sucia** soiled laundry.

ropero closet, wardrobe.

rosa rose. ○ **color de rosa** pink.

rosario rosary.

rosca thread (screw); spiral. ▲ ring (bread or cake). ○ **hacer la rosca** to flatter.

rostro face.

roto (See **romper**) broken *La silla estaba rota.* The chair was broken.—*El compromiso quedó roto.* The engagement was broken. ▲ tear *Tiene Ud. un roto en el pantalón.* You have a tear in your trousers.

rótulo sign.

rozadura chafed spot, sore spot.

rozar to clear (ground) *Empezó a rozar la tierra.* He began to clear the ground. ▲ to graze, rub *El avión rozó ligeramente el suelo.* The airplane grazed the ground.

‖ *No le gustaba rozarse con nadie.* He didn't like to have anything to do with anybody.

rubia [*f*] blonde.

rubio [*adj*] blond(e), fair.

rúbrica flourish, mark, distinctive flourish after a signature.

rudo rude, rough *Aquel hombre era muy rudo.* That man was very rude. ▲ hard *La jornada fué muy ruda.* The journey was very hard.

rueda wheel.

ruego plea, request.

ruido noise *¿Qué ruido es ese?* What's that noise? ▲ comment, discussion *Aquel suceso dió mucho ruido.* That event caused a lot of comment. ‖ *Mucho ruido y pocas nueces.* Much ado about nothing.

ruidoso noisy.

ruina ruin, decline *Aquel negocio fué su ruina.* That business was his ruin. ○ **en ruinas** in ruins *La ciudad quedó en ruinas.* The city was left in ruins.

ruinoso ruinous.

rumba rumba (dance).

rumbo direction *Salió con rumbo a Europa.* He left for Europe. ○ **fiesta de rumbo** lavish party.

rumor [*m*] murmur *Un rumor confuso salió del público.* A confused murmur arose from the crowd. ▲ rumor *Corre el rumor de que va a cambiar la política.* Rumor has it that there'll be a change of policy.

rústico rustic, rural.

ruta route, way.

S

sábado Saturday.

sábana sheet.

saber [*irr*] to know *¿Sabe Ud. español?* Do you know Spanish? ▲ to know how *¿Sabe Ud. nadar?* Do you know how to swim?—*Sabe Ud. cómo llegar a ese lugar?* Do you know how to get to that place? ▲ to taste *Esto sabe mal.* This tastes bad. ▲ to... usually *or* customarily [*Am*] *Sabe venir los domingos.* He usually comes on Sunday. ○ **a saber** namely, i.e. *Son tres: a saber, Enrique, Juan y María.* They are three; namely, Henry, John, and Mary. ○ **demasiado saber** to know only too well *Demasiado sé que es verdad.* I know only too well that

it is true. ○ **saber a** to taste of *La sopa sabe a ajo.* The soup tastes of garlic. ○ **saberse** to become known, be found out *¡Cuidado, puede saberse!* Be careful, you may be found out! ○ **un no sé qué** a certain something *Ella tiene un no sé qué muy agradable.* She has a certain something that is very pleasing. ‖ *¡Qué sé yo!* How do I know? ‖ *¿Quién sabe?* Who knows? ‖ *¡Ya lo sé!* I know (it)!

sabiduría learning, knowledge.

sabio [*adj*] wise *Doña María es una mujer muy sabia.* Mary's a very wise woman. ▲ [*n*] learned *or* wise person.

sablazo borrowing. ○ **dar un sablazo** to make a touch, borrow *Anoche me dió un sablazo de cinco dólares.* Last night he touched me for five dollars.

sable [*m*] saber.

sabor [*m*] taste, flavor *El sabor de este vino es delicioso.* The flavor of this wine is delicious.

○ **dar sabor** to season *No le daba sabor a lo que guisaba.* She didn't season her cooking.

saborear to taste, to relish.

sabroso savory, tasty.

sabueso hound.

sacacorchos [*m sg*] corkscrew.

sacar to draw (out) *Saqué dinero del banco.* I drew some money from the bank. ▲to take out *Saque Ud. las manos de los bolsillos.* Take your hands out of your pockets. ▲to take off *Lo sacaron del equipo.* They took him off the team. ▲to bring out, manufacture *Están sacando nuevos modelos de aeroplanos.* They are bringing out new airplane models. ▲to put out *Sacó la cabeza por la ventana.* He put his head out of the window. ▲to relieve [*Am*] *La medicina le sacó la fiebre.* The medicine relieved his fever. ▲to get *¿De dónde han sacado Uds. esa idea?* Where did you get that idea? ▲to get out *Nos sacó de un apuro.* He got us out of trouble. ▲to win *Saqué un premio en el sorteo.* I won a prize at the drawing. ▲to accomplish *¿Qué saca Ud. con eso?* What do you accomplish by that? ▲to get out, draw out *Le sacaron el secreto.* They got the secret out of him.

○ **sacar a bailar** to invite for a dance *Voy a sacar a bailar a aquella chica.* I'm going to ask that girl to dance. ○ **sacar a relucir** to bring up *Siempre saca a relucir cosas que sería mejor olvidar.* He always brings up things it would be better to forget. ○ **sacar copia** to make a copy *Hay que sacar varias copias de la carta.* It's necessary to make several copies of the letter. ○ **sacar el jugo** to squeeze, work (one) hard *Les saca el jugo a sus empleados.* He's working his employees to the bone. ○ **sacar en claro** to clear up, come to a conclusion *No sacó nada en claro.* He didn't come to any conclusion. ○ **sacar la cuenta** to figure out *Hay que sacar la cuenta.* It's necessary to figure out the bill. ○ **sacar (la pelota)** to serve (the ball); to kick off. ○ **sacarse** to take off [*Am*] *Estaba sacándose los guan-*

tes. He was taking off his gloves. ○ **sacar una fotografía** to take a picture. ○ **sacar ventaja** to take the lead *Mi caballo sacó ventaja en la carrera.* My horse took the lead in the race. ○ **sacar ventaja de** to profit by *Sacó ventaja de ese negocio.* He profited by that business.

sacerdote [*m*] priest.

saco sack, bag *Guarde Ud. eso en el saco.* Keep that in the bag. ▲coat, jacket [*Am*] *Le sienta muy bien ese saco.* That coat looks good on him. ○ **saco de viaje** traveling bag.

sacrificar to sacrifice *Sacrificaron a su hijo.* They sacrificed their son.

sacrificio sacrifice.

sacudir to shake *Salió a la terraza a sacudir la ropa.* She went out on the terrace to shake out the clothes. ▲to jolt *El autobús sacudió a los pasajeros al parar repentinamente.* The bus jolted the passengers when it stopped suddenly. ▲to beat (remove dust) *Hay que sacudir esas alfombras.* Those rugs have to be beaten. ▲to shake off, snap out of *¡Ya es hora de que sacuda Ud. la pereza!* It's time for you to snap out of your laziness!

sagrado sacred, holy.

sainete [*m*] one-act farce; farce *La vida es un sainete.* Life is a farce.

sal [*f*] salt.

sala living room, parlor *El piso tiene una sala grande.* The apartment has a large living room. ○ **sala (de música)** (music) hall.

salado [*adj*] salted, salty *No le gustaba el jamón salado.* He didn't like salty ham. ▲witty *Es un tipo muy salado.* He's a very witty fellow. ▲cute, winsome *Es una chica muy salada.* She's a very cute girl. ▲unlucky [*Am*] *Está salado.* He's unlucky. ▲expensive [*Arg*] *Es muy salado.* It's very expensive.

salario salary, wages.

salchicha sausage.

salchichón [*m*] sausage (large).

saldo balance *¿Cuál es el saldo de mi cuenta?* What is the balance of my account? ▲sale *Hubo un saldo en esa tienda.* There was a sale in that store.

salero salt cellar.

salida exit; departure *La salida de incendios tiene luz roja.* The emergency exit has a red light. ▲departure *Esperemos hasta la salida del barco.* Let's wait till the boat sails. ▲comeback *Tenía muy buenas salidas.* He always had a snappy comeback. ▲ expenditure *Entradas y salidas.* Income and expenditures.

○ **callejón sin salida** dead-end street, blind alley. ○ **dar salida a** to clear out, dispose of *Hay que dar salida a estos artículos.* We must clear out these goods.

salir [*irr*] to go (*or* come) out, leave, get out *Salieron con Juan.* They went out with John. *Le sale mucho el pañuelo del bolsillo.* His handkerchief sticks way out of his pocket. ▲ to come out, be published *¿Ha salido ya el último número de esta revista?* Has the latest issue of this magazine come out yet? ▲ to come off (*or* out), disappear *Estas manchas no salen.* These spots don't come off. ▲ to rise *Quiso ver salir el sol.* He wanted to see the sun rise. ▲ to grow, to come up *Empieza a salir el trigo.* The wheat is beginning to come up. ▲ to begin (games, sports) *A Ud. le toca salir.* It's your turn to begin. ▲ to draw (prize) *¿Qué número salió premiado?* Which number drew the prize? ▲ to cost *Esto me sale muy caro.* This costs me a lot. ▲ to turn out *El niño salió muy listo.* The child turned out to be very bright. ▲ to end [*Am*] *Al salir el verano regresaremos.* We'll return when the season ends.

○ **salir a bailar con** to dance with *Salió a bailar con mi hermana.* He danced with my sister. ○ **salir bien, salir mal** to come out well, come out badly *Salió bien en los exámenes.* He came out well in his examinations. ○ **salir con** to come out with *¿Ahora sale Ud. con eso?* Now you come out with that? ○ **salir de compras** to go shopping. ○ **salir diputado** to be elected a congressman *¿Quienes salieron diputados?* Which congressmen were elected? ○ **salir ganando** to come out ahead, win *¿Quién salió ganando?* Who came out ahead?—*¿Quién sale ganando?* Who's winning? ○ **salirse** to leak *Este cacharro se sale.* This pot leaks. ▲ to leave, go out *Me salí del teatro.* I left the theater. ○ **salirse con la suya** to have one's own way *Siempre se sale con la suya.* He always has his own way.—*Siempre me salgo con la mía.* I always have my own way. ○ **salirse de** to get out of, to dispose of *Voy a ver si me salgo de este negocio.* I'll see if I can get out of this deal.

saliva saliva, spit.

salmón [*m*] salmon.

salón [*m*] living room, hall, salon. ○ **salón de baile** dance hall.

salpicar to spatter *El automóvil le salpicó el traje de barro.* The car spattered his suit with mud.

salsa gravy, sauce. ‖ *Estaba en su propia salsa.* He felt at home. *or* He was in his element.

saltar to jump *Salté de la cama al oír el despertador.* I jumped out of bed when I heard the alarm clock. ▲ to pop out *Saltó el tapón y salió el líquido.* The cork popped out and the liquid spilled. ▲ to bounce, bound *Esta pelota no salta.* This ball doesn't bounce. ▲ to spring *Saltó en su defensa.* He sprang to her defense.

○ **saltar a la vista** to be self-evident *Eso salta a la vista.* That is self-evident. ○ **saltarse** to skip *Me he saltado un renglón.* I skipped a line. ▲ to pop off *Al desabrocharme el saco se me saltó un botón.* A button popped off while I was unbuttoning my coat. ▲ to crack, break *El cristal se saltó son el calor.* The glass cracked from the heat.

salto jump *Este salto es muy peligroso.* This is a very dangerous jump. ○ **dar un salto mortal** to turn a somersault. ○ **de un salto** in a flash *De un salto se plantó en la puerta.* In a flash he was at the door. ○ **salto de agua** waterfall. ○ **salto mortal** somersault.

salud [*f*] health *Su salud era perfecta.* He was in perfect health. ○ **saludos** regards, greetings [*Am*] *Mi familia le envía muchos saludos.* My family sends you their regards. ‖ *¡A su salud!* To your health! ‖ *¡Salud!* Hello! *or* Greetings! *or* Good luck!

saludable healthful.

saludar to greet *Nos saludó de una manera muy fría.* He greeted us very coldly. ▲ to salute (Mil). ‖ *Le saludo a Ud. atentamente.* Sincerely yours. *or* Yours truly.

saludo greeting, salutation, salute *Su saludo fué muy cordial.* His greeting was very cordial.—*Saludo militar.* Military salute.

salvación [*f*] salvation.

salvador, salvadora savior, rescuer.

salvaje [*adj*] savage, wild *En el parque había animales salvajes.* There were wild animals in the park. ▲ [m] savage, uncivilized person *Los salvajes atacaron el fuerte.* The savages attacked the fort.

salvar to save, rescue *Había que salvar a muchas víctimas.* There were many victims to be saved. ▲ to cover, clear, jump over *Salvó la zanja de un salto.* He cleared the ditch with one jump.

salvo except *He revisado el libro salvo el último capítulo.* I have revised the book except for the last chapter.
　○ **ponerse a salvo** to escape, reach safety *Pudo ponerse a salvo del incendio.* He was able to escape from the fire. ○ **salvo que** unless *Salvo que llueva mucho, iremos al campo.* Unless it rains hard, we'll go to the country.

san [adj] (see **santo**) saint *San Francisco.* Saint Francis.

sanar to heal, to cure.

sangre [f] blood.
　○ **a sangre fría** in cold blood *Lo hizo a sangre fría.* He did it in cold blood. ○ **hacer hervir la sangre** to make the blood boil *¡Eso me hace hervir la sangre!* That makes my blood boil! ○ **sangre fría** composure, coolness of mind *Su sangre fría es notable.* His coolness of mind is well known. ○ **subírsele a uno la sangre a la cabeza** to become excited, see red.

sangriento bloody.

sanidad [f] health *Pertenecía a la junta de Sanidad.* He belonged to the Board of Health.

sano healthy *Estaba muy sana.* She was very healthy. ▲ healthful *Esta región tiene un clima muy sano.* This region has a very healthful climate. ▲ honest, good.
　○ **sano y salvo** safe and sound *Al fin le vimos sano y salvo.* At last we saw him safe and sound.

santidad [f] holiness, sanctity.

santo holy, saintly. ▲ [n] saint.

saque ○ **el saque** the kick-off (soccer, football); serve *Ud. tiene el saque.* It's your serve.

sarape [m] blanket [Mex]; type of woven material [Mex].

sardina sardine.

sarna mange; itch (disease).

sartén [m or f] frying pan.

sastre [m] tailor.

satisfacción [f] satisfaction.

satisfacer [irr] to satisfy *No me satisface su trabajo.* His work doesn't satisfy me. ▲ to pay in full *Había*

que satisfacer aquella deuda.* The debt had to be paid in full.
　○ **satisfacerse** to be satisfied, be convinced *Se satisfizo con la explicación.* He was satisfied with the explanation.

satisfactorio satisfactory.

satisfecho (see **satisfacer**) satisfied.

saya skirt.

sazón [f] ripeness, maturity.
　○ **a la sazón** at that time *A la sazón estaba yo en España.* At that time I was in Spain. ○ **en sazón** ripe *La fruta está en sazón.* The fruit is ripe.

sazón almost ripe [Am] *Este plátano está sazón.* This banana is almost ripe.

sazonar to season *La cocinera sazona bien la comida.* The cook seasons the food well. ▲ to ripen (of fruit) *Esa fruta sazona en la primavera.* That fruit ripens in the spring.

se oneself, himself, herself, themselves, yourselves; to (or for) himself, herself, etc; (used for *le*, *les*) to him, to her, etc *Se afeita.* He's shaving himself.—*El se dijo.* He said to himself.—*Se lo doy a Ud.* (*a él, a ellos, etc*). I'm giving it to you (to him, to them, etc). ▲ to each other, to one another *Se escriben todos los días.* They write to each other every day. ▲ (as an indefinite subject) *Se dice.* They say. *or* It's said. ▲ (for passive voice, without agent) *Se construyó una casa.* A house was built.

secante annoying [Arg]. ▲ blotting. ▲ [m] blotter.
　○ **papel secante** blotting paper.

secar to dry *Hay que secar los platos.* It's necessary to dry the dishes.
　○ **secarse** to dry oneself *Procure Ud. secarse bien.* Try to dry yourself thoroughly. ▲ to wither, dry *Las flores se secaron.* The flowers withered.

sección [f] section, division *¿En qué sección trabaja Ud.?* In what section do you work?

seco dry *Tengo la garganta seca.* My throat is dry.—*Aquí no existe la ley seca.* There's no dry law here. ▲ abrupt, curt *Era un hombre muy seco.* He was a very curt man. ▲ dried *Frutas secas.* Dried fruits.
　○ **a secas** only, just *Me llamo Pepe a secas.* My name is just Joe. ▲ curtly *Le contestó a secas.* He answered her curtly. ○ **en seco** high and dry,

aground. ○ **parar en seco** to stop abruptly.

secretaría secretary's office; secretariat.

secretario, secretaria secretary *Fué secretario del Alcalde.* He was the Mayor's secretary.

secreto secret *Guarde Ud. el secreto.* Keep the secret.
○ **un secreto a voces** an open secret *Su casamiento era un secreto a voces.* Her marriage was an open secret.

secuestro kidnapping.

sed [*f*] thirst *Estoy muerto de sed.* I'm dying of thirst.
○ **tener sed** to be thirsty *Tengo sed.* I'm thirsty. ○ **tener sed de** to be hungry for *Tenía sed de noticias.* He was hungry for news.

seda silk.

seguida ○ **en seguida** right away, immediately *Voy en seguida.* I'm going right away.

seguir [*rad-ch III*] to follow, keep up with *No puedo seguirle a Ud.* I can't follow you.—*No vaya tan de prisa porque no puedo seguirle a Ud.* Don't go so fast because I can't keep up with you. ▲ to follow, come after *¿Qué sigue después?* What comes afterwards? ▲ to continue *Siguió hablando más de dos horas.* He kept on talking for more than two hours. ▲ to keep *Siga a la derecha.* Keep to the right.

según according to *La casa está hecha según los planos.* The house is built according to plans. ▲ as *Hágalo según le digo.* Do it as I tell you. ▲ depending on *Saldré o no, según esté el tiempo.* I shall go or stay, depending on the weather. ▲ it (*or* that) depends *Según; si tengo tiempo iré.* It depends; I'll go if I have the time.
○ **según y conforme, según y como** that depends.

segundo [*adj*] second. ▲ [*m*] second *Espéreme un segundo, ahora vuelvo.* Wait a second, I'll be right back.
○ **segunda intención** double meaning *Lo dijo con segunda intención.* What he said had a double meaning.

seguridad [*f*] security *¿Qué seguridad me ofrece Ud.?* What security can you give me?
○ **caja de seguridad** safe-deposit box. ○ **con (toda) seguridad** certainly, surely *Vendrá con toda seguridad.* He'll surely come.

seguro sure, certain *¿Está Ud. seguro de que no vendrá?* Are you sure he won't come? ▲ safe *Este puente es muy seguro.* This bridge is very safe. ▲ secure *¿Está el clavo bien seguro?* Is the nail in firmly? ▲ steady, sure *Su paso no es seguro.* His step is not steady.—*Anda con paso seguro.* He walks with a sure step. ▲ [*m*] safety catch *Puso la pistola en el seguro.* He put the safety catch of his pistol on. ▲ insurance *¿Quiere Ud. hacerse un seguro de vida?* Do you wish to take out a life insurance policy?

seis six.

selección [*f*] selection, choice.

seleccionar to choose *Seleccionaron a los jugadores.* They chose the players.

selecto distinguished, select *Había un público muy selecto.* There was a very distinguished audience.

sellar to stamp *Selle Ud. esos localidades.* Stamp those tickets. ▲ to seal *Sellaba las cartas.* He was sealing the letters.

sello seal *El notario puso su sello en el documento.* The notary placed his seal on the document. ▲ stamp *¿En qué ventanilla venden sellos?* At what window do they sell stamps? ▲ capsule, pill *Compró unos sellos para el dolor de cabeza.* He bought some headache pills.

selva jungle, woods, forest.

semana week *¿En qué día de la semana estamos?* What day of the week is it?
○ **semana inglesa** five-day week. ○ **Semana Santa** Holy Week (Easter).

semanal [*adj*] weekly.

semblante [*m*] look, expression.

sembrar [*rad-ch I*] to sow *En el otoño sembraremos.* We'll sow in the fall. ▲ to spread *Siembra la discordia entre sus compañeros.* He spread discord among his friends.

semejante [*adj*] similar *Las dos historias son muy semejantes.* The two stories are very similar. ▲ such *No creo en semejante cosa.* Don't believe such a thing. ▲ [*m*] fellow-man *Piense que son sus semejantes.* Remember that they're your fellow-men.

semejanza resemblance, similarity.

semilla seed.

senado senate.

senador [*m*] senator.

sencillez [*f*] simplicity *Vestía con mucha sencillez.* She dressed very simply. ▲ naturalness *Atraía por la sencillez de su carácter.* She attracted people because of her naturalness.

sencillo [*adj*] plain *Habla de una manera sencilla.* She speaks plainly. ▲ unaffected *Su amigo es muy sencillo.* Your friend is very unaffected.

senda path.

sendero path, byway.

sensación [f] sensation.

sensato sensible, wise.

sensible sensitive, keen *Tenía el oído muy sensible.* He had a keen sense of hearing.

sentar [rad-ch I] to seat *Voy a sentarle en la última fila.* I'm going to seat him in the last row. ▲ to fit *Aquel traje no le sentaba bien.* That suit didn't fit him well.

○ sentarle a uno bien (or mal) to agree (or disagree) with one *La langosta no le sentó bien.*—The lobster didn't agree with him.—*Este clima me sienta bien.* This climate agrees with me. ○ sentarle mal (or no sentarle bien) a uno not to set well (with one) *Lo que dijo no me sentó bien.* What he said didn't set well with me. ○ sentarse to sit down *Siéntese Ud.* Sit down.

sentencia sentence *El tribunal dictó la sentencia.* The court pronounced (the) sentence.

sentido sincere *Sus palabras eran muy sentidas.* His words were very sincere. ▲ moving *Su discurso era muy sentido.* His address was very moving. ▲ [m] sense (of five senses) *El sentido del olfato.* The sense of smell. ▲ meaning *Esto tiene doble sentido.* This has a double meaning. ▲ direction *Caminaba en sentido contrario.* He was walking in the opposite direction.

○ estar sentido to be offended, hurt *Está sentida por lo que le dijeron.* She is offended because of what they told her. ○ perder el sentido to lose consciousness *Perdió el sentido y cayó al suelo.* He lost consciousness and fell to the ground. ○ sentido común common sense. ○ tener sentido to make sense *No tenía sentido lo que escribía.* What he was writing didn't make sense.

sentimental sentimental.

sentimiento sentiment, feeling *Era persona de buenos sentimientos.* He was a person of good sentiments. ▲ sorrow, grief *Su sentimiento fué muy grande.* His sorrow was very great.

○ persona de malos sentimientos malicious person.

sentir [rad-ch II] to feel *Siento un dolor en las articulaciones.* I feel a pain in my joints. ▲ to sense, feel, hear *Siento pasos.* I hear footsteps. ▲ to regret *Eso es lo que más siento de todo.* That's what I regret most of all. ▲ to be sorry *Siento mucho molestarle.* I'm very sorry to bother you.

○ sentirse to feel *Se sentía enfermo.* He felt ill. ○ sentirse molesto to be annoyed *No tenía porqué sentirse molesto.* He had no reason to be annoyed.

seña sign *Hizo una seña con la mano.* He made a sign with his hand. ▲ trace, sign *No quedaron ni señas del pastel.* Not a trace of the cake remained. ▲ mark *Tiene una seña en la cara.* He has a mark on his face.

○ señas address *Escriba Ud. a estas señas.* Write to this address. ○ señas digitales fingerprints. ○ señas personales personal description.

señal [f] mark *Ponga una señal en esa página.* Put a mark on that page. ▲ signal *La señal de avance fué un disparo.* A shot was the signal to advance.

○ en señal as a deposit *¿Quiere Ud. que deje algún dinero en señal?* Do you want me to leave some money as a deposit? ○ señal de peligro distress signal; danger signal. ○ señales de tráfico traffic signs.

señalar to mark *Señale Ud. esto con tinta.* Mark this with ink. ▲ to point out, mark *Señale Ud. los errores que encuentre.* Point out the errors you find. ▲ to set *Hay que señalar el día de la reunión.* The date of the reunion must be set.

○ señalar con el dedo to point (with the finger).

señor [m] Mr. *¿Está el señor Palacios?* Is Mr. Palacios in? ▲ sir *Sí señor, tiene Ud. razón.* Yes sir, you're right. ▲ man *Me han dicho que es un señor muy fino.* I have heard that he's a very fine man. ▲ gentleman *Hay un señor esperándole.* There's a gentleman waiting for him.

○ el señor de la casa the master of the house. ○ Señor Lord. ○ Nuestro Señor our Lord.

‖ *Tuve un señor disgusto.* I was very disgusted.

señora Mrs. *¿Puedo hablar con la Señora de García?* May I speak to Mrs. García? ▲ lady *Cuando la conocí era una señora de edad.* When I met her she was an elderly lady. ▲ madam *Sí, señora.* Yes, madam.

señorita Miss *¿Conoce Ud. a la Señorita Martínez?* Do you know Miss Martínez? ▲ young lady *Esta señorita no es americana.* This young lady is not an American.

señorito young gentleman; master of the house; playboy [Sp].

separación [f] separation.

separar to separate, set apart *Separe Ud. las niñas de los niños.* Separate the girls from the boys. ▲to divide *Una cortina separa las dos habitaciones.* A curtain divides the two rooms. ▲to move away *Separe Ud. un poco la mesa de la pared.* Move the table away from the wall a bit. ▲to lay aside *Separe estos trajes para que me los envíen.* Lay aside these suits so they can send them to me.
○separarse to separate *El matrimonio decidió separarse.* The couple decided to separate.

septiembre [*m*] September.

séptimo seventh.

sepultar to bury, inter, entomb.

sepultura grave.

sequedad [*f*] aridity, dryness.

ser [*irr*] to be (with predicate noun or pronoun) *Su padre es abogado.* His father's a lawyer.—*La víctima no fuí yo.* The victim wasn't I. ▲ (with predicate adjectives that express an inherent or characteristic quality) *El camino es muy largo.* The road's very long.—*La niña es bonita.* The child's pretty. ▲ (origin) *El señor Pérez es de Madrid.* Mr. Pérez is from Madrid. ▲ (ownership) *Pero no era de Ud.* But it wasn't yours. ▲ (material of which a thing is made) *Era un reloj de oro.* It was a gold watch. ▲ (in impersonal expressions) *Es imposible.* It's impossible.—*No era verdad.* It wasn't true. ▲ (in expressions of time) *¿Qué hora era?* What time was it?—*Eran las cuatro y media.* It was half past four. ▲to take place *La escena es en París.* The scene takes place in Paris. ▲ (with a past participle to form passive voice) *La obra fué escrita por Lope de Vega.* The work was written by Lope de Vega.
○es que the fact is that *Es que va a venir ahora.* The fact is that he's coming right away. ○no sea que because . . . might *Lleve el paraguas no sea que llueva.* Take an umbrella because it might rain. ○¿qué ha sido de . . . ? what's become of . . . ?

serenata serenade.

serenidad [*f*] serenity, calm.

sereno clear, fair *El cielo está muy sereno.* The sky is very clear. ▲calm, serene *Era un hombre sereno.* He was a calm man. ▲ [*m*] night-watchman [*Sp*] *Esta calle no tiene sereno.* This street has no night-watchman. ▲ dew *Hay mucho sereno en las flores.* There is a lot of dew on the flowers.

serie [*f*] series *Pertenece a la serie A.* It belongs to series A.
○en serie mass produced, standardized.

seriedad [*f*] seriousness, gravity, earnestness.

serio serious, solemn *No se ponga Ud. tan serio.* Don't be so solemn. ▲critical *Estos son tiempos muy serios.* These are critical times.
○en serio seriously *Estábamos hablando en serio.* We were speaking seriously.

servicio service *El servicio del ferrocarril es ahora muy malo.* Train service is very bad now. ▲toilet, water-closet [*Am*].
○servicio doméstico domestic help *Es muy difícil conseguir servicio doméstico.* It is very difficult to get any domestic help. ○servicio militar military service.

servidor, servidora servant *Tiene muy buenos servidores.* She has excellent servants.
‖ *Servidor de Ud.* At your service.

servidumbre [*f*] (staff of) servants, attendants; servitude.

servilleta table napkin.

servir [*rad-ch III*] to serve, wait on *Sirva Ud. primero a las señoras.* Serve the ladies first. ▲to serve *Sirvió cuatro años en las fuerzas aéreas.* He served in the Air Corps for four years.
○servir para to be good for *Eso no sirve para nada.* That's good for nothing. ○servirse to help oneself *Tenga la bondad de servirse.* Please help yourself.
‖ *¡Para servir a Ud.!* At your service!

sesenta sixty.

sesión [*f*] session, meeting *¿Dónde se celebrará la sesión?* Where will the meeting take place?

seso brain *Comió un plato de sesos de ternera.* He ate a plate of calf's brains.
○devanarse los sesos to rack one's brains *Hay que devanarse los sesos para comprender este problema.* One has to rack one's brains to understand that problem. ○perder el seso to lose one's head (over) *Perdió el seso por aquella muchacha.* He lost his head over that girl. ○saltarse la tapa de los sesos to blow out one's brains *De un tiro se saltó la tapa de los sesos.* He blew his brains out with one shot. ○sin seso witless, scatterbrained *¡Qué muchacha sin sesos!* What a scatterbrained girl!

setenta seventy.
severidad [*f*] severity, rigor.
severo severe, rigorous.
sexo sex.
sexto sixth.
sexual sexual.
si if, whether *Deseo saber si Ud. viene.* I want to know whether you're coming. ○ **por si acaso** if by chance, just in case *Le dejo esto por si acaso viene.* I'm leaving this just in case he comes. ‖ *¡Si fuera verdad!* If it were only true!
si yes. ○ **sí que** certainly *Eso sí que es raro. That's certainly strange.* ○ **un ... sí y otro no** every other ... *Viene un día sí y otro no.* He comes every other day.
sí [*pron*].
  ○ **de por sí** separately, individually, by oneself *Dió de por sí todo lo que pudo.* He gave all he could by himself. —*Cada uno de por sí haga lo que pueda.* Let each one individually do what he can. ○ **fuera de sí** beside himself, herself, yourself, themselves *Estaban fuera de sí.* They were beside themselves (with anger, anxiety, joy, etc). ○ **sí mismo, misma, mismos, mismas** himself, herself, themselves *Tenía un gran dominio sobre sí mismo.* He had great control of himself (*or* great self-control). ○ **volver en sí** to regain consciousness *No ha vuelto en sí.* He hasn't regained consciousness.
siembra sowing, seeding, planting.
siempre always *Siempre hace el mismo trabajo.* He always does the same work.
  ○ **para siempre** forever. ○ **para siempre jamás** forever and ever. ○ **siempre que** whenever *Siempre que me ve, me saluda.* Whenever he sees me, he greets me. ▲ provided (that) *Siempre que estudie aprobará.* He'll pass provided he studies.
sien [*f*] temple (anatomy).
sierra saw *No corta bien la sierra.* The saw doesn't cut well. ▲ mountain range *Subieron al pico más alto de la sierra.* They climbed to the highest peak of the range.
siesta afternoon nap.
siete seven. ▲ [*m*] tear, rent (in clothing) *Tenía un siete en la chaqueta.* He had a tear in his jacket.
siglo century.
significación [*f*] significance, importance, implication *Ese hecho no tiene ninguna significación.* That fact has no significance whatever.

significado meaning (literal) *¿Cuál es el significado de esta palabra en inglés?* What's the meaning of that word in English?
significar to mean *No sé qué significa esa palabra.* I don't know what that word means.
significativo significant.
signo mark, sign, symbol *Haga Ud. claros los signos de puntuación.* Make the punctuation marks clear.—*El signo de la Cruz.* The sign of the Cross.—*Un signo fonético.* A phonetic symbol.
siguiente next, following *Esperé hasta el día siguiente.* I waited till the following day.
sílaba syllable.
silbar to whistle *Silbe Ud. para ver si nos oyen.* Whistle to see if they hear us. ▲ to boo (whistling indicates disapproval in Spanish-speaking countries) *El público silbó la comedia.* The audience booed the comedy.
silbato whistle (instrument) *Se oía el silbato de la locomotora.* The locomotive's whistle could be heard.
silbido whistle, sound.
silencio silence *Sufrió en silencio aquel agravio.* He suffered that affront in silence.
  ○ **en silencio** quiet *Todo estaba en silencio.* Everything was quiet. ○ **guardar silencio** to keep quiet (make no sound) *Procuren guardar silencio durante las horas de estudio.* Keep quiet during study hours.
  ‖ *¡Silencio!* Quiet! *or* Silence!
silencioso silent, noiseless *¿Quiere Ud. comprar la máquina de escribir silenciosa?* Do you want the noiseless typewriter?
silla chair *Siéntese en esa silla.* Sit down in that chair.
  ○ **silla de montar** saddle.
sillón [*m*] armchair.
  ○ **sillón de ruedas** wheel chair.
silueta silhouette, outline. ▲ figure *Esa muchacha tiene una silueta muy bonita.* That girl has a very nice figure.
simpatía congeniality *Le inspiró mucha simpatía.* He found her very congenial.
simpático nice, pleasant, congenial *Es un muchacho simpático.* He's a nice boy. ▲ congenial *El ambiente allí es muy simpático.* The atmosphere there's very congenial.
simple simple, easy *Aquel trabajo era muy simple.* That work was very simple. ▲ simple, witless *¡Qué hombre más simple!* What a witless man!

▲ [n] simpleton *Es un simple.* He's a simpleton.

simpleza silliness *La simpleza de esa mujer me molesta.* That woman's silliness annoys me. ▲ silly thing *Ese hombre no hace más que simplezas.* That man's always doing silly things. ▲ trifle *Riñeron por una simpleza.* They quarreled over a trifle.

sin without *Llegó sin un centavo.* He arrived without a penny.—*Le espero en la oficina mañana sin falta.* I'll expect you at the office tomorrow without fail. ○ **sin embargo** however, nevertheless.

sinceridad [f] sincerity.

sincero sincere.

singular [adj] singular (grammar). ▲ strange, singular *¡Qué caso tan singular!* What a strange case! ▲ [m] singular *Escriba Ud. el verbo en singular.* Write the verb in the singular.

siniestro sinister, vicious *Era un hombre siniestro.* He was a sinister man.

sino but. ▲ except, but *Nadie sino tú puede hacerlo.* No one except you can do it. ▲ [m] fate, destiny. ○ **no ... sino** not ... but *No es gordo, sino flaco.* He's not fat, but thin. ○ **no sólo ... sino (también)** not only ... but (also) *No sólo era pobre, sino (también) desgraciado.* He was not only poor but also unfortunate.

síntoma symptom.

sinvergüenza [m] scoundrel, rascal.

siquiera at least *Deme siquiera agua fría.* At least give me some cold water. ○ **(ni) siquiera** (not) even *Ni siquiera me habló.* He didn't even speak to me. ○ **(si) siquiera** if only, if at least *Siquiera nos pagaran hoy.* If only they'd pay us today.

sirvienta maid, servant girl.

sirviente [m] servant (domestic).

sistema [m] system.

sitio spot, site *Es un sitio precioso para pasar el verano.* It's a delightful spot to spend the summer. ▲ place, seat *Ocupe Ud. su sitio.* Take your place. ▲ room, space *No hay bastante sitio para todos* There isn't enough room for all. ▲ siege, besieging *El sitio de la ciudad duró tres semanas.* The siege of the city lasted three weeks.

situación [f] site, location *La situación de la colina era muy favorable.* The situation of the hill was very favorable. ▲ situation, standing (in life) *La situación de esa familia es muy buena.* That family's situation is very good. ▲ situation, predicament *No sé lo que hubiera hecho en esa situación.* I don't know what I'd have done in that predicament.

smoking [m] dinner jacket, tuxedo.

soberano [adj] absolute *Tiene por ella un desprecio soberano.* He feels absolute contempt for her. ○ **los soberanos** the sovereigns (the king and queen).

soberbia arrogance, haughtiness.

soberbio arrogant, haughty.

sobornar to bribe.

sobra excess, surplus. ○ **de sobra** more than enough *Tengo de sobra con lo que Ud. me dió.* I have more than enough with what you gave me. ○ **estar de sobra** to be superfluous, be in the way, be in excess *Yo aquí estoy de sobra.* I'm superfluous here. ○ **saber de sobra** to be fully aware *Lo sabe Ud. de sobra.* You're fully aware of that. ○ **sobras** leftovers *Estas croquetas están hechas con sobras.* These croquettes are made of left-overs.

sobrar to be in excess, be more than enough, be left over *Sobró mucha comida.* A great deal of food was left over.—*Sobra comida.* There's more than enough food. ▲ to be superfluous *Me parece que aquí sobro.* It seems to me that I'm superfluous here.

sobre over *El avión pasó sobre la ciudad.* The airplane passed over the city. ▲ on, upon *Había un libro sobre la mesa.* There was a book on the table. ▲ on *Súbase sobre esa silla para alcanzar el cuadro.* Get up on that chair to reach the picture. ▲ about, concerning *Quiero hablarle a Ud. sobre cierto asunto.* I want to speak to you about a certain matter. ▲ [m] envelope *Deme un sobre.* Give me an envelope. ○ **sobre todo** above all *Sobre todo no dejes de escribir.* Above all don't fail to write.

sobrehumano superhuman.

sobrenatural supernatural.

sobresueldo extra income *Tiene un sobresueldo de veinte dólares la semana.* He has an extra income of twenty dollars a week.

sobrina niece.

sobrino nephew.

sobrio sober, temperate; restrained.

socar to tighten [Am] *Este nudo ha quedado muy socado.* This knot's very tight.

social [adj] social.

sociedad [f] society *Le gustaba frecuentar la buena sociedad.* He liked to move in high society. ▲ partnership; corporation.

○ **sociedad anónima** joint stock company, corporation.

socio partner (in business) *Le presento a mi socio, Sr. Avalos.* Meet my partner, Mr. Avalos. ▲ member (of club or society) *¿Es Ud. socio de ese club?* Are you a member of that club?

socorrer to help *Había que socorrer a los náufragos.* It was necessary to help the survivors of a shipwreck.

socorro help, aid *Le agradecí el socorro que me prestó.* I was grateful to him for the help he gave me.

○ **puesto de socorro** first-aid station. ‖ *¡Socorro! ¡Socorro!* Help!

sofá [m] sofa.

sofocado (see **sofocar**) embarrassed, flushed.

sofocar to stifle, suffocate *El calor lo sofocaba.* The heat was stifling him. ▲ to choke, suffocate *El humo lo sofocaba.* The smoke was choking him. ▲ to put out, extinguish *Las bombas sofocaron el incendio.* The fire engines put out the fire.

○ **sofocarse** to get flushed and out of breath *Se sofocó al subir los escaleras.* He got flushed and out of breath on climbing the stairs. ▲ to get excited *Procure Ud. no sofocarse por ese asunto.* Don't get excited over that matter. ▲ to blush, get embarrassed *Al oír aquella palabra, la niña se sofocó.* The girl blushed when she heard that word.

sofoco blushing, embarrassment.

○ **pasar un sofoco** to be in an embarrassing situation.

soga rope *Coja Ud. la soga por la punta.* Catch the end of the rope.

sol [m] sun. ▲ sunlight, sun *Esas plantas necesitan mucho sol.* Those plants require a lot of sunlight. ▲ sol (Peruvian currency unit).

○ **al salir el sol** at sun-up, at sunrise *Al salir el sol se empezó la marcha.* The march began at sun-up. ○ **estar quemado** (*or* **tostado**) **por el sol** to be sunburned (*or* sun-tanned). ○ **hacer sol** to be sunny *Hoy no hace sol.* It's not sunny today. ○ **tomar el sol** to sunbathe *Estuvieron tomando el sol mucho rato.* They took a long sunbath.

solapa lapel.

soldada salary (of servants).

soldado (see **soldar**) soldered, welded *Todavía no han soldado la cañería.* They haven't soldered the pipe yet.

▲ [m] soldier *Los soldados fueron alojados en el pueblo.* The soldiers were billeted in the town. ▲ private (military).

○ **soldado de primera** (**clase**) private first class. ○ **soldado raso** buck private.

soldar [rad-ch I] to solder, weld.

soledad [f] solitude.

solemne solemn.

soler [rad-ch I] to be in the habit of, have the custom of *¿A qué hora suele venir Ud. a la oficina?* What time do you usually come to the office?—*Solíamos hacer excursiones por la montaña.* We used to make trips to the mountains.

solicitar to request, apply for *Hay que solicitar un permiso para visitar ese edificio.* It's necessary to apply for a pass to visit that building.

solicitud [f] solicitude; application (request).

sólido solid, firm *El puente tiene una base muy sólida.* That bridge has a very solid base. ▲ sound *Tenía una cultura muy sólida.* He had a very sound cultural background.

sollozar to sob.

sollozo sob.

solo alone *Cuando venga a verme venga Ud. solo.* When you come to see me, come alone. ▲ lonely *Estoy muy solo.* I'm very lonely. ▲ [m] solo *El tenor cantó muy bien el solo.* The tenor sang the solo very well.

sólo only *El matrimonio tenía un hijo sólo.* The couple had only one son.

soltar [rad-ch I] to loosen *Soltaron las amarras.* They loosened the cables. ▲ to let out *Soltó una exclamación.* He let out an exclamation. ▲ to drop, let go *Soltó el paquete que tenía en la mano.* He let go the package he had in his hand.

○ **soltarse** to loosen, become loose *Se me ha soltado el cordón del zapato.* My shoe lace is loose. ○ **soltar una bofetada** to slap (suddenly or unexpectedly) *Le soltó una bofetada.* She slapped him. ○ **soltar una carcajada** to burst out laughing *Cuando lo oyó soltó la carcajada.* When he heard it he burst out laughing. ○ **soltar una fresca** to give one a piece of one's mind, tell one where to get off *Le voy a soltar una fresca.* I'll give him a piece of my mind.

soltero single (not married).

soltura poise, ease (of movement) *Bailaba con mucha soltura.* She danced effortlessly. ▲ fluency *Habla las len-*

guas *extranjeras con soltura.* He speaks foreign languages fluently.

solución [*f*] solution *Esto no tiene solución.* This doesn't have any solution. ▲ result *¿Qué solución hubo en aquel pleito?* What was the result of that lawsuit? ▲ solution (liquid).

solucionar to solve.

solvencia solvency.

solvente solvent (financially).

sombra shade *Buscó la sombra del árbol.* He sought the shade of the tree. ▲ shadow *Se veía en el suelo la sombra del avión.* The shadow of the airplane could be seen on the ground. ▲ dark, darkness *Estaba escondido en la sombra.* He was hidden in the dark. luck. ▲ wit *Ese chiste tiene mucha sombra.* That joke's very witty. O **a la sombra** in the shadow; [*Slang*] in jail. O **buena sombra** good luck. O **dar sombra** to give shade *Los árboles dan sombra.* The trees give shade. O **hacer sombra** to outshine *Esa mujer le hace sombra a su marido.* That woman outshines her husband. O **mala sombra** bad luck. O **no ser ni su sombra** to be but a shadow of one's former self.

sombrerería hat factory *or* store.

sombrero hat. O **sombrero de copa** silk hat, top hat. O **sombrero de paja** straw hat.

sombrilla parasol.

sombrío gloomy, somber *Tenía un semblante muy sombrío.* He had a very gloomy expression on his face.

someter to subdue *Es muy difícil someter a esa gente.* It's very difficult to subdue those people. ▲ to subject *Someta Ud. esto a nuevo estudio.* Subject this to further study. ▲ to submit, present *Someta Ud. el informe.* Submit the report. O **someterse** to submit *No sé cómo se somete a que le traten así.* I don't know why he submits to such treatment. ▲ to surrender *Se sometieron ante los invasores.* They surrendered to the invading armies.

son [*m*] sound (musical or pleasant) *El son de los violines.* The sound of the violins. ▲ Cuban song and dance. O **¿a qué son?** for what reason? *¿A qué son dice Ud. eso?* For what reason do you say that? O **en son de** as, like, in the manner of *Lo dijo en son de broma.* He said it as a joke. O **sin ton ni son** without rhyme or reason *Habla sin ton ni son.* He talks without rhyme or reason.

sonado (see **sonar**) sensational, scandalous.

sonar [*rad-ch I*] to sound, ring *Sonó la sirena del barco.* The ship's siren sounded. ▲ to strike *Sonaron las diez.* The clock struck ten. ▲ to ring *Me parece que ha sonado el timbre.* I think the bell rang. ▲ to sound familiar *Ese nombre no me suena.* That name doesn't sound familiar. ▲ to be mentioned, be talked about, be in the public eye *Su nombre suena mucho.* His name's always in the public eye. O **sonarse** to blow one's nose.

sondear to sound, take soundings in *Estuvieron sondeando la bahía.* They were taking soundings in the bay. ▲ to sound out *Sondee Ud. sus intenciones.* Sound out his intentions.

sonido sound (something heard).

sonoro sonorous.

sonreír to smile.

sonrisa smile.

sonrojar to make blush. O **sonrojarse** to blush.

soñador [*m*] dreamer.

soñar [*rad-ch I*] to dream *Sueño con mucha frecuencia.* I dream very often. O **ni soñar** not by a long shot *"¿Te lo dió? "¡Ni soñar!"* "Did he give it to you?" "Not by a long shot!"

sopa soup. O **hecho una sopa** drenched to the skin *Llegó a casa hecho una sopa.* He got home drenched to the skin.

soplar to blow *Soplaba mucho viento.* A strong wind was blowing. ▲ to tattle, blab *Le sopla al jefe todo lo que ocurre en la oficina.* He tattles to the boss about everything that goes on in the office.

soplido blow(ing), puff *De un soplido, apagó la vela.* He put out the candle with a puff.

soplo breath, gust (of air), puff *No hay hoy ni un soplo de aire.* There's not a breath of air today. ▲ tip, hint *Cogieron al asesino gracias a un soplo que recibió la policía.* They caught the murderer as a result of a tip received by the police.

soportar to bear, put up with *No hay más remedio que soportar esto.* There's nothing to do but bear it.

sorber to sip.

sorbo sip *Deme un sorbo de agua.* Give me a sip of water.

sordo deaf *Estaba bastante sordo.* He was quite deaf. ▲ muffled, dull *Oyó un ruido sordo.* He heard a muffled noise.

▲ dull *Tenía un dolor sordo en el pecho.* He had a dull pain in his chest.

○ **hacerse el sordo** to turn a deaf ear *Se hizo el sordo a mis peticiones.* He turned a deaf ear to my pleas.

sordomudo deaf and dumb. ▲ [*n*] deaf-mute.

soroche [*m*] altitude sickness, mountain sickness [*Am*].

sorprendente surprising.

sorprender to surprise *Le soprendió aquella noticia.* That news surprised him. ▲ to catch *Su madre le sorprendió robando.* His mother caught him stealing.

○ **sorprenderse** to be surprised *No se sorprenda Ud. por eso.* Don't be surprised by that.

sorpresa surprise *¡Qué sopresa tan agradable el verle!* What a pleasant surprise to see you!

○ **de sorpresa** by surprise *Me ha cogido de sorpresa esa noticia.* That news took me by surprise. ○ **por sorpresa** by surprise *Los detuvieron por sorpresa.* They arrested them by surprise.

sortear to raffle off, draw lots for *Sortearon un reloj.* They raffled off a watch. ▲ to elude, dodge *El torero sortea hábilmente al toro.* The bullfighter dodges the bull skillfully.

sortija ring (circular object).

sosegarse [*rad-ch I*] to compose oneself, calm down *Cuando Ud. se sosiegue, hablaremos.* When you calm down, we'll talk.

sosiego peace, tranquillity.

soso tasteless *Estas legumbres están muy sosas.* These vegetables are tasteless. ▲ insipid *¡Qué persona más sosa!* What an insipid person!

sospecha suspicion.

sospechar to suspect *Sospecho que este trabajo no está bien hecho.* I suspect that this work isn't well done.

sospechoso suspicious.

sostener [*irr*] to hold *Sostenía la botella en la mano.* He held the bottle in his hand. ▲ to maintain, stick to *Lo digo y lo sostengo.* I say it and I stick to it. ▲ to support *Con su trabajo sostenía a su familia.* He supported his family by working.

○ **sostenerse** to support oneself, stand (up) *Estaba tan borracho que no podía sostenerse.* He was so drunk he couldn't stand up.

sótano basement.

su; *pl* **sus** your, his, her, its, their *Su*

pluma. Your pen, his pen, etc.—*Sus plumas.* Your pens, his pens, etc.

suave delicate, soft, gentle, light *El dentista tenía la mano muy suave.* The dentist had a very light hand. ▲ smooth *Es una tela muy suave.* It's a very smooth cloth. ▲ gentle *Soplaba un viento suave.* A very gentle breeze was blowing. ▲ mellow, mild *Este vino es muy suave.* This wine's very mellow. ▲ meek, docile *Este niño tiene un carácter muy suave.* This child's very meek.

suavizar to soften.

subalterno [*adj; n*] subordinate.

subasta auction.

subido (see **subir**) high, bright *Es una corbata de color subido.* It's a bright-colored tie.

subir to go up *Voy a subir por mi abrigo.* I'm going up for my coat. ▲ to bring up *Súbame Ud. el baúl.* Bring up my trunk. ▲ to put on, set on *El mozo le subirá la maleta al tren.* The porter will put your suitcase on the train. ▲ to put up, lift up *Suba Ud. el niño a la silla.* Lift the child up on the chair. ▲ to raise *Tendrá Ud. que subir un poco la voz, es muy sordo.* You'll have to raise your voice a little; he's very deaf. ▲ to add up, amount, come *¿A cuánto sube la cuenta?* How much does the bill come to? ▲ to go up, rise, increase *Los precios han subido mucho.* Prices have gone up a lot.—*Le subió la temperatura.* His temperature rose. ▲ to rise, ascend *El globo subió hasta diez mil pies.* The balloon rose to ten thousand feet. ▲ to rise, advance *Ha subido muy de prisa ese muchacho.* That boy's advanced very rapidly.

○ **subírsele a uno a la cabeza** to go to one's head *Se le ha subido a la cabeza su popularidad.* His popularity's gone to his head.

su(b)scribirse to subscribe *¿Quiere Ud. subscribirse a esta revista?* Do you want to subscribe to this magazine?

su(b)scripción [*f*] subscription.

su(b)stitución [*f*] substitution.

su(b)stituir to replace.

su(b)stituto, su(b)stituta substitute.

subterráneo subway [*Am*].

suceder to succeed *Se cree que su hijo le sucederá.* It's thought that his son'll succeed him. ▲ to happen *Sucedió algo que nadie se explica.* Something happened that can't be explained.

○ **suceda lo que suceda** come what may *Suceda lo que suceda, yo estaré aquí.* Come what may, I'll be here.

sucesivo consecutive, successive.

○ **en lo sucesivo** in the future.

suceso event.

suciedad [*f*] filthiness.

sucio dirty *La calle estaba muy sucia.* The street was very dirty. ▲ dirty, unfair *Hizo una jugada sucia.* He played a dirty trick.

sudamericano [*adj; n*] South American.

sudar to sweat.

sudeste [*m*] southeast.

sudoeste [*m*] southwest.

sudor [*m*] sweat.

suegra mother-in-law.

suegro father-in-law.

suela sole *Las suelas de mis zapatos están rotas.* The soles of my shoes are worn out.

suelo floor *El suelo estaba manchado.* The floor was stained. ▲ soil *Este suelo produce mucho.* This soil's very productive. ▲ ground *Cayó al suelo herido.* He fell to the ground wounded.

suelto loose, untidy *Tenía suelto el cordón de un zapato.* One of his shoelaces was loose. ▲ free, (on the) loose *Ese perro está suelto.* That dog's loose. ▲ odd *Tenemos unos números sueltos de esa revista.* We have some odd copies of that magazine. ▲ single *Número suelto, dos pesos.* Single copy, two pesos. ▲ [*m*] (loose) change *¿Tiene Ud. suelto?* Have you any change? ▲ newspaper report *or* item *¿Ha visto Ud. este suelto en el periódico?* Have you seen this newspaper report?

○ **suelto de lengua** loose-tongued *Era muy suelto de lengua.* He was very loose-tongued.

sueño sleep *Necesita Ud. más sueño.* You need more sleep. ▲ dream *He tenido un sueño muy raro.* I've had a very strange dream.

○ **conciliar el sueño** to get to sleep *No pudo conciliar el sueño.* He couldn't get to sleep. ○ **echar un sueño** to take a nap *A la mitad de la tarde eché un sueño.* I took a nap in the middle of the afternoon. ○ **tener sueño** to be sleepy.

‖ *Tenía el sueño pesado.* He was a very sound sleeper.

suerte [*f*] fate, luck *Quiso la suerte que yo llegara en aquel momento.* As luck would have it, I arrived at that moment. ▲ luck *Ese hombre tiene buena suerte.* That man has good luck.

○ **de suerte que** so (that), and so *¿De suerte que no le ha visto Ud.?* So you haven't seen him? ○ **echar (a) suertes** to draw lots. ○ **por suerte** fortunately *Por suerte o por desgracia ya está Ud.*

aquí. Fortunately or unfortunately you're here now. ○ **tocarle a uno la suerte** to be lucky *¡A mí me tocó la suerte!* I was lucky.

suéter [*m*] sweater [*Am*].

sufragio suffrage, vote.

sufrimiento suffering.

sufrir to suffer *¿De qué dolencia sufre Ud.?* What ails you? ▲ to undergo *Ha sufrido una operación.* He's undergone an operation. ▲ to endure, put up with *¡No le puedo sufrir más!* I can't put up with him any longer!

sufrido (see **sufrir**) serviceable, practical *El traje tiene un color sufrido.* The dress is a practical color. ▲ patient, long-suffering *Es un hombre muy sufrido.* He's a very long-suffering man.

sugerir [*rad-ch II*] to suggest.

sugestionar to influence *Nada podía sugestionarle.* Nothing could influence him. ▲ to hypnotize.

○ **sugestionarse** to be spellbound *Me quedé sugestionado.* I was spellbound.

suicida [*m, f*] suicide (person).

suicidarse to commit suicide.

suicidio suicide (act).

sujetar to hold *Los policías trataron de sujetarle.* The police tried to hold him. ▲ to fasten *Sujete al perro con una cadena.* Fasten the dog with a chain.

○ **sujetarse** to submit, abide (by) *Había que sujetarse a la nueva disposición.* We had to submit to the new regulation.

sujeto (see **sujetar**) fastened *No está bien sujeto el cinturón.* The belt's not well fastened. ▲ [*m*] subject (grammar) *¿Cuál es el sujeto de esa oración?* What's the subject of that sentence? ▲ fellow, guy *¿Quién es ese sujeto?* Who's that fellow?

suma amount, sum *¿Cuánto es la suma total?* What's the total amount?

○ **en suma** in short *En suma, ¿qué es lo que pasó?* In short, what happened?

sumar to add; to amount to.

sumergirse to submerge, dive.

sumidero sewer, sink, drain.

sumo great *He tenido sumo gusto en conocerle.* It's been a great pleasure to know you.

○ **a lo sumo** at most *A lo sumo tardará dos horas.* She'll be delayed two hours at most. ○ **el sumo** the greatest *El Sumo Hacedor.* The Almighty.

suntuoso sumptuous.

superficial superficial *La herida era superficial.* The wound was superficial. —*Sus conocimientos eran muy superficiales.* His knowledge was very superficial. ▲ shallow *¡Qué muchacha tan superficial!* What a shallow girl!

superficie [*f*] surface.

superior superior, better *Esto es de calidad superior.* This is of superior quality. ▲ higher *Tenía un grado superior en el ejército.* He held a higher rank in the army. ▲ above *Vive en el piso superior.* He lives on the floor above. ▲ [*m*] superior *Respete a sus superiores.* Show respect for your superiors.

○ **parte superior** upper part *El libro está en la parte superior del armario.* The book's in the upper part of the cupboard.

superioridad [*f*] superiority.

súplica request; entreaty, supplication.

superstición [*f*] superstition.

superviviente [*m, f*] survivor.

suplente [*adj*] substituting. ▲ [*n*] substitute.

suplicar to implore *Le suplicó que le ayudara.* She implored him to help her. ▲ to beg, request *Le suplico a Ud. que vuelva mañana.* I beg you to come back tomorrow.

suplicio torture *Le sometieron a horribles suplicios.* They subjected him to horrible torture. ▲ ordeal, anguish *Pasó por el suplicio de ver morir a su padre.* He went through the ordeal of seeing his father die.

suponer [*irr*] to suppose, assume *Supuso que ella no quería hacer ese trabajo.* He assumed she didn't want to do that work. ▲ to imagine *Ud. podrá suponer lo que ocurrió.* You can imagine what happened. ▲ to amount to, cost *¿Cuanto supone todo esto?* How much does all this amount to?

suposición [*f*] supposition.

supremo supreme *Tribunal Supremo.* Supreme Court.

supresión [*f*] suppression.

suprimir to suppress, leave out, omit *Suprima Ud. la pimienta en la sopa.* Omit the pepper from the soup. ▲ to abolish *Suprimieron los impuestos sobre la renta.* They abolished income taxes.

supuesto (see **suponer**) assumed; supposed.

○ **por supuesto** of course *Por supuesto, tendrá Ud. el pasaporte en regla.* Of course, you have your passport in order.

sur [*m*] south.

surco furrow.

surgir to make a sudden appearance *Surgió cuando nadie le esperaba.* He appeared when no one expected him. ▲ to arise (as a situation).

suroeste [*m*] southwest.

surtido (see **surtir**) supplied; assorted. ▲ [*m*] assortment.

surtidor [*m*] vertical fountain, spout; sprinkler.

○ **surtidor de gasolina** filling station.

surtir to supply *¿Le ha surtido de todo lo necesario?* Has he supplied you with everything that's necessary?

○ **surtir efecto** to have the desired effect *Surtirá muy buen efecto este artículo.* This article will have the desired effect.

suspender to suspend, stop *Suspendieron el espectáculo por la lluvia.* The show was stopped on account of the rain. ▲ to suspend, hang *Suspendieron el cuadro de un clavo.* They hung the picture on a nail. ▲ to flunk (give a failing mark to) *Lo suspendieron en aritmética.* They flunked him in arithmetic.

suspenso (see **suspender**) hung, suspended. ▲ [*m*] failing grade, flunk.

○ **en suspenso** in suspense *Se quedó en suspenso.* He stopped in suspense. ▲ suspended *Esa ley está en suspenso.* That law's suspended.

sustento support, sustenance, living expenses.

○ **ganarse el sustento** to make a living.

susto fright, scare.

○ **dar un susto** to frighten.

suyo, suya; suyos, suyas your(s), of yours, his, of his, her(s), of hers, their(s), of theirs *Este lápiz no es suyo.* This pencil isn't yours (or his, hers, theirs).—*Son amigos suyos.* They're friends of yours (or of his, of hers, of theirs).

○ **el suyo, la suya; los suyos, las suyas** yours, his, hers, theirs *El mío está aquí. ¿Dónde está el suyo?* Mine's here. Where's yours? ○ **los suyos** his (or her, your, their) folks *Fué con todos los suyos a la playa.* He went with all his folks to the beach.

T

tabaco tobacco; cigar; cigarettes.

taberna saloon, tavern, dive.

tabla board, plank *¿Tiene Ud. una tabla de planchar?* Have you an ironing board? ▲ list, table (of contents, prices, etc) *Quiero ver la tabla de precios.* I want to see the price list.
  ○ **salvarse en una tabla** to have a narrow escape. ○ **tablas** [*f pl*] stage (theater) *Es gente de las tablas.* They belong to the theatrical world. ▲ draw (in a game) *El partido terminó en tablas.* The game ended in a draw.

tablado outdoor stage, platform.

tacha fault *Es una persona sin tacha.* He is a person without any faults.

tachar to cross out *Tache Ud. esa palabra.* Cross out that word.
  ○ **tachar de** to accuse of being *Le tacharon de ladrón.* They accused him of being a thief.

taco taco (Mexican dish) *Quiero un taco de puerco.* I want a pork taco. ▲ heel (of a shoe) [*Am*] *Usa tacos muy altos.* She wears very high heels.
  ○ **echar tacos** to swear, curse [*Sp*]. ○ **taco de billar** billiard cue.

tacón [*m*] heel (of shoe).

táctica tactics; policy, way of doing *Tendremos que emplear otra táctica.* We'll have to use different tactics.

tacto touch, sense of touch *Esta tela es muy suave al tacto.* This cloth is very soft to the touch. ▲ tact *Tiene mucho tacto para tratar a sus amigos.* He's very tactful with his friends.

tajada slice (usually meat).

tal such *Jamás se ha visto tal cosa.* Never has such a thing been seen. ▲ such (a) thing *Ud. me dijo eso y no hay tal cosa.* You told me that, but there's no such thing.
  ○ **con tal que** provided that *Con tal que me lo haga Ud. bien no importa el precio.* Provided you do it well the price doesn't matter. ○ **el tal, la tal** that (contemptuous) *No me gustó la tal comedia.* I didn't like that comedy. ○ **tal como** just as *Siga tal como empezó.* Go on just as you started. ○ **tal cual** as *Me gusta tal cual es.* I like it as it is. ▲ so-so [*Mex*] *"¿Cómo está Ud.?" "Tal cual."* "How are you?" "So-so." ○ **tales y tales** such and such *Me dijo: Pregunte a tales y tales personas ....* He said to me: Ask such and such persons.... ○ **tal para cual**

two of a kind *Son tal para cual.* They're two of a kind. ○ **un tal** a certain *¿Conoce Ud. a un tal Pérez?* Do you know a certain Pérez?
  ‖ *¿Qué tal?* How do you do? *or* How's everything?

talabartería leather workshop, harnessmaker's shop.

taladro drill, bit.

talante [*m*] ○ **mal talante** bad humor, bad disposition.

talento talent, brains.

talla carving *Se ha dedicado a la talla en madera.* She devoted herself to wood carving. ▲ size *Deseo un traje de la talla cuarenta.* I want a suit size forty. ▲ height (of humans) *Un hombre de talla elevada.* A man of great height. ▲ prominence *Un escritor de talla.* A prominent writer.

talle [*m*] waist, figure *Esa muchacha tiene un lindo talle.* That girl has a pretty figure.

taller [*m*] workshop; factory, mill.

tallo stem (of plant).

talón [*m*] heel (of foot). ▲ stub (of a check, receipt) *No pierda Ud. el talón de los cheques.* Don't lose your check stubs.

talonario check book, receipt book, stub book, book of tickets.

tamal [*m*] tamale [*Am*].

tamaño so great, such a big *Es imposible creer tamaña mentira.* It's impossible to believe such a big lie. ▲ [*m*] size *¿De qué tamaño?* What size?

también also, too *El también irá con nosotros.* He also will go with us.

tambor [*m*] drum.

tampoco neither, not either *Yo tampoco la he visto.* I haven't seen her either.

tan [*before adj or adv*] (see **tanto**) so *No le esperaba a Ud. tan temprano.* I didn't expect you so early.

tanate [*m*] bundle [*Am*] *Haré un tanate con esta ropa.* I'll make a bundle of these clothes.

tanda turn *Como somos muchos, almorzaremos por tandas.* Since there are so many of us, we'll take turns at lunch. ▲ batch. ▲ performance, session [*Am*] *Iremos a la primera tanda.* We'll go to the first performance.

tango tango.

tanque [*m*] tank (military); tank (for liquid).

tantear to estimate, consider *Hay que tantear la situación antes de decidir.* The situation must be considered before deciding. ▲ to judge, estimate [Am] *Tantee Ud. el peso de esto.* Estimate the weight of this. ▲ to feel out *Tantéelo Ud. antes de hablarle claro.* Feel him out before speaking plainly to him. ▲ to feel, test *Tanteamos el piso para ver si era fuerte.* We tested the floor to see if it was strong.

tanteo computation, calculation; points, score.

tanto so much *He comido tanto que ya no tengo hambre.* I've eaten so much that I'm no longer hungry.—*No debe Ud. trabajar tanto.* You shouldn't work so much. ▲ so many *Ha ido tantas veces que conoce muy bien el lugar.* He has gone so many times that he knows the place very well.—*Eran tantos que faltó comida.* There were so many that there wasn't enough food. ▲ so long *No tardará tanto si va en auto.* He won't take so long if he goes by car. ▲ so often *Yo no voy tanto al teatro como mi hermano.* I don't go to the theater as often as my brother does. ▲ [m] part [Am] *Mezclaba tres tantos de cal por cinco de arena.* He mixed three parts lime with five of sand. ▲ point (in games) *Ganaron por dos tantos a cero.* They won two to nothing.

○ **entre tanto** meanwhile *Entre tanto sentémonos.* Meanwhile let's sit down. ○ **estar al tanto** to keep informed, be on the alert *Yo estaba al tanto.* I was on the alert. ○ **no ser para tanto** not to be so serious *No es para tanto el asunto.* It's not such a serious matter. ○ **por lo tanto** so, therefore *Es tarde, por lo tanto debemos irnos ya.* It's late so we ought to go now. ○ **tanto como** as much as *Sabe tanto como su hermana.* He knows as much as his sister. ○ **tanto más cuanto que** so much more since *Tanto más cuanto que yo no lo esperaba.* So much more since I didn't expect it. ○ **tanto mejor** so much the better *Si llega Ud. antes, tanto mejor.* If you get there before, so much the better. ○ **tener al tanto de** to keep one posted *or* informed *Téngame al tanto de lo que pase.* Keep me informed of what's happening. ○ **un tanto** rather, somewhat *Llegó un tanto cansado.* He arrived rather tired.

‖ *¡Se lo he pedido tanto!* I've asked him so many times! ‖ *¡Tanto bueno por aquí!* It's good to see you here!

tapa lid *¿Dónde está la tapa de la caja?* Where's the lid of the box? ▲ cover

Las tapas de este libro están manchadas. The covers of this book are stained.

tapado lady's overcoat [Am].

tapar to cover *Tape el café para que no se enfríe.* Cover the coffee so it won't get cold. ▲ to obstruct (*or* block) one's view *No puedo ver porque me tapa esa columna.* I can't see because that pillar blocks my view. ▲ to cover up for *Su madre le tapa todas sus diabluras.* His mother covers up all his deviltries.

○ **taparse** to bundle up, wrap (oneself) up *Tápese bien que hace frío afuera.* Bundle up for it's cold outside. ▲ to cover oneself *Se tapó la cara con las manos.* She covered her face with her hands .

tapete [m] small rug; cover for a table.

tapia wall, brick fence.

tapioca tapioca.

tapiz [m] tapestry; carpet (without pile).

tapón [m] cork, stopper; fuze.

taquigrafía shorthand.

taquilla ticket office, ticket window.

tarantín [m] kitchen utensils [Am] *Hay muchos tarantines en esta cocina.* There are many utensils in this kitchen.

tardanza delay, slowness, lateness, tardiness.

tardar to delay, be long *No tarde mucho.* Don't be long. ▲ to take (time) *Tardaron varios meses en hacer el trabajo.* They took several months to do the work.

○ **a más tardar** at the latest *A más tardar, vendré el sábado.* I'll come Saturday at the latest.

tarde [m] afternoon, early evening *Estaré en casa por la tarde.* I'll be at home in the afternoon. ▲ [adv] late *Más vale tarde que nunca.* Better late than never.

○ **de la tarde** (at a certain hour) in the afternoon. *Venga Ud. a las tres de la tarde.* Come at three in the afternoon. ○ **hacerse tarde** to become (*or* get) late *Se hace tarde y no estamos listas.* It's getting late and we're not ready. ○ **por la tarde** afternoon *Nos veremos el lunes por la tarde.* We'll get together Monday afternoon. ○ **tarde o temprano** sooner or later *Tarde o temprano lo sabrá.* He'll find out sooner or later.

‖ *Buenas tardes.* Good afternoon. *or* Good evening.

tarea task.
○ **por tarea** against time [Am] *Está trabajando por tarea.* He's working against time.
tarifa rates, tariff; list or schedule of prices, taxes, etc.
tarjeta card; visiting card; filing card.
tata [m] papa.
taz ○ **taz con taz** equal, the same, side by side [Am] *Quedaron taz con taz.* They were equal.
taza cup.
tazón [m] bowl (utensil).
té [m] tea *¿Quiere una taza de té?* Do you want a cup of tea?
te you, to you; yourself, to yourself *Te buscan.* They are looking for you.—*Te lo daré cuando lo encuentre.* I'll give it to you when I find it.—*¡Cuidado, no te cortes!* Careful, don't cut yourself!
teatro theater.
techo ceiling; roof.
técnica technique.
tecolote [m] owl [Mex].
tecomate [m] gourd, canteen [Am].
teja roof tile.
tejado roof.
tejer to weave; [Am] to knit.
tela cloth, material *No me gusta la tela de este traje.* I don't like the material in this dress.
○ **tela metálica** screen wire; wire fencing.
telefonear to telephone, phone.
telefonista [m, f] telephone operator.
teléfono telephone.
○ **teléfono automático** dial telephone.
telegrafiar to telegraph, send a telegram.
telégrafo telegraph.
telegrama [m] telegram.
telón [m] theater curtain.
tema [m] subject, topic, theme.
temblar [rad-ch I] to tremble, shiver *Está temblando de frío.* He's shivering with cold. ▲ to quake [Am] *En ese país tiembla mucho.* There are many earthquakes in that country.
temblor [m] tremor.
○ **temblor de tierra** earthquake.
tembloroso trembling.
temer to fear, be afraid of.
temerario rash; unwise.
temible [adj] fearful, terrible.
temor [m] fear.
temperamento temperament.
temperatura temperature.
tempestad [f] storm, tempest.
templado brave, courageous *Es un tipo muy templado.* He's a courageous fellow. ▲ temperate *Francia está en la zona templada.* France is in the temperate zone. ▲ mild *Hoy hace un día templado.* It's a mild day today. ▲ tuned *El violín no está bien templado.* The violin isn't tuned. ▲ tepid, lukewarm *Deme Ud. agua templada.* Give me some tepid water.
templar to tune.
○ **templarle la gaita a uno** to humor one.
templo temple, church.
temporada spell, period of time, season *Pasaremos una temporada en la playa.* We'll spend some time at the beach. ▲ season *¿Ha empezado ya la temporada de ópera?* Has the opera season started yet?
temporal temporary *Tengo un trabajo temporal.* I have a temporary job. ▲ [m] storm *El temporal duró varios días.* The storm lasted several days.
temprano [adj, adv] early.
tenaz tenacious, persevering *Es muy tenaz en sus propósitos.* He's very persevering. ▲ stubborn *La resistencia fué tenaz.* Resistance was stubborn.
tenaza pliers, tongs.
tendencia tendency.
tender [rad-ch I] to stretch, spread out *Estaba tendiendo el mantel sobre la mesa.* She was putting the tablecloth on the table. ▲ to hang (clothes) *Tienda Ud. esa ropa al sol.* Hang that wash out in the sun. ▲ to extend, offer (one's hand) *Al verlo le tendió la mano.* When he saw him he offered him his hand. ▲ to build (engineering) *Tendieron un puente y una línea ferroviaria.* They built a bridge and a railroad.
○ **tenderse** to stretch out, lie full length *Se tendieron sobre la arena.* They stretched out on the sand.
tendero, tendera shopkeeper.
tendón [m] sinew, tendon.
tenedor [m] holder; keeper; fork.
○ **tenedor de libros** bookkeeper.
tener [irr] to have, possess *Tengo un automóvil nuevo.* I have a new car. ▲ to hold *Téngalo Ud. por los brazos.* Hold him by the arms. ▲ to have, contain *Cada caja tiene veinticuatro píldoras.* Each box contains twenty-four pills. ▲ to have, carry, sell *¿Tienen aquí libros en español?* Do you carry Spanish books here? ▲ to have, entertain *Hoy tendremos invitados.* We're going to entertain some guests today. ▲ to be, live (in a place) *Tenemos muchos años de vivir aquí.* We've lived here many years.

○ **no tener razón** to be wrong.
○ **tener . . . años** to be . . . years old
Creo que tiene veinticinco años. I think
he's twenty-five years old. ○ **tener
buena cara** to be looking well *¿Cómo
estás, María? Tienes buena cara.* How
are you, Mary? You're looking well.
▲ to look good *Tiene buena cara ese
pastel.* That cake looks good. ○ **tener
con cuidado** to worry *Su ausencia me
tiene con cuidado.* His absence worries
me. ○ **tener cuidado** to be careful.
○ **tener en cuenta** to take into consideration. ○ **tener gana(s) de** to feel like.
○ **tener frío** to be cold. *Tengo frío.* I'm
cold. ○ **tener gracia** to be funny *¡Tendría gracia que eso pasara!* It would be
funny if that happened. ○ **tener gusto**
to be pleased, be glad *Tengo mucho
gusto en conocerle.* I'm very glad to
meet you. ○ **tener hambre** to be hungry. ○ **tener (la) costumbre de** to be
used to *Tengo costumbre de levantarme
temprano.* I'm used to getting up early
in the morning. ○ **tener miedo** to be
afraid. ○ **tener presente** to bear in mind
*Tendré presente lo que Ud. me ha
dicho.* I'll bear in mind what you've
told me. ○ **tener prisa** to be in a
hurry. ○ **tener que** to have to, be
obliged to *Tengo que irme ya.* I have
to go now. ○ **tener que ver** to have to
do with *Eso no tiene que ver con lo
que digo.* That has nothing to do
with what I'm saying. ○ **tener razón**
to be right. ○ **tener remedio** to be able
to be remedied *or* helped *Esta situación
no tiene remedio.* This situation can't
be helped. ○ **tenerse (en pie)** to keep
on one's feet, stand, remain standing
Apenas podía tenerse en pie. He could
hardly stand.
teniente [*m*] lieutenant.
tenis [*m*] tennis.
tensión [*f*] tension.
tentación [*f*] temptation.
tentar [*rad-ch I*] to touch, feel; to tempt.
tentativa attempt.
teñir [*rad-ch III*] to dye.
tequila tequila (plant, drink) [*Mex*].
tercer [*adj*] (see **tercero**) third *Este es
mi tercer viaje a este país.* This is my
third trip to this country.
tercero [*adj*] third *Vive en el piso tercero.* He lives on the third floor. ▲ [*m*]
third person, mediator *Necesitamos un
tercero para resolver esto.* We need a
third person to decide this. ▲ third one
Era el tercero de su clase. He was
third in his class.

tercio one-third; Spanish Foreign Legion.
terciopelo velvet.
terco stubborn.
terminación [*f*] termination, completion.
terminar (de) to end, finish *Terminó de
hablar.* He finished speaking.
término end.
　○ **en último término** in the last analysis. ○ **poner término a** to put an end to.
○ **término medio** compromise, middle
road. ○ **término municipal** township.
termómetro thermometer.
ternera female calf; calfskin; veal.
ternero male calf.
ternura tenderness, fondness.
terquedad [*f*] stubbornness, obstinacy.
terraza terrace.
terremoto earthquake.
terreno piece of ground, lot; ground, soil.
terrible terrible *Hace un calor terrible.*
It's terribly hot. ▲ wonderful, terrific
Nos divertimos de una manera terrible.
We had a terrific time.
territorio territory.
terrón [*m*] lump (of sugar); clod (of
earth).
terror [*m*] terror.
tertulia conversation, gabfest, gathering.
tesorería treasury.
tesorero, tesorera treasurer.
tesoro treasure.
testamento will (document).
testarudo stubborn, hardheaded.
testificar to testify.
testigo [*n*] witness. ▲ [*m*] testimony.
tetera teapot.
texto text; textbook.
tez [*f*] complexion.
ti [*Fam; used only with a preposition*]
you *Esta carta es para ti.* This letter
is for you.—*No me lo dijo a mí, sino a
ti.* He didn't say it to me, but to you.
tía aunt; old woman.
　○ **no hay tu tía** [*Fam*] there are no
excuses, nothing doing *No hay tu tía;
tienes que ir.* Nothing doing; you have
to go yourself.
tibio tepid, lukewarm.
tiempo time, period, epoch *Esto fué construido en tiempo de la colonia.* This
was built in colonial times. ▲ time *No
sé si tendré tiempo de ir con Ud.* I don't
know whether I'll have time to go with
you. ▲ weather *El tiempo está muy
malo desde ayer.* The weather has been
very bad since yesterday.
　○ **a tiempo** on time *Llegué a tiempo.*
I arrived on time. ○ **con tiempo** in
time *Avíseme con tiempo.* Notify me
in time. ○ **en otro tiempo** formerly.
○ **ganar tiempo** to save time. ○ **hacer**

buen (*or* mal) tiempo to be good (*or* bad) weather. ○ hacer tiempo to while away the time. ○ hace tiempo long ago. ○ hace (*or* hacía) tiempo que it is (*or* was) a long time since *Hace tiempo que estuve allí.* It's a long time since I was there. ○ los buenos tiempos the good old days; one's youth. ○ matar el tiempo to kill time. ○ mucho tiempo a long time. ○ perder el tiempo to waste time. ○ poco tiempo a short time. ○ ¿ (por) cuánto tiempo . . .? (for) how long . . .? *¿Cuánto tiempo duró la representación?* How long did the show last?

tienda shop, store.
   ○ tienda de campaña tent.

tierno tender, soft *Esta carne de vaca está muy tierna.* This beef is very tender. ▲ tender, affectionate *Le lanzó una mirada tierna.* He looked at her affectionately.

tierra earth *¿Cómo parece la tierra desde un avión?* How does the earth look from an airplane? ▲ ground *El avión cayó en tierra.* The plane fell to the ground. ▲ land *Están arando la tierra.* They are plowing the land. ▲ soil, dirt *Ponga tierra en la maceta.* Put some soil in the flowerpot. ▲ native land, country *Pronto regresaré a mi tierra.* Soon I'll return to my country.
   ○ caer por tierra to fall to the ground. ○ echar por tierra to overthrow, ruin *Le echaron por tierra sus proyectos.* They ruined his plans. ○ echar tierra a to forget, hush up *Le echaron tierra al asunto.* They hushed up the matter. ○ por tierra overland, by land *La única manera de llegar allí es por tierra.* The only way to get there is by land.

tigre [*m*] tiger.

tijera ○ cama de tijera day bed, cot.
   ○ tijeras [*pl*] scissors, shears.

timbre [*m*] electric bell; seal, tax stamp.

timidez [*f*] shyness, bashfulness.

tímido timid, shy, bashful.

timo fraud, swindle *Ud. ha sido víctima de un timo.* You've been the victim of a swindle.

timón [*m*] helm; rudder.

tino good aim; tact.
   ○ hablar sin tino to chatter incessantly. ○ sin tino without rhyme or reason, aimlessly.

tinta ink.

tinte [*m*] shade, tint; dyeing; dry cleaning shop.

tinterillo shyster lawyer [*Am*].

tintero inkwell.

○ quedársele a uno algo en el tintero to forget completely *Se me ha quedado en el tintero.* I completely forgot about it.

tinto wine colored.
   ○ café tinto black coffee [*Col*].

tintorería dry cleaning shop; combination laundry and dry cleaning establishment [*Arg*].

tío uncle *Llegó con su tío.* He came with his uncle. ▲ fellow, guy *Me lo dijo el tío ese.* That fellow told me so.

típico typical, characteristic *¿Cuál es el traje típico de esta región?* What is the typical dress here?—*Eso es típico de ellos.* That's typical of them.

tiple [*m*] treble. ▲ [*f*] soprano.

tipo type, pattern *Ese tipo de letra es muy moderno.* That's very modern lettering. ▲ type *Limpie los tipos de la máquina de escribir.* Clean the type on the typewriter.—*Tiene tipo latino.* He's a Latin type. ▲ guy (derogatory), character *¿Quién es ese tipo?* Who's that guy?
   ○ buen tipo good figure *or* physique *Tiene buen tipo.* He has a good physique. ○ mal tipo bad egg *Es muy mal tipo.* He's a bad egg. ▲ poor physique *Tiene mal tipo.* He has a poor physique. ○ tipo de interés rate of interest *Han subido el tipo del interés.* The rate of interest has gone up.

tiquete [*m*] ticket [*Am*].

tira narrow strip.

tirador, tiradora marksman, good shot.

tiranía tyranny.

tirano tyrant.

tirante tight, taut *Ponga la red bien tirante.* Make the net good and tight. ▲ tense *La situación era muy tirante.* The situation was very tense.
   ○ tirantes [*m pl*] suspenders *Compró unos tirantes.* He bought suspenders.

tirar to throw *Tiró la pelota más lejos que todos los otros.* He threw the ball farther than all the others. ▲ to throw away, discard *Este cinturón ya no sirve; hay que tirarlo.* This belt is no longer any good; we have to throw it away. ▲ to shoot, fire (gun) *Estaban tirando al blanco con rifle.* They were shooting at the target with rifles. ▲ to draw *Tire Ud. una línea recta.* Draw a straight line. ▲ to squander, waste *Ha tirado su herencia.* He's wasted his inheritance. ▲ to print *Tirarán muchos ejemplares.* They'll print a large edition.
   ○ tirar a los dados to shoot craps.

○ **tirar coces** to kick *Está tirando coces el caballo.* The horse is kicking. ○ **tirar de** to pull *Tira de la cuerda.* Pull the cord. ○ **tirar de la oreja a Jorge** to gamble *Fueron encarcelados por tirar de la oreja a Jorge.* They were imprisoned for gambling. ○ **tirarse** to throw oneself, hurl oneself *Se tiró por la ventana.* He threw himself out the window. ▲ to jump *Vimos como se tiraban los paracaídistas.* We saw the parachutists jump.

tiritar to shiver.

tiro drive, shot *Su tiro de revés es mejor que su tiro de derecha.* His backhand drive is better than his forehand. ▲ shot *El tiro atravesó la pared.* The shot went through the wall. ▲ team of horses *Caballo de tiro.* Draft horse.

○ **(de) al tiro** right away, immediately [*Am*]. ○ **errar el tiro** to miss the mark *Ha errado Ud. el tiro.* You missed. ○ **ni a tiros** for love or money *No lo haremos ni a tiros.* We won't do it for love or money.

‖ *¡Lindo tiro!* Good shot!

titubear to hesitate, waver *No titubea nunca.* He never hesitates.

título title, name *¿Cuál es el título del libro?* What's the title of the book? ▲ headline (newspaper) *Sólo he leído los títulos.* I've only read the headlines. ▲ diploma, degree, title *Tiene el título de maestra normal.* She has a teacher's diploma.

○ **a título de que** on whose authority *¿A título de qué hace ella eso?* On whose authority is she doing that? ○ **título de propiedad** deed (of property) *¿Dónde están los títulos de su propiedad?* Where are the deeds to your property?

toalla towel *No tengo toalla.* I haven't got a towel.

tobillo ankle.

tocador [*m*] boudoir; dressing table.

tocante a concerning.

tocar to touch *No me toque Ud.* Don't touch me. ▲ to play (an instrument) *Estaba tocando el piano.* He was playing the piano. ▲ to knock *Toqué a la puerta.* I knocked at the door. ▲ to get a share *Nos tocarán partes iguales.* We'll get equal shares. ▲ to draw *Le tocó el número premiado.* He drew the prize-winning number. ▲ to call (at a port) *El barco no tocará en Veracruz.* The ship won't call at Veracruz.

○ **por lo que a mí** (*él, etc*) **toca** as far as I'm (he's, etc) concerned. ○ **tocarle a uno** to be one's turn *Le toca*

jugar. It's his turn to play. ▲ to concern *Eso no le toca a ella.* That doesn't concern her.

tocino bacon.

todavía still *¿Todavía tienes hambre?* Are you still hungry? ▲ yet *Todavía no ha llegado.* He hasn't arrived yet. ▲ even *Ella es todavía más buena que él.* She's even kinder than he is.

○ **todavía no** not yet *Todavía no he comido.* I haven't eaten yet.

todo [*adj*] all *Este pollo es todo huesos.* This chicken's all bones. ▲ full *Pasaron a toda velocidad.* They tore past at full speed. ▲ [*m*] all, the whole *¡Eso es todo!* That's all! ▲ everything *Le gusta probarlo todo.* He likes to try everything.

○ **ante todo** first of all *Ante todo dígame Ud. a qué hora llegan.* First of all tell me what time they're coming. ○ **así y todo** in spite of all *Así y todo me gusta estar aquí.* In spite of all that, I like being here. ○ **a todo** all out, to the limit *Iban a toda correr.* They were going at full speed. ○ **con todo** still, however *Con todo prefiero no ir.* Still, I prefer not to go. ○ **del todo** wholly, completely *Se le olvidó del todo.* He completely forgot. ○ **jugarse el todo por el todo** to bet everything *Se están jugando el todo por el todo.* They're betting everything. ○ **ser el todo** to be the whole *El es el todo del equipo.* He's the whole team. ○ **sobre todo** especially, above all *Me gusta el café, sobre todo si está caliente.* I like coffee, especially if it's hot. ○ **todo bicho viviente** every living soul *Se lo contó a todo bicho viviente.* He told every living soul. ○ **todo cuanto** all that *Todo cuanto Ud. dice me interesa.* All that you tell me interests me. ○ **todo el día** all day *Todo el día estuvo jugando.* He was playing all day. ○ **todo el mundo** everybody *Todo el mundo lo sabe.* Everybody knows it. ○ **todos** everybody *Todos lo quieren.* Everybody likes him. ○ **todos los** every *Todos los años va a la montaña.* He goes to the mountains every year.

‖ *Todos son unos.* They're all the same.

toldo awning; tarpaulin.

tolerancia toleration, tolerance.

tolerante tolerant.

tolerar to overlook, tolerate *Le tolera sus faltas.* She overlooks his faults. ▲ to tolerate *No podemos tolerar eso.* We can't tolerate that.

tomada [*Am*] plug (electrical).

tomar to take *Tomaré el que más me guste.* I'll take the one I happen to like best.—*Tomaremos el avión esta tarde.* We'll take the plane this afternoon.—*No lo tome Ud. en ese sentido.* Don't take it that way. ▲ to drink, eat, have *Tomaremos café al regresar.* We'll have coffee when we return. ▲ to take, hire *Tomemos un taxi.* Let's take a taxi. ▲ to take, adopt *Ha tomado las costumbres de aquel país.* He has adopted the customs of that country. ▲ to take, capture *Tomaron la ciudad por la noche.* They captured the city during the night.

○ **sin tomar aliento** in a great hurry *Vino sin tomar aliento.* He came in a great hurry. ○ **tomar a bien** to take the right way (to put the correct interpretation upon) *Lo tomarán a bien.* They'll take it the right way. ○ **tomar a broma** to take as a joke *Tomémoslo a broma.* Let's take it as a joke. ○ **tomar a mal** to take offense. ○ **tomar a pecho** to take to heart *No lo tome Ud. a pecho.* Don't take it to heart. ○ **tomar asiento** to sit down, take a seat *¿Quiere Ud. tomar asiento?* Won't you sit down? ○ **tomar cariño a** to become attached to, fond of *Me tomaron mucho cariño.* They became very much attached to me. ○ **tomar el gusto** to begin to like *Ya le estoy tomando el gusto a este juego.* I'm beginning to like this game. ○ **tomar el sol** to sun oneself *Salieron para tomar el sol.* They went out to sun themselves. ○ **tomarla con uno** to pick on, ride *La ha tomado conmigo.* He picked on me. ○ **tomar la responsabilidad** to take (assume) responsibility *El tomó la responsabilidad del trabajo.* He assumed the responsibility for the work. ○ **tomar las de Villadiego** to take to one's heels. ○ **tomar nota** to take note *Tomaron nota de todo.* They took note of everything. ○ **tomar por** to consider, take for *Lo toman por tonto.* They take him for a fool. ○ **tomar por, tomar hacia** to turn, go in the direction *Al llegar a la esquina tomó hacia su casa.* When he reached the corner he went in the direction of his house. ○ **tomar precauciones** to take precautions *Están tomando todas las precauciones necesarias.* They're taking all the necessary precautions. ○ **tomarse** to take *Se tomó unas horas para decidirlo.* He took a few hours to decide. ○ **tomarse alas** to take liberties; to get too big for one's breeches. ○ **tomar**

(una or **la) resolución** to resolve, decide *Tomó la resolución de hacerlo.* He decided to do it.

‖ *¡Tome Ud.!* Here you are!

tomate [*m*] tomato.

tomo volume *Esta obra tiene varios tomos.* This work is in several volumes.

tonada tune, song.

tonel [*m*] cask, barrel.

tonelada ton.

tono tone, note *Desafina casi medio tono.* She's nearly a half-note off pitch. ▲ manner *Me lo dijo con mal tono.* He told me in a rude manner. ▲ shade *¿No tiene otro tono de rojo?* Haven't you another shade of red?

○ **bajar el tono** to lower the pitch *Baje Ud. el tono de voz.* Lower your voice. ○ **darse tono** to put on airs *Se da tono de gran persona.* She puts on the airs of a great lady. ○ **en todos los tonos** in every possible way *Se lo he dicho en todos los tonos.* I've told him in every way I know.

tontería foolishness, nonsense *Eso es una tontería.* That's nonsense!

tonto silly, foolish, stupid, dumb *No es tan tonto como Ud. cree.* He's not as dumb as you think. ▲ [*n*] fool *¡Qué tonto!* What a fool!

○ **a tontas y a locas** thoughtlessly, haphazard *Todo lo hace a tontas y a locas.* Everything he does is crazy. ○ **hacerse el tonto** to play the fool. ○ **pasar las horas en tonto** to pass the time doing nothing. ○ **tonto de capirote** blockhead *Es un tonto de capirote.* He's a blockhead.

topar to butt, strike against.

○ **topar con** to stumble upon, find, come upon *Topé con él en la calle.* I came upon him in the street.

toque [*m*] touch *Unos cuantos toques más y estará terminado.* A few more touches and it will be finished.

○ **toque de corneta** bugle-call. ○ **toque de diana** reveille. ○ **toque de tambor** beat of drum.

torbellino whirlwind.

torcer [*rad-ch I*] to twist *Está torciendo el alambre.* He's twisting the wire. ▲ to turn *El camino tuerce hacia el río.* The road turns toward the river.

○ **no dar el brazo a torcer** to be stubborn *Nunca da su brazo a torcer.* He never gives in. ○ **torcerse** to sprain, dislocate *Se ha torcido un pie.* He's sprained his foot.

torcido crooked *Arregle el cuadro que está torcido.* Straighten the picture;

it's crooked. ▲ bent *El clavo está torcido.* The nail is bent. ▲ twisted *Este alambre está torcido.* This wire is twisted. ▲ unlucky [*Am*] *Es muy torcido en el juego.* He's very unlucky at gambling.

torero bullfighter.

tormenta storm.

tormento torment, pain.

tornarse to turn, become *Se tornó muy amargo.* He became very bitter.

torneo tournament.

tornillo screw *Necesitamos un clavo, no un tornillo.* We need a nail, not a screw.

○ **faltarle a uno un tornillo** to have a screw loose *A ese muchacho le falta algún tornillo.* That boy has a screw loose.

toro bull.

torpe slow; stupid.

torre [*f*] tower.

torta cake.

tortilla omelet; [*Mex*] pancake.

tortuga turtle.

tos [*f*] cough.

tosco rough *Es un trabajo muy tosco.* It's a very rough job. ▲ coarse. uncouth *Es un hombre tosco.* He's a coarse fellow.

toser to cough.

tostada toast *En el desayuno tomo café con tostadas.* I have coffee and toast for breakfast.

tostado tanned (by the sun).

tostar [*rad-ch I*] to toast.

tostón [*m*] tostón (coin for half a peso) [*Mex*].

total [*adj; m*] total *¿Cuál es el total de la suma?* What's the total amount?

○ **en total** in a word, in short *En total, lo que pasó fué esto.* In a word, what happened was this: ○ **total que** the upshot of it was that *Total que no podía verla.* The upshot of it all was that I didn't get to see her.

trabajador industrious *Era honrado y trabajador.* He was honest and industrious. ▲ [*n*] worker *Han aumentado el número de trabajadores.* They've increased the number of workers.

trabajar to work *Trabaja en una compañía de transportes.* He works with a transport company. ▲ to work, strive *Ha trabajado mucho para conseguir lo que quería.* He's worked hard to get what he wanted. ▲ to till *Están trabajando la tierra.* They're tilling the land.

trabajo work *El trabajo está muy bien hecho.* The work is very well done.

▲ labor *Van a cambiar la ley del trabajo.* They're going to change the labor laws.

○ **costar mucho trabajo** to be difficult, hard *Me costó mucho trabajo arreglar el asunto.* It was quite a job for me to get the matter straightened out. ○ **pasar trabajos** to experience hardships, have a hard time *Está pasando muchos trabajos.* He's having a hard time. ○ **trabajos forzados** hard labor (penal).

trabar ○ **trabar amistad** to strike up a friendship *Trabaron amistad en un viaje.* They struck up a friendship on a trip. ○ **trabarse la lengua** to stammer *Se le traba la lengua cuando habla ligero.* When he speaks fast he stammers.

tradición [*f*] tradition.

tradicional traditional.

traducción [*f*] translation.

traducir [-*zc*-] to translate *¿Quién tradujo esto?* Who translated this?

traer [*irr*] to bring *He traído una carta para Ud.* I brought a letter for you. ▲ to wear *Ella traía un lindo abrigo.* She wore a lovely coat. ▲ to bring, serve *Espere que traigan el café.* Wait until they serve the coffee. ▲ to carry, have *El periódico hoy trae un artículo sobre el Señor X.* Today's paper has an article on Mr. X. ▲ to have *No traigo la pluma conmigo.* I haven't my pen with me.

○ **traer y llevar** to talk about someone, gossip *Le gusta mucho traer y llevar.* He likes to gossip.

tráfico traffic *En esta ciudad hay poco tráfico.* Traffic is very light in this city.

tragar to swallow.

tragedia tragedy.

trágico tragic.

trago swallow, drink.

○ **echar un trago** to take a drink, to have a shot.

traición [*f*] treason.

traicionar to betray.

traidor [*m*] traitor.

traje [*m*] dress *Llevaba un lindo traje.* She was wearing a pretty dress.

○ **traje de baño** bathing suit. ○ **traje de etiqueta** formal dress *Todos vestían traje de etiqueta.* They were all wearing formal dress. ○ **traje largo** evening dress *Las señoras iban de traje largo.* The ladies were in evening dress. ○ **traje sastre** tailored suit *Siempre usa traje sastre.* She always wears tailored suits.

trámite [m] business transaction.

trampa trap *Pusieron algunas trampas para los ratones.* They set several rat traps.

○ **hacer trampas** to cheat *Hace trampas cuando juega.* He cheats when he plays.

trance [m] ○ **a todo trance** at any cost *Está resuelto a hacerlo a todo trance.* He is determined to do it at any cost. ○ **en trance de** at the point of *Estaba en trance de muerte.* He was at the point of death.

tranquilidad [f] rest, peace, tranquillity.

tranquilizarse to be reassured *Me he tranquilizado con lo que Ud. me ha dicho.* What you have told me has reassured me. ▲ to calm oneself, be calmed *¡Tranquilícese!* Calm yourself!

tranquilo [adj] quiet.

transacción [f] settlement; transaction.

transcurrir to pass, elapse *Transcurrió mucho tiempo sin que le volviera a ver.* A long time passed without her seeing him again.

transeúnte [adj] transient. ▲ [n] passerby.

transferir [rad-ch II] to transfer.

transformar to transform.

transición [f] transition.

transigir to settle, compromise *¡Con eso no transijo!* I won't compromise on that! ▲ to agree *Transigieron en hablarle.* They agreed to talk to him.

tránsito passage *Se prohibe el tránsito.* No thoroughfare.

○ **de tránsito** in transit *Estaba de tránsito.* He was passing through.

transmisión [f] transmission; broadcast(ing) *La transmisión del programa de radio será a las ocho de la noche.* The program will be broadcast at eight P.M.

transmisora broadcasting station.

transmitir to transmit; to broadcast.

transparente transparent. ▲ [m] window shade.

transportar to transport, carry.

transporte [m] transport; transportation.

tranvía [m] street car.

trapero rag picker.

trapo piece of cloth. ▲ rag *Déme Ud. el trapo para limpiar la mesa.* Give me the rag to clean the table.

○ **a todo trapo** to beat the band *Estaban charlando a todo trapo.* They were talking to beat the band. ○ **poner como un trapo** to insult, skin alive.

‖ *Siempre están charlando de trapos.* They're always discussing clothes.

tras after *La policía andaba tras él.* The

police were after him. ▲ behind *Estaba tras la puerta.* It was behind the door. ○ **tras de** behind *Iba tras de ella.* He was walking behind her.

trasero [adj] rear, back *La parte trasera del automóvil.* The rear part of the automobile. ▲ [m] rear, hind part.

trasladar to transfer *La trasladaron a otro departamento.* She was transferred to another department.

○ **trasladarse** to move (change place of residence or work) *Se han trasladado a otra ciudad.* They've moved to another city.

trasnochador [m] night-owl.

trasnochar to be up all night.

traspasar to go through, pierce *El balazo le traspasó el corazón.* The bullet pierced his heart. ▲ to transfer, sell (a business) *Traspasó la tienda muy ventajosamente.* He sold the business very profitably.

traspatio back yard [Am].

trastornado (see **trastornar**) crazy, insane.

trastornar to upset, disturb *Trastornó toda la habitación.* He upset the whole room. ▲ to drive insane *El disgusto la trastornó.* The misfortune drove her insane.

tratado treaty; treatise.

tratamiento medical treatment; courteous form of address.

tratante [m] dealer (in cattle or grain) *Es un tratante en granos.* He's a grain dealer.

tratar to treat *Lo trataron con desprecio.* They treated him with contempt.—*El médico la trató por mucho tiempo.* The doctor treated her for a long time. ▲ to handle *Trate eso con cuidado.* Handle that with care.

○ **tratar de** to deal with (a subject or thing) *Vamos a tratar de ese negocio.* Let's deal with that business. ▲ to try *Trataron de resolver el problema.* They tried to solve the problem. ▲ to call *Lo trató de loco.* She called him a madman. ○ **tratarse (con)** to deal with (person), be on good *or* intimate terms (with) *No me trato con Juan.* I'm not on good terms with John.—*Juan y Pedro no se tratan.* John and Peter are not on good terms. ○ **tratarse de** to be the subject of, be a question of *Se trata de hacerlo lo mejor posible.* It's a question of doing it in the best possible way.

trato treatment *Le dieron a él muy buen trato.* They treated him very well. ▲ behavior, manners *Su trato es muy* *correcto.* His manner is very correct. ▲ pact, agreement, deal (commercial) *Hicieron un trato.* They had an understanding. ▲ close friendship *Parece que tienen mucho trato.* They seem to be very close friends.

○ **tener buen trato** to be pleasant, be nice.

través ○ **a través de** through, across *Fueron a través del bosque.* They went through the woods. ○ **de través** sidewise, out of the corner of the eye *Me miró de través.* He looked at me out of the corner of his eye.

travesía voyage.

travesura prank, antic.

traviesa railroad tie [*Sp*].

travieso mischievous, prankish.

trayecto distance, stretch, line.

traza looks, appearance.

○ **buena traza** good appearance. ○ **mala traza** evil look *Ese hombre tiene mala traza.* That man looks dangerous. ○ **tener trazas** to show signs *Esto no tiene trazas de terminarse.* This doesn't seem to be anywhere near finished. ○ **tener trazas de** to look like *Tiene trazas de mendigo.* He looks like a beggar.

trazar to draw *Trazó un croquis rápidamente.* He quickly drew a sketch. ▲ to draw up *Trazaron planes para el futuro.* They drew up plans for the future.

trazo line, stroke *Con unos trazos de lápiz hizo una caricatura.* With a few strokes of his pencil he made a caricature.

trébol [*m*] clover.

trece thirteen.

trecho space, stretch *Hay un trecho de mal camino.* There's a stretch of bad road.

○ **de trecho en trecho** at intervals *Han plantado árboles de trecho en trecho.* They have planted trees at intervals.

tregua truce, lull *Hubo una tregua en la lucha.* There was a lull in the fighting. ○ **sin tregua** without rest *Trabaja sin tregua.* He works without rest.

treinta thirty.

tremendo terrible, dreadful *Hubo un accidente tremendo.* There was a terrible accident. ▲ huge, tremendous *Ocasionó tremendos gastos.* It entailed tremendous expense.

tren [*m*] train *El tren viene atrasado.* The train is late. ▲ pomp, show *Con ese tren de vida se van a arruinar.* They'll go broke with such extravagant living.

○ **tren correo** mail train. ○ **tren de mercancías** freight train *Pasaron un tren de mercancías.* They passed a freight train. ○ **tren de viajeros** passenger train *Hay un tren de viajeros cada dos horas.* There's a (passenger) train every two hours. ○ **tren expreso** (*or* **rápido**) express train. ○ **tren mixto** freight and passenger train.

trenza braid, tress.

trepar to climb *Trepó al árbol con gran dificultad.* He climbed the tree with great difficulty.

tres three.

triángulo triangle.

tribu [*f*] tribe.

tribuna rostrum, reviewing stand *El orador subió a la tribuna.* The speaker mounted the rostrum. ▲ gallery *Desde las tribunas ovacionaron a los diputados.* The galleries cheered the delegates.

○ **la tribuna** the bar; politics (profession). ○ **tribunas** grandstand *Las tribunas estaban llenas de espectadores.* The grandstand was filled with spectators.

tribunal [*m*] court (of justice); examining board.

○ **llevar alguien a los tribunales** to sue.

tribuno orator.

trigo wheat.

trinchadora sideboard.

trinchante [*m*] carving knife.

trinchar to carve (meat).

trinchera trench; ditch; trench coat.

trineo sled; bob sled.

tripa tripe; intestines; belly.

triple triple, treble.

tripulación [*f*] crew.

triste sad. ▲ sad, sorry *Hizo un triste papel.* He cut a sorry figure. ▲ gloomy, dismal *El día está muy triste.* It's a gloomy day.

tristeza sadness, sorrow.

triunfar to triumph, succeed *Triunfaron sus proyectos.* His plans succeeded. ▲ to win *Ha triunfado en el campeonato.* He won the championship.

○ **triunfar de** to triumph over *Pudo triunfar de toda la oposición.* He was able to triumph over all opposition.

triunfo triumph, victory *El triunfo sobre el enemigo fué completo.* The victory over the enemy was complete. ▲ trump card *Echó un triunfo.* He played a trump.

○ **costar un triunfo** to be exceedingly

difficult *Nos costó un triunfo conseguirlo.* It cost us a lot of effort to get it. *or* It was no easy matter to get it.

triza small piece.
  ○ **hacer trizas** to tear to bits *Hizo trizas el papel.* He tore the paper to bits.

trompa horn; elephant's trunk.

trompeta [*f*] trumpet, bugle.▲ [*m*] bugler.

tronar [*rad-ch I*] to thunder *Ha estado tronando durante toda la noche.* It's been thundering all night long.
  ○ **por lo que pueda tronar** as a precaution *Lo llevaré por lo que pueda tronar.* I'll take it along as a precaution.

tronchado (see **tronchar**) broken.
  ○ **estar tronchado** to be all in.

tronchar to break.
  ○ **troncharse** to split one's sides with laughter [*Slang*].

troncho stalk, stem (of garden plants).

tronco trunk, stalk, stem *El tronco del árbol es muy grueso.* The tree has a large trunk. ▲ team *Un hermoso tronco de caballos tiraba del carro.* The carriage was drawn by a handsome team of horses. ▲ stock *Procede de viejo tronco.* He comes from very old stock.

trono throne.

tropa troop *Las tropas desfilaron por la calle.* The troops marched through the streets.

tropel [*m*] bustle, confusion (of people) *¿Por qué hay tanto tropel en la calle?* Why is there so much confusion in the street?
  ○ **en tropel** boisterously, in a throng *Entraron en la casa en tropel.* They entered the house boisterously. ○ **tropel de caballos** herd of horses.

tropelía excess, excessive act; outrage *Los soldados cometieron tropelías.* The troops committed many outrages.

tropezar [*rad-ch I*] to stumble *Tropezó y cayó al suelo.* He stumbled and fell.
  ○ **tropezar con** to run into, come upon *Tropecé con él en la calle.* I came upon him in the street. ○ **tropezar en** to trip over *Tropecé en el bordillo de la acera.* I tripped over the curb.

tropical tropical.

trópico tropic(al). ▲ [*m*] tropics.

tropiezo obstacle, hitch.

trotar to trot *Los caballos trotaban a través del campo.* The horses were trotting across the field. ▲ to hustle *Me he pasado la mañana trotando.* I've been on the go all morning.

trote [*m*] trot *El caballo tiene muy buen trote.* The horse has a good trot.
  ○ **al trote** in haste *Me llevaba al trote.* He kept me on the run.

trozo piece *Déme Ud. un trozo de pollo.* Give me a piece of chicken. ▲ part *Un trozo de la calle está en mal estado.* A part of the street is in bad shape. ▲ fragment *Está hecho con trozos de tela.* It's made out of odds and ends of cloth. ▲ selection, passage (of books) *Léame un trozo de ese libro.* Read me a selection from that book.
  ○ **trozo de madera** wooden block *El niño juega con trozos de madera.* The child is playing with wooden blocks. ○ **trozo musical** musical selection *Es un lindo trozo musical.* That's a beautiful piece of music.

trucha trout.

trueno thunder *Hubo truenos y relámpagos durante la tormenta.* There was thunder and lightning during the storm.
  ○ **trueno gordo** big scandal *Esa noticia será un trueno gordo.* That news will create a big scandal.

trusa bathing suit [*Antilles*].

tu *pl* **tus** [*adj; Fam*] your *Aquí tienes tus guantes y tu bastón.* Here are your gloves and your cane.

tú [*pron; Fam*] you *María, tú irás conmigo.* Mary, you'll go with me.
  ○ **tratar de tú** to use *tú* in addressing, be on intimate terms with *¿Le trata Ud. de tú?* Are you on intimate terms with him?

tubo tube, pipe.

tuerca nut (hardware)

tuerto one-eyed.

tumba tomb.

tumbar to knock down *Lo tumbó al primer golpe.* He knocked him down with the first punch.
  ○ **tumbarse** to tumble *Se tumbó en la cama.* He tumbled into bed.

tumbo tumble, somersault *Andaba dando tumbos.* He was turning somersaults.

tumor [*m*] tumor.

tumulto mob, noisy crowd.

tuna prickly pear [*Am*].

tunante [*m*] rake, rascal, rogue *¡Es un tunante!* He's a rascal!

túnel [*m*] tunnel.

tupido (see **tupir**) thick; close-woven; stopped up, clogged.

tupir to pack tight *Se me han tupido las narices.* My nose is stopped up.

turba crowd, mob.

turbación [*f*] confusion.

turbar to disturb, upset; to confuse.

turbio muddy *Esta agua está turbia.* This water is muddy. ▲blurred, indistinct *Veo todo turbio.* I see everything blurred.

turista [*m, f*] tourist.

turno turn *Espere que le llegue su turno.* Wait your turn.
○ **de turno** on duty *Estaba de turno aquella noche.* He was on duty that night.

turquesa turquoise.

turrón [*m*] nougat.

tutear to use the familiar *tú* in addressing a person.

tutor, tutora tutor.

tuyo yours, of yours [*Fam*] *¿Es tuyo esto?* Is this yours?—*Creía que eran amigas tuyas.* He thought they were friends of yours.

U

u (for *o*, before *o* or *ho*) or *Elija uno u otro.* Choose one or the other.

último last *¿Quién es el último?* Who's last? ▲final *Fué su última decisión.* It was his final decision. ▲latest *Las últimas noticias son muy buenas.* The latest news is very good.
○ **a la última moda** in the latest style *Va a la última moda.* She dresses in the latest style. ○ **a la última hora** at the last minute. ○ **a últimos de** at the end of *Vendrá a últimos de septiembre.* He'll come at the end of September. ○ **estar a la última** (*or* **a la cuarta**) **pregunta** to be flat-broke *El pobre muchacho está a la última pregunta.* The poor boy's flat-broke. ○ **por última vez** for the last time *Por última vez ¿viene Ud.?* For the last time, are you coming? ○ **por último** finally.

un (see **uno**) a, an; one.

unánime unanimous.

undécimo eleventh.

ungüento ointment.

único only, only one *Es el único que puede arreglar este asunto.* He's the only one who can arrange this matter.—*Es hijo único.* He's an only son.

unidad [*f*] unity *Trabajemos todos por la unidad.* Let's all work for unity. ▲figure *A esa unidad agréguele dos ceros.* Add two zeros to that figure. ▲unit *¿Cuál es la unidad monetaria de su país?* What's the monetary unit of your country?

unión [*f*] union *La unión de esos dos países es probable.* The union of those two countries is likely. ▲union, marriage *Anoche se celebró la unión de Juan y María.* The marriage of John and Mary took place last night. ▲unity *La unión hace la fuerza.* In unity there is strength. ▲joining, joint *La unión de esas tablas está mal hecha.* Those boards are badly joined.

unir to tie together *Una Ud. esas dos cuerdas.* Tie those two strings together. ▲to attach *Una Ud. esa carta al informe.* Attach that letter to the report.
○ **unirse** to unite, join *No quería unirse con nadie en aquel negocio.* He didn't want to be united with anybody in that business. ▲to join *Se unió a los obreros.* He joined the workers.

universal universal.

universidad [*f*] university.

universo universe, world.

uno a, an *Necesito un experto para este trabajo.* I need an expert for this work. ▲one *Sólo uno ha llegado.* Only one has arrived.
○ **cada uno** each one *Pagó a cada uno lo que le debía.* He paid each one what he owed him. ○ **de una a otra parte** from one place to another; from side to side. ○ **uno a uno, uno por uno** one by one *Salgan uno a uno.* Go out one by one. ○ **uno que otro** occasional(ly) *Uno que otro día viene a vernos.* He comes to see us occasionally. ○ **unos a otros** each other, one another *Se miraban unos a otros.* They were looking at one another. ○ **unos cuantos** some, a few *¿Quiere Ud. darme unos cuantos?* Will you give me a few? ○ **unos, unas** some, a few *Deme unas manzanas.* Give me a few apples. ○ **un ... sí y otro no** every other ... *Viene un día sí y otro no.* He comes every other day.

untar to spread *Unte mantequilla a las tostadas.* Spread some butter on the toast. ▲to bribe *Le untaron para que no declarara la verdad.* They bribed him so that he wouldn't tell the truth.
○ **untar con grasa** to grease *Untó la rueda con grasa.* He greased the wheel. ○ **untarse** to grease, smear *Le gustaba untarse la cara con crema.* She liked to use cream on her face.

uña nail, fingernail, toenail *Se rompió la uña.* She broke her fingernail. ▲ claw *El gato sacó las uñas.* The cat showed its claws.

○ **ser uña y carne** to be fast friends.

urbanidad [*f*] (good) manners.

urbano urban.

urgencia urgency, hurry *Lo necesitan con urgencia.* They need it in a hurry.

○ **clínica de urgencia** emergency ward. ○ **cura de urgencia** emergency treatment. ○ **sello de urgencia** special-delivery stamp.

urgente pressing, urgent.

usado (see *usar*) used, second-hand *Quiero comprar un carro usado.* I want to buy a used car.

usanza usage, custom.

usar to use *¿Puedo usar su pluma?* May I use your pen? ▲ to wear *¿Qué número de zapatos usa Ud.?* What size shoe do you wear?

○ **antes de usarse** before using *Agítese antes de usarse.* Shake well before using. ○ **usarse** to be in use *or* fashion *Este año se usa mucho ese color.* This year that color's very fashionable.

uso use *¿Qué uso tiene esta máquina?* What use has this machine?

○ **en buen uso** in good condition *Ese abrigo está todavía en buen uso.* That overcoat's still in good condition.

‖ *Empezó a trabajar apenas tuvo uso de razón.* He began to work when he was very young.

usted (*abbr* **Ud., Vd.**) you *¿Cómo está Ud.?* How are you?

usual usual, customary *Lo usual en estos casos es el traje de smoking.* The tuxedo's customary for such occasions.

útil profitable *El juego es útil y agradable.* The game's both pleasant and profitable. ▲ useful *Era un hombre muy útil.* He was a very useful man.

○ **útiles (de trabajo)** tools, utensils.

utilidad [*f*] usefulness, utility *¿Tiene esto alguna utilidad?* Has this any usefulness?

utilizar to utilize.

uva grape.

V

vaca cow. ▲ beef *Estos filetes ¿son de vaca o de ternera?* Are these steaks beef or veal?

vacación [*f*] vacation.

vacante [*adj*] vacant. ▲ [*f*] vacancy.

vaciar to empty; to drain.

vacilar to reel, stagger *Vacilaba mucho al andar.* He staggered badly when he walked. ▲ to waver, hesitate *¡No vacile Ud.!* Don't hesitate!

vacío void, empty *El granero estaba vacío.* The granary was empty. ▲ unoccupied, vacant *A fin de mes quedará el cuarto vacío.* At the end of the month the room'll be vacant. ▲ vacuous, stupid, empty *Era un hombre vacío.* He was a stupid fellow. ▲ [*m*] empty space, space, vacuum *Se lanzó al vacío.* He jumped into space.

vacuna vaccine.

vadear to wade through, ford.

vado ford.

vagabundo, vagabunda tramp, bum.

vagar to rove, wander.

vago vague, hazy *Tengo una vaga idea.* I have a vague idea. ▲ [*m*] loafer, tramp *No le gusta trabajar, es un vago.* He doesn't like to work; he's a loafer.

vagón [*m*] railway car.

○ **vagón de carga** freight car.

vagoneta dump cart.

vaina nuisance, bother. ▲ scabbard, sheath; pod (of vegetables).

vainilla vanilla.

vaivén [*m*] fluctuation; vibration.

vajilla set of dishes; chinaware.

vale [*m*] note, I.O.U.; sales slip; coupon.

valentía courage.

valer [*irr*] to cost *¿Cuánto vale ese traje?* How much is that dress? ▲ to cause, result in *Aquella tontería le valió muchos disgustos.* That foolishness caused him a lot of trouble. ▲ to be of value *Puede Ud. tirar esos papeles, no valen nada.* You can throw those papers away, they're worthless. ▲ to be worth, be worthy *Ese hombre vale mucho.* That man's very worthy. ▲ [*m*] worth, merit *Es un hombre de mucho valer.* He's a man of great merit.

○ **más valiera** it'd be better *Más me valiera no haberle conocido.* It'd be better for me never to have known him. ○ **no poder valerse** to be helpless *Con las manos heridas no podía valerse.* With his injured hands he was helpless. ○ **valer(le a uno) la pena** to be worth (one's) while *No (me) vale la pena ir.* It's not worth (my) while to go. ○ **valerse de** to make use of, avail

oneself of *Se valió de muchos medios.*
He availed himself of every means at
his disposal.

valiente valiant, brave, courageous.

valija valise, suitcase; briefcase.

valioso [*adj*] valuable.

valla wooden fence.

valle [*m*] valley.

valor [*m*] price *Lo he comprado por la
mitad de su valor.* I bought it at half
price. ▲ value *El valor del dólar equivale a cinco pesos en México.* The dollar's worth five Mexican pesos. ▲ import, importance, meaning *¿ Qué valor
le da Ud. a esas palabras?* What importance do you attach to those words?
▲ courage, gallantry *El soldado demostró mucho valor.* The soldier showed
great courage. ▲ nerve, crust *¿Cómo
tiene Ud. valor para presentarse aquí?*
How do you have the nerve to appear
here?
O **valores** stocks, bonds, securities.

vanidad [*f*] vanity.

vanidoso vain.

vano vain, shallow.
O **en vano** in vain.

vapor [*m*] steam; steamship.
O **al vapor** swiftly, at lightning speed.

vaquero cowboy, cowhand.

vara twig, switch; vara (measure; about
a yard); yardstick.

varar to run aground *La embarcación
varó frente a la costa.* The vessel ran
aground off the coast.
‖ *Se ha varado completamente.* He's
down and out [*Col*].

variable changeable, variable, unstable.

variación [*f*] variation, change.

variedad [*f*] variety, diversity.
O **variedades** vaudeville show.

vario various, varied *Tenía telas de varios
precios.* He had fabrics at various
prices. ▲ several *Hay varios libros en
la mesa.* There are several books on
the table.

varón [*m*] male (of humans).

varonil virile, manly.

vaselina vaseline.

vasija container, receptacle (for liquids).

vaso (drinking) glass.

vasto vast, huge, immense.

¡**vaya un(a) ... !** what a(n) ... ! ¡*Vaya
una idea!* What an idea!

vecindad [*f*] tenants *¿Tiene esta casa
mucha vecindad?* Are there many tenants in this house? ▲ vicinity, neighborhood *Viven en la vecindad.* They
live in the vicinity.

vecindario population of a district, ward,
etc.

vecino neighboring, near-by *Traen las
provisiones del pueblo vecino.* They
bring provisions from the town near-by.
▲ [*n*] neighbor. ▲ tenant *Aquella casa
tenía cincuenta vecinos.* There were
fifty tenants in that house.

vegetación [*f*] vegetation.

vegetal [*adj; m*] vegetable.
O **el reino vegetal** the vegetable
kingdom.

vehemencia vehemence.

veinte twenty.

vejez [*f*] old age.

vela vigil *Le vela duró hasta la madrugada.* The vigil lasted till daybreak.
▲ candle *Encienda Ud. esa vela.* Light
that candle. ▲ sail *Tenía varios barcos
de vela.* He had several sailing ships.
O **a toda vela** under full sail; at full
speed. O **en vela** awake *Pasó la noche
en vela.* He was awake all night.

velada evening party *or* gathering.

velar to stay up, keep watch *Estuvo toda
la noche velando el enfermo.* He kept
watch all night over the sick man. ▲ to
stay awake *Veló toda la noche.* He
stayed awake all night.
O **velar por** to take care of, protect
Vela muy bien por su familia. He
takes very good care of his family.

velo veil; film (thin coat).
O **correr un velo** to drop the matter,
forget about it *Corramos un velo.* Let's
drop it.

velocidad [*f*] velocity, speed.

veloz swift, fast.

vena vein.
O **estar de vena** to be in the mood.

venado deer.

vencer to defeat, vanquish *Vencieron al
enemigo.* They defeated the enemy.
▲ to overcome *No creo que venza esa
pasión.* I don't think he'll overcome
that habit. ▲ to win *Venció nuestro
equipo por dos tantos.* Our team won
by two points. ▲ to prevail *Su opinión
fué la que venció.* It was his opinion
that prevailed. ▲ to become due *La
letra venció ayer.* The bill of exchange
was due yesterday.
O **vencerse** to control (one's feelings).

venda bandage, surgical dressing; roll of
bandage.

vendaje [*m*] bandage, surgical dressing;
bandaging.

vendar to bandage, dress.

vendedor [*m*] vendor, seller, trader.

vender to sell *Vendió todas sus propieda-
des.* He sold all his property.
O **vender a crédito** to sell on credit.
O **vender al contado** to sell for cash.

○ **vender a plazos** to sell on installments ○ **vender(se)** to give oneself away, betray *Su emoción le vendió.* His emotion betrayed him.—*Al hablar sé vendió.* When he spoke he gave himself away. ▲ to accept a bribe, sell out *Le fusilaron por haberse vendido al enemigo.* They shot him for having sold out to the enemy.

veneno poison, venom.

venenoso [*adj*] poisonous, venomous.

venganza revenge, vengeance.

vengar to avenge.

○ **vengarse** to take revenge.

venir [*irr*] to come. *Viene de muy buena familia.* He comes of a very good family. ▲ to fit *Eso le viene muy ancho.* That's too big for her. ▲ to occur *No sé como me vino esa idea.* I don't know how that idea occurred to me.

○ **que viene** next *Le veré la semana que viene.* I'll see you next week. ○ **venir a** (followed by infinitive) to get to, end by *Vino a ser presidente.* He got to be president. ○ **venir a menos** to decline, be in reduced circumstances *Con la muerte del padre esa familia vino a menos.* As a result of the death of the father, that family's in reduced circumstances. ○ **venir a parar** to turn out, terminate *¿En qué vino a parar ese asunto?* How did that matter turn out? ○ **venir a pelo** to be to the point *Lo que dijo no venía a pelo.* What he said wasn't to the point. ○ **venir a ser** to amount to *Eso viene a ser lo mismo.* That amounts to the same thing. ○ **venir a tener** probably have, must have *Viene a tener unos cuatro mil pesos de renta al año.* He must have an income of about four thousand pesos a year. ○ **venir bien** to suit *Me vendrá muy bien una temporada en el campo.* A stay in the country will suit me fine. ○ **venir mal** not to suit, be inconvenient for *Me viene mal ir a esa hora.* It isn't convenient for me to go at that hour. ○ **venirse abajo, venirse a tierra** to fall (through), collapse *Todo aquello se vino a tierra.* The whole thing fell through.

venta sale *Hicimos un contrato de venta.* We made a contract of sale. ▲ sales, selling *Toda la venta se hacía al por mayor.* All the sales were wholesale.

○ **estar a la venta** to be on sale.

ventaja advantage, profit; headway, lead.

○ **llevar ventaja** to be ahead, have a lead.

ventajoso advantageous.

ventana window.

○ **echar la casa por la ventana** to put oneself out, go to a lot of expense. ○ **ventanas de la nariz** nostrils.

ventanilla ticket window; window (of a vehicle).

ventilación [*f*] ventilation.

ventilador [*m*] electric fan; ventilator.

ventilar to air, ventilate *Hay que ventilar esta habitación.* This room must be aired. ▲ to settle *¿Cuándo ventila esta cuenta con el Banco?* When are you going to settle this account with the bank?

ventoso windy.

ventura happiness; happy event. ▲ luck *Tuve la ventura de encontrarlo.* I had the luck to find him.

ver [*irr*] to see *¿Ve Ud. bien con esas gafas?* Can you see well with those glasses? ▲ to look at [*Am*] *No me vea Ud. de esa manera.* Don't look at me that way.

○ **no poder ver** to abhor, detest *No me hables de él, no le puedo ver.* Don't mention his name, I detest him. ○ **no tener que ver con** to have nothing to do with *No tengo nada que ver con él.* I have nothing to do with him. ○ **ver el cielo abierto** to see a great opportunity. ○ **ver las estrellas** to see stars (experience a sudden pain). ○ **verse** to meet, see each other *Hace mucho tiempo que no se ven.* It's been a long time since they saw each other. ▲ to find oneself, be *Me ví en una mala situación.* I found myself in a tough spot.—*Me veo obligado a hacerlo.* I'm forced (*or* I find myself obliged) to do it. ○ **ver visiones** to see things *¡Está Ud. viendo visiones!* You're seeing things!

‖ *¡Allá* (or *Ya) veremos!* Time'll tell! ‖ *¡A ver!* Let's see! ‖ *Hasta más ver.* See you again.

veranear to summer, spend the summer *¿Dónde veranea Ud.?* Where are you spending the summer?

veraneo (summer) vacation, summering *Fuimos de veraneo a la playa.* We spent the summer at the beach.

verano summer.

veras [*f pl*] reality, truth.

○ **de veras** in truth, really, honestly *¡Ahora va de veras!* Now he's really going!—*Se lo digo de veras.* I'm telling you honestly.

verdad [*f*] truth *Le ha dicho la verdad.* He's told you the truth.

○ **a decir verdad** to tell the truth

A decir verdad, yo no creo eso. To tell the truth, I don't believe that. ○ **decir cuatro verdades** to speak one's mind, tell someone a thing or two. ○ **de verdad** really *¿De verdad lo cree Ud.?* Do you really believe it? ○ **ser verdad** to be true *Era verdad lo que decía.* What he said was true. ○**¿verdad (que)?** isn't that so? isn't it true? isn't it? *Es Ud. americano ¿verdad?* Isn't it true that you're an American?—*¿Verdad que no estaba allí?* Isn't it true that he wasn't there? ‖ *¿No es verdad?* or *¿Verdad?* Isn't it so?

verdadero true, staunch *Es un amigo verdadero.* He's a staunch·friend. ▲ **real** *No usaba su nombre verdadero.* He didn't use his real name.

verde [*adj*] green. ▲green, unripe *La fruta estaba demasiado verde.* The fruit was too green. ▲ risqué, off-color *Ese libro es muy verde.* That book's very off-color.

verdor [*m*] greenness, green.

verdura vegetation; leafy vegetables.

vereda path; [*Arg*] sidewalk.

vergonzoso shameful; shy, bashful.

vergüenza shame; shyness, bashfulness. ○ **darle a uno vergüenza** to be ashamed *No me atrevo a decírselo, me da vergüenza.* I don't dare tell him, I'm ashamed. ▲to be (too) bashful *Le da vergüenza declararse.* He's too bashful to propose. ○ **no tener vergüenza** to be shameless *Ese hombre no tiene vergüenza.* That man's shameless. ○ **no tener vergüenza de** not to be too bashful to, not to be ashamed to *Ese niño no tiene vergüenza de cantar delante de la gente.* That boy's not ashamed to sing before people. ○ **tener vergüenza** to be shy *Ese niño tiene mucha vergüenza.* That child's very shy. ▲to be honorable *or* honest *Es un político que tiene vergüenza.* He's an honest politician. ‖ *¡Qué vergüenza!* How shameful!

verso line of poetry; poem.

verter [*rad-ch I*] to spill *Ha vertido el vino.* He's spilled the wine. ▲ to empty *Vierta Ud. esa jarra.* Empty that jug. ▲to translate *Han vertido ese libro al inglés.* They've translated that book into English.

vertiente [*f*] slope; watershed; basin (of a river).

vértigo dizziness.

vestíbulo vestibule; lobby.

vestido (see **vestir**) dressed *Iba muy bien vestido.* He was very well dressed.

▲ [*m*] dress *¿Qué vestido llevo a la comida?* What dress shall I wear to the dinner? ▲garments, clothing.

vestir [*rad-ch III*] to dress. ▲to wear *Vestía uniforme militar.* He was wearing a military uniform. ▲to be fashionable, be dressy *Ese traje viste mucho.* That dress is very fashionable. —*Ese traje viste demasiado.* That outfit's too dressy.

○ **vestirse** to dress *¿Quién le ayuda a Ud. a vestirse?* Who helps you dress? ▲to clothe oneself; to buy clothes *Antes, yo me vestía en Paris.* I used to buy my clothes in Paris.

veterano old, seasoned (of soldiers). ▲ [*m*] veteran; old hand, old-timer.

vez [*f*] turn (in line) *Le llegó a Ud. la vez de entrar.* It was your turn to go in. ▲time *La primera vez que vine a los Estados Unidos fué en 1938.* The first time I came to the United States was in 1938.

○ **a la vez** at once, simultaneously *Todos querían hablar a la vez.* Everybody wanted to talk at once. ○ **alguna que otra vez** occasionally *Le veía alguna que otra vez.* I used to see him occasionally. ○ **alguna vez, algunas veces** sometimes *Algunas veces voy a comer al restaurante.* Sometimes I eat at the restaurant. ○ **a veces** occasionally *A veces le veo en casa de sus amigos.* Occasionally I see him at the home of friends. ○ **cada vez** each time *¡Que lo haga otra persona cada vez!* Let a different person do it each time! ○ **cada vez que** whenever, every time *Cada vez que le encuentro se lo digo.* Whenever I see him I tell him so. ○ **cuantas veces** whenever, every time *Cuantas veces lo veo me habla.* Whenever I see him, he speaks to me. ○ **¿cuántas veces?** how many times? how often? ○ **de una vez** immediately, without delay, right now *¡Hágalo de una vez!* Do it right now! ▲in (*or* at) a gulp *Se lo comió de una vez.* He ate it in a gulp. ○ **de una vez para siempre** once and for all *De una vez para siempre se lo prohibo.* Once and for all I forbid it. ○ **de vez en cuando** once in a while, from time to time *De vez en cuando iba a verla.* I went to see her once in a while. ○ **dos veces** twice. ○ **en vez de** instead of *Voy a tomar pescado en vez de carne.* I'm going to have fish instead of meat. ○ **otra vez** again *¿Por qué ha hecho Ud. eso otra vez?* Why did you do that again? ▲some other time *Otra vez* *almorzaremos juntos.* We'll have lunch together some other time. O **tal vez** perhaps *Tal vez mañana podamos vernos.* Perhaps we can meet tomorrow. O **todas las veces que** whenever, every time *Todas las veces que le veo me pregunta por Ud.* Whenever I see him he asks about you. O **una vez** once *Me invitó a comer una vez.* He invited me to dinner once.—*Había* (or *Era*) *una vez.* . . . Once upon a time there was. . . .

vía track *¿Por qué vía viene el expreso?* Which track does the express train come in on? ▲ route *La vía marítima es algo peligrosa.* The sea route's somewhat dangerous. ▲ via, by way of *Llegamos a Nueva York vía Miami.* We arrived in New York via Miami. ▲method, procedure *Se hizo por la vía ejecutiva.* It was done through executive channels. O **vía pública** thoroughfare, street.

viajar to travel.

viaje [m] trip, travel *¿Cuándo sale Ud. de viaje?* When do you start on your trip?—*Hizo un relato de sus viajes.* He gave an account of his travels. ‖ *¡Buen viaje!* Bon voyage! or Have a good trip!

viajero, viajera traveler *El viajero estaba muy cansado.* The traveler was very tired. ▲ passenger *Se ruega a los viajeros que conserven sus billetes.* Passengers are requested to keep their tickets.

víbora viper.

vibrar to vibrate.

vicio vice. O **quejarse de vicio** to complain habitually.

vicioso licentious, given to vice.

víctima victim.

victoria victory, triumph. O **cantar victoria** to celebrate victory; to crow too soon.

victorioso victorious, triumphant.

vid [f] grapevine.

vida life, human life *Aquel descubrimiento salvó muchas vidas.* That discovery saved many lives. ▲ life, liveliness *El niño tiene mucha vida.* The child's full of life. ▲ life, way of living *Llevaba muy buena vida.* He lived a very good life. ▲ life (being alive) *Estuvo entre la vida y la muerte.* He hovered between life and death. ▲ life, history *Sabe la vida y milagros de todo el mundo.* He knows everybody's life story. O **en mi vida** never in my life *En mi*

vida le he visto. I've never seen him before in my life. O **ganarse la vida** to make (*or* earn) a living *Se gana la vida escribiendo.* He earns his living by writing. O **vida de perros** dog's life.

vidriera glass door, window, *or* partition; show case; show window [*Am*].

vidriero glazier, dealer in glass.

vidrio glass (material); pane of glass. O **pagar los vidrios rotos** to be made the scapegoat.

viejo old *Aquella casa era muy vieja.* That was a very old house. ▲ [m] old man [*Am*] *El viejo caminaba con dificultad.* The old man walked with difficulty. ▲old man, pal [*Am*] *¡Oyeme viejo!* Listen to me, old man! O **los viejos** parents (affectionate) [*Am*] *Tengo que escribirles a los viejos.* I have to write to my parents. O **mi vieja** my old lady (affectionate) [*Am*]. O **mi viejo** my old man (affectionate) [*Am*]. O **viejo verde** old goat *Era un viejo verde.* He was an old goat.

viento wind. O **contra viento y marea** come hell and high water. O **con viento contrario** against the wind. O **ir viento en popa** to go very well *Sus negocios van viento en popa.* His business is going very well.

vientre [m] belly.

viernes [m sg] Friday. O **Viernes Santo** Good Friday.

viga beam (of a building).

vigilancia vigilance, watchfulness.

vigilante watchful. ▲ [m] watchman; [*Arg*] policeman.

vigilar to watch, keep watch, guard, watch over.

vigilia fast, abstaining from food for religious reasons; wakefulness. O **comer de vigilia** to fast (abstain from meat).

vigor [m] vigor, strength *Era un hombre de mucho vigor.* He was a man of great strength. O **en vigor** in effect, in force. O **leyes en vigor** laws in force.

vil vile, mean, despicable.

villa town *Toda la villa estaba alegre en la fiesta.* The whole town was gay at the festival. ▲ villa, country house *En el campo tengo una villa.* I have a villa in the country.

vinagre [m] vinegar. O **cara de vinagre** sour-puss.

vindicar to vindicate.

vino wine.

○ **vino tinto** red wine.

viña vineyard.

violencia violence, strength.

violento impulsive; violent *Tiene un carácter muy violento.* He's very impulsive. ▲ strong *No diga Ud. esas frasas tan violentas.* Don't use such strong language.

○ **sentirse violento** to be embarrassed, feel out of place.

violeta violet; lilac (color).

violín [*m*] violin.

violón [*m*] bass viol.

○ **tocar el violón** to talk through one's hat.

virgen [*adj; f*] virgin.

virtud [*f*] virtue, good quality; efficacy, power.

virtuoso virtuous. ▲ [*n*] virtuoso.

viruela smallpox.

visera eyeshade, visor.

visible [*adj*] visible.

visillo window curtain.

visión [*f*] vision *Tuvo una visión.* He had a vision. ▲ view, opinion *Su visión del problema me parece justa.* His view of the problem seems correct to me. ▲ sight, peculiar looking person *Con aquel traje y aquel sombrero estaba hecha una visión.* With that dress and hat she was a sight.

○ **ver visiones** to be seeing things, be deluded.

visita visit *¿Recibió Ud. la visita de mi amigo?* Did my friend call on you? ▲ visitor, caller *Con tantas visitas no hemos podido hacer nada.* There were so many callers we haven't been able to accomplish anything.

○ **hacer una visita** to pay a call. ○ **pagar la visita** to return the call. ○ **tener visita** to have company *No puede recibirle, tiene visita.* She can't see you, she has company.

visitar to visit, call on *¿Cuándo podré visitarle?* When may I call on you? ▲ to visit, to make a professional visit, make a call *El doctor está visitando a sus enfermos.* The doctor is making his calls. ▲ to inspect *El inspector y los arquitectos han salido a visitar las obras.* The inspector and the architects have gone to inspect the constructions.

víspera eve, day before *Hoy es la víspera de la fiesta.* This is the eve of the holiday.

○ **estar en vísperas de** to be on the eve of, be about to *Estaba en vísperas*

de embarcar para Europa. He was about to sail for Europe.

vista eyesight, vision *Tiene muy buena vista.* He has very good eyesight. ▲ sight *¡No te pongas delante de mi vista!* Get out of my sight! ▲ view, vista *La vista desde la terraza era preciosa.* There was an attractive view from the terrace.

○ **corto de vista** near-sighted *Es muy corto de vista.* He's very near-sighted. ○ **de vista** by sight, without introduction *No me han presentado, lo conozco sólo de vista.* I haven't been introduced to him; I know him only by sight. ○ **echar la vista encima** to lay eyes on (upon). ○ **en vista de** in view of *En vista de esto, yo no puedo comer con Ud. hoy.* In view of this, I cannot eat with you today. ○ **hacer la vista gorda** to wink (at), to overlook. ○ **tener la vista cansada** to have tired eyes; to be far-sighted. ○ **tener vistas a** to face *La casa tiene vistas a la calle.* The house faces the street. ○ **vista cansada** far-sightedness.

‖ *¡Hasta la vista!* So long!

visto (see **ver**) seen.

○ **estar mal visto** to be improper, be disapproved, be bad form *No haga Ud. eso, equí está mal visto.* Don't do that; it's considered bad form here. ○ **estar visto** to be evident, obvious, clear *Está visto que Juan no viene.* It's evident that John isn't coming. ○ **no estar bien visto** to be improper, frowned upon *Eso no está muy bien visto.* That isn't done. ○ **por lo visto** apparently *Por lo visto no se acordó de que tenía que venir.* Apparently he forgot that he was supposed to come. ○ **visto bueno** (abbr **Vo Bo**) approved, O.K. ▲ approval, O.K. *Tiene que llevar el visto bueno del jefe.* He has to have the chief's O.K.

vistoso showy, loud.

vital vital, essential.

vitrina show window [*Am*]; show case [*Sp*].

viuda widow.

viudo widower.

víveres [*m pl*] provisions.

viveza quickness, liveliness *Tiene mucha viveza de ingenio.* He has a quick mind. ▲ vehemence, spirit *Al oírlo contestó con viveza.* When she heard it she replied with spirit.

vivienda dwelling, house.

vivir to live, exist *No sé si vive o ha muerto.* I don't know whether he's

living or dead. ▲ to live, to dwell *Yo
vivo en América.* I live in America.
○ **vivir de** to live on *Vivía de sus
rentas.* He lived on his investments.
‖ *¿Quién vive?* Who's there [*Mil*]?
‖ *¡Viva!* Hurray! ‖ *¡Viva la República!* Long live the Republic!
vivo alive *Por fortuna estoy vivo.* Fortunately I'm alive. ▲ vivid *Los colores
eran muy vivos.* The colors were very
vivid. ▲ intense *La luz a esa altura es
muy viva.* The light at that altitude is
very intense. ▲ acute, quick, keen
Tiene una inteligencia muy viva. He
has a very keen mind. ▲ [*m*] edging,
piping *Llevaba un traje con vivos
verdes.* She was wearing a suit with
green piping. ▲ wise guy *No me gusta
porque es un vivo.* I don't like him because he's a wise guy.
○ **a lo vivo** vividly *Se lo pintó a lo
vivo.* He described it to her vividly.
○ **de viva voz** by word of mouth *Lo
aprendió de viva voz.* He learned it
by word of mouth. ○ **en carne viva**
raw, open (wound) *Tenía la rodilla en
carne viva.* His knee was raw. ○ **tocar
en lo vivo** to cut to the quick.
vocabulario vocabulary.
vocación [*f*] vocation (activity or profession for which one feels an inner calling) *Soy médico pero mi verdadera vocación era la pintura.* I'm a doctor, but
I've always wanted to be a painter.
volado See **volar.**
○ **hacer un volado** to do something
pressing *or* urgent [*Am*] *Tengo que
hacer un volado.* I have something
urgent to do. ○ **volado de genio** quick-
tempered [*Am*].
volante [*m*] steering wheel (of vehicle);
flywheel.
○ **tomar el volante** to take the wheel.
volar [*rad-ch I*] to fly *El avión vuela alto.*
The plane's flying high. ▲ to vanish,
disappear *Mi dinero voló.* My money
vanished. ▲ to blow up *Volaron los
puentes con dinamita.* They blew up
the bridges with dynamite.
○ **volando** quickly, on the run, as fast
as possible *Fué volando.* He went on
the run.
volcán [*m*] volcano.
volcar [*rad-ch I*] to overturn, turn over
*El automóvil volcó al entrar en el
puente.* The car turned over when it
entered the bridge.
voltear to turn (over), whirl *Volteaba en
el trapecio.* He was whirling on the
trapeze.
○ **voltearse** to change party or creed

Se volteó a otro partido. He changed
sides.
volumen [*m*] bulk, volume; volume
(book).
voluntad [*f*] will *Tiene una voluntad de
hierro.* He has a will of iron.
○ **buena voluntad** kindliness, good
will.
voluntario voluntary. ▲ [*m*] volunteer.
voluptuoso voluptuous.
volver [*irr*] to turn (over) *Volvía las
páginas del libro rápidamente.* He was
turning the pages of the book quickly.
▲ to turn *Este camino vuelve a la derecha.* This road turns to the right.
▲ to return, go back *Volvió a su casa
por el mismo camino.* He went back
home by the same route. ▲ to return,
to pay back, to give *or* send back
Vuelva Ud. favor por favor. Return
favor for favor.
○ **volver a** to . . . again *No ha vuelto
a escribirme.* He hasn't written me
again. ○ **volver del revés** to turn upside down; to turn inside out. ○ **volver
en sí** to recover consciousness, come to.
○ **volver la cabeza** to turn one's head
Al oír su nombre volvió la cabeza.
She turned her head when she heard
her name. ○ **volver loco** to drive crazy,
irritate *Me vas a volver loco.* You're
driving me crazy. ○ **volverse** to turn
Se le ha vuelto el pelo muy blanco. His
hair has turned snow-white. ▲ to turn
over *¡Haga el favor de volverse del
lado contrario!* Please turn over on
the other side. ○ **volverse atrás** to
flinch. ▲ to back out *Dijo que vendría,
pero se ha vuelto atrás.* He said he
would come, but he has backed out.
○ **volverse loco** to become crazy, become insane *Se ha vuelto loco.* He's
gone crazy.
vomitar to vomit.
vómito vomiting, vomit.
voraz ravenous *Tenía hambre voraz.* He
was ravenously hungry. ▲ fierce *Un
voraz incendio arrasó el edificio.* A
fierce fire demolished the building.
vos you [*Fam; Am*].
votación [*f*] voting, balloting.
voto vote, ballot; vow.
○ **hacer voto** to make a vow.
voz [*f*] voice.
○ **a media voz** softly *Estaban hablando a media voz.* They were talking
softly. ○ **a voces** (by) shouting *A
voces no consigue Ud. nada.* You won't
get anything by shouting. ○ **correr
la voz** to be rumored *Corre la voz de
que ha desaparecido.* It's rumored

that he has disappeared. ○ **dar voces** to shout, yell *¡No des esas voces!* Don't shout like that! ○ **en voz alta** aloud. ○ **en voz baja** very softly *No hable Ud. en voz tan baja, no le oigo.* Don't speak so softly, I can't hear you. ○ **secreto a voces** open secret. ○ **voz de mando** command *A la voz de mando se pusieron en marcha.* At the command they began to march.

vuelco tumble, overturning.

vuelo flight, trip *De un solo vuelo el avión atravesó el mar.* The airplane made a non-stop flight across the ocean. ▲ width, fullness *Las faldas ahora tienen poco vuelo.* Skirts are narrow this season.

○ **al vuelo** right away, quickly; in flight, on the wing.

vuelta turn, revolution. ▲ curve *¡Cuidado con esa vuelta!* Watch out for that curve! ▲ change *¿Tiene Ud. vuelta de este billete?* Do you have change for this bill?

○ **a la vuelta** upon returning *A la vuelta de mi viaje nos veremos.* We'll see each other when I get back from my trip. ○ **a la vuelta de** around *La casa está a la vuelta de la esquina.*

The house is around the corner. ○ **dar la vuelta a** to turn *Hay que dar dos vueltas a la llave.* You have to turn the key twice. ▲ to go around *Dimos la vuelta a la casa.* We walked around the house. ○ **darse vuelta** to turn around; go to and fro *Haga Ud. el favor de darse vuelta.* Please turn around. ○ **dar una vuelta** to take a stroll, turn *Vamos a dar una vuelta por el parque.* Let's take a turn through the park. ▲ to turn over *El automóvil dió una vuelta.* The car turned over. ○ **dar vueltas** to turn *La tierra da vueltas sobre su eje.* The earth turns on its axis. ▲ to hang around *Anda dando vueltas por ahí sin hacer nada.* He's hanging around here not doing anything. ○ **dar vueltas a** to turn, turn around and around *Déle vueltas a la manivela.* Turn the handle. ○ **poner de vuelta y media** to give a bawling out.

‖ *No hay que darle vueltas.* There are no two ways about it.

vuelto change (money) [*Am*] *Cuente Ud. el vuelto.* Count your change.

vulgar vulgar, coarse; common.

Y

y and.

○ **¿y bien?** all right *Y bien, ¿cuándo nos vamos?* All right, when do we go? ○ **y eso que** and yet, even though *Ud. no ha barrido mi cuarto, y eso que le dije que no dejara de hacerlo.* You haven't swept my room, even though I told you not to fail to do so. ○ **¿y luego?** and then *Y luego, ¿qué pasó?* And then what happened? ○ **¿y qué?** is it true that [*Am*] *¿Y qué se fué para Europa?* Is it true that he went to Europe?

ya already *Ya sabe Ud. lo que yo quiero.* You already know what I want. ▲ now *Ya es tarde.* It's too late now. ▲ at once, right now [*Am*] *Hágalo ya.* Do it right now.

○ **ya lo creo** of course *¿Quiere Ud. venir? ¡Ya lo creo!* Do you want to come? Of course! ○ **ya no** no longer *Ya no tengo ganas.* I no longer feel like it. ○ **ya pronto** presently, any minute now *Ya pronto llegará el tren.* The train will be here any minute now.

○ **ya que** since *Ya que me preguntas, te contestaré.* Since you ask me, I'll tell you. ○ **ya voy** I'm coming! *¡Ya voy! espere un minuto.* I'm coming! Wait a minute!

‖ *¡Ya, ya!* Sure!

yanqui Yankee, any citizen of the U.S.A.

yapa something extra, good measure [*Am*] *Me dieron esto de yapa.* They gave me this for good measure.

yegua mare.

yema bud, shoot; yolk; cushion of fingertip.

yerba herb; grass.

yerno son-in-law.

yerro error, mistake.

yeso plaster.

yeta bad luck, misfortune [*Arg*].

yo I *Soy yo.* It's me. *or* It's I.

○ **yo mismo** I myself *Yo mismo se lo dije.* I told you so myself.

yodo iodine.

yugo yoke (for animals).

yunta team of draft animals.

Z

zacate [m] grass; hay [Am].
zafarse to slip off, come off [Am] Se zafó la rueda. The wheel came off. ▲ to dislocate [Am] Se ha zafado un brazo. He dislocated his arm. ▲ to get out of, avoid No sé como zafarme de ese compromiso. I don't know how to get out of that engagement.
zafio coarse, vulgar.
zaguán [m] entrance, hall, vestibule.
zambo [adj; n] half-breed (Negro and Indian).
zambullida dive, plunge.
zambullir to plunge.
    ○ zambullirse to dive.
zanahoria carrot.
zancudo long-legged. ▲ [m] mosquito [Am].
zangolotear to shake violently [Am].
zanja ditch, trench.
zapatería shoemaker's shop, shoe store.
zapatero shoemaker.

zapatilla slipper.
zapato shoe.
zarco blue-eyed.
zarpar to weigh anchor; to sail, start moving (of a boat).
zarza bramble.
zarzuela musical comedy.
zona district, zone.
zonzo dull, stupid, silly [Am].
zoológico zoological.
zoquete [m] piece of stale bread; chuck, block; blockhead.
zorro fox.
zozobra worry.
zozobrar to capsize, founder, sink.
zumbar to buzz.
zumbido buzz, buzzing.
zumo juice (of fruit); juice (of fruit skin) [Am].
zurcir to darn, mend.
zurdo left-handed.
zurrar to whip, flog.

PART II

English-Spanish

A

a un, una *Do you have a pen, an envelope, and some paper?* ¿Tiene Ud. una pluma, un sobre y papel? ▲un, algún *Is there a bank near here?* ¿Hay algún banco cerca de aquí? ▲una, alguna *Is there a nurse here?* ¿Hay alguna enfermera aquí? ▲por *I make forty dollars a week.* Gano cuarenta dólares por semana. ▲por, cada *The rate of exchange is two pesos a dollar.* El cambio está a dos pesos por dólar. ▲*These eggs are fifty cents a dozen.* Estos huevos son a cincuenta centavos la docena.

abandon abandonar *She abandoned her child.* Abandonó a su hijo.

abbreviate abreviar.

A.B.C. abecé *It's as simple as A.B.C.* Eso es el abecé.

ability habilidad.

abnormal anormal.

abolish abolir, derogar.

abortion aborto.

about [*prep*] de *What's he talking about?* ¿De qué está hablando? ▲concerniente *It isn't anything about you.* No es nada concerniente a Ud. ● [*adv*] casi *Dinner's about ready.* La comida está casi preparada. ▲unos *I have about ten.* Tengo unos diez. ○**about to** a punto de, para *The train's about to leave.* El tren está a punto de partir. ○**what about?** ¿qué hay de? *What about the things you were going to get for me?* ¿Qué hay de las cosas que Ud. me iba a conseguir?

above sobre *How far above sea level are we?* ¿A qué altura estamos sobre el nivel del mar? ○**above all** sobre todo, ante todo *Above all, remember to be on time.* Ante todo, acuérdese de estar a tiempo. ○**to be above** sobrepasar *He's above average height.* Su estatura sobrepasa la normal. ○**to go above** pasar de *Don't go above five dollars.* No pase de cinco dólares.

abreast de ... en fondo *They marched four abreast.* Marchaban de cuatro en fondo. ○**to keep abreast of** estar al corriente de *I can't keep abreast of the news.* No puedo estar al corriente de las noticias.

abroad en el extranjero.

abrupt brusco *(rude);* repentino *(sudden).*

absence falta *Have you a record of her absences?* ¿Lleva Ud. nota de sus faltas? ▲ausencia *Her absence was noticed at the office.* En la oficina notaron su ausencia.

absent ausente *Three members were absent because of illness.* Tres miembros estuvieron ausentes por enfermedad.

absent-minded distraído.

absolute absoluto *His power was absolute.* Su poder era absoluto. ▲puro *That's the absolute truth.* Esta es la pura verdad.

absolutely absolutamente *I'm absolutely certain of my facts.* Estoy absolutamente seguro de mis datos.

absorb absorber *This blotter absorbs ink very well.* Este secante absorbe muy bien la tinta.—*He was so absorbed in his book he didn't hear me come in.* Estaba tan absorto en la lectura que no me oyó entrar.

abstain abstenerse, privarse.

absurd absurdo.

abundance abundancia.
abuse [n] abuso *That's an abuse of authority.* Eso es un abuso de autoridad. ▲maltrato *That child got more abuse than affection.* Ese niño recibió más maltrato que cariño.
abuse [v] abusar de *I advise you not to abuse any of the privileges we have here.* Le aconsejo que no abuse de ninguno de los privilegios que tenemos aquí. ▲insultar *We heard her abuse her sister.* La oímos insultar a su hermana. ▲tratar mal *Do you really feel abused?* ¿De veras siente Ud. que le tratan mal?
abusive abusivo.
academy academia.
accelerate acelerar, apresurar.
accelerator acelerador.
accent [n] acento *Where's the accent in this word?* ¿Dónde lleva el acento esta palabra?—*He speaks English with a Russian accent.* Habla inglés con acento ruso.
accent [v] acentuar *Accent the first syllable of this word.* Acentúe la primera sílaba de esta palabra.
accept aceptar *He accepted the money that I offered him.* Aceptó el dinero que le ofrecí.
acceptance aceptación.
access acceso, entrada.
accessory accesorio *I'd like to get some accessories for the automobile.* Quisiera comprar algunos accesorios para el automóvil. ▲cómplice *The police held him as an accessory.* La policía le detuvo como cómplice.
accident accidente *In case of accident, notify the manager.* En caso de accidente avise al administrador.
  ○**by accident** por casualidad *We met them by accident.* Les encontramos por casualidad.
accidental accidental, casual.
accommodate acomodar *We can only accommodate three more people.* Podemos acomodar sólo a tres personas más.
accommodations alojamiento *We'll have to wire ahead for accommodations.* Tendremos que telegrafiar para reservar alojamiento.
accompany acompañar *May I accompany you home?* ¿La puedo acompañar a casa?
accomplish llevar a cabo, realizar *He accomplished his purpose quickly.* Llevó a cabo su propósito rápidamente.
  ○**accomplished** consumado *He's an*

accomplished linguist. Es un lingüista consumado.
accomplishment realización.
accord acuerdo *His ideas on politics are in accord with mine.* Sus ideas políticas están de acuerdo con las mías.
  ○**of one's own accord** espontáneamente *He wrote to me of his own accord.* Me escribió espontáneamente. ○**with one accord** de común acuerdo. unánimemente.
accordance conformidad, armonía.
accordingly de acuerdo, conforme *He gave us instructions and we acted accordingly.* Hemos obrado de acuerdo con las instrucciones que nos dió.
according to según *We'll make our arrangements according to your plans.* Haremos nuestros arreglos según sus planes.
accordion acordeón.
account relato *His account of the accident's different from hers.* Su relato del accidente es diferente al de ella. ▲cuenta *The company's accounts were in good order.* Las cuentas de la compañía estaban en orden. ▲valor, importancia *This book's of no account.* Este libro no tiene ningún valor.
  ○**on account of** a causa de *The game was postponed on account of rain.* El partido fué pospuesto a causa de la lluvia. ○**on no account** de ninguna manera, por ningún motivo. ○**to account for** explicarse *How do you account for that?* ¿Cómo se explica eso? ○**to take into account** tener en cuenta.
  ‖ *Is the baggage accounted for?* ¿Está completo el equipaje?
accountant contador.
accuracy exactitud, precisión.
accurate exacto.
accuse acusar.
accustom acostumbrar.
  ○**to be accustomed** estar acostumbrado *I'm not accustomed to such treatment.* No estoy acostumbrado a semejante trato.
ache [n] dolor *Have you got a headache?* ¿Tiene dolor de cabeza?
  ●[v] doler *My tooth aches.* Me duele una muela *(molar).* or Me duele un diente *(front tooth).*
achieve llevar a cabo, lograr.
acid [adj, n] ácido.
acknowledge admitir *The court acknowledged my claims.* El tribunal admitió mi demanda. ▲dar las gracias por *They haven't acknowledged*

the wedding presents yet. Todavía no han dado las gracias por los regalos de boda.

acknowledgment reconocimiento *(recognition)*; admisión *(admission).*

acorn bellota.

acoustics acústica.

acquaint ○ **to be acquainted** conocerse *Are you two acquainted?* ¿Se conocen Uds. dos?

acquaintance conocido, amigo *She's an old acquaintance of mine.* Es una vieja conocida mía.

○ **to make one's acquaintance** conocer a uno *I'm very happy to make your acquaintance.* Tengo mucho gusto en conocerle.

acquire adquirir.

acquit absolver.

○ **to acquit oneself well** portarse bien.

acre acre.

across al otro lado de *The restaurant's across the street.* El restaurante está al otro lado de la calle. ▲ a través *There's an obstruction across the road.* Hay un obstáculo a través del camino.

act [*n*] acción *That was a very kind act.* Fué una acción muy amable. ▲ acto *I don't want to miss the first act.* No quiero perder el primer acto. ● [*v*] obrar, actuar *Now's the time to act.* Ahora es el momento de obrar. ▲ portarse *Don't act like a child.* No te portes como un niño. ○ **act of Congress** ley aprobada por el Congreso. ○ **to act as** hacer de *Who's acting as head?* ¿Quién hace de jefe? ○ **to act on** seguir *I'll act on your suggestion.* Seguiré su sugestión. ○ **to act upon** *When will this be acted upon?* ¿Cuándo se decidirá sobre esto? ○ **to be in the act of** *I was in the act of packing.* Estaba haciendo el equipaje.

action acción *He's a man of action.* Es un hombre de acción.

○ **to take action** tomar medidas *Has any action been taken on my case?* ¿Se ha tomado alguna medida en mi caso?

active activo.

activity actividad, movimiento.

○ **social activities** vida social.

actor actor.

actress actriz.

actual real, verdadero *What's the actual cost?* ¿Cuál es el coste real?

actually realmente, en realidad.

acute agudo.

ad See **advertisement.**

adapt adaptar.

add agregar, añadir *Add it to my bill.* Añádalo a mi cuenta.

○ **to add up** sumar *Add up this list of figures.* Sume Ud. esta columna de números.

adding machine máquina de sumar.

addition adición, suma *Is my addition correct?* ¿Está correcta mi suma? ▲ aumento *We need additions to our staff.* Necesitamos un aumento en nuestro personal.

○ **in addition to** además de *In addition to my worries this has to happen.* Además de mis preocupaciones tenía que ocurrir esto.

additional adicional.

address [*n*] dirección, señas *"What's your address?" "My address is 21 Fifth Avenue." "¿*Cuál es su dirección?" "Mi dirección es: Quinta Avenida número 21." ▲ discurso *I have to listen to an address tonight.* Tengo que oír un discurso esta noche. ● [*v*] dirigir *How shall I address the letter?* ¿Cómo tengo que dirigir la carta? ▲ dirigirse a *The speaker addressed the public.* El orador se dirigió al público.

adequate bastante, suficiente.

adhesive tape esparadrapo.

adjacent adyacente, cercano.

adjective adjetivo.

adjoining contiguo.

adjust arreglar, ajustar *Adjust the clock so it'll run faster.* Ajuste el reloj para que adelante. ▲ adaptar, acostumbrar *I can't adjust myself to the climate here.* No me puedo acostumbrar al clima de aquí. ▲ arreglar, atender *The manager adjusts all complaints.* El administrador atiende todas las quejas.

adjutant ayudante.

administer administrar.

administration aplicación *The workers complained about the administration of the law.* Los obreros se quejaron por la aplicación de la ley. ▲ ministerio, gobierno *During his administration a great many new laws were passed.* Durante su gobierno se promulgaron muchas leyes nuevas. ▲ administración *The administration of a new drug curbed the epidemic.* L administración de un nuevo medicamento detuvo la epidemia.

admirable admirable.

admiral almirante.

admiration admiración.

admire admirar.

admission admisión, entrada *How much is the admission?* ¿Cuánto cuesta la entrada? ▲confesión *He made a frank admission.* Hizo una confesión sincera.

‖ *No admission.* Se prohibe la entrada.

admit dejar entrar *Ask for me and you'll be admitted.* Pregunte Ud. por mí y le dejarán entrar. ▲admitir *When were you admitted to that club?* ¿Cuándo se le admitió en ese club? ▲reconocer *I admit that I was wrong.* Reconozco que estaba equivocado.

adopt adoptar.

adore adorar.

adorn adornar.

adult [n] adulto *What's the proper dose for adults?* ¿Cuál es la dosis para adultos?

● [adj] juicioso *She's very adult for her age.* Es muy juiciosa para su edad.

‖ *Adults only.* Sólo para personas mayores.

adultery adulterio.

advance [n] aumento *There's an advance in price after 6 o'clock.* Hay un aumento en los precios después de las seis. ▲adelanto, progreso *What advances have been made in medicine?* ¿Qué progresos se han hecho en medicina?

● [v] avanzar *Advance!* ¡Avancen! ▲promover, ascender *We'll advance him if he proves capable.* Le ascenderemos si demuestra su capacidad. ▲adelantar *Could you advance me some money?* ¿Podría Ud. adelantarme algún dinero?

○ **in advance** por adelantado, con anticipación *Let me know in advance, if you come.* Si vienes, avísame por adelantado.

advantage ventaja *You have the advantage over me.* Ud. me lleva ventaja. ▲provecho, beneficio *This is to your advantage.* Es para su provecho.

○ **to take advantage of** aprovecharse de *I wish to take advantage of your offer.* Deseo aprovecharme de su ofrecimiento. ▲aprovecharse de, engañar *Don't let people take advantage of you.* No deje que se aprovechen de Ud.

advantageous provechoso.

adventure aventura.

adverb adverbio.

advertise avisar, anunciar *The store's advertising a sale.* La tienda anuncia

un saldo. ▲poner un anuncio *They're advertising for a cook.* Han puesto un anuncio solicitando un cocinero.

advertisement anuncio, aviso.

advice consejo *I'll act on your advice.* Seguiré sus consejos.

advisable prudente, aconsejable.

advise avisar, informar *We were advised of the dangers of the trip.* Nos avisaron que el viaje era peligroso. ▲aconsejar *I advise against our going.* Aconsejo que no vayamos.

aerial [n] antena *The aerial on our radio needs fixing.* Hay que reparar la antena de nuestra radio.

● [adj] aéreo *The town was subjected to an aerial attack.* La ciudad fué sometida a un ataque aéreo.

affair negocio, asunto *He handled the affairs of the company badly.* Manejó mal los negocios de la compañía. ▲acontecimiento, suceso *The dance was the biggest affair of the season.* El baile fué el acontecimiento más grande de la temporada.

○ **love affair** aventura amorosa.

affect afectar, conmover *I wasn't a bit affected by the news of his death.* La noticia de su muerte no me afectó nada. ▲afectar, fingir *He affects indifference when you mention her.* Finge indiferencia cuando se alude a ella.

affection afecto, cariño.

affectionate afectuoso.

affectionately afectuosamente.

affirm afirmar.

afford tener con que comprar *I really can't afford to buy this dress.* De veras no tengo con que comprar este vestido. ▲convenir *He can't afford to have his reputation hurt.* No le conviene comprometer su reputación. ▲proporcionar *The trip afforded us the opportunity of seeing the country.* El viaje nos proporcionó la oportunidad de ver el país.

affront [n] afrenta, insulto.

afloat a flote *After the battle our ship was still afloat.* Después de la batalla nuestro buque quedó a flote.

afraid ○ **to be afraid** tener miedo, temer *Don't be afraid.* No tenga miedo.—*I'm afraid I'm going to be late.* Me temo que voy a llegar tarde.

after [adv] detrás *The man walked ahead and the woman came after.* El hombre caminaba delante y la mujer venía detrás.

● [prep] después de *Come any time after nine.* Venga cuando quiera después de las nueve. ▲tras *We came one after the other.* Vinimos uno tras otro. ▲detrás de *The police are after him.* La policía anda detrás de él. ● *[conj]* después que *Wait until after I come back.* Espere hasta después que yo vuelva. ○after all después de todo *You're right, after all.* Después de todo tiene Ud. razón. ○after this en adelante *After this let us know in advance.* En adelante avísenos por anticipado. ○to go after ir por *Will you go after the mail?* ¿Quiere Ud. ir por el correo? ○to look after cuidar de, tener cuidado de *Is there anyone to look after the children?* ¿Hay alguien que cuide de los niños?

afternoon tarde *Can you come this afternoon or tomorrow afternoon?* ¿Puede Ud. venir esta tarde o mañana por la tarde?

afterward(s) después.

again otra vez, de nuevo *Try once again.* Pruebe otra vez. ○again and again una y otra vez, muchas veces *I'll do this again and again.* Haré esto muchas veces. ○never again nunca más *Never again will I make that mistake.* Nunca más cometeré ese error. ‖ *I hope to see you again.* Espero volver a verle.

against contra *Lean it against the wall.* Apóyalo contra la pared. ▲en contra de *Is everyone against him?* ¿Está todo el mundo en contra de él?

age *[n]* edad *What's your age and profession?* ¿Qué edad y qué profesión tiene Ud.? ▲época *This is the age of invention.* Esta es la época de los inventos. ● *[v]* envejecer *He's aged a great deal lately.* Ha envejecido mucho ultimamente. ○of age mayor de edad *He'll come of age next year.* Será mayor de edad el año próximo. ○old age vejez *Save something for your old age.* Ahorre algo para la vejez.

agency agencia.

agent agente *Your agent has already called on me.* Su agente acaba de visitarme. ▲representante *I'm a government agent.* Soy un representante del gobierno.

aggravate *(make worse)* agravar.

ago hace *I was here two months ago.* Estuve aquí hace dos meses. ○a while ago hace un rato *He left a while ago.* Salió hace un rato.

agony agonía.

agree estar de acuerdo *Do you agree with me?* ¿Está Ud. de acuerdo conmigo? ▲concordar *The two statements don't agree.* Las dos declaraciones no concuerdan. ▲convenir *I agree to your terms.* Convengo en sus condiciones.

agreeable agradable *She has an agreeable disposition.* Tiene un carácter agradable. ▲simpático *She's a very agreeable person.* Es una persona muy simpática. ○agreeable to de acuerdo con *Is everyone agreeable to the plan?* ¿Están todos de acuerdo con el plan?

agreement acuerdo, pacto. ○in agreement de acuerdo.

agriculture agricultura.

ahead adelante *Are there many turns up ahead?* ¿Hay muchas vueltas más adelante? ○to be ahead ir a la cabeza, ir delante *Who's ahead?* ¿Quién va a la cabeza? ▲ir adelantado, estar adelantado *I'm ahead in my work.* Voy adelantado en mi trabajo. ‖ *Go ahead.* Pase delante. or Siga Ud.

aid *[n]* ayuda *I'd welcome any aid.* Agradecería cualquier ayuda. ● *[v]* ayudar *Let me aid you.* Déjeme que le ayude.

aim *[n]* puntería *Is your aim good?* ¿Tiene Ud. buena puntería? ▲propósito, mira *What are your aims in life?* ¿Cuáles son sus propósitos en la vida? ● *[v]* apuntar *Aim higher.* Apunte más alto.

air *[n]* aire *I'm going out for some air.* Voy a salir a tomar un poco el aire.— *There's an air of mystery about the whole affair.* Hay un aire de misterio en todo el asunto. ● *[v]* ventilar, airear *Would you please air the room while I'm out?* ¿Quisiera Ud. hacer el favor de ventilar el cuarto mientras estoy fuera? ○by air por vía aérea, por avión *I'd like to go by air, if possible.* Si es posible quisiera ir por avión.

aircraft carrier portaviones.

airfield campo de aviación, campo de aterrizaje.

air force fuerzas aéreas.

air mail correo aéreo.

airplane aeroplano, avión.

airport aeropuerto.

aisle pasillo.

ajar entreabierto, entornado.

alarm [n] alarma *What was that alarm for?* ¿Por qué ha sido esa alarma? ● [v] alarmar *The noise alarmed the whole town.* El ruído alarmó a toda la ciudad. ○ **to be alarmed** alarmarse.

alarm clock despertador.

album álbum.

alcohol alcohol.

alcove alcoba, recámara.

ale cerveza inglesa.

alert [n] alarma *We ran for shelter when we heard the alert.* Corrimos a refugiarnos cuando oímos la alarma. ● [adj] listo, vivo *He's a very alert child.* Es un chico muy listo. ▲ despabilado *The students aren't very alert on Mondays.* Los estudiantes no están muy despabilados los lunes. ○ **to be on the alert** estar sobre aviso, estar alerta.

algebra álgebra.

alien [n] extranjero *There were many aliens in the city.* Había muchos extranjeros en la ciudad. ● [adj] extranjero, ajeno *They adopted alien ways while they were in that country.* Adquirieron costumbres extranjeras mientras estuvieron en ese país. ▲ contrario *Such actions are alien to his character.* Tales actos son contrarios a su carácter.

align alinear.

alike igual, semejante *These places are all alike.* Estos sitios son todos iguales. ▲ del mismo modo, igualmente *We treat all the guests alike.* Tratamos a todos los clientes del mismo modo.

alimony alimentos por razón de divorcio.

alive vivo, viviente *I feel more dead than alive.* Me siento más muerto que vivo. ○ **to keep alive** mantener vivo.

all todo *I've been waiting all day.* He estado esperando todo el día.—*That's all.* Eso es todo.—*Tell me all about it.* Dígamelo todo.—*That's all there is.* Eso es todo lo que hay.—*It's all gone.* Todo se ha acabado. ▲ todos *Did you all go?* ¿Fueron todos Uds.? ○ **all alone** solo *I can't do this all alone.* No lo puedo hacer yo solo. ○ **all at once** de pronto *All at once something happened.* De pronto ocurrió algo. ○ **all over** *Is it all over?* ¿Se ha acabado todo? ○ **all the better** tanto mejor *If that's so, all the better.* Si es así, tanto mejor. ○ **all the same** lo mismo *That's all the same to me.* Me da lo mismo. ○ **at all**

If I go at all I'll be there before eight. Si voy, estaré allí antes de las ocho. ○ **in all** en total *How many are there in all?* ¿Cuántos hay en total? ○ **not at all** nada *I'm not at all tired.* No estoy nada cansado. ▲ de nada *"Thank you." "Not at all." "Gracias." "De nada."* ○ **once and for all** por última vez, ya de una vez *Once and for all, let's get this over with.* Por última vez, dejemos esto terminado. ‖ **All right.** Está bien. *or* Bueno.

allege alegar.

allergy alergia.

alley callejuela, callejón. ○ **blind alley** callejón sin salida. ○ **bowling alley** bolera [Sp], boliche [Am].

alliance alianza.

alligator caimán, [Am] lagarto.

allot distribuir, repartir.

allow permitir, dejar *We're not allowed to leave the camp at night.* No se nos permite salir del campamento por la noche. ○ **to allow for** dejar para *How much should I allow for traveling expenses?* ¿Cuánto tendría que dejar para gastos de viaje?

allowance dieta, abono *How much of an allowance do you get for your traveling expenses?* ¿Qué dietas le dan para sus gastos de viaje? ○ **to make allowance for** tener en cuenta, hacerse cargo de, excusar. ‖ *How much a month does your father give you for an allowance?* ¿Cuánto te da tu padre para tus gastos personales al mes?

allure [v] atraer, tentar.

ally [n] aliado *The Allies won the first World War.* Los aliados ganaron la primera guerra mundial. ○ **to ally oneself, to be allied** aliarse *They allied themselves with powerful neighbors.* Se aliaron con vecinos poderosos.

almanac almanaque, calendario.

almighty todopoderoso. ○ **the Almighty** el Todopoderoso.

almond almendra.

almost casi *Are you almost ready?* ¿Estás casi preparado?

alone solo *Do you live alone?* ¿Vive Ud. solo? ▲ sólo, solamente *You alone can help me.* Sólo Ud. puede ayudarme. ○ **to let alone** dejar en paz *Let me alone.* Déjeme en paz.

along a lo largo de *A fence runs along*

the road. Hay una cerca a lo largo de la carretera.
‖ *Bring her along.* Tráigala consigo. ‖ *Come along with me.* Venga Ud. conmigo. ‖ *Do they get along?* ¿Se llevan? ‖ *How are you getting along?* ¿Cómo le va a Ud.?

aloof apartado, lejos, a distancia.

aloud alto, en voz alta *Read the story aloud.* Lea Ud. el cuento en voz alta.

alphabet alfabeto.

already ya.

also también *You may also come.* También Ud. puede venir.

altar altar.

alter cambiar, modificar.

alternate [*adj*] alterno.

alternative [*n*] alternativa.

although aunque *I'll be there, although I may be late.* Estaré allá, aunque llegue tarde.

altitude altura.

altogether en conjunto, enteramente.

always siempre *Are you always busy?* ¿Está Ud. siempre ocupado?

am See **be**.

amateur aficionado.

amaze asombrar, pasmar *I'm amazed.* Estoy pasmado

ambassador embajador.

ambition ambición *He has no ambition.* No tiene ambición. ▲ aspiración *My greatest ambition is to be an opera singer.* Mi mayor aspiración es ser cantante de ópera.

ambitious ambicioso.

ambulance ambulancia.

ambush [*n*] emboscada.
● [*v*] sorprender.

amend enmendar, corregir.

amendment enmienda.

amends compensación, reparación.
○ **to make amends** compensar, dar cumplida satisfacción.

amiable amable, afable.

amid entre, en medio de.

ammunition munición.

among entre *You're among friends.* Ud. está entre amigos.

amount [*n*] importe, suma *What's the whole amount?* ¿Cuál es el importe total?
● [*v*] subir *What does the bill amount to?* ¿A cuánto sube la cuenta? ‖ *The disturbance didn't amount to anything.* El disturbio no tuvo ninguna importancia.

ample amplio.

amuse divertir *That amuses me very much.* Eso me divierte mucho.

amusement diversión *Are there any amusements here?* ¿Hay aquí algunas diversiones?

an See **a**.

analysis análisis.

analyze analizar.

anarchy anarquía.

anatomy anatomía.

ancestor antepasado.

anchor [*n*] ancla *The boat had no anchor.* El bote no tenía ancla.
● [*v*] anclar *They anchored the ship in the bay.* Anclaron el buque en la bahía.
○ **to weigh anchor** levar el ancla.

ancient antiguo.

and y *The room had only a bed and a chair.* La habitación tenía solamente una cama y una silla.—*Wait and see.* Espere y verá. ▲ e (*before* i *or* hi) *Father and son.* Padre e hijo.
○ **and so forth** etcetera (*abbr* etc.) *I need soap, towels, and so forth.* Necesito jabón, toallas, etc.

angel ángel.

anger [*n*] cólera, enojo.

angle ángulo *Measure each angle of the triangle.* Mida cada ángulo del triángulo. ▲ punto de vista, aspecto *Let's not discuss that angle of the problem.* No discutamos ese aspecto del problema.
○ **at an angle** inclinado, en angulo *She wears her hat at an angle.* Usa el sombrero inclinado.

angry enojado, enfadado, [*Am*] bravo *What are you angry about?* ¿Porqué está Ud. enojado?
○ **to be angry** estar enfadado, estar enojado, [*Am*] estar bravo *Are you angry at him?* ¿Está Ud. enfadado con él? ○ **to get angry** enojarse, enfadarse.

anguish angustia.

animal animal.

animate [*v*] animar.

ankle tobillo.

annex [*n*] anexo.

annex [*v*] anexar.

anniversary aniversario.

announce anunciar *They just announced that on the radio.* Lo acaban de anunciar en la radio. ▲ participar *They just announced their engagement.* Acaban de participar su próximo enlace.

announcement aviso, anuncio.

annoy molestar, incomodar.

annual [*adj*] anual.

another otro *Please give me another cup of coffee.* Haga el favor de darme otra taza de café.

‖ *They saw one another frequently.* Se veían con frecuencia. ‖ *They saw one another.* Se vieron unos a otros.

answer [n] respuesta, contestación *What's your answer?* ¿Cuál es su respuesta? ▲ solución *Where can I find the answer?* ¿Dónde encontraré la solución?
● [v] contestar *Please answer me by return mail.* Haga el favor de contestarme a vuelta de correo.

ant hormiga.

antagonize contrariar.

antarctic [adj, n] antártico.

antenna antena.

anthem ○ **national anthem** himno nacional.

anticipate esperar, prever *There was a larger crowd at the concert than we had anticipated.* Había más gente en el concierto de lo que esperábamos. ▲ anticiparse *The attendants anticipated all our needs.* La servidumbre se anticipó a todo lo que necesitábamos.

antidote antídoto, contraveneno.

antique [n] antigüedad, antigualla.
● [adj] antiguo.

antiseptic [adj, n] antiséptico.

anxiety ansia, ansiedad.

anxious inquieto *I've been anxious about you.* He estado muy inquieto por tí. ▲ ansioso *I'm anxious to succeed.* Estoy ansioso de triunfar.

any alguno *Are there any books around here?* ¿Hay algunos libros por aquí? ▲ algún *I don't like this hat. Do you have any other?* No me gusta este sombrero. ¿Tiene Ud. algún otro? ▲ cualquier *Any policeman can direct you.* Cualquier guardia puede indicarle el camino.
○ **any longer** más, más tiempo *I can't stay any longer.* No puedo quedarme más. ○ **any way** de cualquier modo, de cualquier manera *Do it any way you can.* Hágalo de cualquier manera. ○ **at any time** en cualquier momento. ○ **in any case** en todo caso, de todos modos.
‖ *"Do you have any money?" "I don't have any."* "¿Tiene Ud. dinero?" "No tengo nada."

anybody alguien *Will anybody be at the station to meet me?* ¿Habrá alguien en la estación esperándome? ▲ cualquiera *Anybody can do that.* Cualquiera puede hacer eso.

anyhow de todos modos, de todas maneras *It may rain but I'm going any-how.* Puede ser que llueva pero iré de todos modos.

anyone alguien *If anyone calls, take the message.* Si llama alguien, tome Ud. el recado.

anything algo, alguna cosa *Is there anything for me?* ¿Hay algo para mí? ▲ cualquier cosa *Anything you have will be all right.* Cualquier cosa que Ud. tenga estará bien.
‖ *Can't anything be done?* ¿No se puede hacer nada?

anyway de todos modos, con todo *I didn't want to go anyway.* De todos modos yo no quería ir.

anywhere en alguna parte *Have you seen him anywhere?* ¿Le ha visto Ud. en alguna parte? ▲ en ninguna parte *(in negative sentence) I don't want to go anywhere tonight.* No quiero ir a ninguna parte esta noche. ▲ donde quiera, cualquier parte *We could go anywhere if we had the money.* Podríamos ir a cualquier parte si tuviéramos dinero.

apart separado *The house stands apart from the others.* La casa está separada de las otras. ▲ aparte *Set this apart for me.* Ponga esto aparte para mí.
○ **to take apart** desmontar *Take the machine apart.* Desmonte Ud. la máquina. ○ **to tell apart** distinguir *How do you tell the two apart?* ¿Cómo puede distinguir uno del otro?

apartment piso [Sp], apartamento [Am], departamento [Chile] *We want to rent an apartment in the city.* Queremos alquilar un apartamento en la ciudad.

ape mono.

apiece por persona, cada uno *My brother and I earned six dollars apiece.* Mi hermano y yo ganamos seis dólares cada uno.

apologize disculparse, excusarse *You ought to apologize to her for being so rude.* Debe Ud. disculparse con ella por haber sido tan descortés.

appall espantar, aterrar.

apparatus aparato.

apparent aparente *(seeming);* claro *(clear).*

appeal [n] llamamiento *He made an appeal for justice.* Hizo un llamamiento pidiendo justicia. ▲ apelación *The defendant was granted an appeal.* Al acusado le permitieron la apelación.
● [v] apelar, recurrir *He appealed to his friends for sympathy.* Apeló a la solidaridad de sus amigos. ▲ atraer

Her type appeals to me. El tipo de ella me atrae.

appear salir, aparecer *The paper appears every day.* El periódico sale todos los días. ▲parecer *He appears to be very sick.* Parece muy enfermo.

appearance apariencia, aspecto *Try to improve your appearance.* Trate de mejorar su aspecto.

○to **make an appearance** dejarse ver *At least make an appearance.* Por lo menos déjese Ud. ver un momento.

appease apaciguar, calmar.

appeasement apaciguamiento.

appendix apéndice.

appetite apetito.

appetizer aperitivo.

applause aplauso.

apple manzana.

appliance aparato.

application solicitud *Your application has been received.* Su solicitud ha sido recibida. ▲compresa *Cold applications will relieve the headache.* Compresas frías aliviarán el dolor de cabeza.

○ **application blank** formulario *Fill out this application blank.* Llene este formulario.

apply dirigirse *To whom do I apply?* ¿A quién tengo que dirigirme? ▲aplicar *Apply a hot compress every two hours.* Aplique una compresa caliente cada dos horas.

○to **apply for** solicitar, pedir *I wish to apply for the position.* Quiero pedir el empleo.

‖ *The information doesn't apply.* La información no es pertinente. ‖ *This order applies to all citizens.* Esta orden comprende a todos los cuidadanos.

appoint nombrar, designar.

appointment nombramiento, puesto *She's very happy since she received her appointment.* Está muy feliz desde que recibió su nombramiento. ▲cita *I have an appointment to meet him at six o'clock.* Tengo cita para encontrarle a las seis.

appreciate apreciar.

appreciation reconocimiento *Everyone expressed appreciation for what he had done.* Todos expresaron su reconocimiento por lo que él había hecho. ▲aprecio *She has a deep appreciation for art.* Tiene un profundo aprecio por el arte.

apprehension aprehensión, aprensión.

approach [*n*] acceso *The approaches to*

the bridge are under repair. Los accesos del puente están en reparación. ▲camino, método *Am I using the right approach?* ¿Estoy siguiendo el camino debido?

● [*v*] acercarse *Let's approach carefully.* Acerquémonos con cuidado. ‖ *Is it all right to approach him about this matter?* ¿Está bien que le preguntemos a él acerca de este asunto?

appropriate [*v*] destinar *The government has appropriated more money for road construction.* El gobierno ha destinado más dinero para la construcción de caminos. ▲apropiarse *All my ties have been appropriated by my son.* Mi hijo se ha apropiado de todas mis corbatas.

appropriate [*adj*] apropiado *I don't think that's an appropriate dress for a party.* No creo que ese vestido sea apropiado para una fiesta.

approval aprobación, consentimiento.

approve aprobar.

approximate [*adj*] aproximado.

apricot albaricoque, [*Mex*] chabacano.

April abril.

apron delantal.

apt capaz *He's apt to do anything.* Es capaz de hacer cualquiera cosa. ▲propenso *He's apt to make mistakes.* Está propenso a equivocarse. ▲acertado *Her last remark was very apt.* Su última observación fué muy acertada. ▲competente *He's an apt student.* Es un estudiante competente.

‖ *Don't call this afternoon because I'm apt to be out.* No me llame por teléfono esta tarde porque puede ser que salga.

arbor emparrado.

arch [*n*] arco *The bridge has a tremendous arch.* El puente tiene un arco enorme.

● [*v*] arquear *She arched her eyebrows.* Arqueó las cejas.

○ **fallen arches** pies planos.

architect arquitecto.

architecture arquitectura.

arctic [*adj*] ártico.

ardor ardor.

are See **be.**

area area *What's the area of the park?* ¿Cuál es el área del parque? ▲zona *What area's he working in?* ¿En qué zona trabaja?

argue sostener *I argued that taking the train would save us a lot of time.* Sostenía que ganaríamos mucho tiempo tomando el tren. ▲discutir *Let's not argue the point.* No discutamos ese asunto. ▲convencer, persuadir *You can't argue me into going there again.* Ud. no puede persuadirme de volver allí.

argument argumento *This is a strong argument in his favor.* Este es un argumento muy fuerte en su favor. ▲razonamiento *I don't follow your argument.* No sigo su razonamiento. ▲disputa *They had an argument.* Tuvieron una disputa.
‖ *Let's not have any argument.* No disputemos.

arise surgir *Many difficulties arose in carrying out the plan.* Surgieron muchas dificultades al realizar el plan. ▲sobrevenir *The trouble arose over a question of priority.* Sobrevino la dificultad sobre una cuestión de prioridad.

aristocracy aristocracia.

arithmetic aritmética.

arm brazo *Can you carry the package under your arm?* ¿Puede llevar el paquete debajo del brazo?
● [*v*] armar *They armed the soldiers with pistols.* Armaron a los soldados con pistolas.

armchair butaca, sillón.

armistice armisticio.

armor [*n*] blindaje *These shells can't penetrate the heavy armor of a battleship.* Estos proyectiles no pueden atravesar el grueso blindaje de un acorazado.
● [*v*] blindar *The tanks were heavily armored.* Los tanques estaban muy bien blindados.

armory armería, arsenal.

armpit sobaco, axila.

arms armas *They couldn't fight without arms.* No podían pelear sin armas.
○ **to bear arms** tomar las armas.
○ **to be up in arms** sublevarse *The students were up in arms at the new restrictions.* Los estudiantes se sublevaron ante las nuevas restricciones.
○ **to carry arms** llevar armas, tener armas *In this city you need a license to carry arms.* En esta ciudad se necesita un permiso para llevar armas. ○ **under arms** sobre las armas.

army ejército.

around alrededor de *We'll have to take a walk around the town.* Tendremos que dar un paseo alrededor de la ciudad. ▲alrededor de, más o menos *I have around twenty dollars.* Tengo

alrededor de veinte dólares. ▲a la vuelta de *The store's around the corner.* La tienda está a la vuelta de la esquina. ▲alrededor *Look around you.* Mire a su alrededor.
○ **around here** por aquí *Are there any soldiers around here?* ¿Hay por aquí algunos soldados? ○ **to look around** buscar *I'll have to look around for it.* Tendré que buscarlo por aquí. ○ **to turn around** dar la vuelta *He turned around and spoke to me.* Dió la vuelta y me habló.
‖ *How many miles is it around the lake?* ¿Cuántas millas tiene la vuelta del lago? ‖ *It's somewhere around the house.* Está en algún sitio de la casa.

arouse despertar *I was aroused during the night by fire engines.* Me despertaron los bomberos por la noche.
○ **to arouse suspicion** despertar sospechas.

arrange arreglar *Everything's been arranged.* Todo está arreglado.

arrangement colocación, disposición *The arrangement of the furniture was very inconvenient.* La disposición de los muebles era muy incómoda. ▲arreglo, preparativo *They made arrangements to leave by plane.* Hicieron los preparativos para ir en avión. ▲arreglo musical *How do you like the arrangement of that song?* ¿Qué le parece el arreglo musical de esa canción?

arrears atrasos.

arrest [*n*] detención *The police made two arrests.* La policía hizo dos detenciones.
● [*v*] arrestar, prender *Why have you been arrested?* ¿Por qué ha sido Ud. arrestado?—*They arrested two men.* Prendieron dos hombres. ▲atraer *It arrested my attention.* Me atrajo la atención.
‖ *You're under arrest.* Está Ud. arrestado.

arrival llegada.
○ **new arrival** recién llegado.

arrive llegar *When will I arrive in New York?* ¿Cuándo llegaré a Nueva York?

arrow flecha.

arsenal arsenal.

art arte *This building contains many works of art.* Este edificio encierra muchas obras de arte. ▲técnica *There's an art to it.* Hay una técnica para ello.
○ **art gallery** galería de arte.

artery arteria.

article objeto *I have no articles of value to declare.* No tengo objetos de valor que declarar. ▲ artículo *There was an interesting article about it in the newspaper.* Había en el periódico un artículo interesante acerca de ello.

artificial artificial *The flowers she was wearing were artificial.* Las flores que ella llevaba eran artificiales. ▲ afectado, fingido *Her manner of acting was artificial.* Su manera de actuar era afectada.

artillery artillería.

artist artista.

artistic artístico.

as como *He's late as usual.* Está retrasado como de costumbre. ▲ porque *I must go, as it's late.* Tengo que irme porque es tarde. ▲ cuando *Did you see anyone as you came in?* ¿Vió Ud. a alguien cuando entró? ▲ a medida que *Count the people as they enter.* Cuente la gente a medida que entre. ○ as far as hasta *I'll go with you as far as the door.* Le acompañaré a Ud. hasta la puerta. ○ as if como si *Act as if nothing had happened.* Obre Ud. como si no hubiese pasado nada. ○ as soon as possible cuanto antes, lo más pronto posible *I want to leave as soon as possible.* Quiero salir cuanto antes. ○ as to, as for en cuanto a *As to that, I don't know.* En cuanto a eso, yo no lo sé. ○ as yet aún, todavía *Nothing has happened as yet.* Todavía no ha pasado nada. ○ so as to para, a fin de *We must start early so as to be on time.* Tenemos que salir pronto para llegar a tiempo. ‖ *I regard it as important.* Lo considero de importancia.

ascend ascender, subir.

ascertain averiguar, determinar.

ash(es) ceniza. ○ ash tray cenicero.

ashamed ○ to be ashamed dar vergüenza *I was ashamed to ask for a second helping.* Me daba vergüenza repetir. ▲ tener vergüenza, estar avergonzado *He's ashamed of his English.* Está avergonzado de su inglés.

aside a un lado *All joking aside, I intend to go.* Bromas a un lado, tengo la intención de ir. ○ aside from aparte de *Aside from singing he has no talent.* Aparte de cantar no tiene otros talentos. ○ to put aside dejar a un lado *Let's put our work aside and go and get a*

drink. Dejemos a un lado el trabajo y salgamos a beber algo. ○ to set aside apartar *I think we have enough set aside for the trip.* Creo que hemos apartado suficiente dinero para el viaje.

ask preguntar *Did you ask him his name?* ¿Le preguntó Ud. su nombre? ▲ pedir *He asked for permission to go.* Pidió permiso para ir. ▲ invitar *Ask him in.* Invítele a entrar. ○ to ask about informarse de, pedir información sobre *Mr. X is asking about trains.* El señor X. pide información sobre los trenes. ○ to ask a question hacer una pregunta, preguntar una cosa *May I ask a question?* ¿Puedo hacer una pregunta?

asleep dormido *I must have been asleep.* Debo haberme dormido. *or* Estaría dormido. ○ to fall asleep dormirse, quedarse dormido *He's fallen asleep.* Se ha quedado dormido.

asparagus espárrago.

aspect aspecto *Have you considered every aspect of the problem?* ¿Ha examinado Ud. todos los aspectos del problema? ▲ apariencia *The house has a gloomy aspect.* La casa tiene una apariencia sombría.

asphalt asfalto.

aspire aspirar.

aspirin aspirina.

ass asno, burro.

assassin asesino.

assault [n] asalto. ● [v] asaltar.

assemble reunir *They assembled a great force for the invasion.* Reunieron una gran fuerza para la invasión. ▲ reunirse *A large crowd assembled in the park.* Un gran gentío se reunió en el parque. ▲ montar, armar *He's an expert at assembling airplane motors.* Es experto en montar motores de aeroplano.

assembly asamblea.

assert afirmar, sostener. ○ to assert oneself hacerse sentir, hacer valer sus derechos.

assign indicar, señalar *I'll assign your lessons for tomorrow.* Voy a indicarles la lección para mañana. ▲ asignar *Who was assigned to the new post?* ¿A quién asignaron para el nuevo cargo?

assignment misión *The editor gave him an interesting assignment to cover.* El director del periódico le encargó una misión interesante. ▲ tarea *Our* *teacher gave us a big assignment.* El profesor nos dió una tarea grande. ▲designación *I was surprised at his assignment.* Me causó sorpresa su designación.

assimilate asimilar.

assist ayudar, asistir.

assistance auxilio, ayuda.

assistant ayudante, asistente.

associate [n] consocio *He's been an associate of mine for many years.* Ha sido consocio mío durante muchos años.

associate [v] mezclar *His name has been associated with a recent scandal.* Su nombre ha estado mezclado en un reciente escándalo. ▲asociar *Our two firms have always been associated.* Nuestras dos casas siempre han estado asociadas. ‖ *She never did associate with us very much.* Nunca ha sido muy amiga nuestra.

association asociación, relación *His association with important people helped him to advance.* Su relación con gente de importancia le ayudó a progresar. ▲asociación, sociedad *I don't think I'll join that association.* No creo que me incorporaré a esa asociación. ○ **associations** recuerdo *This picture doesn't bring up any associations for me.* Este cuadro no despierta en mí ningún recuerdo.

assorted surtido *I want a bag of assorted chocolates.* Deseo un paquete de bombones surtidos.

assume asumir *I've always had to assume the family's responsibilities.* Siempre he tenido que asumir las responsabilidades de la familia. ▲suponer, presumir *I assume that dinner will be on time.* Supongo que la comida estará a la hora. ▲darse *She assumed an air of innocence.* Se dió aire de inocente.

assurance seguridad, certeza *He gave us his assurance that he'd pay on time.* Nos dió la seguridad de que pagaría a tiempo.—*He works with complete assurance that he'll succeed.* Trabaja con la completa seguridad de que va a tener éxito.—*I wouldn't want to start this without the assurance that it's necessary.* No quisiera empezar esto sin tener la seguridad de que es necesario.

assure asegurar *That's not so, I assure you.* No es así, se lo aseguro.—*He assured us that he'd be there.* Nos aseguró que estaría allí.

aster aster.

asthma asma.

at en *I'll be at home.* Estaré en casa.—*I'm not good at that.* No soy hábil en eso. ▲de *I was surprised at its size.* Estaba sorprendido de su tamaño.—*What are you laughing at?* ¿De qué se están riendo Uds.? ▲a *The gloves sell at three dollars a pair.* Los guantes se venden a tres dólares el par.—*Be there at ten o'clock.* Esté Ud. allí a las diez.—*Aim at it.* Apunte a eso.—*We haven't arrived at a decision.* No hemos llegado a ninguna decisión. ▲por *In the morning, and at night.* Por la mañana, y por la noche. ▲con *He's mad at me.* Está enfadado conmigo.

○ **at all** nada de *I haven't got any money at all.* No tengo nada de dinero. ○ **at all costs** a toda costa *We must do it at all costs.* Tenemos que hacerlo a toda costa. ○ **at best** a lo más *This car will go only forty-five miles per hour, or at best, fifty.* Este auto marcha sólo a cuarenta y cinco millas por hora, o a lo más a cincuenta. ○ **at first** al principio *At first we didn't like the town.* Al principio no nos gustaba la ciudad. ○ **at last** al fin *At last the train's arrived.* Al fin el tren ha llegado. ○ **at least** al menos, por lo menos *There were at least a hundred people present.* Había presentes por lo menos cien personas. ○ **at most** a lo más *Give me a dozen, or at most twenty.* Déme una docena, o a lo más veinte. ○ **at once** en seguida *I'll leave at once.* Salgo en seguida. ○ **at times** a veces *At times I'm doubtful.* A veces dudo. ○ **at will** a antojo de uno *They come and go at will.* Van y vienen a su antojo. ○ **to be at ease** sentirse bien *I feel at ease in his presence.* Me siento bien en su presencia. ‖ *Be ready to leave at a moment's notice.* Esté preparado para salir a momento en que le avisen.

athlete atleta.

atmosphere atmósfera.

attach enganchar *Attach the trailer to your automobile.* Enganche el carro de remolque a su automóvil. ▲embargar *His creditors attached his salary.* Sus acreedores le embargaron el sueldo. ○ **to attach importance to** dar importancia a *We don't attach much importance to it.* No le damos mucha importancia ○ **to be attached** ser agregado, estaı agregado *For many years he's been attached to the Embassy.* Fué agregado a la Embajada durante muchos años. ▲ estar apegado *He's very much attached to his family.* Esta muy apegado a su familia.

attack [n] ataque *She's had a heart attack.* Ha tenido un ataque al corazón.

  ● [v] atacar *The enemy position has been attacked.* La posición del enemigo ha sido atacada.

attain lograr, obtener.

attempt [n] esfuerzo *He made a courageous attempt to save her.* Hizo un esfuerzo valeroso para salvarla. ▲ tentativa *That was her first attempt at cooking.* Fué su primera tentativa culinaria.

  ● [v] intentar *Don't attempt too much* No intente demasiado.

attend asistir a *Did you attend the meeting?* ¿Asistió Ud. a la reunión? ▲ cuidar *What doctor attended you?* ¿Qué doctoı le cuidó?

  ○ **to attend to** atender, ocuparse *I have some things to attend to.* Tengo algunas cosas a que atender.

attendance presencia *My attendance will hardly be necessary.* Casi no será necesaria mi presencia. ▲ público, auditorio *We've had very poor attendance at these meetings.* Hemos tenido muy poco público en estas reuniones.

attendant sirviente.

attention atención *Please give me your complete attention.* Hagan el favor de escucharme con toda atención.

  ‖ *I can't get anyone's attention.* No puede conseguir que nadie me atienda.

attest atestiguar.

attitude actitud.

attorney abogado

attract atraer.

attraction atracción *Her dancing is the big attraction of the show.* Su baile es la atracción más grande de la función.

  ○ **main attraction** número principal *We got to the circus just in time for the main attraction.* Llegamos al circo precisamente para el número principal.

attractive atractivo, atrayente.

attribute [n] atributo.

attribute [v] atribuir *To what do you attribute your success?* ¿A qué atribuye Ud. su éxito?

auction subasta, remate.

audible audible.

audience auditorio, público.

auditorium auditorio.

August agosto.

aunt tía.

  ○ **aunt and uncle** tíos *I'd like you to meet my aunt and uncle.* Me gustaría presentarle a mis tíos.

author autor.

authority autoridad *What authority do you have to do this?* ¿Qué autoridad tiene Ud. para hacer esto?—*I'm not an authority on that.* No soy una autoridad en eso.

  ○ **authorities** autoridades *I'll speak to the authorities.* Hablaré con las autoridades.

authorize autorizar, facultar.

auto auto.

automatic automático.

  ○ **automatic (pistol)** pistola automática.

automobile automóvil.

autumn otoño.

avail ○ **of no avail** en vano *The doctor's efforts to save his life were of no avail.* Los esfuerzos del médico por salvar su vida fueron en vano.

  ○ **to avail oneself** aprovecharse *Avail yourself of every opportunity.* Aprovéchese de todas las oportunidades.

available disponible.

avenue avenida.

average [n] promedio *The average (age) of the class is fifteen years.* El promedio (de edad) de la clase es de quince años.

  ● [adj] medio *What's the average temperature here?* ¿Cuál es la temperatura media aquí?

  ● [v] hallar el promedio *Average this column of figures for me.* Hálleme el promedio de esta columna de cifras.

  ○ **on the average** por término medio *On the average I go to the movies once a week* Por término medio voy al cine una vez por semana.

aviation aviación.

avocado aguacate, palta [Am].

avoid evitar *Avoid that at all cost.* Eviten eso a toda costa.

  ‖ *He avoided her.* Evitaba encontrarla.

await esperar *We await your reply.* Esperamos su repuesta.

awake [adj] despierto *Are you wide awake?* ¿Está Ud. bien despierto?

  ● [v] despertar *Some airplanes awoke me at five o'clock.* Unos aeroplanos me despertaron a las cinco.

○ **to be awake to** darse cuenta *He's awake to his responsibilities.* Se da cuenta de sus responsabilidades.
aware enterado, sabedor.
away fuera *Have you been away?* ¿Ha estado Ud. fuera?
○ **to give away** dar *We're giving this away free.* Estamos dando esto gratis. ○ **to go away** irse *Go away.* Váyase. ○ **to take away** llevar(se) *Please take this away.* Haga el favor de llevarse esto. ○ **to throw away** tirar *Don't throw anything away.* No tire nada.
‖ *It's thirty kilometers away.* Está a treinta kilómetros.
awe pavor.
awful terrible, tremendo *An awful accident happened yesterday.* Ayer ocurrió un accidente terrible. ▲ horrible *We've been having awful weather.* Hemos tenido un tiempo horrible. ▲ muy malo *He looked awful.* Tenía un aspecto muy malo
‖ *What an awful shame!* ¡Qué lástima!
awhile algún tiempo *The girl will be here for awhile.* La muchacha estará aquí por algún tiempo. ▲ un rato *Let's talk for awhile.* Vamos a charlar un rato.
awkward torpe, chambón *He was awkward in everything he did.* Era torpe en todo lo que hacía. ▲ desgarbado *He's a very awkward fellow.* Es un tipo muy desgarbado. ▲ incómodo *This package is awkward to carry.* Es muy incómodo llevar este paquete. ▲ delicado, embarazoso *It was an awkward situation.* Era una situación delicada.
awning toldo, marquesina.
ax hacha.
axis eje.
axle eje de las ruedas.

B

baby [*n*] nene, criatura, bebé, crío. ▲ niño *She's sewing baby clothes.* Está cosiendo ropa de niño.
● [*v*] mimar *We must baby her until she gets well again.* Tenemos que mimarla hasta que se ponga buena.
bachelor soltero *My brother's a bachelor.* Mi hermano es soltero. ▲ bachiller *He has a bachelor's degree.* Tiene el grado (*or* titulo) de bachiller.
○ **confirmed bachelor** solterón *My uncle's a confirmed bachelor.* Mi tío es un solterón.
back [*n*] espalda *(of person)* *He's carrying the bag on his back.* Lleva el saco a la espalda. ▲ lomo *(of animal).* ▲ respaldo *This chair has a high back.* Esta silla tiene un respaldo alto.
● [*adj*] de atrás *He went out the back door.* Salío por la puerta de atrás.
● [*adv*] de vuelta *I'll be back at four.* Estaré de vuelta a las cuatro.
● [*v*] apoyar *We'll back him in his request.* Le apoyaremos en su petición. ▲ dar marcha atrás *Please back your car slowly.* Por favor, dé marcha atrás despacio.
○ **at the back, in the back** al fondo *He's in the back of the classroom.* El está al fondo de la clase. ○ **back in** allá por *Back in 1850.* Allá por el año de 1850. ○ **back number** número atrasado *The library has the back numbers of this magazine.* La biblioteca tiene los números atrasados de esta revista. ○ **behind one's back** a espaldas de uno *They told stories about her behind her back.* Contaban cosas de ella a sus espaldas. ○ **on one's back** boca arriba *He lay on his back.* Estaba acostado boca arriba. ○ **to back down** volverse atrás *Don't back down on what you said.* No se vuelva atrás en lo que ha dicho. ○ **to get back** volver, regresar *They got back from their journey.* Han vuelto de su viaje. ○ **to give back** devolver *When are you going to give me back the book?* Cuándo me va a devolver el libro? ○ **to go back on** volverse atrás *He went back on me.* Se me volvió atrás. ○ **to hold back** contener *They held the crowd back.* Contuvieron a la multitud. ○ **to hold something back** callarse algo *Tell everything; don't hold anything back.* Dilo todo; no te calles nada. ○ **to pay back** pagar *We must pay back what we owe him.* Debemos pagar lo que le debemos. ○ **to turn one's back on** volver la espalda *He turned his back on them.* Les volvió la espalda.
‖ *What's at the back of what he said?* ¿Con qué intención lo dijo?
backbone espinazo *He hurt his back-*

bone. Se lastimó el espinazo. ▲ agallas *If she had any backbone she wouldn't take those insults.* Si tuviera agallas no aguantaría esos insultos
‖ *He's the backbone of the organization.* Es la piedra angular de la organización.

background fondo *He painted some white flowers on a black background.* Pintó unas flores blancas sobre un fondo negro. ▲ antecedentes *She has a very fine background.* Tiene muy buenos antecedentes.
○ **in the background** en segundo término *She likes to keep in the background.* Le gusta estar en segundo término.

backward [*adj*] tímido *He's very backward about asking for anything.* Es muy tímido para pedir algo. ▲ atrasado *She runs a school for backward children.* Tiene una escuela para niños atrasados.
● [*adv*] al revés *You've got your blouse on backward.* Ud. tiene puesta la blusa al revés.

backwards hacia atrás.
bacon tocino.
bad [*n*] lo malo *We must take the bad along with the good.* Hay que aceptar lo bueno con lo malo.
● [*adj*] mal, malo *It's a bad day to go out.* Es mal día para salir. *or* Está día malo para salir *(of weather).* —*It's not a bad idea.* No es una mala idea. ▲ fuerte *I caught a bad cold in the rain.* Con la lluvia he cogido un fuerte catarro. ▲ mal *I feel bad today.* Me siento mal hoy.
○ **from bad to worse** de mal en peor *His affairs went from bad to worse.* Sus asuntos iban de mal en peor. ○ **to be bad for** hacer daño *a Too much smoking's bad for you.* El fumar demasiado le hará daño. ○ **to go bad** echarse a perder *The butter went bad because of the heat.* La mantequilla se echó a perder por el calor. ○ **too bad** (una) lástima *That's too bad.* Eso es una lástima.

baffle [*v*] desconcertar, confundir.
bag [*n*] bolsa, saco, cartucho *Put these groceries in a bag.* Ponga estos comestibles en una bolsa. ▲ cartera *Hand me my bag and my gloves, please.* Por favor, mi cartera y mis guantes. ▲ maleta *Where shall I check my bags and trunk?* ¿Dónde puedo facturar las maletas y el baúl?

● [*v*] capturar *They bagged a lion.* Capturaron un león.
○ **to bag at the knees** hacer rodilleras *His trousers bag at the knees.* Los pantalones le hacen rodilleras. ○ **to let the cat out of the bag** escapársele a uno un secreto.

baggage equipaje *Take my baggage up to my room.* Suba el equipaje a mi cuarto.
○ **baggage car** furgón (*or* vagón) de equipajes *The baggage car's at the end of the train.* El furgón de equipajes está al final del tren. ○ **baggage room** sala de equipajes *Where's the baggage room?* ¿Dónde está la sala de equipajes?

bail [*n*] fianza *He's out on bail.* Está libre bajo fianza.
● [*v*] poner fianza, salir fiador *His friends bailed him out of jail.* Sus amigos le pusieron una fianza para sacarlo de la cárcel. ▲ achicar *He had to bail the water out of the boat with a can.* Tuvo que achicar el bote con una lata.
○ **to bail out** lanzarse *The pilot bailed out of the plane.* El piloto se lanzó del avión.

bait [*n*] cebo.
bake asar, [*Am*] hornear *We had baked potatoes for dinner.* Hemos comido patatas asadas. ▲ cocer [*Sp*], hornear [*Am*] *The bread was baked this morning.* El pan ha sido cocido esta mañana.

baker panadero.
bakery panadería.
balance [*n*] equilibrio *I lost my balance and fell off the step.* Perdí el equilibrio y me caí del escalón. ▲ resto *Pay the balance in monthly installments.* Pague el resto por mensualidades. ▲ balance *What's my bank balance?* ¿Cuál es mi balance en el banco?
● [*v*] equilibrar *The two weights balance each other.* Los dos pesos se equilibran.
○ **in the balance** en la balanza *His fate hung in the balance.* Su suerte estaba en la balanza.
‖ *Does this account balance?* ¿Está bien el balance de esta cuenta?

balcony balcón.
bald calvo.
bale fardo, bala.
ball ovillo *He rolled the string into a ball.* Hizo un ovillo con la cuerda. ▲ pelota *They played ball all after-*

noon. Jugaron a la pelota toda la tarde.
○ **to be balled up** estar hecho un lío
He got all balled up. Estaba hecho un lío.
‖ *Do you want to play baseball, football, or basketball?* ¿Quiere Ud. jugar al beisbol, al futbol, o al basketball?

ballet ballet.

balloon globo.
○ **balloon tire** neumático de baja presión, neumático de balón.

ballot papeleta para votar.

ballroom salón de baile.

bamboo bambú.

banana plátano, banana.

band lista, franja *The room was decorated with a blue band near the ceiling.* El cuarto estaba decorado con una franja azul cerca del techo. ▲ banda *The band played marches.* La banda tocó marchas. ○ **metal band** fleje, [*Sp*] precinto, [*Am*] zuncho *Put a metal band around this box.* Ponga un zuncho en esta caja. ○ **rubber band** goma *Can you get me a box of rubber bands?* ¿Me puede conseguir una caja de gomas? ○ **to band together** unirse *They banded together against me.* Se unieron contra mí.

bandage [*n*] vendaje.
● [*v*] vendar.

bandit bandido.

bang [*n*] estrépito *I heard a loud bang.* Oí un gran estrépito. ▲ ímpetu *He started off with a bang.* Empezó con mucho ímpetu.
● [*v*] golpear con violencia *She banged the table.* Golpeó la mesa con violencia. ▲ tirar con violencia *He banged the book down on the table.* Tiró el libro sobre la mesa con violencia. ▲ cerrar de golpe *He banged the door.* Cerró la puerta de golpe. ▲ golpear *Stop banging on the piano!* No siga golpeando en el piano. ○ **bangs** flequillo *She wore her hair in bangs.* Se peinaba con flequillo. ○ **to go over with a bang** resultar bomba *The party went over with a bang.* La fiesta resultó bomba.

banish desterrar.

banjo banjo.

bank [*n*] montón *There's a bank of snow near the door.* Hay un montón de nieve cerca de la puerta. ▲ orilla, margen, ribera *He swam to the nearest bank.* Nadó hasta la orilla más cercana. ▲ banco *We should deposit this money in a bank.* Deberíamos depositar este dinero en un banco.— *I'd like to open a bank account.* Quisiera abrir una cuenta en el banco. ▲ banca *(in games) How much is in the bank?* ¿Cuánto hay de banca?
● [*v*] tapar, cubrir *(a fire) Please bank the fire so it'll burn slowly.* Haga el favor de cubrir el fuego para que arda lentamente. ○ **to bank on** estar seguro *You can bank on it.* Puede estar seguro.

banker banquero.

bankruptcy quiebra.

banner bandera.

banquet banquete *They gave a banquet in his honor.* Dieron un banquete en su honor.

baptize bautizar.

bar [*n*] tranca, barra *Put the bar across the window.* Ponga Ud. la tranca a través de la ventana. ▲ barra *Where's the bar of soap?* ¿Dónde está la barra de jabón? ▲ impedimento *Is a foreign accent much of a bar to making friends?* ¿Es un impedimento para hacer amigos el acento extranjero? ▲ compás *He played a few bars of my favorite waltz.* Tocó unos compases de mi vals favorito. ▲ mostrador *He was standing at the bar when I walked in.* Estaba frente al mostrador cuando yo entré. ▲ bar *Meet me in the bar on the corner in an hour.* Encuéntreme en el bar de la esquina dentro de una hora.
● [*v*] trancar *He forgot to bar the gate to the pasture.* Olvidó trancar la portilla de la pradera. ▲ obstruir *The fallen tree barred our way.* El árbol caído obstruía el paso. ▲ excluir *He's been barred from the club.* Le han excluído del club. ○ **bar none** incluyendo a todos, sin excepción. ○ **barred window** ventana enrejada *The jail has barred windows.* La cárcel tiene ventanas enrejadas. ‖ *He was admitted to the bar.* Se licenció para ejercer la abogacía.

barbecue [*n*] barbacoa [*Mex*].
● [*v*] asar en asador, hacer barbacoa.

barbed wire alambre de púas.

barber peluquero, barbero *Where can I find a good barber?* ¿Dónde puedo encontrar un buen peluquero?
○ **barber shop** peluquería, barbería.

bare desnudo, al aire *Don't go out in this weather with bare legs.* No salga Ud. en este tiempo con las piernas desnudas. ▲puro *I'm telling you the bare truth.* Le estoy diciendo la pura verdad. ▲vacío *The apartment was completely bare when we moved in.* El apartamento estaba completamente vacío cuando nos mudamos allí. ▲escaso *He won the race by a bare second.* Ganó la carrera por un segundo escaso.

○ **to bare one's head** descubrirse *When the flag passed, the men bared their heads.* Al pasar la bandera, los hombres se descubrieron.

bareback ○ **to ride bareback** montar en pelo.

barefoot descalzo.

barely escasamente *He had barely enough to live on.* Tenía escasamente lo bastante para vivir.

bargain [n] trato *I'll make a bargain with you.* Haré un trato con Ud. ▲ganga *You'll find many bargains there.* Ud. encontrará allí muchas gangas.

● [v] regatear *We bargained with him before buying.* Estuvimos regateando con él antes de comprar.

‖ *Tomorrow's a bargain day at this store.* Mañana habrá una venta de saldos en esta tienda.

barge lanchón.

baritone [adj; n] barítono.

bark [n] corteza *That tree has a rough bark.* Ese árbol tiene una corteza áspera.

● [v] raspar *I barked my shin.* Me raspé la canilla.

bark [n] ladrido *That dog has a shrill bark.* Ese perro tiene un ladrido agudo.

● [v] ladrar *Make the dog stop barking.* Haga que el perro deje de ladrar.

barley cebada.

barn granero *The barn was filled with hay and grain.* El granero estaba lleno de heno y de grano.

barometer barómetro.

barracks cuartel.

barrel barril *The truck was loaded with barrels of beer.* El camión estaba cargado con barriles de cerveza. ▲cañón *Clean the barrel of this gun.* Limpie el cañón de esta escopeta.

barren árido.

barrier obstáculo, barrera.

base [n] pedestal *The base of the statue was still there.* Todavía estaba allí el pedestal de la estátua. ▲base *The soldiers returned to their base.* Los soldados regresaron a su base.—*Run*

to base before he catches you. Corra a la base antes de que le coja.

● [adj] bajo *That's a very base action.* Esa es una acción muy baja.

● [v] basar *Success is based on honesty.* El éxito está basado en la honradez.

baseball beisbol *(game).*

basement sótano.

bashful tímido.

basic básico.

basin palangana *(for washing).*

basis base.

basket cesta, canasta *He brought a basket of fruit.* Trajo una canasta de fruta.

basketball basketball.

bass *(singer)* bajo.

bass *(fish)* lubina, róbalo.

baste hilvanar *Why don't you baste the seam?* ¿Por qué no hilvana Ud. la costura? ▲lardear *Baste the chicken with butter every half hour.* Lardee Ud. el pollo con mantequilla cada media hora.

bat [n] bate *He hit the ball with the bat.* Dió con el bate a la pelota.

● [v] batear *He batted the ball over the fence.* Bateó la pelota por encima de la cerca.

○ **at bat** bateando *Who's at bat?* ¿Quién está bateando?

bat murciélago *I'm afraid of bats.* Tengo miedo a los murciélagos.

○ **blind as a bat** ciego como un topo *[literally, "as a mole"].*

batch *(of bread)* hornada.

bath baño *Where can I take a bath?* ¿Dónde puedo tomar un baño?

bathe bañar *What time do you usually bathe the baby?* ¿A qué hora baña Ud. al niño usualmente? ▲bañarse *We went bathing in the lake.* Nos bañamos en el lago.

bathing cap gorro de baño.

bathing suit traje de baño.

bathrobe albornoz, bata de baño.

bathroom cuarto de baño.

bath towel toalla de baño.

bathtub bañera, baño, [Am] tina.

batter *(cooking)* batido.

batter down derribar.

battery batería *My radio needs a new battery.* Mi radio necesita una nueva batería.—*We silenced the enemy battery.* Silenciamos la batería enemiga.

○ **assault and battery** agresión.

battle [n] batalla *The battle was fought at the river.* La batalla se libró junto al río.

● [v] batirse *The two armies bat-*

tled all day long. Los dos ejércitos se batieron todo el día. ▲ *luchar He battled against heavy odds.* Luchó en condiciones desiguales.

battlefield campo de batalla.

battleship acorazado.

bay bahía *The boat sailed in the bay.* El barco navegaba por la bahía.

bay ○ *at bay* a raya *He held them at bay.* Los mantuvo a raya.

be ser *The road was built by the prisoners.* El camino fué construido por los prisioneros.—*The plans have been perfected.* Los planes han sido perfeccionados.—*It was a gold watch.* Era un reloj de oro.—*"What time is it?" "It's ten o'clock."* "¿Qué hora es?" "Son las diez."—*They're mine.* Son míos.—*We're from New York.* Somos de Nueva York.—*Be a good boy!* ¡Sé buen chico!—*He's a doctor.* Es médico.—*I wish I were younger!* ¡Ojalá fuese más joven!—*My birthday's July the third.* Mi cumpleaños es el tres de julio.—*Being stubborn won't help you.* El ser terco no le traerá ningún beneficio. ▲ *estar Where's your office?* ¿Dónde está su oficina?—*He's to be there next Tuesday.* Tendrá que estar allí el martes próximo.—*He'll be here tomorrow.* Estará aquí mañana.—*I'm looking for another job.* Estoy buscando otro empleo.—*He was writing a letter.* Estaba escribiendo una carta.—*The house was painted white.* La casa estaba pintada de blanco.—*She's still sick.* Todavía está enferma.—*Your baggage is being checked.* Están facturando su equipaje. ▲ *haber There's a big house on the corner.* Hay una casa grande en la esquina.—*There was a cup on the table.* Había una taza en la mesa.—*The child must be punished.* Hay que castigar al niño.—*I'm sorry I was late this morning.* Siento haber llegado tarde esta mañana. ▲ *tener I'm cold.* Tengo frío.—*You're right.* Tiene razón. ▲ *hacer It's sunny.* Hace sol.—*It's cold.* Hace frío.—*We'll have been here a year this coming Friday.* El viernes que viene hará un año que estamos aquí.—*What are you doing?* ¿Qué hace Ud.?

○ *to be off* ser inexacto *His figures were way off.* Sus cálculos eran muy inexactos.

‖ *It's rumored that they're getting a divorce.* Se dice que van a divorciarse. ‖ *Be quiet!* ¡Cállate! ‖ *Span-*

ish is spoken here. Aquí se habla español. ‖ *The book was written by a friend of mine.* Un amigo mío escribió el libro.

beach [n] playa *Were you at the beach all summer?* ¿Estuvo Ud. en la playa todo el verano?

● [v] varar, poner en seco *We beached the canoe.* Hemos puesto la canoa en seco.

bead cuenta.

beak pico.

beam [n] viga *The beams are beginning to rot.* Las vigas empiezan a pudrirse. ▲ rayo *I was awakened by a beam of light.* Me despertó un rayo de luz.

● [v] destellar de alegría *She beams every time he speaks to her.* Destella de alegría cada vez que le habla.

○ *to be off the beam* no dar pie con bola *You're off the beam this morning.* No da Ud. pie con bola esta mañana.

bean frijol [Am], judía [Sp] *Do they have beans on the menu?* ¿Tienen frijoles en el menú?

bear [n] oso.

bear [v] sostener *This board won't bear your weight.* Esta tabla no sostendrá su peso. ▲ soportar *He bore the pain bravely.* Soportó el dolor con valentía. ▲ sufrir *I can't bear to see them leave.* No puedo sufrir el verlos marchar. ▲ aguantar *I can't bear him.* No puedo aguantarle. ▲ dar *This orchard bears good peaches.* Este huerto da buenos duraznos. ▲ tener *She's borne three children.* Ha tenido tres hijos.

○ *to bear out* probar *This bears out what I said.* Esto prueba lo que dije.

beard barba.

bearing relación *That has no bearing on the matter.* Eso no tiene relación con el asunto. ▲ porte, aire *His military bearing's excellent.* Su porte militar es excelente. ▲ cojinete *The bearings of the car are worn out.* Los cojinetes del automóvil están gastados. ▲ marcación, rumbo *The navigator's taking a bearing.* El oficial de derrota está determinando el rumbo.

○ *to get one's bearings* orientarse, marcarse *Let's get our bearings before we go any further.* Vamos a orientarnos antes de continuar. ○ *to lose one's bearings* aturdirse.

beat [n] ritmo *The beat of the music*
beast bestia.

beat [n] ritmo *The beat of the music wasn't clear.* El ritmo de la música no era claro. ▲ronda *What policeman's on this beat?* ¿Qué policía hace esta ronda?
  ● [v] derrotar *We beat the enemy.* Derrotamos al enemigo. ▲vencer *They were beaten in the game.* Fueron vencidos en el juego. ▲sacudir *Please beat this carpet.* Haga el favor de sacudir esta alfombra. ▲batir *Beat the egg before putting it in.* Bata el huevo antes de añadirlo. ▲latir, palpitar *His heart was beating regularly.* Su corazón latía con regularidad.
  ○ **beaten path** camino(s) trillado(s) *He always sticks to the beaten path.* Siempre sigue los caminos trillados. ○ **to beat back** hacer retroceder *The soldiers beat back the enemy.* Los soldados hicieron retroceder al enemigo. ○ **to beat it** escapar(se) *He beat it.* Se escapó. ○ **to beat time** marcar el compás *He beat time with his foot.* Marcaba el compás con el pie. ○ **to beat to death** matar a golpes *They beat him to death.* Le mataron a golpes.
  ‖ *Beat it!* ¡Lárguese! ‖ *They beat him to it.* Le cogieron la delantera.
beautiful bello, hermoso *What a beautiful day!* ¡Qué día tan hermoso!
beauty belleza *I find great beauty in his music* Encuentro mucha belleza en su música.—*She's a beauty!* ¡Es una belleza!
  ‖ *The fish we caught were beauties.* Los pescados que cogimos eran muy hermosos.
beauty parlor salón de belleza, peluquería.
beaver castor.
because porque *He didn't come because he got sick.* No vino porque se enfermó.
  ○ **because of** a causa de *I didn't buy it because of the high price.* No lo compré a causa de lo elevado del precio.
beckon llamar con señas.
become hacerse *The work's become harder.* El trabajo se ha hecho más difícil.—*He became a lawyer.* Se hizo abogado. ▲ponerse *He became ill.* Se puso enfermo. ▲volverse *He's becoming more aggressive every day.* Se está volviendo cada día más agresivo. ▲llegar a ser *He became a good lawyer.* Llegó a ser un buen abogado. ▲cumplir *When he became twenty-*

one, *he left home.* Cuando cumplió veintiún años se marchó de su casa. ▲sentar bien, quedar bien *The red dress becomes her.* El traje rojo le sienta bien.
  ○ **to become of** ser de *What's to become of her?* ¿Qué será de ella?
becoming [adj] ○ **to be becoming** sentar bien, quedar bien *That hat's very becoming.* Ese sombrero le sienta bien. ○ **to be becoming to** ir con *Such conduct isn't becoming to a man of your position.* Tal conducta no va con un hombre de su posición.
bed cama *My bed hasn't been made.* No han hecho mi cama. ▲lecho *He was on his death bed.* Estaba en su lecho de muerte. ▲base *The machine's set in a bed of concrete.* La máquina está colocada sobre una base de hormigón. ▲firme *The road bed's in bad condition.* El firme de la carretera está en malas condiciones. ▲macizo *Don't step in the flower bed.* No pise Ud. el macizo de flores. ▲cauce *Follow the old river bed for two miles.* Siga el viejo cauce del río dos millas.
  ○ **to get up on the wrong side of the bed** levantarse de mal humor. ○ **to go to bed** acostarse *I went to bed late.* Me acosté tarde.
bedbug chinche.
bedding ropa de cama *Air the bedding.* Ponga al aire la ropa de cama. ▲cama *We used straw for bedding for the horses.* Usábamos paja para la cama de los caballos.
bedroom dormitorio, alcoba.
bedspread colcha, cubrecama.
bee abeja.
  ○ **to have a bee in one's bonnet** estar un poco destornillado.
beech haya.
beef carne de vaca *Do you have beef or pork?* ¿Tiene Ud. carne de vaca o de cerdo?
beefsteak bistec, biftec.
beehive colmena.
beeline ‖ *He made a beeline for home.* Se fué directamente a casa.
been See **be.**
beer cerveza.
beet remolacha.
beetle escarabajo.
before [adv] antes *We should have done this before.* Deberíamos haberlo hecho antes.
  ● [prep] ante, en presencia de *He was taken before the judge.* Fué llevado ante el juez. ▲antes de *The telegram should come before evening.* El

telegrama debe llegar antes de la noche. ▲ antes que *Do this before anything else.* Haga Ud. esto antes que nada.

● [*conj*] antes de *I'll telephone you before I start.* Le telefonearé antes de salir. ▲ antes de que *Let me know before you come.* Avíseme antes de que Ud. venga.

○ **before Christ (B. C.)** antes de Jesucristo (a. de J. C.) *The temple was built in the first century before Christ.* El templo fué construído en el siglo primero antes de Jesucristo.

○ **before long** dentro de poco *They'll come before long.* Vendrán dentro de poco.

‖ *Business before pleasure.* Primero es la obligación que la devoción.

beforehand de antemano.

beg pedir limosna *Begging is a common practice in this country.* El pedir limosna es corriente en este país. ▲ mendigar *That man went begging from door to door.* Aquel hombre iba mendigando de puerta en puerta. ▲ pedir *The children begged for pennies.* Los chicos pedían centavos. ▲ rogar *They begged us to help them.* Nos rogaron que les ayudásemos.

‖ *I beg your pardon! ("Excuse me.")* ¡Perdone! ‖ *I beg your pardon? ("Please repeat.")* ¡Perdone! ¿Qué dijo Ud.?

beggar mendigo, pordiosero.

begin empezar *The performance begins at 8:30 P. M.* La función empieza a las ocho y media de la noche.—*The building was begun many years ago.* El edificio fué empezado hace muchos años. ▲ comenzar *Cigarettes began to disappear from the market.* Los cigarillos comenzaban a desaparecer del mercado.

○ **to begin with** para empezar *To begin with, he's too old.* Para empezar, es demasiado viejo.

beginner principiante.

beginning [*n*] principio.

behalf ○ **in,** *or* **on, behalf of** a favor de, en nombre de.

behave portarse, conducirse *The little boy behaved badly during the whole trip.* El muchacho se portó muy mal durante todo el viaje. ▲ conducirse bien *Behave oneself.* Condúcete bien.

behavior conducta *Her behavior's very strange.* Su conducta es muy rara.

‖ *He was on his very best behavior.* Se comportó de bien como nunca.

behind [*adv*] atrás *They left all the*

other cars behind.* Dejaron atrás a los demás autos.

● [*prep*] detrás de *The car's parked behind the house.* El carro está estacionado detrás de la casa.

○ **behind one's back** a espaldas *He talked about me behind my back.* Habló a espaldas mías. ○ **to be behind time** estar atrasado *The train's behind time.* El tren está atrasado.

○ **to fall behind** atrasarse *He's fallen behind in his work.* Se ha atrasado en su trabajo. ○ **to leave behind** olvidar *Have you left anything behind?* ¿Ha olvidado Ud. algo?

behold contemplar.

beige beige.

being ser *They don't act like human beings.* No se portan como seres humanos.

○ **for the time being** por ahora, de momento *Let the matter rest for the time being.* Deja dormir el asunto por ahora.

belief creencia, opinión.

believe creer *Do you believe what he told us?* ¿Cree Ud. lo que nos dijo? —*I believe so.* Creo que sí.

○ **to believe in** creer en *Do you believe in ghosts?* ¿Ud. cree en fantasmas?

bell campana *The bell rings half an hour before services.* La campana toca media hora antes de los servicios religiosos. ▲ timbre *Ring the bell for the elevator.* Toque el timbre para el ascensor.

○ **stroke of a bell** campanada *I couldn't count the strokes of the bell.* No he podido contar las campanadas.

bellboy botones, muchacho (*or* mozo) de hotel.

bellow [*v*] bufar.

belly vientre.

belong pertenecer *Does this book belong to you?* ¿Le pertenece a Ud. este libro?—*He belongs to the Republican Party.* Pertenece al Partido Republicano. ▲ ser de *Who does this belong to?* ¿De quién es esto?—*This old chair belongs in the kitchen.* Esta silla vieja es de la cocina.

beloved [*adj*, *n*] querido, amado.

below [*adv*] abajo *From the window they saw what happened below.* Desde la ventana veían lo que pasaba abajo. ▲ de abajo *Try the floor below.* Mire en el piso de abajo.

● [*prep*] debajo de *Who has the room below mine?* ¿Quién tiene el cuarto debajo del mío? ▲ bajo *The*

temperature here seldom gets below zero. La temperatura aquí rara vez llega a bajo cero. ▲ por debajo de *He's below average height.* Está por debajo de la altura media.
‖ *Watch out below!* ¡Cuidado!

belt cinturón *Do you wear a belt or suspenders?* ¿Usa Ud. cinturón o tirantes? ▲ correa *Please fix the fan belt in this car.* Haga el favor de arreglar la correa del ventilador del auto.
O *life belt* salvavidas, cinturón de salvamento *Have your life belts ready.* Tengan listos los salvavidas.

bench banco *We sat down on a bench in the park.* Nos sentamos en un banco en el parque. ▲ banco *The carpenter's at his bench eight hours a day.* El carpintero está pegado a su banco ocho horas al día.

bend [n] curva *The house is beyond the bend in the road.* La casa está pasada la curva de la carretera.
● [v] doblar *He bent the rod into a V shape.* Dobló la varilla en forma de V. ▲ doblarse *How much will this bend without breaking?* ¿Cuánto se podrá doblar esto sin que se rompa?
O *to bend down* encorvarse, agacharse *You'll have to bend down to get through here.* Tendrá Ud. que agacharse para pasar por aquí.

beneath debajo de *He was buried beneath the tree.* Fué enterrado debajo del árbol. ▲ inferior a *Don't look on these people as beneath you.* No considere a esta gente inferior a Ud.
‖ *That remark's beneath our notice.* Esa observación ni siquiera merece que la tomemos en cuenta.

benefit [n] beneficio(s) *The new law gave us very little benefit.* La nueva ley nos suministro muy pocos beneficios.—*Will you buy this ticket for the benefit?* ¿Quiere comprar este billete para el beneficio?
● [v] beneficiar, aprovechar *The trip didn't benefit us much.* El viaje no nos ha beneficiado mucho.

bent [n] inclinación *He has a bent for art.* Tiene inclinación por el arte.
● [adj] torcido *These nails are bent too much.* Estos clavos están demasiado torcidos.
O *bent on* resuelto a *In spite of us he's bent on going.* A pesar de nuestra opinión está resuelto a irse.

berth cama *I couldn't get a berth on the midnight train.* No pude conseguir cama en el tren de media noche.

▲ camarote *There are two berths left on this ship.* Quedan dos camarotes en este barco. ▲ amarradero *The ship was anchored in its berth.* El buque estaba anclado en su amarradero.

beside al lado de *Please put this trunk beside the other one.* Haga Ud. el favor de poner este baúl al lado del otro.
O *beside oneself* fuera de sí *He was beside himself with anger.* Estaba fuera de sí de rabia. O *to be beside the point* no venir al caso

besides [adv] además *We need these and others besides.* Necesitamos estos y además otros.
● [prep] además de *Others must help besides him.* Otros deben ayudar además de él.

best [adv] mejor *She knows three languages but speaks French best.* Sabe tres idiomas pero el que mejor habla es el francés.
O *the best* el mejor *We tried to pick out the best plan.* Tratamos de escoger el mejor plan. ▲ lo mejor *We want only the best.* Queremos sólo lo mejor. O *to get the best of* adelantarse, aventajar *We must be careful he doesn't get the best of us.* Tenemos que tener cuidado de que no se nos adelante. O *to make the best of* sacar el mejor partido de *We had few supplies, but we made the best of what we had.* Teníamos pocas provisiones, pero sacamos el mejor partido de ellas.

bestow conferir.

bet [n] apuesta *When are you going to pay up that bet?* ¿Cuándo va a pagar esa apuesta?
● [v] apostar *I bet five dollars on the black horse.* Apuesto cinco dólares al caballo negro.
‖ *You bet!* ¡Y que lo digas!

betray traicionar *He was charged with betraying his country.* Se le acusó de traicionar a su país. ▲ revelar *His remarks betrayed his ignorance.* Lo que decía revelaba su ignorancia.

better [adj] mejor *I want a better room than this one.* Quiero un cuarto mejor que éste.—*I felt better this morning.* Me encontraba mejor esta mañana.
● [adv] mejor *I can't do better than this.* No lo puedo hacer mejor que esto.
● [v] mejorar *We're trying to better living conditions here.* Estamos

tratando de mejorar aquí las condiciones de vida.

○ **better half** media naranja, esposa.
○ **better off** mejor *We'll be better off if we move.* Estaremos mejor si nos mudamos. ○ **so much the better** tanto mejor *So much the better if you pay in advance.* Tanto mejor si Ud. paga por adelantado. ○ **to get better** mejorar *The doctor says he's getting better.* El médico dice que va mejorando. ○ **to get the better of** aprovecharse de *He'll try to get the better of you.* Tratará de aprovecharse de Ud.
‖ *This is for the better.* Más vale así. ‖ *We'd better go before it rains.* Sería mejor que nos fuésemos antes de que llueva.

between (por) entre *They walked between the buildings.* Pasaron entre los edificios. ▲ de *I'll meet you between six and seven.* Le encontraré de seis a siete.
○ **between you and me** entre nosotros, entre Ud. y yo *There's nothing between you and me.* No hay nada entre Ud. y yo. ○ **to come between** interponerse entre *We nearly caught up with him, but the traffic came between us.* Casi le alcanzamos pero el tráfico se interpuso entre nosotros.

beverage brebaje.

beware ○ **to beware of** cuidarse de *Beware of the dog!* ¡Cuídese del perro!
‖ *Beware!* ¡Cuidado!

bewilder dejar perplejo.

beyond más allá de *They live beyond the river.* Viven más allá del río.
‖ *When we arrived he was beyond help.* Cuando llegamos para socorrerle, ya era tarde. ‖ *She's living beyond her means.* Gasta más de lo que tiene.

bias [n] sesgo *I want the skirt cut on the bias.* Quiero la falda cortada al sesgo. ▲ prejuicio *It's wrong to judge her with so much bias.* No es justo juzgarla con tanto prejuicio.
● [v] influir *Her opinions have been biased by her friends.* Sus opiniones han sido influidas por sus amigos.

bib babero.

Bible Biblia.

bicycle [n] bicicleta *My bicycle needs repairs.* Mi bicicleta necesita reparación.
● [v] dar un paseo en bicicleta *Let's bicycle down to the lake.* Vamos a dar un paseo en bicicleta hasta el lago.

bid [n] oferta *His bid was too high to get the contract.* Su oferta fué demasiado elevada para conseguir la contrata.
● [v] mandar, ordenar *He wouldn't do as I bid him.* No quiso hacerlo como se lo mandé. ▲ ofrecer *He bid five dollars for the rug and then she bid ten.* El ofreció cinco dólares por la alfombra y después ella ofreció diez. ▲ declarar *I bid two hearts.* Declaro dos corazones.
○ **to bid good-by** decir adiós.

big grande *They live in a big house.* Viven en una casa grande. ▲ mayor *She's my big sister.* Ella es mi hermana mayor. ▲ importante *A big man will talk at the meeting.* Un hombre importante hablará en el mitin.
○ **to talk big** darse importancia, echárselas de importante *He talks big, but don't believe everything he says.* Se da mucha importancia, pero no crea Ud. todo lo que dice.

bill cuenta *We must pay the bill today.* Tenemos que pagar la cuenta hoy. ▲ billete *Can you change a five-dollar bill?* ¿Me puede cambiar un billete de cinco dólares? ▲ cartel *Post no bills.* Se prohibe fijar carteles.— *What's on the bill at the theater this evening?* ¿Qué hay en el cartel del teatro esta noche? ▲ proyecto de ley *The bill will be voted upon by the House of Representatives.* El proyecto de ley será votado por la Cámara de Diputados. ▲ pico *This bird has a long bill.* Este pájaro tiene un pico largo.
○ **bill of fare** lista de comidas.
○ **bill of health** certificado de sanidad.
○ **bill of lading** manifiesto de embarque.

billboard cartelera.

billfold billetera.

billiards billar.

billion mil millones (1,000,000,000).

bind atar *They bound his hands behind his back.* Le ataron las manos detrás de la espalda. ▲ vendar *You should bind up this cut.* Ud. debería vendar esta cortadura. ▲ encuadernar, empastar *They're binding both volumes of his poetry into one book.* Están empastando los dos volúmenes de su poesía en un solo libro. ▲ obligar *That doesn't bind me.* Eso no me obliga.

biography biografía.
biology biología.

birch abedul.

bird pájaro.

birth nacimiento *What's the date of your birth?* ¿Cuál es la fecha de su nacimiento? ▲origen *The governor was a man of humble birth.* El gobernador era un hombre de humilde origen.

○**by birth** de nacimiento *Are you an American by birth?* ¿Es Ud. norteamericano de nacimiento? ○**to give birth to** dar a luz *She's given birth to twins.* Ha dado a luz gemelos.

birthday cumpleaños.

biscuit galleta de mar, bizcocho.

bishop obispo *(church)*; alfil *(chess)*.

bit pedazo, pedacito *He broke the candy into bits.* Partió el dulce en pedacitos. ▲bocado *This bridle doesn't have a bit.* Estas bridas no tienen el bocado. ▲taladro *I need a bit to drill a hole with.* Necesito un taladro para hacer un agujero. ▲pizca, lo más mínimo *That doesn't make a bit of difference.* Eso no altera en lo más mínimo. ▲poco, poquito *They arrived a bit later than the others.* Llegaron un poco más tarde que los demás.

○**bit by bit** poco a poco *We learned the story bit by bit.* Nos enteramos de la historia poco a poco. ○**to blow to bits** hacer pedazos *The truck was blown to bits.* El camión quedó hecho pedazos.

‖ *May I give you a bit of advice?* ¿Me permite Ud. darle un consejo?

bite [*n*] bocado *I took one bite of the apple.* Tomé un bocado de la manzana. ▲picadura *I have two mosquito bites on my arm.* Tengo dos picaduras de mosquito en el brazo.

● [*v*] morder *Will this dog bite?* ¿Muerde este perro?—*He bit into the apple.* Mordió la manzana. ▲picar *The fish are biting well today.* Los peces están picando bien hoy. ▲cortar *It's a biting-cold day.* Es un día en que el frío corta.

○**biting** mordaz *She often makes biting remarks.* Hace muchas veces observaciones mordaces.

‖ *His bark's worse than his bite.* No es tan fiero como parece.

bitter amargo *This coffee's too bitter.* Este café está demasiado amargo. ▲picante, desapacible *It was bitter-cold.* Hacía un frío desapacible. ▲enconado *He had a bitter quarrel with his brother.* Tuvo una enconada

disputa con su hermano. ▲encarnizado *After the war their bitter hatred continued.* Después de la guerra continuaron sus odios encarnizados.

○**to the bitter end** hasta vencer o morir *He fought to the bitter end.* Luchó hasta vencer o morir.

black luto *She's worn black since her husband died.* Va de luto desde que murió su marido. ▲negro *Do you have a black dress?* ¿Tiene Ud. un traje negro?—*Their future's black.* Su porvenir es negro. ▲obscuro *The night was very black.* La noche era muy obscura.

○**to black out** pintar de negro *This line should be blacked out.* Esta línea hay que pintarla de negro. ▲obscurecer *The house must be blacked out by dark.* Hay que obscurecer la casa al anochecer.

blackberry zarza *(plant)*; mora *(fruit)*.

blackbird mirlo.

blackboard pizarra, encerado.

blacken one's character difamarlo a uno.

blackmail [*n*] chantaje.

● [*v*] chantajear.

blackout apagón, obscurecimiento, blackout.

blacksmith herrero.

blade hoja *(knife)*; pala *(oar, propeller)*.

○**blade of grass** brinza de hierba.

blame echar la culpa *He blamed us for the accident.* Nos echó la culpa del accidente. ▲culpar *He didn't blame us for going ahead.* No nos culpó porque prosiguiéramos.

○**to be to blame** tener la culpa *Who's to blame?* ¿Quién tiene la culpa? ○**to take the blame** echarse la culpa.

‖ *You must blame the taxi for our lateness.* El taxi tiene la culpa de nuestro retraso.

blank blanco *Fill in the blanks.* Llene Ud. los blancos. ▲vacío *He feels that his future is a blank.* El cree que su porvenir es vacío.

○**blank check** cheque en blanco. ○**blank form** formulario.

blanket [*n*] manta *We only had one blanket apiece.* Sólo teníamos una manta cada uno. ▲capa *The ground was covered with a thick blanket of snow.* La tierra estaba cubierta con una capa espesa de nieve.

● [*v*] envolver *A thick fog blanketed the city.* Una niebla densa envolvía a la ciudad.

blast [*n*] ráfaga *A blast of wind*

knocked off my hat. Una ráfaga de viento me llevó el sombrero. ▲ explosión *You could hear the blast for miles.* Se podía oír la explosión a muchas millas.

● [v] volar *From a distance we watched them blasting rocks.* Les observábamos desde lejos volar las rocas. ▲ malograr *That scandal blasted her chances for success.* Aquel escándalo malogró sus probabilidades de éxito.

○ **at full blast** a toda velocidad *The machine was working at full blast.* La máquina estaba funcionando a toda velocidad.

blaze [n] llama *Isn't that fire giving off a good blaze!* ¡No da este fuego buena llama!

● [v] arder *The fire's blazing nicely now.* El fuego está ardiendo ahora muy bien. ▲ abrir, construir *We're going to blaze a new trail.* Vamos a abrir un nuevo sendero.

bleach [v] blanquear, poner blanco.

bleed sangrar *This cut's bleeding a lot.* Esta cortadura está sangrando mucho.

○ **to bleed for** sangrar de dolor por *My heart bleeds for you.* Mi corazón sangra de dolor por tí.

blemish [n] mancha.

blend [n] mezcla *This tobacco's a good blend.* Este tabaco es una buena mezcla.

● [v] combinar *Those two colors blend well.* Esos dos colores combinan bien.

bless bendecir.

blessing bendición.

blind [n] persiana *The house has green blinds.* La casa tiene persianas verdes.

● [adj] ciego *He was blind to the true facts.* Estaba ciego para ver la verdad.

● [v] cegar *The lightning blinded me for a while.* El relámpago me cegó por un momento.

○ **blind alley** callejón sin salida *This is only a blind alley.* Esto es sólo callejón sin selida. ○ **blind man** ciego *We helped the blind man across the street.* Ayudamos al ciego a cruzar la calle. ○ **to be blinded** quedarse ciego, cegar *He was blinded in the accident.* Se quedó ciego a consecuencia del accidente.

‖ *He was too blind to read the letter.* Veiía tan mal que no podía leer la carta.

blister ampolla.

blizzard ventisca.

block [n] tarugo, zoquete, trozo *The child was playing with wooden blocks.* El niño estaba jugando con tarugos de madera. ▲ manzana [Sp], cuadra [Am] *Walk three blocks and then turn right.* Camine Ud. tres manzanas y entonces tuerza a la derecha.

● [v] obstruir *That car's blocking traffic.* Ese automóvil está obstruyendo el tráfico. ▲ planchar *How long will it take you to block my hat?* ¿Cuánto tardará Ud. en planchar mi sombrero?

blond [adj, n] rubio.

blonde [adj, n] rubia.

blood sangre *After the accident there was blood on the ground.* Después del accidente había sangre en el suelo.

○ **blood pressure** presión *I have high blood pressure.* Tengo la presión alta. ○ **blood relatives** parientes por consanguinidad *They're blood relatives.* Son parientes por consanguinidad. ○ **blood test** reacción de la sangre *Have you had your blood test?* ¿Le han hecho ya la reacción de su sangre? ○ **in cold blood** a sangre fría *The crime was committed in cold blood.* El crímen fué cometido a sangre fría.

bloody sangriento.

bloom [v] florecer.

blossom [n] flor, capullo *The blossoms are beginning to fall off the trees.* Las flores empiezan a caer de los árboles.

blot [n] borrón *This book's full of ink blots.* Este libro está lleno de borrones de tinta. ▲ mancha, baldón *Don't forget this will be a blot on your record.* No se olvide que esto será una mancha en su hoja de servicios.

● [v] emborronar *The teacher scolded the little girl for blotting her homework.* La maestra regañó a la niña por emborronar sus cuadernos.

○ **to blot out** quitar la vista, encubrir *The trees blot out the view from here.* Los árboles quitan la vista desde aquí. ▲ arrasar, destruir *After the raid the town was almost blotted out.* Después del raid el pueblo quedó casi arrasado. ○ **to blot up** secar *Blot up the ink you spilled.* Seque la tinta que ha derramado.

‖ *She tried to blot out the memory of the man she loved.* Trató de olvidar al hombre que amaba.

blotter papel secante.

blow [n] golpe *He died from a blow on the head.* Murío de un golpe en la cabeza.

● [v] soplar *The wind'll blow hard tonight.* El viento soplará fuerte esta noche. ▲ sonar *Has the whistle blown?* ¿Ha sonado la sirena? ▲ tocar *Blow the horn three times when you come.* Toque Ud. la bocina tres veces cuando venga.

○ **to blow away** llevarse el viento *The wind'll blow the tent away.* El viento se va a llevar la tienda de campaña. ○ **to blow down** derribar *The wind blew the tree down.* El viento derribó el árbol. ○ **to blow one's nose** sonarse (las narices) *I have to blow my nose.* Tengo que sonarme. ○ **to blow out** apagar *Blow out the candle before you go.* Apague la vela antes de irse. ▲ reventar, estallar *The old tire blew out.* El neumático viejo reventó. ▲ fundir(se) *The fuse blew out.* Se fundió el fusible. ○ **to blow over** pasar *Wait until all this blows over.* Espere hasta que pase todo esto. ○ **to blow up** volar *The enemy will try to blow up the bridge.* El enemigo tratará de volar el puente. ▲ inflar *Please blow up this tire.* Haga el favor de inflar este neumático. ▲ desencadenarse *A storm may blow up this afternoon.* Puede desencadenarse una tormenta esta tarde. ○ **to come to blows** pelear, venir a las manos.

blue azul *She always wears blue.* Va siempre de azul. ▲ triste *Why are you so blue this morning?* ¿Porqué está Ud. tan triste esta mañana?

○ **the blues** esplín [*Sp*], morriña [*Sp*], tristeza *I get the blues when it rains.* Tengo esplín cuando llueve. *or* Me da tristeza cuando llueve.

bluff [n] risco *We climbed to the top of the bluff.* Escalamos hasta la punta del risco.

● [v] farolear *He won't do it, he's only bluffing.* No lo hará, está faroleando únicamente.

○ **to call one's bluff** ver un farol, descubrir una farsa.

blunder equivocación *I made an awful blunder.* Cometí una tremenda equivocación.

blunt [adj] romo *These scissors have a blunt point.* Estas tijeras tienen la punta roma. ▲ descortés, crudo *There's no need for you to be so blunt about it.* No hace falta que sea Ud. tan descortés.

● [v] embotar *If you use the knife that way you'll blunt the edge.* Si usa Ud. así el cuchillo embotará el filo.

blush [n] rubor.

● [v] ruborizarse, sonrojarse.

board [n] tabla *We need some boards to make the top of the box.* Necesitamos algunas tablas para hacer la tapa del cajón. ▲ comida *Is the board good there?* ¿Es buena la comida allí? ▲ junta *The board has made new regulations.* La junta ha establecido nuevas regulaciones.

● [v] subir *He's already boarded the train.* Ya ha subido al tren. ▲ comer *Is there a place to board near your work?* ¿Hay un sitio dónde comer cerca de su trabajo? ○ **ironing board** tabla de planchar *Do you have an ironing board?* ¿Tiene Ud. una tabla de planchar? ○ **on board** a bordo *The whistle's blown. Let's get on board.* Ha sonado la sirena. Subamos a bordo. ○ **room and board** pensión completa *They advertise room and board.* Anuncian pensión completa.

‖ *How many people does she board?* ¿Cuántos huéspedes tiene?

boarder huésped.

boarding house casa de huéspedes.

boardwalk entablado de paseo.

boast jactarse *I get fed up hearing you boast about your connections.* Estoy harto de oírle a Ud. jactarse de sus relaciones.

‖ *Our town boasts the finest race horses in the country.* Nuestro pueblo se vanagloria de poseer los mejores caballos de carrera del país.

boat barca *We can cross the river in this boat.* Podemos cruzar el río en esta barca. ▲ barco *The boat trip'll take five days.* El viaje en barco durará cinco días.

‖ *We're all in the same boat.* Corremos todos la misma suerte.

bob cortar corto *She bobbed her hair.* Ella se cortó corto el pelo.

○ **to bob up** presentarse súbitamente *He's always bobbing up at the wrong time.* Siempre se presenta súbitamente en el momento inoportuno.

bobby pin horquilla, ganchito para el pelo.

body cuerpo *He had a rash on his body.* Tenía una erupción en el cuerpo. ▲ cuerpo, tronco *His legs are too short for his body.* Sus piernas son demasiado cortas para su cuerpo. ▲ ca-

dáver *They buried the two bodies in one grave.* Enterraron los dos cadáveres en una tumba. ▲ formación *A body of troops marched down the street.* Una formación de tropas marchaba calle abajo. ▲ contenido *The body of his speech was technical.* El contenido de su discurso era técnico. ○ in a body en grupo *They all left in a body.* Todos salieron en grupo.
bodyguard guardaespaldas.
bog pantano.
○ to bog down empantanarse.
boil [n] divieso, furúnculo, grano *This boil's painful.* Este divieso es doloroso.
● [v] hervir *In a few minutes the water will boil.* Dentro de pocos minutos hervirá el agua. ▲ cocer *Please boil the egg two minutes.* Haga el favor de cocer el huevo dos minutos. ○ to boil down reducirse *What does all this boil down to?* ¿A qué se reduce todo esto? ○ to boil over salirse *The coffee's boiling over.* Se sale el café.
‖ *That remark made me boil.* Esa observación me indignó.
boiler caldera.
boisterous ruidoso.
bold arrojado, atrevido *He was bold enough to face the enemy alone.* Era bastante atrevido para hacer frente él solo al enemigo. ▲ descarado *He's too bold in his manners.* Es demasiado descarado en sus modales.
bologna salchichón.
bolt [n] tornillo *The nut's loose on this bolt.* La tuerca del tornillo está floja. ▲ cerrojo *Did you push the bolt shut?* ¿Ha corrido Ud. el cerrojo? ▲ pieza *She ordered half a bolt of cloth.* Ella pidió media pieza de paño.
● [v] echar el cerrojo a *You forgot to bolt the door.* Ha olvidado Ud. echar el cerrojo a la puerta. ▲ dispararse *The horse bolted across the field.* El caballo se disparó por el campo. ▲ engullir *Don't bolt your food.* No engullas la comida.
○ bolt of lightning rayo, centella.
bomb [n] bomba *A bomb was dropped by the plane.* El avión dejó caer una bomba.
● [v] bombardear *They bombed the factory last night.* Bombardearon la fábrica anoche.
bomber bombardero, avión de bombardeo.
bombing [n] bombardeo *This city was subjected to a bombing.* Esta ciudad fué sometida a un bombardeo.

bond lazo *There's a firm bond of friendship between them.* Hay un lazo de amistad muy firme entre ellos. ▲ bono *How much have you invested in bonds?* Cuánto ha invertido Ud. en bonos? ▲ contrato *Will you require a written bond for this job?* ¿Será necesario un contrato escrito para este trabajo?
‖ *The employees were bonded by the bank.* Los empleados fueron asegurados por el banco.
bone [n] hueso *He broke two bones.* Se le rompieron dos huesos.
● [v] quitar las espinas a *(of fish)*; quitar los huesos a *(of animal).*
○ fish bone espina *A fish bone caught in his throat.* Se le ha clavado una espina en la garganta. ○ to feel in one's bones darle a uno el corazón *I feel it in my bones that he isn't coming.* Me da el corazón que no viene. ○ to make no bones no andarse con rodeos *He made no bones about what he wanted.* No se anduvo con rodeos en lo que quería.
‖ *I have a bone to pick with you.* Tengo que habérmelas con Ud. ‖ *I'm chilled to the bone.* Estoy helado hasta los huesos.
bonfire hoguera, fogata.
bonnet caperuza.
book [n] libro *I want a book to read on the train.* Quiero un libro para leerlo en el tren. ▲ taco *This book of tickets will save you money.* Este taco de billetes le ahorrará dinero.
● [v] reservar *Have you booked passage on the boat yet?* ¿Ha reservado Ud. ya el pasaje del barco?
○ to keep books llevar los libros *Who kept the books when the accountant was sick?* ¿Quién llevó los libros cuando el contador estuvo enfermo?
‖ *The dance team was booked up two weeks in advance.* La pareja de baile estaba contratada con dos semanas de anticipación. ‖ *We're booked up two weeks in advance (theater, travel reservations).* Lo tenemos todo vendido con dos semanas de anticipación. ‖ *This hotel's completely booked up at present.* Este hotel está tomado completamente al presente.
bookcase librería, estante para libros.
bookend sujetalibros.
bookkeeper tenedor de libros.
booklet folleto.

bookmaker, "bookie" corredor de apuestas.

bookstore librería.

boom estampido *We could hear the boom of the cannons.* Podíamos oír el estampido de los cañones. ▲ auge *He made all his money in the boom.* Hizo todo su dinero en aquel auge.

boost [n] empuje, alza.

boot [n] bota *You can't get rubber boots now.* No se pueden comprar ahora botas de goma.
○ **to boot** *He gave me the horse and ten dollars to boot.* Me dió diez dólares además del caballo.

bootblack limpiabotas.

booth puesto *We visited most of the booths at the fair.* Hemos visitado la mayoría de los puestos en la feria. ▲ cabina telefónica *I'm calling from a booth.* Estoy llamando desde una cabina telefónica.

bootlegging contrabando.

booty botín.

border frontera *Tell me when we reach the border.* Avíseme cuando lleguemos a la frontera. ▲ borde *The border of this rug's worn out.* El borde de esta alfombra está gastado.
○ **to border on** rayar en *His argument borders on the ridiculous.* Su argumento raya en lo ridículo.

bore [n] pelmazo *Don't tell me you're going out again with that bore.* No me diga que va Ud. a salir otra vez con ese pelmazo.
● [v] aburrir *That speech bored me to death.* Ese discurso me aburrió enormemente.
○ **to bore a hole** taladrar, hacer un agujero *We'll have to bore a hole through the wall.* Tendremos que taladrar (*or* hacer un agujero) a través de la pared.

born ○ **to be born** nacer *Were you born in America?* ¿Nació Ud. en los Estados Unidos?

borrow pedir prestado *He's borrowed money at the bank.* Ha pedido dinero prestado al banco.

bosom pecho, seno.

boss [n] jefe *The boss bawled me out for being late again.* El jefe me echó una buena por llegar tarde otra vez. ▲ cacique *The party split when he became boss.* El partido se dividió cuando él se hizo cacique.
● [v] mandar, ordenar *What right have you to boss me around?* ¿Con qué derecho me manda Ud.?

botany botánica.

both ambos, los dos *Both roads will take you to the city.* Los dos caminos le llevan a la ciudad.—*I'll buy both of the books.* Compraré ambos libros.
○ **both ... and** y ... a la vez *It's both good and cheap.* Es bueno y barato a la vez. ▲ tanto ... como *Both boys and girls use this playground.* Tanto los muchachos como las niñas usan este campo de juego. ○ **both of us** nosotros dos *Both of us saw it happen.* Nosotros dos vimos como ocurrió.

bother [n] molestia.
● [v] molestar, incomodar.

bottle [n] botella *He drank the whole bottle of milk.* Se bebió toda la botella de leche. ▲ frasco *I'd like a bottle of ink.* Quisiera un frasco de tinta.
● [v] embotellar *This milk was bottled this morning.* Esta leche ha sido embotellada esta mañana.
○ **to bottle up** reprimir *He bottled up his anger.* Reprimió su cólera.

bottleneck embotellamiento, atascamiento *There was a bottleneck in the work.* Hubo un embotellamiento en el trabajo.

bottom fondo *The coffee grounds were at the bottom of the cup.* Los posos del café estaban en el fondo de la taza.—*The bottom of this chair's broken.* El asiento de esta silla está roto.
○ **at bottom** en el fondo *At bottom he's honest.* En el fondo es honrado.
○ **to get to the bottom of** llegar al fondo de *We'll never get to the bottom of the case.* Nunca podremos llegar al fondo del caso.
‖ *Bottoms up!* ¡Salud!

bough rama.

boulevard bulevar.

bounce [n] bote *This ball still has a lot of bounce.* Esta pelota todavia tiene buen bote.
● [v] rebotar *The ball bounced off the roof.* La pelota rebotó en el tejado. ▲ echar, arrojar, [Am] botar *That drunk ought to be bounced out of here.* Se le debería arrojar a ese borracho de aquí.

bound [n] límite *His pride had no bounds.* Su orgullo no tenía límites.
● [v] limitar *The United States is bounded on the north by Canada.* Los Estados Unidos limitan al norte con el Canadá.
‖ *The ball fell out of bounds.* La pelota cayó fuera del campo.

bound [n] salto *He jumped to safety*

in one bound. De un salto se puso a salvo.

● [v] saltar *The child bounded along the sidewalk.* El niño iba saltando por la acera.

bound ○ **bound up** ligado *His success is bound up with politics.* Su éxito está ligado a la política.

‖ *She's bound to be late.* Es seguro que venga tarde.

bound ‖ *Where are you bound for?* ¿A dónde se dirige Ud.?

boundary límite.

bounty generosidad; prima *(money)*.

bouquet ramo *(flowers)*; aroma *(smell)*.

bow arco *(weapon)*; arco de violín; lazo *(knot)*.

bow [n] reverencia *The conductor made a bow.* El director hizo una reverencia.

● [v] inclinarse *He bowed respectfully on leaving.* Se inclinó respetuosamente al salir. ▲ ceder *I generally bow to my father's wishes.* Generalmente cedo a los deseos de mi padre.

bow proa *(ship)*.

bowels intestinos.

bowl [n] tazón *Can I have another bowl of soup?* ¿Puedo tomar otro tazón de sopa?

● [v] jugar a los bolos *He went bowling last night.* Anoche fué a jugar a los bolos.

○ **to bowl over** dejar de una pieza *I was simply bowled over by his marvelous performance.* Me dejó de una pieza por su ejecución maravillosa.

box cajón *We need a larger box for packing.* Necesitamos un cajón mayor de embalaje. ▲ caja *Please put it in a box.* Haga el favor de ponerlo en una caja.—*She ate a whole box of chocolates.* Se comió una caja de bombones. ▲ palco *The party took a box at the theater.* El grupo tomó un palco en el teatro.

○ **to box up** meter en una caja *Box up what's left.* Meta en una caja lo que queda.

boxcar furgón.

boxer boxeador.

boxing boxeo *Do you like boxing?* Le gusta el boxeo?

box office taquilla.

boy niño *They have two boys and a girl.* Tienen dos niños y una niña. ▲ mozo, muchacho *Boy, please bring me some ice water.* Mozo, haga el favor de traerme agua con hielo.—*The boys are having a game of poker.* Los muchachos van a echar una partida de poker. ▲ chico *Boy, what a night!* ¡Chico, qué noche!

○ **boy scout** explorador, boy scout.

boycott [n] boicoteo.

● [v] boicotear.

brace [n] abrazadera, laña.

● [v] asegurar *Brace the tent. A storm's coming up.* Asegure la tienda de campaña; se acerca una tormenta.

○ **to brace up** fortalecer *I drank some broth to brace me up.* Tomé un caldo para fortalecerme. ○ **to brace oneself** tomar ánimo *Brace yourself for the news.* Tome Ud. ánimo para enterarse de la noticia.

bracelet pulsera.

brag jactarse, fanfarronear.

braid [n] trenza *(hair)*; galón *(fabric)*.

● [v] trenzar.

brain [n] cerebro *She's going to have an operation on her brain.* Se le va a hacer una operación en el cerebro. ▲ seso *You haven't got a brain in your head.* No tiene Ud. nada de seso.

● [v] romper la crisma *If you do that again I'll brain you.* Si vuelve Ud. a hacer eso le voy a romper la crisma.

○ **on the brain** metido en el seso *I've got that song on the brain.* Tengo esa canción metida en el seso. ○ **to rack one's brain** dar vueltas a la cabeza *No matter how I rack my brain I can't remember.* Por más vueltas que le doy en mi cabeza no puedo acordarme.

brainstorm ○ **to have a brainstorm** salirse de quicio, perder la cabeza.

brake freno.

brakeman guardafreno.

bran salvado, afrecho.

branch [n] rama *Several branches were blown off by the wind.* El viento se llevó algunas ramas.—*Our branch of the family comes from the West.* Nuestra rama familiar procede del Oeste. ▲ brazo *No, this is only a branch of the river.* No, sólo es un brazo del río.

● [v] bifurcarse *Wait for us where the road branches to the right.* Espérenos donde el camino se bifurca a la derecha.

‖ *Get the stamps at the branch post office.* Compre los sellos en la sucursal de correos.

brand [n] marca *Have you tried that new brand of coffee?* ¿Ha probado Ud. esa nueva marca de café? ▲ hierro, marca *Whose brand is on that* *cow?* ¿De quién es el hierro de esa vaca?

● [*v*] marcar con hierro *We're going to brand the new horses this afternoon.* Esta tarde vamos a marcar con hierro los potros.

‖ *He was branded as a swindler.* Tenía fama de estafador.

brand-new flamante, lo más nuevo.

brandy coñac.

brass latón *Here's a brass bowl you can use for the flowers.* Aquí tiene un cacharro de latón donde puede colocar las flores. ▲ metal *There's too much brass in the orchestra.* Hay demasiado metal en la orquesta. ▲ cara dura *With all his brass he should get ahead.* Con toda su cara dura ya podría salir adelante.

brassiere sostén.

brave [*adj*] valiente, bravo.

● [*v*] arrostrar.

brawl alboroto, refriega.

bread [*n*] pan *I must cut the bread.* Tengo que cortar el pan.

● [*v*] empanar.

○ **bread line** cola de menesterosos *Many people are on the bread line.* Hay mucha gente en la cola de menesterosos. ○ **loaf of bread** pan *We need two loaves of bread.* Necesitamos dos panes. ○ **to earn one's bread and butter** ganarse el pan *How does he earn his bread and butter?* ¿Cómo se gana el pan?

breadth anchura.

break [*n*] oportunidad *Let's give him a break.* Démosle una oportunidad.

● [*v*] romper *Be careful not to break it.* Ten cuidado de no romperlo. —*He broke with his family.* Rompió con su familia. ▲ romperse *Does it break easily?* ¿Se rompe con facilidad? ▲ quebrantar *We mustn't break the law.* No debemos quebrantar la ley.

○ **jail break** fuga *There was a jail break yesterday.* Hubo una fuga ayer en la cárcel. ○ **to break camp** levantar el campo *We're going to break camp tonight.* Vamos a levantar el campo esta noche. ○ **to break down** estropearse *The car didn't break down until yesterday.* El auto no se estropeó hasta ayer. ▲ echar abajo *They broke down the argument.* Echaron abajo el argumento. ○ **to break into** entrar en *A thief may break into the house.* Un ladrón puede entrar en la casa. ○ **to break off** partir *Please break off a piece for me.* Haga el

favor de partirme un pedazo. ▲ romper *They've broken off relations.* Han roto relaciones. ○ **to break out** estallar *We hope war won't break out.* Esperamos que la guerra no estalle. ○ **to break out with** brotar *The child's breaking out with measles.* Al niño le está brotando el sarampión. ○ **to break the ice** romper el hielo *They were very formal until a joke broke the ice.* Estaban muy ceremoniosos hasta que una broma rompió el hielo. ○ **to break up** disolver *The police are breaking up the meeting.* La policía está disolviendo la reunión. ▲ resquebrajarse *The ice is breaking up.* El hielo se está resquebrajando.

breakdown agotamiento *(nervous)*; interrupción, avería *(mechanical)*.

breakfast [*n*] desayuno.

● [*v*] desayunar.

breast pecho.

breath respiración *Hold your breath to stop the hiccups.* Contenga la respiración para que se le quite el hipo. ▲ soplo *There isn't a breath of air today.* No hay ni un soplo de aire hoy.

○ **out of breath** sin aliento *She ran up the hill and was out of breath.* Subió corriendo a la colina y quedó sin aliento. ○ **to catch one's breath** tomar aliento *Let's stop here and catch our breath.* Detengámonos aquí para tomar aliento. ○ **to save one's breath** ahorrarse las palabras *You might as well save your breath.* Podría Ud. ahorrarse las palabras. ○ **to take a breath** respirar *Now take a deep breath.* Ahora respire Ud. hondo.

breathe respirar *He's breathing regularly.* Respira con regularidad. ▲ revelar *Don't breathe a word of this to anyone.* No revele a nadie ni una palabra de esto.

○ **breathing spell** respiro *When do we get a breathing spell?* ¿Cuándo tenemos un respiro?

breed [*n*] casta, raza.

● [*v*] criar.

○ **to breed hatred** despertar odio.

breeze brisa.

brew [*n*] mezcla.

● [*v*] amenazar *(storm)*; hacer *(tea)*.

‖ *Something's brewing here.* Aquí va a empezar algo.

bribe [*n*] soborno.

● [*v*] sobornar.

brick ladrillo *Their house is made of*

red brick. Su casa está hecha de ladrillo rojo. ‖ *You're a brick.* Vale Ud. lo que pesa.

bride novia.

bridge [n] puente *This boat can go under the bridge.* Este barco puede pasar por debajo del puente.—*Can you see the captain on the bridge?* ¿Puede Ud. ver al capitán en el puente?—*The dentist's making a new bridge for me.* El dentista me está haciendo un puente nuevo. ▲ bridge *Do you play bridge?* ¿Juega Ud. al bridge?

● [v] tender un puente sobre *They intend to bridge this river.* Se proponen tender un puente sobre este río. ▲ llenar *These books will bridge the gaps in the library.* Estos libros llenarán los claros de la biblioteca.

○ to burn one's bridges behind one quemar las naves *He burned his bridges behind him.* Ha quemado sus naves.

brief breve *Please make your speech brief.* Por favor, haga su discurso breve.

○ in brief brevemente, en una palabra *In brief, our plan is this.* Brevemente, nuestro plan es éste.

brief case portafolio, cartera de papeles.

bright claro *We'd better wait for a bright day.* Sería mejor que esperásemos un día claro. ▲ llameante *I like to see a bright fire.* Me gusta ver un fuego llameante. ▲ fuerte *The flower's a bright yellow.* La flor es de un amarillo fuerte. ▲ brillante *He's a bright boy.* Es un muchacho brillante. ▲ inteligente *He wasn't bright enough to catch the idea.* No era bastante inteligente para comprender la idea. ▲ luminoso *Do you have any bright ideas?* ¿Se le ocurre alguna idea luminosa? ▲ alegre *Everyone was bright and cheerful at the party.* Todos estaban alegres y animados en la reunión.

brilliance brillantez.

brilliant brillante.

brim borde *(glass, cup)*; ala *(hat)*.

bring llevar *May I bring a friend with me?* ¿Puedo llevar a un amigo conmigo? ▲ traer *Bring it with you.* Tráigalo con Ud. ▲ valer *How much does this bring in the market?* ¿Cuánto vale esto en el mercado?

○ to bring about efectuar *We hope to bring about a change soon.* Esperamos efectuar un cambio pronto. ○ to bring around convencer *At first*

they didn't agree but we brought 'em around. Al principio no estaban de acuerdo pero les convencimos. ○ to bring back devolver *Please bring the book back with you.* Haga Ud. el favor de devolver el libro. ○ to bring down bajar *Do you think they'll bring down the prices soon?* ¿Cree Ud. que bajarán los precios pronto? ○ to bring forward presentar, poner sobre el tapete *If you have any complaints, bring them forward.* Si Ud. tiene algunas quejas, preséntelas. ○ to bring in dar *Have they brought in the verdict yet?* ¿Han dado ya el veredicto? ▲ recoger *Bring in the clothes before it rains.* Recoja la ropa antes de que llueva. ○ to bring on traer *This bad weather will bring on many colds.* Este mal tiempo traerá muchos catarros. ○ to bring out poner en escena *They're bringing out a new play.* Van a poner en escena una nueva obra. ▲ presentar *He brought out his point forcefully.* Presentó su argumento con energía. ○ to bring over traer *They brought him over to this country.* Le trajeron a este país. ○ to bring to hacer volver en sí, reanimar *Cold water will bring him to.* El agua fría le hará volver en sí. ○ to bring up presentar *I'll bring the plan up at the next meeting.* Presentaré el plan en la próxima reunión. ▲ criar, educar *Their grandmother had to bring them up.* Su abuela tuvo que criarlos.

‖ *His joke brought down the house.* La broma le hizo morirse de risa.

brisk vivo, animado.

bristle cerda.

brittle quebradizo.

broad ancho *The avenue's very broad.* La avenida es muy ancha. ▲ liberal, tolerante *He's very broad in his views.* Tiene ideas muy liberales. ▲ amplio, extenso *He had a broad knowledge of the subject.* Tenía un conocimiento amplio del tema.

○ in broad daylight en pleno día *The crime was committed in broad daylight.* El crimen fué cometido en pleno día.

broadcast [n] emisión *Did you hear the broadcast of the symphony last night?* ¿Oyó Ud. anoche la emisión de la sinfonía?

● [v] perifonear, radiar *The President will broadcast tonight.* El Presidente perifoneará esta noche. ▲ propalar, divulgar *If you tell her she'll*

broadcast it all over the neighborhood.
Si se lo dice a ella, lo divulgará por
todo el vecindario.
O **broadcasting station** radio emisora.
broadcloth paño fino.
broad-minded liberal, tolerante.
broil [v] asar.
bronze bronce.
brook arroyo.
broom escoba.
broth caldo.
brother hermano *She expected her
brother to come soon.* Esperaba que
su hermano viniese pronto.
O **brothers and** (*or* or) **sisters** hermanos *Do you have any brothers or
sisters?* ¿Tiene Ud. hermanos?
brotherhood hermandad.
brother-in-law cuñado.
brow frente.
browbeat intimidar *The poor fellow's
browbeaten.* El pobre se siente in-
timidado.
brown [n] color pardo, color castaño
This brown's too dark. Este color
castaño es demasiado oscuro.
● [adj] moreno *Do you have any
brown bread?* ¿Tiene Ud. pan moreno?
● [v] tostar *The cake was browned
in the oven.* El bizcocho fué tostado al
horno.
‖ *The sun made his skin brown.*
Tiene la piel tostada.
bruise [n] contusión.
● [v] contusionar.
brunet [adj, n] moreno, trigueño.
brunette [adj, n] morena, trigueña.
brush [n] cepillo *This brush has stiff
bristles.* Este cepillo tiene las cerdas
duras. ▲brocha *I need a new brush
to paint the walls.* Me hace falta una
brocha nueva para pintar las paredes.
▲matorrales *The workmen are cutting
the brush.* Los trabajadores están
cortando los matorrales.
● [v] cepillar *Please brush these
clothes for me.* Haga el favor de
cepillarme esta ropa. ▲limpiarse *I
must brush my teeth.* Tengo que limpiarme los dientes.
O **to brush aside** dejar de lado, no
hacer caso de *He brushed my protests
aside.* No hizo caso de mis protestas.
O **to brush away** espantar *He brushed
away the fly.* Espantó la mosca. O **to
brush up** (**on**) repasar *I'm brushing
up on my French.* Estoy repasando
mi francés.

‖ *She brushed past us without seeing us.* Nos rozó al pasar sin vernos.
brute bestia, bruto.
bubble burbuja, ampolla.
bucket cubo.
buckle [n] hebilla *Did you break the
catch on that buckle again?* ¿Ha roto
Ud. de nuevo el broche de la hebilla?
● [v] abrocharse *I can't buckle this
belt.* No puedo abrocharme este cinturón. ▲encorvarse *When it gets wet
it buckles.* Cuando se moja se en-
corva.
O **to buckle down to work** ponerse
a trabajar en serio *It's about time we
buckled down to work.* Ya es hora
que nos pongamos a trabajar en serio.
bud [n] pimpollo, yema, capullo *This
rosebush has many buds.* Este rosal
tiene muchos capullos.
● [v] brotar *Everything's beginning
to bud now.* Todo empieza a brotar
ahora.
budding en embrión *He's a budding author.* Es un autor en embrión.
budget [n] presupuesto *Our budget
won't allow us to buy the piano.*
Nuestro presupuesto no nos permite
comprar el piano.
● [v] arreglarse *You'll have to
learn to budget yourself on your salary.* Ud. tendrá que aprender a arreglarse con su sueldo.
buffalo búfalo.
buffet aparador *You'll find a tablecloth
in the buffet.* Ud. encontrará un
mantel en el aparador. ▲bufet, aparador *They served a buffet supper.*
Sirvieron una cena de bufet.
bug insecto.
bugle la trompeta, la corneta.
bugler el trompeta, el corneta.
build construir *They're building a new
house.* Están construyendo una nueva
casa. ▲hacer *The birds are building
a nest in the tree.* Los pájaros están
haciendo un nido en el árbol. ▲pre-
parar *Please build a fire in the fireplace.* Haga el favor de preparar el
fuego en la chimenea.
O **to build up** acrecentar *The advertising will build up the business.* Los
anuncios acrecentarán el negocio.
▲hacerse *He's trying to build up a
reputation.* Está tratando de hacerse
una reputación.
‖ *He has a good build.* Está bien
formado.
building edificio *Both offices are in one
building.* Las dos oficinas están en
el mismo edificio. ▲construcción *Be-*

hind the house are three small build-ings. Detrás de la casa hay tres pequeñas construcciones.
built-in ‖ *The apartment has built-in bookcases.* El apartamento tiene estantes para libros empotrados en la pared.
bulb bombilla *The bulb in the kitchen's burnt out.* La bombilla de la cocina está fundida. ▲ bulbo *We planted tulip bulbs this year.* Plantamos bulbos de tulipán este año.
bulge [*n*] bulto *What's causing that bulge in your pocket?* ¿Qué es lo que le hace bulto en el bolsillo?
● [*v*] abultarse *Her pocket's bulging.* Su bolsillo se está abultando.
bulk ○ in bulk a granel *They're cheaper if you buy them in bulk.* Son más baratos si los compran a granel. ○ the bulk of la mayor parte de *The bulk of my salary goes for rent and food.* La mayor parte de mi sueldo se va en la renta y en la comida.
bull toro.
bullet bala.
bulletin boletín.
bully [*n*] matón *Don't let that big bully push you around.* No se deje Ud. dominar por ese matón.
● [*v*] intimidar *He bullied me into finishing the job myself.* Me intimidó para que yo mismo terminara el trabajo.
bum vagabundo.
○ to bum around vagabundear *We like to bum around.* Nos gusta vagabundear.
‖ *He bums from others all the time.* Siempre vive de gorra.
bump [*n*] chichón *Where did you get that bump on your head?* ¿Dónde se ha hecho ese chichón en le cabeza?
● [*v*] tropezar *He bumped into the chair.* Tropezó con la silla.
○ to bump into darse de cara con *Guess who I bumped into yesterday?* ¿Adivine Ud. con quién me di de cara ayer? ○ to bump off despachar *They bumped off the other gangster.* Despacharon al otro gangster.
bun bollo.
bunch [*n*] manojo *I'll buy two bunches of flowers.* Voy a comprar dos manojos de flores. ▲ racimo *How much is this bunch of grapes?* ¿Cuánto cuesta este racimo de uvas?
● [*v*] agrupar *All the children were bunched in a corner.* Todos los niños estaban agrupados en un rincón.

‖ *How's the bunch?* ¿Cómo están los amigos?
bundle lío, fardo, atado *Is that bundle too heavy to carry?* ¿Es demasiado pesado ese lío para llevarlo?
○ to bundle up abrigarse *It's cold today; you'd better bundle up.* Hace frío hoy; tiene Ud. que abrigarse.
buoy boya.
burden carga *This housework's a heavy burden.* Esta tarea doméstica es una carga pesada.
○ to be burdened estar cargado *I wish I weren't burdened with so many responsibilities.* Quisiera no estar cargado con tantas responsabilidades.
bureau cómoda *The bottom drawer of the bureau's mine.* El último cajón de la cómoda es el mío. ▲ negociado, departamento *My brother got a job in one of the government bureaus.* Mi hermano consiguió trabajo en un negociado del gobierno.
burglar ladrón.
burial entierro.
burn [*n*] quemadura *This burn's very painful.* Esta quemadura me duele mucho.
● [*v*] quemar *They burned their old papers.* Quemaron sus papeles viejos. ▲ picar *This pepper burns my tongue.* Esta pimienta me pica en la lengua.
○ to burn a hole hacer un agujero *The acid burned a hole in his coat.* El ácido le hizo un agujero en la chaqueta. ○ to burn down quemarse por completo *Their home burned down.* Su casa se quemó por completo. ○ to burn one's fingers quemarse los dedos *Don't interfere or you'll get your fingers burned.* No intervengas porque te vas a coger los dedos. ○ to burn out fundir(se) *This bulb burned out.* Esta bombilla se ha fundido. ○ to burn up quemarse *His books burned up in the fire.* Sus libros se quemaron en el fuego. ○ to burn with anger arder de rabia *He was burning with anger.* Estaba que ardía de rabia.
‖ *The sidewalk's burning hot.* La acera está que quema. ‖ *This burns me up.* Esto me quema la sangre.
burner (*of stove*) mechero.
burst [*n*] explosión *There was a burst of applause after his speech.* Hubo una explosión de aplausos después de su discurso.
● [*v*] estallar *A bomb had burst in the next block.* Una bomba había estallado en la manzana próxima.

▲ reventarse *The tire was so old that it burst.* El neumático era tan viejo que se reventó. ▲ romperse *Last year the dam burst.* El año pasado se rompió la presa.

○ to **burst into** irrumpir en *He burst into the room.* Irrumpió en la habitación. ▲ estallar en *The airplane burst into flames.* El aeroplano estalló en llamas. ▲ echarse a *The man burst into laughter.* El hombre se echó a reír. ○ to **burst out** romper, prorrumpir *She burst out crying.* Rompió a llorar.

bury enterrar *They'll bury the body tomorrow.* Enterrarán el cadáver mañana. ▲ sepultar *Did they bury him at sea?* ¿Le sepultaron en el mar? ▲ enterrar *My passport was buried under the other papers.* Mi pasaporte estaba enterrado entre otros papeles. ○ to **be buried in** thought estar absorto en la meditación. ○ to **bury the hatchet** hacer la paz.

bus autobús, bus, [*Cuba*] guagua *Where can I catch the bus?* ¿Dónde puedo coger el autobús?

bush arbusto.
○ to **beat about the bush** andar por las ramas *Stop beating about the bush and get to the point.* Deje Ud. de andar por las ramas y llegue al punto esencial.

business ocupación, oficio *What's his business?* ¿Cuál es su ocupación? ▲ asunto, cuestión *Let's settle this business right away.* Arreglemos la cuestión ahora mismo. ▲ negocio *My business is going very well.* Mi negocio marcha muy bien. ▲ comercio *He's in business.* Se dedica al comercio. ▲ derecho *He had no business asking such questions.* No tenía el derecho de preguntar tales cosas. ▲ obligación *It's your business to keep the staff satisfied.* Es su obligación tener a los empleados contentos. ▲ propósito *Make it your business to do it right.* Hágase el propósito de hacerlo bien. ‖ *He told us to mind our own business.* Nos dijo que no nos metiésemos en lo que no nos importaba.

bust [*n*] busto *A famous sculptor's doing a bust of the President.* Un famoso escultor está haciendo un busto del Presidente. ▲ pecho *That blouse is too tight across the bust.* Esta blusa es demasiado estrecha de pecho.
bust [*v*] reventarse *The little boy cried*

when his balloon busted. El niño lloró al reventarse el balón.
bustle *(stir)* bullicio.
busy ocupado *This morning I was too busy to read the newspaper.* Esta mañana estaba demasiado ocupado para leer el periódico.—*The operator says the line's busy.* La telefonista dice que la línea está ocupado. ▲ de mucho tráfico *They live on a busy street.* Viven en una calle de mucho tráfico.
busybody chismoso, entremetido.
but pero *We can go with you but we'll have to come back early.* Podemos ir con Ud. pero tenemos que volver temprano. ▲ sino *It's not made of wood, but of leather.* No es de madera sino de cuero. ▲ menos *All are ready but you.* Todos están listos menos Ud. ▲ salvo *There's no other meat but chicken.* No hay otra carne, salvo pollo. ▲ más que *When his mother died he was but a child.* Cuando su madre murió no era más que un niño. ○ **all but** casi *He was so nervous that he all but wrecked the machine.* Estaba tan nervioso que casi rompió la máquina.
‖ *Lord, but it's cold!* ¡Dios mío, qué frío hace! ‖ *There are no buts about it.* No hay pero que valga.
butcher [*n*] carnicero.
● [*v*] matar *This afternoon we're going to butcher two beefs.* Esta tarde vamos a matar dos reses. ▲ hacer una carnicería con *Everybody in that village was butchered.* Se hizo una carnicería con todos los habitantes del pueblo. ▲ destrozar *He really butchers the music.* Verdaderamente destroza la música.
butler mayordomo.
butt culata *They knocked him unconscious with the butt of a gun.* Le privaron del sentido con la culata del fusil. ▲ blanco *He doesn't realize he's the butt of their jokes.* No se da cuenta que él es blanco de sus bromas. ○ **cigarette butt** colilla *Clean up the cigarette butts.* Tire Ud. las colillas. ○ to **butt in** entremeterse *Everytime we talk, her little brother butts in.* Cada vez que hablamos, su hermanito se entremete.
‖ *The goat kept butting his head against the fence.* La cabra siguió topetando contra la valla.
butter [*n*] mantequilla, [*Sp, Arg*] manteca *I want bread and butter with the*

tea. Quiero el té con pan y mantequilla.

● [*v*] untar con mantequilla *Shall I butter your toast?* ¿Quiere que le unte la tostada con mantequilla?

butterfly mariposa.

button [*n*] botón *This button's come off.* Se me ha caído este botón.—*He's wearing a Red Cross button.* Lleva un botón de la Cruz Roja.—*Push the button for the elevator.* Apriete el botón para llamar al ascensor.

● [*v*] abrochar *Button up your overcoat.* Abróchese el sobretodo.

‖ *Button up your lip.* No hable Ud.

buy [*n*] compra *That's a good buy.* Es una buena compra.

● [*v*] comprar *I'll buy our tickets tomorrow.* Compraré nuestros billetes mañana. ▲ sobornar *You can't buy the police of this town.* Ud. no puede sobornar a la policía de esta ciudad. ○ **to buy out** *(a partner)* comprar la parte (de un socio). ○ **to buy up** adquirir *All the trucks have been bought up by the government.* Todos los camiones han sido adquiridos por el gobierno.

buzz [*n*] zumbido *The buzz of those flies gets on my nerves.* El zumbido de esas moscas me crispa los nervios.

● [*v*] zumbar *The mosquitoes kept buzzing all night.* Los mosquitos continuaron zumbando toda la noche.

by por *This book was written by a Frenchman.* Este libro fué escrito por un francés.—*By order of the police.* Por orden de la autoridad.—*It's rented by the hour.* Se alquila por hora. ▲ a *This wood's sawed by a machine.* Esta madera está serrada a máquina. ▲ en *Can we get there by rail?* ¿Podemos ir en tren? ▲ conforme, según *He's not playing by the rules.* No juega según las reglas. ▲ de *I just know him by name.* Sólo le conozco de nombre.—*He travels by night.* Viaja de noche. ▲ con *What do you mean by that?* ¿Qué quiere Ud. decir con eso? ▲ para *Please clean these clothes by Saturday.* Haga el favor de limpiar estos trajes para el sábado. ▲ junto a, cerca de *The hotel's by the sea.* El hotel está junto al mar.

○ **by and by** más tarde, luego *I'll see you by and by.* Le veré más tarde. ○ **by and large** bastante *By and large the results were satisfactory.* Los resultados fueron bastante satisfactorios. ○ **by far** con mucho *This is by far the best hotel in town.* Este es con mucho el mejor hotel de la ciudad. ○ **by oneself** por sí mismo *He did that by himself.* Lo hizo por sí mismo. ○ **by the way** a propósito *By the way, I met a friend of yours yesterday.* A propósito me encontré ayer a un amigo suyo. ○ **close by** por aquí cerca *Is there a restaurant close by?* ¿Hay algún restaurante por aquí cerca? ○ **day by day** día por día *Turn in your reports day by day.* Entregue Ud. los informes día por día.

‖ *She's a cousin by marriage.* Es mi prima política. ‖ *We need a map to go by.* Necesitamos un mapa para guiarnos.

C

cab taxi.

cabin cabaña *We have a cabin in the mountains.* Tenemos una cabaña en las montañas. ▲ camarote *It's so windy on deck I'm going to my cabin.* Hace tanto viento sobre cubierta que me voy al camarote.

cabinet armario *She keeps her best dishes in that cabinet.* Guarda los mejores platos en ese armario. ▲ gabinete *The cabinet met with the President yesterday.* Hubo ayer una reunión de gabinete con el Presidente.

cable [*n*] cable *The bridge collapsed when one of the cables broke.* Se hundió el puente al romperse uno de los cables.—*I want to send a cable.* Quiero mandar un cable.

● [*v*] cablegrafiar *Cable me the minute you arrive.* Cablegrafíe en el momento que Ud. llegue.

cadet cadete.

cafe café *The cafe's just around the corner.* El café está a la vuelta de la esquina.

cage jaula.

cake bizcocho *I'd like cakes with my coffee.* Quisiera bizcochos con el café. ▲ torta, pastel *Do you have chocolate cake?* ¿Tiene Ud. pastel de chocolate? ▲ tortita *Do you have fish cakes today?* ¿Tiene Ud. tortitas de pescado hoy? ▲pastilla *Could I have a towel and a cake of soap?* ¿Podría Ud. darme una toalla y una pastilla de jabón?

calamity calamidad.

calculate calcular *What do you calculate it would cost?* ¿Qué calcula Ud. que costaría? ‖ *You can calculate on getting ten dollars in tips besides your salary.* Puede Ud. contar con diez dólares de propinas además del sueldo.

calculating calculador *She's a calculating woman.* Es una mujer calculadora.

calendar calendario.

calf ternero *The calf was born this morning.* El ternero nació esta mañana. ▲pantorrilla *The boot was tight around the calf.* La bota le estaba apretada en la pantorrilla.

calfskin piel de ternera, becerro *Is that bag made of calfskin?* ¿Es de piel de ternera ese bolso?

call [n] visita *The doctor's out on a call.* El doctor ha ido a hacer una visita. ▲llamada *I'm waiting for a telephone call.* Espero una llamada telefónica. ● [v] llamar *Would you call the porter for me?* ¿Quiere llamar al mozo?—*Please call me at 7 A.M.* Haga el favor de llamarme a las siete de la mañana.—*Has my name been called yet?* ¿Me han llamado ya?—*I don't call this cheap.* No le llamo a esto barato. ▲telefonear *Your friend said he'd call back.* Su amigo dijo que volverá a telefonear.

○ **to call attention** llamar la atención *Please call my attention to any errors that I make.* Haga el favor de llamarme la atención si cometo algún error. ○ **to call away** llamar *I expect to be called away soon.* Espero que me llamarán pronto. ○ **to call down** regañar *I was late and got called down for it.* Llegué tarde y me regañaron por eso. ○ **to call for** ir a buscar *Will you call for me at the hotel?* ¿Irá Ud. a buscarme al hotel? ▲exigir *This job calls for a lot of training.* Este trabajo exige mucha experiencia. ○ **to call in** llamar *If your illness gets worse, call in a specialist.* Si se pone Ud. peor llame a un especialista. ○ **to call off** suspender *The game's been called off.* Se ha suspendido el partido. ○ **to call on** visitar *Someone called on you while you were out.* Vino una persona a visitarle cuando Ud. estaba fuera.

▲pedir *Whenever you need help, feel free to call on me.* Cuando necesite Ud. ayuda, pídamela con toda libertad. ○ **to call out** llamar *The fire department had to be called out.* Tuvieron que llamar a los bomberos. ○ **to call up** llamar por teléfono *I intended to call him up, but I forgot.* Pensaba llamarle por teléfono, pero se me olvidó.

‖ *Were there any calls for me?* ¿Me han llamado por teléfono? ‖ *Last call!* ¡Ultimo turno! ‖ *That was a close call!* ¡Qué poco faltó! ‖ *What do you call this in Spanish?* ¿Cómo se llama esto en español?

calm [adj] tranquilo *The sea's very calm today.* El mar está muy tranquilo hoy.

● [v] tranquilizar *We tried to calm the child.* Tratamos de tranquilizar al niño.

○ **to calm down** tranquilizarse *It took her some time to calm down.* Tardó algún tiempo en tranquilizarse.

camel camello.

camera cámara, máquina fotográfica.

camp [n] colonia *The children left for camp this morning.* Los niños han salido para la colonia esta mañana.

● [v] acampar *On our vacation we're going to camp in the woods.* Durante las vacaciones vamos a acampar en el bosque.—*The regiment camped just outside the town.* El regimiento acampó en las afueras del pueblo.

campaign [n] campaña *Many men were lost in the last campaign.* Murieron muchos hombres en la última campaña.

● [v] hacer una campaña *The club's campaigning for funds.* El club está haciendo una campaña para conseguir fondos.

camphor alcanfor.

can [n] lata *Give me a can of tomatoes.* Déme Ud. una lata de tomates.

● [v] poner en conserva *She's canning peaches.* Ella está poniendo melocotones en conserva. ▲hacer conservas *She does her own canning.* Hace sus conservas.

can poder *Can you give me some help?* ¿Puede Ud. ayudarme?—*Could I look at this?* ¿Podría mirar esto?—*I don't see how it can be true.* No entiendo como puede ser verdad.—*He did everything he could think of.* Hizo todo lo que se le pudo ocurrir.—*When could you start working?* ¿Cuándo podría

Ud. comenzar a trabajar?—*You can go now if you wish.* Puede Ud. ir ahora si quiere.—*Can't we open these windows?* ¿No podemos abrir estas ventanas? ▲saber *He can't read or write.* No sabe leer ni escribir. ▲querer *You can't mean that, can you?* ¿No quiere Ud. decir eso, verdad? ‖ *Can you speak English?* ¿Habla Ud. inglés? ‖ *He can't see without his glasses.* No ve sin anteojos. ‖ *I don't know what the trouble could be.* No sé en qué consiste la dificultad.

canal canal.

canary canario.

cancel [v] cancelar, anular.

cancellation cancelación, anulación.

cancer cáncer.

candidate candidato.

candle vela, bujía.

candlestick candelero.

candy dulces. ○ **chocolate candy** bombones. ○ **hard candy** caramelos.

cane caña; bastón *(walking stick)*.

cannon cañón.

canoe canoa.

can opener abrelatas.

cantaloupe melón.

canvas lienzo *Who painted that canvas?* ¿Quién pintó ese lienzo? ▲lona *I've never worn canvas shoes.* Nunca he usado zapatos de lona.

cap gorra *He was wearing a cap on his head.* Llevaba una gorra puesta. ▲tapón *Put the cap back on the bottle.* Póngale el tapón a la botella.

capable competente *I want a very capable person for that job.* Quiero una persona muy competente para ese puesto. ‖ *Is the hall capable of holding so many people?* ¿Tiene capacidad el salón para tantas personas?

capacity capacidad *His capacity for learning is quite limited.* Su capacidad de aprender es bastante limitada. ▲puesto *In what capacity does she serve?* ¿Qué puesto tiene? ‖ *The theater was filled to capacity.* El teatro estaba completamente lleno.

cape cabo *I enjoyed my trip around the cape.* Me gustó mucho el viaje alrededor del cabo. ▲capa *This cape isn't warm enough.* Esta capa no abriga bastante.

capital capital *Have you ever visited the capital?* ¿Ha visitado Ud. alguna vez la capital?—*He lost all his capital in that investment.* Perdió todo su capital en esa inversión. ▲mayúscula *Do you spell that word with a capital?* ¿Se escribe esa palabra con mayúscula?

capitalist capitalista.

capitol capitolio.

capsule cápsula.

captain capitán.

captive prisionero, cautivo.

capture [n] captura *The capture was made in broad daylight.* La captura se hizo en pleno día. ● [v] capturar *They captured many prisoners.* Capturaron a muchos prisioneros.

car auto, [Am] carro, [Sp] coche *Would you like to ride in my car?* ¿Quiere Ud. venir en mi carro? ▲tranvía *Which car goes downtown?* ¿Qué tranvía va al centro? ○ **dining car** coche comedor. ○ **freight car** vagón, furgón. ○ **sleeping car** coche-cama.

carbon copy copia.

carbon paper papel carbón.

carburetor carburador.

card ficha, tarjeta *We'll keep your card on file.* Archivaremos su ficha. ▲tarjeta *She wasn't home so I left my card.* No estaba en casa así que dejé una tarjeta. ▲carta, naipe *Let's have a game of cards.* Vamos a jugar una partida de cartas. ○ **postal card** tarjeta postal *Did you get my postal card?* ¿Recibió Ud. mi tarjeta postal?

cardboard cartón.

care [n] cuidado *I'll leave my valuables in your care.* Dejaré las cosas de valor a su cuidado. ▲atención *He needs medical care.* Necesita atención médica. ● [v] importar *I don't care what he thinks.* No me importa lo que piensa. ○ **in care of** suplicado para [Sp], recomendado a [Am] *He addressed the letter to me in care of my uncle.* Dirigió la carta a mi tío suplicada para mi. *or* Me dirigió la carta recomendada a mi tío. ○ **to care for** cuidar *The children are well cared for.* Los niños están bien cuidados. ▲querer *Do you care for gravy on your meat?* ¿Quiere Ud. salsa con la carne? ○ **to take care** tener cuidado *Take care not to hurt his feelings.* Tenga cuidado de no herir sus sentimientos. ○ **to take care of** guardar *Take care of my money for me.* Guárdeme el dinero. ▲cuidar *Take care of yourself.* Cuídese Ud.

‖ *His face is full of care.* Se ve muy preocupado. ‖ *I don't care to hear your excuses.* No me interesan sus excusas. *or* No me dé Ud. explicaciones.

career carrera.

careful cuidadoso *He's very careful in his work.* Es muy cuidadoso en su trabajo.
‖ *Be careful!* ¡Tenga cuidado!

careless descuidado *I've never seen men so careless about their clothes.* No he visto nunca hombres más descuidados en su manera de vestir.
‖ *He makes so many careless mistakes.* Comete tantos errores por descuido.

caress [*n*] caricia.
● [*v*] acariciar.

cargo carga, cargamento.

caricature caricatura *That's a very good caricature he drew of you.* Le ha hecho a Ud. una caricatura muy buena.

carpenter carpintero.

carpet [*n*] alfombra *We took up the carpet for the summer.* Quitamos la alfombra durante el verano.
● [*v*] alfombrar *They promised to carpet the room before we moved in.* Prometieron alfombrar la habitación antes de que nos mudásemos.

carriage coche *Let's take a ride in a carriage.* Demos un paseo en coche. ▲ aire *He has the carriage of a soldier.* Tiene un aire marcial.

carrot zanahoria.

carry llevar *The porter will carry the bags.* El mozo llevará las maletas. ▲ soportar *How much weight will this bridge carry?* ¿Cuánto peso soportará este puente? ▲ ser de *His remarks carried great weight.* Sus observaciones eran de mucho peso. ▲ tener *Do you carry men's shirts?* ¿Tienen Uds. camisas de hombre?
○ **to carry arms** llevar armas *It's forbidden to carry arms.* Se prohibe llevar armas. ○ **to carry away** encantar, hechizar *She was carried away by the music.* Estaba encantada con la música. ○ **to carry into effect** llevar a cabo *When will this project be carried into effect?* ¿Cuándo se llevará a cabo este proyecto? ○ **to carry on** ocuparse de *His son carried on his business.* Su hijo se ocupaba de sus negocios. ▲ armar bulla *They carried on until daybreak.* Estuvieron armando bulla hasta la madrugada.
○ **to carry out** llevar a cabo *We'll try*

to carry out your plan. Trataremos de llevar a cabo su plan.

cart [*n*] carretón *He'll bring the groceries in a cart.* Traerá los comestibles en un carretón.
● [*v*] acarrear *This sand has to be carted away.* Hay que acarrear esta arena a otro sitio.

cartoon caricatura.

cartoonist caricaturista.

cartridge cartucho.

carve tallar *Those figures were carved out of wood.* Esas figuras están talladas en madera. ▲ trinchar *Will you carve the turkey?* ¿Quiere Ud. trinchar el pavo?

carving knife trinchante.

case cajón *Leave the bottles in the case.* Deje las botellas en el cajón. ▲ caso *In that case I'll have to change my plans.* En ese caso tendré que cambiar mis planes.—*He presented his case well.* Presentó bien su caso.— *What a case he is!* ¡Es un caso! —*Some cases of typhoid have been reported.* Han informado de algunos casos de tifoidea. ▲ causa, pleito *He's lost his case.* Ha perdido su pleito.
○ **in any case** en todo caso *In any case I'd follow his advice.* En todo caso seguiría su consejo. ○ **in case** en el caso *Wait for me in case I'm late.* Espéreme en el caso que llegue tarde. ○ **in case of** en caso de *In case of illness notify my family.* En caso de enfermedad avise a mi familia. ○ **show case** vitrina *There's a new show case in the store.* Hay una nueva vitrina en la tienda.

cash [*n*] dinero *Is there any cash in the drawer?* ¿Hay algún dinero en caja? ▲ al contado *I'm able to pay cash.* Puedo pagar al contado.
● [*v*] cambiar *Will you cash a check for me?* ¿Quiere Ud. cambiarme un cheque?
○ **to cash in on** aprovecharse de *He wants to cash in on what I did.* Quiere aprovecharse de lo que hice.

cashier cajero.

casket *(coffin)* ataúd.

cast [*n*] reparto *The cast of players hasn't been chosen.* No se ha hecho el reparto.
● [*v*] echar *The fisherman cast his line far out.* El pescador echó el anzuelo muy lejos. ▲ vaciar *They cast the statue in bronze.* Vaciaron la estatua en bronce.
○ **to cast a ballot** votar *I haven't cast my ballot yet.* Todavía no he

votado. ○ **to cast a glance** echar una mirada *I cast a glance in his direction*. Le eché una mirada. ○ **to cast anchor** echar el ancla *We'll cast anchor at daybreak*. Echaremos el ancla al amenecer. ○ **to cast off** soltar las amarras *The captain says we're ready to cast off*. El capitán dice que vamos a soltar las amarras. ○ **to put in a cast** enyesar *His broken arm was put in a cast*. Le han enyesado el brazo roto.
‖ *Who was cast in the leading role?* ¿A quién le han dado el papel principal?

castle castillo.

castor oil aceite de ricino, [*Am*] aceite de castor.

casual ‖ *They had a casual conversation.* Hablaron de cosas sin importancia.

cat gato.

catalog catálogo.

catastrophe catástrofe.

catch [*n*] pesca *(of fish) A good catch of fish was brought in*. Trajeron una buena pesca. ▲ cerradura *The catch on the door's broken*. La cerradura de la puerta está rota. ▲ buen partido *That young man was a good catch for any girl*. Aquel joven era un buen partido para cualquier muchacha.
● [*v*] capturar *The police are trying to catch the criminal*. La policía esta tratando de capturar al criminal. ▲ tomar *I have to catch the 5:15 train*. Tengo que tomar el tren de las cinco y quince. ▲ entender *I didn't catch his name*. No entendí su nombre. ▲ coger [*Should not be used in Argentina, Mexico, or Uruguay. Use* atrapar]. *Be careful not to catch cold*. Tenga cuidado de no coger un catarro. ○ **to catch fire** prender *The wood's so dry that it'll catch fire easily*. La leña esta tan seca que prenderá fácilmente. ○ **to catch hold of** agarrar *Catch hold of the rope*. Agarre Ud. la cuerda. ○ **to catch on** darse cuenta *Do you catch on?* ¿Se da Ud. cuenta? ○ **to catch one's eye** llamar la atención *The neckties in the window caught my eye*. Las corbatas del escaparate me llamaron la atención. ○ **to catch on fire** incendiarse *The car caught on fire when it turned over*. El automóvil se incendió al volcarse. ○ **to catch sight of** echar la vista encima *If you catch sight of him, let us know*. Si le echa Ud. la vista encima, díganoslo. ○ **to catch up with** alcan-

zar *Go on ahead and I'll catch up with you*. Siga Ud. adelante y yo le alcanzaré. ○ **to play catch** jugar a la pelota *Do you want to play catch?* ¿Quiere Ud. jugar a la pelota?

caterpillar oruga.

cathedral catedral.

Catholic [*adj, n*] católico.

catsup salsa de tomate.

cattle ganado.

cauliflower coliflor.

cause [*n*] causa *What's the cause of the delay?* ¿Cuál es la causa de la demora?—*He's defending a good cause*. Defiende una buena causa.
● [*v*] causar *Sorry to cause you this inconvenience*. Siento causarle esta molestia.

cautious cauto, prudente.

cave cueva.
○ **to cave in** hundirse *Watch out! The roof's caving in!* ¡Cuidado! ¡Se está hundiendo el techo!

cease cesar *At midnight the rain ceased.* A media noche cesó la lluvia.

cedar cedro.

ceiling techo, cielo raso.

celebrate celebrar *They're celebrating their wedding anniversary*. Están celebrando el aniversario de su boda. —*Let's celebrate*. Vamos a celebrarlo.

celebrated célebre.

celebration celebración.

celery apio.

cell celda *(of a convent or jail);* calabozo *(of a jail);* célula *(biology).*

cellar sótano.

cellophane celofán.

celluloid celuloide.

cement [*n*] cemento.

cemetery cementerio.

censorship censura.

cent centavo [*Am*], céntimo [*Sp*] *I haven't a cent in change*. No tengo ni un centavo suelto.

center [*n*] centro *Aim for the center of the target*. Apunte Ud. al centro del blanco.—*Isn't this city an industrial center?* ¿No es esta ciudad un centro industrial?
● [*v*] centrar *The typist centered the paper*. La mecanógrafa centró el papel.
‖ *Who's playing center?* ¿Quién juega de centro?

centimeter centímetro.

central [*n*] central *Central doesn't answer*. La central no contesta.
● [*adj*] central *Does this building have central heating?* ¿Tiene este edificio calefacción central? ▲ céntrico

This building's in the central part of town. Este edificio está en la parte céntrica de la ciudad. ▲ principal *He's left out the central point.* Ha omitido el punto principal.

century siglo.

cereal [*adj; n*] cereal.

ceremony ceremonia.

certain seguro *I'm certain they're working.* Estoy seguro de que están trabajando. ▲ cierto *They have to do it within a certain time.* Tiene que hacerlo dentro de un cierto plazo.

certainly ciertamente *It's certainly hot in here.* Ciertamente hace aquí mucho calor. ▲ con mucho gusto *Certainly, I'll do it for you.* Se lo haré, con mucho gusto.

certificate certificado. ·

certify certificar.

chafe rozar.

chafed irritado.

chain [*n*] cadena *My bicycle chain's broken.* La cadena de mi bicicleta está rota. ▲ circuito [*Am*] *He owns a chain of movie houses.* Tiene un circuito de cines.
   ● [*v*] amarrar, atar *Chain that dog.* Amarre ese perro.
   ○ **chain of mountains** cordillera.

chair silla.

chairman presidente.

chalk tiza.

challenge [*n*] desafío *Our team accepted their challenge and beat them.* Nuestro equipo aceptó el desafío y los venció.
   ● [*v*] desafiar *I was flattered when the swimming champ challenged me.* Me sentí halagado cuando el campeón de natación me desafió.

chamber cámara *The Lower Chamber hasn't voted on this matter yet.* La Cámara de Diputados no ha votado sobre este asunto todavía.

chambermaid camarera.

champion campeón.

chance oportunidad *Give me a chance to explain.* Déme Ud. una oportunidad para explicarme. ▲ posibilidad *Is there any chance of catching the train?* ¿Tenemos alguna posibilidad de coger el tren?
   ○ **by chance** por casualidad *I met him by chance.* Le encontré por casualidad. ○ **to take a chance** aventurarse, arriesgarse.

chandelier araña.

change [*n*] cambio *They made many changes in the house.* Han hecho muchos cambios en la casa.—*Here's your change, sir.* Aquí tiene Ud. su cambio, señor.
   ● [*v*] cambiar *We may have to change our plans.* Puede que tengamos que cambiar nuestros planes.—*You've changed a lot since I saw you last.* Usted ha cambiado mucho desde la última vez que le ví.—*Can you change these bills for me?* ¿Puede Ud. cambiarme estos billetes? ▲ mudarse *She's changing her clothes now.* Se está mudando de ropa ahora.
   ○ **for a change** para variar *I'll take vanilla ice cream for a change.* Para variar voy a tomar mantecado. ○ **to change hands** cambiar de dueño *This hotel has changed hands several times.* Este hotel ha cambiado de dueño varias veces. ○ **to change one's mind** cambiar de opinión *I'd thought of staying, but I've changed my mind.* Había pensado quedarme, pero he cambiado de opinión. ○ **to change one's tune** cambiar de disco *He used to talk against the governor, but now he's changed his tune.* Antes hablaba contra el gobernador, pero ahora ha cambiado de disco.
   ‖ *Do you think there'll be a change of weather?* ¿Cree Ud. que cambiará el tiempo?

channel canal *They dredged a channel in the river.* Dragaron un canal en el río. ▲ conducto *Did you send that application through the proper channels?* ¿Envió Ud. esa solicitud por conducto apropiado?

chaos cáos.

chapel capilla.

chaplain capellán.

chapped cortado.

chapter capítulo *I have one more chapter to go in this book.* Me falta sólo un capítulo terminar este libro. ▲ sección, capítulo *The women's chapter of the society meets today.* La sección de mujeres de la sociedad se reune hoy.

character carácter *That boy has character.* Ese muchacho tiene carácter. ▲ condición *I don't like men of his character.* No me gustan los hombres de su condición. ▲ personaje *Who are the principal characters in the novel?* ¿Cuáles son los principales personajes de la novela? ▲ tipo *He's quite a character!* ¡Es un tipo!

characteristic [*n*] característica *Selfishness is one of his characteristics.* El egoísmo es una de sus características.
   ● [*adj*] característico *He solved the*

problem with characteristic accuracy.
Resolvió el problema con su característica exactitud.
charcoal carbón de leña.
charge [n] acusación *He could prove that the charge was false.* Pudo probar que la acusación era falsa.
  ● [v] acusar *What crime is he charged with?* ¿De qué delito se le acusa? ▲ cobrar, pedir *Please give me back two dollars; you charged me too much.* Tiene que hacer el favor de devolverme dos dólares, me ha cobrado de más.—*You're charging too much.* Ud. me pide demasiado. ▲ poner *Charge this to my account.* Ponga Ud. esto a mi cuenta. ▲ embestir *Watch out or the bull will charge at us.* Cuidado con el toro, puede embestir.
  ○ **charge account** cuenta de crédito *I want to open a charge account.* Deseo abrir una cuenta de crédito. ○ **to be in charge** estar encargado *Mr. López is in charge of the office.* El señor López está encargado de la oficina. ○ **to take charge of** hacerse cargo de, encargarse de *Who took charge of the store after he left?* ¿Quién se hizo cargo de la tienda cuando él se fué?
  ‖ *Is there any charge for this service?* ¿Hay que pagar algo por este servicio?
charity limosna *She doesn't want to accept charity.* No quiere admitir limosnas. ▲ sociedad de beneficencia *That charity runs a nursery.* Esa sociedad de beneficencia mantiene una guardería de niños.
charm [n] encanto *Her smile has great charm.* Su sonrisa tiene un gran encanto.
  ● [v] encantar *I was charmed by her smile.* Estaba encantado de su sonrisa.
charming encantador *She was a charming girl.* Era una muchacha encantadora.
chart carta, mapa.
charter título, licencia.
  ○ **to charter a boat** fletar un barco.
chase [n] caza, persecución *We all joined in the chase for the thief.* Todos tomamos parte en la caza del ladrón.
  ● [v] cazar *The cat's chasing a mouse.* El gato está cazando un ratón. ▲ correr tras de *I've been chasing you all morning.* Estoy corriendo tras de Ud. todo la mañana. ▲ echar

Chase him out of here. Echelo de aquí. ▲ ahuyentar *Chase that dog away.* Ahuyente ese perro. ▲ ir corriendo *I've got to chase down to the store before it closes.* Tengo que ir corriendo a la tienda antes de que la cierren.
chat [n] charla, plática.
  ● [v] charlar, platicar.
chatter [v] charlar *She chattered on all afternoon.* Estuvo charlando toda la tarde. ▲ castañetear *His teeth were chattering with cold.* Le castañeteaban los dientes de frío.
chauffeur chofer, chófer.
cheap barato *Do you have anything cheaper than this?* ¿Tiene Ud. algo más barato que esto? ▲ vulgar, cursi *She was very cheap-looking.* Tenía un aire muy vulgar.
  ○ **cheap trick** mala jugada *He played a cheap trick.* El hizo una mala jugada. ○ **to feel cheap** sentirse humillado *His kindness made me feel cheap.* Su amabilidad me hizo sentirme humillado.
cheat [n] tramposo *They all know he's a cheat.* Todos saben que es un tramposo.
  ● [v] engañar *Be careful you're not cheated.* Cuidado que no le engañen.
check [n] cheque *I'll send you a check in the morning.* Le mandaré un cheque mañana por la mañana. ▲ cuenta *Who's going to pay the check?* ¿Quién va a pagar la cuenta? ▲ marca *Put a check beside each price.* Ponga Ud. una marca en cada precio. ▲ talón *(for baggage) Give your check to the baggage man.* Dele Ud. el talón al mozo del equipaje.
  ● [v] examinar *They're ready to check our passports.* Están listos para examinar nuestros pasaportes. ▲ marcar *Check the things that are most important.* Marque Ud. las cosas más importantes. ▲ refrenar *He was about to speak but checked himself.* Estaba a punto de hablar pero se refrenó. ▲ dar a guardar *Check your hat and coat here.* Dé Ud. a guardar el sombrero y el abrigo aquí.
  ○ **to check in** firmar *At the office we check in at nine o'clock.* Firmamos en la oficina a las nueve. ▲ registrarse *Have you checked in at the hotel?* ¿Se ha registrado en el hotel? ○ **to check out** marcharse *I'm checking out; have my bill ready.* Me marcho, tenga Ud. lista la cuenta. ○ **to check through** facturar *I want*

this baggage checked through to New York. Deseo facturar este equipaje hasta Nueva York. ○ **to check up** comprobar *They're checking up on your records now.* Están comprobando su documentos. ○ **to check with** estar de acuerdo con *Does this timetable check with the new schedule?* Está de acuerdo este horario con el nuevo plan? ▲ consultar *Just a moment until we check with the management.* Un momento hasta que consultemos con la dirección.

checkers damas.

check-up *(medical)* reconocimiento médico *Report to the doctor for a check-up.* Preséntese Ud. al doctor para un reconocimiento médico.

cheek mejilla, carrillo *She had a lot of rouge on her cheeks.* Tenía mucho colorete en las mejillas.

‖ *He had his tongue in his cheek when he said it.* Lo dijo de dientes afuera.

cheer [*n*] vivas *They gave a cheer for the president.* Dieron vivas al presidente.—*We could hear the cheers from quite a distance.* Oímos los vivas desde bastante distancia.

● [*v*] aplaudir *The crowd cheered like mad.* La muchedumbre aplaudía con frenesí.

○ **to cheer up** animar *We visit her often to cheer her up.* La visitamos con frecuencia para animarla.—*Cheer up!* ¡Anímate!

cheerful animado, alegre *You seem very cheerful this morning.* Parece que está Ud. muy animado esta mañana.

cheese queso.

chemical [*adj*] químico.

cherry cereza.

chess ajedrez.

chest *(anatomy)* pecho.

chestnut castaña.

chest of drawers cómoda.

chew mascar, masticar.

chicken pollo.

chicken pox varicela, viruelas locas.

chief [*n*] jefe *Where's the office of the chief of police?* ¿Dónde queda la oficina del jefe de policía?

● [*adj*] principal *What's your chief complaint?* ¿Cuál es su queja principal?

child niño, niña.

childhood infancia.

children niños.

chili sauce salsa de chile, salsa de ají.

chill [*n*] frío *There's a chill in the air tonight.* Hace un poco de frío esta

noche. ▲ escalofrío *I have chills.* Tengo escalofríos.

● [*v*] enfriar *The news chilled the enthusiasm of the crowd.* La noticia enfrió el entusiasmo del gentío. ▲ helar *I'm chilled to the bone.* Estoy helado hasta los huesos.

chilly frío.

chimney chimenea *They came to fix the chimney.* Vinieron a arreglar la chimenea. ▲ tubo *Where's the chimney for this lamp?* ¿Dónde está el tubo de esta lámpara?

chin barba, barbilla.

chip astilla *Have you any chips to start the fire?* ¿Tiene Ud. astillas para escender el fuego?

chirp [*v*] gorjear.

chisel escoplo, cincel.

chocolate [*n*] bombón *I want to buy a box of chocolates.* Deseo comprar una caja de bombones. ▲ chocolate *I'd rather have chocolate than coffee.* Prefiero tomar chocolate que café.

● [*adj*] de chocolate *Do you want chocolate ice cream?* ¿Quiere Ud. helado de chocolate?

choice [*n*] elección *The choice was difficult.* La elección era difícil.

● [*adj*] excelente *These are choice cuts of meat.* Estos son excelentes trozos de carne.

‖ *Do we have a choice of desserts?* ¿Tenemos derecho a elegir el postre? ‖ *I had no choice in the matter.* No pude elegir en ese asunto.

choir coro.

choke [*n*] regulador del aire, válvula de obturación *(motors).*

● [*v*] atragantarse *Be careful you don't choke on that fishbone.* Tenga cuidado, no se atragante con esa espina. ▲ ahogar *That large log will choke the fire.* Ese leño grande ahogará el fuego.

○ **to choke to death** estrangular.

cholera el cólera.

choose elegir *I have to choose the lesser of two evils.* Tengo que elegir el menor de los dos males. ▲ escoger *I chose the books carefully.* Escogí los libros cuidadosamente.

chop [*n*] chuleta *This chop's all bone.* Esta chuleta no tiene más que hueso.

● [*v*] cortar *Should I chop more wood?* ¿Corto más leña?

chorus coro *I sing in the school chorus.* Canto en el coro del colegio. ▲ estribillo *Do you know the words of the chorus?* ¿Conoce Ud. la letra del estribillo?

○ in **chorus** a coro *They greeted the teacher in chorus.* Todos saludaron a coro al profesor.
chorus girl corista.
Christian [*adj, n*] cristiano, cristiana.
Christmas Pascua, Navidad *Merry Christmas!* ¡Felices Pascuas!
chronic crónico.
chum amigo, amiga *We've been chums for years.* Somos amigos desde hace años.
church iglesia.
cider sidra.
cigar cigarro, tabaco.
cigarette cigarrillo, pitillo *Do you have a cigarette?* ¿Tiene Ud. un cigarrillo?
cigarette case pitillera *I lost my cigarette case.* Perdí mi pitillera.
cigar store cigarrería, estanco.
cinnamon canela.
circle [*n*] círculo *The sign has a red circle on a white field.* La señal tiene un círculo rojo sobre fondo blanco. ▲ plaza *There's a big circle at the entrance to the park.* Hay una gran plaza a la entrada del parque. ▲ círculo *I have a small circle of friends.* Tengo un pequeño círculo de amigos.
● [*v*] dar vueltas *The airplane circled the field several times.* El aeroplano dió varias vueltas sobre el campo. ▲ poner un círculo en *Please circle the words that are misspelled.* Haga el favor de poner un círculo en las palabras mal escritas.
circuit circuito.
circular [*n*] circular *They send out a circular each month.* Envían una circular todos los meses.
● [*adj*] redondo *She's skating at the circular rink.* Está patinando en la pista redonda.
circulate circular *Lots of rumors are circulating about him.* Circulan muchos rumores acerca de él.
circulation circulación *I've been taking exercises to improve my circulation.* He estado haciendo ejericios para mejorar mi circulación.—*The circulation of that magazine increased considerably.* La circulación de esa revista ha aumentado considerablemente. ‖ *If we had a fan there'd be more circulation of air in here.* Si tuviéramos aquí un ventilador circularía más el aire.
circumference circunferencia.
circumstances circunstancias *Under those circumstances I could hardly blame her.* En esas circunstancias no podía echarle a ella la culpa. ‖ *He's in very good circumstances.* Es un hombre muy bien acomodado.
circus circo.
citizen ciudadano, ciudadana.
city ciudad.
city hall ayuntamiento, municipio.
civil civil *This comes under civil jurisdiction.* Esto es de jurisdicción civil. ▲ civil, cortés, correcto *At least he was civil to us.* Por lo menos se mostró correcto con nosotros. ‖ *He was married under civil law.* Se casó por lo civil.
civilian paisano, paisana.
civilize civilizar.
civil service Funcionarios del Estado, Servicio Civil Oficial.
claim [*n*] demanda *The insurance company paid all claims against it.* La Compañía de Seguros pagó todas las demandas hechas contra ella. ▲ pretensión *You can't justify your claims.* No puede Ud. justificar sus pretensiones.
● [*v*] reclamar *His children claimed half the estate.* Sus hijos reclamaron la mitad de sus bienes. —*Where do I claim my baggage?* ¿Dónde puedo reclamar mi equipaje? ▲ sostener *He claims that the traffic delayed him.* Sostiene que el tráfico lo retrasó.
clam almeja.
clamor [*n*] griterío *Suddenly there was a great clamor in the street.* De pronto hubo un gran griterío en la calle.
● [*v*] gritar *The child kept clamoring for attention.* El niño estaba gritando para que le hicieran caso.
clap [*v*] aplaudir *The audience clapped for five minutes.* El público aplaudió durante cinco minutos.
○ **clap of the hand** palmada *He stopped the noise with a clap of his hand.* Con una palmada paró el ruido. ○ **clap of thunder** trueno *Did you hear that clap of thunder?* ¿Ha oído Ud. ese trueno? ‖ *He clapped his hand over her mouth.* Le tapó la boca con la mano.
clasp [*n*] broche *The clasp on this necklace is broken.* El broche de este collar está roto. ▲ apretón *He gave me a firm clasp of the hand.* Me dió un fuerte apretón de manos.
class [*n*] clase *This law will improve the conditions of the working class.* Esta ley mejorará la condición de la clase trabajadora.—*I have a class at*

nine. Tengo una clase a las nueve.— *Give me a second-class ticket to Mexico City.* Déme Ud. un billete de segunda clase para Ciudad de México. ▲ estilo *That girl has class.* Esa muchacha tiene mucho estilo.

● [v] clasificar *These can be classed as first quality.* Estos se pueden clasificar como de primera calidad. ‖ *We graduated in the same class.* Nos graduamos el mismo año.

classic(al) clásico.

classify clasificar.

claw [n] garra.

clay greda, arcilla.

clean [adj] limpio *This plate isn't clean.* Este plato no está limpio. ▲ moral *The new play's clean and amusing.* La nueva comedia es moral y divertida.

● [v] limpiar *Hasn't the maid cleaned the room yet?* ¿No ha limpiado aún el cuarto la criada?—*These fish were cleaned at the market.* Estos pescados los han limpiado en el mercado. ○ **to clean out** vaciar *I'll look for it when I clean out my trunk.* Lo buscaré cuando vacíe el baúl. ○ **to clean up** arreglarse *I'd like to clean up before dinner.* Me gustaría arreglarme antes de la comida. ▲ terminar *You may go home when you clean up the work.* Se puede Ud. marchar cuando haya terminado el trabajo. ‖ *He licked the platter clean.* Comió todo lo que tenía en el plato.

cleaner's tintorería.

cleaning [n] limpieza *The room needs cleaning.* El cuarto necesita una limpieza.

cleaning fluid quitamanchas.

clear [adj] claro *The water's so clear we can see the bottom.* El agua es tan clara que se ve el fondo.—*I don't have a clear idea of what you mean.* No tengo una idea clara de lo que Ud. quiere decir. ▲ limpio *My conscience is clear.* Mi conciencia está limpia.

● [v] despejar *The skies are clearing now.* El cielo se está despejando. —*Have they cleared the road yet?* ¿Han despejado ya el camino? ▲ salvar *The plane cleared the tree tops.* El avión salvó las copas de los árboles. ○ **to clear away** quitar *Ask her to clear away the dishes.* Pídale que quite los platos. ○ **to clear off** quitar de *Clear everything off the shelf.*

Quite todo del estante.—*Clear those things off your desk.* Quite Ud. esas cosas de su escritorio. ○ **to clear out** vaciar *Please clear out this closet.* Tenga la bondad de vaciar este armario. ○ **to clear up** aclarar *We'll leave as soon as the weather clears up.* Saldremos en cuanto aclare el tiempo.—*Would you mind clearing up a few points for me?* ¿Quiere Ud. aclararme algunos puntos? ▲ solucionar *I want to clear up some affairs before I go.* Antes de marcharme quiero solucionar algunos asuntos. ‖ *From this seat you have a clear view of the stage.* Desde esta butaca se ve muy bien el escenario. ‖ *He got clear out of sight.* Le perdimos de vista. ‖ *He was cleared of the murder.* Retiraron la acusación de asesinato que había contra él.

clerk dependiente *The clerk's looking up the price.* El dependiente está averiguando el precio. ▲ empleado *She's a clerk in that office.* Es una empleada de esa oficina. ▲ actuario, secretario *The clerk kept all the records of the court.* El actuario llevaba todas las actas del juzgado.

clever listo, inteligente.

click [n] ruido *I heard the click of the lock when he came in.* Oí el ruido de la cerradura cuando entró.

● [v] sonar *Her heels clicked against the sidewalk.* Sonaban sus tacones al pisar la acera. ‖ *They clicked from the very beginning.* Desde el primer momento se entendieron muy bien.

client cliente.

cliff risco, acantilado.

climate clima.

climax colmo, culminación.

climb [n] subida *You'll find the climb steep and difficult.* Encontrará Ud. la subida empinada y difícil.

● [v] subir *I prefer not to climb stairs.* Prefiero no subir las escaleras. ○ **to climb down** bajarse *Tell that boy to climb down from the tree.* Dígale a ese chico que se baje del árbol.

clinic clínica.

clip [n] broche *She wore a gold clip on her dress.* Llevaba un broche de oro en el traje. ▲ clip, presilla [Am], sujetapapeles *Fasten these papers together with a clip.* Una Ud. estos papeles con un sujetapapeles.

● [v] unir *I clipped my picture to*

the application. Uní mi fotografía a la solicitud. ▲ recortar *If you find the magazine clip that article out for me.* Si encuentra Ud. la revista recórteme Ud. ese artículo. ▲ cortar *Don't clip my hair too short.* No me corte Ud. el pelo demasiado.

clipping recorte.

clock reloj *What time does the clock say?* ¿Qué hora marca el reloj?

close [*n*] final *At the close of the meeting everybody left.* Al final de la reunión se marchó todo el mundo.

● [*v*] cerrar *Please close the door.* Haga el favor de cerrar la puerta.— *They close the store at six.* Cierran la tienda a las seis. ▲ liquidar *I intend to close my account before I leave.* Pienso liquidar mi cuenta antes de marcharme.

○ **to close out** liquidar *The store around the corner's closing out.* La tienda que está a la vuelta de la esquina está liquidando.

‖ *This matter's closed.* Este asunto está concluído.

close [*adj*] cercano *Do you have any close relatives in this country?* ¿Tiene Ud. algún pariente cercano en este país? ▲ íntimo *I'm staying with some close friends.* Estoy hospedada en casa de unos amigos íntimos. ▲ mal ventilado *It's very close in this room.* Este cuarto está muy mal ventilado. ▲ reñido *The vote was very close.* La votación fué muy reñida. ▲ tupido *That material has a very close weave.* Esa tela tiene una trama muy tupida.

○ **close call** *We just had a close call.* Nos salvamos de milagro. ○ **close shave** *I passed the examination, but it was a close shave.* Pasé el examen por un pelo. ○ **close to** cerca de *The hotel's close to the station.* El hotel está cerca de la estación.

‖ *Give this your close attention.* Preste a esto toda su atención.

closely atentamente *He examined the book closely.* Examinó el libro atentamente. ▲ estrechamente *That matter's closely connected with what we were discussing.* Ese asunto está estrechamente relacionado con lo que estábamos tratando.

closet [*n*] ropero, armario.

‖ *He closeted himself with the president.* Se encerró (*or* conferenció a puerta cerrada) con el presidente.

cloth tela *Do you have a better quality of cloth?* ¿Tiene Ud. una tela de

mejor calidad? ▲ trapo, paño *Wipe off the car with a clean cloth.* Limpie Ud. el auto con un trapo limpio.

clothe vestir *He needs this money to feed and clothe his family.* Necesita este dinero para alimentar y vestir a su familia.

clothes ropa *I want these clothes cleaned and pressed.* Quiero que limpien y planchen esta ropa.

clothesline tendedera.

clothespin pinza de tendedera.

clothing ropa.

cloud [*n*] nube *The plane's flying above the clouds.* El avión vuela sobre las nubes.—*The car left in a cloud of dust.* El auto partió envuelto en una nube de polvo.

● [*v*] nublar *The facts are clouded in my memory.* Los hechos están nublados en mi memoria. ▲ alargarse *Her face clouded when I mentioned his name.* Se le alargó la cara cuando mencioné su nombre.

○ **to cloud up** nublarse *Just after we started on the picnic, it began to cloud up.* En cuanto salimos para la jira, comenzó a nublarse.

cloudy nublado.

clove clavo.

clover trébol.

clown payaso.

club [*n*] porra, garrote *The policeman was forced to use his club.* El policía tuvo que usar su garrote. ▲ club *Are you a member of the club?* ¿Es Ud. miembro del club? ▲ trébol *I played a club.* Jugué un trébol.

● [*v*] golpear *The police said the victim had been clubbed.* La policía dijo que la víctima había sido golpeada.

clue indicio, pista.

clumsy desmañado.

cluster [*n*] racimo (*of grapes*); grupo (*of people*).

● [*v*] agrupar.

clutch [*n*] embrague *It took me a while to learn how to use the clutch.* Tardé un poco en aprender a usar el embrague.

● [*v*] agarrar *The child clutched my hand crossing the street.* El niño me agarró la mano al cruzar la calle.

coach coche, vagón *They added two coaches to the train.* Han añadido dos coches al tren. ▲ entrenador *He's the best coach that team ever had.* Es el mejor entrenador que ha tenido ese equipo.

coal carbón.

coalbin carbonera.
coarse basto, burdo *This cloth is too coarse.* Esta tela es demasiado basta. ▲ grosero *His answer was very coarse.* Su respuesta fué muy grosera.
coast costa.
‖ *The coast is clear.* No hay moros en la costa.
coast guard guardacostas.
coastline costa.
coat [*n*] abrigo, sobretodo, [*Arg*] tapado *You'll need a heavy coat for winter.* Necesitará Ud. un abrigo greso para el invierno. ▲ chaqueta, [*Sp*] americana, [*Am*] saco *The pants and vest fit, but the coat's too small for me.* El pantalón y el chaleco están bien, pero el saco me está pequeño. ▲ mano *This room needs another coat of paint.* Este cuarto necesita otra mano de pintura.
● [*v*] cubrir *The automobile was coated with mud.* El auto estaba cubierto de barro.
coat hanger percha.
coax instar, insistir.
cobbler zapatero.
cockroach cucaracha, [*Chile*] barata.
cocktail cocktail, coctel.
cocoa cacao.
coconut coco.
cod bacalao.
coffee café.
coffee cake rosca, bizcocho.
coffee house café.
coffee pot cafetera.
coffin ataúd.
coil [*n*] rollo *We'd better take that coil of rope along in the boat.* Sería mejor llevar ese rollo de cuerda en el barco.
● [*v*] enroscar *The snake was coiled around the tree.* La serpiente estaba enroscada en el árbol.
coin [*n*] moneda *Drop a coin in the slot.* Eche una moneda en la ranura.
● [*v*] acuñar *The government needs to coin more money.* El gobierno necesita acuñar más moneda.
○ **to toss a coin** echar a cara o cruz.
coincide coincidir.
coincidence coincidencia.
coke cok.
cold [*n*] frío *The cold was so severe that the animals froze.* El frío fué tan intenso que se helaron los animales. ▲ catarro *I've got a cold.* Tengo catarro.
● [*adj*] frío *After that incident, he grew cold towards us.* Después de aquel incidente, se mostró frío con nosotros. ▲ sin sentido *The blow knocked him cold.* El golpe le dejó sin sentido.

○ **in cold blood** a sangre fría *He did it in cold blood.* Lo hizo a sangre fría.
○ **to be cold** tener frío *Drink some coffee and you won't be so cold.* Beba Ud. un poco de café y no tendrá tanto frío.
‖ *It feels cold in here.* Hace frío aquí.
cold cream cold cream, crema de limpiar.
collaborate colaborar.
collar cuello.
collarbone clavícula.
colleague colega, compañero.
collect recoger *Tickets are collected at the gate.* Los billetes se recogen en la entrada. ▲ coleccionar *I'm interested in collecting stamps.* Me interesa coleccionar estampillas. ▲ cobrar *He's going to collect a bill.* Va a cobrar una cuenta. ▲ reunirse *A crowd collected around the wounded man.* Se reunió la multitud alrededor del herido.
○ **to collect oneself** tranquilizarse *He was confused at first, but collected himself quickly.* Estaba azarado al principio, pero se tranquilizó en seguida.
‖ *Give me a chance to collect my thoughts.* Déjeme pensar un momento.
collection colección *The museum has a famous collection of Italian paintings.* El museo tiene una famosa colección de cuadros italianos. ▲ recogida *Mail collections are at nine and three.* Las recogidas del correo son a las nueve y a las tres. ▲ colecta *They took up a collection after the meeting.* Hicieron una colecta después de la reunión.
college universidad.
colon dos puntos (:); colón (*anatomy*).
colonel coronel.
colony colonia *I didn't know that country had so many colonies.* No sabía que ese país tuviera tantas colonias.— *There's a large artists' colony near here.* Hay una gran colonia de artistas cerca de aquí.
color color *We have this pattern in several colors.* Tenemos este dibujo en varios colores.— *Once you get out in the air, your color will improve.* En cuanto esté Ud. al aire libre, tendrá mejor color.— *A red flower was the only touch of color on her dress.* Una flor roja era la única nota de color que llevaba en el traje.
‖ *The news in that paper's generally colored.* Las noticias de ese periódico generalmente son parciales.
colt potro.
column columna *You can recognize the house by its white columns.* Conocerá

Ud. la casa porque tiene unas columnas blancas.—*I wonder where that column of smoke comes from.* ¿De dónde saldrá esa columna de humo?—*The soldiers marched in a column of twos.* Los soldados marchaban en columna de a dos.—*I saw the story in the third column on the first page.* Ví la noticia en la tercera columna de la primera página. ▲ sección *His column on foreign affairs appears in twenty newspapers.* Su sección de política internacional aparece en veinte periódicos.

comb [n] peine *I left my comb on the dresser.* Dejé el peine en el tocador. ▲ peineta [Am], peinecillo [Sp] *She always wears several combs in her hair.* Lleva siempre varias peinetas en el pelo. ▲ panal *They have honey in jars, but not in combs.* Tienen miel en tarros, pero no en panales.

  ○ **to comb one's (own) hair** peinarse *My hair needs combing.* Necesito peinarme.

combination combinación *That color combination isn't becoming to her.* Esa combinación de colores no le sienta.— *We're the only ones who know the combination to the safe.* Somos los únicos que conocemos la combinación de la caja de caudales.

combine [v] combinar.

come venir *Come here!* ¡Venga acá! ▲ llegar *When did he come?* ¿Cuándo llegó? ▲ ser *When do the examinations come?* ¿Cuándo son los exámenes?

  ○ **come (on)** vamos *Come, tell me what you mean.* Vamos, dime lo que quieres decir. ○ **to come about** pasar *How did this come about?* ¿Cómo pasó esto? ○ **to come across** encontrar *Let me know if you come across anything with my name on it.* Si encuentra Ud. algo a mi nombre, avíseme. ○ **to come along** acompañar *Do you mind if we come along?* ¿Le molesta a Ud. que le acompañemos? ▲ andar, marchar *How is your work coming along?* ¿Cómo anda su trabajo? ○ **to come back** volver, regresar *He came back home yesterday.* Volvió a casa ayer. ○ **to come by** pasar por *I'll come by your house tonight.* Pasaré por su casa esta noche. ▲ obtener *How did he come by all that money?* ¿Como obtuvo todo ese dinero? ○ **to come down** bajar *Come down the stairs.* Baje por la escalera. ○ **to come down** with darle a uno *I think I'm coming down with the flu.* Creo que me va a dar la grippe. ○ **to come easy to, come natural to**

tener gran facilidad (*or* aptitud) para *Arithmetic comes easy to him.* Tiene gran aptitud para la aritmética. ○ **to come in handy** ser útil. ○ **to come into** entrar en *Tell him to come into the house.* Dígale que entre en la casa. ○ **to come into style** ponerse de moda *When did this come into style?* ¿Cuándo se puso esto de moda? ○ **to come off** quitar *Is this lid fastened or does it come off?* ¿Es fija esta tapa o se puede quitar? ▲ caerse *One of my buttons came off.* Se me cayó un botón. ○ **to come on** *I feel a cold coming on.* Creo que me va a dar un catarro. ○ **to come out** salir *He'll come out soon.* Saldrá pronto.—*The book hasn't come out yet.* El libro todavía no ha salido. —*Everything came out all right.* Todo salió muy bien. ▲ quitarse *This spot won't come out.* Esta mancha no se quita. ▲ declararse *The governor came out against the bill.* El gobernador se declaró contra el proyecto de ley. ○ **to come through** salir *He came through with flying colors.* Salió triunfante. ○ **to come to** ascender a *The bill comes to two dollars.* La cuenta asciende a dos dólares. ▲ volver en sí *The woman who fainted is coming to.* La mujer que se desmayó está volviendo en sí. ▲ resultar de *Who knows what all this will come to?* ¿Quién sabe qué resultará de todo esto? ○ **to come true** resultar, cumplirse, realizarse *Everything he predicted came true.* Se cumplió todo lo que predijo. ○ **to come up** subir *Won't you come up and have a drink?* ¿Quiere subir a tomar un trago? ▲ salir *The grass didn't come up this spring.* La hierba no salió esta primavera. ▲ presentarse *This problem comes up every day.* Este problema se presenta todos los días. ○ **to come upon** encontrar *I came upon the answer by accident.* Encontré la solución por casualidad.

  ‖ *He has now come around to our point of view.* Ahora está de acuerdo con nosotros. ‖ *Come in!* ¡Adelante! *or* ¡Entre Ud.! ‖ *Does this cloth come in other colors?* ¿Tienen Uds. esta tela en otros colores? ‖ *What's come over you?* ¿Qué tiene? ‖ *What law does this come under?* ¿Qué ley se aplica en este caso?

comedy comedia.

comfort [n] comodidad *They lacked many comforts.* Les faltaban muchas comodidades.

  ● [v] consolar *This news may comfort*

you. Esta noticia puede que te consuele.

‖ *The medicine gave me no comfort.* La medicina no me ha aliviado nada.

comfortable cómodo *This chair's soft and comfortable.* Esta silla es blanda y cómoda.

comical cómico, gracioso.

comics historietas cómicas, muñequitos.

comma coma.

command [*n*] orden *Has he issued his commands yet?* ¿Ha dado ya sus órdenes? ▲ mando *A new officer's taken command of the troops.* Un nuevo oficial ha tomado el mando de las tropas. ● [*v*] ordenar *We were commanded to take to the lifeboats.* Nos ordenaron que ocupáramos los botes salvavidas. ○ **to have a good command of** dominar *Does he have a good command of English?* ¿Domina el inglés?

commander comandante.

commence comenzar.

commend encomendar, alabar.

comment [*n*] comentario, observación *We'll have no comments from you!* ¡No haga Ud. comentarios! ● [*v*] hacer comentarios *She always comments on my clothes.* Siempre hace comentarios sobre mi ropa.

commentator comentador.

commerce comercio.

commercial comercial, mercantil.

commission [*n*] comisión, junta *The commission has promised to take action soon.* La comisión ha prometido actuar pronto. ▲ comisión *My commission's almost as large as my salary.* Mi comisión es casi igual que mi sueldo. ● [*v*] encargar *I've been commissioned to sell the property.* Me han encargado de vender la propiedad. ○ **out of commission** descompuesto *The car's out of commission.* El auto está descompuesto. ○ **to have a commission** ser oficial *Three members of my family have commissions in the army.* Tres de mi familia son oficiales del ejército. ‖ *He was commissioned from the ranks.* De soldado ascendió a oficial.

commissioner comisionado, comisario.

commit encerrar, meter *It's too bad they had to commit her to an asylum.* Es una lástima que hayan tenido que meterla en un manicomio. ▲ perpetrar, cometer *It's not the first crime he's committed.* No es el primer crimen que ha cometido. ○ **to commit oneself** comprometerse *You don't have to commit yourself un-*less *you want to.* No tiene Ud. que comprometerse si no quiere.

committee comisión, comité *Who's on the committee?* ¿Quiénes forman la comisión?

common común *These laws are for the common good.* Estas leyes son para el bien común. ▲ vulgar, ordinario *Her manners were rather common.* Sus modales eran algo vulgares. ○ **common man** hombre del pueblo *He says this is the century of the common man.* Dice que éste es el siglo del hombre del pueblo. ○ **common sense** sentido común *If other problems arise, use your common sense.* Si se presentan otros problemas, use Ud. su sentido común. ○ **in common** en común *The three sisters own the house in common.* Las tres hermanas son dueñas en común de la casa. ‖ *It's common knowledge that you can't believe everything he says.* Es cosa conocida que no se le puede creer todo lo que dice.

commonplace [*adj*] común.

commotion conmoción, tumulto.

communicate comunicar.

communication comunicación *The messenger brought two communications from headquarters.* El enviado trajo dos comunicaciones del cuartel general. —*Our communication lines have been broken by the storms.* Las tormentas han cortado nuestras líneas de comunicación. ○ **in communication** en communicación *We haven't been in communication with them.* No hemos estado en comunicación con ellos.

communion comunión.

communist comunista.

community comunidad.

compact [*n*] polvera *Lend me your compact.* Préstame tu polvera.

compact [*adj*] conciso, breve *His last article was very compact.* Su último artículo era muy conciso. ‖ *That kitchen's very compact.* En esa cocina está todo en muy poco espacio.

companion compañero *We were companions on a trip to Paris.* Fuimos compañeros durante un viaje a Paris.

company visita *I'm expecting company this evening.* Espero visita esta noche. ▲ compañía *What company do you represent?* ¿Qué compañía representa Ud?—*The leading actor's good, but the rest of the company's poor.* El primer actor es bueno, pero el resto de la compañía no vale nada.—*The captain will review his company tomorrow.* El capitán pasará revista a su compañía mañana.

○ **good company** simpático *I find him very good company.* Me parece muy simpático.

comparative comparativo, relativo.

compare comparar *We compared the two methods and chose this one.* Comparamos los dos métodos y escogimos éste. ▲ poderse comparar *This hotel doesn't compare with others I've stayed in.* Este hotel no se puede comparar con los otros en que he estado.

comparison comparación *There's no comparison between the two towns.* No hay comparación entre las dos poblaciones.

compartment compartimiento.

compass brújula, compás *The ship's compass was broken during the storm.* Durante la tempestad la brújula del barco se rompió. ▲ compás *For these drawings you need a compass.* Para hacer estos dibujos necesita Ud. un compás.

compel obligar.

compensate compensar.

compete competir *They'll compete for the prize.* Competirán por el premio. ▲ tomar parte *Are you competing in the contest?* ¿Toma Ud. parte en el concurso?

competent competente, capaz.

competition competencia.

competitor competidor.

complain quejarse *She left work early, complaining of a headache.* Salió del trabajo temprano, quejándose de dolor de cabeza.

complaint queja *If it annoys you so much, file a complaint.* Si le molesta tanto presente Ud. una queja. ▲ malestar *He told the doctor about his complaint.* Le dijo al doctor el malestar que sentía. ▲ reclamación *Refer this woman to the complaint department.* Dirija esta señora a la sección de reclamaciones.

complete [*adj*] completo *Is the list complete?* ¿Está la lista completa?
● [*v*] completar, terminar *You ought to complete the work before you go home.* Debe Ud. terminar el trabajo antes de irse a casa.

complex [*adj*] complejo.

complexion cutis *Being outdoors so much has improved her complexion.* Su cutis ha mejorado mucho desde que pasa tanto tiempo al aire libre. ▲ estado *There doesn't seem to be any change*

in the complexion of our local politics. Parece que no hay cambio en el estado de nuestra política local.

complicate complicar.

compliment [*n*] piropo, galantería *Thanks for the compliment.* Gracias por la galantería.
● [*v*] felicitar *Let me compliment you on your cooking.* Permítame Ud. felicitarla por lo bien que cocina.

comply with cumplir, conformarse a.

compose componer, formar *What's it composed of?* ¿De qué se compone? ▲ componer *He composed that piece several years ago.* Compuso esa pieza hace varios años.

○ **to compose oneself** serenarse, calmarse *Try to compose yourself.* Trate Ud. de serenarse.

composition composición *That symphony's his most famous composition.* Esa sinfonía es su composición más famosa.—*The chemist will analyze the composition of this metal.* El químico analizará la composición de este metal.

comprehend comprender.

compress [*v*] comprimir.

comrade camarada, compañero.

concave cóncavo.

conceal ocultar, esconder.

conceit presunción, engreimiento.

conceited engreído *He's very conceited about his looks.* Está muy engreído porque se cree buen mozo.

conceive imaginar *I can't conceive of her doing that.* No puedo imaginar que ella haga eso. ▲ concebir *Only a genius could conceive such a plan.* Sólo un genio podría concebir tal plan.

concentrate concentrarse *There's so much noise that I can't concentrate.* Hay tanto ruido que no me puedo concentrar. ▲ concentrar *We were all concentrated in one area.* Todos estábamos concentrados en una sola zona.

concentration concentración.

concept concepto.

conception concepción *He's responsible for the conception of the plan.* La concepción del plan es suya. ▲ opinión *According to my conception his ability is highly overrated.* Según mi opinión se exagera mucho acerca de su capacidad.

concern [*n*] angustia, preocupación *She's showing a great deal of concern over her husband.* Demuestra mucha preocupación por su marido. ▲ casa comercial, empresa *How long have you been with this concern?* ¿Cuánto tiempo*

lleva Ud. trabajando para esta empresa?
● [v] importar *This concerns you.* Esto le importa a Ud. ‖ *She said it was no concern of hers.* Dijo que eso no le atañía. ‖ *We're concerned about your health.* Su salud nos inquieta. ‖ *I'm not concerned with the details.* No me interesan los detalles.

concerning acerca de, respecto a *Nothing was said concerning the matter.* No dijeron nada acerca del asunto.

concert concierto.

concert hall salón para conciertos.

concise conciso, breve.

conclude concluir, terminar *The meeting concluded with a vote.* La reunión terminó con una votación. ▲ llegar a la conclusión *They concluded that it must have been suicide.* Llegaron a la conclusión de que debía haber sido un suicidio.

conclusion conclusión *I've come to the same conclusion.* He llegado a la misma conclusión. ▲ final *At the conclusion of the program he played one of his own compositions.* Al final del programa tocó una de sus composiciones.

concrete [n] cemento, hormigón *His new house is built completely of concrete.* Su nueva casa es toda de cemento.
● [adj] definitivo *It's too early for my plans to be very concrete.* Es demasiado pronto para que yo pueda tener planes definitivos.

condemn condenar *You're in no position to condemn her actions.* Ud. no está en condiciones para condenar su conducta.—*Do you think the jury will condemn him?* ¿Cree Ud. que el jurado le condenará?
‖ *This building's been condemned.* Oficialmente se ha prohibido el uso de este edificio.

condense condensar *You'd better buy six more cans of condensed milk.* Convendría que Ud. comprara seis latas más de leche condensada. ▲ condensarse *The room was so hot that the steam condensed on the windows.* Hacía tanto calor en el cuarto que el vapor se condensó sobre los cristales.

condition [n] estado *The house was in poor condition.* La casa estaba en muy mal estado. ▲ condición *I'll accept the offer on three conditions.* Aceptaré la oferta con tres condiciones.
● [v] determinar *His decision was conditioned by his religious beliefs.* Su

decisión fué determinada por sus creencias religiosas.
○ in condition en buenas condiciones *The athlete isn't in condition.* El atleta no está en buenas condiciones.
○ on any condition de ninguna manera *She said she wouldn't attend on any condition.* Dijo que no asistiría de ninguna manera. ○ on condition that con la condición de que *I'll go on condition that I pay my own way.* Iré con la condición de que yo pague mis gastos.

conduct [n] conducta *I don't like his conduct.* No me parece bien su conducta.

conduct [v] conducir *A guide will conduct the party through the museum.* Un guía conducirá el grupo por el museo. —*We need a wire to conduct electricity to the barn.* Necesitamos un flexible para conducir la electricidad al granero. ▲ manejar, llevar, hacerse cargo *Who conducted the business in his absence?* ¿Quién se hizo cargo de los negocios en su ausencia? ▲ dirigir *I wonder who conducts the orchestra tonight?* ¿Quién dirigirá la orquesta esta noche?
○ to conduct oneself comportarse *He conducted himself well during the meeting.* Se comportó muy bien durante la reunión.

conductor director *He's the conductor for the final concert this season.* Será el director del último concierto de la temporada. ▲ revisor, [Am] conductor *The conductor took our tickets as soon as we got on the train.* El revisor nos pidió los billetes en cuanto nos subimos a tren. ▲ combrador, [Am] conductor *Ask the conductor to stop at the next corner.* Pídale al cobrador que pare en la próxima esquina. ▲ conductor *Copper's a better conductor of heat than iron.* El cobre es mejor conductor que el hierro.

cone cono.

confer conferir *They conferred extraordinary powers upon him.* Le confirieron poderes extraordinarios. ▲ conferenciar *They were conferring on the war situation.* Conferenciaban sobre la situación de la guerra.

conference junta, reunión, conversación *He's in conference just now.* Está ahora en una junta. ▲ conferencia *Who's our delegate to the conference?* ¿Quién es nuestro delegado en la conferencia?

confess confesar.

confession confesión.

confidence confianza.

confident seguro.

confidential confidencial.

confine limitar *He confined himself to a few brief remarks.* Se limitó a hacer unas breves observaciones. ○ **to be confined** dar a luz *When does your sister expect to be confined?* ¿Cuándo dará a luz su hermana? ‖ *I was confined to the house with a cold.* Tuve que quedarme en casa por el catarro.

confirm confirmar *No one's confirmed the news yet.* No han confirmado todavía la noticia.—*They gave me flowers when I was confirmed.* Me dieron flores cuando me confirmaron.

conflict [n] conflicto *There was a great conflict of interests.* Había un gran conflicto de intereses.

conflict [v] luchar, chocar *Their ideas are always conflicting.* Sus opiniones siempre chocan.

conform conformarse *He never learned to conform.* No sabe conformarse. ▲ estar de acuerdo *That conforms to the requirements.* Eso está de acuerdo con lo que se requiere.

confuse confundir, desorientar *All this talking confuses me.* Tanta charla me desorienta.

confusion ○ **to throw into confusion** alterar, desorganizar *The accident threw traffic into confusion.* El accidente desorganizo el tráfico.

congenial simpático *She's very congenial.* Es muy simpática.

congratulate felicitar *Let me be the first to congratulate you.* Permítame ser el primero en felicitarle.

congratulations enhorabuena, felicitaciones.

congregation congregación.

congress congreso.

conjunction conjunción. ○ **in conjunction with** en relación con.

connect conectar *Please connect these wires to the battery.* Haga Ud. el favor de conectar estos flexibles con la batería. ▲ enlazar *All the trains connect with busses at the station.* Todos los trenes enlazan con autobuses en la estación. ▲ relacionar *I always connect his name with that event.* Siempre relaciono su nombre con ese acontecimiento. ‖ *What firm are you connected with?* ¿Con qué empresa trabaja Ud.?

connection conexión *There's a loose connection somewhere in the engine.* Hay una conexión floja en alguna parte del motor. ▲ comunicación *The connections with that town are very poor.* Las comunicaciones con ese pueblo son muy malas. ▲ relación *I don't understand the connection between the two statements.* No comprendo la relación que hay entre las dos declaraciones. ‖ *He has excellent connections.* Está muy bien relacionado. ‖ *He's a man with wide connections.* Es un hombre de muchas campanillas.

conquer conquistar.

conscience conciencia.

conscientious concienzudo.

conscious ○ **to be conscious of** darse cuenta de *I wasn't conscious of what I was doing.* No me daba cuenta de lo que hacía. ‖ *He hasn't been conscious since this morning.* No ha recobrado el conocimiento desde esta mañana. *or* No ha vuelto en sí desde esta mañana.

consecrate consagrar.

consecutive consecutivo, sucesivo.

consent [n] permiso *If he's under age, the consent of his parents is required.* Si es menor de edad es preciso conseguir el permiso de sus padres. ● [v] consentir *He consented to stay.* Consintió en quedarse.

consequence consecuencia.

consequently por lo tanto, por consiguiente.

conservative [adj; n] conservador.

conserve conservar.

consider estudiar *We're considering all angles of the proposal.* Estamos estudiando todos los aspectos de la propuesta. ▲ ocuparse de *Don't even consider that.* Ni se ocupe de eso. ▲ considerar *I don't consider him fit for the job.* No le considero capacitado para ocupar el puesto. ▲ tomar en cuenta *He never considers the feelings of others.* Nunca toma en cuenta los sentimientos de los demás.

considerable bastante *I spent considerable time on it.* Tardé bastante tiempo en hacerlo.

consideration consideración *You'd think he'd have some consideration for my feelings.* Cualquiera pensaría que él había de tener un poco más de consideración para con mis sentimientos. —*We'll take the matter under consideration.* Vamos a tomar en consideración el asunto. ▲ retribución *He'll probably expect a consideration for his services.* Probablemente esperará una retribución por sus servicios.

○ **in consideration of** en reconocimiento a *We present this to you in consideration of your services.* Le hacemos este obsequio en reconocimiento a sus servicios. ○ **to take into consideration** tener en cuenta *Take into consideration all the money it cost me.* Tenga Ud. en cuenta todo el dinero que me costó.

consign consignar.

consist consistir.

consistent lógico, razonable.

consommé caldo.

conspiracy conspiración.

constant constante *He was a very constant friend.* Era un amigo muy constante. — *The constant noise kept me awake all night.* El ruido constante me tuvo despierto toda la noche.

constantly constantemente.

constitute constituir *This constitutes our major health problem.* Esto constituye nuestro mayor problema sanitario.

constitution constitución *She has a strong constitution.* Tiene muy buena constitución.—*The President's actions are in full accord with the Constitution.* Las actuaciones del Presidente están completamente de acuerdo con la Constitución.

construct construir.

construction construcción.

consul cónsul.

consult consultar.

consume consumir *How much water does the city consume in a week?* ¿Qué cantidad de agua consume la ciudad por semana?—*The school building was completely consumed by fire.* El edificio de la escuela fué completamente consumido por el fuego. ○ **to be consumed** consumirse *He was consumed with anger.* Se consumía de rabia.

consumption tisis, tuberculosis *She's the third member of her family to die of consumption.* Es la tercera persona en su familia que ha muerto de tisis. ▲ consumo *The consumption of coal increased during the month of February.* El consumo de carbón ha aumentado durante el mes de febrero.

contact [*n*] relación *Have you made any new business contacts?* ¿Ha hecho alguna nueva relación comercial? ● [*v*] ponerse en contacto con *I'll contact you as soon as I arrive.* Me pondré en contacto con Ud. en cuanto llegue. ○ **to come in contact with** ponerse en contacto con, tocar *Don't let your clothes come in contact with the wound.* No deje que la ropa toque la herida.

contain contener *What does the trunk contain?* ¿Qué contiene el baúl? ○ **to contain oneself** contenerse *He contained himself throughout the quarrel.* Se contuvo durante toda la disputa. ‖ *How much does this thermos contain?* ¿Qué capacidad tiene ese termos?

contemplate proyectar *He's contemplating a trip to Europe.* Proyecta un viaje a Europa.

contemporary [*adj; n*] contemporáneo.

contempt desprecio, menosprecio. ○ **contempt of court** contumacia, rebeldía.

contend mantener.

content [*adj*] contento, satisfecho *He was content with what we offered him.* Se quedó contento con lo que le ofrecimos.

content, contents [*n*] contenido *I don't understand the content of this letter.* No comprendo el contenido de esta carta.—*The contents of your trunk must be examined.* Es preciso que registren el contenido de su baúl.

contentment contento, satisfacción.

contest concurso *Prizes will be given to the winners of the contest.* Se darán premios a los que ganen en el concurso. ▲ contienda *There was a bitter contest in the elections.* La contienda fué muy dura en las elecciones.

continent continente.

continual continuo.

continue continuar *The novel will be continued next week.* La novela continuará la semana próxima.

continuous continuo.

contour contorno.

contract [*n*] contrato *I refuse to sign the contract as it stands.* Me niego a firmar el contrato en esas condiciones.

contract [*v*] contratarse *They contracted to do the work.* Se contrataron para hacer el trabajo. ▲ contraer *I'm not responsible for any debts you contract.* No soy responsable de las deudas que Ud. contraiga.—*He contracted a severe illness.* Contrajo una enfermedad grave. ‖ *His pupils contracted in the sunlight.* Se le contrajeron las pupilas con la luz del sol.

contractor contratista.

contradict contradecir.

contradictory contradictorio.

contrary contrario *The results are contrary to my expectations.* Los resul-

tados son contrarios a lo que yo esperaba.
○ on the **contrary** al contrario *On the contrary, nothing could be worse.* Al contrario, nada podría ser peor.
‖ *She's a very contrary child.* La niña tiene espíritu de contradicción.

contrast [*n*] diferencia *There's quite a contrast between what he says and what he does.* Hay mucha diferencia entre lo que dice y lo que hace. ▲ contraste *Red flowers would be a nice contrast with that blue dress.* Unas flores rojas harían un bonito contraste con ese vestido azul.

contrast [*v*] comparar *It isn't fair to contrast my work with an expert's.* No es justo comparar mi trabaja con el de un experto. ▲ hacer contraste *Do you think these colors contrast well?* ¿Cree Ud. que estos colores hagen un buen contraste?

contribute contribuir, prestar *I contributed my time without pay.* Presté mis servicios de balde. ▲ colaborar *He contributes to the local paper.* Colabora en el periódico local.
○ to **contribute** to aumentar *All this noise just contributes to the confusion.* Todo este ruido no hace más que aumentar la confusión.

control [*n*] dirección, [*Am*] control *The control of the business has passed to the son.* El control del negocio ha pasada a manos del hijo.
● [*v*] dominar, [*Am*] controlar *You must learn to control your temper.* Tiene Ud. que aprender a dominar su genio.
○ **controls** control, mandos *Would you mind taking the controls for a while?* ¿Le importaría tomar los mandos por un rato?

controversy controversia, disputa.

convenience comodidad *Our house in the country has every convenience.* Nuestra casa de campo tiene todas las comodidades.
‖ *Call me back at your convenience.* Vuelva a llamarme cuando Ud. lo crea conveniente.

convenient cómodo *The bus service here's convenient.* Es muy cómodo el servicio de autobuses aquí. ▲ oportuno *It was a very convenient accident.* Fué un incidente muy oportuno.

convention convención *The convention wasn't too successful.* La convención no tuvo mucho éxito. ▲ reglas sociales *That isn't in accord with convention.* Eso no está de acuerdo con las reglas sociales.

conventional convencional.

conversation conversación.

convert [*v*] convertir, transformar.

convey transmitir, llevar.

convict [*n*] presidiario, preso *They had convicts working on the road.* Tienen a los presos trabajando en la carretera.

convict [*v*] condenar *He was convicted of murder.* Fué condenado como culpable del asesinato.

convince convencer.

cook [*n*] cocinero *This is our cook's specialty.* Esta es la especialidad de nuestra cocinera.
● [*v*] cocinar, guisar *Start cooking dinner now.* Empiece Ud. a cocinar la comida ahora.
○ to **cook** up inventar *They've cooked up a good story for us.* Nos han inventado un buena fábula.

cookie galleta.

cool [*adj*] fresco *It gets pretty cool here toward evening.* Por la tarde hace bastante fresco aquí. ▲ sereno *I tried to keep cool when he insulted me.* Traté de permanecer sereno cuando me insultó.
● [*v*] enfriar *Don't let this soup cool too long.* No deje Ud. enfriar demasiado la sopa.
○ to **cool** off enfriarse *Stop the engine and let it cool off.* Pare Ud. el motor y deje que se enfríe.
‖ *He was very cool to me.* Me trató con mucha frialdad.

coop gallinero *Two chickens got out of the coop.* Dos pollos se salieron del gallinero.
○ to **coop** up encerrar *It's too hot to keep him cooped up in the house all day.* Hace demasiado calor para tenerlo encerrado en la casa todo el día.

cooperate cooperar.

copper cobre.

copy [*n*] copia *Please make ten copies of this report.* Tenga Ud. la bondad de hacer diez copias de este informe. ▲ manuscrito *I've already sent the copy to the printer.* Ya mandé el manuscrito a la imprenta. ▲ ejemplar *I just bought two copies of his new book.* Acabo de comprar dos ejemplares de su nuevo libro. ▲ número *Do you have the last copy of that magazine?* ¿Tiene Ud. el último número de esa revista?
● [*v*] copiar *Please copy this letter.* Haga el favor de copiar esta carta.

cord cuerda *I don't have enough cord to*

tie up this package. No tengo suficiente cuerda para amarrar este paquete. ▲ cordón *We'll have to get a new cord for the iron.* Tendremos que conseguir un nuevo cordón para la plancha. ▲ carga *Order a cord of wood.* Pida Ud. una carga de leña.
cordial [*adj; n*] cordial.
corduroy pana.
core corazón.
cork [*n*] corcho.
● [*v*] tapar con corcho.
corkscrew tirabuzón [*Am*], sacacorchos [*Sp*].
corn maíz *They planted corn in some fields and wheat in others.* Sembraron maíz en algunos campos y trigo en otros. ▲ callo *He said that those shoes hurt his corns.* Dijo que esos zapatos le lastimaban los callos.
corner [*n*] esquina *I hit my hand on the corner of the table.* Me golpeé la mano en la esquina de la mesa.—*Please stop at the next corner.* Haga el favor parar en la próxima esquina. ▲ rincón *Please bring that chair over from the corner.* Traiga Ud. aquella silla que está en el rincón.
● [*v*] acorralar *The thief was cornered by the police.* El ladrón fué acorralado por la policía. ▲ monopolizar *This dealer's cornered the wheat market.* Este comerciante ha monopolizado el mercado del trigo.
cornstarch almidón de maíz, maicena.
corporal [*n*] cabo.
corporation corporación, sociedad anónima.
corpse cadáver.
corral [*n*] corral.
correct [*adj*] exacto *He got the correct answer to the problem.* Logró dar la solución exacta al problema. ▲ correcto *Her English is not very correct.* Su inglés no es muy correcto. ▲ propio *What's the correct dress for this ceremony?* ¿Cuál es el traje propio para esta ceremonia?
● [*v*] corregir *Please correct my mistakes.* Haga el favor de corregir mis faltas.—*The mother was constantly correcting the child.* La madre estaba corrigiendo constantemente al niño.
correction corrección *Please make the necessary corrections.* Haga el favor de hacer las correcciones necesarias.
‖ *This child needs correction.* Este niño necesita que le corrijan.
correspond estar de acuerdo *What he says and what he does don't correspond.* Lo que dice no está de acuerdo con lo que hace.
○ to **correspond** with escribir a *I hope you won't be too busy to correspond with your old friends.* Espero que no esté Ud. tan ocupado que no pueda escribir a sus viejos amigos.
correspondence correspondencia.
correspondent corresponsal *I'm an American newspaper correspondent.* Soy corresponsal de un periódico americano.
‖ *We've been regular correspondents for two years.* Durante dos años hemos mantenido correspondencia con regularidad.
corridor corredor, pasillo.
corruption corrupción.
corsage ramillete.
cost [*n*] precio *He buys clothes without regard for the cost.* Compra ropa sin mirar el precio. ▲ coste *He was forced to sell his stock at less than cost.* Tuvo que vender sus existencias en menos del coste.
● [*v*] costar *His recklessness cost him his life.* Su temeridad le costó la vida.
○ at **all costs** a toda costa *We have to do it at all costs.* Tenemos que hacerlo a toda costa. ○ at the **cost of** a costa de *He finished his book at the cost of his health.* Terminó su libro a costa de su salud.
costly costoso, caro.
costume disfraz *What costume did he wear to the ball?* ¿Qué disfraz llevó al baile? ▲ traje *She was dressed in skating costume.* Estaba vestida con un traje de patinar.
○ **costumes** vestuario *Who designed the costumes for that play?* ¿Quién diseñó el vestuario para esa comedia?
cot catre.
cottage casita, chalet.
cotton algodón.
couch diván.
cough [*n*] tos *Do you have something that's good for a cough?* ¿Tiene Ud. algo para la tos?
● [*v*] toser *The baby's been coughing all night.* El nene ha tosido toda la noche.
council consejo, junta.
councilman consejal.
counsel consejo *I'm in trouble and I need your counsel.* Me encuentro en un apuro y necesito su consejo. ▲ abogado *He's the counsel for the defense.* Es el abogado de la defensa.
count [*n*] recuento *The count hasn't been taken yet.* No se ha hecho todavía el recuento. ▲ contar *The boxer got up*

on the count of nine. El boxeador se levantó al contar nueve segundos. ▲ conde *What's the proper way to address a count?* ¿Qué tratamiento se le da a un conde? ● [v] contar *Please count your change.* Tenga la bondad de contar su cambio. —*The bill's five dollars, not counting the tax.* La cuenta es cinco dólares, sin contar el impuesto. ▲ contar, importar *In this broad outline, the details don't count.* En este plan general, los detalles no cuentan. ○ **to count on** contar con *We're counting on you.* Contamos con Ud. ▲ depender de *I could never count on him.* Nunca podía depender de él.

countenance cara, aspecto.

counter [n] mostrador, contador *He put the money on the counter.* Puso el dinero sobre el mostrador. ● [adv] contrario *The game was going counter to expectations.* El juego se desarrolló de forma contraria a lo que se esperaba.

counterfeit [n] falsificación *This is a counterfeit of the document.* Esta es una falsificación del documento. ● [adj] falso *This coin's counterfeit.* Esta moneda es falsa.

countess condesa.

country país *What country were you born in?* ¿En qué país nació Ud.? ▲ región *This is good wheat country.* Esta región es buena para el trigo. ▲ campo *The country air will do you good.* El aire del campo le hará bien. ▲ patria *He gave his life for his country.* Dió la vida por su patria.

county condado, distrito territorial, jurisdicción rural.

couple par *I want a couple of eggs.* Quiero un par de huevos. ▲ pareja *Those young people make a very nice couple.* Eso dos jóvenes hacen muy buena pareja.

coupon cupón.

courage valor *It took a lot of courage to say what he did.* Necesitó mucho valor para decir lo que dijo.

course curso *What chemistry courses are being offered at the university?* ¿Qué cursos de química se dan en la universidad?—*The course of the river's been changed by the dam.* La presa ha cambiado el curso del río.—*I heard from him twice in the course of the year.* Tuve dos veces noticias suyas durante el curso del año. ▲ ruta, dirección *The captain says we'll have to change our course.* El capitán dice que

tendremos que cambiar nuestra ruta. ▲ campo *When's the golf course open?* ¿Cuándo está abierto el campo de golf? ▲ plato *They serve a five-course dinner.* Sirven una comida de cinco platos. ○ **a matter of course** la cosa más corriente *He takes everything as a matter of course.* Lo toma todo como la cosa más corriente. ○ **of course** claro, por supuesto *Of course I know what you mean.* Claro que sé lo que Ud. quiere decir.

court [n] patio *We have several rooms facing the court.* Tenemos varios cuartos que dan al patio. ▲ cancha *The court's still too wet for a game.* La cancha está todavía demasiado mojada para jugar. ▲ juzgado *I have to go to court to pay a fine.* Tengo que ir al juzgado para pagar una multa. ▲ tribunal *The case goes from court to court.* El caso pasa de tribunal en tribunal. ▲ corte *The ambassador hasn't been received at court yet.* El Embajador no ha sido aún recibido en la Corte. ● [v] hacer la corte *He used to court her years ago.* Le hacía la corte hace muchos años.

courteous cortés.

courtesy cortesía *I'll go out of courtesy, but I'd rather stay home.* Iré por cortesía, pero preferiría quedarme en casa. ▲ atención *She's always doing little courtesies for everybody.* Siempre tiene pequeñas atenciones con todo el mundo.

cousin primo *The two girls are cousins.* Las dos muchachas son primas.

cover [n] tapa, tapadera *Where are the covers for these boxes?* ¿Dónde están las tapas de estas cajas? ▲ tapas *The cover of this book's been torn off.* Le han arrancado la tapa a este libro. ▲ funda *The apartment must be cleaned and the covers removed from the furniture.* Es preciso limpiar el apartamento y quitarles las fundas a los muebles. ▲ manta, [Am] cobija *I didn't have enough covers last night.* No tuve suficientes mantas anoche. ● [v] cubrir, tapar *The floor was completely covered by a large rug.* El piso estaba completamente cubierto con una gran alfombra. ▲ tapar *Cover the jar.* Tape el tarro. ▲ taparse *She covered her face with her hands.* Se tapó la cara con las manos. ▲ abarcar *This book covers the subject pretty well.* Este libro abarca el tema bastante bien. ▲ recorrer *The express* *train covers the distance in two hours.* El expreso recorre la distancia en dos horas.—*A new salesman's been taken on to cover this territory.* Se ha empleado a un nuevo viajante para recorrer esta zona. ▲ apuntar *He had us covered with a revolver.* Nos apuntaba con un revólver.

O **from cover to cover** de cabo a cabo *I read the book from cover to cover.* Leí el libro de cabo a cabo. O **to be covered by insurance** estar asegurado. O **to cover up** ocultar *He carefully covered up all his mistakes.* Ocultaba cuidadosamente todos sus errores. O **to take cover** ponerse a cubierto.

cow vaca.

coward cobarde.

cowardly cobarde.

cowboy vaquero, gaucho [*Arg*], huaso [*Chile*], llanero [*Ven*], charro [*Mex*].

cozy cómodo, agradable, acogedor.

crab (*shellfish*) cangrejo.

crack [*n*] raja, grieta *Can you fix that crack in the door?* ¿Puede Ud. arreglar esa raja en la puerta? ▲ detonación *I thought I heard the crack of a rifle.* Me pareció oír la detonación de un rifle. ▲ ensayo *Would you like a crack at this job?* ¿Le gustaría a Ud. hacer un ensayo en este trabajo?

● [*adj*] gran *She's a crack typist.* Es una gran mecanógrafa.

● [*v*] rajar *This cup's cracked.* Esta taza está rajada. ▲ forzar *If we can't open the safe we'll have to crack it.* Si no podemos abrir la caja de caudales tendremos que forzarla. ▲ cascar *I can't crack this walnut.* No puedo cascar esta nuez.

O **to crack jokes** decir chistes *He cracked several jokes before beginning his talk.* Dijo varios chistes antes de comenzar su charla. O **to crack up** estrellarse *The plane cracked up near the landing field.* El avión se estrelló cerca del campo de aterrizaje. ‖ *That's a tough nut to crack.* Ese es un asunto muy difícil de pelar (*or* resolver). ‖ *He's always making cracks about me.* Siempre se está burlando de mí.

cracked chiflado *Your cousin's cracked.* Su primo está chiflado.

cracker galleta.

cradle cuna.

crank manivela *Is there a crank in this truck?* ¿Hay una manivela en este camión? ▲ cascarrabias *Our neighbor's such a crank: he's always com-*

plaining. Nuestro vecino es un cascarrabias, siempre está refunfuñando.

crash [*n*] estrépito *What was that loud crash in the kitchen?* ¿Qué estrépito ha sido ése en la cocina? ▲ choque *He broke his leg in the crash.* Se rompió una pierna en el choque.

● [*v*] chocar *Two cars just crashed.* Dos automóviles acaban de chocar.

crater cráter.

crawfish cabrajo, bogavante.

crawl [*v*] marchar lentamente *The car crawled toward the gate.* El automóvil marchó lentamente hacia la entrada. ▲ sentirse humillado *She made the poor boy crawl.* Hizo sentirse humillado al pobre muchacho.

O **to crawl (on all fours)** gatear *The baby's just learning to crawl.* El nene está aprendiendo a gatear. O **to crawl on one's stomach** arrastrarse *He crawled through the grass on his stomach.* Se iba arrastrando por la hierba. O **to make one's flesh crawl** estremecerse *When I heard her scream, it made my flesh crawl.* Al oírla dar aquel grito me estremecí.

crazy extravagante *What a crazy way to do things!* ¡Qué manera más extravagante de hacer las cosas! ▲ loco *This noise is driving me crazy.* Este ruido me está volviendo loco.

cream crema *Do you take cream with your coffee?* ¿Toma Ud. crema en el café? —*Apply this cream twice a day.* Aplíquese esta crema dos veces al día. ▲ crema y nata *They invited the cream of society.* Invitaron a la crema y nata de la sociedad.

crease [*n*] raya *Put a crease in my trousers.* Sáquele Ud. la raya a mis pantalones.

● [*v*] doblar *Crease the paper and tear it in half.* Doble Ud. el papel y pártalo en dos.

create crear.

creation creación.

creative creador.

creature criatura *These poor creatures haven't been fed yet.* A esas pobres criaturas no les han dado de comer todavía. ▲ animal, bicho *We saw many strange creatures in the wood.* Vimos muchos animales raros en el bosque. ▲ tipo *Who's that creature in the green hat?* ¿Quién es ese tipo del sombrero verde?

credit [*n*] mérito, paternidad *He took credit for the plan, although the others did the work.* Se adjudicó la paternidad del plan, aunque otros habían hecho el trabajo. ▲ saldo a favor *The books showed a credit of five dollars in your name.* Los libros arrojan un saldo de cinco dólares a su favor.

● [v] dar crédito a *Can you credit the reports in that newspaper?* ¿Se puede dar crédito a las noticias de ese periódico?

○ on credit a crédito *They're willing to sell us the furniture on credit.* Están dispuestos a vendernos los muebles a crédito. ○ to give credit fiar *Will they give us credit in this store?* ¿Nos fiarán en esta tienda? ▲ reconocer, estar reconocido *We have to give him credit for his work.* Tenemos que reconocerle el trabajo que ha hecho. ‖ *He's a credit to his profession.* Honra su profesión.

creditor acreedor.

creek riachuelo, arroyo.

creed credo.

creep gatear *How old was the baby when he started creeping?* ¿Qué edad tenía el niño cuando comenzó a gatear? ▲ subir silenciosamente *We crept up the steps so as not to wake anybody.* Subimos silenciosamente la escalera para no despertar a nadie. ▲ trepar *Those vines are creeping all over the wall.* Esas enredaderas están trepando por toda la pared.

○ the creeps escalofríos *Just the thought of being alone in this house gives me the creeps.* Solo la idea de estar sola en esta casa me da escalofríos.

cremate incinerar.

crepe crespón.

crescent creciente.

crest cresta.

crew dotación, tripulación *When the ship sank, several of the crew were drowned.* Cuando el barco se fué a pique, se ahogaron unos cuantos de la tripulación. ▲ cuadrilla *We passed a crew of workmen repairing the road.* Pasamos una cuadrilla de obreros que estaban reparando la carretera.

cricket grillo.

crime delito; crimen (*capital crime*).

criminal [adj. n] criminal.

crimson [adj, n] carmesí.

cripple [n] inválido, cojo, [Arg] rengo. ○ to be crippled quedarse inválido, [Arg] quedarse rengo.

crisis crisis.

crisp fresco *I don't like salad unless it's crisp.* No me gusta la ensalada si no es fresca. ▲ tonificante *The air's cool and crisp.* El aire es fresco y tonifi-

cante. ▲ crujiente *Those cookies are nice and crisp.* Esas galletas están muy buenas y crujientes.

critic crítico.

critical crítico.

criticism crítica *He wrote a criticism of the lecture.* Escribió una crítica de la conferencia. ‖ *She has nothing to offer but criticism.* No hace más que criticar.

crochet [v] hacer crochet.

crocodile cocodrilo.

crook (*person*) estafador, ladrón, pícaro.

crooked torcido *This pin's too crooked to use.* Este alfiler está demasiado torcido para usarlo. ▲ deshonesto, sinvergüenza *I wouldn't do business with such a crooked person.* No haría negocios con una persona tan deshonesta.

crop (*harvest*) cosecha.

cross [n] cruz *Put a cross on the map to show where we are.* Ponga Ud. una cruz en el mapa para señalar donde estamos.

● [adj] enojado *He was very cross with his children this morning.* Estaba muy enojado con sus hijos esta mañana.

● [v] cruzar *Is it possible to cross these two species?* ¿Es posible cruzar estas dos especies?—*Cross the street at the corner.* Cruce Ud. la calle en la esquina.

○ to cross one's mind ocurrírsele a uno *It never crossed my mind that he'd object.* Nunca se me ocurrió que él se opusiera. ○ to cross one's path encontrarse con *I've never happened to cross his path.* Nunca he tenido la oportunidad de encontrarme con él. ○ to cross out tachar *Cross out the items you don't want.* Tache Ud. los artículos que no le interesan.

crossing cruce, intersección.

crossword puzzle crucigrama.

crouch [v] agacharse.

crow [n] cuervo *His hair's as black as a crow.* Tiene el pelo como ala de cuervo.

● [v] cantar *I get up soon after I hear the rooster crow.* Me levanto poco después de oír cantar el gallo.—*They're still crowing over their victory.* Todavía cantan victoria.

○ as the crow flies en línea recta.

crowbar palanca de hierro.

crowd [n] gentío, multitud, muchedumbre *A crowd gathered on the street corner.* La multitud se reunió en la esquina. ▲ grupo *He runs around with a different crowd.* Va con otro grupo.

● [v] apiñarse *More and more people*

crowded into the square. La gente se apiñaba en la plaza cada vez más.

○ **to be crowded** estar lleno *The hall was crowded to capacity.* El salón estaba completamente lleno.

crown corona.

crude bruto *Our ship's carrying several tons of crude rubber.* Nuestro barco lleva varias toneladas de caucho en bruto. ▲ *He's awfully crude at times.* A veces es muy tosco.

cruel cruel.

cruelty crueldad.

crumb miga.

crumple arrugar.

crush [n] aglomeración *There was a big crush when they opened the gates.* Hubo mucha aglomeración cuando abrieron las puertas. ● [v] aplastar *The package was crushed in the mail.* En el correo se aplastó el paquete. ▲ abrumar *We were crushed by the announcement.* Nos quedamos abrumados con la noticia.

crust [n] pasta *This pie has a very good crust.* La pasta de esta tarta es muy buena. ▲ corteza *Don't cut the crust off the toast.* No le quite la corteza a las tostadas. ▲ capa *It was so cold last night there's a crust of ice on the lake.* Hizo tanto frío anoche que hay una capa de hielo en el lago.

cry [n] grito *There was a cry of "man overboard!"* Se oyó un grito de "¡hombre al agua!" ▲ llantina [*Sp*], llorada [*Am*] *After a good cry, she felt better.* Después de la llorada se sintió mejor. ● [v] llorar *The baby cried all night.* El niño lloró toda la noche. ▲ gritar *"Stop him!" she cried.* "¡Párenlo!" gritó.

○ **a far cry** una gran diferencia *These accommodations are a far cry from what we wanted.* Hay una gran diferencia entre estos arreglos y lo que queríamos. ○ **to cry out** gritar *The pain was so great that he cried out.* El dolor fué tan grande que gritó.

crystal cristal.

cube cubito *Have we any ice cubes left?* ¿Nos quedan cubitos de hielo?

○ **cube of sugar** terrón de azúcar *How many cubes do you take in your tea?* ¿Cuántos terrones de azúcar toma Ud. en el té?

cucumber pepino.

cue entrada *That actor keeps missing his cues.* Ese actor no coge nunca la entrada. ▲ taco *The cue's on the pool table.* El taco está en la mesa de billar.

○ **to take one's cue** guiarse por *I took my cue from what she said and went early.* Me guié por lo que ella me dijo y salí temprano.

cuff [n] puño *Would you mind sewing a button on my cuff?* ¿Podría Ud. pegarme un botón en el puño? ● [v] abofetear *He cuffed me in the face.* Me abofeteó.

cuff link gemelo.

cultivate cultivar *This soil's so poor it isn't worth cultivating.* Este terreno es tan pobre que no vale la pena cultivarlo. *It'd be worth your while to cultivate her friendship.* Valdría la pena de que cultive Ud. su amistad.

culture cultura, civilización.

cunning gracioso (*cute*); astuto, sagaz (*clever*).

cup taza *The cup isn't full.* No está llena la taza. ▲ copa *He keeps the cups he won on the mantel.* Tiene las copas que ha ganado en la repisa de la chimenea.

cupboard aparador.

curb [n] borde de la acera *Park the car nearer the curb.* Estacione Ud. el auto más pegado al borde de la acera. ▲ freno *Her mother finally put a curb on her wild spending.* Por fin su madre puso freno a sus gastos excesivos. ● [v] dominar, controlar *You'll have to learn to curb your temper.* Tendrá Ud. que aprender a dominar su mal genio.

cure [n] cura *Will the water cure do him any good?* ¿Le sentará bien la cura de aguas? ● [v] curar *We can trust this doctor to cure him.* Podemos confiar en que este doctor lo curará. ▲ corregir *This'll cure him of that habit.* Esto le corregirá esa costumbre. ▲ curar *Is this ham well cured?* ¿Está bien curado este jamón?

curiosity curiosidad.

curious curioso, deseoso *I'm curious to know how everything turned out.* Estoy curioso por saber como salió todo. ▲ raro *What a curious bird!* ¡Qué pájaro tan raro!

curl [n] rizo, [*Am*] crespo *Her curls reach her shoulders.* Los rizos le llegan hasta los hombros. ● [v] rizar *She went to have her hair curled.* Fué a que le rizaran el pelo. ○ **to curl up** enroscarse *The dog curled up and went to sleep.* El perro se enroscó y se durmió.

currant grosella.

currency dinero, billetes *New paper cur-*

rency will be in circulation next week. Pondrán en circulación nuevos billetes la semana que viene. ‖ *The rumor seems to have gained currency.* El rumor parece estar circulando.

current [n] corriente *Does the river have a strong current?* ¿Tiene el río una corriente fuerte?—*The current's been cut off.* Han cortado la corriente. ● [adj] corriente, común *That's a current expression.* Es una expresión corriente. ▲ presente, corriente *You'll be paid during the current month.* Se le pagará durante el presente mes. ▲ de actualidad *He lectured on current events.* Dió una conferencia sobre los sucesos de actualidad.

curse [n] maldición. ● [v] maldecir.

curtain cortina, visillo *I want curtains for all the windows.* Quiero cortinas para todas las ventanas. ▲ telón *The curtain goes up at 8:30.* Se levanta el telón a las ocho y media. ▲ cortina, capa *There was a curtain of smoke over the area.* Había una cortina de humo sobre la zona.

curtain rod barra de cortina.

curve [n] curva *Take it easy going around curves.* Vaya Ud. despacio en las curvas. ● [v] curvar *You'll have to curve the wire to make it fit right.* Tiene Ud. que curvar el alambre para que se adapte bien. ▲ hacer una curva *Look out, the road curves here.* Cuidado, la carretera hace aquí una curva.

curved curvado, curvo.

custard flan.

custom costumbre *Is it your custom to eat breakfast early?* ¿Tiene Ud. la costumbre de desayunarse temprano? ○ **customs** impuestos *Do we have to pay customs on this?* ¿Hay que pagar impuestos sobre esto? ▲ aduana *We were delayed at the customs.* Nos demoramos en la aduana.

custom-made hecho a la medida *He wears only custom-made clothes.* Solamente usa ropa hecha a la medida.

cut [n] cortadura, [Am] cortada *The cut on my finger's nearly healed.* La cortadura que tengo en el dedo está casi curada. ▲ rebaja *He asked us to take a salary cut of ten per cent.* Nos pidió que aceptáramos una rebaja de sueldo del diez por ciento. ▲ parte *Did all of them get their cut?* ¿Recibieron todas la parte que les correspondía? ▲ corte *The cut of that dress is a little old-*

fashioned. El corte de ese traje es un poco pasado de moda. ▲ puerto *The road goes through the cut in the mountains.* La carretera pasa por el puerto. ▲ trozo, clase *What other cuts of meat do you have?* ¿Tiene Ud. otros trozos de carne? ● [adj] tallado *Give me that cut-glass pitcher.* Déme Ud. aquella jarra de cristal tallado. ● [v] cortar *Please cut the meat.* Haga el favor de cortar la carne.— *He cut his hand when he fell.* Al caerse se cortó la mano.—*I must get my hair cut.* Tengo que cortarme el pelo.— *She's cutting a dress for me.* Me está cortando un traje.—*The cards have to be cut before you deal.* Hay que cortar antes de dar las cartas.—*The movie had to be cut in several places.* Tuvieron que cortar la película en varias escenas. ▲ partir *Shall we cut the cake now?* ¿Partimos la torta ahora? ▲ rebajar *Prices will be cut next month.* Rebajarán los precios el mes que viene. ▲ segar *The farmers are cutting the hay.* Los labradores están segando el heno. ▲ hacerse el distraído, [Am] hacerse el desentendido *I didn't mean to cut 'em.* No quise hacerme el distraído. ▲ salirle a uno *The baby's cutting his first two teeth.* Al niño le están saliendo los dos primeros dientes. ▲ suplantar *He used to have a good business but was cut out by competitors.* Tenía anteriormente un buen negocio, pero fué suplantado por los competidores. ○ **cold cuts** fiambres *We're having cold cuts for supper.* Tenemos fiambres para la comida. ○ **cut and dried** preparado de antemano *Everything was cut and dried.* Todo estaba preparado de antemano. ○ **to be cut out for** servir para *He's not cut out for languages.* No sirve para los idiomas. ○ **to cut across** atravesar *It'll save time if we cut across this field.* Economizaremos tiempo si atravesamos esta campo. ○ **to cut class** fumarse la clase [Sp], no ir a clase *He had to cut class in order to meet us.* Para poderse encontrar con nosotros, tuvo que fumarse la clase. ○ **to cut corners** *The job'll take five days if we cut corners.* Tardaremos cinco días en hacer el trabajo si lo abreviamos. ○ **to cut down** cortar *They've cut down most of the trees for firewood.* Han cortado la mayor parte de los árboles para leña. ▲ reducir *The report had to be cut down to half* *its length.* Hubo que reducir el informe a la mitad. ○ *to cut in We were talking very quietly until he cut in.* Estábamos hablando tranquilamente hasta que nos interrumpió. ○ **to cut in ahead of** adelantar *He was going slow and I cut in ahead of him.* Iba despacio y me le adelanté. ○ **to cut into pieces** hacer pedazos, destrozar *The child cut the book into pieces.* El niño hizo pedazos el libro. ○ **to cut off** cortar *Cut off the loose ends.* Corte los cabos sueltos.—*The flood's cut off all communication with the next town.* La inundación ha cortado las comunicaciones con el pueblo vecino.—*I was talking to my sister, but we were cut off.* Estaba hablando con mi hermana, pero nos cortaron. ○ **to cut out** recortar *Please cut out this article.* Haga el favor de recortar este artículo. ▲ dejar de, parar *Tell them to cut out the noise.*

Dígales que dejen de hacer ruido. ○ **to cut short** interrumpir *Our trip was cut short by the bad news.* Nuestro viaje fué interrumpido a causa de la mala noticia. ○ **to cut to the quick** llegar a lo vivo. ○ **to cut up** dividir *This house has been cut up into apartments.* Esta casa se ha divida en apartamentos. ▲ cortar *This meat's cut up before its served.* Esta carne se sirve ya cortada. ▲ angustiar *He was terribly cut up over the loss of his wife.* Estaba muy angustiado a causa de la pérdida de su mujer. ▲ hacer travesuras *Have the children been cutting up?* ¿Han hecho travesuras los niños? ‖ *Cut it out!* ¡Deje Ud. de hacer eso!

cute gracioso *What a cute girl?* ¡Que muchacha tan graciosa!

cyclone ciclón.

cylinder cilindro.

D

dad, daddy papá.

dagger puñal.

daily [*n*] diario, periódico *Two dailies are published in the town.* Se publican dos diarios en el pueblo.
● [*adj*] diario *He's making his daily report.* Está escribiendo su informe diario.
● [*adv*] diariamente, todos los días *An inspection of passports is made daily.* Diariamente se hace una inspección de los pasaportes.

dainty [*adj*] delicado, fino.

dairy lechería.

dam presa.

damage [*n*] daños *How much damage has been done?* ¿Cuáles han sido los daños causados?
● [*v*] estropear, averiar *The accident damaged the car.* El accidente estropeó el automóvil.
○ **damages** indemnización *They collected damages after the accident.* Recaudaron una indemnización después del accidente.

damn [*adj*] maldito *Throw the damn cat out.* Eche afuera al maldito gato.
● [*v*] condenar *All the critics damned her book.* Todos los críticos condenaron su libro.
● [*interj*] ¡caray! *Damn! There goes my shoelace.* ¡Caray! se me ha roto el cordón del zapato.

‖ *Damn it!* ¡Caramba! *or* ¡Maltido sea! ‖ *He's not worth a damn.* No vale un comino.

damp húmedo.

dance [*n*] baile *We're invited to a dance at their home.* Estamos invitados a un baile en su casa.
● [*v*] bailar *Would you like to dance this rhumba?* ¿Le gustaría bailar esta rumba?
○ **dance hall** salón de baile.
‖ *May I have the next dance?* ¿Puedo bailar con Ud. el próximo baile?

dancer bailarín, bailarina.

danger peligro.

dangerous peligroso.

dangle pender, columpiarse.

dare atreverse, arriesgarse *Do you dare go there alone?* ¿Se atreve Ud. a ir sola allá? ▲ desafiar *My friends dared me to do it.* Mis amigos me desafiaron a hacerlo.
‖ *Don't you dare touch me!* ¡Cuidado con tocarme!

dark [*n*] oscuridad *The place is difficult to find in the dark.* Es difícil encontrar el lugar en la oscuridad.
● [*adj*] oscuro *His house is a dark gray.* Su casa es de un gris oscuro. ▲ negro *Those were dark days for me.* Aquellos fueron días negros para mí.
○ **in the dark** al margen *My friend's kept me in the dark about his move-*

ments. Mi amigo me tiene al margen de sus acciones. O **to get dark** oscurecer *It gets dark earlier and earlier.* Oscurece más temprano cada día.

darkness oscuridad.

darling [n] querido.

● [adj] querido. ▲ bonito, lindo *What a darling dress you have on!* ¡Qué vestido tan bonito llevas!

darn [v] zurcir *She's out on the porch darning.* Está afuera en el porche zurciendo.

darn O **darn (it)!** ¡demonios! *Darn (it)!* *I cut my finger.* ¡Demonios! Me he cortado el dedo. O **not to know a darn thing** no saber ni jota.

dart [n] dardo, flecha.

● [v] volar como una flecha.

dash [n] carrera *He won the hundred-yard dash.* Ganó la carrera de cien yardas. ▲ guión *Put a dash between these two words.* Ponga un guión entre estas dos palabras. ▲ poquito *A dash of vinegar's all the salad needs.* Un poquito de vinagre es lo único que le falta a la ensalada.

● [v] echar, tirar, arrojar *She dashed water in his face.* Le echo agua a la cara. ▲ salir corriendo *He dashed to the corner to mail a package.* Salió corriendo hasta la esquina para echar un paquete en el correo.

O **to dash against** estrellarse contra *The waves dashed against the rocks.* Las olas se estrellaban contra las rocas. O **to dash off** hacer de prisa *Dash off these letters before you leave tonight.* Haga de prisa estas cartas antes que Ud. se marche. O **to make a dash for** darse una prisa para *We made a mad dash for the train.* Nos dimos una prisa loca para alcanzar el tren.

date [n] fecha *What's the date today?* ¿A qué fecha estamos hoy? ▲ cita *I have a date for lunch today.* Hoy tengo una cita para almorzar.

● [v] salir con *He's been dating her regularly.* Ha estado saliendo regularmente con ella.

O **out of date** fuera de moda *Her clothes seem out of date.* Su ropa parece estar fuera de moda. O **to date** hasta la fecha *We haven't heard from him to date.* No sabemos nada de él hasta la fecha. O **to date from** datar de *This church dates from the eighteenth century.* Esta iglesia data del sigo diez y ocho. O **up to date** al corriente *I'm not up to date on this subject.* No estoy al corriente en este asunto.

‖ *Who's your date tonight?* ¿Con quién tiene Ud. cita esta noche?

date dátil *How much are dates by the pound?* ¿Cuánto cuesta la libra de dátiles?

daughter hija.

dawn [n] amanecer, madrugada.

‖ *It just dawned on me that he was lying.* Se me occurre que mentía. or Acabo de llegar a la conclusión de que mentía.

day día *We spent three days in the country.* Pasamos tres días en el campo.— *Christmas day's a holiday.* El día de Navidad es fiesta. ▲ época *This is the day of airplanes.* Esta es la época de los aeroplanos.

O **day after day; day in, day out** día tras día *We walk through the town day after day.* Caminamos a través de la ciudad día tras día. O **day after tomorrow** pasado mañana. O **day before yesterday** anteayer, antier. O **from day to day** de día en día *We're learning more about the country from day to day.* De día en día aprendemos más del país. O **day by day** cada día *Day by day I'm getting more used to it.* Cada día me voy acostumbrando más a ello.

‖ *Let's stop work and call it a day.* Dejemos de trabajar y demos por terminado el día. ‖ *My day begins at seven o'clock.* Empiezo a trabajar a las siete.

daybreak amanecer.

daylight luz del día.

daytime O **in the daytime** de día *I sleep in the daytime.* Duermo de día.

daze [v] aturdir *He was dazed by the blow on his head.* El golpe en la cabeza le aturdió.

‖ *He walks around in a daze.* Anda como un sonámbulo.

dazzle encandilar, deslumbrar.

dead muerto *His father's dead.* Su padre ha muerto. ▲ apagado *The furnace is dead.* El horno está apagado.

O **dead-certain** completamente seguro *Are you dead-certain you can do it?* ¿Está Ud. completamente seguro de que puede hacerlo? O **dead-tired** muerto de cansancio *She said she was dead-tired.* Dijo que estaba muerta de cansancio. O **to stop dead** parar en seco.

‖ *She fell in a dead faint.* Cayó desmayada como muerta.

dead end calle sin salida.

dead weight estorbo, lastre *This baggage*

is so much dead weight. Este equipaje no es más que un estorbo.

deaf sordo *He doesn't go to concerts, because he's deaf.* No va a los conciertos porque es sordo. ○ **deaf and dumb** sordo mudo. ‖ *He's deaf to my request for credit.* Cuando le pido crédito se hace el sordo.

deal [*n*] negocio *He made a lot of money in the deal.* Ganó mucho dinero en el negocio. ▲ trato *If they make a deal we're lost.* Si ellos hacen un trato estamos perdidos. ● [*v*] tratar *This bureau deals with passport questions.* Esta oficina trata de asuntos de pasaportes. ▲ traficar *This merchant deals in wines.* Este comerciante trafica en vinos. ▲ asestar *The shortage of gasoline has dealt a heavy blow to our business.* La escasez de gasolina ha asestado un duro golpe a nuestros negocios. ▲ dar *Whose turn is it to deal?* ¿A quién le toca dar? ○ **a good deal** bastante, mucho *I smoke a good deal.* Fumo bastante. ○ **a great deal of** mucho, gran cantidad de. ○ **bad deal** mal negocio. ○ **good deal** buen negocio. ○ **square deal** buen trato. ‖ *He dealt fairly with me.* Fué honrado conmigo.

dealer comerciante, vendedor *The dealer tried his best to sell me a car.* El comerciante hizo lo posible por venderme un carro. ‖ *Who's the dealer for this hand?* ¿A quién le toca dar esta mano?

dear [*n*] querido *Whatever you say, dear.* Lo que tu digas, querida. ● [*adj*] querido *Dear John.* Querido Juan. ▲ caro *These candies are very dear; those are cheap.* Estos dulces son muy caros; aquellos son baratos. ○ **Dear Sir** Muy señor mío. ○ **oh dear!** ¡Dios mío! *Oh dear! we're late again.* ¡Dios mío! llegamos tarde otra vez. ‖ *My sister's very dear to me.* Quiero mucho a mi hermana.

death muerte *I was very sorry to hear of the death of your friend.* Sentí mucho la noticia de la muerte de su amigo. ‖ *I feel worked to death.* Estoy muerto de tanto trabajar.

debate [*n*] discusión, debate. ● [*v*] debatir, discutir.

debit debe.

debt deuda.

decade década.

decay [*n*] decomposición; caries (*teeth*).

● [*v*] descomponerse, pudrirse; picarse, carearse (*of teeth*).

decease muerte.

deceive engañar.

December diciembre.

decent decente *That's not a decent way to treat him.* Ese no es un modo decente de tratarle. *or* Esa no es manera de tratarle. ‖ *Does he make a decent living?* ¿Gana él lo suficiente para vivir decorosamente?

decide decidir.

deciding decisivo.

decision decisión, resolución.

deck [*n*] cubierta *Let's go up on deck.* Subamos a cubierta. ● [*v*] adornar *Let's deck the building with flags.* Adornemos el edificio con banderas. ○ **deck of cards** baraja, [*Am*] naipe *Do you have a deck of cards?* ¿Tiene Ud. una baraja? ○ **to deck out** engalanar *She was decked out with cheap jewelry.* Se había engalanado con baratijas.

declare declarar *They declared war within 24 hours.* Declararon la guerra a las 24 horas.—*You must declare these perfumes at the customs.* Hay que declarar estos perfumes en la aduana. ○ **to declare oneself** declararse *He declared himself against the action.* Se declaró contra la acción.

decline [*n*] baja *We expect a decline in all prices.* Esperamos una baja de todos los precios. ▲ declinación *Has there been any decline in the epidemic?* ¿Ha habido alguna declinación de la epidemia? ● [*v*] rehusar *They declined his invitation.* Rehusaron su invitación. ▲ decaer *His health has declined a lot recently.* Su salud ha decaído mucho últimamente.

decorate decorar.

decoration decoración *The decorations were in very bad taste.* Las decoraciones eran de muy mal gusto. ▲ condecoración *He was awarded a decoration for bravery.* Se le concedió una condecoración por su heroísmo.

decrease [*n*] disminución, descenso *There's been a great decrease in the birth rate.* Ha habido una gran disminución de nacimientos. ● [*v*] disminuir, reducir *How can we decrease expenses?* ¿Como podemos reducir los gastos?

decree [*n*] decreto *When was the decree*

published? ¿Cuando fué publicado el decreto?
● [*v*] decretar, ordenar *The government decreed a holiday.* El gobierno decretó un día de fiesta.
dedicate dedicar.
deed acción, obra *They performed many good deeds.* Hicieron muchas obras buenas.
deem juzgar, estimar.
deep hondo, profundo *This lake's very deep.* Este lago es muy hondo. ▲ oscuro *The sky was a deep blue.* El cielo estaba azul oscuro. ▲ grave *The singer had a deep voice.* El cantante tenía una voz grave.
○ **deep in** metido en *That family's always deep in debt.* Esa familia está siempre metida en deudas.
‖ *He's given the matter deep study.* Ha estudiado profundamente el asunto.
deep-seated arraigado *It's a deep-seated tradition.* Es una tradición arraigada.
deer venado.
default [*v*] faltar, no cumplir *They defaulted on their interest payment.* Faltaron en el pago de los intereses.
‖ *He won the tennis match by default.* Ganó el partido de tenis por no haberse presentado su contrario.
defeat [*n*] derrota *They took their defeat with good grace.* Aceptaron su derrota elegantemente.
● [*v*] vencer *We defeated our opponents in the last game.* Vencimos a nuestros competidores en el último juego.
defect defecto.
defend defender *They decided not to defend the town.* Resolvieron no defender el pueblo.
defendant defensor.
defense defensa *What can you say in your defense?* ¿Qué puede Ud. decir en su defensa?
defer deferir, aplazar.
deficit déficit.
define definir.
definite definitivo.
deform deformar.
defy desafiar.
degrade degradar.
degree grado *At night the temperature sometimes drops ten degrees.* De noche la temperatura baja algunas veces diez grados. ▲ título *What degrees have you received?* ¿Qué títulos ha recibido Ud.?
○ **by degrees** por grados, gradualmente *By degrees he's getting closer to the answer.* Está llegando a la

solución gradualmente. ○ **to a certain degree** hasta cierto punto *That book's useful to a certain degree.* Ese libro es útil hasta cierto punto.
dehydrate deshidratar.
deity deidad, divinidad.
dejected abatido, acongojado.
delay [*n*] demora *The delay caused me to miss the train.* La demora me hizo perder el tren.
● [*v*] demorar *We'll delay the trip for a week.* Demoraremos el viaje por una semana.
delegate [*n*] delegado.
deliberate [*v*] deliberar, pensar.
deliberately con intención *They did it deliberately.* Lo hicieron con intención.
delicate delicado *They performed a delicate operation on his brain.* Le hicieron una operación muy delicada en el cerebro.—*She's too delicate to work.* Está demasiado delicada para trabajar. ▲ exquisito *This wine has a delicate flavor.* Este vino tiene un sabor exquisito. ▲ frágil *These vases are delicate.* Estos floreros son frágiles.
delicious delicioso.
delight [*n*] deleite *Buying clothes is her greatest delight.* Su mayor deleite consiste en comprar ropa.
● [*v*] encantar, deleitar *The film delighted everyone.* La película encantó a todo el mundo.
delightful delicioso *The trip was most delightful.* El viaje fué de lo más delicioso. ▲ encantador *Her manners were delightful.* Tenía modales encantadores.
deliver entregar, repartir *The mailman delivers the first mail at nine o'clock.* El cartero reparte el primer correo a las nueve. ▲ dar *The professor delivered a course of lectures.* El profesor dió una serie de conferencias.
○ **to deliver a baby** asistir a un parto.
delivery entrega *I'll pay the balance on delivery of the goods.* Pagaré el saldo a la entrega de la mercancía.
○ **delivery room** sala de maternidad.
‖ *Do you make deliveries on Saturday?* ¿Reparte Ud. los sábados? ‖ *I didn't like the song but her delivery was good.* No me gusto la canción, pero ella la cantó bien.
delusion decepción.
demand [*n*] petición, reclamo *His constant demands exasperated us.* Sus constantes peticiones nos exasperaron. ▲ demanda *The supply's greater than the demand.* Las existencias son mayores que las demandas.

● [v] exigir *He demands immediate payment.* Exige el pago inmediato. ▲ insistir *When she was sick she demanded that we visit her every day.* Cuando estaba enferma insistió en que la visitáramos diariamente. ○ **to be in demand** ser solicitado *He was in great demand as a speaker.* Era muy solicitado como orador.

democracy democracia.

democratic democrático.

demolish demoler, derrumbar.

demonstrate demostrar *He demonstrated the use of the machine.* Demostró el manejo de la máquina.

den caverna, guarida (*for animals*); estudio, retiro (*for people*).

denote denotar.

denounce denunciar.

dense denso, espeso *We haven't had such a dense fog for a long time.* Hace mucho tiempo que no tenemos una niebla tan espesa. ▲ cerrado, torpe *He's awfully dense about some things.* Es muy torpe para algunas cosas.

dent [n] abolladura *Can you fix the dent in my fender?* ¿Puede Ud. arreglar la abolladura en mi guardafango? ▲ mella *Our warnings never make a dent in him.* Nuestras advertencias no le hacen mella.

● [v] abollar(se) *This metal dents easily.* Este metal se abolla fácilmente.

dentist dentista *Is there a good dentist around here?* ¿Hay un buen dentista por aquí?

deny negar.

depart irse, partir.

department departamento *He works in the bookkeeping department.* Trabaja en el departamento de contabilidad. ▲ ministerio *You'll have to see someone from the State Department.* Es preciso que veas a alguien del Ministerio de Relaciones Exteriores.

department store almacén.

departure partida, salida.

depend ○ **to depend on** depender de *My plans depend on the weather.* Mis planes dependen del tiempo.—*We have to depend on the radio for our news.* Tenemos que depender de la radio para obtener noticias. ▲ confiar en *Can I depend on his keeping his promise?* ¿Puedo confiar en que él cumpla su promesa?

dependent [adj] dependiente.

deposit [n] depósito *I can't pay it all now, so I'll leave a deposit.* No puedo pagarlo todo ahora, dejaré un depósito.

● [v] depositar *I'll have to deposit some money.* Tendré que depositar algún dinero.

depot depósito, almacén *We must get our supplies from the depot.* Tenemos que conseguir nuestras provisiones del depósito. ▲ estación, paradero *What time does the train leave the depot?* ¿A que hora sale el tren de la estación?

depress deprimir.

depression depresión, abatimiento *I wish I could get over these moods of depression.* Quisiera poder vencer estos períodos de abatimiento. ▲ depresión *We lost all our money in the depression.* Perdimos todo nuestro dinero en la depresión.

deprive privar.

depth profundidad *The well's 50 feet in depth.* El pozo tiene 50 pies de profundidad. ▲ fondo *Because of its depth, the stage can accommodate a large cast.* Por tener tanto fondo el escenario puede dar cabida a un gran elenco. ‖ *The music shows great depth of feeling.* La música expresa un sentimiento muy profundo.

descend descender, bajar.

descendant descendiente.

describe describir.

description descripción.

desert desierto *The desert begins a few miles beyond the town.* El desierto comienza unas cuantas millas más allá del pueblo.

deserve merecer.

design [n] proyecto *He's working on a design for a new machine.* Está trabajando en un proyecto para una nueva máquina. ▲ dibujo *The tablecloth has a simple design in the center.* El mantel tiene un dibujo sencillo en el centro. ● [v] diseñar *She designs her own clothes.* Diseña su propia ropa. ▲ proyectar *The architect's designing an addition to the building.* El arquitecto proyecta un anejo para el edificio.

desire [n] deseo *Your desire will soon be fulfilled.* Su deseo se verá realizado pronto. ● [v] desear *What do you desire most of all?* ¿Qué es lo que más desea Ud.?

desk escritorio *Put the papers on this desk.* Ponga los papeles sobre este escritorio. ▲ despacho *Hand your application to the secretary at that desk.* Entregue Ud. su solicitud al secretario en ese despacho.

desolate desolado, desierto, despoblado.

despair [n] desesperación. ● [v] desesperar.

desperate desesperado *Her plight's desperate.* Su situación es desesperada. ▲ peligrosísimo *He's a desperate criminal.* Es un criminal peligrosísimo.

despise despreciar.

despite [*prep*] a pesar de.

dessert postre.

destination destinación, destino.

destiny destino.

destitute desamparado.

destroy destruir *All my papers were destroyed in the fire.* Todos mis documentos fueron destruidos en el incendio.

destroyer destructor; destruidor (*ship*).

destruction destrucción.

detach separar, despegar *Detach the stub before handing in the tickets.* Separe el talón antes de entregar el boleto. ▲ destacar *They detached several soldiers for a special mission.* Destacaron algunos soldados para una misión especial.

detail [*n*] detalle *The details of the trip will be arranged by the guide.* Los detalles del viaje serán arreglados por el guía. ▲ destacamento *A detail of policemen took charge of the investigation.* Un destacamento de policía se hizo cargo de la investigación. ● [*v*] detallar *The story's too long to be detailed here.* El cuento es demasiado largo para detallarlo aquí. ▲ destacar *Policemen were detailed to hold back the crowd.* Destacaron a varios policías para detener a la gente. ○ in detail con detalle(s) *He loves to talk about his travels in great detail.* Le gusta relatar sus viajes con muchos detalles. ○ to go into detail explicar detalladamente *I'll go into detail if you want me to.* Lo explicaré detalladamente si Ud. lo desea.

detain detener *I'm sorry I'm late, but I was detained at the office.* Siento llegar tarde, pero me detuvieron en la oficina.

detective detective.

detention detención.

determine decidir, resolver *We determined to stay on till the end.* Decidimos quedarnos hasta el fin. ▲ determinar *Can you determine the exact height of that hill?* ¿Puede Ud. determinar la altura exacta de aquella colina? ○ determined resuelto *They have a determined look.* Tienen un aire resuelto. ○ to be determined by depender de *My answer will be determined by what happens today.* Mi respuesta dependerá de lo que pase hoy.

detest detestar.

detour [*n*] vuelta, rodeo *We had to take a detour because the bridge was washed away.* Tuvimos que hacer un rodeo porque la corriente se había llevado el puente. ● [*v*] desviar *They detoured traffic because of the accident.* Han desviado el tráfico a causa del accidente.

develop desarrollar *These exercises will develop the strength of your fingers.* Estos ejercicios desarrollarán la fuerza de sus dedos. ▲ revelar, desarrollar *Can you develop these films right away?* ¿Puede Ud. revelar estas películas inmediatamente?

development desarrollo *The development of this business has been rapid.* El desarrollo de este negocio ha sido rápido. ▲ cambio, acontecimiento *If there are any new developments, let me know.* Si hay algún nuevo cambio, hágamelo saber.

device dispositivo, aparato *It's a mechanical device.* Es un dispositivo mecánico. ▲ recurso, ardid *He used an unusual device to accomplish his purpose.* Se valió de un ardid excepcional para alcanzar su propósito.

devil diablo, demonio.

devise idear, proyectar *We'll have to devise some sort of plan.* Tendremos que idear algún plan.

devote dedicar *He's devoting all of his time to writing.* Dedica todo el tiempo a escribir.

devout devoto.

dew rocío.

diagnose diagnosticar.

diagonal [*adj; n*] diagonal.

diagram diagrama.

dial [*n*] cuadrante, esfera *The dial on my watch is dirty.* La esfera de mi reloj está sucia. ● [*v*] marcar *Please dial the number for me.* Márqueme Ud. el número. ‖ *He turned the radio dial.* Dió vuelta a la aguja de la radio.

dialogue diálogo.

diameter diámetro.

diamond [*n*] diamante *I've an ace of diamonds.* Tengo un as de diamantes. ● [*adj*] de diamantes, de brillantes *He gave her a diamond brooch.* Le dió un broche de brillantes.

diaper pañal.

diarrhea diarrea.

diary diario.

dice dados.

dictate dictar *He dictated a letter to his*

secretary. Le dictó una carta a su secretaria.

‖ *I refuse to be dictated to.* Yo no admito que se me mande.

dictation ‖ *Read that dictation back to me.* Léame lo que le he dictado.

dictator dictador.

dictionary diccionario.

die morir, morirse *He died this morning at two o'clock.* Murió esta mañana a las dos. ▲ pararse *The motor died before we got to the top of the hill.* El motor se paró antes de que pudieramos subir a la loma. ▲ morirse *She's dying to meet him.* Se muere por conocerlo. ○ **to die away** desaparecer poco a poco, desvanecerse poco a poco *The sound of the train died away in the distance.* El ruido del tren se desvaneció poco a poco en la distancia. ○ **to die down** acabarse, apagarse *After dinner we let the fire die down.* Después de la comida dejamos que se apague el fuego. ▲ acabarse *After she came in the conversation died down.* Se acabó la conversación cuando ella entró. ○ **to die laughing** morirse de risa *I just about died laughing when I heard that.* Por poco me muero de risa cuando oí eso. ○ **to die off** ir muriendo *The old inhabitants are dying off.* Van muriendo los antiguos habitantes. ○ **to die out** desaparecer, acabarse *The custom of wearing a vest is dying out.* Ya está desapareciendo la moda de llevar chaleco.

diet [*n*] dieta *That's a very strict diet.* Esa dieta es muy estricta.

● [*v*] estar a dieta *I've been dieting for a month.* He estado a dieta durante un mes.

differ diferir *They differ in many respects.* Difieren en muchos aspectos.

‖ *I beg to differ with you.* No estoy de acuerdo con Ud.

different diferente, distinto.

difficult difícil.

difficulty dificultad *He's always getting into difficulties.* Siempre se está metiendo en dificultades.

dig excavar *Dig this hole a little deeper.* Excave Ud. este hoyo un poco más. ▲ sacar *These potatoes are ready to be dug now.* Estas papas están listas para sacarlas.

○ **dig in the ribs** codazo *If he starts talking too much, give him a dig in the ribs.* Si empieza a hablar demasiado, déle un codazo. ○ **to dig in** atrincherarse *The troops have had a good chance to dig in.* Las tropas han tenido

buena oportunidad para atrincherarse. ▲ empeñarse *It's a hard job, but he's digging right in.* Es un trabajo difícil pero no sigue empeñándose en el. ○ **to dig up** excavar, levantar *We can't get through because they're digging up the pavement.* No podemos pasar porque están levantando el pavimento. ▲ desarraigar, arrancar *We'll have to dig up this plant and put it over here.* Tendremos que desarraigar esta planta de aquí y ponerla allá. ▲ desenterrar *The dog's digging up the bones.* El perro está desenterrando los huesos. ▲ averiguar *See what you can dig up about him.* Vea lo que puede averiguar acerca de él. ○ **to make digs** lanzar sátiras *The editor's always making digs at the mayor.* El director del periódico lanza continuamente sátiras contra el alcalde.

digest [*n*] resumen, reseña *Have you read the digest of his latest book?* ¿Ha leído Ud. la reseña de su último libro?

● [*v*] digerir *I have trouble digesting my food.* Me cuesta trabajo digerir lo que como.

digestion digestión.

dignified digno, serio, señorial.

dignity dignidad.

dike dique.

diligent diligente, aplicado.

dilute aguar, diluir *He diluted the wine.* Aguó el vino.

dim [*adj*] débil, mortecino *The lights in the office are very dim.* Las luces de la oficina son muy débiles.

● [*v*] velar, amortiguar *Dim the light.* Amortigüe la luz.

dimension dimensión.

diminish disminuir.

dine comer, cenar *They're dining with the ambassador tonight.* Van a comer con el embajador esta noche.

○ **to dine out** comer fuera *We always dine out on Sundays.* Siempre comemos fuera los domingos.

‖ *Dining on the terrace.* Se sirven cenas en la terraza.

dining car coche-comedor, coche restaurante.

dining room comedor.

dinner cena, comida *Dinner's ready.* La cena está servida.

○ **to have dinner** cenar, comer *Won't you come over and have dinner with us tomorrow night?* ¿Quiere Ud. venir a cenar con nosotros mañana por la noche?

‖ *Come to dinner.* Vengan a comer.

dip [*n*] zambullida *There's still time for*

a dip in the lake. Todavía hay tiempo para una zambullida en el lago.
● [v] meter *Dip your finger in the water to see if it's hot enough.* Meta el dedo en el agua para ver si está suficientemente caliente. ▲ sacar *We used a pail to dip the water out of the tub.* Usamos un balde para sacar el agua de la bañera. ▲ teñir *I think I'll dip these stockings.* Creo que voy a teñir estas medias. ▲ saludar con *They dipped the flag as they passed the reviewing stand.* Saludaron con la bandera al pasar por la tribuna (presidential).

diplomacy diplomacia.

diplomat diplomático.

dipper cazo, cucharón.

direct [adj] directo *This is the most direct route to the city.* Este es el camino más directo a la ciudad. ▲ recto *He's always been direct and honest with me.* Siempre ha sido recto y honrado conmigo.
● [adv] directamente *Let's go direct to the hotel.* Vayamos directamente al hotel.
● [v] dirigir *Can you direct me to the nearest post office?* ¿Puede Ud. dirigirme a la oficina de correos más cercana? ▲ ordenar *I was directed to wait until he returned.* Me ordenaron que esperara hasta que él volviera.
○ **direct opposite** todo lo contrario *The result's the direct opposite of what we expected.* El resultado es todo lo contrario de lo que esperábamos.

direction dirección, rumbo *They went in different directions.* Se marcharon en distintas direcciones. ○ dirección *They've made great progress under his direction.* Han hecho mucho progreso bajo su dirección. ▲ instrucción, dirección *Follow the directions printed on the box.* Siga Ud. las instrucciones indicadas en la caja.

directly directamente *Write directly to the main office.* Escriba directamente a la oficina principal. ▲ exactamente, precisamente *Our house is directly opposite the store.* Nuestra casa está exactamente en frente de la tienda.

director director.

dirt mugre, suciedad *His face was smudged with dirt.* Tenía la cara llena de mugre. ▲ tierra *He filled the flowerpot with dirt.* Llenó la maceta con tierra.

dirty [adj] sucio *The floor of my room's dirty.* El piso de mi cuarto está sucio. ▲ verde *Most of his stories are pretty dirty.* La mayoría de sus cuentos son verdes.
● [v] manchar *All my clothes were dirtied with soot.* Toda mi ropa estaba manchada de hollín.
○ **dirty look** mirada despectiva *He gave us a dirty look.* Nos lanzó una mirada despectiva.

disagreeable desagradable.

disagreement desacuerdo.

disappear desaparecer.

disappoint ○ **disappointing** desilusionante *The new play was rather disappointing.* La nueva comedia fué algo desilusionante. ○ **to be disappointed** quedar desilusionado, estar decepcionado *I was disappointed with the results.* Quedé desilusionado con los resultados. ▲ sentir mucho *I shall be very disappointed if you don't come.* Sentiré mucho que Ud. no venga.

disappointment desengaño, chasco.

disaster desastre.

discharge [n] disparo, descarga *We could hear the discharge of the gun.* Oímos el disparo del arma. ▲ supuración, pus *The doctor inserted a tube to drain off the discharge.* El doctor introdujo una sonda para drenar la supuración.
● [v] desempeñar, cumplir *He's failed to discharge his duties.* Ha dejado de cumplir sus deberes. ▲ dar de alta *I expect to be discharged from the hospital tomorrow.* Espero que mañana me den de alta en el hospital.
○ **to be discharged** dispararse, descargarse *The rifle was discharged accidentally.* El rifle se disparó por un accidente.

discipline [n] disciplina *While learning to fly you'll be under steady discipline.* Mientras Ud. aprenda a volar estará sometido a una disciplina constante. ▲ castigo *If you break the rules you'll be subject to discipline.* Si Ud. infringe las reglas será sometido a un castigo.
● [v] castigar *He disciplines his childen too severely.* Castiga demasiado severamente a sus hijos.

discontent descontento, disgusto.

discontented descontento, disgustado.

discord discordia.

discount descuento, rebaja *I shop there because I get a discount.* Yo compro allá porque me hacen un descuento.
○ **at a discount** a precio rebajado.

discourage desanimar *He did everything to discourage me from going.* Hizo lo posible para desanimarme de ir.
○ **discouraging** desalentador *The re-*

sults are so discouraging. Los resultados son muy desalentadores.
discourse [n] discurso.
discover descubrir.
discreet discreto.
discretion discreción, prudencia.
discuss discutir *Don't discuss the matter.* No discuta Ud. el asunto. ▲ tratar *I'll discuss that point in my next lecture.* Trataré ese punto en mi próxima conferencia.
discussion discusión, debate.
disease enfermedad.
diseased enfermo.
disgrace ignominia, deshonra, vergüenza.
disguise disfraz *He wore an unusual disguise.* Llevaba un disfraz raro.
  ○ **disguised** disfrazado *He passed through the enemy lines disguised as a monk.* Pasó a través de las líneas enemigas disfrazado de monje.
disgust [n] disgusto, desagrado *He looked at me in disgust.* Me miró con desagrado.
  ● [v] repugnar *I'm disgusted with such goings on.* Me repugnan tales actos.
dish plato *He dropped the dish and broke it.* Dejó caer el plato y se rompió.— *What's your favorite dish?* ¿Cuál es su plato favorito?
  ○ **to dish out, to dish up** servir *The cook dished out the food on our plates.* El cocinero nos sirvió la comida en los platos.
dishonest deshonesto, falso.
disinfect desinfectar.
dislike [n] antipatía *I can't overcome my dislike for the city.* No puedo vencer mi antipatía por la ciudad.
  ‖ *I dislike traveling by train.* Me disgusta viajar por tren.
dismal triste.
  ○ **dismal failure** fracaso total *It was a dismal failure.* Fué un fracaso total.
dismiss despedir.
dispatch [v] despachar, enviar.
dispensary dispensario.
dispense dispensar.
disperse dispersar.
displace desplazar.
display [n] exhibición, presentación *At the fair we saw the most beautiful display of flowers.* Vimos en la feria una bellísima presentación de flores. ▲ ostentación *I don't care for a lot of display.* A mí no me gusta la ostentación.
  ● [v] exhibir *They're displaying his pictures at the gallery this week.* Están exhibiendo sus cuadros en la galería esta semana.

disposal disposición.
dispose ○ **to be disposed to** estar dispuesto a *He was disposed to take things very seriously.* Estaba dispuesto a tomar las cosas muy seriamente. ○ **to dispose of** disponer de *They'll leave as soon as they dispose of their furniture.* Partirán en cuanto dispongan de sus muebles. ▲ depositar, disponer de *Where can we dispose of the garbage?* ¿Dónde podemos depositar la basura? ▲ resolver *He disposed of our objections in short order.* Resolvió nuestras quejas rápidamente.
disposition genio *She's a pretty girl, but what an awful disposition!* Es una muchacha bonita, pero ¡qué mal genio tiene!
  ‖ *What disposition will be made of his belongings?* ¿En qué forma se va a disponer de sus bienes?
dispute [n] disputa, discusión *Will you settle the dispute?* ¿Quiere Ud. poner fin a la disputa?
  ● [v] disputar, discutir *I won't dispute with you on that point.* No voy a discutir con Ud. sobre ese punto.
dissipate disipar.
dissolve disolver.
distance [n] distancia *What's the distance from here to the next town?* ¿Cuál es la distancia de aquí al próximo pueblo?
  ○ **from a distance** desde lejos *You can see the tower from a distance.* Se puede ver la torre desde lejos. ○ **in the distance** a lo lejos *The plane disappeared in the distance.* El avión desapareció a lo lejos. ○ **to keep one's distance** mantenerse a distancia.
distant distante *My brother lives in a distant part of the country.* Mi hermano vive en un lugar distante del país. ▲ lejano *She's a distant relative of mine.* Es una lejana parienta mía. ▲ abstraído *She seems very distant today.* Ella parece muy abstraída hoy.
distill destilar.
distinct claro, preciso.
distinction distinción.
distinguish distinguir *It's so dark I can't distinguish anything.* Está tan oscuro que no puedo distinguir nada.
  ○ **to distinguish oneself** distinguirse *He distinguished himself as a musician.* Se distinguió como músico.
distort torcer.
distract distraer.
distress [n] angustia *There isn't really any need for such distress.* Verdaderamente no hay necesidad de tanta an-

gustia. ▲peligro, apuro *The ship was in distress.* El barco estaba en peligro. ●[*v*] angustiar *I was distressed to see her so unhappy.* Me angustió verla tan desventurada.

distribute distribuir.

distribution distribución *The distribution of population in this country is uneven.* Es desigual la distribución de la población en este país. ▲reparto *When's the first distribution of mail?* ¿Cuándo se hace el primer reparto del correo?

district distrito.

distrust [*n*] desconfianza. ●[*v*] desconfiar.

disturb molestar *I don't want to be disturbed until ten.* No quiero que me molesten antes de las diez. ▲desordenar *Someone's disturbed my papers.* Alguien ha desordenado mis papeles. ▲perturbar, inquietar *I'm disturbed to hear the news.* Me he inquietado al enterarme de la noticia.

ditch zanja *They dug a ditch to irrigate the land.* Cavaron una zanja para irrigar la tierra. ▲cuneta (*roadside*) *There's a ditch on each side of the road.* Hay una cuneta a cada lado del camino. ‖ *Let's ditch these people and have some fun.* Vamos a sacudirnos de encima esta gente para poder divertirnos.

dive [*n*] zambullida *What a beautiful dive!* ¡Qué hermosa zambullida! ▲picada *The plane went into a sudden dive.* El avión hizo una picada repentina. ●[*v*] zambullirse *Let's dive in.* Vamos a zambullirnos. ‖ *There'll be a diving contest this afternoon.* Esta tarde habrá un concurso de saltos de palanca. ‖ *I'd like to visit some waterfront dives.* Me gustaría visitar los bajos fondos de los muelles.

divide [*v*] dividir.

dividend dividendo.

divine [*adj*] divino.

diving board trampolín, [*Am*] palanca.

division división.

divorce [*n*] divorcio *I'm finally getting a divorce from him.* Por fin él me va a dar el divorcio. ●[*v*] divorciarse de *She divorced her husband several years ago.* Hace varios años que se divorció de su marido. ○**to divorce oneself from** apartarse de *He divorced himself from his friends.* Se apartó de sus amigos.

dizzy mareado *He felt dizzy after his illness.* Se sentía mareado después de la enfermedad. ▲vertiginoso *He drove the car at a dizzy speed.* Llevaba el carro a una velocidad vertiginosa.

do hacer *He does all his work at night.* Hace todo su trabajo de noche.—*You'd better do as you're told.* Más le valdría hacer lo que le han dicho.—*My pen won't work; what did you do to it?* ¿Qué le ha hecho a mi pluma que no escribe?—*On a bad road like this I can't do more than forty miles an hour.* En un camino tan malo no puedo hacer más de cuarenta millas por hora.—*He gets up early and so do I.* Se levanta temprano y lo mismo hago yo. ▲hacer, escribir *He's doing a magazine article on local customs.* Está haciendo un artículo sobre costumbres locales para una revista. ▲cumplir *Leave him alone; he's doing his duty.* Déjalo solo, que está cumpliendo su deber. ▲pasarse en la cárcel *If we got caught we'd have to do five years.* Si nos pillan tendríamos que pasarnos cinco años en la cárcel. ▲lucir *The corn's doing well this year.* El maíz luce bien este año. ▲estar bien, quedar bien *Do you think this color will do?* ¿Cree Ud. que este color quedará bien? ○**done** hecho *I can't leave before the job's done.* No puedo irme antes de que el trabajo esté hecho. ▲hecho, cocido *In ten minutes the potatoes will be done.* Las papas estarán hechas dentro de diez minutos. ○**done for** gastado *These tires are done for.* Estos neumáticos están ya gastados. ○**done in** agotado, deshecho *I'm done in working in all this heat.* Estoy agotado de trabajar en este calor. ○**to be done for** fastidiarse *If the boss finds this out I'm done for.* Si el jefe se entera de esto me fastidiaré. ○**to be done with** terminar con, acabar con *Are you done with these scissors?* ¿Ha terminado Ud. con estas tijeras? ○**to do away with** suprimir *They plan to do away with most of these regulations.* Piensan suprimir la mayor parte de estos reglamentos. ○**to do harm** perjudicar, hacer daño, ser perjudicial *Will it do any harm if we talk over that matter?* ¿Será perjudicial si hablamos de ese asunto? ○**to do one's best** hacer lo mejor posible. ○**to do someone good, to do something good** hacer bien *A vacation will do you lots of good.* Le hará mucho bien una vacación. ○**to do the dishes** lavar los platos. ○**to do the room** arreglar el cuarto. ○**to do up** hacer, arreglar *He did the package up good and tight.* Hizo el paquete bien apretado. ○ **to do with** tener que ver con *That has nothing to do with the question.* Eso no tiene nada que ver con la cuestión. ○ **to do without** prescindir de *Women couldn't do without make-up.* Las mujeres no podrían prescindir del maquillaje. ‖ *How's your brother doing at his new job?* ¿Cómo le va a su hermano en su nuevo empleo? ‖ *Did you want to see me now?* ¿Quería Ud. verme ahora? ‖ *Don't lean out the window.* No se asome Ud. fuera de la ventana. ‖ *Don't you think I'm right?* ¿No cree Ud. que tengo razón? ‖ *Do you like the food here?* ¿Le gusta la comida de aquí? ‖ *He left for the country, but I didn't.* El se fué para el campo, pero yo no. ‖ *He's out of danger now and is doing as well as can be expected.* Está ya fuera de peligro y todo lo bien que se puede esperar. ‖ *How do you do?* ¿Cómo está Ud.? ‖ *I don't want to trouble you.* No quiero molestarle. ‖ *I do wish we could finish today!* ¡Ojalá que pudiéramos terminar hoy! ‖ *It didn't look like very good weather out, did it?* No parecía hacer muy buen tiempo ¿verdad? ‖ *That'll do now!* ¡Ya basta! ‖ *We could do with a little more help.* No nos vendría mal un poco más de ayuda. ‖ *We have to pay more than you do for cigarettes.* Tenemos que pagar más que Ud. por los cigarillos. ‖ *We'll have to make this do.* Tendremos que conformarnos con esto. ‖ *Where can I get this laundry done?* ¿Dónde me pueden lavar y planchar esta ropa?

dock [*n*] muelle *They're busy repairing the docks.* Están ocupados reparando los muelles.
● [*v*] atracar *What time does the steamer dock?* ¿A qué hora atraca el barco?

dock [*v*] descontar *I was only 15 minutes late but they docked me for an hour.* Llegué solamente quince minutos tarde, pero me descontaron una hora.

doctor [*n*] médico, doctor *Will you please send for a doctor.* Haga el favor de llamar a un médico.
● [*v*] curar, tratar *I'm doctoring a cold.* Me estoy curando un resfriado.
‖ *He's a Doctor of Philosophy in literature.* Tiene su doctorado en letras. *or* Es doctor en letras.

doctrine doctrina.

document documento.

dodge [*n*] treta *What sort of a dodge has* he thought of now? ¿Qué nueva treta ha ideado ahora?
● [*v*] desviar *If I hadn't dodged, the rock would have hit me in the head.* Si no me hubiera desviado, la piedra me habría pegado en la cabeza. ▲ evadir *Stop trying to dodge the issue.* No siga Ud. tratando de evadir el tema.

dog [*n*] perro *Have you fed the dog yet?* ¿Ha dado Ud. de comer al perro ya?
● [*v*] perseguir *They say they'll dog him until he gives in.* Dicen que lo perseguirán hasta que ceda.
‖ *He's going to the dogs.* Está hecho un perdido.

dogged terco, tenaz.

doll muñeca.

dollar dólar.

dome cúpula.

domestic [*adj*] casero *She's always been very domestic.* Ella siempre ha sido muy casera. ▲ doméstico *I'd rather not do domestic work.* Preferiría no hacer trabajos domésticos. ▲ del país *Most of these products are domestic.* La mayoría de estos productos son del país.

dominion dominio.

donate donar, contribuir.

donkey burro.

donor donador.

doom [*n*] destino (*fate*). ▲ muerte *The soldiers marched to their doom.* Los soldados marchaban hacia la muerte.
● [*v*] condenar *The convicts were doomed to die that night.* Los reos fueron condenados a morir esa noche.

door puerta *Please open the door for me.* Haga el favor de abrirme la puerta.
○ **out of doors** al aire libre, a la intemperie. ○ **to show a person the door** echar a alguien *If he becomes insulting, show him the door.* Si se pone insolente, échelo.

doorbell timbre.

doorman portero.

dope narcótico *They were accused of selling dope.* Les acusaron de vender narcóticos. ▲ bobo *No one can understand why she married such a dope.* Nadie puede comprender como se ha casado con semejante bobo. ▲ datos, información *He gave us the right dope about the deal.* Nos dió los datos exactos sobre el asunto.
○ **to be doped** estar narcotizado *He acted as if he'd been doped.* Se condujo como si hubiera estado narcotizado. ○ **to dope out** calcular *I've got it all doped out.* Todo lo tengo calculado.

dormitory dormitorio.

dose [*n*] dosis *That's a big dose for a*

child. Esa es una dosis grande para un niño.

● [*v*] curar *He keeps dosing himself with patent medicine.* Sigue curándose con específicos.

dot [*n*] lunar *Wear your dress with the blue dots.* Póngase el traje de lunares azules.

● [*v*] motear *The water was dotted with little boats.* El agua estaba moteada con botecitos.

○ **dotted line** línea de puntos *Sign on the dotted line.* Firme Ud. en la línea de puntos. ○ **on the dot** en punto *I'll see you at three on the dot.* Le veré a las tres en punto.

double [*n*] doble *He looks enough like you to be your double.* Se parece tanto a Ud. que podría pasar por su doble.

● [*adj*] doble *May I have a double portion of ice cream?* ¿Puede Ud. servirme un helado doble?—*That word has a double meaning.* Esa palabra tiene doble sentido.

● [*adv*] el doble de *His income was double what he expected.* Sus ingresos fueron el doble de lo que esperaba.

● [*v*] duplicar, doblar *He's doubled his capital in two years.* En dos años duplicó su capital. ▲ doblar *They doubled the bid.* Doblaron la oferta. ▲ redoblar *Our efforts must be doubled.* Debemos redoblar nuestros esfuerzos. ▲ apretar *He doubled his fists in anger.* Apretó los puños con rabia.

○ **to double back on** volver sobre *The prisoner must have doubled back on his tracks.* El fugitivo debe haber vuelto sobre sus pasos. ○ **double bed** cama de matrimonio. ○ **double room** habitación para dos personas. ○ **doubles** (*tennis*) dobles *Let's play doubles.* Juguemos dobles. ○ **to double up** estar doblado, estar encogido, doblarse *He's doubled up with pain.* Está encogido de dolor. ‖ *There's only one room, so we must double up.* Sólo hay una habitación, así es que tendremos que compartirla.

double-cross [*v*] engañar, traicionar.

doubt [*n*] duda *There's no doubt about it.* De eso no cabe duda.

● [*v*] dudar *I doubt if the story's true.* Dudo que el cuento sea cierto.

○ **no doubt** sin duda, indudablemente *No doubt the train'll be late.* Sin duda el tren llegará atrasado.

doubtful dudoso *It's doubtful if he'll get well.* Es dudoso que mejore.

○ **doubtful character** persona de poco fiar *He's a doubtful character.* Es una persona de poco fiar.

doubtless sin duda, indudablemente.

dough masa, pasta *Don't make the dough too thin.* No haga la masa demasiado delgada. ▲ pasta (*money*) *I haven't any dough on me.* No tengo pasta en este momento.

dove paloma.

down [*n*] pluma(s), plumón *This pillow's filled with down.* Esta almohada es de pluma(s).

down [*adv*] abajo *They lived down there by the river.* Vivían allá abajo por el río.—*Is the elevator going down?* ¿Va hacia abajo este ascensor?

● [*v*] echarse *He downed his drink quickly.* Se echó el trago rápidamente.

○ **down and out** arruinado *They used to be well off, but now they're down and out.* Estuvieron en buena posición pero ahora están arruinados. ○ **to be down on someone** tener inquina a alguien *The others are down on him because he can't keep his temper.* Le tienen inquina los demás porque no domina su mal genio. ○ **to come down** perdurar *That old song's come down through the ages.* Esa vieja canción ha perdurado a través de los tiempos. ○ **to go down** bajar *Has the rate of exchange gone up or down?* ¿Ha subido o ha bajado el tipo de cambio? ○ **up and down** de arriba abajo, de un lado a otro *He was walking up and down the room.* Se paseaba por el cuarto de un lado a otro. ‖ *The poor fellow's spirits are down.* El pobre chico está bajo de moral. ‖ *Is the sun down yet?* ¿Se ha puesto ya el sol? ‖ *He lived down south two years.* Vivió en el sur durante dos años. ‖ *Let's get down to work.* Pongámonos a trabajar en serio. ‖ *How much will the down payment be?* ¿Cuánto hay que pagar al contado?

downgrade ○ **to be on the downgrade** estar en la pendiente *We're on the downgrade now.* Estamos en la pendiente.

downhill cuesta abajo *Put on the brakes or else the car'll roll downhill.* Eche los frenos, si no rodará el carro cuesta abajo.

downstairs [*n*] planta baja *We'll have the downstairs ready next week.* Tendremos la planta baja lista para la semana entrante.

● [*adv*] abajo *The visitor's waiting downstairs.* La visita está esperando abajo. ▲ escaleras abajo *He tripped and fell downstairs.* Tropezó y cayó escaleras abajo.

○ **downstairs room** cuarto en la planta baja *I'd like to rent a downstairs* *room*. Me gustaría alquilar un cuarto en la planta baja.

downtown [*adv*] al centro *Let's go downtown for our shopping*. Vamos a hacer nuestras compras al centro.

downward hacia abajo.

doze [*v*] dormitar.

dozen docena *Give me a dozen oranges*. Deme una docena de naranjas.

drab gris, triste *It's a drab day*. Es un día gris.

draft [*n*] corriente de aire, [*Am*] chiflón *I'm sitting in a draft*. Estoy sentado en una corriente de aire. ▲ giro *The bank'll cash this draft for you*. El banco le abonará este giro. ▲ tiro *This chimney doesn't have a good draft*. Esta chimenea no tiene buen tiro. ▲ conscripción *The draft's taken half of our employees*. La conscripción ha afectado a la mitad de nuestros empleados. ▲ borrador *He's made a rough draft of his speech*. Hizo un breve borrador de su discurso. ▲ plano *The architect has completed his draft for the house*. El arquitecto ha terminado el plano de la casa. ▲ calado *This boat has a draft of six feet*. Este barco tiene seis pies de calado.

● [*v*] reclutar *They've drafted many men from this town*. Han reclutado a muchos hombres de esta ciudad. ▲ trazar *They drafted the plans in the engineer's office*. Trazaron los planos en el despacho del ingeniero.

○ draft beer cerveza de barril.

drag [*n*] carga *He's been an awful drag on the family*. Ha sido una gran carga para su familia.

● [*v*] arrastrar *Your dress is dragging all over the floor*. Su vestido arrastra por todo el suelo.—*Don't drag the trunk, it marks the floor*. No arrastre Ud. el baúl, que raya el piso. ▲ dragar *Why are they dragging the river?* ¿Para qué están dragando el río?

‖ *The days seem to drag here*. Los días parecen interminables aquí.

drain [*n*] desagüe *The drain's stopped up again*. El desagüe está atascado otra vez.

● [*v*] agotar *That illness is draining away all her strength*. Esa enfermedad está agotando sus fuerzas. ▲ desecar *If they'd drain the swamp, there wouldn't be so many mosquitoes around here*. Si desecaran el pantano no habría tantos mosquitos por aquí.

‖ *War's a great drain on this country's strength*. La guerra está consumiendo los recursos de este país.

drainage desagüe, drenaje.

drama drama.

draw [*n*] empate *The game ended in a draw*. El juego terminó en un empate. ▲ desempate *The opposing team won the draw*. El equipo contrario ganó el desempate.

● [*v*] sacar *Go out and draw a bucket of water*. Salga y saque un cubo de agua.—*They drew different conclusions from the same facts*. Sacaron distintas conclusiones de los mismos hechos. —*I'll have to draw fifty dollars out of the bank*. Tendré que sacar cincuenta dólares del banco. ▲ sacarse *He drew a winning number*. Se sacó uno de los números premiados. ▲ atraer *This concert's sure to draw a big crowd*. Este concierto seguramente atraerá mucha gente. ▲ dibujar *Won't you please draw me a map of the route?* ¿Quiere hacerme el favor de dibujarme un plano del camino? ▲ entrar *The train's just drawing into the station*. El tren está entrando en la estación. ▲ llegar *The campaign's drawing to a close*. La campaña está llegando a su fin.

○ drawing card atracción, gran número *He's a big drawing card wherever he goes*. Es una gran atracción dondequiera que vaya. ○ to draw a line poner un límite. ○ to draw a sigh dar un suspiro *When the examination was over he drew a sigh of relief*. Cuando terminó el examen dió un suspiro de desatrogo. ○ to draw out sonsacar *I did my best to draw him out*. Hice lo que pude para sonsacarle. ○ to draw up acercarse *Just then a taxi drew up*. En ese momento se acercó un taxi. ▲ preparar *As soon as I get the information I'll draw up a report*. En cuanto reciba la información prepararé un informe.

‖ *The scratches were deep enough to draw blood*. Los rasguños fueron lo suficientemente profundos para hacer manar sangre. ‖ *On this river the boats can't draw more than three feet*. En este río los barcos no pueden tener un calado mayor de tres pies. ‖ *This is a good-drawing pipe*. Esta es una pipa de buen tiro.

drawer cajón, gaveta.

drawers calzoncillos.

drawing dibujo.

dread [*n*] miedo, terror.

dreadful espantoso *There was a dreadful storm*. Hubo una tempestad espantosa. ▲ cursi *She wears dreadful clothes*. Lleva una ropa muy cursi.

dream [*n*] sueño *I had a funny dream*

last night. Anoche tuve un sueño divertido.
● [v] soñar *Last night I dreamed I was home.* Soñé anoche que estaba en casa.
O to dream of soñar con *I often dream of you.* A menudo sueño contigo.
‖ *I wouldn't dream of doing it.* No se me ocurriría hacerlo nunca.

dreary triste, melancólico.

drench empapar.

dress [n] vestido, traje *She wants to buy a new dress.* Desea comprar un vestido nuevo.
● [adj] de etiqueta *The reception's a dress affair.* La recepción es de etiqueta.
● [v] vestir *Dress the children.* Vista a los niños. ▲ vestirse *We've got to dress for the reception.* Hay que vestirse para la recepción. ▲ arreglar *They were dressing the Christmas tree for the party.* Arreglaban el árbol para la fiesta de Navidad. ▲ hacer la cura a *When was this wound dressed?* ¿Cuándo se hizo la cura a esta herida? O dressed limpio *Does he sell dressed chickens?* ¿Vende pollos limpios? O to dress up arreglarse *I'll have to dress up to go there.* Tendré que arreglarme para ir allí.
‖ *They gave me a dressing down for being late.* Me regañaron por llegar tarde.

dresser aparador.

dressing salsa *What kind of dressing would you like on your lobster?* ¿Que clase de salsa le gustaría en la langosta? ▲ relleno *She served roast turkey with chestnut dressing.* Sirvió pavo asado con un relleno de castañas. ▲ venda *The nurse changes his dressings every morning.* La enfermera cambia sus vendas todas las mañanas.

dressing gown bata.

dressmaker modista.

dried seco *These leaves are dried and yellow.* Esas hojas están secas y amarillas.

drill [n] taladro *The engineers need another drill.* Los ingenieros necesitan otro taladro.
● [v] entrenar *The officer's drilling his men.* El oficial está entrenando a sus soldados. ▲ perforar *The dentist has to drill this tooth.* Es preciso que el dentista perfore este diente. ▲ hacer ejercicios militares *We drill every day on that field.* Hacemos ejercicios militares en ese campo todos los días.

drink [n] bebida, trago *Can I mix you a drink?* ¿Puedo prepararle una bebida?

● [v] tomar, beber *Drink plenty of water.* Tome Ud. mucha agua. ▲ brindar *Let's drink to your return.* Brindemos por su vuelta.
‖ *May I have a drink of water?* ¿Puéde Ud. darme un poco de agua?

drip [v] gotear.

drive [n] carretera *The drive goes around the lake.* La carretera da la vuelta al lago. ▲ paseo en coche *Let's go for a drive.* Vamos a dar un paseo en coche. ▲ golpe (*golf*) *He has a very powerful drive.* Tiene un golpe muy fuerte. ▲ campaña *Next week there'll be a drive to raise money for the poor.* La semana próxima habrá una campaña para colectar dinero en beneficio de los pobres.
● [v] clavar *Drive that nail into the wall.* Clave Ud. ese clavo en la pared. ▲ impulsar *He was driven to stealing by hunger.* Fué impulsado al robo por el hambre. ▲ llevar *The boss drove me home in his new car.* El jefe me llevó hasta casa en su nuevo auto. ▲ manejar, conducir *Can you drive a truck?* ¿Puede Ud. manejar un camión? ▲ pasear en coche, ir en coche *Let's drive out into the country.* Vamos a pasear en coche por el campo. ▲ hacer trabajar *The foreman drives the workers continually.* El capataz hace trabajar a los obreros constantemente.
O to drive at proponerse *What are you driving at?* ¿Qué es lo que se propone Ud.? O to drive away echar *Drive the dog away.* Eche Ud. al perro de aquí. O to drive back echar hacia atrás, empujar hacia atrás *The crowd was driven back.* Echaron el gentío hacia atrás. ▲ rechazar *The soldiers drove the enemy back.* Los soldados rechazaron al enemigo.
‖ *He drives a hard bargain.* Lleva adelante con empeño un negocio. ‖ *He was a man of considerable drive.* Daba mucho impulso a lo que hacía.

driver chofer, chófer *Where's the driver of the car?* ¿Dónde está el chofer del automóvil?

droop [v] inclinar, bajar, decaer.

drop [n] gota *There's not a drop of water left.* No queda ni una gota de agua. ▲ caramelo *Lemon drops are my favorite candy.* Los caramelos de limón son mis dulces favoritos.
● [v] dejar *For the time being, let's drop the subject.* Por ahora, dejemos ese tema.—*Please drop me at the corner.* Haga el favor de dejarme en la esquina. ▲ dejar caer *I dropped the*

letter in the street. Dejé caer la carta en la calle. ▲ caerse *The pencil dropped out of my hand.* Se me cayó el lápiz de la mano. ▲ bajar *The temperature dropped very rapidly.* La temperatura bajó rápidamente. ▲ omitir *Drop every other letter to read the code.* Para leer la clave hay que omitir una letra sí y otra no. ▲ echar *If I don't pay any dues I'll be dropped from the club.* Si no pago la cuota, me echarán del club. ▲ soltar *She dropped a hint that she wanted to go.* Soltó una indirecta que quería irse.

○ **at the drop of a hat** con cualquier pretexto. ○ **to drop in** *or* **over** venir *Drop in to see me tomorrow.* Venga a verme mañana. ○ **to drop off (to sleep)** quedarse dormido *I dropped off to sleep immediately.* Me quedé dormido inmediatamente.

‖ *From the second floor there's a drop of twenty feet to the ground.* Desde el segundo piso al suelo hay una altura de veinte pies.

drought sequía.

drown ahogarse *Many people have drowned at this beach.* Se ha ahogado mucha gente en esta playa. ▲ inundar *This field was drowned out by the spring rains.* Este campo se inundó con las lluvias de la primavera.

○ **to drown out** ahogar *The noise drowned out his remarks.* El ruido ahogó sus observaciones.

drowsy soñoliento, medio dormido.

drug [*n*] droga, medicina *This drug's sold only on a doctor's prescription.* Esta medicina solamente se vende por prescripción médica.

● [*v*] narcotizar *He thought they had drugged him.* Creía que lo habían narcotizado.

○ **drugged** borracho *I felt drugged with sleep.* Me sentía borracho de sueño.

‖ *This year's grapes are a drug on the market.* Este año las uvas están tiradas. *or* Este año no hay quien quiera las uvas.

druggist boticario, farmacéutico.

drug store botica, farmacia.

drum [*n*] tambor *Do you hear the roll of the drums?* ¿Oye Ud. el redoblar de los tambores? ▲ barril *They unloaded six drums of gasoline.* Descargaron seis barriles de gasolina.

● [*v*] teclear *Please stop drumming on the table.* Por favor deje de teclear sobre la mesa.

‖ *He's trying to drum up more trade.*

Está haciendo diligencias para mejorar sus negocios.

drunk [*n*] borracho *We had trouble with a drunk.* Tuvimos dificultades con un borracho. ▲ borrachera *He looks like he's been on a drunk.* Parece que ha estado de borrachera.

○ **to get drunk** embriagarse, emborracharse *He got drunk at the party.* Se emborrachó en la fiesta.

dry [*adj*] seco *It's been a dry summer.* Ha sido un verano seco.—*I'm dry; let's have a drink.* Estoy seco; tomemos un trago. ▲ aburrido *The lecture was so dry I walked out.* La conferencia era tan aburrida que me salí.

● [*v*] secar *Who's going to dry the dishes?* ¿Quién va a secar los platos? ▲ secarse *The paint dried in five hours.* La pintura se secó en cinco horas.

○ **dry land** tierra firme. ○ **to dry up** secarse *Every summer this stream dries up.* Esta corriente se seca todos los veranos.

dry-goods store mercería, tienda de telas *You can buy buttons in the dry-goods store.* Ud. puede comprar botones en la mercería.

duchess duquesa.

duck [*n*] pato *We're having roast duck for dinner.* Tendremos pato asado para la cena.

● [*v*] bajar, agachar *Duck your head.* Baje la cabeza. ▲ zambullir *Let's duck him in the lake.* Vamos a zambullirlo en el lago.

○ **to duck out** escaparse *Let's duck out of here.* Vamos a escaparnos de aquí. ○ **white duck** dril blanco.

due [*adv*] derecho hacia *Go due west until you come to the river.* Vaya Ud. derecho hacia el oeste hasta que llegue al río.

○ **due to** ocasionado por, causado por *His death was due to an accident.* Su muerte fué ocasionada por un accidente.

‖ *I have three weeks' pay due me.* Me deben tres semanas de sueldo. ‖ *The train's due at noon.* El tren debe llegar al mediodía.

duel [*n*] duelo.

dues cuota *The dues are five dollars a year.* La cuota es de cinco dólares al año.

duke duque.

dull [*adj*] romo *This knife's dull.* Este cuchillo está romo. ▲ triste *If it's a dull day, let's not go.* No vayamos si el día está triste. ▲ sordo *He felt a dull pain in his chest.* Sentía un dolor sordo en el pecho. ▲torpe *Their son's a dull student.* Su hijo es un estudiante torpe. ▲soso *Our neighbors are very dull.* Nuestros vecinos son muy sosos. ▲aburrido *What a dull evening!* ¡Qué noche más aburrida!

● [*v*] estropear *Be careful not to dull the knife.* Tenga cuidado de no estropear el cuchillo.

duly debidamente.

dumb mudo *He became dumb after his sickness.* Quedó mudo después de la enfermedad.

○ **to strike dumb** dejar atónito, pasmar *We were struck dumb by the news.* La noticia nos dejó atónitos.

‖ *I knew you'd do something dumb like that.* Yo sabía que Ud. haría alguna tontería de esa índole.

dummy maniquí *Put the dress on the dummy.* Ponga Ud. el vestido en el maniquí. ▲tonto *He's a dummy.* Es un tonto.

dump [*n*] basurero, vaciadero *Where's the city dump?* ¿Dónde está el basurero de la ciudad? ▲depósito *The ammunition dump's very well guarded.* Está muy bien vigilado el depósito de municiones.

● [*v*] echar *She dumped the coal into the stove.* Echó el carbón en la estufa.

○ **to be down in the dumps** tener murria, estar con murria *I've been down in the dumps all day.* He estado con murria todo el día.

‖ *For many years they've been dumping cheap toys on the market.* Durante muchos años han inundado el mercado de juguetes baratos.

dung excremento, estiércol.

duplicate [*n*] duplicado, copia *Do you have the duplicate?* ¿Tiene la copia.

▲duplicado *Fill this out in duplicate.* Llene esto por duplicado.

duplicate [*v*] igualar *His work'll never be duplicated.* Su obra nunca será igualada.

durable durable, duradero.

duration duración.

during durante *I met him during the war.* Le conocí durante la guerra.

dusk crepúsculo.

‖ *We'll return at dusk.* Regresaremos al oscurecer.

dust [*n*] polvo *She swept the dust under the rug.* Barrió el polvo que había debajo de la alfombra.

● [*v*] quitar el polvo de *Please dust my desk.* Haga el favor de quitar el polvo de mi escritorio.

○ **to bite the dust** morder el polvo.

duty deber *He thought it was his duty to visit his parents.* Creyó que su deber era visitar a sus padres. ▲obligación *Answering the phone is one of my duties.* Una de mis obligaciones es contestar al teléfono. ▲impuesto *How much duty is there on this tobacco?* ¿Cuánto es el impuesto sobre este tabaco?

○ **off duty** libre de servicio *I go off duty at 5:30.* Estoy libre de servicio a las cinco y media. ○ **on duty** de servicio *I'm on duty all night.* Estoy de servicio toda la noche.

dwarf [*n*] enano.

dwell ○ **to dwell on** insistir en.

dwelling vivienda, casa.

dwindle menguar, disminuir.

dye [*n*] tinte *Please get me a package of blue dye.* Hágame el favor de conseguirme un paquete de tinte azul.

● [*v*] teñir *I had my shoes dyed.* Me hice teñir los zapatos.

dynamite dinamita.

dysentery disentería.

E

each cada *How many beds are there to each room?* ¿Cuántas camas hay en cada cuarto? ▲cada uno *These apples are a penny each.* Estas manzanas son a un centavo cada una.

○ **each other** el uno al otro, unos a otros *We don't understand each other.* No nos comprendemos (unos a otros).

‖ *Each one must look out for himself.* Sálvese el que pueda.

eager ansioso *I'm eager to meet your friends.* Estoy ansioso de conocer a sus amigos.

eagle águila.

ear oído *My ear hurts.* Me duele el oído. —*I don't have an ear for music.* No tengo buen oído para la música. ▲oreja *The donkey has long ears.* El burro tiene orejas largas. ▲mazorca (*corn*), espiga (*wheat*) *The ears of wheat are nearly ripe.* Están casi maduras las espigas del trigo.

○ **all ears** todo oídos *Go on with your story, I'm all ears.* Siga Ud. con el cuento, soy todo oídos.

eardrum tímpano.

earlier más temprano *Can't you get up earlier?* ¿No se puede Ud. levantar más temprano?

early [*adj*] primero *When does the early show begin?* Cuándo comienza la primera sesión? [*Sp*] or ¿Cuándo comienza la primera tanda? [*Am*] ▲ pronto, rápido *We expect an early reply.* Esperamos una pronta contestación.

● [*adv*] temprano *Please call me early.* Por favor llámeme temprano.

○ **early life** primeros años, juventud *Tell me something of your early life.* Cuénteme algo sobre su juventud.

○ **early riser** madrugador *He's a very early riser.* Es muy madrugador.

earmuff orejera.

earn ganar *How much do you earn a week?* ¿Cuánto gana usted a la semana?—*His behavior earned him the respect of everyone.* Su comportamiento le ganó el respeto de todos.

earnest serio.

earnings salario.

earphone auricular.

earring pendiente (*long*), arete (*round*).

earth mundo, tierra *There's nothing on earth like it.* No hay nada igual en el mundo. ▲ tierra *These pits must be filled with earth.* Hay que llenar estos hoyos con tierra.

○ **down-to-earth** práctico *He has a down-to-earth attitude.* Tiene un punto de vista práctico. ○ **to get back to earth** volver a la realidad *Stop dreaming and get back to earth!* ¡Deje Ud. de soñar y vuelva a la realidad!

earthquake terremoto.

ease [*n*] naturalidad *He dances with such ease.* Baila con tanta naturalidad.

● [*v*] aliviar *This medicine will ease the pain quickly.* Esta medicina aliviará pronto el dolor.

○ **a life of ease** una vida desahogada *He leads a life of ease.* Llleva una vida muy desahogada. ○ **to ease up** aligerar *The pressure of the work has eased up a little in the past week.* El trabajo se ha aligerado un poco en la última semana.

‖ *Ease the bureau over.* Tumbe Ud. la cómoda con cuidado. ‖ *He always puts his guests completely at ease.* Siempre logra que sus invitados se sientan como en su casa.

easel caballete.

easily fácilmente *I don't make friends easily.* No hago amistades fácilmente. ▲ seguramente *That's easily the best thing I've seen.* Seguramente es lo mejor que he visto. ▲ probablemente

He could easily be late. Probablemente llegará tarde.

east este *I lived in the East for ten years.* Viví en el Este durante diez años.— *Where do I turn east?* ¿Dónde tuerzo hacia el Este? ▲ Oriente *We get most of our tea from the East.* Recibimos del Oriente la mayor parte de nuestro té.

○ **east wind** viento de levante *An east wind usually comes up in the afternoon.* Por lo general se levanta por la tarde un viento de levante.

Easter Pascua Florida.

easy fácil *It is easy?* ¿Es fácil? ▲ con calma *Let's take things easy.* Tomemos las cosas con calma.

○ **easy-going** tranquilo, bonachón *The boss is very easy-going.* El jefe es muy tranquilo.

‖ *He's been living on easy street since his father died.* Vive espléndidamente desde que murió su padre.

eat comer *I want something to eat.* Quiero algo de comer.

○ **to eat out** comer fuera *Shall we eat out tonight?* ¿Comemos fuera esta noche?

eavesdrop atisbar, curiosear.

echo [*n*] eco *He shouted and we heard the echo.* Gritó y oímos el eco.

● [*v*] resonar *The shot echoed through the hills.* El disparo resonó en las colinas. ▲ repetir *Quit echoing every word he says.* Deje de repetir cada palabra que dice él.

eclipse eclipse.

economical económico.

ecstasy éxtasis.

edge [*n*] las afueras *How far is it to the edge of town?* ¿A qué distancia quedan las afueras del pueblo? ▲ borde *Don't fall over the edge.* No se caiga por el borde. ▲ filo *The edge of this razor is dull.* El filo de esta navaja está embotado. ▲ ventaja *I think you have the edge on me.* Creo que tiene Ud. una ventaja sobre mí. or Creo que me lleva Ud. ventaja.

● [*v*] abrirse paso por *The man edged his way through the crowd.* El hombre se abrió paso por entre la multitud.

‖ *I want an edge put on this blade.* Quiero que me afilen esta hoja.

edible comestible.

edit redactar.

edition edición.

editor redactor.

editorial editorial, artículo de fondo *There's a good editorial in today's pa-*

per. Hay un buen editorial en el periódico de hoy.
‖*He has an editorial position.* Tiene un puesto de redactor.

educate educar.

education instrucción *How much education have you had?* ¿Qué instrucción ha recibido Ud.?

eel anguila.

effect [*n*] efecto *What's the effect of this medicine?* ¿Qué efecto produce esta medicina? ▲efecto, resultado *His speech produced the desired effect.* Su discurso produjo el efecto deseado.
● [*v*] efectuar, realizar *He effected the change without difficulty.* Efectuó el cambio sin dificultad.
○ **effects** efectos personales *His effects are still in his room.* Sus efectos personales están todavía en la habitación. ○ **for effect** para producir efecto *She's wearing those clothes for effect.* Lleva esos vestidos para producir efecto. ○ **in effect** en realidad *His career began in effect when he was twelve.* Su carrera comenzó en realidad cuando tenía doce años. ○ **to go into effect** entrar en vigor *When does this regulation go into effect?* ¿Cuándo entra en vigor este reglamento? ○ **to take effect** hacer efecto *This medicine is beginning to take effect.* Esta medicina está empezando a hacer su efecto.

effective de buen efecto *That's a very effective color scheme.* Aquella combinación de colores es de muy buen efecto. ▲en vigor *The new law becomes effective immediately.* La nueva ley entrará en vigor inmediatamente.

efficiency eficiencia.

efficient eficiente.

effort esfuerzo *That job will take all your effort.* Ese empleo necesitará de todo su esfuerzo.—*All her efforts to reach him were in vain.* Todos los esfuerzos de ella para alcanzarle fueron en vano. ▲intento *That book was his first effort in the line of mystery stories.* Ese libro fué su primer intento en el género de novelas policíacas.

egg [*n*] huevo *How much are eggs by the dozen?* ¿Cuánto vale la docena de huevos?
● [*v*] impulsar *He was egged on by his friends.* Fué impulsado por sus amigos.
○ **to put all one's eggs in one basket** jugarse todo a una sola carta.
‖ *He's a bad egg.* Es un sinvergüenza.

eggplant berenjena.

eight ocho.

eighteen diez y ocho.

eighth octavo.

eighty ochenta.

either [*pro*] alguno de los dos *Does either of these roads lead to town?* ¿Va hacia el pueblo alguno de estos dos caminos? ▲cualquiera de los dos *Either one is satisfactory.* Cualquiera de los dos es satisfactorio. ▲ambos, entrambos *There were trees on either side of the road.* Había árboles a ambos lados del camino.
● [*adv*] tampoco *If you don't go I won't either.* Si Ud. no va, yo tampoco.
○ **either...or** o...o *I'll leave either tonight or tomorrow.* Partiré o esta noche o mañana.

elaborate [*adj*] elaborado, con muchos detalles *They made elaborate plans for the party.* Prepararon los planes para la fiesta con muchos detalles.

elaborate [*v*] elaborar.
○ **to elaborate upon** ampliar.

elapse pasar, transcurrir.

elastic [*n*] elástico, goma.
● [*adj*] elástico.

elated exaltado.

elbow codo *He hurt his elbow.* Se lastimó el codo.—*We'll have to get a new elbow for the pipe.* Tendremos que conseguir un nuevo codo para el tubo.
○ **to elbow one's way** abrirse camino a codazos *She elbowed her way through the crowd.* Se abrió camino a codazos por entre la muchedumbre.

elect [*adj*] electo *The president-elect will speak tomorrow.* Mañana hablará el presidente electo.
● [*v*] elegir *Who was elected president?* ¿Quién fué elegido presidente?

election elección.

electric eléctrico.

electrician electricista.

electricity electricidad.

elegant elegante.

element elemento *How many elements can you name?* ¿Cuántos elementos puede Ud. nombrar?
○ **to be in one's element** estar en su propio elemento, estar en su ambiente.

elementary elemental.

elephant elefante.

elevate elevar.

elevator ascensor.

eleven once.

eligible elegible.

eliminate eliminar.

elm olmo.

eloquent elocuente.

else más *There's no one else here.* No

hay nadie más aquí. ▲los demás *Everyone else has gone.* Todos los demás se han ido.
○ **or else** o si no *Hurry or else we'll be late.* Apresúrese o si no llegaremos tarde.
‖ *How else can I manage?* ¿Y qué otra cosa puedo hacer?
elsewhere en otra parte.
embalm embalsamar.
embark embarcar.
embarrass poner en un aprieto *Our presence embarrassed him.* Nuestra presencia le puso en un aprieto. ▲turbar *He was embarrassed by what I said.* Se turbó por lo que dije.
○ **financially embarrassed** con dificultades económicas *She found herself financially embarrassed.* Se encontró en dificultades económicas.
embarrassment turbación.
emblem emblema.
embrace abrazar *He embraced his mother tenderly.* Abrazó a su mamá con ternura. ▲abarcar *Their plan embraces all aspects of the problem.* Su plan abarca todos los aspectos del problema.
embroider bordar *She was embroidering a tablecloth.* Ella estaba bordando un mantel.
embryo embrión.
emerald esmeralda.
emergency emergencia.
emigrant emigrante.
emigrate emigrar.
eminent eminente.
emotion emoción.
emperor emperador.
emphasis énfasis.
emphasize recalcar.
empire imperio.
employ emplear *How many workers are employed here?* ¿Cuántos obreros hay empleados aquí? ▲tener *You have to employ caution in crossing this river.* Tiene Ud. que tener cuidado al cruzar este río.
‖ *In whose employ are you?* ¿Para quién trabaja Ud.?
employee empleado.
employer patrón.
employment empleo.
empress emperatriz.
empty [*adj*] vacío *Do you have an empty box?* ¿Tiene Ud. una caja vacía? ▲vano, inútil *He made a few empty threats.* Hizo unas cuantas amenazas vanas.
● [*v*] vaciar(se) *This tank empties in about three minutes.* Este tanque se vacía en unos tres minutos. ▲desem-

bocar *This stream empties into a big lake.* Este arroyo desemboca en un lago grande.
enable permitir *This inheritance will enable me to buy that house.* Esta herencia me permitirá comprar esa casa.
enamel [*n*] esmalte.
● [*v*] esmaltar.
enchanting encantador.
encircle rodear.
enclose cercar *The property is enclosed.* La propiedad está cercada.
○ **enclosed** cerrado *The house has an enclosed porch.* La casa tiene un porche cerrado. ▲adjunto *Enclosed is the sum you requested.* Adjunto le remito la cantidad que pidió.
encounter [*n*] encuentro.
● [*v*] encontrar, dar con.
encourage estimular, animar *He encouraged our efforts.* Estimuló nuestros esfuerzos. ▲fomentar *Let's not encourage that sort of conduct.* No fomentemos esa clase de conducta.
○ **encouraged** animado *Do you feel more encouraged now?* ¿Se siente Ud. ahora más animado?
encyclopedia enciclopedia.
end [*n*] fin *Who knows what the end will be?* ¿Quién sabe cuál será el fin? ▲final *Is this the end of the street?* ¿Es este el final de la calle? ▲fines *I'll pay you at the end of the month.* Le pagaré a fines de mes.
● [*v*] terminar *When does the performance end?* ¿Cuándo termina la representación?
○ **at the other end** al otro extremo.
○ **loose ends** cabos *A few loose ends remain to be cleared up.* Quedan algunos cabos por atar. ○ **no end** un sin fin *We've had no end of trouble on the trip.* Hemos tenido un sin fin de dificultades en el viaje. ○ **to put an end to** poner fin a *Please put an end to this discussion.* Por favor, ponga Ud. fin a esta discusión.
‖ *It's getting hard to make both ends meet.* Se está haciendo difícil vivir con lo que se tiene.
endeavor [*n*] esfuerzo.
● [*v*] esforzarse.
endless sin fin, infinito.
endorse endosar.
endorsement endoso.
endow dotar.
endurance resistencia, aguante.
enemy enemigo.
energetic enérgico.
energy energía.
enforce hacer cumplir, ejecutar.

engage comprometer *How long have they been engaged?* ¿Cuánto tiempo llevan de comprometidos? ▲ tomar *I've just engaged a new maid.* Acabo de tomar una nueva criada. ▲ trabar contacto con *It was two weeks before we were able to engage the enemy.* Transcurrieron dos semanas antes de que pudiéramos trabar contacto con el enemigo. ○ **to be engaged in** dedicarse a, ocuparse de *He has been engaged in politics for years.* Hace años que se dedica a la política.

engagement compromiso, esponsales *They've just announced their engagement.* Acaban de anunciar su compromiso. ▲ compromiso, cita *I have an engagement this afternoon.* Tengo un compromiso esta tarde. ▲ encuentro *We had a violent engagement with the enemy.* Tuvimos un encuentro violento con el enemigo.

engine motor *The engine needs repairing.* El motor necesita reparaciones. ▲ locomotora *The train has two engines.* El tren lleva dos locomotoras.

engineer [n] ingeniero *Is there an engineer here?* ¿Hay aquí ingeniero? ▲ maquinista *The engineer brought the train to a stop.* El maquinista paró el tren. ● [v] llevar, dirigir *He engineered the scheme very well.* El llevó el plan muy bien.

English inglés.

engrave grabar.

enjoy gozar de *I hope you enjoyed the party.* Espero que haya gozado de la fiesta.—*As a rule he enjoys good health.* Por lo regular goza de muy buena salud. ▲ gustar, tener placer en *I don't enjoy doing this.* No me gusta hacer esto. ○ **to enjoy oneself** divertirse *I enjoyed myself very much.* Me divertí mucho.

enjoyment goce, placer.

enlarge ampliar, agrandar. ○ **to enlarge on** exagerar *Stop enlarging upon your troubles.* Deje Ud. de exagerar sus males.

enlargement ampliación.

enlist alistarse *He enlisted in the navy two days ago.* Se alistó en la marina hace dos días. ▲ sentar plaza *He enlisted in the army.* Sentó plaza en el ejército. ▲ conseguir *He enlisted the help of the teachers in that drive.* Consiguió la ayuda de los maestros en aquella campaña.

enormous enorme.

enough [adj] suficiente *Do you have enough money?* ¿Tiene Ud. suficiente dinero? ● [adv] bastante *He seemed glad enough to do it.* Parecía estar bastante contento en hacerlo. ○ **to be enough** bastar *That's enough!* ¡Basta! ‖ *Enough is enough.* Basta y sobra. ‖ *Sure enough; you're right.* Verdad que sí; tiene Ud. razón.

enrage enfurecer, encolerizar.

enroll matricularse.

entangle enredar.

enter entrar en *He entered the room.* Entró en el cuarto. ▲ ingresar *When did you enter the army?* ¿Cuándo ingresó Ud. en el ejército? ▲ inscribir *Who's entered in the race?* ¿Quiénes se han inscrito para la carrera? ▲ disponer *The cards are entered in alphabetical order.* Las tarjetas están dispuestas por orden alfabético. ○ **to enter into** encajar en *He entered into the spirit of the party.* Encajó en el ambiente de la fiesta.

entertain divertir *He entertained the audience with his jokes.* Divirtió al público con sus chistes. ▲ entretener *Will you please entertain the guest while I dress?* Haga Ud. el favor de entretener al invitado mientras me visto. ▲ convidar *She entertains a lot.* Convida mucho a la gente. ▲ abrigar *Whatever makes you entertain such an idea?* ¿Cómo puede Ud. abrigar tal idea?

entertainment espectáculo.

enthusiasm entusiasmo.

entire entero *I read the entire book in one day.* Leí el libro entero en un día. ▲ todo *The entire trip is pleasant.* Todo el viaje es agradable. ▲ total *Is that the entire cost?* ¿Es ese el coste total?

entitle autorizar *I'm entitled to spend 50 dollars a month.* Estoy autorizado a gastar cincuenta dólares al mes. ○ **entitled** titulado (*of a book*). ‖ *His age entitles him to respect.* Merece que se le respete por su edad.

entrance entrada *Her sudden entrance took us by surprise.* Su entrada repentina nos cogió de sorpresa.—*Where's the entrance?* ¿Dónde queda la entrada?—*Is there an entrance fee?* ¿Hay que pagar entrada?

entrée entrada.

entry entrada *The people cheered the entry of the troops.* La gente vitoreó la entrada de las tropas. ▲ asiento, partida *How many entries are there in this account?* ¿Cuántos asientos hay en esta cuenta? ▲competidor, participante *When the race started there were only ten entries.* Cuando la carrera empezó había solamente diez competidores.

envelop [*v*] *The town was enveloped in smoke.* La ciudad estaba envuelta en humo.

envelope [*n*] sobre.

envy [*n*] envidia.

● [*v*] envidiar.

epidemic epidemia.

equal [*n*] igual *It will be hard to find his equal.* Será difícil encontrar su igual.

● [*adj*] igual *These are two equal objects.* Estos son dos objetos iguales. ▲mismo *All men should have equal rights.* Todos los hombres deben tener los mismos derechos. ▲parejo *They had equal luck.* Tuvieron una suerte pareja. *or* Tuvieron la misma suerte.

● [*v*] equivaler *Does this amount equal your losses?* ¿Equivale esta suma a sus pérdidas? ▲igualar *It'll be hard to equal his record.* Será difícil igualar su record.

○ **equal to** con fuerzas para *I don't feel equal to the trip.* No me siento con fuerzas para el viaje.

equator ecuador.

equip equipar *The soldiers were very well equipped.* Los soldados estaban muy bien equipados.

equipment equipo *Our fishing equipment will all fit into one bag.* Todo nuestro equipo de pesca cabrá en una bolsa.

equivalent [*adj; n*] equivalente.

era época, era.

erase borrar.

eraser borrador.

erect [*adj*] derecho *Stand erect.* Póngase derecho.

● [*v*] erigir *I was a child when they erected that monument.* Era yo niño cuando erigieron aquel monumento.

errand recado, mandado.

error error *There seems to be an error in the bill.* Parece que hay un error en la cuenta.

escalator escalera móvil sin fin, escalera rodante.

escape [*n*] fuga *The escape of the thief shocked us.* La fuga del ladrón nos impresionó.

● [*v*] fugarse *The criminal was able to escape.* El criminal logró fugarse. ▲escaparse *Did anyone escape?* ¿Se escapó alguno? ▲evitar, escapar a *You can't escape the consequences.* No

puede Ud. escapar a las consecuencias. ‖ *He goes to the theater as an escape.* Va al teatro para distraerse. ‖ *Her face is familiar, but her name escapes me.* Su cara me es familiar pero su nombre no me viene a la memoria. ‖ *We had a narrow escape.* Escapamos por un pelo.

especially especialmente *I want this especially.* Quiero esto especialmente. ‖ *Is anything especially wrong?* ¿Sucede algo de particular?

essay ensayo.

essence esencia *That was the essence of his speech.* Eso fué la esencia de su discurso.—*The dessert was flavored with essence of peppermint.* El postre tenía sabor de esencia de menta.

essential [*n*] rudimento, fundamento *He taught the essentials of swimming in one lesson.* Enseñaba los rudimentos de la natación en una lección.

● [*adj*] esencial *Good manners are essential.* Son esenciales los buenos modales.

establish establecer *I should like to establish myself here.* Quisiera establecerme aquí. ▲colocar *Are you comfortably established here?* ¿Está Ud. cómodamente colocado aquí? ▲comprobar *Can you establish your claim?* ¿Puede Ud. comprobar su reclamación?

establishment establecimiento.

estate finca, propiedad *He has a large estate in the country.* Tiene una finca muy grande en el campo. ▲herencia *His estate is valued at $10,000.* Su herencia está valuada en $10,000.

esteem [*n*] estima.

● [*v*] estimar.

estimate [*n*] cálculo *My estimate was pretty close to the exact measurement of the room.* Mi cálculo era muy aproximado a la medida exacta de la habitación. ▲presupuesto, valuación *The painter made us an estimate.* El pintor nos hizo un presupuesto.

● [*v*] estimar *He estimated the damage at close to a thousand dollars.* Estimó que el daño causado llegaba aproximadamente a mil dólares.

etc. etc., etcétera.

etching grabado al agua fuerte.

eternal eterno.

ether éter.

ethics ética.

etiquette etiqueta.

evaporate evaporarse.

even [*adj*] liso *Is the surface even?* ¿Esta lisa la superficie? ▲uniforme *The train traveled at an even speed.* El tren

andaba a una velocidad uniforme.
▲ equitativo *There will be an even distribution of the food.* Habrá una distribución equitativa de víveres. ▲ par *Is this game played by an odd or even number of people?* ¿Interviene en este juego un número par o impar de personas? ▲ exacto *With two more we'll have an even dozen.* Con dos más tendremos una docena exacta. ▲ apacible, tranquilo *He has an even disposition.* Tiene en genio tranquilo. ▲ igual *The two sides were almost even.* Los dos bandos eran casi iguales.
● [adv] hasta *Even the strongest were exhausted.* Hasta los más fuertes estaban agotados. ▲ aún *The clothes were dirty even after they were washed.* La ropa estaba sucia, aún después de lavada. ▲ siquiera *He couldn't even feed himself.* Ni siquiera podía alimentarse por sí mismo. ▲ todavía *He can do even better if he tries.* Lo puedo hacer mejor todavía si quiere.
● [v] igualar *Please even the sleeves of this coat.* Haga el favor de igualar las mangas de este abrigo.
○ even if aun cuando *Even if we went at full sped it would take an hour to get there.* Aun cuando vayamos a toda velocidad tardaríamos una hora en llegar. ○ even so no obstante *Even so I don't agree with you.* No obstante, no estoy de acuerdo con Ud. ○ even though aunque *Even though I don't like this work I must do it.* Aunque no me gusta este trabajo, tengo que hacerlo. ○ even with al nivel de *The snow was even with the window.* La nieve llegaba al nivel de la ventana. ○ to break even cubrir los gastos. ○ to get even vengarse *I'll get even with you.* Me vengaré de Ud. ‖ *After gambling all night I broke even.* Después de jugar toda la noche no gané ni perdí.

evening tarde (*before sunset*); noche (*after sunset*) *We'll see you this evening.* Le veremos esta tarde. ▲ noche *We had a nice evening.* Pasamos una buena noche. ‖ *Good evening!* ¡Buenas tardes! (*before sunset*) ¡Buenas noches! (*after sunset*)

event acontecimiento *I always try to keep up with current events.* Trato siempre de estar informado sobre los acontecimientos del día. ▲ suceso *In this town the arrival of a foreigner is an event.* En este pueblo la llegada de un extranjero es un suceso. ▲ competición

(*sports*) *What's the next event?* ¿Cuál es la próxima competición?
○ course of events curso de los acontecimientos *A thing like this couldn't happen in the normal course of events.* Una cosa como ésta no podía ocurrir en el curso normal de los acontecimientos. ○ in any event en todo caso *I'll be there in any event.* En todo caso estaré allí. ○ in the event of en caso de *In the event of an accident, please notify my father.* En caso de accidente, por favor, notifíquese a mi padre.

eventually eventualmente.

ever alguna vez *Have you ever seen him?* ¿Le ha visto Ud. alguna vez? ▲ nunca *I like this more than ever.* Me gusta esto más que nunca.
○ ever since desde que *I've been taking it easy ever since she left.* Lo he estado tomando todo con calma, desde que ella se fué. ○ for ever and ever por siempre jamás. ‖ *Why did I ever get into this?* ¿Por qué diablos me metí en esto?

every cada *Every time I see him he's busy.* Cada vez que le veo está ocupado.
○ every day todos los días *I see my cousins every day.* Veo a mis primos todos los días. ○ every now and then, every once in a while de vez en cuando *He takes a drink every now and then.* Se toma un trago de vez en cuando. ○ every other ... un ... sí y otro no *They have movies here every other day.* Aquí dan películas un día sí y otro no.

everybody todo el mundo.

everyone todos.

everything todo.

everywhere en todas partes.

evidence evidencia, testimonio *He was convicted on false evidence.* Fué condenado por falso testimonio. ▲ señal, muestra *She gave no evidence of liking me.* Ella no dió muestras de que yo le gustara.

evident evidente.

evil [n] mal *He doesn't know the difference between good and evil.* No sabe la diferencia entre el bien y el mal.
● [adj] malo *He's an evil man.* Es un hombre malo.
○ evils malas consecuencias *He lectured us on the evils of drink.* Nos habló sobre las malas consecuencias de beber.

evil-minded ‖ *She's evil-minded.* Ella tiene mucha malicia.

evolution evolución.

exact exacto.

exactly exactamente.

exaggerate exagerar.

exam examen.

examination examen *How did you make out in your examination?* ¿Como salió Ud. de sus exámenes?—*I've made a careful examination of the situation.* He hecho un examen cuidadoso de la situación.

○ **physical examination** reconocimiento médico *You ought to have a thorough physical examination.* Le debe rían hacer un reconocimiento médico completo.

examine examinar *Let me examine your passport.* Déjeme examinar su pasaporte. ▲ reconocer *Has the doctor examined you yet?* ¿Le ha reconocido ya el médico? ▲ interrogar *When examined in court, he denied everything.* Cuando le interrogaron en el Juzgado lo negó todo.

example ejemplo *Is this a good example of his work?* ¿Es éste un buen ejemplo de su trabajo?—*You ought to set an example for the others.* Debería Ud. dar un ejemplo a los demás. ▲ problema *What's the answer to the third example?* ¿Cuál es la conestación al tercer problema?

○ **for example** por ejemplo *Consider this case, for example.* Considere Ud. este caso, por ejemplo.

‖ *He must be made an example of.* Hay que castigarle para que sirva de ejemplo.

exceed excederse *He exceeded the speed limit.* Se excedió en la velocidad reglamentaria.

exceeding extraordinario *She's a woman of exceeding beauty.* Es una mujer de belleza extraordinaria.

exceedingly sumamente *Your handwriting is exceedingly good.* Su letra es sumamente buena.

excel sobresalir.

excellent excelente.

except excepto *There are no rooms available except on the top floor.* No hay cuartos disponibles excepto en el último piso.

○ **except for** si no fuera por, si no fuera porque *I would have been here sooner except for the fact that I had to walk.* Hubiera llegado antes si no fuera porque tuve que venir andando.

exception excepción.

excess [n] sobrante, lo que sobra *Pour off the excess.* Vierta Ud. lo que sobra. ● [adj] exceso de *Can we take any excess baggage on the plane?* ¿Pode-

mos llevar algún exceso de equipaje en el avion?

○ **to be in excess of** exceder a *The supply of cars was never in excess of the demand.* La oferta de automóviles nunca excedió a la demanda. ○ **to excess** con exceso *You'll get sick if you continue to drink to excess.* Se pondrá Ud. enfermo si sigue tomando con exceso.

excessive excesivo.

exchange [n] cambio *The fight began with a rapid exchange of blows.* La pelea se inició con un cambio rápido de golpes.

● [v] cambiar *I'd like to exchange this book for another one.* Quisiera cambiar este libro por otro. ▲ canjear *Prisoners of war may be exchanged within a year.* Los prisioneros de guerra se podrán canjear dentro de un año.

○ **in exchange for** a cambio de. ○ **rate of exchange** tipo de cambio.

excite excitar, agitar *Don't get excited.* No se excite Ud. ▲ excitar, animar *The kids were excited about the circus.* Los (chicos) pequeños estaban muy excitados a causa del circo. ▲ provocar *The book excited much popular interest.* El libro provocó mucha curiosidad en el público.

○ **exciting** emocionante, interesante *I think that's an exciting story.* Creo que ese cuento es emocionante.

excitement excitación, agitación *What's all the excitement about?* ¿A qué se debe tanta excitación?

exclaim exclamar.

exclamation exclamación.

exclude excluir.

exclusive selecto *This is a very exclusive club.* Este es un club selecto.

○ **exclusive of** aparte de, además de *He makes ten dollars a day exclusive of commissions.* El gana diez pesos diarios aparte de sus comisiones. ○ **exclusive rights** exclusiva *We have exclusive rights to his invention.* Tenemos la exclusiva de su invención.

excursion excursión.

excuse [n] razón *What's your excuse for being late?* ¿Qué razón da Ud. por llegar tarde?

excuse [v] perdonar *Excuse me.* Perdóneme. ▲ dispensar *You'll have to excuse the way the house looks.* Dispense Ud. la apariencia de casa. ▲ disculpar *Please excuse my bad pronunciation, I'm just learning the language.* Por favor disculpe Ud. mi mala pronunciación, apenas he empezado a aprender el idioma.—*He was excused from work yesterday because he was sick.* Le disculparon del trabajo ayer porque estuvo enfermo.

‖ *You may be excused now.* Puede Ud. salir ahora.

execute cumplir *He refused to execute the orders.* Se negó a cumplir las órdenes. ▲ ejecutar *The symphony was magnificently executed.* La sinfonía fué ejecutada magníficamente.—*The murderer was executed this morning.* El asesino fué ejecutado esta mañana. ▲ ejecutar, hacer *He's the artist who executed the sculptures in this park.* Es el artista que hizo las esculturas en este parque. ▲ cumplir, ejecutar *The will was never executed.* El testamento nunca fué cumplido.

execution ejecución.

executive ejecutivo *I think the executive branch of the government is exceeding its powers.* Creo que el poder ejecutivo se está tomando demasiadas atribuciones. ▲ directivo *I'm interested only in getting an executive job.* Solo me interesa un puesto directivo.

O **executive board** consejo de administración, junta directiva *The matter is coming up before the executive board tomorrow.* El asunto será sometido mañana al consejo de administración.

exempt [*adj*] exento *The best students are exempt from the examination.* Los mejores estudiantes están exentos del examen.

● [*v*] exentar, eximir *Those with small incomes were exempted from paying the tax.* Los que tenían pequeños ingresos quedaron exentos de pagar el impuesto.

exercise [*n*] ejercicio *Each exercise should be performed fifty times.* Cada ejercicio debería hacerse cincuenta veces.—*I like to take exercise at least three times a week.* Me gusta hacer ejercicio por lo menos tres veces por semana.—*Do all the exercises at the end of the lesson.* Haga Ud. todos los ejercicios al final de la lección.

● [*v*] hacer ejercicio *We exercised the horses twice a day.* Hacíamos hacer ejercicios a los caballos dos veces al día. ▲ emplear *He has exercised a great deal of ingenuity in this matter.* Ha empleado mucho ingenio en este asunto.

O **exercises** ceremonia *When are they going to hold the graduation exercises?*

¿Cuándo van a celebrar la ceremonia de graduación?

exert usar *He exerted influence to get his job.* Usó su influencia para obtener el empleo. ▲ hacer *He exerted pressure on the edge of the box.* Hizo presión sobre el borde de la caja.

O **to exert oneself** esforzarse *You'll have to exert yourself to finish in time.* Tendrá Ud. que esforzarse para terminar a tiempo.

exhaust agotar *I've exhausted my funds.* He agotado mis fondos.—*His lectures on modern poetry exhausted the subject.* Sus discursos (*or* conferencias) sobre poesía moderna agotaron el tema.

O **exhausted** exhausto, agotado *I'm exhausted after that long trip.* Estoy exhausto después de aquel largo viaje.

O **exhaust pipe** tubo de escape *I'll have to get a new exhaust pipe for the car.* Tendré que conseguir un nuevo tubo de escape para el automóvil.

exhaustion agotamiento.

exhibit [*n*] exposición *Is the art exhibit open to the public yet?* ¿Está ya abierta al público la exposición de arte?

● [*v*] exhibir *His wife loves to exhibit her jewelry.* A su esposa le encanta exhibir sus joyas.

exhibition exhibición *They put on a very interesting exhibition.* Hicieron una exhibición muy interesante. ▲ exposición *He had an exhibition of his paintings at the art gallery last month.* Hizo una exposición de sus cuadros en la galería de arte el mes pasado.

exile [*n*] destierro, exilio. ▲ exilado, desterrado (*person*).

● [*v*] exilar, desterrar.

exist existir *I doubt if such a person exists.* Dudo que exista tal persona.

‖ *How does he manage to exist on what he makes?* ¿Cómo se las arregla para vivir con lo que gana?

existence existencia.

exit salida *Where's the exit?* ¿Dónde está la salida? ▲ mutis *The heroine made a very awkward exit.* La heroína hizo un mutis muy deslucido.

‖ *I tried to make an inconspicuous exit from the party.* Traté de escabullirme de la fiesta.

expand dilatar, dilatarse *Iron expands with heat.* El hierro dilata con el calor. ▲ agrandar, ensanchar, extender *This business has greatly expanded.* Este negocio se ha ensanchado mucho.

expansion expansión.

expect esperar *I never expected to see him again.* Nunca esperaba volver a

verlo.—*I'll expect you at 6 o'clock.* Le espero (*or* esperaré) a las seis. ▲ contar con *You can't expect good weather here at this time of year.* Aquí no se puede contar con buen tiempo en esta época del año. ▲ suponer *I expect you had a hard time finding the house.* Supongo que le ha sido difícil encontrar la casa.
expectant expectante.
expectation expectativa.
expedient [*n*] expediente.
 ● [*adj*] oportuno.
expedition expedición.
expel expulsar.
expenditure gasto.
expense gasto *I'd like to do it but I can't afford the expense.* Me gustaría hacerlo pero no puedo permitirme los gastos. —*He gets a straight salary and expenses in this job.* En este trabajo gana un sueldo fijo con sus gastos pagados.
 O **at one's expense** a costa de uno, a propia costa *He built the whole thing at his own expense.* Construyó todo a su propia costa. ▲ a costa de uno *We had a good laugh at his expense.* Reímos mucho a su costa. O **expense account** cuenta de gastos. O **to go to expense** meterse en gastos *I don't want to go to much expense for this party.* No quiero meterme en muchos gastos en esta fiesta.
expensive caro.
experience [*n*] experiencia *I've learned by experience that this is the best way.* He aprendido por experiencia que éste es el mejor camino a seguir.—*What experience do you have?* ¿Qué experiencia tiene Ud.?
 ● [*v*] pasar por, sufrir *We may experience some difficulties.* Puede que pasemos por algunas dificultades.
experiment [*n*] experimento.
 ● [*v*] experimentar.
expert [*n*] experto *The experts decided the document was a forgery.* Los expertos dictaminaron que el documento era una falsificación.
 ● [*adj*] experto *We need an expert mechanic for this job.* Necesitamos un mecánico experto para este trabajo.
expire expirar.
explain explicar *Could you explain how this machine works?* ¿Puede Ud. explicar como funciona esta máquina? ▲ justificar *I can explain everything.* Lo puedo justificar todo.
explanation explicación.
explicit explícito.

explode volar, hacer explosión.
exploit [*n*] hazaña.
 ● [*v*] explotar.
exploration exploración.
explore explorar.
explorer explorador.
explosion explosión.
explosive explosivo.
export [*n*] exportación *What are the chief exports of your country?* ¿Cuáles son las exportaciones más importantes de su país?—*The export of cotton is highly profitable.* La exportación del algodón da mucho rendimiento.
export [*v*] exportar *We haven't been able to export any spices for several years.* Desde hace varios años no hemos podido exportar ninguna especia.
expose exponer *His lack of discretion exposed him to ridicule.* Su falta de discreción le expuso al ridículo. ▲ revelar *The newspaper exposed his illegal income.* El periódico reveló la fuente ilícita de sus ingresos.
exposé revelación comprometedora.
exposition exposición, exhibición.
exposure exposición *How long an exposure do you think this film should have?* ¿Cuánta exposición cree Ud. que se le debe dar a esta película?—*Try to avoid exposure to the cold.* Procure Ud. evitar la exposición al frío. ▲ fotografía *I have three exposures of the same view.* Tengo tres fotografías de la misma vista.
 ‖ *I'd like a room with a southern exposure.* Deseo un cuarto que dé al sur.
express [*v*] expresar *I want you to feel free to express your opinion.* Quiero que se sienta Ud. con libertad para expresar su opinión.
 O **express train** tren expreso *Is the next train an express?* ¿Es expreso el próximo tren? O **to express oneself** expresarse *I have difficulty in expressing myself in Spanish.* Me es difícil expresarme en español.
expression expresión *That sounds like an old-fashioned expression.* Esa parece una expresión anticuada.—*I can tell what you're thinking by the expression on your face.* Puede decir lo que está Ud. pensando por la expresión de su cara.—*He plays the piano without much expression.* Toca el piano sin mucha expresión. ▲ muestra, expresión *I give you this book as a small expression of my gratitude.* Le doy este libro como una pequeña muestra de mi gratitud.
expressive expresivo.

exquisite exquisito.
extend extender *This estate extends for miles on all sides.* Esta propiedad se extiende en muchas millas a la redonda. ▲ prorrogar *Can you extend this visa?* ¿Puede Ud. prorrogar este visado? ▲ prolongar *They plan to extend the railroad to the border next year.* El año que viene proyectan prolongar el ferrocarril hasta la frontera. ▲ expresar *We extend to you our heartiest congratulations.* Le expresamos nuestras más cordiales felicitaciones.
extension prolongación *The new extension was opened to traffic today.* La nueva prolongación fué abierta al tráfico hoy. ▲ extensión *Please connect me with extension seven.* Comuníqueme con la extensión número siete.
   O **extension cord** extensión *We need an extension cord so we can put the lamp over in the corner.* Necesitamos una extensión para poner la lámpara en el rincón.
extensive extensivo.
extent extensión *He owns a vast extent of land in this area.* Es propietario de una vasta extensión de tierras en esta zona.
   O **to a certain extent** hasta cierto punto.
   ‖ *What's the extent of his holdings in the company?* ¿Cuántas acciones tiene en la compañía?
exterior [adj; n] exterior.
external externo.
extinguish extinguir, apagar.
extra [n] comparsa *He worked for years as an extra before he got his first part.* Trabajó durante años como comparsa antes de conseguir su primer papel. ▲ extra *The newspaper published an extra because of the late war news.* El periódico publicó un extra a causa de las últimas noticias de la guerra.
   ● [adj] de más, adicional *Do you have an extra pencil you could lend me?* ¿Tiene Ud. algún lápiz de más que pueda prestarme?
   O **extra expenses** gastos extraordinarios. O **extra pay** sobrepaga, paga extraordinaria.

extract [n] éxtracto.
extract [v] extraer.
extraction extracción.
extraordinary extraordinario.
extravagant extravagante.
extreme extremo *Such action is only necessary in extreme cases.* Tal acción es necesaria solamente en casos extremos. ▲ extremado *He was reduced to extreme poverty.* Quedó reducido a una pobreza extremada.
   O **to go from one extreme to another** ir de un extremo a otro *He's always going from one extreme to another.* Siempre va de un extremo a otro. O **to go to extremes** tomar medidas extremas, exagerar *Let's not go to extremes.* No exageremos.
   ‖ *We never have any extremes in temperature.* Nunca tenemos temperaturas extremas.
extremely sumamente.
eye ojo *I have something in my eye.* Tengo algo en el ojo.
   O **black eye** ojo amoratado *Have you anything good for a black eye?* ¿Tiene Ud. algo que sirva para un ojo amoratado? O **hook and eye** corchetes *This coat fastens at the top with a hook and eye.* Este abrigo se abrocha en el cuello con corchetes. O **to catch one's eye** llamar la atención a uno *I've been trying to catch your eye for the last half hour.* He estado tratando de llamarle la atención hace ya media hora. O **to keep an eye on** vigilar *Be sure to keep an eye on the children.* No dejes de vigilar a los niños. O **to see eye to eye** estar completamente de acuerdo *I don't see eye to eye with you on this question.* No estoy completamente de acuerdo con Ud. en este asunto.
   ‖ *I never set eyes on her before in my life.* Es la primera vez que la veo en mi vida.
eyebrow ceja.
eyeglasses lentes, gafas.
eyelash pestaña.
eyelid párpado.
eyesight vista.

F

fabric tela.
face [n] cara *When he gets angry he turns red in the face.* Cuando se enfada se le pone roja la cara.

   ● [v] dar a *Our room faces the street.* Nuestro cuarto da a la calle. ▲ ponerse de cara a *Face the wall.* Ponte de cara a la pared. ▲ hacer frente a *Why don't you face the situation like a man?* ¿Por qué no hace Ud. frente a la situación como un hombre? ○ **at face value** al pie de la letra *Don't take this news at its face value.* No tome Ud. esta noticia al pie de la letra. ○ **face down** boca abajo *Put your cards on the table face down.* Ponga Ud. sus cartas en la mesa boca abajo. ○ **face to face** cara a cara *One day I met him face to face.* Un día me lo encontré cara a cara. ○ **face value** valor nominal *The bill's still worth its face value.* El billete conserva todavía su valor nominal. ○ **on the face of it** obviamente, evidentemente *The idea's absurd on the face of it.* Evidentemente la idea es absurda. ○ **to make faces** hacer muecas *Stop making faces at me.* Deja de hacerme muecas. ○ **to one's face** en la cara de uno, en presencia de uno *I'd call him that right to his face.* Se lo llamaría en su cara. ○ **to show one's face** asomar la cara *I'm ashamed, I won't dare show my face.* Estoy tan avergonzado, que no me atrevo a asomar la cara. ○ **with a long face** cariacontecido *Ever since she lost her job she's been going around with a long face.* Desde que perdió su puesto, anda cariacontecida.

facial [*n*] masaje facial *I made an appointment for a facial.* Pedí hora para un masaje facial. ● [*adj*] de la cara, facial *Watch his facial expression when you tell him the news.* Fíjese en la expresión de su cara cuando le dé la noticia.

facility facilidad *He speaks with such facility!* ¡Habla con tanta facilidad! ▲ medio *What facilities do you have here for recreation?* ¿Qué medios tienen Uds. aquí para divertirse?

fact hecho verídico *Is it a fact or is it just your opinion?* ¿Es un hecho verídico o es sólo su opinión? ○ **as a matter of fact** en realidad *As a matter of fact I couldn't go if I wanted to.* En realidad no podría ir aunque quisiera. ○ **facts of life** cosas de la vida *It's time he learned the facts of life.* Es hora de que conozca las cosas de la vida.

faction facción.

factor elemento, factor.

factory fábrica.

faculty facultad *He doesn't seem to have all his faculties.* Parece que no tiene todas sus facultades.—*I'm having lunch with two members of the faculty.* Voy a almorzar con dos miembros de

la facultad.—*He got his degree in the faculty of law.* Se licenció en la facultad de derecho.

fad moda.

fade desteñir(se) *My stockings faded in the wash.* Se han desteñido mis medias al lavarlas. ▲ desvanecerse, debilitarse *As we got further away, the sound of the music faded.* A medida que nos alejábamos se iba desvaneciendo el sonido de la música. ▲ marchitar(se) *These roses faded so quickly!* ¡Estas rosas se marchitaron tan pronto! ○ **to fade away** desvanecerse *The image faded away.* La imagen se desvaneció.

fail malograrse *The crops failed last year.* La cosecha se malogró el año pasado. ▲ no poder *I failed to find the book I was looking for.* No pude encontrar el libro que buscaba. ▲ decaer *The patient's failing rapidly.* El enfermo está decayendo rápidamente. ▲ quebrar *It'll be terrible if the business fails.* Será terrible si el negocio quiebra. ▲ ser suspendido *Five students in the class failed.* Han sido suspendidos cinco alumnos de la clase. ▲ fallar *I won't fail you.* No le fallaré a Ud. ▲ cortarse, interrumpirse *The electricity failed.* Se cortó la electricidad. ○ **without fail** sin falta *Be there without fail.* Esté allí sin falta.

failure fracaso *As a director he was a complete failure.* Como director ha sido un completo fracaso.—*He was very much upset by his failure in the examination.* Estaba muy disgustado por su fracaso en los exámenes. ▲ falta *It was because of his failures that he was dismissed.* Fué por sus faltas que lo han despedido. ▲ interrupción *The failure of telephone service affected everybody.* La interrupción del servicio telefónico afectó a todo el mundo. ▲ quiebra *We lost all our money in the bank failure.* Perdimos todo el dinero en la quiebra de banco. ○ **heart failure** ataque al corazón *He died of heart failure.* Murió de un ataque al corazón. ‖ *His failure to come on time lost him his job.* Perdió su empleo por no llegar puntualmente.

faint [*adj*] vago *I have a faint idea of what you want.* Tengo una idea vaga de lo que Ud. quiere. ▲ pálido *The color's too faint.* El color es demasiado pálido. ▲ desfallecido *I feel faint.* Me siento desfallecido.

● [v] desmayarse *Someone fainted.* Alguien se desmayó.

fair [n] feria *The fair opens next Monday.* La feria se abre el lunes próximo.

fair [adj] justo *They were always fair to me.* Siempre fueron justos conmigo. —*That's fair enough.* Eso es (muy) justo. ▲ razonable, bueno *He offered us a fair price.* Nos ofreció un precio razonable. ▲ bueno *Give me a fair amount of it.* Déme una buena cantidad. ▲ ni bien ni mal, regular *The works only fair.* El trabajo no está ni bien ni mal. ▲ rubio *She has blue eyes and fair hair.* Tiene los ojos azules y el pelo rubio. ▲ claro, bueno *Is the weather fair?* ¿Hace buen tiempo? ▲ limpio *Was that play fair or foul?* ¿Fué la jugada limpia o sucia? ○ **fair** sex bello sexo.

fairy hada.

faith confianza *I've lost faith in you.* He perdido la confianza en Ud. ▲ religión *I don't know what his faith is.* No sé cuál es su religión. ○ **in good faith** de buena fe *We acted in good faith.* Obramos de buena fe.

faithful fiel, leal.

fake [n] estafa *That deal was a fake.* Ese asunto resultó una estafa. ● [v] fingir *He faked experience when he asked for a job.* Cuando pidió empleo fingió tener experiencia.

fall [n] descenso *There was a sudden fall in the temperature last night.* Anoche hubo un descenso repentino de temperatura. ▲ cascada *There are a lot of falls on this river.* Hay muchas cascadas en este río. ▲ caída *She had a fall last winter.* Tuvo una caída el invierno pasado. ▲ caída, toma *They still celebrate the anniversary of the fall of the city.* Aún se celebra el aniversario de la caída de la ciudad. ▲ otoño *I'll be back next fall.* Volveré el otoño que viene. ● [adj] otoñal *I love fall colors.* Me gustan los colores otoñales. ● [v] caer *Did you hear something fall?* ¿Oyó Ud. caer algo?—*This letter would cause trouble if it fell into the wrong hands.* Esta carta causaría mucho daño si cayera en las manos que no debe.—*The sunlight fell directly on his book.* La luz del sol caía directamente sobre su libro.—*The holiday falls on Monday this year.* Este año la fiesta cae en lunes. ▲ caerse *I slipped on the ice and fell.* Me resbalé en el hielo y me caí. ▲ bajar *The curtain's already fallen.* Ya ha bajado el telón.—*It's*

dangerous to cross the bridge unless the river falls.* Es peligroso cruzar el puente si no baja el río.—*His voice fell when he mentioned her name.* Bajó la voz al mencionar su nombre.—*Her eyes fell.* Bajó los ojos. ▲ pasar *His property falls to his wife.* Sus propiedades pasan a su mujer. ○ **fallen** caído *He tripped over a fallen branch.* Tropezó con una rama caída. ○ **fallen arches** pies planos *He wears special shoes because he has fallen arches.* Lleva calzado especial porque tiene los pies planos. ○ **to fall asleep** dormirse *Did you fall asleep?* ¿Se durmió Ud.? ○ **to fall back** retroceder *The enemy fell back ten miles.* El enemigo retrocedió diez millas. ○ **to fall back on** recurrir a *We can always fall back on our savings.* Siempre podemos recurrir a nuestros ahorros. ○ **to fall behind** atrasarse *Don't fall behind in your payments.* No se atrase Ud. en sus pagos. ○ **to fall down** fracasar *Can you be sure he won't fall down on the job?* ¿Tiene Ud. la seguridad de que no fracasará en el trabajo? ○ **to fall for** prenderse de *He fell hard for her.* Se prendió de ella locamente. ○ **to fall in love** enamorarse *They fell in love with each other at first sight.* Se enamoraron desde el primer momento en que se vieron. ○ **to fall off** disminuir *His income's been falling off lately.* Sus ingresos han disminuido últimamente. ▲ caerse *The cover fell off the coffee pot.* Se cayó la tapa de la cafetera. ○ **to fall through** fracasar *The plans for the picnic fell through.* Los planes para la jira fracasaron. ○ **to fall to pieces** caerse a pedazos *This typewriter's ready to fall to pieces.* Esta máquina está que se cae a pedazos. ‖ *His story sounded convincing, so I fell for it.* Su relato parecía convincente y por eso le creí. ‖ *The dinner fell short of our expectations.* Creíamos que la comida sería mejor de lo que resultó. ‖ *Where does the accent fall on this word?* ¿Dónde lleva el acento esta palabra?

false falso *Is this true or false?* ¿Es esto verdadero o falso?—*The tenor hit a false note.* El tenor dió una nota falsa. ○ **false teeth** dentadura postiza. ○ **under false pretenses** con engaño *She got the job under false pretenses.* Consiguió el puesto con engaño.

falsify falsificar.

falter vacilar.

fame fama.

familiar conocido, familiar *It's good to see a familiar face.* Es agradable ver una cara conocida.

○ **to be familiar with** estar familiarizado con *I'm not familiar with your customs.* No estoy familiarizado con las costumbres de Uds. ‖ *If you aren't careful with him he's likely to get familiar.* Si no tiene Ud. cuidado se tomará demasiadas confianzas.

familiarity familiaridad.

family familia *She has to work to support her family.* Tiene que trabajar para mantener a su familia. ● [adj] de familia *That temper of his is a family trait.* Su mal genio es cosa de familia. *or* Su mal genio le viene de familia.

famine hambre.

famous famoso.

fan [n] abanico *She has a lovely Chinese fan.* Tiene un precioso abanico chino. ▲ ventilador *Turn on the fan.* Ponga el ventilador. ▲ aficionado *She's an enthusiastic baseball fan.* Es una aficionada entusiasta del beisbol. ● [v] abanicar *She sat in the rocker and fanned herself.* Se sentó en la mecedora y se abanicó. ▲ soplar *He fanned the embers into a blaze.* Sopló el rescoldo para hacer que llameara.

○ **to fan out** salir *The roads fanned out from the town in all directions.* Los caminos salían del pueblo en todas direcciones. ‖ *The incident fanned the flame of their resentment.* El incidente intensificó su resentimiento.

fanatic fanático.

fan belt correa de ventilador.

fancy [n] fantasía *That whole story's just a fancy.* Toda esa historia no es más que fantasía. ▲ imaginación *It's all your fancy.* Todo es obra de su imaginación. ● [adj] fino, muy bueno *He sent me a basket of fancy fruit for my birthday.* Me envió una cesta de frutas finas para mi cumpleaños. ▲ elegante, de vestir *That dress is too fancy to wear to work.* Ese traje es demasiado elegante para llevarlo al trabajo.

○ **to take a fancy** coger cariño *He's taken quite a fancy to her.* Le ha cogido mucho cariño. ‖ *Fancy meeting you here!* ¡Qué milagro encontrarme aquí con Ud.!

fantastic fantástico.

far lejos *Don't go far.* No vaya Ud. lejos.

—*The store's not far from our house.* La tienda no está lejos de nuestra casa. —*This joke's gone far enough.* Esta broma ha ido demasiado lejos. ▲ muy *You're not far wrong.* No está Ud. muy equivocado. *or* No está Ud. muy lejos de la verdad.

○ **as far as** hasta *We walked together as far as the gate.* Caminamos juntos hasta la entrada. ▲ tan lejos como *We went as far as we could.* Fuimos tan lejos como pudimos. ○ **as far as I know** que yo sepa *As far as I know, he'll arrive this afternoon.* Que yo sepa, llegará esta tarde. ○ **as far as I'm concerned** por lo que a mí toca, en lo que a mí respecta. ○ **by far** con mucho, con una gran diferencia *He's by far the best writer in this country.* Es con mucho el mejor escritor de este país. ○ **far away** muy lejos *Is it far away?* ¿Está muy lejos? ○ **Far East** Lejano Oriente *Have you ever been in the Far East?* ¿Ha estado Ud. alguna vez en el Lejano Oriente? ○ **far into the night** hasta las altas horas de la noche. ○ **far more** mucho más *This is far more important than you realize.* Esto es mucho más importante de lo que Ud. cree. ○ **how far?** ¿a qué distancia? *How far are the mountains from here?* ¿A qué distancia de aquí están las montañas?—*How far off is it?* ¿A qué distancia está? ○ **on the far side of** *His house is on the far side of the woods.* Su casa queda del otro lado del bosque. ○ **so far** hasta ahora *So far you've been pretty lucky.* Hasta ahora ha tenido Ud. bastante suerte. ○ **to be far from** estar muy lejos de *Far be it from me to say such a thing.* Está muy lejos de mí el decir semejante cosa. ‖ *Far from it.* Muy al contrario.

fare precio de billete *What's the fare?* ¿Cuál es el precio del billete? ‖ *I didn't fare very well on my last job.* No me fué muy bien en mi último empleo.

farewell [n] dispedida.

farm [n] finca, granja, [Am] hacienda. ● [v] cultivar, labrar.

farmer labrador, agricultor, granjero.

farmhouse granja.

farther más (lejos) *Move the chair a little farther from the fire.* Aparta Ud. la silla un poco más del fuego. ▲ más *How much farther do we have to go?* ¿Cuánto más tenemos que andar?—*The post office is farther down.* El correo está más allá.

○ **farther than** más lejos que *Your house is farther away than mine.* Su casa está más lejos que la mía.

farthest más lejos *They wanted to see who could throw the farthest.* Querían ver quién podía tirar más lejos. ▲ **a** más distancia *Which one of those mountains is the farthest away?* ¿Cuál de esas montañas queda a más distancia? ▲ más lejano *It's the farthest thing from my mind.* Es la cosa más lejana a mi pensamiento.

fascinate fascinar.

fascist fascista.

fashion moda *She dresses in the latest fashion.* Se viste a la última moda.
○ **after a fashion** un poco *Yes, I play tennis after a fashion.* Si, juego al tenis un poco. ○ **to go out of fashion** pasarse de moda *Long hair's gone out of fashion.* Se ha pasado de moda el pelo largo.

fashionable de moda.

fast [*n*] ayuno *He broke his fast.* Rompió el ayuno.
● [*adj*] rápido *If you take a fast train, you'll get there in two hours.* Si toma Ud. un tren rápido llegará allí en dos horas. ▲ adelantado *My watch is ten minutes fast.* Mi reloj está adelantado diez minutos. ▲ alocado *He travels in fast company.* Anda con un grupo muy alocado. ▲ muy bueno, invariable *They're fast friends.* Son muy buenos amigos. ▲ inflexible *There are no hard and fast rules here.* Aquí no hay reglas rígidas e inflexibles. ▲ fijo, firme *Are these colors fast?* ¿Son estos colores fijos?
● [*adv*] ligero, de prisa *Don't talk so fast, please.* No hable tan de prisa, por favor. ▲ profundamente *I was fast asleep.* Estaba profundamente dormido.
● [*v*] ayunar *Yes, I'm fasting.* Sí, estoy ayunando.
○ **to make fast** amarrar *Make the boat fast to the dock.* Amarre el barco al muelle.
‖ *Give me a cup of coffee and make it fast.* Dáme una taza de café, pronto.

fat [*n*] gordo *There's too much fat on this meat.* Esta carne tiene demasiado gordo. ▲ manteca *What's the best fat for frying?* ¿Cuál es la mejor manteca para freír?
● [*adj*] grasiento *That meat's too fat.* Esa carne es demasiado grasienta. ▲ grueso, gordo *I'm getting too fat.* Me estoy poniendo demasiado grueso. *or* Estoy engordando demasiado.

fatal fatal, mortal.

fate fortuna, suerte.

father padre *How's your father?* ¿Como está su padre?—*We just had a visit from Father Martin.* Acaba de visitarnos el Padre Martín.
‖ *Are your father and mother coming to the party?* ¿Vienen sus padres a la fiesta?

father-in-law suegro.

fatigue [*n*] fatiga.

faucet llave, grifo.

fault culpa *Whose fault was it?* ¿Quién tuvo la culpa?   ▲ defecto, falta *His worst fault is that he talks too much.* Su mayor defecto es que habla demasiado.
○ **to find fault** encontrar defectos *You're always finding fault.* Siempre está Ud. encontrando defectos.

favor [*n*]favor *I want to ask you a favor.* Quiero pedirle un favor.
● [*v*] preferir *Which side do you favor?* ¿Qué partido prefiere Ud.? ▲ parecerse a *The little boy favors his father's side of the family.* El pequeño se parece a la familia de su padre.
○ **to be in favor of** ser partidario de *I'm in favor of immediate action.* Soy partidario de la acción inmediata.
‖ *That's a point in your favor.* Es un tanto a su favor.

favorable favorable.

favorite [*n*] preferido, favorito *The boy's his father's favorite.* El preferido de su padre es el varón.
● [*adj*] preferido *Who's your favorite actress?* ¿Quién es su actríz preferida?

fear [*n*] temor, miedo *He doesn't know the meaning of fear.* No sabe lo que es miedo. ▲ peligro *There's no fear of anything like that happening.* No hay peligro de que pase nada de eso.
● [*v*] temer *You have nothing to fear.* No tiene Ud. nada que temer.
○ **for fear of, for fear that** por el temor de, por temor a que *I hurried home for fear I'd be late for dinner.* Corrí a casa por el temor de llegar tarde a comer.

fearful terrible *There was a fearful storm.* Hubo una tormenta terrible. ▲ miedoso, tímido *The child was very fearful of everyone.* El niño era muy tímido con todo el mundo.

feast [*n*] banquete.
● [*v*] deleitarse.

feat hecho, hazaña.

feather pluma.

feature [*n*] facción *He isn't handsome but he has pleasant features.* No es

guapo pero tiene facciones agradables.
● [v] exhibir *They're featuring spring
styles very early this year.* Este año
están exhibiendo los modelos de primavera muy pronto.
○ **main feature** lo más sobresaliente
This is the main feature in the exhibit.
Esto es lo más sobresaliente de la exposición. ▲ película principal *What
time does the main feature go on?* ¿A
qué hora empieza la película principal?
February febrero.
federal federal.
federation confederación, federación.
fee honorario; cuota (*in clubs*).
feeble débil.
feed [n] pienso *Did you buy the feed for
the horses?* ¿Ha comprado el pienso
para los caballos?
● [v] dar de comer *That child refused
to let anyone feed her.* Esa niña no
consintió que nadie le diera de comer.
—*They fed us well at the hotel.* Nos
dieron bien de comer en el hotel. ▲ alimentar *Resentment fed his anger.* El
resentimiento alimentaba su cólera.
○ **fed up** harto *I'm fed up with this
whole business.* Estoy harto de todo
este asunto.
feel [n] sensación *I don't like the feel of
woolen shirts.* No me agrada la sensación que dan las camisas de lana.
● [v] sentir *He felt a tap on the
shoulder.* Sintió que le tocaban en el
hombro. ▲ tocar *Feel this cloth.* Toque
Ud. esta tela. ▲ tomar, sentir *Are you
going to feel my pulse?* ¿Va Ud. a
tomarme el pulso? ▲ sentir *You know
how it feels to lose an old friend.* Ud.
sabe lo que se siente al perder un viejo
amigo.—*I feel a pain here.* Siento un
dolor aquí.—*I never feel the cold.* No
siento el frío. ▲ sentirse *I feel pretty
well.* Me siento bastante bien. ▲ estar
I feel certain of that. Estoy seguro de
eso. ▲ sufrir *The city didn't feel the
hardships of the war.* La ciudad no
sufrió las penalidades de la guerra.
▲ creer *How do you feel about this?*
¿Qué cree Ud. de esto?
○ **it feels like** parece que *It feels like
it's going to be a nice day today.*
Parece que va a hacer hoy un buen
día. ○ **to feel like** tener ganas de *Do
you feel like taking a walk?* ¿Tiene
Ud. ganas de dar un paseo? ○ **to feel
out** averiguar *Let's feel out the situation before we do anything more.*
Averigüemos la situación antes de
hacer nada más ○ **to feel up to** sentirse con ánimo para *I don't feel up to*

playing tennis right now. Ahora no
me siento con ánimo para jugar al
tenis. ○ **to feel the need of** sentir la
necesidad de *I feel the need of a good
stiff drink.* Siento la necesidad de una
bebida fuerte. ○ **to get the feel of**
coger el tino, coger el truco, coger el
juego *Keep practicing and you'll get
the feel of it.* Practique Ud. más y le
cogerá el tino.
‖ *Does your raincoat feel warm
enough?* ¿Le abriga bastante el impermeable? ‖ *Does this room feel cold
to you?* ¿Siente Ud. frío en este
cuarto? ‖ *Do you feel hungry?* ¡Tiene
Ud. hambre? ‖ *It feels cold in here.*
Hace frío aquí. ‖ *It feels like leather,
but it isn't.* Al tacto parece cuero,
pero no lo es. ‖ *It was so dark I had
to feel my way around the room.* Estaba tan obscuro que tuve que andar
a tientas por el cuarto. ‖ *I feel like a
Coca-Cola.* Me apetece una Coca-Cola.
feeling sensibilidad *I have no feeling in
this leg.* No tengo sensibilidad en esta
pierna.
○ **feelings** sentimientos *I didn't mean
to hurt your feelings.* No tuvé intención de lastimar sus sentimientos.
feet pies *My feet are sore.* Tengo los
pies adoloridos.—*He's over six feet
tall.* Tiene más de seis pies de estatura.
○ **to stand on one's own feet** independizarse *He's old enough to stand on
his own feet.* Tiene ya suficientes años
para independizarse.
‖ *A good rest'll put him back on his
feet again.* Un buen descanso le devolverá la salud.
fellow tipo *Who's that fellow over there?*
¿Quién es aquel tipo que está allí?
▲ hombre *He's a pretty good fellow
when you get to know him.* Es un
buen hombre cuando se le conoce bien.
○ **fellow** citizen conciudadano. ○ **fellow student** compañero, condiscípulo.
○ **poor fellow** pobre hombre *I feel sorry
for him, poor fellow.* Lo siento por él,
pobre hombre.
felt de fieltro *He has an old felt hat he
always wears in the rain.* Tiene un
sombrero viejo de fieltro que se lo
pone siempre cuando llueve.
female [n, adj] hembra.
feminine femenino.
fence [n] empalizada, cerca.
fender guardafango, guardabarros.
ferment [n] agitación *There's a great
political ferment in the country.* Hay
una gran agitación política en el país.

ferment [v] fermentar *This grape juice has fermented.* Este jugo de uva ha fermentado.
fern helecho.
ferry [n] transbordador, ferry.
ferryboat transbordador.
fertile fértil (*of land*); fecundo.
festival fiesta.
fetch traer.
fever fiebre *Do you have a fever?* ¿Tiene Ud. fiebre?—*He nearly died of yellow fever a year ago.* Hace un año que por poco se muere de fiebre amarilla.
few unos cuantos *I only know a few words.* No sé más que unas cuantas palabras. ▲ pocos *Few people realize it, but it's true.* Pocos se dan cuenta, pero es verdad.
○ **few and far between** poquísimos *The fish in this river are few and far between.* Hay poquísimos peces en este río. ○ **fewer** menos *Fewer people come here every year.* Aquí cada año viene menos gente. ○ **quite a few** bastante *Quite a few people are coming around to that way of thinking.* Bastante gente comienza a pensar de ese modo.
fiancé novio.
fiancée novia.
fiber fibra.
fickle variable, inconstante.
fiction novela *She reads nothing but fiction.* No lee más que novelas. ▲ fantasía *Is that story fact or fiction?* ¿Es esa una historia real o es una fantasía?
fiddle violín.
○ **to play second fiddle** ser plato de segunda mesa *I won't play second fiddle for anyone.* No seré plato de segunda mesa en ninguna parte.
field campo *Let's cut across this field.* Atravesemos este campo.—*The teams are coming onto the field.* Los equipos salen al campo. ▲ especialidad *He's the best man in his field.* Es el mejor dentro de su especialidad. ▲ campaña *This writer spent several years in the field with the troops.* Este escritor pasó varios años en campaña con las tropas.
field glasses gemelos.
fierce feroz *He gave me a fierce look.* Me echó una mirada feroz. ▲ horrible *How can you stand that fierce heat all day?* ¿Cómo puede Ud. aguantar ese calor horrible todo el día? ▲ violento *You're going to come up against fierce competition.* Va Ud. a tener una competencia violenta.

fiery ardiente, fogoso, vehemente.
fifth [n] quinto *This bottle holds a fifth of a gallon.* Esta botella contiene un quinto de galón.
❍ [adj] quinto *He's the fifth man in line.* Es el quinto en la fila.
fifty cincuenta *He's in his fifties.* Tiene cincuenta y tantos años.
○ **fifty-fifty** mitad y mitad.
fig higo.
fight [n] pelea *Let's not start a fight.* No comencemos una pelea.
● [v] pelear *Have you been fighting with the boy next door again?* ¿Has peleado con el muchacho de al lado otra vez? ▲ luchar, pelear *I think I'm right, but I'm not going to fight about it.* Creo que tengo razón, pero no voy a pelear por eso. ▲ combatir *You've got to fight that tendency of yours.* Debe Ud. combatir esa tendencia que tiene.
○ **to fight off** luchar con *I fought off my desire to sleep.* Luché con mis deseos de dormir. ○ **to put up a fight** resistir *We put up a good fight but we lost.* Resistimos mucho pero sin embargo perdimos.
‖ *He hasn't got any fight left in him.* No le queda ni el ánimo de reñir.
figure [n] cifra *Add up this column of figures.* Sume Ud. esta columna de cifras. ▲ número *I can't make out these figures.* No entiendo estos números. ▲ tipo, figura, línea *She has a nice figure.* Tiene buen tipo. ▲ figura *He's one of the most important figures in modern literature.* Es una de las figuras más importantes de la literatura moderna.—*How do you like this bronze figure I picked up in my travels?* ¿Le gusta esta figura de bronce que conseguí en uno de mis viajes?—*Figure seven shows all the parts of the motor.* La figura siete muestra todas las partes del motor. ▲ dibujo *The material's white with a little green figure.* La tela es blanca con un pequeño dibujo verde.
● [v] calcular *I figure it's about time we're going.* Calculo que ya es hora de que nos marchemos. ▲ figurar *This didn't figure in my plans.* Esto no figuraba en mis planes.
○ **figured** estampado *He had on a figured necktie.* Llevaba una corbata estampada. ○ **to figure on** contar con *That's something I hadn't figured on.* No había contado con eso. ○ **to figure out** resolver *Can you figure out this*

problem? ¿Puede Ud. resolver este problema? ○ **to figure up** calcular *Figure up how much it amounts to.* Calcule Ud. cuánto resulta.

file [n] archivo *Let's move the file over to the other side of the room.* Mudemos el archivo al otro lado del cuarto. ▲lima *I need a heavy file.* Necesito una lima fuerte.
● [v] archivar *Where should I file this correspondence?* ¿Dónde debo archivar esta correspondencia? ▲limar *I'll have time to file my nails while you're dressing.* Tendré tiempo para limarme las uñas mientras tu te vistes.
○ **in single file** en fila *Line up in single file.* Pónganse en fila. ○ **nail file** lima de uñas. ○ **on file** archivado *Do we have your application on file?* ¿Tenemos su solicitud archivada? ○ **to file out** salir en fila *The children filed out of the room.* Los niños salieron en fila del cuarto.

fill llenar *Fill this bottle full of hot water.* Llene Ud. esta botella con agua caliente.—*There are several jobs here that need to be filled.* Hay varios puestos aquí que hay que llenar. ▲llenarse *The theater was slowly filling with people.* Poco a poco el teatro se llenaba de gente. ▲ocupar completamente *The sofa just fills that end of the room.* El sofá ocupa completamente ese extremo del cuarto. ▲empastar *This tooth'll have to be filled.* Habrá que empastar esta muela. ▲despachar *This order came in yesterday, but hasn't been filled yet.* Este pedido llegó ayer, pero no se ha despachado todavía.
○ **to fill in** rellenar *The ditch has been filled in.* Ha sido rellenada la zanja. ○ **to fill out** llenar *Fill out this blank.* Llene Ud. este formulario. ○ **to fill the bill** llenar los requisitos *Does this fill the bill?* ¿Llena esto los requisitos? ○ **to fill up** llenar *Fill 'er up.* Llénelo. ○ **to have one's fill** hartarse *Have you had your fill of it?* ¿Se ha hartado ya de eso?
‖ *I'm just filling in here temporarily.* Estoy prestando mis servicios aquí provisionalmente.

film [n] capa *This salve will act as a protective film over the burn.* Este ungüento hará de capa protectora sobre la quemadura. ▲película *I don't like modern films.* Las películas modernas no me gustan.—*Do you have*

any film for this camera? ¿Tiene Ud. película para esta cámara?
● [v] hacer una película de, filmar *They filmed the entire ceremony.* Hicieron una película de toda la ceremonia.

filter [n] filtro.
● [v] filtrar.

filth suciedad.

final [n] examen final *How did you make out on your French finals?* ¿Cómo salió en los exámenes finales de francés?
● [adj] último *This is the final lecture of the series.* Esta es la última conferencia de la série. ▲final *Is that your final decision?* ¿Es esa su decisión final?
○ **finals** la final *He was eliminated before he got to the finals.* Fué eliminado antes de llegar a la final.
‖ *I don't want you to go alone; this is final.* No quiero que vayas sola; no hay más que decir.

finally finalmente, por último, en fin.

finances fondos, recursos.

financial financiero.

find [n] hallazgo *I think this new salesman's a real find.* Creo que este nuevo dependiente es un verdadero hallazgo.
● [v] encontrar *I just found a nickel in the street.* Acabo de encontrar un níquel en la calle.—*Can you find your way all right?* ¿Podrá Ud. encontrar el camino sin dificultad?
○ **to find out** averiguar *I finally found out where you were last night.* Por fin averigüé donde estuviste anoche.

fine [n] multa *If he's convicted he'll have to pay a fine.* Si es condenado, tendrá que pagar una multa.
● [adj] fino *Her hair's so fine it doesn't take a good permanent.* Tiene el cabella tan fino que no puede hacerse una buena permanente.—*This pen has a very fine point.* Esta pluma tiene una punta muy fina.—*Grind this coffee very fine.* Muela Ud. este café muy fino. ▲sutil *There's no need of making such fine distinctions.* No hace falta hacer distinciones tan sutiles. ▲magnífico *That was a mighty fine thing for him to do.* Fué una cosa magnífica lo que hizo. ▲lindo *That's a fine way to treat a friend.* Esa es una linda manera de tratar a un amigo. ▲buen *It's a fine day today.* Hace hoy muy buen día. ▲muy

bien *I'm feeling fine, thanks.* Me siento muy bien, gracias.

● [v] multar *The judge fined him five dollars.* Le multó el juez con cinco dólares. *or* El juez le puso una multa de cinco dólares.

○ **finest** mejor *He was given the finest education that money could buy.* Se le dió la mejor instrucción que se puede conseguir con dinero.

‖ *That's fine!* ¡Qué bueno! *or* ¡Es estupendo!

finger dedo *I cut my finger peeling potatoes.* Me corté el dedo pelando papas.

○ **to put one's finger on it** dar con él *I know I have it, but I can't put my finger on it.* Lo tengo, pero no puedo dar con él. *or* Lo tengo pero no sé donde lo puse. ○ **to slip through one's fingers** escapársele a uno de las manos.

fingernail uña.

fingerprint [n] impresión digital, huella digital.

finish [n] final *Were you there to see the finish?* ¿Estuvo Ud. allí para ver el final? ▲ acabado *This table has a nice finish.* Esta mesa tiene un bonito acabado.

● [v] terminar *Let's finish this job tonight.* Terminemos este trabajo esta noche. ▲ acabar *Wait until I finish eating.* Espere que acabe de comer.

fir abeto.

fire [n] fuego *Will you light the fire?* ¿Quiere prender el fuego? ▲ incendio *There was a big fire in the store.* Hubo un gran incendio en la tienda.

● [v] echar, despedir *That man was fired last week.* Despidieron a ese hombre la semana pasada.

○ **to catch on fire** incendiarse *The chimney caught on fire and the house burned down.* Se incendió la chimenea y se quemó toda la casa. ○ **to hang fire** llevar en suspenso *The scheme's been hanging fire for a couple of weeks.* El plan lleva dos semanas en suspenso. ○ **to open fire** abrir fuego *Wait until they open fire.* Esperen hasta que abran fuego. ○ **to play with fire** jugar con fuego *Better be careful, you're playing with fire.* Cuidado, está Ud. jugando con fuego. ○ **to set fire to, to set on fire** prender fuego a *Don't set fire to anything.* Cuidado con prenderle fuego a algo. —*That was no accident; someone set the house on fire.* Eso no fué un acci-

dente; alguien prendió fuego a la casa.

‖ *Don't fire!* ¡No dispare! ‖ *Fire!* ¡Fuego! ‖ *Fire away!* ¡Empiece!

firecracker triquitraque.

fire engine bomba de incendios.

fire escape escalera de salvamento.

fire insurance seguro contra incendios *How much fire insurance do you have?* ¿De cuánto es el seguro contra incendios que tiene Ud.?

fireplace chimenea, hogar.

firewood leña.

firm [n] casa *Whose firm do you represent?* ¿Qué casa representa Ud.? ● [adj] firme *The ground's firm here.* El suelo es firme aquí.—*He has very firm convictions.* Tiene muy firmes convicciones.

‖ *Don't use too firm a grip on the wheel.* No agarre Ud. demasiado fuerte el volante.

first [n] día primero *I get paid on the first.* Cobro el día primero. ▲ primero *He's always the first to complain.* Siempre es el primero en quejarse.

● [adj] primero *Do you remember the first time I came here?* ¿Recuerda Ud. la primera vez que vine aquí?— *The first good rain storm will wash it away.* La primera lluvia fuerte que caiga se lo llevará. ● [adv] primero *I have to go to the store first.* Tengo que ir primero a la tienda.—*First, let me ask you this.* Primero déjame preguntarte esto. ▲ por primera vez *I went there first in 1942.* Fuí allí por primera vez en 1942.

○ **at first** al principio *I didn't like him at first, but I do now.* Al principio no me gustaba, pero ahora, sí. ○ **at first sight** a primera vista *The idea's better than it seems at first sight.* La idea es mejor de lo que parece a primera vista. ○ **not to know the first thing about** no saber nada de *He doesn't know the first thing about hunting.* No sabe nada de caza. ○ **the first thing** lo primero *I'll do this first thing in the morning.* Será lo primero que haga por la mañana.

first aid primeros auxilios.

first class primera clase.

fish [n] pez *(alive).* ▲ pescado *This fish is delicious.* Este pescado está riquísimo.

● [v] pescar *Do you want to go fishing?* ¿Quieres ir a pescar? ○ **to fish for compliments** tratar de

que le alaben a uno, buscar alabanzas.
‖ *Did you catch any fish?* ¿Pescó
algo? ‖ *He fished through his pockets for his keys.* Buscaba la llave
en los bolsillos.
fisherman pescador.
fishhook anzuelo.
fist puño.
fit [*n*] ataque *Every time I mention the
incident he throws a fit.* Cada vez
que menciono el acontecimiento le da
un ataque.
● [*v*] sentar *Does it fit all right?*
¿Le sienta bien? ▲encajar *The picture just fits in this space.* El cuadro
encaja perfectamente en este espacio.
▲servir para *Have you got a key to
fit this lock?* ¿Tiene Ud. una llave
que sirva para esta acerradura? ▲co-
locar *I'm going to have a new lock
fitted on the door.* Voy a hacer colocar una nueva cerradura en la puerta.
○ **not fit to eat** incomible *This fish
isn't fit to eat.* Este pescado está
incomible. ○ **to be fit for** poder hacer
What kind of work is he fit for?
¿Qué clase de trabajo puede hacer?
‖ *This suit's not a good fit.* Este
traje no me está bien.
five cinco.
fix [*n*] lío *He's got himself in a terrible
fix.* Se ha metido en un lío espan-
toso.
● [*v*] componer *Can you fix this?*
¿Puede Ud. componer esto? ▲fijar
*All these prices are fixed by the gov-
ernment.* El gobierno ha fijado todos
estos precios.
○ **to fix a flat** arreglar un pinchazo
Where can we get this flat fixed?
¿Dónde nos pueden arreglar este pinchazo? ‖ *Can you fix me up with a place
to sleep?* ¿Puede Ud. proporcionarme
un sitio donde dormir?
fixture instalación.
flag [*n*] bandera *Didn't you see the red
flag?* ¿No vió Ud. la bandera roja?
‖ *See if you can flag a passing
truck.* Mire a ver si haciendo señales
puedes parar algún camión.
flame [*n*] llama *Heat it in the flame.*
Caliéntelo sobre la llama.
● [*v*] hacer llama *He blew on the
embers until they flamed up.* Sopló
el rescoldo hasta que hizo llama.
flank [*n*] costado, flanco.
● [*v*] ir *or* estar al lado de; flan-
quear *(military).*
flannel franela.
flap [*n*] cartera *(pocket).*

● [*v*] agitarse *(of a flag).*
○ **to flap its wings** aletear.
flash [*n*] instante *It was all over in a
flash.* Todo pasó en un instante.
● [*v*] brillar *The windows flashed
in the sun.* Los cristales brillaban al
sol. ▲pasar como un relámpago *An
idea just flashed through my mind.*
Me acaba de pasar una idea por la
cabeza como un relámpago. ▲deste-
llar *They were flashing signals from
the coast with a lantern.* Desde la
costa destellaban señales con una
linterna. ▲proyectar *Flash the light
in this corner.* Proyecte la luz hacia
este rincón.
○ **flash of light** destello, resplandor.
○ **flash of lightning** relámpago.
flashlight linterna elétrica *Can you lend
me your flashlight?* ¿Puede Ud.
prestarme su linterna eléctrica?
flashy llamativo.
flask frasco.
flat [*n*] apartamiento, [*Sp*] piso *I just
moved into a new flat.* Acabo de
mudarme a un apartamento nuevo.
▲pinchazo *The car ran over some
glass and we had a flat.* El automóvil
pasó sobre unos pedazos de vidrio y
tuvimos un pinchazo.
● [*adj*] plano, horizontal *His house
has a flat roof.* Su casa tiene el
tejado plano. ▲plano *Put the flat
side of it against the wall.* Ponga
Ud. la parte plana contra la pared.
—*What's in that flat package?* ¿Qué
hay en ese paquete plano? ▲llano *Is
the country flat?* ¿Es llano el país?
▲desinflado *The tire's flat.* El neumático está desinflado. ▲chato, [*Am*]
ñato *He has a flat nose.* Tiene la
nariz chata. *or* Es chato. ▲insípido
This drink's pretty flat. Esta bebida
es bastante insípida. ▲muerto *This
beer's flat.* Esta cerveza está muerta.
▲desentonado *Her high notes are a
little flat.* Sus notas altas son un
poco desentonadas. ▲menor *The next
movement's in A-flat.* El movimiento
que sigue es en "la menor."
○ **to fall flat** no tener éxito *My
prize joke fell flat.* Mi chiste favorito
no tuvo éxito.
flatten allanar, aplastar.
flatter adular *You won't get ahead by
flattering me.* Ud. no conseguirá
nada con adularme. ▲favorecer *That
hat certainly flatters you.* Indudablemente ese sombrero le favorece.
flavor [*n*] sabor *The custard is vanilla
flavor.* El flan tiene sabor a vainilla.

● [v] sazonar *What did you use to flavor this soup?* ¿Qué usó Ud. para sazonar esta sopa?

flaw defecto.

flea pulga.

flee huir.

fleet flota.

flesh carne.

flight vuelo *They made a non-stop flight from New York to Madrid.* Hicieron vuelo continuo de Nueva York a Madrid. ▲ huída, fuga *They told him about the flight of the prisoners.* Le hablaron de la fuga de los prisioneros. ▲ piso *My room's two flights up.* Mi cuarto está dos pisos más arriba. ▲ tramo *How many more flights do we have to climb?* ¿Cuántos tramos más tenemos que subir?

○ to put to flight poner en fuga *Our army put the enemy to flight.* Nuestro ejército puso en fuga al enemigo.

flirt [n] coqueta *She's a flirt.* Es una coqueta.

● [v] flirtear *She flirts with every man she meets.* Flirtea con todos los hombres que conoce.

○ to flirt with death jugar con la muerte.

flit revolotear.

float [n] balsa *Let's swim out to the float.* Vamos a nadar hasta la balsa. ▲ corcho *Some floats are missing from the net.* Le faltan algunos corchos a la red. ▲ carroza *Will you be on one of the floats in the parade?* ¿Estará Ud. en una de las carrozas del desfile?

● [v] flotar *He swam out to the log that was floating on the water.* Nadó hasta el madero que flotaba en el agua. ▲ poner a flote *They worked a long time before they were able to float the ship.* Trabajaron mucho tiempo antes de poder poner el barco a flote. ▲ emitir *How big a loan will they have to float?* ¿A cuánto alcanzará el empréstito que van a emitir?

flock [n] rebaño *(animals);* bandada *(birds).*

● [v] congregarse, juntarse.

flood [n] inundación *The town was isolated by the flood.* El pueblo quedó aislado por la inundación.

● [v] inundar *The whole area was flooded when the dam burst.* Toda la región se inundó cuando se rompió la presa.—*The room was flooded with light.* El cuarto estaba inundado de luz.

∥ *She wept floods of tears.* Lloró a mares. *or* Lloró a lágrima viva.

floor [n] piso, suelo *I just swept the floor.* Acabo de barrer el piso. ▲ piso *What floor do you live on?* ¿En qué piso vive Ud.? ▲ palabra *I asked for the floor twice.* He pedido la palabra dos veces.

● [v] derribar *He floored him with a blow.* Lo derribó de un puñetazo.

flop [n] fracaso *The premiere was a flop.* Fué un fracaso el estreno.

● [v] dejarse caer *She flopped down in a chair.* Se dejó caer en la silla.

○ to take a flop caerse *I took a flop on the wet steps.* Me caí en las escaleras mojadas.

florist florista.

flounder *(fish)* [n] lenguado.

flour harina.

flourish prosperar.

flow [n] corriente, flujo.

● [v] fluir.

flower flor.

flowerpot tiesto, maceta.

flu gripe.

fluent fluente, fluido.

fluid [adj, n] flúido, líquido.

flush [adj] igual, parejo *Try to make that shelf flush with the other one.* Trate de poner ese estante parejo al otro.

● [v] ruborizarse *She flushed when they laughed at her.* Se ruborizó cuando se rieron de ella. ▲ limpiar, desatancar *We flushed the pipes with a chemical solution.* Desatancamos la cañería con una solución química.

○ to be flush tener dinero *Remind me some day when I'm flush.* Recuérdamelo algún día, cuando tenga dinero. ○ to be flushed estar emocionado *Our team was flushed with success.* Nuestro equipo estaba muy emocionado con el éxito.

flute flauta.

flutter agitarse, temblar.

fly [n] mosca *The flies around here are terrible.* Son terribles las moscas de aquí.

● [v] volar *The birds are flying south.* Los pájaros vuelan hacia el sur.—*Have you flown before?* Ha volado Ud. anteriormente? ▲ ir en avión *I'd like to fly if possible.* Me gustaría ir en avión si fuese posible. ▲ volar, conducir un avión *He learned to fly in three weeks.* Aprendió a volar en tres semanas.

○ on the fly en marcha *I was late*

and caught the train on the fly. Llegué retrasado y cogí el tren en marcha. ○ **to fly into a temper** enfadarse *There's no need to fly into a temper.* No necesita Ud. enfadarse. ‖ *What flag are they flying?* ¿Qué bandera llevan?

flying boat hidroavión.

foam [n] espuma.

focus [n] foco, centro *The child was the focus of all eyes.* El niño era el centro de todas las miradas. ● [v] enfocar *He focused the light on the picture so we could see it clearer.* Enfocó la luz sobre el cuadro para que pudiéramos verlo mejor. ○ **in focus** enfocado. ○ **out of focus** desenfocado.

fodder [n] forraje.

foe enemigo.

fog neblina, niebla.

fold [n] pliegue *The curtains hung in folds.* Las cortinas colgaban haciendo pliegues. ● [v] doblar *Help me fold these blankets.* Ayúdame a doblar estas mantas. ▲ cruzar *The teacher folded her arms and looked very stern.* La profesora cruzó los brazos y tomó un aire muy severo. ○ **to fold up** liquidar *The company folded up last year for lack of funds.* La compañía liquidó el año pasado a causa de la falta de fondos.

foliage follaje.

folk [adj] popular *He has a large collection of folk music.* Tiene una gran colección de música popular.

folks gente, familia *How are your folks?* ¿Cómo está su gente?

follow seguir *I think there's somebody following us.* Creo que alguien nos viene siguiendo.—*The hot weather was followed by several days of rain.* El calor fué seguido de varios días de lluvia.—*Be sure to follow these instructions exactly.* Siga Ud. estas instrucciones al pie de la letra. ▲ entender, seguir *I can't quite follow your reasoning.* No entiendo muy bien su razonamiento. ▲ estar al corriente de *I haven't been following the news lately.* Últimamente no he estado al corriente de las noticias. ○ **to follow in** seguir *He's following in his father's footsteps.* Sigue los pasos de su padre. ‖ *That doesn't necessarily follow.* Ese no es el resultado necesariamente. ‖ *The formula is as follows.* La fórmula es como sigue.

follower partidario.

following [n] partidarios *This bullfighter has a large following.* Este torero tiene muchos partidarios. ● [adj] siguiente *He came on the following Tuesday.* Llegó el martes siguiente. ○ **the following** lo siguiente *Please write the following.* Haga el favor de escribir lo siguiente.

folly tontería.

fond cariñoso, tierno *She has a fond expression in her eyes when she looks at him.* Tiene una expresión cariñosa en los ojos cuando le mira. ‖ *I'm very fond of olives.* Me gustan muchísimo las aceitunas.

fondness cariño.

food comida *Is the food good there?* ¿Es buena la comida allí? ○ **food for thought** en que pensar *This news gives us food for thought.* Esta noticia nos da en que pensar.

fool [n] tonto, necio *He's a fool if he believes that.* Es un tonto si cree eso. ● [v] bromear *It's time you stopped fooling and got down to business.* Ya es tiempo de dejar de bromear y empezar a trabajar. ▲ engañar *If you think you're fooling me, you're mistaken.* Si cree que me engaña, se equivoca. ○ **to fool around** bromear *Quit fooling around and get to work.* Déjese de bromear y póngase a trabajar. ○ **to fool with** jugar con *Don't fool with that radio while I'm gone.* No juegues con la radio mientras estoy fuera. ‖ *Let me tell you, I'm nobody's fool.* Permítame que le diga que a mí no me engaña nadie.

foolish tonto *Don't be foolish.* No seas tonto. ○ **foolish thing** tontería *I said a very foolish thing.* Dije una gran tontería.

foot [n] pie *I hurt my foot.* Me he hecho daño en el pie.—*He was sitting at the foot of the stairs.* Estaba sentado al pie de la escalera.—*The wall's a foot thick.* La pared tiene un pie de grueso. ● [v] pagar *Who's going to foot the bill?* ¿Quien va a pagar la cuenta? ○ **on foot** a pie *We had to come most of the way on foot.* Tuvimos que venir a pie la mayor parte del camino. ○ **to put one's foot down** proceder enérgicamente, tomar una resolución *This has gone far enough.*

I'm going to put my foot down. Esto ya es demasiado. Voy a tomar una resolución. ○ **to put one's foot in it** meter la pata *I really put my foot in it that time.* Esa vez sí que metí la pata.

football fútbol, football.

for [*prep*] para *Is it hard for you to do this?* ¿Es difícil para Ud. hacer esto?—*This problem's too difficult for me.* Este problema es demasiado difícil para mi.—*That book was too much for me.* Ese libro era demasiado para mi.—*He's tall for his age.* Está alto para su edad.—*Who's he working for now?* ¿Para quién trabaja ahora?—*When does the train leave for New York?* ¿Cuándo sale el tren para Nueva York?—*What does he do for a living?* ¿Qué hace para ganarse la vida?—*I went out for a cup of coffee.* Salí para tomar una taza de café.—*He brought some candy for the child.* Trajo unos dulces para el niño.—*I bought some goods for a dress.* Compré tela para un vestido.—*They said he was good for nothing.* Decían que no servía para nada.—*She's too old for dancing.* Es demasiado vieja para bailar.—*The dog's too old for hunting.* El perro es demasiado viejo para cazar. ▲ por *How much do you want for this book?* ¿Cuánto pide por este libro?—*This restaurant's known for its good food.* Este restaurante es conocido por su buena comida.—*That'll be enough for the time being.* Bastará por ahora.—*He was elected for four years.* Fué elegido por cuatro años.—*At that party there were three women for every man.* En aquella fiesta había tres mujeres por cada hombre.—*I do this for the fun of it.* Lo hago sólo por gusto.—*They respect him for his honesty.* Le respetan por su honradez.—*Pray for us.* Ruegue por nosotros.—*For heaven's sake!* ¡Por Dios!—*She felt only friendship for him.* Sólo sentía amistad por él.—*I voted for him last year.* Voté por él el año pasado.—*I despise him for what he did.* Le desprecio por haber hechlo lo que hizo. ▲ como *What do you use for fuel?* Qué usa Ud. como combustible? ▲ en honor de *We're giving a dinner for him.* Vamos a dar una comida en su honor. ▲ en pro *Are you for or against it?* ¿Está Ud. en pro o en contra? ▲ de *It's time for dinner.* Es hora de comer.

● [*conj*] porque *I think the play'll succeed, for it's what the public wants.* Creo que tendrá éxito la representación porque es lo que desea el público.

○ **as for** en cuanto a *As for me, I don't care what you do.* En cuanto a mí, no me importa lo que haga Ud. ○ **for the first time** por primera vez *I saw him yesterday for the first time.* Lo ví ayer por primera vez. ‖ *He stayed for an hour.* Se quedó una hora. ‖ *He was named for his grandfather.* Le pusieron el mismo nombre que su abuelo. ‖ *It's time for us to go home.* Es hora de que vayamos a casa. ‖ *Would you like to go for a walk?* ¿Le gustaría dar un paseo? ‖ *You'd better send for the doctor.* Es preciso que mande a buscar al médico. ‖ *For one thing, he doesn't know the language.* Empieza por que no conoce el idioma.

forbid prohibir *Is it forbidden to smoke here?* ¿Está prohibido fumar aquí?

force [*n*] violencia *The trees were torn up by the force of the storm.* Los árboles fueron arrancados por la violencia de la tempestad. ▲ **fuerza** *We had to take him by force.* Tuvimos que llevarlo a la fuerza.—*I see the force of your argument.* Comprendo la fuerza de su argumento.—*I go there from force of habit.* Por la fuerza de la costumbre voy allí.—*Which branch of the armed forces were you in?* ¿En qué arma de las fuerzas armadas ha servido Ud.? ● [*v*] forzar *The door's been forced.* La puerta ha sido forzada. ▲ obligar *We were forced to change our tactics.* Nos vimos obligados a cambiar nuestra táctica.—*We forced him to admit that he'd done it.* Le obligamos a confesar que lo había hecho.

○ **forced** forzado, forzoso *The plane made a forced landing.* El avión hizo un aterrizaje forzoso. ○ **police force** servicio de policía.

forearm antebrazo.

forecast [*n*] pronóstico.

● [*v*] pronosticar.

forehead la frente.

foreign extranjero *He studied at a foreign university.* Estudió en una universidad extranjera.

foreigner extranjero *He has a prejudice against foreigners.* Tiene un prejuicio en contra de los extranjeros.

foreman capataz.

forenoon mañana.
foresight previsión.
forest bosque.
forever para siempre *I'm afraid I'll be stuck in this place forever.* Temo que tendré que quedarme aquí para siempre. ▲siempre *He's forever telling the same story.* Siempre está contando la misma historia.
forge [*n*] fragua *(of blacksmith).*
● [*v*] forjar.
forge falsificar *(a check, etc).*
forgery falsificación.
forget olvidar(se) *It's raining, and we forgot to close the windows.* Está lloviendo y nos hemos olvidado de cerrar las ventanas.—*She's forgotten how to do it.* Ha olvidado el modo de hacerlo.
forgive perdonar.
fork tenedor *Could I have a knife and fork, please?* ¿Puede Ud. hacer el favor de darme un cuchillo y un tenedor? ▲bifurcación *Turn left when you get to the fork in the road.* Doble hacia la izquierda cuando llegue Ud. a la bifurcación de la carretera.
forlorn abandonado, desamparado.
form [*n*] forma *Is this a different word or just another form of the same word?* ¿Es ésta una palabra distinta u otra forma de la misma palabra? ▲estilo *I play tennis, but my form is terrible.* Juego al tenis, pero tengo muy mal estilo. ▲formulario *You didn't finish filling out this form.* No acabó Ud. de llenar este formulario.
● [*v*] formar *I haven't formed an opinion on that subject yet.* Todavía no me he formado una opinión sobre ese tema.
○ **as a matter of form** por apariencia *We had to attend just as a matter of form.* Tuvimos que asistir meramente por apariencia. ○ **to be in good form** estar en buena forma. ○ **to form a line** hacer cola *They formed a line to get tickets.* Hacían cola para sacar los billetes.
formal [*n*] baile de etiqueta *We're invited to a formal Saturday night.* Estamos invitados a un baile de etiqueta el sábado por la noche.
● [*adj*] ceremonioso *He's quite formal when he meets a stranger.* Es muy ceremonioso cuando le presentan una persona desconocida. ▲en forma *Did you make a formal agreement with him?* ¿Hizo Ud. un contrato en forma con él?

formation formación.
former primero *Of your two suggestions, I think I prefer the former.* De sus dos sugestiones, creo que prefiero la primera. ▲antiguo *He's a former student of mine.* Es un antiguo alumno mío. ▲ex- *He's a former president of the country.* Es un ex-presidente del país.
formerly anteriormente, antiguamente.
formula fórmula.
forsake dejar, abandonar.
fort fuerte, fortaleza.
forth ○and so forth etcétera *(abbr etc.).* ○ back and forth arriba y abajo *He kept walking back and forth.* Estaba paseando arriba y abajo.
fortunate afortunado.
fortune fortuna.
forty cuarenta.
forward [*v*] reexpedir *Please forward my mail to this address.* Haga el favor de reexpedirme el correo a esta dirección.
○ **to come forward** adelantarse *Six men came forward to volunteer for the work.* Seis hombres se adelantaron para ofrecerse para hacer el trabajo. ○ **to look forward to** esperar con ilusión *I'm looking forward to the party.* Estoy esperando con ilusión la fiesta.
fossil fósil.
foster [*adj*] adoptivo *He was visiting his foster mother.* Estaba visitando a su madre adoptiva.
● [*v*] alentar, fomentar *They did everything they could to foster good relations.* Hicieron todo lo que pudieron para fomentar las buenas relaciones.
foul [*adj*] sucio *It was a foul play.* Era un juego sucio. ▲viciado *The air in here's foul.* El aire aquí está muy viciado.
○ **to have a foul mouth** ser mal hablado *That man has a foul mouth.* Ese hombre es muy mal hablado.
found fundar *This college was founded in 1843.* Este colegio se fundó en 1843.
foundation cimientos *The foundation of this house is beginning to weaken.* Los cimientos de esta casa empiezan a ceder. ▲fundación *He was awarded a scholarship to do research for the foundation.* Se le dió una beca para que hiciera trabajos de investigación para la fundación.
fountain fuente.

fountain pen pluma fuente, pluma estilográfica.
four cuatro.
fourteen catorce.
fourth cuatro *I'll be there on the fourth.* Estaré allí el cuatro. ▲cuarta parte *Three-fourths of the people of this town don't vote.* Tres cuartas partes de la gente de este pueblo no votan.
fowl ave; volatería [*pl*].
fox zorro.
fraction fracción.
fracture [*n*] fractura *The fracture wasn't as serious as we thought.* No fué tan grave la fractura como creíamos.
● [*v*] fracturar *The boy fell off the bicycle and fractured his skull.* El muchacho se cayó de la bicicleta y se fracturó el cráneo.
fragment fragmento.
frail frágil.
frame [*n*] armazón, armadura *The frame of the house should be finished in a day or two.* El armazón de la casa debería acabarse en uno o dos días. ▲marco *I bought a leather frame for the picture.* Compré un marco de cuero para el retrato. ▲armadura *I'd prefer a plain frame on these glasses.* Preferiría una armadura sencilla en estos anteojos. ▲complexión, constitución *He has a heavy frame.* Es de complexión fuerte.
● [*v*] redactar *They framed a constitution for the club.* Redactaron los estatutos para el club. ▲poner marco a *Have you framed those pictures I brought in last week?* Ha puesto Ud. marcos a aquellas fotografías que traje la semana pasada?
○ **frame of mind** estado de ánimo *It's best not to leave her alone in that frame of mind.* Es mejor que no la dejen sola en ese estado de ánimo.
‖ *He was framed on a murder charge.* Se hizo una maniobra para acusarle de asesinato.
frank [*n*] franquicia de correos *Do we have any envelopes without the frank?* ¿Tenemos algunos sobres sin franquicia de correos?
● [*adj*] franco *You're just a little too frank.* Ud. es demasiado franco.
frankfurter salchicha.
fraternal fraternal.
fraternity fraternidad.
fraud fraude.
freak rareza, monstruosidad.
freckle peca.
free [*adj*] libre *This is a free country.*

Este es un país libre.—*Isn't he rather too free with his comments?* ¿No es más bien demasiado libre en sus comentarios?—*You're free of all responsibility.* Ud. está libre de toda responsabilidad.—*I don't have any free time today.* Hoy no tengo ningún tiempo libre. ▲gratis *This is a free sample.* Esta es una muestra gratis. ▲en libertad *They held him for a few hours and then let him go free.* Le detuvieron por unas horas y luego le pusieron en libertad.
● [*v*] libertar *He wants us to free the prisoners.* Quiere que libertemos a los prisioneros. ▲poner en libertad *When will he be freed?* ¿Cuándo será puesto en libertad?
○ **a free hand** plena libertad, carta blanca *Will you give me a free hand in the matter?* ¿Me concederá Ud. plena libertad en este asunto? ○ **free-for-all** pelea general, zafarrancho *The game ended in a free-for-all.* El juego terminó en un zafarrancho. ○ **to be free from** hallarse (*or* estar) libre de *The product's guaranteed free from defects.* Garantizan que el producto se halla libre de defectos.
freedom libertad *That doesn't leave me much freedom of action.* Eso no me deja mucha libertad de acción.
freeze helar *Do you think the pond's frozen hard enough to skate on?* ¿Cree Ud. que el lago está bastante helado para patinar? ▲helarse *My feet are freezing.* Se me hielan los pies.—*He froze with fear when he saw the snake.* Se quedó helado cuando vió la serpiente. ▲congelar *The cold froze the water in the pipes.* El frío congeló el agua de las cañerías. ▲bloquear, congelar *All funds are frozen until further notice.* Todos los fondos están congelados hasta nuevo aviso.
‖ *I'm frozen in my job.* Estoy obligado a continuar en mi empleo.
freight carga *How much freight did you carry last trip?* ¿Cuánta carga llevó en el último viaje? ▲flete *How much is the freight on this box?* ¿Cuánto es el flete de este cajón?
French [*n*] francés *Do you speak French?* ¿Habla Ud. francés?
● [*adj*] francés *Do you like French wine?* ¿Le gusta a Ud. el vino francés?
frenzy frenesí.
frequency frecuencia.
frequent [*adj*] frecuente.

frequent [v] frecuentar.
frequently frecuentemente.
fresh fresco *Are these eggs fresh?* ¿Son estos huevos frescos?—*I like fresh peas better than canned.* Me gustan los guisantes frescos más que en conserva.—*That fellow's very fresh.* Ese tipo es muy fresco. ▲ nuevo *Let's open a fresh deck of cards.* Vamos a usar una baraja nueva. ▲ puro *Let's get some fresh air.* Vamos a tomar un poco de aire puro. ▲ fresco, descansado *After all this work he seems as fresh as when he started.* Después de todo este trabajo, parece estar tan fresco como cuando empezó.
○ **fresh water** agua dulce *I prefer the flavor of fresh-water fish.* Prefiero el sabor del pescado de agua dulce.
fret [v] irritarse.
friction fricción.
Friday viernes.
friend amigo *He's a good friend of mine.* Es un buen amigo mío.
○ **to make friends with** hacerse amigo *I did my best to make friends with him.* Hice todo lo que pude para hacerme amigo suyo.
friendly benévolo, cogedor *He has a very friendly smile.* Tiene una sonrisa muy acogedora. ▲ amistoso *Our country's always had friendly relations with yours.* Nuestro país siempre ha mantenido relaciones amistosas con el suyo.
friendship amistad.
fright susto, miedo.
frighten asustar.
frightful espantoso, terrible.
fringe fleco.
fritter [n] fritura, frito.
frog rana.
from de *I just came from my house.* Acabo de venir de casa.—*Take a clean glass from the cupboard.* Saque Ud. un vaso limpio del aparador.—*Take a book from the shelf.* Tome un libro del estante.—*I live ten miles from the city.* Vivo a diez millas de la ciudad.—*Can you tell him from his brother?* ¿Puede Ud. distinguirlo de su hermano?—*I won't take such insults from anybody.* No toleraré tales insultos de nadie.—*Where do you come from?* ¿De dónde es Ud.? ▲ por *He was tired and nervous from overwork.* Estaba cansado y nervioso por exceso de trabajo.—*From what he says I don't think we should go.* Por lo que dice, no creo que debamos ir. ▲ desde *I saw it from the window.* Lo ví desde la ventana.—*From his point of view he's right.* Desde su punto de vista tiene razón.
○ **from bad to worse** de mal en peor.
○ **from beginning to end** desde el principio al fin. ○ **from day to day** de día en día. ○ **from house to house** de casa en casa.
‖ *He kept me from making a big mistake.* Me impidió cometer un gran error.
front [n] fachada *The front of the house is painted white.* La fachada de la casa está pintada de blanco. ▲ el frente *He was at the front for three months.* Estuvo tres meses en el frente.
○ **front door** puerta principal *Someone's at the front door.* Hay alguien en la puerta principal. ○ **in front of** delante de *Who was that sitting in front of you at the movies?* ¿Quién estaba sentado delante de Ud. en el cine? ▲ frente a *The crowd assembled in front of the post office.* La muchedumbre se reunió frente al correo.
‖ *The picture's in the front of the book.* La fotografía está al principio del libro.
frontier frontera *We crossed the frontier yesterday.* Cruzamos ayer la frontera.
frost escarcha.
frown [v] fruncir el entrecejo *My friend frowned as she read the letter.* Mi amiga frunció el entrecejo al leer la carta.
○ **to frown on** mirar con antipatía *The whole family frowned on the match.* Toda la familia miraba con antipatía a aquel matrimonio.
fruit fruta.
fry freír.
frying pan sartén.
fuel combustible.
fugitive fugitivo.
fulfill cumplir.
full lleno *Give me a full glass of water.* Déme Ud. un vaso lleno de agua.—*That book's full of mistakes.* Ese libro está lleno de errores.—*I'm so full I can't eat any more.* Me siento tan lleno que no puedo comer más. ▲ ancho *The dress has a full skirt.* El traje tiene una falda ancha. ▲ completo *He made a full report.* Hizo un informe completo.
fully enteramente, completamente.
fume [v] hablar con enojo.
○ **fumes** gases, vapores.

fun diversión, gracia *I don't see any fun in it.* No veo ninguna diversión en eso. *or* No le veo la gracia.
  ○ **just for fun** solo por divertirse.
  ○ **to have fun** divertirse *We were just having a little fun.* Nos estábamos divirtiendo un poco. ○ **to make fun of** reirse de.

function [n] función.

fund fondo.

fundamental fundamental.

funeral funeral *(church)*; entierro *(cemetery)*.

funnel embudo *(utensil)*; chimenea *(of a ship)*.

funny gracioso *That's not a very funny story.* No es una historia muy graciosa. ▲ extraño, raro *I have a funny feeling.* Tengo una sensación rara.

fur piel.

furious furioso.

furlough licencia.

furnace caldera.

furnish amueblar *How have you furnished your apartment?* ¿Cómo ha amueblado su apartamento? ▲ proporcionar *We'll furnish you with everything you need.* Le proporcionaremos todo lo que necesita.
  ○ **furnished room** cuarto amueblado.

furniture muebles.

furrow surco.

further [adj] nuevo *Espere nuevas órdenes.* Wait for further orders.
  ● [adv] más *Do you want to study it further?* ¿Quiere Ud. estudiarlo más?

fury furia.

fuse fusible, plomo *The short circuit blew a fuse.* El corto circuito fundió el fusible.

future [n] futuro *Try to do better in the future.* Procure Ud. hacerlo mejor en el futuro. ▲ porvenir *This job has no future.* Este trabajo no tiene porvenir.
  ● [adj] future *Introduce me to your future wife.* Presénteme Ud. a su futura esposa.

G

gag [n] mordaza *The bandits put a gag in his mouth.* Los bandidos le pusieron una mordaza en la boca. ▲ broma *Is this a gag?* ¿Es esta una broma?
  ● [v] amordazar *We found him bound and gagged.* Lo encontramos amarrado y amordazado. ▲ dar asco a uno *The invalid gagged on the heavy food.* Al enfermo le dió asco la comida pesada.

gaiety alegría.

gain [n] ganancia *Their loss is our gain.* Su pérdida supone nuestra ganancia. ▲ aumento *There's been a recent gain in the population of the city.* Ha habido un aumento de población recientemente en la ciudad.
  ● [v] adelantarse *My watch gains ten minutes a day.* Mi reloj se adelanta diez minutos al día. ▲ conquistar, ganar *His sincerity gained the confidence of everyone.* Con su sinceridad ganó la confianza de todos. ▲ mejorar *The doctor reports that the patient's gaining rapidly.* El doctor dice que el enfermo va mejorando rápidamente. ▲ alcanzar *The men have gained the hill beyond the town.* Los hombres han alcanzado la colina que está más allá del pueblo.
  ○ **gains** ganancias *On the last play I lost all my gains.* En la última jugada perdí todas mis ganancias.

gale temporal, ventarrón.

gallant [adj] valiente, valeroso.

gallery galería *We have seats in the gallery.* Tenemos asientos de galería. —*We walked through a long gallery.* Caminamos a través de una larga galería.
  ○ **art gallery** galería de arte. ○ **shooting gallery** galería de tiro al blanco.

gallon galón *Give me five gallons of gas, please.* Déme cinco galones de gasolina, por favor.

gallop [n] galope.
  ● [v] galopar.

gamble [n] riesgo *It's an awful gamble.* Es un gran riesgo.
  ● [v] especular *Don't gamble with other people's money.* No especule con dinero ajeno. ▲ jugar *He loves to gamble but generally loses.* Le gusta jugar pero generalmente pierde. ▲ jugar, arriesgar *He's gambling everything on the success of his son.* Se lo está jugando todo por el éxito de su hijo.

game partida *Let's play a game.* Vamos a jugar una partida. ▲ juego *He*

325

looks upon his work as a game. Considera su trabajo como un juego. ▲ jugada *I saw through his game.* Le ví la jugada. ▲ caza *Is there any big game near here?* ¿Hay caza mayor cerca de aquí? ▲ actividad, asunto *How long have you been in this game?* ¿Cuánto tiempo lleva Ud. dedicado a estas actividades? ‖ *Their team put up a game fight.* Su equipo se defendió con brío. ‖ *I'm game for anything.* Estoy dispuesto a todo. ‖ *He plays a good game.* El juega bien. ‖ *They realized the game was up.* Se dieron cuenta de que habían perdido el juego.

gang [*n*] pandilla *The gangsters of the city were organized in gangs.* Los pistoleros de la ciudad se organizaron en pandillas. ▲ cuadrilla *Two work gangs were repairing the road.* Dos cuadrillas de trabajadores estaban reparando la carretera.

○ **to gang up** organizarse en cuadrilla.

gap abertura, portillo *There's a big gap between the planks.* Hay una gran abertura entre las tablas. ▲ quebrada, barranca *Let's take a hike through the gap.* Demos una caminata por la quebrada.

gape boquear, estar con la boca abierta.

garage garaje.

garbage basura.

garden jardín *These flowers are from our garden.* Estas flores son de nuestro jardín.

○ **botanical garden** jardín botánico. ○ **vegetable garden** huerta *I want to plant a vegetable garden.* Quiero sembrar una huerta.

gargle [*n*] gárgara.

● [*v*] gargarizar, hacer gárgaras.

garlic ajo.

garment prenda de vestir.

garret buhardilla.

garter liga.

gas [*n*] gas *Turn off the gas.* Sierre el gas.—*Did the dentist give you gas?* ¿Le dió gas el dentista?

● [*v*] gasear *He was gassed in the last war.* Fué gaseado en la última guerra.

○ **gas station** puesto de gasolina. ○ **gas stove** cocina de gas. ○ **intestinal gas** gases intestinales. ○ **to gas up** tomar gasolina *Let's stop at the next station and gas up.* Detengámonos en el próximo puesto y tomemos gasolina.

gasoline gasolina.

gasp [*v*] boquear.

gate puerta *The crowd poured out through the gate.* La gente salía en masa por la puerta. ▲ entrada *The game drew a gate of three thousand.* El partido atrajo una entrada de tres mil personas.

○ **gates** compuertas *(water) When the water rises too high, they open the gates.* Abren las compuertas cuando el agua sube demasiado.

gather recoger *He gathered up his things and left.* Recogió sus cosas y partió. ▲ reunirse, congregarse *The crowd gathered around the speaker.* La multitud se congregó alrededor del orador. ▲ deducir *I gather you don't like him.* Deduzco que a Ud. no le gusta. ▲ ganar, aumentar *The car slowly gathered speed.* El automovil ganó velocidad poco a poco. ▲ fruncir *The sleeves are gathered at the cuff.* Las mangas están fruncidas en el puño.

gaudy llamativo, charro, chillón.

gauge [*n*] manómetro de aire *Is there an air gauge here?* ¿Hay un manómetro de aire aquí? ▲ indicador *What does the gasoline gauge say?* ¿Qué marca el indicador de gasolina? ▲ calibrador *Gauges are used to measure the thickness of wire.* Para medir el grosor de los alambres hay que usar calibradores.

● [*v*] medir *The wind must be gauged accurately.* Hay que medir la velocidad del viento con exactitud.

○ **narrow gauge** vía angosta *The railroads of that country are narrow gauge.* Los ferrocarriles de ese país son de vía angosta.

gauze gasa.

gay alegre.

gaze [*n*] mirada fija.

● [*v*] mirar con fijeza, clavar la mirada.

gear engranaje *Be careful or you'll strip the gears.* Cuidado que puede romper los dientes de los engranajes. ▲ equipo *We spent the afternoon cleaning our gear.* Pasamos la tarde limpiando el equipo.

‖ *The car is in gear.* El carro tiene una velocidad puesta.

gem gema, piedra preciosa.

general [*n*] general *Tomorrow the general will take command.* El general tomará el mando mañana.

● [*adj*] general *They hold a general election every year.* Celebran elecciónes generales todos los años.

○ **in general** en general *In general things are all right.* En general las cosas están bien.

generally generalmente.

generate producir, generar.

generation generación.

generator generador.

generous generoso *Be generous; don't think only of his faults.* Sea Ud. generoso, no piense solamente en sus defectos. ▲espléndido, generoso *He's certainly generous with his money.* Verdaderamente es espléndido con su dinero. ▲abundante, amplio *This restaurant serves generous portions.* Este restaurante sirve raciones abundantes.

genial cordial, afable.

genius genio.

gentle cuidadoso *The nurse has very gentle hands.* La enfermera tiene manos muy cuidadosas. ▲leve *There was a gentle knock on the door.* Dieron un golpe leve en la puerta. ▲suave *He was rowing against a gentle current.* Remaba contra una corriente suave. ▲apacible, bondadoso *Isn't he a gentle person?* ¿Verdad que es una persona bondadosa? ▲dócil, manso *That dog is very gentle.* Ese perro es muy dócil.

gentleman caballero *This way, gentlemen!* ¡Por aquí, caballeros!

genuine genuino.

geography geografía.

germ germen.

German alemán, germano.

gesture [n] gesto, ademán *He made a gesture with his hand.* Hizo un ademán con la mano. ▲gesto *His work was merely a gesture of good will.* Su trabajo fué un mero gesto de buena voluntad.

● [v] gesticular, hacer gestos *He gestures when he speaks.* Gesticula cuando habla.

get recibir *When did you get my letter?* ¿Cuando recibió Ud. mi carta? ▲conseguir *Can you get me another pencil?* ¿Puede Ud. conseguirme otro lápiz? —*Can you get him to come to the theater?* ¿Puede Ud. conseguir que venga al teatro?—*They got him elected Mayor.* Consiguieron que le eligieran alcalde. ▲tener *We've got enough.* Tenemos bastante. ▲llegar *I'll get there in an hour.* Llegaré allí dentro de una hora. ▲buscar *I'll go and get the book tomorrow.* Iré a buscar el libro mañana. ▲localizar, dar con *I couldn't get him by phone.*

No pude localizarle por teléfono. ▲hacer llegar *We must get the message to the telegraph office.* Tenemos que hacer llegar el mensaje a la oficina telegráfica. ▲ir por *Wait till I get my hat.* Espéreme mientras voy por mi sombrero.

○ **to get about** mostrarse activo *For an old man he gets about very well.* Para los años que tiene se muestra muy activo. ○ **to get across** hacerse comprender *Finally I was able to get the meaning across.* Por fin me pude hacer comprender. ○ **to get along** llevarse bien *Those two don't get along.* Esos dos no se llevan bien. ▲componérselas *I'll get along somehow.* Me las compondré de algún modo. ▲marcharse *It's late and I'll have to be getting along.* Tengo que marcharme porque es tarde. ○ **to get along in years** envejecer, ponerse viejo *He's certainly getting along in years.* Ya se está poniendo viejo. ○ **to get around** salir mucho, ir a todas partes *He gets around a lot.* Sale mucho. or Va a todas partes. ▲divulgarse, difundirse *The story will get around in a few hours.* El cuento se divulgará en pocas horas. ▲pasar por alto, eludir *Can you get around that regulation?* ¿Puede Ud. eludir esa disposición? ▲manejar *She gets around him.* Ella le maneja bien. ○ **to get at** llegar hasta, alcanzar *I can't get at my luggage.* No puedo llegar hasta donde está mi equipaje. ▲descubrir, averiguar *Some day I'll get at the real reason.* Algún día descubriré la verdadera razón. ○ **to get away** alejarse *I want to get away from the noise.* Quiero alejarme del ruido. ○ **to get away with something** arreglárselas, componérselas *I'm sure I can get away with it.* Estoy seguro que podré arreglármelas. ○ **to get back** regresar, volver *When did you get back?* ¿Cuándo regresó Ud.? ○ **to get back at** desquitarse *How can I get back at him?* ¿Cómo puedo desquitarme con él? ○ **to get by** burlar *Can I get by the guard?* ¿Podré burlar la guardia? ▲pasar *Do you think I can get by with it?* ¿Cree Ud. que podré pasarlo? ▲arreglárselas *I'll get by if I have a place to sleep.* Me las arreglaré si encuentro un lugar donde dormir. ○ **to get fired** ser despedido *I'll get fired if they find out.* Seré despedido si lo descubren. ○ **to get going** poner en marcha *He'll* *be able to get the work going.* El podrá poner el tiabajo en marcha. ○ **to get in** llegar, arribər *What time does the train get in?* ¿A qué hora llega el tren? ▲ meter, entrar *Please get the clothes in before it rains.* Haga el favor de meter la ropa antes de que llueva. ○ **to get in touch with** comunicar con *Get in touch with me.* Comuníquese conmigo. ○ **to get in with** congeniar con *Did you get in with our crowd?* ¿Ha congeniado Ud. con nuestro grupo? ○ **to get off** apearse, bajarse *I want to get off at the next stop.* Quiero apearme en la parada siguiente. ▲ quitar *I can't get my shoes off.* No puedo quitarme los zapatos. ▲ levantarse *Please get off the couch.* Hágame el favor de levantarse del diván. ○ **to get off with** salir con *I'll get off with very light punishment.* Saldré de esto con una pena leve. ○ **to get old, get on in years** envejecer *He's getting old.* Está envejeciendo. ○ **to get on** subir *Don't get on the train yet.* No suba al tren todavía. ▲ proseguir, continuar *Let's get on with the meeting.* Prosigamos con la sesión. ▲ irle a uno, pasarlo *How are you getting on?* ¿Cómo lo pasa Ud.? ▲ llevarse *The three of us get on very well.* Nosotros tres nos llevamos muy bien. ○ **to get out** salir, bajarse *Get out of the car.* Salga del automóvil. ▲ divulgarse, hacerse público *We musn't let this news get out.* No debemos permitir que esta noticia se divulgue. ▲ publicar *They are getting out a new book on that subject.* Van a publicar un nuevo libro sobre ese tema. ○ **to get out of** sacar de *How much did you get out of the deal?* ¿Cuánto sacó Ud. del negocio? ▲ librarse de, salir de *How did you ever get out of it?* ¿Cómo hizo Ud. para salir de aquello? ○ **to get over** curarse *I got over my cold quickly.* Me curé del catarro rápidamente. ▲ salvar, vencer *How did you get over the difficulty?* ¿Cómo salvó Ud. el obstáculo? ▲ hacer comprender, dar a entender *I finally got the point over.* Al fin pude darles a entender lo que quería. ○ **to get ready** prepararse, alistarse *Get ready!* ¡Prepárese! ▲ tener listo, hacer *When are you going to get dinner ready?* ¿Cuándo va a tener Ud. lista la comida? ○ **to get something out** sacar, echar *Get it out of the house.* Sáquelo de la casa. ○ **to get**

to be llegar a ser *They got to be good friends.* Llegaron a ser buenos amigos. ○ **to get together** reunirse *Let's get together tonight at my house.* Reunámonos esta noche en mi casa. ▲ ponerse de acuerdo, entenderse *They never seem to get together on anything.* Por lo visto, nunca se ponen de acuerdo en nada. ○ **to get up** levantarse *I get up at seven every morning.* Todas las mañanas me levanto a las siete. ○ **to get wet** mojarse *I don't want to get my feet wet.* No quiero mojarme los pies. ‖ *How are you getting along?* ¿Cómo le va? ‖ *He got off to a flying start.* Empezó con mucho impulso. ‖ *Do you get the idea?* ¿Lo comprende Ud.? ‖ *I got angry.* Me enfadé. ‖ *I've got to leave early.* Tengo que salir temprano. ‖ *I've got lots of work to do.* Tengo mucho trabajo que hacer. ‖ *All my clothes have gotten dirty since I've been here.* Desde que estoy aquí se me ha ensuciado toda la ropa.

ghost fantasma.
　‖ *He doesn't have a ghost of a chance.* No tiene ni la menor oportunidad.

giant [n] gigante *That man is a giant.* Ese hombre es un gigante.
　● [adj] gigantesco *There will be a giant crop of corn this year.* Este año habrá una gigantesca cosecha de maíz.

gift obsequio, regalo *Thank you for the Christmas gift.* Muchas gracias por su obsequio de navidad. ▲ talento *He has a gift for drawing.* Tiene talento para el dibujo.

giggle [n] risa tonta.
　● [v] reírse tontamente.

gild dorar.

ginger jengibre.

gipsy gitano.

girder viga.

girdle [n] faja.
　● [v] ceñir, cercar.

girl niña *The woman gave birth to a baby girl.* La mujer dió a luz a una niña. ▲ muchacha *Are there any pretty girls in town?* ¿Hay muchachas bonitas en el pueblo? ▲ chica, muchacha *Well, girls, it's time to go.* Bueno, chicas, ya es hora de que nos vayamos. ▲ novia *I just got a letter from my girl.* Acabo de recibir una carta de mi novia. ▲ sirvienta, criada *We pay our girl fifty dollars a month.*

Pagamos a la criada cincuenta dólares mensuales.

give dar *Please give me the letter.* Haga el favor de darme la carta. ▲ pronunciar, decir *Who's giving the main speech?* ¿Quién pronunciará el principal discurso? ▲ hundirse *Be careful! The step might give under your weight!* ¡Tenga cuidado! El escalón se puede hundir con su peso. ○ to **give a damn** *I don't give a damn.* No me importa un comino. ○ to **give away** regalar *I gave my old clothes away.* Regalé mi ropa vieja. ▲ divulgar *Don't give away my secret.* No divulgue Ud. mi secreto. ○ to **give back** devolver *Please give me back my pen.* Haga el favor de devolverme la pluma. ○ to **give in** ceder *After a long argument, I finally gave in.* Después de una larga discusión finalmente cedí. ○ to **give off** despedir, dar *The flowers give off a strong odor.* Las flores despiden un olor fuerte. ○ to **give out** repartir *Who gave out the tickets?* ¿Quién repartió los boletos? ▲ acabarse, agotarse *Our supplies are giving out.* Se están agotando nuestras existencias. ○ to **give up** dejar, abandonar *The maid gave up her job.* La criada dejó el empleo. ▲ darse por vencido *I tried hard but I had to give up.* Hice todo lo que pude pero tuve que darme por vencido. ▲ retirarse de *I'm going to give up business.* Me voy a retirar de los negocios. ▲ romper las relaciones con, renunciar a *After their quarrel she gave him up.* Después del disgusto ella renunció a él. ▲ desahuciar, perder la esperanza *He was so ill, the doctor gave him up.* Estaba tan enfermo que el doctor le desahució. ○ to **give way** ceder *The bridge gave way.* El puente cedió. ▲ retroceder *The crowd gave way.* El gentío retrocedió. ‖ *Who gave away the bride?* ¿Quién llevó a la novia? ‖ *This elastic has a lot of give.* Este elástico da mucho de sí. ‖ *My old coat still gives me service.* Todavía me sirve mi abrigo viejo.

given dado *I must finish in a given time.* Tengo que terminarlo en un tiempo dado.—*Given such a situation what else could I do?* Dada una situación tal ¿qué otra cosa podía hacer? —*He is given to lying.* Es dado a mentir.

glad ○ to **be glad** alegrarse *I'm glad to hear you're better.* Me alegra saber que está Ud. mejor.

glance [n] vistazo *I recognized him at a glance.* Lo reconocí de un vistazo. ○ to **glance off** desviarse al chocar *The bullet glanced off his helmet.* La bala se desvió al chocar con su casco.

gland glándula.

glare [n] resplandor *The sun's glare is strong today.* Hoy está muy fuerte el resplandor del sol. ● [v] deslumbrar *The lights glare terribly.* Las luces deslumbran terriblemente. ▲ mirar ferozmente *The woman glared at us.* La mujer nos miró ferozmente.

glass vidrio *I cut myself on a piece of glass.* Me corté con un pedazo de vidrio. ▲ vaso *May I have a glass of water?* ¿Puede Ud. darme un vaso de agua? ▲ cristal, vidrio *I bought a glass vase.* Compré un florero de cristal. ○ **field glasses** gemelos. ○ **glasses** anteojos, [Sp] gafas *I wear glasses only for reading.* Uso anteojos solamente para leer.

gleam [n] destello, centelleo. ● [v] destellar.

glee júbilo.

glide resbalar, deslizarse *The sleigh glided swiftly over the ice.* El trineo se deslizó rápidamente sobre el hielo. ▲ planear *(aviation) Look how the plane's gliding toward the field!* ¡Mira como planea el avión hacia el aeródromo!

glimpse [n] ojeada, vistazo. ● [v] dar un vistazo.

glitter [n] resplandor *The glitter of the sun hurts my eyes.* El resplandor del sol me lastima los ojos. ● [v] brillar *Water glitters in the sunlight.* El agua brilla a la luz del sol.

globe esfera, globo.

gloomy sombrío *It's a very gloomy day.* Es un día muy sombrío. ▲ triste, melancólico *Why are you so gloomy?* ¿Por qué estás tan triste? ▲ pesimista *Don't be so gloomy about the future.* No seas tan pesimista sobre el porvenir.

glorious glorioso *Our country has a glorious history.* Nuestro país tiene una historia gloriosa. ▲ magnífico *This is certainly a glorious day.* Verdaderamente hace un día magnífico.

glory gloria.

glove guante.

glow [n] encendimiento, calor vivo.
● [v] relucir.
glue cola.
gnat jején.
gnaw roer.
go [n] energía *For an old man, he has a lot of go.* Para su edad avanzada tiene mucha energía.
● [v] ir *Go slow.* Vaya despacio. —*That chair goes in the corner.* Esa silla va en el rincón.—*I am going to go right away.* Me voy a ir en seguida. ▲ caminar, ir *The train is sure going fast.* El tren camina muy ligero. ▲ irse *Let's go.* Vámonos. *When did he go?* ¿Cuándo se fué? ▲ acabarse *The brandy is all gone.* Se ha acabado el coñac. ▲ dejar, vender *The shop keeper let this cloth go for almost nothing.* El tendero dejó esta tela casi por nada. ▲ desaparecer *The pain has gone.* Ha desaparecido el dolor. ▲ estar bien *Whatever he says goes.* Cualquier cosa que diga está bien. ▲ funcionar *This typewriter won't go.* Esta máquina de escribir no funciona. ▲ hacer *When you start to swim, go like this.* Cuando empiece Ud. a nadar, hágalo así. ▲ pasar *Let him go hungry.* Déjele pasar hambre. ▲ salir *Everything goes wrong when I leave.* Cuando me ausento todo va mal. ▲ volverse *I'll go crazy if this keeps up.* Me volveré loco si esto continúa. ▲ ser *The prize will go to the best student.* El premio será para el mejor estudiante. ○ **Go on!** ¡Qué va! *Go on! You don't mean that.* ¡Qué va! Ud. no quiere decir eso. ○ **on the go** en actividad *He's on the go day and night.* Está en actividad día y noche. ○ **to go around** alcanzar para todos *There is barely enough to go around.* Apenas alcanza esto para todos. ○ **to go astray** extraviarse *The letter has gone astray.* Si ha extraviado la carta. ○ **to go away** marcharse, irse *When are you going away?* ¿Cuándo se marcha Ud.?* ○ **to go back** volver *When do you expect to go back?* ¿Cuándo piensa volver? ○ **to go back on** fallar, defraudar *I won't go back on my friends.* Yo no les fallaré a mis amigos. ○ **to go by** usar *He goes by a false name.* Usa un nombre falso. ○ **to go down** bajar *Let's go down to get a cup of coffee.* Bajemos a tomar una taza de café.—*Has the rate of exchange gone up or down?*

¿Ha subido o bajado el tipo del cambio? ▲ ponerse *The sun goes down early in winter.* El sol se pone temprano en invierno. ○ **to go for a walk** dar un paseo *Let's go for a walk.* Vamos a dar un paseo. ○ **to go from bad to worse** ir de mal en peor *Things are going from bad to worse.* Las cosas van de mal en peor. ○ **to go in** entrar en, participar en *Would you like to go in with me on this proposition?* ¿Le gustaría participar en este proyecto conmigo? ○ **to go in for** dedicarse a *Do you go in for sports?* ¿Se dedica Ud. a los deportes? ○ **to go into** discutir *Why go into that now?* ¿Porqué discutir eso ahora? ▲ tocar *Let's not go into that subject now.* No toquemos este asunto ahora. ▲ ventilar *We should go into this matter thoroughly.* Tendremos que ventilar este asunto a fondo. ○ **to go off** dispararse *The pistol went off accidentally.* La pistola se disparó accidentalmente. ▲ llevar a cabo, resultar *The attack went off according to plan.* El ataque se llevó a cabo de acuerdo con el plan. ○ **to go on** ir *Let's go on toward the mountain.* Vamos hacia la montaña. ▲ continuar, seguir *He went on talking.* Continuó hablando.—*Let's go on working hard.* Continuemos trabajando de firme. ○ **to go on board** embarcarse, ir a bordo *You'll have to go on board before six o'clock.* Tendrán que ir a bordo antes de las seis. ○ **to go on with** proseguir, continuar *We'll go on with the discussion after lunch.* Proseguiremos la discusión después del almuerzo. ○ **to go out** salir *I'm going out to dinner.* Voy a salir a comer. ▲ pasar de moda *That song will go out with the war.* Esa canción pasará de moda después de la guerra. ▲ apagarse *Suddenly the lights went out.* De pronto se apagaron las luces. ○ **to go out of one's way** tomarse la molestia *He went out of his way to help me.* Se tomó la molestia para ayudarme. ○ **to go over** examinar, revisar *He went over the problem very carefully.* Examinó el problema muy cuidadosamente. ▲ tener éxito *Do you think this song will go over?* ¿Cree Ud. que esta canción tendrá éxito? ○ **to go slow** atrasarse *My watch goes slow.* Mi reloj se atrasa ○ **to go through** pasar por *The soldiers go through severe training.* Los soldados pasan por un riguroso entrenamiento. ▲aprobarse *Do you think the application will go through?* ¿Cree Ud. que se aprobará la solicitud? ○to go to trouble molestarse *Don't go to any trouble.* No se moleste Ud. ○to go under arruinarse, quebrar *His business went under last year.* Su negocio se arruinó el año pasado. ○to go up subir *Apples have gone up.* Las manzanas han subido. ○to go with salir *They've been going with each other for years.* Salen juntos desde hace años. ▲acompañar, ir con *Do you want me to go with you?* ¿Quiere que la acompañe? ▲ir con, entonar *The curtains don't go with the other furnishings.* Las cortinas no van con los demás muebles. ○to let go soltar *Let go of the rope.* Suelte la cuerda. ○to make a go of ir bien *Did he make a go of his marriage?* ¿Le fué bien en su matrimonio?

‖ *Go ahead.* Siga Ud. ‖ *Tell him to go about his own business.* Dígale que se ocupe de sus cosas y no de las ajenas.

goal meta, [*Am*] gol.

goat cabra.

God Dios *God knows what he'll do next!* ¡Sabe Dios lo que hará después!—*God bless you!* ¡Dios le bendiga!

‖ *God bless you! (sneezing)* ¡Salud!

goggles anteojos.

gold oro.

golden dorado.

golf golf.

gonorrhea gonorrea.

good buen, bueno *He gave me good advice.* Me dió un buen consejo.—*This is a good meal.* Esta es una buena comida.—*Good!* ¡Bueno! ▲competente *He's a good man for that job.* Es un hombre competente para ese trabajo. ▲mucho *I haven't seen him for a good while.* No le he visto en mucho tiempo. ○a good deal mucho *After the operation I had a good deal of pain.* Después de la operación tuve mucho dolor. ○as good as casi *The job is as good as done.* El trabajo está casi terminado. ○better mejor *Give me a better pencil.* Déme Ud. un lápiz que sea mejor. ○for good definitivamente, de una vez para siempre *Let's fix it for good this time.* Vamos a arreglar esto de una vez para siempre. ○good and bien *Make the tea good and strong.* Haga el té bien cargado. ○to be good for durar *That watch is good for a lifetime.* Ese reloj le durará toda la vida. ▲pagar *He is good for the damages to your car.* Él pagará los daños causados a su automóvil. ○to make good cumplir *He always makes good his promises.* Siempre cumple sus promesas. ▲responder de *If I break it, I will make good the damage.* Responderé de los daños si lo rompo. ‖ tener éxito *I'm sure he'll make good in business.* Estoy seguro de que tendrá éxito en los negocios. ○to the good venir bien *Whatever he brings us is to the good.* Nos viene bien cualquier cosa que traiga.

‖ *Did you have a good time?* ¿Se ha divertido Ud.? ‖ *The medicine is good for you.* La medicina le caerá bien. ‖ *I'd like to go and see him, but what good will it do?* Me gustaría ir a verle, pero ¿de qué servirá? ‖ *Be a good boy.* Pórtate bien, chico.

good-by adiós.

good-looking guapo, bien parecido.

goodness bondad *He is known for his goodness.* Es conocido por su bondad.

‖ *Goodness, it's cold!* Ave María, qué frío hace! *or* ¡Cielos, qué frío hace!

goods mercancías *This store has a large stock of goods.* Este establecimiento tiene gran existencia de mercancías. ▲géneros *Cotton goods are very popular this summer.* Los géneros de algodón son muy populares este verano.

goose ganso.

gorge desfiladero, barranco *There is a great gorge two miles from here.* A dos millas de aquí hay un gran desfiladero.

gorge ○to gorge oneself darse un atracón *He gorged himself on sweets.* Se dió un atracón de dulces.

gorgeous magnífico, estupendo, espléndido.

gospel evangelio.

gossip [*n*] chisme *I wouldn't believe that gossip if I were you.* Si yo fuera Ud., no creería ese chisme. ▲chismoso *His wife is an old gossip.* Su mujer es una chismosa.

● [*v*] chismear *That fellow gossips too much.* Ese tío chismea demasiado.

govern gobernar *The president has governed the country well.* El presidente ha gobernado bien el país.

government gobierno.

governor gobernador.

gown vestido *That's a beautiful gown*

you're wearing. Lleva Ud. un hermoso vestido.
○ **dressing gown** bata (de casa).
grab [*v*] agarrar.
grace gracia.
graceful garboso, donairoso.
gracious afable, amable.
grade [*n*] grado *What grade do you teach?* ¿En qué grado enseña Ud.? ▲ clase, calidad *We buy the best grade of milk.* Compramos leche de primera calidad. ▲ notas *He received the highest grades in the class.* Recibió las mejores notas de la clase. ▲ pendiente *There is quite a steep grade on the other side of the hill.* Al otro lado del cerro hay una pendiente muy pronunciada.
● [*v*] clasificar *Oranges are graded by size and quality.* Las naranjas se clasifican según su tamaño y calidad. ▲ nivelar *The workers graded the field.* Los obreros nivelaron el terreno.
○ **down grade** cuesta abajo *Business has been going down grade for the last month.* En el último mes los negocios han ido cuesta abajo. ○ **to make the grade** subir la cuesta *The car had trouble making the grade.* Al automóvil le costó trabajo subir la cuesta. ▲ alcanzar éxito *If you work hard you can make the grade.* Si trabaja duro, alcanzará éxito.
gradual gradual.
graduate [*adj*] de ampliación *He is doing graduate work in science.* Está haciendo estudios científicos de ampliación.
● [*v*] graduarse *When did you graduate from college?* ¿Cuándo se graduó Ud. en la Universidad?
‖ *His brother was a graduate of the University of Madrid.* Su hermano se graduó en la Universidad de Madrid.
graft [*n*] injerto *(surgical).*
● [*v*] injertar.
grain grano *The grain is ready for harvest.* El grano está listo para la cosecha.—*How many grains are there in each pill?* ¿Cuántos granos contiene cada píldora? ▲ veta *This wood has a beautiful grain.* Esta madera tiene una veta hermosa. ▲ pizca *There isn't a grain of truth in the story.* No hay ni pizca de verdad en el cuento.
grammar gramática.
grand magnífico *It was grand weather*

for tennis. Hacía un tiempo magnífico para jugar al tenis.
○ **grand ballroom** gran salón de baile. ○ **grand total** importe total.
grandchild nieto, nieta.
granddaughter nieta.
grandfather abuelo.
grandmother abuela.
grandparents abuelos.
grandson nieto.
granite granito.
grant [*n*] subvención *The school is supported by a government grant.* La escuela tiene una subvención del gobierno.
● [*v*] conceder *Did they grant him permission to leave?* ¿Le concedieron permiso para marcharse?
○ **to take for granted** tomar por cierto, dar por hecho *You take too much for granted.* Ud. toma por ciertas muchas cosas.
grape uva.
grapefruit toronja.
graph gráfica.
grasp [*n*] conocimiento *He has a firm grasp of the subject.* Tiene un buen conocimiento del tema.
● [*v*] comprender *I don't quite grasp your meaning.* No acabo de comprender lo que Ud. quiere decir. ▲ agarrarse *She grasped the strap with both hands.* Se agarró de la correa con las dos manos.
‖ *He has a powerful grasp.* Agarra muy fuerte.
grass hierba, césped, grama *Keep off the grass.* Se prohibe pisar la hierba.
grate [*n*] parrilla *The furnace has a grate.* El horno tiene parrilla.
● [*v*] destrozar *That music grates on my nerves.* Esa música me destroza los nervios. ▲ raspar, rayar *Grate some cheese.* Raye un poco de queso.
grateful agradecido.
gratify complacer *He gratified my desires.* Complació mis deseos. ▲ tener el gusto *I was gratified to meet her.* Tuve el gusto de conocerla.
gratifying serle grato a uno *It is very gratifying to hear of their success.* Me es muy grato tener noticias de su buen éxito.
gratitude gratitud.
grave [*n*] sepulcro, tumba *Her grave was covered with roses.* Su tumba estaba cubierta de rosas.
● [*adj*] grave *The patient's condition is grave.* La condición del enfermo es grave.
gravel grava, cascajo.

gravity gravedad.

gravy salsa.

gray [*adj*] gris *The sky was gray all morning.* El cielo estuvo gris toda la mañana.
● [*v*] encanecer *He's graying fast.* Él está encaneciendo rápidamente.
○ **gray-haired** de pelo cano, canoso.

graze rozar *The bullet grazed his forehead.* La bala le rozó la frente. ▲ apacentar, pacer, pastar *This land is good for grazing cattle.* Este campo es bueno para apacentar el ganado.

grease [*n*] grasa.
● [*v*] engrasar.

great gran *I think that's a great idea.* Creo que eso es una gran idea. ▲ mucho *I was in great pain.* Sentía mucho dolor. ▲ estupendo *He's a great one for telling funny stories.* Es estupendo para contar chistes.
○ **a great deal** mucho *He sings a great deal.* Canta mucho. ○ **great big** gran *He owned a great big estate.* Era propietario de una gran hacienda.

greed codicia.

green verde *Green is not becoming to her.* El verde no le sienta bien a ella.
‖ *He's pretty green at that job.* Es un novato en ese empleo.

greens verduras *You don't eat enough greens.* Ud. no come suficientes verduras.

greeting saludo.

grief sentimiento, dolor.

grievance agravio, motivo de queja.

grieve afligir, lastimar.

grill [*n*] parrilla.
● [*v*] asar a la parrilla.

grim torvo, ceñudo *He had a grim look on his face.* Su cara tenía un aspecto torvo. ▲ horrendo *The battle was grim.* La batalla fué horrenda.

grimy tiznado, sucio.

grin [*n*] mueca.
● [*v*] hacer muecas.

grind [*n*] calvario *A day's work for a miner is a long grind.* Un día de trabajo para un minero es un calvario.
● [*v*] moler *We grind our coffee by hand.* Molemos el café a mano. ▲ rechinar *He ground his teeth in anger.* Rechinó los dientes de rabia.

grip [*n*] maleta *Where can I leave my grip?* ¿Dónde puedo dejar mi maleta?
● [*v*] agarrarse *The sailor gripped the railing.* El marinero se agarró a la barandilla.
‖ *He can't get a grip on himself.* No se puede contener. ‖ *Get a good grip on the rope.* Agarre la cuerda firmemente.

groan [*n*] gemido, quejido.
● [*v*] gemir.

grocer tendero, abacero, [*Cuba*] bodeguero, [*Mex*] abarrotero.

grocery ○ **groceries** comestibles *Let's go and buy some groceries.* Vamos a comprar algunos comestibles. ○ **grocery store** tienda de comestibles, [*Sp*] ultramarinos, [*Mex*] tienda de abarrotes, [*Cuba*] bodega, [*Arg & Chile*] almacén.

groom [*n*] novio *The bride is ready. Where's the groom?* La novia ya está lista. Dónde está el novio?
● [*v*] almohazar *The horse must be groomed.* Hay que almohazar al caballo.

groove acanaladura, estría.

grope tentar.

gross [*n*] gruesa *A gross is twelve dozen.* Una gruesa son doce docenas.
● [*adj*] craso *The accountant made a gross error.* El contador cometió un error craso. ▲ grosero *That's a very gross way of putting it.* Esa es una manera muy grosera de decirlo.
○ **gross income** ingresos totales.

ground [*n*] tierra *This ground is not very fertile.* Esta tierra no es muy fértil. ▲ terreno *The ground was very rocky.* El terreno era muy pedregoso. ▲ razón *What grounds do you have for saying that?* ¿Que razones tiene Ud. para decir eso?
● [*adj*] baja *I don't want a room on the ground floor.* No quiero una habitación en la planta baja.
○ **from the ground up** de abajo arriba. ○ **grounded** fundado *Your opinions are well grounded.* Sus juicios están bien fundados. ▲ versado *They were well grounded in history.* Eran muy versados en historia. ▲ sin volar, en tierra *The plane was grounded by bad weather.* El avión estuvo sin volar a causa de mal tiempo. ▲ conexión con tierra *Is the radio grounded?* ¿Tiene la radio conexión con tierra? ○ **grounds** jardines *A gardener takes care of the grounds.* Un jardinero cuida los jardines. ▲ posos *I don't like coffee grounds in my cup.* No me gustan los posos de café en mi taza. ○ **to gain ground** ganar terreno. ○ **to give ground** ceder terreno *When he insisted, I had to give ground.* Al insistir él, tuve que ceder terreno. ○ **to hold or stand one's ground** mantenerse firme en su

terreno. ○ **to lose ground** perder terreno.

‖ *If I drive, I can cover a lot of ground in one day.* Si vamos en coche podremos hacer un gran recorrido en un día.

group [*n*] grupo *There was a group of men in the street.* Había un grupo de hombres en la calle.

● [*v*] agrupar *Group the words according to meaning.* Agrupe las palabras según su significado.

grove arboleda, alameda.

grow crecer *The little boy grew very fast.* El niño creció muy rápidamente. ▲ aumentar, crecer *The crowd grew rapidly.* La muchedumbre aumentó rápidamente. ▲ cultivar *That farmer grows vegetables.* Ese agricultor cultiva legumbres.

○ **to grow cold or warm** empezar a hacer frío o calor *The weather is growing cold.* Empieza a hacer frío. ○ **to grow up** desarrollarse, crecer *His daughter is growing up rapidly.* Su hija se está desarrollando rápidamente.

‖ *That music grows on me.* Esa música me gusta cada vez más. ‖ *He's a grown-up man now.* Ya es un hombre.

growl [*n*] gruñido.

● [*v*] gruñir, refunfuñar.

growth desarrollo, crecimiento *The dog reached full growth in a year.* El perro alcanzó su desarrollo completo en un año. ▲ tumor *He has a growth on his arm.* Tiene un tumor en el brazo.

‖ *He has a two days' growth of beard.* Tiene una barba de dos días.

grudge envidiar *I don't grudge him his success.* No le envidio su éxito.

○ **to bear a grudge against someone** tener inquina a alguien, tener rabia a alguien.

gruff ceñudo, áspero.

grumble quejarse, refunfuñar.

grunt gruñir.

guarantee [*n*] garantía *This clock has a five-year guarantee.* Este reloj tiene una garantía de cinco años.

● [*v*] garantizar, asegurar *I'll guarantee that you'll enjoy this movie.* Le aseguro que le gustará esta película.

○ **to be guaranteed** estar garantizado *This pen is guaranteed for life.* Esta pluma está garantizada por toda la vida.

guard [*n*] guardia *The guard kept me from passing.* El guardia me impidió pasar.—*For a moment his guard was down.* Descuidó la guardia por un momento. ▲ vigilancia *They kept close guard of the bridge.* Guardaban una estrecha vigilancia del puente.

● [*v*] vigilar *Guard the prisoner carefully.* Vigile con cuidado al prisionero. ▲ tomar precauciones *They tried to guard against the disease spreading.* Trataron de tomar precauciones contra la propagación de la epidemia.

○ **off one's guard** desprevenido, fuera de guardia *You can never catch him off guard.* Nunca le puede Ud. coger desprevenido. ○ **to be on guard** estar en guardia.

guardian guardián, guarda.

guerilla guerrillero.

guess [*n*] suposición, conjetura *That was a good guess.* Esa fué una buena suposición.

● [*v*] acertar, adivinar *Can you guess my age?* ¿Puede Ud. acertar mi edad? ▲ suponer *I guess he's sick.* Supongo que está enfermo.

guest huésped.

guide [*n*] guía *The guide took me around.* El guía me llevó a todas partes.—*Where can I buy a guide to the city?* ¿Dónde puedo comprar una guía de la ciudad?

● [*v*] guiar *He guided the group through the woods.* Guió el grupo a través del bosque. ▲ guiarse, dejarse llevar *Don't be guided by his advice.* No se guíe por sus consejos.

guilt delito, culpa.

guilty culpable *The prisoner was found guilty.* Se halló que el preso era culpable.

‖ *I have a guilty conscience.* Tengo remordimiento de conciencia.

gulf golfo.

gum chicle *Do you have any gum?* ¿Tiene Ud. chicle? ▲ goma *There isn't much gum on these envelopes.* No tienen mucha goma estos sobres. ▲ encía *My gums hurt.* Me duelen las encías.

gun fusil *He spends a lot of time cleaning his gun.* Dedica mucho tiempo a la limpieza de su fusil. ▲ cañonazo *The ship fired a salute of twenty-one guns.* El barco disparó una salva de veintiún cañonazos. ▲ cañón *This is a long-range gun.* Es un cañón de largo alcance.

○ **to stick to one's guns** mantenerse con la suya.

gunner artillero.
gush derramar, verter.
gust ráfaga, racha.

gutter canal, gotera.
gymnasium gimnasio.

H

habit costumbre *I'm trying to break myself of the habit.* Estoy tratando de perder la costumbre.—*I got into that habit while I was abroad.* Adquirí esa costumbre mientras estaba en el extranjero. ○ **to be in the habit of** acostumbrar a *I'm in the habit of sleeping late on Sundays.* Acostumbro dormir hasta tarde los domingos.
habitual habitual.
haggard trasnochado, demacrado.
hail [*n*] granizo *The hail broke the window panes.* El granizo rompió los cristales. ▲ granizada *The soldiers loosed a hail of bullets against the enemy.* Los soldados lanzaron una granizada de balas contra el enemigo. ● [*v*] granizar *We might as well stay here until it stops hailing.* Mejor será que nos quedemos aquí hasta que deje de granizar.
hail [*v*] aclamar *The book's been hailed by all the critics.* El libro ha sido aclamado por todos los críticos. ▲ llamar *I've been trying to hail a cab for the last ten minutes.* Llevo diez minutos tratando de llamar un taxímetro. ○ **to hail from** venir de *What part of the country do you hail from?* ¿De que parte del país viene Ud.?
hailstorm granizada *The hailstorm ruined the tobacco crops.* La granizada destruyó la cosecha de tabaco.
hair pelo *There's a hair on your coat.* Tiene Ud. un pelo en el abrigo.—*He just missed me by a hair.* No me alcanzó por un pelo. ▲ cabello *What color is her hair?* ¿De qué color es el cabello de ella?
haircut corte de pelo.
hairdresser peluquero.
hair net redecilla.
hairpin horquilla, ganchito.
half [*n*] medio *This shirt'll take a yard and a half of material.* Para esta camisa se necesita yarda y media de tela. ▲ mitad *I'll give him half of my share.* Le daré la mitad de mi parte. ● [*adj*] medio *Give me a half pound of those.* Deme Ud. media libra de aquellos.

● [*adv*] medio, a medias *It's only half done.* Está hecho solamente a medias. ▲ medio *I was lying on the couch half asleep.* Estaba echado en el sofá, medio dormido. ○ **half an hour, a half hour** media hora *I'll be back in half an hour.* Volveré dentro de media hora.—*I waited for him a good half hour.* Le esperé media hora larga. ○ **half past** ... las ... y media *We'll be there at half past eight.* Estaremos allí a las ocho y media. ○ **half price** mitad de precio *I got it for half price at a sale.* Lo conseguí en un saldo a mitad de precio. ○ **in half** por la mitad *Shall I cut it in half?* ¿Lo corto por la mitad? ○ **to go halves** ir a medias *Will you go halves with me?* ¿Quiere Ud. ir a medias conmigo?
half-breed [*adj, n*] mestizo.
half-mast media asta.
hall vestíbulo *Please wait in the hall.* Haga el favor de esperar en el vestíbulo. ▲ corredor *It's the second door down the hall.* Es la segunda puerta del corredor. ▲ salón *There were no seats, so we stood at the back of the hall.* Como no quedaban asientos estuvimos de pie en el fondo del salón. ○ **city hall** ayuntamiento *His office is in the city hall.* Su despacho está en el ayuntamiento.
halt hacer alto *The soldiers halted for a short rest.* Los soldados hicieron alto para descansar un rato. ○ **to come to a halt** interrumpirse, pararse *The work finally came to a halt.* Por fin se interrumpió el trabajo. ‖ *Halt! Who's there?* ¡Alto! ¿Quién vive?
halter cabestro.
halting vacilante *Shyness made the child speak in a halting manner.* La timidez hizo que el niño hablara de una manera vacilante.
ham jamón *Bring me a nice piece of ham for dinner.* Tráigame un buen pedazo de jamón para la comida. ‖ *That actor's quite a ham.* Ese actor es un maleta [*Sp*]. Ese actor es muy malo.

hamburger albóndiga, [*Mex*] hamburguesa.

hammer [*n*] martillo *Could I borrow a hammer?* ¿Puedo pedir prestado un un martillo?
● [*v*] martillar *hammer the iron over the anvil.* Martille el hierro sobre el yunque.

hammock hamaca.

hamper [*n*] canasta *Throw those dirty clothes into the hamper.* Tire esa ropa sucia en la canasta.
● [*v*] impedir *He was hampered in getting a job by his lack of experience.* Su falta de experiencia le impidió conseguir un empleo.

hand [*n*] mano *Where can I wash my hands?* ¿Dónde puedo lavarme las manos?—*The affair's in my hands.* El asunto está en mis manos. *or* Tengo el asunto entre manos.—*This is the worst hand I've had all evening.* Esta es la peor mano que me ha tocado en toda la noche. ▲manecilla *The hour hand's broken.* La manecilla que marca las horas está rota. ▲parte *Did you have a hand in this?* ¿Ha tomado Ud. parte en esto? ▲ovación *The audience gave her a big hand.* El público le dió una gran ovación.
● [*v*] pasar *Will you hand me that pencil?* ¿Quiere Ud. pasarme ese lápiz?
○ **at first hand** directamente *I got this information at first hand.* Recibí estos informes directamente. ○ **by hand** a mano *All this sewing had to be done by hand.* Hubo que hacer toda esta costura a mano. ○ **farm hand** peón de granja *I worked a couple of years as a farm hand.* Trabajé un par de años como peón de granja. ○ **in hand** dominado, controlado *The situation's well in hand.* La situación está dominada. ○ **on hand** a mano, disponible *He's never on hand when I want him.* Nunca está a mano cuando lo necesito. ▲ en existencia *We haven't any soap on hand this week.* Esta semana no tenemos jabón en existencia. ○ **on one's hands** entre manos *I've got a lot of work on my hands today.* Hoy tengo mucho trabajo entre manos. ○ **on the other hand** por otra parte *He's a good man, but, on the other hand, he hasn't had much experience.* Es un buen hombre pero, por otra parte, no tiene mucha experiencia. ○ **on the right-hand** (*or* **left-hand**) **side** a la derecha (*or* izquierda) *The house is on the left-hand*

side *as you go up the street.* Yendo calle arriba, la casa está a la izquierda. ○ **to be handed down** pasar de padres a hijos *These jewels have been handed down in our family for generations.* Estas joyas han pasado de padres a hijos en nuestra familia. ○ **to change hands** cambiar de manos, cambiar de dueño *The business has changed hands.* El negocio ha cambiado de manos. ○ **to get out of hand** desmandarse *Don't let the students get out of hand.* No permita que los estudiantes se desmanden. ○ **to hand in** presentar *I'm going to hand in my resignation tomorrow.* Mañana voy a presentar mi dimisión. ○ **to hand out** distribuir *Take these tickets and hand them out.* Tome Ud. estos billetes y distribúyalos. ○ **to have one's hands full** estar ocupadísimo *He certainly has his hands full with that new job.* No hay duda de que está ocupadísimo con ese nuevo trabajo. ○ **to lend a hand** echar una mano, ayudar *Would you lend me a hand in moving that furniture?* ¿Me echaría Ud. una mano para mover estos muebles? ○ **to shake hands with** dar la mano, estrechar la mano *I shook hands with him and left.* Le dí la mano y me fuí.
‖ *Can you take this problem off my hands?* ¿Puede Ud. quitarme de encima este problema?

handbag cartera.

handball pelota.

handbill hoja suelta, prospecto.

handcuffs esposas.

handful puñado.

handicap impedimento, obstáculo *The lame arm'll be a handicap.* El brazo lisiado será un impedimento para su trabajo. ▲handicap *Who's your favorite to win the handicap?* ¿Quién cree Ud. que gane el handicap?
○ **to be handicapped** estar en situación de inferioridad *He's been handicapped all his life.* Ha estado toda su vida en una situación de inferioridad.

handkerchief pañuelo.

handle [*n*] mango *This hoe needs a new handle.* A este azadón le hace falta un mango nuevo.
● [*v*] manejar *handle with care.* Manéjese con cuidado.—*Can you handle a gun?* ¿Sabe Ud. manejar un fusil?—*He handles the car very well.* Maneja muy bien el automóvil. ▲ tocar, manosear *Look at it all you want*

but don't handle it. Mírelo todo lo que quiera pero no lo toque. ▲ saber dominar *He handled the situation very well.* Supo dominar la situación muy bien. ▲ tener *We don't handle that brand.* No tenemos esa marca.

handsome guapo, buen mozo *I don't think he's very handsome.* No me parece que es muy guapo. ▲ excelente *He made me a handsome offer for my farm.* Me hizo una oferta excelente por mi granja.

handwriting letra, escritura.

handy a la mano *Everything in the kitchen is so handy.* Todo en la cocina está a la mano. ▲ útil *This can opener's very handy.* Este abrelatas es muy útil. ▲ hábil *He's very handy at repairing things around the house.* Es muy hábil en reparar las cosas de la casa.

hang colgar *He hung the picture over the fireplace.* Colgó el cuadro encima de la chimenea.—*Is that your hat hanging on the hook?* ¿Es suyo el sombrero que cuelga de la percha? ▲ fijar *We should hang a sign on the door.* Debemos fijar un letrero en la puerta. ▲ bajar, inclinar *Why are you hanging your head?* ¿Por qué baja Ud. la cabeza? ▲ ahorcar *They'll hang him for his crime.* Le ahorcarán por su crimen.

○ **to get the hang of it** coger el tino *Now you're getting the hang of it.* Ahora ya le va Ud. cogiendo el tino. ○ **to hang on** agarrarse, asirse *I hung on as tight as I could.* Me agarré lo más fuertemente que pude. ○ **to hang on to** guardar *Hang on to this money.* Guarde bien este dinero. ○ **to hang out** asomarse demasiado *Don't hang out of the window.* No te asomes demasiado por la ventana. ○ **to hang up** colgar *Hang up your hat and coat.* Cuelgue Ud. su sombrero y su abrigo. ▲ colgar *He hung up on me.* Me colgó (el teléfono).

‖ *He's always hanging around the race track.* Todo el tiempo se lo pasa en el Hipódromo.

hangar hangar.

hanger *(for clothes)* colgador, gancho.

hangover resaca cruda. [*Mex*].

haphazard [*adj*] casual, fortuito.

happen pasar *What happened?* ¿Qué pasó?—*What happened to the typewriter?* ¿Qué le pasó a la máquina de escribir? ▲ ocurrir *Were you there when the accident happened?* ¿Estaba Ud. allí cuando ocurrió el acci-

dente? ▲ suceder *Everything happens to me.* Todas las cosas me suceden a mí. ▲ acontecer *A wonderful thing happened to me last night.* Anoche me aconteció algo maravilloso. ▲ lograr *How did you happen to find me?* ¿Cómo logró Ud. encontrarme? ‖ *I don't happen to agree with you.* El caso es que yo no estoy de acuerdo con Ud. ‖ *It happens that we can't do anything about it.* Da la casualidad que nada podemos hacer acerca de ello.

happily felizmente *They seem to live happily together.* Parece que viven juntos felizmente.—*Happily, no one was injured in the accident.* Felizmente nadie se hizo daño en el accidente.

happiness felicidad.

happy feliz *This is one of the happiest days of my life.* Este es uno de los días mas felices de mi vida.—*The movie had a happy ending.* La película tuvo un epílogo feliz. ▲ contento, alegre *I don't feel very happy.* No estoy muy contento.

harbor [*n*] puerto.

● [*v*] abrigar.

hard duro *I don't like to sleep on a hard bed.* No me gusta dormir en cama dura. ▲ apretado *He tied the rope into a hard knot.* Amarró la cuerda con un nudo apretado. ▲ difícil *I had a hard time getting here.* Me fué difícil llegar aquí. ▲ fuerte *If you like hard work, I'll see that you get it.* Si le gusta un trabajo fuerte yo me encargaré de proporcionárselo. ▲ asiduo *He's a hard worker and does a good job.* Es un trabajador asiduo y además hace un buen trabajo. ▲ severo *He's a hard man.* Es un hombre severo. ▲ injurioso *Those are hard words.* Esas son palabras injuriosas. ▲ duro, fuerte *He's been training for two months and he's as hard as nails.* Se ha entrenado durante dos meses y está fuerte como el hierro.

○ **hard-and-fast** inflexible, riguroso *We have no hard-and-fast rules here.* Aquí no hay reglas inflexibles. ○ **hard of hearing** duro de oído *You'll have to speak louder because he's hard of hearing.* Tendrá Ud. que hablar más alto porque es duro de oído. ○ **hard road** carretera pavimentada. ○ **hard water** agua gorda. ○ **to be hard up** hallarse en apuros, estar a la cuarta pregunta *He's always hard up before pay day.* Siempre se halla en apuros antes del día de pago.

○ **to freeze hard** congelarse bien *The ice cream didn't freeze hard.* El helado no se congeló bien. ○ **to rain hard** llover a cántaros *It was raining hard when he left the house.* Llovía a cántaros cuando salió de la casa. ○ **to try hard** esforzarse mucho *He tried hard to do it right, but failed.* Se esforzó mucho por hacerlo bien, pero fracasó.

hard-boiled duro *I like hard-boiled eggs.* Me gustan los huevos duros. ▲ duro, severo *The boss is pretty hard-boiled.* El jefe es muy duro.

hardly apenas *He had hardly begun to speak when he was interrupted.* Apenas empezó a hablar, cuando le interrumpieron.—*I hardly think so.* Apenas lo creo. ▲ casi *There were hardly any people there when the show started.* Casi no había gente allí cuando comenzó el espectáculo. ‖ *You can hardly expect me to believe that story.* Ud. no esperará que le crea ese cuento.

hardware ferretería.

harm [n] daño *The dry weather's done a lot of harm to the crop.* La sequía ha hecho mucho daño a la cosecha. ● [v] dañar *Be careful not to harm him.* Cuidado de no dañarle. ‖ *He gets mad easily but he wouldn't harm a flea.* Se enoja fácilmente pero no es capaz de matar ni una mosca.

harmony armonía, harmonía *I like the harmony of this composition.* Me agrada la armonía de esta composición.—*There was perfect harmony between the two families.* Había una completa armonía entre las dos familias. ○ **to be in complete harmony** estar completamente de acuerdo *The delegates are in complete harmony on everything.* Los delegados están completamente de acuerdo en todo.

harness [n] arnés. ● [v] guarnicionar.

harp arpa *This symphony requires two harps.* Esta sinfonía requiere dos arpas. ○ **to harp on** machacar sobre *I'm tired of hearing you harp on the same subject.* Estoy cansado de oirle machacar sobre el mismo tema.

harsh áspero.

harvest [n] cosecha. ● [v] cosechar.

hash picadillo *We had the best hash for dinner!* ¡Tuvimos un magnífico pica-dillo para la cena! ▲ lío, confusión *You sure made a hash of this!* ¡Qué lío ha hecho Ud. de esto. ○ **to hash up** enredar, echar a perder *Your intentions may have been good, but you've certainly hashed up everything.* Podrán haber sido buenas sus intenciones, pero lo cierto es que lo ha enredado todo.

haste prisa.

hasten darse prisa.

hasty hecho a la ligera *It's only a hasty job.* Es solo un trabajo hecho a la ligera. ▲ rápido, precipitado *They had to beat a hasty retreat.* Tuvieron que hacer una retirada precipitada. ▲ impulsivo, irreflexivo *He's very hasty in everything he does.* Es muy impulsivo en todo lo que hace. ▲ ligero, irreflexivo *It was a very hasty decision.* Fué una decisión muy ligera.

hat sombrero.

hatch empollar, incubar *Can't these eggs be hatched artificially?* ¿No se pueden incubar estos huevos artificialmente? ▲ tramar, fraguar *I wonder what those two are hatching.* ¿Qué estarán tramando esos dos?

hatchet hacha pequeña.

hate [n] odio *You could see hate in her eyes.* Se notaba el odio en sus ojos. ● [v] aborrecer *She hated her husband because he'd left her.* Aborrecía a su marido porque la había abandonado. ▲ odiar *I hate to get up in the morning.* Odio levantarme por las mañanas.

hatred odio.

haul [n] redada *We brought in a big haul of fish this morning.* Trajimos una buena redada de peces esta mañana. ● [v] tirar de, arrastrar *How are you going to haul it?* ¿Cómo lo va a arrastrar? ○ **to haul the flag down** arriar la bandera.

haunt [v] frecuentar, rondar. ○ **haunted house** casa embrujada.

have tener *I have two tickets to the theater.* Tengo dos billetes para el teatro.—*He has a fine library.* Tiene una excelente biblioteca.—*I had some money with me.* Tenía algún dinero conmigo.—*Do you have any brothers and sisters?* ¿Tiene Ud. hermanos?—*I have the idea clearly in mind.* Tengo la idea clara en mi mente.—*When do you have your vacation?* ¿Cuándo va Ud. a tener sus vacaciones? ▲ desear *What'll you have?* ¿Qué desea

Ud.? ▲tomar *I have piano lessons twice a week.* Tomo lecciones de piano dos veces por semana.—*I've had one drink too many.* He tomado un trago más de la cuenta. ▲echar, tomar *Let's have a drink.* Vamos a echar un trago. *or* Vamos a tomar algo. ▲jugar *Let's have a game.* Vamos a jugar un partido. ▲hacerse *I have my teeth cleaned twice a year.* Me hago hacer una limpieza de dientes dos veces al año. ▲hacer, mandar hacer *I had my typewriter cleaned.* Hice limpiar mi máquina de escribir. ▲hacer que *I'll have the boy take the package.* Haré que el muchacho lleve el paquete. ▲mandar *I had it made to order.* Lo mandé hacer a la medida.—*He has the laundry do his shirts.* Manda sus camisas a la lavandería. ▲querer *I'll have it that way.* Lo quiero así. ▲permitir *I won't have noise in this room any longer.* No permitiré más ruido en este cuarto. ▲haber *Has he done his job well?* ¿Ha hecho bien su trabajo?—*He'll have finished by that time.* Habrá terminado para entonces.—*Has he gone home?* ¿Ha ido a casa?—*If I'd known that, I wouldn't have come at all.* Si hubiera sabido eso, no hubiese venido.

○ **to have a baby** dar a luz *My wife's going to have a baby in June.* Mi esposa va dar a luz en junio. ○ **to have a mind to** pensar, tener intención de *I have a mind to go there tomorrow.* Pienso ir allí mañana. ○ **to have breakfast** desayunar. ○ **to have dinner** comer *Let's have dinner at six o'clock.* Comamos a las seis. ○ **to have it in for** tenérselas juradas a uno *I'll have it in for him if he does it.* Se las tengo juradas si lo hace. ○ **to have it out** poner las cosas en claro, plantear la cuestión *It's better to have it out now than later.* Más vale poner las cosas en claro ahora, que mas tarde. ○ **to have lunch** almorzar. ○ **to have supper** cenar. ○ **to have to** tener que *You don't have to do anything you don't want to.* No tienes que hacer nada que no quieras.—*I had to leave early.* Tuve que salir temprano.—*She has to go home now.* Ella tiene que irse a casa ahora. ○ **to have to do with** tener que ver con *I have nothing to do with it.* No tengo nada que ver con ello.

‖ *Have a cigar.* Sírvase un cigarro.

‖ *I had a hard time getting up this morning.* Me fué difícil levantarme esta mañana. ‖ *We had been a week without a bath.* Llevábamos una semana sin bañarnos. ‖ *Now I have him where I want him.* Ahora sí que le tengo en mi terreno. ‖ *I'd better leave before the rain starts.* Será mejor que me vaya antes que empiece a llover. ‖ *I'd rather wait until the mail comes.* Prefiero esperar hasta que llegue el correo.

haven abrigo, asilo.

havoc estrago.

hawk halcón.

hay heno *They saw field after field of hay.* Vieron campos y campos de heno.

○ **to hit the hay** dormir *I'm tired; let's hit the hay.* Estoy cansado; vamos a dormir. ○ **to make hay while the sun shines** aprovechar la racha.

hay fever fiebre de heno.

haystack hacina de heno.

hazardous arriesgado, peligroso.

he él *Who is he?* ¿Quién es él?

head cabeza [f] *My head hurts.* Me duele la cabeza.—*He has a good head for business.* Tiene buena cabeza para los negocios.—*We want some nails with larger heads.* Queremos algunos clavos con la cabeza más grande.—*You're at the head of the list.* Ud. está a la cabeza de la lista.—*How many head of cattle are on the farm?* ¿Cuántas cabezas de ganado hay en la hacienda? ▲cabeza [m] *Who's the head of the family?* ¿Quién es el cabeza de familia? ▲tapa *We'll have to take off the head of the barrel.* Tendremos que quitar la tapa del barril. ▲principio *Begin at the head of the page.* Empiece por el principio de la página. ▲director *I want to speak to the head of the organization.* Deseo hablar con el director de la organización. ▲nacimiento, cabecera *How far is it to the head of the river?* ¿A qué distancia queda el nacimiento del río?

● [adj] a proa, de proa *A head wind delayed our landing.* El viento de proa retrasó nuestro desembarque.

● [v] estar a la cabeza de, ir a la cabeza *The boy heads his class at school.* El muchacho está a la cabeza de su clase en la escuela. ▲conducir *The pilot headed the plane into the wind.* El piloto condujo el avión de cara al viento. ▲dirigirse *They are heading for the city.* Se dirigen a la ciudad. O **head first** de cabeza *I fell headfirst.* Caí de cabeza. O **head man** jefe *Mr. Smith is the head man.* El señor Smith es el jefe. O **head of hair** cabello, cabellera *She has a fine head of hair.* Tiene un cabello hermoso. O **head-on** de frente *It was a head-on collision.* Fué un choque de frente. O **head over heels** locamente *My friend is head over heels in love.* Mi amigo está locamente enamorado. O **heads** cara *Heads I win, tails I lose.* Cara, yo gano; cruz, pierdo. O **out of one's head** estar fuera de sí *The man is positively out of his head.* El hombre está realmente fuera de sí. O **over one's head** fuera de alcance *That subject is over my head.* Ese asunto está fuera de mi alcance. ▲ por encima de uno *It may be necessary to go over his head on this.* Quizás será necesario saltar por encima de él en este asunto. O **to come to a head** llegar a un punto decisivo *Matters are coming to a head.* Los asuntos van llegando a su punto decisivo. O **to go to one's head** subírsele a uno a la cabeza *The success has gone to his head.* El éxito se le ha subido a la cabeza. O **to hit the nail on the head** dar en el clavo *You hit the nail on the head that time.* Esa vez dió Ud. en el clavo. O **to keep one's head** mantener la calma *Everyone kept his head in the excitement.* Todos mantuvieron la calma en la conmoción. O **to lose one's head** perder los estribos *She got angry and lost her head.* Ella se enfadó y perdió los estribos. O **to put heads together** cambiar impresiones *Let's put our heads together and figure it out.* Cambiemos impresiones para solucionarlo. O **to take it into one's head** metérsele a uno en la cabeza *The maid took it into her head to leave suddenly.* De pronto a la sirvienta se le metió en la cabeza marcharse. O **to turn one's head** envanecer *Their flattery turned his head.* Su adulación le envaneció.

‖ *The lettuce is ten cents a head.* La lechuga es a diez centavos cada una. ‖ *We need two heads of cabbage.* Nos hacen falta dos repollos. ‖ *I can't make head or tail of the story.* No le encuentro ni pies ni cabeza al cuento.

headache dolor de cabeza.

heading encabezamiento; membrete *(stationery)*.

headlight faro, linterna delantera.

headline titular, epígrafe.

headquarters jefatura, cuartel general.

heal sanar.

health salud *How's your health?* ¿Cómo está Ud. de salud?—*Here's to your health.* ¡A su salud!

healthy bien de salud *I feel healthy enough.* Me siento bastante bien de salud. ▲ saludable *This isn't a healthy place to be in.* Este no es un sitio saludable para quedarse.

O **healthier** más saludable *You look healthier now.* Ahora tiene Ud. un aspecto más saludable.

heap [n] montón *Throw all this stuff in a rubbish heap.* Tire Ud. estos cachivaches en el montón de la basura.

O **heaped** repleto *The table was heaped with all kinds of foods.* La mesa estaba repleta de toda clase de manjares. O **in a heap** amontonado *Don't leave these things in a heap.* No dejen esas cosas amontonadas.

hear oír *I hear someone coming.* Oigo que alguien viene.—*I just heard the telephone ring.* Acabo de oír sonar el teléfono.—*Hear me to the end.* Óyeme hasta el final.—*I never heard of such a thing.* Jamás oí cosa igual. —*They offered to put me up for the night, but I wouldn't hear of it.* Me ofrecieron alojarme durante la noche, pero no quise ni oírlas. ▲ escuchar *I hear good music every night.* Todas las noches escucho buena música. ▲ oír decir *I hear that the play was a success.* Oigo decir que la representación tuvo éxito. ▲ saber *What do you hear from home?* ¿Qué sabe Ud. de su casa? ▲ enterarse *Did you hear of his arrival?* ¿Se enteró Ud. de su llegada? ▲ informarse *The judge hears different kinds of cases every day.* El juez se informa de distintos casos todos los días.

‖ *Hearing the good news made me very happy.* Al oír la buena noticia me puse muy contento.

hearing audiencia *The judge gave both sides a hearing.* El juez concedió audiencia a las dos partes.

‖ *The old man's hearing is poor.* El viejo no oye bien.

heart corazón *His heart is weak.* Tiene el corazón débil.—*She has a soft heart.* Ella tiene un corazón blando. —*I haven't the heart to do it.* No tengo corazón para hacerlo. No podría hacerlo.—*I bid two hearts.* Doy dos corazones. ▲ centro *The store was* *located in the heart of town.* La tienda estaba situada en el centro de la ciudad. ▲ compasión *Have a heart.* Tenga Ud. compasión. ▲ fondo, meollo *I intend to go to the heart of this matter.* Intento llegar al fondo de este asunto.

○ **at heart** en el fondo *At heart he's really a nice fellow.* En el fondo es un buen chico. ○ **by heart** de memoria *He learned the poem by heart.* Se aprendío la poesía de memoria. ○ **to break one's heart** destrozarle el corazón *He broke her heart when he left.* Le destrozó el corazón al marcharse. ○ **to do one's heart good** alegrarle el corazón *It does my heart good to see them happy.* Me alegra el corazón verlos felices. ○ **to lose heart** descorazonarse, perder valor *In spite of everything I didn't lose heart.* A pesar de todo, no me descorazoné.— *Don't lose heart.* No pierda valor. ○ **to take something to heart** tomar algo a pecho *Don't take it to heart.* No lo tome a pecho. ‖ *I have my heart in my mouth.* Estoy en ascuas. ‖ *He's a man after my own heart.* Es un hombre de mi gusto.

heart attack ataque al corazón.

heartburn acedía, pirosis, [Am] vinagrera.

hearth hogar.

hearty cordial *We were given a hearty welcome as we stepped off the train.* Nos hicieron un cordial recibimiento al bajar del tren.

○ **hale and hearty** sano y fuerte *My father's still hale and hearty at sixty.* Mi padre está todavía sano y fuerte a los sesenta años. ○ **hearty eater** comilón *He's a hearty eater, but he stays thin.* Es un comilón pero se mantiene delgado. ○ **hearty meal** comilona *We ate a hearty meal when we came back from swimming.* Nos dimos una comilona cuando regresamos de nadar.

heat [n] calor *I can't stand the heat in this room.* No puedo aguantar el calor en este cuarto.—*In July the heat is intense.* En julio el calor es intenso. ▲ calefacción *The heat should be turned on.* Deberían abrir la calefacción. ▲ acaloramiento *In the heat of the argument he struck him.* En el acaloramiento de la discusión le golpeó.

● [v] calentar *She heated the iron.* Calentó la plancha.

heater calentador.

heave [n] empujón *One more heave and we'll have the car out of the mud.* Un empujón más y sacaremos el carro del lodo.

● [v] empujar *Will you help me heave these trunks over in the corner?* ¿Quiere Ud. ayudarme a empujar estos baúles hasta el rincón? ▲ lanzar *How far can you heave this rock?* ¿A qué distancia puede Ud. lanzar esta piedra? ▲ remar *Let's all heave together and we'll reach shore in a few minutes.* Rememos todos juntos y llegaremos a la costa en pocos minutos. ▲ exhalar, dar *She heaved a sigh of relief when he left.* Dió un suspiro de alivio cuando él se marchó.

heaven cielo. ▲ Dios *Heaven forbid!* ¡No quiera Dios! *or* ¡Dios me (te, le, etc) libre! ‖ *Good heaven!* ¡Cielo santo! *or* ¡Dios mío!

heavy pesado *Is that too heavy for you?* ¿Es eso demasiado pesado para Ud.? ▲ fuerte *In the morning there was a heavy rain.* Hubo un aguacero fuerte en la mañana. ▲ duro *My duties are heavy this week.* Mis ocupaciones son muy duras esta semana. ▲ pesado *This book is very heavy reading.* Este libro es muy pesado para leer. ‖ *Is he a heavy drinker?* ¿Es muy bebedor? ‖ *He was tired and fell into a heavy sleep.* Estaba cansado y se durmió profundamente.

hedge [n] seto.

heed atender.

heel [n] talón *I cut my heel on a stone.* Me herí el talón con una piedra.— *There are holes in the heels of these socks.* Estos calcetines tienen agujeros en los talones.

height altura *What is the height of those hills?* ¿Qué altura tienen esos cerros?—*This plane can fly at great heights.* Este avión puede volar a grandes alturas. ▲ pináculo *He has reached the height of success.* Alcanzó el pináculo del éxito. ▲ crisis *The fever has passed its height.* La crisis de la fiebre ha pasado. ▲ colmo *What he said was the height of stupidity.* Fué el colmo de la estupidez lo que dijo.

heir heredero.

heiress heredera.

hell infierno.

hello hola *Hello, how are you?* ¡Hola! ¿Cómo estás? *or* ¡Hola! ¿qué tal?

helm timón.
helmet casco.
help [*n*] ayuda *Do you need any help?* ¿Necesita Ud. ayuda? ▲ socorro *Help!* ¡Socorro! ▲ criados, sirvientes; empleados *(store) It's difficult to get help these days.* En estos tiempos es difícil conseguir empleados. ● [*v*] ayudar *I helped the old man cross the street.* Ayudé al anciano a cruzar la calle. ▲ remediar *Sorry, it can't be helped.* Lo siento pero no se puede remediar. ▲ evitar *I can't help it.* No lo puedo evitar. ▲ auxiliar *Please help me!* ¡Auxílienme! ○ **can't help but** no poder dejar de, no poder menos de *I couldn't help but tell him.* No pude dejar de decírselo. ○ **to help oneself** servirse *Help yourself.* Sírvase Ud.
helper ayundante.
helpful útil.
helping porción.
helpless inútil.
hem dobladillo.
hemisphere hemisferio.
hemp cáñamo.
hen gallina.
hence por lo tanto, en consecuencia *He's guilty, hence he must be punished.* Es culpable, por lo tanto se le debe castigar.
henceforth de aquí en adelante.
her [*pron*] la *I saw her last week.* La ví la semana pasada. ▲ ella *Give this to her.* Déle esto a ella. ● [*adj*] su *Her umbrella's here.* Su paraguas está aquí.
herb heirba.
herd [*n*] manada, hato *Herds of wild horses were roaming about the plains.* Manadas de caballos salvajes andaban errantes por los llanos. ▲ multitud *You can follow the herd if you like.* Ud. puede seguir a la multitud si quiere. ● [*v*] apiñarse *The animals herded together to keep warm.* Los animales se apiñaban unos contra otros para calentarse. ▲ reunir *The dogs help herd the cattle.* Los perros ayudan a reunir el ganado. ▲ meter, apiñar *The people were herded into the subway like cattle.* Metían a la gente en el subterráneo como ganado.
here aquí *Meet me here at six o'clock.* Véame aquí a las seis. ▲ acá *Come here, young man.* Venga Ud. acá, joven. ▲ presente *Only six of the men answered "here".* Sólo seis de los hombres contestaron "presente".

○ **here and there** por todas partes *The stores are scattered here and there throughout the city.* Las tiendas están diseminadas por todas partes de la ciudad.
hereafter en adelante, en lo futuro.
hereditary hereditario.
heretofore hasta ahora, hasta aquí.
herewith adjunto.
heritage herencia.
hermit ermitaño.
hero héroe.
heroine heroína.
herring arenque.
hers suyo *This is hers.* Esto es suyo.
herself ella misma *She did it herself.* Lo hizo ella misma. ▲ la misma *She is not herself today.* Hoy no es la misma. ▲ se *She fell and hurt herself.* Ella se cayó y se lastimó.
hesitate vacilar *The officer in charge hesitated before making the decision.* El comandante vaciló antes de tomar la decisión.—*Don't hesitate to call me up if you need me.* No vacile en llamarme si me necesita.
hiccup hipo.
hidden oculto, secreto *Did he have any hidden reason?* ¿Tenía alguna razón oculta?
hide [*n*] cuero *They are selling hides in the market.* Venden cueros en el mercado. ● [*v*] esconder *He hid his money in a bureau drawer.* Escondió su dinero en un cajón de la cómoda. ▲ ocultar *The tree hides the view.* El árbol oculta la vista.—*Are you hiding anything from me?* ¿Me oculta Ud. algo?
hideous horrible.
high [*n*] subida *Prices have reached a new high.* Los precios han experimentado una nueva subida. ▲ directa *He shifted the gears into high.* Puso los cambios en directa. ● [*adj*] de altura *This building is two hundred feet high.* Este edificio tiene doscientos pies de altura. ▲ elevado *The temperature will be pretty high today.* Hoy estará bastante elevada la temperatura.—*I have a high opinion of him.* Tengo una opinión elevada de él. ▲ alto *This price is too high.* Este precio es demasiado alto. ▲ fuerte *The airplane met high winds.* El avión se encontró con vientos fuertes. ▲ agudo *She sang a high note.* Cantó una nota aguda. ▲ bueno *Why is he in such high spirits today?* ¿Por qué está de tan buen ánimo hoy?

○ **high and dry** plantado *She was left high and dry.* La dejaron plantada. ○ **high and low** por todas partes *I looked high and low but couldn't find it.* Busqué por todas partes pero no pude encontrarlo. ○ **high time** hora *It was high time you did it.* Ya era hora de que lo hicieras. ‖ *He climbed up so high that we couldn't see him.* Subió a tal altura que no lo podíamos ver. ‖ *How high a speed will this car reach?* ¿Cuál es la velocidad máxima que puede alcanzar este automóvil? ‖ *Let's wait till high tide.* Esperemos a que suba la marea. *or* Esperemos la marea alta. ‖ *That house is three stories high.* Esa casa tiene tres pisos.

highchair silla alta.

highly altamente, sumamente.

high school escuela de segunda enseñanza, instituto.

high-strung nervioso.

highway carretera, camino real.

hike caminata *The boys went on a twenty-mile hike today.* Los muchachos dieron hoy una caminata de veinte millas.

hill colina *What's beyond the hill?* ¿Qué hay más allá de la colina?

him le *I've seen him.* Le he visto. ▲ él *Give this to him.* Déle esto (a él).— *"To whom shall I give this?" "To him."* "¿A quién tengo que dar esto?" "A él."

himself él mismo *Did he do it himself?* ¿Lo hizo él mismo? ▲ se *He hurt himself in the leg.* Se lastimó la pierna. ‖ *He was himself at all times.* Era siempre él mismo. *or* Jamás se excitaba.

hinder impedir.

hinge [n] gozne, bisagra *The hinge on the door is broken.* Está rota la bisagra de la puerta. ● [v] depender de *My final decision hinges on what the family says.* Mi última decisión depende de lo que diga la familia.

hint [n] indicio *Can you give me a hint as to how the picture ends?* ¿Me puede Ud. dar un indicio de cómo termina la película? ● [v] insinuar *My father hinted that it was time to go to bed.* Mi padre insinuó que ya era la hora de acostarse. ○ **to take a hint** darse cuenta de la indirecta *Can't you take a hint?* No se da Ud. cuenta de la indirecta?

hip cadera.

hire alquilar *Let's hire the boat for the day.* Alquilemos el bote para todo el día. ▲ emplear *I was hired only temporarily.* Me emplearon sólo temporalmente. ○ **to hire out** alquilar *The store hires out bicycles on Sunday.* La tienda alquila bicicletas los domingos. ‖ *Do you have horses for hire?* ¿Alquila Ud. caballos?

his suyo *This is his.* Esto es suyo. ▲ su *Do you have his address?* ¿Tiene Ud. su dirección?

hiss [v] sisear.

historian historiador.

historic histórico.

history historia *The history of this country is very interesting.* La historia de este país es muy interesante. ▲ libro de historia *He's writing a history.* Está escribiendo un libro de historia.

hit [n] blanco *He made four hits and missed the rest.* Dió en el blanco cuatro veces y erró las demás. ● [v] pegar, dar *The ball hit the fence.* La pelota pegó en la valla. ▲ golpearse *I hit my knee against the door.* Me golpeé la rodilla contra la puerta. ▲ dar *The light hit his eyes.* Le dió la luz en los ojos. ▲ afectar *The news hit me very hard.* La noticia me afectó mucho. ○ **hit or miss** descuidado *He works in a hit or miss fashion.* Es muy descuidado en su manera de trabajar. ○ **to be a hit** ser sensacional *That movie was a hit.* Esa película fué sensacional. ○ **to hit it off** entenderse bien *They hit it off well from the beginning.* Se entendieron bien desde el principio. ○ **to hit on** ocurrírsele algo *How did you hit on that?* ¿Cómo se le ocurrió eso?

hitch [n] impedimento *There's a hitch in our plans.* Hay un impedimento en nuestros planes. ● [v] enganchar *Hitch the horse to the wagon.* Enganche Ud. el caballo al carro.

hive colmena.

hives urticaria, ronchas.

hoard [n] cúmulo *They have a great hoard of silk articles.* Tienen una gran cúmulo de artículos de seda. ▲ tesoro escondido *The old miser has a hoard of money.* El viejo avaro tiene un tesoro escondido. ● [v] acaparar *The government has asked everyone not to hoard food.* El gobierno ha pedido a todos que no acaparen los alimentos.

hobby pasatiempo, afición.

hobo vagabundo.

hock [*v*] empeñar *I've hocked my watch.* He empeñado mi reloj.

hockey hockey.

hoe [*n*] azada.

hog [*n*] cerdo *Do you know where I can buy good hogs?* ¿Sabe Ud. dónde puedo conseguir buenos cerdos? ▲ comilón, tragón *You're an awful hog.* Ud. es un gran comilón.
● [*v*] atribuirse méritos *He hogs all the credit for the work we do together.* El se atribuye todos los méritos por el trabajo que hacemos juntos.
○ **to go the whole hog** gastar hasta el último centavo *He went the whole hog in buying himself a new car.* Gastó hasta el último centavo en comprarse un nuevo automóvil.

hoist [*v*] alzar, elevar; izar (*a flag*).

hold [*v*] tener *She held the baby in her arms.* Tenía el niño en los brazos.— *They held the land under a ten-year lease.* Tenían el terreno arrendado por diez años. ▲ retener *She held the check for a long time.* Retuvo el cheque mucho tiempo. ▲ sostener, apoyar *Hold him, or he'll fall.* Sosténgalo, o se caerá. ▲ aguantar, contener *He held his breath till he got to the surface.* Aguantó la respiración hasta que llegó a la superficie. ▲ sujetar *The pin held her dress in place.* Tenía el vestido sujetado con un alfiler. ▲ estar *He held himself ready for all emergencies.* Estaba preparado para cualquiera emergencia. ▲ acomodar *The car holds five people.* El automóvil acomoda a cinco personas. ▲ contener *This coffee pot can hold four cups.* Esta cafetera puede contener cuarto tazas de café. ▲ ocupar *He held that office for a long time.* El ocupó ese puesto durante mucho tiempo. ▲ celebrarse *The club meetings are held once a week.* Las reuniones del club se celebran una vez por semana. ▲ sostener *I hold that your opinion is unsound.* Sostengo que su opinión es errónea.— *She held high C for a long time.* Sustuvo por largo rato el "do" agudo. ▲ juzgar *The court held him guilty.* La corte le juzgó culpable.
○ **to hold back** refrenarse *I wanted to go but held myself back.* Quería ir pero me refrené. ▲ detener *Hold that crowd back!* ¡Detenga a ese gentío! ○ **to hold on** aguantar *Try to hold on a little longer.* Trate de aguantar un poco más. ▲ detenerse, esperarse *Hold on a minute, I want to talk to you.* Deténgase un momento

que quiero hablarle. ▲ agarrarse *Hold on to him.* Agárrese a él. ○ **to hold on** mantenerse firme en *He'll hold on to his post.* Se mantendrá firme en su puesto. ○ **to hold out** resistir *They held out against the enemy.* Resistieron al enemigo. ○ **to hold over** dejar (en suspenso) *Let's hold this over until the next meeting.* Dejemos esto (en suspenso) hasta la reunión siguiente. ○ **to hold up** parar, detener *The work was held up for three weeks.* El trabajo estuvo parado durante tres semanas. ▲ atracar, asaltar para robar *I was held up last night.* Anoche me atracaron. ▲ soportar *We held up well under the strain.* Soportamos bien la tensión nerviosa.

holder ○ **cigarette holder** boquilla *Where can I buy a cigarette holder?* ¿Dónde puedo comprar una boquilla?

holdup asalto, atraco.

hole agujero *There's a hole in that glove.* En ese guante hay un agujero. —*The mouse ran into his hole.* El ratón se metió en su agujero. ▲ apuro, aprieto *She found herself in a hole financially.* Se encontraba en un apuro de dinero.
‖ *That restaurant is a hole.* Ese es un restaurant de mala muerte. ‖ *The trip made a big hole in her pocketbook.* El viaje le costó un ojo de la cara.

holiday día festivo, día de fiesta *Is today a holiday?* ¿Es hoy día de fiesta? ▲ vacación *I want to take a holiday.* Quiero tomarme unas vacaciones.
○ **holiday season** fiestas *When does the holiday season begin?* ¿Cuándo empiezan las fiestas?

hollow hueco, vacío.

holy sagrado.

home casa *She lives home with her parents.* Ella vive en la casa de sus padres.—*They have a beautiful home in the country.* Tienen una hermosa casa en el campo. ▲ hogar *You can always find a home with us.* Siempre encontrará Ud. un hogar en nuestra casa. ▲ asilo *There's a home for old ladies up on the hill.* En el cerro hay un asilo de ancianas.—*I have to go home.* Tengo que irme a casa.
○ **at home** en casa *I was at home all day yesterday.* Ayer estuve en casa todo el día. ▲ en su casa *Make yourself at home.* Está Ud. en su casa. ○ **home town** pueblo natal, patria chica *He went back to his home town.* Regresó a su pueblo natal.

‖ *He drove his point home.* Logró que se aceptara su punto de vista.

homely feo *She has a homely face but she's a very nice person.* Es fea de cara, pero es una persona muy buena. ▲ simple *He always uses homely expressions.* Siempre usa expresiones simples. ▲ sin gracia *She's a homely person.* Es una persona sin gracia.

homesick nostálgico.

homicide homicido.

honest honrado, honesto *That wouldn't be honest.* Eso no sería honrado. ▲ honrado *He has an honest face.* Tiene cara de honrado. ▲ equitativo *That's an honest bargain.* Ese es un convenio equitativo. ▲ exacto, justo *The scale gives honest weight.* La báscula da el peso exacto.

honestly honradamente.

honesty honradez.

honey miel *I'd like some bread and honey.* Quisiera un poco de pan con miel. ▲ encanto *That's a honey of a dress.* Ese vestido es un encanto. ‖ *Hello, honey!* ¡Ola, simpática! or ¡Ola, corazón!

honeymoon luna de miel.

honor [n] honor *He has won great honor.* Ha alcanzado gran honor.— *It's an honor to be elected.* Es un honor ser elegido.—*You are a man of honor.* Es Ud. un hombre de honor. —*I swear on my honor.* Juro por mi honor. ▲ honra *He's an honor to his family.* El es una honra para su familia. ● [v] honrar *I was honored by the invitation.* Me sentí honrado con la invitación.—*They gave a dinner to honor the heroes.* Celebraron una comida para honrar a los héroes. ▲ aceptar *We can't honor this check.* No podemos aceptar este cheque. ○ **honors** honores *He expects to graduate with honors.* Espera graduarse con honores. ○ **to do the honors** hacer los honores *You do the honors tonight.* Esta noche haga Ud. los honores.

honorable honorable.

honorary honorario.

hood capota.

hoof casco.

hook [n] gancho *Is there a hook to hang my coat on?* ¿Hay un gancho para colgar mi abrigo? ▲ anzuelo *We went fishing with a hook and line.* Fuimos a pescar con caña y anzuelo. ▲ puñetazo *He gave him a left hook to the jaw.* Le soltó un puñetazo en la mandíbula con la izquierda.

● [v] pescar *I hooked a big fish.* Pesqué un pez grande. ▲ abrochar *Help me hook this.* Ayúdeme a abrochar esto. ▲ enganchar *The two parts of this buckle hook together.* Las dos piezas de este broche enganchan. ▲ rodear *He hooked his arm around the post.* Rodeó el poste con el brazo. ○ **hooks and eyes** corchetes *This dress is fastened with hooks and eyes.* Este vestido se abrocha con corchetes.

hook-up circuito.

hop [n] brinco. ● [v] brincar.

hope [n] esperanza *Don't give up hope.* No pierda Ud. la esperanza.—*Is there any hope?* ¿Hay alguna esperanza? ▲ salvación, esperanza *The new player is the only hope of the team.* El nuevo jugador es la única salvación del equipo. ● [v] esperar *I hope you can come.* Espero que pueda Ud. venir. ▲ esperar, confiar *Let's hope for the best.* Esperemos lo mejor.

hopeful esperanzado, lleno de esperanza.

hopeless desahuciado, desesperanzado.

horizon horizonte.

horizontal horizontal.

horn asta, cuerno *Be careful, the bull has sharp horns.* Tenga cuidado que el toro tiene las astas puntiagudas. ▲ trompa *He played a horn solo.* Tocó un solo de trompa. ▲ bocina *Don't blow the horn so much.* No toque Ud. tanto la bocina. ‖ *He's always blowing his own horn.* Siempre está hablando de sí. or Siempre se está vanagloriando.

horrible horrible.

horrid hórrido.

horror horror.

horse caballo *Where can I get a horse?* ¿Dónde puedo conseguir un caballo?— *Let's go to the horse races.* Vamos a las carreras de caballos. ‖ *That's a horse of a different color.* Eso ya es algo diferente.

horseback ○ **on horseback** a caballo *You can get there quicker on horseback.* Ud. puede llegar allí más ligero a caballo. ○ **to ride horseback** montar a caballo *We plan to go horseback riding Sunday.* Proyectamos montar a caballo el domingo.

hose calcetines *The store is having a sale on men's hose.* La tienda tiene una liquidación de calcetines de hombre. ▲ manguera *Get out the hose, and water the garden.* Saque Ud. la manguera y riegue el jardín.

hospitable hospitalario.
hospital hospital.
hospitality hospitalidad.
host anfitrión, dueño de la casa.
hostage rehén.
hostess dueña de la casa.
hostile hostil.
hostilities hostilidades.
hot caliente *Do you have hot water?* ¿Tiene Ud. agua caliente?—*I want a hot dinner.* Quiero una comida caliente.—*His forehead is hot.* Tiene la frente caliente. ▲ picante *I don't like hot foods.* No me gustan las comidas picantes. ▲ violento, furioso *He has a hot temper.* Tiene un genio violento. ▲ fresco, reciente *The dog followed the hot scent.* El perro siguió el rastro fresco. ▲ de cerca *We thought we were hot on the trail.* Creímos que les seguíamos de cerca. ‖ *The sun's awfully hot today.* El sol quema mucho hoy. ‖ *He's in hot water because he has no license.* Se ha metido en un lío por no tener licencia.
hot-blooded de malas pulgas *He's a hot-blooded individual.* Es una persona de malas pulgas.
hot dog perro caliente, salchicha de francfort.
hotel hotel.
hot water bottle bolsa de agua caliente.
hound [n] sabueso.
hour hora *I'll be back in an hour.* Volveré en una hora.—*Are you available at all hours?* ¿Está Ud. disponible a todas horas?—*When do you take your lunch hour?* ¿Cuál es su hora de almorzar? *or* ¿A qué hora almuerza Ud.?—*How many hours of French are you taking?* ¿Cuántas horas de francés toma Ud.?—*This is after hours.* Esto es fuera de horas. ○ **to keep late hours** recogerse tarde, acostarse tarde *He keeps late hours.* Se recoge tarde. *or* Se acuesta tarde. ‖ *He's the man of the hour.* Es el hombre del momento. ‖ *Hours on end.* Horas enteras. ‖ *In the early hours of the morning.* En la madrugada.
hourly a cada hora.
house [n] casa *I want to rent a house.* Quiero alquilar una casa.—*The whole house turned out to greet him.* Todos los de la casa salieron a saludarle.—*Their house sells clothing.* Su casa vende ropa.—*He belongs to the house of Aragon.* Desciende de la casa de Aragón. ▲ público *The whole house enjoyed the play.* Todo el público gozó del espectáculo.

○ **house to house** casa por casa *We made a house to house search.* Hicimos un registro casa por casa. ○ **movie house** cine. ○ **to keep house** mantener casa *I'm not used to keeping house.* No estoy acostumbrado a mantener casa. ○ **upper house** senado *The law was just passed by the upper house.* El senado acaba de aprobar la ley.
● [v] alojar *Where are the visitors to be housed?* ¿Dónde se pueden alojar los invitados?
household familia *The household gathered around the radio.* La familia se agrupó alrededor de la radio. ▲ casa *Everyone chipped in and helped with the household tasks.* Todos arrimaron el hombro y ayudaron en las tareas de la casa.
housekeeper ama de llaves.
housewife ama de casa.
how cómo *How shall I do it?* ¿Cómo lo haré?—*How are you?* ¿Cómo está Ud.?
○ **how is it?** ¿por qué? *How is it you did not come?* ¿Por qué no vino Ud.? ○ **how much?** ¿cuánto? *How much did he pay?* ¿Cuánto pagó? ‖ *How far is it to the river?* ¿Qué distancia hay hasta el río?
however [adv] por muy *However good he may be, I don't want him here.* Por muy bueno que sea, no le quiero aquí. ▲ por mucho *However cold it gets, I won't wear my fur coat.* Por mucho frío que haga no me pondré el abrigo de piel. ▲ como quiera *However you do it, do it well.* Como quiera que lo haga, hágalo bien.
● [conj] no obstante *However, forget it.* No obstante, olvídelo.
howl [n] aullido *At night you can hear the howl of wolves.* De noche se puede oír el aullido de los lobos. ▲ alarido *He let out a howl.* Dió un alarido. ▲ gritos *He was greeted with a howl of protest.* Fué recibido con gritos de protesta.
● [v] aullar *The dog's howling.* El perro está aullando.
○ **to be a howling success** tener un éxito ruidoso *The play was a howling success.* La obra tuvo un éxito ruidoso. ○ **to howl with laughter** chillar de contento *The audience howled with laughter.* El público chillaba de contento.
huddle acurrucarse *The children were huddled in the corner.* Los niños estaban acurrucados en un rincón.
hue matiz.

hug [n] abrazo.
- [v] abrazar.

huge enorme.

hull (of ship) casco.

hum [n] zumbido *They could hardly hear the hum of the motor.* Casi no podían oír el zumbido del motor.
- [v] tararear *What's that tune you're humming?* ¿Cómo se llama esa melodía que Ud. está tarareando?
▲ estar activo *The factory is really humming.* La fábrica está muy activa.
○ **humming** zumbido *The humming of that bee annoys me.* Me molesta el zumbido de esa abeja.

human [n] ser humano *There were more animals than humans on this island.* En esta isla había más animales que seres humanos.
- [adj] humano *I'm only human.* Soy humano.—*It's only human to make mistakes.* Es muy humano equivocarse.
○ **human being** ser humano.

humane humanitario.

humanity humanidad.

humble humilde.

humid húmedo.

humidity humedad.

humiliate humillar.

humor [n] gracia *I don't see any humor in the situation.* No veo ninguna gracia en la situación.—*You're in good humor today.* Hoy está Ud. de buen humor.
- [v] seguir la corriente *You'll have to humor him.* Tendrá Ud. que seguirle la corriente.
‖ *Keep your sense of humor.* Conserve Ud. su sentido de humor. or No pierda Ud. el humor.

humorous divertido.

hunch ○ **to have a hunch** tener un presentimiento *I have a hunch something's wrong.* Tengo el presentimiento que ocurre algo malo.
‖ *He's sitting all hunched up in a corner.* Está acurrucado en un rincón.

hunger hambre *The woman fainted from hunger.* La mujer se desmayó de hambre.
- [adj] de hambre *The child has a hungry look.* El niño tiene cara de hambre.
○ **to be hungry** tener hambre *I'm hungry.* Tengo hambre.
‖ *He hungered for power.* Sentía hambre de poder. ‖ *He's hungry for affection.* Tiene sed de cariño.

hunt [n] cacería *Are you going on the hunt?* ¿Va Ud. a ir a la cacería?
- [v] cazar *Do you like to hunt?* ¿Le gusta a Ud. cazar?—*They're out hunting deer.* Estan cazando ciervos.
▲ perseguir *They hunted the fugitive from city to city.* Persiguieron al fugitivo de ciudad en ciudad. ▲ buscar *I hunted high and low but couldn't find it.* Busqué por todas partes pero no lo pude encontrar.
○ **hunting** caza *There's a great deal of hunting in this forest.* Hay mucha caza en este bosque. ○ **to hunt down** cazar *They hunted him down.* Le persiguieron hasta capturarlo. ○ **to hunt up** inventar *He could always be counted on to hunt up an excuse.* Para inventar excusas, siempre se podía contar con él. ▲ buscar, encontrar *Try to hunt up that telephone number.* Vea de encontrar ese número de teléfono.
‖ *I made a thorough hunt for the missing bracelet.* He buscado por todas partes la pulsera perdida.

hunter cazador.

hurl lanzar.

Hurrah! ¡Viva!

hurricane huracán.

hurry [n] prisa *I'm in a hurry.* Tengo prisa. or Estoy de prisa.—*What's the hurry?* ¿Qué prisa hay?
- [v] apresurarse, darse prisa *Don't hurry.* No se dé Ud. prisa.—*Hurry up!* ¡Dése prisa! ▲ acelerar *Don't hurry the decision.* No acelere Ud. la decisión.
‖ *Hurry them out of here.* Déles prisa para que se vayan.

hurt [adj] ofendida *She has a hurt look.* Tiene cara de ofendida.
- [v] dañarse *He fell and hurt his leg.* Se cayó y se hizo dañó en la pierna. ▲ herir *Where are you hurt?* ¿Dónde está Ud. herido? ▲ lastimarse *Was anyone hurt?* ¿Se ha lastimado alguien? ▲ dolerse *My arm hurts.* Me duele el brazo. ▲ doler *Where does it hurt?* ¿Dónde le duele? ▲ resentir *I hope your feelings aren't hurt.* Espero que no esté Ud. resentido. ▲ perjudicar *This'll hurt business.* Esto perjudicará a los negocios. ▲ causar trastorno *Will it hurt if I'm late?* ¿Causará trastorno si llego tarde?

husband esposo *Is your husband living?* ¿Vive su esposo? ▲ marido *Where's your husband?* ¿Dónde está su marido?

hush [n] silencio *A hush came over the*

crowd. Un silencio se apoderó de la multitud.

‖ *Hush! I can't hear a word he's saying.* Cállese, no puedo oír ninguna palabra de lo que dice.

husk cáscara.

husky fuerte, fornido *What a fine husky boy your son's turned out to be.* Su hijo se ha convertido en un mocetón fornido. ▲ronca *My voice sounds husky since I caught this cold.* Mi voz está ronca desde que me resfrié.

hustle apurarse *Hustle or we'll miss the movie.* Apúrese o perdemos la pelí-

cula. ▲echar *The police hustled the bums out of town.* La policía echó a los vagabundos del pueblo.

○ hustle and bustle a prisa y corriendo.

hut choza, [*Am*] bohío.

hydrant boca de riego.

hygiene higiene.

hymn himno.

hypocrite hipócrita.

hypodermic hipodérmico.

hysterical histérico.

hysterics histeria.

I

I yo *It is I.* Soy yo.—*He's older than I.* Es más viejo que yo.

‖ *I'll do it if he asks me.* Lo haré si me lo pide.

ice [*n*] hielo *Put some ice in the glasses.* Eche Ud. un poco de hielo en los vasos. ▲sorbete, granizado *I'll have an orange ice, please.* Quiero un granizado de naranja, por favor.

● [*v*] enfriar *The drinks ought to be iced.* Hay que enfriar las bebidas. ▲bañar *Ice the cake as soon as it's cool.* Bañe Ud. la torta en cuanto se enfríe.

○ to break the ice romper el hielo *She broke the ice by telling a joke.* Rompió el hielo contando un chiste.

○ to skate on thin ice comprometerse *He's certainly skating on thin ice when he says that.* Indudablemente se está comprometiendo al decir eso.

icebox nevera.

ice cream helado *Would you like to have ice cream for dessert?* ¿Le gustaría de postre un helado?

iced helado *Let's order iced drinks.* Pidamos bebidas heladas.

iceman vendedor de hielo.

icicle carámbano.

icing baño de azucar.

icy helado.

idea idea *Have you any ideas on the subject?* ¿Se le ocurren algunas ideas sobre el asunto? ▲intención, propósito *My idea is to go by train.* Tengo la intención de ir en tren.

‖ *Have you any idea?* ¿Se le ocurre algo? ‖ *That's the idea.* Eso es. ‖ *What an idea!* ¡Vaya una ocurrencia!

ideal [*n*] modelo *His father has always been his ideal.* Su padre le ha servido

siempre de modelo. ▲ideal *He was willing to fight for his ideals.* Siempre estaba dispuesto a luchar por sus ideales.

● [*adj*] ideal, magnífico *This is an ideal place to spend the summer.* Es un sitio ideal para pasar el verano.

identical idéntico.

identification identificación.

idiom modismo.

idiot idiota.

idle desocupado *Are you idle at the moment?* ¿Está Ud. desocupado en este momento? ▲vano, infundado *Stop tormenting yourself with idle fears.* Deje Ud. de atormentarse con temores infundados.

‖ *She does a lot of idle talking.* Habla a tontas y a locas. or Habla disparates.

idol ídolo.

if si *If I had any plans, I'd tell you.* Si tuviera algún plan, se lo diría.—*If anyone asks me, say I'll be right back.* Si alguien pregunta por mí, diga que volveré en seguida.—*See if there's any mail for me.* Mire Ud. si hay correo para mí.

○ as if como si *He talked as if he had been there.* Hablaba como si hubiera estado allí. ○ even if *I'll go even if it rains.* Iré aunque llueva. ○ if only *If I could only get there.* Si pudiera llegar allí.

ignorance ignorancia.

ignorant ignorante.

○ to be ignorant of ignorar. ▲no estar al tanto de *He's ignorant of the details.* No está al tanto de los detalles.

ill enfermo *He's been seriously ill.* Ha estado gravemente enfermo.

O **to be ill at ease** no estar a gusto *He's ill at ease with such people.* No está a gusto con esa gente.

illegal ilegal.

illegitimate ilegítimo.

illiterate analfabeto.

illness enfermedad.

illogical ilógico.

illuminate iluminar.

illusion ilusión.

illustrate ilustrar *The book is illustrated with photographs.* El libro está ilustrado con fotografías.

illustration ilustración.

image imagen *He knelt before the image.* Se arrodilló ante la imagen.— *His description of the town was full of poetical images.* Su descripción de la ciudad estaba llena de imágenes poéticas. ▲ vivo retrato *He's the image of his father.* Es el vivo retrato de su padre.

imaginary imaginario.

imagination imaginación *Don't let your imagination run away with you.* No se deje Ud. llevar por la imaginación.

imagine imaginarse *I can't imagine what you mean.* No me puedo imaginar lo que quiere Ud. decir.—*He was imagining all sorts of things.* Se imaginaba toda clase de cosas. ▲ creer *I imagine so.* Creo que sí.
‖ *I can just imagine!* ¡Sí, me lo figuro!

imitate imitar *His work isn't original; he just imitates what other people have done.* Su obra no es original; meramente imita lo que han hecho otros.

imitation imitación.

immediate inmediato *The immediate result was not what they expected.* El resultado inmediato no fué el que esperaban. ▲ urgente *The need is immediate.* La necesidad es urgente.
O **immediate neighborhood** inmediaciones *There is a river in the immediate neighborhood.* Hay un río en las inmediaciones.
‖ *We must take immediate action.* Hay que obrar inmediatamente.

immediately inmediatamente.

immense inmenso, enorme *The living room has an immense fireplace.* La sala tiene una chimenea inmensa.

immigrant inmigrante.

immigrate inmigrar.

immoral inmoral.

immortal inmortal.

impartial imparcial.

impassable intransitable *This time of year the roads are impassable.* En esta época del año los caminos están intransitables.

impatient impaciente *Don't be impatient.* No sea impaciente.

imperial imperial.

impersonal impersonal.

impetuous impetuoso.

imply dar a entender *He implied he'd take the job if he got enough pay.* Dió a entender que aceptaría el puesto si le pagaban lo suficiente. ▲ significar *That implies a lot of work for us.* Eso significa que tenemos que trabajar mucho.

impolite descortés.

import [n] importación *Imports from foreign countries have been stopped because of the war.* A causa de la guerra se han suspendido las importaciones del extranjero.
● [v] importar *Is this wine imported or domestic?* ¿Es este vino importado o del país?

importance importancia.

important importante *I want to see you about an important matter.* Quiero verle para un asunto importante.— *He was the most important man in town.* Era el hombre más importante de la ciudad. ▲ presuntuoso, engreído *Who's that fellow who seems so important?* ¿Quién es ese tipo tan presuntuoso?

impose imponer *He tried to impose his ideas on us.* Trató de imponernos sus ideas.
O **to impose on** molestar *I hope I'm not imposing on you.* Espero que no le estoy molestando.

impossible imposible *Don't try to do the impossible.* No trate de hacer lo imposible.—*That's impossible.* Eso es imposible. ▲ inaguantable, insufrible *That man is absolutely impossible.* Ese hombre es absolutamente inaguantable. ▲ inservible *These scissors are impossible.* Estas tijeras están inservibles.

impress impresionar *Aren't you impressed?* ¿No está Ud. impresionado? ▲ convencer *We tried to impress on him the importance of the job.* Tratamos de convencerle de la importancia del puesto.

impression impresión *He gives the impression of knowing more than he really does.* Da la impresión de saber más de lo que sabe. ▲ huella *She left the impression of her feet in the cement.* Dejó la huella de sus pies en el cemento.

imprison encarcelar.

improve mejorar *Do you think his health has improved?* ¿Cree Ud. que su salud ha mejorado? ▲ perfeccionar *He improved his knowledge of Spanish.* Perfeccionó su conocimiento del español. ○ **to improve on** perfeccionar *Can you improve on this model?* ¿Puede Ud. perfeccionar este modelo? ▲ mejorar *Can you improve on my suggestion?* ¿Puede Ud. mejorar mi sugestión?

improvement mejoría *Has the patient shown any signs of improvement today?* ¿Ha dado el enfermo alguna señal de mejoría hoy? ▲ mejora *We've put a lot of improvements into the house.* Hemos hecho muchas mejoras en la casa.—*These busses are definitely an improvement on the old ones.* Estos autobuses suponen realmente una mejora sobre los antiguos.

impulse impulso.

in en *There's no heat in my room.* No hay calefacción en mi cuarto.—*The dress is in that pile of clothes.* El vestido está en ese montón de ropa. —*Say it in English.* Dígalo en inglés.—*Is he in the army?* ¿Está en el ejército?—*I can finish this in a week.* Podré terminar esto en una semana. ▲ a *His boys are in college.* Sus hijos van a la universidad. ▲ con *Write in ink.* Escriba Ud. con tinta. ▲ de *He broke it in anger.* Lo rompió de rabia.—*That's the best hotel in New York.* Este es el mejor hotel de Nueva York. ▲ dentro de *I'll be back in a week.* Volveré dentro de una semana. ▲ durante *It gets hot here in the daytime.* Hace mucho calor aquí durante el día. ▲ para *Are you good in arithmetic?* ¿Tiene Ud. aptitud para la aritmética? ▲ por *Cut it in half.* Pártalo por la mitad.—*Please put that in writing.* Haga Ud. el favor de ponerlo por escrito.—*I'll see you in the morning.* Le veré mañana por la mañana.

‖ *Come in!* ¡Adelante! *or* ¡Pase Ud.! ‖ *He always talks in his sleep.* Habla siempre cuando está dormido. ‖ *I'm in poor health.* Estoy mal de salud. ‖ *Who's in?* ¿Quién está?

incense incienso.

inch pulgada *This ruler is fifteen inches long.* Esta regla tiene quince pulgadas de largo.

○ **within an inch of** a punto de *He came within an inch of being run over.* Estuvo a punto de ser atropellado por un automóvil.

‖ *I used up every inch of cloth.* Aproveché hasta el último trozo de la tela.

incident [n] incidente.

incline [n] pendiente *How steep is the incline?* ¿Qué inclinación tiene la pendiente?

● [v] inducir *The incident inclined him to drive more slowly.* Lo ocurrido le indujo a manejar más despacio. ○ **to be inclined** inclinarse *I'm inclined to follow your advice.* Me inclino a seguir su consejo.

inclose cercar *He inclosed his garden with a high hedge.* Cercó su jardín con un seto alto. ▲ incluir *I am inclosing a money order for ten dollars.* Le incluyo a Ud. un giro postal de diez dólares.

include incluir *Include this in my bill.* Incluya Ud. esto en mi cuenta. ▲ comprender *The course includes some laboratory work.* El curso comprende trabajo de laboratorio.

○ **including** incluso *Everyone came, including the president.* Vinieron todos, incluso el presidente.

income ingresos; renta *(other than wages).*

incompetent incompetente.

inconvenience [n] molestia, incomodidad.

● [v] incomodar, estorbar.

increase [n] aumento *Do you expect an increase in salary?* ¿Espera Ud. un aumento de sueldo?

● [v] aumentar *His business has increased a great deal lately.* Sus negocios han aumentado mucho últimamente.—*We have to increase your rent.* Tenemos que aumentarle el alquiler.

incredible increíble.

indeed verdaderamente, claro *Indeed not!* ¡Claro que no!

indefinite indefinido, vago.

independent separado *Her financial interests are independent of her husband's.* Tiene sus bienes separados de los de su marido. ▲ independiente *I used to live with my parents, but now I'm independent.* Antes vivía con mis padres, pero ahora soy independiente.—*Every nation wants to be independent.* Todas las naciones quieren ser independientes.—*You're getting pretty independent.* Se está volviendo muy independiente.—*She's financially independent.* Ella vive de sus rentas.

index [n] índice.

○ **index finger** dedo índice.

indicate indicar *The policeman indicated*

the street we were looking for. El agente nos indicó la calle que buscábamos.—*His expression did not indicate his feelings.* Su expresión no indicaba lo que sentía. ▲ mostrar *This indicates that he is innocent.* Esto·muestra su inocencia.

indifferent indiferente *He is completely indifferent to everything that doesn't concern his work.* Es completamente indiferente a todo lo que no se relaciona con su trabajo. ▲ ni bueno ni malo *That last book of his is an indifferent piece of work.* Su última obra no es ni buena ni mala.

indigestion indigestión.

indignation indignación.

indirect indirecto *The banker asked several indirect questions.* El banquero hizo varias preguntas indirectas.

indiscreet indiscreto.

individual [*n*] persona *He's a peculiar individual.* Es una persona rara. ● [*adj*] original *She has very individual taste in clothes.* Tiene un gusto muy original para vestirse.

indoors en casa *You had better stay indoors today.* Sería mejor que se quedara hoy en casa.

induce inducir, incitar.

indulge mimar *Don't indulge the child so much.* No mime Ud. tanto al niño. ‖ *"Have a drink?" "No thanks, I don't indulge."* "¿Quiere beber algo?" "No gracias, no bebo."

industry industria *Steel is one of the main industries here.* La fabricación del acero es una de las industrias principales de aquí. ▲ diligencia *You might be promoted if you showed more industry.* Si mostrara Ud. mayor diligencia sería ascendido.

inequality desigualdad.

inexperience inexperiencia.

infant criatura.

infantry infantería.

infect infectar *The doctor will clean out that cut for you so it won't get infected.* El médico le limpiará la cortadura para que no se infecte. ▲ contagiar *He infects everybody with his enthusiasm.* Contagia a todo el mundo con su entusiasmo.

infection infección.

infer deducir *We inferred from his remarks that he didn't like his work.* Deducimos de lo que dijo que no le gustaba su trabajo.

inferior [*adj, n*] inferior.

inferiority inferioridad.

infinite infinito.

inflame inflamar *My throat is inflamed.*

Tengo lo garganta inflamada. ▲ enardecer, excitar *The crowd was inflamed by the speech.* Se enardeció el público con el discurso.

inflict infligir.

influence [*n*] influencia *His teacher had a tremendous influence on him.* Su maestro ha ejercido en él mucha influencia.—*Do you have any political influence?* ¿Tiene Ud. influencia política? ● [*v*] influir *I'm not trying to influence you.* No trato de influir en Ud.

inform avisar, informar *I was not informed in time.* No me avisaron a tiempo. ○ **informed** informado, enterado *I'm not very well informed on local politics.* No estoy muy bien informado de la política local.

informal de confianza, familiar *We had an informal party.* Tuvimos una reunión de confianza. ‖ *The inauguration was informal.* No hubo ceremonia alguna en la toma de posesión. ‖ *It was an informal dance.* El baile no fué de etiqueta.

information información *I want some information about train schedules.* Deseo información sobre el horario de trenes.

ingenuity inventiva.

ingratitude ingratitud.

ingredient ingrediente.

inhabit habitar.

inhabitant habitante.

inherit heredar *Who's going to inherit all his money when he dies?* ¿Quién heredará todo su dinero cuando muera?—*She inherited her mother's good looks.* Heredó la belleza de su madre.

inheritance herencia.

initial [*n*] inicial *Please write your initials.* Haga el favor de escribir sus iniciales. ● [*adj*] inicial *His initial investment was small.* Su inversión inicial fué pequeña. ● [*v*] poner las iniciales *Please initial this memorandum.* Haga Ud. el favor de poner sus iniciales en este memorandum.

inject inyectar.

injection inyección.

injure herir *Was he badly injured?* ¿Fué herido gravemente?—*She was injured by my remark.* Se sintió herida por mi observación.

injury herida *He still suffers from the injury he received in the last war.*

Sufre todavía de la herida que recibió en la última guerra.

ink [*n*] tinta *Please write in ink.* Haga el favor de escribir con tinta. ● [*v*] echar tinta, entintar *Don't ink the pad too heavily.* No eches demasiada tinta a la almohadilla.

inkwell tintero.

inland tierra adentro *They traveled inland for three days.* Viajaron tierra adentro durante tres días. ○ **inland navigation** navegación fluvial, navegación interior.

inn posada.

inner interior.

innocent inocente.

inoculate vacunar *Have you been inoculated against diphtheria?* ¿Le han vacunado a Ud. contra la difteria?

inquire preguntar *Let's inquire if he's in.* Vamos a preguntar si está en casa. ▲ indagar *We inquired a great deal before we found out where he was.* Hemos indagado mucho antes de saber donde estaba. ▲ averiguar *Let's inquire into the truth of the matter.* Averigüemos la verdad del asunto.

inquiry averiguación.

insane loco *The poor man went insane.* El pobre se volvió loco. ○ **insane asylum** manicomio.

insanity locura.

insect insecto.

insert añadir *Several new maps have been inserted in the later editions of the book.* A las últimas ediciones del libro se le han añadido varios mapas nuevos.

inside [*n*] interior *May I see the inside of the house?* ¿Puedo ver el interior de la casa? ● [*adj*] interior *Give me an inside room.* Deme Ud. un cuarto interior. ● [*adv*] adentro *Leave it inside.* Déjalo adentro. ○ **inside of** dentro de, en menos de *See that it's done inside of five minutes.* Procure que eso esté hecho en menos de cinco minutos. ○ **inside out** del revés, al revés *She wore her stockings inside out.* Se puso las medias al revés. ○ **to turn inside out** dar la vuelta. ‖ *Let's go inside.* Entremos. ‖ *The theft must have been an inside job.* Uno de la casa debe haber cometido el robo. ‖ *The fruit looked good but the inside was rotten.* La fruta parecía buena pero estaba podrida por dentro.

insignificant insignificante.

insist insistir, porfiar.

inspect inspeccionar.

inspection inspección.

inspector inspector.

inspiration inspiración.

inspire inspirar.

install instalar *The library is going to install a new lighting system.* La biblioteca va a instalar un nuevo sistema de iluminación. ○ **to be installed in** haber tomado posesión de *Are you installed in your new office?* ¿Ha tomado Ud. posesión de su nuevo cargo?

installment plazo *How many more installments do you have to pay on this furniture?* ¿Cuántos plazos más tiene Ud. que pagar sobre estos muebles? ▲ parte *The next installment of this story will come out in the July issue.* La próxima parte de esta novela saldrá en la edición de julio.

instance ocasión *In that instance he was found stealing money.* En esa ocasión se le sorprendió robando dinero. ▲ ejemplo *Give me a particular instance.* Deme Ud. un ejemplo. ○ **for instance** por ejemplo. ○ **in the first instance** en primer lugar.

instant [*n*] momento *Let me know the instant he arrives.* Avíseme en el momento que llegue. *or* Notifíqueme tan pronto como llegue. ○ **this instant** ahora mismo *Come this instant.* Venga ahora mismo. ● [*adj*] inmediato *The play had instant success.* La obra tuvo un éxito inmediato.

instantly al instante.

instead en lugar de eso, de esto, *etc. What do you want instead?* ¿Qué desea en lugar de eso? ○ **instead of** en vez de *Can I pay you later instead of now?* ¿Puedo pagarle más tarde en vez de hacerlo ahora?

institute [*n*] instituto.

institution institución.

instruct enseñar *How do you instruct your pupils?* ¿Cómo enseña Ud. a sus alumnos? ▲ dar órdenes *I have been instructed to deliver the message at once.* Me han dado órdenes de entregar el mensaje inmediatamente.

instruction instrucción, enseñanza.

instructor maestro.

instrument instrumento *Does any one here play an instrument?* ¿Hay aquí alguien que toque algún instrumento? ▲ medio *He'll use any instrument to get what he wants.* Se valdrá de cualquier medio para obtener lo que quiere.

○ **surgical instruments** instrumental quirúrgico.

insult [*n*] insulto *That sounds like an insult.* Eso suena a insulto.

● [*v*] ofender *She felt insulted.* Se sintió ofendida.

insurance seguro.

insure asegurar *The soldiers were picked carefully to insure the success of the expedition.* Seleccionaron con mucho cuidado a los soldados para asegurar el éxito de la expedición.—*My father's life is insured for twenty-five thousand dollars.* La vida de mi padre está asegurada en veinte y cinco mil dólares.

intellectual [*n, adj*] intelectual.

intelligence inteligencia *(brains);* información *(service).*

intelligent inteligente.

intend intentar *What do you intend to do?* ¿Qué intenta Ud. hacer? ▲ querer *I intended you to come.* Quería que vinieras.

‖ *Is this package intended for me?* ¿Es este paquete para mí?

intense intenso.

intent [*n*] intento *He was charged with intent to kill.* Fué acusado de intento de asesinato.

● [*adj*] resuelto, decidido *My brother is very intent on becoming a naval officer.* Mi hermano está muy decidido a hacerse oficial de marina.

intention intención, propósito.

intercept interceptar.

interchange [*n*] intercambio.

● [*v*] cambiar.

intercourse comunicaciónes *The island was cut off from intercourse with the outside world.* La isla quedó sin comunicaciones con el resto del mundo. ▲ relaciones íntimas *He was charged with having intercourse with a minor.* Se le acúso de haber tenido relaciones íntimas con una menor.

interest [*n*] interés *He listened with great interest.* Escuchaba con mucho interés.—*Do you have an interest in the business?* ¿Tiene Ud. algún interés en el negocio?—*How much interest does it pay?* ¿Cuánto da de interés?—*It's to your interest to do this.* Por su propio interés le conviene hacer esto.

● [*v*] interesar *Does this interest you?* ¿Le interesa esto?

○ **business interests** vida comercial, negocios *The business interests in the city want a new bridge.* La vida comercial de la ciudad requiere un nuevo puente. ○ **interests** intereses

While he was away, a lawyer took care of his interests. Durante su ausencia, se ocupó un abogado de sus intereses.

‖ *That book is of no interest to me.* Ese libro no me interesa.

interesting interesante.

interfere meterse *Don't interfere in my affairs.* No se meta en mis asuntos. ▲ intervenir *If they quarrel about it, don't you interfere.* Si se pelean por eso, no intervenga Ud.

○ **to interfere with** estorbar *I hope that won't interfere with my plans.* Espero que eso no estorbará mis planes.

interior [*n, adj*] interior.

intermediate intermedio.

intermission intermedio, descanso.

internal interno.

international internacional.

interpret interpretar.

interpretation interpretación.

interrupt interrumpir.

interruption interrupción.

interval intervalo.

interview [*n*] entrevista.

● [*v*] entrevistar.

intimate [*adj, n*] íntimo.

into *Get into the car and wait for me.* Entre Ud. en el carro y espéreme. —*I got into trouble.* Me metí en un lío. ▲ dentro de *They went into the house.* Entraron a la casa. ▲ *Can you translate that into English?* ¿Puede Ud. traducir eso al inglés?

introduce presentar *I'd like to introduce you to my father.* Me agradaría presentarle a mi padre.—*Who introduced that law?* ¿Quién presentó ese proyecto de ley?

‖ *She's trying to introduce something new in women's clothes.* Está tratando de lanzar una nueva moda femenina.

introduction prefacio, introducción *(to a book);* presentación *(to a person).*

○ **letter of introduction** carta de presentación.

invariable invariable.

invasion invasión.

invent inventar *Who invented this machine?* ¿Quién inventó esta máquina? —*Did you invent that story?* ¿Inventó Ud. esa historia?

invention invento; invención *(fabrication).*

invest invertir.

investigate investigar.

investigation investigación.

investment inversión.

invitation invitación *I did not receive*

your invitation. No recibí su invitación.

invite convidar, invitar *Who is invited for the week end?* ¿A quién se ha invitado para el fin de semana? ▲ provocar *His suggestion invited a lot of criticism.* Su sugestión provocó mucha crítica.
   ○ **inviting** tentador, atractivo *The water's very inviting.* El agua está muy tentadora.

involve ○ **involved** complicado *They have a very involved system of bookkeeping in this office.* En esta oficina tienen un sistema muy complicado de llevar los libros. ○ **to be involved** verse envuelto *He was involved in a scandal.* Se vió envuelto en un escándalo.
   ‖ *This job involves a lot of traveling.* En este trabajo se necesita viajar mucho.

iodine yodo.

iron [*n*] hierro *This stove's made of iron.* Esta estufa es de hierro. ▲ plancha *Have you got an iron I can borrow?* ¿Tiene Ud. una plancha que pueda prestarme?
   ● [*v*] planchar *Iron my dress carefully please.* Haga el favor de plancharme el vestido con cuidado.
   ○ **to iron out** resolver *They ironed out the difficulties.* Resolvieron las dificultades.

ironing board tabla de planchar.

irregular irregular *His behavior was a little irregular.* Su conducta era algo irregular.

irritate molestar, irritar *His foolish questions irritate me.* Me molestan sus preguntas tontas. ▲ irritar *This loose bandage will irritate the wound.* Esta venda floja irritará la herida.

irritation irritación.

island isla.

isolate aislar.

issue [*n*] edición *When does the next issue of the paper come out?* ¿Cuándo sale la próxima edición del periódico? ▲ emisión *Do you approve the issue of government bonds?* ¿Aprueba Ud. la misión de bonds del gobierno? ▲ problema *I don't want to make an issue of it.* No quiero hacer un problema de ello. ▲ tema *What issues are treated in the article?* ¿Qué temas se discuten en el artículo?
   ● [*v*] publicar *When is the paper issued?* ¿Cuándo se publica el periódico?
   ○ **at issue** en cuestión, en litigio *That is the point at issue.* Ese es el punto en cuestión. ○ **to take issue** oponerse, disentir *Why do you always take issue with what I say?* ¿Por qué disiente Ud. siempre de lo que digo?

it lo *I can't do it.* No lo puedo hacer.
   ‖ *Were you on the boat when it left?* ¿Estaba Ud. en el barco cuando zarpó? ‖ *It was that house that I saw yesterday.* Esa es la casa qui ví ayer. ‖ *It is impossible to get there by two o'clock.* Es imposible llegar allí para las dos. ‖ *It's five o'clock.* Son las cinco. ‖ *Is it raining?* ¿Llueve? *or* ¿Está lloviendo? ‖ *It's I.* Soy yo.

itch [*n*] picor, picazón, prurito.
   ● [*v*] picar.

its su *What's its number?* ¿Cuál es su número?
   ‖ *Did the cat drink all its milk?* ¿Se tomó el gato toda la leche? ‖ *Did you explore all of its possibilities?* ¿Examinó Ud. todas las posibilidades?

itself sí mismo *That speaks for itself.* Eso habla por sí mismo. *or* Eso es evidente. ▲ mismo, propio *The motor itself provides the heat.* El propio motor suministra la calefacción. ▲ se *The baby hurt itself.* El niño se ha lastimado.

ivory marfil.

ivy hiedra.

J

jack gato *I need a jack to change my tire.* Necesito un gato para cambiar el neumático. ▲ sota *Play the jack of hearts.* Juegue la sota de corazones.
   ○ **to jack up** alzar con gato *You'll have to jack up the car.* Tiene Ud. que alzar el carro con el gato. ▲ subir *Prices were suddenly jacked up.* Los precios subieron de repente.

jacket chaqueta, saco.

jackknife navaja, cortaplumas.

jail carcel.

jam (*preserves*) mermelada. ○ **jammed** atascado *I can't open the window; it's jammed.* No puedo abrir la ventana; está atascada. ▲ atestado *The station was jammed with people.* La estación estaba atestada de gente.

janitor portero.

January enero.

jar [n] tarro *I want a jar of preserves.* Quiero un tarro de conservas. ▲ sacudida *The fall gave me quite a jar.* La caída me produjo una sacudida. ● [v] mover *Don't jar the table.* No muevas la mesa. ○ **jarring** discordante *Her manner was a jarring note.* Su comportamiento era una nota discordante. ○ **to jar on** irritar *The noise of the city jars on my nerves.* El ruido de la ciudad me irrita los nervios.

jaw quijada, mandíbula.

jazz jazz.

jealous celoso *He's jealous of his younger brother.* Está celoso de su hermano menor.

jelly jalea

jest broma.

Jew judío.

jewel joya, alhaja *I have no jewels to declare.* No tengo joyas que declarar. ▲ piedra preciosa *She has a beautiful pair of jeweled earrings.* Ella tiene un lindo par de pendientes con piedras preciosas. ‖ *My watch has seventeen jewels.* Mi reloj tiene diecisiete rubíes.

jewelry joyería.

jewelry store joyería.

job empleo *Do you want a job?* ¿Desea Ud. un empleo? ▲ deber *My job is to wash the dishes.* Mi deber es lavar los platos. ▲ trabajo *It's going to be an awful job to file these letters.* Va a ser un enorme trabajo archivar estas cartas.

join juntar *Let's join hands.* Juntemos las manos. ▲ acoplar *Join these pipes together.* Acople estos tubos. ▲ juntarse *Where do the roads join?* ¿Dónde se juntan los caminos? ▲ incorporarse, ingresar *When did you join the army?* ¿Cuándo se incorporó Ud. al ejército? ▲ ir con, unirse a *Do you want to join us?* ¿Quiere Ud. ir con nosotros? ‖ *Everybody join in the chorus!* ¡Todos a cantar en coro!

joint [n] empalme, juntura *The pipe is leaking at the joints.* Se sale el agua por los empalmes de la cañería. ▲ coyuntura, articulación *It hurts me in the joints* Me duelen las coyunturas. ▲ buchinche [Cuba] *What's the name of the joint we went to last night?* ¿Cómo se llama el buchinche donde fuimos anoche? ● [adj] mancomunado *My husband and I have a joint bank account.* Mi marido y yo tenemos una cuenta mancomunada en el banco. ○ **to throw out of joint** desarticularse, descoyuntarse *The athlete threw his arm out of joint.* El atleta se desarticuló el brazo.

joke chiste *He's always telling jokes.* Siempre está contando chistes. ▲ broma *This is no time for joking.* Este no es el momento para bromas. ○ **to play a joke** bromear *I was only playing a joke on you.* Solamente estaba bromeando con Ud.

jolly alegre, jovial.

jolt [n] choque *The news gave me an awful jolt.* La noticia me causó un choque tremendo. ● [v] traquetear, dar saltos *Why does the car jolt so?* ¿Por qué da tantos saltos el coche?

journal revista, periódico.

journey [n] jornada, viaje. ● [v] viajar.

joy alegría *She was filled with joy.* Estaba llena de alegría. ▲ gozo *It's a joy to hear him play.* Da gozo oírle tocar.

joyful alegre.

judge [n] juez *Where's the judge?* ¿Dónde está el juez? ▲ perito *I am no judge of art.* No soy perito en arte. ● [v] arbitrar *Who judged the race?* ¿Quién arbitró la carrera? ▲ juzgar *Don't judge me too harshly.* No me juzgue tan severamente.

judgment juicio *He always shows good judgment.* Siempre muestra buen juicio. ▲ fallo *What was the judgment of the court?* ¿Cuál fué el fallo de la Corte? ‖ *Don't pass judgment too quickly.* No juzgue muy a la ligera.

jug jarro.

juice zumo, jugo *I want some orange juice.* Quiero jugo de naranja.

July julio.

jumble [n] revoltillo, enredo.

jump [n] salto *He made a jump of twenty feet.* Dió un salto de veinte pies. ▲ cambio *There's been quite a jump in the temperature.* Ha habido un cambio brusco en la temperatura. ● [v] saltar *See how high you can jump* Vea hasta que altura puede saltar Ud. ○ **to jump at** apresurarse a aceptar, saltar sobre *He jumped at the offer.* Se apresuró a aceptar la oferta. ‖ *Jump on!* ¡Salte Ud.! ‖ *It made him jump to see you.* Tuvo un sobresalto al verlo.

junction cruce.

June junio.

jungle selva.

junior menor *His boss is three years his junior.* Su jefe es tres años menor que él.
● [*adj*] juvenil *Is your son entering the junior tournament?* ¿Tomará parte su hijo en el torneo juvenil?
○ **Jr.** hijo *John Paul Jones, Jr.* John Paul Jones, hijo.

junk broza, desecho *(scraps);* trasto *(furniture);* chatarra, hierro viejo *(metal).*

juror jurado.

jury jurado *The jury returned a verdict of guilty.* El jurado le declaró culpable.

just [*adj*] justo *His decisions are always just.* Sus decisiones son siempre justas. ▲merecido, justo *His punishment was just.* Su castigo era merecido. ▲exacto *He gave a just account of what happened.* Dió un informe exacto de lo que ocurrió.
● [*adv*] apenas *At this rate we'll just get there.* A este paso apenas llegaremos. ▲precisamente, justamente *That's just what I want.* Eso es precisamente lo que quiero. ▲no más que *He's just a little boy.* No es más que un niño. ▲sólo *Just a minute and I'll be with you.* Sólo un minuto y estaré con Ud.
○ just as *He arrived just as I was leaving.* Llegó en el momento en que yo salía. ▲tal como *Write me just as he would.* Escríbame tal como él lo haría. ○ just beyond un poco más allá de. ○ just now ahora mismo.
○ to have just acabar de *They had just arrived in New York.* Acababan de llegar a Nueva York.
‖ *Just a moment.* Un momento. ‖ *Just as you please.* Como Ud. guste. ‖ *Just what do you mean?* ¿Qué es lo que Ud. quiere decir? ‖ *I'm just tired to death.* Me estoy muriendo de cansancio. ‖ *Just imagine! He made a fortune in a year.* ¡Imagínese! Hizo una fortuna en un año. ‖ *Just we two.* Nosotros dos solamente.

justice justicia *Don't expect justice from him.* No espere que le haga justicia.
○ justice of the peace juez de paz.
○ to do justice to hacer justicia a, apreciar *Are you doing justice to his talents?* ¿Hace Ud. justicia a su talento? ▲estar a la altura de *This work doesn't do justice to your abilities.* Este trabajo no está a la altura de sus habilidades.

justify justificar.

jut sobresalir.

juvenile juvenil.

K

keel quilla *When was the keel of that ship laid?* ¿Cuándo pusieron la quilla de ese barco?
○ to keel over desplomarse *I only hit him once and he keeled over.* Solamente le dí un golpe y se desplomó. ▲desmayarse *She suddenly keeled over from the heat.* De repente se desmayó a causa del calor.

keen afilado *This knife would cut better if it had a keener edge.* Este cuchillo cortaría mejor si estuviera más afilado. ▲aguzado *He has a keen mind for mathematics.* Tiene la mente muy aguzada para las matemáticas. ▲perspicaz *Her actions show how keen she is.* Sus acciones demuestran lo perspicaz que es.
○ to be keen about tener entusiasmo por *The boss is very keen about the new program.* El jefe tiene mucho entusiasmo por el nuevo programa.
‖ *He has a keen appetite.* Tiene muy buen apetito.

keep quedarse *May I keep this picture?* ¿Puedo quedarme con esta foto? ▲guardar *I kept this for you.* Guardé esto para Ud.—*Can you keep a secret?* ¿Puede Ud. guardar un secreto?— *Keep dinner warm for me.* Guárdeme la comida caliente. ▲guardarse, quedarse con *Keep the change.* Guárdese el cambio. *or* Quédese con el cambio. ▲seguir *Do I keep to the left or right?* ¿Debo seguir por la izquierda o por la derecha? ▲proseguir, continuar *Keep on the job.* Continúe con su trabajo. ▲mantenerse *Keep in touch with me.* Manténgase en contacto conmigo. ▲conservar(se) *This milk won't keep till tomorrow.* Esta leche no se conservará hasta mañana. ▲llevar *Can you keep accounts?* ¿Puede Ud. llevar la contabilidad? ▲mantener *Do you earn enough to keep your family?* ¿Gana Ud. lo suficiente para mantener a su familia? ▲tener

Why don't you keep boarders? ¿Por qué no tiene Ud. huéspedes? ○ **to earn one's keep** ganarse la vida *Does he earn his keep?* ¿Se gana la vida? ○ **to keep an eye on** vigilar *Keep an eye on my coat.* Vigile Ud. mi abrigo. ○ **to keep cool** tener calma *Keep cool.* Tenga calma. ○ **to keep in stock** tener en existencia *What do you keep in stock?* ¿Qué tiene Ud. en existencia? ○ **to keep on** seguir, continuar *Keep on working.* Siga trabajando.—*Keep on trying.* Continúe Ud. esforzándose. ○ **to keep one's temper** no perder la calma *Keep your temper.* No pierda Ud. la calma. ○ **to keep one's word** cumplir su palabra *I always keep my word.* Siempre cumplo mi palabra. ○ **to keep one waiting** hacer esperar a uno *Sorry to keep you waiting.* Siento hacerle esperar. ○ **to keep on with** continuar con *Keep on with what you're doing.* Continúe Ud. con lo que está haciendo. ○ **to keep out of** no meterse en *I'll try to keep out of trouble.* Trataré de no meterme en líos. ○ **to keep up** sostener *It's expensive to keep up a car.* Resulta caro mantener un automóvil. ○ **to keep up with** ir al paso de *Did you have any trouble keeping up with the others?* ¿Tuvo Ud. alguna dificultad en ir al paso de los demás? ○ **to play for keeps** ir de veras, jugar de veras *We're playing for keeps.* Estamos jugando de veras. ‖ *Keep off the grass.* Prohibido pisar el césped. ‖ *Keep him from eating too much.* Evite que coma demasiado. ‖ *Keep up the good work.* Continúe en su buen trabajo. or Persevere por ese buen camino. ‖ *Does your watch keep good time?* ¿Es exacto su reloj?

kerosene kerosén, keroseno.

ketchup salsa de tomate.

kettle caldera, marmita.

key llave *I've lost the key to my room.* He perdido la llave de mi cuarto. ▲ clave *Do you know the key to the code?* ¿Conoce Ud. la clave del código? —*The symphony's written in the key of G.* La sinfonía está escrita en clave de Sol. ▲ tecla *The typewriter keys are terribly stiff.* Las teclas de la máquina de escribir están muy duras. ○ **key man** principal, el más importante *He's the key man in the plant.* El es el principal de la fábrica. ○ **to be keyed up** estar excitado *He was all keyed up for the race.* Estaba muy excitado por la carrera.

khaki caqui.

kick [n] patada *Give the ball a kick.* Dele una patada al balón. ● [v] dar coces, cocear *I hope this horse doesn't kick.* Espero que este caballo no de coces. ▲ quejarse *He's always kicking about something.* Siempre se está quejando de algo. ▲ dar un puntapié a, dar una patada a *Kick the ball!* ¡Dé Ud. un puntapié a la pelota! ○ **to get a kick out of** gozar con, pasarlo bien con *He gets a big kick out of sports.* Goza mucho con los deportes.

kid [n] cabrito *We'll have to separate the kids from the goats.* Tendremos que separar los cabritos de las cabras. ▲ pequeño, niño *We'll feed the kids first.* Les daremos de comer a los pequeños primero. ● [adj] de cabritilla *She was very proud of her kid gloves.* Estaba muy orgullosa de sus guantes de cabritilla. ● [v] bromear *Are you kidding?* ¿Está Ud. bromeando?

kidney riñón.

kidney bean frijol [Am], judía [Sp], poroto [Am].

kill [n] piezas, caza *The hunters brought home the kill.* Los cazadores se llevaron las piezas a sus casas. ● [v] matar *Be careful with that pistol, you might kill someone.* Tenga cuidado con esa pistola que puede matar a alguien.—*Let's take a walk to kill some time.* Caminemos un rato para matar el tiempo. ▲ ahogar *The committee killed the bill.* El comité ahogó el proyecto de ley. ▲ quitar *Too much salt will kill the flavor of the soup.* Demasiada sal le quitará el sabor a la sopa. ○ **for the kill** para dar muerte *They closed in for the kill.* Le rodearon para darle muerte.

kilogram kilogramo.

kilometer kilómetro.

kind [n] clase *What kind of person is he?* ¿Qué clase de persona es él? ▲ raza *What kind of a dog is he?* ¿De qué raza es ese perro? ▲ especie *It's a kind of medicine he's taking.* Es una especie de medicina que toma. ● [adj] amable *The people here are very kind.* La gente de aquí es muy amable. ○ **all kinds of** toda clase de *I like all kinds of food.* Me gusta toda clase de comida. ○ **in kind** en especie *The farmer pays his workers in kind.* El

agricultor paga a sus trabajadores en especie. O **kind of** más bien *I felt kind of sorry for him.* Sentía más bien lástima por él. || *Be kind enough to help me.* Tenga la bondad de ayudarme.
kindle encender.
kindly [*adj*] bondadoso *Her grandmother is a kindly old lady.* Su abuela es una viejecita bondadosa.
● [*adv*] amablemente *He will be treated kindly.* Será tratado amablemente. ▲ haga el favor de *Kindly mind your own business.* Haga el favor de no meterse en lo que no le importa.
kindness || *She always showed kindness to the children.* Se mostró siempre cariñosa con los niños.
king rey.
kingdom reino.
kiss [*n*] beso.
● [*v*] besar.
kitchen cocina *Do you mind eating in the kitchen?* ¿Le importa a Ud. comer en la cocina?—*Who is in charge of the school kitchen?* ¿Quién está encargado de la cocina de la escuela?
O **kitchen stove** fogón de la cocina, estufa *You'll find it under the kitchen stove.* Lo encontrará debajo del fogón de la cocina.
kitten gatito.
knee rodilla.
kneel arrodillarse.
knife [*n*] cuchillo *Give me the big knife to cut the bread.* Deme el cuchillo grande para cortar el pan.
● [*v*] apuñalar, dar una cuchillada (*or* puñalada) *He was knifed in a street fight.* Le dieron una cuchillada en una pelea callejera.
knit tejer.
knitting needle aguja de tejer.
knob tirador.
knock [*n*] golpe, ruido *Did you hear a knock?* ¿Oyó Ud. un golpe?
● [*v*] llamar a la puerta *Knock before you go in.* Llame a la puerta antes de entrar. ▲ tropezar *Try not to knock against the table.* Trate de no tropezar con la mesa.
O **to knock down** desarmar *Knock down the scaffolding.* Desarmen el andamiaje. ▲ subastar *He knocked down the painting for a hundred dollars.* Subastó el cuadro por cien dólares. ▲ rebajar *Can't you knock down the price a couple of dollars?* ¿No podría rebajar el precio un par de dólares? O **to knock off** suspender *Let's knock off at five o'clock.* Suspendamos el trabajo a las cinco. ▲ rebajar *Knock something off the price.* Rebaje un poco el precio. O **to knock out** poner fuera de combate *He was knocked out in the tenth round.* Fué puesto fuera de combate en el décimo asalto. ▲ agotar *He was knocked out after one game of tennis.* Estaba agotado después de un partido de tenis.
knot [*n*] nudo *Can you untie this knot?* ¿Puede desatar este nudo?—*I can't saw through this knot.* No puedo aserrar este nudo de la madera.—*This ship can make fifteen knots.* Este barco puede hacer quince nudos.
● [*v*] amarrar *He knotted the rope securely.* Amarró la cuerda fuertemente.
know saber *I know he's ill.* Sé que él está enfermo.—*I knew you were coming today.* Sabía que Ud. vendría hoy.—*I know only French and English.* Solamente sé francés e inglés.—*I don't know how to drive a car.* No sé conducir un automóvil. ▲ conocer *Wait until all the facts in the case are known.* Espere hasta que todos los hechos del caso sean conocidos.—*Do you know him by sight?* ¿Le conoce Ud. de vista? ▲ reconocer *I knew him immediately when I met him after two years.* Le reconocí en seguida cuando le ví a los dos años.
|| *What do you know?* ¿Qué hay de nuevo? || *Be sure you know all the facts before you accuse anyone.* Asegúrese de los hechos antes de acusar a nadie.
knowledge conocimiento *Do you have any knowledge of this matter?* ¿Tiene Ud. algún conocimiento de este asunto?
|| *To the best of my knowledge, no.* Según mi leal saber y entender, no.
knuckle articulación de los dedos.
kodak kodak.

L

label [*n*] rótulo, etiqueta.
● [*v*] rotular.
labor [*n*] trabajo *Mining is very heavy labor.* El trabajo en las minas es muy pesado. ▲ proletariado, clase obrera *Labor favors an eight-hour day.* El

proletariado es partidario de la jornada de ocho horas.

● [adj] obrero *Do you know the labor laws?* ¿Conoce Ud. la legislación obrera?

● [v] trabajar *They labored from morning till night.* Trabajaban de la mañana a la noche. ▲ esforzarse *He labored to finish the book before summer.* Se esforzaba en terminar el libro antes del verano. ▲ dar importancia *Don't labor the point.* No le dé importancia al asunto.

○ to be in labor estar de parto *She was in labor nine hours.* Estuvo de parto durante nueve horas. ○ to labor under difficulties trabajar en condiciones difíciles.

laboratory laboratorio.

laborer peón, jornalero.

lace encaje.

lack [n] falta *His lack of knowledge was obvious.* Era evidente su falta de conocimientos.

● [v] no tener, faltar *He lacks enthusiasm.* Le falta entusiasmo.

○ to be lacking faltar *Nothing was lacking to make the party a success.* No faltó detalle para que la fiesta fuese un éxito.

lad mozo, muchacho.

ladder escalera.

lady señora *Is that lady at the door your mother?* ¿Es su madre la señora que está en la puerta?—*Act like a lady.* Condúzcase como una señora.

○ ladies' room lavabo de señoras [Sp], baño de señoras, cuarto de señoras, tocador [Am] *Where is the ladies' room?* ¿Dónde está el lavabo de señoras? ○ lady of the house dueña de la casa *Do you wish to speak to the lady of the house?* ¿Desea Ud. hablar con la dueña de la casa?

lag [n] retraso.

● [v] retrasarse.

lake lago.

lamb cordero.

lame cojo, [Arg] rengo *The little boy is lame.* El niño es cojo. ▲ molido, lastimado *I was lame after the horseback ride.* Estaba molido después de montar a caballo.

○ lame excuse disculpa pobre.

lament [n] lamento.

lamp lámpara.

lampshade pantalla.

lance [v] abrir *The doctor lanced my finger.* El doctor me abrió el dedo.

land [n] tierra *The land here is poor for farming.* La tierra aquí es mala para

el cultivo.—*He inherited a great deal of land.* Heredó muchas tierras.—*When do we expect to reach land?* ¿Cuándo cree Ud. que tocaremos tierra? ▲ campo *He always wanted to get back to the land.* Siempre había deseado volver al campo.

● [v] atracar *The ship should land within the next hour.* El barco debería atracar dentro de una hora. ▲ aterrizar *The pilot landed the plane at night.* El piloto aterrizó de noche. ▲ pisar tierra firme *You don't know how eager I am to land.* Ud. no puede figurarse los deseos que tengo de pisar tierra firme.

○ native land patria *He had a great love for his native land.* Tenía gran amor por su patria.

‖ *He landed on his head.* Se cayó de cabeza.

landlady propietaria, casera.

landlord propietario, casero.

landscape paisaje.

lane senda, vereda.

language idioma *I don't know what language he speaks.* No sé que idioma habla.

lantern linterna, farol.

lap [n] regazo *She held the baby in her lap.* Tenía al niño en su regazo.

● [v] lamer *The kitten lapped up the milk.* El gatito lamía la leche.

lapel solapa.

lard manteca de puerco.

large grande *This room is not large enough.* Este cuarto no es suficientemente grande.

○ at large en general *The country at large is interested in the problem.* El país en general está interesado en el problema. ○ large scale gran escala.

lark alondra.

laryngitis laringitis.

lash [n] azote.

● [v] azotar.

lasso lazo, mangana.

● [v] lazar.

last [n] horma *This shoe has a comfortable last.* Este zapato tiene una horma cómoda.

● [adj] último *He was the last to leave.* Fué el último en marcharse. —*This is my last day here.* Este es mi último día aquí.—*Did you see the name of the last station?* ¿Vió Ud. el nombre de la última estación? ▲ pasado *I saw him last week.* Le ví la semana pasada.

● [v] durar *How long does this ride last?* ¿Cuánto dura este trayecto?

▲ resistir *Do you think you can last another mile?* ¿Cree Ud. que puede Ud. resistir una milla más? ▲ llegar, alcanzar *I don't think my money will last.* No creo que me llegue el dinero. O **at last** por último, finalmente. O **last night** anoche *Last night I went shopping.* Anoche fuí de compras. O **night before last** anteanoche. O **the last thing** lo último *That was the last thing I expected him to do.* Eso era lo último que yo esperaba que hiciera. O **year before last** el año antepasado.

lasting profundo *It created a lasting impression on me.* Me causó una profunda impresión.

latch aldaba, picaporte.

late difunto *Her late husband was fond of sports.* Su difunto esposo era aficionado a los deportes. ▲ tarde *It was late when she came.* Era tarde cuando llegó. O **to be late** llegar tarde *Don't be late for the theater.* No llegue Ud. tarde al teatro.

lately recientemente.

lather [n] espuma.

● [v] enjabonar.

latter reciente, último *He was very successful in the latter part of his life.* Fué muy afortunado en la última parte de su vida. O **the latter** el más reciente, el segundo *Of the two reports, I prefer the latter.* De los dos informes, prefiero el segundo. ▲ éste *The latter's better than the former.* Este es mejor que aquél.

laugh [n] risa.

● [v] reirse. O **to laugh at** reirse de.

laughter risa.

launch [n] lancha.

● [v] botar, echar al agua *Who's going to speak when they launch that new battleship?* ¿Quién será el orador cuando boten ese nuevo acorazado? ▲ lanzar, desencadenar *The offensive was launched at dawn.* Se desencadenó la ofensiva en la madrugada.

launder lavar.

laundry lavandería *These clothes must go to the laundry.* Esta ropa hay que mandarla a la lavandería. ▲ ropa limpia *My laundry just came back.* Acaban de mandarme la ropa limpia. ▲ ropa sucia *They came to take my laundry.* Han venido a buscar la ropa sucia.

laundry man lavandero.

lava lava.

lavatory lavabo, baño *Where's the men's lavatory?* ¿Dónde está el lavabo de caballeros?

lavish [adj] pródigo.

● [v] prodigar.

law ley *Is there a law against speeding?* ¿Hay una ley que prohiba ir a mucha velocidad? ▲ leyes, derecho *He is studying law.* Está estudiando derecho.

‖ *My brother is practicing law.* Mi hermano ejerce como abogado.

lawful lícito, legal.

lawless ilegal.

lawn césped.

lawyer abogado.

laxative laxante.

lay dejar *Lay the book here.* Deje aquí el libro. ▲ poner *Lay the baby on the bed gently.* Ponga cuidadosamente el niño en la cama.—*He didn't lay the bricks carefully.* No ponía los ladrillos con cuidado.—*This hen lays a lot of eggs.* Esta gallina pone muchos huevos. ▲ colocar, situar *He laid the scene of his last play in Europe.* Ha situado la acción de su última comedia en Europa. ▲ preparar *They laid their plans carefully, but failed.* Prepararon sus planes con cuidado, pero fracasaron. ▲ apostar *I lay ten dollars to one that you succeed.* Apuesto diez dólares contra uno a que tiene Ud. éxito. O **to lay aside** ahorrar *He laid aside a good sum of money.* Ha ahorrado mucho dinero. O **to lay down one's life** dar la vida *He laid down his life for his country.* Dió la vida por su país. O **to lay down on the job** abandonarse mucho en el trabajo. O **to lay eyes on** echar la vista encima *I never laid eyes on him.* Nunca le he echado la vista encima. O **to lay in** proveerse de *They laid in supplies for the winter.* Se proveyeron de víveres para el invierno. O **to lay off** despedir *He laid off ten employees today.* Ha despedido hoya diez empleados. O **to lay oneself open** exponerse *He laid himself open to a lot of criticism.* Se expuso a las críticas. O **to lay out** trazar *They laid out the town in the shape of a rectangle.* Trazaron la ciudad en forma rectangular. ▲ gastar *I just laid out ten dollars.* Acabo de gastar diez dólares. O **to lay waste** asolar, devastar *The whole region was laid waste by the storm.* Toda la región fué asolada por la tempestad.

layer capa.

layman profano *I'm a layman in questions of medicine.* Soy un profano en materia médica.

layout trazado *How do you like the layout of this town?* ¿Qué le parece a Ud. el trazado de esta ciudad?

laziness pereza.

lazy perezoso.

lead [*n*] delantera, ventaja *How much of a lead does our candidate have?* ¿Qué delantera lleva nuestro candidato? ▲ papel principal *She has the lead in the play.* Tiene el papel principal de la obra. ▲ sugestión *When I was looking for a job he gave me a good lead.* Cuando estaba buscando trabajo me hizo una buena sugestión.
● [*v*] llevar, conducir *I'll lead the horse to the stable.* Llevaré el caballo a la cuadra. ▲ llevar *This street leads to a dead end.* Esta calle lleva a un callejón sin salida. ▲ causar, dar lugar a *The information led to his arrest.* La información causó su arresto. ▲ ir a la cabeza, ir al frente *The general was leading the parade.* El general iba a la cabeza del desfile. ▲ dirigir *He led the orchestra.* Dirigió la orquesta.
○ **to lead a ... life** llevar una vida ... *He leads a busy life.* Lleva una vida ocupada. ○ **to lead astray** llevar por mal camino. ○ **to lead up to** conducir a *What are these events leading up to?* ¿A qué conducirán estos acontecimientos? ○ **to take the lead** tomar la delantera *The white horse has taken the lead.* El caballo blanco ha tomado la delantera.

lead mina *I need lead for my pencil.* Me hacen falta minas para mi lápiz. ▲ plomo (*metal*).
‖ *They filled him full of lead.* Le acribillaron a balazos.

leader líder *Who are the leaders of the political parties here?* ¿Quiénes son aquí los líderes de los partidos políticos? ▲ director *The leader of the band was a very tall man.* El director de la banda era un hombre muy alto.
‖ *He's a born leader.* Ha nacido para mandar.

leadership dirección.

leaf hoja *I like to see the leaves on the trees change color.* Me gusta ver cambiar de color a las hojas de los árboles. —*The leaves of this book are torn.* Las hojas de ese libro están rotas. ▲ tabla *Add another leaf to the table.* Añádale otra tabla a la mesa.

○ **to turn over a new leaf** cambiar de modo de ser.

league liga, confederación.

leak [*n*] gotera *There's a leak in the roof.* Hay una gotera en el techo. ▲ vía de agua *The boat has a leak.* El buque tiene una vía de agua.
● [*v*] salirse *The pot is leaking.* La olla se sale.
○ **to leak out** descubrirse *Keep your mouth shut or our secret will leak out.* Cállese la boca o nuestro secreto se descubrirá.

lean [*adj*] magro *I like lean meat.* Me gusta la carne magra. ▲ flaco *Who is the tall, lean individual over there?* ¿Quién es ese individuo alto y flaco que está allá? ▲ malo *It's been a lean year for farmers.* Ha sido un año malo para los labradores.
● [*v*] apoyarse *I want to lean on your arm.* Quiero apoyarme en su brazo. ▲ inclinarse *If you lean forward you can see.* Si Ud. se inclina hacia delante, podrá ver. ▲ apoyar *Lean this picture against the wall.* Apoye este cuadro contra la pared. ▲ depender *She leans on her mother in everything.* Depende de su madre para todo.
‖ *She leaned out of the window.* Se asomó a la ventana.

leap [*n*] salto *The frog made a big leap.* La rana dió un gran salto.
● [*v*] saltar *The dog leaped the fence.* El perro saltó la valla.

learn aprender *Are you learning how to type?* ¿Está Ud. aprendiendo a escribir a máquina? ▲ saber *Have you learned of any good restaurant around here?* ¿Sabe Ud. de algún buen restaurant por aquí cerca?
○ **to learn by heart** aprender de memoria.

learned culto, erudito.

lease [*n*] arriendo *Did they sign the lease?* ¿Firmaron el arriendo?
● [*v*] arrendar *I've leased a cottage from him for the summer.* He arrendado una casita suya para el verano.
○ **new lease on life** nuevo plazo de vida *The bill just passed gave the committee a new lease on life.* El decreto que acaban de aprobar dió un nuevo plazo de vida a la comisión.

leash correa.

least menor *The work has to be done in the least possible time.* Hay que hacer el trabajo en el menor tiempo posible.
○ **at least** por lo menos *You might at least have written to me.* Por lo menos podría Ud. haberme escrito. ○ **the least**

lo menos *That is the least you can do.*
Eso es lo menos que puede Ud. hacer.
leather cuero.
leave [*n*] licencia *He went home on leave.*
Fué a su casa con licencia.

● [*v*] dejar *Leave a note saying we called.* Deje Ud. una nota diciendo que hemos venido a verle.—*I left my coat up-stairs.* Me he dejado el abrigo arriba.—*Leave it to me.* Déjelo de mi cuenta.—*I'm leaving my job.* Voy a dejar mi trabajo.—*She'll leave the house to her son.* Dejará la casa a su hijo. ▲ salir *I must leave now to catch my train.* Tengo que salir ahora para coger el tren.

○ **to be left** quedar *Are there any tickets left for tonight?* ¿Quedan billetes para esta noche? ○ **to leave out** omitir *When you copy it, don't leave anything out.* Cuando lo copie Ud., no omita nada.
lecture [*n*] conferencia *That was a pretty interesting lecture.* Fué una conferencia bastante interesante.

● [*v*] hablar *I haven't heard anyone lecture so well in a long time.* Hace mucho que no he oído a nadie hablar tan bien. ▲ regañar *Don't lecture me so much.* No me regañe tanto.

○ **to give a lecture to** reprender, regañar *My father gave us a lecture for being out so late.* Mi padre nos reprendió por haber estado fuera hasta tan tarde.
ledge borde, saliente.
left [*n*] izquierda *Turn to the left.* Tuerza hacia la izquierda.—*Politically he's always been on the left.* Siempre ha sido un político de izquierda.

● [*adj*] izquierdo *Take the other bag with your left hand.* Coja la otra maleta con la mano izquierda.
left-handed zurdo.
leftovers sobras.
leg pierna *I have a pain in my right leg.* Me duele la pierna derecha. ▲ pierna, (*of trousers*) pernera *I've torn the leg of my trousers.* Me he roto la pierna del pantalón. *or* Me he roto la pernera. ▲ pata *The dog hurt his leg.* El perro se ha hecho daño en una pata.—*The leg of the chair is broken.* Se ha roto la pata de la silla.
legal legal.
legend leyenda.
legible legible.
legion legión.
legislation legislación.
legislature legislatura, asamblea.
legitimate legítimo.

leisure horas libres *I don't have much leisure nowadays.* No tengo muchas horas libres en estos días.

○ **at leisure** lentamente, con tranquilidad *He ate his dinner at leisure.* Comió la cena lentamente. ○ **at one's leisure** en los ratos libres *There's no rush; you can write it at your leisure.* No es urgente, puede Ud. escribirlo en los ratos libres. ○ **to be at leisure** estar desocupado *When will you be at leisure to see me?* ¿Cuándo estará Ud. desocupado para verme?
lemon limón.
lemonade limonada.
lend prestar *Can you lend me a dollar?* ¿Puede Ud. prestarme un dólar?

○ **to lend color** dar color *She lent color to the occasion by her presence.* Dió color al acto con su presencia.
length largo *Is the length of the sleeves all right?* ¿Está bien el largo de las mangas? ▲ largo, longitud *The length of the room is twice its width.* El largo del cuarto es doble del ancho.

○ **at length** al fin *At length he came.* Al fin vino. ▲ detalladamente, extensamente *She described the party at length.* Describió la fiesta detalladamente.

‖ *We were surprised at the length of time you were away.* Nos sorprendió el que haya estado Ud. tanto tiempo fuera.
lengthen alargar *Tell the tailor to lengthen these trousers three inches.* Diga al sastre que alargue estos pantalones tres pulgadas.
lengthwise a lo largo.
lengthy largo.
less menos *I have less money than I thought.* Tengo menos dinero de lo que pensaba.—*I've always paid less for my gloves.* Siempre he pagado menos por los guantes.
lesser menor *Which is the lesser of the two evils?* ¿De los dos males, cuál es el menor? ▲ de menos categoría *The speaker is one of the lesser officials of the town.* El orador es uno de los funcionarios de menos categoría en le pueblo.
lesson lección.
let dejar *Will the customs officials let us go through?* ¿Nos dejarán pasar los empleados de la aduana?—*Let me by.* Déjeme pasar. ▲ alquilar *Have you rooms to let?* ¿Tiene Ud. habitaciones para alquilar?

○ **to let alone** dejar en paz *Please let me alone for a while.* Haga el favor de dejarme en paz un rato. ○ **to let down** bajar, descuidar *They let down a lot in their work.* Han bajado mucho en su trabajo. ▲ fallar, no cumplir *I counted on his help but he let me down.* Contaba con su ayuda, pero me falló. ▲ dejar plantado *I'll wait for you, but don't let me down.* Te esperaré, pero no me dejes plantado. ○ **to let go of** vender *Don't let go of your property yet.* No venda Ud. todavía la propiedad. ▲ soltar *Don't let go of the rope till I tell you.* No suelte la cuerda hasta que yo le diga. ○ **to be let off** salir bien librado *The criminal was let off with a light sentence.* El criminal salió bien librado con una condena muy leve. ○ **to let up** cesar *The rain hasn't let up for two days.* La lluvia no ha cesado en dos días.

‖ *Please let me have the menu.* ¿Puede hacer el favor de darme el menú? ‖ *Let's go to the theater.* Vamos al teatro. ‖ *Let's see what can be done.* Veamos lo que se puede hacer.

letter [*n*] carta *Are there any letters for me?* ¿Hay alguna carta para mi? ▲ letra *Have you learned all the letters in the alphabet?* ¿Ha aprendido Ud. todas las letras del alfabeto?

● [*v*] escribir *Letter the sign carefully.* Escriba el letrero con cuidado. ○ **to keep to the letter** seguir al pie de la letra.

lettuce lechuga.

level [*n*] nivel *The level is a very useful instrument.* El nivel es un instrumento muy útil.—*He is below the general level of the class.* Está por debajo del nivel medio de la clase.—*The river rose almost to the level of the dam.* El río llegó casi hasta el nivel de la presa.

● [*adj*] llano *Is the country level or mountainous?* ¿Es el país llano o montañoso?

● [*v*] igualar *Their aim is to level all classes.* Su propósito es igualar todas las clases sociales. ▲ arrasar *The shelling leveled the town.* El bombardeo arrasó la ciudad.

○ **to be level** ser de la misma altura *The book shelves are level with the table.* Las estanterías y la mesa son de la misma altura.

‖ *He has a level head.* Es muy juicioso.

lever palanca.

liable ‖ *Don't rock the boat; it's liable to tip over.* No mueva Ud. la barca porque puede volcar.

liar mentiroso.

liberal generoso *She's very liberal with her money.* Es muy generosa con su dinero. ▲ liberal *The doctor has very liberal views.* El doctor tiene ideas muy liberales.

liberate libertar, librar.

liberty libertad *The prisoner got his liberty.* El prisionero fué puesto en libertad.

○ **to take liberties** tomarse libertades *He took too many liberties when he was here.* Se tomó demasiadas libertades cuando estuvo aquí.

librarian bibliotecario.

lice piojos.

license [*n*] licencia *Have you got your hunting license yet?* ¿Consiguió Ud. ya su licencia de caza?

lick [*v*] lamer *The dog licked the plate.* El perro lamió el plato. ▲ vencer *I had a tough time but I finally licked him.* Me costó mucho trabajo pero al fin lo pude vencer. ▲ pegar *His father licked him when he caught him stealing.* Su padre le pegó cuando le encontró robando.

lid tapa, tapadera.

lie [*n*] mentira *Everything he says is a lie!* ¡Todo lo que dice es mentira!

● [*v*] mentir *There's no doubt that he's lying about it.* No hay duda de que en eso está mintiendo. ▲ echarse *Don't lie on the damp grass.* No se eche sobre la hierba húmeda. ▲ yacer *His body lies in the cemetery.* Su cuerpo yace en el cementerio. ▲ estar, consistir en *This book's appeal lies in its humor.* El mérito del libro está en su humorismo. ▲ estar echado, [*Am*] estar recostado *He lay on the couch and read the paper.* Estaba echado en el diván leyendo el periódico. ▲ estar situado, quedar a *The river lies to your right.* El río queda a su derecha.

○ **to lie down** acostarse *I want to lie down for a few minutes.* Quiero acostarme unos minutos.

‖ *The book is lying on the table.* El libro está sobre la mesa. ‖ *The factory has been lying idle for a year.* La fábrica ha estado parada durante un año.

lieutenant teniente.

life vida *Are there any signs of life in him?* ¿Da señales de vida?—*The average life of a dog is ten years.* Diez años es el termino medio de vida de un perro.—*The children are full of life.* Los niños están llenos de vida.—*Life in the country is dull.* La vida en el campo es muy aburrida. ▲ biografía

He wrote a life of the president. Escribió la biografía del presidente.
lifeboat lancha salvavidas.
life insurance seguro de vida.
life preserver salvavidas.
lift levantar *It's too heavy to lift.* Es demasiado pesado para levantarlo. ▲ disipar *The fog lifted quickly.* La niebla se ha disipado muy rápidamente. ‖ *His letter really gave me a lift.* Su carta me ha reanimado mucho. ‖ *Will you give me a lift here?* ¿Quiere echarme una mano? ‖ *Can you give me a lift to the next town?* ¿Puede Ud. llevarme en su coche hasta el próximo pueblo?
light [n] luz *The light was so strong that he had to shut his eyes.* La luz era tan fuerte que tuvo que cerrar los ojos.— *Please turn on the light.* Haga el favor de encender la luz.—*The investigation brought many facts to light.* La investigación sacó muchos hechos a la luz. ▲ lumbre, fuego *Give me a light.* Deme Ud. lumbre.
● [adj] claro *I want a light blue hat.* Quiero un sombrero azul claro. ▲ ligero, leve *Our losses in the battle were light.* Nuestras pérdidas en la batalla fueron ligeras. ▲ ligero *A light snow fell last night.* Anoche cayó una nevada ligera. —*I had a light lunch today.* Hoy he tomado un almuerzo ligero.—*Please give me some light wine.* Déme Ud. un poco de vino ligero.
● [v] encender *Please light the lamp.* Haga el favor de encender la lámpara. —*Light the fire.* Encienda Ud. el fuego. ○ **lighter** más liviano, menos pesado *The big suitcase is lighter than the little one.* La maleta grande es más liviana que la pequeña. ○ **to be light** hacerse de día *Wake me up as soon as it's light.* Despiérteme en cuanto se haga de día. ○ **to light up** iluminar *The candle lit up the table.* La vela iluminaba la mesa.—*A smile lit up her face.* Una sonrisa iluminó su cara. ‖ *For such a heavy woman she's very light on her feet.* Para lo gorda que es anda con mucha agilidad.
lighthouse faro.
lightning relámpago.
like [n] igual *I've never met his like.* Nunca le he encontrado su igual.
● [v] querer *Would you like another cup of coffee?* ¿Querría Ud. otro taza de café? ▲ gustarle a uno *This is the kind of food I like.* Este es la clase de comida que me gusta.
● [prep] como *He ran like mad.* Corría

como loco.—*He treated me like a brother.* Me trató como un hermano. ○ **to be like** ser propio de *It's not like you to be so irritable.* No es propio de Ud. ser tan irritable. ▲ parecerse *People here are very much like Americans.* La gente de aquí se parece mucho a los norteamericanos. ○ **to feel like** tener ganas de *Do you feel like dancing?* ¿Tiene Ud. ganas de bailar? ‖ *She doesn't hesitate to express her likes and dislikes.* No hesita en decir lo que le gusta y lo que no le gusta.
likely verosímil, verisímil *That's not a likely story.* No es un relato verosímil. ‖ *Are we likely to arrive on time?* ¿Llegaremos a tiempo?
likeness semejanza, parecido *There's a great likeness between the child and his father.* Hay un gran parecido entre el niño y su padre. ▲ retrato *He painted a likeness of my grandmother.* Pintó un retrato de mi abuela.
likewise asimismo.
lily lirio.
limb rama *The lightning split the limb from the tree.* El relámpago desgajó la rama del árbol. ▲ miembro *His limbs are very long for his body.* Sus miembros son muy largos en relación con el cuerpo.
lime cal (*chemical substance*); lima (*fruit*).
limit [n] límite *What are the city limits?* ¿Cuáles son los límites de la ciudad?
● [v] limitar *We have to limit our expenses this month.* Tenemos que limitar nuestros gastos este mes.
limitation limitación.
limp [n] cojera *He has a slight limp.* Tiene una ligera cojera. *or* Es un poco rengo [Arg].
● [adj] deprimido *I feel quite limp from the heat.* Me siento deprimido por el calor.
● [v] cojear *He limped across the room.* Cruzó el cuarto cojeando.
line [n] cuerda *Hang the clothes on the line.* Cuelgue la ropa en la cuerda. ▲ línea *Draw a line between these two points.* Trace una línea entre estos dos puntos.—*How long is this railroad line?* ¿Qué longitud tiene esta línea férrea?—*The bandits cut the telephone lines.* Los bandidos cortaron las líneas telefónicas.—*Which bus line do you use to go home?* ¿Qué línea de autobuses usa Ud. para ir a su casa? ▲ raya *Divide the court with a chalk line.* Divida Ud. el campo con una raya de tiza. ▲ renglón *Skip a line.* Deje un

renglón en blanco. ▲ fila *There's a long line of cars ahead of us.* Hay una fila larga de autos delante de nosotros. ▲ surtido *We have a nice line of dresses.* Tenemos un bonito surtido de trajes. ▲ conversación *He has a very good line.* Tiene una conversación muy persuasiva.

● [*v*] forrar *Her coat is lined with red.* Su abrigo está forrado de rojo. ▲ rayar *Use lined paper.* Use Ud. papel rayado.

○ **along this line** en estos términos, de esta manera *Do it along this line.* Hágalo de esta manera. ○ **in line** disciplinado *He managed to keep the whole party in line.* Consiguió mantener el partido disciplinado. ○ **in line with** de acuerdo con *What you are doing is not in line with our policy.* Lo que hace no está de acuerdo con nuestras normas. ○ **to be in one's line** ser de la especialidad de uno *This is not in my line.* Eso no es de mi especialidad. ○ **to bring into line** poner de acuerdo *Try to bring the whole committee into line.* Trate de poner de acuerdo a la comisión. ○ **to line up** alinearse *They lined up in front of the post office.* Se alinearon en frente de la oficina de correos. ○ **to stand in line** hacer cola *I had to stand in line to get cigarettes.* Tuve que hacer cola para conseguir cigarrillos.

‖ *Drop me a line if you have time.* Mándeme unas líneas si tiene tiempo. ‖ *I like the lines of your dress.* Me gusta la línea de su traje.

linen [*n*] ropa blanca *What laundry do you send your linen to?* ¿A qué lavandería envía Ud. su ropa blanca?

● [*adj*] de lino, de hilo *Where can I buy linen handkerchiefs?* ¿Dónde puedo comprar pañuelos de hilo?

liner (*ship*) vapor.

linger demorarse.

lining forro.

link [*n*] eslabón.

lion león.

lip labio *Your lip is swollen.* Tiene Ud. un labio hinchado. ▲ pico *The lip of the pitcher is broken.* El pico de la jarra está roto.

lipstick barra de labios, lápiz de labios.

liquid [*n*; *adj*] líquido.

liquor licor(es), bebidas alcohólicas.

list [*n*] lista *Is my name written on the list?* ¿Está mi nombre escrito en la lista?

● [*v*] hacer una lista de *Please list the places I should visit.* Haga el favor

de hacer una lista de los lugares que debo visitar.

listen (to) oír *I like to listen to good music.* Me gusta oír buena música. ▲ escuchar *Listen to what I'm telling you.* Escuche lo que le digo.

liter litro

literal literal.

literary literario.

literature obras literarias *The library has collected the best literature.* La biblioteca ha reunido las mejores obras literarias. ▲ literatura *He's taking a course in English literature.* Está estudiando un curso de literatura inglesa.

litter camada (*animals*); camilla (*stretcher*).

little pequeño *This dress is for a little girl.* Este traje es para una niña pequeña. ▲ poco *He has little influence.* Tiene poca influencia.

○ **a little** un poco de *I can speak a little French.* Hablo un poco de francés. ▲ un poco *I can swim a little.* Nado un poco. ○ **little by little** poco a poco. ○ **little piece** pedacito *Give me a little piece of cake.* Déme un pedacito de torta. ○ **little while** ratito *I'll come in a little while.* Iré dentro de un ratito.

live [*v*] vivir *The doctor said that the patient would live.* El doctor dice que el enfermo vivirá.—*How can people live on this food?* ¿Cómo puede vivir la gente con esta alimentación?—*I expect to live here for two months.* Espero vivir aquí dos meses. ▲ tener *He lived a happy life.* Tuvo una vida feliz.

○ **to live up to** llenar *He did not live up to my hopes.* No llenó mis esperanzas.

‖ *It will take years to live down the gossip.* Esa murmuración tardará años en borrarse.

live [*adj*] vivo *Is that a live snake?* ¿Está viva esa culebra? ▲ cargado de electricidad *Don't touch that, it's a live wire.* No toque eso, es un alambre cargado de electricidad. ▲ vital *It's a live issue in some places.* Es una cuestión vital en algunos sitios.

○ **live coals** ascuas *Roast it over the live coals.* Aselo sobre las ascuas.

livelihood vida.

lively vivo, animado *She's a lively girl.* Es una muchacha muy animada.

‖ *Step lively!* ¡Vayan de prisa!

liver hígado.

living [*n*] sustento *Can he make a living*

for his family? ¿Puede ganar el sustento de su familia?

● [*adj*] vivo *Haven't you ever studied a living language?* ¿Ha estudiado Ud. alguna vez una lengua viva?—*He's the living image of his grandfather.* Es la viva imagen de su abuelo.

living room sala.

load [*n*] carga *That is too great a load for the donkey.* Es una carga demasiado pesada para el burro.

● [*v*] cargar *Are the men loading or unloading the vessel?* ¿Están los hombres cargando o descargando el barco?—*The gun was loaded.* El fusil estaba cargado. ▲ abrumar *They loaded us with work.* Nos abrumaron de trabajo.

loaf [*n*] pan *Slice three loaves for sandwiches.* Corte Ud. tres panes para emparedados.

● [*v*] holgazanear *We spent the whole day loafing.* Estuvimos todo el día holgazaneando.

○ **meat loaf** carne en molde *We had meat loaf for dinner.* Cenamos carne en molde.

loan [*n*] préstamo *It was nice of you to arrange that loan for me.* Ha sido Ud. muy amable en conseguirme ese préstamo.

● [*v*] prestar *Can you loan me the book when you finish it?* ¿Puede Ud. prestarme el libro una vez que lo haya leído?

loathe detestar, abominar.

lobby vestíbulo.

lobster langosta.

local local *You'll need only a local anesthetic for that operation.* No necesitará más que una anestesia local para esa operación. ▲ regional, local *This is a local custom.* Esa es una costumbre regional.

○ **local train** tren ordinario, tren correo.

locality localidad.

locate situar *Where is the house located?* ¿Dónde está situada la casa? ▲ hallar *Can you locate the hill on this map?* ¿Puede Ud. hallar la colina en este mapa?

location situación.

lock [*n*] cerradura *He cut a hole in the door for the lock.* Hizo un agujero en la puerta para colocar la cerradura. ▲ candado *Do you have a lock for a trunk?* ¿Tiene Ud. un candado para un baúl? ▲ mechón *She kept a lock of the baby's hair.* Guardó un mechón del pelo del niño. ▲ esclusa *The ship*

has to stay in the locks an hour. El barco estará en las esclusas una hora.

● [*v*] cerrar con llave *Be sure to lock the door when you leave.* Fíjese en cerrar la puerta con llave cuando salga. ▲ encerrar *Lock these prisoners in their cells.* Encierre a estos prisioneros en sus celdas.

locomotive locomotora.

lodge [*n*] posada *We stopped at the lodge overnight.* Nos alojamos en la posada por la noche. ▲ logia *What lodge do you belong to?* ¿A qué logia pertenece Ud.?

● [*v*] alojarse *The bullet lodged in his lung.* La bala se alojó en su pulmón.

○ **to lodge a complaint** dar queja *He lodged his complaint with the mayor.* Dió queja al alcalde.

log tronco; libro de bitácora (*navigation*).

logic lógica.

logical lógico.

loin lomo *Give me some loin of pork.* Déme lomo de cerdo.

lone solitario, solo.

lonely solitario *He lives a lonely life.* Lleva una vida solitaria. ▲ sólo *Aren't you lonely without your friends?* ¿Se siente Ud. sólo sin sus amigos? ▲ solitario *This must be a lonely place in the winter.* Este debe ser un lugar solitario en invierno.

lonesome solo y triste.

look [*n*] mirada *Take a look at this report.* Echele una mirada a este informe.

● [*v*] parecer *It looks all right to me.* Me parece muy bien.—*It looks like snow.* Parece que va a nevar. ▲ estar *She looks very pretty today.* Está muy bonita hoy.

○ **to look after** cuidar *Did you get someone to look after the child?* ¿Ha encontrado Ud. a alguien que cuide al niño ○ **to look at** mirar *Look at the beautiful sunset!* ¡Mira la hermosa puesta de sol! ○ **to look for** buscar *We are looking for an apartment.* Estamos buscando un apartamento.— *He's always looking for trouble.* Siempre está buscando camorra. ○ **to look forward to** aguardar con impaciencia, esperar con ilusión *We are looking forward to our vacation.* Estamos aguardando las vacaciones con impaciencia. ○ **to look into** estudiar *We will look into the matter.* Estudiaremos el asunto. ○ **to look on** mirar *The others played but he just looked on.* Los demás jugaban, pero él no hacía más que mirar. ○ **to look out on** dar a *The big window looks out on a garden.* La ventana grande da a un jardín. ○ **to look** to buscar *He always looked to his father for help.* Siempre buscaba la ayuda de su padre. ○ **to look up** venir a ver, ir a ver *Look me up when you come back.* Venga a verme cuando Ud. vuelva. ▲ buscar *Look up his telephone number.* Busque Ud. el número de su teléfono. ▲ mejorar *Things are looking up.* Las cosas van mejorando. ○ **to look up to** respetar, estimar *I can't help looking up to him.* No puedo menos de respetarle. ‖ *Look out!* ¡Cuidado!

looking glass espejo.

looks aspecto, aire *I don't like his looks.* No me gusta su aspecto.

loop [*n*] lazada (*rope*); curva, vuelta (*road*).
● [*v*] dar una vuelta.

loose flojo *There's a loose button on your shirt.* Tiene un botón flojo en la camisa.—*Put a loose bandage on his arm.* Póngale una venda floja en el brazo. ▲ suelto *The dog is loose again.* El perro está suelto otra vez.—*Look for it among the loose papers on my desk.* Búsquelo entre los papeles sueltos que hay en mi escritorio.—*Do you sell coffee in packages or loose?* ¿Vende Ud. el café en paquetes o suelto? ▲ libre *He made a loose translation of the original.* Hizo una traducción libre del original. ▲ licencioso *She leads a loose life.* Lleva una vida licenciosa. ○ **loose character** perdido *That man is a loose character.* Aquel hombre es un perdido. ○ **to cut loose** soltarse el pelo *He certainly cut loose at that party.* Realmente se soltó el pelo en aquella fiesta. ○ **to cut loose from** independizarse de *I finally cut loose from my family.* Por fin me independicé de mi familia. ‖ *She's known for her loose tongue.* Tiene fama de chismosa. ‖ *He has a loose tooth.* Tiene un diente que se mueve.

loosen soltar.

lord señor.
○ **House of Lords** Cámara de los Lores.

lose perder *I've lost my purse again.* He perdido mi bolsa otra vez.—*Try to lose your accent.* Procure perder su acento. —*He lost his wife five years ago.* Perdió a su esposa hace cinco años.—*The horse lost the race.* El caballo perdió la carrera.—*I don't want to lose any more time here.* No quiero perder más

tiempo aquí. ▲ hacer perder *That speech lost him the election* Ese discurso le hizo perder la elección.
○ **lost** perdido *Where is the Lost and Found Department?* ¿Dónde queda la sección de objetos perdidos? ○ **to lose heart** desanimarse. ○ **to lose one's heart** enamorarse. ○ **to lose one's mind** volverse loco. ○ **to lose one's temper** perder los estribos, enfadarse. ○ **to lose one's way** perderse, extraviarse *He lost his way in the woods.* Se perdió en el bosque. ○ **to lose time** atrasarse *Has your watch been losing time since you had it fixed?* ¿Se ha seguido atrasando su reloj desde que se lo arreglaron?

loss pérdida *The loss of his wife was a great blow.* La pérdida de su esposa fué un gran golpe.—*The drought caused a great loss of crops.* La sequía causó grandes pérdidas en la cosecha. —*There was no reason for the loss of time.* No había razón que justificara la pérdida de tiempo.
○ **at a loss** perdiendo, con pérdida *He sold his house at a loss.* Vendió su casa perdiendo. ○ **to be at a loss** no saber como *I am at a loss to explain his absence.* No sé cómo explicar su ausencia.

lot grupo *They are a fine lot of soldiers.* Forman un grupo de buenos soldados. ▲ lote *He bought a lot at the edge of town.* Compró un lote en las afueras del pueblo.—*I'll send the books in three different lots.* Mandaré los libros en tres lotes diferentes. ○ **a lot** mucho *She's a lot better than people think.* Es mucho mejor de lo que la gente piensa. ○ **a lot of** mucho *The trucks make a lot of noise.* Los camiones hacen mucho ruido. ○ **to draw lots** echar a suertes *They drew lots to see who would go first.* Echaron a suertes para ver quién iba primero.

lotion loción.

loud [*adj*] fuerte *We heard a loud noise.* Oímos un ruido fuerte.—*There were loud criticisms in the press.* Hubo fuertes críticas en la prensa. ▲ chillón *His ties are always too loud.* Sus corbatas son siempre demasiado chillonas.
● [*adv*] alto *Please speak loud enough to be heard.* Por favor hable bastante alto para que le puedan oír.

loud-speaker altoparlante, altavoz.

louse piojo.

love [*n*] amor *His love probably won't last.* Probablemente su amor no durará. ▲ recuerdo *Give my love to all my* *friends.* Déles recuerdos a todos mis amigos.

● [*v*] querer *Do you love your mother very much?* ¿Quiere Ud. mucho a su madre? ▲ gustarle a uno *I love apples.* Me gustan las manzanas.

○ **to fall in love** enamorarse *He fell in love with the captain's daughter.* Se enamoró de la hija del capitán.

lovely bello, hermoso *There is a lovely view from the bridge.* Hay una hermosa vista desde el puente.

lover amante.

low bajo *The tide is low in the morning.* La marea está baja por la mañana.— *The temperature is very low today.* La temperatura es muy baja hoy.—*The singer has a very low voice.* El cantante tiene una voz muy baja.—*That plane is flying too low.* Ese avión vuela demasiado bajo. ▲ débil *She gave a low moan.* Dió un débil quejido. ▲ humilde *He is not ashamed of his low birth.* No se avergüenza de su humilde cuna.

○ **low (gear)** primera (velocidad) *Put the car in low to climb the hill.* Ponga el automóvil en primera para subir la cuesta. ○ **low opinion** mala opinión *I have a low opinion of him.* Tengo mala opinión de él. ○ **to feel low** sentirse abatido, sentirse deprimido *I feel very low today.* Hoy me siento muy deprimido.

‖ *The temperature hit an all time low.* Fué la temperatura más baja registrada.

lower [*adj*] más bajo *Have you a room on a lower floor?* ¿Tiene Ud. un cuarto en un piso más bajo?

● [*v*] arriar *They are lowering the flag.* Están arriando la bandera. ▲ poner más bajo *Please lower that shelf in the bookcase.* Haga el favor de poner más baja esa tabla de la estantería. ▲ bajar *Can't you lower your voice?* ¿No puede Ud. bajar la voz?

loyal leal.

loyalty lealtad.

lubricant lubricante.

lubricate lubricar.

luck suerte *He said his failure was due to bad luck.* Dijo que su fracaso se debió a su mala suerte.—*He's always had luck in business.* Siempre ha tenido suerte en los negocios.

lucky afortunado, con suerte.

luggage equipaje.

lumber madera *Where can I buy lumber and nails?* ¿Dónde puedo comprar madera y clavos?

lump bola, grumo *There are lumps in the cream.* La crema tiene bolas. ▲ terrón (*sugar*) *Put two lumps of sugar in my tea, please.* Haga el favor de poner dos terrones en mi té.

○ **lump on the head** chichón *He has a lump on his head where he bumped into the door.* Se pegó con la puerta y le salió un chichón.

‖ *He paid for the work in a lump sum.* Pago el trabajo de una sola vez. ‖ *Shall we lump it all on one bill?* ¿Lo ponemos todo en una sola cuenta?

lunch [*n*] almuerzo *It's almost time for lunch.* Es casi la hora del almuerzo.

● [*v*] almorzar *Will you lunch with me?* ¿Quiere Ud. almorzar conmigo?

lung pulmón.

luxury lujo.

M

macaroni macarrones.

machine máquina.

machine gun ametralladora.

machinery maquinaria *The machinery is out of order.* La maquinaria no funciona.

mad enfadado, enojado *He's mad at me for something I did to him.* Está enfadado conmigo por algo que le hice. ▲ loco *The heat drove him mad.* Le volvió loco el calor. ▲ rabioso *Watch out for the mad dog.* Tenga cuidado con el perro rabioso.

○ **like mad** como loco, como un loco *He drove like mad.* Manejaba como un loco. ○ **to be mad about** tener locura por *My husband is mad about ice cream.* Mi marido tiene locura por el helado. ○ **to get mad** enfadarse *There's no reason to get mad.* No hay razón para enfadarse.

‖ *That was a mad thing to do.* Fué una locura hacer eso.

madam señora.

magazine revista.

magic mágia.

magical mágico.

magistrate magistrado.

magnet imán.

magnetic magnético.

magnificent magnífico.

magnify ampliar, aumentar de tamaño.

mahogany caoba.

maid criada, sirvienta *Where can I get a maid?* ¿Dónde puedo encontrar una sirvienta?
○ old maid solterona *Two old maids live there.* Dos solteronas viven allí.

maiden [*adj*] soltera *I have a maiden aunt.* Tengo una tía soltera.
○ maiden voyage primer viaje *This is the ship's maiden voyage.* Este es el primer viaje que hace el barco.

mail [*n*] cerreo *Did I get any mail this morning?* ¿Tuve correo esta mañana?
● [*v*] echar al correo *Where can I mail this letter?* ¿Dónde puedo echar esta carta al correo?

mailbox buzón.

mailman cartero.

main [*n*] cañería madre *The water main has burst.* Se ha reventado la cañería madre del agua.
● [*adj*] principal *Where's the main street?* ¿Dónde queda la calle principal?
○ in the main en general *I agree with him in the main.* En general estoy de acuerdo con él.

maintain mantener, sostener.

maintenance mantenimiento.

major [*n*] comandante *Has anyone seen the major?* ¿Ha visto alguien al comandante? ▲ especialidad *What was your major in college?* ¿Cuál fué su especialidad en la universidad?
● [*adj*] principal *It was the major event of the year.* Fué el principal acontecimiento del año. ▲ mayor *The piece is in a major key.* La pieza está en clave mayor.

majority mayoría.

make [*n*] modelo *He has a car of an old make.* Tiene un automóvil de modelo antiguo. ▲ marca *What make car have you?* ¿De qué marca es su automóvil?
● [*v*] hacer *He made a bookcase for his apartment.* Hizo una librería para su apartamento.—*They made that man president of the club.* A ese hombre le hicieron presidente del club.—*Don't make me do that.* No me haga hacer eso.—*Are they willing to make peace?* ¿Están dispuestos a hacer las paces?
—*That car can make eighty miles an hour.* Ese auto puede hacer ochenta millas por hora. ▲ cometer *He hardly ever makes a mistake.* Rara vez comete errores. ▲ adquirir, hacerse *He made his reputation early in life.* Desde muy joven adquirió buena reputación.

▲ ganar *How much do you make a week?* ¿Cuánto gana Ud. por semana? ▲ hacer, ganar *Who made the highest score?* ¿Quién hizo el mayor número de tantos? ▲ ir *That makes the tenth load today.* Con ésta van diez cargas hoy. ▲ calcular *I make it to be eight o'clock.* Calculo que son las ocho. ▲ llegar *Can we make our destination by evening?* ¿Podemos llegar a nuestro destino para la noche? ▲ alcanzar *Do you think we'll make the train?* ¿Cree Ud. que alcanzaremos el tren?
○ to make a fool of poner en ridículo. ○ to make a hit causar buena impresión. ○ to make a living ganarse la vida. ○ to make a move moverse. ○ to make a point of dar importancia a *Does he make a point of being on time?* ¿Da importancia a la puntualidad? ○ to make a record establecer un record. ○ to make a success of tener éxito en *He's making a success of his business.* Tiene éxito en su negocio. ○ to make a wish desear, pensar en algo que se desea. ○ to make believe fingir, hacer creer *She's only making believe that she doesn't know.* Solamente está fingiendo que no lo sabe. ○ to make clear poner en claro, aclarar. ○ to make fast amarrar. ○ to make for ir hacia *Let's make for that tree.* Vayamos hacia aquel árbol. ▲ hacer *Her company made for a pleasant afternoon.* Su compañía hizo la tarde agradable. ○ to make friends conquistar amigos. ○ to make fun of burlarse de. ○ to make good time ganar tiempo *We can make good time on this road.* Podemos ganar tiempo por esta carretera. ○ to make headway adelantar. ○ to make into convertir en. ○ to make it right arreglar, pagar. ○ to make known hacer saber. ○ to make love enamorar. ○ to make of sacar de *What do you make of this?* ¿Qué saca Ud. de esto? ▲ pensar de *I don't know what to make of it.* No sé que pensar de eso. ○ to make off with irse con, llevarse *Don't make off with my book.* No te vayas con mi libro. ○ to make oneself sick enfermarse *He made himself sick by drinking too much.* Se enfermó por beber demasiado. ○ to make out entender *Can you make out what he means?* ¿Puede Ud. entender lo que dice? ▲ llenar *Have you made out the check yet?* ¿Ha llenado Ud. ya el cheque? ▲ hacer *Please make out our bill.* Háganos la cuenta, por favor. ▲ hacer ver *They tried to make out that we were to*

blame. Trataron de hacer ver que éramos culpables. ▲ arreglárselas, salir bien *Don't worry, I'll make out.* No se apure Ud., ya me las arreglaré. ○ **to make over** reformar *She's having her old coat made over.* Ha mandado que le reformen su abrigo viejo. ○ **to make ready** preparar, alistar. ○ **to make room for** dar lugar, hacer lugar. ○ **to make sense** tener sentido *Does this make sense?* ¿Tiene sentido esto? ○ **to make sick** fastidiar *Their complaints make me sick.* Sus quejas me fastidian. ▲ enfermar *This food makes me sick.* Esta comida me enferma. ○ **to make sure** cerciorarse. ○ **to make terms** arreglarse. ○ **to make the acquaintance of** conocer a. ○ **to make up** hacer, preparar *We must make up a list of employees.* Tenemos que hacer una lista de los empleados. ▲ inventar *Is it true, or did he make that story up?* ¿Es verdad ese cuento o se lo inventó él? ▲ hacer las paces, reconciliarse *Do you think they'll make up?* ¿Cree Ud. que harán las paces? ▲ pagar, compensar *I want to make up my share of the bill.* Quiero pagar lo que me toca de la cuenta. ▲ pintarse *She takes a lot of time to make up.* Tarda mucho en pintarse. ○ **to make up one's mind** resolverse, determinar. ○ **to make use of** servirse de, hacer uso de. ○ **to make way** abrir paso.
‖ *Did you make up your quarrel?* ¿Hicístes las paces? ‖ *He makes a good carpenter.* Hace bien de carpintero. ‖ *How did you make out in that matter?* ¿Cómo te fué en ese asunto? ‖ *My mind is made up.* Estoy resuelto. *Do you think we can make it through the doorway?* ¿Cree Ud. que podremos pasar por la puerta? ‖ *The writer was made by his first book.* El escritor se consagró con su primer libro.
make-believe [*adj*] fingido, falso.
maker fabricante.
make-up cosméticos *She never uses make-up.* Ella nunca usa cosméticos.
malaria paludismo, malaria.
male macho *Is the dog male or female?* ¿Es este perro macho o hembra?
malice malicia.
malicious malicioso.
mamma mamá.
man [*n*] hombre *How many men are there here?* ¿Cuántos hombres hay aquí? —*What a man!* ¡Qué hombre!—*I need a man to mow the lawn.* Necesito un hombre para cortar el césped.—*He spoke like a man.* Habló como un

hombre. ▲ hombre, caballero *Where's the men's room?* ¿Dónde está el lavabo de caballeros? ▲ uno *A man has to get used to this climate.* Uno tiene que acostumbrarse a este clima.
● [*v*] tripular *He's having trouble manning his ship.* Encuentra dificultades para tripular el barco.
○ **man and wife** marido y mujer. ○ **to a man** unánimamente, por unanimidad, como un solo hombre.
‖ *Men have used that road for hundreds of years.* Este camino se viene usando desde hace siglos.
manage manejar *They say he's difficult, but I can manage him.* Dicen que él es difícil, pero yo puedo manejarlo. ▲ llevar, cargar *Can you manage those packages by yourself?* ¿Puede Ud. llevar solo todos esos paquetes? ▲ arreglárselas, componérselas *I'll manage, thanks.* Yo me las arreglaré, gracias.
management administración, dirección *I'll complain to the management about the poor service.* Me quejaré del mal servicio a la dirección.
manager gerente, director, administrador *I want to see the manager.* Quiero hablar con el gerente. ▲ administrador *He doesn't make much money, but his wife is a good manager.* No gana mucho pero su mujer es buena administradora.
mane crin (*horse*), melena (*lion*).
maneuver maniobra.
manger pesebre.
manhood virilidad.
mania manía.
manifest manifiesto.
mankind la humanidad.
manly varonil.
manner manera *He answered in a sharp manner.* Contestó de una manera brusca.
○ **in a manner of speaking** hasta cierto punto, en cierto modo. ○ **manners** costumbres *Their manners are different from ours.* Sus costumbres son diferentes de las nuestras. ▲ modales, costumbres *We must be careful of our manners.* Debemos cuidar nuestros modales.
mansion mansión.
manual [*adj; n*] manual.
manufacture [*n*] fabricación *He's invented a new method of manufacture.* Ha inventado un nuevo procedimiento de fabricación.
● [*v*] fabricar *What do you manufacture here?* ¿Qué fabrica Ud. aquí? ▲ inventar *He'll be able to manufacture a*

story for the occasion. Ya inventará algún cuento para el caso.

manure abono.

many muchos *I have many reasons for doing so.* Tengo muchas razones para proceder así.—*There weren't very many at his house.* No había muchos en su casa.

○ **a good many** mucho *He knows a good many people in this city.* Conoce a mucha gente en esta ciudad. ○ **a great many** muchísimos, un gran número de *A great many people use that bank.* Muchísimas personas utilizan ese banco. ○ **as many** tantos como *I have as many books as he does.* Tengo tantos libros como él. ○ **how many** cuántos *How many tickets do you want?* ¿Cuántos boletos quiere? ○ **many a time** a menudo, muchas veces *I've passed you on the street many a time.* Le he encontrado en la calle muchas veces. ○ **too many** de más, de sobra *He has two cars too many.* Tiene dos autos de más. ○ **twice as many** dos veces más *He has twice as many as I.* Tiene dos veces más que yo.

map [n] mapa *Can you show me the town on the map?* ¿Puede Ud. mostrarme el pueblo en el mapa?

● [v] levantar un plano de, hacer un mapa de *My assistant is mapping the coastline.* Mi ayudante está levantando un plano de la costa. ▲ planear, hacer planes de *The guide is mapping our route now.* El guía está ahora planeando nuestro itinerario.

maple arce.

○ **maple syrup** jarabe de arce.

mar estropear, echar a perder.

marble mármol.

March marzo *I plan to stay through March.* Pienso quedarme hasta fines de marzo.

march [n] marcha *We had a tough march this morning.* Esta mañana hicimos una marcha penosa.—*The band started the concert with a march.* La banda comenzó el concierto con una marcha. —*The march of events.* La marcha de los acontecimientos.

● [v] marchar *We marched five miles.* Marchamos cinco millas. ▲ hacer marchar *They march the prisoners every afternoon.* Todas las tardes hacen marchar a los presos.

○ **to march by** desfilar *Did you see the soldiers march by?* ¿Vió Ud. desfilar a los soldados?

mare yegua.

margarine margarina.

margin margen.

marine [adj] marino.

maritime marítimo.

mark [n] seña, señal, marca *Make a mark after the names of those present.* Ponga una seña en los nombres de los que están presentes. ▲ propósito, fin *Do you think he'll reach the mark he's set for himself?* ¿Cree Ud. que alcanzará el fin que se propone?

● [v] calificar *When will you have our exams marked?* ¿Cuándo habrá calificado Ud. nuestros exámenes? ▲ marcar, señalar *I've marked the important parts of the notice.* He marcado las partes importantes de la noticia.

○ **to mark down** apuntar, anotar *I've marked down the items I want.* He apuntado las cosas que quiero. ▲ rebajar (los precios) *We shall have to mark down the prices on these coats.* Tendremos que rebajar los precios de estos abrigos. ○ **to mark time** matar el tiempo, pasar el tiempo *I am just marking time in this job.* No hago más que matar el tiempo en este empleo.

‖ *His guess was wide of the mark.* Su suposición estaba alejada de la verdad. ‖ *On your mark; get set; go!* Preparados. *or* Listos. *or* ¡Ya! ‖ *What does the price mark say?* ¿Cuanto marca la etiqueta? *or* ¿Qué precio tiene marcado?

market [n] mercado *The market is very lively today.* El mercado está muy animado hoy.—*Is there a good market for cotton cloth in this city?* ¿Hay un buen mercado para los tejidos de algodón en esta ciudad? ▲ comprador *He's trying to find a market for his house.* Está tratando de encontrar un comprador para su casa.

● [v] poner a la venta *He'll market the fruit this month.* Este mes pondrá la fruta a la venta.

○ **on the market** en la bolsa *Is there anything new on the market today?* ¿Hay alguna novedad hoy en la bolsa? ○ **to be in the market for** estar dispuesto a comprar *Are you in the market for a good car?* ¿Está Ud. dispuesto a comprar un buen automóvil? ○ **to do marketing** hacer compras, mercar *She does her marketing in the morning.* Hace sus compras por la mañana.

‖ *The coffee market is off today.* Los valores del café han bajado hoy.

marmalade mermelada.

maroon [v] abandonar, aislar.

marriage matrimonio.

marry casarse *Do you know when she's getting married?* ¿Sabe Ud. cuándo se casa ella? ▲ casar *He married his daughter to an old friend.* Casó a su hija con un viejo amigo.
marsh pantano.
marshal mariscal.
marvelous maravilloso.
masculine masculino.
mash majar, machacar.
○ **mashed potatoes** puré de papas [*Am*], puré de patatas [*Sp*].
mask máscara, careta.
mason albañil; masón (*lodge*).
mass [*n*] masa *Look at that mass of molten iron!* ¡Mira aquella masa de hierro fundido! ▲ montón *There was a mass of flowers on the stage.* Había un montón de flores en el escenario. ▲ misa *Are you going to mass this morning?* ¿Va Ud. a misa esta mañana?
● [*v*] congregar, reunir *All the delegates were massed together on the platform.* Todos los delegados se hallaban congregados en la tribuna.
○ **great mass** mayoría *The great mass of these farmers have small farms.* La mayoría de estos granjeros tienen granjas pequeñas. ○ **mass meeting** mitin popular. ○ **mass production** producción en serie. ○ **the masses** las masas, el pueblo.
massacre matanza.
mast mástil.
master [*n*] señor *Is the master of the house in?* ¿Está el señor de la casa? ▲ amo, dueño *He always tries to be master of the situation.* Siempre trata de ser el amo de la situación. ▲ capitán *The master of the ship is on the top deck.* El capitán del barco está en la cubierta superior.
● [*v*] dominar *I find this language difficult to master.* Encuentro que este idioma es difícil de dominar.
○ **master key** llave maestra. ○ **master of ceremonies** maestro de ceremonias. ○ **master switch** conmutador principal.
masterpiece obra maestra.
mat felpudo, estera *Wipe your feet on the mat.* Límpiese los pies en el felpudo.
○ **matted** enredado *My hair is all matted from the wind.* El viento me ha enredado todo el pelo.
match [*n*] fósforo, cerilla *Have you got a match?* ¿Tiene Ud. un fósforo? ▲ igual *He met his match.* Se encontró con su igual. ▲ partido *Would you like to see a tennis match?* ¿Le gustaría ver un partido de tenis? ▲ pareja

They're a good match. Hacen una buena pareja.
● [*v*] igualar *Can we match their speed?* ¿Podemos igualar su velocidad? ‖ *I'll match you for the drinks.* Les juego las bebidas. ‖ *I'm no match for him.* Yo no puedo competir con él. ‖ *These colors aren't a good match.* Estos colores no casan.
matchbox caja de fósforos.
mate compañero *Have you seen the mate to my brown shoe?* ¿Ha visto Ud. el compañero de mi zapato marrón? ▲ consorte, marida *or* mujer *She had a hard time finding a mate.* Le fué difícil conseguir consorte. ▲ primer oficial *The captain told the mate to take over.* El capitán le dijo al primer oficial que se encargara del mando.
‖ *Those two are very well mated.* Esos dos hacen una buena pareja.
material [*n*] tela, material *Do you have enough of this material to make me a suit?* ¿Tiene Ud. suficiente tela de ésta para hacerme un traje? ▲ material, datos *He's collecting material for a book.* Está reuniendo datos para escribir un libro.
● [*adj*] material *It's a material and not a spiritual problem.* Es un problema material y no espiritual.—*Give him enough to take care of his material needs.* Dele lo suficiente para satisfacer sus necesidades materiales.
○ **materials** material *What materials do you need to make a bookcase?* ¿Qué material necesita Ud. para hacer una librería? ○ **material witness** testigo presencial, testigo de presencia. ○ **raw material** materia prima *The factory is short of raw materials.* Escasean las materias primas en la fábrica. ○ **writing materials** efectos de escritorio *Do you carry writing materials here?* ¿Vende Ud. efectos de escritorio?
‖ *He had nothing material to say.* No tenía materialmente nada que decir.
maternal maternal.
maternity maternidad.
mathematics matemáticas.
matron ama de llaves *I'd like to speak to the matron.* Quisiera hablar con el ama de llaves.
matter materia *He has no gray matter.* No tiene materia gris. ▲ material *This reading matter will last me a week.* Con este material de lectura tendré para una semana. ▲ tema *The subject matter of his talk is very interesting.* El tema de su discurso es muy interesante. ▲ asunto *Will you look into the*

matter? ¿Quiere Ud. estudiar el asunto? ▲ cosa *You take matters too seriously.* Ud. toma las cosas muy en serio. ▲ cosa, asunto *You are only making matters worse.* Lo único que hace Ud. es empeorar las cosas. ▲ causa *His leaving is a matter of great concern to us.* Su marcha es causa de mucha preocupación para nosotros. ○ **as a matter of fact** en realidad. ○ **for that matter** en cuanto a eso. ○ **printed matter** impresos *Must I declare this printed matter?* ¿Debo declarar estos impresos? ‖ *It doesn't matter.* No importa. ‖ *What's the matter?* ¿Qué sucede? *or* ¿Qué pasa? ‖ *What's the matter with going home?* ¿Qué inconveniente hay en ir a casa? ‖ *What's the matter with you?* ¿Qué le pasa? *or* ¿Qué tiene?

mattress colchón.

mature [*adj*] juicioso *He seems like a mature sort of person.* Da la impresión de ser una persona juiciosa. ● [*v*] madurar *They did not act until their plans matured.* No actuaron hasta que maduraron los planes. ▲ desarrollarse *After his fourteenth birthday he matured very rapidly.* Después de cumplir los catorce años se desarrolló rápidamente. ▲ vencer *The bond will be worth twenty-five dollars when it matures.* El bono valdrá veintecinco dólares cuando venza.

maximum [*adj; n*] máximo.

May mayo *I was born in May.* Nací en mayo.

may poder *That may be true.* Puede que eso sea verdad.—*You might try to reach him at home.* Podría Ud. tratar de ponerse en comunicación con él en su casa.—*I may go if my money holds out.* Puede que vaya si me queda dinero. ‖ *May I have this dance?* ¿Quiere Ud. concederme este baile?

maybe tal vez, quizás.

mayonnaise mayonesa.

mayor alcalde.

me me *He gave me some candy.* Me dió unos cuantos dulces.—*Give me some of that.* Deme Ud. un poco de aquello. ▲ mí *Is this for me?* ¿Es esto para mí?

meadow pradera.

meal comida *We eat three meals a day.* Hacemos tres comidas al día. ▲ harina *This pudding is made of corn meal.* Este pudín es de harina de maíz. ‖ *Where can I get a good meal?* ¿Dónde se puede comer bien?

mean [*adj*] malo *Her husband was very mean to her.* Su marido era malo con ella. ▲ avaro, egoísta *I'd borrow some of his books if he weren't so mean about it.* Le pediría prestados algunos libros si no fuera tan avaro. ▲ indigno *I felt mean about hurting her feelings that way.* Me sentí indigno por haberla ofendido de ese modo. ● [*v*] proponerse, intentar *Do you mean to see him before you go?* ¿Se propone Ud. verle antes de partir? ▲ quiere decir *Do you mean this for me?* ¿Quiere Ud. decir que ésto es para mí?—*What do you mean by that?* ¿Qué quiere decir Ud. con eso? ▲ tener objeto *What's this meant for?* ¿Qué objeto tiene esto? ▲ significar *What do those signs mean?* ¿Qué significan esos anuncios? ▲ tener importancia, tener significación *This means a lot to me.* Esto tiene gran importancia para mí. ○ **to mean well** tener buenas intenciones. ‖ *Be careful; that's a mean animal.* Tenga Ud. cuidado; ese animal tiene muy mal genio. ‖ *I sure feel mean this morning.* Me siento de mal humor esta mañana. ‖ *It was mean of him not to greet his sister-in-law.* Fué una desconsideración de su parte no saludar a su cuñada. ‖ *She's a pretty girl, but she has a mean temper.* Es una bonita muchacha, pero tiene mal genio.

meaning sentido *I don't get the meaning of this poem.* No comprendo el sentido de este poema. ▲ significado *What's the meaning of this word?* ¿Cuál es el significado de esta palabra? ‖ *What's the meaning of this?* ¿Qué significa esto?

means medios *I have no means of transportation.* No tengo medios de transporte. ▲ dinero *She married a man of means.* Se casó con un hombre de dinero. ○ **by all means** a todo trance, sin falta. ○ **by means of** por medio, de debido a. ○ **by no means** de ningún modo, de ninguna manera.

meantime, meanwhile [*adv*] mientras tanto, entretanto.

measles sarampión.

measure [*n*] medida *This is a liquid measure.* Esta es una medida para líquidos.—*We'll have to take strong measures.* Tendremos que tomar medidas enérgicas. ▲ compás *Begin singing after four measures.* Comience a cantar después de cuatro compases. ● [*v*] medir *The tailor has measured my suit.* El sastre me ha medido el traje.

○ **full measure** medida exacta *I always get full measure at that store.* Siempre me dan la medida exacta en esa tienda. ○ **in some measure** hasta cierto punto.

measurement medida *The dressmaker took her measurements.* La costurera le tomó las medidas.

meat carne *Do you have any meat today?* ¿Tiene Ud. carne hoy? ▲ contenido *There's very little meat in that book.* Ese libro tiene muy poco contenido. ○ **meat market** carnicería.

mechanic mecánico.

mechanical mecánico.

medal medalla.

meddle meterse, entrometerse.

medical médico.

medicine medicina *Did the doctor give you any medicine for your cold?* ¿Le ha dado el médico alguna medicina para el catarro? ○ **medicine chest** botiquín. ○ **to take one's medicine** pagar las consecuencias.

meditate meditar.

medium [n] medio *We sold a lot of our products through the medium of advertising.* Vendimos muchos de nuestros productos por medio de anuncios. ● [adj] *This is the medium size.* Este es el tamaño medio. ● [adv] medio *I'd like my steak medium rare.* Me gustaría el bistec medio crudo. ○ **happy medium** término medio *If we could only strike a happy medium!* ¡Si pudiéramos llegar a un término medio! ○ **medium-sized** de tamaño mediano *I want medium-sized pajamas.* Quiero pijamas de tamaño mediano.

meek manso, humilde.

meet [n] concurso, competencia *Are you going to the swimming meet?* ¿Va Ud. al concurso de natación? ● [v] encontrar *Did you meet anyone on the road?* ¿Encontró Ud. alguien en el camino? ▲ encontrar, hallar *She met her death in a street accident.* Halló la muerte en un accidente callejero. ▲ encontrar, recibir a alguien *Is anybody going to meet them at the train?* ¿Va alguien a recibirlos a la estación? ▲ encontrarse, confluir *The rivers meet below the town.* Los ríos confluyen más allá del pueblo. ▲ conocer *I want you to meet my father.* Quiero que conozca a mi padre. *or* Quiero presentarle a mi padre. ▲ reunirse *The court will not meet again until next week.* El tribunal no volverá a reunirse hasta la semana próxi-

ma. ▲ empalmar *Will the bus meet the train?* ¿Empalmará el omnibús con el tren? ▲ hacer frente a *We have enough to meet this month's expenses.* Tenemos suficiente dinero para hacer frente a los gastos de este mes. ▲ satisfacer *Can you meet their demands?* ¿Puede Ud. satisfacer sus exigencias? ‖ *I met with an accident.* Tuve un accidente.

meeting sesión, junta *Tonight there will be a meeting of the Spanish Club.* Esta noche habrá sesión en el Club Español. ▲ mitin *Who's going to address the meeting?* ¿Quién va a hablar en el mitin? *or* ¿Quién va a dirigir la palabra en el mitin? ‖ *He proposed to her immediately after their meeting.* Le propuso matrimonio inmediatamente después de haberla conocido.

melancholy melancólico.

mellow blando, suave, meloso.

melody melodía.

melon melón.

melt derretir *The sun has melted the snow.* El sol ha derretido la nieve. ▲ derretirse *The ice in my glass has all melted.* Se ha derretido completamente el hielo de mi vaso. ▲ desvanecerse, disolverse *The crowd melted away when the police came.* La muchedumbre se disolvió cuando llegó la policía.

member socio, miembro *Only members allowed.* Sólo para socios.

membership afiliados *What's the membership of this club?* ¿Cuántos afiliados tiene este club? ‖ *Do you have your membership card?* ¿Tiene su tarjeta de socio?

membrane membrana.

memorandum memorándum.

memorial [n] monumento conmemorativo. ● [adj] conmemorativo.

memory memoria *My memory for names is not very good.* No tengo buena memoria para los nombres.—*This monument is in memory of George Washington.* Este monumento es en memoria de George Washington. ▲ recuerdo *I'll have pleasant memories of this town.* Tendré gratos recuerdos de este pueblo. ‖ *That never happened before, in my memory.* Que yo recuerde, eso nunca ha sucedido.

menace [n] amenaza. ● [v] amenazar.

mend remendar *Where can I get these pants mended?* ¿Dónde puedo mandar remendar estos pantalones? ▲ resta-

blecerse *He's mending slowly after his operation.* Está restableciéndose poco a poco después de la operación.
○ **on the mend** mejorando *It looks as if their relations are on the mend.* Parece que sus relaciones van mejorando. ○ **to mend one's ways** reformarse *She told him he'd better mend his ways.* Ella le dijo que fuera mejor que se reformara.

mental mental.

mention [*n*] mención *Have you heard any mention of him recently?* ¿Ha oído Ud. que hagan mención de él últimamente?
● [*v*] mencionar *He didn't mention the price.* No mencionó el precio.
‖ *Don't mention it.* No hay de que.

menu menú, lista de platos.

merchandise mercadería.

merchant [*n*] comerciante *Who are the leading merchants in town?* ¿Quiénes son los comerciantes más importantes de esta ciudad?
● [*adj*] mercante *Our merchant ships usually dock here.* Nuestros barcos mercantes suelen atracar aquí.
○ **merchant marine** marina mercante.

merchantman buque mercante.

merciful misericordioso.

mercury mercurio.

mercy misericordia, clemencia.

mere mero, puro *This is a mere formality.* Esto no es más que una mera formalidad.

merely solamente, meramente.

merge unir, fundir.

meridian meridiano.

merit [*n*] mérito *His painting was of little merit.* Sus cuadros tenían muy poco mérito.
● [*v*] merecer *I think he merits a raise in salary.* Creo que merece un aumento de sueldo.

merry alegre *She's a very merry person.* Es una persona muy alegre. ▲ feliz *Merry Christmas!* ¡Felices Pascuas!

mess lío *What a mess!* ¡Que lío! ▲ comida *The soldiers complain about the mess.* Los soldados se quejan de la comida. ▲ cantidad *I caught a fine mess of fish last night.* Anoche cogí una buena cantidad de pescado.
● [*v*] enredar *You're always messing things up.* Siempre lo enreda todo.
○ **in a mess** desarreglado, revuelto *The house is in a complete mess.* La casa está completamente desarreglada.
○ **to mess up** ensuciar *I'm sorry the dog messed up your floor.* Siento que el perro le haya ensuciada el piso.

message recado, mensaje *I want to leave a message.* Quiero dejar un recado.
○ **to take a message** dar un recado.

messenger mensajero.

metal [*n*] metal.

meteor meteoro.

meter metro.

method método.

microphone micrófono.

microscope microscopio.

midday mediodía.

middle [*n*] centro, medio *Set the vase in the middle of the table.* Ponga Ud. el florero en el centro de la mesa. ▲ mediados *I'm going about the middle of August.* Iré a mediados de agosto. ▲ cintura *He's put on weight around the middle.* Ha aumentado de cintura.
● [*adj*] medio *He's a man of middle height.* Es un hombre de estatura media.
○ **in the middle of** en pleno *I'm in the middle of my work.* Estoy en pleno trabajo.
‖ *You'll find them in the middle room.* Los encontrará Ud. en el cuarto de en medio.

middle-aged de edad madura.

middle class clase media.

midnight media noche.

midst ○ **in the midst of** en medio de.

midwife partera, comadrona.

might poder, fuerza *He pulled with all his might.* Tiró con todas sus fuerzas.

mighty poderoso *He made a mighty effort.* Hizo un poderoso esfuerzo.
‖ *He's done mighty little work today.* Ha hecho poquísimo trabajo hoy.
‖ *That's a mighty good thing.* Es una gran cosa. ‖ *I'm mighty glad to meet you.* Tengo mucho gusto en conocerle.

mild suave *She has a very mild disposition.* Ella tiene un carácter muy suave. ▲ templado *It's very mild today.* Hoy hace un día muy templado. ▲ blando, fresco *I'm quite fond of mild cheese.* Me gusta mucho el queso blando.

mildew añublo, moho.

mile milla.

military militar.

milk [*n*] leche *I want two liters of milk.* Quiero dos litros de leche.
● [*v*] ordeñar *Do you know how to milk a cow?* ¿Sabe Ud. ordeñar vacas? ▲ chupar *The officials milked the treasury year after year.* Los funcionarios chupaban año tras año del erario público.
‖ *He lacks the milk of human kindness.* Es muy poco humano.

milkman lechero.

mill [n] molino *There's a flour mill just above the bridge.* Hay un molino un poco más allá del puente. ▲ molinillo *Do you have a coffee mill at home?* ¿Tiene Ud. un molinillo de café en su casa? ▲ fábrica *How many people work in the mill?* ¿Cuántas personas trabajan en la fábrica?

● [v] moler *The baker mills his own flour.* El panadero muele su propia harina.

○ **to go through the mill** pasar por muchas cosas en la vida. ○ **to mill around** moverse con impaciencia *The crowd milled around waiting for the parade to begin.* La multitud se movía con impaciencia esperando que comenzara el desfile.

miller molinero.

millimeter milímetro.

million millón.

mimeograph mimeógrafo.

mind [n] mente, inteligencia *He has a very quick mind.* Tiene una mente muy ágil. ▲ memoria *My mind isn't clear on what happened.* Mi memoria no está clara sobre lo que pasó.

● [v] tener cuidado *Mind how you cross the street.* Tenga Ud. cuidado al cruzar la calle. ▲ cuidar *Mind the store while I'm gone.* Cuide Ud. la tienda en mi ausencia. ▲ obedecer, guiarse por, hacer caso *You have to mind the traffic rules here.* Aquí hay que obedecer las reglas del tráfico.

○ **never mind** no se moleste *Never mind, I'll do it myself.* No se moleste Ud., lo haré yo mismo. ▲ no importa *Never mind what he says.* No le importe lo que diga. ○ **to be out of one's mind** estar como loco *She's out of her mind with worry.* Está como loca de ansiedad. ○ **to call to mind** recordar, traer a la memoria *That calls to mind a story I know.* Eso me trae a la memoria un cuento que sé. ○ **to change one's mind** mudar (or cambiar) de opinión *I thought I'd go along with them, but changed my mind.* Pensé ir con ellos, pero mudé de opinión. ○ **to have a mind** estar por, tener ganas de *I've a mind to come along.* Estoy por acompañarles. ○ **to have in mind** pensar en *Have you anyone in mind for the job?* ¿Piensa Ud. en alguien para ese puesto? ○ **to keep in mind** tener presente *I'll keep you in mind.* Le tendré presente. ○ **to know one's mind** saber lo que uno quiere *He doesn't know his own mind.* El mismo no sabe lo que quiere. ○ **to lose one's mind** volverse loco, perder el juicio *I thought I'd lose my mind with all that noise.* Creí que me iba a volver loco con todo aquel ruido. ○ **to make up one's mind** decidir, resolver *Have you made up your mind about him yet?* ¿Ya ha decidido Ud. acerca de él? ○ **to my mind** a mi parecer *To my mind that job will take at least a week.* A mi parecer se tardará por lo menos una semana en hacer ese trabajo. ○ **to set one's mind on** estar resuelto a *She has her mind set on going shopping today.* Está resuelta a ir de compras hoy. ○ **to slip one's mind** escaparse de la memoria, olvidarse *I planned to do it, but it slipped my mind.* Pensaba hacerlo, pero se me olvidó.

‖ *Are you sure you don't mind?* ¿Está Ud. seguro que no le importa? ‖ *Keep your mind on your work.* Ponga Ud. atención en su trabajo. ‖ *Mind your own business!* No se meta Ud. en lo que no le importa. ‖ *What's on your mind?* ("What do you want?") ¿Qué desea Ud.?

mine [n] mina *Who owns this coal mine?* ¿De quien es esta mina de carbón?

● [v] extraer minerales *What do they mine here?* ¿Qué mineral extraen de aquí?

mine mío *Those books are all mine.* Esos libros son todos míos. ▲ el mío, la mía *Your room is on the right and mine is on the left.* Su cuarto queda a la derecha, el mío a la izquierda.

‖ *He's a friend of mine.* Es un amigo mío.

miner minero.

mineral [adj; n] mineral.

mingle mezclarse.

minimum [adj; n] mínimo.

minister [n] pastor protestante, ministro *We have a new minister.* Tenemos un nuevo pastor protestante. ▲ ministro *I want to see the American minister.* Deseo ver al ministro americano.

● [v] atender *The nurse ministers to the patient's wants.* La enfermera atiende a los deseos del enfermo.

minor [n] menor de edad *No liquor will be served to minors.* No se venderán bebidas alcohólicas a menores de edad.

● [adj] de poca importancia *Don't bother me with those minor matters.* No me moleste Ud. con esas cosas de poca importancia.

mint [n] menta *I like mint in my ice tea.* Me gusta la menta en mi té helado.

▲ pastilla de menta *Have some mints.* Tome Ud. algunos pastillas de menta. ▲ casa de la moneda *My uncle works in the mint.* Mi tió trabaja en la casa de la moneda. ▲ dineral, cantidad grande de dinero *That guy made a mint of money in the clothing business.* Ese individuo ha hecho un dineral en el negocio de ropa.

● [*v*] acuñar *I understand the government has stopped minting gold coins.* Tengo entendido que el gobierno ha dejado de acuñar monedas de oro.

minus menos, sin *How much will the ticket cost minus the tax?* ¿Cuánto costará la entrada menos el impuesto? ‖ *She's a minus quantity.* Ella es un cero a la izquierda.

minute [*n*] minuto *I'll be back in five minutes.* Regresaré en cinco minutos.—*The ship's five degrees and forty minutes off its course.* El barco se ha desviado de su ruta cinco grados y cuarenta minutos. ▲ momento *Wait a minute.* Espere un momento.

○ **minutes** acta *Who's taking the minutes of the meeting?* ¿Quién hace el acta de la reunión? ○ **up to the minute** de última hora *The news in this paper is up to the minute.* Las noticias de este periódico son de última hora. ‖ *Call the hotel the minute you arrive.* Llame Ud. al hotel en cuanto llegue.

minute [*adj*] menudo, diminuto *It's hard to read the minute print in this book.* Es difícil leer la letra menuda de este libro.

miracle milagro.

mirror [*n*] espejo *I'd like to buy a small mirror.* Quisiera comprar un espejo pequeño.

● [*v*] reflejar *The trees on the bank are mirrored in the lake.* Los árboles de la orilla se reflejan en el lago.

mischief traversura.

miser avaro.

miserable desdichado *I've never seen a man so miserable.* Nunca he visto un hombre tan desdichado. ▲ pésimo, muy mal *I feel miserable.* Me siento muy mal.

misery miseria.

mislead extraviar *Our guide misled us and we got lost.* El guía nos extravió y nos perdimos. ▲ descaminar *His companions misled him.* Sus compañeros le descaminaron.

misprint errata, error de imprenta.

miss [*n*] señorita *Will you wait on me,*

Miss? ¿Quiere Ud. atenderme, señorita?

● [*v*] perder *Do you think I'll miss my train?* ¿Cree Ud. que perderé el tren? —*He never misses a chance to do a little business.* Nunca pierde la oportunidad de hacer algún negocio. ▲ no encontrar *I missed him at the hotel.* No lo encontré en el hotel. ▲ equivocarse, dejar de encontrar *You can't miss the house if you follow this street.* No puede Ud. equivocarse de casa si sigue por esta calle. ▲ errar *You can't miss.* No puede Ud. errar. ▲ salirse de *The speaker misses the point entirely.* El orador se sale del tema completamente. ▲ hacer falta, echar de menos *I'll miss you.* Me hará Ud. falta. *or* Le echaré de menos. ▲ dejar de *Don't miss the museum before you leave town.* No deje de visitar el museo antes de partir de la ciudad.

○ **to be missing** faltar *Is anything missing from your wallet?* ¿Le falta algo en su cartera? ‖ *I missed what you said.* Se me escapó lo que Ud. dijo. ‖ *The truck just missed hitting the boy in the street.* El camión por poco atropelló al niño en la calle.

mission misión.

missionary misionero.

mist niebla, neblina.

mistake [*n*] error, culpa, falta *Sorry, my mistake.* Lo siento, ha sido culpa mía. ▲ equivocación, error *There must be some mistake.* Debe haber alguna equivocación.

● [*v*] confundir *You can't mistake it.* No lo puede Ud. confundir. ▲ interpretar mal *Please don't mistake me.* Por favor no me interprete Ud. mal. ▲ tomar *I mistook her for a friend of mine.* La tomé por una amiga mía.

○ **by mistake** sin querer *Did you do this by mistake?* ¿Hizo Ud. esto sin querer? ○ **to make a mistake** equivocarse, cometer un error. ‖ *This is the right answer; make no mistake about it.* Esta es la solución correcta, no le quepa a Ud. duda.

mistaken equivocado *This is a case of mistaken identity.* Esto es un caso de identificación equivocada.

○ **to be mistaken** estar equivocado *You must be mistaken.* Ud. debe estar equivocado.

mister señor *Hey, mister, have you got a match?* Oiga, señor, ¿tiene Ud. un fósforo?

mistress señora, dueña *The mistress of*

the house is very charming. La dueña de la casa es muy agradable. ▲ amante, concubina *She was the king's mistress.* Era la amante del rey. ‖ *She was mistress of the situation.* Ella dominaba la situación.

misunderstand entender mal.

misunderstanding equivocación *He came too early because of a misunderstanding.* Por una equivocación llegó demasiado temprano. ▲ desavenencia, mal entendido *They haven't spoken since their misunderstanding.* Ellos no se hablan desde que tuvieron aquel mal entendido.

mittens mitones, manoplas.

mix mezclar *Don't mix too much sand with the concrete.* No mezcle Ud. demasiada arena con el cemento. ▲ preparar *Who's mixing the drinks?* ¿Quién está preparando las bebidas? ▲ relacionarse, llevarse *They don't mix well with other people.* No se llevan bien con la gente. ▲ combinar, ir bien *These two foods don't mix well.* Estos dos alimentos no van bien juntos. ○ **to mix up** confundir *Don't mix me up.* No me confunda Ud. ○ **to get mixed up** in mezclarse en *I don't want to get mixed up in their arguments.* No quiero mezclarme en sus disputas.

mixed ○ **mixed chorus** coro mixto. ○ **mixed drinks** bebidas mezcladas.

mixture mezcla, mixtura.

mix-up confusión.

moan [n] quejido.

mob [n] multitud, muchedumbre, gentío *There was a mob of people in the city.* Había una gran muchedumbre en la ciudad. ● [v] asaltar *The singer was mobbed by autograph hunters.* La cantante fué asaltada por los coleccionistas de autógrafos. ▲ apoderarse *The crowd tried to mob the prisoner.* La muchedumbre intentó apoderarse del detenido.

mobilize mobilizar.

mock burlar.

mode modo.

model [n] modelo *He's making a model of the bridge.* Está haciendo un modelo del puente.—*That car's last year's model.* Ese automóvil es un modelo del año pasado. ● [adj] modelo, ejemplar *Ours is a model town.* La nuestra es una ciudad modelo. ● [v] planear *We're modeling our house after that picture.* Estamos

planeando nuestra casa según esa fotografía.

moderate [adj] moderado.

moderation moderación.

modern moderno.

modest modesto.

moist húmedo.

molasses melaza.

mold [n] moho *This bread is covered with mold.* Este pan está cubierto de moho. ▲ molde *You use these molds for jelly.* Puede usar estos moldes para la jalea. ● [v] moldear *His character was molded by his experience.* La experiencia moldeó su carácter.

mole topo *The moles have ruined our garden.* Los topos nos han arruinado la huerta. ▲ lunar *He has a mole on his face.* Tiene un lunar en la cara.

molest molestar.

moment momento, instante *Wait a moment.* Espere Ud. un momento. ○ **at a moment's notice** de un momento a otro *Be ready to leave at a moment's notice.* Esté preparado para partir de un momento a otro. ○ **at the moment** por ahora *I can't answer your question at the moment.* Por ahora me es imposible contestar a su pregunta.

monarch monarca.

Monday lunes.

money dinero *Where can I change my American money?* ¿Dónde puedo cambiar mi dinero americano?

money order giro postal *Where can I get this money order cashed?* ¿Dónde puedo hacer efectivo este giro postal?

monk monje, fraile.

monkey [n] mono. ● [v] meterse a arreglar *Don't monkey with the radio.* No te metas a arreglar la radio.

monopoly monopolio.

monotonous monótono.

monster monstruo.

month mes.

monthly [adv] mensualmente.

mood humor, genio.

moon luna *Is there a full moon tonight?* ¿Hay luna llena esta noche?

moor [v] amarrar.

Moor moro (*Mohammedan*).

mop [n] estropajo *Where's the mop?* ¿Dónde está el estropajo? ● [v] fregar *What can I mop the floor with?* ¿Con qué friego el piso? ○ **to mop up** secar, limpiar *Mop up the water on the floor.* Seque el agua del piso.

moral [n] moraleja *I don't get the moral*

of this story. No le veo la moraleja al cuento.

● [*adj*] moral, ético *That's not a very moral thing to do.* No es muy ético el hacer eso.

morale moral, estado de ánimo.

more más *I need more money than I have on me.* Necesito más dinero de lo que llevo encima.—*The more the merrier.* Cuantos más, mejor.—*This cost me more than I expected.* Esto me ha costado más de lo que esperaba.

○ **more and more** cada vez más *He likes her more and more.* La quiere cada vez más. ○ **more or less** más o menos *I believe that the report is more or less true.* Creo que el informe es más o menos cierto. ○ **once more** una vez más *Try once more.* Pruebe Ud. una vez más. ○ **what's more** además, es más *What's more, I don't believe you.* Además, no le creo a Ud.

‖ *I don't care any more.* Ya no me importa.

moreover además, además de eso.

morning [*n*] mañana *I'll see you in the morning.* Le veré en la mañana. *or* Le veré por la mañana.

● [*adj*] de mañana *Is there a morning train?* ¿Hay un tren de la mañana? *or* ¿Hay un tren por la mañana?

○ **morning paper** diario de la mañana. ‖ *Good morning.* Buenos días.

morphine morfina.

morsel bocado.

mortal mortal.

mortar mortero.

mortgage [*n*] hipoteca.

● [*v*] hipotecar.

○ **to pay off a mortgage** redimir una hipoteca.

mosquito mosquito.

mosquito net mosquitero.

moss musgo.

most lo máximo, lo más *That's the most I can pay.* Eso es lo máximo (*or* más) que puedo pagar. ▲ la mayoría *What do most people do here in the evening?* ¿Qué hace aquí la mayoría de la gente por la noche? ▲ casi todo, mayor parte *She's already been to most of the stores in town.* Ya ha estado en casi todas las tiendas de la ciudad.—*He's brighter than most of the others.* Es más inteligente que la mayor parte de los demás. ▲ mayor *You can get there most easily by bus.* Puede Ud. llegar allí con mayor facilidad en autobús. ▲ de lo más *The talk was most interesting.* El discurso fué de lo más interesante. ▲ el más, la más, lo más *She is*

the most beautiful girl I've ever seen. Es la muchacha más linda que he visto en mi vida.

○ **at most** todo lo más *The hotel is four blocks from here, at most.* Todo lo más que hay de aquí al hotel son cuatro cuadras. ○ **for the most part** por lo general *For the most part he does a good job.* Por lo general hace un buen trabajo. ○ **the very most** lo más que *That's the very most I can do.* Eso es lo más que puedo hacer. ○ **to make the most of** aprovechar lo mejor posible *We'd better make the most of the time we have.* Más nos valdría aprovechar el tiempo lo mejor posible.

mostly en su mayor parte, por lo común.

moth polilla.

mother [*n*] madre *Do you live with your mother?* ¿Vive Ud. con su madre?

● [*adj*] materno *What's your mother tongue?* ¿Cuál es su lengua materna?

● [*v*] cuidar como una madre, cuidar como a un hijo *She mothered him all through his illness.* Le cuidó como a un hijo durante su enfermedad.

○ **mother country** madre patria *Did the colonies send representatives to the mother country?* ¿Han enviado las colonias representantes a la madre patria? ○ **mother-in-law** suegra.

motion [*n*] movimiento *The motion of the boat has made me seasick.* El movimiento del barco me ha mareado. ▲ proposición, moción *I want to make a motion.* Quiero presentar una moción.

● [*v*] hacer señas *Will you motion to that bus to pick us up?* ¿Quiere Ud. hacer señas a ese autobús para que nos recoja? ▲ indicar *I motioned to him to take a seat.* Le indiqué que tomara asiento.

motionless inmóvil.

motive motivo *What was the motive for the crime?* ¿Cuál fué el motivo del siento?

○ **motive power** fuerza motriz.

motor motor.

motorcycle motocicleta.

mould See **mold.**

mound túmulo, montón.

mount [*n*] monte *Have you seen Mount Everest?* ¿Ha visto Ud. el monte Everest?

● [*v*] subir *He mounted the platform.* Subió a la plataforma. ▲ subir, aumentar *Our debts are mounting fast.* Nuestras deudas aumentan rapidamente.—*Their profits have mounted up considerably.* Sus beneficios han aumentado considerablemente.

○ **to mount a horse** montar a caballo. ‖ *This old horse is my favorite mount.* Este viejo caballo es mi favorito para montar.

mountain montaña, monte *How high is that mountain?* ¿Qué altura tiene esa montaña? ▲ montón *I've got a mountain of work to do.* Tengo un montón de cosas que hacer.

mountainous montañoso.

mouse ratón.

mouth boca *I've got a bad taste in my mouth.* Tengo mal sabor de boca. ▲ entrada *The dog stopped at the mouth of the cave.* El perro se detuvo a la entrada el la cueva. ▲ embocadura, desembocadura *How far is it to the mouth of the river?* ¿A qué distancia queda la desembocadura del río?

○ **down in the mouth** cariacontecido *Why are you so down in the mouth?* ¿Por qué está Ud. tan cariacontecido? *or* ¿Por qué está Ud. tan cabizbajo?

○ **from mouth to mouth** de boca en boca *The story passed from mouth to mouth.* La historia pasó de boca en boca. ○ **to keep one's mouth shut** tener la boca cerrada, guardar un secreto *He can't keep his mouth shut.* No sabe nunca tener la boca cerrada.

move [*n*] paso *He can't make a move without his partner.* No puede dar un paso sin su socio. ▲ turno *Whose move is it now?* ¿De quién es el turno ahora? ▲ acción *That was a wasted move.* Esá fué una acción inútil. ▲ paso, movimiento *He made a move toward the door.* Dió un paso hacia la puerta. ▲ jugada *The chess player made a fine move.* El jugador de ajedrez hizo una buena jugada.

● [*v*] mover *Move your car back a little.* Mueva su coche hacia atrás un poco. ▲ moverse *I can't move.* No me puede mover. ▲ circular *The police are keeping the crowds moving.* La policía hace circular a la multitud. ▲ marchar *The new director's got things moving.* El nuevo director hace marchar las cosas. ▲ funcionar, moverse *This machine moves only by hand.* Esta máquina funciona solamente a mano. ▲ mudarse *Do you know where they're moving to?* ¿Sabe Ud. dónde se mudan? ▲ emocionar *I am very much moved by what you say.* Me emociona mucha lo que Ud. dice. ▲ alternar con, andar con, tratarse con *They like to think that they move in the best circles.* Se hacen la ilusión de que alternan con la mejor sociedad. ▲ proponer *I move that*

we accept him as a member. Propongo que le aceptemos como socio. ▲ tener salida *These coats are not moving as they did last year.* Estos abrigos no tienen la salida que tuvieron el año pasado.

○ **to be on the move** estar de acá para allá *They're forever on the move.* Siempre están de acá para allá. ○ **to move along** ir a gran velocidad *Our train is really moving along.* Nuestro tren realmente va a gran velocidad. ○ **to move away** quitar, poner en otro sitio *Move the table away please.* Quite Ud. la mesa de aquí por favor. ○ **to move off** alejarse *He moved a few feet off.* Se alejó unos metros.

movie película *Let's go to a movie.* Vamos a ver una película. *or* Vamos al cine.

mow segar.

Mr. señor, Sr. *How are you, Mr. Jones?* ¿Qué tal, Sr. Jones?—*Dear Mr. García.* Muy señor mío (*formal*). *or* Querido sr. García (*familiar*).

Mrs. señora, sra. *This is for Mrs. Smith.* Esto es para la señora Smith.

much mucho *Did you spend much last night?* ¿Gastó Ud. mucho anoche?— *I don't have much faith in what they say.* No tengo mucha fe en lo que dicen.—*Thank you very much.* Muchas gracias.

○ **how much** cuánto *How much will it cost me?* ¿Cuánto me costará? ○ **so much** tanto *I don't think that car is worth so much.* No creo que ese coche valga tanto.

mud fango, cieno, barro *Don't step in the mud.* No pise Ud. en el barro.

muff [*n*] manguito.

muffler bufando.

mulatto mulato.

mule mula.

multiply multiplicar.

mumps paperas.

murder [*n*] asesinato *The prisoner had committed murder.* El preso había cometido un asesinato.

● [*v*] asesinar.

murderer asesino.

murmur [*n*] murmullo.

● [*v*] murmurar.

muscle músculo.

museum museo.

mushroom seta, hongo.

music música *Where's the music coming from?* ¿De dónde viene la música?

○ **to face the music** hacer frente a la situación.

musical musical.

muslin muselina.

must tener que *We must do what we can to help him.* Tenemos que hacer lo que podamos para ayudarle. ▲ deber *He must be there by now.* Ya debe estar allí.

mustache bigote.

mustard mostaza.

mute mudo.

mutiny [*n*] motín, sublevación.
● [*v*] amotinarse, sublevarse.

mutter refunfuñar, gruñir.

mutton carnero.

mutual mutuo.

my (see I, me) mi *This is my picture.* Este es mi retrato. ▲ mío *That's my pen!* ¡Esa pluma es mía! ▲ mis *Are these my gloves?* ¿Son éstos mis guantes? ▲ caramba, caray *My, it's hot!* ¡Caray qué calor hace!

myself yo mismo *I'll do this myself.* Esto lo haré yo mismo. ▲ el mismo *I'm not myself today.* Hoy no soy el mismo. ▲ mi *As for myself, I don't know.* En cuánto a mí, no lo sé. ▲ me *I cut myself shaving this morning.* Me corté afeitándome esta mañana.
○ by myself, all by myself completamente solo [*Sp*], ingrime y solo [*Am*] *I took the trip all by myself.* Hice el viaje completamente solo.

mystery misterio.

N

nag [*n*] jaca.
● [*v*] regañar, machacar.

nail [*n*] clavo *This nail's bent.* Este clavo está torcido. ▲ uña *I've broken my nail.* Me he roto la uña.
● [*v*] clavar *Have you nailed the top on the box yet?* ¿Ha clavado Ud. ya la tapa del cajón?
○ to hit the nail on the head dar en el clavo.

nail file lima para las uñas.

nail polish esmalte para las uñas.

naked desnudo.

name [*n*] nombre *Give me the names of the employees.* Déme Ud. los nombres de los empleados. ▲ nombre, fama *That company has a good name.* Esa compañía tiene buena fama. ▲ título *What's the name of that book?* ¿Cuál es el título de ese libro?
● [*v*] poner . . . a *We named the dog Fido.* Al perro le pusimos Fido. ▲ nombrar *Can you name all the players?* ¿Puede Ud. nombrar a todos los jugadores?
○ by name de nombre *I know him only by name.* Le conozco solamente de nombre. ○ in name only solamente de nombre. ○ in the name of en nombre de *Open the door in the name of the law.* Abra la puerta en nombre de la ley. ○ to be named after llamarse lo mismo que *Is the baby named after his father?* ¿Se llama el niño lo mismo que el padre? ○ to one's name a nombre de uno *I haven't a cent to my name.* No tengo ni un centavo a mi nombre.
‖ *What's your name?* ¿Cómo se llama Ud.? ‖ *He was named in the will.* Su nombre figuraba en el testamento.

namely a saber.

nap [*n*] sueñecillo, siesta.
○ to catch one napping cogerle a uno desprevenido.

napkin servilleta.

narcotic narcótico.

narrative narración.

narrow [*adj*] estrecho *This is a narrow road.* Este es un camino estrecho.— *His decision showed a narrow interpretation of the law.* Su resolución mostró una estrecha interpretación de la ley. ▲ estrecho, limitado *His views on the subject are very narrow.* Su punto de vista con respecto al asunto es muy limitado.
● [*v*] estrecharse *The road narrows just beyond the bridge.* El camino se estrecha al otro lado del puente.
○ to narrow down reducirse *The question narrows down to this: do you want to go or not?* La pregunta se reduce a esto: ¿Quiere Ud. ir o no?
‖ *We had a narrow escape yesterday.* Ayer nos salvamos de milagro.

nasty antipático *He's a nasty boy.* Es un muchacho antipático. ▲ obsceno, mal pensado *What a nasty mind you've got!* ¡Qué mente más obscena tiene Ud! *or* ¡Qué mal pensado es Ud.!
○ nasty weather mal tiempo.

nation nación *Five nations were represented at the conference.* Cinco naciones estaban representadas en la conferencia. ▲ país *The whole nation will be affected by that new law.* Esa nueva ley afectará a todo el país.

national nacional.

nationality nacionalidad.

native [*n*] indígena *What kind of clothes do the natives wear?* ¿Qué clase de trajes llevan los indígenas?

● [adj] materno *What's your native language?* ¿Cuál es su lengua materna? ▲ oriundo *Olive oil's native to Spain.* Al aceite de oliva es oriundo de España.

natural natural *There's a natural lake there.* Hay un lago natural en ese lugar.—*He died a natural death.* Falleció de muerte natural.—*He's a very natural person.* Es una persona muy natural. ▲ natural, innato *He has a natural talent for painting.* Tiene un talento natural para la pintura. ‖ *That was the natural thing to say.* Decir eso era lo natural.

naturalist naturalista.

naturally naturalmente, por supuesto.

nature naturaleza *You can't go against nature.* No puede Ud. ir contra la naturaleza. ▲ naturaleza, modo de ser *It's not his nature to forget.* No está en su naturaleza olvidar. ▲ índole *What was the nature of the crime?* ¿Cuál fué la índole del crimen? O by nature por naturaleza *He's a lazy person by nature.* Es un perezoso por naturaleza.

naughty díscolo, desobediente.

nausea náusea.

naval naval.

navigate navegar.

navigator navegante.

navy marina de guerra, armada.

near [adj] cercano *He's a near relative.* Es un pariente cercano. ● [prep] cerca de *Is there a hotel near here?* ¿Hay un hotel cerca de aquí? O near at hand próximo, cerca *The hour of attack's near at hand.* La hora del ataque está próxima. O to come near estar a punto de, estar próximo a *I came near getting lost.* Estuve a punto de perderme. O to draw near acercarse *The harvest season's drawing near.* Se acerca la estación de la siega.

nearby cerca *Is there a tobacco store nearby?* ¿Hay un estanco cerca?

nearly aproximadamente, casi.

neat aseado, limpio.

necessary necesario.

necessity necesidad.

neck nuca *He broke his neck playing football.* Se rompió la nuca jugando al futbol. ▲ cuello *Pick up the bottle by the neck.* Agarre la botella por el cuello.—*She wore a dress with a high neck.* Llevaba un vestido con un cuello alto. O neck and neck al mismo tiempo *The two horses finished neck and neck.* Los dos caballos llegaron al mismo tiempo.

necktie corbata.

need [n] necesidad *There's a great need for nurses.* Hay una gran necesidad de enfermeras. ● [v] necesitar *I need money.* Necesito dinero.—*He needs to get a haircut.* Necesita un corte de pelo. ▲ hacer falta *These clothes need to be washed.* Hace falta lavar esta ropa. O if need be si hubiese necesidad, si fuera necesario *I'll go myself if need be.* Iré yo mismo si fuera necesario. O to be in need of tener necesidad de *He's in need of a vacation.* Tiene necesidad de unas vacaciones.

needle aguja *Have you a needle and thread?* ¿Tiene Ud. hilo y aguja?— *Change the needle before playing that record.* Cambie la aguja antes de tocar ese disco. ▲ brújula *The needle's pointing toward the north.* La brújula señala al norte. O pine needles hojas de pino, pinochas *We made a bed of pine needles.* Hicimos un lecho con hojas de pino.

needless inútil, innecesario.

needy necesitado.

negative [n] negativo *Can you lend me the negative of that picture?* ¿Puede Ud. prestarme el negativo de esa fotografía? ● [adj] negativo *Was the result of your examination negative?* ¿Fué negativo el resultado de su examen?— *You have such a negative approach to life!* ¡Tiene Ud. una actitud negativa ante la vida! ▲ mediocre, nulo *She has a negative personality.* Tiene una personalidad mediocre. O in the negative negativamente *He replied in the negative.* El respondió negativamente.

neglect [n] abandono, descuido *The house shows signs of neglect.* La casa da señales de abandono. ● [v] descuidar *He's been neglecting his work lately.* Ha estado descuidando su trabajo últimamente. ▲ olvidarse *I neglected to lock the door.* Me olvidé de cerrar la puerta con llave.

negligence negligencia, descuido.

negotiation negociación.

Negro [n] negro.

neighbor vecino *He's my next-door neighbor.* Es mi vecino de al lado.

neighborhood vecindad, barrio.

neither ninguno de los dos *Neither of us can be there.* Ninguno de los dos puede estar allí.

O **neither . . . nor** ni . . . ni *Neither he nor I feel like doing it.* Ni él ni yo tenemos ganas de hacerlo.—*I could neither see nor hear the speaker.* No pude ni ver ni oír al orador.

nephew sobrino.

nerve nervio. ▲ valor *Try not to lose your nerve.* Procure no perder el valor. ‖ *He's got a lot of nerve.* Es un fresco.

nervous nervioso.

nest nido.

net [*n*] red *The nets were loaded with fish.* Las redes estaban llenas de pescados.

● [*adj*] neto *The net weight's two pounds.* Tiene un peso neto de dos libras.—*We made a net profit of one hundred dollars.* Obtuvimos un beneficio neto de cien dólares. ▲ neto, líquido *What was your net profit last year?* ¿Cuáles fueron sus ganancias líquidas el año pasado?

O **mosquito net** mosquitero *It's safer to sleep under a mosquito net in this climate.* En este clima es más seguro dormir con mosquitero.

‖ *The firm netted a good profit.* La firma obtuvo unas buenas ganancias líquidas.

neutral [*adj*] neutral.

never nunca, jamás *I never said any such thing.* Yo nunca dije tal cosa.

‖ *He never even opened the book.* Ni siquiera abrió el libro.

nevertheless no obstante, sin embargo.

new nuevo *This building's new.* Este edificio es nuevo.—*I feel like a new man.* Me siento como nuevo.

‖ *What's new?* ¿Qué hay de nuevo?

news noticias *What's the latest news?* ¿Cuáles son las últimas noticias? ▲ nuevo *That's news to me.* Eso es nuevo para mí.

O **to break the news** dar la noticia *Who's going to break the news to him?* ¿Quién va a darle la noticia?

newsboy vendedor de periódicos.

newspaper periódico.

newsstand puesto de periódicos.

next [*adj*] siguiente, de al lado *The next house is mine.* La casa de al lado es la mía. ▲ próximo *The next train leaves in half an hour.* El próximo tren sale dentro de media hora.—*I'll tell him that the next time I see him.* Le diré eso la próxima vez que le vea.

● [*adv*] después *What shall I do next?* ¿Qué hago después?

O **next door** al lado *Who lives next door?* ¿Quién vive al lado? O **next**

door to al lado de *We live next door to the school.* Vivimos al lado de la escuela. O **next to** al lado *She sat next to me at the theater.* Ella se sentó a mi lado en el teatro.

‖ *What next?* ¿Y ahora qué? or ¿Y luego qué? ‖ *This is the next best thing.* Esto es lo mejor que le sigue. or Esta es la mejor alternativa. ‖ *I was next in line.* Luego seguía yo. ‖ *Who's next?* ¿A quién le toca? or ¿Quién sigue?

nice agradable *Did you have a nice time?* ¿Pasó un rato agradable? or ¿Se divirtió Ud.? ▲ bonito *She wears nice clothes.* Ella usa bonitos trajes.

‖ *It's nice and warm here.* Aquí hace un calor agradable.

nick [*n*] muesca.

● [*v*] hacer muescas en.

O **in the nick of time** en el momento preciso, a buen tiempo.

nickel níquel.

nickname apodo, mote.

niece sobrina.

night noche *Good night.* Buenas noches. —*He spent the night on the train.* Pasó la noche en el tren.

O **to make a night of it** pasar una buena noche.

night club cabaret.

nine nueve.

nineteen diecinueve.

ninety noventa.

ninth noveno.

no no *Answer yes or no.* Conteste Ud. sí o no.

‖ *No Smoking.* Prohibido Fumar. or Se Prohibe Fumar. ‖ *No sooner said than done.* Dicho y hecho.

noble [*adj, n*] noble.

nobody nadie.

nod [*v*] afirmar con la cabeza.

noise ruido.

noisy ruidoso.

nomination nombramiento.

none ningún, ninguno *They have none of the opportunities you have.* Ellos no tienen ninguna de las oportunidades que tiene Ud.

O **none of it** nada de eso, nada de ello *They told him of the plan, but he'd have none of it.* Le hablaron del plan, pero él no quiso saber nada de ello.

nonsense tontería.

noon mediodía.

nor ni *I'm neither for it nor against it.* No estoy ni en favor ni en contra de ello.

normal normal.

north norte *Which way's north?* ¿Dónde queda el norte?

northern del norte, al norte.

nose nariz. ▲ nariz, proa *The airplane has a cannon mounted in the nose.* El aeroplano tiene un cañón emplazado en la nariz.

○ **a nose for news** olfato para las noticias *That reporter has a good nose for news.* Ese reportero tiene buen olfato para las noticias.

not no *He's not going to be home today.* El no estará hoy en casa.—*Not everyone can go to college.* No todos pueden ir a la Universidad.

notable [*adj, n*] notable.

notary notario.

note [*n*] anotación *His notes on the lecture are very good.* Sus anotaciones sobre la conferencia son muy buenas. ▲ nota *Today's paper has a note about the ship's arrival.* El periódico de hoy da una nota sobre la llegada del barco. —*He just had time to write a short note.* Sólo tuvo tiempo de escribir una breve nota.—*There was a note of anxiety in her voice.* En su voz había una nota de ansiedad.—*She sang the high notes very well.* Ella dió muy bien las notas altas. ▲ pagaré *I took a note for the amount of money he owed me.* Acepté un pagaré por la cantidad que me debía.

● [*v*] darse cuenta *He noted that there was a mistake.* Se dió cuenta que había una equivocación.

○ **notes** guión, apuntes, notas *He can't give a speech without using notes.* No puede hacer un discurso sin guión. ○ **to compare notes** comparar resultados. ○ **to make a note of** tomar nota de. ○ **to take notes** tomar notas.

notebook cuaderno, libreta.

noted célebre.

nothing no . . . nada *I have nothing to do.* No tengo nada que hacer.

○ **nothing less than** nada menos que, por lo menos.

notice [*n*] atención *That paragraph escaped my notice.* Aquel párrafo escapó a mi atención. ▲ aviso *The police posted a notice about the missing persons.* La policía fijó un aviso acerca de las personas desaparecidas.—*The office will be closed until further notice.* La oficina permanecerá cerrada hasta nuevo aviso. ▲ crítica *Did you see the notices about the new play?* ¿Vió Ud. las críticas sobre la nueva comedia?

● [*v*] darse cuenta de *I didn't notice the sign until you spoke of it.* No me

dí cuenta del letrero hasta que Ud. lo mencionó. ▲ fijarse en *I want you to notice this.* Quiero que se fije en esto.

○ **at a moment's notice** en el momento, en cualquier momento *I can be ready at a moment's notice.* Puedo estar listo en cualquier momento. ○ **to serve notice** notificar *The store's served notice that all bills must be paid tomorrow.* El establecimiento ha notificado que todas las cuentas deben saldarse mañana.

‖ *One must give two weeks' notice before leaving.* Hay que avisar con dos semanas de anticipación antes de irse.

notify notificar.

notion noción.

notorious notorio.

noun nombre, substantivo.

novel [*n*] novela.

November noviembre.

now ahora *The doctor can see you now.* El doctor puede verle ahora.—*Now that the rain has stopped we can leave.* Ahora que ha cesado la lluvia podemos marcharnos. ▲ ahora bien *Now, you listen to me!* ¡Ahora bien, escúcheme!

○ **by now** ya *He ought to be there by now.* Debe haber llegado allí ya. ○ **from now on** de ahora en adelante *From now on the work'll be difficult.* De ahora en adelante el trabajo será difícil. ○ **just now** ahora mismo *I saw him on the street just now.* Le ví en la calle ahora mismo. ○ **now and then** de vez en cuando *I hear from him now and then.* Tengo noticias suyas de vez en cuando. ○ **now that** ahora que *Now that you mention it, I do remember seeing her.* Ahora que Ud. menciona eso, recuerdo haberla visto.

nuisance lata, fastidio.

numb [*adj*] aterido, entumecido.

number [*n*] número *What's the number of your house?* ¿Cuál es el número de su casa?—*There were five numbers on the program.* Había cinco números en el programa. ▲ ejemplar, número *The latest number of the magazine came today.* Hoy llegó el último número de la revista.

● [*v*] numerar *He numbered the pages carefully.* Numeró las páginas cuidadosamente. ▲ ascender a *The population numbered 2,000 in 1940.* La población ascendió a 2.000 habitantes en 1940.

○ **a number of** varios *He owns a number of houses.* Tiene varias casas.

‖ *His days are numbered.* Tiene los días contados. ‖ *I've got your number.*

Ya te he calado.
numerous numeroso.
nun monja.
nurse [n] enfermera *I want a nurse.* Quiero una enfermera. ▲niñera *The nurse took the children for a walk.* La niñera llevó a los niños de paseo. ● [v].cuidar *They nursed him through his illness.* Le cuidaron durante su enfermedad. ▲curarse *I'm nursing a cold.* Me estoy curando de un resfriado. ▲amamantar *She was nursing the baby when I came in.* Estaba amamantando al nene cuando entré. ▲guardar *He's nursing a grudge against me.* Me guarda rencor.
nut nuez *That store sells candy and nuts.* En esa tienda se venden dulces y nueces. ▲tuerca *This board's held in place by a nut and bolt.* Esta tabla queda fija con perno y tuerca. ▲loco, chiflado *He's a nut.* Es un chiflado. ○**to go nuts** volverse loco *If this keeps up, I'll go nuts.* Si esto sigue así, me volveré loco.
nylon nilón.

O

oak roble.
oath juramento.
oats avena.
obedient obediente.
obey obedecer *He wants to be obeyed immediately.* Quiere que le obedezcan inmediatamente.
object [n] objeto *What's that strange-looking object?* ¿Qué es ese objeto tan raro?—*What's the object of that?* ¿Qué objeto tiene eso? ▲propósito *My object is to become an aviator.* Mi propósito es hacerme aviador. ○**object lesson** lección práctica *Let this be an object lesson to you.* Que ésto le sirva de lección práctica. ‖ *I hate to be an object of sympathy.* Detesto ser compadecido.
object [v] oponerse *Would you object to his marriage?* ¿Se opondría Ud. a su matrimonio?
objection objeción.
obligation obligación.
oblige obligar *His contract obliged him to go through with it.* Su contrato le obligó a hacerlo. ▲complacer *I'm always glad to oblige you.* Siempre me es grato complacerle. ○**to be obliged to** tener que *She was obliged to go to work.* Tuvo que trabajar. ‖ *Much obliged.* Muy agradecido.
observation observación.
observe advertir, darse cuenta de *Did you observe her reaction?* ¿Se dió Ud. cuenta de su reacción? ▲celebrar, guardar *What holidays do you observe?* ¿Qué fiestas celebra Ud.? ▲observar *The students were observing bacteria under the microscope.* Los estudiantes observaban los microbios al microscopio. ▲cumplir, observar, obedecer *Observe the rules.* Cumpla las reglas.
obstacle obstáculo.
obstinate terco, obstinado.
obtain obtener, adquirir.
obvious obvio, evidente.
occasion [n] ocasión *Were you there on that occasion?* ¿Estuvo Ud. allí en esa ocasión? ● [v] causar, ocasionar *What do you suppose occasioned that remark?* ¿Qué cree Ud. que ha podido causar esa observación? ○**to be the occasion for** ser motivo de, ser causa de *His motion was the occasion for a heated debate.* Su moción fué causa de un acalorado debate.
occasionally a veces, de vez en cuando.
occupation ocupación, trabajo, oficio.
occupy ocupar *Every seat was occupied.* Todos los asientos estaban ocupados.—*What room do you occupy?* ¿Qué cuarto ocupa Ud.?—*Is this seat occupied?* ¿Está ocupado este asiento?—*What position do you occupy?* ¿Qué posición ocupa Ud.?—*I'm occupied at the moment.* En estos momentos estoy ocupado. ▲ocupar, tomar *School occupies all my time.* La escuela me toma todo el tiempo. ▲ocupar, apoderarse de *The enemy occupied the town.* El enemigo ocupó el pueblo.
ocean océano, mar *How near are we to the ocean?* ¿A qué distancia estamos del mar?
o'clock ○**at ... o'clock** a la(s) ... *The train leaves at seven o'clock.* El tren sale a las siete.
odd raro *He's an odd person.* Es una persona rara. ▲impar *The committee has to have an odd number of members.* La comisión tiene que tener un número impar de miembros. ▲desparejado, suelto *Have you run across an odd glove?* ¿Ha encontrado Ud. por casualidad un guante suelto? ▲suelto *He*

had to do some odd jobs. Tuvo que hacer algunos trabajos sueltos.

odor olor.

of de *We're within ten miles of our destination.* Estamos a diez millas de nuestro destino.—*He's a man of means.* Es un hombre de recursos.—*I've never heard of him.* No he oído nunca hablar de él.—*None of us has ever been there.* Jamás ha estado allí ninguno de nosotros.—*I'm getting tired of this delay.* Me estoy cansando de esta tardanza.—*My house is on the other side of the church.* Mi casa está al otro lado de la iglesia.—*There's a hole in the roof of this house.* Hay un agujero en el tejado de esta casa.—*Could I have a glass of water, please?* Puede darme un vaso de agua, por favor.—*Please give me a piece of that cake.* Déme, por favor, un pedazo de esa torta.—*Three of the prisoners escaped.* Se escaparon tres de los prisioneros.—*Where's the driver of this car?* ¿Dónde está el conductor de este coche? ▲ acerca de *I don't know him personally but I've heard of him.* No le conozco personalmente, pero he oído hablar acerca de él. ▲ con *I've been dreaming of this for a long time.* He estado soñando con esto desde hace mucho tiempo. ▲ en *He must be thinking of her.* Debe estar pensando en ella.

○ **of his, of yours, of theirs** suyo *I met a friend of yours yesterday.* Me encontré ayer con un amigo suyo. ○ **of mine** mío.

‖ *So nice of you to come!* ¡Qué amable ha sido Ud. en venir! ‖ *Call me at a quarter of eight.* Llámeme a las ocho menos cuarto.

off ○ **a mile off** a una milla de distancia. ○ **off and on** de vez en cuando, a intervalos. ○ **to be well off** tener dinero, estar acomodado. ○ **way off** muy lejos.

‖ *Are you taking a week off?* ¿Va Ud. a dejar de trabajar por una semana? ‖ *I'm to have a week off soon.* Voy a tener pronto una semana de vacaciones. ‖ *June's still three months off.* Todavía faltan tres meses para junio. ‖ *It's all off.* No hay nada de lo dicho. ‖ *It's an off year for crops.* No es un buen año para la cosecha. ‖ *Keep off the grass.* No pise el césped. ‖ *Leave the top off.* Déjelo destapado. or No ponga la tapa. ‖ *The power's off.* No hay corriente. ‖ *There's a button off your dress.* Le falta un botón a su vestido. ‖ *The ship anchored three miles off shore.* El barco ancló a tres

millas de la costa. ‖ *The trip's off.* Se ha suspendido el viaje. or Hemos desistido del viaje.

offend ofender.

offense ofensa *It was hard to forgive such an offense.* Era difícil perdonar tal ofensa. ▲ culpa, delito *What offense did he commit?* ¿Qué delito ha cometido?

offer [n] oferta *They made him a good offer.* Le hicieron una buena oferta.

● [v] ofrecer *I'm willing to offer one hundred dollars for it.* Estoy dispuesto a ofrecer cien dólares por ello.— *Did they offer any resistance?* ¿Ofrecieron resistencia?

‖ *May I offer my congratulations?* ¿Me permite Ud. que le felicite?

office oficina *You can see me in my office.* Me puede ver en mi oficina. ▲ cargo *What office does he hold?* ¿Qué cargo desempeña? ▲ personal, gente de la oficina *He invited the whole office.* Invitó a toda la gente de la oficina.

officer oficial *Were you an officer in the army?* ¿Fué Ud. oficial del ejército? ▲ directivo *Yesterday this club elected its officers.* Ayer eligió este club sus directivos.

○ **police officer** policía, agente de policía *Where can I find a police officer?* Dónde puedo hallar policía?

official [n] funcionario *He's a government official.* Es un funcionario público.

● [adj] oficial *Is this official business?* ¿Es un asunto oficial?

often a menudo, con frecuencia *Does this happen often?* ¿Pasa esto a menudo?

○ **how often** ¿cada cuánto tiempo? ¿con qué frecuencia? *How often do trains leave?* ¿Con qué frecuencia salen los trenes?

oil [n] aceite *What kind of oil's in that can?* ¿Qué clase de aceite hay en esa lata? ▲ óleo, cuadro al óleo *I prefer oils to water colors.* Prefiero los cuadros al óleo a las acuarelas.

● [v] engrasar, aceitar *This machine needs oiling.* Es necesario engrasar esta máquina.

O.K. bien *Everything's O.K. now.* Todo está bien ahora.

old viejo *I'm too old for that.* Soy demasiado viejo para eso.—*Wear old clothes.* Lleve ropa vieja. ▲ antiguo *He's an old student of mine.* Es un antiguo discípulo mío.

○ **old man** viejo, anciano *His grandfather's a very old man.* Su abuelo es muy viejo.

‖ *How old are you?* ¿Cuántos años tiene Ud.? *or* ¿Qué edad tiene Ud.? ‖ *He has an old head on his shoulders.* Es muy joven para lo juicioso que es. ‖ *I'm thirty years old.* Tengo treinta años.

olive aceituna, oliva.

olive oil aceite de oliva.

omelet tortilla.

omit omitir.

on a, hacia *It's on the left.* Está a la izquierda. ▲ a *The bell rings on the hour.* El timbre suena exactamente a la hora.—*On the contrary.* Al contrario. ▲ acerca, sobre *What are your ideas on the subject?* ¿Que opina Ud. sobre el asunto? ▲ de, sobre *It's a book on biology.* Es un libro de biología. ▲ de *When are you on duty?* ¿Cuándo está Ud. de servicio?—*I got this on good authority.* Lo supe de buena tinta. *or* Lo supe de buena fuente.—*I'm going away on my vacation next Monday.* Me voy de vacaciones el lunes próximo.— *He got on his feet.* Se puso de pie. ▲ en *Who's on the team?* ¿Quiénes están en el equipo?—*The house is on fire.* La casa está en llamas. *or* La casa está ardiendo. ▲ por cuenta (de) *This is on me.* Esto corre por mi cuenta. ▲ sobre, encima de *Put it on the table.* Póngalo sobre la mesa. ▲ sobre, en *Put it on ice.* Póngalo en hielo.

○ **on credit** al fiado *Do you sell on credit?* ¿Vende Ud. al fiado? ○ **on end** de pie *Stand the book on end.* Ponga Ud. el libro de pie. ○ **on foot** a pie *Can we go on foot?* ¿Podemos ir a pie? ‖ *Wait until later on.* Espere Ud. hasta más adelante. ‖ *Have you got your coat on?* ¿Se ha puesto Ud. el abrigo? ‖ *Is the race on yet?* ¿Ha comenzado ya la carrera? ‖ *Is the cover on the pot?* ¿Tiene el puchero la tapadera puesta? ‖ *Do you have a room on the court?* ¿Tiene Ud. un cuarto que dé al patio? ‖ *The joke's on him.* Le han gastado una broma. ‖ *Do you have it on order?* ¿Lo tiene Ud. pedido? *or* ¿Lo ha encargado Ud.? ‖ *I bought it on the installment plan.* Lo compré a plazos. ‖ *Move on!* ¡Circulen! ‖ *When do you start on your trip?* ¿Cuándo empieza Ud. su viaje? ‖ *He went on an errand.* Salió para hacer un recado. ‖ *Are you open on Saturday?* ¿Abre Ud. los sábados?

once una vez *Let's try to make the call once more.* Tratemos de llamar una **vez** más.—*If you once read it, you'll* never forget it. Si lo lee Ud. una vez, nunca lo olvidará. ▲ en otro tiempo, antiguamente *I was in the army once.* Estuve en el ejército en otro tiempo.

○ **at once** en seguida, inmediatamente *Come at once.* Venga Ud. en seguida. ○ **once in a while** de vez en cuando *You might be nice to me once in a while.* Podrías ser amable conmigo de vez en cuando.

one uno *One or two will be enough.* Uno o dos será bastante.—*One of us can buy the tickets while the others wait here.* Uno de nosotros puede comprar los billetes mientras los demás esperan aquí.—*One has to make the best of it.* Uno tiene que sacar el mejor partido posible. ▲ alguno *If there is one, it should be around here.* Si hay alguno, debería estar cerca de aquí. ▲ un *I have one thought.* No tengo más que un pensamiento.

○ **one at a time** de uno en uno, uno de cada vez. ○ **one by one** uno a uno. ‖ *I prefer the more expensive one.* Prefiero el más caro. ‖ *One has to be careful with fire.* Hay que tener cuidado con el fuego. ‖ *We're all one as to that idea.* Todos tenemos la misma idea.

onion cebolla.

only [*adj*] único *He's the only one there.* Es el único que está allí.

● [*adv*] únicamente *This is only for you.* Esto es únicamente para Ud. ▲ solamente *I only want a little.* Solamente quiero un poco. ● [*conj*] sólo que, pero *I was going to buy it, only you told me not to.* Iba a comprarlo, pero Ud. me dijo que no. ‖ *I'd be only too glad to help you.* Me gustaría mucho ayudarle. ‖ *If you could only help me.* Si pudiera Ud. ayudarme. ‖ *I got here only a moment ago.* No hace más que un momento que llegué.

open [*n*] campo abierto *He walked out into the open.* Salieron a campo abierto.

● [*adj*] abierto *Is the door open?* ¿Está abierta la puerta?—*Do you stay open on Sundays?* ¿Está abierto los domingos?—*Is the road open?* ¿Está abierta la carretera?—*Is the park open to the public?* ¿Está el parque abierto al público?—*The newspaper was open at page five.* El periódico estaba abierto por la página quinta. ▲ franco, sincero *Can't you be more open?* ¿No puede Ud. ser más franco? ▲ sin resolver,

pendiente *That's still an open question.*
Esa es una cuestión todavía sin resolver. ▲en pie *Is your offer still
open?* ¿Está todavía en pie la oferta?
● [v] abrir *Open the door, please.*
Haga el favor de abrir la puerta.—
What time do you open the shop? ¿A
qué hora abre Ud. la tienda?—*They
opened the road to traffic.* Abrieron al
tráfico la carretera. ▲comenzar, empezar *When will they open the meeting?* ¿Cuándo comenzará la reunión?
○ open air aire libre *I love to walk
in the open air.* Me gusta pasear al
aire libre. ○ to open onto dar a *What
do the windows open onto?* ¿A dónde
dan las ventanas? ○ to open up abrir
Open up the package. Abra Ud. el
paquete. ▲abrirse *All the flowers
opened up over night.* Todas las flores
se abrieron durante la noche.
‖ *That's an open secret.* Eso es un
secreto a voces. ‖ *He's always open
to reason.* Siempre atiende a razones.
‖ *When does the fishing season open?*
¿Cuándo se levanta la veda para pescar?

opening [n] abertura *That skirt opening
isn't big enough.* La abertura de esta
falda no es bastante grande. ▲brecha
They made an opening in the wall.
Hicieron una brecha en el muro. ▲va-
cante *Is there an opening in this office?*
¿Hay alguna vacante en esta oficina?
▲claro *The house is in an opening in
the woods.* La casa está en un claro
en el bosque. ▲oportunidad *He never
gave us an opening to bring up the
subject.* Nunca nos dió oportunidad
para plantear la cuestión. ▲inaugura-
ción, apertura *Will you be at the opening of the exhibition?* ¿Estará Ud. en
la inauguración de la exposición?
● [adj] de introducción *I liked the
opening number on the program.* Me
gustó mucho el número de introducción
del programa.

opera ópera.

operate hacer funcionar *How do you
operate this machine?* ¿Cómo se hace
funcionar esta máquina? ▲operar,
hacer una operación *The doctor says
it's necessary to operate.* El médico
dice que es necesario operar.
○ to operate on operar *She's so ill
they're going to have to operate on
her.* Está tan enferma que van a tener
que operarla.

operation funcionamiento *He supervises
the operation of the machines.* Inspec-

ciona el funcionamiento de las máqui-
nas. ▲trabajo *Fixing it will be a
simple operation.* El arreglarlo será
una trabajo sencillo. ▲operación *They
kept the military operations a secret.*
Mantuvieron en secreto las operaciones
militares.—*Do I have to have an operation?* ¿Me tienen que hacer una operación?
○ to be in operation estar funcionando. ○ to go into operation entrar
en vigor *When does that rule go into
operation?* ¿Cuándo entra en vigor ese
reglamento?

operator telefonista (*telephone*); operario
(*machine*); ascensorista (*elevator*).

opinion opinión.

opportunity oportunidad.

opposite [n] contrario *This is the opposite of what I expected.* Esto es lo
contrario de lo que esperaba.
● [adj] contrario, opuesto *You should
go in the opposite direction.* Debe Ud.
ir en la dirección opuesta.
● [prep] enfrente *What's that building opposite here?* ¿Qué es ese edificio
de enfrente?

opposition oposición.

oppression opresión.

or o *Could I have two or three more
cookies?* ¿Puede darme dos o tres
galletas más?—*Hurry or we'll be late.*
Apúrese o llegaremos tarde. ▲u (before o or ho) *Choose one or the other.*
Elija uno u otro.

orange naranja.

orangeade naranjada.

orchard huerto.

orchestra orquesta (*musicians*); [Sp]
patio de butacas, [Mex] lunetario
(*part of theater*).
○ orchestra seat butaca, [Mex] lu-
neta.

order [n] orden [m] *Put these papers in
order.* Ponga Ud. en orden estos papeles.—*Are these papers in order?* ¿Estan
en orden estos papeles?—*In what order
should these cards go?* ¿En qué orden
han de ir estas tarjetas?—*You'll have
to keep order in this hall.* Ud. tendrá
que mantener el orden en esta sala.
▲orden [f] *Did the captain give you
that order?* ¿Le ha dado el capitán
esa orden?—*He joined the Franciscan
order.* Entró en la orden franciscana.
▲pedido *Did you fill the order?* ¿Ha
enviado Ud. el pedido?
● [v] ordenar *He ordered their arrest.*
Ordenó que fueran arrestados. ▲man-
dar *Who ordered you to do this?*

¿Quién le mandó hacer eso? ▲pedir *This is not what I ordered.* Esto no es lo que pedí. ▲encargar *May I order dinner now?* ¿Puedo encargar la comida ahora?

○ in **order** reglamentario *Is this motion in order?* ¿Es reglamentaria esta proposición? ○ in **order** to para, a fin de *I came all the way just in order to see you.* He venido desde tan lejos solamente para verle a Ud. ○ to be in **order** estar en regla *Everything's in order.* Todo está en regla. ○ to **order** around mandar *Stop ordering me around.* Deja de mandarme tanto. ‖ *Is the machinery out of order?* ¿No funciona la maquinaria?

orderly [*adj*] ordenado.

ordinary ordinario, corriente.

organ órgano *He plays the organ in our church.* Toca el órgano en nuestra iglesia.—*This newspaper's the organ of our party.* Este periódico es órgano de nuestro partido.

○ sense **organs** órganos de los sentidos.

organization organización.

organize organizar.

Oriental [*adj, n*] oriental.

origin origen.

original [*n*] original *Is this the original?* ¿Es éste el original?

● [*adj*] primero, primitivo *Who were the original inhabitants?* ¿Quiénes fueron los primeros habitantes? ▲original *That's an original idea.* Esa es una idea original.

originally al principio.

other otro *Sorry, I have other things to do.* Dispénseme, tengo otras cosas que hacer.—*I don't want this one but the other.* No deseo éste, sino el otro.— *Where are the others?* ¿Dónde están los otros?

○ every **other** day un día si otro no. ○ **other** one otro *Give me the other one.* Déme Ud. el otro. ○ the **other** day el otro día.

otherwise de otro modo *He couldn't do otherwise.* No lo pudo hacer de otro modo. ▲si no *You'd better hurry; otherwise you'll be late.* Tiene que darse prisa, si no va a llegar tarde.

ought deber, tener que *He ought to leave before it rains.* Debe salir antes de que llueva. ▲deber *You ought to be ashamed of yourself.* Debía de darle a Ud. vergüenza.

ounce onza.

our nuestro *Where are our seats?* ¿Dónde están nuestros asientos?

ours nuestro *This is ours.* Esto es nuestro.

ourselves nosotros mismos *Let's do it ourselves.* Vamos hacerlo nosotros mismos.

‖ *We fell and hurt ourselves.* Nos caímos y nos hicimos daño.

out [*adv*] fuera *We went to see him yesterday, but he was out.* Fuimos a verle ayer, pero estaba fuera.

● [*prep*] por *Please throw the bottle out the window.* Haga el favor de tirar la botella por la ventana.

○ **out-and-out** perfecto, completo *You're an out-and-out liar.* Eres un perfecto mentiroso. ○ **out** for en plan *He's out for a good time.* Está en plan de divertirse. ○ **out** of por *I did it out of gratitude.* Lo hice por agradecimiento. ○ **out** of fashion pasado de moda. ○ **out** of place fuera de lugar, impropio *That remark was quite out of place.* Ese comentario estaba muy fuera de lugar. ▲fuera de sitio *This book's out of place.* Este libro está fuera de su sitio. ○ **out** of the question imposible *My staying here's out of the question.* Es imposible que me esté aquí. ○ **out**-of-the-way apartado *He lives in an out-of-the-way place.* Vive en un sitio muy apartado. ○ **out** of work sin trabajo. ○ to be **out** of no tener, estar sin *We're all out of cigarettes.* No tenemos cigarillos. ○ to be **out** of step no llevar el paso.

‖ *Have your tickets out.* Tengan Uds. sus billetes preparados. ‖ *The store's out of my way.* No paso por esa tienda. ‖ *Where will I be out of the way?* ¿Dónde me puedo poner que no le moleste? ‖ *Well, out with it!* ¡Caray, hable Ud. sin rodeos! ‖ *The secret's out.* Se ha revelado el secreto. ‖ *What flowers are out now?* ¿Qué flores hay ahora? ‖ *I'm out three dollars.* Me faltan tres dólares.

outdoors al aire libre *The children are playing outdoors.* Los chicos están jugando al aire libre. ▲allá fuera, fuera de la casa *"Where's your mother?" "She's outdoors."* "¿Dónde está tu madre?" "Está allá fuera."

outfit [*n*] traje *I can't afford a new outfit this spring.* No me puedo comprar un nuevo traje esta primavera.

● [*v*] equipar *The team was outfitted by one of the local stores.* Una de las tiendas del barrio equipó a los jugadores.

outlet desagüe *The outlet's clogged up.* El desagüe está obstruido. ▲enchufe (*electrical*) *We need another outlet in* *this room.* Nos hace falta otro enchufe en este cuarto. ▲ salida *Do you think there'll be much of an outlet for this product?* ¿Cree Ud. que tendrá mucha salida este producto?

outline [*n*] silueta, contorno *She drew the outline of the building from memory.* Dibujó de memoria la silueta del edificio. ▲ resumen *Here's a brief outline of his speech.* Aquí tiene Ud. un pequeño resumen de su discurso.

● [*v*] hacer un resumen *Don't bother to outline every chapter.* No se moleste en hacer un resumen de cada capítulo.

outrage [*n*] atrocidad.

outside [*n*] parte de fuera, exterior *Is there a label on the outside of the box?* ¿Hay un rótulo en la parte de fuera de la caja?

● [*adj*] exterior *Do you have an outside room?* ¿Tiene Ud. un cuarto exterior?

● [*adv*] fuera *Wait outside.* Espere fuera.

● [*prep*] fuera de *Is this outside your jurisdiction?* ¿Está esto fuera de su jurisdicción?

○ **on the outside** por fuera.

‖ *The outside of the house is green.* La casa está pintada de verde por fuera.

outsider forastero, extraño.

outstanding destacado.

outward [*adj*] externo, exterior *To all outward appearances they were friends.* Según todas las apariencias eran amigos.

● [*adv*] fuera *They tried to move outward from the crowd.* Trataron de salir fuera de la multitud.

over sobre *The ventilator's over my head.* El ventilador está sobre mi cabeza. ▲ por *It's silly to fight over it.* Es tonto pelearse por eso.—*She threw a shawl over her shoulders.* Se echó un chal por los hombros. ▲ de *We'll laugh over this some day.* Algún día nos reiremos de esto. ▲ a más de *Is it over three miles?* ¿Está a más de tres millas? ▲ encima de *Are you going to wear a coat over your dress?* ¿Va Ud. a llevar un abrigo encima del traje? ▲ en *Don't trip over the rug.* No tropiece en la alfombra.

○ **all over** por todo *He traveled all over the country.* Ha viajado por todo el país. ○ **over again** otra vez *Do it over again.* Hágalo Ud. otra vez. ○ **over and over (again)** repetidas veces, una y otra vez *He heard it over*

and over again. Lo leyó repetidas veces. ○ **over that way** en esa dirección *It's ten miles over that way.* Está a diez millas en esa dirección. ○ **over there** allí *What's going on over there?* ¿Que pasa allí? ○ **to be over** terminar, acabar *What time was the play over?* ¿A qué hora ha terminado la comedia? ‖ *The horse jumped over the fence.* El caballo saltó la valla. ‖ *Think it over.* Piense en eso. *or* Piénselo bien.

overalls mono de mecánico, [*Am*] mameluco.

overboard ‖ *Man overboard!* ¡Hombre al agua!

overcome vencer *They had to overcome a great deal of prejudice.* Tuvieron que vencer muchos prejuicios. ▲ agotar, rendir *She was overcome by the heat.* Estaba agotada por el calor.

overdo exagerar *Exercise is all right if you don't overdo it.* El ejercicio está bien si no se exagera.

○ **to be overdone** estar muy hecho *I ordered a rare steak; this is overdone.* He pedido un filete bastante crudo y éste está muy hecho.

overdue retrasado.

overhear oír por casualidad.

overlook dar a, mirar *Our house overlooks the river.* Nuestra casa da al río. ▲ olvidar, pasar por alto *We overlooked her name when we sent out the invitations.* Se nos olvidó su nombre cuando enviamos las invitaciones. ▲ tolerar, pasar *I'll overlook it this time, but don't let it happen again.* Lo toleraré por esta vez, pero que no pase de nuevo.

overnight ○ **to stop overnight** pasar la noche, pernoctar *I intend to stop there overnight.* Tengo intención de pasar allí la noche.

oversight descuido *He claimed that the mistake was due to an oversight.* Sostenía que la falta fué por un descuido.

oversleep [*v*] dormir demasiado.

overtake alcanzar *Do you think we can overtake them before they get across the border?* ¿Cree Ud. que podremos alcanzarlos antes de que pasan la frontera?

overtime horas extraordinarias *I don't want to work overtime.* No quiero trabajar horas extraordinarias.

overwork [*v*] trabajar demasiado.

○ **to be overworked** estar agotado de tanto trabajar, estar exhausto por el trabajo.

owe deber *How much do I owe you?* ¿Cuánto le debo?

owl lechuza, buho.

own [*adj*] propio *He didn't recognize his own father.* No reconoció a su propio padre.
• [*v*] tener *Do you own any land?* ¿Tiene Ud. tierras?
○ **my own** mío *It's not my own.* No es el mío.

║ *Are these your own things?* ¿Son éstas sus cosas? ║ *Who owns this property?* ¿De quién es esta propiedad?
owner propietario *Who's the owner?* ¿Quién es el propietario?
ox buey.
oyster ostra.

P

pace [*n*] paso *We must quicken our pace.* Tenemos que acelerar el paso.
• [*v*] pasearse *Why are you pacing up and down?* ¿Por qué se pasea de un lado a otro?
○ **to keep pace with** correr parejas con.

pack [*n*] carga *The donkeys were carrying heavy packs.* Los burros llevaban cargas pesadas. ▲ montón *That story is a pack of lies.* Ese cuento es un montón de mentiras. ▲ manada *A pack of wolves attacked our sheep.* Una manada de lobos atacó a nuestras ovejas. ▲ compresa *The ice pack made his throat feel better.* La compresa de hielo le alivió la garganta.
• [*v*] empaquetar *Have you packed your books yet?* ¿Ha empaquetado Ud. ya sus libros?
○ **pack of cards** baraja *Where is that new pack of cards?* ¿Dónde está esa baraja nueva? ○ **to be packed** estar abarrotado, estar atestado *The theater was packed long before the performance began.* El teatro estaba atestado mucho antes de empezar la función. ○ **to pack down** apisonar *They're packing the earth down.* Están apisonando la tierra. ○ **to pack in boxes** encajonar *The fruit will be packed in boxes for shipping.* La fruta será encajonada para el embarque. ○ **to pack off** enviar, despachar *He packed his wife off to the country.* Despachó a su mujer al campo. ○ **to pack up** hacer el equipaje, [*Am*] empacar *He packed up his things and left.* Hizo su equipaje y partió.

package paquete *Has a package arrived for me?* ¿Ha llegado un paquete para mí?

pad [*n*] bloc de papel *Here is a pad to keep notes on.* Aquí hay un bloc de papel para tomar notas.
○ **padded** relleno *I don't like men's suits with the shoulders padded.* No me gustan los trajes de hombre con las hombreras rellenas. ○ **to be padded** tener paja *The company's reports were*

padded. Los informes de la compañía tenían mucha paja.
page [*n*] página *The book is 200 pages long.* El libro tiene 200 páginas.
page [*v*] ║ *If you want me, page me in the dining room.* Si me necesita, que me llamen en el comedor.
pail cubo, balde.
pain [*n*] dolor *I have a pain in my side.* Tengo un dolor en el costado.
• [*v*] doler *Does your foot pain you?* ¿Le duele el pie?—*It pains me to tell you the bad news.* Me duele darle las malas noticias.
○ **to take pains** esmerarse, poner esmero *Take pains to do your work well.* Esmérese en su trabajo para hacerlo bien.
painful doloroso *The operation was very painful.* La operación fué muy dolorosa. ▲ penoso *It is my painful duty to tell you that the work has to be done all over again.* Tengo el penoso deber de comunicarle a Ud. que tiene que hacer su trabajo de nuevo.
painless sin dolor.
paint [*n*] pintura *Look out, that's fresh paint!* ¡Cuidado, la pintura está fresca!
• [*v*] pintar *He paints very well.* Pinta muy bien.
painting pintura, cuadro.
pair par *Where can I get a pair of shoes?* ¿Dónde puedo conseguir un par de zapatos? ▲ pareja *They make a nice pair.* Hacen una buena pareja.
○ **to pair off** emparejarse *The boys and girls paired off for the dance.* Los muchachos y las muchachas se emparejaron para el baile.
pajamas pijama.
pal compañero *We've been pals for years.* Hemos sido compañeros muchos años.
palace palacio.
pale [*adj*] pálido.
palm palma *I have a splinter in the palm of my hand.* Tengo una astilla en la palma de la mano.
palm tree palmera.
pamphlet folleto.
pan cacerola, olla *Put a pan of water on*

the stove. Ponga Ud. una cacerola con agua en la lumbre.

pancake panquec, panqueque [*both Am*].

panel panel, tablero.

pang dolor. ▲remordimiento *He suffered the pangs of conscience.* Tuvo remordimientos de conciencia.

panic pánico, terror.

pansy pensamiento.

pant [*v*] jadear.

pantry despensa.

pants pantalones.

papa papá.

paper [*n*] papel *Have you some good writing paper?* ¿Tiene Ud. buen papel de escribir? ▲periódico *Where is the morning paper?* ¿Dónde está el periódico de la mañana? ▲artículo *He's written a very good paper on the production of rubber.* Ha escrito un artículo muy buene sobre la produccíon del caucho.
● [*v*] empapelar *This room hasn't been papered in five years.* Hace cinco años que este cuarto no ha sido empapelado.
○ **on paper** en teoría, sobre el papel *My profits were just on paper.* Mis ganancias sólo lo fueron en teoría.
○ **paper clip** sujetapapeles, [*Am*] presilla. ○ **paper money** papel moneda.

parachute paracaídas.

parade [*n*] parada, desfile.
● [*v*] desfilar, formar en parada.

paradise paraíso.

paragraph párrafo.

parallel paralelo *The road runs parallel to the river.* La carretera va paralela al río.
○ **to draw a parallel** establecer un paralelo.

paralyze paralizar.

parcel paquete, bulto *I am expecting a parcel from the store.* Estoy esperando un paquete de la tienda.
○ **parcel post** servicio de paquetes postales.

parch secar, abrasar *The grass is parched this summer.* Este verano se ha abrasado la hierba.

pardon [*n*] indulto, perdón *The president granted him a pardon.* El presidente le concedió el indulto.
● [*v*] perdonar *Pardon me, could you tell me the time please?* Perdone, ¿Podría Ud. decirme la hora, por favor? ▲indultar *The governor refused to pardon him.* El gobernador se negó a indultarle.
‖ *I beg your pardon* ("*Excuse me*"). Perdone Ud. *or* Dispense Ud. ‖ *I beg your pardon* ("*I didn't understand*

you"). No le he entendido. *or* Quiere hacer el favor de repetirlo.

pare pelar, mondar.

parents padres *My parents are still living.* Mis padres viven aún.

parish parroquia.

park [*n*] parque *The city has many beautiful parks.* La ciudad tiene muchos parques hermosos.
● [*v*] estacionar, dejar *Where can we park the car?* ¿Dónde podemos dejar el auto? ▲dejar, poner *You can park your things here.* Puede Ud. poner sus cosas aquí.
○ **parking** estacionamiento *No parking.* Prohibido el estacionamiento.

Parliament Parlamento.

parlor salón, sala.

parrot papagayo, loro.

parson párroco.

part [*n*] parte *What part of town do you live in?* ¿En qué parte de la ciudad vive Ud.?—*Mix two parts of rum with one part of lemon juice.* Mézclense dos partes de rón con una de jugo de limón.—*The fence is part wood and part stone.* La cerca es parte de madera y parte de piedra. ▲papel *The actor plays his part well.* El actor hace su papel bien. ▲repuesto, pieza de respuesto *Where can I get some new parts for the car?* ¿Dónde puedo conseguir algunos repuestos nuevos para el automóvil? ▲parte, lado *In arguments he always takes his brother's part.* En las discusiones siempre se pone de parte de su hermano. ▲raya del pelo *The part in your hair isn't straight.* No está derecha la raya de su pelo.
● [*v*] romperse *The cables parted under the strain.* Los cables se rompieron bajo el peso. ▲separarse *We parted without ceremony.* Nos separamos sin cumplidos.
○ **for the most part** por lo general.
○ **part-time work** trabajo por horas.
○ **to part with** desprenderse de *I wouldn't part with that book at any price.* No me desprendería de ese libro a ningún precio. ○ **to take part** tomar parte, participar *He refused to take part in the game.* Rehusó participar en el juego.

partial parcial *I can only make a partial payment.* Solamente puedo hacer un pago parcial.
‖ *He's partial to blondes.* Es aficionado a las rubias.

participate participar.

particle partícula.

particular [n] detalle *This work is complete in every particular.* No falta detalle en este trabajo.
● [adj] particular *He also has his own particular work to do.* Tiene además su trabajo particular que hacer.—*Is he a particular friend of yours?* ¿Es un amigo particular suyo?
O **in particular** en particular *I remember one person in particular.* Me acuerdo en particular de una persona. ‖ *He's very particular about his appearance.* Cuida mucho de su apariencia. ‖ *I can't get a ticket for that particular train.* No puedo conseguir billete para ese tren.

parting partida, despedida.

partition partición, división.

partly en parte, en cierto modo.

partner compañero *He was my partner in the card game.* Era mi compañero en la partida de cartas. ▲ socio *My partner and I just closed a deal.* Acabamos de cerrar el trato, mi socio y yo.

partridge perdiz.

party fiesta *Let's have a party for him before he goes.* Démosle una fiesta antes de que se marche. ▲ grupo *A party of soldiers arrived in a car.* Un grupo de soldados llegó en automóvil. ▲ partido *Which party won the last election?* ¿Qué partido ganó las últimas elecciones? ▲ parte *Both parties failed to appear.* No comparecieron las partes interesadas.
O **dinner party** comida, cena *I went to a big dinner party last night.* Anoche fuí a una gran cena. ‖ *They couldn't prove he was a party to the crime.* No pudieron probar su participación en el crimen.

pass [n] pase, permiso *You'll need a pass to get by the gate.* Necesitará Ud. un pase para pasar por la puerta. ▲ paso *You can't get through the mountain pass at this time of year.* No puede Ud. franquear el paso de la montaña en esta época del año.
● [v] pasar *Will you please pass the bread?* ¿Quiere pasarme el pan, por favor?—*Pass the rope through here and tie it firmly.* Pase la cuerda por aquí y amárrela fuertemente.—*The days pass quickly when you're busy.* Los días pasan rápidamente cuando uno está ocupado.—*I had very poor cards and decided to pass.* No tenía juego y decidí pasar. ▲ pasar por *I pass the bank every day on the way to work.* Todos los días cuando voy al trabajo paso por el banco. ▲ atravesar,

cruzar, pasar por *How long will it take us to pass through the tunnel?* ¿Cuánto tiempo tardaremos en atravesar el túnel? ▲ pasar, aprobar *Did you pass your examination?* ¿Pasó el examen?—*The senate passed the bill yesterday.* El Senado aprobó la ley ayer. ▲ pronunciar *The court passed sentence today.* Hoy pronunció su sentencia el tribunal.
O **to let pass** dejar pasar, pasar por alto *He shouldn't have said that, but let it pass.* No ha debido decir eso, pero dejémoslo pasar. O **to pass around** circular *The story passed around that we were to leave immediately.* Circuló el rumor de que nos marchábamos inmediatamente. O **to pass away** fallecer *Her mother passed away last week.* Su madre falleció la semana pasada. O **to pass off** pasar, hacer pasar *He tried to pass off this fake money on me.* Trató de pasarme esta moneda falsa. O **to pass out** desmayarse, caer redondo *If you give her another drink she'll pass out.* Si le da Ud. otra copa caerá redondo. O **to pass up** pasar por alto *You ought not to pass up an opportunity like that.* No debía Ud. pasar por alto una ocasión como esa.

passage pasillo *Put the light on in the passage.* Encienda la luz del pasillo. ▲ pasaje *I want to book passage on the next ship.* Deseo tomar pasaje en el próximo barco.—*The priest read a passage from the Bible.* El cura leyó un pasaje de la Biblia.

passenger pasajero.

passing [n] muerte *We mourned his passing.* Sentimos su muerte.
● [adj] pasajero, transitorio *This is just a passing fancy.* Esto es solamente un capricho pasajero.

passion pasión *She has a passion for men.* Tiene pasión por los hombres. ▲ cólera, rabia *She flew into a passion.* De repente se encendió en cólera. ‖ *She has a passion for pretty clothes.* A ella le encanta la ropa bonita.

passport pasaporte.

past [n] pasado *Do you know anything about her past?* ¿Sabe Ud. algo de su pasado?
● [adj] pasado *We've been expecting rain for the past week.* Desde la semana pasada estamos esperando que llueva.
O **in the past** antes *It has been very difficult to get tickets in the past.* Antes era muy difícil conseguir boletos.

‖ *I wouldn't put it past him.* Le creo **capaz** de hacer eso. ‖ *It's past noon, let's eat.* Comamos, que son las doce pasadas.

paste [*n*] pasta de pegar *Has anyone seen the paste?* ¿Ha visto alguien la pasta de pegar?
● [*v*] pegar *Paste these labels on the jars.* Pegue estas etiquetas a los tarros.

pastime pasatiempo.

pastor pastor protestante.

pastry pastelería, pasteles.

pasture pasto, dehesa.

pat [*n*] palmada *She gave the child a pat on the shoulder.* Le dió al niño una palmada en el hombro.
● [*v*] acariciar, dar palmadas *I don't like people to pat my cheek.* No me gusta que la gente me acaricie la cara.

patch [*n*] remiendo *The only way you can fix that is to put a patch on it.* La única manera de arreglar esto es poniéndole un remiendo. ▲ parche *He wore a patch on his eye.* Llevaba un parche en un ojo. ▲ mechón *He has a patch of gray in his hair.* Tiene un mechón blanco en el pelo.
● [*v*] remendar *Mother had to patch the seat of his pants.* Mi madre tuvo que remendarle los fondillos.
○ **to patch things up** hacer las paces, reconciliarse *They patched things up after their fight.* Han hecho las paces después de la pelea.

patent patente.

paternal paternal.

path sendero, camino *Take the path that runs along the river.* Tome el camino que va a lo largo del río.
○ **in the path of** en la dirección de, en el camino de *We were directly in the path of the storm.* Nos encontrábamos exactamente en la dirección del huracán.

pathetic patético, conmovedor.

patience paciencia.

patient [*n*] enfermo, paciente *How is the patient this morning?* ¿Cómo está el enfermo esta mañana?
● [*adj*] paciente *He'd be a better teacher if he were more patient.* Sería mejor profesor si fuera más paciente.

patriot patriota.

patriotic patriótico.

patrol [*n*] patrulla *The captain sent out a patrol to scout the terrain.* El capitán envió una patrulla para reconocer el terreno.
● [*v*] hacer la ronda, patrullar *That watchman patrols this street.* Aquel sereno hace la ronda en esta calle.

patron parroquiano, cliente.

pattern dibujo *This rug has a nice pattern.* Esta alfombra tiene un bonito dibujo. ▲ patrón, molde *Where did you get the pattern for your new dress?* ¿Dónde consiguió Ud. el patrón de su nuevo vestido?
‖ *I've always tried to pattern myself after my father.* He tratado siempre de imitar a mi padre.

pause [*n*] descanso, parada *After a brief pause she continued her work.* Después de un breve descanso continuó su trabajo.
● [*v*] hacer una pausa *He paused before continuing his story.* Hizo una pausa antes de continuar el relato.

pave pavimentar *They've finally paved our street.* Por fin han pavimentado nuestra calle.
○ **to pave the way for someone** preparar el camino a alguien.

pavement pavimento, empedrado.

paw pata.

pawn empeñar, dar en prenda.

pay [*n*] paga, sueldo *What pay do you get in your new job?* ¿Qué sueldo cobra Ud. en su nuevo empleo?
● [*v*] pagar *How much did you pay for your car?* ¿Cuánto pagó Ud. por su auto? ▲ valer la pena *It doesn't pay to spend much time on this work.* No vale la pena gastar demasiado tiempo en este trabajo.
○ **paid up** pagado, cancelado *The bills are all paid up.* Todas las facturas están canceladas. ○ **to pay attention** prestar atención. ○ **to pay a visit** hacer una visita *We ought to pay him a visit before he leaves.* Deberíamos hacerle una visita antes de que se marche. ○ **to pay back** devolver *Give me a dollar now and I'll pay you back on Monday.* Déme Ud. un dólar ahora y se lo devolveré el lunes. ○ **to pay cash, to pay down** pagar al contado. ○ **to pay off** pagar *Pay him off and get rid of him.* Páguele y despídalo.
‖ *This machine will pay for itself in no time.* El rendimiento de esta máquina cubrirá los gastos en poco tiempo. ‖ *I went there to pay my respects.* Fuí allí a ofrecer mis respetos.

payment pago.

pea guisante [*Sp*], chícharo [*Mex*], arveja, alverja [*S. A.*].

peace paz.

peaceful tranquilo, pacífico.

peach melocotón.

peacock pavo real.

peak cima, cúspide.

peal estruendo, estrépito.

peanut cacahuete, maní.

pear pera.

pearl perla.

peasant campesino, labriego.

peck (at) picotear.

peculiar peculiar, raro.

pedal pedal.

peel [n] cáscara, pellejo.

● [v] pelar *Peel me an apple.* Pélame una manzana. ▲ pelarse, despellejarse *My face is peeling.* Se me está despellejando la cara.

peep [n] mirada, ojeada *Have a peep at the baby.* Eche Ud. una ojeada al niño.

● [v] atisbar *He's peeping through the curtains.* Está atisbando a través de las cortinas.

‖ *I don't want to hear another peep out of you.* No quiero ni oírles chistar.

peg clavija.

pen pluma *My pen's dry; can you spare some ink?* Mi pluma está seca; ¿tiene Ud. tinta?

O **fountain pen** pluma fuente, estilográfica.

pen O**pig pen** chiquero. O**to pen up** acorralar.

penalty castigo (*punishment*); multa (*fine*).

penance penitencia.

pencil lápiz.

peninsula península.

penitent [*adj; n*] penitente.

penny centavo.

pension [n] pensión *He gets a government pension.* Recibe una pensión del gobierno.

● [v] pensionar *The company pensioned him for life.* La compañía le pensionó por vida.

pensive pensativo.

people gente *Were there many people at the meeting?* ¿Había mucha gente en la reunión? ▲ pueblo *The government doesn't have the support of the people.* El gobierno no tiene el apoyo del pueblo.

pepper pimiento *I cut some peppers for the salad.* Corté unos pimientos para la ensalada. ▲ pimienta *Pass me the pepper, please.* Páseme la pimienta, por favor.

per por *How much do they charge per person?* ¿Cuánto cobran por persona? ‖ *How much is sugar per pound?* ¿Cuánto vale la libra de azúcar?

perceive percibir.

per cent por ciento.

perch [n] percha; perca (*fish*).

perfect [*adj*] perfecto *She gave a perfect performance.* Tuvo una actuación perfecta. ‖ *He's a perfect stranger to me.* Me es totalmente desconocido.

perfect [v] perfeccionar *The method hasn't been perfected yet.* Aún no se ha perfeccionado el método.

perfection perfección.

perform hacer *That magician can perform miracles.* Ese mago puede hacer milagros. ▲ ejecutar *The doctor is performing a difficult operation.* El cirujano está ejecutando una operación delicada.

performance función, representación *Did you enjoy the performance?* ¿Le gustó la representación? ▲ desempeño *She's been careless in the performance of her job.* Se ha descuidado en el desempeño de su cargo. ▲ rendimiento *What is the plane's performance at high altitude?* ¿Cuál es el rendimiento del avión a gran altura?

‖ *The new actor gave a wonderful performance.* El nuevo actor interpretó admirablemente su papel.

perfume perfume.

perhaps quizás *Perhaps it'll rain today.* Quizás llueva hoy.

peril peligro.

period período *This country has enjoyed a long period of peace.* Este país ha disfrutado de un largo período de paz. ▲ punto *You forgot to put a period here.* Se le olvidó a Ud. poner un punto aquí. ▲ hora *I have no classes the third period.* No tengo clases en la tercera hora. ▲ tiempo *He worked here for a short period.* Trabajó aquí por poco tiempo.

perish perecer.

permanent [n] permanente *My hair needs a permanent.* Mi pelo necesita una permanente.

● [*adj*] estable, permanente *Is your job permanent?* ¿Es su trabajo estable?

permission permiso *I got permission to leave early.* Me dieron permiso para salir temprano.

permit [n] permiso *You'll have to get a permit to visit that factory.* Necesitará Ud. un permiso para visitar esa fábrica.

permit [v] permitir *Such behavior shouldn't be permitted.* No se debe ría permitir semejante comportamiento.

perpendicular [*adj; n*] perpendicular.

perpetual perpetuo.

persecute perseguir.

persecution persecución.

persist insistir.
person persona *What sort of person is she?* ¿Qué clase de persona es ella? O **in person** personalmente, en persona *Please deliver this to him in person.* Haga el favor de entregarle esto personalmente.
personal personal *He asked too many personal questions.* Hizo demasiadas preguntas personales.
‖ *He made a personal appearance at the movie theater.* Se presentó en persona en el cine.
personality modo de ser *I don't like his personality.* No me gusta su modo de ser. ▲ personaje *He's a famous personality of the screen.* Es un personaje famoso del cine.
persuade persuadir.
persuasion persuasión.
pertain pertenecer.
pervert [n] pervertido.
pervert [v] pervertir.
pestilence pestilencia.
pet [n] animal (doméstico) *Pets are forbidden in this house.* No se admiten animales en esta casa.
● [v] consentir, mimar *He's been petted by everybody, all his life.* Siempre ha sido mimado por todo el mundo.
petal pétalo.
petition [n] petición.
● [v] suplicar.
petroleum petróleo.
petticoat enaguas [Sp], fustán [Am], fondo [Am].
petty mezquino *Don't be so petty.* No sea tan mezquino.
O **petty cash** gastos menores de caja.
O **petty thing** pequeñeces *Overlook petty things!* ¡No se pare Ud. en pequeñeces!
pheasant faisán.
philosophy filosofía.
phone [n] teléfono.
● [v] telefonear *I must phone the doctor.* Tengo que telefonear al doctor.
O **phone call** llamada telefónica *I want to make a phone call.* Quiero hacer una llamada telefónica.
phonograph fonógrafo.
photograph [n] retrato, fotografía *You'll need a passport photograph.* Necesitará Ud. una fotografía para su pasaporte.
● [v] retratar, fotografiar *He photographed these buildings for the exhibit.* Fotografió estos edificios para la exposición.
photographer fotógrafo.

phrase frase *You can omit that phrase.* Puede omitir esa frase. ▲ expresión *That's a common phrase in this country.* Esa es una expresión corriente en este país.
‖ *Can you phrase your question differently?* ¿Puede Ud. hacer su pregunta en otra forma?
physic purgante.
physical físico.
physician médico.
physics física.
piano piano.
pick [n] pico *The men were working with picks and shovels.* Los hombres trabajaban con picos y palas.
pick [v] coger, [Am] cortar *Is the fruit ripe enough to pick?* ¿Está suficientemente madura la fruta para cogerla? ▲ escoger *I picked a winner that time.* Esa vez escogí un ganador. ▲ abrir con ganzúa, [Am] falsear *We'll have to pick the lock to get into the house.* Habrá que abrir la cerradura con ganzúa para entrar en la casa.
O **to pick a quarrel** buscar camorra.
O **to pick on** elegir *The officer picked on me to do the job.* El oficial me eligió a mí para hacer el trabajo. ▲ meterse con *Pick on someone your own size.* Métase Ud. con alguien de su igual. O **to pick one's teeth** mondarse (*or* limpiarse) los dientes *He knows he shouldn't pick his teeth in public.* El sabe que no debe mondarse los dientes en público. O **to pick out** escoger *He picked out a very nice gift for his wife.* Escogió un regalo muy bonito para su esposa. O **to pick to pieces** hacer trizas *They picked his argument to pieces.* Hicieron trizas su argumento. O **to pick up** recoger *Please pick up the papers.* Recoja Ud. los papeles, por favor. ▲ ganar *The train will pick up speed in a minute.* El tren ganará velocidad en seguida.
‖ *He tried to pick up a girl on the train.* Trató de hacer una conquista en el tren.
pickle encurtido, pepinillo (en vinagre).
‖ *He found himself in quite a pickle.* Se encontró en un lío.
picnic picnic, jira campestre.
O **to go on a picnic** ir de campo, ir de jira campestre.
picture [n] cuadro *They have some beautiful pictures for sale.* Tienen en venta unos hermosos cuadros. ▲ fotografía, retrato *I haven't had my picture taken for years.* No me había hecho sacar una fotografía desde hace años. ▲ pelí-

cula *I like to see a good picture once in a while.* Me gusta ver una buena película de vez en cuando.

● [*v*] imaginarse *I can't quite picture you as a politician.* No me lo puedo imaginar a Ud. como un político.

pie pastel, tarta *Have you any apple pie today?* ¿Tienen Uds. hoy tarta de manzana?

piece pieza *There's a piece missing from the chess set.* Le falta una pieza del juego de ajedrez.—*What is the name of the piece the orchestra is playing?* ¿Cuál es el nombre de la pieza que está tocando la orquesta? ▲ pedazo, trozo *Write your name on this piece of paper.* Escriba Ud. su nombre en este pedazo de papel. ▲ moneda *I just found a fifty-cent piece.* Acabo de encontrar una moneda de cincuenta centavos.

○ **to fall to pieces** hacerse pedazos *It just fell to pieces all at once.* Se hizo pedazos de una vez.

pier muelle.

pierce perforar.

piety piedad.

pig cerdo, puerco, cochino, marrano, [*Am*] chancho.

pigeon paloma.

pile [*n*] pila, rimero *There's a pile of letters on my desk.* Hay una pila de cartas en mi escritorio. ▲ montón *He has piles of money.* Tiene un montón de dinero. ▲ pilote *The piles on this bridge are rotten.* Los pilotes de este puente están podridos.

● [*v*] apilar *Let's pile up these boxes.* Apilemos estas cajas.

piles almorranas, hemorroides.

pill píldora.

pillar pilar, columna.

○ **from pillar to post** de la Ceca a la Meca *He goes from pillar to post.* Anda de la Ceca a la Meca.

pillow almohada.

pillowcase funda (de almohada).

pilot [*n*] piloto.

● [*v*] pilotear.

pimple grano, barro.

pin [*n*] prendedor, broche *She wore a silver pin on her coat.* Llevaba un prendedor de plata en el abrigo.

● [*v*] prenderse *Pin the flower on your lapel.* Préndase la flor en la solapa. ▲ fijar *Will you pin this notice up, please?* ¿Quiere Ud. fijar este aviso, por favor?

○ **pinned** aprisionado *The two men were pinned under the wreckage.* Los dos hombres estaban aprisionados debajo de los escombros. ○ **safety pin** im-

perdible [*Sp*], alfiler de gancho [*Am*]. ○ **straight pin** alfiler. ○ **to pin down** hacer concretar *You can't pin him down to facts.* No se le puede hacer concretar los hechos.

pinch [*n*] pellizco *He gave me a pinch on the arm.* Me dió un pellizco en el brazo. ▲ pizca *This stew needs a pinch of salt.* Este guisado necesita una pizca de sal.

● [*v*] pellizcar *Stop pinching me.* Déjese de pellizcarme. ▲ cogerse *I pinched my finger in the door.* Me cogí el dedo en la puerta.

pine pino.

pineapple piña.

pingpong pingpong.

pink [*adj*] rosado.

● [*n*] color de rosa.

pint pinta.

pioneer pionero, iniciador.

pious piadoso.

pipe tubo, cañería. *There's a leak in that pipe.* En esa cañería hay un escape. ▲ pipa *Do you smoke a pipe?* ¿Fuma Ud. en pipa?

● [*v*] traer por cañería *They pipe the water here from a spring.* Traen el agua por cañería desde el manantial.

pistol pistola.

pit hoyo *We'll burn our rubbish in the pit.* Quemaremos la basura en el hoyo. ▲ hueso *Be careful not to swallow the pit of the cherry.* Tenga cuidado de no tragarse el hueso de la cereza.

○ **pit of the stomach** boca del estómago.

pitch [*n*] tono *That singer doesn't have the right pitch.* Ese cantante no da el tono exacto.

● [*v*] lanzar, tirar *Pitch the ball to me.* Tíreme la pelota. ▲ armar *Where shall we pitch the tent?* ¿Dónde armaremos la tienda?

○ **to pitch in** poner manos a la obra *Pitch in and get some work done.* Manos a la obra y hagamos algún trabajo.

pitcher jarro, [*Am*] pichel *Send me up a pitcher of ice-water.* Mándeme un jarro de agua helada. ▲ lanzador, [*Am*] picher *Who is the pitcher for today's game?* ¿Quién es el picher en el partido de hoy?

pitiful lastimoso.

pity [*n*] lástima *It's a pity we can't go with you.* Es lástima que no podamos ir con Ud. ▲ lástima, compasión *I don't feel any pity for him.* No siento ninguna lástima por él.

● [v] compadecer *He wants people to pity him.* Quiere que la gente lo compadezca.

place sitio, lugar *Be sure to put it back in the same place.* Acuérdese de volver a ponerlo en su sitio. ▲ parte *The play is weak in several places.* La comedia es floja en algunas partes. ▲ puesto *She should be put in her place.* Hay que ponerla en su puesto. ● [v] colocar, poner *The table can be placed over there for now.* Por ahora, se puede colocar la mesa allí.—*The girl was placed in the office as a secretary.* Colocaron a la muchacha de secretaria en la oficina.

○ in the first place en primer lugar. ○ to take place tener lugar, ocurrir *That must have taken place while I was away.* Eso debe haber ocurrido cuando yo estaba ausente.

‖ *I've lost my place in the book I was reading.* He perdido la página del libro que estaba leyendo. ‖ *It's not my place to report the incident.* No me toca a mí informar sobre el incidente. ‖ *Nothing can take the place of a square meal.* No hay nada como una buena comida. ‖ *I'm sure I've met him before, but I can't quite place him.* Estoy seguro de haberle visto antes, pero no puedo recordar exactamente quién es.

placid apacible.

plague plaga.

plain [n] llano *I've lived most of my life on the plains.* He vivido la mayor parte de mi vida en los llanos.

● [adj] corriente *She's plain-looking but she has a lot of character.* Su tipo es muy corriente pero tiene mucho carácter. ▲ sencillo *We have a very plain house.* Tenemos una casa muy sencilla.

‖ *I'll put it in the plainest language I can.* Se lo diré lo más claro que pueda. ‖ *It's in plain sight.* Está a la vista. ‖ *It's quite plain that he's going to be late.* Desde luego llegará tarde.

plan [n] plano *Do you have a plan of the house?* ¿Tiene Ud. un plano de la casa? ▲ plan *What are your plans for tomorrow?* ¿Cuáles son sus planes para mañana?

● [v] planear, pensar *Where do you plan to spend the summer?* ¿Dónde piensa Ud. pasar el verano? ▲ planear, proyectar *I planned the whole thing this way.* Planeé todo en esta forma.

○ to plan on contar con *You'd better not plan on it.* Es mejor que no cuente Ud. con ello.

plane [n] aeroplano, avión *Have you ever been up in a plane?* ¿Ha subido Ud. alguna vez en aeroplano?

● [adj] plano *That's not a plane surface.* Esto no es una superficie plana.

planet planeta.

plank tablón.

plant [n] planta *No plants will grow in this cold climate.* No crece ninguna planta en este clima tan frío. ▲ fábrica, planta *The manager offered to show me around the plant.* El director ofreció mostrarme toda la fábrica.

● [v] sembrar, plantar *The seeds I planted last week are just beginning to come up.* Comienzan a nacer las semillas que sembré la semana pasada.

plaster [n] estuco, repello *The plaster on the walls is all cracked.* Está agrietado el estuco de las paredes.

● [v] revocar, repellar *Have they finished plastering the walls?* ¿Han terminado de revocar las paredes?

○ in a plaster cast enyesado *She has her arm in a plaster cast.* Tiene el brazo enyesado. ○ mustard plaster sinapismo, cataplasma de mostaza *I need a mustard plaster for my cold.* Necesito una cataplasma de mostaza para mi catarro.

‖ *Her clothes were plastered with mud.* Su ropa estaba toda enlodada.

plastic plástico, sintético.

plastics materiales plásticos.

plate [n] plato *Pass your plate and I'll give you some more food.* Pase su plato y le daré más comida.—*This plate of meat will be enough.* Bastará con este plato de carne. ▲ plancha, lámina *The sides of the truck have steel plates on them.* Los lados del camión llevan planchas de acero.

○ plated chapeado, enchapado *I have a gold-plated watch.* Tengo un reloj enchapado de oro.

platform plataforma.

platter fuente.

play [n] representación, obra teatral *Are there any good plays in town?* ¿Representan alguna buena obra en la ciudad? ▲ juego *There's a lot of play in this steering wheel.* Este volante tiene bastante juego.

● [v] jugar *The boys are playing in the yard.* Los muchachos están jugando en el patio.—*He played his highest card.* Jugó su carta más alta. ▲ bromear *You mustn't take it to heart because he was just playing.* No debe tomarlo a pecho, pues sólo estaba bromeando. ▲ hacer el papel de *He plays (the part of*) *the king.* Hace el papel de rey. ▲ tocar *The orchestra is playing now.* Ahora está tocando la orquesta.

○ **to be played out** estar agotado *or* rendido *After a hard day's work he's played out.* Está agotado después de un día de trabajo duro. ○ **to play a joke** hacer una broma, gastar una broma *He played a joke on his friend.* Le gastó una broma a su amigo. ○ **to play around** divertirse *You've been playing around long enough.* Ha estado Ud. divirtiéndose bastante tiempo. ▲ estar perdiendo el tiempo *Stop playing around and get to work.* Deje de estar perdiendo el tiempo y póngase a trabajar. ○ **to play fair** jugar limpio. ○ **to play on** estimular *The movies always play on your emotions.* Las películas siempre estimulan las emociones. ○ **to play up** elogiar, ensalzar *He played up the good things about the job instead of the bad ones.* Sólo elogiaba las ventajas del empleo en lugar de mencionar sus inconvenientes.

player jugador.

playground patio de recreo.

playmate compañero de juego.

plea declaración *What was the plea of the accused?* ¿Cuál fué la declaración del acusado? ▲ alegato *The lawyer made a plea in defense of his client.* El abogado presentó un alegato en defensa de su cliente. ‖ *The church made a plea for more money.* La iglesia solicitó más dinero.

plead suplicar, pedir (*beg*); defender (*a lawsuit*). ○ **to plead guilty (not guilty)** declararse culpable (inocente).

pleasant agradable.

please agradar, gustar *Does this please you or do you want something else?* ¿Le gusta esto o desea otra cosa? ▲ complacer, contentar *She's a hard person to please.* Es una persona difícil de contentar. ▲ gustar *Do as you please; it makes no difference to me.* Haga Ud. como guste; a mí me da lo mismo. ‖ *Please shut the door.* Cierre la puerta, por favor.

pleasing complaciente.

pleasure placer.

pledge [*n*] compromiso para ayudar *Have you signed your pledge to the Red Cross?* ¿Ha firmado su compromiso para ayudar a la Cruz Roja? ● [*v*] prometer *We pledge our support to your organization.* Prometemos nuestro apoyo a su organización. ○ **to pledge allegiance** prestar juramento *Have you pledged allegiance to the flag?* ¿Ha prestado Ud. juramento a la bandera?

plentiful copioso, abundante.

plenty bastante *I have plenty of matches, thanks.* Tengo bastantes fósforos, gracias. ▲ mucho *There's plenty more in the kitchen.* Hay mucho más en la cocina. ‖ *That dress is plenty big enough on you.* Ese vestido le queda bastante grande.

pliers alicates, tenazas.

plight apuro, aprieto.

plot [*n*] conspiración, complot *He was mixed up in a plot against the President.* Se hallaba complicado en una conspiración contra el Presidente. ▲ trama *Did the play have a good plot?* ¿Era buena la trama de la pieza? ● [*v*] conspirar *Who's plotting against us now?* ¿Quién está conspirando contra nosotros ahora? ○ **plot of land** solar, lote *I'm going to buy a plot of land in the country.* Voy a comprar un lote de terreno en el campo.

plow [*n*] arado. ● [*v*] arar.

pluck [*n*] valor, ánimo *For a sick man he has a lot of pluck.* Tiene mucho ánimo por ser un hombre enfermo. ● [*v*] desplumar *Have the chickens been plucked?* ¿Han desplumado los pollos?

plug tapón; enchufe (*electricity*).

plum ciruela.

plume pluma.

plump rollizo, regordete.

plunge zambullir, zambullirse.

plural plural.

plus más.

pneumonia neumonía.

poached escalfado *I want some poached eggs on toast.* Quiero huevos escalfados en tostadas.

pocket [*n*] bolsillo *Will you keep this in your pocket for me?* ¿Quiere Ud. guardarme esto en su bolsillo? ● [*v*].guardarse *He paid the bill with my money and pocketed the change.* Pagó la cuenta con mi dinero y se guardó la vuelta. ○ **air pocket** bolsa de aire. ○ **pocket knife** cortaplumas, cuchilla.

pocketbook cartera.

poem verso, poema.

poet poeta.

poetry poesía.

point [*n*] punta *He broke the point of his knife.* Rompió la punta du su cuchillo. —*The boat we saw has sailed around the point.* El barco que vimos ha navegado alrededor de la punta. ▲punto *I disagree on almost every point.* Estoy en desacuerdo con casi todos los puntos. ▲punto, lugar *The train stopped at a point halfway between the two stations.* El tren se paró en un lugar a medio camino entre las dos estaciones. ▲rumbo (*of mariner's compass*). ▲tanto, punto *Our team made 23 points.* Nuestro equipo hizo veintitres tantos. ● [*v*] apuntar *The gun's pointed north.* El cañón apunta hacia el norte. ▲señalar *He pointed to where the house is located.* Señaló hacia donde está la casa.

○ **decimal point** coma *Where should we put the decimal point?* ¿Dónde debemos poner la coma? ○ **on the point of** a punto de *We were on the point of leaving when some visitors arrived.* Estábamos a punto de salir cuando llegaron unas visitas. ○ **point of view** punto de vista. ○ **to be beside the point** no venir al caso, estar fuera del tema. ○ **to make a point of** esmerarse *He makes a point of being polite.* Se esmera en ser cortés. ○ **to point out** indicar, mostrar *Point out the place you told me about.* Muéstreme el lugar de que me habló. ○ **to point toward** indicar, mostrar *All the signs point toward a hard winter.* Todo indica que vamos a tener un invierno muy crudo. ○ **to the point** al grano *Let's get to the point!* ¡Vamos al grano! ‖ *His answer shows that he missed the real point of the argument.* Su respuesta indica que no ha comprendido el verdadero sentido del argumento. ‖ *Don't you think the job has its good points?* ¿No cree Ud. que el trabajo tiene su lado (*or* aspecto) bueno?

poise [*n*] aplomo, serenidad.

poison [*n*] veneno *This bottle contains poison.* Esta botella contiene veneno. ● [*v*] envenenar *Our dog has been poisoned.* Han envenenado a nuestro perro. ○ **poison gas** gas asfixiante.

poisonous venenoso.

poke [*n*] puyón [*Am*], empujón *He gave me a poke in the back.* Me dió un empujón en la espalda. ● [*v*] puyar [*Am*], dar codazos *Stop poking me with your elbow.* Deje de estarme puyando con el codo. ○ **to poke fun at** burlarse de. ○ **to poke up** atizar *Poke up the fire.* Atice el fuego. ‖ *She pokes her nose into everybody's business.* Se mete en todo.

pole poste, palo; polo (*geography*). ○ **The North Pole** El Polo Norte. ○ **The South Pole** El Polo Sur.

police [*n*] policía *The police were called in to stop the fight.* Llamaron a la policía para que pusiera fin a la pelea. ● [*v*] vigilar *This street is well-policed, at night especially.* Esta calle está bien vigilada, especialmente de noche. ○ **police station** comisaría, prefectura, delegación de policía, [*Am*] estación de policía.

policeman agente de policía.

policy política *Their foreign policy has changed in recent years.* Han cambiado su política exterior en los últimos años. ▲costumbre, norma *It's the policy of our company never to cash checks.* Nuestra compañía tiene la costumbre de no cambiar nunca cheques. ○ **insurance policy** póliza de seguro.

polish [*n*] barniz *Where can I buy some polish for the furniture?* ¿Dónde puedo comprar barniz para los muebles? ● [*v*] lustrar, limpiar *I must get my shoes polished.* Necesito lustrar mis zapatos.

polite cortés.

political político.

politician político.

politics política.

poll encuesta *We'll have to take a poll to see what the public opinion is.* Hay que hacer una encuesta para conocer la opinión pública.

polls (*voting place*) colegio electoral [*Sp*].

pollute contaminar.

pomp pompa.

pond charca.

ponderous pesado.

pony jaca, caballito, [*Arg*] petiso.

pool [*n*] charco *There was a pool of water on the floor.* Había un charco en el piso. ▲chapó *Let's play a game of pool.* Juguemos una partida de chapó. ● [*v*] reunir *We pooled our money to buy a car.* Reunimos nuestro dinero para comprar un carro. ○ **swimming pool** piscina.

poor pobre *Many poor people live in this neighborhood.* En este barrio vive mucha gente pobre.—*The poor fellow is blind.* El pobre hombre es ciego. ▲ malo *This is poor soil for potatoes.* Esta tierra es mala para las patatas. ○ the **poor** los pobres *We are taking up a collection for the poor.* Estamos haciendo una colecta para los pobres.

pop [*n*] papá *His pop takes him to the movies every Saturday.* Su papá le lleva al cine todos los sábados. ▲ taponazo *The bottle opened with a loud pop.* Se abrió la botella de un fuerte taponazo.
● [*v*] asomar de repente *She popped her head out of the window.* De repente asomó la cabeza fuera de la ventana.
○ **pop corn** palomitas de maíz, cancha. ○ **soda pop** bebida gaseosa. ○ to **pop the question** pedir la mano *She doubted that it was his intention to pop the question.* Dudaba que él tuviera la intención de pedirle la mano.

poplar álamo.
popular popular.
population población.
porcelain porcelana.
porch porche, portal.
pore [*n*] poro *After a hot bath your pores are open.* Después de un baño caliente se abren los poros.
pore [*v*] leer (*or* estudiar) atentamente *He is poring over his book.* Estudia atentamente en su libro. *or* Lee atentamente su libro.
pork puerco.
port puerto *When do you expect this ship to get into port?* ¿Cuándo espera Ud. que este barco toque puerto?
○ **port side** babor *Man overboard, on the port side!* ¡Hombre al agua, por babor!
port oporto *Port is my favorite wine.* Oporto es mi vino favorito
portable portátil.
porter maletero, mozo de cuerda, cargador.
portion parte, porción.
portrait retrato.
position posición *If you are not comfortable, change your position.* Cambie de posición si no está cómodo. ▲ sitio *From this position you can see the whole field.* Desde este sitio se puede ver todo el campo. ▲ puesto, empleo *He has a good position with a wholesale house.* Tiene un buen empleo en un casa de venta al por mayor. ▲ posición, situación *This places me in a very difficult position.* Esto me coloca en una posición muy difícil. ▲ opinión

What's your position in regard to this new law? ¿Cuál es su opinión respecto a la nueva ley?
positive positivo; seguro (*certain*).
possess poseer.
possession posesión *This island is a possession of the United States.* Esta isla es una posesión de los Estados Unidos. ▲ posesión, poder *I have in my possession a book with your name on it.* Tengo en mi poder un libro con su nombre escrito.
○ **possessions** bienes *He gave away all his possessions before he went into the army.* Donó todos sus bienes antes de entrar en el ejército.
possibility posibilidad.
possible posible *Be here by nine, if possible.* Esté Ud. aquí a las nueve, si le es posible.
possibly posiblemente.
post [*n*] poste, pilar *The fence needs some new posts.* La cerca necesita unos postes nuevos. ▲ puesto *He guarded his post.* Guardó su puesto. ▲ puesto, cargo *He has just been appointed to a new post in the government.* Acaba de ser designado para un nuevo puesto en el gobierno. ▲ campamento, guarnición *The whole post was notified of the change in rules.* Se comunicó al campamento la modificación del reglamento.
● [*v*] apostar *Troops were posted to guard the bridge.* Se apostaron fuerzas para guardar el puente. ▲ fijar, colocar *Post it on the bulletin board.* Fíjelo en el tablero de anuncios. ▲ fijar *Post no bills.* No se fijen carteles.
postage franqueo.
postal postal.
poster cartel.
postman cartero.
postmark sello de la oficina de correos.
post office correos, oficina de correo.
postpone posponer.
posture postura.
pot olla *There is a pot of soup on the stove.* Hay una olla de sopa sobre la lumbre.
○ **flower pot** tiesto, maceta. ○ **pot of tea**, tea pot tetera.
potato patata [*Sp*], papa [*Am*].
pottery cerámica.
pouch saquito, faltriquera.
poultry aves de corral.
pound [*n*] libra *Give me a pound of tobacco, please.* Deme una libra de tobaco, por favor. ▲ libra esterlina *He owes me six pounds.* Me debe seis libras esterlinas.
pound [*v*] aporrear, golpear *We pounded*

on *the door for five minutes.* Estuvimos aporreando la puerta durante cinco minutos.

pour echar *Pour the water into these glasses.* Eche el agua en estos vasos. ▲ servir *Please pour me a cup of coffee.* Sírvame una taza de café, por favor. ▲ llover a cántaros *Don't go out, it's pouring.* No salgas, está lloviendo a cántaros.

○ **to pour out** vaciar *He poured out the water in the pitcher.* Vació la jarra de agua.

poverty pobreza.

powder [*n*] polvos *I need some powder and lipstick.* Necesito polvos y lápiz de labios. ▲ pólvora *There's enough powder here to blow up the whole town.* Aquí hay suficiente pólvora para volar el pueblo entero.

● [*v*] empolvarse *Pardon me, I have to go powder my nose.* Perdóneme, tengo que ir a empolvarme.

power potencia, fuerza motriz *How much power does this machine have?* ¿Qué potencia tiene esta máquina? ▲ potencia *That country was once a great world power.* Ese país fué una vez una gran potencia mundial. ▲ poder *I'll do everything in my power.* Haré todo lo que esté en my poder.

○ **horsepower** caballo de fuerza. ○ **in power** en el poder *This party won't be in power much longer.* Este partido no permanecerá mucho en el poder.

powerful poderoso.

practical práctico.

practically practicamente, de una manera práctica *Try to do things more practically.* Trate de hacer las cosas de una manera más práctica.

‖ *We're practically there.* Estamos ya casi llegando.

practice práctica *I'm a little out of practice.* Estoy un poco fuera de práctica. *or* Estoy un poco desentrenado. ▲ costumbre *We make it a practice to get to work on time.* Tenemos por costumbre llegar a tiempo al trabajo. ▲ clientela *That doctor has a rather small practice.* Ese médico tiene una clientela más bien pequeña.

● [*v*] hacer ejercicios, practicar, estudiar *He's practicing on the piano.* Está haciendo ejercicios de piano. ▲ ejercer *He practiced law for five years.* Ejerció la abogacía durante cinco años.

○ **in practice** en la práctica.

praise [*n*] elogio, alabanza.

● [*v*] alabar, elogiar.

pray rezar, orar.

prayer oración, plegaria.

preach predicar.

preacher predicador.

precede preceder.

precinct distrito.

precious valioso, precioso.

precipice precipicio.

precise preciso.

precision precisión.

predecessor predecesor.

predict predecir, pronosticar.

preface prefacio.

prefer preferir.

preference preferencia.

pregnant preñada, encinta, embarazada.

○ **pregnant with** repleto de, lleno de.

prejudice prejuicio (*bias*); perjuicio (*harm*).

● [*v*] prejuzgar.

preliminary preliminar.

premium prima.

○ **at a premium** difícil de obtener; sobre la par.

preparation producto, preparación *Can you recommend a good preparation for dry hair?* ¿Puede recomendarme un buen producto para el pelo seco? ▲ preparativo *Have you made all the preparations for the trip?* ¿Ha hecho todos los preparativos para el viaje?

prepare preparar, prepararse.

prepay pagar por adelantado.

prescribe prescribir *We must do what the law prescribes.* Debemos hacer lo que prescribe la ley. ▲ recetar *The doctor prescribed quinine.* El doctor recetó quinina.

prescription receta.

presence presencia.

present [*n*] presente *The future can't be any worse than the present.* El futuro no puede ser peor que el presente. ▲ regalo, presente *Did you give him a present for his birthday?* ¿Le hizo Ud. un regalo para su cumpleaños?

○ **at present** ahora *He's too busy to see you at present.* Está demasiado ocupado para verle a Ud. ahora. ○ **for the present** ahora *That'll be enough for the present.* Eso bastará por ahora. ○ **to be present** asistir *How many people are expected to be present?* ¿Cuántas personas se espera que asistan?

‖ *What's your present address?* ¿Qué dirección tiene Ud. ahora?

present [*v*] presentar *The soldiers presented a good appearance.* Los soldados presentaban buen aspecto. ▲ regalar

They presented him with a gold watch. Le regalaron un reloj de oro.

preserve [v] preservar *To preserve this meat it must be kept on ice.* Para preservar esta carne hay que guardarla en hielo. ‖ *Do you like strawberry preserves?* ¿Le gustan las fresas en conserva?

preside presidir.

president presidente.

press [n] prensa *There are three steel presses in the factory.* Hay tres prensas de acero en la fábrica.—*Will the press be admitted to the conference?* ¿Se admitirá a la prensa en la conferencia? ▲ tirada *The edition's ready to go to press.* Esta edición está lista para la tirada. ● [v] planchar *Where can I get my suit pressed?* ¿Dónde me pueden planchar el traje? ▲ apretar, tocar *Press the button and see what happens.* Apriete el botón y vea lo que pasa. ▲ empujar, agolparse *The crowd pressed against the gates.* La muchedumbre se agolpaba contra las puertas. ▲ insistir en *or* sobre *I wouldn't press the matter any further if I were you.* Yo en su caso no insistiría más sobre el asunto. ○ **pressing** urgente *I have a pressing engagement elsewhere.* Tengo un compromiso urgente en otro sitio.

pressure presión *Check the tire pressure.* Mire como estan de presión los neumáticos. ▲ urgencia, prisa *I don't work well under pressure.* No trabajo bien con prisa.

pretense pretensión.

pretty [adj] bonito *She's a very pretty girl.* Es una muchacha muy bonita. ● [adv] bastante *I've been pretty busy since I saw you last.* He estado bastante ocupado desde la última vez que le ví a Ud.

prevail prevalecer, predominar.

prevent impedir, evitar.

previous previo.

price [n] precio.

prick [n] punzada. ● [v] punzar, pinchar, [Am] puyar.

pride [n] orgullo *His pride won't let him admit he's wrong.* Su orgullo no le permitirá admitir que está equivocado. ○ **to pride oneself** enorgullecerse *He prides himself on his taste.* Se enorgullece de su buen gusto.

priest sacerdote, cura.

primary [adj] primario, primero.

prime [n] flor *That man's in the prime of*

life. Ese hombre está en la flor de la vida. ● [adj] capital *That job's of prime importance.* Ese trabajo es de capital importancia. ● [v] preparar, alistar *The troops were primed for action.* Las tropas estaban ya preparadas para la acción.

primitive primitivo.

prince príncipe.

princess princesa.

principal [n] capital, [Sp] principal *The principal was five hundred dollars.* El capital era de quinientos dólares. ▲ director *The principal called the teachers into his office.* El director llamó a los profesores a su despacho. ● [adj] principal *This is one of the principal arguments against it.* Este es uno de los principales argumentos en contra.

principle principio *I admire a man who has such principles.* Admiro a un hombre que tenga talés principios. ▲ teoría *What principle does this machine work on?* ¿En qué teoría se basa el funcionamiento de esta máquina? ○ **in principle** en principio.

print [n] tipo, letra *The print in this book's too small.* La letra de este libro es demasiado pequeña. ▲ grabado *The museum has a fine collection of prints.* El museo tiene una magnífica colección de grabados. ▲ estampado *We're selling a lot of cotton prints.* Estamos vendiendo muchos estampados de algodón. ▲ copia *How many prints do you want from this negative?* ¿Cuántas copias quiere Ud. de este negativo? ● [v] imprimir, tirar *Where was this book printed?* ¿Dónde imprimieron este libro? ▲ publicar *The letter was printed in yesterday's paper.* Ayer se publicó la carta en el periódico. ▲ escribir en letra de imprenta *Please print your name.* Escriba su nombre en letras de imprenta, por favor. ‖ *That book's hard to get because it's out of print.* Es difícil conseguir ese libro porque la deción está agotada.

printer impresor.

prior previo, anterior. ○ **prior to** antes de.

prison cárcel, prisión.

prisoner preso *A prisoner's just escaped.* Acaba de escaparse un preso. ▲ prisionero *How many prisoners were taken in the last battle?* ¿Cuántos prisioneros se capturaron en la última batalla?

privacy ‖ *Can't we have any privacy*

around here? ¿No podemos estar solos por aquí?

private [*n*] soldado raso *He was a private in the last war.* Fué soldado raso en la última guerra.

● [*adj*] particular *This is a private beach.* Esta es una playa particular. ○ **in private** en privado.

privilege privilegio.

privileged privilegiado.

prize [*n*] premio *There'll be a fifty-dollar prize for the best short story.* Habrá un premio de cincuenta dólares para el mejor cuento.

● [*adj*] premiado *The prize story was written by a friend of mine.* El cuento premiado fué escrito por un amigo mío. ▲ mejor, que merece premio *That's the prize movie of the year.* Esa es la mejor película del año.

○ **prized** preciado, estimado *This is one of my most prized possessions.* Esta es una de mis posesiones más preciadas.

probable probable.

probably probablemente.

problem problema.

procedure proceder, procedimiento.

proceed proceder, continuar.

proceeds producto.

process proceso.

procession procesión.

proclaim proclamar.

proclamation proclamación.

procure lograr, conseguir.

produce [*n*] productos *There's no market for our produce.* No hay mercado para nuestros productos.

produce [*v*] presentar *Can you produce the facts to prove your argument?* ¿Puede Ud. presentar las pruebas que justifiquen su alegato? ▲ producir *How many planes does the factory produce a month?* ¿Cuántos aviones produce la fábrica al mes? ▲ producir, provocar *The purpose of the medicine is to produce a high fever.* El objeto de la medicina es provocar una fiebre alta. ▲ montar *How much will it cost to produce the play?* ¿Cuánto costará montar la comedia?

production película, producción teatral *Who's directing this production?* ¿Quién está dirigiendo esta película? ▲ producción *Production at the factory's slowing up.* Está disminuyendo la producción de la fábrica.

productive productivo.

profane profano.

profession profesión *What's your profession?* ¿Cuál es su profesión? ▲ pro-

fesión, protesta *I'm not sure of her professions of friendship.* Dudo de sus protestas de amistad.

professional [*adj, n*] profesional.

professor profesor.

profile perfil.

profit [*n*] beneficio, ganancia *The profits from the business will be divided equally.* Los beneficios del negocio se dividirán equitativamente.

● [*v*] aprovechar, sacar provecho *I hope he profits by this experience.* Espero que saque provecho de esta experiencia.

profitable provechoso.

profound profundo.

profuse profuso.

program programa.

progress [*n*] progreso(s) *That country's made great progress recently.* Ese país ha hecho muchos progresos últimamente.

○ **in progress** en curso, en marcha *This work's still in progress.* El trabajo está aún en marcha.

progress [*v*] progresar *We've progressed since those days.* Hemos progresado desde aquellos días. ▲ marchar, andar *How are things progressing?* ¿Cómo marchan las cosas?

progressive [*adj*] progresivo.

prohibit prohibir.

prohibition prohibición.

project [*n*] proyecto *Let's work on this project.* Trabajemos en este proyecto.

project [*v*] proyectar *Moving pictures here are projected on the wall.* Las películas aquí son proyectadas en la pared. ▲ sobresalir, resaltar *That balcony projects too far from the wall.* Ese balcón sobresale demasiado de la pared.

projection proyección.

prolong prolongar.

prominent prominente, eminente.

promise [*n*] promesa *You've broken your promise.* Ha faltado Ud. a su promesa.

● [*v*] prometer *We promised the child a present.* Le hemos prometido un regalo al niño.

‖ *The new airplanes show great promise.* Los nuevos aviones prometen mucho.

promote ascender, promover; fomentar (*help to grow*).

promotion ascenso, promoción.

prompt [*v*] impulsar *What prompted you to say that?* ¿Qué le impulsó a decir eso?

‖ *She sent a prompt reply to my letter.* Me contestó pronto la carta.

pronoun pronombre.

pronounce pronunciar *How do you pronounce this word?* ¿Cómo pronuncia Ud. esta palabra? ▲ declarar *The judge pronounced him guilty of murder.* El juez le declaró culpable de asesinato.

pronunciation pronunciación.

proof prueba *What proof do you have that he's the man we want?* ¿Qué pruebas tiene Ud. de que él es el que buscamos?

   ○ **fire-proof** a prueba de incendio, contra incendio.

proofread ‖ *We finished proofreading the book.* Hemos terminado la corrección de pruebas del libro.

propaganda propaganda.

propagate propagar.

propeller hélice.

proper propio *His office is not in the building proper.* La oficina no está en el propio edificio. ▲ correcto *What's the proper way to address a business letter?* ¿Cuál es la manera correcta de dirigir una carta comercial?

properly propiamente, apropiadamente.

property propiedad.

prophecy profecía.

prophet profeta.

proportion proporción.

proposal propuesta.

propose proponer matrimonio *When did he propose to her?* ¿Cuándo le propuso matrimonio? ▲ proponer *Who was proposed for chairman?* ¿Quién fué propuesto para presidente? ▲ proponerse, tener intención de *Do you propose to take a vacation this summer?* ¿Tiene Ud. intención de tomar vacaciones este verano?

proposition proposición, propuesta *Will you consider my proposition?* ¿Considerará Ud. mi propuesta?

   ‖ *Going to war's a serious proposition.* El ir a la guerra es cosa seria. ‖ *Thus far it's been a paying proposition.* Hasta ahora este negocio ha sido lucrativo. ‖ *That fellow seems to be a tough proposition.* Ese tipo parece ser muy difícil. *or* Ese tipo parece ser cosa seria.

proprietor propietario, dueño.

prose [n] prosa.

prosecute proseguir (*carry on*); acusar (*law*).

prosecution prosecución.

prospect perspectiva.

prosperity prosperidad.

prostitute [n] prostituta.

protect proteger.

protection protección.

protector protector.

protest [n] protesta *He ignored her protest.* Ignoró su protesta.

   ○ **under protest** contra la voluntad de uno *I'll go only under protest.* Iré contra mi voluntad.

   ● [v] quejarse, protestar *Let's protest to the landlord about the noise.* Quejémonos al casero del ruido. ▲ protestar *The accused protested his innocence.* El acusado protestó su inocencia.

Protestant [adj; n] protestante.

protrude sobresalir.

proud orgulloso.

prove probar, demostrar *I can prove I didn't do it.* Puedo probar que no lo hice.

   ‖ *The movie proved to be very bad.* La película resultó muy mala.

proverb proverbio.

provide poner, proporcionar, proveer *If you provide the materials I'll build you a bookcase.* Si Ud. pone el material yo le construiré un estante. ▲ establecer *The rules provide that you can't leave the camp without permission.* El reglamento establece que no se puede salir del campamento sin permiso.

   ○ **provided** con tal que *I'll go, provided you come with me.* Iré con tal que Ud. me acompañe. ○ **to provide for** asegurar *The family was provided for in the will.* La familia estaba asegurada en el testamento. ▲ proveer lo necesario para *He provided for his child's education.* Proveyó lo necesario para la educación de su hijo.

province provincia *He comes from the provinces.* Viene de las provincias. ▲ incumbencia, competencia *Administrative problems aren't within my province.* No son de mi incumbencia los problemas administrativos.

provision provisión *We need many provisions for the trip.* Necesitamos muchas provisiones para el viaje. ▲ preparativo *What provisions have been made for his visit?* ¿Qué preparativos se han hecho para su visita? ▲ estipulación *The provisions of the contract are not in our favor.* Las estipulaciones del contrato no nos favorecen.

provoke provocar *That game always provokes an argument.* Ese juego provoca siempre pleitos. ▲ irritar *That fellow provokes me.* Ese tipo me irrita.

prudence prudencia.

prudent prudente.

prune ciruela pasa.

psalm salmo.

psychologist psicólogo.

psychology psicología.

public [n] público *Is this building open to the public?* ¿Está abierto al público este edificio?
● [adj] público *This is a public meeting and admission's free.* Esta es una reunión pública y la entrada es gratis.

publication publicación.

publish publicar.

publisher editor.

pudding pudín, budín.

puddle charco.

puff [n] bocanada *Did you see that puff of smoke?* ¿Vió esa bocanada de humo?
● [v] jadear *He always puffs when he runs.* Siempre jadea cuando corre.
○ **powder puff** mota, borla. ○ **puff of wind** ráfaga. ○ **to be puffed up** hincharse (*to be swollen*); engreirse (*to be proud*).

pull [n] tirón *If you give too hard a pull, the rope'll break.* Si da Ud. un tirón demasiado fuerte se romperá la cuerda.
▲ influencia, [Sp] mano, [Am] cuello *You have to have a lot of pull to get a job here.* Hay que tener mucha mano para conseguir un puesto aquí.
● [v] sacar, extraer *This tooth must be pulled.* Hay que sacar esta muela.
▲ tirar (de) *If you pull this cord, the driver will stop the bus.* Si tira Ud. de este cordón, el conductor parará el bus. ○ **to pull down** bajar *Pull the shades down.* Baje Ud. los transparentes.
▲ derribar, tumbar *They're going to pull the building down and build another.* Van a derribar el edificio para construir otro. ○ **to pull in** tirar de *Let's pull in the line.* Tiremos de la cuerda.
▲ llegar *We pulled in at three o'clock in the morning.* Llegamos a las tres de la mañana. ○ **to pull off** sacar(se), quitar(se) *Help me pull off my sweater.* Ayúdeme a quitarme el suéter. ○ **to pull oneself together** arreglarse *Pull yourself together and let's get going.* Arréglese y vámonos. ○ **to pull out** salir *The train pulled out on time.* El tren salió a tiempo. ○ **to pull through** salir adelante, resistir *She was pretty sick and we were afraid she might not pull through.* Estaba muy enferma y temíamos que no saliera adelante. ○ **to pull to pieces** hacer pedazos, desbaratar *The dog pulled the cushion to pieces.* El perro hizo pedazos el cojín. ○ **to pull up** arrancar *They pulled the plants up by the roots.* Arrancaron las

plantas de raíz. ▲ arrimar, acercar *Pull up a chair, I'd like to talk to you.* Arrime una silla, quiero hablarle. ▲ parar *The car pulled up in front of the house.* El auto paró enfrente de la casa. ‖ *He pulled a mean trick on me.* Me hizo una mala jugada. ‖ *Pull over to the curb.* Arrime su carro a la acera.

pulley polea.

pulp pulpa.

pulpit púlpito.

pulse pulso *I'm going to take your pulse.* Voy a tomarle el pulso.

pump [n] bomba *Is there a pump in the house?* ¿Hay una bomba en la casa?
● [v] bombear *You'll have to pump water for a bath.* Tiene que bombear agua para bañarse.
○ **to pump up** inflar *This tire needs pumping up.* Hay que inflar esta llanta.

pumpkin calabaza, [Am] ayote, [Arg] zapallo.

punch [n] ponche *Will you have some fruit punch?* ¿Quiero Ud. tomar ponche de frutas?

punch [n] puñetazo *He gave me a punch in the ribs.* Me dió un puñetazo en las costillas. ▲ vigor, fuerza *His speech didn't have any punch.* A su discurso le faltó vigor.
● [v] dar un puñetazo *I'll punch you in the nose.* Le daré un puñetazo en la nariz. ▲ picar, marcar *The conductor forgot to punch my ticket.* El conductor olvidó picar mi boleto.

punctual puntual.

puncture [n] pinchazo, punzada.
● [v] pinchar.

punish castigar.

punishment castigo, pena *The punishment for this crime is death.* Este crimen tiene pena de muerte.
‖ *The car took a lot of punishment on the last trip.* Se ha estropeado mucho el coche en el último viaje.

pupil (*student*) discípulo, alumno.

puppy cachorro, perrito.

purchase [n] compra *I have a few purchases to make in this store.* Tengo que hacer unas compras en esta tienda.
● [v] comprar *I'm trying to purchase some land in this street.* Estoy tratando de comprar un terreno en esta calle.

pure puro *The dress is pure silk.* El vestido es de pura seda.
‖ *Is the water pure enough to drink?* ¿Es buena el agua para beber?

purge [n] purga.

purify purificar.
purple [*n*] púrpura.
● [*adj*] morado.
purpose objeto, propósito *What's your purpose in coming here?* ¿Qué objeto tiene su venida aquí? *or* ¿A qué vino Ud. aquí?
○ **on purpose** a propósito *I asked on purpose to see what you'd say.* Lo pregunté a propósito para ver que decían Uds.
purse bolso, [*Am*] bolsa *How much money have you in your purse?* ¿Cuánto dinero tiene Ud. en la bolsa? ▲ premio *The purse was divided among the winners.* El premio se repartió entre los ganadores.
pursue perseguir *They pursued the enemy as far as the river.* Persiguieron al enemigo hasta el río.
pus pus.
push [*n*] empujón *Give the car a push.* Dé un empujón al coche.
● [*v*] empujar *Push the table over by the window.* Empuje la mesa hasta la ventana. ▲ llevar adelante, dar impulso a *I intend to push my claim.* Intento llevar adelante mi reclamación.
○ **to push off** alejarse, separarse *The boat pushed off from shore.* El barco se alejó de la orilla.
‖ *He pushed his way into the elevator.* Se metió en el ascensor empujando.
put poner *Put your suitcase over here.* Ponga su maleta aquí. ▲ exponer *The report puts the facts very clearly.* El informe expone los hechos con mucha claridad.
○ **to put an end** *or* **stop to** poner fin a *The news put an end to our hopes.* La noticia puso fin a nuestras esperanzas.
○ **to put aside** *or* **away** ahorrar, apartar *She's been putting aside a little money each month.* Ha estado apartando un poco de dinero cada mes.
○ **to put back** poner otra vez *Put the book back where you found it.* Ponga el libro otra vez donde lo encontró.
○ **to put down** apuntar *Put down your name and address.* Apunte Ud. su nombre y dirección. ▲ dominar *The revolt was put down with little trouble.* La revolución fué dominada fácilmente. ○ **to put in an appearance** hacer acto de presencia, aparecer. ○ **to put in order** poner en orden. ○ **to put in writing** poner por escrito. ○ **to put off** dejar *Let's put off the decision until*

tomorrow. Dejemos la decisión para mañana. ○ **to put on** ponerse *Wait till I put on my coat.* Espere que me ponga el abrigo. ▲ afectar *That accent isn't real, it's put on.* Ese acento no es natural, es afectado. ○ **to put on airs** darse importancia. ○ **to put oneself out** molestarse *Don't put yourself out on my account.* No se moleste Ud. por mí. ○ **to put out** apagar *Put out the lights before you leave.* Apague Ud. las luces antes de marcharse. ▲ publicar *This publisher puts out some very good books.* Esta imprenta publica muy buenos libros. ○ **to put to a vote** someter a votación. ○ **to put to bed** acostar *I have to put the kids to bed.* Tengo que acostar a los niños. ○ **to put to death** ejecutar *He's already been put to death.* Yo lo han ejecutado. ○ **to put to expense** hacer gastar *This'll put me to considerable expense.* Esto me hará gastar mucho. ○ **to put to use** emplear *You can be sure this money will be put to good use.* Puede Ud. tener la seguridad de que este dinero será bien empleado. ○ **to put up** construir *This building was put up in six months.* Este edificio se construyó en seis meses. ▲ dar alojamiento a, alojar *Can you put up two guests for the night?* ¿Puede dar alojamiento a dos huéspedes esta noche? ○ **to put up for sale** poner a la venta. ○ **to put up with** soportar, aguantar *I can't put up with this noise any longer.* No puedo aguantar más este ruido.
‖ *You can't put anything over on him.* No se le puede dar gato por liebre. *or* No se le puede engañar.
‖ *The bill was put through Congress last week.* El congreso aprobó el proyecto de ley la semana pasada. ‖ *Can this idea be put across?* ¿Podrá lanzarse esta idea con éxito? ‖ *Will you put the newspaper back together?* ¿Quiere arreglar el periódico como estaba?
puzzle [*n*] rompecabezas *Can you solve this puzzle?* ¿Puede Ud. resolver este rompecabezas? ▲ enigma *It's a puzzle to me how she gets her work done.* Es un enigma para mí como logra ella hacer su trabajo.
● [*v*] dejar perplejo *What he said puzzled us.* Nos dejó perplejos lo que dijo.
○ **to puzzle out** resolver, descifrar.
pyramid pirámide.

Q

quack [n] charlatán, sacamuelas *That doctor is a quack.* Ese médico es un charlatán.

quack [v] graznar *Do you hear the ducks quacking?* ¿Oye Ud. como graznan los patos?

quail codorniz.

quake terremoto, temblor *Back in '36 we had a terrible quake.* En 1936 tuvimos un violento terremoto.

qualification preparación *What are your qualifications?* ¿Qué preparación tiene Ud.? ▲ requisito, requerimiento *What are the qualifications for this job?* ¿Cuáles son los requisitos para este empleo?

qualify modificar *I think you should qualify your statement.* Creo que debe Ud. modificar su declaración.

○ **qualified** preparado *We think he is qualified for the position.* Pensamos que es una persona preparada para el cargo.

‖ *If you pass the examination you'll qualify for the job.* Si pasa el examen se le considerará calificado para el empleo.

quality calidad *Prices vary according to the quality of the goods.* Los precios varían según la calidad de los artículos.

quantity cantidad *Quantities of coal have been found in this region.* Se han hallado grandes cantidades de carbón en esta región.

quarantine [n] cuarentena *He was in quarantine for two weeks.* Estuvo en cuarentena por dos semanas.

● [v] aislar *The doctor quarantined the whole family.* El médico aisló a toda la familia.

quarrel [n] disgusto *They haven't been friends since their quarrel.* Dejaron de ser amigos desde que tuvieron aquel disgusto.

● [v] disputar, reñir *I don't want to quarrel with you.* No quiero reñir con Ud.

quarry cantera *There's a marble quarry not far from here.* Hay una cantera de mármol no muy lejos de aquí.

quart See Appendix.

quarter [n] cuarta parte *Each son received a quarter of the estate.* Cada hijo recibió una cuarta parte del patrimonio. ▲ cuarto de dólar, veinticinco centavos *It costs a quarter to get into the show.* Cuesta veinticinco centavos la entrada a la función. ▲ cuarto *The train leaves at a quarter to three.* El tren sale a las tres menos cuarto. ▲ círculo, lugar *He has a very bad reputation in certain quarters.* Tiene muy mala fama en ciertos círculos. ▲ cuartel *We gave no quarter to the enemy.* No se le dió cuartel al enemigo.

● [v] acantonar, alojar *The soldiers were quartered in an old house near the fort.* Alojaron a los soldados en una casa vieja cerca del fuerte.

○ **quarters** morada, vivienda *His quarters are near the camp.* Su vivienda está cerca del campamento.

queen reina.

queer extraño, raro.

quench apagar.

question [n] pregunta *They asked a lot of questions.* Hicieron muchas preguntas. ▲ cuestión *It's a question of knowing what to do.* Es cuestión de saber lo que hay que hacer.

● [v] dudar *I question the sincerity of what he says.* Dudo de la sinceridad de lo que dice.

○ **beyond question** indudable, fuera de duda *His honesty is beyond all question.* Su honradez está fuera de toda duda. ○ **questioning** interrogatorio *The questioning is going on now.* El interrogatorio se está efectuando ahora. ○ **to be beside the question** no venir al caso, estar fuera del tema *What you say is beside the question.* Lo que Ud. dice no viene al caso. ○ **to be out of the question** no haber que pensar en, ser inadmisible *To take a vacation is out of the question.* No hay que pensar en tomar una vacación. ○ **without question** indiscutiblemente *He'll be there tomorrow without question.* Indiscutiblemente estará mañana allí.

‖ *It's entirely out of the question.* Es del todo imposible. ‖ *There can be no question about what they meant.* No cabe la menor duda acerca de lo que querían decir.

quick [adj] rápido *He is a man of quick decisions.* Es un hombre de decisiones rápidas.—*His answer was quick and to the point.* Su respuesta fué rápida y precisa.

● [adv] pronto *I'll be there as quick as I can.* Estaré allí lo más pronto que pueda.

quickly rápidamente.

quiet [n] tranquilidad *I'm looking for*

peace and quiet. Busco paz y tranquilidad.
● [*adj*] quieto, tranquilo *I live in a quiet neighborhood.* Vivo en un barrio muy tranquilo. ▲ silencioso, callado *He's so quiet you never know he's around.* El es tan silencioso que nunca se sabe que está por aquí.
● [*v*] aquietar, calmar *His speech quieted the crowd.* Su discurso calmó a la multitud.
○ to keep *or* be quiet callarse, no hacer ruido. ○ to quiet down calmarse *After a while the baby quieted down.* Después de un rato el niño se calmó.
‖ *Quiet, please!* ¡Silencio, por favor!
quilt edredón.
quinine quinina.
quit dejar de *Quit bothering the dog.* Deje de molestar al perro. ▲ renunciar a, dejar *He quit his job yesterday.* Ayer dejó su empleo.

quite completamente *Are you quite sure that you can go?* ¿Está Ud. completamente seguro de que puede ir? ▲ exactamente, realmente *That's not quite what I wanted.* Eso no es exactamente lo que quería. ▲ realmente *The news was quite a surprise to us.* La noticia fué realmente una sorpresa para nosotros. ▲ bastante *I live quite near here.* Vivo bastante cerca de aquí.—*I'm quite well, thank you.* Estoy bastante bien, gracias.
quiver [*v*] temblar.
quote citar *She's always quoting poetry.* Siempre está citando versos. ▲ cotizar *I cannot quote prices on these articles.* No le puedo cotizar precios en estos artículos. ▲ mencionar *or* citar el nombre de uno *You can quote us all as being in favor of the plan.* Puede Ud. citar nuestros nombres a favor del plan.

R

rabbit conejo, coneja.
race [*n*] carrera *The races will be held next week.* Las carreras se celebrarán la semana próxima.—*It was a race to get to the station on time.* Hubo que ir a la carrera para llegar a la estación a tiempo. ▲ regata *Which boat won the race?* ¿Qué barco ganó la regata? ▲ raza *He hates the whole human race.* Aborrece a toda la raza humana.
● [*v*] echar una carrera *Let's race to the barn.* Vamos a echar una carrera hasta el granero. ▲ tomar parte en la regata *How many boats are racing?* ¿Cuántos barcos van a tomar parte en la regata?
‖ *The car raced past the farm.* El automóvil pasó a toda velocidad por delante de la hacienda.
rack red *Put your baggage up on the rack.* Ponga su equipaje en la red.
○ to rack one's brains devanarse los sesos.
racket bulla, estruendo (*noise*); raqueta (*tennis*).
radiant radiante.
radiator radiador.
radio [*n*] la radio [*Sp*], el radio [*Am*] *Will he speak over the radio?* ¿Hablará por la radio?
● [*v*] radiar *The news was radioed to us.* Nos han radiado la noticia.
○ radio set aparato de radio *The radio set will come tomorrow.* Llegará mañana el aparato de radio.

radish rábano.
rag trapo.
○ in rags en harapos.
rage rabia, ira.
rail baranda *Hold on to the rail.* Agárrese a la baranda. ▲ riel *The train had to stop because one of the rails was damaged.* El tren tuvo que detenerse porque uno de los rieles estabo roto.
○ by rail por ferrocarril.
railing baranda.
railroad ferrocarril.
○ railroad track rieles, vía *Don't walk on the railroad track.* No camine por la vía.
rain [*n*] lluvia *The rains started late this year.* Este año han empezado tarde las lluvias.
● [*v*] llover *It rained hard this morning.* Llovió mucho esta mañana.
‖ *Only a few drops of rain have fallen.* Sólo han caído cuatro gotas.
rainbow arco iris.
raincoat impermeable.
rainstorm aguacero.
rainy lluvioso.
raise [*n*] aumento *He asked for a raise in pay.* Pidió un aumento de sueldo. ▲ criar *They raised a big family.* Criaron muchos hijos. ▲ cultivar (*vegetable products*); criar (*animals*) *This farmer raises wheat and hogs.* Este labrador cultiva el trigo y cria puercos. ▲ recoger, recaudar *How large a sum did they raise?* ¿Cuánto dinero recogieron?

▲reclutar *The country raised a large army.* El país reclutó un gran ejército. ▲subir *He has raised prices since we were here.* Ha subido los precios desde que estuvimos aquí. ▲izar *The soldiers raised the flag.* Los soldados izaron la bandera. ▲quitarse *When she came by he raised his hat.* Cuando ella se acercó él se quitó el sombrero.
● [v] levantar *If you want a ticket, please raise your hand.* El que quiera un billete que levante la mano.—*Don't raise your voice.* No levante la voz.
raisin pasa.
rake [n] rastrillo.
● [v] rastrillar.
rally [n] reunión, mitin.
● [v] reunir *The captain rallied his scattered troops.* El capitán reunió sus tropas dispersas.—*The government's rallying all its energies to defeat the enemy.* El gobierno está reuniendo todas sus fuerzas para derrotar al enemigo. ⸕ rehacerse, reponerse *The invalid rallied after his operation.* El enfermo se fué rehaciendo después de la operación.
ranch hacienda.
range [n] escala *What is his range of prices?* ¿Cuál es su escala de precios? ▲pastos *They drove the horses out to the range.* Sacaron los caballos a los pastos. ▲cocina *Light the range.* Encienda Ud. la cocina.
● [v] ir *Prices range from one to five dollars.* Los precios van desde uno a cinco dólares.
○ range of mountains cordillera, cadena de montañas. ○ rifle range tiro al blanco. ○ to be within range estar a tiro *Wait till the deer is within range.* Espere a que el venado esté en línea de tiro.
‖ *Are we out of range of hearing?* ¿Estamos bastante lejos para que no nos oigan?
rank [n] fila *Only the first rank had guns.* Solamente la primera fila tenía fúsiles. ▲grado *He has the rank of captain.* Tiene el grado de capitán.
○ rank and file tropa *This order is for the rank and file.* Esta orden es para la tropa.
‖ *This city ranks low in importance.* Esta ciudad es de poca importancia.
‖ *That tobacco you're smoking is rank.* Ese tabaco que Ud. fuma apesta.
rap [n] golpe.
● [v] golpear.
rapid rápido *He made a rapid journey.* Hizo un viaje rápido.

○ **rapids** rápidos del río *The rapids are stronger this year than last.* Los rápidos del río son más fuertes este año que el pasado.
rapidly rápidamente.
rare raro.
○ rare meat carne medio cruda.
rash [n] erupción (*skin*).
rash [adj] imprudente (*reckless*).
raspberry frambuesa.
rat rata.
rate [n] velocidad *This car can go at the rate of sixty miles per hour.* Este automóvil puede ir a una velocidad de sesenta millas por hora. ▲tarifa *The postage rate is six cents per ounce.* La tarifa postal es de seis centavos por onza.
● [v] merecer *He rates a reward for that.* Merece un premio por eso.
○ at any rate en todo caso *He arrived today; at any rate his baggage is here.* Llegó hoy; en todo caso aquí está su equipaje. ○ at the rate of a razón de *You can pay the bill at the rate of five dollars per week.* Ud. puede pagar la cuenta a razón de cinco dólares por semana. ○ at this (that) rate a este paso. ○ first-rate de primera *This book is definitely first-rate.* Sin duda es un libro de primera.
‖ *He charges more than the regular rate.* Cobra más de lo debido. ‖*What is the rate of exchange?* ¿A cómo está el cambio? ‖ *He rates high in my estimation.* Le tengo en gran estima.
‖ *I feel first-rate.* Me siento de lo mejor.
rather un poco, algo *It is rather cold on deck.* Hace un poco de frío sobre cubierta. ▲más bien, mejor dicho *He was running or, rather, walking fast.* Iba corriendo o mejor dicho, andando de prisa.
○ rather than más bien que, antes que *Let's go there rather than hurt her feelings.* Vamos allá antes que se ofenda.
‖ *I'd rather have ice cream.* Preferiría tomar helado.
rattle [n] sonajero *Give the baby his rattle.* Dale el sonajero al niño.
● [v] batir *The window rattled all night.* La ventana estuvo batiendo toda la noche.
rave delirar *He raved like a madman.* Deliraba como un loco.
○ to rave about comentar con admiración *Everyone raved about my gown.* Todos comentaron mi traje con admiración.

raw crudo *This meat is nearly raw.* Esta carne está casi cruda. ▲ en rama *The ship is carrying raw cotton.* El vapor lleva algodón en rama. ▲ novato, bisoño *He had only raw soldiers to use for the work.* No tenía más que soldados bisoños para el trabajo. ▲ desapacible *There's a raw wind today.* Hoy hace un viento muy desapacible. ▲ despellejado *Her face is raw because of the wind.* Tiene la cara despellejada por el viento. ○ **raw material** materia prima *The raw materials must be shipped in.* Las materias primas tienen que ser importadas. ○ **raw place** matadura *The horse has a raw place on its back.* El caballo tiene una matadura en el lomo.

ray rayo.

rayon rayón, seda artificial.

razor navaja de afeitar. ○ **razor blade** hoja de afeitar, navajilla.

reach alcanzar *Can you reach the sugar?* ¿Puede Ud. alcanzar el azúcar? ▲ llegar hasta *Her gown reaches the floor.* El traje le llega hasta el suelo. ▲ llegar *Tell me when we reach the city.* Avíseme cuando lleguemos a la ciudad. ○ **in reach of** al alcance de *Is it in reach of the dog?* ¿Está al alcance del perro? ○ **out of reach** fuera del alcance *The job he wanted was out of his reach.* El puesto que quería estaba fuera de su alcance.

react reaccionar.

reaction reacción.

read leer *Please read the instructions.* Haga el favor de leer las instrucciones.—*Please read it to me.* Haga el favor de leérmelo. ▲ sonar *This reads like a fairy tale.* Esto suena a cuento de hadas.

reader lector (*person*); libro de lectura (*book*).

ready preparado *When will dinner be ready?* ¿Cuándo estará preparada la comida? ▲ listo, preparado *I'll be ready in ten minutes.* Estaré listo dentro de diez minutos. ▲ dispuesto *I am ready to go anywhere I am sent.* Estoy dispuesto a ir a donde me manden. ○ **ready-made** hecho *I bought a ready-made suit.* Compré un traje hecho.

real verdadero *Is this real marble or imitation?* ¿Es mármol verdadero o imitación?—*What was his real reason?* ¿Cuál era la razón verdadera que tenía? ▲ real *That never happens in real life.* Eso nunca sucede en la vida real. ○ **real silk** seda natural.

reality realidad.

realize darse cuenta de, comprender *I did not realize that you were interested in that.* No me dí cuenta de que Ud. estaba interesado en eso. ▲ realizar *He has never realized his desire to own a house.* Nunca ha realizado su deseo de tener casa propia. ▲ ganar, obtener *He has realized a profit.* Ha obtenido ganancias.

really verdaderamente, en realidad *He is really younger than he looks.* En realidad es más joven de lo que parece. ‖ *Really!* or *Well, really!* ¿De veras? ¡Vaya, que cosa! or ¿De verdad? ¡No me lo digas!

rear [n] parte de atrás, parte de detrás *Please move to the rear of the bus.* Por favor, pasen a la parte de detrás del autobús. ● [adj] de atrás *You'll have to use the rear door while the house is being painted.* Tendrá que usar la puerta de atrás mientras pintan la casa. ● [v] criar *I was born and reared on a farm.* Nací y me crié en una granja. ▲ encabritarse *Her horse reared suddenly and threw her.* El caballo se encabritó de pronto y la tiró.

reason [n] razón *I can't figure out the reason why he did it.* No me explico por qué razón lo hizo.—*He was stubborn, but we brought him to reason.* Estaba testarudo pero le hicimos entrar en razón. ▲ motivo *I have reason to think that we will never see him again.* Tengo motivos para pensar que nunca volveremos a verle. ● [v] razonar *The child cannot reason.* El niño no puede razonar. ▲ discutir *We reasoned with her until she changed her mind.* Discutimos con ella hasta que cambió de modo de pensar. ○ **to lose one's reason** perder la razón *If this goes on, I'll lose my reason.* Si sigue esto, voy a perder la razón. ○ **to reason out** resolver *I tried to reason it out.* Traté de resolverlo. ○ **to stand to reason** ser lógico. ‖ *Please listen to reason.* Sea Ud. razonable.

reasonable razonable, justo.

rebel [n] rebelde *He was always a rebel.* Siempre fué rebelde.

rebel [v] rebelarse *Didn't anyone rebel against his decision?* ¿No se rebeló nadie contra su decisión?

recall recordar *Your face is familiar, but I can't recall your name.* Su cara me es familiar, pero no puedo recordar su nombre. ▲ retirar *The ambassador was recalled.* Retiraron el embajador.

receipt [*n*] recibo *Be sure to get a receipt when you deliver the package.* No olvide Ud. de pedir un recibo cuando entregue el paquete.

● [*v*] poner el recibí *Please receipt this bill.* Haga Ud. el favor de poner el recibí en esta cuenta.

○ **receipts** ingresos, entradas *Our receipts will just pay for our expenses.* Los ingresos cubren exactamente nuestros gastos.

receive recibir *Have you received the letter?* ¿Ha recibido Ud. la carta?— *The speech was well received by the audience.* El discurso fué bien recibido por el auditorio.—*He was on hand to receive the guests.* Estaba allí para recibir a los convidados.

receiver receptor.

recent reciente.

reception recibimiento (*greeting*); recepción (*party*).

recess recreo (*rest*); nicho (*niche*).

recipe receta.

recite recitar.

reckless imprudente, temerario.

reckon creer *I reckon I'll go to supper now.* Creo que voy a cenar ahora.

○ **reckon up** calcular *Have you reckoned up the expense?* ¿Ha calculado Ud. los gastos? ○ **reckon with** contar con *They didn't reckon with their father's opposition.* No contaron con la oposición de su padre.

recognize reconocer *I recognize him by his voice.* Le reconozco por la voz.— *Have they recognized the new government?* ¿Han reconocido el nuevo gobierno? ▲ dar la palabra *Wait till the chairman recognizes you.* Espere hasta que el presidente le dé la palabra. ▲ percibir, reconocer *No one recognized his genius while he was alive.* Ninguno reconoció su genio mientras vivió.

recommend recomendar *Can you recommend a good restaurant?* ¿Puede Ud. recomendarme un buen restaurante?

recommendation recomendación.

reconcile reconciliar *Were they reconciled after their quarrel?* ¿Se han reconciliado después de la pelea?

○ **to become reconciled** resignarse *Has he become reconciled to his misfortune?* ¿Se ha resignado con su suerte?

record [*n*] registro *They looked for his name in the church records.* Buscaron su nombre en los registros de la iglesia. ▲ record *He broke all speed records.* Batió todos los records de velocidad. ▲ disco *Do you have many jazz records?* ¿Tiene Ud. muchos discos de jazz? ▲ antecedentes *He has a criminal record.* Tiene antecedentes penales.

● [*adj*] extraordinario *We had a record crop this year.* Hemos tenido una cosecha extraordinaria este año.

○ **on record** registrado *This is the worst earthquake on record.* Este es el temblor más fuerte que se ha registrado. ○ **to keep a record** apuntar, llevar cuenta *Keep a careful record of all expenses.* Apunte cuidadosamente todos los gastos.

‖ *Let me go on record against this idea.* Que conste que estoy en contra de esta idea.

record [*v*] llevar el registro *Where do they record births?* ¿Dónde llevan el registro de los nacimientos? ▲ grabar *What company records your songs?* ¿Qué compañía graba los discos de sus canciones?

recover restablecerse *How long did it take you to recover from your operation?* ¿Cuánto tiempo tardó Ud. en restablecerse de la operación? ▲ recobrar *I recovered my match within a week.* Recobré mi reloj en menos de una semana.

○ **to recover oneself** recobrar la serenidad *He lost his temper but soon recovered himself.* Sen enfadó, pero en seguida recobró la serenidad.

recreation recreo.

recruit [*n*] recluta.

● [*v*] reclutar.

red rojo.

Red Cross Cruz Roja.

redeem salvar *Generosity is his only redeeming feature.* La generosidad es la única cualidad que le salva. ▲ desempeñar *Did you redeem your watch?* ¿Ha desempeñado el reloj?

red tape papeleo.

reduce reducir *They're selling out all their stock at reduced prices.* Están vendiendo las existencias a precios reducidos. ▲ adelgazar *I'm on a reducing diet.* Sigo un régimen para adelgazar.

○ **to be reduced to** verse obligado a *They were reduced to begging.* Se vieron obligados a pedir limosna.

reduction reducción.

refer referirse *This law refers only to aliens.* Esa ley se refiere sólo a los extranjeros.

○ **to refer to** hablar de *I won't have you refer to my friend that way.* No

quiero que hable Ud. de mi amigo de esa manera.
‖ *Can you refer me to a good book on the subject?* ¿Me puede Ud. indicar un buen libro sobre esa materia?
reference referencia.
refine refinar.
reflect reflejar.
reform [n] reforma *They mayor has made many reforms.* El alcalde ha hecho muchas reformas.
● [v] corregir, reformar *Don't try to reform him.* No trate de corregirle.
○ **reform school** reformatorio *These boys should be sent to a reform school.* Habría que mandar a estos muchachos a un reformatorio.
refrain [n] estribillo.
● [v] reprimir. ▲ evitar *They have to refrain from making so much noise.* Tienen que evitar hacer tanto ruido.
refresh refrescar.
refreshment refresco.
refrigerator refrigerador, refrigeradora, nevera.
refuge refugio.
refugee refugiado.
refund [n] reembolso, reintegro.
● [v] reembolsar, devolver.
refuse [n] basura *Throw it out with the rest of the refuse.* Tírelo con el resto de la basura.
refuse [v] rechazar, no querer aceptar *I offered him a drink, but he refused it.* Le ofrecí un trago, pero no quiso aceptarlo. ▲ negarse a *The committee refused to accept his resignation.* La junta se negó a aceptar su dimisión. ▲ rechazar, decir que no *She has refused him again.* Le ha dicho que no otra vez.
regard [n] consideración, respeto *Show some regard for your parents.* Tenga Ud. consideración con sus padres.
● [v] considerar *He is regarded as a great pianist.* Es considerado como un gran pianista.
○ **regarding** acerca de. ○ **regards** memorias, recuerdos *Send my regards to your mother.* Envíele recuerdos de mi parte a su madre. ○ **with regard to, in regard to** con respecto a.
regardless sin tener en cuenta, sin hacer caso.
region región.
register [n] registro *Write your name in the register.* Escriba su nombre en el registro.
● [v] certificar *He got a registered letter.* Ha recibido una carta certificada. ▲ matricularse *Have you regis-*

tered for the course yet? ¿Se ha matriculado ya en ese curso? ▲ registrar, inscribir *They're registered in the hotel.* Están registrados en el hotel.
○ **cash register** caja registradora.
regret [n] pena *He was tormented by regret.* Estaba atormentado por la pena.
● [v] sentir *I've always regretted not having traveled.* Siempre he sentido no haber viajado.
○ **to send regrets** excusarse *Everyone sent their regrets.* Todos se excusaron.
‖ *I have no regrets for what I've done.* No siento lo que he hecho.
regular regular, corriente *This is the regular procedure.* Este es el procedimiento corriente. ▲ metódico *He lives a very regular life.* Lleva una vida muy metódica. ▲ regular *Is there regular bus service to town?* ¿Hay un servicio regular de autobuses a la ciudad? ▲ verdadero *That storm was a regular flood.* Esa tormenta fué un verdadero diluvio.
regularly con regularidad.
regulate regular.
regulation regla, reglamento.
rehearsal ensayo.
rehearse ensayar.
reign [n] reinado.
● [v] reinar.
rein rienda.
reject [v] rechazar.
rejoice gozar, regocijarse.
relate relatar, contar *Can you relate some of your adventures?* ¿Puede Ud. contar algunas de sus aventuras?
○ **to be related to** estar emparentado con *Are you related to that man?* ¿Está Ud. emparentado con ese hombre?
relation pariente *They invited all their friends and relations to the wedding.* Convidaron a todos sus amigos y parientes a la boda. ▲ relación *Our relations with the mayor are excellent.* Estamos en muy buenas relaciones con el alcalde.
○ **in relation to** con relación a, con respecto a *You must judge his work in relation to the circumstances.* Hay que juzgar su trabajo con relación a las circunstancias. ○ **to have no relation to** no tener nada que ver con *That scene has no relation to the rest of the play.* Esta escena no tiene nada que ver con el resto de la obra.
relative [n] pariente *They are close relatives.* Son parientes cercanos.
● [adj] relativo *Everything in life is relative.* Todo es relativo en la vida.

○ **to be relative to** depender de *The merits of this proposal are relative to particular conditions.* Las ventajas de esta proposición dependen de condiciones especiales.

relax descansar.

release [*v*] soltar *Release the brake.* Suelte el freno. ▲ relevar *You're released from your promise.* Queda relevado de su promesa.

reliable seguro, digno de confianza.

relic reliquia.

relief alivio *Did you get any relief from the medicine I gave you?* ¿Ha notado Ud. alivio con la medicina que le dí? ▲ descanso *I'll finish the work while you take your relief.* Terminaré el trabajo mientras Ud. se toma descanso. ▲ socorros *Relief has been sent to the flooded villages.* Han enviado socorros a los pueblos inundados. ▲ socorro de paro *If he loses his job, they'll have to go on relief.* Si pierde su puesto tendrán que pedir socorro de paro.

relieve quitar *Can you give me something to relieve this headache?* ¿Me puede dar algo que me quite este dolor de cabeza? ▲ sustituir *Will you relieve me for a few minutes?* ¿Quiere Ud. sustituirme unos minutos? ▲ disminuir *What can we do to relieve the monotony?* ¿Qué podemos hacer para disminuir la monotonía?

religion religión.

religious religioso.

rely ○ **to rely on** depender de, contar con *I'd hate to rely on him for anything I want done in a hurry.* Me molestaría tener que depender de él para algo que se tenga que hacer con prisa.

remain quedar *Will he remain in school another year?* ¿Se quedará en la escuela otro año? or ¿Se quedará en la escuela un año más? ▲ quedar, faltar *Nothing else remains to be done.* No queda nada más que hacer.

remainder resto.

remains restos, sobras *Clear away the remains of dinner.* Quite los restos de la comida. ▲ restos *Where did they bury his remains?* ¿Dónde han enterrado sus restos?

remark [*n*] observación *That was an unkind remark.* Esa ha sido una observación molesta (*or* dura).
● [*v*] hacer comentarios *He remarked on her appearance.* Hizo comentarios sobre su aspecto.

remarkable notable.

remedy [*n*] remedio *Try this remedy for* your cough. Pruebe este remedio para la tos.
● [*v*] remediar *Complaining won't remedy the situation.* Quejándose, no se remediará la situación.

remember acordarse de *Do you remember when he said that?* ¿Se acuerda Ud. de cuando dijo eso?—*Remember to turn out the lights.* Acuérdese de apagar las luces. ▲ recordar *I can't remember his name.* No puedo recordar su nombre. ▲ tener presente, incluir *I'll remember you in my will.* Le tendré presente en mi testamento. ▲ dar recuerdos *Remember me to your mother.* Déle recuerdos de mi parte a su madre. ‖ *He always remembers us at Christmas.* Siempre nos felicita en Navidad. *or* Siempre se acuerda de nosotros en Navidad.

remembrance recuerdo.

remind recordar *She reminds me of my mother.* Me recuerda a mi madre.— *If you don't remind me, I'll forget.* Si Ud. no me lo recuerda, se me olvidará. ▲ venir a la memoria *I am reminded of an amusing story.* Me viene a la memoria un cuento gracioso.

remit remitir.

remnant retal *I bought a silk remnant for a blouse.* He comprado un retal de seda para una blusa.

remorse remordimiento.

remote remoto.

remove quitar *Remove the lamp from the table.* Quite la lámpara de la mesa. ▲ quitarse *Please remove your hats.* Hagan el favor de quitarse el sombrero. ▲ extirpar *They operated on him to remove a growth.* Le hicieron una operación para extirparle un tumor. ▲ suprimir *Try to remove the cause of the disease.* Procuren suprimir la causa de la enfermedad.

render dejar, volver *The shock rendered him speechless.* La impresión le dejó mudo. ▲ prestar *For services rendered, ten dollars.* Por servicios prestados, diez dólares.
○ **to render assistance** prestar ayuda *You have rendered invaluable assistance.* Ha prestado Ud. una ayuda inestimable.

renew renovar.

rent [*n*] alquiler *How much rent do you pay for the apartment?* ¿Cuánto paga Ud. de alquiler por su piso?
● [*v*] alquilar *He rented a house for the summer.* Alquiló una casa durante el verano.—*He rents boats to tourists.* Alquila barcas a los turistas. ▲ alqui-

larse *This car rents for a dollar an hour.* Este auto se alquila a un dólar la hora.

repair [*n*] reparación *A complete repair job will take ten days.* Se tardarán diez días en hacer todas las reparaciones.
● [*v*] componer *Can you repair my shoes in a hurry?* ¿Puede Ud. componerme los zapatos muy de prisa? ▲ reparar, remediar *We can't repair the damage done by that law.* No podemos reparar el daño hecho por esa ley.

repairman reparador.

repeal [*v*] derogar.

repeat repetir *He repeated what he had just said.* Repitió lo que acababa de decir.—*Repeat this after me.* Repita Ud. lo que yo diga. ▲ volver a representar *The play will be repeated next week.* Volverán a representar la comedia la semana que viene.

repel rechazar.

repent arrepentirse.

repetition repetición.

replace reemplazar *We haven't been able to get anyone to replace her.* No hemos encontrado a nadie que la reemplace. ▲ volver a colocar *Replace those books on the shelf when you're done with them.* Vuelva a colocar esos libros en el estante cuando termine de usarlos.

reply [*n*] respuesta *What can you say in reply to this?* ¿Qué respuesta puede Ud. dar a esto?
● [*v*] contestar *He replied that they would be glad to go.* Contestó que tendrían mucho gusto en ir. ▲ responder *I refuse to reply to these charges.* Me niego a responder a estas acusaciones.

report [*n*] informe *He gave the report in person.* Dió su informe en persona. ▲ rumor *I've heard a report that you're leaving.* He oído el rumor de que Ud. se va. ▲ estampido, escopetazo *The gun went off with a loud report.* Al dispararse la escopeta dió un estampido muy fuerte.
● [*v*] hacer un informe, informar *I will report on this matter tomorrow.* Mañana haré un informe sobre este asunto. ▲ dar cuenta de *He reported that everything was in order.* Dió cuenta de que todo estaba como debía. ▲ decir *It is reported that you're wasting money.* Se dice que Ud. malgasta el dinero. ▲ hacer un reportaje *He reported the fire for his paper.* Hizo un reportaje sobre el incendio para su periódico. ▲ denunciar *They reported*

him to the police. Le denunciaron a la policía.
○ **to report for duty** presentarse *Report for duty Monday morning.* Preséntese Ud. el lunes por la mañana.

reporter repórter, reportero.

repose [*n*] reposo.
● [*v*] reposar.

represent representar *He's represented us in Congress for years.* Nos ha representado en el parlamento durante muchos años.—*What does this symbol represent?* ¿Qué representa este símbolo?

representative diputado, [*Am*] representante *Who's the representative from your district?* ¿Quién es el diputado de su distrito? ▲ típico *This sketch is representative of his style.* Este dibujo es típico de su estilo.

reproach [*n*] reproche *They met him with tears and reproaches.* Le recibieron con lágrimas y reproches.
● [*v*] reprochar *My mother is always reproaching me for my extravagance.* Mi madre siempre me reprocha que derrocho el dinero.

reproduce reproducir.

republic república.

reputation reputación, fama.

request [*n*] petición *Please file a written request.* Haga el favor de presentar una petición escrita.—*I'm writing you at the request of a friend.* Le escribo a Ud. a petición de un amigo.
● [*v*] pedir *He requested us to take care of his child.* Nos pidió que cuidásemos de su hijo.

require requerir *You are required by law to appear in person.* La ley requiere que Ud. se presente en persona. ▲ necesitar *How much do you require?* ¿Cuánto necesita Ud?

requirement exigencia *He doesn't give her enough money to meet all her requirements.* No le da bastante dinero para satisfacer todas sus exigencias. ▲ requisito, condición *Our college won't admit him until he meets all the requirements.* No será admitido en nuestra universidad hasta que llene todos los requisitos.

research investigación.

resemble parecerse (a).

reservation reserva *I accept your suggestion without reservation.* Acepto su sugestión sin reservas.
‖ *We telegraphed ahead to the hotel for reservations.* Telegrafiamos al hotel con anticipación pidiendo habitaciones.

reserve [*n*] reserva *We'll have to fall*

back on our reserves. Tendremos que recurrir a nuestras reservas.—*You're among friends, so you can speak without reserve.* Está Ud. entre amigos, puede hablar sin reserva.
● [*v*] reservar *Is this seat reserved?* ¿Está reservado este asiento?
○ **reserved** reservado *I found him very reserved.* Me pareció muy reservado.

reservoir depósito.

reside residir.

residence residencia, domicilio.

resign dimitir, renunciar *He resigned because they refused to give him a raise.* Dimitió porque no le quisieron ascender. ▲ resignar *I'll have to resign myself to being alone while you're away.* Me tendré que resignar a estar solo mientras estés fuera.

resignation dimisión, renuncia *We heard that he was going to hand in his resignation.* Hemos oído que iba a presentar su dimisión. ▲ resignación *He accepted the loss of his property with resignation.* Aceptó la pérdida de sus bienes con resignación.

resist resistir.

resistance resistencia.

resolute resuelto.

resolution resolución.

resolve [*v*] resolver.

resort [*n*] lugar (de veraneo) *This resort has a fine beach for the children.* Este lugar tiene una playa estupenda para los niños. ▲ recurso *As a last resort he tried to bribe them.* Como último recurso trató de sobornarlos. ○ **to resort to** recurrir a *We'll have to resort to force if he won't come quietly.* Tendremos que recurrir a la fuerza si no quiere venir por las buenas.

resound resonar.

resource recurso.

respect [*n*] respeto *He has the respect of everyone he works with.* Tiene el respeto de todos los que trabajan con él. ● [*v*] respetar *I respect your opinion.* Respeto su opinión.—*They should respect our rights.* Deben respetar nuestros derechos. ○ **in many respects** en muchos puntos *In many respects I agree with you.* En muchos puntos estoy de acuerdo con Ud. ○ **in what respect** desde qué punto de vista *In what respect is this true?* ¿Desde qué punto de vista es esto verdad? ○ **with** (*or* **in**) **respect to** tocante a, con respecto a *With respect to this question, I still feel the same way.* Con respecto a esta cuestión sigo pensando lo mismo.

‖ *Have some respect for other people's opinions.* Respete Ud. las opiniones de los demás.

respectable respetable.

respectful respetuoso.

respectfully respetuosamente.
‖ *Respectfully yours* Su atto. y s. s. (Su atento y seguro servidor).

respective respectivo.

respond responder.

response respuesta, contestación.

responsibility responsabilidad.

responsible responsable *He was declared not responsible for his acts.* Se le ha declarado no responsable de sus actos. ▲ de responsabilidad *It is a most responsible position.* Es un puesto de mucha responsabilidad. ▲ de fiar *I consider him a thoroughly responsible individual.* Le tengo por una persona muy de fiar. ○ **responsible for** causa de *His strategy was responsible for the victory.* Su estrategia fué causa de la victoria.
‖ *He is responsible only to the president.* Sólo tiene que dar cuenta de sus actos al presidente.

rest [*n*] descanso *A little rest would do you a lot of good.* Un pequeño descanso le sentará muy bien. ● [*v*] descansar *Rest awhile.* Descanse Ud. un rato.—*Let the matter rest.* Deje descansar el asunto. ▲ dejar descansar *Rest your eyes for a few days.* Deje que sus ojos descansen unos días. ▲ apoyar *She rested her head on the pillow.* Apoyó la cabeza en la almohada. ▲ apoyarse *The ladder is resting against the house.* La escalera está apoyada contra la casa.—*This argument rests on insufficient evidence.* Este razonamiento se apoya en pruebas insuficientes. ▲ estar *Rest assured that I will take care of it.* Puede Ud. estar seguro de que yo me ocuparé de todo. ○ **(as) for the rest** por lo demás *For the rest, I'm satisfied with the present situation.* Por lo demás, estoy satisfecho con esta situación. ○ **at rest** parado *Wait till the pointer is at rest.* Espere Ud. hasta que el indicador esté parado. ○ **the rest** los demás, los otros *Where are the rest of the boys?* ¿Dónde están los otros muchachos? ▲ el resto *I'll do the rest of the job.* Haré el resto del trabajo. ▲ lo demás *I understood a little and guessed the rest.* Entendí un poco y adiviné lo demás.
‖ *The power rests with him.* El tiene

el poder. ‖ *This will put your mind at rest.* Esto le tranquilizará a Ud.

restaurant restaurante *Where's a good cheap restaurant?* ¿Dónde hay un restaurante bueno y barato?

restless inquieto.

restore restaurar.

restrain dominar, contener *I had to restrain myself from insulting him.* Me tuve que dominar para no insultarle.

restrict no dar libertad *My parents restricted me too much when I was young.* Mis padres no me dieron bastante libertad cuando era muchacho. ‖ *The school library is restricted to students.* La biblioteca de la escuela es sólo para el uso de los estudiantes.

result [n] resultado *The results were very satisfactory.* Los resultados eran muy satisfactorios.
• [v] terminar *The elections resulted in victory for the opposition.* La elección terminó con la victoria de la oposición. ‖ *A lot of trouble resulted from the gossip.* Esa murmuración causó muchos disgustos.

retail al por menor.

retain retener.

retire retirarse.

retreat [n] retiro.
• [v] retirarse.

return [n] vuelta, regreso *I'll take the matter up on my return.* Trataré el asunto a mi vuelta. ▲ provecho, rédito *How much of a return did you get on your investment?* ¿Qué réditos obtuvo Ud. de su inversión?
• [adj] de vuelta *I didn't use the return half of the ticket.* No he usado el billete de vuelta.
• [v] devolver *Will you return it when you are through?* ¿Lo devolverá Ud. cuando haya terminado? ▲ reelegir *He has been returned to Congress several times.* Ha sido reelegido varias veces miembro del parlamento. ▲ regresar, volver *When did he return home?* ¿Cuándo volvió a su casa?
○ **by return mail** a vuelta de correo *Try to answer these letters by return mail.* Procure contestar estas cartas a vuelta de correo. ○ **returns** resultados *Have the election returns come in yet?* ¿Han llegado ya los resultados de las elecciónes. ‖ *Many happy returns of the day.* Feliz cumpleaños.

reveal revelar.

revelation revelación.

revenge vengaza.

revenue rentas públicas.

reverence reverencia, veneración.

reverse [n] contrario *The facts are just the reverse of what he told you.* Los hechos son lo contrario de lo que él le dijo.
• [v] revocar *Do you think the judge will reverse his decision?* ¿Cree Ud. que el juez revocará su decisión? ▲ dar vuelta *We reversed our seat in the train so we could stretch our feet.* Dimos vuelta a nuestro asiento en el tren para poder estirar las piernas.
○ **reverses** contratiempos, reveses *Our business met with reverses this year.* Hemos tenido muchos reveses en los negocios este año. ○ **to put (a car) in reverse** meter la marcha atrás.

review [n] repaso *I hope we have a review in history.* Ojalá tengamos un repaso en historia. ▲ revista *Today there will be a review of the troops.* Hoy pasarán revista a las tropas.— *Let's get tickets for the review.* Vamos a comprar billetes para la revista.
• [v] hacer la crítica de *Who's reviewing the play for the paper?* ¿Quién hará la crítica de la obra para el periódico? ▲ repasar *We reviewed our class-notes for the test.* Repasamos nuestros apuntes para el examen.

revise revisar.

revive hacer volver en sí, reanimar *The doctor's trying to revive the lady who fainted.* El doctor trata de hacer volver en sí a la señora que se desmayó. ▲ restablecer *The president helped revive business.* El presidente ayudó a restablecer los negocios.

revolt [n] sublevación, rebelión.
• [v] sublevarse.

revolution revolución.

revolve girar, dar vueltas.
○ **revolving door** puerta giratoria *We went through the revolving door.* Pasamos por la puerta giratoria.

revolver revólver.

reward [n] gratificación *You may get it back if you offer a reward.* Puede que se lo devuelvan si ofrece una gratificación. ▲ recompensa *You deserve a reward for all your hard work.* Merece Ud. una recompensa por haber trabajado tanto.
• [v] premiar, recompensar *He was rewarded with a promotion.* Le recompensaron con un ascenso.

rheumatism reumatismo.

rhumba rumba.

rhyme rima.

rhythm ritmo.

rib costilla.

ribbon cinta *I bought a yard of white ribbon.* Compré una yarda de cinta blanca.

rice arroz *Please give me a pound of rice.* Haga el favor de darme una libra de arroz.

rich rico *He was adopted by a very rich family.* Una familia riquísima le adoptó. ▲ fuerte *I have to be careful about rich foods.* Tengo que tener cuidado con las comidas fuertes. ▲ fértil, bueno *This is very rich wheat land.* Son unos campos de trigo muy buenos. ○ **to be rich** in tener mucho *Spinach is rich in iron.* Las espinacas tienen mucho hierro.

riches riqueza.

rid librar *If you'd keep the door closed we could rid the house of these flies.* Si tuviera Ud. cerrada la puerta podríamos librar la casa de las moscas. ○ **to get rid of** quitarse *Rest is what you need to get rid of that cold.* Ud. necesita descanso para quitarse ese catarro. ▲ librarse de *Can't you get rid of that nuisance?* ¿No se puede Ud. librar de ese estorbo?

ridden (*See* ride) montado *He has ridden horses all his life.* Ha montado a caballo su vida. ‖ *How far have you ridden?* ¿Qué distancia lleva Ud. recorrida?

riddle acertijo.

ride [*n*] paseo *We went for a ride in his car.* Dimos un paseo en su auto. ▲ viaje *It's a short bus ride.* Es un viaje corto en autobús.
● [*v*] montar, andar *Do you know how to ride a bike?* ¿Sabe Ud. montar en bicicleta? ▲ pasear, ir *We rode in a beautiful car.* Fuimos en un auto espléndido. ▲ molestar *Oh, stop riding me.* Oh, deje de molestarme. ▲ tener una marcha *This car rides smoothly.* Este auto tiene una marcha muy suave. ‖ *He gave me a ride in his car the whole way.* Me llevó en su auto todo el camino.

rider jinete.

ridicule [*n*] burla *They greeted his suggestion with ridicule.* Recibieron su sugestión con burlas.
● [*v*] ridiculizar, poner en ridículo.

ridiculous ridículo.

rifle rifle.

right [*n*] el bien *You seem to have no idea of right and wrong.* Parece que Ud. no distingue el bien del mal. ▲ derecho *I have a right to go if I want to.* Tengo derecho a ir si quiero.
● [*adj*] correcto *This is the right an-*swer. Esta es la contestación correcta. ▲ bueno *We'll leave tomorrow if the weather is right.* Nos iremos mañana si el tiempo está bueno. ▲ derecho *He wears a ring on his right hand.* Lleva un anillo en la mano derecha.
● [*adv*] bien *Do it right or not at all.* Hágalo. Ud. bien o no lo haga. ▲ mismo *The book's right there on the shelf.* El libro está ahí mismo en el estante. ○ **all right** bien *He does his work all right.* Hace su trabajo bien.—*Everything will turn out all right.* Todo saldrá bien. ▲ está bien, bueno *All right, I'll do it if you want me to.* Bueno, lo haré si Ud. quiere. ○ **in . . . right mind** en . . . cabales *You're not in your right mind.* No está Ud. en sus cabales. ○ **on the right** de la derecha *Take the road on the right.* Tome Ud. el camino de la derecha. ○ **right angle** ángulo recto. ○ **right away** ahora mismo *Let's go right away or we'll be late.* Vamos ahora mismo, si no llegaremos tarde. ○ **right now** en este momento *I'm busy right now.* En este momento estoy ocupado. ○ **right side** el derecho *Which is the right side of this material?* ¿Cuál es el derecho de esta tela? ○ **to be right** tener razón *He's right about everything.* Tiene razón en todo. ○ **to right a wrong** corregir un abuso.
‖ *Go right ahead.* Siga Ud. ‖ *I'll be right there.* Ahora mismo voy. ‖ *It serves him right.* Se ha llevado lo que merecía. ‖ *Is this the right way to do it?* ¿Se hace de esta manera? *or* ¿Es así?‖ *That's right.* Eso es. ‖ *The bullet went right through his arm.* La bala le atravesó el brazo. ‖ *They fought right to the end.* Lucharon hasta el fin. ‖ *This one is the right size.* Este está bien de tamaño. ‖ *You did not do the right thing by him.* No se ha portado como debía con él.

rigid rígido.

rind corteza.

ring [*n*] anillo *This ring is too small even for my little finger.* Este anillo me está pequeño hasta en el dedo meñique. ▲ círculo *They formed a ring around the speaker.* Se colocaron en círculo alrededor del orador. ▲ ring, cuadrilátero *We had seats near the ring.* Estábamos sentados cerca del ring. ▲ boxeo *He has just retired from the ring.* Acaba de retirarse del boxeo. ▲ organización *They broke up the ring of spies.* Destruyeron la organización de espionaje.

○ **napkin ring** servilletero.

ring [n] timbre *His voice has a familiar ring.* Su voz tiene un timbre familiar.

● [v] sonar *The phone rang.* Sonó el teléfono. ▲ tocar *Ring the bell.* Toque el timbre. ▲ resonar *The hall rang with applause.* Los aplausos resonaron en el salón. ▲ parecer *His offer rings true.* Su proposición parece sincera. ○ **to give a ring** llamar por teléfono *Give me a ring tomorrow.* Llámeme mañana. ○ **to ring out** sonar *Two shots rang out.* Sonaron dos detonaciones. ○ **to ring up** llamar por teléfono *Ring him up some night next week.* Llámele una noche de la semana próxima.

rinse enjuagar.

riot [n] tumulto, motín *He was injured in the riot.* Le hirieron en el motín.

● [v] amotinarse *The people rioted in the streets.* La gente se amotinó en las calles.

‖ *That movie is a riot.* Esa película es divertidísima.

rip [n] rasgón *You have a rip in your sleeve.* Tiene Ud. un rasgón en la manga.

● [v] rasgar *I ripped my pants climbing the fence.* Me rasgué el pantalón al saltar la cerca. ▲ descoser *Rip the hem and I'll shorten the skirt for you.* Descosa Ud. el dobladillo y le acortaré la falda.

ripe maduro *The strawberries should be ripe in another week or two.* Las fresas estarán maduras dentro de una o dos semanas.

‖ *He lived to a ripe old age.* Vivió hasta una edad muy avanzada. ‖ *The time is ripe for action.* Ha llegado el momento de actuar.

ripple [n] rizo, onda.

● [v] rizar, ondear.

rise [n] subida *The people protested against the rise in prices.* La gente protestó de la subida de los precios. ▲ elevación del terreno, altura *The house is on a little rise.* La casa está situada en una pequeña elevación del terreno.

● [v] crecer *The river's rising fast.* El río está creciendo rápidamente. ▲ Levantarse *When will the curtain rise?* ¿A qué hora levantaran el telón? ▲ Ponerse de pie *The men all rose as we came in.* Los hombres se pusieron de pie cuando entramos. ▲ subir *Prices are still rising.* Los precios siguen subiendo. ▲ ascender *He rose to an important post.* Ascendió a un puesto importante. ▲ salir *The sun rises early*

at this time of year. El sol sale temprano en esta época del año.

○ **to give rise to** dar origen a, originar *The rumor gave rise to a lot of unnecessary worry.* El rumor originó muchas preocupaciones innecesarias. ○ **to rise to the occasion** hacer frente a, estar a la altura de *You can depend on her to rise to the occasion.* Puede Ud. confiar en que ella sabrá hacer frente a las circunstancias.

risk [n] riesgo.

● [v] arriesgarse.

rite rito.

rival [n] rival.

● [v] competir *Her beauty rivaled that of the queen's.* Su hermosura competía con la de la reina.

river río.

rivet [n] remache.

● [v] remachar.

roach cucaracha.

road carretera, camino *The road is getting steadily worse.* La carretera es cada vez peor. ▲ camino, vía *He's well on the road to recovery.* Está en camino de restablecerse.

○ **to go on the road** representar en provincias. *When does the show go on the road?* ¿Cuándo representarán esa obra en provincias?

roam vagar.

roar [n] rugido *The lion let out a roar.* El león lanzó un rugido. ▲ estruendo *Do you hear the roar of the motors?* ¿Oye Ud. el estruendo de los motores?

● [v] rugir *The lion was roaring in his cage.* El léon rugía en la jaula.

‖ *They roared with laughter.* Se morían de risa.

roast [n] carne para asar *Buy a big roast.* Compre Ud. un pedazo grande de carne para asar.

● [adj] asado *Do you like roast duck?* ¿Le gusta a Ud. el pato asado?

● [v] asar *That chicken should be roasted longer.* Ese pollo hay que asarlo más. *I'm roasting in here, how about you?* Me estoy asando aquí dentro, ¿Y Ud.?

roast beef rosbif, carne de vaca asada.

rob robar *They'll rob you of everything you've got.* Le robarán todo lo que tiene Ud.

robber ladrón.

robbery robo.

robe bata *(dressing gown).*

robin petirrojo.

rock [n] roca *Their house is built on solid rock.* Su casa está construida sobre la roca. ▲ escollo *The ship was* *wrecked on a rock.* El barco naufragó contra un escollo. ▲ piedra *That's no pebble, that's a rock.* No es una china, es una piedra.

rock [*v*] vibrar, temblar *The earthquake made the whole house rock.* El temblor hizo vibrar la casa entera. ▲ mecer *Rock the baby to sleep.* Meza el niño hasta que se duerma. ▲ balancearse, mecerse *Stop rocking in that chair.* Deja de mecerte en la silla.

rod varilla, barra *We need new curtain rods.* Necesitamos varillas nuevas para las cortinas. ▲ caña *I bought a new fishing rod.* He comprado una nueva caña de pescar.

roll [*n*] rollo *Did you buy a roll of wrapping paper?* ¿Compró Ud. un rollo de papel de envolver? ▲ lista *Have they called the roll yet?* ¿ Han pasado ya la lista? ▲ fajo *He took out a big roll of bills.* Sacó un gran fajo de billetes. ▲ panecillo *I like coffee and rolls for breakfast.* Me gusta desayunar café y panecillos.

● [*v*] hacer rodar *Roll the barrel over here.* Haga rodar el barril hasta aquí. ▲ rodar *The ball rolled down the hill.* La pelota rodó cuesta abajo. ▲ enrollar hacer *He rolls his own cigarettes.* El mismo hace sus cigarillos. ▲ pasar el rodillo *The court needs rolling.* Hay que pasar el rodillo por el campo de tenis. ▲ balancearse, moverse *The ship rolled heavily.* El barco se balanceaba mucho.

○ **roll by** pasar *I get more homesick as the months roll by.* Tengo más nostalgia a medida que pasan les meses. ○ **to roll along** andar, ir *This car rolls along smoothly.* Este auto anda suavemente. ○ **to roll into a ball** hacer una bola *Roll the paper into a ball for the kitten to play with.* Haga una bola de papel para que el gatito juegue con ella. ○ **to roll out** extender (con el rollo) *Roll the dough out thin.* Extienda la masa muy delgada. ○ **to roll up** enrollar *We rolled up the rug.* Enrollamos la alfombra. ▲ remangarse *Roll up your shirt sleeves a little bit.* Remánguese Ud. un poco las mangas de la camisa.

‖ *Roll over.* Dése la vuelta.

roller rueda (*caster*).

romance amor *He was the one romance in her life.* Fué el único amor de su vida. ▲ novela romántica *She was reading a romance.* Estaba leyendo una novela romántica. ▲ diversión *There isn't much romance in washing*

dishes. No es muy divertido lavar los platos.

romantic romántico.

roof tejado *The tin roof's only temporary.* El tejado de lata es provisional.

○ **roof of the mouth** paladar *I burned the roof of my mouth.* Me quemé el paladar. ○ **to be roofed with** tener el tejado de *The cottage is roofed with slate.* La quinta tiene el tejado de pizarra.

room [*n*] cuarto, habitación *Where can I rent a furnished room?* ¿Dónde puedo alquilar un cuarto amueblado? ▲ sitio *Is there room for one more?* ¿Hay sitio para uno más?

● [*v*] alojarse *Where is he rooming?* ¿Dónde se aloja?

○ **room and board** pensión completa *What do they charge for room and board?* ¿Cuánto piden por la pensión completa?

‖ *I see a lot of room for improvement.* Me parece que se podría mejorar mucho.

rooming house pensión.

rooster gallo.

root raíz *This tree has very deep roots.* Este árbol tiene las raices muy profundas. ▲ origen *Let's get at the root of the matter.* Vayamos al origen del asunto.

○ **by the roots** de raíz *The hurricane pulled up the trees by the roots.* El huracán arrancó los árboles de raíz. ○ **to take root** arraigar *Has the rosebush taken root yet?* ¿Arraigó ya el rosal?

rope cuerda, soga *He slid down the rope.* Se deslizó por la cuerda.

○ **to give (one) rope** dar libertad, dejar suelto *His father gave him too much rope.* Su padre le dejó demasiado suelto. ○ **to know the ropes** Estar al tanto de las cosas.

rose rosa *They presented the singer with a bouquet of roses.* Le regalaron a la cantante un ramo de rosas.

○ **bed of roses** lecho de rosas *His life is no bed of roses!* ¡Su vida no es un lecho de rosas!

rosebush rosal *How do you like my rosebushes?* ¿Le gustan a Ud. mis rosales?

rosy rosado.

rot pudrir(se).

rotation rotación

rotten podrido *The peaches in the bottom of the basket are rotten.* Los melocotones del fondo del cesto están podridos. ▲ malo *That was a rotten trick* Esa fué una mala jugada.

rouge colorete.

rough [*adj*] tempestuoso, agitado *The water's pretty rough today.* El agua está hoy muy agitada. ▲ quebrado *How well can this truck take rough ground?* ¿Marcha bien este camión por un terreno quebrado? ▲ áspero *The bark of this tree is very rough.* La corteza de este árbol es muy aspera. ▲ sin pulimentar *This table is made of rough planks.* Esta mesa está hecha de tablas sin pulimentar. ▲ aproximado *This will give you a rough idea.* Esto le dará una idea aproximada. ▲ duro, malo *They had a rough time of it.* Las pasaron muy duras *or* Pasaron una mala temporada. ▲ brusco *The teacher was rough with the students.* El maestro era brusco con sus alumnos. ● [*adv*] duramente, con dureza *Treat him rough!* ¡Trátale con dureza! ○ **rough** draft borrador *Here's a rough draft of my speech.* Aquí está el borrador de mi discurso. ○ **to rough** it vivir sin comodidades *He didn't enjoy roughing it last summer.* No le gustó vivir sin comodidades el verano pasado.

round [*n*] asalto *In what round was the boxer knocked out?* ¿En qué asalto quedó fuera de combate el boxeador? ▲ ronda *He ordered another round of drinks.* Pidió otra ronda. ▲ recorrido *The newsboy is on his rounds.* El chico de los periódicos está haciendo su recorrido. ● [*adj*] redondo *They have a round table in the living room.* Tienen una mesa redonda en la sala. ▲ *I'm speaking in round numbers.* Habla en números redondos. ▲ lleno *What nice, round, rosy cheeks!* ¡Qué mejillas más llenas y rosadas! ● [*v*] dar la vuelta a *As soon as you round the corner you will see the store.* En cuanto dé la vuelta a la esquina verá Ud. la tienda. ● [*prep*] a la vuelta de *He's just coming round the corner.* Ahora mismo llega a la vuelta de la esquina. ▲ alrededor *The handkerchief has lace round the edge.* El pañuelo tiene un borde de encaje. ○ **all the year round** Todo el año *I live here all the year round.* Vivo aquí todo el año. ○ **to go round** dar la vuelta a *I'll go round the block with you.* Daré la vuelta a la manzana con Ud. ○ **to go round and round** dar vueltas *They were waltzing round and round.* Daban vueltas bailando el vals. ○ **to**

round off redondear *Round off the corners a little.* Redondee un poco las esquinas. ○ **to round out** completar *I need this to round out my collection.* Me falta esto para completar mi colección. ‖ *Is there enough candy to go round?* ¿Hay bastantes dulces para todos? ‖ *That story sure made the rounds.* Ese cuento ha corrido por todas partes. **round trip** viaje de ida y vuelta. ○ **round-trip ticket** boleto de ida y vuelta [*Am*], billete de ida y vuelta [*Sp*].

rouse despertar.

route ruta, vía.

routine [*n*] marcha *You've been disturbing the office routine.* Ha estado Ud. dificultando la marcha de la oficina. ● [*adj*] rutinario *That's just a routine job.* Es un trabajo rutinario.

row [*n*] pelea, bochinche *We had quite a row on our street last night.* Anoche se armó un bochinche bastante grande en nuestra calle.

row [*n*] fila *They stood in a row awaiting their turn.* Estaban en fila esperando su turno.

row [*v*] remar *You'll have to row too.* También tiene Ud. que remar. ‖ *Row me across the river.* Lléveme al otro lado del río.

royal real, regio.

rub [*n*] fricción *The nurse gave him an alcohol rub.* La enfermera le dió una fricción con alcohol. ● [*v*] rozar *The back of the chair's rubbing (against) the wall.* El respaldo de la silla roza (contra) la pared. ▲ frotar *He rubbed his hands together.* Se frotó las manos. ▲ restregar *Better rub the clothes hard or they won't get clean.* Hay que restregar bien la ropa porque si no, no quedará limpia. ○ **to rub in** machacar *I know I'm wrong, don't rub it in.* Sé que no tengo razón, no machaques más. ○ **to rub out** borrar *You forgot to rub out your name.* Se ha olvidado Ud. de borrar su nombre.

rubber caucho, [*Am*] hule *They used a lot of rubber in these tires.* Han usado mucho caucho en estos neumáticos.

rubbers zapatos de hule [*Mex and C.A.*], chanclos [*Sp*], zapatones [*Colom*].

rubbish basura.

rude descortés *Don't be so rude!* ¡No sea Ud. tan descortés!

ruffle [*n*] volante.

rug alfombra *I like oriental rugs.* Me gustan las alfombras orientales.

ruin [*n*] ruina *He caused the ruin of his family.* Causó la ruina de su familia. —*You'll be the ruin of me.* Tu vas a ser mi ruina.

● [*v*] estropear *This material's ruined.* Esta tela está estropeada. ▲ dañar *The frost will ruin the crop.* La escarcha va a dañar la cosecha. ▲ arruinar *He's ruining his health.* Está arruinando su salud.

○ ruins ruinas *Did you ever visit the ruins of the Coliseum?* ¿Ha visitado Ud. las ruinas del Coliseo? ▲ ruinas, escombros *They were hunting for bodies among the ruins.* `Buscaban cadáveres entre los encombros. ○ to be ruined arruinarse *He was ruined in the bank failure.* Se arruinó en la quiebra del banco.

rule [*n*] regla *What are the rules of the game?* ¿Cuáles son las reglas del juego? ▲ dominio, mando *This island has been under foreign rule for years.* Hace muchos años que esta isla está bajo el dominio extranjero.

● [*v*] rayar. *I want a tablet of ruled writing paper.* Necesito un bloc de papel rayado. ▲ llevar, guiar *He's ruled by his emotions.* Se deja llevar por sus emociones. ▲ regir, gobernar *The same family has been ruling for generations.* La misma familia gobierna hace muchos años.

○ as a rule por regla general *As a rule I don't drink.* Por regla general no bebo. ○ to rule out excluir *This doesn't entirely rule out the other possibility.* Esto no excluye enteramente la otra posibilidad. ∙

‖ *That sort of thing is the rule around here.* Eso es lo que se hace por aquí.

ruler regla *Measure this line with a ruler.* Mida esta línea con una regla. ▲ gobernante *The new ruler of this country is well liked.* El nuevo gobernante de este país es muy querido.

rum ron.

rumble [*n*] ruido sordo.

● [*v*] retumbar.

rumor [*n*] rumor.

run [*n*] carrera *He's coming on the run.* Viene a la carrera. ▲*There's a run in your stocking.* Tiene Ud. una carrera en la media. ▲ viaje *The truck goes a hundred miles on each run.* El camión hace cien millas en cada viaje. ▲ racha *That run of luck pulled him*

out of debt. Esa racha de suerte lo sacó de sus deudas.

● [*v*] correr *You'll have to run if you want to catch the train.* Tiene que correr si quiere coger el tren. ▲ *I let the water run down my back.* Dejé que el agua me corriera por la espalda. ▲ trepar *Ivy is running up the wall.* La yedra trepa por la pared. ▲ pasar *The road runs right by my house.* El camino pasa por delante de mi casa. ▲ andar, marchar *That engine hasn't run well since we bought it.* Ese motor no anda bien desde que lo compramos. ▲ manejar *Can you run a washing machine?* ¿Sabe Ud. manejar una máquina de lavar? ▲ estar en vigor *This law runs until next year.* Esta ley estará en vigor hasta el año próximo. ▲ llegar *My horse ran last.* Mi caballo llegó el último. ▲ clavarse *I ran a splinter into my finger.* Me clavé una astilla en el dedo. ▲ pasar *Run the rope through this ring.* Pase la soga por esta anilla. ▲ correrse, desteñirse *These colors are guaranteed not to run.* Se garantiza que estos colores no se corran. ▲ decir *How does the first line run?* ¿Qué dice el primer renglón? ▲ hacerse carreras *Do rayon stockings run worse than silk?* ¿Se le hacen más carreras a las medias de rayón que a las de seda natural?

○ in the long run a la larga *You're bound to succeed in the long run.* Es seguro que a la larga tendrá Ud. éxito. ○ run down agotado de salud *She looks terribly run down.* Parece muy agotada. ▲ abandonado *The house is run down.* La casa está muy abandonada. ○ to have a running nose estar mocoso *The baby's nose has been running for the last few days.* El niño está mocoso en estos días. ○ to run across (or into) encontrar *When did you last run across him?* ¿Cuál fué la última vez que le encontró Ud? ○ to run a risk correr un riesgo. ○ to run around with ir en compañía de, andar con *He's running around with a fast crowd.* Anda por ahí con unos juerguistas. ○ to run away huir, escaparse *My dog ran away.* Mi perro se escapó. ▲ huir *He ran away when he saw me.* Huyó al verme. ○ to run away with llevarse *He ran away with my best suit.* Se llevó mi mejor traje. ○ to run down acabarse la cuerda, pararse *Wind up the clock before it runs down.* Dé cuerda al reloj antes de que se pare. ▲ atropellar *He was run down by a truck.* Fué atropellado por un camión. ▲ hablar mal de *She ran her sister down to all her friends.* Habló mal de su hermana a todos sus amigos. ○ **to run dry** secarse *The well never runs dry.* El pozo nunca se seca. ○ **to run for** presentarse *Who ran for president that year?* ¿Qué candidatos se presentaron para la presidencia aquel año? ▲ ser candidato para, aspirar a *Do you think he will run for mayor?* ¿Cree Ud. que será uno de los candidatos para la alcaldía? ○ **to run in the family** ser de familia *That trait runs in the family.* Este es un rasgo de familia. ○ **to run into** chocar con *The car ran into a tree.* El auto chocó con un árbol. ○ **to run off** fugarse *She ran off with a soldier.* Se fugó con un soldado. ○ **to run out** acabarse *Our supply of sugar has run out.* El azúcar se nos ha acabado. ▲ echar *They ran him out of the country.* Le echaron del país. ○ **to run out of** acabársele a uno *We ran out of ammunition.* Se nos han acabado las municiones. ○ **to run over** derramarse, salirse *The bathtub is running over.* Se está derramando el agua del baño. ▲ repasar *Run over your part before the rehearsal.* Repase su papel antes del ensayo. ○ **to run short** andar escaso *I'm running short of cash.* Ando escaso de dinero. ○ **to run wild** volverse salvaje *They're letting their children run wild.* Están dejando que sus hijos se vuelvan unos salvajes. ‖ *The run of that play is amazing.* Es asombroso el número de veces que se ha dado esa obra. ‖ *There's a run on these goods.* Hay una gran demanda de estos artículos. ‖ *That's out of the usual run.* Esto está fuera de lo corriente. ‖ *That play has been running a year.* Esa obra la están dando desde hace un año. ‖ *Don't leave the faucet running.* No deje el grifo abierto. ‖ *In what sizes do these dresses run?* ¿En qué tallas se hacen estos

vestidos? ‖ *Along what lines do his interests run?* ¿Qué cosas son las que le interesan? ‖ *Don't let your imagination run away with you.* No se deje llevar por su imaginación.

rung peldaño, travesaño *Is the top rung strong enough?* ¿Es bastante fuerte el peldaño superior?

runner corredor *There were five runners in the race.* Hubo cinco corredores en la carrera. ▲ patín *One of the runners of my sled is broken.* Uno de los patines de mi trineo está roto.

running board estribo.

rush [n] aglomeración *At 5 o'clock there's always a rush.* A las cinco siempre hay mucha aglomeración. ▲ prisa *What's your rush?* ¿Por qué tiene tanta prisa? ▲ junco *That swamp was full of rushes.* Ese pantano estaba lleno de juncos. ▲ ruido *You could hear the rush of water.* Se oía el ruido de la corriente.
● [v] darse prisa *They rushed to the bank.* Se dieron prisa para llegar al banco. ▲ enviar con rapidez, inmediatamente *Rush him to the hospital.* Envíele inmediatamente al hospital. ○ **to rush through** hacer de prisa *They rushed through their work.* Hicieron de prisa el trabajo. ‖ *This is the rush season in our business.* Esta es la época en que tenemos más negocios. ‖ *It was a rush job.* Era un trabajo que había que hacer de prisa. ‖ *The blood rushed to his face.* Se sonrojó *or* Se puso colorado.

rust [n] orín, herrumbre *The knives are covered with rust.* Los cuchillos están cubiertos de herrumbre.
● [v] oxidarse *Oil the parts or they will rust.* Lubrique las piezas porque si no se oxidarán.

rusty mohoso, herrumbroso.

rut surco, rodada *This road is full of ruts.* Este camino está lleno de surcos. ○ **to be in a rut** no progresar.

rye centeno.

S

sack saco *I want a sack of potatoes.* Quiero un saco de patatas. ○ **to get the sack** echar, despedir *How many in the office got the sack?* ¿A cuántos echaron de la oficina?

sacred sagrado.

sacrifice [n] sacrificio.
● [v] sacrificar.

sad triste *What happened to him was very sad.* Fué muy triste lo que le sucedió. ▲ pobre *That's a sad excuse.* Esa es una pobre excusa. ▲ desgraciado, triste *Have you heard the sad news of his death?* ¿Se ha enterado de la triste noticia de su muerte? ○ **to make sad** entristecerse *It makes* *me sad to see you looking so unhappy.* Me entristece verla tan afligida.

saddle [n] silla de montar.

● [v] ensillar.

sadness tristeza.

safe [n] caja fuerte, caja de caudales *Please put this in the safe.* Haga el favor de poner esto en la caja de caudales.

● [adj] seguro *Is the bridge safe?* ¿Es seguro el puente? ▲ *He's safe in jail.* Está seguro en la cárcel. ▲ a salvo *You are safe now.* Ahora está Ud. a salvo. ▲ bien fundado *That's a safe guess.* Esa es una suposición bien fundada.

○ **safe and sound** sano y salvo. ○ **be on the safe side** para mayor seguridad. *Let's take ten dollars with us just to be on the safe side.* Llevemos diez dólares para mayor seguridad.

safely sin peligro, a salvo.

○ **to arrive safely** llegar sin novedad.

safety [n] protección, seguridad *This is for your safety.* Esto es para su protección.

● de seguridad *Miners use safety lamps.* Los mineros usan lámparas de seguridad.

safety pin imperdible.

sail [n] vela *That boat has very pretty sails.* Ese barco tiene muy bonitas velas.

● [v] zarpar, hacerse a la mar *When do we sail?* ¿Cuándo zarpamos? ▲ navegar *This boat is sailing slowly.* Este barco navega lentamente. ▲ embarcarse *We sail for Europe today.* Hoy nos embarcamos para Europa. ▲ llevar, gobernar *Can you sail a boat?* ¿Puede Ud. llevar un barco?

○ **to go for a sail** dar un paseo por mar.

sailor marinero.

saint santo.

sake razón *This is for the sake of economy.* Esto es por razón de economía.

○ **for my sake** por mí. ○ **for your sake** por su bien, por consideración a Ud.

‖ *For God's sake!* ¡Por Dios!

salad ensalada.

salary salario, sueldo.

sale venta *Our sales doubled this year.* Nuestras ventas se duplicaron este año. ▲ saldo *When are you holding a sale?* ¿Cuándo va Ud. a tener un saldo?

salesgirl vendedora.

salesman vendedor.

salmon salmón.

salon salón.

saloon taberna, cantina.

salt [n] sal *I want some salt for my meat.* Quiero sal para la carne.

● [adj] salado *I like to swim in salt water.* Me gusta nadar en agua salada.

○ **salt pork** cerdo en salazón *Do you have salt pork?* ¿Tiene Ud. cerdo en salazón? ○ **to put salt** poner sal *Did you put salt in the soup?* ¿Ha puesto Ud. sal en la sopa? ○ **to salt away** guardar, conservar *I understand he's salted away a good deal for his old age.* Tengo entendido que ha guardado mucho dinero para su vejez. ○ **to take with a grain of salt** tomar con reserva, no tomar en serio *I always take what she says with a grain of salt.* Siempre tomo lo que ella dice con reserva.

salt shaker salero de mesa.

salute saludar.

salve emplasto, ungüento.

same mismo *Can you go and be back on the same day?* ¿Puede Ud. ir y volver en el mismo día? — *He's not the same as he was ten years ago.* Ya no es el mismo que era hace diez años. — *I got up and he did the same.* Me levanté y él hizo lo mismo. ▲ igual *Is this the same as the other chair?* ¿Es esta silla igual a la otra?

○ **all the same** lo mismo *That's all the same to me.* A mí me da lo mismo. ▲ no obstante, a pesar de todo *All the same, I want to see it.* No obstante, quiero verlo.

sample [n] muestra. *Here's a sample of the material I want.* Aquí hay una muestra de la tela que quiero.

● [v] probar *Won't you sample some of this wine?* ¿No quiere Ud. probar un poco de este vino?

sand arena.

sandal sandalia.

sandwich emparedado, sandwich.

sandy arenoso.

sane cuerdo, sano.

sanitarium sanatorio.

sanitary higiénico.

sap [n] savia *This branch has no sap.* Esta rama no tiene savia. ▲ estúpido, topo *He's an awful sap.* ¡Es un estúpido! *or* ¡Es un topo!

● [v] agotar *That work sapped our strength.* Aquel trabajo agotó nuestras fuerzas.

sapphire zafiro.

sarcasm sarcasmo.

sat *See* sit.

sateen satén.

satin raso.

satire sátira.

satisfaction satisfacción.

satisfactory satisfactorio *Is everything satisfactory?* ¿Es todo satisfactorio?

satisfy satisfacer *I am not satisfied with my new apartment.* No estoy satisfecho con mi nuevo apartamiento.— *Does this answer satisfy you?* ¿Le satisface esta respuesta? ○ **to be satisfied** estar seguro, estar convencido *I'm not satisfied that he's guilty.* No estoy convencido de que sea culpable. ○ **to satisfy one's thirst** apagar la sed, quitar la sed *Will this glass of beer satisfy your thirst?* ¿Le quitará la sed este vaso de cerveza?

Saturday sábado.

sauce salsa.

saucer platillo, paila [*Am*].

sauerkraut col agria.

sausage salchicha.

savage salvaje.

save guardar *Could you save this for me?* ¿Puede Ud. guardarme esto? ▲ reservar *Is this seat being saved for anybody?* ¿Está reservado este asiento? ▲ cuidar, cuidarse *Save your voice.* Cuídese la voz. ▲ salvar *He saved her life.* Le salvó la vida. ▲ ahorrar, evitar *You can save yourself the trouble.* Puede Ud. ahorrarse la molestia. ▲ coleccionar *He saves stamps.* El colecciona sellos.

saving [*n*] ahorro.

savings ahorros. ○ **savings bank** caja de ahorros.

savor [*n*] sabor, dejo.

saw [*n*] sierra, serrucho *Could I borrow a saw?* ¿Podría pedir prestado un serrucho? ● [*v*] aserrar *He sawed the logs in half.* Aserró los leños por la mitad.

say [*n*] opinión *I insist on having my say.* Insisto en expresar mi opinión. ● [*v*] decir *What did you say?* ¿Qué dijo Ud.? — *I said what I thought.* Dije lo que pensaba. — *They say it's going to rain tonight.* Dicen que va a llover esta noche. — *I'll meet you, say in an hour.* Me encontraré con Ud., digamos dentro de una hora. — *What was said at the meeting?* ¿Qué dijeron en la reunión? ‖ *He has the whole say around here.* El único que opina aquí es él.

scald [*v*] escaldar.

scale [*n*] escama *The fish has shiny scales.* El pez tiene las escamas brillantes. ▲ escala, graduación *The scale on this barometer is hard to read.* Es difícil leer la escala en este barómetro. ▲ escala *What is the wage scale in this factory?* ¿Cuál es la escala de jornales en esta fábrica? — *This map has a scale of one inch to a hundred miles.* La escala de este mapa es de una pulgada por cien millas. ● [*v*] escamar *Please scale the fish.* Haga el favor de escamar el pescado. ▲ escalar *They scaled the cliff with difficulty.* Escalaron la peña con dificultad. ○ **on a large scale** en gran escala *They've planned improvements on a large scale.* Han proyectado hacer mejoras en gran escala. ○ **platform scale** báscula. ○ **scales** balanza *Put the meat on the scales.* Ponga Ud. la carne en la balanza. ○ **to practice scales** hacer escalas *She practiced scales all day.* Tocaba escalas todo el día. ○ **to scale down** reducir, rebajar *All their prices have been scaled down.* Todos sus precios han sido rebajados.

scalp cuero cabelludo.

scandal escándalo.

scar cicatriz.

scarce escaso *Apples are scarce this year.* Las manzanas están escasas este año.

scare [*n*] susto. ● [*v*] asustar.

scarf bufanda.

scarlet escarlata. ○ **scarlet fever** escarlatina.

scatter esparcir, echar *The boy scattered the papers all over the room.* El niño esparció los periódicos por toda la habitación. ▲ dispersar *Wait until the crowd scatters.* Espere Ud. hasta que la multitud se disperse. ○ **scattered** en desorden *I found everything scattered around.* Encontré todo en desorden.

scenario argumento escénico, libreto.

scene vista, paisaje *That's a beautiful scene.* Esa es una hermosa vista. ▲ escena *This is the third scene of the second act.* Esta es la tercera escena del segundo acto. ○ **behind the scenes** entre bastidores *I met him behind the scenes.* Le encontré entre bastidores. ▲ bajo cuerda, entre bastidores *The details were worked out behind the scenes.* Se acordaron los pormenores bajo cuerda. ○ **to make a scene** hacer escenas *Don't make a scene.* No haga Ud. escenas. ‖ *Where's the scene of the play?* ¿Dónde transcurre la acción de la obra?

scenery paisaje; decoración (*theater*).

scent [n] olor *These flowers have a wonderful scent.* Estas flores tienen un olor maravilloso. ▲ olfato *His hunting dogs have very keen scent.* Sus perros de caza tienen un olfato muy agudo. ● [v] husmear, rastrear *The dogs have scented the fox.* Los perros han husmeado la zorra.

schedule programa, plan; horario (*train*).

scheme [n] proyecto, esquema. ● [v] proyectar, idear.

scholar escolar, estudiante; sabio, erudito, hombre de letras (*learned man*).

scholarship beca *He won a scholarship for a year's study abroad.* Ganó una beca para estudiar un año en el extranjero.

school escuela *Do you go to school?* ¿Asiste Ud. a la escuela? — *He went to the School of Mines.* Fué a la Escuela de Minas. — *The whole school turned out to welcome him back.* Toda la escuela le dió la bienvenida a su regreso.—*He belongs to a new school of thought.* Pertenece a una nueva escuela de ideas. ▲ las clases *When is school out?* ¿Cuándo se terminan las clases? ▲ banco *We were directly above a school of fish.* Estábamos exactamente encima de un banco de peces. ○ **school books** libros de texto. ○ **to school** enseñar *He was schooled to control his temper.* Se le enseñó a dominar el mal genio.

science ciencia.

scientific científico.

scientist hombre de ciencia.

scissors tijeras.

scold [v] regañar.

scope alcance; plan (*coverage*). ○ **to be within the scope of** estar comprendido en, estar al alcance de.

scorch [v] chamuscar.

score [n] tantos *What's our score?* ¿Como estamos de tantos? ▲ partitura *He never uses a score when he conducts.* Nunca usa la partitura cuando dirige. ▲ veintena (*twenty*). ● [v] hacer tantos *He scored five points.* Hizo cinco tantos. ▲ marcar los tantos *How does one score this game?* ¿Cómo se marcan los tantos en este juego? ▲ instrumentar *This work is scored for piano and orchestra.* Esta obra está instrumentada para piano y orquesta. ○ **to settle the score** desquitarse *I'll settle the score with him.* Voy a desquitarme con él.

scorn [n] desprecio.

● [v] despreciar.

scotch whisky *A scotch and soda, please.* Un whisky con soda, por favor.

scout [n] explorador. ● [v] explorar.

scramble [n] rebatiña *There was a terrific scramble to buy up the best stock.* Había una rebatiña terrible para adquirir el mejor surtido. ● [v] trepar *The monkey scrambled up the tree to get the fruit.* El mono trepó al árbol para coger la fruta. ○ **scrambled eggs** huevos revueltos *I'd like some scrambled eggs and bacon.* Quisiera huevos revueltos con tocino.

scrap [n] pizca *There isn't a scrap of food in the icebox.* No hay pizca de comida en la nevera. ▲ riña *Did you hear about the scrap the neighbors had last night?* ¿Oyó Ud. la riña que tuvieron anoche los vecinos? ● [v] reñir, pelear *Why are they always scrapping?* ¿Por qué están riñendo siempre? ▲ desechar *The government plans to scrap some of the older planes.* El gobierno se propone desechar algunos de los aviones más viejos. ○ **scrap metal** chatarra, hierro viejo *They'll probably turn these old cars into scrap metal.* Probablemente harán chatarra de estos viejos coches. ○ **scrap paper** papel borrador. ○ **scraps** sobras *Give the scraps to the dog.* Dé Ud. las sobras al perro.

scrape [n] lío, enredo *He's always getting into scrapes.* Siempre está metiéndose en líos. ● [v] raspar *How can we scrape the paint off the door?* ¿Cómo podemos raspar la pintura de la puerta? ▲ restregar *Don't scrape your feet on the floor.* No restriegue los pies en el piso. ▲ rasguñar, arañar *He scraped his knee.* Se rasguñó la rodilla. ○ **to scrape together** juntar poco a poco.

scratch [n] raspadura *Who made this scratch on the desk?* ¿Quién hizo esta raspadura en el escritorio? ▲ rasguño *Where did you get that scratch on your cheek?* ¿Dónde se hizo Ud. ese rasguño en la mejilla? ● [v] raspar, rayar *Be careful not to scratch the furniture.* Tenga cuidado de no raspar los muebles. ▲ arañar *This pen scratches the paper.* Esta pluma araña el papel. ○ **from scratch** sin nada *That man started his business from scratch.* Ese hombre empezó su negocio sin nada. O **scratch out** quitar, suprimir *You'd better scratch out that paragraph.* Mejor será que quite Ud. ese párrafo.

scream [n] grito *I thought I heard a scream.* Creí haber oído un grito.

● [v] gritar *Don't scream!* ¡No grite Ud.! ▲ reventar de risa *Everybody simply screamed at his jokes.* Todos reventaban de risa con sus chistes. ‖ *That movie is a scream.* Esa película es divertidísima.

screen [n] tela metálica *We'd better get the holes in the screen fixed.* Sería mejor arreglar los agujeros de la tela metálica. ▲ biombo *You can change your clothes in back of that screen.* Puede cambiarse la ropa detrás de ese biombo. ▲ pantalla *(motion picture) I don't like to sit too close to the screen.* No me gusta sentarme demasiado cerca a la pantalla.

● [v] ocultarse *They tried to screen themselves from public notice.* Trataron de ocultarse de la vista del público.

screw [n] tornillo *These screws need tightening.* Hace falta apretar estos tornillos.

● [v] atornillar *Screw in the bolt.* Atornille el perno. ▲ enroscar *Screw the nut on carefully.* Enrosque bien la tuerca.

screwdriver destornillador.

scripture Escritura, Biblia.

scrub fregar, restregar.

scrubwoman fregona.

scrupulous escrupuloso.

sculptor escultor.

sculpture escultura.

sea mar *How far are we from the sea?* ¿A qué distancia estamos del mar? — *Have you ever been to the Red Sea?* ¿Ha estado Ud. alguna vez en el Mar Rojo?

O **at sea** confuso *Her answers left me completely at sea.* Sus contestaciones me dejaron completamente confuso. O **to be at sea** navegar *They have been at sea for the past three weeks.* Han estado navegando las tres últimas semanas. O **to go to sea** zarpar *When is that boat going to sea?* ¿Cuando va a zarpar ese barco? ▲ hacerse a la mar, comenzar a navegar *He went to sea before he was twenty.* Comenzó a navegar antes de cumplir los veinte años.

seacoast costa, costa marítima.

seal [n] sello *I like the seal on your ring very much.* Me gusta mucho el sello de su anillo. ▲ foca *Let's feed the seals.* Vamos a dar de comer a las focas.

● [v] cerrar *Let me add a few words before you seal the letter.* Déjeme añadir unas palabras antes de que cierre Ud. la carta. ▲ decidir, determinar *The court's decision sealed the prisoner's fate.* La sentencia decidió la suerte del prisionero.

seam costura.

seaman marinero.

search [n] registro *We'll have to make a thorough search.* Tendremos que hacer un registro minucioso.

● [v] buscar *I've searched everywhere for her.* La he buscado por todas partes. ▲ registrar *We'll have to search you.* Tendremos que registrarle.

O **in search of** en busca de *He went in search of gold.* Salió en busca de oro.

season [n] estación *Fall is my favorite season.* El otoño es mi estación favorita. ▲ temporada *This is the best season for hiking.* Esta es la mejor temporada para hacer excursiones a pié. — *The hotelkeeper said this was their best season in many years.* El hotelero dijo que ésta había sido la mejor temporada desde hacía muchos años.

● [v] curar *Has this wood been seasoned long enough?* ¿Ha sido curada suficientemente esta madera? ▲ sazonar, condimentar *The food is too heavily seasoned.* La comida está demasiado sazonada. O **in season of** temporada, de estación *Are strawberries in season yet?* ¿Están de temporada las fresas? O **seasoned** fogueado *Those men are seasoned soldiers.* Esos hombres, son soldados fogueados.

seasoning condimento.

seat [n] asiento *This seat needs fixing.* Este asiento necesita compostura. — *I beg your pardon, sir, I believe this is my seat.* Perdóneme, señor, creo que éste es mi asiento. — *He has a seat in Congress.* Tiene asiento en el Parlamento. ▲ localidad *I want two seats for the play.* Quiero dos localidades para la función. ▲ residencia *Where's the seat of government?* ¿Dónde esta la residencia del gobierno?

● [v] sentarse, tomar asiento *May I be seated?* ¿Puedo sentarme? ▲ tener capacidad para *This theater seats several hundred people.* Este teatro tiene capacidad para varios cientos de personas.

○ **seat of one's pants** fondillos *The seat of my pants is torn.* Llevo los fondillos rotos. ○ **to take a seat** tomar asiento, sentarse *Tell him to take a seat.* Dígale que tome asiento.

second [n] segundo *He ran a hundred yards in ten seconds.* Hizo las cien yardas en diez segundos. — *Wait a second.* Aguarde un segundo. ▲ defectuoso, inferior, [*Cuba*] segunda *These stockings are seconds.* Estas medias son defectuosas.

● [adj] segundo *He's second in command.* Es el segundo en mando.

● [v] apoyar, secundar *I second the motion.* Apoyo la moción. ▲ secundar *He seconded everything she did.* Secundó todo lo que ella hizo.

○ **second-hand** de segunda mano, de ocasión. ○ **second-rate** de segunda clase, de segunda categoría. ○ **to have a second helping** repetir de una cosa *May I have a second helping?* ¿Puedo repetir de esto? *or* ¿Me permite repetir? ‖ *Upon second thought I've decided to stay.* Después de pensarlo bien, he decidido quedarme.

secret [n] secreto *Can you keep a secret?* ¿Puede Ud. guardar un secreto?

● [adj] secreto *It was a secret agreement.* Fué un acuerdo secreto.

secretary secretario *I want a secretary.* Quiero una secretaria. ▲ papelera, escritorio *He bought a new secretary.* Compró una papelera nueva. ▲ ministro *He's the Secretary of the Treasury.* Es el Ministro de Hacienda.

section parte *Cut the cake into equal sections.* Corte Ud. el pastel en partes iguales. ▲ sección *What section of the class is he in?* ¿En qué sección de la clase está él? — *The part I'm referring to is in Chapter 1, Section 3.* La parte a que me refiero se encuentra en el capítulo 1, sección 3. ▲ barrio *I was brought up in this section of town.* Me crié en este barrio de la ciudad.

secure [adj] seguro *Is this bolt secure?* ¿Es seguro este cerrojo? — *I feel secure in my new job.* Me siento seguro en mi nuevo empleo.

● [v] asegurar *Secure the latch before you leave.* Asegure Ud. la aldaba antes de irse. ▲ garantizar *Is your loan secured?* ¿Está garantizado su préstamo? ▲ obtener, conseguir *Can you secure a seat on the plane for me?* ¿Puede Ud. conseguirme un asiento en el avión?

security seguridad, garantía.
seduce seducir.

see ver *May I see your pass?* ¿Puedo ver su pase? — *We've just seen a good movie.* Acabamos de ver una buena película. — *Can you see in this light?* ¿Puede Ud. ver con esta luz? — *See what can be done about it.* Vea Ud. lo que se puede hacer sobre ello.— *I'd like to see more of you.* Me gustaría verle más a menudo. — *Come to see me tomorrow.* Venga a verme mañana. — *I don't see it that way.* Yo no lo veo de esa manera. — *He's seen a lot in his time.* Ha visto mucho en sus tiempos.

▲ ver, presenciar *Who saw the accident?* ¿Quién vió el accidente? ▲ encargarse de *Please see that this letter is mailed.* Encárguese Ud. de que se eche esta carta al correo. ▲ comprender *I see what you mean.* Comprendo lo que Ud. quiere decir. ▲ rendir *These boots have seen plenty of service.* Estas botas han rendido muy buen servicio.

○ **to see someone off** despedir a alguien *Will anyone see her off?* ¿Vendrá alguien a despedirla? ○ **to see someone to** acompañar a alguien *Let me see you to the door.* Permítame que le acompañe hasta la puerta. ○ **to see through** llevar a cabo, ver hasta el fin *I intend to see the project through.* Me propongo llevar a cabo el proyecto. ▲ ver a través de *I can see through his politeness.* Puedo verle el juego a través de sus cortesías. ▲ **to see to** encargarse, cuidar de *I'll see to the arrangements.* Me encargaré de los preparativos.

‖ *See you again.* Hasta la vista. ‖ *Did they see her through the trouble?* ¿La ayudaron ellos a salir del paso?

seed [n] semilla *This store sells all kinds of seeds.* Esta tienda vende toda clase de semillas.

● [v] quitar la semilla, despepitar *These raisins have been seeded.* A estas pasas les han quitado las semillas. ▲ sembrar *When did you seed the lawn?* ¿Cuándo sembró Ud. el césped?

○ **to go to seed** dar grano, granar *The plant has gone to seed.* La planta ha granado.

seek buscar *I didn't seek this job.* Yo no he buscado este empleo. ▲ tratar *He seeks to persuade everybody.* Trata de convencer a todo el mundo.

○ **sought after** solicitado *He's much sought after.* Es una persona muy solicitada.

seem parecer *I seem to be interrupting.* Me parece que estoy interrumpiendo.

— *How does that seem to you?* ¿Qué le parece a Ud. eso?

seize agarrar *He seized the reins and mounted the horse.* Agarró las riendas y saltó sobre el caballo. ▲ confiscar *The authorities seized all property owned by enemy aliens.* Las autoridades confiscaron todas las propiedades que pertenecían a nuestros enemigos. ▲ aprovechar *He seized every opportunity that came his way.* Aprovechaba todas las oportunidades que se le presentaban. ▲ detener *The police seized everyone in the place.* La policía detuvo a todo el mundo en el lugar. ▲ apoderarse de, capturar *We seized the town after a short battle.* Nos apoderamos del pueblo después de una corta batalla.

seldom raramente, rara vez.

select [*adj*] escogido *These are select peaches.* Estos son melocotones escogidos. ▲ selecto *She went to a select school.* Asistió a una escuela selecta. ● [*v*] elegir *Please select a few of the best oranges for me.* Haga el favor de elegirme algunas naranjas de las mejores.

selection selección.

self ‖ *His better self won out.* Pudo en él más su lado bueno.

selfish egoísta.

self-starting de arranque eléctrico, de arranque automático *It's a self-starting motor.* Es un motor de arranque eléctrico.

self-supporting ‖ *She's self-supporting.* Se mantiene a sí misma.

sell vender *I sold the piano for two hundred dollars.* Vendí el piano por [*or* en] doscientos dólares. — *They sell furniture.* Venden muebles. ○ to sell one on an idea convencer *If you had been more tactful you might have sold him on the idea.* Si Ud. hubiera tenido más tacto, quizás le habría convencido. ○ to sell out traicionar, vender *Someone sold us out to the enemy.* Alguien nos vendió al enemigo. ▲ liquidar, vender *They sold out their whole stock before closing.* Liquidaron sus existencias antes de cerrar.

semester semestre.

semicolon punto y coma.

senate senado.

senator senador.

send mandar, poner *I want to send a telegram.* Quiero mandar un telegrama. ▲ enviar, mandar *Could you*

send this to me? ¿Podría Ud. mandarme esto? ○ to send for llamar *We will send for you when we need you.* Le llamaremos cuando le necesitemos. ○ to send in hacer, entrar, hacer pasar *Send him in.* Hágale entrar *or* Que entre. ‖ *They sent him to prison for five years.* Le condenaron a cinco años de cárcel.

sensation sensación.

sensational sensacional.

sense [*n*] sentido *Have you lost your sense of hearing?* ¿Ha perdido Ud. el sentido del oído? — *He doesn't have any sense of responsibility.* No tiene ningún sentido de la responsabilidad. — *In what sense do you mean what you just said?* ¿Qué sentido le da Ud. a lo que acaba de decir? — *That doesn't make sense.* Eso no tiene sentido. ▲ juicio *He has sense enough to stay out of trouble.* Tiene suficiente juicio para no provocar dificultades. ● [*v*] sospechar *Do you sense something unusual?* ¿Sospecha Ud. algo extraordinario?

sensible sensato, cuerdo.

sentence [*n*] frase *I didn't understand that last sentence.* No entendí esa última frase. ▲ sentencia *The sentence which the judge gave was unjust.* La sentencia que pronunció el juez era injusta. ● [*v*] condenar, sentenciar *He was sentenced to five years in prison.* Le condenaron a cinco años de cárcel.

sentiment sentimiento.

sentimental sentimental.

separate [*adj*] separado, aparte *We want separate rooms if possible.* Queremos cuartos separados si es posible. ▲ por separado *I'd like to make a separate settlement.* Me gustaría hacer un arreglo por separado. **separate** [*v*] dividir *Separate the class into five sections.* Divida Ud. la clase en cinco secciones. ▲ separar *We'd better separate the two boys who are fighting.* Es mejor que separemos a los dos niños que están peleando. ▲ separarse *When did she separate from her husband?* ¿Cuándo se separó ella de su marido? ○ to be separated estar separado *We don't want to be separated.* No queremos estar separados.

September septiembre.

serene sereno, sosegado.

sergeant sargento.

series serie.

serious verdadero *Did you make a serious attempt to find him?* ¿Hizo Ud. un verdadero esfuerzo por encontrarle? ▲ serio *Why are you so serious?* ¿Por qué está Ud. tan serio? ▲ grave *Is his illness serious?* ¿Es grave su enfermedad?

sermon sermón.

servant criado *I want to hire a servant.* Quiero tomar un criado. ▲ funcionario *He made his career as a public servant.* Hizo su carrera como funcionario público.

serve servir *Please serve dinner now.* Haga el favor de servir le comida ahora. — *How long did you serve in that capacity?* ¿Cuánto tiempo sirvió Ud. en ese cargo? — *Can I serve you in any way?* ¿Puedo servirle en algo? ▲ merecer *It serves you right.* Lo tiene Ud. muy merecido. ▲ cumplir *He is serving a life term in prison.* Está cumpliendo condena perpetua. ▲ hacer *He served the summons on us.* Nos hizo una citación judicial. ▲ servir, sacar *Whose turn is it to serve (tennis)?* ¿A quién le toca servir?

service servicio *I'd like to offer my services.* Me gustaría ofrecer mis servicios. — *I want to complain about the service.* Quiero quejarme del servicio. — *He enlisted in the service.* Se alistó en el servicio. ▲ servicio religioso *When do they hold services?* ¿Cuándo celebran servicios religiosos? ▲ saque, servicio *He has an excellent service (tennis).* Tiene un saque magnífico. ○ Civil Service administración pública, servicio público *Has she a civil service job?* ¿Tiene ella un puesto en la administración pública? ○ service station puesto de gasolina, estación de servicio *Let's stop at the next service station.* Paremos en el próximo puesto de gasolina. ○ to be of service ser útil *Will this book be of service to you?* ¿Le será útil a Ud. este libro? ○ to be serviced reparar *I'm leaving my car here to be serviced.* Dejo mi automóvil aquí para que lo reparen. ‖ *I'm at your service.* Estoy a sus órdenes.

session sesión.

set [n] colección *Do you have the complete set of his works?* ¿Tiene Ud. la colección completa de sus obras? ▲ juego *I want a chess set.* Quiero un juego de ajedrez. ▲ medio *He doesn't fit in our set.* El no encaja en nuestro medio. ▲ equipo, aparato *My radio set needs a new tube.* A mi aparato de radio le hace falta una nueva válvula. ● [adj] terco, obstinado *He's very set in his ways.* Es muy terco. ▲ dispuesto *Are you all set to go?* ¿Tiene Ud. todo dispuesto para marcharse? ● [v] poner, colocar *Set it over there.* Póngalo allí. ▲ poner *I want to set my watch.* Quiero poner mi reloj en hora. — *The prisoner will be set free.* El prisionero será puesto en libertad. — *I set my heart on going today.* He puesto todo mi empeño en marcharme hoy. — *They set him to counting the money.* Le pusieron a contar el dinero. — *Can you set words to this music?* Puede Ud. ponerle letra a esta música? ▲ componer *Set this paragraph in italics.* Componga Ud. este párrafo en cursivas. ▲ fijar *He set the price at fifty dollars.* Fijó el precio en cincuenta dólares. ▲ dar *Try to set an example.* Procure Ud. dar ejemplo. ▲ cuajar *Has the pudding set yet?* ¿Se ha cuajado ya el budín? ▲ ponerse *The sun sets at six o'clock tonight.* Esta tarde el sol se pone a las seis. ▲ empollar *Is the hen setting?* ¿Está empollando la gallina? ○ sets decoraciones *Who designed the sets for the play?* ¿Quién hizo las decoraciones para el espectáculo? ○ to set aside apartar, separar *Set this aside for me.* Aparte Ud. esto para mí. ▲ desechar, rechazar *The judge's decision was set aside.* La decisión del juez fué desechada. ○ to set back hacer retroceder, regular *Fascism has set Italy back fifty years.* El fascismo ha hecho retroceder cincuenta años a Italia. ○ to set down poner por escrito *Set down the main arguments.* Ponga por escrito los argumentos principales. ▲ aterrizar *He set the plane down in the center of the runway.* Aterrizó el avión en medio de la pista de aterrizaje. ○ to set forth exponer, dar a conocer *He set forth his position quite clearly.* Expuso su posición con toda claridad. ○ to set in comenzar *The rainy season set in early this year.* La estación de lluvias comenzó temprano este año. ○ to set off salir *We're setting off on our hike tomorrow morning.* Saldremos de caminata mañana por la mañana. ▲ hacer resaltar, realzar *A red belt will set off the colors of this dress nicely.* Un cinturón rojo hará resaltar los colores del vestido. ▲ hacer estallar *He set off the fire cracker.* Hizo estallar el triquitraque. ○ to set one straight on aclararse *Set me straight on this.*

Acláreme esto. ○ **to set out** salir *They were lucky for having set out on time.* Tuvieron bastante suerte por haber salido a tiempo. ○ **to set up** poner, establecer *When did they set up housekeeping?* ¿Cuándo pusieron casa? ▲ inaugurar *When will the exposition be set up?* ¿Cuándo se inaugurará la exposición? ▲ armar, montar *Set up the tent.* Arme la tienda. ▲ edificar *I intend to set up a house on this spot.* Pienso edificar una casa en este lugar. ▲ hacerse pasar, presumir *He sets himself up as an important fellow.* Se hace pasar por una persona importante. ‖ *His eyes are set far apart.* Tiene los ojos muy separados. ‖ *The trunk is so heavy I have to set it down.* Es tan pesado el baúl que tengo que ponerlo en el suelo.

settle establecer *In what part of the country did they settle?* ¿En qué parte del país se han establecido? ▲ colocarse, instalarse *He settled himself in that chair.* Se instaló en esa silla. ▲ posarse *Wait until the tea leaves settle to the bottom.* Aguarde a que las hojas del té se posen en el fondo. ▲ ceder *The road has settled a little.* El camino ha cedido un poco. ▲ solucionar *Can you settle this question?* ¿Puede Ud. solucionar esta cuestión? ▲ satisfacer *All legitimate claims will be settled.* Todas las reclamaciones legítimas serán satisfechas. ○ **settled** firme *He seems to be very settled in his convictions.* Parece ser muy firme en sus convicciones. ○ **to settle down** sentar la cabeza *Hasn't he settled down yet?* ¿No ha sentado todavía la cabeza? ▲ establecerse *He's settled down in New York.* Se ha establecido en Nueva York. ▲ ponerse a hacer *The boy couldn't settle down to his homework.* El niño no podía ponerse a hacer los deberes. ○ **to settle on** ponerse de acuerdo *They settled on the terms of the treaty.* Se pusieron de acuerdo sobre los términos del tratado.

settlement acuerdo *Haven't they reached a settlement yet?* ¿No han llegado todavía a un acuerdo? ▲ arreglo, ajuste *They made a friendly settlement.* Hicieron un arreglo amistoso. ▲ caserío *You'll find a native settlement about ten miles upstream.* Encontrará Ud. un caserío a unas diez millas río arriba.

seven siete.
seventeen diecisiete.

seventh séptimo.
seventy setenta.
several varios.
severe grave *He just got over a severe illness.* Acaba de pasar una enfermedad grave. ▲ duro *Are the winters here severe?* ¿Son muy duros aquí los inviernos? ▲ severo *Don't be so severe with the child.* No sea Ud. tan severo con el niño. ▲ sencillo *The dress has very severe lines.* Es un vestido de líneas muy sencillas. ‖ *This motor will have to undergo a severe test.* Hay que examinar escrupulosamente este motor.

sew coser *She makes her living by sewing.* Se gana la vida cosiendo. — *Please sew the buttons on.* Haga el favor de coser los botones. ‖ *Sew up the seam.* Haga Ud. esta costura.

sewer alcantarilla, cloaca.
sewing costura. ○ **sewing machine** máquina de coser.
sex sexo.
shack choza, cabaña.

shade [n] sombra *Let's stay in the shade.* Quedémonos a la sombra. — *Light and shade are well balanced in this painting.* Las sombras y los claros están bien combinados en este cuadro. ▲ tono *Can you match this shade of red?* ¿Puede Ud. darme un tono rojo como éste? ▲ transparente *Pull down the shades.* Baje los transparentes. ● [v] resguardarse, protegerse *Shade your eyes from the glare.* Protéjase Ud. los ojos del resplandor. ▲ sombrear *Shade this part a little more.* Sombree Ud. esta parte un poco más.

shadow [n] sombra *That tree casts a long shadow.* Ese árbol da una gran sombra. — *He clings to him like his shadow.* Le sigue como su sombra. — *He's just a shadow of his former self.* No es más que una sombra de lo que fué. ▲ asomo, sombra *There is not a shadow of doubt about the truth of the story.* No hay ni asomo de duda acerca de la verdad del relato. ● [v] seguir los pasos *They hired someone to shadow him.* Contrataron a una persona para seguirle los pasos.

shake [n] movimiento *He answered with a shake of his head.* Contestó con un movimiento de cabeza. ● [v] sacudir *He took the child by the shoulders and shook him.* Agarró al niño por los hombros y le sacudió. ▲ agitar *Shake well before using.* Agítese antes de usarlo. ▲ tiritar *He was* *shaking with cold.* Estaba tiritando de frío. ▲temblar *That accident made me shake with fright.* Aquel accidente me hizo temblar de miedo. ▲conmoverse *I was deeply shaken by her death.* Me conmovió profundamente su muerte.

○ **to shake hands** estrechar la mano. ○ **to shake off** sobreponerse *He shook off his sorrow and continued his work.* Se sobrepuso a su dolor y continuó su trabajo. ▲quitarse *The mud will shake off your shoes easily when it dries.* Se quitará fácilmente el barro de sus zapatos cuando se seque. ▲desprender *The wind has shaken all the leaves off the trees.* El viento ha desprendido todas la hojas de los árboles. ○ **to shake out, to shake off** sacudir *Shake the dust out of that rug.* Sacuda el polvo de esa alformbra. ○ **to shake out of** sacar de *The news shook him out of his indifference.* Las noticias le sacaron de su indiferencia.

‖ *He was badly shaken up by the accident.* Recibió una fuerte sacudida en el accidente.

shall ‖ *Shall I wait?* ¿Espero? or ¿Debo esperar? ‖ *Shall I close the window?* ¿Cierro la ventana? ‖ *I shall do it.* Lo haré. ‖ *Let's have dinner now, shall we?* ¿Le parece que comamos ahora? or Vamos a comer ahora ¿le parece? ‖ *"Thou shalt not kill."* "No matarás." ‖ *They shall not pass.* No pasarán.

shallow superficial, poco profundo.

shame vergüenza *He'll never live down the shame of his disgrace.* Jamás podrá sobrevivir la vergüenza de su desgracia. ▲lástima *Isn't it a shame he couldn't come?* ¿No es una lástima que no pudo venir?

○ **in shame** avergonzado *He hid his face in shame.* Escondió la cara avergonzado.

shampoo champú, shampoo.

shape [*n*] forma *His head has a very funny shape.* Su cabeza tiene une forma muy rara. ▲estado *What shape is the car in?* ¿En qué estado está el coche?

● [*v*] modelar, dar forma *He shaped the clay into a bust.* Modeló un busto con la arcilla.

○ **in shape** en orden, arreglado *Is the room in shape?* ¿Está la habitación arreglada? ○ **to shape up** marchar, ir *How are things shaping up?* ¿Cómo van las cosas?

‖ *I'm in bad shape.* Me siento mal (*health*). or Estoy en mala situación (*circumstances*).

share [*n*] acción *How many shares of stock do you hold in that company?* ¿Cuántas acciones tiene Ud. en esa compañía? ▲parte *You'll have to do your share.* Tendrá Ud. que hacer su parte.—*You'll have to pay your share of the bill.* Tendrá Ud. que pagar su parte de la cuenta.

● [*v*] compartir *May I share your seat?* ¿Puedo compartir con Ud. el asiento? ▲repartir *Let's share the pie.* Vamos a repartir el pastel. ▲compartir, participar *They shared the secret.* Participaron del secreto.

sharp afilado *Is there a sharp knife in the drawer?* ¿Hay un cuchillo afilado en la vageta? ▲agudo *He's got a sharp mind.* Tiene una mente muy aguda. —*I have a sharp pain in my side.* Tengo un dolor agudo en el costado. ▲acerbo, duro *What you say is a very sharp criticism.* Lo que Ud. dice es una crítica muy acerba. ▲en punto *We have to be there at five o'clock sharp.* Tenemos que estar allí a las cinco en punto.

○ **sharp-sighted** perspicaz. ○ **sharp-witted** agudo de ingenio.

‖ *The air is very sharp this morning.* Hoy corta mucho el aire.

sharpen afilar.

shatter destrozar, hacer pedazos.

shave afeitar *They had to shave his head for the operation.* Tuvieron que afeitarle la cabeza para operarle. ▲afeitarse *I have to shave before dressing.* Tengo que afeitarme antes de vestirme. ▲raspar *If you shave the soap, it will melt faster.* Si raspa Ud. el jabón se derretirá más pronto.

○ **to shave off** acepillar *Use a plane to shave off the edge of the door.* Use Ud. un cepillo para acepillar el borde de la puerta.

‖ *I went to the barber for a haircut and shave.* Fuí a la barbería para cortarme el pelo y afeitarme.

shawl chal, pañolón, mantón.

she ella *She is not the one I met.* Ella no es la persona que yo conocí.—*Find out what she wants.* Averigüe qué es lo que ella quiere. ▲hembra *Is the puppy a he or a she?* ¿Es un perrito macho o hembra?

shed cobertizo, [*Am*] galpón.

sheep oveja *How many sheep have you?* ¿Cuántas ovejas tiene Ud.?

○ **black sheep** oveja negra, garbanzo negro *He's the black sheep of the family.* El es la oveja negra de la familia.

or El es el garbanzo negro de la familia.

sheet pliego, hoja *I want a hundred sheets of paper.* Quiero cien pliegos de papel. ▲ sábana *Put clean sheets on the bed.* Ponga Ud. sábanas limpias en la cama.

shelf estante.

shell [*n*] concha *He has a pretty collection of shells.* Tiene una linda colección de conchas. ▲ cáscara *I can't break the shell of this coconut.* No puedo romper la cáscara de este coco. ▲ proyectil *A shell nearly hit him.* Por poco le alcanza un proyectil. ● [*v*] desgranar, desvainar *Are the peas all shelled?* ¿Están desgranados todos los guisantes? ▲ bombardear *We shelled the enemy positions for hours.* Bombardeamos las posiciones del enemigo durante horas.

shelter [*n*] albergue *He only wants shelter for tonight.* Quiere solamente albergue para esta noche. ▲ refugio *Where's the shelter?* ¿Dónde está el refugio? ● [*v*] albergar *Who sheltered the refugees?* ¿Quién albergó a los refugiados?

shepherd pastor.

sherbet sorbete.

sherry jerez.

shield [*n*] escudo. ● [*v*] proteger, amparar. ○ **police shield** chapa de policía.

shift [*n*] tanda, turno *Which shift do you work on?* ¿En qué turno trabaja Ud.? ▲ cambio *There's a shift in the plans.* Hay un cambio en los planes. ● [*v*] cambiar de dirección *The wind has shifted.* El viento ha cambiado de dirección. ▲ cambiar, meter *You'd better shift into second.* Es mejor que cambie Ud. a segunda. *or* Es preferible que meta Ud. la segunda. ▲ mudar *They shifted the furniture from one room to another.* Mudaron los muebles de una habitación a otra. ○ **to shift for oneself** arreglárselas solo *You'll have to shift for yourself now.* Ahora tendrá que arreglárselas solo.

shin espinilla.

shine [*n*] brillo *Your shoes haven't got enough shine on them.* No se les ha sacado bastante brillo a sus zapatos. ● [*v*] brillar *Her face is shining with joy.* Su rostro brilla de alegría. ▲ alumbrar, proyectar *Shine the light over here.* Proyecte la luz hacia aquí. ▲ lustrar, limpiar *I want my shoes shined.* Quiero lustrarme los zapatos. ▲ sobresalir, distinguirse *He shone in*

his studies. Sobresalió en sus estudios. ‖ *The sun isn't shining very hard today.* Hoy no hay mucho sol. ‖ *We'll come, rain or shine.* Vendremos, llueva o haga buen tiempo.

shiny brillante.

ship [*n*] barco *When does the ship leave?* ¿Cuándo zarpe el barco? ▲ aeronave, avión *He was piloting a two-motored ship.* Piloteaba un avión bimotor. ● [*v*] embarcar *I want to ship this.* Quiero embarcar esto. ○ **to ship water** hacer agua *This rowboat ships water.* Este bote hace agua.

shipment embarque, cargamento, remesa.

shipwreck naufragio.

shirt camisa.

shiver tiritar.

shock choque, shock *The wounded man is suffering from shock.* E! herido padece un choque traumático. ▲ choque *When the two trains collided there was a terrible shock.* Al topar los dos trenes se projudo un terrible choque. ▲ corriente, descarga *Don't touch that wire or you'll get a shock.* No toque Ud. ese alambre que le dará una corriente. ▲ emoción, impresión *His death was a great shock to us all.* Su muerte nos causó a todos una gran impresión. ○ **to be shocked** escandalizarse *I'm shocked to hear you say that.* Me escandaliza oírle decir eso.

shoe [*n*] zapato *I want a pair of shoes.* Quiero un par de zapatos. ● [*v*] herrar *Who's going to shoe the horse?* ¿Quién va a herrar el caballo? ○ **in someone else's shoes** en el pellejo de otro *Put yourself in his shoes.* Póngase Ud. en su pellejo.

shoe horn calzador.

shoelace cordón de zapato.

shoemaker zapatero.

shoe polish betún, pasta, crema para los zapatos.

shoot [*n*] tallo, renuevo, vástago *The new shoots are coming up fast.* Están brotando rápidamente los nueves tallos. ● [*v*] disparar, tirar *Don't shoot!* ¡No dispare Ud.! ▲ hacer, disparar *He shot a million questions at us.* Nos hizo un millón de preguntas. ▲ salir disparado *The car shot down the street.* El automóvil salió disparado calle abajo. ▲ tomar *I wish I could learn to shoot action pictures.* Me gustaría aprender a tomar instantáneas fotográficas. ○ **to shoot up** crecer *How fast that child has shot up in the last year!* ¡Con que rapidez ha crecido ese niño en este último año!

‖ *Sharp pains are shooting up and down my leg.* Siento punzadas por toda la pierna. ‖ *Just at the last moment he managed to shoot a goal.* En el último momento metió un goal.

shop [*n*] tienda *I'm going to the shop next to the movies.* Voy a la tienda de al lado del cine.

● [*v*] ir de compras *Let's go shopping.* Vamos de compras.

○ **tobacco shop** estanco, [*Am*] tabaquería, cigarrería *I'm looking for a tobacco shop.* Estoy buscando una tabaquería. ○ **to shop around** ir de tiendas *I want to shop around before I buy the present.* Quiero ir de tiendas antes de comprar el regalo. ○ **to talk shop** hablar de los quehaceres *or* negocios de uno.

‖ *You'll have to take this to a shoe repair shop.* Tendrá Ud. que llevar esto al zapatero.

shore orilla *How far is it to the other shore?* ¿Qué distancia hay a la otra orilla? ▲ tierra *Let's pull the boat farther up on shore.* Arrastremos el bote más hacia tierra. ▲ costa, playa *I want to go to the shore for a vacation.* Quiero ir de vacaciones a la playa.

‖ *I'm on shore leave.* Estoy en tierra con permiso.

short [*adj*] corto *I want my hair cut short.* Quiero que me corte el pelo corto.—*This coat is too short.* Este abrigo es demasiado corto. ▲ tosco, brusco *You are too short with the child.* Ud. es demasiado tosco con el niño.

● [*adj*] repentinamente *He stopped short when he saw us.* Se detuvo repentinamente al vernos.

○ **in a short time** dentro de poco *I'll be back in a short time.* Volveré dentro de poco. ○ **in short** en una palabra, en suma, en resumen *I have neither the time, nor the inclination; in short, I refuse.* No tengo tiempo ni ganas; en una palabra, rehuso. ○ **short circuit** corto circuito. ○ **short cut** atajo *Is there a short cut home?* ¿Hay algún atajo de aquí a casa? ○ **short of** falto de *We have run short of supplies.* Estamos faltos de existencias. ○ **to cut short** interrumpir *Her mother's illness cut their vacation short.* La enfermedad de su madre les interrumpió las vacaciones. ○ **to fall short** no alcanzar *The factory fell short of its goal.* La fábrica no alcanzó el rendimiento fijado. ○ **to fall short of one's**

expectation defraudar una esperanza *The picture fell short of our expectations.* El cuadro defraudó nuestras esperanzas. ○ **to run short** quedarse falto, hallarse falto *We ran short of paper.* Nos quedamos faltos de papel. ▲ escasear *Our supplies were running short.* Nuestras existencias estaban escaseando.

‖ *His action is nothing short of criminal.* Su acción es realmente criminal. ‖ *Nothing short of an operation can save him.* Sólo una operación le podrá salvar. ‖ *They stopped just short of the railroad tracks.* Pararon justamente antes de llegar a la vía.

shorten acortar, abreviar.

shorthand taquigrafía.

shortly en breve, dentro de poco *We're leaving for the country shortly.* Nos iremos al campo dentro de poco.

shorts (*underwear*) calzoncillos *He asked for six pairs of shorts.* Pidió seis pares de calzoncillos.

short story cuento.

shot [*n*] disparo *Did you hear a shot?* Oyó Ud. un disparo? ▲ tiro *He took a shot at the sniper.* Disparó un tiro al tirador emboscado.—*Good shot!* ¡Buen tiro! ▲ tirador *He's a good shot.* Es un buen tirador. ▲ instantánea *That's a good shot of the mountain.* Esa es una buena instantánea de la montaña. ▲ trago, sorbo *I want a shot of whisky.* Quiero un trago de whisky.

should ‖ *I should like to start early.* Me gustaría empezar temprano. ‖ *I told them that I should be able to come in time.* Les dije que podría llegar a tiempo. ‖ *What should I do?* ¿Qué debería yo hacer? ‖ *How should I know?* ¿Cómo iba yo a saber? ‖ *If it should turn out nice, we will go.* Iremos si hace buen tiempo.

shoulder [*n*] hombro *My shoulder hurts.* Me duele el hombro. ▲ paseo de carretera *The shoulder of the road is slippery.* El paseo de la carretera está resbaladizo.

● [*v*] cargar al hombro, llevar a hombros *He shouldered the pack.* Cargó el fardo al hombro. ▲ cargar con, asumir *Who'll shoulder the blame for this?* ¿Quién cargará con la culpa de esto? ○ **shoulder pad** hombrera. ○ **straight from the shoulder** sin rodeo, cara a cara *He gave it to him straight from the shoulder.* Se lo dijo sin rodeos. ○ **to give the cold shoulder** tratar con frialdad *Why did you give him the cold* *shoulder?* ¿Por qué le trató Ud. con frialdad?

‖ *We shouldered our way through the mob.* Nos abrimos paso a empellones por entre la muchedumbre.

shout [n] grito *Did you hear a shout just now?* ¿Oyó Ud. un grito ahora mismo? ● [v] gritar *You don't have to shout.* No hay necesidad de gritar.

shove [n] empujón, empellón *He gave the child a shove.* Le dió un empujón al niño.

● [v] empujar *We shoved the rowboat into the water.* Empujamos el bote agua adentro.

○ **to shove off** marcharse, irse *Well, it's time I shoved off.* Ya es hora de que me marche. ○ **to shove someone around** *Quit shoving me around.* Deje de empujarme de un lado para otro.

shovel pala.

show [n] espectáculo, función *At what time does the show go on?* ¿A qué hora empieza el espectáculo? ▲ ostentación *She made too much of a show of her jewels.* Hizo demasiada ostentación de sus joyas.

● [v] indicar *Could you show me the way?* ¿Podría Ud. indicarme el camino? ▲ enseñar, mostrar *Have you shown this to anyone?* ¿Ha enseñado Ud. esto a alguien?—*Show me how to do it.* Enséñeme como hacerlo. ▲ mostrar *His work showed great care.* Su trabajo mostraba mucho esmero. ▲ mostrarse *He showed great kindness to me when I was in trouble.* Se mostró generoso conmigo en momentos difíciles. ▲ probar, justificar *They weren't able to show why they needed more time.* No pudieron probar porqué necesitaban más tiempo. ▲ representar, dar *What are they showing at the theater?* ¿Qué están representando en el teatro?

○ **to show off** presumir *Don't you think he shows off a good deal?* ¿No cree Ud. que el presume demasiado? ○ **to show up** presentarse, aparecer *He never showed up.* Nunca se presentó. ▲ destacarse *This color shows up well against the dark background.* Este color se destaca bien contra el fondo obscuro. ▲ descubrir, exponer *I intend to show up your dishonesty.* Tengo intención de exponer su falta de honradez.

‖ *Does my slip show?* ¿Se me ve el refajo? ‖ *You made an awful show of yourself at that party.* Dió Ud. un espectáculo horrible en esa fiesta.

showcase escaparate, vidriera, vitrina.

shower [n] chubasco, aguacero *Wait until the shower is over.* Aguarde hasta que pase el chubasco. ▲ ducha *You can take a shower here after the game.* Puede darse una ducha aquí después del partido. ▲ lluvia *We were caught in a shower of sparks from the burning building.* Nos cayó una lluvia de chispas del edificio en llamas.

● [v] inundar *Their friends showered them with presents.* Sus amigos les inundaron de regalos.

shrewd astuto, perspicaz.

shrill agudo, penetrante.

shrimp camarón.

shrink encogerse.

shrub arbusto, mata.

shrug ○ **to shrug one's shoulders** encogerse de hombros.

shuffle arrastrar *Stop shuffling and walk properly.* Deje Ud. de arrastrar los pies y camine correctamente.

○ **to shuffle the cards** barajar *Whose turn is it to shuffle the cards?* ¿A quién le toca barajar?

shun evitar, rehuir.

shut cerrar *Is it shut tight?* ¿Está bien cerrado?—*Shut the door and sit down.* Cierre la puerta y siéntese.

○ **to be shut out of** quedarse fuera de *Don't forget your key, or you'll be shut out of the house.* No olvide Ud. la llave, o se quedará Ud. fuera de la casa. ○ **to shut down** cerrar, clausurar *For how long will the factory be shut down?* ¿Por cuánto tiempo va a estar cerrada la fábrica? ○ **to shut in** encerrar *They shut the dog in the house.* Encerraron al perro en la casa. ○ **to shut off** cerrar *Shut off the water.* Cierre la llave del agua. ○ **to shut up** cerrar *When they went to the country, they shut up their house.* Al irse al campo cerraron la casa. ▲ callarse *We told him to shut up.* Le dijimos que se callara.

shutter persiana.

shy tímido.

sick enfermo *He's sick in bed with pneumonia.* Está enfermo en cama con pulmonía.—*I'm going to get sick.* Me voy a poner enfermo. ▲ enfermizo *The child has a sick look.* El niño tiene un aspecto enfermizo. ▲ aburrido, cansado *I'm sick of working.* Estoy aburrido de trabajar.

○ **the sick** los enfermos *Who takes care of the sick?* ¿Quién está al cuidado de los enfermos?

|| *The soldier was given sick leave.* Se le dió licencia al soldado por enfermedad.

side [*n*] lado *The label is on one side of the box.* El rótulo está en un lado de la caja.—*They crossed to the other side of the river.* Cruzaron al otro lado del río.—*Look at every side of the matter.* Vea todos los lados de la cuestión.—*He has no relatives living on his father's side.* No le queda ningún pariente del lado paterno. ▲ parte *His store is on the east side.* Su tienda está en la parte este. ▲ costado *I have a pain in my side.* Tengo un dolor en el costado.— *It's an error on your side.* Es una equivocación de su párte. ▲ partido *Whose side are you on?* ¿Por quién toma Ud. partido? ● [*adj*] lateral *Please use the side door.* Haga el favor de utilizar la puerta lateral. ○ on all sides por todas partes. ○ on the side *He makes some money working on the side.* Aparte de su trabajo se gana algún dinero. ○ right side lado derecho *I can't tell the right side from the wrong.* No puedo distinguir el lado derecho del revés. ○ side issue cuestión secundaria *The point you are bringing up is a side issue.* Lo que Ud. plantea es una cuestión secundaria. ○ side of a hill ladera *They ran down the side of the hill.* Bajaron corriendo por la ladera. ○ to side with one ponerse del lado de alguien, tomar partido por *She used to side with us in our discussions.* Ella acostumbraba ponerse de nuestro lado en las discusiones. ○ to take sides tomar partido *It's difficult to take sides on this question.* Es difícil tomar partido en este asunto. || *This side up!* ¡Esta parte arriba! *or* ¡Este lado para arriba!

side dish plato de entrada, entremés.

sidewalk acera, [*Mex*] banqueta, [*Am*] vereda.

siege asedio, sitio.

siesta siesta.

sigh [*n*] suspiro. ● [*v*] suspirar.

sight [*n*] vista *I have poor sight.* Tengo mala vista.—*Don't lose sight of that man.* No pierda Ud. de vista a ese hombre.—*At first sight I didn't recognize you.* A primera vista no le reconocí. ▲ escena, espectáculo *It was a terrible sight.* Era un espectáculo horrible. ▲ lugar interesante, objeto de interés *Did you see the sights in New York?* ¿Ha visitado Ud. los lugares interesantes de Nueva York? ● [*v*] divisar *When do you expect to sight land?* ¿Cuándo esperan divisar tierra? ○ by sight de vista *I know him only by sight.* Le conozco solamente de vista. ○ in sight a la vista, visible *There was no one in sight.* No había nadie a la vista. ○ to catch sight of ver, alcanzar a ver *I caught sight of you in the crowd.* Le ví entre el gentío. || *They had orders to shoot him on sight.* Tenían órdenes de disparar sobre él a primera vista.

sightseeing || *Let's take a sightseeing bus.* Tomemos el ómnibus para turistas.

sign [*n*] letrero, cartel *What does that sign say?* ¿Qué dice ese letrero? ▲ indicio huella *Have you seen any sign of my friend?* ¿Ha visto Ud. algún indicio de mi amigo? ▲ seña *The waiter gave us a sign to follow him.* El mozo nos hizo seña para que le siguiéramos. ▲ señal *Does he show any signs of improvement?* ¿Muestra algunas señales de mejoría? ▲ muestra *Have you seen any sign of affection between them?* ¿Ha visto Ud. alguna muestra de cariño entre ellos? ● [*v*] firmar *He forgot to sign the letter.* Se le olvidó firmar la carta. ○ to sign away firmar la cesión o el traspaso *He signed away all his property to the bank.* Firmó al banco la cesión de todas sus propiedades. ○ to sign off terminar las emisiones *Radio stations here sign off early in the evening.* Aquí las estaciones de radio terminan sus emisiones temprano por la noche. ○ to sign on contratar, alistar, enrolar *The ship in the harbor is still signing on men.* El barco en el puerto está aún contratando tripulantes. ○ to sign over traspasar *He signed over control of the business to his son.* Traspasó la dirección del negocio a su hijo. ○ to sign up firmar *He signed up for three years.* Firmó por tres años. ▲ inscribirse, alistarse *He signed up for volunteer work.* Se alistó para hacer trabajo voluntario. ▲ contratar *The team signed up a new player.* El equipo ha contratado un nuevo jugador.

signal [*n*] señal *I'll give you the signal when we are ready to leave.* Le haré una señal cuando estemos listos para salir. ● [*v*] hacer señales *Signal that taxi!* ¡Haga Ud. señales a aquel taxi!

signature firma.

significant significante, significativo.

signify significar, dar a entender.

silence silencio *Silence!* ¡Silencio!—*His silence about the price surprised us.* Su silencio acerca del precio nos sorprendió. ● [v] hacer callar *He silenced the audience and went on speaking.* Hizo callar al público y continuó hablando.

silent silencioso, callado *Why are you so silent?* ¿Por qué está Ud. tan callado? —*She's too silent to be good company.* Es demasiado callada para hacer buena compañía. ▲ callado *The newspapers were silent about the accident.* Los periódicos se mantuvieron callados acerca del accidente.

silk seda.

silly tonto.

silver [n] plata *This country produces a great deal of silver.* Este país produce mucha plata. ▲ cubiertos de plata *She received some beautiful silver for a wedding present.* Recibió como regalo de boda unos lindos cubiertos de plata. ▲ dinero suelto, sencillo [Am] *Can you give me some silver for these bills?* ¿Puede Ud. cambiarme estos billetes por dinero suelto? ● [adj] de plata *She's wearing a silver ring.* Lleva un anillo de plata. ▲ blanco *Her hair is all silver.* Tiene todo el pelo blanco. ● [v] azogar, platear *The mirror needs to be silvered.* Es necessario azogar el espejo. ○ **sterling silver** plata de ley.

silverware cubiertos de plata.

similar semejante, similar.

simple sencillo *His manners are simple.* Tiene modales sencillos. — *That's a simple matter.* Ese es un asunto sencillo. ▲ fácil, sencillo *The work here is fairly simple.* El trabajo aquí es bastante fácil. ▲ simple *He had a simple fracture of the arm.* Tenía una simple fractura en el brazo. ▲ simple, torpe *I may seem simple, but I don't understand it.* Pareceré torpe, pero no lo comprendo. ‖ *These are the simple facts.* Estos son escuetamente los hechos.

simplicity sencillez.

simply sencillamente, simplemente.

sin pecado.

since desde *I've had no fun since I got here.* No me he divertido desde que llegué aquí.—*He hasn't been here since Monday.* No ha estado aquí desde el lunes. ▲ puesto que *Since you don't believe me, look for yourself.* Puesto

que no me cree, compruébelo Ud. mismo. ○ **ever since** desde entonces *He broke his leg and has had it in a cast ever since.* Se rompió la pierna y la tiene enyesada desde entonces. ‖ *How long has it been since you last saw her?* ¿Cuánto tiempo hace desde la última vez que la vió?

sincere sincero.

sincerely sinceramente. ‖ *Yours sincerely.* Le saluda atentamente. *or* Su atento y seguro servidor.

sincerity sinceridad.

sing cantar *I can't sing very well.* No puedo cantar muy bien.—*The canaries have been singing all morning.* Los canarios han estado cantando toda la mañana. ▲ cantar, arrullar *Try singing the baby to sleep.* Procure arrular al niño para que se duerma. ▲ silbar *Bullets were singing all around us.* Las balas silbaban en derredor nuestro.

singer cantante.

single solo *I haven't a single thing to eat.* No tengo un solo bocado de comida. ▲ sencillo, para uno *I want a single room if possible.* Quiero una habitación para uno, si es posible. ▲ soltero *Are you married or single?* ¿Es Ud. casado o soltero? ○ **singles** individuales *Let's play singles.* Juguemos individuales. ○ **to single out** escoger, señalar *They singled him out for honorable mention.* Le señalaron para una mención honorífica.

singular singular.

sink [n] fregadero, [Am] *The sink's full of dirty dishes.* El fregadero está lleno de platos sucios. ● [v] hundirse *I'm afraid the boat'll sink if we take more than seven people.* Temo que este bote se hunda si aceptamos más de siete personas. ▲ esconderse *Take that picture before the sun sinks behind the clouds.* Tome Ud. esa fotografía antes de que el sol se esconda detrás de las nubes. ▲ abrir, excavar *Can you suggest a good place to sink a well?* ¿Puede Ud. sugerir un buen sitio para abrir un pozo? ▲ invertir sin provecho *He sank all his money in the business.* Invirtió sin provecho todo su dinero en el negocio. ○ **to sink in** dejar caer *He paused a few minutes to let his remarks sink in.* Hizo una pausa para dejar caer sus observaciones. ○ **to sink into** entrar en, penetrar *I hope that lesson has sunk* *into your head.* Espero que esa leccion se le habrá entrado en la cabeza.

sinus seno.

sip [*n*] sorbo, trago.

● [*v*] sorber, chupar.

sir señor *Yes, sir.* Sí, señor.

siren sirena.

sirloin lomo de vaca, lomo de res.

sister hermana *Do you have any sisters?* ¿Tiene Ud. hermanas? ▲ hermana, monja *Two sisters from the convent came to ask for a donation.* Dos monjas del convento vinieron a pedir un donativo. ○ **sister ship** barco gemelo.

sister-in-law cuñada.

sit sentarse *Where are we sitting tonight?* ¿Dónde nos sentamos esta noche? ▲ posar *She made arrangements to sit for her portrait.* Convino en posar para su retrato.—*There are some pigeons sitting on the fence.* Hay unas palomas posadas en la cerca. ▲ celebrar sesión, estar en audiencia *The court is sitting.* El tribunal está celebrando sesión. ○ **to be sitting** estar sentado *They were sitting when we arrived.* Estaban sentados cuando llegamos. ○ **to be sitting on** estar colocado en *That vase has been on the shelf for years.* Ese jarrón ha estado colocado en el estante durante años. ○ **to sit down** sentarse *Sit down there.* Siéntese allí. ○ **to sit in on** tomar parte, participar de *He sat in on all the conferences that day.* Tomó parte en todas las conferencias ese día. ○ **to sit out** dejar de, pasar por alto *Let's sit this dance out.* Dejemos de bailar esta pieza.—aguantar *I couldn't sit that play out.* No pude aguantar la función hasta el final. ○ **to sit up** incorporarse *He sat up suddenly.* De repente se incorporó. ▲ sentarse *The baby had been sitting up since he was five months old.* El niño se sentaba desde que tenía cinco meses. ▲ estarse levantado *We sat up all night talking.* Estuvimos levantados toda la noche hablando.

situated situado.

situation situación.

six seis.

sixteen dieciséis.

sixth sexto.

sixty sesenta.

size tamaño, número *What size are the shoes?* ¿De qué tamaño son las zapatos? ▲ tamaño *Try this for size.* Pruébese esto para ver el tamaño. ▲ extensión *What's the size of the property?* ¿Cuál es la extensión de la propiedad? ▲ estatura *He's a medium-sized man.* Es un hombre de mediana estatura. ○ **to size up** darse cuenta de, justipreciar *I sized up the situation at a glance.* Me dí cuenta de la situación a primera vista.

skate [*n*] patín.

● [*v*] patinar.

skater patinador.

skating rink pista de patinar.

skeleton esqueleto.

skeptical escéptico.

sketch [*n*] croquis *Draw me a sketch of the first floor.* Hágame un croquis del primer piso. ▲ tipo cómico *He's quite a sketch.* Es un tipo muy cómico.

● [*v*] hacer croquis, dibujar *This is a good place to sketch.* Este es un buen lugar para hacer croquis.

skill habilidad, destreza.

skilled diestro, experto.

skin piel *She has a very white skin.* Tiene una piel muy blanca.—*These shoes are made of alligator skin.* Estos zapatos son de piel de cocodrilo. ▲ piel, corteza *The best part of a potato is near the skin.* Lo mejor de la patata está cerca de la piel.

● [*v*] desollar *The hunter was skinning the deer.* El cazador estaba desollando el ciervo.

○ **by the skin of one's teeth** por un pelo *I made the train by the skin of my teeth.* Alcancé el tren por un pelo.

skip saltar *The little girl skipped down the sidewalk.* La niña iba saltando por la acera. ▲ saltarse, pasar por alto *Skip that chapter.* Sáltese Ud. ese capítulo.

skirt falda, [*Arg*] pollera *Her skirt's too long.* Su falda es demasiado larga.

skull cráneo.

skunk zorrillo, mofeta.

sky cielo *How does the sky look today?* ¿Cómo está el cielo hoy?—*The sky is overcast.* El cielo está nublado.

○ **out of a clear sky** de buenas a primeras *He quit his job out of a clear sky.* Abandonó su empleo de buenas a primeras. ○ **to the skies** por las nubes *He praised her to the skies.* La puso por las nubes.

skyscraper rascacielo.

slack flojo *That rope is very slack.* Esa cuerda está muy floja.—*Business is slack.* Los negocios están flojos. ▲ descuidado, negligente *She's very slack in her work.* Es muy descuidada en su trabajo.

slacken aminorar, disminuir *Slacken your*

speed! ¡Disminuya la velocidad!
▲ ceder, cejar *Don't slacken your efforts until you've gotten what you want.* No ceda en su empeño hasta que haya conseguido lo que quiere.

slacks pantalones.

slander [*n*] calumnia.
● [*v*] calumniar.

slang caló, jerga, argot.

slap [*n*] palmada, bofetada.
● [*v*] dar una palmada, dar una bofetada.

slash tirar tajos y reveses (*sword*); azotar, dar latigazos (*whip*).

slaughter [*n*] mantaza.
● [*v*] matar; hacer una carnicería (*butcher*).
○ **slaughter house** matadero.

slave esclavo.

sled trineo.

sleep [*n*] sueño.
● [*v*] dormir *Did you sleep well?* Durmió Ud. bien?—*I slept well, thanks.* Dormí bien, gracias.
○ **to be sleepy** tener sueño. ○ **to sleep away** pasar el tiempo durmiendo *He slept the afternoon away.* Se pasó la tarde durmiendo. ○ **to sleep off** dormir la mona *Go home and sleep off your drunk.* Vaya Ud. a su casa a dormir la mona.
‖ *I must get some sleep.* Debo dormir algo.

sleeping car coche dormitorio, [*Am*] pullman.

sleet [*n*] cellisca.
● [*v*] cellisquear.

slender delgado.

slice [*n*] tajada, rebanada.
● [*v*] rebanar; cortar en lonchas, cortar en tajadas (*meat*).

slide deslizarse, resbalar.

slight [*n*] desprecio, desaire *She resented the slight.* Ella se ofendió por el desaire.
● [*adj*] leve, ligero *I have a slight cold.* Tengo un catarro ligero. ▲ pequeño *There's a slight difference.* Hay una pequeña diferencia. ▲ delicado *She has a rather slight figure.* Tiene una figura más bien delicada.
❷ [*v*] desairar *I didn't intend to slight you.* No fué mi intención desairarle.

slim delgado.

slip [*n*] combinación *She sent me a beautiful lace slip for my birthday.* Para mi cumpleaños me envió una preciosa combinación de encaje. ▲ imprudencia, pata *Did I make a slip? ¿Cometí* una imprudencia? *or ¿Metí la pata?* ▲ trozo, tira *He wrote the message on*

a slip of paper. Escribió el mensaje en un trozo de papel. ▲ esqueje, gajo *This rose bush grew from a slip.* Este rosal creció de un esqueje.
● [*v*] echar *He slipped the letter into the mailbox.* Echó la carta en el buzón. ▲ deslizar *The drawer slips in easily.* La gaveta se desliza fácilmente. ▲ resbalar *Don't slip on the ice.* No se resbale sobre el hielo. ▲ ponerse *Wait until I slip into a coat.* Espere Ud. hasta que me ponga el abrigo. ▲ escapar *escabullirse Don't let the chance slip.* No deje escapar la oportunidad. ▲ olvidarse *The matter slipped my mind completely.* El asunto se me olvidó completamente.
○ **pillow slip** funda *Please wash the pillow slips.* Haga el favor de lavar las fundas. ○ **to give the slip** dar esquinazo *The thief gave his pursuers the slip.* El ladrón les dió el esquinazo a los que le perseguían. ▲ dejar plantado *She gave me that slip.* Me dejó plantado. ○ **to slip away** escabullirse *Let's slip away quietly.* Escabullámonos silenciosamente. ○ **to slip one's clothes** on vestirse de prisa. ○ **to slip up** meter la pata, colarse *I slipped up badly, didn't I?* Metí la pata, ¿verdad?

slipper zapatilla, pantufla, chinela.

slippery resbaladizo, resbaloso.

slope [*n*] declive *The hill has about a thirty degree slope.* La colina tiene cerca de treinta grados de declive. ▲ pendiente *They raced down the slope.* Bajaron la pendiente corriendo.
● [*v*] estar inclinado *The floor slopes badly.* El piso está muy inclinado.

sloppy chapucero *He's a sloppy writer.* Es un escritor chapucero. ▲ desaliñado *She's very sloppy in her appearance.* Es una mujer muy desaliñada.

slot ranura.

slow lento *Is it a slow train? ¿Es un tren lento?—Cook the soup on a slow fire.* Ponga a hervir la sopa a fuego lento. ▲ blando, mojado (*horse racing*) *The horses are racing on a slow track today.* Los caballos están corriendo hoy en una pista blanda. ▲ retrasado *The teacher is in charge of a class of slow pupils.* La maestra tiene a su cargo una clase de alumnos retrasados. ▲ despacio, lento *Don't drive so slow.* No maneje tan despacio [*Am*]. *or* No conduzca Ud. tan despacio [*Sp*].
○ **slow-witted** torpe, estúpido. ○ **to be slow** atrasar *My watch is an hour slow.* Mi reloj atrasa una hora. ○ **to slow down** ir más despacio *Slow down!*

¡Vaya más despacio! ▲ retardar *It looks as if he's trying to slow down the negotiations.* Parece que está tratando de retardar las negociaciones. ○ **to slow up** ir más despacio *Slow up when you come to a crossing.* Vaya más despacio al llegar a los cruces.

slowly despacio *Can't you drive a little more slowly?* ¿No puede Ud. conducir un poco más despacio? ▲ lentamente *He walks slowly.* Anda lentamente.

sluggish indolente, dejado.

slums barrios bajos.

sly astuto, taimado.

smack [n] manotada *He gave me a smack in the face.* Me dió una manotada en la cara.
● [v] chocar *The car smacked into a tree.* El coche chocó contra un árbol.

small pequeña *The room is quite small.* El cuarto es bastante pequeño.—*Her folks are small farmers.* Es de familia de pequeños agricultores. ▲ menudo *Please gather some small wood.* Haga el favor de recoger leña menuda.—*Chop it up small.* Píquelo muy menudo. ▲ mezquino, ruin *That was an awfully small thing to do.* Fué muy ruin hacer eso.
○ **small arms** armas portátiles. ○ **small change** menudo, suelto *I haven't any small change.* No tengo suelto. *or* No tengo menudo. ○ **small fry** pequeño, pequeñajo; gente menuda (*unimportant people*). ○ **small letters** minúsculas *Print it all in small letters.* Imprímalo todo en minúsculas. ○ **small print** tipo pequeño.
‖ *This is a small matter.* Esto no tiene importancia. *or* Es cosa de muy poca importancia.

smallpox viruelas.

smart [adj] listo *She's a very smart child for her age.* Es una niña muy lista para su edad. ▲ elegante *She wears very smart clothes, don't you think?* Lleva vestidos muy elegantes, ¿verdad?
● [v] escocer *This burn's beginning to smart.* Esta quemadura empieza a escocerme.

smash aplastar, hacer pedazos, hacer añicos.

smear [v] untar, ensuciar, tiznar.

smell [n] olfato *The dog has very keen hearing and smell.* El perro tiene el oído y el olfato muy aguzados. ▲ olor *What is that smell?* ¿Qué olor es ése? —*I don't like the smell.* No me gusta el olor.
● [v] oler *Do you smell smoke?* ¿Huele Ud. humo?—*That perfume smells good.* Ese perfume huele bien.
○ **to smell a rat** darse cuenta de que hay gato encerrado, oler el poste *As soon as she mentioned it, I smelled a rat.* Tan pronto lo mencionó, me dí cuenta de que había gato encerrado. ○ **to take a good smell** oler fuerte *Take a good smell and tell me what you think that is in the bottle.* Huela fuerte y dígame que cree Ud. que hay dentro de la botella.

smile [n] sonrisa *He always has a smile on his face.* Siempre tiene la sonrisa en los labios.—*You have a pretty smile.* Ud. tiene una bonita sonrisa.
● [v] sonreír *I like the way she smiles.* Me gusta su manera de sonreír. ▲ sonreirse *She smiled unhappily.* Se sonreía tristemente.

smoke [n] humo *Open the windows; there's too much smoke in here.* Abra las ventanas; aquí hay demasiado humo.
● [v] fumar *Do you smoke?* ¿Fuma Ud.?—*I smoke cigars.* Fumo cigarros. —*No smoking.* Prohibido fumar. ▲ despedir humo *That stove smokes too much.* Esa estufa despide demasiado humo. ▲ ahumar *The fishermen here smoke most of their fish.* Los pescadores aquí ahuman la mayor parte del pescado.
○ **smoke screen** cortina de humo *The ship retired under a smoke screen.* El barco se retiró bajo una cortina de humo.
‖ *I'm dying for a smoke.* Me muero por fumar.

smooth [adj] llano *Is this road smooth?* ¿Es este camino llano? ▲ tranquilo *The sea was very smooth.* El mar estaba muy tranquilo.—*We had a very smooth ride.* Dimos un tranquilo paseo en coche. ▲ suave *This is a smooth wine.* Este es un vino suave. ▲ lisonjero *He's a smooth salesman.* Es un vendedor lisonjero.
● [v] alisar *Smooth out the paper before you wrap the package.* Alise el papel antes de envolver el paquete. ▲ preparar, allanar *Send him ahead to smooth the way.* Mándele por delante para preparar el terreno.

smother sofocar.

snail caracol.

snake culebra, serpiente.

snap [n] corchete *I have to sew snaps on my dress.* Tengo que coser unos corchetes en mi traje. ▲ instantánea *I want to take a few snaps of you.*

Quiero tomar unas instantáneas de Ud. ○ **to snap out of something** despabilarse *Snap out of your laziness and do something!* ¡Despabílese, haga algo! ‖ *Snap out of it!* ¡Déjese de eso! ‖ *That's a snap!* ¡Es muy fácil!

snapshot instantánea.

sneakers zapatos de tenis.

sneeze [*n*] estornudo.
● [*v*] estornudar.

snore [*n*] ronquido.
● [*v*] roncar.

snow [*n*] nieve *How deep is the snow?* ¿Cuánte nieve hay? *or* ¿Qué altura tiene la nieve? ▲ nevada *This is the first snow of the year.* Esta es la primera nevada del año.
● [*v*] nevar *It snowed a lot last winter.* Nevó mucho el invierno pasado. —*It's snowing.* Está nevando. ○ **to snow in** estar incomunicado *o* detenido por la nieve *They were snowed in for a whole week.* Estuvieron incomunicados por la nieve toda una semana. ○ **to snow under** agobiar, abrumar *We were snowed under with bills.* Estábamos abrumados de deudas.

snowfall nevada.

so [*adv*] así *So they say.* Así dicen.— *I think so.* Así lo creo. *or* Creo que sí. —*I've heard so.* Lo he oído decir. *or* Eso es lo que he oído.—*I suppose so.* Así me parece. *or* Supongo que sí.— *It's all right now. I hope it will remain so.* Está bien ahora. Espero que continúe así. ▲ cierto *That's not so!* ¡Eso no es cierto!—*Is that so?* ¿Es cierto eso?—*I think he left a letter. So he did.* Creo que él dejó una carta. Es cierto. ▲ tan *Why are you so gloomy?* ¿Por qué está Ud. tan triste? ▲ muy *You're so clever!* ¡Es Ud. muy listo! *or* ¡Qué listo es Ud.! ▲ mucho *I'm so glad to meet you!* ¡Mucho gusto en conocerle! ▲ También *If I can do it, so can you.* Si yo lo puedo hacer, también puede Ud.—*They're very nice, and so are their children.* Son muy simpáticos, y también lo son sus hijos. ▲ tanto *I'd better not go out, my head aches so.* Me duele tanto la cabeza que es mejor que no salga. ▲ ya *The door's open. So I see.* La puerta está abierta. Ya lo veo. ▲ así es *I'm not feeling well, so I don't think I'd better go.* No me siento bien, así es que no creo que debo ir.
● [*interj*] conque *So you've finally come home!* ¡Conque por fin vuelve Ud. a casa!
○ **and so** así es *They left early, and so I missed them.* Se fueron temprano,

así es que no pude verlos. ○ **and so forth** y así por el estilo, y así de lo demás. ○ **and so on, and so forth** etcétera, etcétera. ○ **it so happens** da la casualidad *It so happens that I am responsible for the work.* Da la casualidad de que yo soy responsable del trabajo. ○ **just so** de esta manera *Do it just so.* Hágalo de esta manera. ▲ al pelo, perfectamente *She does everything just so.* Todo lo hace al pelo. ○ **or so** poco más o menos, o cosa así *I need a pound or so of sugar.* Necesito poco más o menos una libra de azúcar. ○ **so and so** tal por cual, fulano de tal. ○ **so as to** de modo que, de suerte que para *Say it so as not to hurt her.* Digáselo de modo que no se ofenda. ▲ para, a fin de *I did some of the work so as to make things easier for her.* Hice parte del trabajo a fin de facilitarle su labor. ○ **so . . . as to** tan . . . como para que *I hope the suits aren't all so worn as to be useless.* Espero que los trajes no estén tan usados como para que no puedan usarse. ○ **so-called** supuesto; así llamado. ○ **so far** hasta aquí, hasta ahora *So far I'm bored.* Hasta ahora me estoy aburriendo. ○ **so far as I know** que yo sepa *So far as I know, I have nothing to declare.* Que yo sepa, no tengo nada que declarar. ○ **so much** tanto *Not so much pepper, please.* No tanta pimienta, por favor. —*He ran so much, he got all out of breath.* Corrió tanto que se quedó sin aliento. ○ **so, so** así, así; medianamente, regular. ○ **so that** a fin de que, para que *I fixed things so that you could come.* Arreglé las cosas a fin de que Ud. pudiera venir. ○ **so . . . that** tan . . . que *I am so tired that I can hardly stand up.* Estoy tan cansado que apenas puedo tenerme en pie.
‖ *How so?* ¿Cómo es eso? ‖ *I'm so glad to know it!* ¡Cuánto me alegro saberlo! ‖ *Is it so?* ¿Verdad? *or* ¿Es cierto? ‖ *I hope so.* Así lo espero. ‖ *I told you so.* Ya se lo dije a Ud. ‖ *So far so good.* Hasta ahora todo bien. ‖ *So long!* ¡Hasta luego! *or* ¡Hasta la vista! ‖ *So what?* ¿Y qué? ‖ *Thanks so much.* Muchísimas gracias. ‖ *Who said so? I said so.* ¿Quién dijo eso? Lo dije yo. ‖ *Why so?* ¿Por qué así?

soak empapar, remojar.

soap jabón.
○ **shaving soap** jabón de afeitar.
○ **toilet soap** jabón de tocador.

sob [*n*] sollozo *I was wakened by the*

child's sobs. Me despertaron los sollozos del niño.
● [*v*] sollozar, llorar *The baby sobbed himself to sleep.* El nene lloró hasta dormirse.
○ **sob story** cuento de lástima *She tried to take us in with a sob story.* Trató de engañarnos con su cuento de lástima.
sober sobrio.
social social.
socialist socialista.
society sociedad.
sock [*n*] calcetín *I want three pairs of socks.* Quiero tres pares de calcetines.
sock [*n*] puñetazo *I'd like to give him a sock on the jaw.* Me gustaría darle un puñetazo en la mandíbula.
● [*v*] dar puñetazos *If you do it again, I'll sock you.* Si lo vuelves a hacer, te daré un puñetazo.
socket enchufe, portalámpara.
soda sosa (*sodium*); soda (*water*); gaseosa (*pop*).
○ **ice-cream soda** ice-cream soda, refresco de gaseosa con helado. ○ **soda fountain** mostrador de refrescos, fuente de soda. ○ **soda water** agua de Seltz, agua de sifón, soda.
sofa sofá, canapé.
soft blando *This pillow is too soft for my taste.* Esta almohada es demasiado blanda para mi gusto.—*You're too soft to be an executive.* Es Ud. demasiado blando para mandar. ▲ fino, no grueso *That material is not soft enough for a dress.* Esa tela no es lo suficientemente fina para un vestido. ▲ suave *She has very soft skin.* Tiene un cutis muy suave. ▲ fofo *I'll get soft if I don't have any exercise.* Si no hago ejercicio voy a ponerme fofo.
○ **soft-boiled** eggs huevos pasados por agua. ○ **soft drink** refresco. ○ **soft-hearted** de buen corazón. ○ **soft-spoken** de hablar meloso, de hablar suave. ○ **soft water** agua fina, agua delgada.
‖ *Make the radio softer.* Baje un poco la radio.
soften ablandar (*make softer*); suavizar (*make smooth*).
softly sin ruido, con cuidado *Walk softly so as not to wake up the baby.* Ande con cuidado para no despertar al bebé.
‖ *Speak softly.* Hable bajo.
soil [*n*] tierra *What will grow in this soil?* ¿Qué se puede cultivar en esta tierra?
soil [*v*] ○ **soiled**, sucio, manchado *My clothes are soiled.* Mi ropa está sucia.
○ **to get soiled** emporcarse, ensuciarse

Don't let it get soiled. No deje Ud. que se ensucie.
soldier soldado.
sole [*n*] suela *I need new soles on these shoes.* Necesito suelas nuevas en estos zapatos. ▲ lenguado *We had fillet of sole for lunch.* Comimos filete de lenguado en el almuerzo.
● [*adj*] único *Are we the sole occupants?* ¿Somos los únicos ocupantes?
● [*v*] poner suelas *These shoes need to be soled.* Hace falta poner suelas a estos zapatos.
○ **sole** for the sole purpose of con el fin exclusivo de *He reads for the sole purpose of amusing himself.* Sólo lee con el fin exclusivo de distraerse.
solemn solemne.
solicit solicitar.
solid [*n*] sólido *The doctor told him not to eat solids for a few days.* El doctor le dijo que no comiera sólidos durante unos días.
● [*adj*] sólido *Is the ice solid?* ¿Está sólido el hielo? ▲ firme, sólido *This chair doesn't feel very solid to me.* Esta silla no me parece muy firme. ▲ macizo *Is the beam solid or hollow?* ¿Es la viga maciza o hueca? ▲ entero, todo *He talked to me for a solid hour.* Me habló durante toda una hora. ▲ liso *I want a solid blue material.* Quiero una tela azul lisa. ▲ recto *He seems to be a solid sort of person.* Parece ser un hombre recto.
some algo *Take some meat.* Tome Ud. algo de carne. *or* Tome Ud. carne. ▲ poco *Give me some more water.* Déme un poco más de agua. ▲ cierto *He's a man of some reputation.* Es un hombre de cierta fama.—*Some types are better suited to this purpose.* Ciertos tipos de personas cuadran mejor para este fin. ▲ algún *I've been working for some time.* He estado trabajando por algún tiempo.—*I hope I can see you again some day.* Espero verle de nuevo algún día.—*I've seen you some place.* Le he visto a Ud. en algún sitio.—*There must be some way of finding out.* Debe haber alguna manera de averiguarlo. ▲ unos, algunos *Could I have some oranges?* ¿Puede Ud. darme unas naranjas? ▲ algunos *Take some of these books.* Tome algunos de estos libros.—*Some of you may disagree with me.* Quizás algunos de Uds. no estén de acuerdo conmigo. ▲ unos *Some friends were looking for you.* Unos amigos vinieron a buscarle.
○ **some ... and some** unos ... y otros

Some will go by train and some by boat.
Unos irán por tierra y otros por mar.
○ **some of** de *I want some of that material.* Quiero de esa tela. ○ **some . . . or
other** uno . . . u otro *Try to get some
typist or other to do the job.* Consiga
una u otra mecanógrafa para que haga
el trabajo. ▲ uno de esos *It's in some
book or other on that shelf.* Está en
uno de esos libros de la estantería.
○ **to some extent** hasta cierto punto *To
some extent that's true.* Hasta cierto
punto eso es verdad.
‖ *She's some girl!* ¡Vaya una muchacha! ‖ *That's some house they live
in!* ¡Vaya la casa en que viven!
somebody alguien, alguna persona.
○ **somebody else** algún otro.
somehow de algún modo.
○ **somehow or other** de un modo u
otro.
someone alguien.
some place en alguna parte.
something algo *He knows something
about medicine.* Sabe algo de medicina.
—*Is something the matter?* ¿Sucede
algo?—*If you want something, ring the
bell.* Si quiere Ud. algo, toque el
timbre.—*That's really something.* Eso
sí que es algo.—*There's something
peculiar here.* Aquí hay algo extraño.
—*There's something in what you say.*
Hay algo en lo que Ud. dice. ▲ algo, un
poco *He's something of a musician.*
Tiene algo de músico.
○ **something else** algo más *There's
something else I want.* Hay algo más
que yo quiero. ○ **something or other**
algo, una u otra cosa *I'm sure I've forgotten something or other.* Estoy seguro que he olvidado algo.
sometime algún día *Can I have a date
with you sometime?* ¿Podríamos salir
juntos algún día? ▲ durante, en el
curso de *It happened sometime last
October.* Sucedió durante el pasado
octubre.
sometimes a veces *I get mixed up sometimes.* A veces me atolondro. ▲ algunas veces *Sometimes I wonder if it's
worth while to work so hard.* Algunas
veces dudo si vale la pena trabajar tan
duro.
○ **sometimes . . . sometimes** a veces
. . . otras veces *Sometimes I sleep late,
sometimes I get up early.* A veces duermo hasta muy tarde, otras veces me
levanto temprano.
somewhat algo *This differs somewhat
from the usual type.* Esto difiere
algo del tipo corriente. ▲ un poco,

algo *That is somewhat too expensive.*
Eso es algo caro.—*This puts it somewhat more plainly.* Esto lo explica
algo más claramente.
somewhere alguna parte *Haven't we seen
each other somewhere before?* ¿No nos
hemos visto antes en alguna parte?
son hijo.
song canción *That's a pretty song.* Esa
es una bonita canción.
○ **for a song** por una bicoca, por
una nada *We bought the chair for a
song.* Compramos la silla por una
bicoca.
‖ *The crowd burst into song.* La
multitud se puso a cantar.
son-in-law yerno.
sonnet soneto.
soon pronto *I'll be back soon.* Volveré
pronto.—*Come again soon.* Vuelva Ud.
pronto.—*It's too soon to tell what's the
matter with him.* Es demasiado pronto
para saber lo que tiene.
○ **as soon as** tan pronto como *I told
you as soon as I knew myself.* Se lo
dije tan pronto como lo supe. ○ **as
soon as possible** cuanto antes, lo antes
posible. ○ **no sooner . . . than** apenas
. . . cuando *He no sooner said her name
than she came in sight.* Apenas pronunció su nombre cuando apareció ella.
○ **soon after** poco después que *He came
soon after I left.* Vino poco después
de que yo me marché. ○ **sooner or later**
tarde o temprano *I'll have to see him
sooner or later.* Tendré que verle
tarde o temprano.
‖ *The sooner the better.* Cuanto antes mejor. ‖ *He said he'd just as soon
stay home as not.* Dijo que lo mismo
le daba quedarse o no quedarse en casa.
‖ *I'd sooner die than give in.* Prefiero
morir antes que ceder.
soot hollín.
soothe calmar, tranquilizar.
sore [*n*] llaga, erosión *There is a sore on
my foot.* Tengo una llaga en el pie.
● [*adj*] mal *My throat is sore.* Estoy
mal de la garganta. *or* Me duele la garganta. ▲ lastimado *That's the sore toe.*
Ese es el dedo lastimado.
○ **to be sore** doler *This bruise is sore
to the touch.* Esta herida duele al
tocarla. ○ **to get sore** ofenderse *Don't
get sore; I didn't mean anything.* No
se ofenda que no quise decir nada. ○ **to
make sore** desesperar, ofender *That
makes me sore.* Eso me desespera.
sore throat inflamación de la garganta,
dolor de garganta.
sort tipo *She has beauty of a different*

sort. Su belleza es de otro tipo.—*She's not the sort of girl you can forget easily.* No es el tipo de muchacha que se olvida fácilmente. ▲ clase *They have books of all sorts.* Tienen libros de todas clases.—*What sort of man is he?* ¿Qué clase de hombre es? ▲ especie *It's a sort of gift some people have.* Es una especie de don que tiene alguna gente.

○ **all sorts** toda clase *I need all sorts of things.* Necesito toda clase de cosas. ○ **a sort of** cierto *You cannot help but feel a sort of admiration for a man like that.* Uno no puede menos que sentir cierta admiración por un hombre como ese. ○ **nothing of the sort** nada de eso *You'll do nothing of the sort.* Ud. no hará nada de eso. ○ **sort of** más bien *I'm sort of glad things happened the way they did.* Estoy más bien contento por la manera como ocurrieron las cosas. ▲ en cierto modo *I'd sort of like to go.* En cierto modo me gustaría ir. ○ **to sort out** clasificar, ordenar por clases *I must sort out the mail.* Tengo que clasificar la correspondencia.

soul alma.

sound [*n*] sonido *I thought I heard a funny sound.* Creí oír un sonido extraño.—*Is that sound always represented by the same letter?* ¿Está ese sonido siempre representado por la misma letra? ▲ estrecho *Let's go for a sail on the sound.* Vamos a navegar por el estrecho.

● [*adj*] firme *The floor is old but very sound.* El piso es viejo pero muy firme. ▲ sano *Did you get home safe and sound?* ¿Llegó Ud. a su casa sano y salvo? ▲ bueno *His constitution is still sound.* Su estado de salud es bueno todavía. ▲ seguro *Do you think that this is a sound business?* ¿Cree Ud. que éste es un negocio seguro? ▲ sólido, razonable, de peso *That's a sound argument.* Ese es un argumento de peso. ▲ legítimo *Have you got sound title to the property?* ¿Tiene Ud. un título legítimo de la propiedad?

● [*v*] sonar *That shot sounded very close.* Ese tiro sonó muy cerca.—*His name sounds just like hers.* Su nombre suena muy parecido al de ella. ▲ tocar, sonar *The bugle sounded retreat.* El corneta tocó retreta. ▲ parecer *It sounds impossible.* Parece imposible. ▲ sondear *They sounded the lake.* Sondearon el lago.

○ **to sound someone out** sondear, tan-

tear *I sounded him out on his ideas.* Le tanteé para ver que ideas tenía.

‖ *How does that sound to you?* ¿Qué le parece eso? ‖ *I had a sound sleep last night.* Anoche dormí profundamente. ‖ *She didn't know we were within sound of her voice.* Ella no sabía que podíamos oírla desde donde estábamos.

soup sopa.

soup plate plato sopero, plato hondo.

sour agrio, ácido.

source fuente *What is your source of information?* ¿Cuál es su fuente de información? ▲ motivo *His success has been a source of great pride to all of us.* Su éxito ha sido motivo de gran orgullo para todos nosotros. ▲ origen, causa *Have you found the source of the trouble?* ¿Ha encontrado Ud. el origen de este disgusto? ▲ nacimiento, manantial *Where is the source of this river?* ¿Dónde está el nacimiento de este río?

○ **source book** libro de consulta, libro de referencia.

south [*n*] sur *This farm runs about a mile from North to South.* La extensión de la finca de norte a sur es de una milla. —*We traveled through the south of France.* Hemos viajado por el sur de Francia.

● [*adj*] *It's on the south side.* Está en el lado sur.—*There's a south wind.* Sopla viento sur.

‖ *He lives a block south of here.* Vive a una manzana de aquí hacia el sur.

southeast sudeste.

southern meridional *Southern Europe.* Europa meridional. ▲ al sur, del sur *I'd prefer a room with a southern exposure.* Preferiría un cuarto que dé al sur.

southwest sudoeste.

souvenir recuerdo.

sovereign soberano.

sow [*n*] puerca, marrana.

sow [*v*] sembrar.

soybean soya.

space [*n*] espacio *Is there any space for my luggage?* ¿Hay espacio para mi equipaje?—*Leave a double space after each sentence.* Deje doble espacio después de cada frase.—*He just sat there staring out into space.* Estaba sentado con la mirada fija en el espacio.—*He did the work in the space of a day.* Hizo el trabajo en el espacio de un día. —*How much space does the building occupy?* ¿Cuánto espacio ocupa el edificio?—*Write small to save space.*

Escriba Ud. apretado para ahorrar espacio.

● [v] espaciar, separar *The posts are spaced a foot apart.* Los postes están separados un pie de distancia entre sí.

spade [n] pala, azada *I have to get this spade fixed.* Tengo que dar a arreglar esta pala. ▲ espada *I have two spades and three hearts.* Tengo dos espadas y tres corazones.

● [v] cavar con pala, remover la tierra *Will you help me spade my garden?* ¿Quiere Ud. ayudarme a remover la tierra de mi jardín?

○ **to call a spade a spade** llamar al pan, pan y al vino, vino.

span [v] atravesar, extenderse sobre *The bridge spans the river at its narrowest point.* El puente atraviesa el río por su punto más estrecho.

○ **bridge span** ojo de puente, tramo, luz. ○ **life span** promedio de vida *What is the life span of a man?* ¿Cuál es el promedio de vida de un hombre?

Spaniard español.

Spanish español.

spank zurrar, pegar, dar una paliza.

spanking zurra, paliza.

spare [n] rueda de repuesto *Hand me the spare, please.* Haga el favor de darme la rueda de repuesto.

● [adj] disponible *I haven't a spare minute.* No tengo un minuto disponible.

● [v] perdonar, salvar *Luckily his life was spared.* Por fortuna se le perdonó la vida. ▲ ahorrar *Spare me the details.* Ahórreme los detalles.—*You can spare yourself the trouble.* Puede Ud. ahorrarse la molestia. ▲ escatimar *I've spared no expense in building the house.* No escatimé gastos al edificar la casa. ▲ prestar *I can spare you some money.* Le puedo prestar algún dinero. ▲ sobrar *Can you spare a cigarette?* ¿Le sobra un cigarrillo? *or* ¿Me puede dar Ud. un cigarrillo? ▲ conceder *Can you spare a minute?* ¿Puede Ud. concederme un minuto?

○ **spare parts** piezas de repuesto *Do you have any spare parts for your radio?* ¿Tiene Ud. piezas de repuesto para su radio? ○ **spare time** momentos libres, rato de ocio *I'll do it in my spare time.* Lo haré en los momentos que tengo libres. ○ **to spare** de tiempo *I got to the station with five minutes to spare.* Llegué a la estación con cinco minutos de tiempo.

‖ *I'll try to spare your feelings.* Procuraré abstenerme para no herir sus sentimientos. ‖ *I'll take it if you can spare it.* Lo tomaré si Ud. no lo necesita.

spark chispa.

sparkle [n] fulgor, brillo, destello.

● [v] relucir, brillar (*shine*); chispear, echar chispas (*spark*).

sparkling chispeante, brillante; vivaz (*lively*).

○ **sparkling wine** vino espumoso.

sparrow gorrión.

speak hablar *Do you speak Spanish?* ¿Habla Ud. español?—*We were just speaking of you.* Precisamente estábamos hablando de Ud.—*Who spoke last night?* ¿Quién habló anoche?— *To speak plainly, you're a thief.* Hablando claramente, es Ud. un ladrón. ▲ decir *Go ahead and speak your piece.* Ande, diga lo que quiere decir.

○ **generally speaking** generalmente *Generally speaking, he is home every evening.* Generalmente está en casa todas las noches. ○ **so to speak** por decirlo así. ○ **to speak for** hablar en nombre de *I'm speaking for my friend.* Hablo en nombre de mi amigo. ▲ comprometer *Next Saturday is already spoken for.* El sábado que viene ya está comprometido.

‖ *Speak out!* ¡Hable claro! ‖ *It speaks for itself.* Habla por sí mismo. ‖ *We're not on speaking terms.* No nos hablamos.

speaker orador, conferencista.

spear lanza.

special especial *I have a special reason.* Tengo una razón especial.—*Have you anything special in mind for tonight?* ¿Tiene Ud. pensado algo especial para esta noche?—*Is there any special train for the weekend?* ¿Hay algún tren especial para fin de semana?

special delivery entrega inmediata, urgente.

specialist especialista.

specialize especializar.

specialty especialidad.

species especie.

specific específico.

specify especificar.

specimen muestra, espécimen.

speck motita.

spectacle espectáculo.

spectacles gafas, anteojos, lentes.

spectator espectador.

speech discurso *That was a very good speech.* Ese discurso fué muy bueno. ▲ modo de hablar *You can often tell where a person comes from by his speech.* Con frecuencia se puede saber de donde es una persona por su modo de hablar.

speechless mudo, sin habla.

speed velocidad *This car has four speeds.* Este automóvil tiene cuatro velocidades.—*The train is moving at a very slow speed.* El tren marcha a muy poca velocidad.—*Speed limit 30 miles per hour.* Velocidad máxima treinta millas por hora. ▲ rapidez *The job will be finished with all speed.* El trabajo se terminará con la mayor rapidez. ▲ prisa *Do it with all speed.* Hágalo a toda prisa. ○ **to speed up** acelerar *Speed up the work.* Acelere Ud. el trabajo. ‖ *We sped home as fast as we could.* Nos apresuramos a ir a casa lo más rápidamente que pudimos.

spell [n] ataque *He had a coughing spell.* Tuvo un ataque de tos. ▲ racha *This hot spell won't last long.* Esta racha de calor no durará mucho. ▲ intervalo *He worked in that office for a short spell.* Trabajó en esa oficina por un corto intervalo. ● [v] deletrear *He doesn't know how to spell yet.* Todavía no sabe deletrear. ‖ *It's spelled the same, but pronounced differently.* Se escribe lo mismo, pero se pronuncia de otra manera. ‖ *How do you spell your name?* ¿Cómo se escribe su nombre?

spelling deletreo; ortografía (*orthography*).

spend gastar *I haven't much to spend.* No tengo mucho que gastar. ▲ pasar *I want to spend the night here.* Quiero pasar la noche aquí.

sphere esfera.

spice especia.

spick-and-span nuevo, flamante.

spider araña.

spill derramar *Who spilled the milk?* ¿Quién derramó la leche?

spin [v] hilar.

spinach espinaca.

spine espinazo, columna vertebral.

spirit espíritu.

spiritual espiritual.

spit [n] saliva *The baseball player rubbed his hands with spit.* El jugador de beisbol se restregó las manos con saliva. ▲ asador *I like meat roasted on a spit.* Me gusta la carne al asador. ● [v] escupir *No spitting.* Se prohibe escupir. ○ **to spit out** escupir *If it tastes bad, spit it out.* Si sabe mal, escúpalo.

spite [n] despecho *She did that just for spite.* Lo hizo sólo por despecho.

○ **in spite of** a pesar de, a despecho de *I failed in spite of all my efforts.* Fracasé a pesar de todos mis esfuerzos. ‖ *I'll do it in spite of him.* Mal que le pese lo haré. ‖ *They're just spiting themselves by not going there.* Son ellos mismos los que se fastidian no yendo allí.

splash [n] salpicadura. ● [v] salpicar, chapotear.

splendid espléndido *This is splendid weather for swimming.* Hace un tiempo espléndido para nadar. ▲ lujoso *Their house is a little too splendid for my taste.* Para mi gusto su casa es demasiado lujosa.

splendor esplendor.

splinter [n] astilla. ● [v] astillar, hacer astillas.

split [n] escisión *There was a split in the party after elections.* Hubo una escisión en el partido después de las elecciones. ● [v] dividir, repartir *Let's split the profits.* Dividamos las ganancias. ○ **splitting** tremendo, terrible *I have a splitting headache.* Tengo un tremendo dolor de cabeza. ○ **to split hairs** pararse en pelillos. ○ **to split one's sides** with laughter desternillarse de risa.

spoil echar a perder *He spoiled my plans.* Echó a perder mis planes. ▲ echarse a perder *Food spoils quickly in hot weather.* La comida se echa a perder muy pronto con el calor. ○ **spoiled** consentido, mimado *He's a very spoiled child.* Es un niño muy consentido. ○ **spoils** botín *They got their share of the spoils.* Recibieron su parte del botín.

spoke radio, rayo *This wheel has a broken spoke.* Esta rueda tiene un radio roto.

spokesman portavoz.

sponge esponja.

sponger gorrista, sablista.

sponsor [n] patrocinador *The only one who voted in favor of that law was its sponsor.* El único que votó en favor de esa ley fué su patrocinador. ● [v] costear, suscribir *Which program will you sponsor?* ¿Qué programa de radio costeará Ud.? ▲ patrocinar *It would be a great favor to us if you'd sponsor the bill.* Nos haría un gran favor si patrocinara Ud. el proyecto de ley. ‖ *Who's the sponsor of that new radio program?* ¿Quién es el que costea ese nuevo programa de radio?

spontaneous espontáneo.

spool carrete.

spoon cuchara.

sport [n] deporte *Do you like sports?* ¿Le gustan a Ud. los deportes? ‖ *This is fine sport.* Esto es muy divertido. ‖ *She's a poor sport.* No sabe perder. ‖ *He's a good sport; he never gets angry.* Tiene mucha correa; nunca se enfada.

sports [adj] de sport *I have to wear sports clothes.* Tengo que llevar ropa de sport. ▲ deportivo *I always read the sports page first.* Lo primero que leo siempre es la página deportiva.

spot [n] mancha *Can you get these spots out of my pants?* ¿Puede Ud. quitarme estas manchas del pantalón? ▲ lugar, punto *Show me the exact spot you mean.* Enséñeme el lugar exacto a que se refiere Ud. ▲ lugar *I was right on the spot when the accident happened.* Estaba precisamente en el lugar cuando do ocurrió el accidente. ● [v] reconocer, distinguir *I spotted you in the crowd as soon as I saw your hat.* Le reconocí entre el gentío tan pronto divisé su sombrero. ○ **on the spot** en el acto, al punto *They hired him on the spot.* Le emplearon en el acto. ▲ en una situación comprometida *That really put me on the spot.* Eso me puso verdaderamente en una situación comprometida.

spotlight reflector, proyector. ○ **to be in the spotlight** estar en candelero, estar en posición conspicua.

spout [n] borbotón, chorro; pico (*of teapot*); espita (*beer barrel*). ● [v] borbotar, salir a borbotones, correr a chorros.

sprain [n] torcedura *Is that sprain very painful?* ¿Le duele mucho esa torcedura? ● [v] torcerse *She sprained her ankle.* Se torció el tobillo.

spray [n] rociada. ● [v] rociar.

spread [n] propagación *They tried to check the spread of the disease.* Trataron de evitar la propagación de la enfermedad. ● [v] extender *Spread the rug out and let me look at it.* Extienda la alfombra y déjeme verla. ▲ extenderse *The fire spread rapidly.* El incendio se extendió rápidamente. ▲ propagar *Spread the news.* Propague la noticia. ▲ poner, untar *Spread the honey on the bread.* Untele miel al pan. ▲ espaciar, distribuir *He repaid me in small amounts, spread over several years.* Me pagó en pequeños plazos distribuidos a lo largo de varios años. ○ **bed spread** colcha, cubrecama. ○ **to spread the table** poner la mesa.

spring [n] resorte, muelle *The spring seems to be broken.* Parece ser que el resorte está roto. ▲ manantial *Let's have a drink of nice cool spring water.* Bebamos un poco de agua fresca del manantial. ▲ primavera *We won't be leaving town before spring.* No saldremos de la ciudad antes de la primavera. ● [v] lanzarse *The cat sprang at the mouse.* El gato se lanzó sobre el ratón. ○ **bedspring** muelle de cama, colchón de muelles *Do you know where I can buy a good bedspring?* ¿Sabe Ud. dónde puedo comprar un buen muelle de cama? ○ **to spring up** aparecer, surgir *Towns began to spring up all along the river.* Empezaron a surgir poblaciones a lo largo del río. ‖ *He sprang to his feet.* De un salto se puso en pie. ‖ *The teacher sprang that test on us without warning.* El maestro nos dio ese examen sin previo aviso. *or* El maestro nos dio una sorpresa con ese examen.

sprinkle [v] rociar (*spray*); lloviznar (*rain*).

sprinkler regadera.

sprout brotar, germinar.

spry ágil.

spur [n] espuela. ○ **on the spur of the moment** de repente, al impulso, sin pensarlo del momento.

spy [n] espía. ● [v] espiar.

squab pichón.

square [n] plaza *How far are we from the square?* ¿A qué distancia estamos de la plaza? ▲ cuadrado *They cut the cake into small squares.* Cortaron el bizcocho en cuadritos. ● [adj] cuadrado *How many square feet does the building cover?* ¿Cuántos pies cuadrados ocupa el edificio?—*I want a square box.* Quiero una caja cuadrada. ▲ honrado, íntegro *He's a pretty square fellow.* Es un chico bastante honrado. ● [v] arreglar, ajustar *I'll square things with you later.* Más adelante arreglaremos cuentas. ○ **carpenter's square** escuadra de carpintero. ○ **square deal** juego limpio, buen trato. ○ **square meal** comida abundante, comida completa *You can get a square meal there for very little money.* Por poco dinero puede Ud.

conseguir una comida abundante en ese lugar.

squash [n] calabaza, [Am] ayote *We had squash for lunch.* Comimos calabaza en el almuerzo.

● [v] despachurrar, aplastar *I'm afraid I squashed the cake.* Temo haber despachurrado el pastel.

squeak [n] chirrido.

● [v] chirriar.

squeeze [v] apretar, estrujar *He squeezed her hand until she screamed.* Le apretó la mano hasta hacerla gritar. ▲ exprimir *Squeeze some lemons for the lemonade.* Exprima unos limones para la limonada.

○ to squeeze through abrirse paso forzadamente por *He squeezed his way through the crowd.* Se abrió paso forzadamente por entre la multitud.

squirrel ardilla.

stab [n] punzada *As he turned he felt a sudden stab of pain in his side.* Al volverse sintió repentinamente una punzada de dolor en el costado.

● [v] apuñalar, dar de puñaladas *He was stabbed to death.* Lo mataron a puñaladas. *or* Murió apuñalado.

○ stab in the back puñalada trapera.

stable [n] caballeriza *Where are the stables?* ¿Dónde están las caballerizas?

stable [adj] equilibrado, juicioso *She's a pretty stable person.* Es una persona bien equilibrada. ▲ estable *They haven't had a stable government for centuries.* Hace siglos que no han tenido un gobierno estable.

stack [n] pila, montón.

● [v] apilar, amontonar.

staff cayado, báculo (*stick*). ▲ personal *The staff of that office is very efficient.* El personal de esa oficina es muy eficiente.

○ editorial staff cuerpo de redacción.

○ general staff estado mayor.

stage [n] período *He's in an advanced stage in his studies.* Está en un período avanzado de sus estudios. ▲ escenario *I can't see the stage from this seat.* No puedo ver el escenario desde este asiento. ▲ teatro *My sister is trying to get on the stage.* Mi hermana está tratando de actuar en el teatro.

● [v] representar *The plot was good but the play was poorly staged.* El asunto era bueno pero la comedia estuvo mal representada.

stagger zigzaguear, hacer eses, tambalearse; colocar al tres, bolillo (*arrange in zigzag order*).

stain [n] mancha.

● [v] manchar.

stairs escalera *Take the stairs to your right.* Tome la escalera a la derecha.

stale rancio, viejo.

stalk tallo (*flower*); caña (*wheat*).

stall [n] pesebre *Put the horse in the stall.* Ponga el caballo en el pesebre. ▲ tenderete, puesto *They're putting up the stalls for the fair.* Están instalando los tenderetes para la feria.

● [v] atascar *The motor's stalled again, damn it!* ¡Demonio! Se ha atascado de nuevo el motor. ▲ entretener *Stall the police until I can get away.* Entretenga a la policía hasta que yo pueda escaparme.

○ to stall for time demorar intencionadamente.

stammer [v] tartamudear.

stamp [n] estampilla, sello *I want five two-cent stamps.* Déme cinco estampillas de dos centavos. ▲ sello *Please buy me a rubber stamp.* Haga el favor de comprarme un sello de goma.

● [v] pisar, golpear con los pies *Stamp on that cigarette butt.* Pise Ud. esa colilla. ▲ patalear *Teach the child not to stamp his feet.* Enséñele al niño a que no patalee. ▲ marcar, sellar *Please stamp this "fragile".* Haga el favor de marcar esto con la palabra "frágil". ▲ poner sello, franquear *Did you stamp the envelope?* ¿Ha puesto un sello en el sobre?

stand [n] velador, mesita *Put the magazines on the stand.* Ponga las revistas sobre el velador. ▲ tribuna, plataforma *The president and his family were on the stand.* El presidente y su familia estaban en la tribuna. ▲ puesto, tiendecilla ambulante *He has a vegetable stand.* Tiene un puesto de verduras. ▲ resistencia *The Forty-sixth Division made a gallant stand.* La 46 división ofreció una resistencia heroica.

● [v] levantarse, [Am] pararse *The audience stood when they saw the conductor come in.* Se levantó la concurrencia al entrar el director de la orquesta. ▲ estar de pie *The ladder's standing in the corner.* La escalera está de pie en el rincón. ▲ estar situado *The house stands in an open field.* La casa está situada en campo abierto. ▲ quedarse *Stand where you are.* Quédese donde está. ▲ estar *The old clock has stood on that shelf for years.* El viejo reloj ha estado en ese estante durante años. *The front door stood wide open.* La puerta principal estaba abierta de par en par.—*As things now stand I'll have to go.* En vista de como están las cosas ahora tendré que irme. ▲ reposar *Let the milk stand overnight.* Deje reposar la leche durante la noche. ▲ resistir *This cloth won't stand much washing.* Esta tela no resistirá mucho el lavado. ▲ soportar, aguantar *I can't stand your friend.* No puedo soportar a su amigo. ▲ poner de pie *He stood the box in the corner.* Puso la caja de pie en el rincón. ▲ poner *Stand it over there.* Póngalo allí. ○ as it stands tal como está *How much for it as it stands?* ¿Cuánto quiere Ud. por ello, tal como está? ○ to stand a chance tener probabilidad *I'm afraid you don't stand a chance of getting a job here.* Me parece que no tiene ninguna probabilidad de conseguir un puesto aquí. ○ to stand alone ser el único *In this opinion I do not stand alone.* No soy el único que piensa así. ○ to stand aside apartarse, ponerse a un lado *Stand aside, please.* Apártese, por favor. ○ to stand back retroceder, retirarse *Stand back and give her air.* Retírense, no le quiten el aire. ○ to stand by estar cerca *He was standing by the door when we arrived.* Estaba cerca de la puerta cuando llegamos. ▲ hallarse presente, asistir *I stood by during the operation.* Me hallaba presente durante la operación. ▲ estar al lado de uno *I'll always stand by you in case of trouble.* Estaré siempre a su lado en cualquier dificultad. ▲ estar atento *Stand by for the latest news.* Esté Ud. atento a las noticias de última hora. ▲ hacer honor a, mantener *You can count on him to stand by his word.* Puede Ud. confiar en que él mantendrá su palabra. ○ to stand fast no ceder, mantenerse firme *The others gave in, but she stood fast.* Los otros cedieron, pero ella se mantuvo firme. ○ to stand for tolerar *I don't have to stand for such behavior.* No tengo por qué tolerar tal comportamiento.—*I can't stand for things like that.* No puedo tolerar tales cosas. ▲ representar *In this code each number stands for a letter.* En esta clave cada número representa una letra. ▲ estar de lado de, ser partidario de, estar por *He stands for democracy.* Es partidario de la democracia. ○ to stand in the way hallarse en el camino, obstruir el paso. ○ to stand off mantenerse distanciado, mantenerse a distancia. ○ to stand on insistir en *I'm going to stand on my rights.* Voy

a insistir en mis derechos. ○ to stand on one's own feet valerse de sí mismo. ○ to stand on tiptoe ponerse de puntillas. ○ to stand out resistir *They stood out against the enemy for months.* Resistieron al enemigo durante meses. ▲ destacarse *Her clothes make her stand out in a crowd.* Se destaca de los demás por su manera de vestir. ○ to stand to reason ser lógico *It stands to reason that she wouldn't do that.* Es lógico que ella no haga eso. ○ to stand up levantarse, ponerse en pie *Don't bother standing up.* No se moleste en levantarse. ▲ resistir *Do you think these shoes will stand up under hard wear?* ¿Cree Ud. que estos zapatos resistirán mucho uso? ▲ dejar plantado *She stood me up at the last minute.* Me dejó plantado en el último momento. ○ to stand up for sacar la cara por, salir en defensa de *If we don't stand up for him, nobody will.* Si nosotros no sacamos la cara por él, nadie lo hará. ○ to stand up to rebelarse, resistir *Why don't you stand up to your father once in a while?* ¿Por qué no se rebela Ud. contra su padre de vez en cuando? ‖ *Where do you stand in this matter?* ¿Cuál es su actitud con respecto a este asunto? ‖ *What I said the other day still stands.* Sostengo lo que dije el otro día. ‖ *How do you stand in the draft?* ¿Cuál es su situación con referencia al servicio militar? ‖ *Stand out of the way!* ¡Quítese Ud. de en medio! ‖ *His ears stand out from his head.* Tiene las orejas muy separadas. ‖ *Stand still!* ¡No se mueva Ud.! ‖ *It's difficult to know just what he stands for.* Es difícil saber exactamente cuáles son sus principios. ‖ *I'm tired of standing here waiting.* Estoy cansado de esperar aquí de pie.

standard [n] norma *Who sets the standard of work here?* ¿Quién da la norma del trabajo a hacer aquí? ▲ nivel *Our standard of living is lower than yours.* Nuestro nivel de vida es más bajo que él de Uds. ● [adj] corriente *This is the standard size.* Este es el tamaño corriente.— *This is the standard price.* Este es el precio corriente. ○ gold standard patrón oro. ○ standard rate precio de tasa. ○ standard weight peso legal.

standing reputación, crédito *This is a firm of good standing.* Esta es una casa de buena reputación. ○ of long standing de mucho tiempo

Their friendship is of long standing.
Son amigos de mucho tiempo. ○ **standing army** ejército permanente.
star [*n*] estrella *The sky is full of stars tonight.* Esta noche el cielo está lleno de estrellas.—*She's the star of that picture.* Es la estrella de esa película.
● [*v*] figurar como estrella *She's starred in every picture she's been in.* Ha figurado como estrella en todas las películas en que ha tomado parte.
○ **starred** marcado con asterisco *Omit the starred passages.* Suprima Ud. los pasajes marcados con asteriscos.
‖ *This is the star pupil of the class.* Este es el alumno más sobresaliente de la clase.
starch [*n*] fécula *You have too much starch in your diet.* Ud. tiene demasiada fécula en su dieta. ▲ almidón *Don't put too much starch in the collars.* No ponga Ud. demasiado almidón en los cuellos.
● [*v*] almidonar *Did you remember to starch the shirts?* ¿Se acordó Ud. de almidonar las camisas?
stare [*v*] mirar fijamente, clavar la mirada.
start [*n*] principio *It was a failure from start to finish.* Fué un fracaso desde el principio hasta el fin.
● [*v*] comenzar *Has the performance started yet?* ¿Ha comenzado ya la función? ▲ empezar (a) *It's starting to rain.* Está empezando a llover.— *The baby started crying.* El niño empezó a llorar.—*We start work tomorrow.* Empezaremos el trabajo mañana. ▲ partir, ponerse en camino *We started off early in the morning.* Partimos de madrugada. ▲ lanzar *Who started that rumor?* ¿Quién lanzó ese rumor? ▲ poner en marcha *Start the engine.* Ponga el motor en marcha. ▲ causar *What started the fire?* ¿Qué fué lo que causó el incendio?
○ **to get one's start** empezar *He got his start in a small office.* Empezó en una pequeña oficina. ○ **to give (one) a start** darle a uno un susto *You gave me quite a start.* Me dió un gran susto.
‖ *He gave me my start in life.* Fué con su ayuda que yo empecé.
startle espantar, asustar.
starve morir de hambre; matar *or* hacer morir de hambre (*starve somebody*).
state [*n*] estado *I'm worried about the state of her health.* Estoy preocupado por el estado de su salud.—*The rail-*

roads are owned by the state. Los ferrocarriles son propiedad del Estado. —*We have to go through three states to get to our summer home.* Tenemos que atravesar tres estados para llegar a nuestra casa de verano. ▲ situacion *This is a fine state of affairs!* ¡Bonita situación es ésta!—*Anything is better than the present state of things.* Cualquier cosa es mejor que la presente situación.—*He works in the State Department.* Trabaja en el Ministerio de Estado.
● [*v*] decir *State your business.* Diga Ud. lo que quiere. *or* ¿Qué desea? ▲ declarar *He stated that she had not been present on that day.* Declaró que ella no había estado presente aquel día.
statement *Do you wish to make any statement to the press?* ¿Quiere Ud. hacer alguna declaración a la prensa?
○ **statement of account** estado de cuentas.
stateroom camarote.
static [*n*] perturbaciones atmosféricas (*radio*).
station [*n*] estación *Where's the railroad station?* ¿Dónde está la estación del ferrocarril?—*Get off at the next station.* Apéese en la estación siguiente. —*What stations can you get on your radio?* ¿Qué estaciones puede Ud. oír con su radio?—*There's an agricultural experiment station near here.* Cerca de aquí hay una estación de experimentación agrícola.
● [*v*] destinar *Where are you stationed?* ¿Dónde está Ud. destinado? ▲ apostar *The police stationed a man at the door.* La policía apostó un hombre en la puerta.
○ **police station** comisaría, estación de policía *I want the police station.* Quiero comunicarme con la comisaría.
stationary estacionario, fijo.
stationery papel de escribir.
statistics estadística.
statue estatua.
status condición; estado legal (*legal position*).
stay [*n*] unos días, temporada, estancia *We had a very pleasant stay at their house.* Pasamos unos días muy agradables en su casa.
● [*v*] permanecer, quedarse *I intend to stay for a week.* Pienso permanecer una semana. ▲ quedarse *I'm sorry we can't stay any longer.* Siento que no podamos quedarnos más tiempo.—*Stay with him.* Quédate con él. ▲ quedar *When I fix a thing, it stays fixed.*

Cuando arreglo una cosa, queda arreglada. ▲ parar, hospedarse *I always stay in his house when I'm in town.* Cuando estoy en la ciudad siempre paro en su casa. ▲ alojarse *Where are you staying?* ¿Dónde se aloja Ud.? ▲ vivir *I'm staying with friends.* Vivo con unos amigos.

○ to stay away estar ausente *You've stayed away a long time.* Ha estado Ud. ausente mucho tiempo. ○ to stay in quedarse en casa, no salir. ○ to stay out of no meterse en. ○ to stay up acostarse tarde *Don't stay up late.* No te acuestes tarde.

steady [adj] firme *This needs a steady hand.* Esto necesita una mano firme. —*Is the ladder steady enough?* ¿Es bastante firme la escalera? ▲ estable, permanente *He got a steady job.* Ha conseguido un empleo estable. ▲ regular *We kept up a fairly steady pace.* Conservamos una marcha bastante regular. ▲ habitual *I'm a steady customer of this store.* Soy un parroquiano habitual de esta tienda. ▲ constante *He's made steady progress.* Ha hecho progresos constantes.—*She's a steady person.* Es una persona constante.

● [v] sostener *Steady the ladder so I won't fall.* Sostenga la escalera para que no me caiga.

○ to steady oneself conservar el equilibrio *She tried to steady herself by grabbing the railing.* Trató de conservar el equilibrio agarrándose a la barandilla.

steak bistec, biftec.

steal [n] plagio *That song hit is a steal from an old folk song.* Esa canción de moda es un plagio de una vieja canción popular.

● [v] robar *I didn't steal anything from you.* No le he robado nada a Ud. —*He stole my book.* Me robó el libro. ▲ entrar a hurtadillas *The children stole into the room.* Los niños entraron a hurtadillas en el cuarto.

○ to steal away escabullirse *They stole away through the woods.* Se escabulleron a través de los bosques. ○ to steal the show llevarse los aplausos *The new actress stole the show.* La nueva actriz se llevó todos los aplausos.

steam [n] vapor *Does it run by steam or electricity?* ¿Funciona a vapor o por electricidad?

○ steam heat calefacción a vapor *Is there steam heat in their new house?*

¿Hay calefacción a vapor en su nueva casa? ○ to steam out zarpar *He watched the ship steam out of the harbor.* Observaba el vapor mientras zarpaba del puerto.

‖ *Do you think he can do the job under his own steam?* ¿Cree Ud. que él puede hacer el trabajo por sí mismo?

steamer vapor, barco.

steel [n] acero *The bridge is made of steel.* El puente está hecho de acero.

● [adj] de acero *The bullet bounced off his steel helmet.* La bala rebotó en su casco de acero.

● [v] fortalecerse *Steel yourself for what's coming.* Fortalézcase Ud. para lo que ha de venir.

steep escarpado, empinado *That slope is steeper than it looks.* Esa cuesta es más empinada de lo que parece. ▲ exorbitante *That's a steep price for that house.* Ese es un precio exorbitante por esa casa.

steer [v] gobernar, dirigir (*ship*); conducir, manejar (*car*).

stem [n] tallo, rabo *Do you want long stems on these flowers?* ¿Quiere Ud. estas flores con los tallos largos?

stem [v] detener, parar *Can't we do something to stem that campaign in the papers?* ¿No podemos hacer algo para detener esa campaña en los periódicos?

○ from stem to stern de proa a popa.

stenographer estenógrafo, taquígrafo.

step [n] paso *He took one step forward.* Dio un paso adelante.—*I don't know the steps of that dance.* No conozco los pasos de ese baile.—*We thought we heard steps.* Creíamos haber oído pasos.—*Keep in step with me.* Lleve el paso conmigo.—*That was the wrong step to take.* Ese fué un paso en falso. —*This is a great step forward.* Este es un gran paso hacia adelante.—*They had to retrace their steps.* Tuvieron que volver sobre sus pasos. ▲ escalón *I sat down on the top step.* Me senté en el último escalón.

● [v] poner el pie, pisar *I stepped in a puddle.* Pisé en un charco.

○ step by step paso a paso. ○ steps escalones *He ran up the steps to the porch.* Subió corriendo los escalones del porche. ○ to step aside ponerse a un lado *Step aside.* Póngase a un lado. ○ to step back retirarse *Step back a little.* Retírese Ud. un poco. ○ to step in entrar *I just stepped in for a moment.* Entré por un momento nada más. ○ to step into intervenir *He*

451

stepped into the situation just in time. Intervino a tiempo en la situación. ○ **to step off** bajarse, apearse *He just stepped off the train.* Acaba de apearse del tren. ○ **to step on** pisar *Don't step on the flowers.* No pise Ud. las flores. ○ **to step up** subir *Step up here!* ¡Suba aquí! ▲ aumentar *Try to step up the sale of gloves.* Procure aumentar la venta de guantes. ○ **to take steps** tomar medidas *I'll have to take steps to stop that gossip.* Tendré que tomar medidas para poner fin a ese chisme.
‖ *He's out of step with the times.* No está a tono con estos tiempos. ‖ *Step on it!* ¡Dése prisa! ‖ *She took a step in the right direction.* Dió un buen paso. ‖ *Step right up for your tickets.* Pasen a recoger sus billetes. ‖ *Watch your step!* ¡Fíjese donde pisa! or ¡Tenga Ud. cuidado! ‖ *What's the next step?* ¿Qué hacemos ahora?

stepbrother hermanastro.
stepchild hijastro.
stepdaughter hijastra.
stepfather padrastro.
stepmother madrastra.
stepsister hermanastra.
stepson hijastro.
sterile (*barren*) estéril.
sterilize esterilizar.
stern [*n*] popa *Sit in the stern while I row.* Siéntese en la popa mientras yo remo.
● [*adj*] duro *You shouldn't be so stern with him.* No debe Ud. ser tan duro con él.
stew [*n*] guisado *Who wants a second helping of stew?* ¿Quién quiere repetir del guisado?
stick [*n*] palo *I hit him with a stick.* Le golpeé con un palo. ▲ bastón *He knocked on the door with his stick.* Llamó a la puerta con su bastón ▲ pedazo *Do you want a stick of gum?* ¿Quiere Ud. un pedazo de goma de mascar?
● [*v*] prenderse *Stick this pin in your lapel* Préndase Ud. este alfiler en la solapa. ▲ ponerse *She stuck a flower in her hair.* Se puso una flor en el pelo. ▲ pinchar *That pin is sticking me.* Me está pinchando ese alfiler. ▲ meter *Don't stick your nose into other people's business.* No meta Ud. la nariz en asuntos ajenos. ▲ poner *Stick it over behind the couch.* Póngalo detrás de la cama turca. ▲ atenerse *Stick to the original.* Aténgase Ud. al original.

▲ atrancarse *This door sticks in hot weather.* Esta puerta se atranca con el calor. ▲ pegar *Stick it together with glue.* Péguelo con cola.—*This glue doesn't stick.* Esta goma no pega. ▲ pegarse *The paper sticks to my fingers.* El papel se me pega a los dedos. ○ **stick** of candy alfeñique. ○ **sticks** leña menuda *Pick up the sticks in the yard.* Recoja Ud. la leña menuda en el patio. ○ **stick up** atraco. ○ **stuck-up** presuntuoso, presumido *He's very stuck-up.* Es muy presumido. ○ **to stick it out** aguantar *Try and stick it out a little longer.* Procure Ud. aguantar un poco más. ○ **to stick out** sacar *Don't stick out your tongue at people.* No saques la lengua a la gente. ▲ sobresalir *There's something sticking out of the window.* Hay algo que sobresale de la ventana. ○ **to stick to** seguir en, no abandonar *Stick to your job.* No abandone su trabajo. ▲ persistir en *He stuck to his story.* Persistía en su versión. ○ **to stick together** mantenerse junto *Let's stick together.* Mantengámonos juntos. ○ **to stick up** sobresalir *Watch out for that pipe sticking up over there.* Cuidado con esa tubería que sobresale allá adelante. ▲ tomar partido, sacar la cara *He always sticks up for you.* Siempre saca la cara por Ud.
‖ *Stick them up!* ¡Manos arriba!
sticky pegajoso *What a sticky day!* ¡Qué día tan pegajoso!—*My fingers are sticky from the honey.* La miel me ha puesto los dedos pegajosos.
stiff duro *Use a stiff brush.* Use un cepillo duro. ▲ tieso *Don't be so stiff.* No esté Ud. tan tieso. ▲ difícil, duro *Is it a stiff examination?* ¿Es un examen difícil? ▲ antipático *What a big stiff!* ¡Qué tío tan antipático! ▲ agujetas *My legs feel stiff.* Tengo agujetas en las piernas.
○ **stiff breeze** brisa fuerte, viento fuerte. ○ **stiff drink** bebida fuerte *Please pour me a stiff drink.* Sírvame Ud. una bebida fuerte. ○ **stiff neck** tortícolis. ○ **stiff price** precio elevado or caro. ○ **to be (become) stiff** endurecerse *Stir the pudding until it's stiff.* Mueva el budín hasta que se endurezca.
‖ *He was scared stiff.* Estaba muerto de miedo.
stifle sofocar *I'm stifling in this room.* Me estoy sofocando en este cuarto. ▲ contener *He tried to stifle his cough.* Trató de contener la tos.
still [*n*] alambique *That rum came from*

this still. Ese ron ha sido destilado en este alambique.
● [*adj*] quieto *The air is very still.* El aire está muy quieto. *or* No corre ningún viento.—*Hold still a minute.* Estese quieto un momento. ▲ silencioso *The whole house was still.* Toda la casa estaba silenciosa.
● [*adv*] todavía *I am still waiting to hear from him.* Todavía estoy esperando noticias de él.—*There's still a lot of work to be done.* Queda todavía mucho trabajo por hacer. ▲ aún *He asked for still more books.* Pidió aún más libros.
● [*conj*] no obstante, sin embargo *Still, I think you did the right thing.* No obstante, yo creo que Ud. hizo lo correcto.
○ to **stand still** no moverse, permanecer quieto.
‖ *I still don't understand what you meant.* Sigo sin comprender lo que Ud. ha querido decir. ‖ *It's still raining.* Continúa lloviendo. ‖ *Keep still about this.* No diga nada de esto.
stilt zanco.
stimulant estimulante.
stimulate estimular.
sting [*n*] picadura *The sting was very painful.* La picadura era muy dolorosa.
● [*v*] picar *He was stung on the arm by a bee.* Una abeja le picó en el brazo.
○ to **be stung by** sentirse herido por *He was stung by her remark.* Se sintió herido por lo que ella le dijo.
stink [*n*] hedor.
● [*v*] heder, apestar.
stipulate estipular, especificar.
stir [*n*] conmoción *There was a stir in the crowd when the speaker approached the platform.* Hubo una conmoción en el público cuando el orador se acercó a la tribuna.
● [*v*] moverse *I can't stir from this chair; I ate too much.* No puedo moverme de esta silla; he comido demasiado. ▲ provocar, excitar *He's always stirring up everybody with his arguments.* Siempre está provocando a todo el mundo con sus opiniones. ▲ mover, menear, dar vueltas *If you'd stirred the cereal it wouldn't have stuck to the pot.* Si hubiera Ud. meneado el cereal no se hubiera pegado a la olla.
○ to **stir up** atizar, avivar *Stir up the fire!* ¡Atice el fuego!
stirrup estribo.
stitch [*n*] puntada *What sort of stitch is this?* ¿Qué clase de puntada es ésta?

● [*v*] coser *These handkerchiefs were stitched by hand.* Estos pañuelos fueron cosidos a mano.
‖ *I didn't have a stitch on.* Estaba completamente desnudo.
stock [*n*] surtido *Do you have a good stock of men's wear?* ¿Tiene Ud. un buen surtido de ropa de caballero? ▲ acción *I advise you not to buy those stocks.* Le aconsejo que no compre Ud. esas acciones. ▲ raza *Are these animals of healthy stock?* ¿Son estos animales de buena raza? ▲ ganado *He keeps all kinds of stock on his ranch.* Tiene toda clase de ganado en su hacienda.
● [*v*] tener en existencia *We don't stock that brand.* No tenemos en existencia esa marca.
○ **in stock** en existencia *What do you have in stock?* ¿Qué tiene Ud. en existencia? ○ **stock broker** corredor de bolsa. ○ **stock list** cotización de bolsa. ○ **stock market** bolsa *Do you speculate in the stock market?* ¿Especula Ud. en la bolsa? ○ to **be out of stock** estar faltos de surtido, haberse agotado las existencias *We're temporarily out of stock.* Se nos han agotado de momento las existencias. ○ to **be stocked up** estar abastecido, estar equipado *Are you well stocked up for the winter?* ¿Está Ud. bien equipado para el invierno? ○ to **lay in a stock** proveerse, surtirse, hacer, provisión. ○ to **put stock in** tener fe en *I don't put much stock in his promise.* No tengo mucha fe en su promesa. ○ to **take stock** hacer inventario *Next week we're taking stock.* La próxima semana vamos a hacer inventario. ▲ hacer un estudio, examinar *Why don't you first take stock of the situation?* ¿Por qué no hace antes un estudio de la situación?
stockings medias *I want three pairs of stockings.* Quiero tres pares de medias.
stomach estómago.
○ **on an empty stomach** en ayunas.
stone [*n*] piedra.
● [*v*] apedrear.
○ **precious stones** piedras preciosas.
‖ *The old man's stone-deaf.* El viejo está completamente sordo. *or* El viejo está como una tapia.
stool banquillo, taburete.
stop [*n*] parada *Get off the bus at the next stop.* Apéese del omnibus en la próxima parada.
● [*v*] parar *Stop the car.* Pare el automóvil. ▲ suspender *Why have you stopped my pay?* ¿Por qué me ha sus-

pendido Ud. el sueldo? ▲detener *If anyone tries to stop you, let me know.* Si alguien trata de detenerle, hágamelo saber. ▲impedir *You can't stop me from thinking about it.* No puede Ud. impedir que piense en ello. ▲dejar de *I've stopped worrying about it.* He dejado de preocuparme de eso. ▲pararse *My watch just stopped.* Mi reloj se acaba de parar.—*I stopped for a drink on the way.* Me paré en el camino para tomar un trago.

○ **stop sign** señal de parada. ○ **to put a stop to** poner término a, poner fin a *You'll have to put a stop to this unpleasant situation.* Tendrá Ud. que poner término a esta situación desagradable. ○ **to stop** *someone from doing something* impedir que, hacer que alguien deje de *Can't you stop him from talking that way?* ¿No puede Ud. procurar que deje de hablar en esa forma? ○ **to stop off** detenerse un rato *Let's stop off at the beach.* Detengámonos un rato en la playa. ○ **to stop over** detenerse, quedarse *Stop over at my place for a few days when you return.* Quédese unos días en mi casa a su regreso. ○ **to stop payment** suspender los pagos. ○ **to stop short** pararse repentinamente *He stopped short and turned around.* Se paró repentinamente y dió la vuelta. ○ **to stop up** tapar, obturar *This hole should be stopped up.* Hay que tapar este agujero.

‖ *We stopped at a hotel overnight.* Pasamos la noche en un hotel.

storage guardamuebles *We put all our things in storage for the summer.* En verano ponemos todas nuestras cosas en un guardamuebles. ▲almacenaje *How much did you pay for storage?* ¿Cuánto ha pagado Ud. por almacenaje?

store [*n*] tienda *I know a store where you can buy that.* Conozco una tienda donde puede Ud. comprar eso. ▲provisión *We've quite a store of food in the bin.* Tenemos una gran provisión de comestibles en la despensa.

● [*v*] guardar *Where shall I store the potatoes?* ¿Dónde guardaré las patatas?

○ **department store** almacén *Where's a good department store?* ¿Dónde hay un buen almacén? ○ **in store for** lo que le espera *I wonder what's in store for us.* ¿Qué será lo que nos espera? ○ **to set store by** confiarse en *I don't set much store by what she says.* No confío mucho en lo que ella dice. ○ **to store**

away acumular *He has a lot of money stored away.* Tiene mucho dinero acumulado.

‖ *You'll see what the boss has in store for you.* Ya verá Ud. lo que el patrón le tiene reservado.

storeroom bodega.

stork cigüeña.

storm [*n*] tormenta, tempestad *We had a big storm yesterday.* Ayer tuvimos una gran tormenta.

● [*v*] asaltar *We stormed the enemy positions.* Asaltamos las posiciones enemigas.

stormy tempestuoso, borrascoso.

story relato, información *The whole story of the case is in the paper.* El periódico trae toda la información sobre el caso. ▲cuento *I read an interesting story yesterday.* Ayer leí un cuento interesante. ▲chisme, hablilla *Have you heard the new story going around about her?* ¿Ha oído Ud. el nuevo chisme que se cuenta de ella? ▲versión, relato *Their stories don't agree.* Sus relatos no coinciden. ▲chiste *(joke) This is a funny story indeed.* Realmente este es un chiste divertidísimo.

○ **as the story goes** según se dice. ○ **to make a long story short** en resumidas cuentas. ○ **true story** historia verídica, anécdota verídica.

story piso *She lives on the second story.* Vive en el segundo piso.

stout gordo, corpulento.

stove hornilla, hornillo *Put the beans on the stove.* Ponga Ud. los frijoles sobre la hornilla. ▲estufa *It's nice sitting around the stove on a winter day.* Verdad que es agradable sentarse alrededor de la estufa en un día de invierno.

straight [*adj*] recto *It's a straight road.* Es un camino recto. ▲derecho *Stand up straight.* Póngase derecho. ▲bien puesto *Is my hat on straight?* ¿Tengo bien puesto el sombrero? ▲solo *I'll take my whiskey straight.* Tomaré mi whiskey solo. ▲honrado *He's always been straight with me.* Siempre ha sido honrado conmigo. ▲seguido *We worked fifteen hours straight.* Trabajamos quince horas seguidas.

● [*adv*] directamente *Go straight home.* Vaya directamente a casa.

○ **straight ticket** candidatura completa *My father always votes a straight ticket.* Mi padre vota siempre la candidatura completa.

‖ *He gave me the information straight from the shoulder.* Me dió la información sin ambajes ni rodeos. ‖ *I could hardly keep a straight face.* Apenas pude contener la risa.

straighten colocar bien, poner bien *Why don't you straighten your tie?* ¿Por qué no se coloca bien la corbata? ▲ poner en orden *It'll take me about a week or so to straighten out my affairs.* Necesito más o menos una semana para poner en orden mis cosas.

strain [*n*] disposición hereditaria *There's a strain of madness in his family.* Hay en su familia una disposición hereditaria a la locura. ▲ indicio *There's a strain of meanness in him.* Hay un indicio de maldad en él.

● [*v*] tirar con fuerza *The dog was straining at the leash.* El perro tiraba con fuerza de la correa. ▲ hacerse daño *Don't strain yourself lifting that trunk.* No se haga Ud. daño levantando ese baúl. ▲ colar *Will you strain the tea, please?* ¿Quiere Ud. hacer el favor de colar el té?

‖ *This small print is a strain on the eyes.* Este tipo de letra menuda cansa los ojos.

strait estrecho.

strand [*n*] hebra, hilo (*thread or rope*); sarta (*of pearls*).

○ **to be stranded** encallar(se) (*ship*).

strange extraño *This house looks strange, though I'm sure I've been here before.* Esta casa me parece extraña; aunque estoy seguro de haber estado aquí antes. ▲ raro *He's a strange character.* Es una persona rara.

‖ *I think it's very strange that he hasn't written yet.* Me extraña mucho que no haya escrito todavía. ‖ *Strange to say he still believes in fairy tales.* Parece mentira, pero todavía cree en los cuentos de hadas.

stranger forastero, extranjero *He's a stranger in this town.* Es un forastero en este pueblo. ▲ desconocido *She's a complete stranger to me.* Me es completamente desconocida.

‖ *You're certainly quite a stranger around here.* Verdaderamente se vende Ud. caro visitándonos.

strangle estrangular.

strap correa.

straw paja, pajilla, [*Mex*] popote *Will you ask the waitress to bring me a straw?* ¿Quiere Ud. decir a la camarera que me traiga una paja? ▲ paja *Do you like my new straw hat?* ¿Le gusta mi nuevo sombrero de paja?

○ **the last straw** el acabóse, el colmo *That's the last straw! I'm going home*

to mother. ¡Eso ya es el colmo! Me voy a casa de mi madre.

strawberry fresa.

stray [*adj*] callejero, vagabundo *There are too many stray dogs in this city.* Hay muchos perros callejeros en esta ciudad.

● [*v*] desviarse, extraviarse *The pilot strayed off his course.* El piloto se desvió de su ruta.

○ **to stray away** escaparse *The cat strayed away from home.* El gato se escapó de la casa.

streak [*n*] señal, huella *The tears have left streaks on her face.* Tiene señales de haber llorado. ▲ lado, fondo *That person has a serious streak you'd never suspect.* Aunque no se crea, esa persona tiene un fondo serio. ▲ racha *We've had a streak of awfully hot weather.* Hemos tenido una racha de tiempo muy caluroso.

○ **streak of dirt** tizne *Wash that streak of dirt off your face.* Límpiese ese tizne de la cara.

‖ *The plane streaked across the sky.* El avión cruzó el espacio como una centella.

stream corriente, río, arroyo *Where can we cross the stream?* ¿Por dónde podemos cruzar la corriente? ▲ desfile continuo *There's been a stream of cars on the highway all day.* Ha habido en la carretera un desfile continuo de automóviles todo el día.

○ **to stream out** salir en avalancha, salir a torrentes *The people streamed out of the theater when the show ended.* El público salió en avalancha del teatro al terminar el espectáculo.

street calle *Be careful when you cross the street.* Tenga cuidado al cruzar la calle.

○ **main street** calle mayor, calle principal. ○ **one-way street** una sola dirección. ○ **on the street** en la calle *I ran into him on the street the other day.* Le encontré en la calle el otro día. *or* Tropecé con él en la calle el otro día.

streetcar tranvía *You can get a streetcar on this corner.* Ud. puede tomar un tranvía en esta esquina.

strength fuerza(s) *I haven't the strength to lift that box.* No tengo bastante(s) fuerza(s) para levantar ese cajón. ▲ fuerzas *We haven't tried to judge the strength of the enemy.* No hemos tratado de calcular las fuerzas del enemigo.—*I'm afraid this medicine has lost its strength.* Temo que esta medicina haya perdido su fuerza. ▲ resistencia *Steel has more strength than almost any other metal.* El acero tiene más resistencia que casi todos los metales. ○ **on the strength of** en virtud de, en fuerza de *We hired those five men on the strength of your recommendation.* Empleamos a esos cinco hombres en virtud de su recomendación.

stress [*n*] esfuerzo (*effort*); énfasis (*emphasis*).
● [*v*] recalcar, subrayar.
○ **to lay stress on** dar importancia a.

stretch [*n*] trecho *The next stretch of road is not bad.* El próximo trecho de la carretera no es malo.
● [*v*] tender *He stretched the rope between the trees.* Tendió la cuerda entre los árboles. ▲ extender *The wheat fields stretch out for miles and miles.* Los trigales se extienden por millas y millas. ▲ estirarse, desperezarse *Stop yawning and stretching.* Deje de bostezar y de estirarse. ▲ ensanchar *Can you stretch my shoes?* ¿Puede Ud. ensancharme los zapatos? ▲ dar de sí *Will this sweater stretch when I wash it?* ¿Dará de sí este suéter al lavarlo?
○ **at a stretch** de un tirón *I can walk about three miles at a stretch.* Puedo caminar más o menos tres millas de un tirón. ○ **to stretch a point** hacer la vista gorda *The judge stretched a point and let the man go.* El juez hizo la vista gorda y le puso en libertad. ○ **to stretch out** echarse a lo largo *He stretched out on the couch.* Se echó a lo largo sobre la cama turca. ▲ alargar *He stretched out his hand to pick up a book.* Alargó la mano para coger un libro.

stretcher camilla.
strict estricto.
stride [*n*] zancada, tranco *You take such long strides I can't keep up with you.* Da Ud. tales zancadas que no le puedo seguir.
● [*v*] dar zancadas, andar a trancos *We saw him striding down the street.* Le vimos dando zancadas por la calle.
○ **to hit one's stride** ponerse en forma *It was a few weeks before he hit his stride.* Pasaron algunas semanas hasta que él volviera a ponerse en forma. ○ **to make great** (*or* **rapid**) **strides** hacer grandes progresos *We weren't surprised to hear that you made great strides in your new job.* No nos sorprendió oír que Ud. ha hecho grandes progresos en su nuevo empleo. ○ **to take in one's stride.** Tomarlo tranquilamente, tomarle como si nada. *Anyone else would have been very upset, but he took it in his stride.* Cualquiera otra persona se hubiera alterado mucho, pero él lo tomó tranquilamente.

strife conflicto, disputa.
strike [*n*] huelga *How long did the miners' strike last?* ¿Cuánto tiempo duró la huelga de los mineros?
● [*v*] pegar *He struck him in self defense.* Le pegó en defensa propia. ▲ chocar con *The ship struck a rock.* El barco chocó con una roca. ▲ atropellar *He was struck by a car.* Fué atropellado por un auto. ▲ caer *That tree's been struck by lightning.* Cayó un rayo en ese árbol. ▲ dar la hora *Did the clock strike?* ¿Dió la hora el reloj? ▲ dar *It just struck seven.* Acaban de dar las siete. ▲ encender *Strike a match and look at the time.* Encienda un fósforo y mire que hora es. ▲ producir *That speech struck a wrong note.* Ese discurso produjo un mal efecto.
○ **to be on strike** estar en huelga *Why are they on strike?* ¿Por qué están en huelga? ○ **to go on strike** declararse en huelga, ir a la huelga *They promised not to go on strike.* Prometieron no declararse en huelga. ○ **to strike a bargain** llegar a un acuerdo, cerrar un trato *We finally struck a bargain.* Por fin llegamos a un acuerdo. ○ **to strike off** tachar, borrar *Strike his name off the list.* Tache su nombre de la lista. ○ **to strike oil** encontrar petróleo *Has anyone ever struck oil around here?* ¿Han encontrado petróleo por aquí alguna vez? ○ **to strike one's eye** llamar la atención *It's just the first thing that struck my eye.* Es precisamente la primera cosa que me llamó la atención. ○ **to strike out** suprimir *Strike out the last paragraph.* Suprima el último párrafo. ○ **to strike the colors** arriar la bandera. ○ **to strike up** comenzar *The band struck up the national anthem.* La banda comenzó a tocar el hinmo nacional. ○ **to strike up a friendship** comenzar una amistad *The two of them struck up a friendship very quickly.* Los dos comenzaron una amistad muy rápidamente.
‖ *How does that suggestion strike you?* ¿Qué le parece esa idea? ‖ *That idea just struck me.* Se me acaba de ocurrir esa idea.

striker huelguista.
string cuerda, cordel *The string is too short.* Esta cuerda es demasiado corta.

▲ fila *There's a long string of busses waiting.* Hay una larga fila de autobuses esperando. ▲ serie, sarta *He asked a long string of questions.* Hizo una larga serie de preguntas.
● [v] enhebrar *Where can I have my amber beads strung?* ¿Dónde podrán enhebrarme las cuentas de ámbar? ▲ tender *They strung the electric wire from pole to pole.* Tendieron el cable eléctrico de poste en poste.
○ string of pearls collar de perlas *She's wearing a beautiful string of pearls.* Lleva un lindo collar de perlas. ○ to pull strings valerse de influencias *I never was good at pulling strings.* Nunca supe valerme de influencias. ○ to string out *The policemen were strung out along the sidewalk.* Se colocó un cordón de policía a lo largo de la acera.
‖ *She has three men on the string.* Tiene tres pretendientes. ‖ *There are no strings attached to the offer.* En esta oferta no hay ninguna reserva.
string bean judía verde, frijol verde, habichuela verde.
strip [n] tira, franja *Paste a strip of paper around the box.* Pegue una tira de papel alrededor de la caja.
● [v] desnudarse *The doctor wants you to strip to the waist.* El médico quiere que se desnude hasta la cintura. ▲ despojar *He was stripped of all his possessions.* Le despojaron de todos sus bienes. ▲ descortezar, quitar la corteza *Who's been stripping the bark from this tree?* ¿Quién ha estado quitando la corteza de este árbol?
stripe raya, lista.
stripes galones (*military*).
strive esforzarse, empeñarse en.
stroke [n] brazada *I saw her swim and I think she has an excellent stroke.* La ví nadar y creo que tiene una brazada excelente. ▲ ataque *I'm worried; my father had another stroke last night.* Estoy preocupado; mi padre ha sufrido anoche otro ataque.
● [v] acariciar *Stroke the dog and he'll become friendly.* Acaricie Ud. el perro y se hará su amigo.
○ stroke of luck suerte *It was a stroke of luck to get this apartment.* Fué una suerte conseguir este apartamento.
‖ *He arrived at the stroke of four.* Llegó cuando daban las cuatro. ‖ *He hasn't done a stroke of work for months.* No ha dado ni golpe en dos meses.

stroll [n] paseo.
● [v] pasear.
○ to go for a stroll dar un paseo, pasearse.
strong fuerte *He has strong hands.* Tiene manos fuertes.—*This party isn't very strong yet.* Este partido todavía no es muy fuerte.—*He showed a strong desire to see it.* Mostró un fuerte deseo de verlo.—*This drink is too strong.* Esta bebida es demasiado fuerte. ▲ resistente *Is this ladder strong enough to hold me?* ¿Es esta escalera lo bastante resistente para aguantarme?
○ strong tea té cargado.
structure estructura.
struggle [n] lucha.
● [v] luchar.
‖ *Struggle for life.* Lucha por la vida.
stub [n] cabo *I can't write with this pencil stub.* No puedo escribir con este cabo de lápiz.
○ ticket stub contraseña de salida, talón. ○ to stub one's toe tropezar *I stubbed my toe on a rock.* He tropezado con una piedra.
stubborn terco, testarudo, contumaz.
stucco estuco.
student alumno *That's one of my best students.* Ese es uno de mis mejores alumnos. ▲ estudiante *He's a student at the University.* Es un estudiante en la Universidad.
‖ *She's a serious student of the subject.* Ella estudia el tema a fondo.
studio estudio.
study [n] estudio *This book requires careful study.* Este libro requiere un estudio cuidadoso.—*He has published several studies in that field.* Ha publicado varios estudios sobre ese tema.
● [v] estudiar *I've studied the situation carefully.* He estudiado la situación cuidadosamente.—*Have you studied your part?* ¿Ha estudiado Ud. su papel?—*I'm studying medicine at the University.* Estoy estudiando medicina en la Universidad.
stuff [n] eso *What's that stuff you're eating?* ¿Qué es eso que come Ud.? ▲ cosas *Get your stuff out of my room.* Llévese sus cosas de mi cuarto.—*I don't like the stuff he's been writing lately.* No me gustan las cosas que ha estado escribiendo últimamente.
● [v] llenar *She keeps her handbag stuffed full of junk.* Tiene su bolso lleno de cosas inútiles. ▲ rellenar *Did you stuff the chicken?* ¿Rellenó Ud. el pollo? ▲ meter, embutir *He*

stuffed his things in a suitcase. Metió sus cosas en una maleta. ▲ disecar *He stuffs animals for the museum.* Diseca animales para el museo. ‖ *That book's good stuff.* Ese libro es muy bueno. ‖ *We'll see what kind of stuff he has in him.* Ya veremos de que clase de madera es.

stuffing relleno.

stumble tropezar.

stump tronco *Be careful not to hit that stump.* Tenga Ud. cuidado de no tropezar con ese tronco. ‖ *This problem has me stumped.* Este problema me tiene en un brete.

stun aturdir.

stupid tonto, estúpido.

sturdy fuerte, robusto.

stutter tartamudear.

style manera, estilo *She does everything in elegant style.* Hace todas las cosas de una manera elegante. ▲ moda *It's the latest style.* Es la última moda. ▲ estilo *My style isn't so good.* Mi estilo no es tan bueno. O **style of address** tratamiento, título de cortesía.

stylish elegante *She's very stylish.* Es muy elegante.

suave fino, de modales corteses, afable.

subdue dominar, sojuzgar.

subject [n] tema *This is a good subject for conversation.* Este es un buen tema para conversar. ▲ asignaturas, materias *What subjects did you study in school last year?* ¿Qué asignaturas estudió Ud. en la escuela el año pasado? ▲ súbdito *He's a British subject.* Es súbdito británico. O **subject to** sujeto a *These rates are subject to change without notice.* Estos precios están sujetos a cambio sin previo aviso. ▲ bajo, sujeto a *We're all subject to the same laws.* Todos nosotros estamos bajo las mismas leyes. O **to be subject to** someterse a *All of my actions are subject to his approval.* Todo lo que yo haga tiene que someterse a su aprobación.

subject [v] exponer *Such behavior will subject you to criticism.* Tal comportamiento le expondrá a críticas. ▲ someter *The thief was subjected to severe punishment.* El ladrón fué sometido a un castigo severo.

sublet subarrendar, subalquilar.

submarine submarino.

submit someter.

subordinate [n] subordinado. ● [v] subordinar.

subscribe suscribir.

O **to subscribe to** suscribirse, abonarse a.

subscription suscripción.

substance sustancia.

substantial sustancial, sustancioso.

substitute [n] sustituto. ● [v] reemplazar, sustituir.

subtle sutil.

subtract sustraer, restar.

suburb suburbio.

subversive subversivo.

subway metro, subterráneo.

succeed lograr *Did you succeed in getting him on the phone?* ¿Logró Ud. hablar con él por teléfono? ▲ tener éxito *The plan didn't succeed equally well in all cases.* El proyecto nu tuvo el mismo éxito en todos los casos. ▲ suceder *Who succeeded him in office?* ¿Quién le sucedió en el cargo?

success éxito *Did you have any success with him?* ¿Tuvo Ud. algún éxito con él?—*His play was an instant success.* La comedia alcanzó un éxito inmediato.

successful afortunado, próspero *He hasn't been successful in business.* No ha sido afortunado en los negocios. ▲ de éxito, de fama *He's a successful writer.* Es un escritor de éxito.

succession sucesión.

successive sucesivo.

such tal *Such statements are exaggerated.* Tales declaraciones son exageradas.—*Conduct such as this is inexcusable.* Tal comportamiento no tiene excusa.—*There's no such thing.* No hay tal cosa. ▲ semejante *I've never seen such beauty.* Nunca he visto belleza semejante. ▲ así *Such is life!* ¡Así es la vida! ▲ tan, tanto *It's been such a long time since we last met.* Hace tanto tiempo desde que nos vimos la última vez. O **such ... as la ...** que *I'll give you such information as is necessary.* Le daré la información que Ud. necesite. O **such as** tal como *Her conduct was such as might have been expected under the circumstances.* Su comportamiento fué tal como era de esperar en aquellas circunstancias. ▲ tal como, tales como *It's too cold here for certain fruit trees, such as the peach.* Hace demasiado frío aquí para ciertos árboles frutales, tal como el durazno. O **such that** tal que *He said it in such a way that I couldn't help laughing.* Lo dijo de tal modo que no pude menos que reírme. ▲ de tal manera que, en tales condiciones que *The road is such that it can be traveled only on foot.* El camino está en tales condiciones que sólo se puede recorrer a pie.

suck chupar.

sudden repentino, súbito *He died a sudden death.* Murió de repente. *or* Falleció de muerte repentina.

○ **all of a sudden** de repente *All of a sudden I remembered that I had to mail a letter.* De repente me acordé que tenía que echar una carta al correo.

suddenly de repente, repentinamente.

suds jabonadura, espuma.

sue demandar, entablar demanda.

suffer sufrir *Did you suffer much after your operation?* ¿Sufrió mucho Ud. después de su operación?—*The buildings along the river suffered severe damage from the flood.* Los edificios a lo largo del río sufrieron grandes daños a consecuencia de la inundación. ▲ sentir *Are you suffering any pain?* ¿Siente Ud. algún dolor?

suffice bastar.

sufficient suficiente.

suffocate sofocar, asfixiar.

suffrage sufragio.

sugar azúcar.

suggest sugerir *Can you suggest anyone for the job?* ¿Puede Ud. sugerir a alguien para el puesto?—*Does this suggest anything to you?* ¿Le sugiere a Ud. algo esto? ▲ insinuar *Are you suggesting that I'm wrong?* ¿Insinúa Ud. que estoy equivocado? ▲ proponer *I suggest that we go swimming today.* Propongo que vayamos a nadar hoy.

suggestion sugestión, sugerencia.

suicide suicidio (*act*); suicida (*person*).

suit [*n*] traje *This suit doesn't fit him very well.* Este traje no le sienta muy bien. ▲ pleito *Who's the lawyer handling the suit?* ¿Quién es el abogado encargado del pleito?

● [*v*] satisfacer, agradar *Does the program suit you?* ¿Le satisface el programa? ▲ venir bien, convenir *Does nine o'clock suit you?* ¿Le viene bien a las nueve? ▲ ir, caer *This color doesn't suit you.* Este color no le va bien a Ud. ▲ adaptar al gusto *Try to suit the play to the audience.* Trate de adaptar la comedia al gusto del público.

○ **to follow suit** (*cards*) jugar el mismo palo.

‖ *Suit yourself.* Haga lo que quiera.

suitable apropiado, adecuado.

suitcase maleta.

sum suma *I want to deposit a large sum of money.* Quiero depositar una suma grande de dinero.

○ **sum total** todo *And that's the sum total of my experience with him.* Y esa es toda mi experiencia con él. ○ **to sum up** resumir *He summed up the situation in very few words.* Resumió la situación en pocas palabras. ○ **total sum** suma total, importe total.

summary resumen, compendio.

summer verano.

○ **to spend the summer** veranear.

summit cima, cumbre.

summons citación.

sun [*n*] sol *The sun just went down.* Acaba de ponerse el sol.—*I've been out in the sun all day.* He estado todo el día al sol.

● [*v*] tomar el sol *We spent the whole day sunning (ourselves).* Estuvimos todo el día tomando el sol.

‖ *In summertime the sun rises early and sets late.* En verano el sol sale temprano y se pone tarde.

sunburn quemadura de sol.

Sunday domingo.

sunglasses gafas de sol, anteojos para el sol.

sunny asoleado, soleado *This is a fine sunny room.* Este es un cuarto bien asoleado.

‖ *It's very sunny today.* Hoy hace mucho sol.

sunrise amanecer, salida del sol.

sunset crepúsculo, puesta de sol.

sunshine luz del sol.

superficial superficial.

superfluous superfluo.

superintendent portero, conserje (*building*); capataz, superintendente (*factory*).

○ **superintendent of schools** director general de primera y segunda enseñanza.

superior superior.

superstition superstición.

supervise supervisar, vigilar y dirigir.

supper cena *Supper is ready.* La cena está lista.

supply [*n*] provisión *We need a fresh supply of potatoes.* Necesitamos una nueva provisión de patatas. ▲ abastecimiento *Our troops are getting their supplies without much difficulty.* Nuestras fuerzas están recibiendo sus abastecimientos sin mucha dificultad. ▲ existencia *The supply of silk stockings can't meet the demand.* La existencia de medias de seda no puede satisfacer la demanda. ▲ surtido *We've just received a good supply of novelties.*

Acabamos de recibir un buen surtido de bisutería.
● [v] suplir *The store has enough shoes on hand to supply any normal demand.* La tienda dispone de zapatos suficientes para suplir cualquier demanda normal. ▲ proporcionar, proveer de *That company supplies us with ice.* Esa compañía nos proporciona el hielo. ○ supplies provisiones *We're running out of supplies.* Se nos están acabando las provisiones.

support [n] soporte, sostén *This lamp has a strong support.* Esta lámpara tiene un soporte sólido. ▲ sustento, mantenimiento *Several relatives depend on him for their support.* Varios parientes dependen de él para su mantenimiento. ● [v] aguantar, resistir *That bridge isn't strong enough to support so much weight.* Ese puente no es lo bastante fuerte para aguantar tanto peso. ▲ mantener *Are you supporting a family?* ¿Mantiene Ud. una familia? ▲ apoyar *I'll support your claims.* Yo apoyaré sus peticiones. ○ in support of en apoyo de, a favor *I've spoken in support of this idea before.* La he hablado antes a favor de esta idea.

suppose suponer *Let's suppose he turns up, what then?* Supongamos que se presente, y entonces ¿qué?—*I suppose so.* Supongo que sí.—*Supposing it rains, can we use that road?* Suponiendo que llueva, ¿podremos utilizar ese camino? ▲ tener por, considerar *He's supposed to be the richest man in town.* Se le tiene por el hombre más rico del pueblo. ○ to be supposed to deber de *I'm supposed to go home early tonight.* Debo de ir a casa temprano esta noche. ‖ *It's to be supposed that he will do it.* Es de creer que lo hará. ‖ *Suppose you wait till tomorrow?* ¿Le parece esperar hasta mañana?

supreme supremo.
suppress suprimir.
sure [adj] seguro *This method is slow but sure.* Este método es lento pero seguro.—*He's sure to be back by nine o'clock.* Está seguro que regresará a las nueve. ● [adv] claro, por supuesto *Sure, I'll do it.* Claro que lo haré. ▲ ciertamente, seguro que *I'd sure like to see them, but I won't have time.* Seguro que me gustaría verles, pero no tendré tiempo. ○ for sure con seguridad *Do you*

know that for sure? ¿Sabe Ud. eso con seguridad? ○ sure enough efectivamente *You said it would rain, and sure enough it did.* Ud. dijo que llovería, y efectivamente así fué. ○ to be sure estar seguro *Are you sure of that?* ¿Está Ud. seguro de eso? ▲ no haber duda, no caber duda *It's a bad day to be sure, but we've seen worse.* No cabe duda de que hace mal día, pero los hemos tenido peores. ○ to be sure and wear your overcoat. No deje de ponerse su abrigo. ○ to make sure asegurarse *Make sure of the facts before you write the paper.* Asegúrese de los hechos antes de escribir el tema.

surely ciertamente, seguramente, sin duda.
surety seguridad, fianza.
surf resaca, marejada.
surface superficie.
surgeon cirujano.
surgery cirugía.
surname apellido.
surpass sobrepasar, superar.
surplus sobrante, superávit.
surprise [n] sorpresa *I've got a surprise for you in this package.* Tengo una sorpresa para Ud. en este paquete.—*Your behavior took me by surprise.* Su comportamiento me cogió de sorpresa. ● [v] sorprender *We surprised the boys stealing apples.* Sorprendimos a los muchachos robando manzanas.—*Are you surprised that I came?* ¿Le sorprende a Ud. que haya venido?
surrender [n] rendición, capitulación. ● [v] rendir, capitular.
surround rodear.
surroundings ambiente, medio ambiente *She comes from poor surroundings.* Viene de un ambiente pobre. ▲ alrededores, cercanías *The surroundings of the city are beautiful.* Las cercanías de la ciudad son muy hermosas.
survey [n] examen, estudio *Let's make a survey of the food situation.* Hagamos un examen de la situación alimenticia. ● [v] medir, deslindar *Before this land can be sold it must be surveyed.* Antes de poder vender esta tierra es necesario medirla.
surveying agrimensura *(land).*
surveyor agrimensor.
survive sobrevivir.
suspect [n] persona sospechosa.
suspect [v] sospechar.
suspend colgar, suspender *These decorations will be suspended from the ceil-*

ing. Estos adornos se colgarán del techo. ▲ reservar *I would prefer to suspend judgment until we know all the facts.* Preferiría reservarme la opinión hasta que conozcamos todos los hechos. ▲ suspender *The company's director was suspended from office.* El director de la compañia fué suspendido en sus funciones.

suspenders tirantes.

suspense suspensión.
○ **to keep in suspense** dejar en la incertidumbre.

suspicion sospecha, recelo.
○ **to be above suspicion** Estar sobre toda sospecha.

sustain sustentar, mantener.

swallow [*n*] golondrina.
● [*v*] tragar.

swamp [*n*] pantano *There are many mosquitoes here because of the swamp.* Aquí hay muchos mosquitos a causa del pantano.
● [*v*] hundir, hacer zozobrar *Be careful not to swamp the boat.* Tenga cuidado de no hundir el bote.
○ **to be swamped** estar abrumado *I've been swamped with work.* He estado abrumado de trabajo.

swampy pantanoso.

swan cisne.

swarm (*of bees*) enjambre.

sway [*n*] bamboleo, movimiento, vaivén *The sway of the train makes me sick.* El movimiento del tren me enferma.
● [*v*] bambolearse *Look at the way that car is swaying.* Mire como se bambolea aquel auto.

swear jurar *That fellow has a bad habit of swearing.* Ese tipo tiene la mala costumbre de jurar.—*She swears she's telling the truth.* Jura que está diciendo la verdad.
○ **to swear in** jurar, prestar juramento, tomar posesión. ○ **to swear off** renunciar a, renegar de.

sweat [*n*] sudor.
● [*v*] sudar.

sweater suéter.

sweep barrer *Will you sweep this room?* ¿Quiere Ud. barrer este cuarto?
○ **to sweep away** arrastrar.
‖ *He made a clean sweep of his debts.* Liquidó completamente todas sus deudas.

sweet dulce *Do you have any sweet oranges?* ¿Tiene Ud. naranjas dulces? —*Her voice is very sweet.* Tiene la voz muy dulce. ▲ fresco *Is the milk still sweet?* ¿Está todavía fresca la leche? ▲ amable *She has a very sweet disposition.* Tiene un carácter muy amable.
○ **sweets** dulces *I don't care much for sweets.* No me gustan mucho los dulces.

sweetbread páncreas.

sweetheart novio, novia.

sweet potato batata [*Sp*], camote [*Am*], boniato.

swell [*adj*] estupendo, excelente *He's a swell fellow.* Es un tipo estupendo.
● [*v*] hinchar *His wrist was swollen.* Tenía la muñeca hinchada. ▲ aumentar *Their numbers are swelling fast.* Aumentan rápidamente en número. ▲ crecer *The river is badly swollen after the spring rains.* El río está muy crecido después de las lluvias de primavera.
○ **to get a swelled head** envanecerse, engreirse *Don't get a swelled head.* No vaya Ud. a envanecerse. *or* ¡Que no se le suba a la cabeza! ○ **to swell up** hincharse *My foot is beginning to swell up.* Se me está hinchando el pie.

swelling hinchazón, inflamación.

swift rápido, veloz.

swim [*n*] nadada [*Am*] *I'm going out for a swim.* Voy a dar una nadada. *or* Voy a nadar un rato.
● [*v*] nadar *Do you know how to swim?* ¿Sabe Ud. nadar? ▲ cruzar a nado *We'll have to swim the river.* Tendremos que cruzar el río a nado.
○ **to make the head swim** hacer perder la cabeza *The blow made my head swim.* El golpe me aturdió.

swine marrano, puerco, cerdo.

swing [*n*] columpio *They're sitting in the swing.* Están sentados en el columpio.
● [*v*] mecer, balancear *She swings her arms when she walks.* Balancea los brazos cuando camina.
○ **in full swing** en plena actividad *The factory is in full swing.* La fábrica está en plena actividad.

switch [*n*] varita, varilla *I'm going to cut a switch to use on my horse.* Voy a cortar una varita para darle a mi caballo.
● [*v*] cambiar de sitio *Let's switch the furniture around.* Cambiemos los muebles de sitio.
○ **electric switch** llave de la luz, conmutador. ○ **railroad switch** aguja de ferrocarril.
‖ *Be careful that the cow doesn't switch her tail in your face.* Tenga cuidado que la vaca no le de con la cola en la cara.

switchboard centralilla (*telephone*); cua-

461

dro conmutador, cuadro de distribución (*electricity*).
sword espada.
syllable sílaba.
symbol símbolo.
sympathize condolocerse, compadecerse.
▲ convenir, estar de acuerdo *I don't sympathize with his point of view.* No estoy de acuerdo con su punto de vista.
sympathy lástima *I don't have any sympathy for such a fool.* No le tengo ninguna lástima a semejante loco. ▲ pésame, condolencia *We sent them a letter of sympathy.* Les escribimos dándoles el pésame.
symphony sinfonía.

symptom síntoma.
synonym sinónimo.
synthetic sintético.
syphilis sífilis.
syphilitic sifilítico.
syringe jeringa.
syrup jarabe (*cough syrup*); almíbar (*pancake syrup*).
system sistema *Do you have a good communication system in this country?* ¿Tienen Uds. un buen sistema de comunicaciones en este país? ▲ método *What's your teaching system?* ¿Que método de enseñanza emplea Ud.?
systematic sistemático.

T

table [*n*] mesa *Push the table against the wall.* Empuje la mesa contra la pared.
○ **table of contents** índice, tabla de materias *He's looking it up in the table of contents.* Lo está buscando en el índice. ○ **to table** dar carpetazo, aplazar *They tabled the motion.* Dieron carpetazo a la moción.
tablecloth mantel.
tablespoon cuchara.
tablet tableta, pastilla (*pill*).
tack [*n*] tachuela *I need four tacks to fasten the poster.* Me hacen falta cuatro tachuelas para clavar el cartel.
● [*v*] clavar *Tack his picture on the wall.* Clave su retrato en la pared. ▲ apuntar *The belt's tacked on to the dress.* El cinturón está apuntado al traje.
tackle [*v*] agarrar *The policeman tackled the thief.* El policía agarró al ladrón. ▲ abordar *It's about time we tackled that problem.* Ya es hora de que abordemos el problema.
○ **fishing tackle** avíos de pescar.
tact tacto.
tag [*n*] rótulo, etiqueta.
tail rabo, cola *The dog wagged his tail.* El perro meneaba la cola. ○ **at the tail end** al final *We arrived at the tail end of the first act.* Llegamos al final del primer acto. ○ **tails** cruz *Tails, you lose.* Cruz y pierde Ud. ○ **heads or tails** cara o cruz.
‖ *His lecture was so confusing, we couldn't make head or tail of it.* Su conferencia era tan confusa, que no tenía ni pies ni cabeza.
tailor [*n*] sastre *Where can I find a good*

tailor? ¿Dónde puedo encontrar un buen sastre?
● [*v*] cortar *This skirt's well tailored.* Esta falda está bien cortada.
take [*v*] coger *She took the baby in her arms.* Cogió al niño en brazos. ▲ coger, llevarse *Don't take my hat.* No se lleve mi sombrero.—*Who took my pen?* ¿Quién cogió mi pluma? ▲ llevar *Take this letter to the post office.* Lleve esta carta al correo.—*Who's taking her to the station?* ¿Quién la va a llevar a la estación?—*Where will that road take us?* ¿A dónde lleva ese camino? ▲ tomar *I'll take the room with bath.* Tomaré el cuarto con baño.—*Did the doctor take your temperature?* ¿Le ha tomado el doctor la temperatura?— *The soldiers took the town in two hours.* Los soldados tomaron el pueblo en dos horas.—*Take a seat, please.* Tome asiento, por favor. ▲ sacar, tomar *Are you allowed to take pictures here?* ¿Se pueden sacar fotografías aquí? ▲ aceptar *Do you take checks?* ¿Aceptan Uds. cheques? ▲ seguir *Take my advice and stay home tonight.* Siga Ud. mi consejo y quédese en casa esta noche. ▲ durar *How long will the trip take?* ¿Cuánto durará el viaje? ▲ tardar *How long will it take to press my suit?* ¿Cuánto tardará en plancharme el traje? ▲ hacer falta, necesitarse *It'll take three men to move this safe.* Harán falta tres hombres para mover la caja de caudales. ▲ ganar *Who do you think'll take the tennis match?* ¿Quién cree Ud. que ganará el partido de tenis? ▲ soportar, sufrir *It won't be pleasant, but you'll have to take it.* No

será agradable, pero tendrá Ud. que soportarlo. ▲ aguantar, tolerar *I can't take any more from him.* No puedo aguantarle más. ○ **to take a bath** bañarse *I'd like to take a bath before dinner.* Me gustaría bañarme antes de comer. ○ **to take advantage of** aprovechar *Thanks, I'll take advantage of your offer.* Gracias, aprovecharé su oferta. ▲ aprovecharse de *He took advantage of his position.* Se aprovechó de su posición. ○ **to take after** parecerse a *Who do you take after, your father or your mother?* ¿A quién se parece Ud. a su madre o a su padre? ○ **to take a nap** dormir la siesta *I always take a nap after dinner.* Siempre duermo la siesta después de comer. ○ **to take a seat** sentarse *Take a seat, please.* Siéntese, por favor. ○ **to take a walk** dar un paseo *Would you like to take a walk in the park?* ¿Le gustaría a Ud. dar un paseo por el parque? ○ **to take back** retractarse de, retirar *I take back what I said a minute ago.* Me retracto de lo que dije hace un minuto. ▲ recoger, llevarse *I won't need your book, so why don't you take it back?* No me hace falta su libro, ¿por qué no se lo lleva Ud.? ○ **to take care of** cuidar *Take care of yourself.* Cuídese Ud. ○ **to take charge of** encargarse de *Who's taking charge of the office while you're away?* ¿Quién se encarga de la oficina mientras está Ud. ausente? ○ **to take down** bajar, descolgar *Take the picture down.* Descuelgue Ud. el cuadro. ▲ tomar nota de *Will you take this down please?* ¿Quiere tomar nota de esto, por favor? ○ **to take for** tomar a uno por *Sorry, I took you for someone else.* Perdón, le tomé a Ud. por otra persona. ○ **to take for granted** dar por sentado *I took it for granted that he wanted the job.* Dí por sentado que quería la colocación. ○ **to take in** visitar *We haven't enough time to take in all the museums.* No tenemos suficiente tiempo para visitar todos los museos. ▲ ganar *How much do you take in every month?* ¿Cuánto gana Ud. al mes? ▲ engañar *He certainly took us in with his stories.* Indudablemente nos engañó con sus cuentos. ▲ estrechar, reducir, hacer más pequeño *Will you take this dress in at the waist?* ¿Me puede estrechar la cintura de este vestido? ○ **to take it** suponer, asumir *I take it you're in trouble.* Supongo que está Ud. en dificultades. ○ **to take it easy** tomar con

calma *Take it easy, there's no hurry.* Tómela con calma, no hay prisa. ▲ no apurarse *Take it easy, don't get so excited.* No se apure, no se excite. ○ **to take off** quitarse *Take off your hat and stay a while.* Quítese Ud. el sombrero y quédese un rato. ▲ despegar *When does the plane take off?* ¿Cuándo despega el avión? ▲ imitar *My friend can take off almost any actor you name.* Mi amigo puede imitar a casi todos los actores que Ud. nombre. ○ **to take offense** ofenderse *You shouldn't take offense at what was said.* No debiera ofenderse por lo que han dicho. ○ **to take on** emplear, tomar *I hear the factory's taking on new men.* Me dicen que la fabrica está empleando nuevos obreros. ▲ empezar *We took on a new job yesterday.* Ayer empezamos un nuevo trabajo. ▲ desafiar *I'll take you on for some tennis.* Le desafío a Ud. a una partida de tenis. ○ **to take one's time** hacerlo despacio, hacerlo con calma *Can I take my time?* ¿Puedo hacerlo con calma? ○ **to take out** sacar *Take the fruit out of the bag.* Saque la fruta del saco. ▲ quitar *Can you take this spot out of my blouse?* ¿Me puede quitar esta mancha de la blusa? ○ **to take place** ocurrir, tener lugar *Where did the accident take place?* ¿Dónde ocurrió el accidente? ○ **to take sick** caer enfermo *When did he take sick?* ¿Cuándo cayó enfermo? ○ **to take the blame** hacerse responsable, tomar la responsabilidad *I won't take the blame for his mistake.* No me quiero hacer responsable de su error. ○ **to take to** tomar cariño *They took to him as soon as they met him.* Le tomaron cariño desde el momento en que le conocieron. ○ **to take up** tomar, estudiar *I think I'll take up French this year.* Creo que voy a estudiar francés este año. ▲ tomar la palabra *I'll take you up on that.* Le tomo la palabra en eso. ▲ consultar *You'll have to take up that matter with someone else.* Tendrá Ud. que consultar ese asunto con otra persona. ○ **to take up with** relacionarse *I wouldn't take up with those people if I were you.* Yo, en su lugar, no me relacionaría con esa gente.
‖ *Take my hand.* Dame la mano. ‖ *Will you let us take your car?* ¿Nos deja usar su coche? ‖ *Don't take on so!* ¡No se ponga así! ‖ *Well, don't take it out on me!* ¡No se desahogue Ud. riñéndome!

taken tomado, ocupado *Is this seat taken?* ¿Está ocupado este asiento?

talcum powder polvos de talco.

tale cuento.

talent aptitud.

talk [*n*] discurso *His talk was long and dull.* Su discurso fué largo y aburrido. ▲ rumor, comentario *Her actions have caused a lot of talk.* Sus actos han provocado muchos comentarios. ● [*v*] hablar *Don't you think he talks too much?* ¿No cree Ud. que él habla demasiado? ○ **talk of the town** comidilla del pueblo *Their house is the talk of the town.* Su casa es la comidilla del pueblo. ○ **to talk back** replicar *For once he dared to talk back to her.* Por una vez se atrevió a replicarle. ○ **to talk into** convencer de *Do you suppose we can talk them into coming with us?* ¿Cree Ud. que podremos convencerles de que vengan con nosotros? ○ **to talk over** discutir, tratar acerca de *Let's talk this over.* Discutamos este asunto.

tall alto *Her husband's that tall man over there.* Su marido es aquel hombre alto que está allí. ‖ *That's a pretty tall order, but I'll try to do it.* Eso es mucho pedir, pero intentaré hacerlo. ‖ *"How tall are you?" "I'm six feet tall."* "¿Qué altura tiene Ud.?" "Tengo seis pies de altura."

tame [*adj*] domesticado *The squirrels are so tame they'll eat out of your hand.* Las ardillas están tan domesticadas que comen en la mano. ▲ soso *The movie's tame compared to the play.* La película es muy sosa comparada con la comedia. ● [*v*] domesticar *They tamed a monkey.* Domesticaron un mono.

tan [*adj*] color canela *She wore a tan blouse and a brown skirt.* Llevaba una blusa color canela y una falda marrón. ● [*v*] curtir *These hides have to be tanned.* Hay que curtir estas pieles. ▲ tostarse *She has a dark skin that tans easily.* Tiene la piel oscura y se tuesta muy fácilmente.

tangle [*n*] enredo. ● [*v*] enredar.

tank tanque.

tap [*n*] golpe *Don't drive it in too hard; just give it a few taps.* No lo clave mucho, déle sólo unos golpes. ▲ grifo *Better get the plumber to fix that tap in the bathtub.* Es mejor que llamemos al cañero para que arregle el grifo del baño.

● [*v*] dar golpecitos *We tapped on the window.* Dimos unos golpecitos en la ventana. ▲ intervenir *The police tapped their telephone wires.* La policía ha intervenido su teléfono.

tape [*n*] cinta.

tapestry tapiz.

tar [*n*] alquitrán. ● [*v*] alquitranar.

target blanco.

tariff tarifa, impuesto.

tarnish [*v*] deslustrarse, enmohecerse.

tart [*n*] tarta *Let's have strawberry tarts for dessert.* Vamos a tomar de postre tartas de fresa. ● [*adj*] agrio *This rhubarb's too tart for me.* Este ruibarbo está demasiado agrio para mí.

task tarea.

tassel borla.

taste [*n*] sabor, gusto *This meat has a strange taste.* Esta carne tiene un gusto raro. ● [*v*] probar *Just taste this coffee.* Pruebe este café. ▲ saber *This wine tastes sour.* Este vino sabe agrio. ▲ probar bocado *She hasn't tasted anything since yesterday.* No ha probado bocado desde ayer. ○ **in poor taste** de mal gusto *That remark was in very poor taste.* Esa observación fué de muy mal gusto. ‖ *Give me a taste of that ice cream.* Déme a probar de ese helado.

tavern taberna.

tax [*n*] impuesto, contribución *I hope I can get my taxes in on time this year.* Espero poder pagar mis impuestos a tiempo este año. ▲ esfuerzo *Reading this small print is a great tax on the eyes.* El leer esta letra tan pequeña es un esfuerzo muy grande para los ojos. ● [*v*] poner impuestos *I think they're taxing us too much for the property.* Creo que nos están poniendo demasiados impuestos sobre la propiedad. ▲ agotar *This heat's taxing my strength.* Este calor me está agotando la fuerzas. ○ **tax collector** cobrador, recaudador de impuestos *or* contribuciones.

taxi [*n*] taxi, taxímetro.

taxpayer contribuyente.

tea té.

teach enseñar *Will you teach me Spanish?* ¿Me quiere Ud. enseñar español? —*Who taught you how to drive a car?* ¿Quién le enseñó a Ud. conducir automóviles?

teacher maestro.

team [n] equipo *They make a very good team for that work.* Constituyen un buen equipo para ese trabajo.
  ○ **to team up** unirse, asociarse *We'll go places if we team up with them.* Llegaremos lejos si nos asociamos con ellos.

teapot tetera.

tear [n] lágrima *Tears won't do you any good.* De nada te servirán las lágrimas.

tear [n] rasgadura, roto *Can the tear in this blanket be repaired?* ¿Se puede remendar el roto de esta sábana?
  ● [v] romper *My shirt's torn at the elbows.* Tengo la camisa rota por los codos.
  ○ **to tear down** derribar *They're going to tear down that old hotel next month.* Van a derribar ese hotel viejo el mes próximo. ○ **to tear out** arrancar *I see a page has been torn out of this book.* Veo que han arrancado una página de este libro. ○ **to tear up** romper *I hope you tore up my last letter.* Espero que haya roto Ud. mi última carta.

tease embromar, fastidiar *We've been teasing him about his accent.* Hemos estado embromándole por su acento. ▲ molestar *The children teased me for candy.* Los niños me estaban molestando para que me diera dulces.

teaspoon cucharita.

technical técnico.

teeth dientes, dentadura *I have to get my teeth fixed.* Tengo que arreglarme los dientes.

telegram telegrama *I want to send a telegram to Montreal.* Quiero enviar un telegrama a Montreal.

telegraph [adj] de telégrafo(s) *Where's the telegraph office?* ¿Dónde está la oficina de telégrafos?
  ● [v] telegrafiar *I'm going to telegraph my folks for some money.* Voy a telegrafiar a mi familia para pedirles dinero.

telephone [n] teléfono *Can I use your telephone, please?* ¿Puedo usar su teléfono, por favor?
  ● [v] telefonear *Did anyone telephone me?* ¿Me ha telefoneado alguien?

telephone book guía de teléfonos, [Am] directorio telefónico.

telephone booth cabina del teléfono.

tell decir *Tell me your name.* Dígame su nombre.—*Tell them not to make so much noise.* Dígales que no hagan tanto ruido.—*I told you so.* Ya se lo dije. ▲ contar *Tell me all about it.* Cuéntemelo Ud. todo, ▲ distinguir *How do you tell one of the twins from the other?* ¿Cómo distingue Ud. a los dos gemelos?
  ○ **to tell off** poner en su sitio *I'm going to tell him off one of these days.* Le voy a poner en su sitio uno de estos días.

teller cajero.

temper [n] mal genio *Control your temper.* Domine su mal genio.
  ○ **to lose one's temper** perder la paciencia *She lost her temper and spanked the child.* Perdió la paciencia y le dió unos azotes al chico.

temperamental nervioso, emocional.

temperate moderado.

temperature temperatura *What's the temperature today?* ¿Qué temperatura tenemos hoy?

temporary temporal.

temptation tentación.

ten diez.

tenant inquilino.

tend ser en general *This kind of apple tends to be sour.* Las manzanas de esta clase en general son agrias. ▲ tender, propender *Prices tend to increase now because of the war.* Los precios propenden a subir ahora a causa de la guerra.
  ○ **to tend to** atender *Stop talking and tend to your work.* Deje Ud. de hablar y atienda su trabajo.

tender [adj] tierno *The meat's so tender you can cut it with a fork.* La carne está tan tierna que se puede cortar con un tenedor.—*She watched the children with a tender expression in her eyes.* Miraba a los niños con una expresión tierna en sus ojos. ▲ dolorido *His arm's still tender where he hurt it.* Tiene el brazo dolorido todavía en el sitio en que se lastimó.
  ● [v] presentar *The chairman's planning to tender his resignation at the next meeting.* El presidente va a presentar su dimisión en la reunión próxima.

tennis tenis.

tense [adj] tenso *His nerves were tense from the strain.* Tenía los nervios tensos por el esfuerzo.

tension tensión.

tent tienda de campaña, [Am] carpa.

tenth [n] día diez *I get paid on the tenth of the month.* Me pagan el día diez del mes.
  ● [adj] décimo *She lives on the tenth floor.* Vive en el décimo piso.

term [n] nombre *Do you know the term for this part of the machine?* ¿Sabe

Ud. cuál es el nombre de esta parte de la máquina? ▲ semestre *When does the new term begin at school?* ¿Cuándo comienza el nuevo semestre en la escuela? ▲ período *His jail term was five years.* Su período de prisión fué por cinco años.
● [v] llamar *He's what might be termed a wealthy man.* Es lo que se llama un potentado.
○ terms condiciones de venta *What are the terms on this automobile?* ¿Cuáles son las condiciones de venta de este automóvil? ○ to be on good terms estar en buenas relaciones *I've been on very good terms with him up until lately.* He tenido buenas relaciones con él hasta hace poco. ○ to come to terms llegar a un arreglo. *We've been trying to come to terms with them for months now.* Estamos tratando de llegar a un arreglo con ellos desde hace meses.

terrace terraza.

terrible terrible *Wasn't that a terrible storm last night?* ¿Verdad que fué terrible la tormenta de anoche?

terrify aterrar, espantar.

territory territorio.

terror espanto, terror.

test [n] examen *You'll have to take a test before you can get your driving license.* Tendrá Ud. que pasar un examen antes de que le den el permiso de conducir. ▲ prueba *We'll hire you for a week's test.* Le tomaremos a prueba por una semana.
● [v] analizar, examinar *I think we'd better test this water before we use it.* Creo que es mejor analizar esta agua antes de usarla.

testify declarar.

textbook texto, libro de texto.

than que *Have you something better than this?* ¿Tiene Ud. algo mejor que esto?

thank dar las gracias *We thanked her for the gift.* Le dimos las gracias por su regalo. ○ thanks gracias *Thanks for coming.* Gracias por haber venido. ○ thanks to gracias a *Thanks to him I was able to get my trunks all right.* Gracias a él, pude conseguir mis baúles fácilmente. ‖ *Thank you.* Gracias.

thankful agradecido.

that [pron] ese *That's the book I've been looking for.* Ese es el libro que buscaba. ▲ eso *That's what I want.* Eso es lo que yo quiero. ▲ que *Who's the lady that just came in?* ¿Quién es la señora que **acaba** de entrar?—*When was the*

last time (that) I saw you? ¿Cuándo fué la última vez que le ví?
● [adj] ese *Do you like that painting?* ¿Le gusta ese cuadro? ▲ aquel *Just look at that magnificent view.* Fíjese en aquella magnífica vista.
● [conj] que *I'm sorry (that) this happened.* Siento que haya ocurrido esto.
○ so that para que *Let's finish this today so that we can do something else tomorrow.* Acabemos hoy ésto para que podamos hacer otra cosa mañana. ○ that much tanto *I don't want that much milk.* No quiero tanta leche.

thaw [n] deshielo.
● [v] deshelarse.

the el *The sky's cloudy today.* El cielo está nublado hoy. ▲ ese *He's the man for the job.* Es el hombre indicado para ese trabajo.
○ the ... the ... cuanto ... tanto... *The sooner we're paid, the better.* Cuanto antes nos paguen, tanto mejor.

theater teatro.

theft robo.

their su, de ellos *Do you know their address?* ¿Sabe Ud. su dirección? or ¿Sabe Ud. la dirección de ellos?

theirs de ellos *Is this boat yours or theirs?* ¿Es suyo este bote o de ellos? ○ of theirs suyo *Are you a friend of theirs?* ¿Es Ud. amigo suyo?

them ellos *Let them decide.* Deje que decidan ellos.

theme tema.

themselves ellos mismos *They did it themselves.* Lo hicieron ellos mismos. ▲ se *Don't let the children hurt themselves playing.* No permita que los niños se lastimen jugando.
○ by themselves ellos mismos *Did they really do all that work by themselves?* ¿Realmente hicieron todo el trabajo ellos mismos?

then entonces, luego, después *Then what happened?* Y después ¿qué pasó? ▲ además *Then there's the trunk that we have to take down to the lobby.* Además está el baúl que tenemos que bajar al vestíbulo.
○ by then para entonces *Wait until next Tuesday; I hope to know by then.* Aguarde hasta el próximo martes; que para entonces espero saber algo. ○ now and then de vez en cuando *We go to the movies now and then.* Vamos al cine de vez en cuando. ○ then and there en seguida *I knew then and there that it was the house to buy.* En seguida me dí cuenta que era la casa que convenía comprar.

theory teoría.

there allí *I've never been there.* Nunca he estado allí. ▲ ahí *Her house is right there.* Su casa está ahí al lado. ▲ allá *Can you get there by car?* ¿Se puede ir allá en automóvil? ▲ en eso *You're wrong there.* En eso está Ud. equivocado. ▲ ¡vaya! *There! I wouldn't worry so much.* ¡Vaya! no me preocuparía tanto. ○ **there are** hay *There are a few good hotels in town.* En la ciudad hay algunos hoteles buenos. ○ **to be all there** estar en sus cabales *Don't be surprised at the way he acts; he's not all there.* No se sorprenda por su conducta, no está en sus cabales.

therefore por lo tanto.

thermometer termómetro.

these [*pron*] éstos *Do you want those roses or these?* ¿Quiere Ud. esas rosas o éstas? ● [*adj*] estos *Have you met all these people?* ¿Conoce Ud. a todas estas personas?

they ellos *Where are they?* ¿Dónde están ellos? ‖ *They give concerts here in the summer.* Durante el verano se dan conciertos aquí.

thick grueso *Is the ice thick enough for skating?* ¿Está suficientemente grueso el hielo para patinar? ▲ de espesor *I need a piece of wood about three inches thick.* Necesito un trozo de madera como de tres pulgadas de espesor. ▲ espeso *I don't like such thick soup.* No me gusta la sopa tan espesa. ▲ fuerte *He has a very thick accent.* Tiene un acento muy fuerte. ▲ torpe, [*Am*] tupido *He's too thick to know what you're talking about.* Es demasiado torpe para enterarse de lo que está Ud. hablando. ○ **through thick and thin** a toda prueba *He stood by us through thick and thin.* Nos fué fiel a toda prueba. ○ **to be thick with** tener intimidad con *They've been very thick with that family for years.* Hace años que tienen mucha intimidad con esa familia.

thief ladrón.

thigh muslo.

thimble dedal.

thin [*adj*] delgado *Cut the bread thin.* Corte el pan delgado. ▲ flaco *You're too thin; you ought to eat more.* Está Ud. muy flaco, debiera comer más. ▲ claro, [*Am*] ralo *This soup's too thin.* Esta sopa está muy clara.

● [*v*] ponerse ralo *My hair's thinning.* El pelo se me está poniendo ralo. ‖ *That's a pretty thin excuse.* Esa no es una excusa suficiente.

thing cosa *What are those things you're carrying there?* ¿Qué son esas cosas que lleva Ud. ahí?—*We've heard a lot of nice things about you.* Hemos oído muchas cosas buenas de Ud.—*How are things?* ¿Cómo van las cosas? ○ **a thing or two** algo *He certainly knows a thing or two about business.* Ciertamente sabe algo de negocios. ○ **of all things** sorpresa *Well, of all things, what are you doing here?* Bueno, que sorpresa, ¿qué hace Ud. aquí? ○ **the poor thing** el pobre, la pobre *When her parents died, the poor thing didn't know what to do.* Cuando murieron sus padres, la pobre no sabía que hacer. ○ **things** cosas *I have to go now; did you see where I put my things?* Tengo que irme ahora; ¿se fijó Ud. dónde dejé mis cosas? ○ **to see things** ver visiones *I think you've been seeing things since you heard that story.* Creo que está Ud. viendo visiones desde que oyó esa historia. ‖ *She says she's in love, and I think it's the real thing.* Dice que está enamorada y creo que lo está muy de veras. ‖ *That job's the very thing I want.* Ese empleo es justamente lo que deseo. ‖ *We haven't done a thing all week.* No hemos hecho nada en toda la semana. ‖ *There's not a thing wrong with me.* No me pasa nada. ‖ *Bring that thing over here.* Tráigame eso.

think pensar *What are you thinking about?* ¿En qué piensa Ud.?—*What do you think of that guy?* ¿Qué piensa Ud. de ese tipo?—*I thought you weren't coming along.* Pensé que Ud. no venía con nosotros. ▲ creer *I think so, too.* Eso creo. *or* Yo también lo creo.—*"Are they leaving today?" "I think so."* ¿Se van hoy? "Creo que sí." ▲ parecerle a uno *What do you think of going to the movies tonight?* ¿Le parece que vayamos al cine esta noche? ▲ recordar, acordarse *I can't think of his address.* No me puedo acordar de su dirección. ○ **to think better of** tener mejor opinión acerca de *We think better of him since we've learned the facts.* Tenemos mejor opinión acerca de él desde que conocemos los hechos. ▲ pensar mejor *You're taking a big chance, and I'd think better of it, if I were you.* Ud. va a correr un gran riesgo; yo, en

su lugar, lo pensaría mejor. ○ **to think
twice** pensar dos veces *I'd think twice
about that, if I were you.* Si yo fuera
Ud., lo pensaría dos veces. ○ **to think
up** inventar *You'd better think up a
good excuse for being late.* Mejor es
que invente una buena excusa por
haber llegado tarde.

third [*n*] tercio, tercera parte *A third of
that'll be sufficient.* Un tercio de eso
será suficiente.—*I can do a third of
the work.* Puedo hacer una tercera
parte del trabajo.
● [*adj*] tercer *I didn't care for the
third act of the play.* No me gustó el
tercer acto de la función.

thirst sed.

thirsty ○ **to be thirsty** tener sed. ○ **to
make one thirsty** Darle a uno sed *These
sandwiches make me thirsty.* Estos
emparedados me han dado mucha sed.

thirteen trece.

thirty treinta.

this [*pron*] esto *What's this?* ¿Qué es
esto? ▲ éste *Who's this?* ¿Quién es
éste?
● [*adj*] este *Do you know this man?*
¿Conoce Ud. a este hombre?—*I like
this room.* Me gusta esta habitación.
● [*adv*] tan *Since it's this late already,
why go at all?* Puesto que ya es tan
tarde ¿para qué ir?
○ **this far** hasta aquí *As long as
we've come this far, we might as well
go on.* Puesto que hemos llegado hasta
aquí, creo que podríamos seguir adelante. ○ **this much** tanto, todo esto *I
can't eat this much.* No puedo comer
tanto.

thorn espina.

thorough completo, cuidadoso *I'll make a
thorough investigation.* Haré una investigación cuidadosa. ▲ concienzudo
That fellow's very thorough in everything he does. Ese hombre es muy
concienzudo en todo lo que hace.

thoroughfare ‖ *No thoroughfare.* Prohibido el paso.

thoroughly enteramente, completamente.

those [*pron*] ésos *Give me some of those.*
Déme Ud. algunas de ésas.
● [*adj*] esos *Those children are making too much noise.* Esos niños están
haciendo mucho ruido. ▲ aquellos
What's the name of those mountains?
¿Cómo se llaman aquellas montañas?

though aunque *I'll attend, though I may
be late.* Asistiré, aunque puede ser
que llegue tarde. ▲ aunque, a pesar de
que *I asked her to the party, though*

we're not good friends. La invité a la
fiesta, aunque no somos muy amigos.
○ **as though** como si *It looks as
though it may rain.* Parece que va a
llover.

thought [*n*] pensamiento *I was trying to
guess his thoughts.* Trataba de adivinar
sus pensamientos. ▲ consideración *We'll
have to give some thought to this matter.* Tendremos que tomar en consideración este asunto. *or* Tendremos
que pensar un poco en este asunto.
▲ consideración *Can't you show a little
thought for the others?* ¿No puede Ud.
tener un poco de consideración con los
demás?
○ **to be well thought of** estar bien
considerado *He's well thought of, don't
you think?* ¿No cree Ud. que está bien
considerado?

thoughtful pensativo *He was thoughtful
for a long time before he answered.*
Se quedó pensativo un largo rato antes
de contestar. ▲ meditado *This is a very
thoughtful article.* Es un artículo muy
meditado. ▲ considerado *He's always
been very thoughtful of his parents.*
Siempre ha sido muy considerado con
sus padres.

thousand mil.

thread [*n*] hilo *If you'll get a needle and
thread, I'll sew your button on.* Si consigue una aguja y un hilo yo le coseré
el botón. ▲ rosca *We can't use this
screw; the thread's damaged.* No podemos usar este tornillo, tiene la rosca
estropeada.
● [*v*] enhebrar *I'll thread the needle
for you.* Le enhebraré la aguja.

threat amenaza.

threaten amenazar *He threatened to leave
if he didn't get a raise.* Amenazó con
irse si no le aumentaban el sueldo.
—*It's threatening to rain.* Amenaza
lluvia.

three tres.

thrifty económico.

thrill [*n*] emoción *We got quite a thrill
out of seeing the President.* Sentimos
mucha emoción al ver al Presidente.
● [*v*] emocionar *I was thrilled by the
music.* La música me emocionó.

thrive prosperar.

throat garganta *I have a sore throat.*
Tengo dolor de garganta.
○ **lump in the throat** nudo en la garganta *Every time I see this town, I get
a lump in my throat.* Siempre que veo
esta ciudad se me hace un nudo en la
garganta. ○ **to stick in one's throat**
clavársele (*or* quedársele) a uno algo

en la garganta *The fishbone stuck in his throat.* Se le clavó la espina en la garganta.
‖ *Don't jump down my throat!* Bueno, bueno, no me chilles. ‖ *I tried to apologize but the words stuck in my throat.* Quise disculparme, pero no pude pronunciar palabra.

throb [*n*] latido, palpitación.

● [*v*] latir, palpitar.

throttle [*n*] acelerador de mano.

● [*v*] (*strangle*) ahogar.

through por *Who's the lady coming through the door?* ¿Quién es la señora que entra por la puerta? ▲ a través de *We came in through the garden.* Vinimos a través del jardín. ▲ por medio de,, através de *I got the information through him.* Obtuve la información por medio de él. ▲ a causa de *Through his negligence the work'll have to be held up two weeks.* A causa de su negligencia el trabajo se retrasará dos semanas.

○ through and through de punta a cabo *He knows his business through and through.* Conoce su trabajo de punta a cabo. ○ through train tren directo. ○ to be through with terminar *Are you through with this book?* ¿Ha terminado Ud. este libro? ○ to fall through fracasar *The plans were drawn up, but the deal fell through.* Se habían hecho los planes, pero la negociación fracasó. ○ to get through terminar *I think I can get through this work tonight.* Creo que podré terminar este trabajo esta noche.
‖ *He got where he is through lots of hard work.* Ha llegado a ser lo que es después de mucho trabajar.

throughout durante *It rained throughout the night.* Llovió durante toda la noche. ▲ en todo *This writer's famous throughout the world.* Este escritor es famoso en todo el mundo.

throw [*n*] tirada, tiro *That was some throw.* Ese fué un buen tiro.

● [*v*] tirar, derribar *Be careful your horse doesn't throw you.* Tenga Ud. cuidado de que el caballo no le tire. ▲ tirar *Who threw that?* ¿Quién tiró eso?

○ to throw away tirar *Throw these papers away.* Tire estos papeles. ○ to throw on echarse *I'll throw a coat on and go down to the store.* Me echaré un abrigo y bajaré a la tienda. ○ to throw oneself at asediar *Oh, stop throwing yourself at him.* Oh! No le asedie Ud. más. ○ to throw out echar

We'd better pay our rent soon or they'll throw us out on the street. Tenemos que pagar en seguida el alquiler o nos echarán a la calle. ○ to throw over dejar *He threw her over for a blonde.* La dejó por una rubia. ○ to throw up renunciar a *Don't let her throw up her job.* No la deje Ud. que renuncie a su empleo. ▲ vomitar *I throw up every time I ride on the train.* Vomito siempre que viajo en tren. ▲ echar en cara *That's the second time you've thrown it up to me.* Esta es la segunda vez que me lo echas en cara.
‖ *Throw that light this way, please.* Alumbre hacia aquí, por favor. ‖ *Everything was thrown into disorder.* Todo estaba tirado en desorden.

thumb [*n*] pulgar, dedo gordo *I burned my thumb with a match.* Me quemé el pulgar con un fósforo.

○ to be thumbs down estar desanimado *Everybody was thumbs down on the picnic.* Todos estaban desanimados para ir de romería.
‖ *He's too much under the thumb of his wife.* Está demasiado dominado por su mujer. *or* Su mujer lo tiene en un puño. ‖ *I'm so upset today I'm all thumbs.* Estoy tan nervioso hoy que todo se me cae de las manos.

thunder [*n*] trueno *Don't be afraid of thunder.* No se asuste de los truenos. ▲ estruendo *The speaker couldn't be heard above the thunder of applause.* No se podía oír al orador entre el estruendo de los aplausos.

● [*v*] tronar *It's beginning to thunder.* Comienza a tronar.
‖ *The train thundered over the bridge.* El tren pasó con estrépito por el puente.

thunderstorm tormenta.

Thursday jueves.

thus así, de este modo.

tick [*n*] tic tac (*sound*); garrapata (*bug*).

ticket billete, [*C.A.*] tiquete *I want a round-trip ticket for Chicago.* Quiero un billete de ida y vuelta para Chicago. ▲ candidatura *Are there any women candidates on the ticket?* ¿Hay algunas mujeres en la candidatura?

tickle [*n*] picor *I have an annoying tickle in my throat.* Tengo un picor de garganta muy molesto.

● [*v*] hacer cosquillas *We tickled the baby to make her laugh.* Hicimos cosquillas a la niña para que se riera.
‖ *We were tickled to hear the news*

of your promotion. Nos agradó mucho saber la noticia de su ascenso.

ticklish ○ **to be ticklish** tener cosquillas.

tide [*n*] marea.

○ **high tide** pleamar, marea alta.
○ **low tide** bajamar, marea baja. ○ **to tide over** llegar *Will this money tide you over until payday?* ¿Le llegará este dinero hasta el día de pago?

tidy [*adj*] limpio, aseado, ordenado.

● [*v*] limpiar, arreglar.

tie [*n*] corbata *Is my tie all right?* ¿Tengo bien puesta la corbata? ▲ lazo *Our family ties are very strong.* Los lazos que unen a mi familia son muy fuertes.

● [*v*] amarrar, atar *Please tie this for me.* Por favor áteme esto.

○ **to tie the score** empatar *I don't think we can tie the score now.* No creo que podamos empatar ahora. ○ **to be tied up** estar ocupado *Are you tied up this evening?* ¿Estará Ud. ocupado esta noche?

‖ *They've been tied down ever since the baby was born.* No pueden salir mucho desde que nació su niño.

tiger tigre.

tight tirante *Pull the rope tight.* Ponga la cuerda tirante. ▲ estrecho *This suit's too tight for me.* Me está demasiado estrecho este traje. ▲ apretado *These shoes are too tight on me.* Estos zapatos me están muy apretados. ▲ tacaño, agarrado *He's plenty tight with his money.* Es muy agarrado. ▲ borracho *Boy, was I tight last night after that party!* Chico, ¡cómo estaba de borracho anoche después de la fiesta!

○ **tight spot** dificultad *I've been in tight spots before.* He pasado por dificultades antes de ahora. ○ **to hold tight** agarrarse bien *Hold on tight to the rail, or you'll fall.* Agárrese bien a la baranda porque se puede caer. ○ **to sit tight** estarse quieto *Sit tight; it'll only take a minute.* Estése quieto; es sólo un momento.

‖ *I have to tie my shoelaces tighter.* Tengo que apretarme más los cordones de los zapatos.

tighten apretar.

tile azulejo (*wall*); teja (*roof*).

till [*prep*] hasta *Let's work till ten tonight.* Trabajemos hoy hasta las diez de la noche.

● [*conj*] hasta que *Wait till I come back.* Espéreme hasta que vuelva.

till [*v*] cultivar *That soil hasn't been tilled for at least five years.* Ese

terreno no ha sido cultivado desde hace por lo menos cinco años.

tilt [*n*] inclinación.

● [*v*] inclinar.

time [*n*] hora *What time is it?* ¿Qué hora es? ▲ vez *This is the last time I'll ever come here.* Esta es la última vez que vengo aquí. ▲ tiempo *It's been a long time since I've seen you.* Ha pasado mucho tiempo desde la última vez que le vi.—*I wonder if we'll have time to see them before they go.* No sé si tendremos tiempo de verles antes de que se marchen. ▲ rato *Did you have a nice time?* ¿Pasó Ud. un rato agradable? ▲ horas de trabajo *We'll have to make up our time on Sunday.* Tendremos que completar las horas de trabajo el domingo. ▲ sueldo *You can get your time at the pay window now.* Puede recoger ahora su sueldo en la ventanilla de pagos. ▲ época, tiempo *I'd like to know more about the time in which he lived.* Me gustaría saber más sobre la época en que vivió.

○ **at the same time** al mismo tiempo *You're right, but at the same time something can be said for him too.* Ud. tiene razón, pero al mismo tiempo se puede decir algo a su favor también. ○ **from time to time** de vez en cuando. ○ **in no time** en muy poco tiempo, en un momento *We can finish the job in no time at all.* Podemos terminar el trabajo en muy poco tiempo. ○ **in time** a tiempo *Do you think we'll be in time to catch the train?* ¿Cree Ud. que llegaremos a tiempo para coger el tren? ○ **on time** a la hora *Is the noon express on time?* ¿Va a llegar a la hora el expreso de las doce? ▲ a plazos *Do you want to pay cash for this radio, or will you take it on time?* ¿Quiere pagar al contado este radio, o lo pagará a plazos? ○ **time after time** una y otra vez *He made the same mistake time after time.* Ha cometido el mismo error una y otra vez. ○ **time and time again** muchas veces *You've pulled that trick time and time again.* Ud. ha gastado esa broma muchas veces. ○ **times** por *two times two equals four.* Dos por dos son cuatro. ▲ tiempos *I had a pretty good job when times were better.* En tiempos mejores tuve un empleo bastante bueno. ○ **to have no time for** no tolerar *We have no time for such nonsense.* Aquí no se tolera semejante tontería. ○ **to keep time** seguir el compás, llevar el compás *That couple isn't* *keeping time with the music.* Esa pareja no sigue el compás de la música. ○ **well timed** oportuno *That speech wasn't very well timed, was it?* Ese discurso no fué muy oportuno, ¿verdad? ‖ *I didn't get up to that point because I timed my speech poorly.* No toqué ese tema porque calculé muy mal el tiempo que había de durar mi discurso.

timely oportuno.

time table guia, [*Am*] horario.

timid tímido.

tinge [*n*] tinte.

tingle [*v*] picar, hormiguear.

tint [*n*] matiz, tono *Her hair has a reddish tint.* Su pelo tiene un tono rojizo. ● [*v*] teñir *She tinted her white dress blue.* Tiñó de azul su traje blanco.

tiny chiquito, menudo.

tip [*n*] extremo *The best swimming's at the northern tip of the island.* El mejor sitio para nadar está en el extremo norte de la isla. ▲ propina *How large a tip should I give the waiter?* ¿Cuánto debo dar al camarero de propina? ▲ punta *I have it on the tip of my tongue.* Lo tengo en la punta de la lengua.

● [*v*] dar propina *Did you tip the porter that carried our bags?* ¿Le dió Ud. propina al mozo que trajo nuestras maletas? ▲ ladear *You're apt to fall over if you tip your chair like that.* Se puede Ud. caer si ladea la silla de esa manera.

○ **to tip off** informar bajo cuerda *The police were tipped off as to where the thieves were hiding.* La policía fué informada bajo cuerda de donde se escondían los ladrones. ○ **to tip over** dar la vuelta a, volcar *The waves tipped our canoe over.* Las olas dieron la vuelta a nuestra canoa.

tiptoe ○ **on tiptoe** de puntillas *She was walking on tiptoe so as not to wake him.* Andaba de puntillas para no despertarlo.

tire [*n*] llanta, cubierta, neumático *Check my tires.* Repase los neumáticos. *or* Mire a ver cómo están de aire las llantas.

tire [*v*] cansar *I'm afraid the trip'll tire me out too much.* Temo que el viaje me va a cansar demasiado.—*Are you tired?* ¿Está Ud. cansado?—*I'm tired of this place.* Estoy cansado de este lugar.

○ **to make (someone) tired** abu-

rrir (le) a uno *You make me tired.* Me aburres.

tiresome pesado, aburrido.

tissue paper papel de seda.

title título *Do you know the title of that book?* ¿Sabe Ud. cuál es el título de ese libro? ▲ campeonato *Who do you think'll win the tennis title this year?* ¿Quién cree Ud. que ganará el campeonato de tenis este año? ▲ título de propiedad *Do you have title to this house?* ¿Tiene Ud. el título de propiedad de esta casa?

to [*prep*] a *Let's go to the movies.* Vamos al cine.—*We won 6 to 2.* Ganamos 6 a 2. ▲ en *His work's gone from bad to worse.* Su trabajo ha ido de mal en peor.—*Apply this cream to your face.* Póngase esta crema en la cara. ▲ con *You're very kind to me.* Es Ud. muy amable conmigo.—*To our great surprise he turned up anyway.* Con gran sorpresa nuestra se presentó. ▲ de *What do you say to this?* ¿Qué dice Ud. de esto?—*Is this apartment to your liking?* ¿Es de su gusto este apartamento? ▲ según *To my way of thinking, you don't know what you're talking about.* Según mi modo de pensar no sabe Ud. de lo que está hablando. ▲ a, para *I came here especially to see you.* He venido aquí especialmente para verle. ▲ para *It's ten minutes to four.* Faltan diez minutos para las cuatro. *or* Son las cuatro menos diez.

○ **to come to** volver en sí *Throw some water in her face and she'll come to.* Echele un poco de agua en la cara y volverá en sí. ‖ *Explain that to me.* Explíquemelo. ‖ *The dog chewed the pillow to pieces.* El perro hizo trizas la almohada. ‖ *This novel's true to life.* Esta novela es realista. *or* Esta novela es de gran realismo. ‖ *We plan to stay here for two weeks.* Proyectamos quedarnos aquí dos semanas.

toast [*n*] tostadas (*bread*); brindis (*drink*).

toaster tostador.

tobacco tabaco *Do you have any tobacco?* ¿Tiene Ud. tabaco?

today hoy *What do you have on the menu today?* ¿Qué tienen hoy en el menú?

toe dedo del pie *My toes are frozen.* Tengo los dedos de los pies helados.

○ **on one's toes** de pie, [*Am*] parado *In this job you've got to be on your toes all day long.* En este trabajo hay que estar de pie todo el día.

together juntos *They work together very well.* Trabajan muy bien juntos.

○ **to get together** reunirse *Do you suppose we can get together some evening?* ¿Cree Ud. que podremos reunirnos alguna noche?

‖ *The price of this ticket together with tax is 52 dollars.* El precio de este billete, incluído el impuesto, es de 52 dólares.

toilet excusado, retrete, baño *Where's the toilet?* ¿Dónde está el excusado?

toilet paper papel higiénico.

token muestra, prueba *We gave her a gift as a token of our affection.* Le hicimos un regalo como muestra de nuestro cariño.

tolerance tolerancia.

tolerant tolerante.

toll bridge pontazgo.

tomato tomate, [*Mex*] jitomate.

tomb tumba.

tombstone lápida.

tommy gun pistola ametralladora.

tomorrow mañana *I'll be back tomorrow.* Volveré mañana.—*I'll see you tomorrow morning.* Le veré mañana por la mañana.

ton tonelada.

tone [*n*] sonido *I don't like the tone of this radio.* No me gusta el sonido de esta radio. ▲ tono *She spoke in an angry tone.* Hablaba en un tono irritado.—*The room was decorated in a soft blue tone.* La habitación estaba decorada en un tono azul pálido.

○ **to tone down** suavizar *He had to tone down his speech before he could give it over the radio.* Tuvo que suavizar su discurso antes de darlo por la radio.

tongs tenazas.

tongue lengua *How do you hold your tongue to make that sound?* ¿Cómo coloca la lengua para producir ese sonido?—*What's your native tongue?* ¿Cuál es su lengua materna?

○ **on the tip of one's tongue** en la punta de la lengua *Just a minute; I have his name on the tip of my tongue.* Un momento, tengo su nombre en la punta de la lengua. ○ **to hold one's tongue** callar, no decir nada.

tonic tónico.

tonight esta noche *What shall we do tonight?* ¿Qué haremos esta noche? —*Have you seen tonight's paper?* ¿Ha visto el periódico de esta noche?

too también *May I come too?* ¿Puedo ir yo también? ▲ demasiado *The soup's too hot.* La sopa está demasiado caliente.—*You're going too far.* Va Ud. demasiado lejos.

○ **all too** demasiado *Our stay there was all too short.* Nuestra estancia allí fué demasiado corta.

‖ *Too bad!* ¡Qué lástima!

tool herramienta *Could I borrow your tools?* ¿Podría Ud. prestarme sus herramientas? ▲ instrumento *The mayor's only a tool of the party.* El alcalde es solamente un instrumento del partido.

○ **tool chest** caja de herramientas.

tooth muela (*molar*), diente (*front tooth*) *This tooth hurts.* Me duele esta muela. ▲ diente *This saw has a broken tooth.* Esta sierra tiene un diente roto.

toothache dolor de muelas.

toothbrush cepillo de dientes.

toothpaste pasta para los dientes, pasta dentífrica.

top [*n*] cima, cumbre *How far is the top of the mountain?* ¿A qué distancia está la cima de la montaña? ▲ capota *Are you going to put down the top of your automobile?* ¿Va Ud. a bajar la capota del automóvil? ▲ trompo *The boy got a new top for his birthday.* Al niño le regalaron un trompo nuevo el día de su cumpleaños.

● [*adj*] máximo *We drove at top speed all the way.* Llevamos el coche a la velocidad máxima durante todo el trayecto. ▲ último *He lives on the top floor.* Vive en el último piso.

○ **from top to bottom** de arriba abajo *We searched the house from top to bottom.* Registramos la casa de arriba abajo. ○ **on top of** encima de, sobre *I'm sure my wallet was on top of the dresser.* Estoy seguro que mi cartera estaba encima de la cómoda. ○ **top man** principal *Who's the top man here?* ¿Quién es el principal aquí? ○ **top of a tree, treetop** copa de árbol. ○ **tops** el mejor, lo mejor *You're tops with me.* Para mí eres lo mejor. ○ **to top off** rematar, terminar *Let's top off the dinner with some brandy.* Rematemos la comida con una copa de coñac.

‖ *He topped my score by at least ten points.* Me aventajó por lo menos en diez tantos. ‖ *Boy, I'm sitting on top of the world!* ¡Hombre, me siento dueño del mundo! ‖ *You don't have to shout at the top of your voice.* No es necesario que grites tanto. ‖ *I'm glad you came out on top.* Me alegro que haya sido Ud. el primero. *or* Me alegro que haya ganado. ¶ *I slept like a top all night.* Toda la noche dormí como un tronco.

topcoat abrigo de entretiempo.

topic tópico, asunto.

torch antorcha.

torment [*n*] tormento.

torment [*v*] atormentar.

tornado tornado, huracán.

torpedo torpedo.

torrent torrente. ¶ It rained in torrents. Llovía a cántaros.

torture [*n*] tortura. ● [*v*] lastimar *These shoes torture me.* Estos zapatos me lastiman.

toss [*v*] tirar, lanzar *Toss me the ball.* Tíreme la pelota. ▲ lanzar *The bullfighter was tossed in the air by the bull.* El toro lanzó al torero por el aire. ○ **to toss about** jugar con, sacudir *The tornado tossed the plane about like a feather.* El huracán jugaba con el avión como si fuese una pluma. ▲ dar vueltas *She tossed about in bed.* Daba vueltas en la cama. ○ **to toss (up) a coin** echar a cara o cruz *Let's toss a coin.* Echémoslo a cara o cruz.

total [*n*] total *Add it up and give me the total.* Haga la suma y dígame el total. ● [*adj*] total, completo *The house was a total loss.* Fué total la destrucción de la casa. ○ **to total up** sumar, hacer la suma (de) *Let's total up our expenses for the month.* Hagamos la suma de los gastos del mes.

totter tambalearse.

touch [*n*] tacto *That cloth feels nice to the touch.* Esa tela es agradable al tacto. ▲ brochazo, toque *This chair needs a few more touches of paint.* Esta silla necesita unos cuantos brochazos más de pintura. ▲ pizca, poquito *This soup needs a touch of salt.* Esta sopa necesita una pizca de sal. ▲ nota *There was a touch of humor in his speech.* Tuvo una nota de humorismo en su discurso. ● [*v*] tocar *Please don't touch those books.* Por favor no toque esos libros. —*His pants almost touch the ground.* Sus pantalones casi tocan el suelo. ▲ afectar *The depression didn't touch him at all.* La depresión no le afectó nada. ▲ conmover *His story really touched us.* Su relato realmente nos conmovió. ○ **in touch** en comunicación, en contacto *Keep in touch with me.* Mantén-

gase en comunicación conmigo. ○ **to touch at** hacer escala en *What ports did your boat touch on your trip?* ¿En qué puertos hizo escala su barco durante el viaje? ○ **to touch off** provocar *Her remarks touched off a violent argument.* Sus observaciones provocaron una violenta discusión. ○ **to touch on** tocar, referirse a *What subjects did he touch on in the lecture?* ¿Qué temas tocó en su discurso? ○ **touched** tocado, loco *Don't mind him, he's a little touched.* No le haga caso, está un poco tocado. ○ **touching** conmovedor *How touching!* ¡Qué conmovedor! ¶ *I felt a gentle touch on my arm.* Sentí que me tocaban suavemente en el brazo.

tough duro, correoso *This meat's very tough.* Esta carne está muy dura. ○ **tough luck** mala suerte.

tour [*n*] jira. ● [*v*] viajar, hacer una jira.

tourist turista.

tournament torneo.

tow [*v*] remolcar.

toward hacia.

towel toalla.

tower torre.

town pueblo *I'd rather live in a town than a city.* Prefiero vivir en un pueblo que en una ciudad. ▲ ciudad *I won't be in town this week-end.* No estaré en la ciudad este fin de semana. ¶ *Let's do the town.* Vamos de parranda po rel pueblo. *or* por la ciudad.

toy [*n*] juguete.

trace [*n*] huella, rastro *Did you see any traces of a dog around here?* ¿Ha visto Ud. las huellas de un perro por aquí? ▲ rastro *He left without a trace.* Se marchó sin dejar ni rastro. ▲ señal *There are plenty of traces of a camp here.* Hay muchas señales de que existe un campamento por aquí. ▲ algo *I smell a trace of liquor on your breath.* Le noto algo de olor a licor en el aliento. ● [*v*] marcar, señalar *Trace the route in pencil on the map.* Marque Ud. el camino con lápiz en el mapa. ¶ *I'm going to have that letter traced.* Voy a averiguar el paradero de esa carta.

track [*v*] seguir la pista a *The police are trying to track the criminal.* La policía está tratando de seguirle la pista al criminal. ○ **race track** hipódromo (*horses*), pista (*athletes*). ○ **to keep track of**

acordarse de, ocuparse de *I hope you don't expect me to keep track of all the details.* Espero que no pretenderá que me ocupe de todos los detalles. ○ **to lose track of** perder la pista *I'm afraid I've completely lost track of him.* Temo que le he perdido la pista por completo. ○ **to make tracks** irse pronto, irse de prisa *It's getting rather late, so we'd better make tracks for home.* Se está haciendo tarde, de modo que es mejor que nos vayamos pronto a casa. ○ **to track down** averiguar el origen de *Could you track that story down for me?* ¿Podría Ud. averiguarme el origen de esa historia? ○ **to track up** dejar pisadas en *Clean off your shoes, you're tracking up the kitchen.* Límpiese los zapatos, está dejando pisadas en la cocina. ○ **tracks** huellas, pisadas *Let's follow his tracks to see where he went.* Sigamos sus huellas para ver adonde fué. ▲ rieles, vía *Wait for the train before you cross the tracks.* Espere que pase el tren antes de cruzar la vía. ‖ *What you say is way off the track.* Lo que Ud. dice no tiene nada que ver con esto. ‖ *You're on the right track.* Va Ud. por buen camino.

tract extensión *That man owns a large tract of land.* Ese hombre posee una gran extensión de terreno.

tractor tractor.

trade [n] comercio *Is there any trade across the border?* ¿Hay comercio a través de la frontera? ▲ oficio *What's your trade?* ¿Cuál es su oficio? ▲ canje, cambio *Let's make a trade.* Hágamos un cambio. ▲ clientela *I think my product will appeal to your trade.* Creo que mi producto tendrá éxito entre su clientela. ● [v] comprar *I don't trade at that store.* No compro en esa tienda. ▲ cambiar *My brother and I traded ties.* Mi hermano y yo cambiamos las corbatas. ○ **to trade in** cambiar *I want to trade this car in for a new one.* Quiero cambiar este automóvil por uno nuevo. ○ **to trade on** aprovecharse de *He's been trading on the family name for years.* Se ha aprovechado desde hace años del nombre de su familia.

trademark marca de fábrica.

tradition tradición.

traffic tráfico.

traffic light luz de tráfico.

tragedy tragedia.

trail [n] sendero, vereda *The trail*

through the woods will be made into a road. El sendero que atraviesa el bosque será convertido en carretera. ▲ huellas, rastro *The invaders have left a bloody trail behind them.* Los invasores han dejado huellas sangrientas tras ellos. ● [v] seguir la pista, rastrear *The police are trailing the criminal.* La policía le sigue la pista al criminal. ▲ arrastrar *Your coat's trailing on the ground.* Su abrigo está arrastrando por el suelo. ▲ rezagarse, ir rezagado *That boy's always trailing along behind his brother.* Aquel muchacho siempre va rezagado detrás de su hermano. ○ **to trail off** desvanecerse, extinguirse *The smoke from the train trailed off into the distance.* El humo del tren se desvanecía en la distancia.

train [n] tren *When does this train leave?* ¿Cuándo sale este tren? ● [v] entrenarse *I hope you've been training for our tennis match.* Espero que se haya entrenado Ud. para nuestra partida de tenis. ○ **to be trained** tener práctica, estar preparado *Have you been trained in business?* ¿Ha tenido Ud. práctica en los negocios? ○ **train of thought** hilo del pensamiento, hilo de las ideas *I'm sorry I've interrupted your train of thought.* Lamento haberle hecho perder el hilo de sus ideas.

training instrucción (*education*); entrenamiento (*sports*).

traitor traidor.

tramp [n] vagabundo *There's a tramp at the back door asking for food.* Hay un vagabundo que pide comida en la puerta trasera. ▲ ruido de pisadas *We heard the tramp of soldiers' feet.* Oímos el ruido de las pisadas de los soldados. ● [v] patear, pasearse pateando, andar pesadamente *Someone's tramping around in the room overhead.* Alguien se pasea pateando por todo el cuarto de arriba.

tranquil tranquilo.

transfer [n] traspaso, traslado *Have you arranged for my transfer to the new job?* ¿Ha arreglado Ud. mi traslado al nuevo trabajo? ▲ boleto de transbordo, transferencia *Could I have a transfer?* ¿Me podría dar un boleto de transbordo?

transfer [v] trasladar *He asked to be transferred to another town.* Pidió que le trasladaran a otra ciudad.

transfusion transfusión.

transient [*adj*] pasajero.
transit tránsito.
transition transición.
translate traducir *How do you translate this?* ¿Cómo se traduce esto?
translation translación, traducción.
transport [*n*] transporte *This ship's a war transport.* Este barco es un transporte de guerra.
transport [*v*] transportar *All our supplies are transported by planes.* Todas nuestras provisiones son transportadas en aviones.
transportation transporte.
trap [*n*] trampa, cepo *This is a bear trap.* Esta es una trampa para osos.
● [*v*] atrapar *The police have trapped the thief in that old house.* La policía atrapó al ladrón en aquella casa vieja.
○ **mouse trap** ratonera.
trash basura.
travel [*n*] tráfico *Travel on this road's always light.* El tráfico en esta carretera siempre es escaso.
● [*v*] viajar *I prefer to travel by plane.* Prefiero viajar en avión.
▲ correr *Boy, is that car traveling!* ¡Chico, como corre ese automóvil!
○ **travels** viajes *Make him tell you about his travels.* Dígale que le hable de sus viajes.
traveler viajero.
tray bandeja, azafate, [*Am*] charola.
treacherous traicionero.
tread [*n*] cubierta *The tread on my tires is badly worn.* Está muy gastada la cubierta de mis neumáticos.
● [*v*] pisar *Don't tread on the snake in the grass.* No pise sobre la culebra en la yerba.
○ **to tread water** pedalear en el agua.
treason traición.
treasurer tesorero.
treasury tesorería.
treat [*n*] placer *It'll be a treat to hear the new concert.* Será un placer oír el nuevo concierto.
● [*v*] tratar *Has the doctor been treating you long?* ¿Hace mucho tiempo que le está tratando el médico?—*You're not treating me fairly.* Ud. no me trata justamente. ▲ tratar (de) *Can you recommend a book that treats current social problems?* ¿Puede Ud. recomendarme algún libro que trate de problemas sociales de actualidad? ▲ tomar *You shouldn't treat that as a laughing matter.* Usted no debe tomar esto de broma. ▲ convidar *How about treating me for a change?* ¿Por qué no me convida Ud. una vez para cambiar?

¶ *I insist, the dinner's my treat.* Insisto, a mí me toca convidarle a comer. ‖ *How's the world been treating you?* ¿Cómo le va? *or* ¿Que es de su vida?
treatment tratamiento.
treaty tratado, pacto.
tree árbol.
tremble [*v*] temblar.
tremendous tremendo, formidable.
trench trinchera.
trench coat trinchera.
trespass [*v*] ‖ *Trespassing on that property's not allowed.* Se prohibe pasar por esta propiedad. ‖ *No trespassing!* ¡Prohibido el paso!
trial prueba *We'll take this machine on trial.* Tomaremos esta máquina a prueba. ▲ proceso, juicio *You'll be given a fair trial.* Se le hará a Ud. justicia en el proceso. ▲ mortificación *You know, you've been a great trial to me.* Sabes que has sido para mí una gran mortificación.
○ **to give a trial** probar *Why don't you give this automobile a trial?* ¿Por qué no prueba Ud. este automóvil?
triangle triángulo.
tribe tribu.
tributary tributario.
tribute tributo.
trick [*n*] maña *She's full of tricks, isn't she?* Está llena de mañas, ¿no es cierto?—*She's got a trick of frowning when she's thinking.* Tiene la maña de fruncir el ceño cuando piensa.—*There's a trick to making a pie.* Se necesíta maña para hacer una tarta. ▲ jugada *That's a mean trick to play on me.* Esa es una mala jugada que me hacen. ▲ truco *He knows some pretty good tricks with cards.* Sabe hacer muy buenos trucos con las cartas. ▲ baza *Who took the last trick?* ¿Quién hizo la última baza?
● [*v*] engañar *Just my luck, tricked again!* ¡Qué mala suerte, me engañaron otra vez! ▲ embaucar, engañar *Are you trying to trick me into saying this?* ¿Está Ud. tratando de embaucarme para que yo diga esto?
○ **to do the trick** resolver el problema, dar en el clavo *Your idea will do the trick.* Su idea resolverá el problema.
trickle [*v*] escurrir, gotear.
trifle [*n*] baratija *Here's a little trifle I picked up in China.* Esta es una baratija que traje de China. ▲ bagatela *This ring cost me only a trifle.* Este anillo me costó sólo una bagatela.

▲ poco, poquito *This book's a trifle too serious for me.* Este libro es un poquito serio para mí.
● [v] jugar *You'd better not trifle with that girl's affections.* No debe jugar con los sentimientos de esa muchacha.

trigger gatillo, percutor.

trim [n] buenas condiciones *Are you in trim for the race?* ¿Está Ud. en buenas condiciones para la carrera?
● [v] emparejar, igualar *Let's trim the bushes in the yard.* Vamos a emparejar los arbustos del patio. ▲ cortar un poco *She had her hair trimmed.* Le cortaron un poco el pelo.
‖ *You're wearing a very trim-looking suit.* Lleva Ud. un traje de muy buen estilo.

trip [n] viaje *How was your trip?* ¿Cómo le fué de viaje?
● [v] tropezar *Don't trip on the stairs.* No tropiece Ud. en la escalera. ▲ brincar *She trips along her way as though she were happy.* Va brincando por el camino como si estuviera muy contenta. ▲ poner la zancadilla *Who tripped me?* ¿Quién me puso la zancadilla?

triumph [n] triunfo.
triumphant triunfante.
trivial trivial.
trolley tranvía.
troop [n] tropa *The enemy troops have surrendered.* Se han rendido las tropas del enemigo. ▲ compañía (*actors*).
● [v] apiñarse *The crowd trooped through the streets.* La multitud se apiñaba en las calles.
trophy trofeo.
tropical tropical.
tropics trópico.
trot [n] trote.
● [v] trotar.
trouble [n] apuro, dificultad *I'm in trouble.* Estoy en un apuro. ▲ lío *Did you get into trouble?* ¿Se metió Ud. en algún lío? ▲ dificultades *I've had trouble with this man before.* He tenido antes dificultades con este hombre. ▲ molestia *No trouble at all!* ¡No es molestia! ▲ barullo *The boys are causing a lot of trouble here.* Los muchachos están armando aquí mucho barullo. ▲ camorra *Are you asking for trouble?* ¿Está Ud. buscando camorra?
● [v] molestar, incomodar *Sorry to trouble you.* Siento molestarle. ▲ molestar *My arm's been troubling me ever since the accident.* Me molesta el brazo desde el accidente.—*May I trouble you*

for a match? ¿Le puedo molestar para pedirle un fósforo?
○ **troubled** preocupado *I've been troubled about your health lately.* Ultimamente he estado preocupado por (*or* con respecto a) su salud.
‖ *What's the trouble?* ¿Qué le pasa? *or* ¿Qué sucede? ‖ *Don't put yourself to any trouble.* No se moleste Ud. ‖ *Thanks for the trouble.* Gracias por tomarse la molestia.
trough abrevadero, [*Am*] bebedero.
trousers pantalones.
trout trucha.
truce tregua.
truck camión.
truck driver chofer de camión.
trudge caminar con dificultad.
true verdadero *He's a true scientist.* Es un verdadero hombre de ciencia. ▲ leal, verdadero *You'll find him a true friend.* Ud. se dará cuenta de que es un amigo leal. ▲ verídico, cierto *Is that story true?* ¿Es verídica esa historia? ▲ cierto, verdad *Is it true that you got a new car?* ¿Es cierto que Ud. compró un nuevo automóvil? ▲ seguro *These dark clouds are a true sign of rain.* Estos nubarrones son anuncio seguro de lluvia. ▲ fiel *He's always true to his word.* Siempre es fiel a su palabra.
○ **true north** norte verdadero.
truly sinceramente, de verdad *I'm truly sorry for what happened.* Siento sinceramente lo ocurrido.
‖ *Yours very truly.* De Ud. atento y S. S. (De Ud. atento y seguro servidor). *or* Suyo affmo. (Suyo afectísimo).
trump (*card playing*) [n] triunfo.
● [v] triunfar.
trumpet trompeta.
trunk tronco *Nail the notice on the trunk of that tree.* Fije Ud. el aviso en el tronco de ese árbol. ▲ baúl *Has my trunk come yet?* ¿Ha llegado ya mi baúl? ▲ (*of body*) tronco.
○ **trunks** calzoneta [*Am*], pantalón de baño *These trunks are too tight.* Esta calzoneta me queda muy ajustada.
trust [n] confianza *He holds a position of great trust.* Tiene un puesto de mucha confianza.
● [v] tener confianza en *Don't you trust me?* ¿No tiene Ud. confianza en mí? ▲ confiar *They trusted the money to his care.* Le confiaron el dinero. ▲ confiar, esperar *I trust you slept well.* Espero que haya dormido bien. ▲ dar crédito *Can you trust me until payday?*

¿Puede darme crédito hasta el día de pago?
O **in trust** en depósito *Shall I hold this money in trust for you?* ¿Le guardo este dinero en depósito?
trustee síndico.
truth verdad *That's the truth.* Esa es la verdad.
try [*n*] intento *Let's take another try at getting up this hill.* Hagamos un nuevo intento para subir la loma.
● [*v*] tratar *Let's try to get there on time.* Tratemos de llegar a tiempo. ▲ probar *Did you try the key?* ¿Probó Ud. la llave? ▲ tomar *I think I'll try some soup.* Creo que tomaré un poco de sopa. ▲ juzgar *Who's going to try your case?* ¿Quién va a juzgar el caso de Ud.?
O **to try on** probarse *I'd like to try that suit on again.* Me gustaría probarme ese traje otra vez. O **to try one's patience** exasperar *Sometimes you try my patience too much.* A veces Ud. me exaspera. O **to try out** hacer una prueba *With his voice, he ought to try out for radio.* Con su voz, debe hacer una prueba en la radio.
‖ *You'll be fairly tried.* A Ud. se le hará justicia.
trying difícil *This has been a trying day.* Este ha sido un día difícil.
tub baño (*bathtub*), tina (*washtub*, [*Am*] *bathtub*).
tube tubo.
tuberculosis tuberculosis.
tuck [*n*] alforza *I'm going to take a tuck in my sleeves.* Voy a hacer una alforza en las mangas.
● [*v*] meter *Tuck this package in your pocket.* Métase este paquete en la bolsa.
O **to tuck in** remeter *Tuck the blankets in carefully when you go to bed.* Remeta las mantas con cuidado cuando se acueste.
Tuesday martes.
tuft manojo (*grass*); penacho (*feathers*).
tug [*n*] remolcador *A tug pulled the barge up the river.* Un remolcador arrastró la barcaza río arriba. ▲ tirón *Give the rope a good tug.* Dé un buen tirón a la cuerda.
● [*v*] tirar de *The dog tugged at his leash.* El perro tiró de la correa.
tulip tulipán.
tumble [*n*] tumbo, caída.
● [*v*] caer, derribar.
O **to tumble down** derrumbarse (*building*); caerse (*person*).
tumor tumor.

tumult tumulto.
tune [*n*] melodía, tonada *What's that tune you're singing?* ¿Cuál es esa melodía que está cantando?
● [*v*] afinar *Has your violin been tuned?* ¿Está afinado su violín?
O **out of tune** desafinado *The piano's out of tune.* El piano está desafinado.
O **to tune in** sintonizar.
tunnel túnel.
turbulent turbulento.
turf césped (*grass*).
turkey pavo, [*Mex*] guajolote.
turn [*n*] vuelta *Give the wheel a turn.* Dé una vuelta a la rueda. ▲ turno *You'll have to wait your turn in line.* Tiene que esperar su turno en fila. ▲ aspecto *I've heard that story before, but you gave it a new turn.* Conocía ya ese cuento pero Ud. le dió un nuevo aspecto. ▲ susto *You gave me quite a turn.* Me dió Ud. un gran susto.
● [*v*] dar vuelta *Try to turn the key.* Trate de dar vuelta a la llave. ▲ volverse *He turned and motioned to us to follow him.* Se volvió y nos indicó que le siguiéramos. ▲ doblar *She just turned the corner.* Acaba de doblar la esquina. ▲ revolver *That spoiled cheese is enough to turn one's stomach.* Ese queso descompuesto es capaz de revolverle a uno el estómago. ▲ torcer *She turned her ankle.* Se torció el tobillo. ▲ ponerse *She turned pale when she heard the news.* Se puso pálida cuando oyó la noticia. ▲ cambiar *Looks like the wind's turning.* Parece que el viento está cambiando.
O **at every turn** en todo momento *He met with resistance at every turn.* En todo momento encontró resistencia. O **in turn** por turno *Each one of you tell me your story in turn.* Cada uno de Uds. por turno me contará su historia. O **to a turn** perfectamente *This meat's cooked to a turn.* Esta carne está cocinada perfectamente. O **to take a turn** dar una vuelta *Let's take a turn around the park.* Démos una vuelta por el parque. O **to take a turn for the better** mejorar *He was very ill, but he's taking a turn for the better.* Estaba muy enfermo, pero ya está mejorando. O **to take a turn for the worse** empeorar. O **to turn around** dar vuelta a *Let's turn the table around.* Démosle vuelta a la mesa. O **to turn aside** desviarse *He turned aside to talk to me.* Se desvió para hablar conmigo. O **to turn away** rechazar *We had to turn hundreds of people away.* Hemos

tenido que rechazar a centenares de personas. ○ to turn back regresar. ○ to turn down doblar *Turn down the blanket.* Doble la manta. ▲ rechazar *My application for a job was turned down.* Mi solicitud para un empleo fué rechazada. ○ to turn gray encanecer *Her hair's turning gray.* Está encaneciendo. ○ to turn in dar la vuelta y entrar *Turn in at the next farm.* Dé la vuelta y entre en la próxima finca. ▲ acostarse *We ought to turn in early tonight.* Debemos acostarnos temprano esta noche. ▲ entregar *Let's turn these old clothes in to the Red Cross.* Entreguemos esta ropa vieja a la Cruz Roja. ○ to turn into cambiar por *You can always turn your bonds into cash.* Siempre se pueden cambiar los bonos por dinero. ○ to turn off cerrar la llave de (*gas, water*); apagar (*light*). ○ to turn on abrir (*gas, water*); encender (*light*). ▲ volverse contra *I didn't expect you'd turn on me also.* No esperaba que Ud. también se volviera contra mí. ▲ depender de *All our plans turn on whether he gets back in time.* Todos nuestros planes dependen de que él regrese a tiempo. ○ to turn one's nose up at mirar con desprecio. ○ to turn out apagar *Turn out the lights.* Apague Ud. las luces. ▲ resultar *How did the party turn out?* ¿Como resultó la fiesta? ▲ echar *I've been turned out of my room.* Me echaron de mi cuarto. ▲ levantarse *What time do you turn out in the morning?* ¿A qué hora se levanta Ud. por la mañana? ▲ venir, acudir *A large crowd turned out for the meeting.* Un gran gentío acudió al mitin. ▲ fabricar, producir *This company turns out fine products.* Esta compañía fabrica buenos productos. ○ to turn over volcar *Watch out! We almost turned over that time.* ¡Cuidado! Esta vez casi volcamos. ▲ transferir, traspasar *He turned his business over to his son.* Le transfirió sus negocios a su hijo. ○ to turn over a new leaf empezar vida nueva, enmendarse. ○ to turn tail volver la espalda *The little boy turned tail and ran.* El niñito volvió la espalda y echó a correr. ○ to turn the tables devolver la pelota. ○ to turn the tide cambiar el curso *The arrival of fresh troops turned the tide of battle.* La llegada de tropas de refresco cambió el curso de la batalla. ○ to turn to recurrir a, acudir a *I have no one to turn to.* No tengo a quien recurrir. ▲ buscar en *You'll find*

those figures if you turn to page fifty. Ud. encontrará esas cifras si busca en la página cincuenta. ○ to turn up poner más alto *Turn the radio up, will you?* ¿Quiere poner más alto el radio? ▲ aparecer *He's always turning up when least expected.* Siempre aparece cuando menos se le espera. ▲ salir, presentarse *Maybe something will turn up next week.* Puede que algo se presente la semana próxima. ○ to turn up, into, *or* down doblar por, [*Am*] cruzar para *Blow your horn when you turn up the avenue.* Toque la bocina cuando doble por la avenida.

‖ *You're talking out of turn.* Está Ud. hablando de cosas que no le corresponden. ‖ *My head's turning.* Se me va la cabeza. ‖ *She claims she's turning thirty.* Asegura que va a cumplir treinta años. ‖ *He never lets praise turn his head.* Nunca deja que los elogios se le suban a la cabeza. ‖ *You're just turning my words around.* Está Ud. dando otro sentido a mis palabras.

turnip nabo.
turpentine trementina.
turret torrecilla, torreta.
turtle tortuga.
tuxedo smoking.
tweezers pinzas.
twelve doce.
twenty veinte.
twice dos veces *I've been here twice already.* Ya he estado aquí dos veces. ‖ *That's twice as much as I want.* Eso es el doble de lo que quiero.
twig ramita.
twilight crepúsculo.
twin gemelo, mellizo *I can't tell those twins apart.* No puedo distinguir a esos gemelos.
twin beds camas gemelas.
twine [*n*] quita, [*Am*] pita. ● [*v*] retorcer, enroscar.
twinkle [*n*] brillo *Can you see the twinkle of that light through the fog?* ¿Puede Ud. ver el brillo de aquella luz a través de la niebla? ● [*v*] brillar *His eyes twinkled when he spoke.* Le brillaban los ojos cuando hablaba.
twirl [*v*] girar, dar vueltas a.
twist [*v*] torcer.
two dos *Can you lend me two dollars?* ¿Me puede Ud. prestar dos dólares? ○ by twos de dos en dos *Let's go by twos.* Vámonos de dos en dos. ○ in two en dos *Let's cut this cake in two.* Partamos esta torta en dos.

type [*n*] tipo *I don't like that type of girl.* No me agrada ese tipo de muchacha. ▲ tipo de letra *The type in this book's too small.* El tipo de letra de este libro es demasiado pequeño. ▲ clase, estilo *What type of shoes do you want?* ¿Qué clase de zapatos desea Ud.?

● [*v*] escribir a máquina *Can you type?* ¿Sabe Ud. escribir a máquina? ‖ *She's the motherly type.* Es muy maternal.

typewriter máquina de escribir.

typical típico.

U

ugly feo *The painting looks ugly to me.* Me parece feo el cuadro. ▲ malo *That man has an ugly disposition.* Ese hombre tiene mal carácter.

ulcer úlcera.

ultimate último.

ultraviolet ultravioleta, ultraviolado.

umbrella paraguas.

umpire árbitro, juez.

unable incapaz.

○ to be **unable** no poder, no ser capaz de, verse en la imposibilidad de.

unacceptable inaceptable.

unanimous unánime.

unauthorized desautorizado, sin autorización.

unavoidable inevitable, ineludible.

unaware que ignora, no enterado.

○ to be **unaware** of ignorar, no saber, no estar enterado de.

uncertain incierto *We're uncertain about the future.* Estamos inciertos respecto al futuro. ▲ inseguro, variable *In springtime the weather's uncertain.* En (la) primavera el tiempo es variable.

○ to be **uncertain** no estar seguro *We're uncertain how things'll turn out.* No estamos seguros de como saldrán las cosas.

uncertainty incertidumbre.

uncivil descortés, desatento.

unclaimed sin reclamar.

uncle tío.

○ **aunt and uncle** tíos.

uncomfortable incómodo, molesto.

unconditional incondicional.

unconscious inconsciente, sin conocimiento.

under [*adj*] inferior *The under side of the boat needs painting.* Se necesita pintar la parte inferior del barco.

● [*prep*] debajo de *Slip the letter under the door.* Meta la carta por debajo de la puerta. ▲ bajo *Is everything under control?* ¿Está todo bajo control? *or* ¿Está todo en orden?

○ to be **under** an obligation deber favores. ○ **under** arms sobre las armas. ○ **under discussion** en discusión *The matter's under discussion.* El asunto está en discusión. ○ **under oath** bajo juramento. ○ **under the circumstances** dadas las circunstancias *Under the circumstances I'll accept your apology.* Dadas las circunstancias aceptaré su excusa. ‖ *He goes under an assumed name.* Lleva un nombre falso. ‖ *Within an hour the firemen had the blaze under control.* Los bomberos dominaron el fuego en una hora.

under-age menor de edad.

undergo sufrir, padecer, experimentar.

underneath [*adv*] por debajo *The box is wooden on top and iron underneath.* La caja es de madera por arriba y de hierro por debajo.

● [*prep*] debajo de *The garage is underneath the house.* El garage está debajo de la casa.

undershirt camiseta.

understand comprender, entender *I don't understand what you mean.* No comprendo lo que quiere Ud. decir. ▲ entender *I understand you're going away.* Tengo entendido que se va Ud. ‖ *Let it be clearly understood that I've warned you.* Conste que se lo he advertido. ‖ *That's not as I understand it.* Eso no es lo que yo tengo entendido. ‖ *That's understood.* Eso se entiende. ‖ *She makes herself understood.* Ella se hace entender.

undertake emprender *I hope you're not planning to undertake such a long trip alone.* Espero que no estará Ud. pensando emprender solo un viaje tan largo. ▲ comprometerse a, encargarse de *I undertook to do the work for him.* Me comprometí a hacerle el trabajo.

underwear ropa interior.

undo desatar *Help me undo this package.* Ayúdeme a desatar este paquete. ▲ deshacer *Take care or you'll undo everything that I've done.* Tenga cuidado porque si no deshará todo lo que yo he hecho.

○ **undone** por hacer, sin hacer *The work remained undone.* Quedó el trabajo sin hacer.

undoubtedly sin duda, indudablemente.

undress desnudarse, devestirse.

uneasiness inquietud, desasosiego.

uneasy inquieto, intranquilo *Why are you so uneasy?* ¿Por qué está Ud. tan inquieto?
○ **to make uneasy** inquietar *That news makes me uneasy.* Esa noticia me inquieta.

unemployed desocupado, sin trabajo.

unemployment falta de trabajo.

unexpected inesperado.

unfit inepto, no apto.
○ **to be unfit for** no servir para.

unfortunate desafortunado, infeliz.

unfriendly poco amistoso, seco, nada amable (*unpleasant*); hostil (*hostile*).

unhappy infeliz, desdichado.

unhealthy malsano, insalubre *This place is unhealthy.* Este lugar es malsano. ▲ enfermizo *He has an unhealthy look.* Tiene un aspecto enfermizo.

uniform [*adj, n*] uniforme.

unimportant poco importante, sin importancia.

union unión *In union there is strength.* La unión hace la fuerza. ▲ sindicato *Is there a labor union in the factory?* ¿Hay un sindicato de obreros en la fábrica?

unit unidad.

unite unir.

universal universal.

universe universo.

university universidad.

unjust injusto.

unkind poco amable, duro.

unknown desconocido.

unless a menos que, a no ser que.

unlike diferente, distinto.

unload descargar.

unlock abrir *Unlock the door.* Abra la puerta.

unlucky de mala suerte, desafortunado.

unnecessary innecesario.

unpleasant desagradable.

unsettled indeciso *She's unsettled as to whether she'll go or not.* Está indecisa si ir o no. ▲ pendiente *The worker's disputes are still unsettled.* Siguen pendientes las cuestiones obreras. ▲ inseguro, instable, fluctuante *The weather's very unsettled.* El tiempo está muy inseguro.
○ **unsettled account** cuenta sin saldar.

untie desatar.

until [*prep*] hasta *It rained until four o'clock.* Llovió hasta las cuatro.

● [*conj*] hasta que *Wait until you hear from me.* Espere hasta que yo le avise.

untrue falso, infiel.

unusual raro, poco corriente *This is unusual weather.* Hace un tiempo poco corriente. ▲ extraordinario *He certainly had an unusual experience.* Ha tenido una aventura extraordinaria.

unwilling de mala gana, de mala voluntad.

unworthy indigno.

up arriba *What are you doing up there?* ¿Qué está Ud. haciendo allá arriba? ▲ levantado *He wasn't up yet when we called.* Todavía no se había levantado cuando le llamamos.
○ **to be up to** ser conforme a, igual a *This isn't up to standard.* Esto no es conforme a la norma. ○ **to burn up** quemar *Burn up those papers.* Queme esos papeles. ○ **to run up against** pasar por *He ran up against a lot of trouble before he was elected.* Pasó por muchas dificultades antes de ser elegido. ○ **up against** it en apuros *That family's really up against it.* Esa familia está realmente en apuros. ○ **up and down** de arriba abajo, de acá para allá *We were just walking up and down.* Estuvimos caminando de acá para allá. ○ **up to** capez de *Do you feel up to making this trip?* ¿Se siente Ud. capaz de hacer este viaje? ○ **up to date** hasta hoy, hasta la fecha *Up to date we haven't been able to finish our work.* Hasta la fecha no hemos podido terminar nuestro trabajo. ○ **up-to-date** al día, moderno, de última moda *These clothes aren't up-to-date.* Esta ropa no es de última moda.
‖ *He's well up on mathematics.* Está fuerte en matemáticas. ‖ *It's up to you to decide where to go.* Le toca a Ud. decidir a donde vamos. ‖ *Put the umbrella up; it's raining.* Está lloviendo; abra Ud. el paraguas. ‖ *What are you up to now?* ¿Qué está haciendo? *or* ¿Qué se trae Ud. entre manos ahora?* ‖ *We're well up in our work.* Llevamos muy adelantado el trabajo. ‖ *What's up?* ¿Qué sucede? *or* ¿Qué pasa?* ‖ *Your time's up.* Ya se le acabó el plazo. ‖ *The new mayor's an up-and-coming politician.* El nuevo alcalde es un político que promete mucho.

upgrade ‖ *Business is on the upgrade.* Los negocios van para arriba.

uphold sostener, apoyar.

uplift [*v*] levantar, exaltar.

upon See on.

upper de arriba, superior *I'd just as soon*

take the upper berth. Me da lo mismo tomar la cama de arriba.

upright erecto, recto *How long must we keep an upright position?* ¿Cuánto tiempo debemos quedarnos en posición erecta? ▲ honrado *She married an upright young man.* Se casó con un joven honrado.

uproar tumulto, alboroto.

uproot desarraigar, arrancar de raíz.

upset [*n*] sopresa *Their victory was quite an upset.* Su victoria fué verdaderamente una sorpresa.

upset [*adj*] mal, desarreglo *What should I take for an upset stomach?* ¿Qué puedo tomar para un mal de estómago? ● [*v*] volcar, voltear *Be careful not to upset the pitcher of water.* Tenga cuidado de no volcar el jarro de agua. ▲ perturbar, contrariar, trastornar *The bad news upset him greatly.* Las malas noticias le contrariaron enormemente. ▲ desarreglar *Don't upset things around here.* No desarregle las cosas por aquí.

upside down patas arriba *The chair's upside down.* La silla está patas arriba. ▲ al revés *You've put the tablecloth upside down.* Ha puesto Ud. el mantel al revés. ▲ revuelto, en desorden *Everything's upside down in this room.* Todo está revuelto en esta habitación.

upstairs arriba, los altos *I live upstairs.* Vivo arriba.

upward hacia arriba.

urge [*n*] impulso, deseo *He felt a great urge to go back home.* Sintió un gran impulso de volver a casa. ● [*v*] instar *We urged him to take a vacation.* Le instamos a que tomara unas vacaciones.

urgent urgente.

urinate orinar.

urine orina.

us nos *My friend has invited both of us to the concert.* Mi amigo nos ha invitado a los dos al concierto. ▲ nosotros *This gift is for us.* Este regalo es para nosotros.

use uso *He's lost the use of his right arm.* Ha perdido el uso del brazo derecho. ▲ manejo, uso *Are you sure you know the proper use of this machine?* ¿Está

Ud. seguro de conocer el manejo de esta máquina? ○ **in use** en uso *This type of machine is now in use.* Este tipo de máquina ya está en uso. ○ **to be of no use** ser inútil, no servir para nada *That book is of no use to me.* Ese libro no me sirve para nada. ○ **to have no use for** *I have no use for that man at all.* Ese hombre no me gusta para nada. ○ **to make use of** aprovechar *Make good use of this opportunity.* Aproveche bien esta ocasión. ‖ *What's the use of arguing?* ¿Para qué discutir? *or* ¿De qué sirve discutir? ‖ *Oh, what's the use!* ¡Para qué preocuparse!

use [*v*] usar *May I use your telephone?* ¿Puedo usar su teléfono? ○ **to be used to** acostumbrar *Are you used to driving in heavy traffic?* ¿Está Ud. acostumbrado a conducir con mucho tráfico? ○ **to use up** gastar *I've used up all my money.* Me he gastado todo el dinero.

useful útil.

useless inútil.

usher acomodador.

usual usual, acostumbrado, de costumbre *Let's go home the usual way.* Vamos a casa por el camino de costumbre. ○ **as usual** como siempre, como de costumbre, sin novedad *Everything here is the same as usual.* Aquí todo está como de costumbre.

usually usualmente, por lo regular, por lo común.

utensil utensilio.

utility utilidad.

utmost sumo *This is of the utmost importance.* Esto es de suma importancia. ○ **to do one's utmost** hacer uno lo más que pueda *He did his utmost to succeed.* Hizo lo más que pudo para triunfar. ○ **to the utmost** a más no poder *He enjoyed himself to the utmost.* Se divirtió a más no poder.

utter [*adj*] completo *We were left in utter darkness.* Nos dejaron en completa oscuridad.

utter [*v*] proferir, dar *He uttered a cry of pain.* Dió un grito de dolor.

V

vacancy vacante.

vacant vacante, desocupado *Are there any vacant apartments for rent?* ¿Hay algún apartamiento desocupado para alquilar? ▲ vacío, libre *Can you find me*

a vacant seat? Puede Ud. encontrarme un asiento libre?

vacation vacación(es).

vaccinate vacunar.

vaccination vacuna.

vague vago, indefinido.
vain vano.
  O **in vain** en vano, en balde.
valid válido, valedero.
valise valija.
valley valle.
valor valor, valentía.
valuable valioso *They gave us valuable information.* Nos dieron una información valioso.
  O **valuables** objetos de valor.
  ‖ *How valuable is this jewelry?* ¿Qué valor tienen estas joyas?
value [*n*] valor *What's the value of the American dollar in this country?* ¿Qué valor tiene el dólar americano en este país?
  ● [*v*] valuar, valorar *What do you value your property at?* En cuánto valora Ud. su propiedad? ▲ estimar, apreciar *I value highly his friendship.* Estimo en mucho su amistad.
valve válvula.
vane O **weather vane** valeta.
vanilla vainilla.
vanish desvanecerse.
vanity vanidad.
vapor vapor.
variable variable.
variety variedad.
various varios, diversos.
varnish [*n*] barniz.
  ● [*v*] barnizar.
vary variar, cambiar.
vase florero.
vaseline vaselina.
vast vasto.
vault bóveda.
  O **bank vault** caja de caudales.
veal carne de ternera.
vegetable legumbre, verdura.
vehicle vehículo.
veil [*n*] velo.
  ● [*v*] velar.
vein vena.
velocity velocidad.
velvet terciopelo.
venetian blinds persianas.
vengeance venganza.
venom veneno.
vent respiradero, salida.
ventilate ventilar.
ventilation ventilación.
ventilator ventilador.
venture [*n*] riesgo, ventura.
  ● [*v*] aventurar, arriesgar.
verb verbo.
verdict veredicto, fallo.
verge borde.
  O **to be on the verge of** estar al borde de.

verify verificar, comprobar.
verse verso.
version versión.
vertical vertical.
very [*adj*] mismo *The very day I arrived war was declared.* Se declaró la guerra el mismo día que llegué. ▲ solo, simple *The very thought of leaving is unpleasant to me.* La sola idea de marcharme me disgusta.
  ● [*adv*] muy *He's a very nice person.* Es una persona muy simpática.
  ‖ *That's the very thing I need.* Eso es precisamente lo que necesito.
vessel vasija (*container*); barco (*ship*).
  O **blood vessel** vaso sanguíneo.
vest chaleco.
vestibule vestíbulo.
veteran veterano.
veterinary veterinario.
veto veto.
vex irritar, molestar.
via por la vía de, por.
vibrate vibrar.
vice vicio.
vice versa viceversa.
vicinity vecindad.
vicious depravado, malvado (*people*); mañoso, malo (*animal*).
victim víctima.
victor vencedor.
victorious victorioso.
victory victoria.
view [*n*] vista *This room has a fine view of the park.* Este cuarto tiene una linda vista del parque. ▲ opinión *What is your view on the subject?* ¿Qué opina Ud. sobre el asunto? or ¿Cuál es su opinión sobre el asunto?
  ● [*v*] mirar *The sergeant viewed the recruits with disgust.* El sargento miraba con mala cara a los reclutas.
  O **in view of** en vista de. O **on view** en exhibición, expuesto *The picture will be on view the end of the week.* El cuadro estará en exhibición a fines de la semana. O **with a view to** pensando en, con miras a *I'm saving money with a view to the future.* Estoy ahorrando dinero con miras al futuro.
viewpoint punto de vista.
vigor vigor.
vigorous vigoroso.
vile bajo, vil.
village aldea, pueblo.
villain villano.
vine vid, parra.
vinegar vinagre.
vineyard viña, viñedo.
violate violar.
violation violación.

violence violencia.
violent violento.
violet violeta.
violin violín.
virgin virgen.
virtue virtud.
visa visa, visado.
visible visible.
vision visión.
visit [n] visita.
 ● [v] visitar.
visitor visita, visitante.
vital vital.
vitamin vitamina.
vivid vivo.
vocabulary vocabulario.
vocal vocal.
vocation ocupación, oficio, profesión.
voice voz.
void [n] vacío (*emptiness*).
 ● [adj] nulo, sin efecto (*null*).
 ● [v] anular.
volcano volcan.

volley salva, descarga, andanada.
volt voltio.
volume volumen.
voluntary voluntario.
volunteer [n, adj] voluntario.
 ● [v] ofrecerse a hacer algo, ofrecerse para servir como voluntario.
vomit vomitar.
vote [n] voto *This candidate got 2000 votes.* Este candidato tuvo 2000 votos. ▲ votación *Let's decide this by a vote.* Decidamos esto por votación.
 ● [v] votar *Have you voted in this election?* ¿Ha votado Ud. en estas elecciones?
vow [n] voto, promesa.
 ● [v] hacer voto.
vowel vocal.
voyage viaje por mar.
vulgar vulgar.
vulnerable vulnerable.
vulture buitre.

#

wade vadear.
wafer barquillo (*biscuit*); oblea (*medicine*).
wag mover, menear.
wage ● daily wage jornal. ○ to wage war hacer guerra. ○ wages sueldo, salario *What wages does this factory pay?* ¿Qué sueldos paga esta fábrica?
wagon carro de cuatro ruedas [Sp], carretón [Am].
waist cintura.
wait [n] espera *There'll be an hour's wait.* Habrá que hacer una espera de una hora.
 ● [v] esperar *I'll wait for you until five o'clock.* Le esperaré hasta las cinco.
 ○ to lie in wait estar en acecho. ○ to wait on atender *Is anyone waiting on you?* ¿Le atiende alguien? ○ to wait up esperar desvelándose *My parents waited up for me last night.* Anoche mis padres se desvelaron esperando me.
waiter camarero, mozo.
waiting room sala de espera.
waitress camarera.
wake [n] estela *We crossed the wake of the ship.* Cruzamos la estela del barco.
wake [v] despertar *Please wake me at seven o'clock.* Por favor, despiérteme a las siete.
 ○ to wake up abrir los ojos *It's high time you woke up to the facts.* Es hora de que Ud. abra los ojos a la realidad.
waken despertar *I don't want to be wakened till nine o'clock.* No quiero que me despierten hasta las nueve.
walk [n] paseo *Let's go for a walk in the park.* Vamos a dar un paseo por el parque. ▲ paseo, camino *They planted flowers on both sides of the walk.* Sembraron flores a ambos lados del camino. ▲ modo de andar *You can always tell him by his walk.* Siempre se le conoce por el modo de andar.
 ● [v] caminar, andar, ir a pie *Do you think we can walk it in an hour?* ¿Cree Ud. que podremos llegar en una hora yendo a pie?
 ○ long walk caminata *It's a long walk from here to the station.* Hay una caminata de aquí a la estación. ○ to walk the streets andar por las calles. ○ to walk up and down pasearse de arriba abajo.
 ‖ *Walk the horses.* Pongan los caballos al paso.
wall [n] pared *Hang the picture on this wall.* Cuelgue Ud. el cuadro en esta pared. ▲ tapia *He built a high wall around his garden.* Construyó una tapia alta alrededor de su jardín.
 ● [v] tapiar *They've just walled up the entrance to the cave.* Acaban de tapiar le entrada de la cueva.

‖ *We have our backs to the wall.* Estamos entre la espalda y la pared.
wallet cartera.
walnut nuez (*nut*); nogal (*tree*).
waltz vals.
wander vagar.
want [*n*] necesidad *My wants are very simple.* Tengo pocas necesidades.
● [*v*] querer *I want to go swimming.* Quiero ir a nadar. ▲ buscar *He was wanted by the police.* Lo buscaba la policía.
○ **to be in want** estar necesitado.
war guerra.
○ **at war** en guerra.
wardrobe ropero, guardarropa (*clothes*); armario (*closet*).
warehouse almacén, depósito.
warm [*adj*] calor *It gets very warm here in the afternoon.* Hace mucho calor aquí por las tardes. ▲ caluroso, afectuoso, cariñoso *She sends you warm greetings.* Le envía cariñosos saludos. ▲ cálido *She looks best in warm colors.* Le quedan mejor los colores cálidos. ▲ caliente *The room is warm.* El cuarto está caliente.
● [*v*] confortar *His kind words warmed our hearts.* Sus palabras amables confortaron nuestro espíritu.
○ **to be warm** hacer calor *It's not warm today.* Hoy no hace calor. ▲ tener calor *I'm too warm in this dress.* Tengo demasiado calor con este traje. ▲ **to warm oneself** calentarse *Come in and warm yourself by the fire.* Entre Ud. y caliéntese cerca del fuego. ○ **to warm up** calentar *We'll have supper as soon as the soup is warmed up.* Comeremos en cuanto calienten la sopa. ▲ entrar en calor *The players are warming up before the game.* Los jugadores están entrando en calor antes del juego. ▲ entrar en confianza [*Am*], encontrarse a gusto *He was shy at first, but soon warmed up to us.* Estaba cohibido al principio, pero en seguida entró en confianza. ○ **warm clothes** ropa de abrigo.
warmth calor moderado (*weather*); cordialidad (*feeling*).
warn advertir.
warp torcer, combar, alabear.
warrant [*v*] justificar.
wash [*n*] ropa (lavada) *The wash hasn't come back from the laundry.* No han traído la ropa de la lavandería.
● [*v*] lavar *Who's going to wash the dishes?* ¿Quién va a lavar los platos? ▲ batir, golpear *Listen to the waves washing against the boat.* Oiga como golpean las olas contra el barco.
○ **to be washed up** haber fracasado *Our vacation plans are all washed up.* Han fracasado nuestros planes para las vacaciones. ○ **to wash away** llevarse *Last spring the flood washed away the dam.* La inundación se llevó la presa la primavera pasada. ○ **to wash up** arrojar, llevar *A lot of shells were washed up on the beach.* Había muchas conchas en la playa arrojadas por las olas. ▲ lavarse, arreglarse *Let's wash up before dinner.* Arreglémonos antes de comer.
washcloth trapo, estropajo.
wasp avispa.
waste [*n*] desperdicio, desechos *Put all the waste in the garbage can.* Ponga todos los desechos en la lata de la basura.
● [*v*] perder *He wastes a lot of time talking.* Pierde mucho tiempo hablando.
○ **a waste of money** gasto inútil, despilfarro, tirar el dinero *This seems like a waste of money.* Eso es tirar el dinero. *or* Esto parece un gasto inútil. ○ **to go to waste** echarse a perder *The food went to waste because it wasn't put on ice.* La comida se echó a perder porque no la pusieron en hielo. ○ **to lay waste** asolar, arruinar *The army laid waste the entire area.* El ejército asoló toda la zona. ○ **to waste away** consumirse *He wasted away during his illness.* Se consumió durante la enfermedad. ○ **waste paper** papel de desecho.
wastebasket cesto para papeles [*Sp*], papelera [*Am*].
watch [*n*] reloj *My watch is fast.* Tengo el reloj adelantado. ▲ servicio, guardia *Every sailor on this ship has to stand a four-hour watch.* Todos los marineros en este barco tienen que hacer cuatro horas de guardia.
● [*v*] observar *We watched the planes land at the airport.* Observamos el aterrizaje de los aviones en el aeropuerto.
○ **to watch out for** tener cuidado con *Watch out for cars when you cross the street.* Tenga cuidado con los automóviles al cruzar la calle. ▲ velar por *Don't worry; he's watching out for his own interests.* No se preocupe, él vela por sus intereses. ○ **to watch over** guardar *The dog watched over the sheep all night.* El perro guardó las ovejas toda la noche.

‖ *Watch your step!* ¡Tenga cuidado! or ¡Mire donde pisa!

watchman vigilante, sereno.

water [*n*] agua *Please give me a glass of water.* Déme un vaso de agua, por favor.

● [*v*] dar de beber a *Don't forget to water the horses.* No se le olvide dar de beber a los caballos. ▲ regar *When did you water the flowers?* ¿Cuándo regó Ud. las flores? ▲ aguar *This wine tastes like it was watered.* Parece que este vino está aguado.

○ by water por barco *The only way you can get there is by water.* La única manera de llegar allí es por barco. ○ water color acuarela. ○ water pipe cañería.

‖ *That argument doesn't hold water.* Ese argumento se cae por su base. ‖ *The smoke made my eyes water.* El humo me hizo llorar. ‖ *The smell of the food made my mouth water.* Con el olor de la comida se me hizo la boca agua.

waterfall cascada, catarata.

waterproof impermeable.

wave [*n*] ola, onda *Be careful of the waves when you go swimming.* Tenga cuidado con las olas cuando vaya a nadar. ▲ onda *She was afraid that the train would spoil her waves.* Temía que la lluvia le estropeara las ondas.

● [*v*] ondear *They watched the flags waving in the breeze.* Miraban las banderas ondeando en el aire. ▲ hacer señas, agitar las manos *We waved to attract his attention.* Agitamos las manos (*or* Le hicimos señas) para llamarle la atención.

○ heat wave ola de calor. ○ wave length longitud de onda *On what wave length is Station WLW found?* ¿A qué longitud de onda se encuentra la estación WLW?

wax cera.

way camino *Is this the right way to town?* ¿Es éste el camino que va al pueblo? ▲ modo *I don't like the way he acts.* No me gusta su modo de comportarse. ▲ aspecto *In some ways this plan is better than the other one.* En algunos aspectos este plan es mejor que el otro. ▲ manera *He still hasn't found a way to make a living.* Todavía no ha encontrado una manera de ganarse la vida.

○ across the way enfrente de, frente a *His house is just across the way from ours.* Su casa está exactamente enfrente de la nuestra. ○ a long way muy

lejos *These students are a long way from home.* Estos estudiantes están muy lejos de sus casas. ○ by the way a propósito *By the way, are you coming with us tonight?* A propósito, ¿viene Ud. con nosotros esta noche? ○ by way of por el camino de *We'll come back by way of the mountain road.* Volveremos por el camino de la montaña. ○ in a way hasta cierto punto *In a way we're lucky to be here.* Hasta cierto punto tenemos suerte de estar aquí. ○ out-of-the-way apartado, retirado *He lives on an out-of-the-way street.* Vive en una calle retirada. ○ to be in the way estorbar *He tried to help but he was just in the way.* Trató de prestar ayuda pero no hizo más que estorbar. ○ under way en camino, en marcha *The work is under way.* El trabajo está en marcha. ○ way off a lo lejos *I see them way off.* Los veo a lo lejos. ○ ways distancia *The village is quite a way off.* El pueblo queda a bastante distancia. ○ ways and means medios *We discussed ways and means of putting the plan into operation.* Discutimos los medios para poner en marcha el plan.

‖ *He has a way with children.* Le cae muy bien a los niños. ‖ *He's in a bad way after the party last night.* Está en malas condiciones después de la fiesta de anoche. ‖ *I finally got that back work out of the way.* Al fin me quité de encima ese trabajo atrasado. ‖ *We gave the other car the right of way.* Dimos la vía al otro autómovil [*Am*]. *or* Dejamos paso al otro autómovil. ‖ *What have you got in the way of portable radios?* ¿Qué tiene Ud. en radios portátiles?

we nosotros.

weak débil.

wealth riqueza.

wealthy rico.

weapon arma.

wear [*n*] ropa, trajes *Do you sell men's wear?* ¿Venden Uds. ropa para caballeros?

● [*v*] llevar, usar *What are you wearing to dinner tonight?* ¿Qué traje llevará Ud. en la comida esta noche? ▲ durar *This coat will wear longer than a cheap one.* Este abrigo durará más que uno barato. ▲ hacer *The eraser wore a hole in the paper.* El borrador hizo un agujero en el papel.

○ evening wear traje de noche. ○ to wear off pasar, desaparecer *The effect of the drug will wear off in a few*

hours. El efecto de la droga desaparecerá en unas horas. ○ **to wear out** gastar *He wears out shoes very fast.* Gasta muy pronto los zapatos. ▲ agotar *He was worn out after the conference.* Estaba agotado después de la reunión. ○ **wear and tear** desgaste por el uso *This suit shows wear and tear.* Este traje muestra el desgaste ocasionado por el uso.
‖ *There's still some good wear left in this suit.* Todavía está en buen uso este traje.

weary cansado, rendido.

weather tiempo *We've had a lot of rainy weather lately.* Hemos tenido un tiempo muy lluvioso últimamente.
○ **to be under the weather** sentirse mal.

weave [*v*] tejer.

web tela (*cloth*); tela de araña (*spider*).

wed casar, casarse, contraer matrimonio.

wedding matrimonio, boda.

wedge cuña.

Wednesday miércoles.

weed [*n*] maleza, mala hierba.
● [*v*] escardar, desyerbar, desherbar.

week semana.

weekday día de trabajo.

weekend fin de semana.

weekly semanal.

weep llorar.

weigh pesar *Please weigh this package for me.* Haga el favor de pesarme este paquete.
○ **to weigh anchor** levar anclas. ○ **to weigh on** preocupar *The responsibility of his job doesn't weigh on him much.* La responsabilidad de su puesto no le preocupa mucho.

weight [*n*] peso *The weight of the trunk is 200 pounds.* El peso del baúl es de 200 libras.—*You've just lifted a weight off my mind.* Acaba de quitarme un peso de encima. ▲ importancia *Don't attach too much weight to what he says.* No le de Ud. mucha importancia a lo que dice.
● [*v*] poner peso *Make them balance by weighting this side.* Equilíbrelos poniendo peso de este lado.

welcome [*n*] bienvenida, recibimiento *They gave us a warm welcome when we came back.* Nos hicieron un cariñoso recibimiento cuando volvimos.
● [*v*] acoger, recibir bien *They welcomed us to the club.* Nos acogieron muy bien en el club.
○ **Welcome!** ¡Bienvenido!
‖ *"Thank you." "You're welcome."* "Gracias." "De nada." ‖ *You're wel-*

come to use my car. Mi auto está a su disposición.

weld soldar.

welfare bienestar.
○ **Welfare Department** Beneficencia.

well [*n*] pozo *Get some water from the well.* Traiga Ud. un poco de agua del pozo.

well [*adj*] sano *He doesn't look like a well man.* No parece un hombre sano.
● [*adv*] bien *They do their work very well.* Hacen su trabajo muy bien.— *Is your father feeling well these days?* ¿Se siente bien su padre en estos días? —*Do you want your steak well done?* ¿Desea Ud. el bistec bien cocido?—*He could very well have gone by train.* Bien podía haber ido en tren.
● [*interj*] bueno *Well, just as you say.* Bueno, como Ud. diga.
○ **as well** también *She sings and plays the piano as well.* Canta y también toca el piano. ○ **as well as** y además, y también *She bought a hat as well as a new dress.* Compró un sombrero y además un vestido nuevo. ○ **how well** que tal *How well did you enjoy your vacation?* ¿Qué tal pasó Ud. las vacaciones? ○ **just as well** mejor *It was just as well that you came.* Es mejor que haya Ud. venido. ○ **to think well of** tener buena impresión de *Do you think well of his work?* ¿Tiene Ud. buena impresión de su trabajo? ○ **well over** bastante más de *The play attracted well over a thousand people.* La representación atrajo a bastante más de mil personas.

west oeste, poniente *The road leads to the west.* El camino se dirige hacia el oeste.

western occidental, oeste *They live in the western part of the state.* Viven en la parte occidental del estado.

wet [*adj*] mojado *You better take off your wet clothes.* Es mejor que se quite la ropa mojada. ▲ fresco *Be careful of the wet paint.* Tenga cuidado con la pintura fresca.
● [*v*] mojar *They wet the street to keep the dust down.* Mojaron la calle para quitar el polvo.
○ **to get wet** mojarse.

whale ballena.

wharf muelle.

what [*pron*] qué *What do you want for supper?* ¿Qué quiere Ud. de comida? ▲ lo que *He always says what he thinks.* Siempre dice lo que piensa.
● [*adj*] *What things are missing?* ¿Qué cosas faltan?—*What nonsense!*

¡Qué tontería!—*We knew what ships were in the harbor.* Sabíamos que barcos estaban en el puerto.
● [*interj*] ¡Cómo! *What! Isn't he here yet?* ¡Cómo! ¿No está aquí todavía?
○ and what not y cualquier ctra cosa *You can buy supplies and what not at the village store.* Se pueden comprar las provisiones y cualquier otra cosa en la tienda del pueblo. ○ but what que *I never doubted but what he'd do it.* Nunca dudé que lo hiciera. ○ what . . . for por qué *What are you hurrying for?* ¿Por qué se apresura Ud.? ○ what if y si *What if your friends don't get here at all?* ¿Y si sus amigos no vienen? ○ what of que hay de *What of that job you asked for?* ¿Qué hay de aquel empleo que pidió Ud.? ○ what's more además *I disagree with him, and what's more, I've told him so.* No estoy de acuerdo con él, y además se lo he dicho. ○ what with entre *What with the children and the housework she had little time left.* Entre los niños y las tareas de la casa se le va casi todo el tiempo.
‖ *I'll tell you what, let's go to the movies tonight.* Mira vamos al cine esta noche.

whatever [*pron*] lo que *Do whatever you want, I don't care.* Haga Ud. lo que quiera, a mí no me importa.
● [*adj*] cuanto, todo el . . . que *She lost whatever respect she had for him.* Perdió todo el respeto que le tenía. ▲ ninguno *He has no money whatever.* No tiene ningún dinero.

wheat trigo.

wheel [*n*] rueda *The front wheels of the car need to be tightened.* Hay que apretar las ruedas de delante del auto.
● [*v*] conducir, llevar *They were wheeling the baby carriage through the park.* Conducían el coche del bebé por el parque.
○ to wheel around *or* about volverse rápidamente *He wheeled around to speak to me.* Se volvió rápidamente para hablarme.

when cuando *When can I see you again?* ¿Cuándo le puedo volver a ver? ▲ en que *There are times when I enjoy being alone.* Hay ocasiones en que me gusta estar solo.

whenever siempre que *Come to see us whenever you have time.* Venga a vernos siempre que tenga tiempo. ▲ cómo *Whenever did you find time to write?* ¿Cómo ha podido Ud. tener tiempo para escribir?

where donde, por donde *Go where you*

please, *I won't stop you.* Vaya donde quiera, yo no se lo impediré. ▲ dónde *Where's the nearest hotel?* ¿Dónde queda el hotel más cercano? ▲ donde, en donde *The house where I used to live is on this street.* La casa en donde vivía está en esta calle. ▲ adonde *The nurses will be sent where they are needed.* Enviarán a las enfermeras adonde sea preciso.
○ where . . . from de dónde *Where does your friend come from?* ¿De dónde es su amigo?

wherever dondequiera que.

whether si *I don't know whether they will come.* No sé si vendrán.

which [*pron*] cuál *Which one did you pick out?* ¿Cuál ha elegido Ud.? ▲ que *Please return the book which you borrowed.* Haga el favor de devolverme el libro que le he prestado.
● [*adj*] qué *Which instrument do you play best?* ¿Qué instrumento toca Ud. mejor?
○ which is which cuál es cuál, quién es quién. ○ which way por dónde *Which way did she go?* ¿Por dónde se fué ella?

whichever cualquiera, cualquiera que.

while [*n*] rato *You'll have to wait a while before you can see him.* Tendrá Ud. que esperar un rato antes de verle.
● [*conj*] mientras *Let's see a movie while we have time.* Veamos una película mientras tenemos tiempo. ▲ mientras que, en cambio *Some of the students are serious, while others are not.* Algunos de los estudiantes son serios, mientras que otros no lo son.
○ to be worth one's while valer la pena *It's not worth your while to do this.* No vale la pena hacer esto.

whine [*v*] gemir.

whip [*n*] látigo.
● [*v*] azotar.

whirl [*v*] girar, remolinar, remolinear.

whirlpool vórtice, vorágine.

whirlwind torbellino, remolino.

whisk broom escobilla.

whiskey whisky.

whisper [*v*] decir al oído, cuchichear.

whistle [*n*] silbido.
● [*v*] silbar.

white blanco.
○ white of egg clara de huevo.

who quién *Who used the book last?* ¿Quién fué el último que usó el libro? ▲ que *The man who just came in is the owner of the store.* El hombre que acaba de entrar es el dueño del almacén.

whoever cualquiera que, quienquiera que.
whole [n] totalidad *Look at this matter as a whole.* Considere Ud. este asunto en su totalidad.
● [adj] todo *The whole office was dismissed at noon.* Despidieron a toda la oficina al mediodía. ▲ entero *Is the plate broken or still whole?* ¿Se rompió el plato o está todavía entero?
○ on the whole en general *On the whole, I agree with you.* En general estoy de acuerdo con Ud. ○ whole lot gran cantidad *I ate a whole lot of cookies.* Me comí una gran cantidad de galletas.
‖ *I don't like the whole business.* No me gusta nada eso. *or* Ese asunto no me gusta nada.
wholesale al por mayor.
wholesome sano, saludable.
whole-wheat bread pan integral.
wholly enteramente.
whom quien, cual *This is the man of whom I was speaking.* Este es el hombre de quien hablaba.
whose de quién *Whose watch is this?* ¿De quién es este reloj? ▲ cuyo *Is this the man whose picture you saw?* ¿Es este el hombre cuyo retrato vió Ud.?
why [adj] por qué *Why is the train so crowded this morning?* ¿Por qué está tan lleno el tren esta mañana?
● [interj] pues, cómo *Why, no!* ¡Cómo, no!
● [conj] por el cual, por el que *I can't imagine any reason why he refused to come.* No se me ocurre ninguna razón por la que no haya querido venir.
○ why certainly por supuesto, desde luego. ○ whys and wherefores el como y el porqué.
wicked malo, malvado.
wide [adj] ancho *Is the street wide enough for two-way traffic?* ¿Es bastante ancha la calle para el tráfico en dos direcciones? ▲ extenso, amplio *This newspaper has a wide circulation.* Este periódico tiene una extensa circulación.
● [adv] de par en par *Open the window wide.* Abra Ud. la ventana de par en par.
○ wide open en descubierto *You left yourself wide open.* Quedó Ud. en descubierto.
‖ *Your last shot was wide of the target.* Su último tiro dió lejos del blanco.
widen ensanchar.
widow viuda.
widower viudo.
width ancho, anchura.

wife esposa, señora, mujer.
wig peluca.
wild salvaje *Are there wild animals in the woods?* ¿Hay animales salvajes en el bosque? ▲ silvestre *She's in the woods gathering wild flowers.* Está en el bosque cogiendo flores silvestres. ▲ bárbaro *We had a wild time at the party last night.* Nos divertimos de una manera bárbara en la fiesta anoche.
○ to run wild desbocarse (horse); correr fuera de control de los mandos (car); volverse salvaje (children). ○ wild shot tiro errado.
wilderness desierto.
will [n] voluntad *That man certainly has a strong will.* No cabe duda que ese hombre tiene mucha voluntad. ▲ testamento *He died without leaving a will.* Murió sin dejar testamento.
● [v] querer *Will you reserve a room for me tomorrow?* ¿Quiere Ud. reservarme un cuatro para mañana?—*Won't you come in for a moment?* ¿No quiere Ud. entrar un momento? ▲ deber *The orders read: you will proceed at once to the next town.* La orden dice: debe Ud. seguir inmediatamente al próximo pueblo. ▲ testar, hacer testamento *He willed everything to his children.* Testó a favor de sus hijos.
○ at will a voluntad. ○ with a will con mucha voluntad.
‖ *He'll go for days without smoking a cigarette.* Pasa días enteros sin fumar un cigarrillo. ‖ *I'll meet you at the corner.* Le encontraré en la esquina. ‖ *I won't be but a minute.* No me quedaré más que un minuto. ‖ *This machine won't work.* Esta máquina no funciona. ‖ *This theater will hold a thousand people.* En este teatro se pueden acomodar mil personas.
willing ○ to be willing estar dispuesto.
willow sauce.
wilt marchitar.
win ganar *He won first prize in the contest.* Ganó el primer premio en el concurso.
‖ *We finally won him over to our way of thinking.* Por fin logramos convencerle.
wind [n] viento *There was a violent wind during the storm last night.* Durante la tormenta de anoche hubo un viento muy fuerte. ▲ respiración *His wind is bad because he smokes too much.* Su respiración es deficiente porque fuma demasiado.
● [v] dejar sin aliento *That run up-*

stairs winded me. El subir la escalera corriendo me dejó sin aliento.

○ **into the wind** contra el viento *The plane flew into the wind.* Condujo el avión contra el viento. ○ **to get wind of** olfatear el rastro *The dogs got wind of the deer.* Los perros olfatearon el rastro del venado. ▲ descubrir, husmear *I got wind of their plans yesterday.* Descubrí sus planes ayer. ○ **to take the wind out of one's sails** *It certainly took the wind out of his sails when he lost his job.* Se desanimó de veras cuando perdío su empleo. ‖ *Something's in the wind.* Algo se está tramando.

wind [v] dar cuerda a *I forgot to wind my watch.* Se me olvidó darle cuerda al reloj. ▲ torcer *The road winds through the mountains.* El camino tuerce por las montañas.

○ **to wind oneself** enroscarse *The snake wound itself around a tree.* La serpiente se enroscó en un árbol. ○ **to wind up** enrollar *Wind up the string.* Enrolle la cuerda. ▲ terminar *Let's wind up our work and go home.* Terminemos nuestro trabajo y vámonos a casa. ▲ resolver, arreglar *He had two weeks to wind up his affairs.* Tenía dos semanas para resolver sus asuntos.

window ventana.

window sill repisa de ventana.

windshield parabrisas.

windy ventoso.

wine vino.

wing ala *The pigeon broke its wing.* La paloma se rompió el ala. ▲ bastidor (*of a theater*).

○ **on the wing** al vuelo. ○ **under one's wing** bajo la protección de uno *She took the newcomer under her wing.* Tomó a la recién llegada bajo su protección.

wink [n] guiño.

● [v] guiñar.

winter invierno.

wipe secar (*to dry*); limpiar (*to clean*).

wire [n] alambre *He bought a roll of copper wire.* Compró un rollo de alambre de cobre. ▲ hilo *The telephone wires were blown down by the storm.* La tempestad echó abajo los hilos del teléfono. ▲ telegrama *Send him a wire to tell him we're coming.* Envíele un telegrama para decirle que iremos.

● [v] telegrafiar *I'll wire if I can.* Si puedo, telegrafiaré.

○ **by wire** por telégrafo *You'll have to send this message by wire.* Tendrá que mandar este mensaje por telégrafo. ○ **to pull wires** mover hilos *He had to*

pull a lot of wires to get that job. Tuvo que mover muchos hilos para conseguir aquel puesto. ‖ *Is the house wired for electricity?* ¿Tiene instalación eléctrica esta casa?

wireless [n] telégrafo sin hilos, teléfono sin hilos.

wisdom sabiduría (*learning*); juicio (*judgment*).

wise sensato, juicioso *He made a wise choice.* Hizo una elección juiciosa. ▲ listo *He's a pretty wise fellow.* Es un tipo muy listo.

○ **to get wise to** caer en cuenta, darse cuenta *He never got wise to the joke they played on him.* Nunca se dió cuenta de la broma que le hicieron. ○ **to put one wise** poner al tanto.

wish [n] deseo *Her wish came true.* Se realizó su deseo. ▲ voto *We sent him our best wishes.* Le enviamos nuestros mejores votos.

● [v] gustar, desear *I wish I could stay here longer.* Me gustaría quedarme aquí más tiempo. ▲ desear *We wished him luck on his trip.* Le deseamos mucha suerte en su viaje.

○ **to wish (off) on** endosar *Who wished this job on me?* ¿Quién me endosó esta tarea?

wit agudeza, ingenio.

witch bruja.

with con *I want a room with bath.* Quiero un cuarto con baño.—*With him, it's all a matter of money.* Con él es todo cuestión de dinero.—*Why did you break up with him?* ¿Por qué rompió Ud. con él?—*He took a lot of money with him.* Llevó mucho dinero consigo.—*He went to the movies with me.* Fué al cine conmigo. ▲ de *Do you know that man with the straw hat?* ¿Conoce Ud. aquel hombre del sombrero de paja? ▲ en *The new treatment has worked wonders with the child.* El nuevo tratamiento ha obrado maravillas en el niño. ▲ entre *That girl is very popular with her classmates.* Esa muchacha es muy popular entre sus compañeras. ‖ *With that remark, he left the room.* Dicho eso, salió del cuarto. ‖ *He's in love with her.* Está enamorado de ella.

withdraw retirar, retirarse.

wither marchitar.

withhold suspender (*payment*). ▲ negarse a conceder *The government has withheld permission to travel abroad.* El gobierno se ha negado a conceder permisos para viajar al extranjero.

within dentro de, en el interior de *Speeding is forbidden within the city limits.*

Se prohibe el exceso de velocidad dentro de los límites de la ciudad. ▲ dentro de *I'll be back within a few hours.* Volveré dentro de unas horas. ○ **within walking distance** *Are we within walking distance of the beach?* ¿Estamos bastante cerca de la playa para ir a pie? ‖ *Please stay within call.* Haga el favor de quedarse donde pueda oírme. ‖ *The letters came within a few days of each other.* Las cartas llegaron con pocos días de diferencia.

without [*adv*] por fuera *The house needs painting within and without.* La casa necesita pintura por dentro y por fuera. ● [*prep*] sin *Can I get into the theater without a ticket?* ¿Puedo entrar en el teatro sin boleto? ‖ *I won't go without you.* Yo no iré si no va Ud.

withstand resistir, aguantar.

witness [*n*] testigo.

witty ingenioso, agudo.

wolf lobo.

woman mujer. ○ **woman doctor** doctora.

wonder [*n*] admiración *They watched the plane with wonder.* Contemplaban el avión con admiración. ▲ maravilla *That teacher works wonders with children.* Ese maestro hace maravillas con los niños. ● [*v*] preguntarse *I was just wondering what you were doing.* Acababa de preguntarme lo que Ud. estaría haciendo. ○ **for a wonder** por un milagro *He's got a clean shirt on today, for a wonder.* Por milagro lleva hoy una camisa limpia. ○ **no wonder** no es extraño *No wonder it's cold, the window is open.* No es extraño que haga frío, la ventana está abierta. ‖ *It's a wonder that you got here at all.* Es prodigioso que al fin haya venido Ud.

wonderful maravilloso.

wood madera (*lumber*); leña (*firewood*).

wooden de madera.

woods bosque.

wool lana.

woolen de lana.

word [*n*] palabra *How do you spell that word?* ¿Como se escribe esa palabra? ▲ noticia *Have you had any word from your son lately?* ¿Ha recibido Ud. noticias de su hijo recientemente? ▲ orden *The word was given that we would*

attack at dawn. Nos dieron la orden de atacar al amanecer. ● [*v*] redactar *How do you want to word the telegram?* ¿Cómo quiere redactar el telegrama? ○ **by word of mouth** de palabra *We got the message by word of mouth.* Recibimos de palabra la noticia. ○ **man of his word** hombre de palabra. ○ **to put in a good word for** recomendar a *Will you put in a good word for me with the boss?* ¿Quiere Ud. recomendarme al jefe? ○ **to take a person at his word** tomar la palabra a una persona. ○ **words** letra *I remember the tune, but I forget the words.* Me acuerdo de la melodía, pero he olvidado la letra. ‖ *May I have a word with you?* ¿Puedo hablarle un momento?

work [*n*] trabajo *What kind of work do you do?* ¿Qué clase de trabajo hace Ud.? ▲ obra *That bridge is a nice piece of work.* Ese puente es una buena obra arquitectónica.—*All of his works are very popular.* Todas sus obras son muy populares.—*That's a work of art.* Es una obra de arte. ● [*v*] trabajar *I'm not working this summer.* No trabajo este verano.—*Work the dough thoroughly with your hands.* Trabaje bien la masa con las manos. ▲ hacer trabajar *He works his employees very hard.* Hace trabajar mucho a sus empleados. ▲ colocar *They finally worked the box into place.* Por fin lograron colocar la caja en su sitio. ▲ intercalar *Can you work this quotation into your speech?* ¿Puede Ud. intercalar esta cita en su discurso? ▲ funcionar *The elevator isn't working.* El ascensor no funciona. ▲ dar resultado *We tried to use the plan, but it didn't work.* Tratamos de utilizar el plan, pero no dió ningún resultado. ○ **to work loose** aflojarse *We almost had an accident when the steering wheel worked loose.* Casi sufrimos un accidente cuando se aflojó el volante. ○ **to work one's way** abrirse paso *We worked our way through the crowd.* Nos abrimos paso a través del gentío. ○ **to work out** preparar, planear *The captain is working out a plan of attack.* El capitán está preparando un plan de ataque. ▲ resolver *It took us a long time to work out the problem.* Tardamos mucho en resolver el problema. ▲ resultar *How do you think this idea would work out?* ¿Cómo le parece que resultaría esta idea? ○ **to**

work up excitar, estimular *All that exercise worked up my appetite.* Tanto ejercicio estimuló mi apetito.
‖ *He's doing government work.* Está trabajando para el gobierno.. ‖ *He worked his way through college.* Se costeó sus estudios universitarios trabajando.

worker trabajador, obrero.

workman trabajador, obrero.

world mundo *He's travelled all over the world.* Ha viajado por todo el mundo.
O **a world of good** la mar de bien *It'll do him a world of good to get away from home.* Le hará la mar de bien salir fuera de su casa. O **for the world** por nada del mundo *I wouldn't hurt him for the world.* Por nada del mundo quisiera hacerle daño.
‖ *My father thinks the world of you.* Mi padre tiene un alto concepto de Ud. ‖ *Where in the world have you been?* ¿Dónde ha estado Ud. metido?

worm gusano.

worn agotado (*tired*); usado (*used*). ▲ ajado *Her face is tired and worn.* Su cara está cansada y ajada.

worry [*n*] preocupación *Most of his worries are about money.* La mayor parte de sus preocupaciones son de dinero.
● [*v*] preocupar *Your actions worry your parents.* Su conducta preocupa a sus padres. ▲ preocuparse *They worry a lot about their children.* Se preocupan mucho por sus hijos. ▲ molestar *Don't worry me.* No me moleste.
O **to be worried** estar preocupado *We were worried when you didn't get here on time.* Estábamos preocupados porque Ud. no llegó a tiempo.

worse peor *The patient felt worse this morning.* El enfermo se sentía peor esta mañana.
O **to get worse** empeorar *The road got worse as we went along.* A medida que avanzábamos la carretera empeoraba. O **worse and worse** de mal en peor *Her condition got worse and worse.* Su estado iba de mal en peor. O **worse than ever** más que nunca *It's snowing worse than ever.* Está nevando más que nunca. ▲ peor que nunca *He was sick but now he's worse than ever.* Estuvo enfermo y ahora está peor que nunca.
‖ *These tires are none the worse for wear.* Estos neumáticos no están tan mal para lo que se han usado.

worship [*v*] adorar.

worst [*n*] peor *But wait, I haven't told*

you the worst. Espere Ud., no le he dicho lo peor.
● [*adj*] peor *This was the worst accident in the city's history.* Este ha sido el peor accidente que registra la historia de la ciudad.
O **at worst** a lo más *At worst, the storm may last a week.* A lo más la tempestad puede durar una semana. O **if worst comes to worst** en el peor de los casos *If worst comes to worst, we can always sell our property.* En el peor de los casos podremos vender nuestra propiedad. O **to get the worst of** salir perdiendo. ‖ *He felt worst about leaving his children.* Lo que más sintió fué tener que dejar a sus hijos.

worth [*n*] valor, mérito *He was never aware of his secretary's worth.* Nunca se dió cuenta del mérito de su secretaria.
O **money's worth** valor *We certainly got our money's worth out of our car.* Seguramente hemos sacado ya el valor del carro. O **to be worth** compensar *Will the result be worth all this trouble?* ¿Compensará el resultado tanta molestia? ▲ valer *That horse is worth five hundred dollars.* Ese caballo vale quinientos dólares. O **to be worth while** valer la pena.
‖ *Give me fifty cents worth of candy.* Déme cincuenta centavos de dulces. ‖ *He's worth a million dollars.* Tiene una fortuna de un millón de dólares.

worthless sin valor, sin ningún valor, falto de mérito.

worthy digno *I don't feel worthy of all that praise.* No me siento digno de tanto elogio. ▲ meritorio *Contributing to the Red Cross is helping a worthy cause.* Dar dinero para la Cruz Roja es ayudar a una causa meritoria.
O **to be worthy** merecer, valer la pena *This plan is not worthy of further consideration.* Este plan no merece más consideración.

would ‖ *He said he would go if I would.* Dijo que si yo iba él iría también. ‖ *He wouldn't take the job for any amount of money.* No quería aceptar el cargo a ningún precio. ‖ *I thought that would happen.* Supuse que sucedería eso. ‖ *He would study for hours without stopping.* Estudiaba las horas sin descansar.

wound [*n*] herida *Has the wound in his leg healed?* ¿Se le ha curado la herida de la pierna?
● [*v*] herir *She was wounded by his indifference.* Su indiferencia la hirió.

wounded herido.

wrap envolver *Will you wrap this package?* ¿Quiere Ud. envolver este paquete?

wreath corona (*funeral*); guirnalda (*decoration*).

wreck [*n*] destrucción, ruina *The cyclone left the town in a wreck.* El ciclón ha dejado la ciudad en ruinas.

● [*v*] destrozar, destruir *The robbers wrecked the store.* Los ladrones destrozaron la tienda.

○ **automobile wreck** accidente de automóvil.   ○ **shipwreck** naufragio. ○ **train wreck** accidente ferroviario. ○ **wrecked** arruinado *His health was wrecked after the war.* Su salud ha quedado arruinnada después de la guerra.

‖ *I'm a wreck after all that work.* Estoy matado después de tanto trabajo.

wrench llave para tuercas.

○ **monkey wrench** llave inglesa.

wrestle luchar, luchar a brazo partido.

wrestling lucha.

wretched miserable, desdichado, calamitoso.

wring retorcer.

wrinkle [*n*] arruga.

● [*v*] arrugar.

wrist muñeca.

wrist watch reloj de pulsera.

write escribir *Write your name at the bottom of the page.* Escriba su nombre al pie de la página.

○ **to write down** apuntar *Write*

down that telephone number before you forget it. Apunte Ud. ese número del teléfono antes de que se le olvide. ▲ poner por escrito *Write down your complaints.* Ponga por escrito sus quejas.   ○ **to write off** condonar, cancelar *The bank wrote off his debts.* El banco condonó sus deudas.   ○ **to write up** escribir sobre *Write up an account of your war experiences.* Escriba una crónica sobre sus experiencias en la guerra.

writer escritor.

wrong [*adj*] equivocado *The operator gave me the wrong number.* La telefonista me dió el número equivocado. ▲ incorrecto *Did I say the wrong thing?* ¿He dicho alguna cosa incorrecta?

● [*adv*] mal *I added these figures up wrong.* He sumado mal estas cantidades.—*Did I do wrong to wait so long?* ¿He hecho mal esperando tanto?

● [*v*] ofender, agraviar *They think that they've been wronged.* Se consideran ofendidos.

○ **to be in the wrong** ser culpable *He admitted he was in the wrong and paid the fine.* Admitió que era culpable y pagó la multa.   ○ **to be wrong** no tener razón, estar equivocado *You're wrong.* Ud. no tiene razón.   ○ **wrong side** (*of material*) revés.

‖ *I got lost because I took the wrong road.* Me perdí porque me equivoqué de camino. ‖ *Something's wrong with the telephone.* Algo le pasa al teléfono.

X

x-ray rayos X (*Roentgen ray*); radiografía (*picture*).

Y

Yankee yanqui.

yard yarda *How much is this material by the yard?* ¿A cómo es la yarda de esta tela? ▲ patio *Does this house have a yard where the children can play?* ¿Tiene esta casa un patio en el que puedan jugar los niños?

yarn hilo, hilado.

yawn [*n*] bostezo.

● [*v*] bostezar.

year año *I hope to be back next year.* Espero regresar el año próximo.

○ **years** edad, años *She's beginning*

to show her years. Ya se le empiezan a ver los años.

yearly [*adj*] anual.

● [*adv*] anualmente, cada, año.

yearn anhelar.

yeast levadura.

yell [*n*] grito, alarido *When he cut himself he let out a yell.* Dió un grito cuando se cortó.

● [*v*] gritar, dar alaridos *When I hit him he started yelling.* Cuando le pegué empezó a gritar.

‖ *I hear someone yelling for help.* Oigo que alguien pide auxilio a gritos.

yellow [*n, adj*] amarillo. ○ **yellow fever** fiebre amarilla.

yes sí.

yesterday ayer.

yet todavía, aún *He hasn't arrived yet.* No ha llegado todavía. ▲ sin embargo, con todo *He's a sick man and yet he continues to work.* Es un hombre enfermo y, sin embargo, sigue trabajando. ○ **as yet** hasta ahora, todavía. ○ **not yet** todavía no, aun no.

yield [*n*] cosecha *What is the annual yield of potatoes from this land?* ¿Cuál es la cosecha anual de patatas que produce esta tierra?
● [*v*] producir *This mine yields a good supply of copper.* Esta mina produce una gran cantidad de cobre. ▲ rendirse *The enemy finally yielded to our infantry.* Al fin el enemigo se rindió a nuestra infantería.

yonder allá.

you usted (Ud.), ustedes (Uds.) *What do you want?* ¿Qué quiere Ud.? ▲ tu, vosotros *You're a good boy.* Tu eres un buen chico. ▲ le, la, te, les, las *Let me help you with your overcoat.* Permítame que le ayude a ponerse el abrigo. ▲ te, os *I love you, darling.* Yo te amo, querida. ▲ uno *You can't help but laugh at his jokes.* Uno no puede menos que reírse de sus chistes. ▲ se *You can never tell what may happen.* Nunca se sabe lo que puede pasar.

young [*n*] cachorros, crías *Look at that lioness with her young.* Mira esa leona con sus cachorros.
● [*adj*] joven *You are very young for your age.* Está Ud. muy joven para su edad. ○ **young fellow** joven. ○ **young girl** chica, mozuela, muchacha. ○ **young lady** señorita. ‖ *The night's still young.* Todavía es temprano.

younger más joven. ○ **younger brother** hermano menor.

your su *Is this your seat?* ¿Es este su asiento? ▲ sus *These are your shirts.* Estas son sus camisas. ▲ tu, [*plural*] tus *What have you done with your doll?* ¿Qué has hecho con tu muñeca? ▲ vuestro, [*plural*] vuestros *You can go now and play with your little friends.* Podéis salir ahora a jugar con vuestros amiguitos.

yours el suyo, el de Ud.; [*plural*] los suyos, los de Uds. *My tie looks like yours.* Mi corbata se parece a la suya. ▲ el tuyo, el vuestro; [*plural*] los tuyos, los vuestros *I want to buy a hat where you bought yours.* Quiero comprar un sombrero donde compraste el tuyo.

youth joven, muchacho *He's a mere youth.* No es nada más que un muchacho. ▲ juventud *How does she keep her youth?* ¿Cómo hace ella para conservar su juventud?

youthful juvenil.

Z

zeal celo.

zealous celoso.

zero cero.

zigzag [*n*] zigzag *The lightning made a zigzag across the sky.* El relámpago hizo un zigzag en el cielo.
● [*v*] zigzaguear *The road zigzags back and forth.* El camino zigzaguea de un lado a otro.

zinc zinc.

zipper cremallera, [*Am*] cierre relámpago *This bag has a zipper.* Esta bolsa tiene cremallera.

zone zona, región.

APPENDIX
Countries, Cities, and Nationalities

Note.—Names indented in the first two columns are names of principal cities, or of regions where so designated. Capital cities are marked with an asterisk (*).

Spanish	English	Spanish	English
Africa	Africa	africano	African
Alaska	Alaska		
*Juneau	*Juneau		
Alemania	Germany	alemán	German
*Berlín	*Berlin		
Hamburgo	Hamburg		
Colonia	Cologne		
Bremen	Bremen		
América del Norte	North America	norteamericano	North American
América del Sur	South America	sudamericano	South American
Argentina	Argentina	argentino	Argentinian
*Buenos Aires	*Buenos Aires		
Rosario	Rosario		
Santa Fé	Santa Fé		
Mendoza	Mendoza		
Córdoba	Cordoba		
Australia	Australia	australiano	Australian
*Canberra	*Canberra		
Sidney	Sydney		
Melbourne	Melbourne		
Austria	Austria	austriaco	Austrian
*Viena	*Vienna		
Bélgica	Belgium	belga	Belgian
*Bruselas	*Brussels		
Amberes	Antwerp		
Lieja	Liege		
Birmania	Burma	birmano	Burmese
*Rangún	*Rangoon		
Mandalai	Mandalay		
Bolivia	Bolivia	boliviano	Bolivian
*La Paz	*La Paz		
Brasil	Brazil	brasileño	Brazilian
*Río de Janeiro	*Rio de Janeiro		
San Pablo	Sao Paulo		
Pernambuco	Pernambuco		
Canadá	Canada	canadiense	Canadian
*Ottawa	*Ottawa		
Toronto	Toronto		
Montreal	Montreal		
Quebec	Quebec		

494

Spanish	English	Spanish	English
Centro América	Central America	centroamericano	Central American
Checoeslovaquia	Czechoslovakia	checo, checoeslovaco	Czechoslovakian
*Praga	*Prague		
Chile	Chile	chileno	Chilean
*Santiago	*Santiago		
Valparaiso	Valparaiso		
China	China	chino	Chinese
*Chungkín	*Chungking		
Pekín	Peking		
Shangái	Shanghai		
Nankín	Nanking		
Cantón	Canton		
Hongkong	Hongkong		
Tientsin	Tientsin		
Colombia	Colombia	colombiano	Colombian
*Bogotá	*Bogota		
Barranquilla	Barranquilla		
Corea	Korea	coreano	Korean
*Seúl	*Seoul		
Costa Rica	Costa Rica	costarricense	Costa Rican
*San José	*San Jose		
Cuba	Cuba	cubano	Cuban
*Habana	*Havana		
Santiago	Santiago		
Dinamarca	Denmark	danés	Dane
*Copenhague	*Copenhagen		
Ecuador	Ecuador	ecuatoriano	Ecuadorian
*Quito	*Quito		
Guayaquil	Guayaquil		
Egipto	Egypt	egipcio	Egyptian
*Cairo	*Cairo		
Alejandría	Alexandria		
Escandinavia	Scandinavia	escandinavo	Scandinavian
España	Spain	español	Spaniard
Regions:			
Andalucía	Andalucia	andaluz	
Aragón	Aragon	aragonés	
Asturias	Asturias	asturiano	
Baleares	Balearic Isles	baleárico	
Canarias	Canary Isles	canario	
Castilla	Castille	castellano	
Cataluña	Catalonia	catalán	
Extremadura	Extremadura	extremeño	
Galicia	Galicia	gallego	
León	Leon	leonés	
Murcia	Murcia	murciano	
Navarra	Navarre	navarro	
Valencia	Valencia	valenciano	
Vascongadas (province)	Basque (province)	vasco	Basque
Cities:			
*Madrid	*Madrid		
Barcelona	Barcelona		
Valencia	Valencia		
Bilbao	Bilbao		

Spanish	English	Spanish	English
España (Cont.)			
Cities:			
Sevilla	Seville		
Zaragoza	Saragossa		
Córdoba	Cordoba		
Málaga	Malaga		
Cádiz	Cadiz		
Estados Unidos	United States	estadounidiense, norteamericano	American
*Washington	*Washington		
Nueva York	New York		
Chicago	Chicago		
Filadelfia	Philadelphia		
Detroit	Detroit		
Los Angeles	Los Angeles		
Cleveland	Cleveland		
Baltimore	Baltimore		
Saint Louis	St. Louis		
Boston	Boston		
Pittsburgo	Pittsburgh		
San Francisco	San Francisco		
Milwaukee	Milwaukee		
Bufalo	Buffalo		
Nueva Orleans	New Orleans		
Etiopía	Ethiopia	etíope	Ethiopian
*Addis Abeba	*Addis Ababa		
Europa	Europe	europeo	European
Filipinas	Philippines	filipino	Filipino
*Manila	*Manila		
Finlandia	Finland	finlandés	Finn
*Helsinki	*Helsinki		
Flandes	Flanders	flamenco	Fleming
Francia	France	francés	Frenchman
*Paris	*Paris		
Marsella	Marseille		
Burdeos	Bordeaux		
Lyon	Lyons		
Tolosa	Toulouse		
Gran Bretaña	Great Britain	británico	Britisher, Briton
*Londres	*London		
Glasgow	Glasgow		
Manchester	Manchester		
Liverpool	Liverpool		
Belfast	Belfast		
Cardiff	Cardiff		
Buckingham	Buckingham		
Grecia	Greece	griego	Greek
*Atenas	*Athens		
Guatemala	Guatemala	guatemalteco	Guatemalan
*Guatemala	*Guatemala		
Haití	Haiti	haitiano	Haitian
*Port-au-Prince	*Port-au-Prince		
Hispanoamérica	Spanish America	hispanoamericano	Spanish American

Spanish	English	Spanish	English
Holanda	Holland	holandés	Dutchman
*Amsterdam	*Amsterdam		
*La Haya	*The Hague		
Roterdam	Rotterdam		
Honduras	Honduras	hondureño	Honduran
*Tegucigalpa	*Tegucigalpa		
Hungría ·	Hungary	húngaro	Hungarian
*Budapest	*Budapest		
India	India	indio	Indian
*Delhi	*Delhi		
Calcuta	Calcutta		
Bombay	Bombay		
Indo China	Indo-China	indochino	Indo-Chinese
*Hanoi	*Hanoi		
Inglaterra	England	inglés	Englishman
Irak	Iraq	iraquense	Iraqi
*Bagdad	*Bagdad		
Irlanda	Ireland (Eire)	irlandés	Irishman
*Dublin	*Dublin		
Italia	Italy	italiano	Italian
*Roma	*Rome		
Milan	Milan		
Turín	Turin		
Génova	Genoa		
Nápoles	Naples		
Japón	Japan	japonés	Japanese
*Tokio	*Tokyo		
Yokohama	Yokohama		
Nagoya	Nagoya		
Nagasaki	Nagasaki		
Líbano	Lebanon	Libanés	Lebanese
*Beirut	*Beirut		
Malasia	Malaysia	malayo	Malay, Malaysian
Manchuria	Manchuria	manchú	Manchurian
*Mukden	*Mukden		
Marruecos	Morocco	marroquí	Moroccan
*Rabat	*Rabat		
Méjico	Mexico	mejicano	Mexican
*Méjico D.F.	*Mexico D.F.		
Monterrey	Monterrey		
Puebla	Puebla		
Veracruz	Veracruz		
Tampico	Tampico		
Nicaragua	Nicaragua	nicaraguense	Nicaraguan
*Managua	*Managua		
Norteamérica	North America	norteamericano	North American
Noruega	Norway	noruego	Norwegian
*Oslo	*Oslo		
Nueva Zelandia	New Zealand	neozelandés	New Zealander
*Wellington	*Wellington		
Oceanía	Oceania		

Spanish	English	Spanish	English
Océano Atlántico	Atlantic Ocean		
Océano Pacífico	Pacific Ocean		
Panamá *Panamá Colón	Panama *Panama Colon	panameño	Panamanian
Paraguay *Asunción	Paraguay *Asuncion	paraguayo	Paraguayan
Perú *Lima Callao Arequipa	Peru *Lima Callao Arequipa	peruano	Peruvian
Polonia *Varsovia Cracovia	Poland *Warsaw Cracow	polaco	Pole
Portugal *Lisboa Oporto	Portugal *Lisbon Oporto	portugués	Portuguese
Prusia	Prussia	prusiano	Prussian
Puerto Rico *San Juan	Puerto Rico *San Juan	puertorriqueño	Puerto Rican
Reino Unido (El)	The United Kingdom		
República Dominicana *Santo Domingo	Dominican Republic *Santo Domingo	dominicano	Dominican
Rumanía *Bucarest	Rumania *Bucharest	rumano	Rumanian
Rusia *Moscú Leningrado Kiev Odesa Stalingrado	Russia *Moscow Leningrad Kiev Odessa Stalingrad	ruso	Russian
Salvador (El) *San Salvador	Salvador (El) *San Salvador	salvadoreño	Salvadorian
Siam (Thailand) *Bangkok	Siam (Thailand) *Bangkok	siamés	Siamese
Siria *Damasco	Syria *Damascus	sirio	Syrian
Suecia *Estokolmo Gotemburgo	Sweden *Stockholm Gothenburg	sueco	Swede
Suiza *Berna Ginebra	Switzerland *Berne Geneva	suizo	Swiss
Turquía *Angora Istambul (Constantinopla)	Turkey *Ankara Istambul (Constantinople)	turco	Turk
Unión Soviética (URSS)	Soviet Union (USSR)	soviético	Soviet

Spanish	English	Spanish	English
Unión Sudafricana *Pretoria El Cabo	South Africa *Pretoria Capetown	sudafricano	South African
Uruguay *Montevideo	Uruguay *Montevideo	uruguayo	Uruguayan
Venezuela *Caracas La Guayra	Venezuela *Caracas La Guayra	venezolano	Venezuelan
Yugoeslavia *Belgrado	Yugoslavia *Belgrade	yugoeslavo	Yugoslavian

Weights and Measures

Spanish	English Equivalent	Abbreviation
tonelada métrica	2,200 pounds	tm.
quintal métrico	220 pounds	qm.
kilo	2.2 pounds	kg.
gramo	0.035 ounce	g.
hectolitro	26.5 gallons	hl.
litro	1.06 quarts	l.
kilómetro	0.62 mile	km.
metro	1.1 yards or 39.37 inches	m.
centímetro	0.39 inch	cm.
milímetro	0.039 inch	mm.

TABLE OF EQUIVALENTS

1 tm. = 1,000 kg.
1 qm. = 100 kg.
1 kg. = 1,000 g.
1 hl. = 100 l.
1 km. = 1,000 m.
1 m. = 100 cm.
1 m. = 1,000 mm.
100°C = 180°F
0°C = 32°F

TABLE OF APPROXIMATE CONVERSIONS

Inches to centimeters:	Multiply by 10 and divide by 4.
Yards to meters:	Multiply by 9 and divide by 10.
Miles to kilometers:	Multiply by 8 and divide by 5.
Gallons to liters:	Multiply by 4 and subtract 1/5 of the number of gallons.
Pounds to kilograms:	Multiply by 5 and divide by 11.

To change degrees C to degrees F, multiply by 9/5 and add 32:
$$(C \times 9/5) + 32 = F$$

To change degrees F to degrees C, subtract 32 and multiply by 5/9:
$$(F - 32) \times 5/9 = C$$

~ Numbers ~

Cardinal		Ordinal
uno (*or* un), una	1	primero, -a (*contr.* primer)
dos	2	segundo, -a
tres	3	tercero, -a (*contr.* tercer)
cuatro	4	cuarto, -a
cinco	5	quinto, -a
seis	6	sexto, -a
siete	7	séptimo, -a
ocho	8	octavo, -a
nueve	9	noveno, -a (*or* nono, -a)
diez	10	décimo, -a
once	11	undécimo, -a
doce	12	duodécimo, -a
trece	13	décimotercio, -a
catorce	14	décimocuarto, -a
quince	15	décimoquinto, -a
diez y seis (*or* dieciseis)	16	décimosexto, -a
diez y siete (*or* diecisiete)	17	décimoséptimo, -a
diez y ocho (*or* dieciocho)	18	décimoctavo, -a
diez y nueve (*or* diecinueve)	19	décimonono, -a
veinte	20	vigésimo, -a
veinte y uno, -a; veintiuno, -a; *or* veintiún	21	vigésimoprimo, -a
veinte y dos (*or* veintidos)	22	vigésimosegundo, -a
veinte y tres (*or* veintitres)	23	vigésimotercio, -a
veinte y cuatro (*or* veinticuatro)	24	vigésimocuarto, -a
veinte y cinco (*or* veinticinco)	25	vigésimoquinto, -a
veinte y seis (*or* veintiseis)	26	vigésimosexto, -a
veinte y siete (*or* veintisiete)	27	vigésimoséptimo, -a
veinte y ocho (*or* veintiocho)	28	vigésimoctavo, -a
veinte y nueve (*or* veintinueve)	29	vigésimonono, -a
treinta	30	trigésimo, -a
treinta y uno	31	trigésimoprimo, -a
cuarenta	40	cuadragésimo, -a
cincuenta	50	quincuagésimo, -a
sesenta	60	sexagésimo, -a
setenta	70	septuagésimo, -a
ochenta	80	octogésimo, -a
noventa	90	nonagésimo, -a

NUMBERS—Continued

Cardinal		Ordinal
ciento (or cien)	100	centésimo, -a (or centeno, -a)
ciento uno	101	centésimoprimo, -a
doscientos, -as	200	ducentésimo, -a
trescientos, -as	300	tricentésimo, -a
cuatrocientos, -as	400	cuadringentésimo, -a
quinientos, -as	500	quingentésimo, -a
seiscientos, -as	600	sexcentésimo, -a
setecientos, -as	700	septingentésimo, -a
ochoscientos, -as	800	octingentésimo, -a
novecientos, -as	900	noningentésimo, -a
mil	1,000	milésimo, -a
diez mil	10,000	décimo milésimo, -a
cien mil	100,000	centésimo milésimo, -a
quinientos mil	500,000	quingentésimo milésimo, -a
un millón	1,000,000	millonésimo, -a

National Holidays

Argentina	May 25, July 9
Bolivia	August 6, February 3
Brazil	September 7, November 15
Chile	September 18
Colombia	July 20, August 7
Costa Rica	September 15, May 1
Cuba	May 20, October 10
Dominican Republic	February 27, January 26
Ecuador	August 10, October 9
Guatemala	September 15, June 30
Haiti	January 1
Honduras	September 15
Mexico	September 15 and 16, May 5
Nicaragua	September 15
Panama	November 3, November 28
Paraguay	May 14, November 25
Peru	July 28, December 9
Salvador (El)	September 15
Spain	May 2, April 14
United States (The)	July 4, February 22
Uruguay	August 25, May 25
Venezuela	July 5, October 28

October 12, Día de la Raza (Discovery of America), observed in all Latin America and Spain

Important Signs

ALTO	STOP
DESPACIO	GO SLOW
DESVIO	DETOUR
PRECAUCION	CAUTION
PELIGRO	DANGER
SENTIDO UNICO	ONE-WAY STREET
NO HAY PASO	NO THOROUGHFARE
NO HAY SALIDA	DEAD END
CONSERVE SU DERECHA	KEEP TO THE RIGHT
CONSERVE SU IZQUIERDA	KEEP TO THE LEFT
VIRAJE RAPIDO or CURVA PELIGROSA	DANGEROUS CURVE
FERROCARRIL	RAILROAD
PASO A NIVEL	GRADE CROSSING
PUENTE	BRIDGE
DEPRESION	DIP
CRUCE	CROSSROAD
CABLES A ALTA TENSION	HIGH TENSION LINES
SENORES or HOMBRES or CABALLEROS	MEN
SENORAS or MUJERES or DAMAS	WOMEN
LAVABOS or LAVATORIO	LAVATORY
SE PROHIBE ESCUPIR or PROHIBIDO ESCUPIR	NO SPITTING
SE PROHIBE FUMAR or PROHIBIDO FUMAR	NO SMOKING
SE PROHIBE LA ENTRADA or PROHIBIDO EL PASO	KEEP OUT
ABIERTO	OPEN
CERRADO	CLOSED
ENTRADA	ENTRANCE
SALIDA	EXIT

Useful Expressions

GENERAL

¿Me permite Ud. una palabra?
May I speak to you for a moment?

¡Oiga!
Listen!

¡Una palabra, señorita!
May I have a word with you, Miss?

Tengo que hablarle.
I have to talk to you.

¿Podría Ud. decirme . . .?
Can you tell me . . .?

Con mucho gusto.
With pleasure.

¿Tendría Ud. la amabilidad de indicarme si . . .?
Would you be so kind as to tell me if . . .?

No se lo podría decir.
I couldn't tell you.

¿Sabe Ud. quién (cómo, porqué) . . .?
Do you know who (how, why) . . .?

No lo sé.
I don't know.

¿Es verdad que . . . ?
Is it true that . . . ?

No estoy enterado.
I don't know anything about it.

Exacto.
Exactly.

¡Quién sabe!
Who knows!

Fuera de duda, Sin duda.
Without a doubt.

Sí y no.
Yes and no.

Tenga Ud. la bondad de . . . .
Please (be so kind as to) . . . .

De buen agrado.
With pleasure.

¿No le parece a Ud. que . . . ?
Don't you think that . . . ?

¿Qué le parece a Ud.?
What do you think?

La cosa salta a los ojos.
That's evident.

Soy del parecer de Ud.
I'm of your opinion.

No me parece mala idea.
I don't think it's a bad idea.

¿Está Ud. seguro que . . . ?
Are you sure that . . . ?

Naturalmente.
Naturally.

¡Quién lo duda!
Who doubts it!

Si no estoy mal informado . . . .
If I'm not misinformed . . . .

No estoy seguro.
I'm not sure.

Así parece.
So it seems.

Puede ser.
It can be.

Se dice, pero . . . .
They say so, but . . . .

¿Qué quiere Ud. decir?
What do you mean?

Ud. sabe lo que quiero decir.
You know what I mean.

¿Qué quiere decir eso en español?
What does this mean in Spanish?

Quiere decir . . . .
It means . . . .

¿Cómo se dice eso en español?
How do you say that in Spanish?

Eso se dice de diversos modos.
You say it (It's said) in different ways.

504

GENERAL—Continued

Eso se dice . . . en español.	They say . . . in Spanish.
¿Qué quiere decir eso?	What does that mean?
¿Qué quiere decir la palabra . . . ?	What does the word . . . mean?
Intentaré explicárselo.	I'll try to explain it to you.
¿Para qué sirve esto?	What's this used for?
No se lo puedo decır.	I can't tell you.
Eso sirve para	That's used for . . . .
¿Puedo contar con Ud.?	Can I count on you?
Seguramente.	Surely.
Lo siento, pero he cambiado de idea.	I'm sorry, but I've changed my mind.
¿Cómo se explica que . . . ?	How do you explain the fact that . . . ?
Es facil de comprender.	It's easy to understand.
¿Se acuerda Ud. de . . . ?	Do you remember . . . ?
¡Ya lo creo que me acuerdo!	Of course I remember!
Francamente, no me acuerdo.	Frankly, I don't remember.
¿Me entiende Ud.?	Do you understand me?
Por supuesto.	Of course.
¿No me ha entendido Ud.?	Didn't you understand me?
Ud. dispense, pero no le he entendido.	Excuse me, but I didn't understand you.
Tenga la bondad de repetir la pregunta.	Please repeat the question.
¿Decía Ud.?	What were you saying?
Voy a repetirlo de nuevo.	I'll repeat it.
¡Ah! ya comprendo.	Oh, now I understand.
Tenga la bondad de hablar un poco más despacio.	Please speak a little more slowly.
Perdón, caballero (señora, señorita).	Excuse me, Sir (Madam, Miss).
Mil perdones.	Please excuse me (lit., "A thousand pardons")
No sabe Ud. cuánto lo siento.	You don't know how sorry I am.
No vale la pena.	It's not worth it.
No ha sido nada.	Think nothing of it.
No es nada.	It's nothing.
No tiene importancia.	It's of no importance.
Gracias.	Thanks.
Mil gracias.	Many (lit., "A thousand") thanks.
Un millón de gracias.	Many (lit., "A million") thanks.
No hay de que darlas.	There's nothing to thank me for.
Ud. es muy amable.	You're very kind.
Agradecidísimo.	Much obliged.
No hay de que.	Don't mention it.
Para servir a Ud.	At your service.

FINDING ONE'S WAY

¿Puede decirme donde está la oficina de correos?	Can you tell me where the post office is?
Tenga la bondad de decirme por donde se va a la estación.	Please tell me how to get to the station.
¿Cada cuánto tiempo pasa el omnibus?	How often does the bus go by?
¿Está cerca de aquí la calle Mayor?	Is Main Street near here?
¿Para aquí el tranvía?	Does the street car stop here?
¡Taxi!	Taxi!
¿Está Ud. libre?	Is it taken? (*taxi*)
¡Alto! que hemos pasado.	Stop, we've gone too far.
No, le dije que el número 90.	No, it was number 90 that I said.
¿Qué le debo?	How much?

ON THE ROAD

¿Cuál es el camino más corto para ir a Puebla?	What's the shortest way to go to Puebla?
¿Hay un puesto de gasolina por aquí?	Is there a gas station around here?
¿Qué camino debo tomar?	Which road must I take?
¿Está en buen estado aquel camino?	Is that road in good condition?
¿Está pavimentado o es de tierra?	Is it paved or is it a dirt road?
¿Cuántas millas hay de aquí a Monterrey?	How many miles is it from here to Monterrey?
¿Está muy lejos?	Is it very far?

TELLING TIME

¿Qué hora es?	What time is it?
¿Tiene Ud. la bondad de decirme la hora?	Will you please tell me the time?
¿Qué hora tiene Ud.?	What time do you have?
Son las diez de la mañana (noche).	It's 10 A.M. (P.M.).
Mi reloj marca las cinco.	My watch says 5 o'clock.
Son las tres y diez.	It's 3:10.
Son las seis y media.	It's 6:30.
Son las dos menos cuarto.	It's a quarter of two.
No son todavía las cuatro.	It's not four yet.
Van a dar las tres.	It's about to strike 3 o'clock.
¿A qué hora sale el tren?	What time does the train leave?
¿A qué hora quiere Ud. que vaya a buscarle?	What time do you want me to call for you?
A las nueve en punto.	At 9 o'clock sharp.
Cerca de las nueve.	About 9 o'clock.
Hacia las nueve.	Around 9 o'clock.
A las nueve a más tardar.	9 o'clock at the latest.

Spanish and Spanish-American Dishes

Spanish	English
Diversos	*Miscellaneous*
ajaco (*Am*)	boiled meat, chicken, pepper, with avocado and other vegetables
arroz con pollo	chicken with rice
chile con carne	chile con carne
cocido	boiled meat with ham, bacon, sausage, and vegetables
empanada	meat pie
enchilada (*Mex*)	corncake with meat, cheese, and chile
estofado	meat stew
guisado de ternera	veal stew
humita (*Chile*)	cake of fresh corn, tomato, pimento, sugar, and grease
locro (*Am*)	stew of ground corn or wheat, meat, and spices
paella valenciana	chicken, ham, sausage, and shellfish with rice
puchero	boiled meat with vegetables
sancocho (*Ecuador*)	stew of meat, yucca, bananas, etc
Sopas	*Soups*
caldo	bouillon, broth, consommé
caldo de pollo	chicken broth
caldo gallego	pottage Galician style
gaspacho	Andalusian cold dish made of bread, oil, garlic, onions, vinegar, and red pepper
pancho villa (*Chile*)	bean soup with egg
potaje	pottage
sopa de camarones (*Peru*)	shrimp soup
sopa de fideos	noodle soup
sopa de legumbres, menestra	vegetable soup
sopa de rabo de buey	oxtail soup
Entremeses	*Hors d'oeuvres*
aceitunas	olives
anchoa	anchovy
caviar	caviar
encurtidos	pickles
ensalada	salad

507

Spanish	English
Aves y caza	*Fowl and game*
conejo	rabbit
faisán	pheasant
guajalote (*Mex*)	turkey
liebre	hare
mole de guajalote (*Mex*)	turkey with special chile sauce
pato	duck
pavo	turkey
pavo asado	roast turkey
pavo relleno	stuffed turkey
pechuga de pollo	breast of chicken
perdiz	partridge
pollo, (*Arg*) gallina	chicken
pollo a la parrilla	broiled chicken
pollo a la reina	chicken a la king
venado	venison

Spanish	English
Pescado	*Fish*
abadejo	cod
atún, bonito	tunafish
bacalao	dried cod
bacalao a la Vizcaina	codfish Biscayan style
besugo	sea bream
caballa	mackerel
escabeche	pickled fish
lenguado	sole
merluza	hake
perca	perch
robalo	haddock
rodaballo	flounder
salmón	salmon
sardina	sardine
trucha	trout

Spanish	English
Mariscos	*Shellfish*
almejas	clams
camarones	shrimps
cangrejo	crab
langosta	lobster
ostras, ostiones	oysters

Spanish	English
Carne	*Meat*
albondiga	meatball
biftec	beefsteak
biftec a la minuta	minute steak
carne a la parrilla	broiled meat
carne asada	roast meat
bien asada	well done
poco asada	medium
medio cruda	rare
carne de puerco	pork
carne de vaca	beef
carne fiambre	cold meat
carnero	mutton
chorizo	sausage
chuleta	chop
cordero	lamb
filete	tenderloin
fricandó	larded veal, roasted and glazed in its own juice
hígado	liver
jamón	ham
jigote	meat hash with butter
mortadela	bologna
picadillo	hash
riñones	kidneys
ropa vieja	meat boiled and fried
rosbif	roast beef
salchicha	sausage
salchichón	salami
sesos	brains
ternera	veal
tocino	bacon
Huevos	*Eggs*
a la ranchera	fried with chile sauce
al plato	shirred
duros	hard-boiled
escalfados	poached
fritos, estrellados	fried
no muy cocidos	medium
revueltos	scrambled
tortilla	omelette
tortilla de cebolla	onion omelette
tortilla de patatas	potato omelette

Spanish	English
Legumbres, verduras y cereales	*Vegetables and cereals*
alcachofa	artichoke
apio	celery
arroz	rice
atole (*Mex*)	corn gruel
avena	oatmeal
batata, (*Am*) boniato, camote	sweet potato
berenjena	eggplant
berro	water cress
calabaza	squash, pumpkin
cebolla	onion
chupe	potato stew
col, repollo	cabbage
coliflor	cauliflower
escarola	endive
espárragos	asparagus
espinacas	spinach
frijoles, (*Sp*) judías	beans
frijoles refritos	beans fried after being boiled
gaches	porridge
garbanzos	chickpeas
guisantes	peas
habichuelas verdes, judías verdes, frijoles verdes	string beans
lechuga	lettuce
lentejas	lentils
mazamorra (*Arg*)	hulled and crushed corn served cold with milk
ñame	yam
papa (*Am*), patata (*Sp*)	potato
papas a la Guancayina (*Peru*)	potato salad
papas fritas	fried potatoes
pepinos	cucumbers
perejil	parsley
pimientos	peppers
pinole (*Mex*)	toasted cornmeal
puré de papa	mashed potatoes
rábanos	radishes
setas, hongos	mushrooms
tamales	tamales
tomate	tomato
tortilla (*Mex*)	corn griddle cake
verduras	green leafy vegetables
zanahorias	carrots

Spanish	English
Pan	*Bread*
bollo	sweet roll
cazabe	manioc bread
pan blanco	white bread
pan con mantequilla	bread and butter
pan de centeno	rye bread
pan de maíz	corn bread
panecillo	roll
pan francés	French bread
pan integral	whole-wheat bread
pan moreno	brown bread
rebanada	slice of bread
tostada	toast
Postre	*Dessert*
almendrado, macarron	macaroon
budín, pudín	pudding
buñuelo	fritter
compota	preserved fruit
confitura	jam
flan	caramel custard
guayaba	guava
helado, mantecado	ice cream
jalea	jelly
mazapán	almond paste
merengue	meringue
mermelada	marmalade
natilla	Spanish custard
pastel, torta	cake
queso	cheese
requesón	cottage cheese
sorbete	sherbet
tapioca	tapioca
tarta	tart, pie
turrón de Alicante	nougat
turrón de Jijona	almond paste and honey
yemas	candied yolks of eggs
Fruta	*Fruit*
aguacate (*Am*), palta (*Am*)	avocado
albaricoque	apricot
cereza	cherry

Spanish	English
Fruta (Cont.)	*Fruit (Cont.)*
chayote (*Mex*)	chayote (pear-shaped fruit)
chirimoya	sweetsop (similar to custard apple)
ciruela	plum
ciruela pasa	prune
frambuesa	raspberry
fresa	strawberry
granada	pomegranate
higo	fig
mandarina	mandarin
mango	mango
manzana	apple
melocotón, (*Am*) durazno	peach
melón	melon
mora	mulberry
naranja	orange
papaya	papaya
pasa	raisin
pasa de Corintc	currant
pera	pear
piña, ananás	pineapple
plátano, banana	banana
sandia	watermelon
toronja	grapefruit
uvas	grapes
Nueces	*Nuts*
almendra	almond
avellana	hazel nut
castaña	chestnut
maní, cacahuete	peanut
nuez	walnut
pacana	pecan
piñón	piñón, pine nut
Condimentos	*Seasonings*
aceite	oil
ají, chile	hot pepper
ajo	garlic
azúcar	sugar
canela	cinnamon
clavo	clove

Spanish	English
Condimentos (Cont.)	*Seasonings (Cont.)*
jengibre	ginger
macias	mace
mayonesa	mayonnaise
mole *(Mex)*	red-pepper sauce
mostaza	mustard
nuez moscada	nutmeg
pimienta	pepper (black or white)
pimiento	pepper (red)
sal	salt
salsa	sauce
salsa de tomate	tomato sauce
vinagre	vinegar

Spanish	English
Bebidas	*Drinks*
agua	water
agua de Seltz, soda	soda water
agua mineral	mineral water
anís	anise
aperitivo	aperitif
café	coffee
café con leche	coffee with milk
café solo	black coffee
cerveza	beer
champaña	champagne
chicha *(Am)*	fermented maize or pineapple beverage
cocktel	cocktail
coñac, cognac	brandy
gaseosa	pop, soda
ginebra	gin
guarapo	cane cider
leche	milk
leche condensada	condensed milk
leche malteada	malted milk
leche pasteurizada	pasteurized milk
limonada	lemonade
naranjada	orangeade
ponche	punch
pulque *(Mex)*	maguey wine
ron	rum
sidra	cider
té	tea
vino	wine
vino blanco	white wine
vino de Borgoña	Burgundy wine
vino de Burdeos	Bordeaux wine
vino tinto	red wine
Jerez	sherry
Oporto	port
yerba mate *(Am)*	maté, Paraguay tea

513

A CATALOGUE OF SELECTED DOVER BOOKS
IN ALL FIELDS OF INTEREST

A CATALOGUE OF SELECTED DOVER BOOKS
IN ALL FIELDS OF INTEREST

AMERICA'S OLD MASTERS, James T. Flexner. Four men emerged unexpectedly from provincial 18th century America to leadership in European art: Benjamin West, J. S. Copley, C. R. Peale, Gilbert Stuart. Brilliant coverage of lives and contributions. Revised, 1967 edition. 69 plates. 365pp. of text.

21806-6 Paperbound $2.75

FIRST FLOWERS OF OUR WILDERNESS: AMERICAN PAINTING, THE COLONIAL PERIOD, James T. Flexner. Painters, and regional painting traditions from earliest Colonial times up to the emergence of Copley, West and Peale Sr., Foster, Gustavus Hesselius, Feke, John Smibert and many anonymous painters in the primitive manner. Engaging presentation, with 162 illustrations. xxii + 368pp.

22180-6 Paperbound $3.50

THE LIGHT OF DISTANT SKIES: AMERICAN PAINTING, 1760-1835, James T. Flexner. The great generation of early American painters goes to Europe to learn and to teach: West, Copley, Gilbert Stuart and others. Allston, Trumbull, Morse; also contemporary American painters—primitives, derivatives, academics—who remained in America. 102 illustrations. xiii + 306pp. 22179-2 Paperbound $3.00

A HISTORY OF THE RISE AND PROGRESS OF THE ARTS OF DESIGN IN THE UNITED STATES, William Dunlap. Much the richest mine of information on early American painters, sculptors, architects, engravers, miniaturists, etc. The only source of information for scores of artists, the major primary source for many others. Unabridged reprint of rare original 1834 edition, with new introduction by James T. Flexner, and 394 new illustrations. Edited by Rita Weiss. 6⅝ x 9⅝.

21695-0, 21696-9, 21697-7 Three volumes, Paperbound $13.50

EPOCHS OF CHINESE AND JAPANESE ART, Ernest F. Fenollosa. From primitive Chinese art to the 20th century, thorough history, explanation of every important art period and form, including Japanese woodcuts; main stress on China and Japan, but Tibet, Korea also included. Still unexcelled for its detailed, rich coverage of cultural background, aesthetic elements, diffusion studies, particularly of the historical period. 2nd, 1913 edition. 242 illustrations. lii + 439pp. of text.

20364-6, 20365-4 Two volumes, Paperbound $5.00

THE GENTLE ART OF MAKING ENEMIES, James A. M. Whistler. Greatest wit of his day deflates Oscar Wilde, Ruskin, Swinburne; strikes back at inane critics, exhibitions, art journalism; aesthetics of impressionist revolution in most striking form. Highly readable classic by great painter. Reproduction of edition designed by Whistler. Introduction by Alfred Werner. xxxvi + 334pp.

21875-9 Paperbound $2.25

ALPHABETS AND ORNAMENTS, Ernst Lehner. Well-known pictorial source for decorative alphabets, script examples, cartouches, frames, decorative title pages, calligraphic initials, borders, similar material. 14th to 19th century, mostly European. Useful in almost any graphic arts designing, varied styles. 750 illustrations. 256pp. 7 x 10.
21905-4 Paperbound $4.00

PAINTING: A CREATIVE APPROACH, Norman Colquhoun. For the beginner simple guide provides an instructive approach to painting: major stumbling blocks for beginner; overcoming them, technical points; paints and pigments; oil painting; watercolor and other media and color. New section on "plastic" paints. Glossary. Formerly *Paint Your Own Pictures*. 221pp.
22000-1 Paperbound $1.75

THE ENJOYMENT AND USE OF COLOR, Walter Sargent. Explanation of the relations between colors themselves and between colors in nature and art, including hundreds of little-known facts about color values, intensities, effects of high and low illumination, complementary colors. Many practical hints for painters, references to great masters. 7 color plates, 29 illustrations. x + 274pp.
20944-X Paperbound $2.50

THE NOTEBOOKS OF LEONARDO DA VINCI, compiled and edited by Jean Paul Richter. 1566 extracts from original manuscripts reveal the full range of Leonardo's versatile genius: all his writings on painting, sculpture, architecture, anatomy, astronomy, geography, topography, physiology, mining, music, etc., in both Italian and English, with 186 plates of manuscript pages and more than 500 additional drawings. Includes studies for the Last Supper, the lost Sforza monument, and other works. Total of xlvii + 866pp. 7⅞ x 10¾.
22572-0, 22573-9 Two volumes, Paperbound $10.00

MONTGOMERY WARD CATALOGUE OF 1895. Tea gowns, yards of flannel and pillow-case lace, stereoscopes, books of gospel hymns, the New Improved Singer Sewing Machine, side saddles, milk skimmers, straight-edged razors, high-button shoes, spittoons, and on and on . . . listing some 25,000 items, practically all illustrated. Essential to the shoppers of the 1890's, it is our truest record of the spirit of the period. Unaltered reprint of Issue No. 57, Spring and Summer 1895. Introduction by Boris Emmet. Innumerable illustrations. xiii + 624pp. 8½ x 11⅝.
22377-9 Paperbound $6.95

THE CRYSTAL PALACE EXHIBITION ILLUSTRATED CATALOGUE (LONDON, 1851). One of the wonders of the modern world—the Crystal Palace Exhibition in which all the nations of the civilized world exhibited their achievements in the arts and sciences—presented in an equally important illustrated catalogue. More than 1700 items pictured with accompanying text—ceramics, textiles, cast-iron work, carpets, pianos, sleds, razors, wall-papers, billiard tables, beehives, silverware and hundreds of other artifacts—represent the focal point of Victorian culture in the Western World. Probably the largest collection of Victorian decorative art ever assembled— indispensable for antiquarians and designers. Unabridged republication of the Art-Journal Catalogue of the Great Exhibition of 1851, with all terminal essays. New introduction by John Gloag, F.S.A. xxxiv + 426pp. 9 x 12.
22503-8 Paperbound $4.50

"ESSENTIAL GRAMMAR" SERIES

All you really need to know about modern, colloquial grammar. Many educational shortcuts help you learn faster, understand better. Detailed cognate lists teach you to recognize similarities between English and foreign words and roots—make learning vocabulary easy and interesting. Excellent for independent study or as a supplement to record courses.

ESSENTIAL FRENCH GRAMMAR, Seymour Resnick. 2500-item cognate list. 159pp.
(EBE) 20419-7 Paperbound $1.25

ESSENTIAL GERMAN GRAMMAR, Guy Stern and Everett F. Bleiler. Unusual shortcuts on noun declension, word order, compound verbs. 124pp.
(EBE) 20422-7 Paperbound $1.25

ESSENTIAL ITALIAN GRAMMAR, Olga Ragusa. 111pp.
(EBE) 20779-X Paperbound $1.25

ESSENTIAL JAPANESE GRAMMAR, Everett F. Bleiler. In Romaji transcription; no characters needed. Japanese grammar is regular and simple. 156pp.
21027-8 Paperbound $1.25

ESSENTIAL PORTUGUESE GRAMMAR, Alexander da R. Prista. vi + 114pp.
21650-0 Paperbound $1.25

ESSENTIAL SPANISH GRAMMAR, Seymour Resnick. 2500 word cognate list. 115pp.
(EBE) 20780-3 Paperbound $1.25

ESSENTIAL ENGLISH GRAMMAR, Philip Gucker. Combines best features of modern, functional and traditional approaches. For refresher, class use, home study. x + 177pp.
21649-7 Paperbound $1.25

A PHRASE AND SENTENCE DICTIONARY OF SPOKEN SPANISH. Prepared for U. S. War Department by U. S. linguists. As above, unit is idiom, phrase or sentence rather than word. English-Spanish and Spanish-English sections contain modern equivalents of over 18,000 sentences. Introduction and appendix as above. iv + 513pp.
20495-2 Paperbound $2.00

A PHRASE AND SENTENCE DICTIONARY OF SPOKEN RUSSIAN. Dictionary prepared for U. S. War Department by U. S. linguists. Basic unit is not the word, but the idiom, phrase or sentence. English-Russian and Russian-English sections contain modern equivalents for over 30,000 phrases. Grammatical introduction covers phonetics, writing, syntax. Appendix of word lists for food, numbers, geographical names, etc. vi + 573 pp. 6⅛ x 9¼.
20496-0 Paperbound $3.00

CONVERSATIONAL CHINESE FOR BEGINNERS, Morris Swadesh. Phonetic system, beginner's course in Pai Hua Mandarin Chinese covering most important, most useful speech patterns. Emphasis on modern colloquial usage. Formerly *Chinese in Your Pocket*. xvi + 158pp.
21123-1 Paperbound $1.50

THE ARCHITECTURE OF COUNTRY HOUSES, Andrew J. Downing. Together with Vaux's *Villas and Cottages* this is the basic book for Hudson River Gothic architecture of the middle Victorian period. Full, sound discussions of general aspects of housing, architecture, style, decoration, furnishing, together with scores of detailed house plans, illustrations of specific buildings, accompanied by full text. Perhaps the most influential single American architectural book. 1850 edition. Introduction by J. Stewart Johnson. 321 figures, 34 architectural designs. xvi + 560pp.
22003-6 Paperbound $4.00

LOST EXAMPLES OF COLONIAL ARCHITECTURE, John Mead Howells. Full-page photographs of buildings that have disappeared or been so altered as to be denatured, including many designed by major early American architects. 245 plates. xvii + 248pp. 7⅞ x 10¾.
21143-6 Paperbound $3.00

DOMESTIC ARCHITECTURE OF THE AMERICAN COLONIES AND OF THE EARLY REPUBLIC, Fiske Kimball. Foremost architect and restorer of Williamsburg and Monticello covers nearly 200 homes between 1620-1825. Architectural details, construction, style features, special fixtures, floor plans, etc. Generally considered finest work in its area. 219 illustrations of houses, doorways, windows, capital mantels. xx + 314pp. 7⅞ x 10¾.
21743-4 Paperbound $3.50

EARLY AMERICAN ROOMS: 1650-1858, edited by Russell Hawes Kettell. Tour of 12 rooms, each representative of a different era in American history and each furnished, decorated, designed and occupied in the style of the era. 72 plans and elevations, 8-page color section, etc., show fabrics, wall papers, arrangements, etc. Full descriptive text. xvii + 200pp. of text. 8⅜ x 11¼.
21633-0 Paperbound $5.00

THE FITZWILLIAM VIRGINAL BOOK, edited by J. Fuller Maitland and W. B. Squire. Full modern printing of famous early 17th-century ms. volume of 300 works by Morley, Byrd, Bull, Gibbons, etc. For piano or other modern keyboard instrument; easy to read format. xxxvi + 938pp. 8⅜ x 11.
21068-5, 21069-3 Two volumes, Paperbound $8.00

HARPSICHORD MUSIC, Johann Sebastian Bach. Bach Gesellschaft edition. A rich selection of Bach's masterpieces for the harpsichord: the six English Suites, six French Suites, the six Partitas (Clavierübung part I), the Goldberg Variations (Clavierübung part IV), the fifteen Two-Part Inventions and the fifteen Three-Part Sinfonias. Clearly reproduced on large sheets with ample margins; eminently playable. vi + 312pp. 8⅛ x 11.
22360-4 Paperbound $5.00

THE MUSIC OF BACH: AN INTRODUCTION, Charles Sanford Terry. A fine, nontechnical introduction to Bach's music, both instrumental and vocal. Covers organ music, chamber music, passion music, other types. Analyzes themes, developments, innovations. x + 114pp.
21075-8 Paperbound $1.25

BEETHOVEN AND HIS NINE SYMPHONIES, Sir George Grove. Noted British musicologist provides best history, analysis, commentary on symphonies. Very thorough, rigorously accurate; necessary to both advanced student and amateur music lover. 436 musical passages. vii + 407 pp.
20334-4 Paperbound $2.25

JOHANN SEBASTIAN BACH, Philipp Spitta. One of the great classics of musicology, this definitive analysis of Bach's music (and life) has never been surpassed. Lucid, nontechnical analyses of hundreds of pieces (30 pages devoted to St. Matthew Passion, 26 to B Minor Mass). Also includes major analysis of 18th-century music. 450 musical examples. 40-page musical supplement. Total of xx + 1799pp.

(EUK) 22278-0, 22279-9 Two volumes, Clothbound $15.00

MOZART AND HIS PIANO CONCERTOS, Cuthbert Girdlestone. The only full-length study of an important area of Mozart's creativity. Provides detailed analyses of all 23 concertos, traces inspirational sources. 417 musical examples. Second edition. 509pp.

(USO) 21271-8 Paperbound $3.50

THE PERFECT WAGNERITE: A COMMENTARY ON THE NIBLUNG'S RING, George Bernard Shaw. Brilliant and still relevant criticism in remarkable essays on Wagner's Ring cycle, Shaw's ideas on political and social ideology behind the plots, role of Leitmotifs, vocal requisites, etc. Prefaces. xxi + 136pp.

21707-8 Paperbound $1.50

DON GIOVANNI, W. A. Mozart. Complete libretto, modern English translation; biographies of composer and librettist; accounts of early performances and critical reaction. Lavishly illustrated. All the material you need to understand and appreciate this great work. Dover Opera Guide and Libretto Series; translated and introduced by Ellen Bleiler. 92 illustrations. 209pp.

21134-7 Paperbound $1.50

HIGH FIDELITY SYSTEMS: A LAYMAN'S GUIDE, Roy F. Allison. All the basic information you need for setting up your own audio system: high fidelity and stereo record players, tape records, F.M. Connections, adjusting tone arm, cartridge, checking needle alignment, positioning speakers, phasing speakers, adjusting hums, trouble-shooting, maintenance, and similar topics. Enlarged 1965 edition. More than 50 charts, diagrams, photos. iv + 91pp. 21514-8 Paperbound $1.25

REPRODUCTION OF SOUND, Edgar Villchur. Thorough coverage for laymen of high fidelity systems, reproducing systems in general, needles, amplifiers, preamps, loudspeakers, feedback, explaining physical background. "A rare talent for making technicalities vividly comprehensible," R. Darrell, *High Fidelity*. 69 figures. iv + 92pp. 21515-6 Paperbound $1.00

HEAR ME TALKIN' TO YA: THE STORY OF JAZZ AS TOLD BY THE MEN WHO MADE IT, Nat Shapiro and Nat Hentoff. Louis Armstrong, Fats Waller, Jo Jones, Clarence Williams, Billy Holiday, Duke Ellington, Jelly Roll Morton and dozens of other jazz greats tell how it was in Chicago's South Side, New Orleans, depression Harlem and the modern West Coast as jazz was born and grew. xvi + 429pp.

21726-4 Paperbound $2.50

FABLES OF AESOP, translated by Sir Roger L'Estrange. A reproduction of the very rare 1931 Paris edition; a selection of the most interesting fables, together with 50 imaginative drawings by Alexander Calder. v + 128pp. 6½x9¼.

21780-9 Paperbound $1.25

POEMS OF ANNE BRADSTREET, edited with an introduction by Robert Hutchinson. A new selection of poems by America's first poet and perhaps the first significant woman poet in the English language. 48 poems display her development in works of considerable variety—love poems, domestic poems, religious meditations, formal elegies, "quaternions," etc. Notes, bibliography. viii + 222pp.

22160-1 Paperbound $2.00

THREE GOTHIC NOVELS: THE CASTLE OF OTRANTO BY HORACE WALPOLE; VATHEK BY WILLIAM BECKFORD; THE VAMPYRE BY JOHN POLIDORI, WITH FRAGMENT OF A NOVEL BY LORD BYRON, edited by E. F. Bleiler. The first Gothic novel, by Walpole; the finest Oriental tale in English, by Beckford; powerful Romantic supernatural story in versions by Polidori and Byron. All extremely important in history of literature; all still exciting, packed with supernatural thrills, ghosts, haunted castles, magic, etc. xl + 291pp.

21232-7 Paperbound $2.00

THE BEST TALES OF HOFFMANN, E. T. A. Hoffmann. 10 of Hoffmann's most important stories, in modern re-editings of standard translations: Nutcracker and the King of Mice, Signor Formica, Automata, The Sandman, Rath Krespel, The Golden Flowerpot, Master Martin the Cooper, The Mines of Falun, The King's Betrothed, A New Year's Eve Adventure. 7 illustrations by Hoffmann. Edited by E. F. Bleiler. xxxix + 419pp. 21793-0 Paperbound $2.50

GHOST AND HORROR STORIES OF AMBROSE BIERCE, Ambrose Bierce. 23 strikingly modern stories of the horrors latent in the human mind: The Eyes of the Panther, The Damned Thing, An Occurrence at Owl Creek Bridge, An Inhabitant of Carcosa, etc., plus the dream-essay, Visions of the Night. Edited by E. F. Bleiler. xxii + 199pp. 20767-6 Paperbound $1.50

BEST GHOST STORIES OF J. S. LeFANU, J. Sheridan LeFanu. Finest stories by Victorian master often considered greatest supernatural writer of all. Carmilla, Green Tea, The Haunted Baronet, The Familiar, and 12 others. Most never before available in the U. S. A. Edited by E. F. Bleiler. 8 illustrations from Victorian publications. xvii + 467pp. 20415-4 Paperbound $2.50

THE TIME STREAM, THE GREATEST ADVENTURE, AND THE PURPLE SAPPHIRE— THREE SCIENCE FICTION NOVELS, John Taine (Eric Temple Bell). Great American mathematician was also foremost science fiction novelist of the 1920's. *The Time Stream,* one of all-time classics, uses concepts of circular time; *The Greatest Adventure,* incredibly ancient biological experiments from Antarctica threaten to escape; The *Purple Sapphire,* superscience, lost races in Central Tibet, survivors of the Great Race. 4 illustrations by Frank R. Paul. v + 532pp.

21180-0 Paperbound $3.00

SEVEN SCIENCE FICTION NOVELS, H. G. Wells. The standard collection of the great novels. Complete, unabridged. *First Men in the Moon, Island of Dr. Moreau, War of the Worlds, Food of the Gods, Invisible Man, Time Machine, In the Days of the Comet.* Not only science fiction fans, but every educated person owes it to himself to read these novels. 1015pp. 20264-X Clothbound $5.00

THE PHILOSOPHY OF THE UPANISHADS, Paul Deussen. Clear, detailed statement of upanishadic system of thought, generally considered among best available. History of these works, full exposition of system emergent from them, parallel concepts in the West. Translated by A. S. Geden. xiv + 429pp.

21616-0 Paperbound $3.00

LANGUAGE, TRUTH AND LOGIC, Alfred J. Ayer. Famous, remarkably clear introduction to the Vienna and Cambridge schools of Logical Positivism; function of philosophy, elimination of metaphysical thought, nature of analysis, similar topics. "Wish I had written it myself," Bertrand Russell. 2nd, 1946 edition. 160pp.

20010-8 Paperbound $1.35

THE GUIDE FOR THE PERPLEXED, Moses Maimonides. Great classic of medieval Judaism, major attempt to reconcile revealed religion (Pentateuch, commentaries) and Aristotelian philosophy. Enormously important in all Western thought. Unabridged Friedländer translation. 50-page introduction. lix + 414pp.

(USO) 20351-4 Paperbound $2.50

OCCULT AND SUPERNATURAL PHENOMENA, D. H. Rawcliffe. Full, serious study of the most persistent delusions of mankind: crystal gazing, mediumistic trance, stigmata, lycanthropy, fire walking, dowsing, telepathy, ghosts, ESP, etc., and their relation to common forms of abnormal psychology. Formerly *Illusions and Delusions of the Supernatural and the Occult.* iii + 551pp.   20503-7 Paperbound $3.50

THE EGYPTIAN BOOK OF THE DEAD: THE PAPYRUS OF ANI, E. A. Wallis Budge. Full hieroglyphic text, interlinear transliteration of sounds, word for word translation, then smooth, connected translation; Theban recension. Basic work in Ancient Egyptian civilization; now even more significant than ever for historical importance, dilation of consciousness, etc. clvi + 377pp. 6½ x 9¼.

21866-X Paperbound $3.75

PSYCHOLOGY OF MUSIC, Carl E. Seashore. Basic, thorough survey of everything known about psychology of music up to 1940's; essential reading for psychologists, musicologists. Physical acoustics; auditory apparatus; relationship of physical sound to perceived sound; role of the mind in sorting, altering, suppressing, creating sound sensations; musical learning, testing for ability, absolute pitch, other topics. Records of Caruso, Menuhin analyzed. 88 figures. xix + 408pp.

21851-1 Paperbound $2.75

THE I CHING (THE BOOK OF CHANGES), translated by James Legge. Complete translated text plus appendices by Confucius, of perhaps the most penetrating divination book ever compiled. Indispensable to all study of early Oriental civilizations. 3 plates. xxiii + 448pp.   21062-6 Paperbound $2.75

THE UPANISHADS, translated by Max Müller. Twelve classical upanishads: Chandogya, Kena, Aitareya, Kaushitaki, Isa, Katha, Mundaka, Taittiriyaka, Brhadaranyaka, Svetasvatara, Prasna, Maitriyana. 160-page introduction, analysis by Prof. Müller. Total of 826pp.   20398-0, 20399-9 Two volumes, Paperbound $5.00

LAST AND FIRST MEN AND STAR MAKER, TWO SCIENCE FICTION NOVELS, Olaf Stapledon. Greatest future histories in science fiction. In the first, human intelligence is the "hero," through strange paths of evolution, interplanetary invasions, incredible technologies, near extinctions and reemergences. Star Maker describes the quest of a band of star rovers for intelligence itself, through time and space: weird inhuman civilizations, crustacean minds, symbiotic worlds, etc. Complete, unabridged. v + 438pp. 21962-3 Paperbound $2.00

THREE PROPHETIC NOVELS, H. G. WELLS. Stages of a consistently planned future for mankind. *When the Sleeper Wakes,* and *A Story of the Days to Come,* anticipate *Brave New World* and *1984,* in the 21st Century; *The Time Machine,* only complete version in print, shows farther future and the end of mankind. All show Wells's greatest gifts as storyteller and novelist. Edited by E. F. Bleiler. x + 335pp. (USO) 20605-X Paperbound $2.00

THE DEVIL'S DICTIONARY, Ambrose Bierce. America's own Oscar Wilde—Ambrose Bierce—offers his barbed iconoclastic wisdom in over 1,000 definitions hailed by H. L. Mencken as "some of the most gorgeous witticisms in the English language." 145pp. 20487-1 Paperbound $1.25

MAX AND MORITZ, Wilhelm Busch. Great children's classic, father of comic strip, of two bad boys, Max and Moritz. Also Ker and Plunk (Plisch und Plumm), Cat and Mouse, Deceitful Henry, Ice-Peter, The Boy and the Pipe, and five other pieces. Original German, with English translation. Edited by H. Arthur Klein; translations by various hands and H. Arthur Klein. vi + 216pp. 20181-3 Paperbound $1.50

PIGS IS PIGS AND OTHER FAVORITES, Ellis Parker Butler. The title story is one of the best humor short stories, as Mike Flannery obfuscates biology and English. Also included, That Pup of Murchison's, The Great American Pie Company, and Perkins of Portland. 14 illustrations. v + 109pp. 21532-6 Paperbound $1.00

THE PETERKIN PAPERS, Lucretia P. Hale. It takes genius to be as stupidly mad as the Peterkins, as they decide to become wise, celebrate the "Fourth," keep a cow, and otherwise strain the resources of the Lady from Philadelphia. Basic book of American humor. 153 illustrations. 219pp. 20794-3 Paperbound $1.25

PERRAULT'S FAIRY TALES, translated by A. E. Johnson and S. R. Littlewood, with 34 full-page illustrations by Gustave Doré. All the original Perrault stories—Cinderella, Sleeping Beauty, Bluebeard, Little Red Riding Hood, Puss in Boots, Tom Thumb, etc.—with their witty verse morals and the magnificent illustrations of Doré. One of the five or six great books of European fairy tales. viii + 117pp. 8⅛ x 11. 22311-6 Paperbound $2.00

OLD HUNGARIAN FAIRY TALES, Baroness Orczy. Favorites translated and adapted by author of the *Scarlet Pimpernel.* Eight fairy tales include "The Suitors of Princess Fire-Fly," "The Twin Hunchbacks," "Mr. Cuttlefish's Love Story," and "The Enchanted Cat." This little volume of magic and adventure will captivate children as it has for generations. 90 drawings by Montagu Barstow. 96pp. (USO) 22293-4 Paperbound $1.95

JIM WHITEWOLF: THE LIFE OF A KIOWA APACHE INDIAN, Charles S. Brant, editor. Spans transition between native life and acculturation period, 1880 on. Kiowa culture, personal life pattern, religion and the supernatural, the Ghost Dance, breakdown in the White Man's world, similar material. 1 map. xii + 144pp.

22015-X Paperbound $1.75

THE NATIVE TRIBES OF CENTRAL AUSTRALIA, Baldwin Spencer and F. J. Gillen. Basic book in anthropology, devoted to full coverage of the Arunta and Warramunga tribes; the source for knowledge about kinship systems, material and social culture, religion, etc. Still unsurpassed. 121 photographs, 89 drawings. xviii + 669pp.

21775-2 Paperbound $5.00

MALAY MAGIC, Walter W. Skeat. Classic (1900); still the definitive work on the folklore and popular religion of the Malay peninsula. Describes marriage rites, birth spirits and ceremonies, medicine, dances, games, war and weapons, etc. Extensive quotes from original sources, many magic charms translated into English. 35 illustrations. Preface by Charles Otto Blagden. xxiv + 685pp.

21760-4 Paperbound $3.50

HEAVENS ON EARTH: UTOPIAN COMMUNITIES IN AMERICA, 1680-1880, Mark Holloway. The finest nontechnical account of American utopias, from the early Woman in the Wilderness, Ephrata, Rappites to the enormous mid 19th-century efflorescence; Shakers, New Harmony, Equity Stores, Fourier's Phalanxes, Oneida, Amana, Fruitlands, etc. "Entertaining and very instructive." *Times Literary Supplement*. 15 illustrations. 246pp.

21593-8 Paperbound $2.00

LONDON LABOUR AND THE LONDON POOR, Henry Mayhew. Earliest (c. 1850) sociological study in English, describing myriad subcultures of London poor. Particularly remarkable for the thousands of pages of direct testimony taken from the lips of London prostitutes, thieves, beggars, street sellers, chimney-sweepers, street-musicians, "mudlarks," "pure-finders," rag-gatherers, "running-patterers," dock laborers, cab-men, and hundreds of others, quoted directly in this massive work. An extraordinarily vital picture of London emerges. 110 illustrations. Total of lxxvi + 1951pp. 6⅝ x 10.

21934-8, 21935-6, 21936-4, 21937-2 Four volumes, Paperbound $14.00

HISTORY OF THE LATER ROMAN EMPIRE, J. B. Bury. Eloquent, detailed reconstruction of Western and Byzantine Roman Empire by a major historian, from the death of Theodosius I (395 A.D.) to the death of Justinian (565). Extensive quotations from contemporary sources; full coverage of important Roman and foreign figures of the time. xxxiv + 965pp. 21829-5 Record, book, album. Monaural. $2.75

AN INTELLECTUAL AND CULTURAL HISTORY OF THE WESTERN WORLD, Harry Elmer Barnes. Monumental study, tracing the development of the accomplishments that make up human culture. Every aspect of man's achievement surveyed from its origins in the Paleolithic to the present day (1964); social structures, ideas, economic systems, art, literature, technology, mathematics, the sciences, medicine, religion, jurisprudence, etc. Evaluations of the contributions of scores of great men. 1964 edition, revised and edited by scholars in the many fields represented. Total of xxix + 1381pp. 21275-0, 21276-9, 21277-7 Three volumes, Paperbound $7.75

INCIDENTS OF TRAVEL IN YUCATAN, John L. Stephens. Classic (1843) exploration of jungles of Yucatan, looking for evidences of Maya civilization. Stephens found many ruins; comments on travel adventures, Mexican and Indian culture. 127 striking illustrations by F. Catherwood. Total of 669 pp.

20926-1, 20927-X Two volumes, Paperbound $5.00

INCIDENTS OF TRAVEL IN CENTRAL AMERICA, CHIAPAS, AND YUCATAN, John L. Stephens. An exciting travel journal and an important classic of archeology. Narrative relates his almost single-handed discovery of the Mayan culture, and exploration of the ruined cities of Copan, Palenque, Utatlan and others; the monuments they dug from the earth, the temples buried in the jungle, the customs of poverty-stricken Indians living a stone's throw from the ruined palaces. 115 drawings by F. Catherwood. Portrait of Stephens. xii + 812pp.

22404-X, 22405-8 Two volumes, Paperbound $6.00

A NEW VOYAGE ROUND THE WORLD, William Dampier. Late 17-century naturalist joined the pirates of the Spanish Main to gather information; remarkably vivid account of buccaneers, pirates; detailed, accurate account of botany, zoology, ethnography of lands visited. Probably the most important early English voyage, enormous implications for British exploration, trade, colonial policy. Also most interesting reading. Argonaut edition, introduction by Sir Albert Gray. New introduction by Percy Adams. 6 plates, 7 illustrations. xlvii + 376pp. 6½ x 9¼.

21900-3 Paperbound $3.00

INTERNATIONAL AIRLINE PHRASE BOOK IN SIX LANGUAGES, Joseph W. Bátor. Important phrases and sentences in English paralleled with French, German, Portuguese, Italian, Spanish equivalents, covering all possible airport-travel situations; created for airline personnel as well as tourist by Language Chief, Pan American Airlines. xiv + 204pp.

22017-6 Paperbound $2.00

STAGE COACH AND TAVERN DAYS, Alice Morse Earle. Detailed, lively account of the early days of taverns; their uses and importance in the social, political and military life; furnishings and decorations; locations; food and drink; tavern signs, etc. Second half covers every aspect of early travel; the roads, coaches, drivers, etc. Nostalgic, charming, packed with fascinating material. 157 illustrations, mostly photographs. xiv + 449pp.

22518-6 Paperbound $4.00

NORSE DISCOVERIES AND EXPLORATIONS IN NORTH AMERICA, Hjalmar R. Holand. The perplexing Kensington Stone, found in Minnesota at the end of the 19th century. Is it a record of a Scandinavian expedition to North America in the 14th century? Or is it one of the most successful hoaxes in history. A scientific detective investigation. Formerly *Westward from Vinland*. 31 photographs, 17 figures. x + 354pp.

22014-1 Paperbound $2.75

A BOOK OF OLD MAPS, compiled and edited by Emerson D. Fite and Archibald Freeman. 74 old maps offer an unusual survey of the discovery, settlement and growth of America down to the close of the Revolutionary war: maps showing Norse settlements in Greenland, the explorations of Columbus, Verrazano, Cabot, Champlain, Joliet, Drake, Hudson, etc., campaigns of Revolutionary war battles, and much more. Each map is accompanied by a brief historical essay. xvi + 299pp. 11 x 13¾.

22084-2 Paperbound $6.00

EINSTEIN'S THEORY OF RELATIVITY, Max Born. Relativity theory analyzed, explained for intelligent layman or student with some physical, mathematical background. Includes Lorentz, Minkowski, and others. Excellent verbal account for teachers. Generally considered the finest non-technical account. vii + 376pp.

60769-0 Paperbound $2.50

PHYSICAL PRINCIPLES OF THE QUANTUM THEORY, Werner Heisenberg. Nobel Laureate discusses quantum theory, uncertainty principle, wave mechanics, work of Dirac, Schroedinger, Compton, Wilson, Einstein, etc. Middle, non-mathematical level for physicist, chemist not specializing in quantum; mathematical appendix for specialists. Translated by C. Eckart and F. Hoyt. 19 figures. viii + 184pp.

60113-7 Paperbound $2.00

PRINCIPLES OF QUANTUM MECHANICS, William V. Houston. For student with working knowledge of elementary mathematical physics; uses Schroedinger's wave mechanics. Evidence for quantum theory, postulates of quantum mechanics, applications in spectroscopy, collision problems, electrons, similar topics. 21 figures. 288pp.

60524-8 Paperbound $3.00

ATOMIC SPECTRA AND ATOMIC STRUCTURE, Gerhard Herzberg. One of the best introductions to atomic spectra and their relationship to structure; especially suited to specialists in other fields who require a comprehensive basic knowledge. Treatment is physical rather than mathematical. 2nd edition. Translated by J. W. T. Spinks. 80 illustrations. xiv + 257pp.

60115-3 Paperbound $2.00

ATOMIC PHYSICS: AN ATOMIC DESCRIPTION OF PHYSICAL PHENOMENA, Gaylord P. Harnwell and William E. Stephens. One of the best introductions to modern quantum ideas. Emphasis on the extension of classical physics into the realms of atomic phenomena and the evolution of quantum concepts. 156 problems. 173 figures and tables. xi + 401pp.

61584-7 Paperbound $2.50

ATOMS, MOLECULES AND QUANTA, Arthur E. Ruark and Harold C. Urey. 1964 edition of work that has been a favorite of students and teachers for 30 years. Origins and major experimental data of quantum theory, development of concepts of atomic and molecular structure prior to new mechanics, laws and basic ideas of quantum mechanics, wave mechanics, matrix mechanics, general theory of quantum dynamics. Very thorough, lucid presentation for advanced students. 230 figures. Total of xxiii + 810pp.

61106-X, 61107-8 Two volumes, Paperbound $6.00

INVESTIGATIONS ON THE THEORY OF THE BROWNIAN MOVEMENT, Albert Einstein. Five papers (1905-1908) investigating the dynamics of Brownian motion and evolving an elementary theory of interest to mathematicians, chemists and physical scientists. Notes by R. Fürth, the editor, discuss the history of study of Brownian movement, elucidate the text and analyze the significance of the papers. Translated by A. D. Cowper. 3 figures. iv + 122pp.

60304-0 Paperbound $1.50

FUNDAMENTAL FORMULAS OF PHYSICS, edited by Donald H. Menzel. Most useful reference and study work, ranges from simplest to most highly sophisticated operations. Individual chapters, with full texts explaining formulae, prepared by leading authorities cover basic mathematical formulas, statistics, nomograms, physical constants, classical mechanics, special theory of relativity, general theory of relativity, hydrodynamics and aerodynamics, boundary value problems in mathematical physics, heat and thermodynamics, statistical mechanics, kinetic theory of gases, viscosity, thermal conduction, electromagnetism, electronics, acoustics, geometrical optics, physical optics, electron optics, molecular spectra, atomic spectra, quantum mechanics, nuclear theory, cosmic rays and high energy phenomena, particle accelerators, solid state, magnetism, etc. Special chapters also cover physical chemistry, astrophysics, celestian mechanics, meteorology, and biophysics. Indispensable part of library of every scientist. Total of xli + 787pp.
60595-7, 60596-5 Two volumes, Paperbound $5.00

INTRODUCTION TO EXPERIMENTAL PHYSICS, William B. Fretter. Detailed coverage of techniques and equipment: measurements, vacuum tubes, pulse circuits, rectifiers, oscillators, magnet design, particle counters, nuclear emulsions, cloud chambers, accelerators, spectroscopy, magnetic resonance, x-ray diffraction, low temperature, etc. One of few books to cover laboratory hazards, design of exploratory experiments, measurements. 298 figures. xii + 349pp.
(EUK) 61890-0 Paperbound $2.50

CONCEPTS AND METHODS OF THEORETICAL PHYSICS, Robert Bruce Lindsay. Introduction to methods of theoretical physics, emphasizing development of physical concepts and analysis of methods. Part I proceeds from single particle to collections of particles to statistical method. Part II covers application of field concept to material and non-material media. Numerous exercises and examples. 76 illustrations. x + 515pp.
62354-8 Paperbound $4.00

AN ELEMENTARY TREATISE ON THEORETICAL MECHANICS, Sir James Jeans. Great scientific expositor in remarkably clear presentation of basic classical material: rest, motion, forces acting on particle, statics, motion of particle under variable force, motion of rigid bodies, coordinates, etc. Emphasizes explanation of fundamental physical principles rather than mathematics or applications. Hundreds of problems worked in text. 156 figures. x + 364pp. 61839-0 Paperbound $2.50

THEORETICAL MECHANICS: AN INTRODUCTION TO MATHEMATICAL PHYSICS, Joseph S. Ames and Francis D. Murnaghan. Mathematically rigorous introduction to vector and tensor methods, dynamics, harmonic vibrations, gyroscopic theory, principle of least constraint, Lorentz-Einstein transformation. 159 problems; many fully-worked examples. 39 figures. ix + 462pp. 60461-6 Paperbound $3.00

THE PRINCIPLE OF RELATIVITY, Albert Einstein, Hendrick A. Lorentz, Hermann Minkowski and Hermann Weyl. Eleven original papers on the special and general theory of relativity, all unabridged. Seven papers by Einstein, two by Lorentz, one each by Minkowski and Weyl. "A thrill to read again the original papers by these giants," School Science and Mathematics. Translated by W. Perret and G. B. Jeffery. Notes by A. Sommerfeld. 7 diagrams. viii + 216pp.
60081-5 Paperbound $2.00

MICROSCOPY FOR CHEMISTS, Harold F. Schaeffer. Thorough text; operation of microscope, optics, photomicrographs, hot stage, polarized light, chemical procedures for organic and inorganic reactions. 32 specific experiments cover specific analyses: industrial, metals, other important subjects. 136 figures. 264pp.

61682-7 Paperbound $2.50

THE ELECTRONIC THEORY OF ACIDS AND BASES, by William F. Luder and Saverio Zuffanti. Full, newly revised (1961) presentation of a still controversial theory. Historical background, atomic orbitals and valence, electrophilic and electrodotic reagents, acidic and basic radicals, titrations, displacement, acid catalysis, etc., are discussed. xi + 165pp.

60201-X Paperbound $2.00

OPTICKS, Sir Isaac Newton. A survey of 18th-century knowledge on all aspects of light as well as a description of Newton's experiments with spectroscopy, colors, lenses, reflection, refraction, theory of waves, etc. in language the layman can follow. Foreword by Albert Einstein. Introduction by Sir Edmund Whittaker. Preface by I. Bernard Cohen. cxxvi + 406pp.

60205-2 Paperbound $3.50

LIGHT: PRINCIPLES AND EXPERIMENTS, George S. Monk. Thorough coverage, for student with background in physics and math, of physical and geometric optics. Also includes 23 experiments on optical systems, instruments, etc. "Probably the best intermediate text on optics in the English language," *Physics Forum*. 275 figures. xi + 489pp.

60341-5 Paperbound $3.50

PIEZOELECTRICITY: AN INTRODUCTION TO THE THEORY AND APPLICATIONS OF ELECTROMECHANICAL PHENOMENA IN CRYSTALS, Walter G. Cady. Revised 1963 edition of most complete, most systematic coverage of field. Fundamental theory of crystal electricity, concepts of piezoelectricity, including comparisons of various current theories; resonators; oscillators; properties, etc., of Rochelle salt; ferroelectric crystals; applications; pyroelectricity, similar topics. "A great work," *Nature*. Many illustrations. Total of xxx + 840pp.

61094-2, 61095-0 Two volumes, Paperbound $6.00

PHYSICAL OPTICS, Robert W. Wood. A classic in the field, this is a valuable source for students of physical optics and excellent background material for a study of electromagnetic theory. Partial contents: nature and rectilinear propagation of light, reflection from plane and curved surfaces, refraction, absorption and dispersion, origin of spectra, interference, diffraction, polarization, Raman effect, optical properties of metals, resonance radiation and fluorescence of atoms, magneto-optics, electro-optics, thermal radiation. 462 diagrams, 17 plates. xvi + 846pp.

61808-0 Paperbound $4.25

MIRRORS, PRISMS AND LENSES: A TEXTBOOK OF GEOMETRICAL OPTICS, James P. C. Southall. Introductory-level account of modern optical instrument theory, covering unusually wide range: lights and shadows, reflection of light and plane mirrors, refraction, astigmatic lenses, compound systems, aperture and field of optical system, the eye, dispersion and achromatism, rays of finite slope, the microscope, much more. Strong emphasis on earlier, elementary portions of field, utilizing simplest mathematics wherever possible. Problems. 329 figures. xxiv + 806pp.

61234-1 Paperbound $3.75

MATHEMATICAL FOUNDATIONS OF STATISTICAL MECHANICS, A. I. Khinchin. Introduction to modern statistical mechanics: phase space, ergodic problems, theory of probability, central limit theorem, ideal monatomic gas, foundation of thermodynamics, dispersion and distribution of sum functions. Provides mathematically rigorous treatment and excellent analytical tools. Translated by George Gamow. viii + 179pp. 60147-1 Paperbound $2.00

INTRODUCTION TO PHYSICAL STATISTICS, Robert B. Lindsay. Elementary probability theory, laws of thermodynamics, classical Maxwell-Boltzmann statistics, classical statistical mechanics, quantum mechanics, other areas of physics that can be studied statistically. Full coverage of methods; basic background theory. ix + 306pp. 61882-X Paperbound $2.75

DIALOGUES CONCERNING TWO NEW SCIENCES, Galileo Galilei. Written near the end of Galileo's life and encompassing 30 years of experiment and thought, these dialogues deal with geometric demonstrations of fracture of solid bodies, cohesion, leverage, speed of light and sound, pendulums, falling bodies, accelerated motion, etc. Translated by Henry Crew and Alfonso de Salvio. Introduction by Antonio Favaro. xxiii + 300pp. 60099-8 Paperbound $2.25

FOUNDATIONS OF SCIENCE: THE PHILOSOPHY OF THEORY AND EXPERIMENT, Norman R. Campbell. Fundamental concepts of science examined on middle level: acceptance of propositions and axioms, presuppositions of scientific thought, scientific law, multiplication of probabilities, nature of experiment, application of mathematics, measurement, numerical laws and theories, error, etc. Stress on physics, but holds for other sciences. "Unreservedly recommended," *Nature* (England). Formerly *Physics: The Elements.* ix + 565pp. 60372-5 Paperbound $4.00

THE PHASE RULE AND ITS APPLICATIONS, Alexander Findlay, A. N. Campbell and N. O. Smith. Findlay's well-known classic, updated (1951). Full standard text and thorough reference, particularly useful for graduate students. Covers chemical phenomena of one, two, three, four and multiple component systems. "Should rank as the standard work in English on the subject," *Nature.* 236 figures. xii + 494pp. 60091-2 Paperbound $3.50

THERMODYNAMICS, Enrico Fermi. A classic of modern science. Clear, organized treatment of systems, first and second laws, entropy, thermodynamic potentials, gaseous reactions, dilute solutions, entropy constant. No math beyond calculus is needed, but readers are assumed to be familiar with fundamentals of thermometry, calorimetry. 22 illustrations. 25 problems. x + 160pp.
60361-X Paperbound $2.00

TREATISE ON THERMODYNAMICS, Max Planck. Classic, still recognized as one of the best introductions to thermodynamics. Based on Planck's original papers, it presents a concise and logical view of the entire field, building physical and chemical laws from basic empirical facts. Planck considers fundamental definitions, first and second principles of thermodynamics, and applications to special states of equilibrium. Numerous worked examples. Translated by Alexander Ogg. 5 figures. xiv + 297pp. 60219-2 Paperbound $2.50

THE THEORY OF SOUND, J. W. S. Rayleigh. Still valuable classic by the great Nobel Laureate. Standard compendium summing up previous research and Rayleigh's original contributions. Covers harmonic vibrations, vibrating systems, vibrations of strings, membranes, plates, curved shells, tubes, solid bodies, refraction of plane waves, general equations. New historical introduction and bibliography by R. B. Lindsay, Brown University. 97 figures. lviii + 984pp.

60292-3, 60293-1 Two volumes, Paperbound $6.00

ELECTROMAGNETIC THEORY: A CRITICAL EXAMINATION OF FUNDAMENTALS, Alfred O'Rahilly. Critical analysis and restructuring of the basic theories and ideas of classical electromagnetics. Analysis is carried out through study of the primary treatises of Maxwell, Lorentz, Einstein, Weyl, etc., which established the theory. Expansive reference to and direct quotation from these treatises. Formerly *Electromagnetics*. Total of xvii + 884pp.

60126-9, 60127-7 Two volumes, Paperbound $4.50

ELEMENTARY CONCEPTS OF TOPOLOGY, Paul Alexandroff. Elegent, intuitive approach to topology, from the basic concepts of set-theoretic topology to the concept of Betti groups. Stresses concepts of complex, cycle and homology. Shows how concepts of topology are useful in math and physics. Introduction by David Hilbert. Translated by Alan E. Farley. 25 figures. iv + 57pp.

60747-X Paperbound $1.25

THE ELEMENTS OF NON-EUCLIDEAN GEOMETRY, Duncan M. Y. Sommerville. Presentation of the development of non-Euclidean geometry in logical order, from a fundamental analysis of the concept of parallelism to such advanced topics as inversion, transformations, pseudosphere, geodesic representation, relation between parataxy and parallelism, etc. Knowledge of only high-school algebra and geometry is presupposed. 126 problems, 129 figures. xvi + 274pp.

60460-8 Paperbound $2.00

NON-EUCLIDEAN GEOMETRY: A CRITICAL AND HISTORICAL STUDY OF ITS DEVELOPMENT, Roberto Bonola. Standard survey, clear, penetrating, discussing many systems not usually represented in general studies. Easily followed by nonspecialist. Translated by H. Carslaw. Bound in are two most important texts: Bolyai's "The Science of Absolute Space" and Lobachevski's "The Theory of Parallels," translated by G. B. Halsted. Introduction by F. Enriques. 181 diagrams. Total of 431pp.

60027-0 Paperbound $2.75

ELEMENTS OF NUMBER THEORY, Ivan M. Vinogradov. By stressing demonstrations and problems, this modern text can be understood by students without advanced math backgrounds. "A very welcome addition," *Bulletin, American Mathematical Society*. Translated by Saul Kravetz. Over 200 fully-worked problems. 100 numerical exercises. viii + 227pp.

60259-1 Paperbound $2.50

THEORY OF SETS, E. Kamke. Lucid introduction to theory of sets, surveying discoveries of Cantor, Russell, Weierstrass, Zermelo, Bernstein, Dedekind, etc. Knowledge of college algebra is sufficient background. "Exceptionally well written," *School Science and Mathematics*. Translated by Frederick Bagemihl. vii + 144pp.

60141-2 Paperbound $1.75

THE PSYCHOLOGY OF INVENTION IN THE MATHEMATICAL FIELD, Jacques Hadamard. Important French mathematician examines psychological origin of ideas, role of the unconscious, importance of visualization, etc. Based on own experiences and reports by Dalton, Pascal, Descartes, Einstein, Poincaré, Helmholtz, etc. xiii + 145pp.   20107-4 Paperbound $1.50

INTRODUCTION TO CHEMICAL PHYSICS, John C. Slater. A work intended to bridge the gap between chemistry and physics. Text divided into three parts: Thermodynamics, Statistical Mechanics, and Kinetic Theory; Gases, Liquids and Solids; and Atoms, Molecules and the Structure of Matter, which form the basis of the approach. Level is advanced undergraduate to graduate, but theoretical physics held to minimum. 40 tables, 118 figures. xiv + 522pp.
62562-1 Paperbound $4.00

POLAR MOLECULES, Pieter Debye. Explains some of the Nobel Laureate's most important theories on dielectrics, including fundamental electrostatic field relations, polarization and molecular structure, measurements of polarity, constitution of simple polar molecules, anomalous dispersion for radio frequencies, electrical saturation effects, connections with quantum theory, energy levels and wave mechanics, rotating molecules. 33 figures. 172pp.   60064-5 Paperbound $2.00

THE CONTINUUM AND OTHER TYPES OF SERIAL ORDER, Edward V. Huntington. Highly respected systematic account of modern theory of the continuum as a type of serial order. Based on the Dedekind-Cantor ordinal theory. Mathematics held to an elementary level. vii + 82pp.   60130-7 Paperbound $1.00

CONTRIBUTIONS TO THE FOUNDING OF THE THEORY OF TRANSFINITE NUMBERS, Georg Cantor. The famous articles of 1895-1897 which founded a new branch of mathematics, translated with 82-page introduction by P. Jourdain. Not only a great classic but still one of the best introductions for the student. ix + 211pp.
60045-9 Paperbound $2.00

ESSAYS ON THE THEORY OF NUMBERS, Richard Dedekind. Two classic essays, on the theory of irrationals, giving an arithmetic and rigorous foundation; and on transfinite numbers and properties of natural numbers. Translated by W. W. Beman. iii + 115pp.   21010-3 Paperbound $1.50

GEOMETRY OF FOUR DIMENSIONS, H. P. Manning. Part verbal, part mathematical development of fourth dimensional geometry. Historical introduction. Detailed treatment is by synthetic method, approaching subject through Euclidean geometry. No knowledge of higher mathematics necessary. 76 figures. ix + 348pp.
60182-X Paperbound $3.00

AN INTRODUCTION TO THE GEOMETRY OF N DIMENSIONS, Duncan M. Y. Sommerville. The only work in English devoted to higher-dimensional geometry. Both metric and projective properties of n-dimensional geometry are covered. Covers fundamental ideas of incidence, parallelism, perpendicularity, angles between linear space, enumerative geometry, analytical geometry, polytopes, analysis situs, hyperspacial figures. 60 diagrams. xvii + 196pp.   60494-2 Paperbound $1.50

INTRODUCTION TO SYMBOLIC LOGIC AND ITS APPLICATION, Rudolf Carnap. Clear, comprehensive, rigorous introduction. Analysis of several logical languages. Investigation of applications to physics, mathematics, similar areas. Translated by Wiliam H. Meyer and John Wilkinson. xiv + 214pp.

60453-5 Paperbound $2.25

SYMBOLIC LOGIC, Clarence I. Lewis and Cooper H. Langford. Probably the most cited book in the literature, with much material not otherwise obtainable. Paradoxes, logic of extensions and intensions, converse substitution, matrix system, strict limitations, existence of terms, truth value systems, similar material. vii + 518pp.

60170-6 Paperbound $2.75

VECTOR AND TENSOR ANALYSIS, George E. Hay. Clear introduction; starts with simple definitions, finishes with mastery of oriented Cartesian vectors, Christoffel symbols, solenoidal tensors, and applications. Many worked problems show applications. 66 figures. viii + 193pp.

60109-9 Paperbound $2.00

GUIDE TO THE LITERATURE OF MATHEMATICS AND PHYSICS, INCLUDING RELATED WORKS ON ENGINEERING SCIENCE, Nathan Grier Parke III. This up-to-date guide puts a library catalog at your fingertips. Over 5000 entries in many languages under 120 subject headings, including many recently available Russian works. Citations are as full as possible, and cross-references and suggestions for further investigation are provided. Extensive listing of bibliographical aids. 2nd revised edition. Complete indices. xviii + 436pp.

60447-0 Paperbound $2.75

INTRODUCTION TO ELLIPTIC FUNCTIONS WITH APPLICATIONS, Frank Bowman. Concise, practical introduction, from familiar trigonometric function to Jacobian elliptic functions to applications in electricity and hydrodynamics. Legendre's standard forms for elliptic integrals, conformal representation, etc., fully covered. Requires knowledge of basic principles of differentiation and integration only. 157 problems and examples, 56 figures. 115pp. 60922-7 Paperbound $1.50

THEORY OF FUNCTIONS OF A COMPLEX VARIABLE, A. R. Forsyth. Standard, classic presentation of theory of functions, stressing multiple-valued functions and related topics: theory of multiform and uniform periodic functions, Weierstrass's results with additiontheorem functions. Riemann functions and surfaces, algebraic functions, Schwarz's proof of the existence-theorem, theory of conformal mapping, etc. 125 figures, 1 plate. Total of xxviii + 855pp. 6⅛ x 9¼.

61378-X, 61379-8 Two volumes, Paperbound $5.00

THEORY OF THE INTEGRAL, Stanislaw Saks. Excellent introduction, covering all standard topics: set theory, theory of measure, functions with general properties, and theory of integration emphasizing the Lebesgue integral. Only a minimal background in elementary analysis needed. Translated by L. C. Young. 2nd revised edition. xv + 343pp.

61151-5 Paperbound $3.00

THE THEORY OF FUNCTIONS, *Konrad Knopp. Characterized as "an excellent introduction . . . remarkably readable, concise, clear, rigorous" by the* Journal of the American Statistical Association *college text.*

A Treatise on the Differential Geometry of Curves and Surfaces, Luther P. Eisenhart. Detailed, concrete introductory treatise on differential geometry, developed from author's graduate courses at Princeton University. Thorough explanation of the geometry of curves and surfaces, concentrating on problems most helpful to students. 683 problems, 30 diagrams. xiv + 474pp.

60667-8 Paperbound $2.75

An Essay on the Foundations of Geometry, Bertrand Russell. A mathematical and physical analysis of the place of the a priori in geometric knowledge. Includes critical review of 19th-century work in non-Euclidean geometry as well as illuminating insights of one of the great minds of our time. New foreword by Morris Kline. xx + 201pp.

60233-8 Paperbound $2.00

Introduction to the Theory of Numbers, Leonard E. Dickson. Thorough, comprehensive approach with adequate coverage of classical literature, yet simple enough for beginners. Divisibility, congruences, quadratic residues, binary quadratic forms, primes, least residues, Fermat's theorem, Gauss's lemma, and other important topics. 249 problems, 1 figure. viii + 183pp.

60342-3 Paperbound $2.00

An Elementary Introduction to the Theory of Probability, B. V. Gnedenko and A. Ya. Khinchin. Introduction to facts and principles of probability theory. Extremely thorough within its range. Mathematics employed held to elementary level. Excellent, highly accurate layman's introduction. Translated from the fifth Russian edition by Leo Y. Boron. xii + 130pp.

60155-2 Paperbound $1.75

Selected Papers on Noise and Stochastic Processes, edited by Nelson Wax. Six papers which serve as an introduction to advanced noise theory and fluctuation phenomena, or as a reference tool for electrical engineers whose work involves noise characteristics, Brownian motion, statistical mechanics. Papers are by Chandrasekhar, Doob, Kac, Ming, Ornstein, Rice, and Uhlenbeck. Exact facsimile of the papers as they appeared in scientific journals. 19 figures. v + 337pp. 6⅛ x 9¼.

60262-1 Paperbound $3.00

Statistics Manual, Edwin L. Crow, Frances A. Davis and Margaret W. Maxfield. Comprehensive, practical collection of classical and modern methods of making statistical inferences, prepared by U. S. Naval Ordnance Test Station. Formulae, explanations, methods of application are given, with stress on use. Basic knowledge of statistics is assumed. 21 tables, 11 charts, 95 illustrations. xvii + 288pp.

60599-X Paperbound $2.00

Mathematical Foundations of Information Theory, A. I. Khinchin. Comprehensive introduction to work of Shannon, McMillan, Feinstein and Khinchin, placing these investigations on a rigorous mathematical basis. Covers entropy concept in probability theory, uniqueness theorem, Shannon's inequality, ergodic sources, the E property, martingale concept, noise, Feinstein's fundamental lemma, Shanon's first and second theorems. Translated by R. A. Silverman and M. D. Friedman. iii + 120pp.

60434-9 Paperbound $1.75

AN INTRODUCTION TO FOURIER METHODS AND THE LAPLACE TRANSFORMATION, Philip Franklin. Introductory study of theory and applications of Fourier series and Laplace transforms, for engineers, physicists, applied mathematicians, physical science teachers and students. Only a previous knowledge of elementary calculus is assumed. Methods are related to physical problems in heat flow, vibrations, eletcrical transmission, electromagnetic radiation, etc. 828 problems with answers. Formerly *Fourier Methods.* x + 289pp. 60452-7 Paperbound $2.50

INFINITE SEQUENCES AND SERIES, Konrad Knopp. Careful presentation of fundamentals of the theory by one of the finest modern expositors of higher mathematics. Covers functions of real and complex variables, arbitrary and null sequences, convergence and divergence. Cauchy's limit theorem, tests for infinite series, power series, numerical and closed evaluation of series. Translated by Frederick Bagemihl. v + 186pp. 60153-6 Paperbound $2.00

INTRODUCTION TO THE DIFFERENTIAL EQUATIONS OF PHYSICS, Ludwig Hopf. No math background beyond elementary calculus is needed to follow this classroom or self-study introduction to ordinary and partial differential equations. Approach is through classical physics. Translated by Walter Nef. 48 figures. v + 154pp. 60120-X Paperbound $1.45

DIFFERENTIAL EQUATIONS FOR ENGINEERS, Philip Franklin. For engineers, physicists, applied mathematicians. Theory and application: solution of ordinary differential equations and partial derivatives, analytic functions. Fourier series, Abel's theorem, Cauchy Riemann differential equations, etc. Over 400 problems deal with electricity, vibratory systems, heat, radio; solutions. Formerly *Differential Equations for Electrical Engineers.* 41 illustrations. vii + 299pp. 60601-5 Paperbound $2.00

THEORY OF FUNCTIONS, PART II. Single- and multiple-valued functions; full presentation of the most characteristic and important types. Proofs fully worked out. Translated by Frederick Bagemihl. x + 150pp. 60157-9 Paperbound $1.50

PROBLEM BOOK IN THE THEORY OF FUNCTIONS, I. More than 300 elementary problems for independent use or for use with "Theory of Functions, I." 85pp. of detailed solutions. Translated by Lipman Bers. viii + 126pp. 60158-7 Paperbound $1.50

PROBLEM BOOK IN THE THEORY OF FUNCTIONS, II. More than 230 problems in the advanced theory. Designed to be used with "Theory of Functions, II" or with any comparable text. Full solutions. Translated by Frederick Bagemihl. 138pp. 60159-5 Paperbound $1.50

INTRODUCTION TO THE THEORY OF EQUATIONS, Florian Cajori. Classic introduction by leading historian of science covers the fundamental theories as reached by Gauss, Abel, Galois and Kronecker. Basics of equation study are followed by symmetric functions of roots, elimination, homographic and Tschirnhausen transformations, resolvents of Lagrange, cyclic equations, Abelian equations, the work of Galois, the algebraic solution of general equations, and much more. Numerous exercises include answers. ix + 239pp. 62184-7 Paperbound $2.75

A COURSE IN MATHEMATICAL ANALYSIS, Edouard Goursat. *The entire "Cours d'analyse" for students with one year of calculus, offering an exceptionally wide range of subject matter on analysis and applied mathematics. Available for the first time in English. Definitive treatment.*

VOLUME I: Applications to geometry, expansion in series, definite integrals, derivatives and differentials. Translated by Earle R. Hedrick. 52 figures. viii + 548pp.   60554-X Paperbound $3.00

VOLUME II, PART I: Functions of a complex variable, conformal representations, doubly periodic functions, natural boundaries, etc. Translated by Earle R. Hedrick and Otto Dunkel. 38 figures. x + 259pp.   60555-8 Paperbound $2.25

VOLUME II, PART II: Differential equations, Cauchy-Lipschitz method, non-linear differential equations, simultaneous equations, etc. Translated by Earle R. Hedrick and Otto Dunkel. 1 figure. viii + 300pp.   60556-6 Paperbound $2.50

VOLUME III, PART I: Variation of solutions, partial differential equations of the second order. Poincaré's theorem, periodic solutions, asymptotic series, wave propagation, Dirichlet's problem in space, Newtonian potential, etc. Translated by Howard G. Bergmann. 15 figures. x + 329pp.   61176-0 Paperbound $3.00

VOLUME III, PART II: Integral equations and calculus of variations: Fredholm's equation, Hilbert-Schmidt theorem, symmetric kernels, Euler's equation, transversals, extreme fields, Weierstrass's theory, etc. Translated by Howard G. Bergmann. Note on Conformal Representation by Paul Montel. 13 figures. xi + 389pp.
61177-9 Paperbound $3.00

ELEMENTARY STATISTICS: WITH APPLICATIONS IN MEDICINE AND THE BIOLOGICAL SCIENCES, Frederick E. Croxton. Presentation of all fundamental techniques and methods of elementary statistics assuming average knowledge of mathematics only. Useful to readers in all fields, but many examples drawn from characteristic data in medicine and biological sciences. vii + 376pp.
60506-X Paperbound $2.25

ELEMENTS OF THE THEORY OF FUNCTIONS. A general background text that explores complex numbers, linear functions, sets and sequences, conformal mapping. Detailed proofs. Translated by Frederick Bagemihl. 140pp.
60154-4 Paperbound $1.50

THEORY OF FUNCTIONS, PART I. Provides full demonstrations, rigorously set forth, of the general foundations of the theory: integral theorems, series, the expansion of analytic functions. Translated by Federick Bagemihl. vii + 146pp.
60156-0 Paperbound $1.50

INTRODUCTION TO THE THEORY OF FOURIER'S SERIES AND INTEGRALS, Horatio S. Carslaw. A basic introduction to the theory of infinite series and integrals, with special reference to Fourier's series and integrals. Based on the classic Riemann integral and dealing with only ordinary functions, this is an important class text. 84 examples. xiii + 368pp.   60048-3 Paperbound $3.00

ALMOST PERIODIC FUNCTIONS, A. S. Besicovitch. Thorough summary of Bohr's theory of almost periodic functions citing new shorter proofs, extending the theory, and describing contributions of Wiener, Weyl, de la Vallée, Poussin, Stepanoff, Bochner and the author. xiii + 180pp. 60018-1 Paperbound $1.75

AN INTRODUCTION TO THE STUDY OF STELLAR STRUCTURE, S. Chandrasekhar. A rigorous examination, using both classical and modern mathematical methods, of the relationship between loss of energy, the mass, and the radius of stars in a steady state. 38 figures. 509pp. 60413-6 Paperbound $3.25

INTRODUCTION TO THE THEORY OF GROUP'S OF FINITE ORDER, Robert D. Carmichael. Progresses in easy steps from sets, groups, permutations, isomorphism through the important types of groups. No higher mathematics is necessary. 783 exercises and problems. xiv + 447pp. 60300-8 Paperbound $3.50

THE SOLUBILITY OF NONELECTROLYTES, Joel H. Hildebrand and Robert L. Scott. Classic, pioneering work discusses in detail ideal and nonideal solutions, intermolecular forces, structure of liquids, athermal mixing, hydrogen bonding, equations describing mixtures of gases, high polymer solutions, surface phenomena, etc. Originally published in the American Chemical Society Monograph series. New authors' preface and new paper (1964). 148 figures, 88 tables. xiv + 488pp. 61125-6 Paperbound $3.00

INTRODUCTION TO APPLIED MATHEMATICS, Francis D. Murnaghan. Introduction to advanced mathematical techniques—vector and matrix analysis, partial differential equations, integral equations, Laplace transform theory, Fourier series, boundary-value problems, etc.—particularly useful to physicists and engineers. 41 figures. ix + 389pp. 61042-X Paperbound $2.25

ELEMENTARY MATHEMATICS FROM AN ADVANCED STANDPOINT: VOLUME I—ARITHMETIC, ALGEBRA, ANALYSIS, Felix Klein. Second-level approach, illuminated by graphical and geometrical interpretation. Covers natural and complex numbers, real equations with real unknowns, equations in the field of complex quantities, logarithmic and exponential functions, goniometric functions, infinitesimal calculus, transcendence of e and π. Concept of function introduced immediately. Translated by E. R. Hedrick and C. A. Noble. 125 figures. ix + 274pp. (USO) 60150-1 Paperbound $2.25

ELEMENTARY MATHEMATICS FROM AN ADVANCED STANDPOINT: VOLUME II—GEOMETRY, Feliex Klein. Using analytical formulas, Klein clarifies the precise formulation of geometric facts in chapters on manifolds, geometric and higher point transformations, foundations. "Nothing comparable," Mathematics Teacher. Translated by E. R. Hedrick and C. A. Noble. 141 figures. ix + 214pp. (USO) 60151-X Paperbound $2.25

ENGINEERING MATHEMATICS, Kenneth S. Miller. Most useful mathematical techniques for graduate students in engineering, physics, covering linear differential equations, series, random functions, integrals, Fourier series, Laplace transform, network theory, etc. "Sound and teachable," Science. 89 figures. xii + 417pp. 6 x 8½. 61121-3 Paperbound $3.00

MATHEMATICAL PUZZLES FOR BEGINNERS AND ENTHUSIASTS, Geoffrey Mott-Smith. 189 puzzles from easy to difficult—involving arithmetic, logic, algebra, properties of digits, probability, etc.—for enjoyment and mental stimulus. Explanation of mathematical principles behind the puzzles. 135 illustrations. viii + 248pp.
20198-8 Paperbound $1.25

PAPER FOLDING FOR BEGINNERS, William D. Murray and Francis J. Rigney. Easiest book on the market, clearest instructions on making interesting, beautiful origami. Sail boats, cups, roosters, frogs that move legs, bonbon boxes, standing birds, etc. 40 projects; more than 275 diagrams and photographs. 94pp.
20713-7 Paperbound $1.00

TRICKS AND GAMES ON THE POOL TABLE, Fred Herrmann. 79 tricks and games—some solitaires, some for two or more players, some competitive games—to entertain you between formal games. Mystifying shots and throws, unusual caroms, tricks involving such props as cork, coins, a hat, etc. Formerly *Fun on the Pool Table*. 77 figures. 95pp.
21814-7 Paperbound $1.00

HAND SHADOWS TO BE THROWN UPON THE WALL: A SERIES OF NOVEL AND AMUSING FIGURES FORMED BY THE HAND, Henry Bursill. Delightful picturebook from great-grandfather's day shows how to make 18 different hand shadows: a bird that flies, duck that quacks, dog that wags his tail, camel, goose, deer, boy, turtle, etc. Only book of its sort. vi + 33pp. 6½ x 9¼. 21779-5 Paperbound $1.00

WHITTLING AND WOODCARVING, E. J. Tangerman. 18th printing of best book on market. "If you can cut a potato you can carve" toys and puzzles, chains, chessmen, caricatures, masks, frames, woodcut blocks, surface patterns, much more. Information on tools, woods, techniques. Also goes into serious wood sculpture from Middle Ages to present, East and West. 464 photos, figures. x + 293pp.
20965-2 Paperbound $2.00

HISTORY OF PHILOSOPHY, Julián Marias. Possibly the clearest, most easily followed, best planned, most useful one-volume history of philosophy on the market; neither skimpy nor overfull. Full details on system of every major philosopher and dozens of less important thinkers from pre-Socratics up to Existentialism and later. Strong on many European figures usually omitted. Has gone through dozens of editions in Europe. 1966 edition, translated by Stanley Appelbaum and Clarence Strowbridge. xviii + 505pp.
21739-6 Paperbound $2.75

YOGA: A SCIENTIFIC EVALUATION, Kovoor T. Behanan. Scientific but non-technical study of physiological results of yoga exercises; done under auspices of Yale U. Relations to Indian thought, to psychoanalysis, etc. 16 photos. xxiii + 270pp.
20505-3 Paperbound $2.50

Prices subject to change without notice.
Available at your book dealer or write for free catalogue to Dept. GI, Dover Publications, Inc., 180 Varick St., N. Y., N. Y. 10014. Dover publishes more than 150 books each year on science, elementary and advanced mathematics, biology, music, art, literary history, social sciences and other areas.